AMERICAN
DECADES
1970-1979

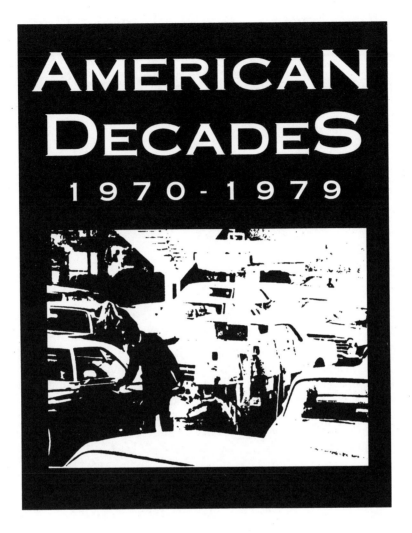

AMERICAN DECADES
1970-1979

EDITED BY

VICTOR BONDI

A MANLY, INC. BOOK

Gale Research Inc. • DETROIT • WASHINGTON, D.C. • LONDON

AMERICAN DECADES
1970-1979

Matthew J. Bruccoli and Richard Layman, *Editorial Directors*

Printed in the United States of America

Library of Congress Catalog Card Number   94-073501
ISBN 0-8103-8882-0

10 9 8 7 6 5

CONTENTS

INTRODUCTION

The Nondecade? It is easy to dismiss the 1970s as the decade that never happened. The political and cultural trends of the 1960s continued to dominate life in the United States at least until President Richard Nixon's resignation in 1974; the political and cultural trends of the 1980s were manifested with increasing visibility for the remainder of the decade. Feminism, drugs, progressive education, busing, pornography, exotic religions, paranoia, welfare, ethnic politics, long hair, blue jeans, platform shoes, and amphetamines lingered from the 1960s. Conservativism, cowboys, televangelists, flag-waving, energy saving, rising cost of living, teen moms, pickup trucks, overseas investments, Sun Belt shift, cocaine, sound bites, and acid rain anticipated the 1980s. The 1970s, it seems, have little to define them except, perhaps, their nothingness. Peter Carroll, one of the earliest historians of the age, even titled his study *It Seemed Like Nothing Happened* (1982). Historical events, of course, occurred. The Kent State shootings, the Christmas bombing of Hanoi and Haiphong, the resignation of Nixon, the energy crisis, and the Iran hostage crisis all transpired during the course of the decade, but they are events identified with the spirit of the revolutionary 1960s or the avaricious 1980s.

Symbols. The 1970s, in fact, have few icons, few symbols to define it, in the manner in which the blue eagle defines the 1930s or the peace symbol the 1960s — unless, perhaps, it was the N. G. Slater Company's ubiquitous smiley face. Two blank eyes and an ever-optimistic grin superimposed on a yellow sun, the smiley face was an image found on lapel buttons, bumper stickers, T-shirts, wall posters, and toilet seats in the 1970s. It is an almost absurdist icon, seemingly meaningless, and yet the perfect expression of the era. While other times featured dramatic events, the 1970s was the decade defined by two deep-seated ideological crises. In the 1970s a belief in the justice of U.S. overseas expansion and a confidence in the merit of a U.S. domestic reform movement were challenged and, to a great extent, found wanting. These concepts were fundamental to U.S. liberalism, and it was a decade of trauma for U.S. liberalism like none before: the assumptions of anticommunism abandoned, the tenets of the civil rights movement challenged, the programs of the Great Society discarded, the philosophy of progressivism

forsaken. It was a decade which saw the shattering of basic, historically grounded assumptions regarding the United States and its citizens. Such a decade presented Americans with an opportunity to construct new philosophies and adopt new symbols — and they chose the smiley face — blissful, welcoming, optimistic. The smiley face is the perfect expression of such a traumatic decade, precisely because it so resolutely denies the injuries of the time. A nation in the midst of a collective repression, profoundly shaken, and yet acting as if nothing happened — the 1970s.

Vietnam and Its Aftereffects. The most obvious blow to certain common assumptions, at least regarding U.S. politics and economics, was the defeat of the United States in the Vietnam War. Yet, true to the era, there was relatively little analysis of the defeat. The Nixon administration implicitly and explicitly obscured the dimensions of the Vietnam failure, implicitly by abandoning the geopolitical assumptions that involved the United States in Vietnam in the first place; explicitly by producing a "peace treaty" in 1973 that did little more than cover the U.S. retreat from Vietnam. Nixon was one of the most perceptive of the cold warriors in recognizing that the ideological rationale behind Vietnam was invalidated by history. The world had changed since the war began. The authoritarianism of Communist states softened. Tensions between the Chinese and Soviets had escalated, and the willingness of the Eastern Bloc to engage in trade with foreign nations increased. By the time of his 1969 inauguration, Nixon was prepared to seek détente with the Soviets and negotiations with the Chinese. He did not dramatically change U.S. policy in Vietnam — in fact, he escalated the war, drawing it out for another four years. His Vietnam policy, however, was predicated upon his vision of a new world order. The axioms of Nixon's war against Vietnam — we must fight the war to maintain our credibility abroad; we must conduct peace negotiations from a position of strength — were political cover against the Republican right wing for his new geopolitical initiatives. But fate intervened. Nixon resigned, and Gerald Ford, who shared Nixon's ideology but lacked his political skill, replaced him. Ford lost the presidency in the next election when he failed to attract the unified support of both the conservative and moderate wings of his party.

Limits. The trauma of Vietnam forced Americans to question two basic assumptions about their place in the world. The first was a type of historical arrogance, a belief held by Americans since the 1840s that the United States was God's chosen nation, destined to teach a benighted world a better form of government. The U.S. experiment with "nation building" in Vietnam merely extended a colonialist policy already exercised in the Caribbean, the Philippines, and China. That since World War II both China and Vietnam rejected such efforts suggested to many Americans that, at best, U.S. democracy was not universally applicable, or, at worst, that God himself had withdrawn approval from his formerly divine mission.

A second assumption, closely tied to the first, held that American corporate capitalism was the best method of economic organization in an inefficient world. Operating with this assumption in mind, U.S. politicians, financiers, and industrialists had established a blueprint for the post–World War II reconstruction of the world economy at the Bretton Woods conference in 1944. U.S. capitalism was expected to direct the global economy based upon free-market access to the raw materials, a positive trading balance, and financial transactions stabilized by U.S. currency. By 1971 Bretton Woods was dead, the United States developed huge trading imbalances, and the global economy was fractured into trading blocs. Nixon accelerated these trends, abandoned American leadership of a global economy, deregulated world currencies, imposed a temporary 10 percent fee on imports, and obscured this shift in policy with domestic wage and price controls. He understood what many Americans did not: the strategy of containment, the Cold War, and the war in Vietnam had badly overextended U.S. resources and crippled U.S. competitiveness with nonmilitary nations such as Japan and Germany. Vietnam forced Americans to abandon grand designs for the world economy and concentrate on maintaining competitiveness in an increasingly competitive world; it forced, in other words, a recognition of limits in a nation that had historically seen its horizons as limitless.

Twilight of Liberalism. Prior to the 1970s Americans had been as expansive in their expectation of social improvement as they had been in foreign policy or economics. These expectations were closely allied: U.S. liberalism assumed that a rising economy would resolve most social problems painlessly; a rising economy demanded market expansion; market expansion necessitated opening closed Communist economies. Most Americans also presumed they could have guns and butter, that the postwar prosperity was so great, so permanent, that the government could finance both New Deal–style assistance programs (President Lyndon Johnson's Great Society) and the anti-Communist crusade. It could not. Johnson had already pared back his domestic programs before he left office; Nixon was inclined to advance these programs,

but he lacked money, congressional consensus, and, ultimately, the energy he demonstrated in foreign affairs. In the 1970s, although domestic reforms remained in place, they languished, disintegrating along with the U.S. economy. Expansion abroad had drawn to a close; so, too, had social reform at home.

Pop Culture Politics. What made these developments distinctive to the 1970s was that they were almost universally ignored or denied. Nixon's public image was so negative that his response to the ideological crises in U.S. politics and economics was overlooked. The domestic reforms of the 1960s collapsed along with the U.S. economy. Americans responded by simply abandoning politics, reform, and liberal ideology. Voter apathy soared. Especially when compared to the activism of the 1960s, the 1970s were an age of political and ideological passivity. Americans turned their attention from public issues to private concerns. The most prominent political movement of the era, feminism, emphasized that "the personal is political," and the most representative political figure of the decade, Jimmy Carter, cultivated an ingenuous intimacy that compensated for his lack of ideological consistency. While there was no broadly based national discussion of the meaning of defeat in Vietnam, stocktaking took place through the medium of popular books, oral histories, and novels such as Ron Kovic's *Born on the Fourth of July,* Michael Herr's *Dispatches,* and Philip Caputo's *A Rumor of War;* through probing, visceral films such as *The Deer Hunter, Coming Home,* and *Apocalypse Now;* through stage plays such as David Rabe's *Streamers;* and through television programs such as *M*A*S*H.* Issues of domestic reform were similarly displaced to pop culture. The Memphis State Tigers, failing to defeat the UCLA Bruins in the 1973 NCAA basketball playoffs, succeeding in unifying a city polarized by racial divisions since 1968. Helen Reddy's 1972 Grammy-winning pop hit, "I Am Woman," became an anthem for feminists. The politics of race, gender, and class were debated as often on situation comedies such as *All in the Family, The Mary Tyler Moore Show,* or *One Day at a Time* as they were in political forums — generally with more telling effect. The more relevant magazines, films, and television became, the more politics and ideology became a variant of style and taste. On television feminism became a temperament rather than a philosophy, radicalism a gesture rather than a belief. Watergate was an uninterrupted media drama rather than a constitutional crisis, slavery a miniseries rather than a historical legacy. As politics and ideology were displaced into the entertainment media, they became entertainment; as they became entertainment, they became ephemeral. The 1970s made the 1960s a media event; Americans tired of it, and switched channels.

From Marches to Malls. What style and taste there was in the 1970s appears to be, in retrospect, almost unremittingly bad. The 1970s began in a drug-addled mix of psychedelic colors and brown shag carpeting; they ended in overpriced denim and white polyester vamping. Without a unified national political and economic ideology, there was no foundation for the stylistic focus, and so the 1970s were a decade of pastiche, failed experimentation, and infinitely disposable flash. Designers sold innovations — unisex clothing, the midi, platform shoes, nylon shirts, and Lurex blouses imprinted with photographs of mountains and forests — but for the most part, Americans were not buying. It was an age of aesthetic democracy: with authority challenged on all fronts, style originated in the street. The antistyle of the hippies became high style; and haute couture was forced to champion military surplus, blue jeans, and cowboy boots. Television went populist, embracing CB radios, Billy Beer, and outlaw truckers with sidekick chimpanzees. The best U.S. films rejected convention and expressed a gritty, cynical realism. Disco bubbled up from the gay and Latino underground, punk from the cellars of New York and London. Architects were influenced by Las Vegas; male literary lions by insurrectionary, articulate women; theatergoers by the dancers in *A Chorus Line.* Established arbiters of taste, in danger of being superseded, co-opted the new aesthetic democracy and watered it down: they added sequins to blue jeans; took Robert Venturi's populist architecture and pressed it into the service of the corporation; replaced the gritty realism of Robert Altman, Francis Ford Coppola, and John Cassavetes with the big-screen-as-television conventions of Steven Spielberg and George Lucas; obscured the disco of Sylvester and made the Bee Gees stars; put the Ramones and punk in suits, turned down the guitars, and created the Knack and new wave rock. There was money to be made in culture in the 1970s, and while U.S. capitalism was faltering in the production of steel and automobiles, U.S. music, cinema, and television were sweeping the globe. The entrepreneurs of the age — Ted Turner, David Geffen, Bill Graham, and Robert Stigwood — specialized in discovering underground culture, refining it, and marketing it for a mass audience. Such entrepreneurs were instrumental in taking American culture from the streets and putting it into that shrine of American bad taste, the suburban shopping mall.

Villains. A decade characterized by such bad taste was also filled with bad men. The 1970s were certainly peopled by low-rent vulgarians and cookie-cutter villains: Idi Amin, Ugandan dictator and internationally acclaimed cannibal; Larry Flynt, who managed to distinguish himself as tasteless even among pornographers; G. Gordon Liddy, the Watergate burglar who defied feminists and proved that true masculinity is the capacity to withstand the heat of a candle flame and eat a diet of fricasseed rat; members of Congress, such as Bob Sikes, Wilber Mills, and Wayne Hays, who reaffirmed Capitol Hill traditions of skirt chasing, boozing, and bribery during a decade of reform; Ohio State football coach Woody Hayes, who exhibited his winning attitude by throwing fits on the sidelines and abusing the players; Clifford Irving, the

author who demonstrated that reality should never get in the way of a good nonfiction book; Howard Hughes, the object of Irving's fascination and a trend-setting eccentric, who, along with Harold Geneen, chairman of ITT, insisted that multinational capitalism leave no political intrigue untouched and no civic virtue uncorrupted; scores of celebrities, businessmen, and politicians determined to augment their notoriety through shameless self-promotion and ill-considered gestures of solidarity with the oppressed; armies of therapists, motivationists, and feel-good intellectuals endlessly hawking paperbacks and personal guides, educational reform plans, artistic manifestos, and stress-reducing tapes filled with the sounds of bird whistles and whale bellows.

Heroes. Not everyone was a villain, of course. The 1970s had its share of heroes. In contrast to the actions of the Watergate conspirators, the high-minded, extraordinary behavior of a bipartisan group of figures, including Sam Ervin, Elliot Richardson, John Sirica, Peter Rodino, and Leon Jaworski, restored a guarded public confidence in American government. Ralph Nader and Cesar Chavez tirelessly defended the interests of U.S. consumers and farmworkers, while journalists such as Tom Wicker and Gloria Steinem publicized the plight of the marginalized and downtrodden with sympathy and intelligence. Dr. Donald A. Henderson of the World Health Organization oversaw the eradication of smallpox. Muhammad Ali returned from political adversity to become once again "the Greatest." Coach John Wooden led the UCLA Bruins to an unprecedented number of NCAA basketball championships in twelve out of his last fourteen seasons. Billie Jean King became a tennis champion and an inspiration to women. Such visible, symbolic heroes, however, were the exception in the 1970s. More often, real heroes took a low-key approach to problems, working at the local level for small victories and incremental progress. Church activists, environmental lawyers, rape-crisis counselors, teachers' assistants, and common citizens of every temperament took the national activism of the 1960s and brought it to their local communities. Typical of such heroes was twenty-seven-year-old housewife Lois Gibbs of Love Canal, New York, a residential neighborhood near Niagara Falls. When noxious fluids began seeping into basements causing homeowners and their families to fall ill, she organized a grass-roots campaign which exposed the area as a toxic waste site. Because of her rallying efforts, the federal government designated Love Canal an emergency area, and the state of New York paid to have residents moved. Her efforts in the 1970s demonstrated the conviction so many had in the 1960s that one person could make a difference.

Weirdos. Perhaps because the media of the 1970s so ruthlessly scrutinized U.S. culture, several highly unusual, eccentric — sometimes weird — people shared the spotlight (albeit temporarily) with the heroes and villains of the decade. There was the mysterious hijacker D. B. Cooper, who jumped out of an airplane over the Northwest with thousands of dollars in stolen money and was never seen again; Evel Knievel, the Elvis-bedecked motorcycle stuntman who jumped over anything for money — including Idaho's Snake River Canyon; Dr. Renee Richards, the male physician turned female athlete who whipped her fearsome first serve over the net at the U.S. Open only after winning a court case against sexual discrimination; Bobby Fischer, the chess player who proceeded from the championship to eccentric obscurity; the New York Dolls, the cross-dresser's answer to the Rolling Stones, who leaped into the music press with strange tunes about Frankenstein and science-fiction freaks. In a decade characterized by growing weirdness, such instances paled in comparison with the case of Patricia Hearst, the nineteen-year-old publishing heiress who was kidnapped in 1974 by the bizarre revolutionary group the Symbionese Liberation Army (SLA). Reportedly locked in a closet and brainwashed, Hearst emerged as the fiery radical "Tania" and helped the SLA liberate money from California banks. After she was captured by the FBI the next year, her trial became one of the great media events of the decade. The case became inspiration for a subplot in the 1976 Oscar-winning film *Network*, which was centered around the character of Howard Beale, a "madman of the airwaves," whose frustrated chant, "I'm as mad as hell, and I'm not going to take this anymore!" became a real-life campaign slogan during the election year. The winner of that election, of course, was Jimmy Carter, who as president in 1979 pardoned Patty Hearst. Such was the circuitous route history would take in the strange and bizarre 1970s.

California. So many of the decade's weirdos had California addresses that the state soon became associated — in the minds of many elsewhere in the United States — with the strange and bizarre; but no other single locale so embodied the decade as did the Golden State. In the early 1970s California was the place to find hippie communes, solar-powered homes, Joni Mitchell, *Rolling Stone*, and Richard Nixon. In the middle 1970s California was the site of the Loud family that disintegrated on PBS, religious cults, porn stars, the Eagles, *High Times*, and Jerry Brown. In the late 1970s California was the home of singles-only apartments, cocaine, *TV Guide*, Fleetwood Mac, and Ronald Reagan. The culture, fads, and trends of the 1970s, of course, were not limited to California, but the state seemed to embrace such things with singular zeal. Hot tubs and saunas could be found in the Upper Midwest, but southern Californians made them the center of social life; New York treated its mystics and gurus as crackpots, but Marin County made them respected businesspeople. Embracing the ridiculous, however, was a humorous tendency in a state given to innovation and experimentation. Californians pioneered hippie capitalism, media multinationalism, the fitness-wear and health-food industries, and the development of computers. No wonder Americans went West: the nation's population shifted to the Sun Belt;

Motown Records moved from Detroit to L.A.; the respected Swiss psychiatrist Elizabeth Kübler-Ross moved there to open a healing center; and in the Oscar-winning *Annie Hall*, Woody Allen's New York–based hero, Alvy Singer, loses his friends — and his girl — to sunny California.

Narcissism. California was also associated with the *Me decade*, a descriptive term coined by author Tom Wolfe in 1976. Wolfe, among others, was sharply critical of the selfishness and narcissism of the decade, especially that of the therapists and gurus seemingly omnipresent in California. The decade was marked by a preoccupation with self. Magazines, paperbacks, pop music, television, and movies were filled with discussions of sensitivity and feelings. Looking good, feeling right, and eating healthily were ritualistic preoccupations of millions. Folksingers moved from protest songs to confessional ballads. The psychologist Heinz Kohut made the narcissistic personality the focus of his clinical study; cultural critics such as Christopher Lasch and Daniel Bell inveighed against narcissism in culture; even artists such as Vito Acconci, busy puncturing, pulling, coloring, and otherwise mutilating his skin in the name of "body art," gave expression to the period's self-obsession.

Paranoia. The 1970s were also anxious, even paranoid. Conspiracies abounded. Films such as *The Parallax View*, *The Conversation*, *Three Days of the Condor*, and *Marathon Man* were pervaded by shadow maneuverings and sinister figures. Paranoia was central to the novels of Thomas Pynchon and Kurt Vonnegut. Some researchers suggested hidden conspiracies in the assassination of John Kennedy, the disappearances of ships and airplanes, and the building of the pyramids of Egypt. Even the O'Jays' pop hit "Backstabbers" expressed the fear of betrayal. Life did give real cause for alarm. Watergate boosted national anxiety, and paranoia was at the heart of the scandal. Nixon's suspicion that he would be betrayed by his own subordinates led to the installation of the infamous taping system within the White House; his unfounded fear that the Democrats would use the same dirty tricks against him that he was using against them provided the impetus for the Watergate burglary; his anxieties regarding the public exposure of broad administrative misdeeds led to the Watergate cover-up. And the upshot of the scandal was that the government was covering things up, breaking the law, lying. Other revelations of governmental skulduggery followed. As they had long suspected, 1960s activists found out that their organizations had been infiltrated and subverted by agents of the FBI, CIA, and local police. The FBI assembled dossiers on thousands of Americans and illegally wiretapped such prominent figures as Martin Luther King, Jr., and Supreme Court justice William O. Douglas. Congressional hearings in the middle of the decade revealed that the CIA and National Security Agency (NSA) had monitored overseas calls, subverted foreign governments, and contracted with the Mafia. The government conducted secret drug tests and medical experiments on thousands of unwitting subjects, the most sensational example of which was the Tuskegee Syphilis Study of the 1940s, revealed to the public in 1972. The U.S. Public Health Service had allowed African-American men to die from syphilis in order to study the disease's effects, rather than cure them of the malady. Given such practices, Americans in the 1970s had cause to keep looking over their shoulders.

Realism. Because the 1970s were the crisis decade for established American political, economic, and social assumptions, it was also a decade wherein Americans attempted to construct new, more realistic, ideologies. The exposure of government misdeeds exemplified the willingness of some political figures to resist the more brutal effects of governmental power and demonstrated their confidence that U.S. institutions were capable of honesty and reform. Members of Congress and of the Ford and Carter administrations tried to scale back the power of federal bureaucracies such as the CIA, FBI, and NSA. Congress undertook sweeping reforms of itself, designed to limit the influence of wealthy individuals and corporations. Domestic-policy specialists in the Nixon, Ford, and Carter administrations attempted to construct a realistic fiscal program. The Nixon administration attempted to abandon the foreign policy of the Cold War, an effort extended under Ford and Carter, and all three presidents tried to restructure the relationship between U.S. government and business to meet the challenges of a transformed global economy. These experiments make the 1970s a rewarding period for historical study, but they also dramatically reveal the limits placed by the public on institutional and ideological innovation, because all of these innovations failed. They failed primarily because the American public did not embrace them, preferring to support established institutions. Politicians who attempted to speak frankly to the public concerning the changed conditions of life in the United States in the 1970s usually paid a heavy political price. Daniel Patrick Moynihan, William Simon, Henry Kissinger, James Schlesinger, Stansfield Turner, and Andrew Young all attempted, at one time or another, to address the limits of U.S. domestic or foreign power, and all were rebuffed by the public for their remarks. The most obvious victim of this process was Jimmy Carter, whose 1979 energy address bluntly discussed the economic woes of the United States, as well as the prospects for a more realistic economy. His defeat in 1980 was fundamentally a repudiation of his candor, as well as a repudiation of détente, economic realism, and limited domestic reform — political concepts substantially shared by all three presidential administrations in the 1970s. Nixon, Ford, and Carter all promised to continue the American standard of living found in the postwar period, but only if Americans accepted certain compromises: geopolitical equality with the Soviets and the Chinese; economic equality with Eu-

rope and Japan; and tightening the scale of governmental assistance. Americans rejected these compromises and found in Ronald Reagan a political temperament unalloyed by compromise. President Reagan demanded victory in the Cold War (even if it were not militarily or economically achievable); U.S. global leadership (regardless of balance of trade); maintenance of governmental assistance to the middle class alone. The 1970s pop-culture attraction to nostalgia illuminates the political temperament: rather than change with the times, Americans preferred to retreat into an idealized imagined past with unassailable truths. Containing almost no ideological innovations, the conservatism of the late 1970s reasserted traditional verities regardless of contemporary realities. Thus in the 1980s the problems of the 1970s were not resolved so much as simply dismissed — the energy crisis, for example, merited almost no discussion in the 1980s, despite the fact that the structural weaknesses behind the crisis in the 1970s remained. But the problems of the 1990s — the economically destabilizing cost of defense expenditures, balance of trade and the administration of the global economy, the scale of domestic reform, the politics of race — resemble those of the 1970s because these problems remain unaddressed by the American people. The 1970s are perhaps the most crucial decade in the postwar period because the decade's problems promise to be — in the next decade — those which Americans can no longer avoid.

PLAN OF THIS VOLUME

This is one of nine volumes in the *American Decades* series. Each volume will chronicle a single twentieth-century decade from thirteen separate perspectives, broadly covering American life. The volumes begin with a chronology of world events outside of the United States, which provides a context for American experience. Following are chapters, arranged in alphabetical order, on thirteen categories of American endeavor ranging from business to medicine, from the arts to sports. Each of these chapters contains the following elements: first, a table of contents for the chapter; second, a chronology of significant events in the field; third, Topics in the News, a series, beginning with an overview, of short essays describing current events; fourth, anecdotal sidebars of interesting and entertaining, though not necessarily important, information; fifth, Headline Makers, short biographical accounts of key people during the decade; sixth, People in the News, brief notices of significant accomplishments by people who mattered; seventh, Awards of note in the field (where applicable); eighth, Deaths during the decade of people in the field; and ninth, a list of Publications during or specifically about the decade in the field. In addition, there is a general bibliography at the end of this volume, followed by an index of photographs and an index of subjects.

ACKNOWLEDGMENTS

This book was produced by Manly, Inc.

Production coordinator is James W. Hipp. Photography editor is Bruce Andrew Bowlin. Photographic copy work was performed by Joseph M. Bruccoli. Layout and graphics supervisor is Penney L. Haughton. Copyediting supervisor is Denise W. Edwards. Typesetting supervisor is Kathleen M. Flanagan. Systems manager is George F. Dodge. Julie E. Frick is editorial associate. The production staff includes Phyllis A. Avant, Ann M. Cheschi, Melody W. Clegg, Patricia Coate, Brigitte B. de Guzman, Sarah A. Estes, Joyce Fowler, Laurel M. Gladden, Stephanie C. Hatchell, Kathy Lawler Merlette, Jeff Miller, Pamela D. Norton, Delores I. Plastow, Laura S. Pleicones, Patricia F. Salisbury, and William L. Thomas, Jr.

Walter W. Ross and Robert S. McConnell did library research. They were assisted by the following librarians at the Thomas Cooper Library of the University of South Carolina: Linda Holderfield and the interlibrary-loan staff; reference-department head Virginia Weathers; reference librarians Marilee Birchfield, Stefanie Buck, Cathy Eckman, Rebecca Feind, Jill Holman, Karen Joseph, Jean Rhyne, Kwamine Washington, and Connie Widney; circulation-department head Caroline ("Tucky") Taylor; and acquisitions-searching supervisor David Haggard.

AMERICAN
DECADES
1970-1979

WORLD EVENTS: SELECTED OCCURRENCES OUTSIDE THE UNITED STATES

1970

- Nadine Gordimer's novel *A Guest of Honor* is published.

- Yukio Mishima's novel *Runaway Horses* is published.

- Graham Greene's novel *Travels with My Aunt* is published.

- John Fowles's novel *The French Lieutenant's Woman* is published.

- Marcel Ophuls's documentary *The Sorrow and the Pity* premieres.

- West German chancellor Willy Brandt, following a policy of *Ostpolitik*, signs nonaggression pacts with the Soviet Union and Poland and begins negotiations with East Germany.

- Citizens of East Pakistan vote for autonomy from Pakistan.

- Soviet cosmonauts set a new duration record (seventeen days) for spaceflight.

12 Jan.	The Biafran independence movement capitulates to the Nigerian government after a secessionist struggle lasting thirty-one months.
16 Jan.	Col. Muammar el-Gadhafi assumes the post of premier of Libya.
10 Feb.	One person is killed and twenty-three are injured in an Arab terrorist attack in Munich, West Germany.
21 Feb.	On route from Zürich to Tel Aviv, a Swissair jetliner explodes and crashes, killing forty-seven. Arab terrorists are suspected in the blast.
1 Mar.	Rhodesia declares its independence from Britain.
4 Mar.	Fifty-seven sailors are feared lost when the French submarine *Eurydice* disappears in the Mediterranean.
15 Mar.	Expo '70 opens in Osaka, Japan.
18 Mar.	The Cambodian government of Prince Norodom Sihanouk is overthrown in a military coup led by Gen. Lon Nol.
8 Apr.	Gas explosions in Osaka, Japan, kill 72 persons and injure 282.
30 Apr.	U.S. and South Vietnamese combat troops invade Cambodia.
31 May	An estimated seventy thousand people are killed and seven hundred thousand are left homeless following an earthquake in Peru.

7 June	Swiss voters reject a proposal to expel some three hundred thousand foreign workers.
8 June	Argentine president Juan Carlos Ongania is deposed in a military coup.
19 June	In an electoral upset the British Conservative Party defeats the Labour PartyLabour Party, Great Britain. Conservative Party head Edward Heath replaces Harold Wilson as prime minister.
24–27 June	In the heaviest fighting since the 1967 war, Israeli and Syrian troops engage in pitched battles on the Golan Heights.
29 June	The last U.S. and South Vietnamese combat troops leave Cambodia.
21 July	The Aswan High Dam project is completed in Egypt.
27 July	Portuguese dictator Antonio Salazar dies at age eighty-one after nearly forty years in power.
7 Aug.	A U.S.-negotiated cease-fire between Israel and the Arab states goes into effect; peace negotiations begin at the United Nations.
6 Sept.	Four New York–bound airliners, carrying over six hundred people, are hijacked by Palestinian terrorists. One plane is diverted to London, and three planes are flown to Jordan. On 9 September another jetliner is hijacked and flown to Jordan. Three days later the passengers are freed and three of the airplanes are blown up.
16 Sept.	King Hussein of Jordan declares martial law.
24 Sept.	The Soviet unmanned spacecraft *Luna 16* returns to Earth with a collection of Moon rocks.
14 Oct.	Anwar as-Sadat is elected president of the United Arab Republic (Egypt).
24 Oct.	Salvador Allende Gossens, leader of the Socialist Party, is elected president of Chile.
5 Nov.	The Arab-Israeli cease-fire is extended.
13 Nov.	Cyclones and tidal waves destroy coastal East Pakistan; two hundred thousand people are estimated killed and three million people displaced.
25 Nov.	Japanese novelist Yukio Mishima harangues one thousand Japanese troops on the disgrace of defeat in World War II and challenges them to join him in a coup; when they refuse, he commits suicide.
26 Nov.	Pope Paul VI narrowly escapes assassination in the Philippines.
1 Dec.	The Italian parliament approves that country's first divorce law.
4 Dec.	In order to combat an outbreak of kidnapping and lawlessness, the Irish government assumes emergency powers.
11 Dec.	The United States and the Soviet Union sign a treaty on fishing rights off the coast of the Middle Atlantic states.
16 Dec.	Meeting in The Hague, Netherlands, fifty nations sign an agreement making air hijacking a crime subject to severe punishment.

1971

- E. M. Forster's novel *Maurice* is published posthumously.

- Anthony Powell's novel *Books Do Furnish A Room* is published.

- Benjamin Britten's opera *Owen Wingrave* premieres.

- Federico Fellini's film *The Clowns* premieres.

- A cholera epidemic sweeps Bangladesh and leads to worldwide concern.

- Three Soviet cosmonauts are found dead in their returning spacecraft.

- The British Parliament votes to join the European Common Market.

- A worldwide monetary crisis results in the devaluation of the American dollar.

- Mount Etna produces its most spectacular eruption in forty-three years.

- New international efforts are made to control biological weapons.

- The shah of Iran celebrates the twenty-five hundredth anniversary of the Persian empire with a gala, attended by over fifty heads of state, at Persepolis, the ancient Persian capital.

2 Jan. In Glasgow, Scotland, a crowd barrier at a soccer stadium collapses, killing sixty-six and wounding over one hundred.

25 Jan. President Milton Obote of Uganda is overthrown in a military coup. Gen. Idi Amin seizes power.

4 Feb. Rolls-Royce, the British automobile and airplane engine manufacturer, declares bankruptcy.

6 Feb. The British send six hundred troops to Northern Ireland to stem renewed sectarian violence.

8 Feb. South Vietnamese troops, with American air cover, invade Laos in an attempt to cut North Vietnamese supply lines.

9 Feb. The European Economic Community establishes a plan to unify member currencies over a ten-year period.

14 Feb. The Persian Gulf oil states receive $10 billion from twenty-three Western oil companies in return for five-year oil rights.

19 Feb. The Soviet newspaper *Pravda* warns Soviet Jews against espousing Zionism.

21 Feb. The 380-mile Karakoram highway is formally opened, linking China to Pakistan.

28 Feb. Male voters in Liechtenstein reject woman suffrage, leaving it the only Western nation denying women the right to vote.

7 Mar. The Arab-Israeli cease-fire expires.

11 Mar. Prime Minister Indira Gandhi of India wins a huge majority in national elections.

25 Mar. President Mohammad Yahya Khan of Pakistan sends troops to East Pakistan and declares martial law.

4 Apr. In local elections Salvador Allende Gossens's left-wing coalition wins 49.7 percent of Chileans' votes.

27 Apr. Park Chung Hee wins a third term as South Korean president.

3 May Erich Honecker replaces Walter Ulbricht as East German Communist Party leader.

19 May The Soviet Union and Canada sign a friendship agreement.

20 May	In Leningrad nine Soviet Jews are sent to prison camp for "anti-Soviet activity."
21 June	The International Court of Justice at The Hague rules that South Africa must end its administration of South-West Africa.
22 July	Sudanese leader Jaafar Mohammad Nimeiri crushes a three-day military coup.
30 July	A midair collision over Honshu, Japan, kills 162 people.
9 Aug.	India and the Soviet Union sign a friendship treaty.
15 Aug.	Bahrain declares its independence from Britain.
22 Aug.	Gen. Juan José Torres of Bolivia is ousted from the presidency in a military coup.
18 Sept.	Israel and Egypt exchange rocket fire over the Suez Canal.
21 Sept.	Adam Malik of Indonesia is elected president of the twenty-sixth UN General Assembly. Bahrain, Bhutan, and Qatar are accepted for membership.
24 Sept.	Britain expels 105 Soviets suspected of espionage.
3 Oct.	Nguyen Van Thieu wins reelection as president of South Vietnam. He was unopposed in the election.
20–21 Oct.	West German chancellor Willy Brandt wins the Nobel Peace Prize. Chilean poet Pablo Neruda wins the Nobel Prize for literature.
25 Oct.	With U.S. support the United Nations votes to admit the People's Republic of China and to expel Taiwan.
10 Nov.	Fidel Castro begins a twenty-five-day visit to Chile.
19 Nov.	In Tokyo 1 person is killed and 1,785 are arrested during demonstrations over the return of Okinawa to Japan.
2 Dec.	Following demonstrations in Santiago over food shortages and the visit of Fidel Castro, Chilean president Salvador Allende Gossens decrees a state of emergency.
3 Dec.	War breaks out between India and Pakistan when Pakistan attacks Indian airfields. The two nations had been feuding over East Pakistan's moves toward independence. On 6 December India recognizes the independence of East Pakistan, now called Bangladesh. On 17 December a cease-fire is declared in the Indian-Pakistani War. On 20 December President Yahya Khan of Pakistan resigns and is replaced by Zulfikar Ali Bhutto.

1972

- Aleksandr Solzhenitsyn's novel *August 1914* is published.

- Italo Calvino's novel *Invisible Cities* is published.

- Tom Stoppard's play *Jumpers* premieres in London.

- Luis Buñuel's film *The Discreet Charm of the Bourgeoisie* premieres.

- Five weeks of fighting between the Tutsi and Hutu peoples in Burundi result in an estimated one hundred thousand deaths.

- Japan, Australia, and New Zealand establish diplomatic relations with the People's Republic of China.

- East and West Germany begin to normalize relations.

- North and South Korea attempt to normalize relations.

22 Jan.　Britain, Norway, Denmark, and Ireland seek admission to the European Economic Community.

24 Jan.　The Soviet Union becomes the first major power to recognize Bangladesh.

30 Jan.　In Northern Ireland thirteen die in renewed rioting.

13 Feb.　The Soviet Union wins eight gold medals as the Winter Olympics in Sapporo, Japan, are concluded.

12 Mar.　Indira Gandhi's Congress Party wins 70 percent of assembly seats in Indian national elections.

30 Mar.　Northern Ireland's prime minister and his cabinet resign following the British Parliament's adoption of a bill enabling Britain to rule Northern Ireland directly.

31 Mar.　North Vietnam launches a military offensive against South Vietnam across the demilitarized zone.

10 Apr.　Seventy nations sign a treaty banning the accumulation of biological warfare weapons.

15 May　The United States returns Okinawa to Japan.

17 May　The West German parliament approves nonaggression treaties with the Soviet Union and Poland.

21 May　A disturbed Hungarian refugee damages part of Michelangelo's *Pieta* at Saint Peter's Basilica in Rome.

1 June　Iraq and Syria seize the assets of Iraq Petroleum Company, a consortium of Western firms.

13 June　Israeli and Egyptian planes engage in air battles.

3 July　India and Pakistan sign a wide-ranging peace agreement.

18 July　Egypt expels Soviet military advisers and experts.

24 July　UN secretary-general Kurt Waldheim appeals to the United States to end its bombing of North Vietnam.

3 Aug.　Due to a dockworkers' strike, Britain declares a state of emergency.

16 Aug.　King Hassan II of Morocco survives an assassination attempt. The next day the Moroccan minister of defense, Gen. Mohammed Oufkir, commits suicide.

26 Aug.　Seven thousand athletes from 120 nations open the twentieth Summer Olympics in Munich, West Germany.

1 Sept.　After matches held in Reykjavík, Iceland, American Bobby Fischer defeats Boris Spassky of the U.S.S.R., winning the world chess championship.

5 Sept.　Eleven members of the Israeli Olympic squad are murdered by Arab terrorists in Munich, West Germany. Five terrorists and a policeman are killed in a subsequent airport shoot-out. Israel responds on 8 September with air raids against ten Arab guerrilla bases in Syria and Lebanon. The Olympic games conduct a memorial service on 6 September and conclude on 11 September.

17 Sept.　According to Uganda, Tanzania has launched an invasion with one thousand troops.

23 Sept.　Following a renewal of terrorism, President Ferdinand Marcos imposes martial law in the Philippines.

26 Sept. Voters in Norway reject membership in the European Economic Community.

2 Oct. Danish voters approve membership in the European Economic Community.

13 Oct. An Aeroflot flight crashes in Moscow, killing 176 people.

17 Oct. Martial law is declared in South Korea.

24 Oct. Political opponents of President Allende Gossens stage a "day of silence" to protest his Chilean government.

29 Oct. Following the hijacking of a German airline, Arab guerrillas win release of three Olympic terrorists.

30 Oct. Prime Minister Pierre Trudeau loses his parliamentary majority in Canadian general elections.

2 Nov. Following three weeks of strikes, President Allende Gossens of Chile restructures his cabinet.

4 Nov. The Bangladesh national assembly approves a new constitution.

17 Nov. After seventeen years of exile, former dictator Juan D. Perón returns to Argentina.

21 Nov. In the Golan Heights the heaviest fighting in two years breaks out between Israel and Syria.

1 Dec. The Irish Parliament passes a bill designed to crack down on the Irish Republican Army.

14 Dec. After a twenty-eight-day visit, Juan Perón leaves Argentina, refusing to accept the nomination for the presidency.

23 Dec. In Managua, Nicaragua, ten thousand people die and 80 percent of the city is destroyed as the result of an earthquake.

1973

- Iris Murdoch's novel *The Black Prince* is published.

- Octavio Paz's volumes of poetry *The Bow and the Lyre* and *Alternating Current* are published.

- Lindsay Anderson's film *O Lucky Man* premieres.

- Ingmar Bergman's film *Scenes from a Marriage* premieres.

- Robin Hardy's film *The Wicker Man* premieres.

- The Soviet Union agrees to abide by the Universal Copyright Convention and to cease publishing pirate editions of Western works.

17 Jan. Philippine president Ferdinand Marcos announces the indefinite continuation of martial law.

11 Feb. Gen. Alfredo Stroessner wins a fifth term as president of Paraguay.

21 Feb. Israeli jets shoot down a Libyan airliner over the Sinai Peninsula; 106 are killed.

2 Mar. One Belgian and two U.S. diplomats are murdered by Palestinian terrorists in Khartoum, Sudan.

12 Mar. China releases John T. Downey, a Central Intelligence Agency agent held in China since 1952.

17 Mar.	Following a bomb attack on the barracks of the presidential guard, President Lon Nol of Cambodia declares a state of emergency.
8 Apr.	Artist Pablo Picasso dies.
21 Apr.	The United Nations Security Council condemns Israel for military attacks in Lebanon and all acts of violence against human life.
11 May	A new sixteen-member cabinet, headed by Premier Joop den Uyl, is sworn in, ending a 163-day political crisis in the Netherlands.
15 May	In Paris gold reaches $128.50 an ounce — a new high.
1 June	The Greek Council of Ministers abolishes the monarchy and proclaims a republic.
7–11 June	West German chancellor Willy Brandt visits Israel.
8 June	Spanish dictator Francisco Franco appoints Adm. Luis Carrero Blanco premier of Spain, but he remains chief of state.
29 June	Troops loyal to Chilean president Salvador Allende Gossens crush an attempted coup.
3 July	The thirty-five-nation Conference on Security and Cooperation in Europe begins meetings in Helsinki, Finland.
10 July	Britain grants the Bahamas independence.
17 July	King Mohammad Zahir Shah of Afghanistan is overthrown in a military coup.
21 July	France test-detonates a nuclear device in the Pacific.
2 Aug.	Thirty-two members of the British Commonwealth begin a nine-day conference in Ottawa, Canada.
5 Aug.	Arab terrorists attack the airport in Athens, Greece, killing three and injuring fifty-five.
19 Aug.	George Papadopoulos is sworn in as the first president of Greece.
28 Aug.	Indian officials agree to repatriate ninety thousand Pakistani prisoners taken in the 1971 Indian-Pakistani War.
1 Sept.	Libya nationalizes 51 percent of all assets of oil companies located within the country.
5 Sept.	The fourth Conference of Nonaligned Nations meets in Algiers, Algeria.
11 Sept.	The Chilean government of Salvador Allende Gossens is overthrown by a military junta. Gossens is killed in the coup.
18 Sept.	The twenty-eighth meeting of the United Nations General Assembly votes to admit the Bahamas, East Germany, and West Germany as members.
23 Sept.	Juan Perón is elected president of Argentina.
29 Sept.	The Austrian government announces it will no longer permit the group emigration of Soviet Jews. In return Arab terrorists agree to release one Austrian and two Soviet Jews.
6 Oct.	War breaks out between Israel and the combined forces of Egypt and Syria.
16 Oct.	The Organization of Petroleum Exporting Countries (OPEC), led by the Arab states, announces an embargo on all oil destined for the United States and the Western industrialized countries.
24 Oct.	A cease-fire in the Middle East goes into effect.

27 Oct. In response to the United States forces being placed on worldwide military alert, the United Nations Security Council agrees, with Soviet concurrence, to send a peacekeeping force to the Middle East.

7 Nov. The United States and Egypt reestablish diplomatic relations, suspended since 1967.

11 Nov. Israel and Egypt sign a formal cease-fire.

25 Nov. George Papadopoulos is overthrown as president of Greece in a bloodless military coup.

29 Nov. Egyptian-Israeli peace talks collapse; machine-gun and mortar attacks between the two sides resume.

17 Dec. Arab terrorists attack a U.S. aircraft in Rome, killing thirty-one persons.

20 Dec. In Madrid, Spanish premier Luis Carrero Blanco is assassinated in a car explosion.

21 Dec. In Geneva the Arab-Israeli peace conference begins.

1974

- Patrick White's novel *The Eye of the Storm* is published.
- Graham Greene's novel *The Honorary Consul* is published.
- Philip Larkin's volume of poetry *High Windows* is published.
- Tom Stoppard's play *Travesties* premieres.
- David Hare's play *Knuckles* premieres.
- Federico Fellini's film *Amarcord* premieres.
- Louis Malle's film *Lacombe, Lucien* premieres.
- John le Carré's novel *Tinker, Tailor, Soldier, Spy*
- Aleksandr Solzhenitsyn's *The Gulag Archipelago* is published in English.
- During the summer, civil war in Cyprus provokes an international confrontation between Greece and Turkey.
- In June American president Richard Nixon conducts a whirlwind tour of the Middle East and the Soviet Union.
- During the summer, floods in India and Bangladesh kill fourteen hundred people.
- The Soviet Union conducts several Soyuz space-station missions.
- Bangladesh, Grenada, and Guinea-Bissau are admitted to the United Nations.
- The Palestine Liberation Organization (PLO) gains substantial support in the United Nations.
- India and Pakistan move to normalize relations.
- The Reverend F. Donald Coggan becomes the 101st archbishop of Canterbury.
- In Ethiopia Emperor Haile Selassie attempts to placate a rebellious military by appointing Edalkachew Makonnen premier and increasing army wages.

18 Jan.	Israel and Egypt sign an accord on military disengagement.
19 Jan.	Five Soviet citizens are expelled from China for espionage.
3 Feb.	Communist Party chairman Mao Tse-tung launches a new cultural revolution in China.
13 Feb.	Nobel Prize–winning novelist Aleksandr Solzhenitsyn is deported from the Soviet Union.
22 Feb.	Pakistan recognizes Bangladesh, formerly East Pakistan.
28 Feb.	Neither the ruling Conservative Party nor the Labour Party gains a majority in British parliamentary elections.
3 Mar.	When a Turkish jumbo jet crashes outside of Paris, 346 people are killed in the worst air disaster in history.
4 Mar.	Liberal Party head Edward Heath resigns as British prime minister and is replaced by Labour Party leader Harold Wilson. The new government ends a two-month-old coal strike on 6 March.
10 Mar.	Premier Golda Meir and a new cabinet assume power in Israel.
2 Apr.	President of France Georges Pompidou dies at age sixty-two.
9 Apr.	India, Pakistan, and Bangladesh sign an agreement to repatriate all Pakistani prisoners of war.
12 Apr.	Israel raids several villages in southern Lebanon following an Arab terrorist attack on Qiryat Shemona which killed eighteen.
15 Apr.	President Hamani Diori of Niger is overthrown in a military coup.
22 Apr.	Israel's Labor Party nominates Yitzhak Rabin to replace Golda Meir, who resigned on 10 April as premier.
25 Apr.	Army officers in Portugal announce the end of forty years of authoritarian rule.
6 May	Assuming responsibility for a spy scandal, West German chancellor Willy Brandt resigns. Helmut Schmidt is elected the new chancellor on 16 May.
9 May	Canadian prime minister Pierre Trudeau loses a vote of confidence. The House of Commons schedules parliamentary elections for 8 July.
18 May	India explodes a nuclear weapon.
19 May	Finance Minister Valéry Giscard d'Estaing is elected president of France.
28 May	Prime Minister Gough Whitlam and the Labour Party win the Australian parliamentary election.
29 May	Following the resignation of the coalition government of Northern Ireland, a fifteen-day general strike ends. Great Britain assumes temporary governmental control over the province.
31 May	Israel and Syria sign a troop disengagement agreement.
3 June	The Israeli parliament installs Yitzhak Rabin as the head of a new three-party coalition government.
16 June	The United States and Syria announce that they will resume diplomatic relations.
17 June	China and France conduct separate atmospheric nuclear tests.

24 June	Prime Minister Harold Wilson announces that Great Britain recently conducted underground nuclear tests.
27 June	France and Iran sign a developmental agreement that includes the sale of nuclear reactors to Iran.
28 June	More than two hundred people die in a landslide ninety-five miles east of Bogota, Colombia.
1 July	Following the death of her husband, Juan D. Perón, seventy-eight, Isabel Perón assumes the presidency of Argentina.
7 July	West Germany wins the World Cup, defeating the Netherlands 2–1.
8 July	Pierre Trudeau and the Liberal Party win a majority in Canada's parliamentary elections.
15 July	In Cyprus the military overthrows the government of Archbishop Makarios.
20 July	Turkish troops invade Cyprus by air and sea.
14 Aug.	Greece withdraws from the North Atlantic Treaty Organization (NATO).
15 Aug.	Mrs. Park Chung Hee, wife of South Korea's president, is killed in an assassination attempt on her husband.
19 Aug.	United States ambassador Rodger P. Davies, fifty-three, is killed in Cyprus.
4 Sept.	The United States and East Germany establish formal diplomatic relations.
10 Sept.	The Republic of Guinea-Bissau, formerly Portuguese Guinea, is granted independence by Portugal.
12 Sept.	Emperor Haile Selassie of Ethiopia (1930–1934, 1941–1974) is deposed in a military coup.
17 Sept.	Abdelaziz Bouteflika, foreign minister of Algeria, is elected president of the twenty-ninth General Assembly of the United Nations.
8 Oct.	Eisaku Sato, former prime minister of Japan, and Sean MacBride of Ireland, United Nations commissioner for South-West Africa, win the 1974 Nobel Peace Prize.
10 Oct.	Prime Minister Harold Wilson wins a three-seat majority for the Labour Party in Great Britain's second general election of 1974.
14 Oct.	A draft resolution approved by the United Nations General Assembly invites the Palestine Liberation Organization to participate in United Nations deliberations.
20 Oct.	A proposal calling for the deportation of half of the foreign population of Switzerland is rejected by Swiss voters.
21 Oct.	Mexico announces the discovery of oil fields in southeastern Mexico.
28 Oct.	Arab heads of state meeting in Rabat, Morocco, call for the creation of an independent Palestinian state.
30 Oct.	A Security Council resolution expelling South Africa from the United Nations is vetoed by the United States, Britain, and France.
12 Nov.	The United Nations General Assembly suspends South Africa from participation in the remainder of the 1974 session.
16 Nov.	The United Nations creates the World Food Conference to administer worldwide antihunger programs.

18 Nov.	Premier Konstantinos Karamanlis and his New Democracy Party win the first Greek parliamentary elections held in ten years.
22 Nov.	The United Nations General Assembly grants observer status to the Palestine Liberation Organization.
26 Nov.	Following a series of alleged financial scandals, Japanese prime minister Kakuei Tanaka resigns, to be replaced on 9 December by Takeo Miki.
5 Dec.	Premier Aldo Moro wins a vote of confidence from the Italian senate.
7 Dec.	Archbishop Makarios returns to Cyprus and resumes control of the government.
8 Dec.	In a national referendum Greek citizens vote to abolish the monarchy.
11 Dec.	Following prolonged fighting, the white minority government of Rhodesia and black nationalists agree to a cease-fire.
25 Dec.	A cyclone destroys 90 percent of Darwin, Australia, and kills fifty people.
28 Dec.	In northern Pakistan fifty-two hundred people are killed in an earthquake.
29 Dec.	The government of Nicaragua agrees with leftist guerrillas to an exchange of political prisoners.

1975

- V. S. Naipaul's novel *Guerrillas* is published.
- Paul Scott's novel *A Division of Spoils,* which completes the Raj quartet, is published.
- Gabriel García Márquez's novel *Autumn of the Patriarch* is published.
- Mario Vargas Llosa's novel *Conversation in the Cathedral* is published.
- Werner Herzog's film *Every Man for Himself and God Against All* premieres.
- Harold Pinter's play *No Man's Land* premieres.
- Ending five hundred years of colonial rule, Portugal grants independence to Angola, Mozambique, the Cape Verde Islands, and lesser African possessions.
- The Soviet Union continues to send cosmonauts to its orbiting space station, setting new records for manned spaceflight.
- The United States and the Soviet Union conduct the joint *Apollo–Soyuz* space mission — the first time manned spacecraft from different nations rendezvous in space.
- The United Nations declares 1975 International Women's Year.

17 Jan.	The People's Republic of China adopts a new constitution.
11 Feb.	Margaret Thatcher becomes the first woman to head a British political party when she is elected leader of the Conservatives.
12 Feb.	A South Korean national referendum approves the government of Park Chung Hee.
13 Feb.	Turkish Cypriots declare a separate state in the northern section of Cyprus.
25 Feb.	The Greek government arrests twenty-five military officers charged with plotting a coup.

27 Feb.   A Philippine national referendum supports the martial law declared by President Ferdinand Marcos.

28 Feb.   The European Economic Community signs a trade pact with forty-six developing nations in Africa, the Pacific, and the Caribbean.

2 Mar.   Shah Mohammed Reza Pahlavi dissolves the political system in Iran and declares it a one-party state for the next two years.

4 Mar.   Ethiopia's military government nationalizes all rural land.

11 Mar.   Portugal's provisional government defeats a military coup.

25 Mar.   King Faisal of Saudi Arabia is assassinated by a nephew and is succeeded by his half brother Khalid.

13 Apr.   President Ngarta Tombalbaye, who led Chad to independence in 1960, is killed in a military coup.

14 Apr.   Voters in Sikkim approve referendums abolishing the monarchy and merging with India.

17 Apr.   The capital of Cambodia, Phnom Penh, falls to the Communist army of the Khmer Rouge, ending a five-year civil war.

22 Apr.   A bloodless coup in Honduras ousts Gen. Oswaldo López Arellano.

30 Apr.   The capital of South Vietnam, Saigon, falls to the Communist army of the North Vietnamese, ending the Vietnam War.

11 May   The European Economic Community and Israel sign a trade and cooperation pact.

13–14 May   Cambodia seizes the U.S. merchant ship *Mayaguez*. Following a rescue effort by the U.S. military, the ship and crew are released.

15 May   Following weeks of violence, Portugal declares martial law in Angola.

28 May   Meeting in Lagos, Nigeria, officials of fifteen west African nations agree to form the Economic Community of West African States.

5 June   Egypt formally opens the Suez Canal, closed since the 1967 Arab-Israeli War.

7 June   UN discussions between Greek and Turkish Cypriot leaders end without an agreement on the future of the island.

9 June   Greece adopts a new constitution.

10 June   Uganda's president Idi Amin releases British citizen Denis Hills, whom Amin had condemned to death for his criticism of Amin.

13 June   Iraq and Iran sign a treaty of reconciliation, fixing national boundaries and ending Iranian support of Iraq's Kurdish rebels.

17 June   The Italian Communist Party polls 33.4 percent of the vote in regional elections.

26 June   Following her conviction for illegal election practices, India's prime minister Indira Gandhi declares a state of emergency and imprisons her political foes.

29 June   The Organization of American States votes to end the ban on diplomatic and commercial relations with Cuba.

4 Aug.   The Japanese Red Army seizes the United States Embassy in Kuala Lumpur, Malaysia, demanding the release of five comrades imprisoned in Japan in exchange for the fifty-three American hostages. On 8 August their terms are met, and the Americans are released.

6 Aug.	The Indian Parliament approves retroactive changes in the election law under which Prime Minister Gandhi was convicted of campaign violations.
15 Aug.	Sheik Mujibar Rahman, president of Bangladesh, is assassinated in a military coup.
18 Aug.	China and Cambodia sign an agreement on economic cooperation.
29 Aug.	Juan Velasco Alvarado, president of Peru, is overthrown in a military coup.
1 Sept.	Guillermo Rodriguez Lara, president of Ecuador, defeats a military coup.
2 Sept.	The nation with the world's fourth largest foreign-aid budget, Canada, announces that it will concentrate its resources on the world's forty poorest countries.
4 Sept.	Israel and Egypt sign an interim agreement on the disposition of the Sinai Peninsula and the Suez Canal.
6 Sept.	An earthquake in eastern Turkey kills 2,312 people.
9 Sept.	After five years of exile in China, Prince Norodom Sihanouk, deposed leader of Cambodia, returns to his nation.
16 Sept.	Papua New Guinea is granted independence and commonwealth status by Great Britain.
1 Oct.	The Organization of Petroleum Exporting Countries raises crude oil prices 10 percent.
16 Oct.	After a month-long leave of absence, Isabel Perón returns to the presidency of Argentina.
21 Oct.	A nationwide postal strike in Canada begins.
7 Nov.	Citing retroactive changes in the election code, India's supreme court reverses an earlier conviction of Prime Minister Indira Gandhi for election fraud.
10 Nov.	By a vote of seventy-two to thirty-five, the United Nations approves a resolution that condemns Zionism as a form of racism.
11 Nov.	For the first time in history the governor-general of Australia, Sir John Kerr, removes the prime minister and dissolves parliament.
25 Nov.	After three hundred years of colonial rule, Suriname is granted independence by the Netherlands.
3 Dec.	The Pathet Lao announce the abolition of the monarchy and the creation of a coalition government in Laos.
5 Dec.	Britain ends the practice of detaining suspected terrorists from Northern Ireland without trial.
14 Dec.	In Beilin, Holland, twenty-three captives are released by terrorists demanding the independence of South Moluccas from Indonesia.
21 Dec.	An attempted coup against the Argentine government of Isabel Perón is thwarted.

1976

- Tom Stoppard's play *Dirty Linen and New-Found-Land* premieres.
- François Truffaut's film *Small Change* premieres.
- Nicholas Roeg's film *The Man Who Fell to Earth* premieres.

- Lina Wertmuller's film *Seven Beauties* premieres.

- Manuel Puig's novel *Kiss of the Spider Woman* is published.

- Muriel Spark's novel *The Takeover* is published.

- Chaos and political maneuvers for power follow the deaths in China of both Mao Tse-tung and Chou En-lai.

- Civil war between Communist and non-Communist factions in Angola breaks out.

- Civil war and sectarian violence plague Beirut and other areas of Lebanon. Syria intervenes with armed troops.

- India normalizes relations with China.

- The supersonic Concorde begins transatlantic service.

- Britain and Iceland engage in a brief "cod war" — a dispute over North Atlantic fishing rights.

- Vietnam formally reunifies.

- The Seychelles become independent.

- Negotiations are conducted to turn Rhodesia over to black majority rule.

- Liechtensteiner women gain the right to vote in local elections.

1 Jan.   Venezuela nationalizes its oil industries.

7 Jan.   Prime Minister Aldo Moro's Italian cabinet resigns.

10 Feb.   Aldo Moro forms a one-party minority government in Italy.

26 Feb.   With the agreement of Spain, Morocco and Mauritania annex the territory of the former Spanish Sahara.

5 Mar.   Britain's secretary of state for Northern Ireland, Merlyn Rees, dismisses the seventy-eight-seat Northern Ireland Convention and announces that Britain will govern Northern Ireland directly.

16 Mar.   Prime Minister Harold Wilson of Britain resigns to be succeeded by Foreign Secretary James Callaghan on 5 April.

24 Mar.   President Isabel Perón of Argentina is overthrown in a military coup. Lt. Gen. Jorge Videla assumes power.

25 Apr.   Socialists win a plurality of votes in Portugal's first free parliamentary elections in fifty years.

30 Apr.   The Italian government of Aldo Moro collapses.

5 May   Delegates from 153 nations meet in Nairobi, Kenya, for the fourth United Nations Conference on Trade and Development.

15–19 May   Violent anti-Israeli riots by Arabs result in the deaths of three protesters.

20–21 May   North Atlantic Treaty Organization foreign ministers meet in Oslo, Norway.

16 June   Rioting breaks out in South Africa following protests against the use of the Afrikaans language in South African schools. Three days later, when the riots subside, more than one hundred persons, most of them black, will have died.

22 June   Following national elections, Italian Communists gain forty-nine seats in the chamber of deputies and twenty-three seats in the senate.

23 June	The United States vetoes the admission of Angola to the United Nations.
3 July	Israeli commandos raid Entebbe Airport in Uganda and free ninety-one passengers and twelve crew members of an Air France jet hijacked by Palestinian terrorists on 27 June.
27 July	In Japan former prime minister Kakuei Tanaka is arrested for financial misconduct.
30 July	In Italy Prime Minister Giulio Andreotti leads a new minority government.
7 Aug.	Uganda and Kenya sign a treaty restoring diplomatic relations.
11 Aug.	Palestinian terrorists kill four and wound thirty in the airport in Istanbul, Turkey.
12 Aug.	Thirty-five to forty persons are killed following a week of rioting in South Africa.
20 Aug.	Right-wing extremists murder forty-six people in Argentina in retaliation for the assassination of a retired army general.
1 Sept.	Political upheaval following a proposal to increase prison sentences for members of the Irish Republican Army results in the declaration of a state of emergency.
21 Sept.	The thirty-first session of the United Nations General Assembly elects H. S. Amerasinghe of Sri Lanka as president.
3 Oct.	Chancellor Helmut Schmidt's Social Democratic Party wins a narrow majority in West German parliamentary elections.
22 Oct.	President Cearbhall O. Dalaigh of Ireland resigns to be succeeded on 9 November by Patrick J. Hillery.
1 Nov.	President Michel Micombero of Burundi is overthrown in a bloodless military coup. Col. Jean-Baptiste Bagaza assumes power.
15 Nov.	In Quebec's provincial elections René Lévesque's separatist Parti Québécois wins a majority.
26 Nov.	Roman Catholicism is no longer recognized as the state religion of Italy.
15 Dec.	Prime Minister Michael Manley of Jamaica leads his People's National Party to overwhelming victory in parliamentary elections.
17 Dec.	The Organization of Petroleum Exporting Countries announces a 5 percent increase in wholesale oil prices from Saudi Arabia and the United Arab Emirates and a 10 percent increase in the cost of oil from the other eleven organization members.
20 Dec.	Prime Minister Yitzhak Rabin of Israel dissolves parliament and calls for elections.

1977

- Günter Grass's novel *Der Butt* is published.
- Margaret Drabble's novel *The Ice Age* is published.
- John le Carré's novel *The Honourable Schoolboy* is published.
- Hugh Leonard's play *Da* premieres.
- Kenji Mizoguchi's film *A Geisha* premieres.
- Andrej Wajda's film *Man of Marble* premieres.

- Great Britain grants independence to the Solomon Islands.

- Brazil moves toward military rule.

- The Soviet Union begins a round of diplomatic overtures in black Africa.

- Djibouti becomes an independent republic.

- Political violence and instability plague Turkey.

6 Jan. In Czechoslovakia 240 prominent intellectuals sign Charter 77, demanding human rights as spelled out in the Helsinki accords of 1975.

18 Jan. Indian prime minister Indira Gandhi announces parliamentary elections in March, the first held since a state of emergency was declared in 1975.

24 Jan. Discussions over black majority rule in Rhodesia break down.

9 Feb. Spain and the Soviet Union resume diplomatic relations, suspended since the Spanish Civil War.

23 Feb. Following President Carter's criticism of his human rights record, Ugandan president Idi Amin forbids two hundred Americans from leaving Uganda. On 1 March he rescinds the travel ban.

7 Mar. At the opening of the fifty-nine nation Arab-African conference in Cairo, Saudi Arabia announces $1 billion in assistance to black Africa.

20 Mar. In a surprising defeat Indira Gandhi and her Congress Party lose the Indian parliamentary election. Morarji R. Desai of the Janata Party succeeds Gandhi as prime minister.

27 Mar. In the Canary Islands two jumbo jets collide, killing more than 570 people, in the worst air disaster in history.

21 Apr. Following weeks of political unrest, Pakistani prime minister Zulfikar Ali Bhutto imposes martial law in three cities.

30 Apr. An oil spill from a platform in the North Sea is finally capped, after twenty thousand metric tons of crude oil had been released.

5–9 May Leaders of five Western nations and Japan meet in London for economic discussions.

17 May Menachem Begin's Likud Party wins an upset victory over the Labour Party in Israeli parliamentary elections.

3 June In Paris discussions regarding the world economic order between wealthy and poor nations end inconclusively.

11 June Dutch marines storm a hijacked train in northern Holland, where South Molluccan terrorists, seeking independence from Indonesia, held fifty-one hostages, some of whom were schoolchildren. Six terrorists and two hostages are killed in the raid.

5 July The forty-eight member Organization of African Unity ends a four-day conference in Libreville, Gabon.

31 July Riots break out during an antinuclear rally in Creys-Malville, France.

26 Aug. The province of Quebec passes Bill 101, making French the official — and principal — language of the province.

3 Sept. Former Pakistani prime minister Zulfikar Ali Bhutto is arrested and charged with conspiracy to murder his political opponents.

15 Sept. South African police arrest twelve hundred black students mourning the mysterious prison death of black nationalist leader Steven Biko on 12 September. His burial, on 25 September, is attended by representatives of thirteen Western nations.

20 Sept. President Idi Amin of Uganda bans, as "security risks," twenty-seven religious organizations from his country.

26 Sept. After ten days of heavy fighting between Israeli-backed Christians and Palestinians on Lebanon's southern border, a cease-fire is declared.

28 Sept. The mysterious Pol Pot, only recently identified as the leader of the Cambodian Communist Party, arrives in Peking for discussions.

3 Oct. Former Indian prime minister Indira Gandhi is arrested on two counts of corruption in office; the charges are later dropped.

10 Oct. Mairead Corrigan and Betty William, two peace activists from Northern Ireland, are named winners of the 1976 Nobel Peace Prize; Amnesty International, the human rights organization, wins the 1977 prize.

31 Oct. In the United Nations Security Council the Western nations veto a UN resolution seeking to impose strict economic sanctions against South Africa. The United Nations does pass an arms embargo on 4 November.

13 Nov. Charging that the U.S.S.R. and Cuba supported Ethiopia in its land dispute with Somalia, Somalia expels all Soviet advisers and breaks diplomatic relations with Cuba.

20 Nov. In a breakthrough for Middle Eastern peace, Egyptian president Anwar as-Sadat journeys to Jerusalem and addresses the Israeli parliament.

5 Dec. Hard-line Arab states, meeting in Tripoli, Libya, denounce Egyptian president Sadat's peace overtures to Israel.

26 Dec. President Sadat of Egypt and Israeli prime minister Begin continue peace discussions in Egypt.

31 Dec. Cambodia and Vietnam break off diplomatic relations.

1978

- David Malouf's novel *An Imaginary Life* is published.
- Georges Simenon's novel *The Girl with a Squint* is published.
- Iris Murdoch's novel *The Sea, The Sea* is published.
- Harold Pinter's play *Betrayal* premieres.
- Tom Stoppard's play *Night and Day* premieres.
- David Hare's play *Plenty* premieres.
- Franco Brusati's film *Bread and Chocolate* premieres.
- The cosmonauts of *Soyuz 27* spend a record ninety-six days in space.
- The United Nations hosts a monthlong conference on disarmament.
- Indochinese "boat people" seek asylum in Malaysia, Thailand, and the United States.

4 Jan. Gen. Augusto Pinochet of Chile confirms his dictatorship by plebiscite.

10 Jan.	Following the assassination of Pedro Joaquin Chamorro, publisher of the antigovernment newspaper *La Prensa,* rioting engulfs Managua, Nicaragua.
20 Jan.	President Suharto of Indonesia bans several newspapers and moves to suppress student dissent.
24 Jan.	Fragments of a radioactive Soviet satellite crash into a remote area of Canada's Northwest Territories.
7 Feb.	A nationwide general strike that began on 23 January ends in Managua, Nicaragua. On 12 February members of the Sandinista National Liberation Front announce they are preparing for civil war.
16 Mar.	Former Italian premier Aldo Moro, leader of the Christian Democratic Party, is kidnapped in Rome by Red Brigades terrorists. The Italian government refuses to release fifteen imprisoned terrorists in return for Moro, and his corpse is discovered on 9 May.
17 Mar.	The *Amoco Cadiz* runs aground near Brest, France, spilling oil along the Brittany coast in the worst oil spill in history.
18 Mar.	Former Pakistani prime minister Zulfikar Ali Bhutto is sentenced to death for having ordered an assassination attempt on a political opponent.
24 Mar.	Ethiopia declares it has reestablished full control over the southeastern Ogaden region after an eight-month conflict with Somalia.
3 Apr.	China and the European Economic Community sign a five-year trade agreement.
9 Apr.	Following the first parliamentary elections since 1972, antigovernment demonstrators are arrested and charged with sedition in the Philippines.
21 Apr.	In Florence, Italy, paintings valued at over $1 million, including Peter Paul Rubens's masterpiece *The Three Graces,* are stolen.
30 Apr.	A military coup takes place in Kabul, Afghanistan. Nur Mohammad Taraki heads the new regime.
4 May	South African troops raid guerrilla bases of the South-West Africa People's Organization located in Angola.
11 May	Antigovernment riots, led by Muslim fundamentalists, sweep Iran.
15 May	Peruvians angered at an austerity program implemented by the military government and the International Monetary Fund riot. On 19 May elections are canceled. On 22 May a two-day general strike is called.
18 May	Italy legalizes abortion.
22 May	Belgian troops rescue twenty-five hundred Europeans trapped in fighting between Zaire and the Congo.
23 June	Following a fifteen-week trial, twenty-nine members of the Red Brigades are sentenced to prison in Turin, Italy.
25 June	Argentina defeats the Netherlands, 3–1, to win the World Cup soccer championship.
3 July	China terminates all economic assistance to Vietnam.
14 July	Soviet dissident Anatoly B. Scharansky is sentenced to thirteen years in prison for espionage. Scharansky had been a leading critic of the Soviet policy toward Jewish emigration.

19 July	After many business relocate to English-speaking Ontario, Quebec modifies Bill 101 — the 1977 law mandating the use of French in Quebec.
25 July	In England the first successful birth of a human test-tube baby occurs.
10 Aug.	The ten provincial premiers of Canada unanimously reject Prime Minister Pierre Trudeau's plan for a new Canadian constitution.
12 Aug.	Japan and China sign a ten-year treaty of peace.
22 Aug.	In Managua, Nicaragua, twenty-five Sandinista guerrillas seize the National Palace, killing six guards and wounding dozens of others. Holding hundreds hostage, they secure the release of fifty-nine prisoners, five hundred thousand dollars in ransom, and safe passage to Panama. In September fighting breaks out between Sandinistas and government troops in several provincial towns.
8 Sept.	Following massive antigovernment demonstrations in twelve cities and hundreds of deaths in Tehran, Shah Mohammad Reza Pahlavi declares martial law in Iran.
17 Sept.	Israeli prime minister Menachem Begin, Egyptian president Anwar as-Sadat, and U.S. president Jimmy Carter conclude eleven days of peace negotiations at Camp David, Maryland. The discussions end with the signing of a framework for a formal peace treaty to be concluded before the end of the year.
20 Sept.	Italian Red Brigades leader Corrado Alunni is sentenced to twelve years in prison for illegal possession of firearms.
26 Sept.	China and Vietnam end diplomatic talks after China accuses Vietnam of a troop buildup on its border.
28 Sept.	Pieter Willem Botha succeeds B. J. Vorster as prime minister of South Africa.
12 Oct.	Border clashes between Uganda and Tanzania occur over a disputed area known as the Kagera Salient.
31 Oct.	In Iran forty thousand petroleum workers go on strike, halving Iranian oil exports.
2 Nov.	Two Soviet cosmonauts set a new 139-day spaceflight record.
3 Nov.	Vietnam and the Soviet Union sign a twenty-five-year peace treaty.
5 Nov.	Former prime minister Indira Gandhi wins election to India's lower house of parliament.
5 Dec.	Afghanistan and the Soviet Union sign a twenty-year treaty of friendship.
27–30 Dec.	The shah of Iran attempts to quell revolutionary activity by passing the government to Shahpur Bakhtiar, a leading government critic. The Bakhtiar effort fails, and on 30 December he is expelled from the opposition National Front.

1979

- Milan Kundera's novel *The Book of Laughter and Forgetting* is published.

- V. S. Naipaul's novel *A Bend in the River* is published.

- Es'kia Mpthalhele's novel *Chirundu* is published.

- John le Carré's novel *Smiley's People* is published.

- Rolf Schneider's novel *November* is published.

- Luchino Visconti's film *The Innocent* premieres.

- Volker Schlondorff's film *The Tin Drum* premieres.

- Rainer Werner Fassbinder's films *The Marriage of Maria Braun* and *Third Generation* premiere.

- Caryl Churchill's play *Cloud Nine* premieres.

- Brian Clark's play *Whose Life Is It Anyway?* premieres.

- Peter Shaffer's play *Amadeus* premieres.

- Hugh Leonard's play *A Life* premieres.

- Rhodesia continues to move toward black majority rule.

1 Jan.   The United States and China establish formal diplomatic relations.

7 Jan.   The Cambodian capital of Phnom Penh falls to the Kampuchean United Front, ousting the Khmer Rouge regime of Pol Pot.

16 Jan.   Shah Mohammed Reza Pahlavi of Iran leaves his nation for a "vacation," widely presumed to be political exile.

19 Jan.   President Anastasio Somoza Debayle rejects a plebiscite, supervised by the Organization of American States, designed to end the civil war in Nicaragua.

1 Feb.   After fifteen years in exile, the Ayatollah Ruhollah Khomeini returns to Iran from France to establish a fundamentalist Islamic state.

17 Feb.   Following repeated border clashes, several hundred thousand Chinese troops invade Vietnam.

22 Feb.   Following the assassination of U.S. ambassador Adolph Dubs, and because of an increasing Soviet presence, the United States cuts aid to Afghanistan.

24 Feb.   Fighting breaks out along the border of North and South Yemen.

5 Mar.   China announces the withdrawal of its troops from Vietnam.

13 Mar.   On the small Caribbean island of Grenada, Prime Minister Eric Gairy is ousted in a bloodless coup by Maurice Bishop, leader of the New Jewel Movement.

14 Mar.   India and the Soviet Union sign treaties of economic and scientific cooperation.

18 Mar.   Kurdish rebels in Iraq's northwestern province attack government troops.

26 Mar.   In Washington, D.C., Israel and Egypt sign a peace treaty ending thirty-one years of war.

26 Mar.   Canadian prime minister Pierre Elliott Trudeau dissolves Parliament and sets national elections for 22 May.

27 Mar.   In Afghanistan the pro-Communist Revolutionary Council names Hafizullah Amin prime minister.

28 Mar.   The British House of Commons votes no confidence in the government of Prime Minister James Callaghan, who resigns. Elections are set for 3 May.

29 Mar.   North and South Yemen provisionally agree to end their border conflict and unite under one government.

31 Mar.   The eighteen-nation Arab League denounces Egypt for its peace treaty with Israel.

4 Apr.	Former prime minister Zulfikar Ali Bhutto of Pakistan is hanged on charges of conspiring to murder a political opponent. Hundreds are arrested the next day in antigovernment protests.
11 Apr.	Tanzanian troops capture the Ugandan capital of Kampala, deposing Ugandan president Idi Amin and installing a new government under Yusufu Lule.
12 Apr.	In Geneva five years of international negotiations conclude in the General Agreement on Tariffs and Trade, reducing world tariffs by an average of 33 percent.
27 Apr.	The United States exchanges two Soviet spies in return for five leading Soviet dissidents, including Aleksandr Ginzburg.
3 May	The Conservative Party defeats the Labour Party in British national elections, making Conservative leader Margaret Thatcher the nation's first woman prime minister.
8 May	Police in El Salvador kill twenty-three and wound seventy during antigovernment demonstrations in San Salvador.
22 May	In Canadian national elections the Progressive Conservative Party wins a plurality of votes. Progressive Conservative leader Joe Clark replaces Liberal Party head Pierre Elliott Trudeau as prime minister.
24 May	President Carlos Humberto Romero of El Salvador suspends the constitution and declares a thirty-day state of siege.
2–10 June	Pope John Paul II visits his native Poland.
20 June	President Yusufu Lule of Uganda is ousted in a bloodless coup by Godfrey Binaisa.
11 July	The International Whaling Commission, meeting in London, bans hunting in the Red Sea, the Arabian Sea, and most of the Indian Ocean for ten years.
16 July	Iraqi president Ahmad Hassan al-Bakr resigns, citing poor health, and appoints Saddam Hussein, chairman of the Revolutionary Command Council and the armed forces, as his successor.
17 July	President Anastasio Somoza Debayle of Nicaragua resigns and goes into exile. Two days later the Sandinista rebels take the capital of Managua, ending the Nicaraguan civil war.
23 July	Ayatollah Ruhollah Khomeini bans music broadcasting in Iran, arguing that it has corrupted Iranian youth. The prohibition follows other bans against men and women swimming together, most Western movies, alcohol, and singing by women.
13 Aug.	China announces a new program to limit population growth by discouraging couples from having more than one child.
18 Aug.	Muslim rebels in Afghanistan announce the formation of an insurgent government.
19 Aug.	Two Soviet cosmonauts set a new 175-day spaceflight record.
27 Aug.	The Irish Republican Army explodes a bomb on a fishing boat off the Irish coast, killing Earl Mountbatten of Burma, cousin to Queen Elizabeth of Britain.
13 Sept.	In Peking's Tiananmen Square nearly one thousand people attend a protest against Communist Party privileges.

21 Sept. Britain and France announce the cancelation of the supersonic Concorde program. Citing prohibitive expenses, they parcel out the remaining seven unsold aircraft to Air France and British Airways.

12 Oct. President Fidel Castro of Cuba addresses the United Nations, denouncing the United States and calling for grants and loans for developing nations.

15 Oct. The military government of Gen. Carlos Humberto Romero of El Salvador is overthrown in a military coup.

24 Oct. The deposed shah of Iran is admitted to a New York hospital for a gallbladder operation and cancer treatments.

26 Oct. President Park Chung Hee of South Korea is assassinated by the head of the South Korean Central Intelligence Agency.

4 Nov. Iranian militants storm the United States embassy in Tehran, seizing ninety hostages and precipitating an international crisis which will result in UN economic sanctions against Iran and an increasing U.S. military presence in the Persian Gulf.

20 Nov. Several hundred armed Islamic extremists seize the Grand Mosque in Mecca. More than 150 people die when Saudi troops retake the mosque.

21 Nov. In Pakistan Islamic extremists angered at reports that the United States and Israel were involved in the seizure of the Grand Mosque in Mecca attack the U.S. embassy in Islamabad.

3 Dec. Puerto Rican nationalists kill two American sailors outside the Sabana Seca naval communications center. On 9 December another attack occurs outside the Roosevelt Roads naval base.

13 Dec. The Canadian supreme court rules that portions of Quebec's Bill 101, mandating the use of French language in the province, are unconstitutional.

14 Dec. A vote of no confidence in the Canadian House of Commons topples the Progressive Conservative government of Joe Clark. New elections are scheduled for February 1980.

15 Dec. The shah of Iran leaves the United States to take up residence in Panama.

27 Dec. Following a Soviet-inspired military coup that results in the execution of President Hafizullah Amin, the Soviet Union invades Afghanistan with tens of thousands of troops.

THE ARTS

by JIM ZRIMSEK

CONTENTS

Sidebars and tables are listed in italics.

1970

Movies
Airport, starring Burt Lancaster and Dean Martin; *Catch-22*, directed by Mike Nichols; *Diary of a Mad Housewife*, starring Carrie Snodgress and Richard Benjamin; *Five Easy Pieces*, starring Jack Nicholson and Karen Black; *Little Big Man*, directed by Arthur Penn and starring Dustin Hoffman and Faye Dunaway; *Love Story*, starring Ryan O'Neal and Ali McGraw; *M*A*S*H*, directed by Robert Altman and starring Donald Sutherland and Elliott Gould; *Patton*, starring George C. Scott.

Fiction
Richard Bach, *Jonathan Livingston Seagull;* Saul Bellow, *Mr. Sammler's Planet;* Thomas Berger, *Vital Parts;* James Dickey, *Deliverance;* Joan Didion, *Play It as It Lays;* Lois Gould, *Such Good Friends;* Jerzy Kosinski, *Being There;* Toni Morrison, *The Bluest Eye;* William Saroyan, *Days of Life and Death;* Erich Segal, *Love Story;* Irwin Shaw, *Rich Man, Poor Man;* Leon Uris, *QBVII.*

Popular Songs
The Beatles, "Let It Be" and "The Long and Winding Road"; the Carpenters, "Close to You"; the Guess Who, "American Woman"; the Jackson Five, "I Want You Back," "ABC," "I'll Be There," and "The Love You Save"; Led Zeppelin, "Whole Lotta Love"; Melanie, "Lay Down (Candles in the Rain)"; the Partridge Family, "I Think I Love You"; Diana Ross, "Ain't No Mountain High Enough"; Carly Simon, "That's the Way I Always Heard It Should Be"; Simon and Garfunkel, "Bridge Over Troubled Water"; Sly and the Family Stone, "Thank You (Falettin' Me Be Mice Elf Agin)" and "Everybody Is a Star"; Smokey Robinson and the Miracles, "Tears of a Clown"; Edwin Starr, "War."

- An "information" exhibition, highlighting the fusion of art, text, sound, light, and video, is held in New York City at the Museum of Modern Art.

- "American Top 40," a weekly countdown of hits on the pop music charts hosted by Casey Kasem, debuts on nationwide radio.

- The recording industry introduces quadriphonic discs.

- Crosby, Stills, Nash and Young record "Ohio," protesting the killing of four students by the National Guard at Kent State University.

- The film and soundtrack album *Woodstock* are released.

- Jimi Hendrix chokes to death after a heavy dose of drugs and alcohol; Janis Joplin dies less than three weeks later of a drug overdose.

5 Feb.
Who Cares?, choreographed by George Balanchine and featuring the music of George Gershwin, is performed for the first time by the New York City Ballet.

25 Feb.
Two Vincent Van Gogh paintings are auctioned for a record $2.175 million in New York City.

10 Mar.
The National Endowment for the Arts grants $706,000 to twelve symphony and opera companies.

11 July
The Twentieth Annual Marlboro Music Festival opens in Marlboro, Vermont.

29 Sept.
Paul Mellon donates Paul Cézanne's *The Artist's Father*, valued at $1.5 million, to the National Gallery of Art, Washington, D.C.

30 Nov.
In the first concert ever held in New York City's Saint Patrick's Cathedral, Leopold Stokowski conducts the Metropolitan Opera Orchestra.

11 Dec.
The Soviet Union cancels the planned 1971 U.S. tour of the Bolshoi Ballet and opera companies, citing provocation by Zionists.

1971

Movies

Billy Jack, directed by and starring Tom Laughlin; *Carnal Knowledge,* directed by Mike Nichols and starring Jack Nicholson, Art Garfunkel, Ann-Margret, and Candace Bergen; *A Clockwork Orange,* directed by Stanley Kubrick; *Dirty Harry,* starring Clint Eastwood; *The French Connection,* directed by William Friedkin and starring Gene Hackman; *The Hospital,* starring George C. Scott; *Klute,* starring Jane Fonda and Donald Sutherland; *The Last Picture Show,* directed by Peter Bogdanovich and starring Jeff Bridges, Cybill Shepherd, and Cloris Leachman; *McCabe and Mrs. Miller,* directed by Robert Altman and starring Warren Beatty and Julie Christie; *Play Misty for Me,* starring Clint Eastwood; *Shaft,* directed by Gordon Parks and starring Richard Roundtree.

Fiction

William Peter Blatty, *The Exorcist;* E. L. Doctorow, *The Book of Daniel;* James P. Donleavy, *The Onion Eaters;* Ernest J. Gaines, *The Autobiography of Miss Jane Pittman;* Bernard Malamud, *The Tenants;* Mary McCarthy, *Birds of America;* Walker Percy, *Love in the Ruins;* Harold Robbins, *The Betsy;* John Updike, *Rabbit Redux.*

Popular Songs

The Bee Gees, "How Can You Mend a Broken Heart?"; Cher, "Gypsies, Tramps and Thieves"; Alice Cooper, "Eighteen"; the Doors, "Riders on the Storm"; Marvin Gaye, "What's Goin' On"; Hamilton, Joe, Frank and Reynolds, "Don't Pull Your Love"; George Harrison, "My Sweet Lord"; Isaac Hayes, "Theme from Shaft"; Janis Joplin, "Me and Bobby McGee"; Carole King, "It's Too Late" and "I Feel the Earth Move"; Led Zeppelin, "Black Dog" and "Stairway to Heaven"; John Lennon, "Imagine"; Paul and Linda McCartney, "Uncle Albert/Admiral Halsey"; Melanie, "Brand New Key"; the Osmonds, "One Bad Apple"; the Rolling Stones, "Brown Sugar"; Sly and the Family Stone, "Family Affair"; Rod Stewart, "Maggie May" and "Reason to Believe"; the Temptations, "Just My Imagination"; Three Dog Night, "Joy to the World."

- Margaret Harris becomes the first black woman to lead a major orchestra, conducting the Chicago Symphony.

- Alan Jay Lerner, Dorothy Fields, and Duke Ellington are among the first to be inducted into the Songwriter's Hall of Fame.

- George Harrison organizes the Concert for Bangladesh, a benefit concert to aid victims of starvation in that region.

17 May

The rock musical *Godspell* opens on Broadway.

July

The first major microfiche collection of books — the Library of American Civilization — is delivered to subscribers.

3 July

Jim Morrison, lead singer of the Doors, dies of a suspected drug overdose.

11 July

Thousands pay tribute to the late jazz trumpeter Louis Armstrong at a public funeral in New Orleans.

8 Sept.

The Kennedy Center for the Performing Arts opens in Washington, D.C.

12 Oct.

The rock musical *Jesus Christ Superstar,* written by Andrew Lloyd Webber and Tim Rice, produced by Robert Stigwood, and starring Yvonne Elliman and Ben Vereen, opens on Broadway.

1972

Movies

Cabaret, directed by Bob Fosse and starring Liza Minnelli, Michael York, and Joel Grey; *Deliverance,* starring Jon Voight and Burt Reynolds; *The Godfather,* directed by Francis Ford Coppola and starring Marlon Brando, Al Pacino, James Caan, Robert Duvall, Diane Keaton, and Talia Shire; *Lady Sings the Blues,* starring Diana Ross, Billy Dee Williams, and Richard Pryor; *The Poseidon Adventure,* directed by Irwin Allen and starring Gene Hackman; *Sounder,* starring Cicely Tyson and Paul Winfield; *Superfly,* directed by Gordon Parks and starring Ron O'Neal.

Fiction

Louis Auchincloss, *I Come as a Thief;* James Baldwin, *No Name in the Street;* Michael Crichton, *The Terminal Man;* John W. Gardner, *The Sunlight Dialogues;* Ira Levin, *The Stepford Wives;* Arthur Mizener, *The Saddest Story;* Chaim Potok, *My Name Is Asher Lev;* Irving Wallace, *The Ward;* Eudora Welty, *The Optimist's Daughter;* Herman Wouk, *The Winds of War.*

Popular Songs

America, "A Horse With No Name"; Chuck Berry, "My Ding-a-Ling"; the Chi-Lites, "Oh Girl"; Mac Davis, "Baby Don't Get Hooked on Me"; Sammy Davis, Jr., "The Candy Man"; Donna Fargo, "The Happiest Girl in the Whole USA"; Roberta Flack, "The First Time Ever I Saw Your Face"; Al Green, "Let's Stay Together"; Looking Glass, "Brandy (You're a Fine Girl)"; Curtis Mayfield, "Freddie's Dead"; Don McLean, "American Pie"; Johnny Nash, "I Can See Clearly Now"; Nilsson, "Without You"; the O'Jays, "Back Stabbers"; Gilbert O'Sullivan, "Alone Again Naturally"; Billy Paul, "Me and Mrs. Jones"; Elvis Presley, "Burnin' Love"; Helen Reddy, "I Am Woman"; the Spinners, "I'll Be Around"; the Staple Singers, "I'll Take You There"; the Temptations, "Papa Was a Rollin' Stone"; Bill Withers, "Lean on Me"; Neil Young, "Heart of Gold."

- The rock musical *Hair* ends its Broadway run after 1,742 performances.

- New York City radio station WCBS-FM becomes the first to adopt an oldies format.

- In New York City the exhibition "Sharp-Focus Realism" is held at the Sidney Janis Gallery.

- Don McLean's "American Pie" becomes the longest song ever to hit number one, clocking in at eight minutes.

14 Feb. The musical *Grease* opens on Broadway.

17 June *Fiddler on the Roof* becomes the longest-running show in Broadway history, with 3,225 performances.

22 Aug. American audiences are exposed for the first time to British comedy troupe Monty Python with the release of their film *And Now for Something Completely Different.*

16 Oct. Henry Lewis becomes the first African-American to conduct the New York Metropolitan Opera House Orchestra.

23 Oct. *Pippin,* directed by Bob Fosse and starring Ben Vereen and Jill Clayburgh, opens on Broadway.

1973

Movies

American Graffiti, directed by George Lucas and starring Richard Dreyfuss, Ron Howard, Cindy Williams, Harrison Ford, and Suzanne Somers; *Badlands*, directed by Terence Malick and starring Martin Sheen and Sissy Spacek; *The Exorcist*, directed by William Friedkin and starring Ellen Burstyn and Linda Blair; *The Harder They Come*, starring Jimmy Cliff; *The Last Detail*, directed by Hal Ashby and starring Jack Nicholson; *Mean Streets*, directed by Martin Scorcese and starring Harvey Keitel and Robert De Niro; *Paper Moon*, directed by Peter Bogdanovich and starring Ryan O'Neal and Tatum O'Neal; *Serpico*, starring Al Pacino; *Sleeper*, directed by Woody Allen and starring Allen and Diane Keaton; *The Sting*, starring Robert Redford, Paul Newman, and Robert Shaw; *The Way We Were*, starring Barbra Streisand and Robert Redford; *What's Up, Doc?*, starring Barbra Streisand and Ryan O'Neal.

Fiction

Thomas Berger, *Regiment of Women*; John Cheever, *The World of Apples*; Alice Childress, *A Hero Ain't Nothin' But a Sandwich*; Leon Forrest, *There Is a Tree More Ancient Than Eden*; Erica Jong, *Fear of Flying*; Jerzy Kosinski, *The Devil Tree*; Bernard Malamud, *Rembrandt's Hat*; Iris Murdoch, *The Black Prince*; Marge Piercy, *Small Changes*; Thomas Pynchon, *Gravity's Rainbow*; Paul Theroux, *Saint Jack*; Kurt Vonnegut, Jr., *Breakfast of Champions*.

Popular Songs

The Carpenters, "Top of the World"; Cher, "Half Breed"; Jim Croce, "Bad Bad Leroy Brown" and "Time in a Bottle"; Roberta Flack, "Killing Me Softly"; Gladys Knight and the Pips, "Midnight Train to Georgia"; Grand Funk Railroad, "We're an American Band"; Elton John, "Crocodile Rock" and "Goodbye Yellow Brick Road"; Eddie Kendricks, "Keep on Truckin' "; Vicki Lawrence, "The Night the Lights Went Out in Georgia"; Curtis Mayfield, "Superfly"; Maureen McGovern, "The Morning After"; the O'Jays, "Love Train"; Paul McCartney and Wings, "My Love" and "Live and Let Die"; Billy Preston, "Will It Go Round in Circles"; Charlie Rich, "The Most Beautiful Girl in the World"; the Rolling Stones, "Angie"; Diana Ross, "Touch Me in the Morning"; Carly Simon, "You're So Vain"; Ringo Starr, "Photograph"; Stories, "Brother Louie"; Tony Orlando and Dawn, "Tie a Yellow Ribbon"; Barry White, "I'm Gonna Love You Just a Little More, Baby"; Stevie Wonder, "Superstition" and "You Are the Sunshine of My Life."

- Jasper Johns's *Double White Map* is sold for $240,000, the highest price ever paid to a living American artist at that time.

- A new Friday night television concert series, *Midnight Special*, debuts with Helen Reddy as host.

- The International Dance Council is established under the auspices of UNESCO.

- *Enter the Dragon*, starring martial artist Bruce Lee, is released, sparking a nationwide Kung Fu craze.

6 Feb.

The New York Times reports that the Soviet Union has agreed to loan forty-one paintings by European masters to show in U.S. galleries.

25 Feb.

Stephen Sondheim's *A Little Night Music*, featuring the song "Send in the Clowns," opens on Broadway.

Mar.

Pink Floyd releases their landmark album *The Dark Side of the Moon*. It remains on the *Billboard* Top 200 Albums chart for 741 weeks — 14 1/4 years.

4 Apr.

Elvis Presley's Hawaiian concert, taped earlier in the year, is televised to a huge audience.

2 May Forty-seven artworks from the Norton Simon Collection are sold in New York City for $6.7 million.

10 May Harold Lawrence, manager of the London Symphony Orchestra, is named to succeed Helen Thompson as manager of the New York Philharmonic.

1974

Movies *Airport 1975*, starring Charlton Heston, Karen Black, George Kennedy, and Helen Reddy; *Alice Doesn't Live Here Anymore*, directed by Martin Scorcese and starring Ellen Burstyn, Kris Kristofferson, and Jodie Foster; *Blazing Saddles*, directed by Mel Brooks and starring Cleavon Little and Gene Wilder; *Chinatown*, directed by Roman Polanski and starring Jack Nicholson and Faye Dunaway; *Claudine*, starring Diahann Carroll and James Earl Jones; *The Conversation*, directed by Francis Ford Coppola and starring Gene Hackman; *Death Wish*, starring Charles Bronson; *Earthquake*, starring Charlton Heston and George Kennedy; *The Godfather Part II*, directed by Francis Ford Coppola and starring Al Pacino, Robert De Niro, Robert Duvall, Talia Shire, and Diane Keaton; *The Great Gatsby*, starring Robert Redford, Mia Farrow, and Karen Black; *Lenny*, directed by Bob Fosse and starring Dustin Hoffman; *The Towering Inferno*, directed by Irwin Allen and starring Paul Newman and Steve McQueen; *Uptown Saturday Night*, directed by Sidney Poitier and starring Poitier, Bill Cosby, and Richard Pryor; *Young Frankenstein*, directed by Mel Brooks and starring Gene Wilder.

Fiction James Baldwin, *If Beale Street Could Talk*; Donald Barthelme, *Guilty Pleasures*; Peter Benchley, *Jaws*; Joseph Heller, *Something Happened*; James Michener, *Centennial*; Albert Murray, *Train Whistle Guitar*; Cornelius Ryan, *A Bridge Too Far*; John Updike, *Buchanan Dying*; Irving Wallace, *The Fan Club*.

Popular Songs Paul Anka, "You're Havin' My Baby"; Bachman-Turner Overdrive, "You Ain't Seen Nothin' Yet" and "Takin' Care of Business"; Bo Donaldson and the Heywoods, "Billy, Don't Be a Hero"; Brownsville Station, "Smokin' in the Boys' Room"; Harry Chapin, "Cat's in the Cradle"; Cher, "Dark Lady"; Eric Clapton, "I Shot the Sheriff"; Dionne Warwick and the Spinners, "Then Came You"; Carl Douglas, "Kung Fu Fighting"; Roberta Flack, "Feel Like Makin' Love"; Grand Funk Railroad, "The Loco-Motion"; Hues Corporation, "Rock the Boat"; Terry Jacks, "Seasons in the Sun"; Elton John, "Don't Let the Sun Go Down on Me" and "The Bitch Is Back"; Gordon Lightfoot, "Sundown"; George McCrae, "Rock Your Baby"; Olivia Newton-John, "I Honestly Love You"; Paper Lace, "The Night Chicago Died"; Paul McCartney and Wings, "Band on the Run"; Ray Stevens, "The Streak"; Barbra Streisand, "The Way We Were"; The Stylistics, "You Make Me Feel Brand New"; Barry White, "Can't Get Enough of Your Love, Babe."

- "Open Circuits," an international conference on video art, is held in New York City at the Museum of Modern Art.

- *People*, an offshoot of *Time* magazine focusing on celebrities and "real life" stories, begins publishing. Mia Farrow, star of *The Great Gatsby*, is pictured on the cover of the first issue.

- The Ramones, a band in the "garage" tradition whose fast, loud three-chord sound will usher in the American punk rock movement, begins playing at the New York City club CBGB.

- Disco, a beat-driven dance music already popular in the black and gay communities, begins to find mainstream success with hits such as "Rock the Boat," "Rock Your Baby," and "Kung Fu Fighting."

12 Feb. The rock club The Bottom Line opens in New York City.

19 Feb. Dick Clark launches the American Music Awards.

6 Mar. The film rights to Bob Woodward and Carl Bernstein's best-selling investigation of Watergate, *All the President's Men,* are sold for $450,000.

18 Apr. Allen Ginsberg wins the National Book Award for Poetry.

16 May Leonard Bernstein's *The Dybbuk,* choreographed by Jerome Robbins, is premiered by the New York City Ballet.

9 Sept. The Senate approves a copyright reform bill requiring jukebox operators to pay royalties to composers and music publishers.

1975

Movies   *Barry Lyndon,* directed by Stanley Kubrick and starring Ryan O'Neal; *Cooley High,* directed by Michael Schultz; *Dog Day Afternoon,* directed by Sydney Lumet and starring Al Pacino; *Jaws,* directed by Steven Spielberg and starring Robert Shaw, Roy Scheider, and Richard Dreyfuss; *Love and Death,* directed by Woody Allen and starring Allen and Diane Keaton; *Mahogany,* starring Diana Ross and Billy Dee Williams; *Nashville,* directed by Robert Altman; *One Flew Over the Cuckoo's Nest,* directed by Milos Forman and starring Jack Nicholson and Louise Fletcher; *The Rocky Horror Picture Show,* starring Tim Curry, Susan Sarandon, and Barry Bostwick; *Shampoo,* starring Warren Beatty, Julie Christie, and Goldie Hawn; *Tommy,* directed by Ken Russell and starring Roger Daltrey and Ann-Margret.

Fiction   Saul Bellow, *Humboldt's Gift;* Thomas Berger, *Sneaky People;* E. L. Doctorow, *Ragtime;* Jerzy Kosinski, *Cockpit;* Larry McMurtry, *Terms of Endearment;* Toni Morrison, *Sula;* Vladimir Nabokov, *Tyrants Destroyed;* Reynolds Price, *The Surface of Earth;* Judith Rossner, *Looking for Mr. Goodbar;* John Updike, *A Month of Sundays;* Joseph Wambaugh, *The Choirboys.*

Popular Songs   America, "Sister Golden Hair"; the Bee Gees, "Jive Talkin' "; David Bowie, "Fame"; Glen Campbell, "Rhinestone Cowboy"; the Captain and Tennille, "Love Will Keep Us Together"; John Denver, "Thank God I'm a Country Boy"; the Doobie Brothers, "Black Water"; the Eagles, "Best of My Love" and "One of These Nights"; Earth Wind & Fire, "Shining Star"; Fleetwood Mac, "Rhiannon"; Grand Funk Railroad, "Bad Time"; Elton John, "Island Girl" and "Philadelphia Freedom"; KC and the Sunshine Band, "Get Down Tonight" and "That's the Way (I Like It)"; Labelle, "Lady Marmalade"; Led Zeppelin, "Kashmir"; Barry Manilow, "Mandy"; Van McCoy, "The Hustle"; Michael Murphey, "Wildfire"; Olivia Newton-John, "Have You Never Been Mellow"; Ohio Players, "Fire"; Ozark Mountain Daredevils, "Jackie Blue"; Paul McCartney and Wings, "Listen to What the Man Said"; Pilot, "Magic"; Queen, "Killer Queen"; Minnie Ripperton, "Lovin' You"; Linda Ronstadt, "You're No Good"; Neil Sedaka, "Bad Blood" and "Laughter in the Rain"; Silver Connection, "Fly Robin Fly"; Donna Summer, "Love to Love You Baby"; Sweet, "Ballroom Blitz" and "Fox on the Run"; 10cc, "I'm Not in Love"; Tony Orlando and Dawn, "He Don't Love You (Like I Love You)"; Dwight Twilley Band, "I'm on Fire"

- Elton John's *Captain Fantastic and the Browndirt Cowboy* becomes the first album to debut at number one on the *Billboard* album chart. His follow-up release, *Rock of the Westies,* also debuts at number one.

- Bruce Springsteen becomes the first and only rock performer to appear on the covers of *Time* and *Newsweek* in the same week, amid the hype for his album *Born to Run.*

- *The Rocky Horror Picture Show,* an offbeat musical about a Transylvanian transvestite, is released and soon gains cult status.

5 Jan. The all-black musical *The Wiz* opens on Broadway, eventually tallying 1,672 performances.

17 Apr. President Gerald Ford becomes the first U.S. president since Abraham Lincoln to attend a performance at Washington's Ford Theater.

5 Sept. The United States and the Soviet Union agree to five major art exchanges over the next five years.

1976

Movies *All the President's Men,* starring Robert Redford and Dustin Hoffman; *Carrie,* directed by Brian DePalma and starring Sissy Spacek and John Travolta; *Car Wash,* directed by Michael Schultz and starring Richard Pryor; *Family Plot,* directed by Alfred Hitchcock; *Logan's Run,* starring Michael York and Farrah Fawcett; *Network,* directed by Sidney Lumet and starring Faye Dunaway, William Holden, Peter Finch, and Robert Duvall; *The Omen,* starring Gregory Peck and Lee Remick; *Rocky,* starring Sylvester Stallone and Talia Shire; *A Star Is Born,* starring Barbra Streisand and Kris Kristofferson; *Taxi Driver,* directed by Martin Scorcese and starring Robert De Niro, Harvey Keitel, Cybill Shepherd, and Jodie Foster.

Fiction John Gardner, *October Light;* Ira Levin, *The Boys from Brazil;* Marge Piercy, *Woman on the Edge of Time;* Paul Theroux, *The Family Arsenal;* Leon Uris, *Trinity;* Gore Vidal, *1876;* Kurt Vonnegut, *Slapstick;* Alice Walker, *Meridian;* Irving Wallace, *The R Document.*

Popular Songs Aerosmith, "Dream On"; Bay City Rollers, "Saturday Night"; The Bee Gees, "You Should Be Dancing"; Bellamy Brothers, "Let Your Love Flow"; Chicago, "If You Leave Me Now"; The Four Seasons, "December 1963 (Oh, What a Night)"; Elton John and Kiki Dee, "Don't Go Breakin' My Heart"; Gordon Lightfoot, "The Wreck of the Edmund Fitzgerald"; Barry Manilow, "I Write the Songs"; C. W. McCall, "Convoy"; Steve Miller Band, "Rock 'n Me"; Paul McCartney and Wings, "Silly Love Songs"; Queen, "Bohemian Rhapsody"; Vickie Sue Robinson, "Turn the Beat Around"; Diana Ross, "Love Hangover" and "Theme from *Mahogany*"; Paul Simon, "50 Ways to Leave Your Lover"; Starland Vocal Band, "Afternoon Delight"; Rod Stewart, "Tonight's the Night"; Johnnie Taylor, "Disco Lady"; Andrea True Connection, "More More More"; Wild Cherry, "Play That Funky Music"

- "Women Artists: 1550–1950," a retrospective exhibit, begins a national tour at the Los Angeles County Museum of Art.

- Conductor Arthur Fiedler and pianist Arthur Rubinstein are awarded the Medal of Freedom by President Gerald Ford. Rubinstein later retires from recitals due to blindness.

- Ragtime composer Scott Joplin, whose rags were popularized by the film *The Sting,* is awarded a posthumous Pulitzer Prize.

- Elton John performs an entire week of sold-out concerts in Madison Square Garden, breaking all attendance records for the venue.

- Peter Frampton's *Frampton Comes Alive!* becomes the biggest-selling live album ever released.

- The Recording Industry Association of America creates the Platinum Award for singles selling one million copies and albums selling two million copies. The first platinum single is "Disco Lady" by Johnnie Taylor; the first platinum album is *The Eagles/Their Greatest Hits 1971–1975.*

- Lasers are used in a rock show for the first time, by the Who.

- The exhibit "Two Centuries of Black American Art" opens at the Los Angeles County Museum of Art.

- Saul Bellow wins the Nobel Prize for literature.

12 Jan. The National Endowment for the Arts awards grants totaling over $8 million to one hundred orchestras.

30 Jan. The first "Live from Lincoln Center" telecast features the New York Philharmonic with Andre Previn as conductor and Van Cliburn as pianist.

18 May An all-star concert, the highlight of a $6.5 million fund-raising drive to restore Carnegie Hall in New York City, features Leonard Bernstein, Vladimir Horowitz, and Isaac Stern.

24 June Joseph Papp's New York Shakespeare Festival opens, featuring *Henry V* with Paul Rudd and Meryl Streep.

30 June *Swan Lake,* performed by the American Ballet Theater at Lincoln Center, becomes the first full-length ballet to be telecast live.

4 July The works of ten U.S. sculptors are unveiled along a 455-mile stretch of interstate highway in Nebraska.

21 July *Guys and Dolls* is revived on Broadway with an all-black cast.

4 Aug. Gian Carlo Menotti's Symphony No. 1, commissioned for the bicentennial, premieres in New York City.

6 Oct. Jackson Pollock's last privately owned painting, *Lavender Mist,* is sold to the National Gallery of Art for $2 million.

6 Nov. *Gone With the Wind* is broadcast on network television for the first time, setting a new Nielsen ratings record.

1977

Movies

Annie Hall, directed by Woody Allen and starring Allen and Diane Keaton; *Close Encounters of the Third Kind,* directed by Steven Spielberg and starring Richard Dreyfuss; *The Goodbye Girl,* directed by Herbert Ross and starring Richard Dreyfuss and Marsha Mason; *Julia,* directed by Fred Zinneman and starring Jane Fonda, Vanessa Redgrave, and Jason Robards; *New York, New York,* directed by Martin Scorcese and starring Robert De Niro and Liza Minnelli; *Saturday Night Fever,* starring John Travolta; *Smokey and the Bandit,* starring Burt Reynolds and Sally Field; *Star Wars,* directed by George Lucas and starring Mark Hamill, Harrison Ford, and Carrie Fisher; *The Turning Point,* directed by Herbert Ross and starring Anne Bancroft, Shirley MacLaine, and Mikhail Baryshnikov.

Fiction

Louis Auchincloss, *The Dark Lady;* John Cheever, *Falconer;* Richard Condon, *The Abandoned Woman;* Robert Coover, *The Public Burning;* Sarah Davidson, *Loose Change;* Joan Didion, *A Book of Common Prayer;* Leon Forrest, *The Bloodworth Orphans;* Marilyn French, *The Women's Room;* Jerzy Kosinski, *Blind Date;* James Alan McPherson, *Elbow Room;* Toni Morrison, *Song of Solomon;* Paul Theroux, *Consul's File.*

Popular Songs

Abba, "Dancing Queen"; Debby Boone, "You Light Up My Life"; Bill Conti, "Gonna Fly Now (Theme from *Rocky*)"; the Eagles, "Fly Like an Eagle" and "Hotel California"; Emotions, "Best of My Love"; Fleetwood Mac, "Dreams"; Andy Gibb, "I Just Want to Be Your Everything"; Hall and Oates, "Rich Girl"; Thelma Houston, "Don't Leave Me This Way"; Mary MacGregor, "Torn Between Two Lovers"; Meco, "*Star Wars* Theme"; Rose Royce, "Car Wash"; Barbra Streisand, "Love Theme from *A Star Is Born* (Evergreen)"; Stevie Wonder, "Sir Duke."

- The national tour "Treasures of Tutankhamen," featuring Egyptian artifacts from King Tut's tomb, draws the largest attendance in history for an art show.

- Studio 54, the first celebrity disco, opens in New York City.

- Fleetwood Mac's album *Rumours* sells over eight million copies, holds the number one album slot on the *Billboard* chart for thirty-one weeks, and becomes the first album to produce four Top 10 singles. It remains on the chart for 3 1/2 years.

20 Feb.

Alex Haley's *Roots* is listed by *The New York Times* as the top-selling book in the country for twenty consecutive weeks.

21 Apr.

The musical *Annie,* produced by Mike Nichols, opens on Broadway, eventually notching 2,377 performances.

26 May

Beatlemania, a mixed-media concert featuring Beatles songs performed by Beatles look-alikes, opens in New York City.

26 June

Elvis Presley makes his last concert appearance, in Indianapolis.

30 June

The Newport Jazz Festival announces a move to Saratoga Springs, New York, citing prohibitive costs.

19 Aug.

Elvis Presley dies of heart failure at age forty-two.

15 Oct.

The Metropolitan Opera performs *La Boheme,* marking its first live television broadcast. Renata Scotto and Luciano Pavarotti star.

1978

22 Nov.	The J. Paul Getty Museum in California reportedly pays between $3.5 and $5 million for a fourth-century bronze, a record price for sculpture.

Movies
The Buddy Holly Story, starring Gary Busey; *Coming Home,* directed by Hal Ashby and starring Jane Fonda and Jon Voight; *Days of Heaven,* directed by Terence Malick and starring Richard Gere; *The Deer Hunter,* directed by Michael Cimino and starring Robert De Niro, Meryl Streep, and Christopher Walken; *Grease,* starring John Travolta and Olivia Newton-John; *Heaven Can Wait,* directed by Warren Beatty and starring Beatty and Julie Christie; *Interiors,* directed by Woody Allen and starring Diane Keaton and Geraldine Page; *Midnight Express,* starring Brad Davis; *National Lampoon's Animal House,* starring John Belushi; *An Unmarried Woman,* starring Jill Clayburgh.

Fiction
Louis Auchincloss, *The Country Cousin;* John Cheever, *The Stories of John Cheever;* Ernest J. Gaines, *In My Father's House;* John Irving, *The World According to Garp;* Judith Krantz, *Scruples;* Herman Wouk, *War and Remembrance.*

Popular Songs
The Bee Gees, "How Deep Is Your Love," "Night Fever," and "Stayin' Alive"; the Commodores, "Three Times a Lady"; Yvonne Elliman, "If I Can't Have You"; Exile, "Kiss You All Over"; Andy Gibb, "(Love Is) Thicker Than Water" and "Shadow Dancing"; Billy Joel, "Just the Way You Are"; Paul McCartney and Wings, "With a Little Luck"; Gerry Rafferty, "Baker Street"; the Rolling Stones, "Miss You"; Donna Summer, "Last Dance" and "MacArthur Park"; A Taste of Honey, "Boogie Oogie Oogie"; John Travolta and Olivia Newton-John, "You're the One That I Want"; Frankie Valli, "Grease"; Village People, "Macho Man" and "Y.M.C.A."

- The National Gallery of Art in Washington, D.C., opens the East Building, dedicated to modern art.

- Richard Rodgers and Arthur Rubinstein are honored at the Kennedy Center in New York City.

- Isaac Bashevis Singer wins the Nobel Prize for literature, the second American writer to win in three years.

- Christina Crawford creates a stir with the best-seller *Mommie Dearest,* a scathing portrait of her late mother, actress Joan Crawford.

Jan.	The English punk rock band the Sex Pistols breaks up in the middle of its first American tour when singer Johnny Rotten quits the band.
4 Jan.	The top-selling paperback in the country, *Close Encounters of the Third Kind,* is a novelization of a film script.
13 Apr.	An elaborate financial plan is announced to save Radio City Music Hall in New York City, known for its Rockettes dancers and Music Hall Symphony.
24 Apr.	The Soviet press agency Tass reports that painter Andrew Wyeth has been elected honorary member of the Soviet Academy of Arts.
9 May	*Ain't Misbehavin',* an all-black musical featuring the music of Fats Waller, opens on Broadway, eventually racking up 1,604 performances.
20 July	John D. Rockefeller III bequeaths his American art collection to the Fine Arts Museum in San Francisco and to the Asia Society in New York City.

27 Dec.   Three paintings by Paul Cézanne, valued at between $2.5 and $3 million, are discovered to be missing from the Art Institute in Chicago.

1979

Movies   *Alien*, starring Sigourney Weaver; *All That Jazz*, directed by Bob Fosse and starring Roy Scheider and Jessica Lange; *Apocalypse Now*, directed by Francis Ford Coppola and starring Martin Sheen, Robert Duvall, and Marlon Brando; *The China Syndrome*, starring Jane Fonda, Jack Lemmon, and Michael Douglas; *Kramer vs. Kramer*, starring Dustin Hoffman and Meryl Streep; *Manhattan*, directed by Woody Allen and starring Allen, Diane Keaton, and Meryl Streep; *Norma Rae*, starring Sally Field; *Rock 'n' Roll High School*, starring the Ramones; *10*, directed by Blake Edwards and starring Dudley Moore, Bo Derek, and Julie Andrews.

Fiction   Jerzy Kosinski, *Passion Play;* Norman Mailer, *The Executioner's Song;* Bernard Malamud, *Dubin's Lives;* Philip Roth, *The Ghost Writer;* Isaac Bashevis Singer, *Old Love;* William Styron, *Sophie's Choice;* John Updike, *Too Far to Go;* Alice Walker, *Goodnight, Willie Lee, I'll See You in the Morning.*

Popular Songs   Herb Alpert, "Rise"; the Bee Gees, "Tragedy"; Blondie, "Heart of Glass"; Chic, "Good Times" and "Le Freak"; the Doobie Brothers, "What a Fool Believes"; Gloria Gaynor, "I Will Survive"; Michael Jackson, "Don't Stop Til You Get Enough"; the Knack, "My Sharona"; M, "Pop Musik"; Peaches and Herb, "Reunited"; Sister Sledge, "We Are Family"; Rod Stewart, "Do Ya Think I'm Sexy"; Donna Summer, "Bad Girls," "Hot Stuff," and "No More Tears (Enough Is Enough)"; Anita Ward, "Ring My Bell."

- Aaron Copland is honored at the Kennedy Center in New York City.

- The first digitally recorded album — Ry Cooder's *Bop Till You Drop* — is released.

- Chuck Berry serves a four-month prison term for income-tax evasion.

- Eleven people are trampled to death at a Who concert in Cincinnati when fans rush to find unassigned seating.

16 Mar.   *The China Syndrome*, a film depicting the shutdown of an unsafe nuclear reactor, opens just twelve days before a malfunction of a reactor at Three Mile Island in Pennsylvania leads to a near meltdown.

15 Sept.   Massachusetts adopts the nation's first lottery in support of the arts.

25 Sept.   The musical *Evita*, written by Andrew Lloyd Webber and Tim Rice and produced by Robert Stigwood, opens on Broadway, eventually running 1,567 performances.

25 Sept.   *Icebergs*, a long-lost painting by nineteenth-century landscape artist Frederick Edwin Church, is auctioned for a record $2.5 million.

OVERVIEW

Aftershocks. As the 1970s dawned, American society was still reeling from the political and social upheavals of the 1960s and the artistic explosions that accompanied them. Artists and their public alike were experiencing a period of freedom and taboo-breaking unprecedented in American history. Change was occurring so rapidly, in fact, that it earned sociologist Alvin Toffler's tag "future shock." When the smoke cleared there seemed to be little left that artists had not tried or audiences had not seen. Tom Wolfe declared that the novel was dead. Pop art had peaked. The commercial theater, as evidenced by the dearth of new Broadway hits, seemed equally exhausted of ideas. And popular music, one of the great unifying cultural forces of the 1960s, began to lose its impact as fans subdivided into small factions. Thus art in the 1970s became defined by fragmentation of artists and their audiences, the retreat from collective movements in favor of personal statements, and the desire to create new art forms by fusing existing forms.

What Next? In the wake of the artistic innovations of the 1960s, movements and art forms that had seemed groundbreaking or revolutionary played themselves out. Artists began to move in different directions. As the black and women's movements gathered momentum, some minorities used art to express new feelings of empowerment and identity. Others agreed with Wolfe that the 1970s were the "me decade." Exhausted by the revolutionary changes of the 1960s and disillusioned by the implosion of their utopian ideals, artists rejected statements as irrelevant and instead concentrated on personal artistic goals. Still others, and much of the art audience at large, took refuge in nostalgia, seeking comfort in images that reflected the "lost innocence" of a pre-1960s America. Whatever they embraced, many artists sensed that reaching a single mass audience was increasingly unlikely or even undesirable and that their commercial appeal, especially in the face of the nation's economic setbacks, was limited. The age of the artist as superstar seemed over. Unlike the 1950s and 1960s, which produced many celebrities in art, music, literature, and drama, the 1970s progressed with the majority of its biggest talents working far from the mainstream and appreciated by a select, usually underground, audience.

Redefinition. Despite the supposed death of many art forms, there were definite signs of new life throughout the decade. Dance achieved a new level of popularity with the public. Many fine artists were invigorated by the fusion of existing art forms into new ones. New styles of music, most notably disco and punk rock, surfaced from the urban underground. Playwrights were nurtured in Off-Broadway venues, allowing their unique talents to develop without overexposure or the need for yearly hits. The same attitude seemed to inspire a new generation of filmmakers, who turned away from Hollywood traditions in favor of pursuing highly personal visions. The result was that, for the first and perhaps the only time in American history, filmmakers became the most influential artists of their time. And, most important, the high visibility of the black and women's movements allowed minority artists to emerge as serious voices with which to be reckoned. As the decade neared its end, the tide turned, and the American public once again began to embrace commercialized culture, much of which had originated as highly personal or underground art but had eventually been absorbed into the mainstream.

Blacks. The 1970s will rightly be remembered as the decade when black artists and entertainers first came into their own, fostering a sense of pride and identity in the black community. As the decade began, soul music was flourishing as a popular musical form, and black pop artists were creating socially relevant music for a largely interracial audience. Several "blaxploitation" movies were marketed as commercial cinema created by and for blacks. Richard Pryor became a star in a string of successful comedy films. As Ben Vereen gained celebrity in stage musicals, James Earl Jones, Cicely Tyson, and Paul Winfield emerged as esteemed film actors. On Broadway all-black productions were finding large audiences. Plays by Ed Bullins, Ntozake Shange, Charles Walker, and Joseph A. Walker sought to raise black consciousness, as did novels by Leon Forrest, Ernest J. Gaines, and Albert Murray. Fiction writer James Alan McPherson and poet Maya Angelou won prizes for their works. The black artistic phenomenon of the decade was Alex Haley's historical narrative *Roots,* which won a special Pulitzer and became the best-seller of 1976. But interestingly, despite these many achievements, the black movement appeared to be losing momentum as the decade neared its end. Though the disco craze was propelled largely by black artists, it was intended for entertainment, not enlightenment.

Women. With the growing strength of the women's movement, many black women artists found themselves straddling a fence in the 1970s. Some wanted to communicate a feminist message of independence and self-realization while still addressing the black experience. Black performers Phoebe Snow and Joan Armatrading became part of a growing group of women singers writing their own material in the 1970s, a group which also included Janis Ian, Carole King, and Carly Simon. King became the most commercially successful female songwriter in history with her *Tapestry* album. Simon's "That's the Way I Always Heard It Should Be," Ian's "At Seventeen," and Helen Reddy's "I Am Woman" became feminist anthems. Poet-songwriter-vocalist Patti Smith was a main innovator of the punk-rock movement. Laurie Anderson made her name with avant-garde performances that merged music, video, and spoken words. Judy Chicago produced feminist art that celebrated female history and sexuality. In films actresses were seeking parts that reflected a feminist sensibility and were becoming role models in the process. Jane Fonda personified the radicalized screen woman of the 1970s, but she had strong company in Ellen Burstyn, Faye Dunaway, Barbra Streisand, Jill Clayburgh, Diane Keaton, Liza Minnelli, and British star Glenda Jackson. Meanwhile, popular novelists such as Erica Jong touched responsive chords among female readers with characters who sought independence, sexual freedom, and self-actualization.

Postmodern Fragments. Even as minorities struggled to redefine themselves and find new identities in the 1970s, so did the creators of fine art. Some turned to the burgeoning environmental movement for inspiration. They began merging nature with synthetic forms, creating high-concept works that were part sculpture, part architecture, and part organic. The idea these artists were seeking to convey was that there should be no statement in the work and that the creative process was as important as the finished product. Photo-realist painters and sculptors had a similar notion. In attempting to duplicate a face, body, or scene with photographic reality, they sought to make the act of painting or sculpture itself the subject of the piece. Fusion artists combined music, art, and dramatic elements within one work. Performance and body artists used their own skin and voices as their media. These artists stressed the concept of the piece over its outcome or final form. By manipulating time, urging viewer participation, or combining elements such as light, sound, video, dance, or spoken words, performance and body artists created a new kind of live theater that deliberately sought to provoke jarring or disquieting audience response.

Selling Out. Because they rejected the notion of their art as a commodity, many artists of the 1970s were able to explore avant-garde forms in a fearless and playful way that freed them from convention. But many American art lovers greeted such experiments with a mixture of bewilderment and distaste. Photography became the decade's most collected art form, and art buyers retreated toward established painters such as Picasso and Jackson Pollock. Although fusionists, muralists, realists, environmentalists, and theatrical artists rejected the artistic marketplace and the art-buying public, by the end of the decade Americans had begun to buy and collect salable art again, often at record prices. New artists hungry for recognition responded eagerly, preparing the art community for the commercial wave of the 1980s.

Nostalgia. Americans were gripped by a wave of nostalgia in the mid 1970s that affected movies, music, theater, dance, and even art. Andrew Wyeth enjoyed a resurgence of popularity, as did music from the 1950s and early 1960s, revisited in the films *American Graffiti* (1973) and *Grease* (1978). Other films harkened back to the 1920s, 1930s, and 1940s, and the accompanying nostalgia soundtracks (especially *The Sting* [1973]) sold in the millions. Don McLean's "American Pie" retraced the early days of rock 'n' roll. Big-band music made a comeback, and so did old Broadway musicals; the 1970s was the decade of revivals. Some speculated that the craze for "the good old days" was a reaction to the excesses and upheavals of the 1960s. Others saw the motivation as escape from the present-day troubles of Watergate, Vietnam, the energy crisis, and the recession. Whatever the reason, everything old was new again in the 1970s.

Dance Fever. While fine art struggled to redefine itself in the 1970s, dance came into its own as a popular art form, embraced by the public as never before. By the time John Travolta electrified audiences with his slick dance moves in *Saturday Night Fever* (1977) and *Grease*, Americans were already gyrating on disco dance floors. Ballet gained a wide following after the 1974 defection of Soviet dancer Mikhail Baryshnikov. His athletic grace and good looks made him a superstar with the American Ballet Theater and with the public, who began attending dance programs in record numbers. Twyla Tharp's imaginative pop choreography brought her national attention. Director Bob Fosse took choreography to new heights in film on the Broadway stage. Michael Bennett created *A Chorus Line* (1975), a musical about a group of struggling young dancers that went on to become the longest-running show on Broadway.

Theater's Growing Pains. The commercial theater struggled throughout the 1970s. The value-questioning dramas (such as those of Edward Albee, for example) and "shock-rock" musicals (*Hair*) of the 1960s had already lost much of their impact. As with art, there was a sense that every issue had already been exhausted, every taboo broken. Shifting public tastes, the ailing economy, and a lack of new publicized playwrights all contributed to an alarming scarcity of quality productions in the early 1970s. In fact, there were so few new plays of merit that no Pulitzer Prize was given for drama in 1972 or 1974.

Musical hits were just as rare, and most of these were revivals. Even Stephen Sondheim, a composer of the innovative musicals *Company* (1970), *Follies* (1971), and *A Little Night Music* (1973), met with only sporadic success. In the unstable commercial climate of the early 1970s it seemed the most promising new theater talent was being developed and nurtured Off-Broadway and Off-Off-Broadway. Like their fine-art contemporaries, playwrights found great opportunity for experimentation and innovation far from the commercial arena. Sam Shepard's plays flourished Off-Broadway, and David Mamet found a local following in Chicago. Joseph Papp's New York Shakespeare Festival proved a fertile testing ground for new writers, including David Rabe. Many of the decade's best productions were developed in such festivals or created in workshops.

Gold Mines. Inevitably, cost-conscious Broadway producers began hunting for new material in the Off-Broadway theater. Strong word-of-mouth promotion of Rabe's *Streamers* (1975) and Mamet's *American Buffalo* (1977) led to Broadway productions, and Al Pacino starred in a new production of Rabe's *The Basic Training of Pavlo Hummel* (1971). The raiding of Off-Broadway really erupted when *A Chorus Line,* originally developed in workshops and then presented at the New York Shakespeare Festival, became a smash hit. Within a year Broadway was again flourishing, with originals (*Annie* [1977], Sondheim's *Sweeney Todd* [1979]), imports (*Evita*), and hybrids of old music with new books (*Ain't Misbehavin'* [1979]). Pulitzer Prizes started going to hit plays again; even Shepard won a Pulitzer. Ironically, the underground innovators, so crucial in revitalizing the American theater, had become the new commercial mainstream by the end of the decade.

Literature in Limbo. Like fine art and theater, American literature by the start of the 1970s had already provided two decades of near-constant innovation and revolutionary movements. Although literary lions such as John Cheever, John Updike, Saul Bellow, Bernard Malamud, Norman Mailer, and Thomas Pynchon continued to publish important works throughout the 1970s (if sporadically), they were now considered to be the establishment and were no longer major innovators. In fact, many writers felt that further innovation was impossible, that the novel was dead as an art form. Literature seemed directionless. Yet the dearth of new literary stars meant that a larger number of writers could be heard from, particularly minorities. Many critics embraced Latin American writers such as Jorge Luis Borges, Gabriel García Marquez, and Carlos Fuentes for their use of history and mysticism. Several strong black novelists also emerged, especially Toni Morrison and Alice Walker, who were acclaimed for contributing fresh female voices to male-dominated black literature. Novels by Jong, Judith Rossner, Marilyn French, and Marge Piercy featured realistic female characters exploring their identity and sexuality.

Best-sellers. On the other hand, fiction sold in the 1970s. The American public consumed new novels as never before, making authors household names. Harold Robbins and Judith Krantz specialized in trash fiction, which frothed with sex, money, and power. Women gobbled up the romance novels of Barbara Cartland and Phyllis A. Whitney. Espionage and global intrigue proved popular subjects, too, in the writings of Robert Ludlum, Leon Uris, and Irving Wallace. James Michener, Herman Wouk, and Irwin Shaw made best-sellers out of historical drama, and Stephen King emerged as a most prolific author of horror fiction. The runaway best-seller of the late 1970s was Colleen McCullough's *The Thorn Birds,* a sweeping romantic saga. Best-selling fiction proved to be the basis for some of the most popular films of the 1970s, including *The Exorcist* (1973), *Jaws* (1975), and *Love Story* (1970), as well as highly rated television miniseries such as *Rich Man, Poor Man.*

Sci-Fi Boom. Just as interest in and funding for the space program began drying up in the early 1970s, Americans became obsessed with fantasy and science fiction. J. R. R. Tolkien's *The Lord of the Rings* (1973) was a cult favorite among high schoolers as well as a continuous source of inspiration for rock songs. Science-fiction writers Isaac Asimov, Ray Bradbury, and Robert A. Heinlein were enormously popular, as was Frank Herbert's epic *Dune.* Erik Von Daniken's speculative books *Chariots of the Gods* and *In Search of Ancient Astronauts* became huge best-sellers. Unidentified flying objects (UFOs) were such a big topic, especially for the young, that pop star David Bowie had great success marketing himself as a space alien on stage, on record, and in film (*The Man Who Fell to Earth* [1976]). Science-fiction films were popular throughout the decade, from the *Planet of the Apes* (1968) sequels to *Logan's Run* (1976), but the true breakthrough came with *Star Wars* (1977). A rash of space-oriented imitators soon followed.

Films as Art. American movies were not just movies anymore in the 1970s; they were art. In fact, film directors were the most important artists to emerge during the decade, representing to the 1970s what Abstract Expressionist painters and Beat poets did to the 1950s. The collapse of the Hollywood studio system and its production code during the 1960s had made possible a new degree of freedom and permissiveness in movies. Toward the end of that decade a new group of young filmmakers, influenced by French, British, and Italian directors, began carving out an American art cinema for the first time. Though their films were box-office successes, these directors and those they inspired in the 1970s seemed less concerned with commercialism than their own personal vision. Critics and audiences began to think of the new directors as the authors (or auteurs) of their films. The film innovators of the early 1970s had unique and recognizable narrative and visual styles, but their works were unified by a level of realism unprecedented in American movies. Uncompromising in their portrayal of sex, language, and violence (however stylized), the auteurs turned a spotlight on the eroding core of society and placed vividly drawn characters at odds with an increasingly alien postmodern world. Several new male stars emerged during this era who embodied the confused, angry, or disillusioned American antihero.

Blockbusters. Although the 1970s were a golden age for film art, they were also the heyday of the blockbuster commercial film. *The Godfather* broke the box-office record in 1972. *The Sting* was almost as big; *The Exorcist* was even bigger. Disaster films racked up huge grosses as well, helping to revitalize the special-effects industry. Audiences also turned out in droves to see horror films, science fiction, Vietnam dramas, Mel Brooks and Woody Allen comedies, violent action pictures, "buddy" movies, and X-rated fare. All were superseded by the runaway success of two releases made by two young directors — Steven Spielberg and George Lucas. Spielberg's *Jaws* was a true phenomenon, but Lucas's *Star Wars* was otherworldly in revolutionizing computerized special effects and changing concepts of movie merchandising, touching off a wave of science-fiction blockbusters that continued through the 1980s. Almost every big movie of the 1970s spawned a sequel, a trend that would continue unabated in Hollywood throughout the following decades. Spielberg and Lucas had created a new demand by the public and film producers for ever-bigger blockbusters. While the success of these movies was undoubtedly a boon to the film industry in general, it all but ended the auteurism that in the early 1970s had created a new art form.

Pop Splinters. While it still thrived in the early 1970s, soul, with its cool style and stunning arrangements, was the brightest spot in popular music. But as soul artists became increasingly concerned with black issues, its unifying impact diminished. Audiences began to segregate again, looking for music that expressed their specific tastes. Rock fans stunned by the deaths of Jimi Hendrix, Janis Joplin, and Jim Morrison looked for new heroes in different places. Guitar afficionados turned to British stars Eric Clapton, Jeff Beck, or Led Zeppelin's virtuoso Jimmy Page. Fans of rock poetry followed art rockers Pink Floyd and Genesis or singer-songwriters James Taylor and Paul Simon. Fans of the hard rock that had flourished in the psychedelic years embraced the wild theatrics of Alice Cooper and Black Sabbath or the hellraising of southern rockers such as the Allman Brothers and Lynyrd Skynyrd. Bubblegum enthusiasts preferred the Carpenters and the Osmonds while the more venturesome sampled the gender-bending pop of Elton John and David Bowie. Mellower listeners followed the California sounds of the Eagles, Linda Ronstadt, and Fleetwood Mac. By the mid 1970s pop music had reached its nadir of energy and creativity, with more and more bands playing it safe in the mainstream, retreading past hits, or producing classically influenced works so inflated with pretension they qualified as neither rock nor art.

Disco and Punk. The two most significant musical movements of the 1970s could not have sounded more different, yet they were born in the same place — the New York underground. Disco, featuring a pulsing, sexual dance beat under catchy melodies and lush, percussive arrangements, first flourished in black, Latino, and gay nightclubs, where dance music had long been common. Most disco songs were one-shot singles that emphasized the production, or the whole sound, over the vocalist. Their only message was escapism — all sex and pure fun. The catchiness and erotic appeal of the best disco music was undeniable, and hits began to appear on the radio in 1974. Meanwhile, the punk rock movement had a much different history. Its roots were the 1960s "garage" bands, avant-garde groups such as the Velvet Underground, and the high-energy urban rock of the New York Dolls and the Stooges. In the mid 1970s a new group of artists, fed up with the overblown mainstream sounds that dominated popular music, began playing a fast, loud, and lean style of music in small New York clubs. Punk rock, as exemplified by the music of Patti Smith, Television, and the Ramones, was essentially a throwback to the threechord, three-verse rock 'n' roll of the 1950s but was played at a higher speed and volume and usually incorporated images of alienation, rebellion, and violence. While the British punk bands that emerged during this time — the Clash and the Sex Pistols in particular — screamed their political and social rage, many of their American counterparts increasingly preferred high-camp humor and the sheer novelty of being different.

Commercialization. Disco exploded in the mid to late 1970s, dominating the radio and eventually the movies by the end of the decade. The Bee Gees were the kings of disco, and Donna Summer was its superdiva queen. Her blend of funk and pop did produce some strong records, as did the raucous styles of the Ohio Players and Chic. But by the end of the decade disco had become so commercialized that its original erotic appeal was largely diluted, as well as its sense of playful escapism. Those sensibilites seemed replaced by a surface glitz and glamour that too often simply shouted bad taste. Punk seemed too political, or its fashion too alienating, to reach a wide audience. But an arty offshoot of punk, New Wave, began to break out of the underground in the late 1970s, especially on college radio. By 1979, a wave of quirky bands such as Talking Heads, the Pretenders, and the Cars had hit the American airwaves. But their slick pop sounds were a far cry from the alienated rebellion of the New York punk scene.

Country's Popularity. The good-old-boy paternalism and conservatism of country music existed seemingly out of time during the late 1960s, far from the social and cultural revolutions happening in the rest of the United States. The country-music establishment in Nashville kept a firm control over artists, production, and publishing rights. Its goal, via increasingly slick and mainstream production and heavy promotion, was crossover success in the pop market. This effort proved successful, as a virtual hayride of new pop artists had coast-to-coast country hits: John Denver, Olivia Newton-John, Charlie Rich, Anne Murray, Linda Ronstadt, and others. The new commercial atmosphere and recording style bothered many traditional country artists, however, and some rebelled against the established Nashville order. Willie Nelson relocated to Texas, while Waylon Jennings renegotiated his contract to secure complete artistic freedom — unheard-of at the time. Nelson and Jennings's "outlaw" movement marked a welcome return to an older, purer country sound advocated also by the Association of Country Entertainers, which was increasingly angered by the success of noncountry outsiders. Yet, despite these purist efforts, country music became ever-more commercialized as the 1970s ended, with ever-bigger budgets and production. Even if the old guard had been ousted, popular country images were alive and well on television shows and in movies. As the creation of Opryland might have suggested earlier in the decade (and as Ronald Reagan's election to the presidency hinted in 1980), conservative America had gone country, and liberated Nashville had gone Hollywood.

TOPICS IN THE NEWS

THE ART OF NOTHING

Pluralism. The artistic movements that had flourished in the 1960s and unified the art community — Pop art, op art, and minimalism — were all but exhausted as the new decade began. Art had entered a postmodern, chaotic phase, fragmenting into many styles that often incorporated elements from other arts in an effort to create new forms. Gradually the decade saw abstractionist art, and geometric minimalism give way to new forms that were more narrative in function. The sense that art was played out commercially and aesthetically worked to the advantage of artists who just wanted to "do their own thing." Freed from the constraints of a single style or movement, some artists used their work autobiographically; others, including some minority artists, used their work to make political statements. Many simply felt that the idea of art expressing any statement, personal or political, had become outdated and irrelevant. Therefore much of the art of the 1970s was highly conceptual, referring to nothing but itself.

Minorities. In the liberated climate of the 1970s some minorities used their art to express new feelings of pride and identity. A wave of mural painting spread through the inner cities in the 1970s, created largely by black and Latino artists. Such murals often depicted cultural histories or political images that evoked peace and empowerment. Here the idea was to unite (and therefore better) the community rather than create a salable product. One of the strongest of these works was *We Are Not a Minority* (1978), a large wall painting in East Los Angeles that depicted Che Guevara pointing accusingly at the viewer.

Judy Chicago in her china-painting studio. The design for the Sojourner Truth plate in *The Dinner Party* ensemble is on the wall above her head.

Black painters found homes for their work in the pages of the new quarterly magazine *Black Art* and support from the newly founded organization Women, Students, and Artists for Black Art Liberation. These artists often incorporated African symbols and colors (red, black, and green) in their work. Charles Searles depicted the vivid life of the African marketplace in *Filas for Sale* (1972) and evoked the spirit of ritual dance in *Dancer Series* (1975). Kofi Kayiga and Everald Brown were also inspired by black folk imagery. In *Black Face and Arm Unit* (1971), sculptor Ben Jones addressed the importance of body adornment and masks in African culture. Bettye Saar's mixed-media piece *The Liberation of Aunt Jemima* (1972) was both political and slyly satiric: the traditional Mammy figure is outfitted with both a broom and a rifle, suggesting that the one-time subservient black had become a revolutionary.

Feminist Art. In New York in the early 1970s a group of women artists began to protest their exclusion from male mainstays such as the Whitney Museum and the Museum of Modern Art. After sharing their work at informal gatherings and small showings, they created A.I.R. Gallery and founded *Heresies,* a feminist publication on art and politics. Judy Chicago and Miriam Schapiro founded the Feminist Art Program at the California Institute of the Arts, the first program of its kind. Schapiro, along with Faith Ringgold and Harmony Hammond, subtly invoked feminist responses by using traditional "women's" materials — cloth, thread, lace, and beads — in her work. Dottie Attie and Pat Steir drew from art history, using image fragments from the masters to make their own statements. Steir's *Word Unspoken* (1974) and *Rose A* (1975–1976) repeated the feminine symbol of a rose, which was then obliterated by an X. Sylvia Sleigh offered feminist inversions of classic erotic masterpieces, and Edwina Sandys' bronze sculpture *Christa* (1975) depicted the crucified savior as a woman. Nancy Spero and May Stevens were both influenced by Marxist theory. Spero's collage *Torture in Chile* (1974) was an open protest against the treatment of women in the Buen Pastor jail. On panels using both verbal and visual elements, Joan Snyder's *Small Symphony for Women* (1974) offered a feminine answer to questions about artistic sensibility. In the late 1970s photographer Cindy Sherman used playful "film stills" to comment on stereotypical images of women.

Judy Chicago. In 1979 artist Judy Chicago, with the help of five hundred others, created *The Dinner Party,* the best-known feminist work of the decade. A huge, triangular dinner table featured place settings for 30 mythological and historical women; porcelain tiles in the center noted 999 more. Each setting's unique goblet, plate, and table runner suggested a triple communion with a female deity, and an accompanying text offered revisions of Genesis (with a goddess as supreme creator) and Revelation (with a postapocalyptic world healed by feminist values). Chicago used elaborate embroidery and hand-

Christo's design for *Valley Curtain*

painted china to comment on the rising and falling of women's freedom and potential throughout history. Like the work of Schapiro, *The Dinner Party* sought to reclaim these "feminine" arts; its suggestive imagery also openly celebrated female sexuality. Though detractors claimed the piece worked better as a political than an artistic statement, there was no denying its impact. Chicago's conceptual project was similar to other major works of the 1970s (especially site sculpture) in its evocation of its own arduous process: *The Dinner Party* took five years to complete.

Site Sculpture. Also called land art or earthworks, this type of work seemed to be born of the ecological movement of the early 1970s. Land art, which placed synthetic forms in nature, invited comparison of two forms while commenting on each. Marry Miss's *Untitled* (1973) featured five heavy plank walls across a Hudson River landfill. In works such as *The Beginnings of a Complex* (1977), Alice Aycock took a more architectural approach. Using forms that ranged from wooden towers to mazelike tunnels, Aycock encouraged, then frustrated, exploration by the viewer. Robert Smithson in 1970 created *Spiral Jetty* (1970), a sixty-foot-long landfill of black rock, salt crystal, and earth that curled from the shore and out into the water of Utah's Great Salt Lake. Its gradual erosion and disintegration were part of the artist's concept. Michael Heizer's *City Complex One* (1972–1976) was a twenty-three-foot-tall mound of earth with a concrete framing

By the time of his death in 1979, Arthur Fiedler had conducted the Boston Pops Orchestra for fifty years — a record for a conductor. Fiedler was affectionately known to his masses of fans as "Mr. Pops" and as the man who had brought classical music to millions of Americans. His programs were a mix of classics (Beethoven), semiclassics (Stravinsky), show tunes, and pop songs. The Pops was the first classical orchestra to play a Beatles tune.

Fiedler was often criticized for catering to lowbrow and middlebrow musical tastes, but he scoffed at such classical snobbery: "There's no boundary line in music. All music is good except the boring kind." He enjoyed his public image as a crusty, lovable curmudgeon. "My aim has been to give audiences a good time," he once remarked. "I'd have trained seals if people wanted them."

Fiedler came to the Boston Symphony in 1915 as a violinist and became the Pops conductor in 1930. He continued to conduct into his eighties, even after suffering several heart attacks. His reward was becoming the best-selling classical artist of all time. Boston Pops recordings sold an incredible fifty million copies, and their recording of "Jalousie" became the first million-selling album by a symphony orchestra.

Fiedler's highest career mark also turned out to be his swan song. On 4 July 1976 he conducted a Bicentennial concert on the bank of the Charles River. A crowd of four hundred thousand listened to rousing versions of Tchaikovsky's *1812 Overture* and Sousa's "Stars and Stripes Forever" while watching a dazzling fireworks display.

In July 1979 Fiedler succumbed to heart failure at age eighty-two, just two months after returning for his fiftieth season. On 15 July an estimated one hundred thousand people turned out for a memorial concert by the Boston Pops — a fitting last tribute for the "maestro of the masses."

Source: "Middlebrow Maestro," *Newsweek,* 94 (23 July 1979): 89.

that looked both industrial and artificial in appearance, suggesting both integration and separation of form.

Serra. In the late 1960s sculptor Richard Serra began creating "Props," gigantic pieces in which heavy sheets of lead and steel plate were balanced precariously against each other. The lack of support suggested imminent disorder and violence despite the outward and temporary poise of the piece. In *Shift* (1970–1972) Serra set six large concrete sections at angles into a contoured landscape, inviting the viewer to experience the art as an extension of its natural surrounding and also as a physical activity. His most notable work was the totalitarian urban sculpture *Tilted Arc* (1981), a wall of three steel plates 120 feet long and 12 feet high across New York City's Federal Plaza. Because the giant wall had to be bypassed in order to access the plaza, Serra invited (or, rather, forced) continuous perception of, reaction to, and interaction with the piece. Since his artistic goal was "dislocating the decorative function of the plaza," Serra no doubt delighted in protests and petitions himself calling for its removal.

Christo. The best-known of the land artists was Christo, who gained notoriety by wrapping natural or man-made objects (islands, bridges) with giant pieces of synthetic material or hanging material in natural settings. *Valley Curtain* (1971) was a hanging of a huge, translucent orange curtain across a canyon in Colorado. The nylon material was 1,250 feet long and 350 feet high, eerily dwarfing the canyon floor below. It hung for twenty-eight hours before eventually being ripped down by strong winds. In 1976 Christo created *Running Fence,* an 18-foot-high construction of nylon fabric, steel poles, and cables that crossed 24 miles and parts of two counties in California. In order to get permits for the second piece, Christo spent hours in California courts and attracted considerable press attention. He considered the legal process for *Running Fence,* which hung for only two weeks, to be part of the artwork.

Photo-realism. Photo-realist artists worked from photographs as the direct models for their work. In using mundane or commonplace subject matter and then recreating it painstakingly, the photo-realists were reacting against the irony and wit of Pop and op art. Chuck Close specialized in portraits such as *Kent* (1971), whose detail included pores of the face being painted. Close sought to neutralize any emotional response by directing the viewer's focus to the painted surface itself rather than the person originally photographed. As with Christo, the process of the art became its true subject. Richard Estes' urban-landscape paintings prompted much the same response: the viewer, tricked into believing the work is a photograph, looked beyond the image to its creation, attempting to see how the effect was achieved. Duane Hansen and John de Andrea took the same approach to sculpture. Hansen's figures were hauntingly lifelike, clothed and posed to become common "types." The viewer was first unnerved by believing the sculpture to be a living person, then amused by recognition of the "type." Andrea sculpted eerily real-looking nudes in an attempt to invoke erotic responses.

Photography. Photography, like performance and video art in the 1970s, appealed to many because of its immediacy and the apparent lack of separation between the subject and the audience. Since the subject of a pho-

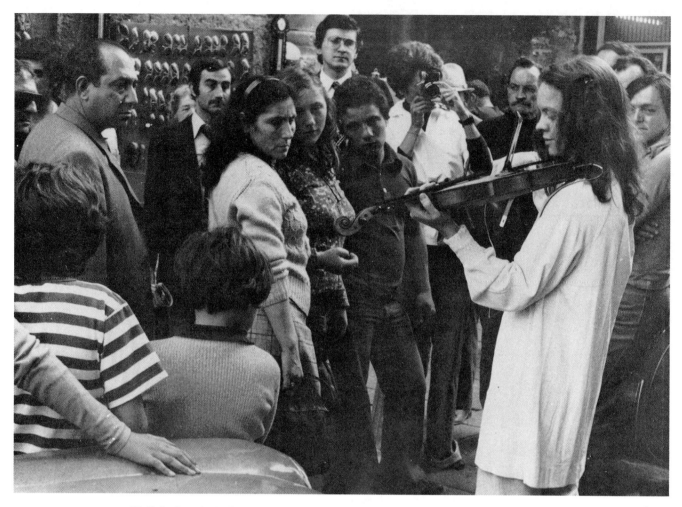

Violinist Laurie Anderson, her feet embedded in ice, performing her "Duets on Ice"

tograph generally dictated its form, photographers were able to use their work to manipulate the viewer's perception of reality. Roger Cutforth, in an idea similar to that of the land artists, juxtaposed images that reflected evolving light patterns to trace the impact of time on nature. John Hilliard's photos heightened focus in order to create continuity between images. Jan Dibbets sought to emphasize gaps between the possible range of the viewer's perception and the limited range of the camera's. Duane Michals's images drew attention to what was outside the range of the lens. By using disrupted fragments of similar photos, Michael Badura commented on the truth of the photographic image itself. Toward the end of the decade, however, many photographers began to drift toward straightforward representation again, rejecting concept as an ingredient.

Performance Art. Performance art grew out of the Happenings and absurdist theater popular in the late 1960s. As the concept of art as a process heightened, artists began using themselves or others as the artistic medium in pieces that relied on the immediacy and voyeuristic aspects of live theater. In *Doomed* (1975) artist Chris Burden invited his audience to become part of the performance and outcome of the piece. Lying on the

floor of a room under a wall clock and behind a glass partition, Burden simply waited — for forty-five hours — to see what, if anything, his audience would do. The vigil, and the performance, ended when someone (apparently concerned) placed a glass of water on the floor next to him. Laurie Anderson's *Duets on Ice* (1974) featured the artist playing the violin while wearing skates that were embedded in blocks of ice. The piece ended when the ice melted. Related to performance art was body art, in which the manipulation of the artist's body was the sole focus of the piece. Vito Acconci was a noted body artist who engaged in acts of self-directed aggression that bordered on mutilation. Again, the subject of the art was its own immediacy and outcome — when and how much was enough to complete the piece could only be resolved in its performance. Like many other art forms of the 1970s, body art seemed blatantly noncommercial and, often, blatantly narcissistic.

Fusions. Some performance artists worked in multimedia, presenting their concepts through song, dance, video, and other forms, often fusing them into one theatrical entertainment. Laurie Anderson became known for her playful performances, which not only drew attention to the forms being used but also evoked emotional responses through manipulation of words and alien, high-tech images. In *Refried Beans for Instants* (1976) Anderson used simultaneous media (tape, film, slides, inscriptions, and musical instruments) to create an episodic structure in which songs, stories, and images constantly interrupted each other. In "Spaces" (1970), a multimedia exhibit at the Museum of Modern Art, the artist group Pulsa used the museum's sculpture garden as the setting for a sound and light show whose subject was viewer responses to television cameras, computer equipment, strobe lights, and loudspeakers. Video artists such as Peter Campus fused theater and technology by interacting with pretaped material in live performances. Like performance art, video art created a sense of both immediacy and impermanence, but it also allowed the artist to become a spectator of the work. Philip Glass and Robert Wilson developed their avant-garde opera *Einstein at the Beach* (1976) by fusing largely improvised elements of dance, music, lighting, and design. Artists of the 1970s also found a new form in story art, which combined verbal and graphic elements without an overall structural intent. Peter Hutchinson and Bill Beckley used printed anecdotes as counterpoint to bold images that were completely unrelated. Like the works of land and body artists, the work's integration came not from its form but from its self-referential concept.

Audience Response. Not surprisingly, much of the public was baffled and alienated by such high-concept artistic experiments. With so many artists working in noncommercial forms, photography became the most collected art form during the 1970s. Amid a nationwide wave of nostalgia the public began to rediscover an appetite for classical art as a commodity. The traveling exhibit of artifacts from King Tut's tomb, *Treasures of Tutankhamen,* became a huge success. Art, from Andrew Wyeth and Man Ray to Picasso and Jackson Pollock, began to sell for record prices at auctions. Sotheby's auction house netted some $21 million in just one month in 1979, close to their entire 1967–1968 turnover. And in a single day 264 works by 146 American painters sold for almost $7 million, a record for a sale of U.S. art. New York museums in 1979 beefed up their exhibition schedules with retrospectives. Meanwhile, as the decade neared its end, corporate funding of the arts was skyrocketing. Contributions by 1979 stood at more than $250 million, up from $22 million only fifteen years earlier and twice the figure provided by the National Endowment for the Arts. Corporations were also purchasing more art for their own collections and displaying it, particularly modern art, in lobbies and boardrooms. While some traditionalists, such as Jasper Johns, complained about corporate sponsorship of exhibits, many newer artists responded eagerly to the quickening of the market, paving the way for a large resurgence of commercialism in art in the 1980s.

Sources:
Milton W. Brown, Sam Hunter, John Jacobus, Naomi Rosenblum, and David M. Sokol, *American Art* (New York: Abrams, 1979);

"The Corporation as Art Patron: A Growth Stock," *ARTnews* (May 1979): 40–46;

Jean-Luc Daval, *Photography: History of an Art* (New York: Rizzoli International Publications, 1982);

"Going ... Going ... Gone!," *Time,* 114 (31 December 1979): 46–50;

"Guess Who's Coming to Dinner," *Newsweek,* 93 (2 April 1979): 92–93;

Hunter and Jacobus, *Modern Art: Painting Sculpture Architecture* (New York: Abrams, 1977);

Peter Selz, *Art in Our Times: A Pictorial History 1890–1980* (New York: Abrams, 1981);

"With a Song in My Art," *Art in America* (March/April 1979): 110–113.

DANCE TAKES OFF

New Energy. The 1960s were an important era for dance, with innovative work from New York City Ballet choreographers George Balanchine and Jerome Robbins, the emergence of Rudolf Nureyev as a major star, and the critical and popular acclaim of Martha Graham's company. But dance (especially ballet) was a minority art, considered too highbrow for mainstream American tastes and little viewed outside of New York. That image changed abruptly in the 1970s. With bursts of new energy from Broadway (Bob Fosse and *A Chorus Line*), movies (John Travolta), popular music (disco), and modern dance and ballet (Mikhail Baryshnikov, Twyla Tharp), dance was suddenly everywhere. By the end of the 1970s it had taken its place as one of the most popular art forms in the United States.

Boom. Attendance at U.S. dance programs was about one million in 1964–1965. Attendance shot up dramatically in the early 1970s, reaching eight million by 1973, then leaping to an incredible twenty million by the 1978–1979 season. Officials of the National Endowment for the Arts estimated in 1964–1965 that only 32 percent of the audience for dance was outside New York City; by 1978–1979 that figure was 80 percent. By the late 1970s there were more than 125 professional dance companies operating across the United States, compared to only a handful in the mid 1960s. The American Ballet Theater had a record paid attendance of more than five hundred thousand during the 1978–1979 season, up more than three hundred thousand from the previous decade. And children — including droves of boys — were signing up for dance classes in record numbers.

Baryshnikov. The 1974 defection of former Bolshoi Ballet star Mikhail Baryshnikov was largely credited with the popular resurgence of ballet in the United States, and with good reason. Baryshnikov's athletic grace, good looks, and amiable persona combined to make him big at the box office and a new superstar. His pyrotechnic style redefined the role of the male dancer in ballet and helped dancers to be correctly seen as athletes as much as artists. Because of Baryshnikov, other male dancers such as Fernando Bujones and Aleksandr Godunov (who defected in 1979) enjoyed greater success. With Baryshnikov as their major new star, the American Ballet Theater rebounded in the mid 1970s, with sold-out houses and long ticket lines for the first time in its history. Baryshnikov's simultaneous *Time* and *Newsweek* covers in May 1975 were the proof, if anyone still needed it, that dance had finally arrived in the United States. The success two years later of the ballet-themed film *The Turning Point,* for which Baryshnikov received an Oscar nomination, only sealed the reputation of dance. In 1979, after a year of dancing for Balanchine and the New York City Ballet, Baryshnikov became the director of the American Ballet Theater.

Accessibility. There were other causes for the dance surge of the 1970s, however, as evidenced by its huge increase in popularity before Baryshnikov's defection. Tours by major companies earlier in the decade made dance accessible to large segments of the country it normally never reached. Substantial grants from the federal government and organizations such as the Ford Foundation, plus increased funding for college dance programs, meant dance productions were more accessible. The National Endowment for the Arts spent almost $4 million on dance in 1973 alone. Meanwhile, modern dance and ballet began to take on a new identity as an American (rather than European) art form as more companies experimented with newer, jazzier, and more athletic dances. The continuing work of Robbins, Balanchine, and Graham, whose company was a hit in London, and star performers such as Gelsey Kirkland created a new appreciation of dance among American audiences.

Regional Shift. Even when there were no tours, American audiences had thriving new regional companies to satisfy their dance cravings. Anatole Chujoy formed the National Association for Regional Ballet to foster intercompany collaboration and festivals and saw more than one hundred companies join. The Dance Theater of Harlem, originally formed by Arthur Mitchell in 1968 to increase opportunity for black dancers, toured throughout the 1970s. Cleveland and Washington were among the U.S. cities to launch successful companies during the decade. The San Francisco Ballet, after a record-low attendance of 45 percent of capacity in 1974, rebounded to 92 percent of capacity after a successful marketing campaign. The blossoming of regional dance companies fostered the development of American talent, reducing the reliance on imported stars.

Choreographers. Several innovative choreographers emerged in the 1970s, including Merce Cunningham, who originally danced under Martha Graham. In frequent collaborations with the avant-garde composer John Cage, Cunningham developed dance as an expression of the body parallel to, rather than dependent on, the accompanying music. *Travelogue* (1979) subverted the dance's logic and sequence by using an accompaniment that changed from performance to performance. Paul Taylor, who worked under Cunningham and Graham, formed his own company to develop new, highly personal pieces. Taylor's dances displayed an impressive range of

BARYSHNIKOV DEFECTS

Russian-born dancer Mikhail Baryshnikov was twenty-six when he arrived in Canada in 1974 as part of a touring troupe of the Kirov and Bolshoi ballets. Unhappy that his government would not allow him to dance with other companies throughout the world (his lifetime ambition), Baryshnikov decided to defect to the West. On 29 June 1974 he abruptly left his troupe and sought political asylum with the Canadian government.

There was an instant furor in the American press. Baryshnikov made his American debut in New York with the American Ballet Theater (ABT) in July, dancing *Giselle* with Natalia Makarova, who had defected in 1970. His reception was nothing short of adulation. Within a week he was a superstar, selling out houses, earning thirty-minute standing ovations, and giving the ABT the biggest box-office season in its history. He also caused a stir when he persuaded ballerina Gelsey Kirkland to leave the New York City Ballet to dance with him.

Baryshnikov was everywhere in the next three years. He danced in more than twenty roles, including *The Nutcracker* and Twyla Tharp's dynamic hit *Push Comes to Shove.* When he appeared in *Don Quixote,* the ABT sold a record fifty-two thousand dollars worth of tickets in the first day of its spring season. In May 1975 he appeared on the covers of *Time* and *Newsweek* simultaneously. He was Oscar-nominated for his appearance in the film *The Turning Point* (1977). In 1978 *Time* called him "the John Travolta of high culture." With his athletic style Baryshnikov had singlehandedly redefined the role of the male dancer in ballet and created an unprecedented level of interest in dance across the United States. He had become an American phenomenon.

But Baryshnikov was not satisfied. He was homesick, for one thing, and the glamour of stardom was not the challenge he sought anymore. So he "defected" again — this time to George Balanchine's New York City Ballet. He danced for a year in twenty-two new ballets by Balanchine and Jerome Robbins, earning mixed critical and popular response. He was unsure of his next move when he was offered the directorship of the ABT in 1979. Now thirty-two and needing another challenge, Baryshnikov "defected" a third time, moving into the 1980s as dancer-director for one of the most prestigious ballet companies in the world.

Source: Barbara Aria, *Misha: The Mikhail Baryshnikov Story* (New York: St. Martin's Press, 1989).

A *Chorus Line,* the most innovative and energizing Broadway hit of the 1970s, was born of despair and disillusionment. Early in 1974 Tony Stevens and Michon Peacock, weary of bad parts, bad shows, and the lack of respect given most dancers, turned to choreographer-director Michael Bennett with the thought of forming a new dance company. The purpose was to write, direct, produce, design, and choreograph new shows that would showcase company members. Bennett was intrigued. He began contacting dancers who might be interested in such a venture and who might have ideas about future material. A meeting was called.

It turned out to be a highly unusual meeting, one that would forever change the lives of its participants. For twelve hours, a large group of assembled dancers, at Bennett's urging, poured out their life stories, some comic, some tragic, most a mixture of the two. Bennett taped the confessions, sensing that here was the raw material for something new on the musical stage. When the meeting ended, everyone was high on the idea of a collaborative dance company, even if the details were uncertain.

Bennett had other ideas. He had had some Broadway success, most recently rewriting, directing, and choreographing the musical *Seesaw.* But he was impatient to make his mark with something unique, something completely his own. The taped stories suggested an answer. He decided to work them into the form of a musical about the lives of dancers.

He began by interviewing more dancers and by hiring Nick Dante to write a rough book from the tapes. He then asked Joseph Papp, the producer of the New York Shakespeare Festival, to sponsor a workshop. Papp agreed, excited by the material Bennett had presented so far. Bennett knew that the festival was an excellent environment in which to develop unusual material and that Papp took pride in "discovering" such properties. With a producer behind him Bennett put the fledgling project into workshop.

The show developed slowly, in bits and pieces. Everyone in the company contributed material. Some of the dancers performed their own monologues; others were assigned segments rewritten and restructured by Dante and Bennett. The successful composer Marvin Hamlisch was brought in to write the music, and he too had to improvise in rehearsal.

It was decided that the story would involve an audition in which struggling, aspiring dancers would gradually be cut down to eight finalists — the chorus line.

As a second workshop developed, the show became an unusual blur of reality (the original life-based monologues) and theater (the songs and dances). Bennett heightened this effect by the way he dealt with his cast, giving special treatment to dancer Donna McKechnie in order to add distance between her character and others in the line, and coming down hard on Sammy Williams to increase his character's feeling of alienation.

The real-life tensions and deeply personal material made *A Chorus Line* unique; never before had a show been assembled completely through improvisation and suggestions from its cast. And Bennett's basic idea — to let each dancer tell his or her story to the audience — had never been tried before. This intimate exploration was given the perfect ironic twist in the finale, in which all the individuals of the line came together to sing "One." The audience, after sharing the struggles of each dancer, now saw them in their familiar form — robotic sychronization.

The show was set to open at the New York Shakespeare Festival. Papp finally saw a run-through and declared, "It's the greatest thing I've ever seen." Even so, Bennett brought in Neil Simon to lighten the drama with some last-minute jokes. *A Chorus Line* opened at the festival 23 April 1975. The critics raved, and strong word of mouth brought the show to Broadway's Shubert Theater 25 July. After eighteen months of work, *A Chorus Line* had arrived.

The show won the 1976 Pulitzer Prize in drama and a total of nine Tonys, including best musical, best director (Bennett), best score (Hamlisch), best book (Dante), best actress (McKechnie), best supporting actor (Williams), and others. A smash hit, the show ran for well over a decade on Broadway, spawned numerous road companies, and went on to earn its creators millions in royalties. Even the original dancers received royalties for their writing contributions. It was a triumphant outcome for such an inauspicious beginning.

Source: Denny Martin Flinn, *What They Did for Love: The Untold Story Behind the Making of* A Chorus Line (New York: Bantam, 1979).

By 1977 disco had already been pumping across American dance floors for more than three years, propelled by number one hits such as the Bee Gees' "Jive Talkin'" and "You Should Be Dancing." But producer Robert Stigwood (best-known for producing *Jesus Christ Superstar* on Broadway in 1971) felt there was still plenty of life left in the popular dance craze. He certainly guessed right when he tapped British-born songsters the Bee Gees to supply the music and television heartthrob John Travolta (popular as Vinnie Barbarino on *Welcome Back, Kotter*) to star in his dance drama *Saturday Night Fever.*

By the time the film was released in December 1977, the first single, "How Deep Is Your Love," was already number one. It remained in the Top 10 for seventeen consecutive weeks, at that time the longest-running Top 10 single in Billboard history. The follow-up, "Stayin' Alive," hit number one in early February 1978. The third single, "Night Fever," was even more successful, staying at the top of the charts for eight weeks. In the spring of 1978 the Bee Gees became the first group since the Beatles to log three songs in the Top 10 simultaneously and to have the top two songs in the country. At the same time, the Bee Gees' younger brother, Andy Gibb, and singers Yvonne Elliman and Samantha Sang were riding high on the charts, with material cowritten or coproduced by one or all of the Gibb brothers. For three consecutive weeks in early 1978 the Bee Gees were responsible for writing, producing, or performing five of the Top 10 records in the United States. Barry Gibb also broke John Lennon and Paul McCartney's record by writing four consecutive number-one songs.

Saturday Night Fever went on to gross $72 million, becoming (at that time) the ninth highest-grossing movie in history. John Travolta was rocketed to stardom, picking up an Oscar nomination for best actor. In a major controversy none of the music from the film was nominated. Nonetheless, the soundtrack became the biggest-selling album of all time (a record it would maintain until Michael Jackson's *Thriller* in 1983). It was also the first album to ever produce four number one singles. Because of the Gibb brothers' efforts, their record company, RSO, was able to set its own industry record of six consecutive number ones and twenty-one consecutive weeks at number one.

The movie and soundtrack were such phenomena that they forever altered the marketing of movie songs and music-oriented films. After *Saturday Night Fever* it became common to feature several hit singles in one film and to sell movies based on the hit potential of their soundtrack albums. A wave of music-oriented movies soon followed, starting with the 1978 Stigwood-Allan Carr production of *Grease*, which starred Travolta and produced another soundtrack smash for RSO. Other music-inspired films in 1978 and 1979 included *American Hot Wax, The Buddy Holly Story, Reynaldo and Clara, Thank God It's Friday, The Wiz, FM, I Wanna Hold Your Hand, The Last Waltz, Can't Stop the Music, The Rose, The Kids Are Alright, Rust Never Sleeps, Rock 'n' Roll High School, More American Graffiti, Hair, The Warriors,* and *National Lampoon's Animal House.*

Saturday Night Fever seemed to be a success too great for its creators to repeat. After *Grease* Stigwood produced *Evita* on Broadway, but he could not sustain his hit-making reputation in the 1980s. RSO's success died with the disco craze. Travolta made a series of flops after *Grease* and lapsed into obscurity for much of the following decade. The Bee Gees had another hit album (and another three number one songs) in 1979, but their appearance in the RSO film fiasco *Sgt. Pepper's Lonely Hearts Club Band* (1978) with Peter Frampton set the tone for their 1980s endeavors. Although they continued to have success as producers, the group did not hit the Top 10 again until 1989. It was to be a long ten years for the most popular musical act of the 1970s.

Source: Fred Bronson, *The Billboard Book of Number One Hits* (New York: Billboard Publications, 1988).

---

focus, from humorous satires to dark, disquieting explorations of human relationships. Taylor's company was the training ground for a dancer who emerged as the most prominent modern dance choreographer of the 1970s — Twyla Tharp.

Tharp. With her successful dance troupe, Tharp introduced a highly creative, highly experimental style of dance that drew from a variety of popular social dance forms. In *Sue's Leg* she used jazz elements to create dances of controlled anarchy, which were intricately structured but appeared fluid and effortless. *Baker's Dozen* (1979) also featured eccentric, high-energy moves tinged with a tongue-in-cheek nostalgia. Her trademarks — fast steps, popular music, cheeky humor, and flippant tone — led to assignments with the Joffrey Ballet (*Deuce Coupe*, 1973) and the American Ballet Theater.

Scene from *A Chorus Line*

The second collaboration, *Push Comes to Shove* (1976), became her biggest success of the decade. The show, developed as a virtuoso vehicle for Baryshnikov, was a playful classical ballet set to ragtime music. Tharp and Baryshnikov became innovators of a new fusion between ballet and modern dance.

Sources:

Barbara Aria, *Misha: The Mikhail Baryshnikov Story* (New York: St. Martin's Press, 1989);

"Ballet Leaps into the Big Leagues in America," *U.S. News and World Report* (12 February 1979): 71–73;

Mary Clarke and Clement Crisp, *The History of Dance* (New York: Crown Publishers, 1981);

"Dance: The Growth Industry of the Arts," *U.S. News and World Report*, 76 (21 January 1974): 80–81.

DRAMA IN TRANSITION

Crisis. The commercial theater in the United States reached a point of creative and financial crisis in the early 1970s. In a sense, theater as a vital and expanding art form had been on the wane throughout the 1960s, despite many excellent new plays and commercial hits. The finest American dramatists — Tennessee Williams and Arthur Miller in particular — had long since peaked (during the 1950s). Edward Albee, who had ignited audiences with his shattering confrontational dramas in the early 1960s, was having trouble sustaining that reputation. The heyday of the musical had passed, too; there had been few memorable musicals after about 1965. The-

ater in the late 1960s had been sustained by a public appetite for previously taboo sexual material and for absurdism, but the novelty had worn off by 1970. That year saw the smallest number of productions on Broadway in its history, and the situation barely improved as the decade progressed. Broadway shows were reported as losing more than $5 million during the 1972–1973 season. Film and television had increasingly become the arenas for new dramatic efforts, and many dramatic writers were working in those media. As the experimental fervor of 1960s drama faded and the youth counterculture began to disintegrate, there seemed to be no new subjects and no new forms. By the mid 1970s most big Broadway hits were nostalgic revivals of old shows.

Sondheim and Fosse. The most creative forces on Broadway in the early 1970s were director-choreographer Bob Fosse and composer Stephen Sondheim. Each was an innovator; each parted from traditional forms. Their efforts helped transform the modern musical into a form closer to concert than traditional story. Sondheim's *Company* (1970) was a loosely tied series of vignettes on marriage that had little plot. His challenge was to write songs that would unify the theme but not develop out of character or plot. His *Follies* (1971) was a study in memory and fantasy in which the action of the past, present, and "what if" occurred onstage simultaneously. In *A Little Night Music* (1973) Sondheim experimented with a mix of musical and opera styles, with songs performed in waltz tempo. Fosse, by contrast, was a razzle-dazzle showman who used erotic dance numbers and costumes to create a decadent stage world. *Pippin* (1972) used illusion and humorous violence to explore the main character's sexual search for identity. *Chicago* (1976) used burlesque and vaudeville stylings to comment on the media and legal sideshow surrounding a murder. *Dancin'* (1978) celebrated Fosse's true theatrical passion, becoming the first musical made up exclusively of dance numbers. Fosse's choreography helped make a major star of dancer Ben Vereen, who won an Antoinette Perry award (Tony) for his work in *Pippin*.

Off-Broadway. Between 1969 and 1980 all but one of the Tony-winning plays and all but one of the Pulitzer Prize–winning plays were first produced Off-Broadway. A few of the best new dramatists (John Guare, Lanford Wilson) did achieve Broadway success. But the Off-Broadway theater, like the underground art and music scenes of the 1970s, became the place for new playwrights to try out and develop unusual and experimental work. Many new works were developed in improvisational workshops, with actors and directors acting in collaboration with dramatists. The 1970s became the era of the company, in which new shows could be tried out in Off-Broadway showcases for potential producers. The decade's biggest hit, *A Chorus Line,* developed in workshops out of interviews with and "confessions" of the cast members. Philip Glass and Robert Wilson's avant-garde opera *Einstein on the Beach* (1976) was also written and choreographed primarily in rehearsal.

New Themes. In the 1960s major dramas tended to explore destructive and apocalyptic modern forces that were symbolic of the era's turbulence: war, corruption, violence, crime, discrimination, and racism. Plays of the 1970s were equally representative of their times. Less confrontational and more introspective, the new works featured isolated individuals attempting to improvise life amid the fallout of a broken society. While drama of the 1960s tended to be a theater of ideas, 1970s drama became more mature, literate, and character driven. Characters frequently demonstrated apathy, indecision, regret, angst, fatalism, and a nostalgia for "the way things used to be." Playwrights experimented with shifts of time and focus, simultaneous action, improvisation, and audience participation. Political and social issues were still addressed, but with a greater sense of irony, acceptance, and empathy. Homosexuality, for example, was depicted less as a crisis or problem and more as an integrated fact of life. In Lanford Wilson's *Fifth of July,* Albert Innaurato's *Gemini,* Michael Cristofer's *The Shadow Box,* and David Rabe's *Streamers* (1975), gay characters were presented without fanfare, and in Terence McNally's *The Ritz* and Martin Sherman's *Bent* they openly celebrated their identity and pride.

Minorities. Some plays by black dramatists tended to be more militant. Ed Bullins was committed to a harsh depiction of the black experience. Bullins won a New York Drama Critics Circle Award for *The Taking of Miss*

EINSTEIN ON THE BEACH

The 4 1/2-hour avant-garde opera *Einstein on the Beach* was conceived after a performance of a 12 1/2-hour avant-garde piece, director Robert Wilson's *Life and Times of Josef Stalin.* Composer Philip Glass, long an admirer of Wilson, suggested the two collaborate on a musical work for the stage.

During subsequent meetings Albert Einstein became the indirect subject of the new work, simply because his image appealed to Glass and Wilson. They soon developed an unusual visual scheme to span their four acts: every scene would be focused around either a train, a trial, or a field with a spaceship.

While Glass worked on the complex musical score, Wilson choreographed the dances. Both saw the work as a "portrait opera" in which images associated with Einstein would gradually accumulate into a picture of him, without the use of plot or narrative structure. They wanted the audience to complete the piece by filling in gaps with their own ideas or preconceptions about Einstein.

Collaborating with Glass and Johnson was fourteen-year-old Christopher Knowles, whom Johnson knew as an unusual and visionary writer. Some of Knowles's writing was incorporated into the piece. Much of the writing and composing took place in workshops, developed to include performers' ideas. Rehearsals were grueling because the piece involved dance, music, and production effects and because of its unusual length.

Einstein on the Beach made a six-country tour of Europe to overwhelming response. Strong word of mouth brought it back to the United States, where it debuted at the Metropolitan Opera in 1976. A Met administrator who seemed baffled by both the opera and its eclectic audience was told by Glass: "You'd better find out who they are, because if this place expects to be running in 25 years, that's your audience out there."

Critics hailed the work as visionary and Glass as a gifted composer. Originally recorded in 1977, a multialbum recording of *Einstein on the Beach* was reissued by CBS in 1979, again to considerable acclaim.

Source: Philip Glass and Robert T. Jones, *Music by Philip Glass* (New York: Harper & Row, 1987).

Janie (1974), which depicted the rape of a white woman by a black man. Steve Carter's *Eden* (1975) explored the prejudice of one black man against another in a stark ghetto setting. Charles Gordone won the Pulitzer Prize for *No Place to Be Somebody* in 1970, and Joseph A. Walker was awarded a Tony for *The River Niger* (1973). Lonnie Elder III, Leslie Lee, and Charles Fuller also contributed major plays on black themes. Many of these works were produced by the Negro Ensemble Company, which became the representative black theater company in the country. To expand further the dramatic opportunities for minorities, the New York Shakespeare Public Theater established black and Hispanic Shakespeare companies. Black productions helped Broadway pull out of its musical slump as well; hits included *Ain't Misbehavin'*, *Purlie*, *The Wiz*, *Raisin*, *Bubbling Brown Sugar*, *Your Arms Too Short to Box with God*, and revivals of *Guys and Dolls* and *Porgy and Bess*. Women also found strong dramatic voices in the 1970s, writing plays that expressed self-knowledge and self-determination. The best-known work was Ntozake Shange's *For Colored Girls Who Have Considered Suicide When the Rainbow Is Enuf*, in which women heal themselves and each other by finding God in their own image. Nancy Ford and Gretchen Cryer's feminist musical *I'm Getting My Act Together and Taking It on the Road* opened on Broadway in 1978. Susan Griffin, Eve Merriam, and Marsha Norman were other major feminist playwrights.

New Voices. The strongest new dramatists to emerge in the 1970s were Sam Shepard, Rabe, and David Mamet. Shepard evoked a sense of myth in his plays, which usually depicted outcasts and cultural burnouts in sinister, nightmarish situations. In plays like *The Tooth of Crime* (1973) and *Curse of the Starving Class* (1978), action and plot were incidental; Shepard used imperfect structures and unresolved endings to heighten character development. His plays were considered too unconventional for Broadway, although he did win a Pulitzer Prize for *Buried Child* (1979). Rabe's plays explored social guilt complexes that developed in the late 1960s over U.S. involvement in the Vietnam War. The military plays *Sticks and Bones* (1972), *The Basic Training of Pavlo Hummel* (1971), and *Streamers* all became Broadway successes. Mamet developed his skills as a playwright in the Chicago theater, where *Sexual Perversity in Chicago* (1974) attracted critical attention. *American Buffalo* (1977), which won the New York Drama Critics Circle Award, displayed Mamet's ear for tough urban dialect and his trademark use of language as a form of violence. Other major playwrights included Lanford Wilson (*The Hot Baltimore*, *Fifth of July*), who used disparate characters to create collages of American life. John Guare specialized in farces of insanity and murder such as *The House of Blue Leaves* (1971), while Christopher Durang experimented with satires and burlesques.

Papp's Influence. Producer Joseph Papp's Public Theater in New York had long been a testing ground for future Broadway dramas and musicals. Papp had an unusually sharp eye for potential in Off-Broadway works. In

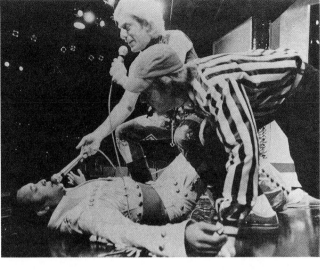

Scene from Sam Shepard's *The Tooth of Crime*

1954 he established the annual New York Shakespeare Festival, which came to be known as "Shakespeare in the Park." Since he was also a Broadway producer, Papp shrewdly used the festival not only for Shakespeare plays but also for promising new productions he could transfer directly onto Broadway. By 1974 Papp had built the festival into the largest nonprofit theater company in the United States. His festival discoveries included Jason Miller's *That Championship Season*, which eventually won a Tony and a Pulitzer Prize for best drama; *For Colored Girls Who Have Considered Suicide When the Rainbow Is Enuf*; the Tony-winning musical *Two Gentlemen of Verona*; and *Sticks and Bones*, which won the 1972 Tony for best play. Papp's real paydirt was *A Chorus Line* (1976), which he sponsored in its original workshop then premiered at the Shakespeare festival. It went on to become the longest-running show in Broadway history.

Revitalized. The success of *A Chorus Line* revitalized the Broadway musical. It was still running, along with new hits such as *Annie* (1977), *Evita* (1979), and Sondheim's *Sweeney Todd* (1979), as the decade ended. Because of Papp, Broadway producers learned to use Off-Broadway theaters as a source of potential talent. After Fosse's *Pippin* broadened its success with television advertising, other plays began using television to market themselves. Producers learned to package new material for sale to film and television and to transfer London hits (such as *Evita*) to Broadway. Meanwhile, serious prizewinning dramas such as *The Shadow Box*, *The Gin Game*, and *The Elephant Man* became major hits. By 1977 *Variety* reported that Broadway plays had set box-office records during the 1976–1977 season, and the 1978–1979 season showed profits of more than $40 million. The theater crisis of the 1970s was over, ready for a commercial boom in the 1980s.

Sources:
Gerald M. Berkowitz, *New Broadways: Theater Across America 1950–1980* (Totowa, N.J.: Rowman & Littlefield, 1982);

Helen Krich Chinay and Linda Walsh Jenkins, *Women in American Theater* (New York: Crown Publishers, 1981);

Otis L. Guernsey, Jr., *Broadway: Song and Story* (New York: Dodd, Mead, 1985);

Errol Hill, ed., *The Theater of Black Americans* (New York: Applause Theater Book Publishers, 1980);

Ted Hoffman, ed., *Famous American Plays of the 1970s* (New York: Dell, 1981);

Ethan Mordden, *The American Theatre* (New York: Oxford University Press, 1981).

FICTION IN LIMBO

Literary Lions. The quarter century after World War II had been an innovative and exciting period for American writing. Authors such as John Cheever, Saul Bellow, John Updike, Gore Vidal, Truman Capote, Kurt Vonnegut, Thomas Pynchon, Norman Mailer, Jack Kerouac, J. D. Salinger, John Barth, Bernard Malamud, Jerzy Kosinski, Joseph Heller, Donald Barthelme, and Philip Roth had expanded the possibilities of the modern novel. By the 1960s experimentation had reached new levels, with novelists using improvisation, journalistic technique, black humor, and self-commentary in their works. By the 1970s the expansive possibilities in American literature seemed to collapse. The writers of the postwar era, once hailed as innovators, became lions of the literary world, that is, the new establishment. Some declared that after so many experiments the novel was dead as an art form. Clearly, new blood was needed to invigorate American fiction. As the 1970s progressed, critics and readers alike looked to minority writers for that new energy.

Black Authors. The 1960s had seen a new renaissance in poetry and fiction, with strong works from James Baldwin, John A. Williams, and Lance Jeffers, among others. A black literary press and network of black essayists and critics unified their efforts through publications such as *Black World.* This unity eroded in the 1970s. Although several new male writers gained prominence in the 1970s, most notably Leon Forrest (*There Is a Tree More Ancient Than Eden, The Bloodworth Orphans*), Ernest J. Gaines (*The Autobiography of Miss Jane Pittman, In My Father's House*), Albert Murray (*Train Whistle Guitar*), and James Alan McPherson (*Elbow Room*), the decade's most memorable black novels were written by women. Toni Morrison emerged as a powerful writer with *The Bluest Eye* (1970), whose black protagonist dreams of having the features of a white girl. In *Sula* (1974) the main character breaks away from her family in order to discover herself, damning herself in the eyes of her community. Morrison's strongest work was *Song of Solomon* (1977), a complex study of black family life and the search for love and meaning in family history. Alice Walker's *Meridian* (1976) presented its heroine's search for self as a struggle for racial and gender identity. In *A Hero Ain't Nothin But a Sandwich* (1973) Alice Childress presented urban ghetto life with (like Morrison and Walker) a strong sense of social commitment.

"LA COTE BASQUE" SCANDAL

Shortly after the success of his influential "non-fiction novel" *In Cold Blood* in 1966, Truman Capote began publicizing his next project, a novel about modern society that he promised would make all his previous works look like mere child's play.

That novel, *Answered Prayers,* was originally contracted for publication in 1971, but Capote continually missed his deadline: he was apparently too busy basking in his celebrity status and partying with his high-society friends. It seemed he might never write the great novel he had so long promised to deliver.

Finally, in the fall of 1975, parts of his unfinished manuscript appeared as an excerpt in *New York* magazine. Instantly, Capote's jet-set world was set on its collective ear. Titled "La Cote Basque," the story was a vicious caricature of Capote's closest society chums, including Babe Paley and Slim Hayward.

As the chapter progressed, thinly disguised versions of several dozen illustrious public figures were dissected, exposed, harpooned, and discarded. Paley and Hayward were livid; both refused to speak to Capote — their long-beloved companion and confidant — ever again. The author protested, claiming artistic license, but nobody backed down. Capote was ostracized.

In 1976 two additional chapters were published, and the furor died away. For Capote, however, the pieces formed almost an epitaph, socially and creatively. Although he published a story collection in 1980, Capote never finished *Answered Prayers,* the book he had long prayed would seal his reputation as a writer of genius. Sadly, the allusion of the title — that more tears are shed over answered prayers than unanswered ones — turned out to be a self-fulfilling prophecy.

Source: Gerald Clarke, *Capote: A Biography* (New York: Ballantine, 1988).

Feminist Fiction. The 1970s produced an unprecedented number of major novels on feminist themes. Erica Jong's novel *Fear of Flying* (1973) was revolutionary in its explicit handling of a female character's sexual adventures and equally frank about her family and career conflicts. The heroine seeks liberation from her safe but dull marriage but ultimately finds no ideal solution. The protagonist of Judith Rossner's *Looking for Mr. Goodbar* (1975) also cannot reconcile her ambitions, her sense of suffocation within her family, and her attraction to sexual danger. The wives in Marge Piercy's *Small Changes* (1973) and Marilyn French's *The Women's Room* (1977) feel oppressed by their domineering husbands and eventually leave to explore the possibilities of self-reliance. Both novels, as well as Lisa Alther's *Kinflicks* (1976), postulate female friendship and lesbian relationships as alternatives to traditional marriage. Rita Mae Brown's *Rubyfruit Jungle* presented a lesbian heroine who unabashedly challenges a hostile world to love her. Lois Gould's *Such Good Friends* (1970) presents the betrayal of both a husband and a woman's closest friends that leaves the heroine no other choice but to start a new life from scratch. Other novels on feminist themes include Sarah Davidson's *Loose Change* (1977) and Piercy's *Women on the Edge of Time* (1976).

Hispanic Writers. Many critics in the 1970s hailed the works of Latin American writers for providing a distinctive new energy to a turgid decade. Argentine author Jorge Luis Borges had in the 1950s and 1960s become the first Latin American writer to achieve an international reputation. Following his footsteps into the 1970s were Carlos Fuentes, Gabriel García Marquez, and Mario Vargas Llosa. Fuentes explored the Mexican narrative tradition in the historical novel *Terra Nostra* (1975), using elements of mystery, myth, and ritual to create a layered sense of time and character. Marquez's reputation was made with the 1970 English translation of his 1967 Colombian novel *One Hundred Years of Solitude*, which eventually became the best-selling Latin American novel in the United States. Like Fuentes, Marquez infused his stories, such as *The Autumn of the Patriarch* (1975), with a lyric sense of ancestry and mystical possibility. Llosa's works reflected a stronger political sense, but also a broad humor, as in *Captain Pantoja and the Special Service* (1973), his most popular novel.

New Voices. Several new American novelists received serious critical attention. Although experiments seemed difficult in the 1970s, E. L. Doctorow created an interesting mix of imagined characters and historical figures in *Ragtime* (1975). His lyrical prose style suggested a musical comedy in the form of a novel. In 1976 *Ragtime* became the first winner of the National Book Critics Circle Award for fiction. John Irving's *The World According to Garp* (1978) adopted a witty and irreverent style and an episodic narrative that advanced from three nonlinear points of view. Most readers and critics found Irving's humor refreshing. Both novels touched on some of the decade's most repeated fictional themes — the illusory nature of reality, the malaise and indifference of the American culture, and the confusion of unresolved personal issues.

Lions Roar. Throughout the decade, and especially at its close, many of the previous generation's major novelists roared back with strong works. Pynchon contributed *Gravity's Rainbow* (1973), hailed by many as the American *Ulysses*. Bellow received the Pulitzer and the Nobel

The 1975 fiction best-seller

prizes for *Humboldt's Gift* (1976). Cheever seemed to be everywhere in the late 1970s, first with *Falconer* (1977) and the following year with his prize-winning collection *The Stories of John Cheever*. In 1979 several major novels were published, including Roth's *The Ghost Writer*, Malamud's *Dubin's Lives*, William Styron's *Sophie's Choice*, and Mailer's *The Executioner's Song*, which was publicized as a "nonfiction novel." It appeared that after a decade of being in limbo, the American novel might be making a comeback in the 1980s.

Best-sellers. American best-sellers thrived during the 1970s. American readers could not seem to get enough of steamy sex, corporate greed, fabulous wealth, and global intrigue depicted in blockbusters such as Sidney Sheldon's *Bloodline* (1978) and Harold Robbins' *The Betsy* (1971). Horror fiction (William Peter Blatty's *The Exorcist*, Stephen King's *Carrie* [1974] and *The Shining* [1977]), historical sagas (Herman Wouk's *The Winds of War* [1971], James Michener's *Centennial*, John Jakes's American Bicentennial Series [1974], and James Clavell's *Shogun* [1975]), and romance novels (Erich Segal's *Love Story* [1970] and Colleen McCullough's *The Thorn Birds* [1977]) proved to be big sellers, too. As the 1970s saw more big novels becoming big movies (*The Godfather, Jaws*) and television miniseries (with Irwin Shaw's *Rich Man, Poor Man* [1970] and Alex Haley's *Roots* [1976] kicking off the trend), fiction sales revved up to unprecedented levels. Sheldon negotiated a $7.5 million deal for five books, and Irving Wallace $2.2 million for three. After the blockbuster success of *Scruples* (1978), Judith Krantz was paid an unheard-of $400,000 for just the outline of her next book, *Princess Daisy* (1980), and wound up with a record advance payment of more than $3 million. The paperback rights to Mario Puzo's *Fools Die* were sold for a record $2.5 million. In 1978 Peter Benchley earned an unprecedented $2.15 million for the movie rights to his unfinished novel *The Island*. By the late 1970s new books by best-selling authors were being planned simultaneously as hardcovers, paperbacks, and movies or miniseries. Perhaps inevitably, the book-to-movie process began to reverse itself, with novelizations of blockbuster films (*The Omen* [1976], *Close Encounters of the Third Kind* [1977]) becoming best-sellers after the success of the movies.

Sources:

"Bestsellers: A Lusty Tale of Power, Money, and Ambition," *Newsweek*, 92 (28 August 1978): 84–87;

Jeffrey Helterman and Richard Layman, eds., *American Novelists Since World War II* (Detroit: Gale, 1978);

Frederick R. Karl, *American Fictions 1940–1980: A Comprehensive History and Critical Evaluation* (New York: Harper & Row, 1983);

Leonard S. Klein, ed., *Latin American Literature in the 20th Century: A Guide* (New York: Ungar, 1986);

Richard A. Long and Eugenia W. Colliers, eds., *Afro-American Writing: An Anthology of Prose and Poetry* (University Park: Pennsylvania State University Press, 1985);

Catherine Rainwater and William J. Scheik, eds., *Contemporary American Women Writers: Narrative Strategies* (Lexington: University Press of Kentucky, 1985).

FILM AND THE BLACK EXPERIENCE

Precursors. For decades blacks in films, when seen at all, had been used in subservient roles, primarily as servants to white characters. Only occasionally were black characters given integral story lines in white dramas, as in *Show Boat* (1936), *Imitation of Life* (1934), or *Pinky* (1949), and black-centered dramas such as *Carmen Jones* (1954) were even rarer. But in the late 1950s and early 1960s Sidney Poitier revolutionized Hollywood by becoming the first black feature film star. Poitier specialized in earnest portrayals of calm, patient, well-groomed, highly intelligent, and most of all socially acceptable black men — the kind of black men that seemed safe and even soothing to a suspicious white America. He proved so popular that by 1968 he was the top box-office draw in the country. But Poitier was a mainstream Hollywood star, marketed to a white audience, particularly to those who wanted to seem correct by embracing integration. Black audiences were hungry for more representation in film, both in front of the camera and behind it. As the Black Power movement bloomed in the late 1960s, the time at last seemed ripe for movies reflecting the reality of their lives.

Pamela Grier in *Coffy*, 1973

"Blaxploitation." The early 1970s witnessed a wave of films made by blacks for a black audience. Most of them presented urban ghetto life in a gritty, uncompromising style that incorporated profanity, violence, and explicit sexuality. In many of these films the societal tables were turned; white characters, when used at all, were presented as evil bigots or simply as louts and simpletons, all of whom were completely dispensable. The underlying message was usually a separatist one: blacks and whites could not, and should not, coexist. This sometimes took the form of antiwhite revenge, as in *The Liberation of L. B. Jones* (1970). At the same time, black characters freely embraced white capitalist values. The heroes of the new black films were generally cool, fearless superstuds with flashy clothes, sleek cars, and big guns who treated women as casually as money. In *Shaft* (1970), directed by Gordon Parks, Richard Roundtree personified black male virility as a private eye who takes on street hoods, the police force, and the Mafia with equal aplomb. In 1971 Parks directed *Superfly* (1972), featuring Ron O'Neal as Priest, a dope pusher who outwits the cops and the system while keeping a huge stash of money for himself. Melvin Van Peebles directed himself as a pimp hero in the 1971 release *Sweet Sweetback's Baadasssss Song*, and former football star Jim Brown portrayed a series of studs in films like *The Slams* (1973) and *Slaughter* (1971). Women got their turn, too, in *Cleopatra Jones* (1973), with Tamara Dobson as a secret agent, and in

In the late 1970s a strange but relatively minor film musical called *The Rocky Horror Picture Show* developed a cult following whose like will probably never be duplicated — or even approached — by the fans of any other film. Redefining the term *audience participation,* fans of *The Rocky Horror Picture Show* turned showings of the film into multicultural and multimedia events. Audiences at a typical screening were likely (and expected) to dress as the film's characters, shout the movie's (or their own) lines at the screen, sing and dance along with the musical numbers, and throw rice or fire water pistols into the air, en masse, at key points throughout the show.

Why all the excitement? Why such slavish devotion to a low-budget movie about an interplanetary convention, a transvestite mad scientist, and a mysterious string of sci-fi seductions and slayings? The film began as an English rock opera by Richard O'Brien originally titled *They Came from Denton High.* When it was later staged in London it was retitled *The Rocky Horror Show* and starred Tim Curry and Meat Loaf. In 1974 the show was produced at the Roxy Theater in Hollywood, where it was such a hit that club owner Lou Adler convinced 20th Century–Fox to make a movie of it. The resulting film, shot in England for about $1.5 million, flopped on its American release in 1975. A Broadway version the same year was equally disastrous.

Despite the bad box office, *The Rocky Horror Picture Show* had developed an underground reputation (especially in the gay community), and the film reopened as a midnight movie at New York's Waverly Theater. Other midnight screenings followed in other cities, and the movie's bizarre and unprecedented cult following began to spread. To uninitiated viewers who perhaps hoped to see the movie itself, the experience of *The Rocky Horror Picture Show* could be irritating or even frightening, since the wildly flamboyant audiences took over the whole show. But they were a diverse audience (cultists included college students, gays, sci-fi addicts, old movie fans, transvestites, punk rockers, and social misfits), usually creative and always high-spirited. *Rocky Horror* freaks were true performance artists, interacting completely with the film and the audience while training the "virgin" newcomers.

The film itself had its moments, especially Curry's deliciously decadent portrayal of Dr. Frank N. Furter, the "transexual transvestite from Transylvania." A few musical numbers — the raucous "Time Warp" and Meat Loaf's big motorcycle number — were traditional showstoppers. But most of the film was simply bad camp, making it perfect fodder for cult worship and the cheerful jeering of repeat audiences. Its wild excess and half-horror/half-drag makeup added to its appeal as a kind of weekly Halloween dress-up party. The phenomenal *Rocky Horror Picture Show* continued to run in midnight shows at theaters across the United States through the rest of the 1970s and through the 1980s and 1990s as well.

Source: Danny Peary, *Cult Movies* (New York: Dell, 1981).

Coffy (1973), in which Pam Grier's superheroine sought revenge on a dope pusher.

Moneymakers. Starved for any sort of black images on their movie screens, however stereotyped or absurd, black audiences turned out in droves to see the new films. *Shaft, Superfly,* and *Sweet Sweetback's Baadasssss Song,* made on shoestring budgets of less than $500,000 each, turned huge profits, earning as much as $20 million each. Hollywood began to take notice. Concerned by shrinking audiences and tepid box-office returns on big-budget vehicles, producers in the early 1970s were looking for ways to fill the urban theaters once frequented by white audiences who had migrated to suburbs and to television viewing. Black films proved to be an unforeseen gold mine both for the white Hollywood establishment and for dozens of black writers, actors, and directors who now found themselves, at long last, in demand. Of four hundred feature films released in 1970, only fourteen were black oriented; by 1972 almost a quarter of all new films in development had black characters or themes. And by 1972 it was calculated that blacks made up almost half the total moviegoing audience. Film screens became inundated with black products, much of it increasingly ludicrous and exploitative, including titles such as *Blacula* (1972), *Blackenstein* (1973), *Black the Ripper* (1973), *Blackfather* (1973), *Black Caesar* (1973), *Black Belt Jones* (1974), and *Black Christ.*

Backlash. Many blacks saw little redeeming value — artistic or cultural — in the new films. The community's intellectuals and political leaders protested, criticizing the violence, reverse racism, and creation of new stereotypes simply borrowed from white culture. Junius Griffin, head of the National Association for the Advancement of Colored People's (NAACP) Hollywood branch, sniped, "We must insist that our children are not constantly exposed to a steady diet of . . . pimps, dope pushers, gangsters,

Raymond St. Jacques and Godfrey Cambridge, *Cotton Comes to Harlem*, 1970

and super males with vast physical prowess but no cognitive skills." Tony Brown, dean of Howard University's School of Communications, agreed, charging that the "blaxploitation" films "are a phenomenon of self-hate. Those blacks that contribute to the making of these films, no matter how much they rationalize it, are guilty of nothing less than treason." There were many complaints about the treatment of women and, to a lesser extent, gays in the new black films. In fact, the portrayal of women as discardable and interchangeable sex objects hardly reflected their traditionally strong role in black society. Countering charges that his films condescended to blacks and glorified violence and drug use, Parks commented that black audiences needed fantasy and escapist entertainment as much as white audiences. O'Neal defended *Superfly* by pointing out that the film at least depicted real urban street life. But whatever their position, many actors and directors working in "blaxploitation" films professed a desire to explore new themes and more challenging subjects.

Serious Dramas. The 1970s produced several strong black dramatic films and exceptional dramatic stars. James Earl Jones emerged as a leading classical actor in the film production of *The Great White Hope* (1970), which confronted the subject of interracial marriage. He also portrayed Diahann Carroll's working-class suitor in *Claudine* (1974), the story of an independent black woman struggling to raise her children on welfare. Diana Ross stunned audiences with her harsh portrayal of Billie Holliday in *Lady Sings the Blues* (1972), which also featured Billy Dee Williams and Richard Pryor. Cicely Tyson and Paul Winfield paired up in *Sounder* (1972), an honest and sensitive story of a struggling black family in the rural South of the 1930s. They reteamed in *A Hero Ain't Nothin' But a Sandwich* (1978) as the heads of a struggling ghetto family. Poitier directed himself as a former Union soldier in the black Western *Buck and the Preacher* (1972), in which he and costar Harry Belafonte lead a group of former slaves to safety. Many blacks disheartened by the "blaxploitation" films embraced these dramas for their dignity, integrity, and concern with serious social issues.

Comedies. Poitier remained active during the 1970s, primarily as a director. In addition to *They Call Me Mr. Tibbs* (1970), a sequel to *In the Heat of the Night* (1967), Poitier directed a series of raucous comedies costarring Bill Cosby that became big hits with black and white audiences in the mid 1970s: *Uptown Saturday Night*

(1974), *Let's Do It Again* (1975), and *A Piece of the Action* (1977). These films were pure fun and echoed Ossie Davis's ground-breaking comedy *Cotton Comes to Harlem* (1970), the first black-directed feature film. Even more successful were two films directed by Michael Schultz, *Cooley High* (1975) and *Car Wash* (1976). *Cooley High* was a black coming-of-age buddy film set in the early 1960s whose easy ensemble style caused it to be dubbed "the black *American Graffiti*." *Car Wash* reminded many of Robert Altman's films with its multiple story lines, wacky characters, and anecdotal style. Pryor, by the mid 1970s already successful in several films (including *Car Wash* and *Uptown Saturday Night*), became a major star in mainstream hits such as *Silver Streak* (1976), *Which Way Is Up* (1977), *Greased Lightning* (1977), *Blue Collar* (1978), and *California Suite* (1978). His popularity with white audiences eventually rivaled that of Poitier in the 1960s. Unlike the safe Poitier, however, Pryor retained his ribald style and manic personality, especially in his live concert films *Richard Pryor's Live and Smokin'* (1971) and *Richard Pryor Live in Concert* (1979).

Sources:

Donald Boyle, *Blacks in American Films and Television: An Encyclopedia* (New York: Garland, 1988);

Gary Null, *Black Hollywood: The Black Performer in Motion Pictures* (Secaucus, N.J.: Citadel, 1975);

Lindsay Patterson, ed., *Black Films and Film-Makers* (New York: Dodd, Mead, 1975).

FILM AND THE WOMEN'S MOVEMENT

Background. Hollywood's golden age of the 1930s and 1940s had been a showplace for tough, career-minded women. Bette Davis, Katharine Hepburn, Joan Crawford, Barbara Stanwyck, Jean Arthur, and Rosalind Russell were seen as models of feminine independence. But in the 1950s and early 1960s the cinematic image of women had softened, becoming more romanticized or more sexually exploitative. Heroines such as Doris Day, Jane Wyman, Audrey Hepburn, Deborah Kerr, and June Allyson were appealing to many, but their decorative, often virginal roles hardly reflected women's real lives. Nor did sexpots such as Sophia Loren, Marilyn Monroe, Kim Novak, and Brigitte Bardot. In the 1960s the image of women began to shift, becoming more three-dimensional again. Emerging stars such as Anne Bancroft, Patricia Neal, Natalie Wood, Shirley MacLaine, Joanne Woodward, and British imports Vanessa Redgrave and Julie Christie fleshed out characters that reflected the tough choices and conflicts women faced in everyday modern life. Campy sex kittens such as Jane Fonda and the femmes fatales of the James Bond films were still big box office, but the glossy, artificial Hollywood image of women was fading. Even the biggest box-office star of the mid 1960s, virginal Julie Andrews, generally played independent women who pursued their own dreams. As the women's movement began to gather

Billy Green Bush, Alfred Lutter, and Ellen Burstyn in *Alice Doesn't Live Here Anymore* (1974)

steam in the United States in the late 1960s, women on film began to mirror society's changing attitudes.

Changing Roles. The biggest effect the women's movement had on society (and on films) in the 1970s was in challenging the rigid distinctions in gender roles — for both women and men. As women abandoned their traditional homemaker roles and entered the workforce in record numbers, many men felt alienated, confused, and even threatened, creating the sense that a battle of the sexes was going on. Women also began to be more vocal about what they wanted from life and from men, financially, spiritually, and sexually. This new spirit of self-determination and sexual liberation was reflected in several films of the 1970s, perhaps most pointedly in Frank Perry's *Diary of a Mad Housewife* (1970). Its heroine, oppressed by her boorish and social-climbing husband, vacillates between her desire to express herself through painting and her genuine love for her family. Sexually unfulfilled, she seeks release through an affair with a young writer who turns out to be as arrogant as her spouse. Though she abandons the affair and eventually seeks psychiatric advice, at the end it is unclear what future path she will choose, or indeed what path she wants. Similarly, in *A Woman Under the Influence* (1974) Gena Rowlands is a housewife who descends into madness trying to please her violent husband. Woodward's bored housewife confronts a midlife crisis in *Summer Wishes, Winter Dreams* (1973) when she admits she has been unfulfilled by her husband and disappointed in her children. Glenda Jackson in *Hedda* (1975) is a bored pregnant woman revolted by her husband. And in *Up the Sandbox* (1972) the friends of a pregnant wife played by Barbra Streisand encourage her to fantasize about her life options. The problems presented by new and alternative choices for women (and men) were typical of 1970s films, and their ambiguous endings were usually less than happy.

Career Women. In *Cabaret* (1972) Liza Minnelli plays a pregnant woman who decides against having the child partly because her relationship with the father is unlikely to be fulfilling (he is gay) and partly because her dream of succeeding as a singer is so important to her. Streisand's political activist in *The Way We Were* (1973) wistfully turns her back on a longtime relationship with the strength of a woman who knows she will never be defined by her association with a man. In *An Unmarried Woman* (1978) Jill Clayburgh plays a jilted divorcée who ultimately passes up a new romance in favor of her career in an art gallery. A woman moves out on her cheating husband in *Blume in Love* (1970) in order to improve herself and learn to get along without men. "Liberated" by the death of her husband, the heroine of *Alice Doesn't Live Here Anymore* (1974) hits the road to become a singer and is ambivalent about committing to her new boyfriend. And a supposedly fulfilled wife and mother reflects back on her choices in *The Turning Point* (1979) and winds up regretting that she did not pursue a career in ballet. The prostitutes of *Klute* and *McCabe and Mrs. Miller* (both 1971) are depicted as completely independent businesswomen who do not need a personal realtionship with men. In some films women's career goals bordered on obsession. In *Stevie* (1978) a woman poet neglects her private life in favor of her art. In *Norma Rae* (1979) the title character refuses to compromise her goal of unionizing a small-town factory, even when it places a strain on her bewildered and neglected family. Faye Dunaway's ratings-minded television producer becomes driven by success to the point of fanaticism in *Network* (1976). And the nurse in *One Flew Over the Cuckoo's Nest* (1975) is a woman obsessed with the power and control she has over her patients.

Sexual Freedom. Film heroines of the 1970s explored their sexuality with a directness unheard-of even in the "anything goes" films of the 1960s. Women were unapologetic and forthright about their sexual needs and desires. In *Cabaret* the decadent and promiscuous Sally Bowles just wanted to have fun, and Glenda Jackson's characters in *Women in Love* (1970), *Sunday Bloody Sunday* (1971), and *A Touch of Class* (1973) approached sex as a pleasurable pastime. Liberating journeys of sexual self-discovery were also chronicled in *An Unmarried Woman* and *Alice Doesn't Live Here Anymore*. Diane Keaton brought an intriguing sense of confusion and neurosis to her late-1970s characters as they explored their sexual and emotional choices. Her restless searches were often comic, as in the Woody Allen films *Annie Hall* (1977) and *Manhattan* (1979), but in *Looking for Mr. Goodbar* (1977) and Allen's *Interiors* (1978) they became disturbing and even dangerous.

Fonda. Jane Fonda personified the liberated, radicalized woman in films throughout the 1970s. Although as late as 1968 (with the sci-fi camp epic *Barbarella*) her image was one of a sex kitten, she transformed herself into an acting force with her portrayal of a tough, embittered marathon dancer in *They Shoot Horses, Don't They?* (1969). She followed that film with *Klute*, bril-

liantly etching the picture of an intelligent high-priced call girl who was determined to challenge and understand herself (especially in scenes with her psychiatrist). Fonda's high profile political stances made her a controversial figure in the early 1970s, especially after she traveled to North Vietnam in protest over U.S. involvement there, earning her the enmity of conservatives and the nickname Hanoi Jane. Her film career suffered, but in the late 1970s she rebounded with a series of strong films featuring women gradually radicalized by strong political and social forces. In *Julia* (1977) she played playwright Lillian Hellman, who becomes involved in the 1930s European fight against fascism. Her repressed housewife in *Coming Home* (1978) is transformed politically and sexually by her involvement with an embittered Vietnam veteran. And in *The China Syndrome* (1979) covering a near-meltdown of a nuclear-power plant brings enlightenment and fulfillment to a television reporter. Fonda even filmed Henrik Ibsen's prefeminist drama *A Doll's House* (1973), which concludes with an unhappy housewife abandoning her home and marriage. In her choice of material (if not screenwriters or directors), Fonda often championed women, who authored the original texts from which *Julia* and *Coming Home* (and, in 1984, the television movie *The Dollmaker*) were filmed.

Bonding. Not every woman on American screens in the 1970s was concerned only with sex or career, however. A few films explored female friendship, a subject largely untouched by Hollywood since the 1930s and 1940s. *Julia* was arguably the best of these, providing a refreshing picture of the love and trust between two lifelong friends. The flip side of this was offered by *The Turning Point*, in which cat fighting and competition seemed more retroactive than modern. *Girlfriends* (1977) was refreshingly realistic, and women as friends were also portrayed warmly and wisely in *An Unmarried Woman, Coming Home, Alice Doesn't Live Here Anymore,* and *I Never Promised You a Rose Garden* (1977). Most intriguing was Robert Altman's 1977 film *Three Women*, whose isolated characters and setting suggested a society that could do without men altogether.

Victims. The idea of trust between women was inverted, nightmarishly, in *The Stepford Wives* (1974), in which a network of female alliances is gradually destroyed by a plot that turns them all into docile, subservient robots. Perhaps the first truly feminist horror film, *The Stepford Wives* played off the threat many men perceived from liberated women and their friendships. As the decade progressed and terrorized women became increasingly common in movies, it seemed that some filmmakers preferred women in their old role as victims, or wished to punish them — as in *Looking for Mr. Goodbar, Straw Dogs* (1971), and *Lipstick* (1976) — for their newfound sexual freedom. Julie Christie was terrorized and finally impregnated by an android in *The Demon Seed* (1977). Sissy Spacek was victimized by her crazed mother and mean schoolmates in *Carrie* (1976). Jamie Lee Curtis was stalked by a vicious killer in *Halloween* (1978), which touched off a wave of stalker and slasher films that continued through the 1980s.

Outcry. Not everyone was pleased with the new screen roles for women. In fact, by the mid 1970s Hollywood actresses were complaining openly about the lack of quality parts. Despite the social progress and occasionally exciting scripts about "real" women, the shortage of roles became so severe that in 1976 Ellen Burstyn talked of boycotting the Academy Awards best actress category, since there seemed to be no one to fill it. The problem seemed to be establishment directors, writers, and producers, unable to conceive of women outside their traditional roles (wives, mothers, mistresses, secretaries, nurses, and prostitutes). Since there were still few women directors (Elaine May, Lina Wertmuller, and Claudia Weill were among the exceptions) or even screenwriters, films still lacked a uniquely feminine voice. Another problem was the public's growing thirst in the late 1970s for big-budget action and adventure films, which usually relegated women to the sidelines. Even the vanguard of auteur filmmakers concentrated largely on men, presumably preferring male angst and bonding to female. Women's films, tending to be smaller in budget and scope than men's, seemed destined to be produced for television, where the majority of the female audience was now concentrated.

Sensitive Males. One of the ironic effects of the women's movement was that many of the traditionally sensitive roles once reserved for women were, by the late 1970s, being played by men. The 1970s man, typified by Woody Allen, Alan Alda, Donald Sutherland, Jack Lemmon, Richard Benjamin, Michael York, Ryan O'Neal, Jon Voight, Richard Dreyfuss, and others, was gentle, thoughtful, intelligent, emotional, caring, and romantic — all the qualities women thought men were missing. Even macho stars showed a sensitive side in 1970s movies, from Burt Reynolds in *The End* (1978) and *Starting Over* (1979) to Sylvester Stallone in *Rocky* (1976) to Marlon Brando in *Last Tango in Paris* (1973). Dustin Hoffman's enlightened single father in *Kramer vs. Kramer* (1979) was the role model for the "new man," but he also played variations of this character in *Straw Dogs* and *Marathon Man* (1976). Voight exemplified the new man in *Coming Home*. Wimps, nebbishes, pacifists, neurotics, and liberals were in. Traditional tough guys and action heroes, temporarily eclipsed, would regain popularity in the late 1970s and the 1980s.

Sources:

Leslie Halliwell, *Film Guide* (New York: Scribners, 1979);

Molly Haskell, *From Reverence to Rape: The Treatment of Women in the Movies* (Chicago: University of Chicago Press, 1987);

Pauline Kael, *Reeling* (Boston: Little, Brown, 1976);

Kael, *When the Lights Go Down* (New York: Holt, Rinehart & Winston, 1980).

Marlon Brando as Vito Corleone being shot by a rival gang member in *The Godfather* (1972)

FILM AUTEURS

Background. In the mid to late 1960s a group of young film directors began, quite independently of one another, to form the beginnings of an American art cinema. Serving as their inspiration were the rich and challenging films by Italian, Swedish, British, and especially French directors. In France in the late 1950s directors François Truffaut] and Jean-Luc Godard, themselves inspired by American filmmaking, formulated the auteur theory, in which the director is the primary creative force of a film. This theory held that the various works of one director are thematically, if not structurally, linked. What interested American directors about the French films was their form, which often featured unusual camera angles, cuts, and movements and were often narratively and visually disjointed. Truffaut's *Jules and Jim* (1962) and *The 400 Blows* (1959) and Godard's *Breathless* (1959) embodied this bold new filmmaking style. The Americans were also influenced by Ingmar Bergman's moody allegories, Federico Fellini's blend of fantasy and reality, and Richard Lester and Tony Richardson's kooky, freewheeling style. As traditional commercial movie ventures began failing in the late 1960s and as the public taste shifted toward more adult themes, the time seemed ripe for auteurism in American movies.

Pioneers. The first American directors to emerge as auteurs were Mike Nichols, Arthur Penn, and Stanley Kubrick. Nichols, formerly a director of Broadway comedies, broke cinematic ground in his debut film *Who's Afraid of Virginia Woolf?* (1966). Incorporating zoom shots, hand-held cameras, painful close-ups, and other tricks, he was able to transform a talky stage play into a vivid film. He expanded his cinematic technique with *The Graduate* (1967), which became the classic statement on alienated youth as well as a film textbook. Penn revolutionized screen violence with *Bonnie and Clyde* (1967), employing split-second cuts, slow motion, and jaunty

Pornography was big business in the early 1970s. Smut peddlers — from bookstore owners to theater operators to stage-show managers — were making a killing. Annual sales of "dirty paperbacks" had topped $200 million, and receipts from hard-core movies were estimated at $800 million per year. But outraged Americans began fighting back, mounting an antiobscenity backlash that reached the heights of the Supreme Court.

A 1971 postal obscenity law had curbed somewhat the use of the mails to deliver and transport pornography, but apparently it had not been enough. In Washington, D.C., police raided a warehouse containing thousands of pornographic books. Authorities shut down a sex bookstore in Georgia, and other similar stores were picketed and protested in Florida and North Carolina. The Nebraska legislature considered a bill that would close any establishment convicted twice of dealing in pornography.

Meanwhile, federal grand juries in Washington, D.C., and Memphis, Tennessee, charged film distributors and theater owners with interstate transport of obscene films. Authorities in Huntsville, Alabama, closed three X-rated movie theaters, while officials in Des Moines, Iowa, considered an ordinance that would prohibit showings of X-rated films in drive-in theaters. A pornographic movie theater in Detroit was picketed by angry neighbors. Police in Newport Beach, California, seized one thousand reels of film and arrested the distributor.

Theatrical shows also felt the backlash. Miami authorities raided, then shut down, a theater in which nude performers simulated sex. San Francisco police did the same in bars featuring live sex acts, and a city ordinance there prohibited public display of signs or pictures advertising nude performers. New York Mayor John Lindsay ordered a crackdown on peep shows, especially in the Times Square area.

The most notorious case involved the 1973 film *Deep Throat*, which with grosses of over $3 million had become the most successful pornographic film in history. Its star, Linda Lovelace, had become a national celebrity. Public outcries led to a New York criminal court ruling that found the film "indisputably and irredeemably obscene," banned further showings, and extracted fines of one hundred thousand dollars. Federal officials also filed a court action to condemn *Deep Throat*.

A similar case concerned the 1971 Mike Nichols film *Carnal Knowledge*. A Georgia theater operator was convicted on obscenity charges for showing the film, which was not X-rated and was considered a major Hollywood release (and even a work of art by many).

On 21 June 1973 the U.S. Supreme Court ruled that local and not national standards must prevail in future pornography decisions. Hailed as a victory by antismut groups, the ruling resulted in the closing of dozens of adult bookstores across the country and caused scores of theater operators to switch from X-rated to more conservative features. The FBI clamped down on interstate shipments of pornographic films and publications. In New York police confiscated thousands of hard-core film prints and closed fifteen bookstores in Times Square. Six Chicago theater operators were indicted for showing *Deep Throat*. Two adult theaters were closed in New Orleans, four in Phoenix, and similar campaigns were mounted in Atlanta, Miami, and Washington, D.C.

Meanwhile, publishers, filmmakers, distributors, and theater and shop owners decried the decision as censorship and a violation of the First Amendment right to free speech. Their protests went largely ignored. Although the Supreme Court overturned the *Carnal Knowledge* conviction in 1974, ruling that the film was not obscene, it was a minor victory. Business for pornographic movies and books continued to decline throughout the 1970s. By the 1980s most of the X-rated film business was in videocassettes.

Sources: "Crackdown on Smut: How It's Faring," *U.S. News and World Report*, 75 (30 July 1973): 24–26;

"Smut, Pornography, Obscenity: Signs the Tide Is Turning," *U.S. News and World Report*, 74 (7 May 1973): 39–44.

---

period music to romanticize his heroes. The film would later inspire Sam Peckinpah's almost balletic treatment of mass violence in *The Wild Bunch* (1969) and *Straw Dogs*. Kubrick's *2001: A Space Odyssey* (1968) became popular with young audiences because of its wildly colorful images, but it was also the first successful American film without any traditional narrative structure. The director's insistence on slow, ponderous shots, dreamlike visual metaphors, and abrupt shifts in action mark the film as a true original. Nichols continued his narrative inventiveness in the black comedies *Catch-22* (1970) and *Carnal Knowledge* (1971), and Penn went on to make the tragicomic saga *Little Big Man* (1970). Kubrick infused the outrageous and alienating violence of *A Clockwork Orange* (1971) with a wickedly comic tone.

Realism. Films of the 1970s were markedly different from movies of earlier eras in their visual style and mood. Rejecting the traditional Hollywood gloss, films began to take on the gritty and even ugly look of their most common subject — reality of modern American life. After the commercial excesses and conceits of the 1950s and 1960s, filmmakers and their audiences wanted realism, however painful or harrowing. The new group of directors, striving for a personal vision instead of a typical commercial product, released uncompromising works whose originality caught the public's mood. Most moviegoers found the new films' depiction of sex, violence, and profanity refreshing and honest, or at least novel; others thought it shocking and in bad taste. As the new directors relentlessly explored themes of cynicism, despair, alienation, anger, and apathy in their characters, some viewers were bewildered or just plain nostalgic for the sheer entertainment value of old Hollywood.

Altman. The huge commercial success of his war comedy *M*A*S*H* (1970) gave Robert Altman a great deal of creative freedom in subsequent films. *M*A*S*H* was the first movie to mix absurdist humor with the horror and bloodshed of war. The film demonstrated several Altman trademarks: filling the screen with objects, sound, and motion; using a telephoto lens to bring all the action into focus; and interweaving narratives in a loose and casual manner that lends them the appearance of spontaneity. In his follow-up, *McCabe and Mrs. Miller,* he experimented with grainy, muted colors, dim lighting, and a fragmented editing style to underline his characters' bleak isolation. *Nashville* (1975) most typified Altman's collagelike approach to filmmaking. Using interconnecting stories, two dozen characters, and a feast of cultural images, the director deliberately drew attention to the process of the film and opens the story to multiple interpretations.

Coppola. Francis Ford Coppola made what were arguably the most influential films of the 1970s — *The Godfather* (1972) and *The Godfather Part II* (1974). Unlike Altman, however, his assignment was to film a bestselling novel and deliver it as a salable product. To do this Coppola chose a style that would allow viewers access to the inner workings of a Mafia family but also ensure enough distance so that they could observe and reflect on the action. In both films assured pacing led the viewer carefully through the story but not to any particular conclusions or judgments. The images were often violent but strangely beautiful, reverent toward religion and family. Coppola's two other 1970s films were equally compelling. *The Conversation* (1974) was a study of urban paranoia in which a violent crime is presented in fragments but is never spelled out. Reality was important only as it affected the main character or was interpreted by the

THE 20 TOP-GROSSING MOVIES OF THE 1970S

(as of 31 December 1980)

1. *Star Wars* (1977)	$175,685,000
2. *Jaws* (1975)	$133,435,000
3 *Grease* (1978)	$96,300,000
4. *The Exorcist* (1973)	$88,500,000
5. *The Godfather* (1972)	$86,275,000
6. *Superman: The Movie* (1978)	$82,500,000
7. *The Sting* (1973)	$78,963,000
8. *Close Encounters of the Third Kind* (1977)	$77,000,000
9. *Saturday Night Fever* (1977)	$74,100,000
10. *National Lampoon's Animal House* (1978)	$74,000,000
11. *Smokey and the Bandit* (1977)	$61,055,000
12. *Kramer vs. Kramer* (1979)	$60,528,000
13. *One Flew Over the Cuckoo's Nest* (1975)	$59,000,000
14. *Star Trek* (1979)	$56,000,000
15. *American Graffiti* (1973)	$55,886,000
16. *Jaws 2* (1978)	$55,608,000
17. *Rocky* (1976)	$54,000,000
18. *Every Which Way But Loose* (1977)	$51,800,000
19. *Love Story* (1970)	$50,000,000
20. *The Towering Inferno* (1974)	$49,400,000

Source: *The World Almanac and Book of Facts* (New York: Newspaper Enterprise Association, 1981).

viewer. Coppola spent four years making his eerie, nightmarish Vietnam epic *Apocalypse Now* (1979), suffering a nervous breakdown in the process. The final film was a haunting, if flawed, journey into the soul of its protagonist.

Fosse. A razzle-dazzle choreographer and former dancer, Bob Fosse brought much of his flamboyant stage style to his 1970s films. His obsession with decadence worked perfectly in *Cabaret*, set in the colorful but sinister Berlin of the 1930s. Fosse used the leering, mocking stage numbers to comment on the growing threat of Nazism, while developing the somewhat sad personal story of unhappy lovers. The blend of satiric music, sharp editing, and bawdy humor gave *Cabaret* a distinctly modern edge. The same could be said of his other 1970s films, *Lenny* (1974) and *All That Jazz* (1979), which like *Cabaret* featured characters desperate for understanding. *Lenny* adopted a documentary approach, incorporating interviews and black-and-white photography, to lend an authenticity to the tragic story of comic Lenny Bruce. *All That Jazz* was more erratic, combining realism with wild dance numbers and a final, Fellini-like dream sequence that depicts the director's own death.

Scorcese. *Mean Streets* (1973) and *Taxi Driver* (1976) established Martin Scorcese as an important filmmaker of the 1970s. His trademarks were a restless energy and self-conscious visuals that comment on the psychological situations within the film. Scorcese specialized in stories of urban violence featuring manic and antagonistic characters. *Mean Streets* focused on four young men growing up in New York's Little Italy and drew attention for its spontaneous acting and realistic visual style. *Taxi Driver*, the story of a paranoid obsessive who is driven to extreme violence, was less flamboyant but more terrifying, drawing viewers into the main character's isolation and rage. Both films featured Robert De Niro and Harvey Keitel, whose unsettling energies were perfect for Scorcese's work. In other films Scorcese experimented, adopting a loose and sunny vision for *Alice Doesn't Live Here Anymore* and a highly stylized artifice for *New York, New York* (1977), also with De Niro.

Allen. Most of Woody Allen's 1970s films were comedies, but he was also an interesting film director. His earlier films were generally broad farces enlivened by Allen's trademark neurotic urban humor. *Annie Hall* marked a departure for him. In this romantic comedy Allen employed subtitles, cartoons, split-screen effects, and characters who talked directly to the audience. The effect was both funny and fresh, and after *Interiors* (1978), an extremely moody drama in the style of Bergman, Allen produced one of his finest movies, *Manhattan*, another bittersweet comedy celebrating the strange highs and lows of New York life. Here Allen blended striking black-and-white visuals with George Gershwin music to create a mood that was both intellectual and romantic.

Diane Keaton and Woody Allen in *Annie Hall* (1977)

Others. Hal Ashby, John Cassavetes, Sidney Lumet, Paul Mazursky, Peter Bogdanovich, and Terence Malick were among the most interesting directors of the 1970s. Ashby often applied an ironic touch to projects such as *Harold and Maude* (1971), *Shampoo* (1975), *The Last Detail* (1973), *Coming Home*, and *Being There* (1979). Cassavetes's improvisational approach in films like *Husbands* (1970) and *A Woman Under the Influence* created a sense of documentary realism. Lumet turned in several films with strong social messages, among them *Serpico* (1973), *Dog Day Afternoon* (1979), and *Network*. Mazursky specialized in the plight of modern romance in such efforts as *Blume in Love* (1973), *Harry and Tonto* (1974), and *An Unmarried Woman*. Bogdanovich seemed to be one of the most promising new directors of the early 1970s after the success of his moody, black-and-white ensemble drama *The Last Picture Show* (1971). *What's Up Doc?* (1972) and *Paper Moon* (1973) were entertaining follow-ups, but later attempts to direct period pieces failed. Terence Malick made a striking impression with *Badlands* (1973), an artful road movie about a serial killer and his girlfriend, and with the visually stunning *Days of Heaven* (1978).

Auteur Actors. The auteur directors of the 1970s helped a generation of young actors push the limits of their talents. Like the British film and stage heroes of the late 1950s and early 1960s, American screens were full of angry young men. Playing antiheroes who were fighting the established social order or the system, the new film actors embodied cynicism, desperation, loneliness, and anger. One of the best was Dustin Hoffman, who had already become a star in the late 1960s in *The Graduate* and *Midnight Cowboy* (1969). Hoffman sought to be a character actor rather than a leading man, which explained the great variety in his 1970s roles — a one-hundred-year-old Indian in *Little Big Man*, a passive husband in *Straw Dogs*, and an aggressive journalist in *All the President's Men* (1976). His best roles came in Fosse's *Lenny*, in which he portrayed the revolutionary comic Lenny Bruce, and in *Kramer vs. Kramer* as a father coping to raise his young son when his wife leaves him. Gene Hackman (*The French Connection* [1971], *The Conversation*), George C. Scott (*Patton* [1970], *The Hospital* [1971]), Jon Voight (*Deliverance, Coming Home*), Warren Beatty (*McCabe and Mrs. Miller, Shampoo, Heaven Can Wait* [1978]), Jack Lemmon (*Save the Tiger* [1973], *The China Syndrome*), and Marlon Brando (*The Godfather, Last Tango in Paris*) also had challenging roles as cynical and dissipirited men.

New Faces. Three young stars revolutionized film acting in the early 1970s: Jack Nicholson, Al Pacino, and Robert De Niro. After his breakthrough as a hippie lawyer in *Easy Rider* (1969), Nicholson challenged audiences and establishment authority with antihero roles *Five Easy Pieces* (1970) and *Carnal Knowledge*. In *The Last Detail* he was a ribald sailor challenging military authority while on leave. His character Jake Gittes in *Chinatown* (1974) was a cynic who refused to play by the rules. The manic energy of his mental patient in *One Flew Over the Cuckoo's Nest* was destroyed when it threatened authority. Previously a stage actor, Pacino first achieved fame as the brooding and brutal Michael Corleone in *The Godfather* films. He used barely controlled anger and desperation to portray a rebellious young cop in *Serpico*, a manic bank robber in *Dog Day Afternoon*, and a caustic attorney in . . . *And Justice for All* (1979). Like Nicholson, Pacino became a hit with audiences for constantly challenging, even mocking, authority. De Niro's 1970s characters were more frightening. He first attracted attention as the uncontrollable lout Johnny Boy in Scorsese's *Mean Streets* then won an Oscar for portraying the young Vito Corleone in *The Godfather Part II*. He later played frustrated, alienated characters in *New York, New York* and *The Deer Hunter* (1978). His finest 1970s role was Travis Bickle, the obsessive loner turned urban vigilante in *Taxi Driver*. De Niro's screen persona was both repelling and fascinating, simultaneously inviting and rejecting audience sympathy.

Personal Styles. One of the more interesting things about the auteur directors and their stars was the identity they carried with them from film to film. Audiences expected artful urban violence from Scorsese and compelling jerks from De Niro. Nicholson mastered the crazy-like-a-fox wise guy, while Fosse perfected dazzling decadence. Coppola's stories had an almost religious tone of fear and dread, as opposed to Altman's upbeat collages of Americana. Pacino's trademark was his explosive anger, and viewers looked forward to it as much as they did Allen's nerdy asides. All of this lent a sense of artistic commitment in their films that lasted for much of the decade. Auteurism began to fade late in the 1970s, however, as some directors' pet projects (*Apocalypse Now; All That Jazz; New York, New York;* and Altman's *A Wedding*, 1978) met with indifference at the box office. When director Michael Cimino, hailed as a visionary after *The Deer Hunter*, filmed the $40 million fiasco *Heaven's Gate* (1980), producers became reluctant to finance such per-

Ron Howard and Cindy Williams in a scene from *American Graffiti* (1973), a movie about teenagers of the 1960s

sonal films, and auteurism was on the wane in Hollywood.

Spielberg and Lucas. Ironically, the two men who helped put an end to auteurism in the 1970s were auteurs in their own right. George Lucas and Steven Spielberg, with their blockbuster hits *Star Wars* (1977), *Jaws* (1975), and *Close Encounters of the Third Kind*, led Hollywood to abandon its idiosyncratic art in favor of widescreen, high-tech adventure spectacles. Neither intended anything of the sort, and in fact each was attempting to do something specific and personal when their films became blockbusters. Lucas, whose earlier film *American Graffiti* (1973) was a model of ensemble acting and nostalgic comedy, had long wanted to make the space adventure *Star Wars*, but he never considered it the commercial product it later became. Likewise, Spielberg built on the small-scale success of *The Sugarland Express* (1974) in crafting a superb suspense film from the best-seller *Jaws*, that broke all box-office records. And *Close Encounters of the Third Kind* was based on a highly personal vision, despite its later popularity.

Sources:

Pauline Kael, *When the Lights Go Down* (New York: Holt, Rinehart & Winston, 1980);

Robert Phillip Kolker, *A Cinema of Loneliness: Penn, Kubrick, Coppola, Scorsese, Altman* (New York: Oxford University Press, 1980);

Axel Madsen, *The New Hollywood: American Movies in the Seventies* (New York: Crowell, 1975);

David Thomson, *Overexposures: The Crisis in American Filmmaking* (New York: Morrow, 1981).

FILM FADS AND FASHIONS

Slump. Hollywood was in trouble as the 1970s began. Audiences had been shrinking throughout the previous decade as television viewing increased. The collapse of the studio system meant that producers had to finance films independently, magnifying the importance of each film's success or failure at the box office. The production code had also disappeared, and now that movies were free to explore previously taboo adult themes, the old-fashioned, big-budget Hollywood epics began to bomb. *Hello, Dolly!* (1969), an overblown version of the stage hit, lost $16 million. By the late 1960s only one film in six was making a profit, and by 1971 weekly movie attendance in the United States had reached a low of 17.5 million, down from 80 million customers a week in Hollywood's peak year of 1946. Richard D. Zanuck, head of 20th Century–Fox, resigned in late 1970 in the face of the studio's $21.3 million deficit. When *Easy Rider,* produced for a mere $400,000, grossed over $30 million, several producers jumped on the youth bandwagon, churning out sleazy rock 'n' roll movies with hippie heroes. This fad quickly died, however, proving that youthful audiences, who were the bulk of moviegoers by the early 1970s, did have taste. By 1973 the "blaxploitation" craze was beginning to burn itself out. The future of movies seemed more uncertain than ever.

Richard Pryor with Diana Ross as Billie Holiday in *Lady Sings the Blues* (1972)

Trendsetters. The success of *The Godfather* in 1972 changed Hollywood's downward spiral. Within a year it had broken the previous box-office record held for seven years by *The Sound of Music* (1965). It also generated a new phenomena in movies — a demand by producers and the public for sequels and for cheaply made ripoffs. In 1973 *American Graffiti* grossed over $50 million, and *The Sting* (1973) made more than $75 million, both helped by the giant success of their soundtrack albums and both contributing to a nationwide nostalgia craze. A film about a young girl's possession by Satan, *The Exorcist* raked in over $85 million. It also spawned imitators; *The Omen* showed the Antichrist born into society as a young boy, and *Audrey Rose* (1977) featured a young girl's horrific visions of a dead child. But all of these were outdone by an even bigger hit in 1975: Steven Spielberg's *Jaws,* about a giant shark that terrorized a resort community. *Jaws* earned $133 million and touched off a rash of films in which ordinary citizens were terrorized by huge bears, alligators, and other creatures of the wild. One of the biggest box-office hits of all time was George Lucas's *Star Wars,* grossing an otherworldly $175 million. *Star Wars* became such a phenomenon that it set off a sci-fi movie craze in the late 1970s (*Superman: The Movie* [1978], *Alien* [1979], *The Black Hole* [1979], *Star Trek: The Motion Picture* [1979]) and forever changed the concept of movie marketing. *Star Wars* also remained the largest-grossing film of all time until 1982, when Spielberg's *E.T.: The Extra-Terrestrial* soared even higher.

Disaster Films. In 1970 a bomb on a jetliner in *Airport* unleashed an explosion of new blockbusters: the all-star disaster movies. These films had almost no plot, and their characters existed only to be placed in jeopardy on crippled jets (*Airport 1975, Airport '77,* and *The Concorde: Airport '79*), on bombed ocean liners (*Juggernaut* [1974]), in burning buildings (*The Towering Inferno* [1974]), or in

the path of natural disasters (*Avalanche* [1978], *Meteor* [1979], *The Swarm* [1978]). *Earthquake* (1974) and *Rollercoaster* (1977) featured the added thrill of Sensurround, a gimmick that caused theater seats to vibrate. The success of the disaster films revitalized the special-effects industry and also the careers of many Hollywood stars of the golden age, who now found employment clinging to burning wreckage. The most prolific stars of the disaster cycle were Charlton Heston and George Kennedy, who both appeared in *Earthquake* and *Airport 1975.* Irwin Allen was the most active director, contributing *The Poseidon Adventure, The Towering Inferno,* and others. But by the end of the decade, with sequels like *Beyond the Poseidon Adventure* (1979) failing, the cycle seemed to be played out. After *When Time Ran Out . . .* in 1980, there seemed nothing left to destroy anyway.

Humanity Threatened. Many attributed the spectacular success of disaster films to a jittery American public, who sought release from real-life disasters (Vietnam, Watergate, the energy crisis, the recession) by watching mass destruction in theaters. Producers read this paranoia well, responding with a barrage of sci-fi films that depicted ecological, nuclear, viral, alien, and even supernatural threats to humanity. The underlying message was that society and technology had been allowed to run amok. The *Planet of the Apes* sequels were the leading examples of this trend — humanity ousting itself through nuclear folly. Heston starred in *Soylent Green* (1973), which dealt with overpopulation and a food shortage so severe that the only things left to eat were other humans. Overpopulation was solved in *Logan's Run* (1976) by killing anyone over the age of thirty. *Westworld* (1973) and *Futureworld* (1976) depicted masses of people being terrorized by malfunctioning robots. Nuclear radiation re-

John Travolta in *Saturday Night Fever* (1977)

sulted in terrifyingly large fish in *The Neptune Factor* (1975), rats in *Food of the Gods* (1976), and rabbits in *Night of the Lepus* (1972). In *The Andromeda Strain* (1970) a strange virus infects a village, causing scientists to panic. *The Omega Man* (1971) featured Heston as the sole healthy survivor of germ warfare, and *Silent Running* (1971) and *Zardoz* (1973) depicted earth in the future as a nuclear-devastated wasteland. *Alien* and *The Black Hole* explored the threats of outer space. Equally grisly were the present-day *Coma* (1978), in which patients at a large hospital were deliberately put into comas so their organs could be sold, and *The Demon Seed*, in which a computer rapes and impregnates a woman. *The Exorcist* and *The Omen* raised perhaps the eeriest threat — Satan himself.

Nostalgia. American moviegoers weary of horror, disaster, and sci-fi took refuge in nostalgia. *Love Story* (1970) first touched off the wave when its sob story about a young wife's death indicated a return to screen romance. *The Last Picture Show* and *American Graffiti* started a craze for images of the late 1950s and early 1960s that was followed up in *Grease, The Lords of Flatbush* (1974), *Ode to Billy Joe* (1976), *The Buddy Holly Story* (1978), *American Hot Wax* (1978), and others. Peter Bogdanovich made tributes to 1930s films in *What's Up, Doc?* and *At Long Last Love* (1975). The use of Scott Joplin rags in *The Sting* heightened nostalgia, as did the evocative imagery of *Chinatown, The Long Goodbye* (1973), *The Last Tycoon* (1977), *Funny Lady* (1975), *Lucky Lady* (1975), *Cabaret, Sounder,* and *The Day of the Locust* (1975). The 1920s were evoked in *The Great Gatsby* (1974) and *Bugsy Malone* (1976). *Lady Sings the Blues, The Way We Were* (1972), and *New York, New York* followed their characters through several decades. Sensing a public need, M-G-M released two retrospectives of their golden age musicals called *That's Entertainment* (1974), and *That's Entertainment, Part 2* (1976). For moviegoing Americans, apparently the past — any past — was preferable to the troubled present.

Vietnam. One recent historical era treated seriously in late-1970s films was the Vietnam War, but it was hardly viewed nostalgically. Though the last American troops were not withdrawn from South Vietnam until 1972, by 1978 filmmakers were attempting to deal with the personal, social, and political traumas the war had created. *The Deer Hunter*, released in late 1978, was the most acclaimed of these films. It portrayed a close-knit group of friends in a small town whose lives are transformed by their war experiences and featured a controversial sequence in which several soldiers are forced by their North Vietnamese captors to play Russian roulette. In *Coming Home* two veterans struggle to deal with the war's punishing costs: an embittered paraplegic regains his identity through protest, and a disillusioned former officer commits suicide when his faith in the war and in himself is destroyed. *Apocalypse Now* was the most visionary, and the most nightmarish, of these films. A retelling of Joseph Conrad's *Heart of Darkness* set in Vietnam, the film surreally portrayed the inner journey of a man seeking answers in the midst of war's chaos.

Sex and Violence. American movies reached a new level of sexual explicitness and violence in the 1970s. Sam Peckinpah ushered in an almost lyric style of film violence in *The Wild Bunch* (1969) and followed it up with such artistic bloodbaths as *Straw Dogs, The Getaway* (1972), and *Pat Garrett and Billy the Kid* (1973). *M*A*S*H* set a new standard for documentary realism in wartime violence, which reached its peak in the Vietnam films late in the decade. Martin Scorcese patented a new, raw style of urban violence best seen in *Mean Streets* and *Taxi Driver*. The bloodshed in *The Godfather* and its sequels was shocking but also artfully controlled, which could not be said of the revenge fantasies *Death Wish* (1974), *Walking Tall* (1973), or *Billy Jack* (1971). And audiences loved the cartoonish violence of disaster films and the late 1970s wave of horror/stalker/slasher films such as *The Texas Chainsaw Massacre* (1974), *Carrie,* and *Halloween*. Sex was rampant, too, finally freed from the timid taboos of the 1950s and 1960s. Nude scenes were commonplace even in the most prestigious films, and audiences became almost blasé about seeing big stars rip their clothes off. Sex was everywhere, from the pathetic fumblings of *Carnal Knowledge* to the arty pairings of *Last Tango in Paris*, from the afternoon delights of *Shampoo* to the brutal backseats of *Saturday Night Fever*. Always an underground industry in prior years, pornographic movies became big box-office hits in the 1970s. Hard-core movies such as *Behind the Green Door* (1971) and *Deep Throat* (1973) even produced their own stars, such as Linda Lovelace, Harry Reems, and Marilyn Chambers.

Buddies, Tough Guys, and Good Old Boys. Despite the consciousness-raising of the women's movement, it was still men who were the big box-office draws in the 1970s. Buddy films, which paired male stars as best friends, included *Husbands, M*A*S*H, The Fortune*

(1975), *California Split* (1974), *The Sting, Harry and Walter Go to New York* (1976), *The Last Detail, Carnal Knowledge, Scarecrow* (1973), and others. One of the decade's top stars was tough guy Clint Eastwood, whose *Dirty Harry* (1971) films and freewheeling adventure movies (*Every Which Way But Loose,* 1978) were huge hits. Charles Bronson was a smash in *Death Wish* (and its sequels, and Joe Don Baker starred in *Walking Tall.* Tom Laughlin became a combination hippie–martial arts superhero as *Billy Jack.* After Burt Reynolds posed nude in *Cosmopolitan* magazine in 1972, he became Hollywood's reigning "good old boy" in *The Longest Yard* (1974), *Smokey and the Bandit* (1977), and *Hooper* (1978). Robert Redford was the biggest heartthrob in the movies after appearing in *The Sting, The Candidate* (1972), *The Way We Were,* and *The Great Gatsby.* And Warren Beatty continued to ooze commercial sex appeal in such high-libido hits as *Shampoo* and *Heaven Can Wait.*

Comedies. The 1970s were a rich era for screen comedy. While Woody Allen seemed to want to make more serious films, Mel Brooks planted his feet firmly in parody, producing two classic comedies, both in 1974. *Blazing Saddles* spoofed Hollywood Westerns, throwing in every possible cliché, pun, and sight gag, including a black sheriff. *Young Frankenstein* skewered 1930s horror films with a feast of one-liners and mock-gothic visuals. Comedy machine Neil Simon continued his 1960s success by churning out hits that included *The Sunshine Boys* (1975), *The Goodbye Girl* (1977), *Murder by Death* (1976), and *California Suite* (1978). Monty Python, a wacky British comedy troupe, hit American screens in 1972 with *And Now for Something Completely Different* and followed up with the medieval spoof *Monty Python and the Holy Grail* (1975). By far the biggest comedy hit of the 1970s was *National Lampoon's Animal House* (1978), which featured television's *Saturday Night Live* star John Belushi as a fat frat boy and set off a craze for toga parties. Meanwhile, his television costar Bill Murray scored a big hit with *Meatballs* (1979). Blake Edwards's *Pink Panther* (1964) sequels enjoyed great success, as did Allen's anarchically silly *Bananas* (1971), *Sleeper* (1973), and *Love and Death* (1975).

Rebound and Repeats. After the success of *The Godfather Part II,* producers seemed to want to film sequels of every hit. The decade was peppered with second helpings of *The French Connection, Rocky, The Exorcist,* and *Jaws,* most of which made money. *Billy Jack* gave birth to two sequels, *Airport* to three. *American Graffiti* sired *More American Graffiti* (1979), and *Love Story* spawned *Oliver's Story* (1978). And the first sequel to the phenomenal *Star Wars* was on the way. It was clear by the end of the decade that Hollywood, spurred by a few unexpected hits, had fully rebounded. As the 1970s surged into the 1980s, big-budget blockbusters were back on top.

Sources:
Leslie Halliwell, *Film Guide* (New York: Scribners, 1979);

The Who album cover (1971)

Axel Madsen, *The New Hollywood: American Movies in the Seventies* (New York: Crowell, 1975);

David Thomson, *Overexposures: The Crisis in American Filmmaking* (New York: Morrow, 1981).

POP AND ROCK MUSIC STYLES

1960s Influence. By the end of the 1960s rock and pop music reflected the explosive change and growth that was happening in society at large. Bands and musicians as diverse as the Kinks, Jim Morrison, and John Fogerty were pushing the boundaries of the music, creating new forms ("rock operas" and concept or theme albums), and marrying music to fashion and image to an unprecedented degree. Meanwhile, an increasingly pervasive media was covering the younger generation as never before — their tastes, their fads, their political opinions. Talented guitarists such as Jimi Hendrix and Eric Clapton were hailed as gods, while black- or blues-inspired vocalists such as Janis Joplin and Mick Jagger lent credibility to rock singing. Innovation in the studio (the Beatles) and scorching pyrotechnics onstage (the Who) combined to give rock the new aura of art. And the soaring popularity of soul, rhythm and blues, and jazz styles among white and black audiences made color seem both empowering ("Black is beautiful") and irrelevant, as millions turned on to the sounds of Motown artists, Sly Stone, and Aretha Franklin. Rock music reached a zenith of creativity, influence, and range even as it united youthful audiences with its social, political, and cultural relevance.

What Happened? As the 1960s became the 1970s, the sense of cultural unity built around rock music began to erode. Like artists and writers of the period, musicians felt that the limits had been reached, that the universal

Bob Dylan album cover (1974)

Carole King album cover (1971)

high was over. The Beatles broke up, then in succession Hendrix, Joplin, and Morrison died. Millions of young Americans, disappointed by the failure of social revolution and their own utopian ideals, turned inward to more personal goals. This new era of self-importance (and self-indulgence) was labeled the me decade by Tom Wolfe and "The Culture of Narcissism" by Christopher Lasch. The rock audience fragmented into smaller groups, each preferring its own favorite sound and style — soul versus hard rock, radio pop versus reggae, funk versus southern boogie, jazz rock versus singer-songwriters. In some cases such diversity made for exciting new music; more often, though, the new rock music sounded stale, homogenized, and largely interchangeable. Rock music made more money than ever in the 1970s, but it failed to seize the public imagination through blockbuster albums, corporate-sponsored tours, and progressive radio formats. By middecade it had never sounded more tired.

Album Rock. The burgeoning sense of rock as an art form in the late 1960s left its mark on rock in the 1970s: the album, not the single, was the new yardstick of serious rock. Although many artists contributed pompous, long-winded concept albums during the decade, many classics were produced. British bands such as the Who and the Rolling Stones were at the forefront of album rock in the early 1970s, the Who issuing *Who's Next* (1971) and the double set *Quadrophenia* (1973) and the Stones releasing *Sticky Fingers* (1971) and their double album *Exile on Main Street* (1972). Bob Dylan, meandering through most of his records since 1966, came back in 1974 with *Blood on the Tracks*. Led Zeppelin's untitled 1971 release (often called "ZoSo") is considered among their best recordings, while Aerosmith's *Toys in the Attic* (1975) is a prime example of hard rock. Pink Floyd's

Dark Side of the Moon (1973) proved so definitive a statement that it remained on the charts for fifteen years. The year 1970 produced several lasting albums, including Rod Stewart's *Every Picture Tells a Story,* Van Morrison's *Moondance,* Creedence Clearwater Revival's *Cosmos Factory,* and Velvet Underground's *Loaded.* David Bowie's *Ziggy Stardust* (1972) epitomized glam (glamour) rock. Bruce Springsteen's *Born to Run* and Patti Smith's *Horses* (both 1975) turned out to be highly influential, as did the debut albums *The Ramones[ramones]* (1976) and *The Clash* (1977). Reggae produced an enduring soundtrack in *The Harder They Come* (1973), as soul did in *Superfly* (1972). Other soul classics were Marvin Gaye's *What's Goin' On* and Sly Stone's possible answer *There's a Riot Goin' On* (both 1971).

Singer-Songwriters. The singer-songwriters were an offshoot of the hippie sensibility of the late 1960s. Folksingers such as Joan Baez and Judy Collins, who used music for political and social protest or enlightenment, gradually gave way to singers with more personal agendas. Joni Mitchell made the transition, as did Neil Young and Paul Simon when they left successful groups (Crosby, Stills, Nash and Young; Simon and Garfunkel) to become solo acts. Their writing began to express emotions of frustration, confusion, and loss that were tempered by a sense of irony and humor. The style of most singer-songwriters was highly confessional, which could be both refreshingly candid and irritatingly self-indulgent. Randy Newman contributed straight-faced satires. Leonard Cohen tackled romance with wit and sophistication. Van Morrison howled through the depths of loneliness. Dylan reemerged singing about uneasy commitments. Women had huge success, particularly in the early 1970s, as singers of their own material. Carole King's *Tapestry*

(1970), an album of upbeat but cynical folk pop, sold in the millions. Carly Simon ("That's the Way I've Always Heard It Should Be," "You're So Vain") and Janis Ian ("At Seventeen") recorded classic feminist songs, and Phoebe Snow and Joan Armatrading added a black woman's point of view. As the music moved further from folk, individual personalities emerged. Cat Stevens tried political pop, while Al Stewart engaged in wistful wishing. Jim Croce, Harry Chapin, and Billy Joel stuck to storytelling. Jackson Browne and Warren Zevon waxed poetic about love. And Springsteen just wanted to rock.

Progressive Rock. Also called art rock, progressive was a style rooted in England, where a sense of history and class distinction made popular the influence of classical sources on rock music. Borrowing motifs from classical composers and imagery from myths, legends, and poetry, British bands such as Emerson, Lake, and Palmer; the Moody Blues; King Crimson; Yes; and Genesis displayed their technical virtuosity in ambitious songs and dense albums. During the decade almost every band dabbled in progressive rock at some point, from Deep Purple to Jethro Tull. Led Zeppelin made constant use of mystic imagery in their songs (from "Ramble On" to "Kashmir"), and the spacey, otherworldly sound perfected by Pink Floyd on *Dark Side of the Moon* was progressive rock at its most popular. The style, with its heavy use of synthesizers, was close in spirit to the "head" music popularized by late 1960s San Francisco bands such as the Jefferson Airplane. Later progressive-oriented British bands included Queen, ELO, Supertramp, and the Alan Parsons Project, while the American wave was headed by Kansas, Styx, and Boston.

Heavy Metal. Heavy metal was a style typified by aggressive guitar riffs played at a generally loud volume and high speed. Metal songs featured strong sexual overtones and sometimes violent imagery. However dark or decadent the subject matter, there was a wild, celebratory energy to the best hard rock that made it ideal for teenagers who loved to play "air guitar" (or "air drums," for that matter). Like progressive rock, heavy metal was an outgrowth of the psychedelic rock that flourished in the late 1960s, particularly that produced by British bands such as the Rolling Stones and Cream. Rather than inflate the music with arty frills, however, heavy metal bands tried to strip it down to its raw basics. Deep Purple, Ted Nugent, AC/DC, Uriah Heep, Montrose, Jethro Tull, and Thin Lizzy were among the leading exemplars of the style. Some metal artists, most notably Alice Cooper, Kiss, and Black Sabbath, used stage theatrics and dark and violent images to paint themselves as modern Lucifers. Aerosmith, though originally accused of being a Rolling Stones ripoff, helped define the florid fashion (leather, headbands, scarves) later associated with heavy metal. Led Zeppelin tempered the grungy sound of metal with strong blues shadings, Jimmy Page's innovative guitar solos, and lead singer Robert Plant's macho swagger and plaintive vocals. By the time of their fourth studio album,

"JESUS" ROCK

Even as heavy metal flirted with Satan in the 1970s, pop music was being touched by God. George Harrison was the first to knock on heaven's door when he released "My Sweet Lord" in 1970. The following year, the Canadian group Ocean ascended the charts with "Put Your Hand in the Hand (of the Man from Galilee)." Two 1971 Broadway musicals were based on Jesus parables — *Godspell* and *Jesus Christ Superstar* — and each produced a hit. "Day by Day" arose from Godspell, while Yvonne Elliman and Helen Reddy both confessed, "I Don't Know How to Love Him." Other holy hits during the early 1970s included the movie theme "One Tin Soldier" (from *Billy Jack*) and the Doobie Brothers' eulogy "Jesus Is Just Alright." Apollo 100 turned a traditional hymn into a pop instrumental with "Joy," and Sister Janet Mead made a hit out of "Lord's Prayer." Such songs were close kin to the peace, love, and ecology anthems of the time ("Give Peace a Chance," "Mercy Mercy Me," "I'd Like to Teach the World to Sing"). As the me decade progressed, however, the public seemed more attuned to Judas Priest than Jesus Christ, and religious rock faded. But in 1977 Debby Boone single-handedly revived the trend when she claimed that she sang her Grammy-winning megahit "You Light Up My Life," the longest-running number one single of the decade, directly to God.

Source: Joel Whitburn, *The Billboard Book of Top 40 Hits* (New York: Billboard Publications, 1985).

with its FM hit "Stairway to Heaven," Zeppelin had established themselves as the biggest and most innovative heavy metal band of the 1970s. Later in the decade, Los Angeles rockers Van Halen adopted a tongue-in-cheek, almost self-parodied style of macho rock they continued to popularize in the 1980s.

Anthem Rock. Not as hard as the metal bands were the purveyors of "anthem" rock, which promoted a partying, AM-radio kind of rebellion. Everyone from Aerosmith ("Dream On") to Queen ("Bohemian Rhapsody") to Slade ("Mama Weer All Crazee Now") contributed to the fist clenching and banner waving. Alice Cooper was represented with his teen anthems "Eighteen" and "School's Out." Brownsville Station celebrated "Smokin' in the Boys' Room," Sweet promised and delivered "Action," and Gary Glitter contributed the cheerfully moronic "Rock and Roll Part 2." The bands most representative of this distinctly teenage subgroup were Grand Funk Railroad, Bachman Turner Overdrive (BTO), the

Kiss album cover (1977)

Guess Who, and Three Dog Night. All of them generally dabbled in hard rock, but their sensibilities were less aggressive. Grand Funk Railroad's anthem was "We're an American Band." The Guess Who's trademark was the 1970 hit "American Woman." One of its original members, Randy Bachman, left soon after to form BTO, whose anthems included "You Ain't Seen Nothin Yet" and "Takin' Care of Business." Three Dog Night had a stranger repetoire, running from social commentary to Joe Cocker-ish pop. Their signature songs, however, were the antiparty anthem "Mama Told Me Not to Come" and the sublimely silly "Joy to the World." A few more sophisticated entries into the form included the MC5 ("High School") and Britain's Mott the Hoople.

Glam Rock. Less a style of music than a fashion, glam rock (also known as glitter rock) was a short-lived movement that spotlighted a growing number of artists who specialized in rock as theater. Though shock-rock artists such as Alice Cooper and Kiss shared some of glam's exhibitionist tendencies, most of the inspiration came, again, from England. In the late 1960s Marc Bolan and T-Rex mixed their decadent pop sound with glamorous costuming that flirted with androgyny. Picking up on their theatricality, Mott the Hoople pushed it further by adding drag touches to their image. Their biggest hit was "All the Young Dudes," which became an underground anthem in the gay community. The song was written by David Bowie, who exploded onto the rock scene with a series of arty albums and expensive tours in which he assumed the persona of a pop space alien, Ziggy Stardust, complete with makeup, an orange shag haircut, and glittery costumes. Bowie's gender-bending pushed the limits

of camp and of rock theatricality. Artistically, his chameleon posturing allowed him to explore the possibilities of rock as pure image. Elton John adopted some of Bowie's androgynous and bisexual posing but went on to create his own style of costumed camp that was far less decadent. John's romantic sensibility and slick, unfailing musical instinct created a highly infectious and undeniably catchy brand of pop. By the mid 1970s he was rock's biggest superstar, pounding his piano in outrageous get-ups, selling out stadiums, and ruling the radio. English compatriots Queen, ELO, and Slade also made the charts with glam-rock anthems. In the rock underground, meanwhile, Roxy Music's Brian Eno (who later produced albums for Bowie) played with glamour-boy artifice, while Lou Reed and Iggy Pop (both on albums produced by Bowie) flirted with the darker sides of glitter's bisexuality. The New York Dolls slapped a campy drag look over their sly and street-tough rock 'n' roll, inspiring Kiss and the entire punk rock generation to form fast and loud bands.

Southern Rock. Like heavy metal, southern rock attempted a return to basics. Boogie bands, as they were also called, promoted themselves as cheerfully crude hell-raisers and good old boys, the inheritors of the Confederacy. Their music had roots in country and western and rhythm and blues styles but added the heavy guitar sound of hard rock. Common lyrical themes included whiskey, guns, and women. The pioneers of southern rock were the Allman Brothers, who broke through with a live album featuring Duane Allman's snaky slide guitar. Allman's death in 1971 altered the band's direction, but there were a host of successors, including the Charlie Daniels Band, the Marshall Tucker Band, the Outlaws, Molly Hatchet, Johnny and Edgar Winter, .38 Special, and Black Oak Arkansas. Lynyrd Skynyrd was probably the most prominent of all, thanks to scorching live performances and a series of radio hits like "Gimme Three Steps" and "Freebird." Then, in 1977 lead singer Ronnie Van Zant and three of the band's guitarists were killed in a plane crash, and the southern rock rebellion began to wane.

Jazz Rock. By the late 1960s groups such as Chicago; Santana; Billy Preston; and Blood, Sweat and Tears were commonly incorporating jazz sounds into their pop recordings. But a new group of innovators expanded jazz into the rock arena. Miles Davis added rock instrumentals and electronic keyboards to his early 1970s records. The Mahavishnu Orchestra mixed well-rehearsed melodies and harmonies with more traditional jazz stylings. Chick Corea adopted a lyric West Coast sound, and Herbie Hancock experimented first with electronic, then with rock, fusion. Weather Report relied on an improvisational sound. Later in the decade, artists such as Spyro Gyra, Chuck Mangione, George Benson, Jeff Lorber Fusion, the Crusaders, and Steely Dan added a distinct pop aura to the music, which set off a wave of popularity but diluted its influences. As popsters Billy

Captain and Tennille album cover (1975)

David Cassidy album cover (1975)

Joel and Gerry Rafferty dabbled in the hybrid sound it ceased to be jazz or rock altogether.

Corporate Rock. Many of the creators of progressive, glitter, heavy metal, and southern rock became superstar acts, mounting gargantuan live tours, releasing mammoth concept albums and double albums, and mass marketing promotional items such as T-shirts, tour jackets, and posters. The imagery of 1970s rock — from pyramids and holograms to sci-fi and fantasy landscapes to skulls and Satan — proved easy to sell, especially to teenagers. This gave rise for the first time to the idea of rock as a largely corporate product rather than a movement or an art form. As the decade progressed and bands were distinguished as much by their logos as by their music, an army of groups with interchangeable names seemed to invade the market: Foghat, Styx, Triumph, Foreigner, Toto, Nazareth, Boston, Kansas, Journey. The ultimate in promoted rock came with the release of Peter Frampton's live double album *Frampton Comes Alive!,* which sold four million copies and introduced America to the blockbuster album. A host of other multimillion sellers soon followed.

California Rock. Fleetwood Mac soon topped Frampton's record sales with their multiplatinum *Rumours* (1977), the first album ever to produce four Top 10 singles. Fleetwood Mac exemplified the "California sound" of the 1970s, mixing soft, artful ballads with harder-edged rockers. The Eagles' trademark, on records such as *Hotel California* (1976) and *The Long Run,* was decidedly mellow, a kind of burnt-out, spaced-out rock tinged with country and blues. Led by Don Henley, Glenn Frey, and Joe Walsh, the Eagles became one of the most successful bands of the decade. Another West Coast artist, pop crooner Linda Ronstadt, also favored blues and country sounds in songs like "Blue Bayou." The slick, highly commercial production on Ronstadt's albums contributed to her huge success. San Francisco rocker Steve Miller had a long streak of twangy journeyman hits in the 1970s, and Los Angeles singer-songwriter Jackson Browne hit the charts as well with his smooth, uneventful pop rock. Other immensely popular California acts included Loggins and Messina and the Doobie Brothers, whose boogie style on hits like "Black Water" owed something to the southern rock sound. The best of the California rockers was Steely Dan, whose jazz-based sound produced several influential albums and singles in the early 1970s.

Top 40 Pop. All the California rockers scored big on the pop charts throughout the 1970s. The United States, it seemed, wanted to mellow out after the violence of Vietnam and the letdowns of the recession and Watergate. Besides Ronstadt (and Fleetwood Mac superstar Stevie Nicks), the biggest female vocalists of the decade were Barbra Streisand, Diana Ross, Helen Reddy, Anne Murray, Carly Simon, Roberta Flack, and Olivia Newton-John, all of whom specialized in laid-back ballads. It was no different for male vocalists: James Taylor, Neil Sedaka, Barry Manilow, John Denver, Leo Sayer, and Harry Chapin all topped the charts regularly with easy-listening material. The softest, sweetest, and most successful balladeers of all were the Carpenters, who in the early 1970s sold millions of wholesome, smiley, squeaky-clean pop records.

Television Pop. Almost as pure were the Osmonds, five brothers promoted as the "white Jackson Five" but actually closer in spirit to the Cowsills or the Archies. Originally popularized on *The Andy Williams Show* in the

MAJOR GRAMMY AWARD WINNERS, 1977

(presented 23 February 1978)

Record of the Year	*Hotel California*, The Eagles
Song of the Year	"Love Theme from *A Star Is Born* (Evergreen)," Barbra Streisand, and "You Light Up My Life," Debby Boone
Album of the Year	*Rumours*, Fleetwood Mac
Pop Vocalist, Female	Barbra Streisand
Pop Vocalist, Male	James Taylor
New Artist	Debby Boone
Comedy Performance	Steve Martin, *Let's Get Small*
Movie Soundtrack	John Williams, *Star Wars*

Source: Norm N. Nite, *Rock On Almanac: The First Four Decades of Rock n Roll* (New York: Harper & Row, 1989).

---

late 1960s, the Osmonds had amazing success with their bubblegum hits. The Partridge Family, though equally successful, was not even a real group: only television mom Shirley Jones and real-life stepson David Cassidy sang on their records. David's stepbrother Shaun Cassidy had some success on the charts later in the decade with his wholesome cover versions of old pop songs (and on television's *Hardy Boys* series). Completing the group of "TV pop" were Tony Orlando and Dawn and the Captain and Tennille, joining Sonny and Cher as Top 40 acts given their own weekly variety series. By middecade themes from television series were regularly making the pop charts, including the themes from *Welcome Back, Kotter; SWAT; Charlie's Angels;* and *Happy Days.* Meanwhile, an independent record distributor found that heavy television advertising could pump new life into the previous year's Top 40 hits. K-Tel International's pop collections, which crammed as many as twelve songs on a side, sold in the millions.

No Heroes. Rock 'n' roll purists, numbed by the banality and pomposity of American rock and pop in the 1970s, searched constantly for signs of hope that the music would rebound. After the Beatles broke up many looked to the solo careers of the former members for inspiration but were generally disappointed. John Lennon released several strong albums, then retreated. George Harrison dabbled in mystical pop rock, and Ringo Starr, despite some Top 40 success, was not vital on his own. The most successful was Paul McCartney, but his efforts with Wings were increasingly mainstream. Other fans looked to the Rolling Stones to carry the rock 'n' roll torch, and they responded with excellent new material until they began to drift into self-indulgence in the mid 1970s. Meanwhile, the search went on for new Janis Joplins, new Jim Morrisons, new Jimi Hendrixes, new Bob Dylans. Early in the decade Rod Stewart showed promise as a raucous, Joplin-style vocalist, but by middecade he faded into commercial pop. Eric Clapton was embraced by guitar fans for his technical abilities, but he was hardly a showman. After the breakup of Creedence Clearwater Revival, fans looked forward to John Fogerty's solo career, but it barely materialized. Neil Young's bitter, honest songwriting and unusual singing earned a large cult following but little more. Van Morrison likewise never broke from his own deeply personal cycle of work, despite his sharp talent. Frank Zappa, whose arty, satiric decadence defied categorization, was worshiped by only a small contingent. Dylan himself surprised the rock world with two excellent comeback albums, then meandered off again. For many cult fans, including rock journalists, Springsteen's arrival in 1973 was transcendent. With his marathon live shows of energetic rock and vivid narrative songs (especially on his album *Born to Run*), Springsteen was hailed in the press as the future of rock 'n' roll in 1975. But despite the hype the public was apathetic. The breakup of the Beatles and the 1977 death of Elvis Presley only heightened a sad idea for rock purists. Apparently a single band or hero could no longer ignite — or unite — the pop music world.

Sources:

Greil Marcus, *Stranded: Rock and Roll for a Desert Island* (New York: Knopf, 1979);

Jim Miller, ed., *The Rolling Stone Illustrated History of Rock and Roll* (New York: Random House, 1980);

David P. Szatmary, *Rockin' in Time: A Social History of Rock and Roll* (Englewood Cliffs, N.J.: Prentice-Hall, 1987).

THE PULSE OF BLACK MUSIC

Unity. Black music had flourished during the late 1960s and was still peaking as the 1970s began. Its popularity with black and white audiences alike had caused a unity among the pop and rock audience that was unprecedented. Rock fans reponded to Aretha ("Lady Soul") Franklin and Otis Redding, while soul followers connected to Jimi Hendrix and Sly and the Family Stone. As audiences began to splinter in the early 1970s, black music continued to set new trends, to be the strongest and purest force in pop music during that era. Lady Soul Franklin released the classics "Rock Steady" and "Spanish Harlem." Al Green typified the sexy soul sound, mixing an urban rhythm and blues influence with touches of gospel on a string of emotionally naked hits such as "Let's Stay Together" and "I'm Still in Love With You." Barry White pushed sexy soul to another level with his steamy innuendo on "I'm Gonna Love You Just a Little More Baby" and "Can't Get Enough of Your Love, Babe." The Staple Singers' gospel-influenced style produced classics in "Respect Yourself" and "I'll Take You There." Bill Withers revealed blues roots on "Ain't No Sunshine" and "Lean on Me." A host of fabulous one-shot or two-shot female artists (Freda Payne, Honey Cone, Jean Knight) showed a refreshing and sexy feminist streak. These and other early-1970s one-shot hits ("Too Late to Turn Back Now," "Everybody Plays the Fool," "Ain't No Woman Like the One I've Got") would later find seemingly endless oldies stations across the country.

Motown. Though its heyday was perhaps already past by the 1970s, Motown continued to record classic black pop and soul. Marvin Gaye ("Let's Get It On"), the Temptations ("Just My Imagination"), Smokey Robinson and the Miracles ("The Tears of a Clown"), and Gladys Knight and the Pips ("Midnight Train to Georgia," "Best Thing That Ever Happened to Me") all made the charts during this period. The Four Tops left the label in 1972, and the Supremes split up as the decade began, but Motown got a burst of youthful energy when its new sensation, the Jackson Five, logged four number ones in 1970: "I Want You Back," "ABC," "The Love You Save," and "I'll Be There." Originally from Gary, Indiana, the young quintet began performing when singer Michael Jackson was only five years old. Before long they were opening at Chicago's Regal Club for superstar Motown acts, and they were signed to a record deal by producer Berry Gordy soon after. They continued to make hits throughout the early 1970s but eventually left Motown in 1976.

Relevance. Several Motown artists, like other soul singers in the early 1970s, began to record music with socially and politically relevant themes. As the black artistic renaissance continued to give artists, writers, and directors a new sense of identity and empowerment, soul music seemed a natural place for its expression. Some of the new music was pure fun: Isaac Hayes asked "Who's the black dick who's a sex machine for all the chicks?" (Answer: "Shaft.") But much of it had a darker edge. The Temptations had begun the trend in the late 1960s with a series of socially conscious hits: "Cloud Nine," "Runaway Child Running Wild," and "Ball of Confusion." In 1971 two artists released strong statements of social and personal disunity. Gaye, known for his upbeat Motown hits, revealed himself as a concerned, mature album artist with the release of *What's Goin' On*. Unified in sound as well as concept, the songs explored ecology, war, poverty, and racism, becoming earnest and haunting pleas for peace, social justice, and a more stable environment. Sly and the Family Stone released a dark-edged, brooding album that shocked many of the band's listeners. Sly's previous output had been celebratory, and one of the racially unifying forces of the late 1960s. *There's a Riot*

Al Green album cover (1972)

Goin' On (1971) abandoned that exultant spirit for a harsh look at the realities of black life and Sly's personal experience. The single "Family Affair" attempted to confront the problems Sly was having with his career and his band, which included illness, drugs, canceled concerts, and management battles.

Chill. Like "blaxploitation" filmmakers, many soul artists turned away from integrationist goals in their music in the early 1970s to connect with the black audience, releasing material that dealt with tough issues. The Temptations recorded "Papa Was a Rolling Stone," an uncompromising look at black family life. Edwin Starr screamed "War, what is it good for?" (Answer: "absolutely nothing.") Curtis Mayfield's soundtrack to the movie *Superfly*, with its chilling hit "Freddie's Dead," was a stinging antidrug testament. Every song seemed to have a warning about the times and about the untrustworthy souls populating them. The O'Jays decried "Back Stabbers" and "Shifty, Shady, Jealous Kind of People." In "Smiling Faces Sometimes," the Undisputed Truth sang "beware of the handshake that hides a snake." "Some people," sang the Dramatics in "What You See Is What You Get," "are made of lies." War spoke ominously of "Slipping Into Darkness," and Stevie Wonder expressed "Superstition" and railed against the miseries of "Living for the City." Wonder released several albums in the early 1970s that confronted social issues, including *Innervisions* and *Talking Book*. The troubled tone of these recordings were vivid proof that the utopian spirit of the 1960s was over.

Philadelphia. Not all soul music of the early 1970s was ominous or downbeat. Love songs and dance songs also flourished, due in large measure to Philadelphia producers Thom Bell, Kenny Gamble, and Leon Huff. The thirty-two single hits they collectively made during that period included classics for Billy Paul ("Me and Mrs. Jones") and Harold Melvin and Blue Notes ("If You Don't Know Me By Now"). But the bulk of their output was with the Spinners, the O'Jays, the Stylistics, and the Chi-Lites. The Spinners' "I'll Be Around" and the O'Jays' "Love Train" featured a new type of dance beat that would later become the basis of disco. The love songs of the Stylistics ("You Are Everything," "You Make Me Feel Brand New") and Chi-Lites ("Have You Seen Her," "Oh Girl") had a sweeter, more plaintive sound that was often melancholy and used a falsetto vocal style. The so-called Philadelphia sound pioneered by Bell, Gamble, and Huff became the most influential black style of the 1970s, as important to what followed as Berry Gordy was to Motown in the 1960s.

Funk. As soul music fragmented and became more political, an alternative group of black artists was creating fresh urban dance sounds that would merge to form the funk movement. Kool and the Gang was one of the style's early purveyors. On songs such as "Jungle Boogie" and "Funky Stuff" they threw wild horns, uneven bass lines, and party whoops into an explosion of sound. Earth, Wind and Fire's Maurice White mixed jazz, soul, and folk ingredients to create a cosmic sound that was more commercial and more elegant than other funk artists, and the group had a major hit with "Shining Star." Thumbing his nose at this overdelicacy, George Clinton in 1968 formed Funkadelic, a group that sought to create an alternative "funk nation." The album *One Nation Under a Groove* (1973) set the tone: in-joke language, tribal rythms, and wild melodies. The campy, space-age fashion of funk promoted by Clinton was reminiscent of glitter rock's alien invasion. An offshoot group, Parliament, was formed by Clinton in 1974. Parliament's raucous, uninhibited "Flashlight" became funk's dance-party anthem.

Mainstream. By the mid 1970s black music had become almost as bland and diluted as white mainstream pop. Though funk was innovative, it remained a largely underground movement. Roberta Flack was representative of the state of soul as the decade wore on — pretty, but without energy or passion. Billy Preston's jazz-pop compositions sounded like commercialized Ray Charles. Diana Ross touched banality with hits like "Touch Me in the Morning" and "Theme from Mahogany." Wonder, though obviously a talented composer, began to seem like a self-parody as he walked off annually with armloads of Grammys for happy albums such as *Songs in the Key of Life* and happy songs such as "You Are the Sunshine of My Life." Sly and the Family Stone had dispersed; Green and Franklin had faltered. Most of Motown's classic 1960s acts had left the company. The time had clearly arrived for a new sound.

Disco. Disco was a shot in the arm to black music, restoring a dance groove to a faltering style. First popularized in cities at black, Latino, and gay clubs, disco had an overtly sexual sound, its beat pulsing steadily beneath supremely catchy melodies and dense, multilayered production. The style and sound were purely escapist, and the primary message was sex. Flashing lights and a hot, crowded dance floor heightened the fantasies evoked by the songs. The best disco was produced by black artists, who began to have commercial success during the summer of 1974 with hits such as "Rock the Boat" and "Rock Your Baby." The following summer, with Van McCoy's "The Hustle," it became a true phenomenon, and new black artists were at the forefront. The Ohio Players' funk-influenced sound produced a smash with "Fire," which they followed with "Love Rollercoaster." Vickie Sue Robinson's "Turn the Beat Around," Hot Chocolate's "You Sexy Thing," the Miracles' "Love Machine Pt. 1," the Sylvers' "Boogie Fever," the Andrea True Connection's "More More More," Rose Royce's "Car Wash," Thelma Houston's "Don't Leave Me This Way," Gaye's "Got to Give It Up," and the Emotions' "Best of My Love," were some of the better disco songs of the next two years. And Chic, with its funky party hits "Dance Dance Dance," "Good Times," and "Le Freak," were innovative disco artists. But by late 1977 some of the original drive and eroticism of the music was being eroded by the sheer number of artists jumping on the bandwagon.

Imitators. Inevitably, a host of white artists soon began recording disco music, some of them long-established acts whose embracing of the style was dubious, if not disastrous. In 1975 the Bee Gees, with "Jive Talkin," and KC and the Sunshine Band, with "Get Down Tonight," were the first white groups to succeed commercially with the sound, as well as Elton John with his disco-tinged hit "Philadelphia Freedom." KC and the Sunshine Band was an attempt at an interracial pop group à la Sly and the Family Stone, but KC was no Sly. Nevertheless, the group enjoyed a string of catchy disco ditties, including "That's the Way I Like It,"That's the Way I Like It" (KC and the Sunshine Band)[That's the Way I Like It] "Keep It Comin' Love," and "Shake Your Booty." The Village People teased audiences with not-so-subtle gay overtones on hits like "Macho Man," "YMCA," and "In the Navy." Soon the fad began to take on elements of the surreal, with chart toppers that included European groups Silver Connection ("Fly Robin Fly" and "Get Up and Boogie") and Abba ("Dancing Queen"). In 1977, with the unprecedented success of the Bee Gees and *Saturday Night Fever*, it seemed as if white pop stars had taken over disco completely.

Divas. Disco, because it catered to escapist fantasy and was not geared to live performing, tended to produce few superstars (the Bee Gees notwithstanding). But Donna Summer had a good claim to the throne of the disco movement at the end of the decade. Sultry and sexy, Summer first hit with "Love to Love You Baby" (1976), a seventeen-minute vinyl aphrodisiac. Her full-throttle vocals propelled a dance version of "MacArthur Park" to number one two years later, and "Last Dance" became another smash. But it was her 1979 album *Bad Girls* that crowned her the true queen of the dance floor. Hot, funky, nasty, and above all fun, the record proved there was still life in disco. Fellow divas at the end of the 1970s included A Taste of Honey ("Boogie Oogie Oogie"), Amii Stewart ("Knock on Wood"), Anita Ward ("Ring My Bell"), and especially Gloria Gaynor ("I Will Survive") and Sister Sledge ("We Are Family"), whose life-affirming hits became anthems for the gay community.

Fever. Disco seemed to strike a nerve with the public, or rather seemed to soothe one. Americans, soured and exhausted by the crises of Vietnam, Watergate, and the economy, just wanted to escape. Disco afforded that release and indulged their fantasies. By 1978 the phenomenon was so hot that thirty-six million adults had invaded twenty-thousand disco clubs nationwide. There were submovements, such as roller disco; movies, such as *Can't Stop the Music* (1980) and *Thank God, It's Friday* (1978); and designer disco fashions. In 1978 more than two hundred radio stations had converted to an all-disco format. There seemed to be no stopping disco. Yet by the end of the decade the music had already lost much of its original power, as every major artist from the Rolling Stones ("Miss You") to Rod Stewart ("Do Ya Think I'm Sexy") released a disco song. The airwaves had become choked with hopeless banalities such as "Disco Duck," "A Fifth of Beethoven," and the disco-tinged "Theme from *SWAT*." The music had become so commercial that in 1979 the inevitable happened. An antidisco backlash gathered steam, spearheaded by Chicago disc jockey Steve Dahl and joined by millions of rock 'n' roll fans who were tired of the empty-headed beat.

Sources:

Fred Bronson, *The Billboard Book of Number One Hits* (New York: Billboard Publications, 1988);

"Disco Takes Over," *Newsweek*, 93 (2 April 1979): 56–64;

Jim Miller, ed., *The Rolling Stone Illustrated History of Rock and Roll* (New York: Random House, 1980).

Punk idol Sid Vicious

THE PUNK ROCK AND NEW WAVE MOVEMENTS

Rebellion. Punk rock combusted in the mid 1970s from the smoldering energies of several different music styles and in reaction to the bland corporate rock then popular. The punk and new wave movements had a violent, nihilistic image that did not always reflect the wide diversity of musical styles (and fashions) they encompassed. Their influences ranged from avant-garde art rock to 1950s rock 'n' roll to Jamaican reggae, but the collective force of their impact made them easy to categorize. The representative effect was a primitive, stripped-down assault of guitars, bass, and drums played fast and loud. To rock fans weary of mainstream excess, punk rock was a revelation. To those who liked the status quo, it was alienating noise. Either way, punk could not have cared less; the only thing that mattered was that the musical rebellion had finally arrived. It was user-friendly, too, and more utopian than it cared to admit: the simplicity of punk meant that anyone who wanted to could play, regardless of talent or experience. Punk was a do-it-yourself movement that was about seizing the moment, discarding history, breaking the rules, inventing new ones, and taking a stand (even a wrong one) whenever possible. In other words, like all rock 'n' roll, it was about being young.

Origins. Punk first arose in New York's East Village, which had a history of underground movements, from jazz to Beat poetry to avant-garde art. The Velvet Underground, an alternative band led by Lou Reed and John Cale, was promoted into brief notoriety by artist Andy Warhol in the late 1960s. Deliberately raw and abrasive, studiedly experimental and strange, the Velvets made an uncompromising but uncommercial series of primitive art albums that inspired legions of followers. The Stooges were among them. With the flamboyant, often self-abusive Iggy Pop as lead singer, the Stooges specialized in thrashy, trashy guitar rock ripe with themes of youthful alienation and rebellion. Borrowing bits from these bands as well as other grunge bands such as the MC5 and Mott the Hoople, the New York Dolls played a fast, funny street rock with the added cheek of drag fashion. Before their breakups in 1973 and 1974, the Stooges and the Dolls, along with Lou Reed as a solo artist, had inspired a New York underground rock scene.

New Artists. In 1974 poet and guitarist Tom Verlaine persuaded a Bowery bar owner to open his club to rock acts, and CBGB was born. Verlaine was soon fronting an arty band called Television, in which he set his unusual voice to unusual lyrics. Another poet rocker was Patti Smith, who expanded her backup from guitarist Lenny Kaye to a full-fledged band in 1975 and recorded the groundbreaking prepunk album *Horses*. With Television and Smith playing regularly at CBGB and another club, Max's Kansas City, other bands joined the growing movement. The Ramones were the definitive New York punk band, unleashing a barrage of hilariously primitive three-chord songs like "Blitzkrieg Bop," "Beat on the Brat," and "Now I Wanna Sniff Some Glue." That the group was technically limited was its entire selling point; they cheerfully took up the banner of punk's "spokesmorons." Richard Hell and the Voidoids created an anthem to alienation in "Blank Generation." Blondie, fronted by singer Deborah Harry, added a pop sound and a flirty sexuality to the new music. David Byrne, a former design student, formed the Talking Heads, whose neurotic-intellectual lyrics and quirky vocals, rhythms, and melodies put them at the forefront of punk's offshoot movement: new wave.

England. Journalists wrote that the Ramones' 1976 British tour ignited the punk rock movement in England, and they may have been one of its catalysts. The real impetus was the country's social and economic climate in the mid 1970s. Rampant unemployment, especially among the young, had heightened class distinctions, isolating the poor and increasing street violence. English punk rock was an eruption of pent-up rage, directed at royalty, the establishment, the police, and economic conditions. British punk was antieverything; it aimed for anarchy and nihilism. The Sex Pistols, formed in late 1975 and promoted by Malcolm McLaren in London clubs, became the definitive punk band in the late 1970s. With the force of chainsaws they screamed through numbers such as "Anarchy in the U.K." and "God Save the Queen" (both banned from BBC radio and both big chart hits) with a sneering fury that was altogether new, even for rock 'n' roll. Singer Johnny Rotten and bassist Sid Vicious adopted a look of spiky hair and ripped clothing to accentuate the group's ferocious image. They had a two-word message: "No future." Denying hope or ambition, dismissing their influences (especially 1950s and 1960s rock 'n' rollers) as "old farts," and rejecting any and all ideas of commerciality, the Pistols were true innovators. The implied question, where to go from there, they found irrelevant as well. But other bands, excited by possibilities in the new music, disagreed.

Movement. The Pistols opened the floodgates for fast, loud bands. The sneering stance of some, such as the Stranglers and the Damned, appeared to be mere posturing. Still, there was no denying the force and spite of Billy Idol avowing (in response to the Who's 1960s anthem "My Generation"), "your generation don't mean a thing to me." That was particularly ironic in light of the Jam, who borrowed heavily from the Who's mod stylings in their songs and image. Other bands preferred plain, ordinary, cheerful subversion, from the Buzzcocks' "Orgasm Addict" to X-Ray Spex's "Oh Bondage, Up Yours." It was the Clash who took the form the Pistols pioneered and tried to give it substance. Their music was angry, too (songs included "White Riot" and "I'm So Bored With the U.S.A."), but group leaders Joe Strummer and Mick Jones wanted to use the music as a force for political change, not mere nihilism. They were also interested in expanding punk's form, especially using elements of reggae. (Reggae, created by Jamaican artists such as Jimmy Cliff, Peter Tosh, Toots and the Maytals, and especially Bob Marley and the Wailers, had been popular for several years in England, leading to a brief ska movement.) The Clash's self-titled debut album was one of punk rock's most powerful statements.

New Wave. Some of the forerunners of American new wave music were British artists who began to gain popularity in the United States in the 1970s. "Pub rockers" such as Ian Dury, Dave Edmunds, and Nick Lowe played in a stripped-down rockabilly style. Graham Parker's rhythm and blues pop songs were howls of pain and frustration. The Police were heavily influenced by reggae. American singer Chrissie Hynde formed the Pretenders with three English musicians, playing crisp and spirited pop. Joe Jackson's early music was driven by his hangdog, loner energy. Squeeze and the Boomtown Rats had a more accessible pop sound. The most influential to emerge from the British new wave was Elvis Costello, whose straight image contrasted with angry songs about betrayal and loss. Lyrically complex but musically simple and forceful, Costello was hailed as a "new wave Dylan," the poet laureate of punk.

Concepts. Equally important was a wave of art rockers led by Roxy Music's Brian Eno and Bryan Ferry. Ferry's lounge-crooner style and Eno's dense, ambient production values simultaneously celebrated and deflated their own pretension. Such self-referential concepts were familiar to art and literature but relatively new to popular music, and they influenced many American new wavers, including the Talking Heads, who began using Eno as a producer on their albums. Avant-garde composers (Philip Glass, Steve Reich, John Cage), fringe pop artists (David Bowie), performance artists (Laurie Anderson), and poets (William Burroughs, Allen Ginsberg) were also heroes for the artier groups, creating an overlapping audience between fans of one art form and another. Artists collaborated by producing records for each other (Bowie for Iggy Pop and Lou Reed, Eno for Bowie). Perhaps predictably, a wave of deliberately ironic "concept" groups began to invade the new wave: Devo (whose robotics celebrated dehumanization), the B-52s (whose 1960s stylings celebrated camp), and the Residents (whose faceless raspings celebrated emptiness). This led even further, to "No Wave" artists such as Nina Hagen, the Slits, the Plasmatics, and Teenage Jesus and the Jerks, whose sound abandoned all pretense of popular music and expressed, instead, only the concept of being alien.

Do It Yourself. One of the appealing aspects of the punk and new wave movement was their complete disassociation from the mainstream. The media gave them little coverage (beyond its obvious shock value), and major labels, other than the Warner Bros. subsidiary Sire, were justifiably concerned about the music's lack of commercial appeal. Punk received little to no radio play, and subsequently it had to be hunted for — especially since every locale had its own band scene and most of those bands were cutting demos, extended plays (EPs), and one-shot singles. Fans of the music loved the punk culture largely because it was underground; it bonded them into an alternative "family," especially as they became targets of criticism and even violence from those who were angered and alienated by punk. Their world was a network, even a vernacular, of independent labels, do-it-yourself fanzines and handbills, alternative record stores, and thrift shops. Punk and new wave tastes — in clothes, in movies, and in the music itself — ranged from aggression and alienation (the stereotypical mohawk haircuts and safety pins) to pure camp (any outmoded image from the 1950s and 1960s). Despite their small onstage numbers, women were both accepted as and expected to be equal participants. Despite its popular image as a violent subculture, punk was in actuality almost utopian in its embrace of a misfit society. Punk affirmed the new, the bizarre, the amateur, the subversive, even the truly frightening — as long as it was not mainstream. To the punk and new wave sensibilities, which celebrated the concept of difference as much as they did music, the only sin was to be commercial.

Changes. Punk rock's most productive year was 1977, in which the Sex Pistols, the Clash, the Talking Heads, the Ramones, Blondie, Television, and Elvis Costello all released some of their best recordings. But beginning in 1978 much of the initial drive and energy of the movement began to disperse. The Sex Pistols broke up in the middle of their first American tour in 1978. Shortly thereafter, Sid Vicious was arrested for the stabbing death of his American girlfriend Nancy Spungen, then died himself early in 1979 of a drug overdose. Johnny Rotten announced that punk was dead and reinvented himself as avant-garde musician John Lydon. Brian Eno and the Talking Heads continued to have fruitful collab-

Country music producer Billy Sherrill

orations, but Television disbanded after their 1978 album. Patti Smith retired from recording and performing after a 1979 tour to marry former MC5 leader Fred Smith. The Ramones were hilarious in Roger Corman's cult punk comedy *Rock 'n' Roll High School* (in which they helped defeat the music-hating principal and helped blow up the school), but as the decade ended they seemed to falter with an album produced by Phil Spector. Many in the punk scene seemed to feel that the music and movement were being corrupted by new interest from major record companies and, finally, the media.

Commercialization. A sure sign of things to come was the early success of the Cars, who were conceived as a new wave band but managed several Top 40 hits in 1979 from their debut album. Their success opened the door to the major-label signing of a host of quirky new bands with skinny ties, arty attitudes, and the word *the* in their names (the Pop, the Shirts, the Shoes). By the summer of 1979 the United States got the Knack, whose power-pop hit "My Sharona" topped the charts for six weeks. Also in 1979 Blondie hit number one (the first of four times) with their disco song "Heart of Glass." In 1980 the Pretenders, Devo, and Gary Numan all had big hits as well. By the early 1980s pop radio was full of "weird" singers (Boy George, Cyndi Lauper) and "arty" bands (Duran Duran, Human League) that would have been considered punk or new wave only a few years earlier but were now achieving wild success in the mainstream. Even some of the most subversive 1970s artists — the Clash, Elvis Costello, and the Talking Heads — began to make the pop charts in the 1980s. Punks antagonized by this commercialization ended the decade by once more going underground, again stripping the music down to its raw basics of noise, anger, and speed. This new style of punk, hardcore, lay buried in the musical underground during the 1980s, only to find itself mined in 1990 as the new

The Band

sound of commercial radio — grunge. Whatever Johnny Rotten's 1979 declarations, punk rock was most definitely not dead.

Sources:

Jim Miller, ed., *The Rolling Stone Illustrated History of Rock and Roll* (New York: Random House, 1980);

David P. Szatmary, *Rockin in Time: A Social History of Rock and Roll* (Englewood Cliffs, N.J.: Prentice-Hall, 1987).

THE RESURGENCE OF COUNTRY MUSIC

Counterculture. Country music, with its inherent appeal for the rural heartland, had always existed apart from more sophisticated (and more fickle) musical trends of urban America. Part of this difference was purely regional, but it was also the result of Nashville's established traditions. Country records were generally low-budget efforts, promoted to a small number of radio stations. Live venues (the Grand Ole Opry, country fairs and festivals, small taverns) existed completely apart from the stadium-scale theatrics of rock 'n' roll. Thus the counterculture of the late 1960s — pot smoking, peace marches, the black and women's movements, explosive artistic experimentation — had barely caused a ripple in the coun-

try music scene. Nashville was seen by most of U.S. youth as part of the establishment, and though country music had traditionally maintained something of a rebel (i.e., Confederate) image, that raw fever was little in evidence during the 1960s. The hard line of Nashville conservatism (the so-called silent majority) was well represented in songs such as Sgt. Barry Sadler's "Ballad of the Green Berets" and Merle Haggard's defiant "Okie from Muskogee" (which drew the admiration of President Richard Nixon). Country music, while never overtly political, remained firmly rooted in patriotic, anti-Communist, conservative values of the 1950s (for example, Tammy Wynette's "Stand by Your Man"), to the point where the social revolutions consuming the rest of the nation might just as well have not even existed.

Commercial Appeal. Some country performers, whatever their politics, had remained faithful to the traditional country sound — pedal-steel guitars, fiddles — and its outlaw image. But by the late 1960s few artists remained who had not adapted to the lush, commercial "Nashville sound" popularized by producers Owen Bradley and Chet Atkins. Their arrangements provided singers such as Patsy Cline and Wynette with a background

Cover for the defining album of the country music "Outlaw" movement

of strings and layered harmonies. Country music had found a comfortable niche in mainstream popularity, its image bolstered by big crossover hits such as "King of the Road," "Harper Valley PTA," and "Rose Garden." Even rebel Johnny Cash scored a crossover smash with "A Boy Named Sue," and onetime purist Buck Owens found his sound watered down for commercial distillation on television's *Hee Haw*. Glen Campbell sang his hits "Wichita Lineman," "Gentle on My Mind," and "By the Time I Get to Phoenix" on his weekly show. Television during the 1960s cheerfully promoted country music as the happy home of amiable rubes on shows such as *Green Acres, Petticoat Junction, the Beverly Hillbillies,* and *The Glen Campbell Hour*. As Nashville solidified its establishment status in the late 1960s, its original style and spirit — honky-tonk blues, rockabilly, bluegrass picking — were driven underground.

Crossover. Some attempts had been made by rock artists during this period to expand the range of country music. The Byrds; the Band; Creedence Clearwater Revival; and Crosby, Stills, Nash and Young had experimented with country styles, and Bob Dylan had recorded *Nashville Skyline* (1969) in the country music capital. The Byrds' Gram Parsons, with his partner Emmylou Harris, was the most serious rock artist to attempt a switch to country. As the 1970s progressed, southern rock bands such as the Allman Brothers and Lynyrd Skynyrd found popularity with hell-raising Confederate images. But generally these efforts were ignored by Nashville and its slick new production machine. It was the pop — not the rock — audience that country bigwigs now coveted. *Crossover* became the key concept behind most recording efforts, as new artists like Charlie Rich ("The Most Beau-

tiful Girl in the World"), Charley Pride ("Kiss an Angel Good Mornin' "), and Donna Fargo ("The Happiest Girl in the Whole U.S.A.") began to have major hits on both the pop and the country charts. Producer Billy Sherrill (who produced Rich, Wynette, and Tanya Tucker) was at the forefront of the crossover boom. He recognized, like most of Nashville by now, that the key to big hits was strong songwriting, and he handpicked material from the many long-established independent music publishers that thrived in the city. But to Sherrill and other like-minded producers and executives, songwriters were merely commodities, like the singers they packaged.

Outlaws. Two of the best new songwriters to arrive in Nashville in the late 1960s, Kris Kristofferson and Willie Nelson, were also two of the first to rebel against the Nashville establishment in the early 1970s. Kristofferson (with "Help Me Make It Through the Night" and "Me and Bobby McGee") and Nelson (with "Crazy" and "The Party's Over") had achieved some success writing for others, but neither had achieved much attention as performers. Both were disgusted by the slick pop of the new Nashville. Kristofferson, ironically, left the scene for a film career in Hollywood. Nelson declared his independence by relocating to Texas in 1971 and organizing the Dripping Springs festival. Waylon Jennings was another singer-songwriter who chafed under his restrictive contract. In 1972 he renegotiated with RCA for complete artistic control of his albums and forged a new partnership with producer Tompall Glaser. Jennings's gritty roadhouse image and straight-ahead cowboy sound were packaged on his 1973 album *Honky Tonk Heroes,* recorded at Glaser's new Hillbilly Central Studio. Jennings's success touched off a wave of similar rebellions at other labels, as artists realized they could hire their own promoters, managers, agents, and producers outside the Nashville system. In 1975 RCA released a synthetic, studio-created duet between Jennings and Nelson, "Good-Hearted Woman." Its success and the popularity of Nelson's *Red Headed Stranger* album that same year (featuring "Blue Eyes Cryin' in the Rain") paved the way for RCA's 1976 compilation album *Wanted! The Outlaws,* which featured Jennings, Nelson, Glaser, and Jennings's wife Jessi Colter. Rather unexpectedly, *Wanted! The Outlaws* became the first platinum country album, and Waylon and Willie went on to sweep the 1976 Country Music Awards. The outlaw movement had touched a Nashville nerve.

Infighting. When the outlaws emerged from country music's underground, Nashville had never seemed more commercial. Opryland, opened in 1972, had by 1974 transplanted the Grand Ole Opry's music into the money-driven world of its giant amusement park. Nontraditional performers were ruling the country charts, from John Denver ("Thank God I'm a Country Boy," "Rocky Mountain High," "Take Me Home, Country Roads") to Linda Ronstadt ("Heart Like a Wheel," "When Will I Be Loved," "You're No Good") to Anne

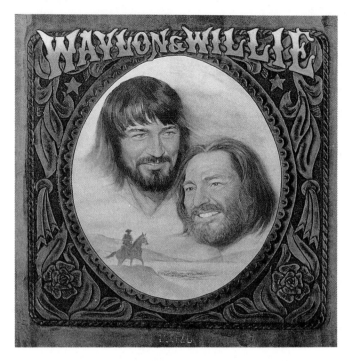

Waylon Jennings and Willie Nelson's 1978 album

Murray ("Snowbird," "Danny's Song," "Love Song"). They were also walking off with an alarming number of Country Music Association awards. The last straw for many traditional country artists was Olivia Newton-John, the Australian vocalist who had first found success in Nashville with hits such as "If Not for You," "Let Me Be There," and "If You Love Me (Let Me Know)." When she snubbed the CMA Awards in 1974 (presumably preferring traditional pop), an angry group of artists led by Merle Haggard (and also including George Jones, Johnny Paycheck, Hank Snow, Dolly Parton, Wynette, and Bill Anderson) decided to form the Association of Country Entertainers (ACE) a group restricted to purely country performers. The success of the outlaw performers and the efforts of ACE seemed to indicate that the time was ripe for a return to traditional country styles. Instead, as the late 1970s arrived, country music became bigger business than ever.

Mainstream. During the course of the decade, country record sales had risen to between 10 percent and 12 percent of the total market. New York corporate offices beefed up their divisions in Nashville; Columbia Records increased its Nashville staff from nine to thirty-three during the 1970s. Meanwhile, legal battles over writer advances had caused the demise of the city's independent music publishers, who had long been under the control of the Nashville establishment. Corporations outside the system now owned most of the material recorded there, and independent producers had arrived with new money and new technology to displace the old guard. Jennings and Nelson, no doubt because of their hell-raising images, were adopted by southern rock fans and had ever-bigger hits, including their duet "Mamas, Don't Let Your Babies Grow Up to Be Cowboys" and Jennings's "Luckenback, Texas." Country's new good-old-boy image spread like a brushfire in the mid to late 1970s via television (*Carter Country, BJ and the Bear*), movies (*Smokey and the Bandit* [1977], *Convoy* [1978], *Every Which Way But Loose* [1977]), and even a nationwide CB radio craze. Jimmy Carter's presidency did much to bolster the commercial potential of the South, as did the sudden success of Dolly Parton. Once the partner of singer Porter Waggoner, Parton became a solo act in 1974 and soon found amazing popularity through television appearances and songs such as "Here You Come Again." Like Owens and Kristofferson, Parton started out a country purist then quickly abandoned the music's traditions in favor of a mainstream career in movies. By 1980 Parton's commercial appeal was sealed in the movie *9 to 5.* Meanwhile, Loretta Lynn's career was celebrated in *Coal Miner's Daughter,* Nelson went "On the Road Again" in *Honeysuckle Rose,* and Jennings recorded the theme song to the television series *The Dukes of Hazzard.* That same year the mechanical bull of *Urban Cowboy* hit the big screen, and even suspicious city folk succumbed to country's commercial charm. And with the 1980 election of Ronald Reagan, it appeared that country's political conservatism was still intact: the ultrapatriotic "Ballad of the Green Berets" was back in style.

Sources:

Patrick Carr, ed., *The Illustrated History of Country Music* (Garden City, N.Y.: Doubleday, 1979);

Paul Kingsbury and Alan Axelrod, eds., *Country: The Music and the Musicians* (New York: Abbeville Press Publishers, 1988).

HEADLINE MAKERS

WOODY ALLEN

1935-

DIRECTOR, ACTOR, WRITER

Early Success. After an apprenticeship in the early 1960s that included work as a gag writer, Woody Allen first gained attention with his stand-up comedy routines in clubs, in college campus shows, and on recorded albums. His reputation as a funnyman was secured after he wrote and appeared in the hit 1965 film *What's New, Pussycat?* The following year his play *Don't Drink the Water* hit Broadway, while his irreverent debut as a movie director, *What's Up, Tiger Lily?*, played in theaters. In writings for *Playboy* and *Esquire* during this period, Allen played on the comic pretense of being a sophisticated bachelor around town. He expanded his cult audience in 1969 with the Broadway success *Play It Again, Sam* and the hit film *Take the Money and Run.*

Persona. By the 1970s Allen's comic persona was well-established. With a highly nervous expression and a hesitant, almost stammering delivery, he excelled in portrayals of a mock-intellectual urban nebbish. His sad face, self-deprecation, romantic frustration, and pacifism drew comparisons with Charlie Chaplin, while Allen's mockery (of self and others), Jewish humor, and lecherous energy paralleled Groucho Marx. "Great humor," Allen remarked, "is intellectual without trying to be." He created audience identification by parodying his own cowardice, physical awkwardness, and pretensions to intelligence and became an embodiment of the 1970s "sensitive male." Early 1970s comedies like *Bananas* (1971) and *Everything You Always Wanted to Know About Sex* (1972) established his trademark preoccupations with God, sex, and death and also featured appearances by his onetime wife Louise Lasser.

Keaton. Allen's most frequent costar in his 1970s comedies was Diane Keaton, who also appeared in *The Godfather* films. Projecting both daffiness and warmth, Keaton became Allen's perfect comic foil. *Play It Again, Sam* (1972) featured Allen as a neurotic film critic who

tries to woo Keaton with romantic advice from the ghost of Humphrey Bogart. In *Sleeper* (1973) Keaton is a frivolous society woman forced to go on the lam with Allen, who played a man deep-frozen after an operation and then thawed two hundred years in the future. Allen parodied everything from *War and Peace* to Ingmar Bergman in his next film, *Love and Death* (1975). His Russian pacifist character carries an unrequited passion for his promiscuous and shallow cousin, played by Keaton.

Annie Hall. The classic Allen-Keaton vehicle was *Annie Hall* (1977), which marked a huge step in Allen's artistic growth as a filmmaker. Based loosely on Allen's own fizzled romance with Keaton, the film portrayed the bittersweet relationship between a neurotic New York comic and an insecure but life-loving Midwestern girl. The film's original title, Anhedonia, referred to the inability of Allen's character to enjoy himself, which led to the movie couple's breakup. Both fresh and funny, *Annie Hall* surprised many critics and moviegoers with its sweetness, honesty, and cinematic originality (using split screens, subtitles, cartoons, and characters speaking to the audience or to people in other scenes). The experiment paid off: the film was chosen the year's best by thirty-two reviewers as well as by the New York Film Critics Circle and the National Society of Film Critics. It received Academy Awards for Best Picture, Best Actress (Keaton), Best Director, and Best Screenplay. Allen, who won the last two awards, did not bother to attend the ceremony, apparently disdaining Hollywood as much as his Alvy Singer character did.

Growth. Allen followed up *Annie Hall* with *Interiors* (1978), a deadly serious homage to Bergman, whom the director obviously revered. The film received mixed responses — most people seemed to miss the comedy — but Allen was again nominated for an Academy Award for Best Director. His next film, *Manhattan* (1979), marked a return to form. *Newsweek* hailed it as a masterpiece, and most critics seemed to agree. *Manhattan* was less inventive than *Annie Hall* but was in some ways more interesting, a moodily comic and bittersweet examination of New York intellectual and romantic life. Allen again wooed Keaton, who this time portrayed a highly neurotic (and pretentious) woman. *Manhattan* earned Allen another Oscar nomination for screenwriting. In *Annie Hall,*

Interiors, and *Manhattan,* Allen began to examine themes that would continue to surface in his later work, particularly the relationship between art and life and his characters' struggle between their true selves and their desired self-images.

Later Work. In addition to his Oscars, Allen won the O. Henry Award in 1977 for the best short story of the year ("The Kugelmass Episode"). This success was typical of his 1980s work, which took on almost a journeyman quality. In a series of films starring girlfriend Mia Farrow, Allen continued to mix comedies (*Broadway Danny Rose, Zelig*) with painful dramas (*Another Woman, September*). The high point of his 1980s career came with *Hannah and Her Sisters* (1986), which lovingly portrayed a cross-section of neurotics, intellectuals, and romantic losers. The film received Academy Award nominations for Best Picture, Best Director, and Best Screenplay. After his breakup with Farrow, a subsequent exchange of charges of child sexual abuse, and an affair with one of Farrow's adopted daughters, Allen reteamed briefly with Keaton for *Manhattan Murder Mystery* (1993) and went on to direct *Bullets Over Broadway* (1994), his most acclaimed work in years.

Sources:
Eric Lax, *Woody Allen: A Biography* (New York: Knopf, 1991);

Maurice Yacowar, *Loser Take All: The Comic Art of Woody Allen* (New York: Ungar, 1979).

SAUL BELLOW

1915-

WRITER

Themes. During his years at the University of Chicago and Northwestern University in the 1930s, young Saul Bellow knew instinctively the academic life was not for him. He felt it was too narrow, too dictatorial; only as a writer could he find the freedom and independence he craved to explore his imagination and interpret the world. Bellow was well-read, and his attachment to books led to employment writing book notices in New York. He soon turned to fiction writing and achieved some attention with his first novel, *Dangling Man* (1943). The book established what was to become typical in Bellow's work over the years: a sensitive protagonist who feels he does not belong or is out of step with the world, searching for some sense of personal destiny or self-realization. This theme paralleled the author's own struggle during his long career for such understanding. *The Victim* (1947) established Bellow as a Jewish writer, a label he often resented as limiting and insulting. Bellow maintained that his characters and their quest for transcendence were more universal than specifically ethnic.

Attention. Bellow's 1953 novel *The Adventures of Augie March* received the National Book Award and brought him serious attention as an important postwar novelist. Drawing from his Chicago upbringing, Bellow explored the choices facing a young man who seeks a fate worthy of his own sense of "special destiny." His painful self-exploration leads him to a common Bellow conclusion: Augie finally must reject the search altogether, turn his back on intellect and reason, in favor of the simple joys of life, of love, and of commonplace experience. Bellow's style — long, dense sentences, deluges of detail and allusions, jumps in time, and multiplicity of memory — allowed the author to explore his characters' (and his own) complex thoughts and emphasized their subjective take on reality. *Seize the Day* (1956) continues the theme with a loser hero who realizes that only his reconnection to others in the world around him can resurrect his deadened spirit. Bellow had come to feel that writers and critics, like his fictional heroes, also must become attuned to human frailty and nuance. The mixed reviews of *Augie March* and *Seize the Day* led to his stinging attacks on critics, who he now saw as rigid and unimaginative in their insistence on literary tradition.

Defiance. With his next novel, *Henderson the Rain King* (1959), Bellow sought to defy every traditional tenet of writing. Its protagonist deserts his dull married life to pursue the desires of his heart and learns, after a series of African adventures, that his simple existence back home was more important than his insistence on a planned destiny. Bellow had less luck with his own life; *The Noble Savage,* a literary journal he cofounded with his friend Jack Ludwig, fizzled after five issues when Ludwig had an affair with Bellow's wife. The pain of this betrayal was the source and inspiration for Bellow's next — and, many feel, best — novel, *Herzog* (1964). The narrator, Moses Herzog, pours out simultaneously his personal anguish and his frustration with the deplorable state of civilization in the form of letters addressed to everyone he can think of, from his mother to the president to God. Again, the character seeks freedom in truth and learns that, ultimately, one can only be healed and find meaning through the acceptance of self and others as they are, and in sharing one's fate and suffering with the rest of humanity. This time the critics raved. *Herzog* was on *The New York Times* best-seller list for a year and received the National Book Award. Bellow had found acceptance.

Maturity. Or had he? When Bellow's 1968 short-story collection was greeted less than favorably, he again railed at the narrow hypocrisy of critics, this time in lecture appearances. Some of his anger and frustration emerged in his next novel, *Mr. Sammler's Planet* (1970). Imagining himself as an elderly curmudgeon, alienated and embittered by the modern world, Bellow for the first time seemed to reject the possibility of transcendence or even hope. Sammler's one remaining purpose before his death is simply to reexamine his life so as to square himself with God and accept the truth of his own failure. Over the course of two days he does so and is left only with the small dignity of his attempt, finally, to measure up. Despite the book's mature content it received mixed reviews, but Bellow again won the National Book Award in 1971. His next work found a slightly more appreciative audience. In *Humboldt's Gift* (1976) Bellow again intermingled past and present events as the narrator, Charlie Citrine, reviews his life. This time his character admits that he was more betrayed by himself than by others and condemns himself for his losses. Citrine confronts the memory of his mentor and friend Von Humboldt Fleischer, whose ultimate gift is the opportunity for the narrator to make peace with himself in the face of death — to transcend his past and his failings by simply being. *Humboldt's Gift* was, of all Bellow's novels, the truest examination of the author's life, imagination, and frustration. Despite its typically mixed critical response, Bellow was awarded the Pulitzer. He subsequently won the Nobel Prize for literature.

Seeker. Despite a generally favorable reception for *To Jerusalem and Back* (1976), his observation of modern Israel and the history of Islam, Bellow again used lectures to air his diatribes against the dehumanization of the United States and critics as intellectual tyrants. This was ironic given the shift of late-1970s critics, especially younger reviewers, toward a new appreciation of Bellow as a serious artist. Bellow struggled on in his search for spiritual truth with *The Dean's December* (1982), a fictionalized meditation on the author's life and career and an indictment of present-day Chicago. For the first time in his fiction, Bellow tempered criticism of the world with solutions and action for its problems. If reviewers were displeased with the book's sterility and pessimism, the bitterness of *More Die of Heartbreak* (1987) was more alarming. By now Bellow's protagonist had become trapped by his own memory and recognized that he had failed himself utterly. *The Bellarosa Connection* (1989) marked a return to Bellow's best form, revealing a spirit still very much alive, still searching for truth and transcendence.

Source:
Ruth Miller, *Saul Bellow: A Biography of the Imagination* (New York: St. Martin's Press, 1991).

FRANCIS FORD COPPOLA

1939-

DIRECTOR, SCREENWRITER

Apprentice. When he saw Sergei Eisenstein's *Ten Days That Shook the World*, sixteen-year-old Francis Ford Coppola decided to become a filmmaker. His success in college as the director of campus shows led to his enrollment in UCLA's film school. Needing money for his education, Coppola took jobs shooting low-budget nudie films and quickie features for B-movie king Roger Corman. The most notable of these were the gory *Dementia 13* and *The Terror*, with Jack Nicholson. While working as a writer for the successful film group Seven Arts, Coppola wrote his first full-length screenplay, *You're a Big Boy Now.* Coppola, always aggressive and forever a risk taker, managed to persuade some major talent (including Geraldine Page and Julie Harris) to accept supporting roles in the film, which gained some attention on its release in 1966. When *Finian's Rainbow* (1967), his first directorial effort for a major studio, became a disaster, Coppola vowed to turn his back on the Hollywood system and make his own films his own way.

Idealist. *The Rain People,* finally released in 1969, was a utopian experiment in filmmaking. Coppola, his cast (including Robert Duvall and James Caan), and his crew (including new protégé George Lucas) modeled the film after its subject: an improvised cross-country trip. The results were mixed, but Coppola was determined to continue the experiment by opening American Zoetrope, an independent film studio near San Francisco that would devote itself to artistic and visionary work. He persuaded Seven Arts to put up the money for Lucas's debut feature *THX 1138* (1971), but when angry executives saw the cold, uncommercial results they pulled the plug on American Zoetrope's funding. Coppola, now five hundred thousand dollars in debt, watched his filmmaking dreams collapse. Ironically, a highly commercial Hollywood success reversed his fortune. *Patton,* which Coppola had scripted in 1965, was finally released early in 1970 and became a huge hit. Coppola eventually won an Oscar for his screenplay and was made an offer he could not refuse: the chance to direct a low-budget gangster movie for Paramount.

The Godfather. Coppola had not wanted to make *The Godfather,* but once committed he exercised his clout to get the cast he wanted. He insisted on Al Pacino as Michael Corleone (despite Pacino's dismal screen tests) as well as Robert Duvall, James Caan, and Marlon Brando, whose casting Paramount bitterly opposed. Collaborating with Mario Puzo, author of the original novel, Coppola drew on his own New York Italian upbringing to expand and deepen the story's religious themes and family details. Though the crew lacked faith in his ability (sometimes to the verge of mutiny), Coppola's sense of detail and character came through strongly, impressing the top brass at Paramount. They beefed up the film's budget significantly, and word of mouth began to spread. The publicity surrounding *The Godfather* incurred the wrath of the Italian American Civil Rights League and some members of the real-life Mafia, but the film itself proved to be a cinematic event, setting box-office records and winning Oscars for Best Picture, Best Actor (Brando refused his award), and best screenplay for Coppola (he lost best director to Bob Fosse). Having made the biggest moneymaker in history, Coppola had won the freedom to make any film he wished.

Peak. Coppola's next project, *The Conversation,* was the only film he made for the Director's Company, an independent venture formed with Peter Bogdanovich and William Friedkin (later disbanded). *The Conversation* used innovative sound recording and editing techniques to present the subjective reality of a wiretapper who eventually becomes the victim of his own increasing paranoia. Artistic and intelligent but also highly disturbing, the film was not a commercial success but did gain extra publicity when the Watergate scandal hit the papers just days after completion of shooting. It went on to win best picture at the Cannes Film Festival as well as Oscar nominations for Coppola as both producer and screenwriter. He also found time to write the script for *The Great Gatsby* (1974) and to produce George Lucas's runaway 1973 hit *American Graffiti* (another nomination). He finished 1974 with *The Godfather Part II,* a dark and complex sequel that contrasted the rise to power of the young Vito Corleone (Robert De Niro) with the complete moral downfall of his son (Pacino) decades later. *The Godfather Part II* won six Oscars, including Best Picture (the first sequel ever to do so) and best director and best screenplay for Coppola.

Apocalypse. An associate of Coppola theorized that the often moody and manic director could function only under conditions of chaos and disaster. This proved to be true in the creation of his next film, *Apocalypse Now.* In the four years that it took him to complete the film, Coppola would suffer a complete nervous breakdown, partly brought on by long months shooting in the jungles of the Philippines. His star, Martin Sheen, suffered both a mental collapse and a heart attack during filming, but that was not the only nightmare for either of them. Bad weather, including a typhoon, destroyed sets and equipment; special-effects sequences (especially explosions and fires) backfired, and the Filipino military impeded more than assisted production. Surrounded by a swirl of negative publicity, Coppola spent a year shooting 250 hours of film and exceeded his initial budget by millions. He then spent almost two years editing what had become his creative millstone. "My nerves are shot, my heart is broken, my imagination is dead," he was to say of this period. Despite some acclaim (and a record-setting advertising budget), *Apocalypse Now* barely recouped its cost and was judged by many critics an ambitious failure. Many close to Coppola claimed he emerged from the experience a completely changed man and artist.

Experiments. Coppola's post-Apocalypse career was erratic. *One From the Heart* (1982), a highly stylized musical, bankrupted his resurrected American Zoetrope Studio. Reviews were mixed on two youth-oriented films, *The Outsiders* and *Rumble Fish* (both 1983). Though the former made money and the latter garnered some critical raves, most felt that Coppola was floundering as a director. Nor did his next film, *The Cotton Club* (1984), do much to salvage his reputation: an unqualified flop, the movie went over budget by millions and bankrupted its

producer, Robert Evans. *Peggy Sue Got Married* (1986) was a commercial success but hardly bore Coppola's mark as director. *Gardens of Stone* (1987) and *Tucker: The Man and His Dream* (1988) were expensive bombs. *The Godfather Part III* (1990), despite several Oscar nominations, was considered by many to be too little too late. His flashy adaptation of *Bram Stoker's Dracula* (1992), however, was an unqualified success, suggesting that there might be new blood in Coppola's waning career.

Source:
Michael Goodwin and Naomi Wise, *On the Edge: The Life and Times of Francis Coppola* (New York: Morrow, 1989).

JANE FONDA

1937-

ACTRESS

Ingenue. Throughout the 1960s Jane Fonda was known primarily as actor Henry Fonda's daughter, as a pretty ingenue in light sex comedies such as *Sunday in New York* (1963) and as director Roger Vadim's protégé in arty skin flicks such as *Barbarella* (1968). All that was to change in the decade that followed. As worldwide political situations intensified, particularly the war in Vietnam, Fonda became increasingly radicalized. A major influence on her in the late 1960s was her friend Vanessa Redgrave, who had often taken strong anti-American political stances. Fonda began to see herself and her role in Hollywood differently. She split with Vadim, then stunned audiences and critics with her portrayal of a bitter, downtrodden marathon dancer in *They Shoot Horses, Don't They?* After traveling to Europe and India to "search for herself," Fonda returned to the United States with a radically different agenda, declaring, "I've wasted the first 32 years of my life."

Radical. In 1970 Fonda participated in some very public protests on behalf of human rights causes, particularly the downtrodden American Indian. She visited Indian groups after their 1970 takeover of Alcatraz Island and joined another group in a march to reclaim Indian land. Angered over U.S. involvement in Vietnam, Fonda also attempted to organize "enlightenment" talks with soldiers in army bases, leading to several arrests for trespassing on government property. She caused further controversy with her open use of marijuana (Fonda to interviewer Rex Reed: "You don't mind if I turn on, do you?"). A search of her luggage for drugs at an Ohio airport led to her arrest for assaulting a police officer. Fonda also publicly supported the Black Panthers' Marxist, revolutionary agenda and in 1971 openly condemned "the system" after Black Panther George Jackson was charged with the murder of a guard in Soledad prison. Fonda also embraced the feminist movement, participating in rallies on behalf of welfare mothers.

Hanoi Jane. Fonda received unprecedented publicity with her 1972 trip to North Vietnam. She had come to believe that the U.S. government was lying to the American people about the extent of its involvement in the war and that hundreds of thousands of innocent Vietnamese were being killed in U.S. bombings. In Hanoi, the North Vietnamese capital, Fonda giddily posed for pictures riding a North Vietnamese antiaircraft gun. She also made broadcasts for Radio Hanoi denouncing American soldiers as war criminals and murderers. Her statements were broadcast to army bases throughout Vietnam, allegedly leading to the torture of some American prisoners of war who refused to support Fonda's position. Fonda dismissed such reports, but many outraged U.S. citizens accused her of treason, demanding prosecution or public apology (and even hanging her in effigy).

Graylist. Fonda won an Academy Award for Best Actress early in 1972 for her brilliant portrayal of a high-priced call girl in *Klute*. Her largely improvised scenes in a psychiatrist's office earned critical raves, but Fonda's political antics, particularly the Hanoi debacle, led to a "graylist" of her in Hollywood. For Oscar night she had planned to make a political speech lambasting the government over Vietnam, but father Henry talked her into saying a simple thank-you. Even so, Fonda was offered few choice roles after *Klute* and wound up accepting parts in several foreign-produced films. One of these was *A Doll's House*, based on the Henrik Ibsen play and featuring Fonda as a newly liberated wife. Despite her Hollywood struggles, Fonda continued her high-profile activism and in 1973 married 1960s-radical-turned-politician Tom Hayden.

Comeback. *Fun with Dick and Jane*, released early in 1977, featured Fonda and George Segal as stylish white-collar criminals on a spree. The film was a hit and proved Fonda could be sexy and funny again. She went on to star in a string of demanding, high-quality roles that earned her three consecutive Oscar nominations, another Oscar, and the respect of the film community and moviegoing public. Most of her late-1970s roles had strong feminist and political overtones. In *Julia* she was playwright Lillian Hellman, gradually radicalized into anti-Fascist actions by her longtime friend, played by Vanessa Redgrave. In *Coming Home* her drab military housewife was gradually radicalized by a paraplegic soldier into antiwar activism and personal and sexual liberation. In *The China Syndrome* her demure, underchallenged reporter was suddenly radicalized into antinuclear action during the near-meltdown of a power plant's reactor core. Other roles included her strong, independent ranch owner in *Comes a Horseman* (1978) and another feisty reporter in *The Electric Horseman* (1979). By the end of the 1970s Fonda had become an on-screen role model for the women's movement and for political enlightenment and one of the most admired public figures in the United States.

Image. After *The China Syndrome* and the real-life near-meltdown at Three Mile Island, she and Hayden organized a fifty-two-city campaign against "corporate power." But as her acting career flourished with films such as the quietly feminist *9 to 5* (1980) and *On Golden Pond* (1981), Fonda began to change her image again. As the 1980s wore on, she launched a new career as an exercise queen. Her workout videos became huge sellers, their success eclipsing even her best film projects, such as *The Morning After* (1986) or her quietly feminist 1984 television movie *The Dollmaker*. Her 1970s radicalism appeared forgotten, at least until 1988. When she tried to make the film *Stanley and Iris* in a small Connecticut town, long-harbored resentment by the townspeople erupted against her, causing Fonda to state publicly that she had acted rashly in Hanoi and had also been greatly uninformed about many of her 1970s causes. After meeting with local citizens Fonda was able to complete the film. Her public contrition also apparently erased the longtime stigma of "Hanoi Jane." Soon after, she announced her retirement from acting and subsequently married multimillionaire television mogul Ted Turner.

Source:
Christopher Anderson, *Citizen Jane: The Turbulent Life of Jane Fonda* (New York: Holt, 1990).

BOB FOSSE

1927-1987

DIRECTOR, CHOREOGRAPHER, DANCER

Dancer. Bob Fosse began his unusual career as a dancer in the late 1940s, touring with companies of *Call Me Mister* and *Make Mine Manhattan*. After playing the lead in a summer-stock production of *Pal Joey*, then choreographing a showcase called *Talent 52*, Fosse was given a screen test by M-G-M and went on to appear in the film *Kiss Me Kate* (1953). This appearance, in a highly original dance number, led to Fosse's first job as a choreographer, the Jerome Robbins–directed Broadway hit *The Pajama Game* (1954). Soon after, he met the talented dancer Gwen Verdon, and the two proceeded to collaborate on several hit shows, including *Damn Yankees* (1955, film 1958), *New Girl in Town* (1957), and *Redhead* (1959). (Fosse and Verdon married soon after.) He was also frequently sought out as the "doctor" on shows in trouble, especially *How to Succeed in Business Without Really Trying* and *Little Me* (both 1962).

Style. Fosse's best collaboration with Verdon, *Sweet Charity* (1966, film 1969), demonstrated their perfect compatibility as a creative team and also flaunted his trademark style as a choreographer. Strongly influenced by choreographer Jack Cole, Fosse staged dance numbers that were highly stylized, using staccato movements and erotic suggestion. The "Steam Heat" number from *The Pajama Game* and "Hey Big Spender" from *Sweet Charity* were trademark Fosse numbers — jazzy, machinelike motion and cocky, angular, even grotesque poses. He favored style over substance (his patented knee slides and spread-finger hands), and minimalistic costuming (all black, accentuated by hats and gloves). A perfectionist, Fosse liked detail in his choreography and would position his dancers down to the angles of their feet or their little fingers. As his career progressed, Fosse became increasingly fascinated with expressing sexuality and decadence through dance.

Cabaret. After the box-office failure of his first directed film, *Sweet Charity,* Fosse feared his career was finished. But when no established director wanted to touch the taboo subjects (Nazi violence, homosexuality) in filming the stage musical *Cabaret,* Fosse eagerly tackled the job. Working in and around West Berlin, Fosse made the material completely his own, mixing the personal saga of the madcap Sally Bowles and her bisexual friend Brian (played by Liza Minnelli and Michael York) with the decadent world of the cabaret in which Sally performs. Both are subtly juxtaposed with the rise of Nazism taking place in Germany simultaneously. The mix was perfect: bawdy, wicked song and dance numbers, genuine romantic pathos, and a vaguely sinister atmosphere add up to a highly original and timeless film. *Cabaret* won eight Oscars, including one for Fosse's direction.

Pinnacle. Fosse's peak year was 1973. In addition to his *Cabaret* Oscar, he nabbed Tonys for his direction and choreography of the Broadway musical *Pippin,* the eerily magical and sexually decadent story of the son of King Charlemagne on a journey of self-discovery. Like *Cabaret, Pippin* featured exaggerated, grotesque makeup and costuming and erotic dance numbers. Fosse's experiment — to place the story and music at the service of choreography — paid off when *Pippin* (helped by a television advertising campaign) became Fosse's longest-running Broadway show. That same year he won an Emmy for directing and choreographing Minnelli's television special *Liza with a Z,* which garnered high ratings and featured groundbreaking production numbers. In 1973 Fosse seemed to be everywhere.

Follow-Up. In *Lenny* (1974), an exploration of the life of controversial comic Lenny Bruce, Fosse experimented with a mock-documentary filmmaking style. He identified with Bruce's attempt to liberate inhibited audiences with shocking and challenging material. Fosse suffered a heart attack while editing *Lenny* and rehearsing the successful Broadway musical *Chicago* (1975), which starred Verdon as notorious murderess Roxie Hart. *Chicago* was a cynical, stylized homage to 1920s-era burlesque and vaudeville. In the fascinating but disturbing film *All That Jazz* (1979), he used the heart attack (including a filmed bypass operation) to kill off the main character, an obsessive, womanizing, workaholic director clearly based on Fosse. His other 1970s stage musical was the innovative *Dancin'* (1978), which featured three acts constructed purely of dance numbers, eliminating story, song, and characters.

Last Work. Fosse's work in the 1980s received mixed responses. His film *Star 80* (1983) explored the violent, obsessive relationship between Playboy-model-turned-actress Dorothy Stratten and Paul Snider, the husband who brutally murdered her in 1980. Audiences and critics did not respond to the tough, gruesome subject matter. Nor did they appear to enjoy the jazz ballet *Big Deal* (1986), Fosse's last Broadway show. A revival of *Sweet Charity* in 1986 was more successful, but just as the touring company was about to be launched, Fosse died of a heart attack on 23 September 1987.

Sources:

Martin Gottfried, *All His Jazz: The Life and Death of Bob Fosse* (New York: Bantam Books, 1990);

Kevin Boyd Grubb, *Razzle Dazzle: The Life and Work of Bob Fosse* (New York: St. Martin's Press, 1989).

TONI MORRISON

1931-

WRITER

Teacher. Toni Morrison never planned to become an author. Born Chloe Anthony Wofford in Lorain, Ohio, she changed her first name to Toni while attending Howard University and acquired her last name after a later marriage. Morrison excelled in the classics and received a master's degree from Cornell in 1955, after which she began teaching English at Texas Southern University and then at Howard. There she became influenced by a small group of poets and fiction writers, who encouraged her to work on a short story — the first she had ever attempted — about a young black girl's yearning for the white ideal of beauty and perfection. The story, which later became her first novel, was set aside while Morrison pursued a publishing career in the 1960s.

Champion. Morrison's editing talent and linguistic skill allowed her to move swiftly in her new career at Random House. She was promoted from textbook editor to senior editor in 1967 and soon became a specialist in black fiction. During eighteen years with the company, Morrison championed new writers such as Gayl Jones, Angela Davis, and Toni Cade Bambara. Meanwhile, she turned to writing again and found, to her surprise, that she had a natural ability with character. She expanded her short story into *The Bluest Eye,* drawing on her upbringing and neighborhood memories to create a strong portrait of black family life. Critics hailed Morrison as a significant new voice in fiction.

Themes. One of Morrison's motivations to write was the desire to create three-dimensional portrayals of African-Americans. Her philosophy, "there are no boring black people," served her well as she drew from life experience in her work. Her fiction emphasized the importance of history and myth, instilled in the author by her grandmother and by the unique characters she encountered growing up in an all-black neighborhood. Morrison was fascinated by the complications of black life and strove to create in her writing strong relationships between people and the earth, community, work, family, and each other. As she developed her talent, Morrison realized that writing was "the one thing I have no intention of doing without."

Breakthrough. *Sula* reflected society's (and the black community's) shift from the mass struggles of the 1960s to the more personal ones of the 1970s. The title character, in her search for an individual identity, refuses to follow the codes and standards of her neighborhood and the black community at large. The story also explored the bond of friendship between African-American women. Although *Sula* was acclaimed, Morrison's true breakthrough came with *Song of Solomon*. The author used fantasy, allegory, and fable to illuminate the main character's search for his personal heritage. Morrison made his struggle for self-discovery a universal experience and in the process found best-seller status. *Song of Solomon* received the National Book Critics Circle Award for fiction and the American Academy and Institute of Art and Letters and Letters prize. Soon after, she was appointed by President Jimmy Carter to the National Council on the Arts.

Success. Morrison lectured at Yale University from 1975 through 1977 and was appointed associate professor at the State University of New York, Purchase. Her literary success continued in the 1980s with the publication of *Tar Baby* (1981), which landed Morrison on the cover of *Newsweek*. Her follow-up, *Beloved* (1987), was a modern slave narrative and is considered her finest work. Although it missed winning the National Book Award (in a controversial decision many claimed was racist), *Beloved* received the Pulitzer Prize in fiction. In 1989 Morrison became a humanities professor at Princeton University. In 1993 she won the Nobel Prize for literature.

Source:
Wilfred D. Samuels and Clenora Hudson-Weems, *Toni Morrison* (Boston: Twayne, 1990).

AL PACINO

1940-

ACTOR

Theater. Al Pacino burst onto the New York theater scene in the late 1960s. He received an Obie nomination (for Off-Broadway productions) for *Why Is a Crooked Letter* (1966), competing against George C. Scott and eventual winner Dustin Hoffman. He won the award two years later for his portrayal of a savage young hoodlum in *The Indian Wants the Bronx*. By 1969 his angry energy had won him several important roles and a Tony award for best supporting actor in *Does a Tiger Wear a Necktie?* Hollywood began to take notice of Pacino's talent for playing urban outsiders and cast him as a junkie in *Panic in Needle Park* (1969). Although many critics and viewers noted certain similarities to Hoffman, Pacino's acting had a unique edge that reminded Lee Strasberg, head of the New York Actors' Studio, of a young Marlon Brando.

Corleone. Director Francis Ford Coppola saw Pacino onstage in New York and felt he would be perfect for the young and alienated Michael Corleone in the upcoming film production of *The Godfather* (1972). Paramount executives felt otherwise; Pacino's screen tests were repeatedly disastrous. Coppola stood firm, and Pacino was cast. Though he was in awe of costar Brando, Pacino was determined to make his role the center of the film. His nervous uncertainty added to Michael's enigmatic character and shaped his transition from ambivalent family outsider to chilling inheritor of the Corleone throne of violence and power. Critics hailed his stunning performance, and though the film studio promoted Brando as the movie's star (he won an Academy Award for Best Actor), Pacino emerged with a supporting nomination and the lion's share of the public attention.

Follow-Up. In 1972 Pacino returned to the stage in David Rabe's acclaimed drama *The Basic Training of Pavlo Hummel*. He followed that with his virtuoso portrayal of a New York cop fighting corruption in *Serpico* (1973). With Sidney Lumet directing, Pacino became his character, donning accents and disguises at will and using his unique urban energy to connect with masses of film viewers. After *Serpico* cemented his image as a hothead rebel, Pacino returned to the role of Michael Corleone in *The Godfather Part II* (1974). Many critics felt that the film — and Pacino's acting — was superior to the original. *Serpico* and *The Godfather* sequel earned Pacino two additional Oscar nominations. In only a few short years he had emerged from Hoffman's shadow to establish himself, along with Jack Nicholson, as a definitive 1970s antihero.

Peak. Pacino's ability to immerse himself completely in a role paid off in his brilliant, Oscar-nominated portrayal of Sonny, the bungling bank robber in *Dog Day Afternoon*. His manic desperation became both heroic and tragic as the film progressed, and his unraveling character tries to hold everything — the hostages, the police, his wife, his male lover — in balance. Pacino's chant of "Attica! Attica!" became his antiestablishment war cry and elevated him to the level of pop superstar. He was not content to work only in films, however, and soon returned to the Broadway stage. In 1977 Pacino re-created his role as an alienated young soldier in *Pavlo Hummel*, earning further critical raves and a Tony award as best actor.

Reemergence. Despite an Oscar nomination for the 1979 film *...And Justice for All*, in which he played an angry lawyer battling the system, Pacino's film career struggled after its mid-1970s peak. He turned down several important roles, including *Lenny, Kramer vs. Kramer* (old rival Hoffman grabbed those), *Coming Home, Apocalypse Now,* and *Days of Heaven.* A planned film of Ron Kovic's Vietnam autobiography, *Born on the Fourth of July* (seemingly an ideal role for Pacino), fell through. Most of his 1980s films, with the exception of *Scarface* (1983), bombed. After the failure of *Revolution* in 1985, Pacino stopped making movies for several years. He had better luck in the theater, receiving great reviews for his role in David Mamet's *American Buffalo* in 1983. Finally, in 1989 the film hit *Sea of Love* revitalized his career, leading to acclaimed roles in *Dick Tracy* (1990), *The Godfather Part III* (1990), *Glengarry Glen Ross* (1992), and *Scent of a Woman* (1992), for which Pacino at last won an Oscar.

Source:

Andrew Yule, *Life on the Wire: The Life and Art of Al Pacino* (New York: Donald I. Fine, 1991).

RICHARD PRYOR

1940-

ACTOR, COMEDIAN

Early Career. In the early 1960s Richard Pryor was among several black comedians who were gaining acceptance with white audiences in clubs and on television. Redd Foxx, Nipsey Russell, Flip Wilson, and Slappy White all achieved some popularity, but all were eclipsed by the major success of comics Bill Cosby and Dick Gregory. Early television appearances such as the *Rudy Vallee Show* gave Pryor some exposure, but he tried too hard to imitate the smooth, nonracial hipness of Cosby and topical humor of White, Russell, and Gregory. Gradually, feeding off his resentment of racism and natural hatred of the television medium, Pryor began to develop his own style — and a growing reputation for being volatile and difficult to manage.

Energy. By the late 1960s Pryor had begun to incorporate some of his later trademarks into his work, especially his randy street humor and his manic, live-wire nervous energy. As he became increasingly alienated from show business, Pryor decided to use his comedy to "tell it like it is." His offstage antics (liquor, drugs, and women) eventually took their toll onstage, leading to a breakdown during a Las Vegas performance in 1967. Pryor regrouped, working in films (*Wild in the Streets* [1968], and releasing an album featuring his raunchy material and several new signature characters (the black preacher and belligerent curmudgeon Mudbone). But his success, even in topical projects such as the television movie *Carter's*

Army (1969), was not satisfying, so Pryor turned to writing racially challenging screenplays in the early 1970s.

Characters. Pryor seemed to use his new material as an emotional catharsis in the 1970s. His comedy acts became a theater of real life, incorporating wildly colorful characters and street language. He enjoyed blurring the distinction between comedy and character acting and translated the mixture of the two into a burgeoning screen career. Some of his films, *Hit!* (1973) and *Wattstax* (1973), were mainly "blaxploitation" fare, but in *Lady Sings the Blues,* Pryor was acclaimed for his junkie character Piano Man. Television appearances on *Sanford and Son,* the *Flip Wilson Show,* and two Lily Tomlin specials added to his cult appeal, and film roles such as Sidney Poitier's *Uptown Saturday Night* helped establish his comic persona as a madman consumed by inner demons. Although he lost the lead in the comedy classic *Blazing Saddles* to Cleavon Little, Pryor was given screen credit for cowriting the script and won a Writers' Guild of America Award.

Success. The mid 1970s were key years in Pryor's exploding career. He seemed to be everywhere: selling out Washington's Kennedy Center in 1974, releasing million-selling comedy albums, winning Grammys in 1975, 1976, and 1977, and hosting the cutting-edge comedy program *Saturday Night Live* (on five-second tape delay) and the Academy Awards. He continued to champion black awareness, donating one thousand tickets for an evening with *Roots* author Alex Haley to the NAACP and five thousand dollars to the Kwanza organization. Successful films such as *Car Wash, Bingo Long's Traveling All-Stars and Motor Kings,* and *Silver Streak* (all 1976) cemented his new mainstream status. The last film also established his long-standing partnership with Gene Wilder and led to his first starring roles.

Superstar. In 1976 Pryor signed a $3 million deal with Universal Pictures, the highest in history for a black performer. In *Which Way Is Up?* (1977) Pryor tackled three roles in the story of a man who sells out for success. *Greased Lightning* (1977), directed by Michael Schultz (*Car Wash, Cooley High*) featured Pryor in his first serious lead as Wendell Scott, the first black race-car champion. Both films were critical and popular hits. *Blue Collar* (1978) teamed Pryor with Harvey Keitel and Yaphet Kotto in the hard-hitting story of Detroit autoworkers organizing a robbery, and Neil Simon's *California Suite* paired Pryor with Cosby. Although a television series and the big-budget musical *The Wiz* both flopped in 1978, Pryor's live comedy performances were sellouts, and his 1979 concert film, *Richard Pryor Live,* was a $30 million smash.

Burnout. *Stir Crazy,* a Poitier-directed comedy with Pryor and Wilder, was a big hit in early 1980. Shortly after its release, Pryor was badly burned while freebasing cocaine. He returned to films after his recovery, including *Bustin' Loose* (1981), *Some Kind of Hero* (1982), and *Su-*

perman III (1983), in which Pryor played a comic villain. His reputation did not appear to be permanently damaged, but his career never regained the heights it reached in the 1970s. Perhaps his volatility and flirtation with danger and controversy had caught up with him. At his peak of popularity he had told an interviewer, "I'm proof there's a God, because I'm supposed to be dead by now."

Sources:

Jim Haskins, *Richard Pryor: A Man and His Madness* (New York: Beaufort Books, 1984);

John A. Williams and Dennis A. Williams, *If I Stop I'll Die: The Comedy and Tragedy of Richard Pryor* (New York: Thunder's Mouth Press, 1991).

STEPHEN SONDHEIM

1930-

COMPOSER, LYRICIST

Musicals. Young Stephen Sondheim's path was made clear when, at age twelve, he was befriended by a family friend, the esteemed lyricist Oscar Hammerstein II. Hammerstein taught him all he knew about songwriting, and by the late 1940s Sondheim was working as a production assistant on Broadway musicals such as *South Pacific* (1949) and *The King and I* (1951). He then won a two-year fellowship to study with avant-garde composer Milton Babbitt, who helped him analyze popular songs and classics. In 1953 plans for Sondheim's first full-length musical composition, *Saturday Night*, were cut short by the death of the producer, so Sondheim turned to scriptwriting for the television series *Topper*. A chance encounter with playwright Arthur Laurents led to Sondheim's meeting with Leonard Bernstein, who was composing the music to *West Side Story*. Impressed with the lyrics to *Saturday Night*, Bernstein asked Sondheim to collaborate on the new songs. The result was a Broadway (and Hollywood) classic, featuring Sondheim's versatile and witty lyric-writing style on songs such as "America," "Tonight," "Maria," and "I Feel Pretty."

Growth. *Gypsy* (1959), a collaboration with composer Jule Styne, was a runaway hit, featuring more classic Sondheim lyrics ("Everything's Coming Up Roses," "Let Me Entertain You," "Rose's Turn"). By now his style was established: his lyrics were intelligent and complex but always effortless and always integrated into the character singing them. Sondheim's Broadway success did not completely satisfy him, however. He wanted to write both music and lyrics, and he was given that opportunity with *A Funny Thing Happened on the Way to the Forum* (1962), which won a Tony for best musical and became Sondheim's biggest commercial success. It was also his first collaboration with director-producer Harold Prince,

who was to work with Sondheim on all of his musicals in the 1970s.

Innovation. After several failures in the mid 1960s, Sondheim returned to Broadway in 1970 with *Company*, a concept musical that used a plotless series of vignettes to comment on modern marriage. With *Company* Sondheim broke from the musical tradition of writing hits, instead keeping each song firmly integrated into its context in the show. Sondheim won Tonys for his lyrics and score, and the show won a New York Drama Critics Circle prize for best musical. Equally innovative was *Follies* (1971), a nostalgic revue that employed flashbacks and simultaneous past and present action among two couples. A spectacle about the ghosts of lost tradition and the sadness of memory, *Follies* won the Drama Critics award and won Sondheim a Tony for his unusual music and lyrics.

Acclaim. With *A Little Night Music* (1973) Sondheim became the first artist to receive Tonys for three consecutive years as composer and lyricist. *A Little Night Music* was hailed as his greatest work to date, producing his first hit ("Send in the Clowns") and refuting his reputation for writing unhummable scores. Based loosely on Ingmar Bergman's film *Smiles of a Summer Night* (1955), the show was delicate and enchanting in mood, using sophisticated songs as interior monologues for the characters. Sondheim composed the music in traditional waltz time in order to create the effect of an operetta. "Send in the Clowns" won a Grammy, as did the original cast album. By 1973 Sondheim was being credited with rejuvenating the once-dying Broadway musical almost singlehandedly. On 11 March of that year he was honored with a gala four-hour musical tribute featuring more than forty Sondheim songs.

Departures. In 1976 *Pacific Overtures* mixed Broadway musical traditions with those of the Japanese Kabuki theater. Using native Japanese music, haiku chants, and Oriental choreography, costuming, and sets, the show was daring and original, a radical departure from anything even Sondheim had tried before. Although *Overtures* won a citation for best musical from the Drama Critics Circle, it closed after a short run. Far more successful with Broadway audiences was *Sweeney Todd* (1979), a Grand Guignol opera about "the demon barber of Fleet Street." A mix of the darkly comic and wildly gothic, *Sweeney Todd* was hailed by most critics as sensational and brilliant. It went on to win six Tonys, including Sondheim's musical score, and the original cast album snared a Grammy.

Later Success. Sondheim's highly original musical *Sunday in the Park with George* (1984) featured a minimum of plot, character, or dance. Instead, music underscored the gradual piecing together, through lighting and staging, of Seurat's painting *La Grande Jatte*. The show won the New York Drama Critics Circle award and a Pulitzer Prize in drama. Although many considered *Sun-*

day in the Park with George to be Sondheim's best work, he also achieved major successes with *Into the Woods* (1987) and *Passion*, which was a Tony winner in 1994.

Sources:

David Ewen, *American Songwriters* (New York: Wilson, 1987);

"Words and Music by Sondheim," *Newsweek*, 81 (23 April 1973): 54–64.

DONNA SUMMER

1949-

SINGER, SONGWRITER

Europe. Born Ladonna Gaines in the Boston area, Donna Summer got her first taste for singing in her church choir. Her idols ranged from gospel legend Mahalia Jackson to rock singer Janis Joplin, and soon Summer was singing with a local rock band. Dropping out of high school, she headed to Europe, where she appeared in the German production of *Hair.* Summer sang and acted in other European musicals and performed regularly with the Vienna Folk Opera. In Munich in 1975 writer-producers Giorgio Moroder and Pete Bellote tapped Summer to record a hot new disco-based number, which was released later that year in the United States. "Love to Love You Baby" became an instant classic, most notably because of Summer's repeated orgasmic moans. The song was featured as the title track on her debut album and helped launch the disco revolution.

Range. Summer specialized in disco songs but made a point of trying to expand that range. "I was totally aware I had more going for me," she said later, and some critics agreed, noting her soulful, full-throttle vocal style. By 1977 Summer had racked up three hit albums for Casablanca Records, including *I Remember Yesterday,* on which she explored a wide pop range, from Tin Pan Alley to Motown. She was also proud of her songwriting, displayed in the autobiographical miniopera *Once Upon a Time* (1977). After scoring another hit with "I Feel Love," Summer appeared as an aspiring singer in the 1978 dance-oriented film *Thank God It's Friday.* The movie's theme song, "Last Dance," won an Academy Award for Best Song in early 1979, and Summer won a Grammy for Best Female R&B Vocal Performance. She also nabbed three American Music Awards and a citation from *Billboard* magazine as the top-selling disco artist of 1978, which was partly due to her huge success with a recording of "MacArthur Park" from *I Remember Yesterday.*

Superstar. Well aware of her reputation as disco's first lady of lust, Summer began expanding her concert repetoire with rock songs. Her 1979 double album *Bad Girls* was also an attempt to show off her songwriting and her stylistic range. The record featured rock, blues, ballad, and pop styles, but it was the disco material (not surprisingly) that took off on the charts. "Hot Stuff" and the title track were both number ones in the summer of 1979, a year in which Summer seemed to be everywhere. After "Dim All the Lights" became the album's third smash, Summer teamed with rival diva Barbra Streisand on the hit "No More Tears (Enough Is Enough)." By the end of the year Summer was named by *Billboard* as its number one singles artist and number two album artist. Her duet with Streisand seemed to clinch what she had already proved: Summer had become disco's one true superstar.

Later Career. The disco hits continued: "On the Radio" and "The Wanderer" hit the Top 5 early in 1980. But as the disco craze faded in the 1980s, Summer happily embraced other styles. Her gospel song "He's a Rebel" won her a Grammy in 1983 for Best Inspirational Performance, and she won the award again the following year for "Forgive Me." Although she had more big hits in "Love Is in Control (Finger on the Trigger)" and "She Works Hard for the Money" in the early 1980s, Summer seemed relieved to have left Casablanca and a style she claimed "had been choking me to death for three years." But perhaps she could never outrun her 1970s reputation. She next hit the Top 10 in 1989 with "This Time I Know It's for Real," a disco song.

Sources:

Michael Bane, *Who's Who in Rock* (New York: Facts on File, 1981);

Irwin Stambler, *The Encyclopedia of Pop, Rock & Soul* (New York: St. Martin's Press, 1989).

STEVIE WONDER

1950-

SINGER, COMPOSER

Prodigy. As a child Steveland Morris had played harmonica, banged toy drums, and sang in the church choir, but no one was prepared for his Motown audition. When producer Berry Gordy saw that Morris, then age ten, and blind since birth, had mastered piano, organ, harmonica, and drums, he signed the young prodigy to a contract and changed his name to Little Stevie Wonder. In 1962 his first rhythm and blues album, *Little Stevie Wonder: The Twelve-Year-Old Genius,* was released. "Fingertips Pt. 2," a raucous live cut, became Wonder's first number one hit. He enjoyed an integrated audience during the 1960s, and the Rolling Stones were his opening act in 1964. Wonder's contributions to the Motown hit factory during his teens included the standards "Uptight" (1966), "I Was Made to Love Her" (1967), "For Once in My Life" (1968), and "My Cherie Amour" (1969). He cowrote all of these songs, which demonstrated his wide musical range and natural instrumental ability.

Independence. By the release in 1970 of *Signed, Sealed and Delivered,* which he produced, Wonder was expressing his desire to break free of Motown's signature style to pursue his own musical ideas. On *Where I'm Coming From* (1970), Wonder cowrote all the songs with Syreeta Wright, whom he married in 1971. That year, Wonder turned twenty-one and gained control of his large trust fund. He built a $250,000 recording studio in New York in order to experiment with Moog and ARP synthesizers and negotiated a new contract with Motown that allowed them to distribute his records but gave Wonder complete artistic freedom. In 1972 he recorded the first of his one-man albums (on which he played all the instruments), *Music of My Mind.* The album marked Wonder's new maturity as a recording artist.

Success. *Talking Book* (1972) produced two classic number one songs, "Superstition" and "You Are the Sunshine of My Life." It was also one of the first successful albums to rely heavily on the synthesizer. Wonder opened for the Rolling Stones on their American tour in the summer of 1972, and in early 1973 he performed at Carnegie Hall in New York. *Innervisions,* a deeply personal album, sealed Wonder's reputation as the most innovative black pop artist of the 1970s with relevant songs such as "Higher Ground" and the dark, gritty "Living for the City." His career was almost cut short by a car accident in August 1973, after which Wonder was comatose for almost a week. He recovered sufficiently to tour Europe in early 1974, followed by a Madison Square Garden concert in March. That same month Wonder received four Grammy Awards, including album of the year.

Superstar. After his near-fatal accident, Wonder began to enlarge the religious and mystical themes that had often pervaded his music. His 1974 release, *Fulfillingness' First Finale,* mixed cosmic messages with Wonder's now-signature sound: overdubbing, expansive use of synthesizers, twangy rhythm and blues arrangements. In early 1975 Wonder again won four Grammys; his award sweeps were beginning to seem inevitable. Late that year he signed a seven-year, $13-million contract with Motown, at that time a record in the recording industry. His first release under the new deal, *Songs in the Key of Life* (1976), was his biggest success to date, selling more than two million copies. In twenty-one new songs, including the hits "I Wish" and "Sir Duke," Wonder expanded his spiritual themes to cover seemingly everything, from God to brotherly love to the black experience. For his seemingly endless reach Wonder was rewarded with four more Grammys in 1977.

Mainstream. After his ethereal, highly experimental double album *Journey Through the Secret Life of Plants* (1979) received a lukewarm response, Wonder returned to romantic ballads for *Hotter Than July* (1980). He continued to have hits throughout the 1980s, including "Part-time Lover" (1985) and "Ebony and Ivory" (1982), a duet with Paul McCartney that urged racial harmony. The peak of his 1980s career was an Academy Award for the 1984 song "I Just Called to Say I Love You," featured in the film *The Woman in Red.* With his Oscar, Wonder ceased to be the wildly innovative young artist of the 1970s and became instead simply a pop institution.

Sources:

David Ewen, *American Songwriters* (New York: Wilson, 1987);

Jim Miller, ed., *The Rolling Stone Illustrated History of Rock and Roll* (New York: Random House, 1980).

PEOPLE IN THE NEWS

Black soprano **Marian Anderson** was honored on her seventy-fifth birthday, 27 February 1977, with a concert at Carnegie Hall attended by First Lady **Rosalyn Carter.**

William Armstrong received the Newberry Medal for Children's Literature on 22 January 1970 for his novel *Sounder.*

On 3 May 1976 **Saul Bellow** was awarded the Pulitzer Prize for his novel *Humboldt's Gift.* In October of that year he became the first American writer since John Steinbeck in 1962 to win the Nobel Prize for literature.

After almost twenty years of recording, rock 'n' roller **Chuck Berry** scored his first — and only — number one hit with the novelty song "My Ding-a-Ling" in October 1972.

In March 1970 three women won National Book Awards: **Elizabeth Bishop** for her poetry collection, **Lillian Hellman** for her memoir *An Unfinished Woman,* and **Joyce Carol Oates** for her novel *Them.*

Writer **Jorge Luis Borges** was awarded the first twenty-five-thousand-dollar Inter-American literature prize on 22 August 1970 for representing Latin American culture.

Pierre Boulez conducted **Elliott Carter's** *A Symphony for Three Orchestras* in its world premiere by the New York Philharmonic on 17 February 1977. In May of that year Boulez left the philharmonic to accept a position in Paris.

In March 1970 **Joyce Brown** became the first black woman to conduct the opening of a Broadway musical, *Purlie.*

Sarah Caldwell, founder of the Boston Opera Company, became the first woman to conduct at the Metropolitan Opera House on 13 January 1976.

Actress **Bette Davis** became the first woman film star to receive the AAMPAS Life Achievement Award in a ceremony held in March 1977.

On 7 May 1971 band leader **Duke Ellington** signed a contract for a five-week tour of the Soviet Union.

Actress-activist **Jane Fonda** married politician-activist **Tom Hayden** in Los Angeles on 20 January 1973.

Aleksandr Godunov, a dancer for the Bolshoi Ballet, defected to the United States while on tour in August 1979.

Choreographer **Martha Graham,** at age eighty-two, received the Medal of Freedom on 14 October 1976. In July of that year The Martha Graham Dance Company became the first modern dance troupe to perform at London's Royal Opera House.

On 18 April 1977 *Roots* author **Alex Haley** won a special Pulitzer Prize for his "important contribution to the literature of slavery." On 22 April novelists **Margaret Walker Alexander** and **Harold Courlander** charged that Haley plagiarized passages from their novels *Jubilee* and *The African.* On 22 September 1978 plagiarism charges against Haley were settled out of court..

Composer **Marvin Hamlisch** became the first individual ever to win three Academy Awards in one night on 2 April 1974. He won in all three music categories: Best Original Score (*The Way We Were*), Best Original Song ("The Way We Were"), and Best Adaptation Score (*The Sting*). **Francis Ford Coppola** won three Oscars the following year for *The Godfather Part II.*

On 29 September 1976 industrialist **Armand Hammer** bought Rembrandt's *Juno* for $3.25 million, setting a new record price for a Rembrandt painting.

In May 1978 **Ruth Carter Johnson** was elected the first woman trustee of the National Gallery of Art in Washington, D.C., replacing **Paul Mellon.**

Pop songwriter and performer **Carole King** won four Grammy Awards on 14 March 1972, three for her album *Tapestry* and one for writing the **James Taylor** hit "You've Got a Friend."

John Lennon was denied permanent-resident status by the United States in March 1973 because of a 1968 conviction of marijuana possession.

In February 1974 novelist **Norman Mailer** signed a contract with Little, Brown to write a work about "the whole human experience" for a record advance payment of $1 million.

Playwright **David Mamet** won the New York Drama Critics Circle Award for his play *American Buffalo* on 25 May 1977.

Paul McCartney announced on 10 April 1970 that he was leaving the Beatles, citing personal reasons. On 12 December 1970 McCartney started legal proceedings to sever ties with the group.

American pianist **Garrick Ohlsson**, age twenty-two, won the Eighth International Chopin Festival in Warsaw, Poland, on 22 October 1970.

In February 1978 film director **Roman Polanski** fled California on a morals charge stemming from his involvement with a thirteen-year-old girl.

Elvis Presley sued his wife **Priscilla Presley** for divorce on 8 January 1973. Their divorce became final on 11 September that year.

In the Night, choreographed by **Jerome Robbins** and featuring the music of Frédéric Chopin, was performed for the first time by the New York City Ballet on 29 January 1970.

Composer **Richard Rodgers** gave a $1-million endowment to the American Academy and Institute of Arts and Letters in April 1977.

Pop vocalist **Diana Ross** made her last appearance with the Supremes on 15 January 1970 in Las Vegas.

Novelist **Philip Roth** and jazz musician **Duke Ellington** were voted into the National Institute of Arts and Letters on 24 February 1970.

In January 1978 opera star **Beverly Sills** announced she was retiring from performing. Later that year she announced she was assuming the directorship of the New York City Opera.

In the first concert ever held in New York City's Saint Patrick's Cathedral, **Leopold Stokowski** conducted the Metropolitan Opera Orchestra on 30 November 1970.

Actress **Elizabeth Taylor** divorced actor **Richard Burton** on 26 June 1974. They remarried 10 October 1975. They divorced again the following year.

In May 1974 screenwriter **Dalton Trumbo** received an Oscar for the 1957 film *The Brave One* twenty-seven years after being blacklisted in Hollywood for his refusal to cooperate with Sen. Joseph McCarthy's investigation into American communism.

Sid Vicious, former member of the punk rock band the Sex Pistols, was arrested on 13 October 1978 in New York City for the stabbing death of his girlfriend **Nancy Spungen**.

On 10 January 1971 Wesleyan University professor **Richard Wilbur** and **Mona Van Duyn** were selected to receive the Bollingen Prize for distinguished work in poetry.

Alec Wildenstein of New York's Wildenstein Gallery paid a record $5.5 million for a painting, buying a Diego Velázquez portrait at a London art auction on 27 November 1970.

AWARDS

PULITZER PRIZES

1970
Fiction: *Collected Stories*, by **Jean Stafford**

Drama: *No Place to Be Somebody*, by **Charles Gordone**

Poetry: *Untitled Subjects*, by **Richard Howard**

Music: *Time's Ecomium*, by **Charles Wuorinen**

1971
Fiction: no award

Drama: *The Effect of Gamma Rays on Man-in-the-Moon Marigolds*, by **Paul Zindel**

Poetry: *The Carrier of Ladders*, by **William S. Merwin**

Music: *Synchronisms No. 6*, by **Mario Davidovsky**

1972
Fiction: *Angle of Repose*, by **Wallace Stegner**

Drama: no award

Poetry: *Collected Poems*, by **James Wright**

Music: *Windows*, by **Jacob Druckman**

1973
Fiction: *The Optimist's Daughter*, by **Eudora Welty**

Drama: *That Championship Season*, by **Jason Miller**

Poetry: *Up Country*, by **Maxine W. Kumin**

Music: *String Quartet III*, by **Elliott Carter**

1974
Fiction: no award

Drama: no award

Poetry: *The Dolphin*, by **Robert Lowell**

Music: *Notturno*, by **Donald Martino**

1975
Fiction: *The Killer Angels*, by **Michael Shaara**

Drama: *Seascape*, by **Edward Albee**

Poetry: *Turtle Island*, by **Gary Snyder**

Music: *From the Diary of Virginia Woolf*, by **Dominick Argento**

1976
Fiction: *Humboldt's Gift*, by **Saul Bellow**

Drama: *A Chorus Line*, by **Michael Bennett, Nicholas Dante, Marvin Hamlisch, James Kirkwood,** and **Edward Kleban**

Poetry: *Self-Portrait in a Convex Mirror*, by **John Ashbery**

Music: *Air Music*, by **Ned Rorem**

1977
Fiction: no award

Drama: *The Shadow Box*, by **Michael Cristofer**

Poetry: *Divine Comedies*, by **James Merrill**

Music: *Visions of Terror and Wonder*, by **Richard Warrick**

1978
Fiction: *Elbow Room*, by **James Alan McPherson**

Drama: *The Gin Game*, by **Donald L. Colburn**

Poetry: *Collected Poems*, by **Howard Nemerov**

Music: *Deja Vu*, by **Michael Colgrass**

1979
Fiction: *The Stories of John Cheever*, by **John Cheever**

Drama: *Buried Child*, by **Sam Shepard**

Poetry: *Now and Then: Poems 1976-1978*, by **Robert Penn Warren**

Music: *Aftertones of Infinity*, by **Joseph Schwantner**

ANTOINETTE PERRY AWARDS (TONYS)

1970

Play: *Borstal Boy*, **Frank McMahon**

Actor, Dramatic Star: **Fritz Weaver**, *Child's Play*

Actress, Dramatic Star: **Tammy Grimes**, *Private Lives*

Musical: *Applause*

Actor, Musical Star: **Cleavon Little**, *Purlie*

Actress, Musical Star: **Lauren Bacall**, *Applause*

1971

Play: *Sleuth*, **Anthony Shaffer**

Actor, Dramatic Star: **Brian Bedford**, *The School for Wives*

Actress, Dramatic Star: **Maureen Stapleton**, *Gingerbread Lady*

Musical: *Company*

Actor, Musical Star: **Hal Linden**, *The Rothschilds*

Actress, Musical Star: **Helen Gallagher**, *No No Nanette*

1972

Play: *Sticks and Bones*, **David Rabe**

Actor, Dramatic Star: **Cliff Gorman**, *Lenny*

Actress, Dramatic Star: **Sada Thompson**, *Twigs*

Musical: *Two Gentlemen of Verona*

Actor, Musical Star: **Phil Silvers**, *A Funny Thing Happened on the Way to the Forum*

Actress, Musical Star: **Alexis Smith**, *Follies*

1973

Play: *That Championship Season*, **Jason Miller**

Actor, Dramatic Star: **Alan Bates**, *Butley*

Actress, Dramatic Star: **Julie Harris**, *The Last of Mrs. Lincoln*

Musical: *A Little Night Music*

Actor, Musical Star: **Ben Vereen**, *Pippin*

Actress, Musical Star: **Glynis Johns**, *A Little Night Music*

1974

Play: *The River Niger*, **Joseph A. Walker**

Actor, Dramatic Star: **Michael Moriarty**, *Find Your Way Home*

Actress, Dramatic Star: **Colleen Dewhurst**, *A Moon for the Misbegotten*

Musical: *Raisin*

Actor, Musical Star: **Christopher Plummer**, *Cyrano*

Actress, Musical Star: **Virginia Capers**, *Raisin*

1975

Play: *Equus*, **Peter Shaffer**

Actor, Dramatic Star: **John Kani**, *Sizwe Banzi*; **Winston Ntshona**, *The Island* (tie)

Actress, Dramatic Star: **Ellen Burstyn**, *Same Time Next Year*

Musical: *The Wiz*

Actor, Musical Star: **John Cullum**, *Shenandoah*

Actress, Musical Star: **Angela Lansbury**, *Gypsy*

1976

Play: *Travesties*, **Tom Stoppard**

Actor, Dramatic Star: **John Wood**, *Travesties*

Actress, Dramatic Star: **Irene Worth**, *Sweet Bird of Youth*

Musical: *A Chorus Line*

Actor, Musical Star: **George Rose**, *My Fair Lady*

Actress, Musical Star: **Donna McKechnie**, *A Chorus Line*

1977

Play: *The Shadow Box*, **Michael Cristofer**

Actor, Dramatic Star: **Al Pacino**, *The Basic Training of Pavlo Hummel*

Actress, Dramatic Star: **Julie Harris**, *The Belle of Amherst*

Musical: *Annie*

Actor, Dramatic Star: **Barry Bostwick**, *The Robber Bridegroom*

Actress, Dramatic Star: **Dorothy Loudon**, *Annie*

1978

Play: *Da*, **Hugh Leonard**

Actor, Dramatic Star: **Barnard Hughes**, *Da*

Actress, Dramatic Star: **Jessica Tandy**, *The Gin Game*

Musical: *Ain't Misbehavin'*

Actor, Musical Star: **John Cullum**, *On the Twentieth Century*

Actress, Musical Star: **Liza Minnelli**, *The Act*

1979

Play: *The Elephant Man*, **Bernard Pomerance**

Actor, Dramatic Star: **Tom Conti**, *Whose Life Is It, Anyway?*

Actress, Dramatic Star: **Constance Cummings,** *Wings;* **Carole Shelley,** *The Elephant Man* (tie)

Musical: *Sweeney Todd*

Actor, Musical Star: **Len Cariou,** *Sweeney Todd*

Actress, Musical Star: **Angela Lansbury,** *Sweeney Todd*

ACADEMY OF MOTION PICTURE ARTS AND SCIENCES AWARDS (THE OSCARS)

1970

Actor: **George C. Scott,** *Patton*

Actress: **Glenda Jackson,** *Women in Love*

Picture: *Patton,* **20th Century–Fox**

1971

Actor: **Gene Hackman,** *The French Connection*

Actress: **Jane Fonda,** *Klute*

Picture: *The French Connection,* **20th Century–Fox**

1972

Actor: **Marlon Brando,** *The Godfather*

Actress: **Liza Minnelli,** *Cabaret*

Picture: *The Godfather,* **Paramount**

1973

Actor: **Jack Lemmon,** *Save the Tiger*

Actress: **Glenda Jackson,** *A Touch of Class*

Picture: *The Sting,* **Universal**

1974

Actor: **Art Carney,** *Harry and Tonto*

Actress: **Ellen Burstyn,** *Alice Doesn't Live Here Anymore*

Picture: *The Godfather Part II,* **Paramount**

1975

Actor: **Jack Nicholson,** *One Flew Over the Cuckoo's Nest*

Actress: **Louise Fletcher,** *One Flew Over the Cuckoo's Nest*IOne Flew Over the Cuckoo's Nest~ (movie)[One Flew Over]

Picture: *One Flew Over the Cuckoo's Nest,*IOne Flew Over the Cuckoo's Nest~ (movie)[One Flew Over] **United Artists**

1976

Actor: **Peter Finch,** *Network*

Actress: **Faye Dunaway,** *Network*

Picture: *Rocky,* **United Artists**

1977

Actor: **Richard Dreyfuss,** *The Goodbye Girl*

Actress: **Diane Keaton,** *Annie Hall*

Picture: *Annie Hall,* **United Artists**

1978

Actor: **Jon Voight,** *Coming Home*

Actress: **Jane Fonda,** *Coming Home*

Picture: *The Deer Hunter,* **Universal**

1979

Actor: **Dustin Hoffman,** *Kramer vs. Kramer*

Actress: **Sally Field,** *Norma Rae*

Picture: *Kramer vs. Kramer,* **Columbia**

DEATHS

William ("Bud") Abbott, 78, famed as half of comedy team Abbott and Costello, 24 April 1974.

Julian ("Cannonball") Adderley, 46, jazz saxophonist, 8 August 1975.

Kurt Adler, 70, Czech-born pianist-conductor for the Metropolitan Opera, 21 September 1977.

Samuel Adler, 81, abstract painter and sculptor, 12 November 1979.

Conrad Aiken, 84, poet, 17 August 1973.

Duane Allman, 24, rock guitarist with the Allman Brothers Band, 29 October 1971.

Eddie ("Rochester") Anderson, 71, radio and film performer, 28 February 1977.

Leroy Anderson, 66, composer-conductor, 18 May 1975.

William ("Bronco Billy") Anderson, 88, star of Western silent films, 20 January 1971.

Louis Armstrong, 71, New Orleans jazz trumpeter and bandleader known to the world as Satchmo, 6 July 1971.

W. H. Auden, 66, Pulitzer Prize–winning poet, 28 September 1973.

Gene Austin, 71, vocalist of the 1920s, 24 January 1972.

Angela Baddeley, 71, British-born film actress best known for television's *Upstairs Downstairs,* 22 February 1976.

Josephine Baker, 68, dancer famed in the 1920s, 12 April 1975.

Barney Balaban, 83, president and chairman of Paramount Pictures (1936–1966), 7 March 1971.

Faith Baldwin, 84, popular author of eighty-five books of light fiction, 19 March 1978.

Florence Ballard, 32, original member of the Supremes, 22 February 1976.

John Barbirolli, 70, British-born conductor of the New York Philharmonic (1937–1944), 29 July 1970.

Ed Begley, 69, Tony- and Oscar-winning stage and film actor (*Inherit the Wind, Sweet Bird of Youth*), 28 April 1970.

S. N. Behrman, 80, playwright (*No Time for Comedy*), 9 June 1973.

Jack Benny, 80, film and television performer, 26 December 1974.

Sally Benson, 71, writer (*Meet Me in St. Louis*), 19 July 1972.

Thomas Hart Benton, 85, realist painter, 19 January 1975.

Edgar Bergen, 75, ventriloquist famed for act with dummy Charlie McCarthy, 30 September 1978.

Busby Berkeley, 80, Hollywood choreographer of 1930s musicals, 14 March 1976.

John Berryman, 57, poet, winner of a Pulitzer Prize and a National Book Award, 7 January 1972.

Joan Blondell, 70, popular film actress of the 1930s, 26 December 1979.

Kermit Bloomgarden, 71, Broadway producer (*The Music Man, Death of a Salesman*), 20 September 1976.

Marc Bolan, 28, British leader of the band T-Rex, 16 September 1977.

Stephen Boyd, 48, film actor (*Ben-Hur*), 2 June 1977.

Charles Boyer, 78, French-born romantic film actor (*Gaslight, Fanny*), 26 August 1978.

John Bray, 99, inventor of an animated cartoon process used by most early animators, including Walt Disney, 10 October 1978.

Walter Brennan, 80, three-time Oscar-winning film actor, 21 September 1974.

Joe E. Brown, 80, rubber-faced screen actor (*Some Like It Hot*), 6 July 1973.

Pearl S. Buck, 80, Pulitzer Prize and Nobel Prize–winning novelist (*The Good Earth*), 6 March 1973.

Chester ("Howlin' Wolf") Burnett, 65, blues singer and guitarist, 10 January 1976.

Dorsey Burnette, 46, rock 'n' roll guitarist, 19 August 1979.

Spring Byington, 77, Broadway and Hollywood comedic actress, 7 September 1971.

James M. Cain, 85, popular writer of detective fiction, 27 October 1977.

Alexander Calder, 78, artist, sculptor, and creator of abstract mobiles and stabiles, 11 November 1976.

Maria Callas, 53, temperamental opera soprano, 16 September 1977.

Godfrey Cambridge, 43, popular black actor, 29 November 1976.

Leo G. Carroll, 80, British-born character actor best known for appearances in Alfred Hitchcock films, 16 October 1972.

Pablo Casals, 96, cellist, 22 October 1973.

John Cazale, 42, film actor (*Dog Day Afternoon, The Deer Hunter*), 12 March 1978.

Samuel Chamberlain, 79, photographer and artist, 10 January 1975.

James Chapin, 87, environmental realist painter of Americana, 12 July 1975.

Charlie Chaplin, 88, British-born silent-film star immortalized as "The Little Tramp," 25 December 1977.

Ilka Chase, 72, Broadway actress, 15 February 1978.

Maurice Chevalier, 83, French-born singer and film actor (*Gigi, Fanny*), 1 January 1972.

Agatha Christie, 85, popular author of mystery novels, 12 January 1976.

Lee J. Cobb, 64, film actor, 11 February 1976.

Eddie Condon, 67, jazz guitarist band leader, helped establish Chicago style of jazz in the 1920s, 4 August 1973.

Chester Conklin, 85, comedian of "Keystone Kops" silent films, 11 October 1971.

Gladys Cooper, 82, British-born film star (*Rebecca, Now Voyager, My Fair Lady*), 17 November 1971.

Katharine Cornell, 81, Broadway actress, 9 June 1974.

Noel Coward, 73, British playwright (*Private Lives, Blithe Spirit, Design for Living*) and actor, 26 March 1973.

James Gould Cozzens, 74, Pulitzer Prize–winning novelist (*Guard of Honor*), 9 August 1978.

Joan Crawford, 71, for five decades an indomitable Hollywood star (*Mildred Pierce, Humoresque, The Women, Grand Hotel*), 10 May 1977.

Jim Croce, 30, singer-songwriter, 20 September 1973.

Bing Crosby, 76, popular crooner and film actor (*Going My Way*), 14 October 1977.

Dan Dailey, 62, film actor, 17 October 1978.

Bobby Darin, 37, singer and film actor famed for his recording of "Mack the Knife," 20 December 1973.

Patrick Dennis, 55, novelist (*Auntie Mame*), 6 November 1976.

William Dieterle, 79, German-born stage and screen director (*The Life of Emile Zola, The Story of Louis Pasteur*), 18 February 1976.

John Dos Passos, 74, popular author of over thirty novels, including *U.S.A.*, 28 September 1970.

Aaron Douglas, 79, leading painter of the Harlem Renaissance, 2 February 1979.

Eddie Dowling, 81, Pulitzer Prize–winning theatrical performer, producer, director, and writer, 18 February 1976.

Andre Eglevsky, 60, dancer during the 1950s with the New York City Ballet, 4 December 1977.

Duke Ellington, 75, legendary jazz composer, pianist, and bandleader, 24 May 1974.

Cass Elliott, 30, singer with the Mamas and the Papas, 29 July 1974.

Max Ernst, 84, painter and sculptor prominent in the Surrealist and Dadaist art movements, 1 April 1976.

Ruth Etting, 80, Broadway and radio star of the 1930s, 24 September 1978.

Edith Evans, 88, British stage and film actress, 14 October 1976.

Percy Faith, 67, music arranger, conductor, and composer, 9 Feb 1976.

James T. Farrell, 75, novelist known for Studs Lonigan trilogy, 22 August 1979.

John Ferren, 64, geometric abstractionist and Abstract Expressionist artist, 24 July 1970.

Arthur Fiedler, 84, conductor for fifty years of the Boston Pops Orchestra, 10 July 1979.

Betty Field, 55, film actress, 13 September 1973.

Dorothy Fields, 68, Broadway lyricist-librettist, 28 March 1974.

Peter Finch, 60, British-born film actor, posthumous Oscar winner for *Network*, 14 January 1977.

Martha Foley, 80, cofounder of *Story* magazine and editor of annual *Best American Short Stories* anthologies, 5 September 1977.

John Ford, 78, four-time Oscar-winning director (*The Informer, The Grapes of Wrath, How Green Was My Valley, The Quiet Man*), also known for Westerns (*Stagecoach, The Searchers*), 31 August 1973.

Mary Ford, 53, singer with guitarist Les Paul, 30 September 1977.

E. M. Forster, 91, British novelist (*A Room with a View, A Passage to India, Howard's End*), 7 June 1970.

Arthur Freed, 78, producer of M-G-M musicals (*An

American in Paris, Singin' in the Rain, Gigi), 12 April 1973.

William ("Lefty") Frizzell, 47, country-music singing star, 19 July 1975.

Fortune Gallo, 91, founder of San Carlo Opera Company in New York (1910) and popularizer of grand opera, 28 March 1970.

Erle Stanley Gardner, 80, author of more than 140 books including the Perry Mason series, the best-selling American writer of the twentieth century, 11 March 1970.

Erroll Garner, 53, jazz pianist and composer ("Misty"), 2 January 1977.

Billy Gilbert, 77, actor and voice of Walt Disney cartoon characters, 23 September 1971.

Samuel Goldwyn, 91, film producer (*Wuthering Heights, The Best Years of Our Lives*), 31 January 1974.

Vladimir Golschmann, 78, conductor of the Saint Louis Symphony (1931–1957), 1 March 1972.

Max Gordon, 86, theater producer (*The Women, Born Yesterday*), 2 November 1978.

Alfred Gottlieb, 70, abstract painter and member of the New York school of Abstract Expressionism, 4 March 1974.

Betty Grable, 56, film actress famed for her World War II pinup poster, 2 July 1973.

Ferde Grofe, 80, pianist, conductor, composer of the *Grand Canyon Suite;* violinist with the Los Angeles Symphony Orchestra, 3 April 1972.

Vince Guaraldi, 47, composer and conductor famed for the television special *A Charlie Brown Christmas,* 6 February 1976.

Peggy Guggenheim, 81, expatriate owner of one of the foremost modern-art collections, 23 December 1979.

Jed Harris, 79, Broadway director and producer, 15 November 1979.

Paul Hartman, 69, Tony-winning dancer and actor (*Red, Hot and Blue*), 2 October 1973.

Lawrence Harvey, 45, British-born film actor (*Room at the Top, Darling, The Manchurian Candidate, Summer and Smoke*), 25 November 1973.

Jack Hawkins, 62, film actor (*Ben-Hur, The Bridge Over the River Kwai, Lawrence of Arabia*), 18 July 1973.

Howard Hawks, 81, film director (*Bringing Up Baby, Red River*), 26 December 1977.

Sussue Hayakawa, 83, Japanese-born film actor (*The Bridge Over the River Kwai*), 23 November 1973.

Leland Hayward, 68, theatrical agent (Clark Gable, Judy Garland), producer (*South Pacific, The Sound of Music*), and literary agent (Ernest Hemingway), 18 March 1971.

Susan Hayward, 56, Oscar-winning film actress (*I Want to Live!, I'll Cry Tomorrow*), 14 March 1975.

Van Heflin, 60, Oscar-winning character actor (*Johnny Eager*), 23 July 1971.

Jimi Hendrix, 27, legendary rock guitarist, 18 September 1970.

Bernard Herrman, 64, composer of memorable film scores (Alfred Hitchcock's *Psycho, Vertigo, North by Northwest,* Martin Scorcese's *Taxi Driver*), 24 December 1975.

Arthur Hornblow, Jr., 83, Hollywood and Broadway producer, 17 July 1976.

Edward Everett Horton, 83, Hollywood character actor, 29 September 1970.

Moe Howard, 78, original member of the Three Stooges comedy team, 4 May 1975.

James Wong Howe, 76, Oscar-winning Hollywood cinematographer (*Hud*), 12 July 1976.

Howard Hughes, 70, millionaire industrialist and sometime film producer (*The Outlaw*), 5 April 1976.

Ivory Joe Hunter, 63, country, blues, and popular song composer and pianist, 8 November 1974.

William Inge, 60, Pulitzer Prize–winning playwright (*Picnic, Come Back Little Sheba,, Bus Stop*) and Oscar-winning screenwriter (*Splendor in the Grass*), 10 June 1973.

Mahalia Jackson, 70, popular gospel singer, 26 January 1972.

Hall Johnson, 82, choral director, composer, and arranger, founded the Hall Johnson Negro Choir (1925), 30 April 1970.

Nunnally Johnson, 79, screenwriter, 25 March 1977.

James Jones, 55, novelist (*From Here to Eternity*), 9 May 1977.

Janis Joplin, 27, legendary blues-influenced rock singer, 3 October 1970.

Louis Jordan, 66, French-born film actor (*Gigi*), 4 February 1975.

Arthur Judson, 93, manager of the New York Philharmonic and Philadelphia orchestras, 28 January 1975.

MacKinlay Kantor, 73, Pulitzer Prize–winning novelist (*Andersonville*), 11 October 1977.

Emmett Kelly, 80, beloved clown of Ringling Brothers and Barnum and Bailey Circus, 28 March 1979.

Rockwell Kent, 88, landscape and graphics artist, 13 March 1971.

Stan Kenton, 67, big-band leader, 25 August 1979.

Alexander Kipnis, 87, Ukranian-born opera interpreter of Richard Wagner, 14 May 1978.

Gene Krupa, 64, jazz drummer and bandleader, who

revolutionized drum solos with the Benny Goodman Orchestra, 16 October 1973.

Fritz Lang, 85, German-born film director (*M, Metropolis*) who migrated to Hollywood, 2 August 1976.

Walter Lang, 73, film director (*The King and I*), 8 February 1972.

Robert Laurent, 79, modern sculptor, 20 April 1970.

Marjorie Lawrence, 71, Wagnerian soprano star of the Metropolitan Opera, 13 January 1979.

Gypsy Rose Lee, 56, queen of the burlesque stage immortalized in the musical *Gypsy*, 26 April 1970.

Manfred B. Lee, 65, author of the Ellery Queen detective novels, 2 April 1971.

Lotte Lehmann, 78, German-born opera soprano, 26 August 1976.

Margaret Leighton, 53, Tony winning stage actress (*The Night of the Iguana*), 13 January 1976.

Oscar Levant, 72, composer and pianist who also appeared in films (*Humoresque, An American in Paris*), 14 August 1972.

Ted Lewis, 80, singer and nightclub entertainer, 25 August 1971.

Harold Lloyd, 77, silent-film comedy star, 8 March 1971.

Guy Lombardo, 75, bandleader famed for his New Year's Eve rendition of "Auld Lang Syne," 5 November 1977.

Vincent Lopez, 79, pianist and bandleader, 20 September 1975.

Robert Lowell, 60, Pulitzer Prize–winning poet, 12 September 1977.

Paul Lukas, 76, Oscar-winning film and stage actor (*Watch on the Rhine*), 15 August 1971.

Alfred Lunt, 84, stage actor famed for dramatic pairings with Lynn Fontanne, 3 August 1977.

Moms Mabley, 78, black comedienne, 23 May 1975.

Jean Madeira, 53, contralto with the Metropolitan Opera (1948–1971), 10 July 1972.

Anna Magnani, 65, Italian-born film actress (*The Rose Tattoo*), 26 September 1973.

Marjorie Main, 85, character actress best known as Ma Kettle, 10 April 1975.

Fredric March, 76, Oscar-winning film actor (*The Best Years of Our Lives*), 14 April 1975.

Groucho Marx, 86, famed as a member of the Marx Brothers in vaudeville and in comedy films, 20 August 1977.

Zeppo Marx, 78, last surviving member of the Marx Brothers, 30 November 1979.

Henry Mattson, 84, seascape and landscape artist, 8 September 1971.

Phyllis McGinley, 72, Pulitzer Prize–winning writer of light verse, 22 February 1978.

Ruth McKenney, 60, author of *The New Yorker* sketches collected and published as *My Sister Eileen*, 25 July 1972.

Johnny Mercer, 66, Oscar-winning singer and composer ("Moon River," "On the Atchison, Topeka and Santa Fe," "In the Cool Cool Cool of the Evening"), 25 June 1976.

Benjamin Franklin Miessner, 85, inventor of electronic musical devices and perfecter of the Wurlitzer organ, 25 March 1976.

Sal Mineo, 37, film actor (*Rebel Without a Cause*), 13 February 1976.

Charlie Mingus, 56, jazz musician, composer, and bandleader, 5 January 1979.

Keith Moon, 32, drummer for the rock band the Who, 7 September 1978.

Marianne Moore, 84, Pulitzer Prize–winning poet, 5 February 1972.

Agnes Moorehead, 67, character actress best known for her portrayals in Orson Welles films (*Citizen Kane, The Magnificent Ambersons*) and for television's *Bewitched*, 30 April 1974.

Jim Morrison, 27, lead singer of the rock group the Doors, 3 July 1971.

Zero Mostel, 62, Tony-winning actor (*Fiddler on the Roof, A Funny Thing Happened on the Way to the Forum, Rhinoceros*), 8 September 1977.

Vladimir Nabokov, 78, Russian-born writer of innovative American fiction (*Lolita, Pale Fire*), 2 July 1977.

Ogden Nash, 68, humorist and poet, 19 May 1971.

Ozzie Nelson, 69, bandleader best-known for television's *The Adventures of Ozzie and Harriet*, 3 June 1975.

Pablo Neruda, 69, Nobel Prize–winning Latin American poet, 23 September 1973.

Alfred Newman, 68, film composer (*The King and I, Love Is a Many Splendored Thing*), 17 February 1970.

Barnett Newman, 65, painter and sculptor influential in Abstract Expressionist and Minimalist movements, 3 July 1970.

Anaïs Nin, 73, diarist and erotic novelist, 14 January 1977.

Sterling North, 68, poet, short-story writer, novelist, and writer of children's books (*Rascal*), 22 December 1974.

Merle Oberon, 68, Indian-born film actress best known for portraying Cathy in *Wuthering Heights*, 11 November 1979.

Phil Ochs, 35, Vietnam-era protest singer, 9 April 1976.

John O'Hara, 65, popular author (*Appointment in Samarra*) and winner of the National Book Award (*Ten North Frederick*), 11 April 1970.

Edward ("Kid") Ory, 86, Dixieland jazz trombonist, 29 January 1973.

Gordon Parks, 44, film director (*Shaft, Superfly*), 3 April 1979.

Louella Parsons, 91, Hollywood gossip columnist, 9 December 1972.

Irene Rice Pereira, 63, abstract artist who experimented with geometric forms, color, and light, 11 January 1971.

S. J. Perelman, 75, humorist and author, 17 October 1979.

Pablo Picasso, 91, the world's best-known painter and famed for his Surrealist style, 8 April 1973.

Mary Pickford, 86, silent-film actress known as "America's Sweetheart" during the 1910s and 1920s, 29 May 1979.

Waldo Pierce, 85, Impressionist painter, 8 March 1970.

Walter Piston, 82, Pulitzer Prize–winning composer, 12 November 1976.

Lily Pons, 71, soprano for the Metropolitan Opera for thirty years, 13 February 1976.

Ezra Pound, 87, influential poet of the 1920s, 1 November 1972.

Elvis Presley, 42, the famed "King of Rock 'n' Roll" and best-selling solo recording artist in history, 16 August 1977.

Louis Prima, 67, jazz trumpeter and bandleader, 24 August 1978.

Joseph Rank, 83, British film executive and founder of Rank Organization, Britain's largest film distributor, 29 March 1972.

Terence Rattigan, 66, British playwright (*Separate Tables*), 30 November 1977.

Man Ray, 86, painter, sculptor, photographer, and leader of Dadaist movement, 18 November 1976.

Andy Razaf, 77, composer-lyricist best known for "Ain't Misbehavin," 3 February 1973.

Carol Reed, 80, British film director (*The Third Man, Oliver!*), 25 April 1976.

Minnie Riperton, 30, pop vocalist ("Lovin' You"), 12 July 1979.

Tex Ritter, 68, country-music performer and cowboy-film star, 2 January 1974.

Thelma Ritter, 63, character actress in dozens of Hollywood films (*All About Eve, Rear Window*), 5 February 1969.

Paul Robeson, 77, black stage actor famed for his portrayal of the character of Eugene O'Neill's *The Emperor Jones*, 23 January 1976.

Edward G. Robinson, film actor best known for gangster roles (*Little Caesar*), 26 January 1973.

Norman Rockwell, 84, popular painter of Americana, 8 November 1978.

Richard Rodgers, 77, song composer with lyricists Lorenz Hart and Oscar Hammerstein II, 30 December 1979.

Walter Rollins, 66, songwriter best known for "Frosty the Snowman," 2 January 1973.

Roberto Rossellini, 71, Italian film director, 3 June 1977.

Mark Rothko, 66, pioneer of Abstract Expressionist painting, 25 February 1970.

Rosalind Russell, 63, film actress (*His Girl Friday, Auntie Mame, The Women*), 28 November 1976.

Margaret Rutherford, 80, Oscar-winning character actress (*The VIPs*) best known for portraying Miss Marple, 22 May 1972.

Robert Ryan, 63, film actor, 11 July 1973.

George Sanders, 65, Oscar-winning British film actor famed for his portrayals of waspish cads (*Rebecca, All About Eve*), 25 April 1972.

Thomas Schippers, 47, conducted a record number of opening-night performances at the Metropolitan Opera, 16 December 1977.

Max Schuster, 73, publisher, editor, and founder of Simon and Schuster, 20 December 1970.

George Seaton, 68, film director, producer, and screenwriter, 28 July 1979.

Jean Seberg, 40, film actress who was launched in Jean-Luc Godard's *Breathless*, 31 August 1979.

Robert Shaw, 51, British-born film actor (*The Sting, Jaws*), 28 August 1978.

Ted Shawn, 80, dancer and choreographer, 9 January 1972.

Herman Shumlin, 80, Broadway producer, 14 June 1979.

Cornelia Otis Skinner, 78, actress and author known for wit and satiric humor, 9 July 1979.

Spyros Skouras, 78, president of 20th Century–Fox film studio (1942–1962), 16 August 1971.

Louis Slobodkin, 72, sculptor, author, designer, and illustrator of over fifty children's books, 8 May 1975.

Betty Smith, 67, author (*A Tree Grows in Brooklyn*), 17 January 1972.

Edward Steichen, 93, America's best-known photographer, 25 March 1973.

William Steinberg, 78, German-born musical director with the Pittsburgh and Boston Symphony orchestras and principal guest conductor with the New York Philharmonic, 16 May 1978.

Max Steiner, 83, film composer (*King Kong, Gone With the Wind, Now Voyager, Mildred Pierce*), 28 December 1971.

William Grant Still, 83, black composer of *Afro-American Symphony* and the first black conductor of a major orchestra, 3 December 1978.

Leopold Stokowski, 95, conductor of the Philadelphia Orchestra, 13 September 1977.

Robert Stolz, 88, Oscar-winning composer and conductor, 27 June 1975.

Rex Stout, 88, best-selling novelist and creator of Nero Wolfe, 27 October 1975.

Paul Strand, 85, photographer, 31 March 1976.

Jacqueline Susann, 53, whose novel *Valley of the Dolls* sold seventeen million copies, 21 September 1974.

Dalton Trumbo, 70, Oscar-winning screenwriter and victim of the 1950s Hollywood blacklist, 10 September 1976.

Richard Tucker, 61, famed tenor with the Metropolitan Opera, 8 January 1975.

Mark Van Doren, 78, Pulitzer Prize–winning novelist and poet, 10 December 1972.

Gene Vincent, 36, rockabilly singer ("Be Bop a Lula"), 12 October 1971.

Aaron ("T-Bone") Walker, 64, blues singer and guitarist, 16 March 1975.

Jack Warner, 86, founder with his brothers of Warner Bros. film studio, 9 September 1978.

Ethel Waters, 80, blues singer and film actress (*The Member of the Wedding*), 1 September 1977.

John Wayne, 72, archetypal hero of film Westerns (*Red River, Stagecoach, The Searchers*) and Oscar winner for *True Grit,* 11 June 1979.

William Wellman, 79, film director (*The Public Enemy, Wings, Beau Geste*), 9 December 1975.

Perc Westmore, 65, Hollywood makeup artist, 30 September 1970.

Thornton Wilder, 78, playwright (*Our Town, The Skin of Our Teeth*), 7 December 1975.

Michael Wilding, 66, British stage and film actor, 8 July 1979.

Bob Wills, 70, country musician / fiddle player, 13 May 1975.

Walter Winchell, 74, father of the modern show-business gossip column, 20 February 1972.

P. G. Wodehouse, 93, British-born satiric novelist, 14 February 1975.

Gig Young, 60, Oscar-winning film actor (*They Shoot Horses, Don't They?*), 19 October 1978.

Darryl F. Zanuck, 77, cofounder and president of 20th Century–Fox film studio, 22 December 1979.

Adolph Zukor, 103, Paramount Pictures mogul, 10 June 1976.

PUBLICATIONS

Carl Belz, *The Story of Rock* (New York: Oxford University Press, 1972);

Joachim Ernst Berendt, *Jazz, A Photo History* (New York: Schirmer, 1979);

Gerald Bordman, *American Musical Theater: A Chronicle* (New York: Oxford University Press, 1978);

Milton W. Brown, Sam Hunter, John Jacobus, Naomi Rosenblum, and David M. Sokol, *American Art* (New York: Abrams, 1979);

Gary Busnar, *It's Rock 'n' Roll* (New York: Messner, 1979);

John Cage, *Empty Words* (Middletown, Conn.: Wesleyan University Press, 1979);

Patrick Carr, ed., *The Illustrated History of Country Music* (Garden City, N.Y.: Doubleday, 1979);

Steve Chapple, *Rock 'n' Roll is Here to Pay* (Chicago: Nelson-Hall, 1977);

Allen Edwards, *Flawed Words and Stubborn Sounds: A Conversation with Elliott Carter* (New York: Norton, 1972);

Bob Greene, *Billion Dollar Baby* (New York: Atheneum, 1974);

Lloyd Grossman, *A Social History of Rock Music: From the Greasers to Glitter Rock* (New York: McKay, 1976);

Leslie Halliwell, *Film Guide* (New York: Scribners, 1979);

Charles Hamm, *Contemporary Music and Music Cultures* (Englewood Cliffs, N.J.: Prentice-Hall, 1975);

Charles B. Harris, *Contemporary American Novelists of the Absurd* (New Haven, Conn.: College & University Press, 1971);

Jeffrey Helterman and Richard Layman, eds., *American Novelists Since World War II* (Detroit: Gale, 1978);

Hunter and Jacobus, *Modern Art: Painting Sculpture Architecture* (New York: Abrams, 1977);

Pauline Kael, *Reeling* (Boston: Little, Brown, 1976);

Alfred Kazin, *Bright Book of Life* (Boston: Little, Brown, 1973);

Hilton Kramer, *The Art of the Avant-Garde: An Art Chronicle of 1956–1972* (London: Secker & Warburg, 1974);

Axel Madsen, *The New Hollywood: American Movies in the Seventies* (New York: Crowell, 1975);

Edward Mape, *Blacks in American Film* (Metuchen, N.J.: Scarecrow Press, 1972);

Greil Marcus, *Mystery Train: Visions of America in Rock 'n' Roll Music* (New York: Dutton, 1975);

Doug, McClelland, *The Golden Age of "B" Movies* (Nashville, Tenn.: Charterhouse, 1978);

Joan Mellen, *Big Bad Wolves: Masculinity in American Film* (New York: Pantheon, 1977);

Donald Miles, *The American Novel in the Twentieth Century* (New York: Barnes & Noble, 1978);

Gregoire Muller, *The New Avant Garde: Issues for the Art of the Seventies* (New York: Praeger, 1972);

Eleanor C. Munro, *Originals: American Women Artists* (New York: Simon & Schuster, 1979);

Gary Null, *Black Hollywood: The Black Performer in Motion Pictures* (Secaucus, N.J.: Citadel, 1975);

Michael Nyman, *Experimental Music: Cage and Beyond* (London: Studio Vista, 1974);

Lindsay Patterson, *Black Films and Film-Makers* (New York: Dodd, Mead, 1975);

William Harwood Peden, *The American Short Story: Continuity and Change, 1940–1975* (Boston: Houghton Mifflin, 1975);

Rupert Pincus-Witten, *Postminimalism* (New York: Out of London Press, 1977);

Rock Art: Fifty-two Record Album Covers (Seaside, Cal.: Comma Books, 1977);

The Rolling Stone Illustrated History of Rock & Roll (New York: Rolling Stone Press, 1976);

Paul Rosenfeld, *Discoveries of a Music Critic* (New York: Vienna House, 1972);

David Shapiro, *Social Realism: Art as a Weapon* (New York: Ungar, 1973);

Donald Spoto, *Camerado: Hollywood and the American Man* (New York: New American Library, 1978);

Tony Tanner, *Adultery in the Novel: Contract and Aggression* (Baltimore: Johns Hopkins University Press, 1979);

Tanner, *City of Words: American Fiction, 1950–1970* (New York: Harper & Row, 1971);

Frank Tirro, *Jazz: A History* (New York: Norton, 1977);

Floyd C. Watkins, *The Death of Art: Black and White in the Recent Southern Novel* (Athens: University of Georgia Press, 1970);

Paul Whiteman, *Jazz* (New York: Arno, 1974);

Art in America, periodical;

ARTnews, periodical;

Billboard, periodical;

Creem, periodical;

Film Comment, periodical;

Films in Review, periodical;

Publishers Weekly, periodical;

Rolling Stone, periodical;

Variety, periodical.

Twyla Tharp dancers in *Baker's Dozen*, 1979

BUSINESS AND THE ECONOMY

by JAMES W. HIPP AND LEONARD BUSHKOFF

CONTENTS

Sidebars and tables are listed in italics.

1970

- Inflation and unemployment inflict serious damage on American prosperity.

- German and Japanese automakers make significant inroads on the American domestic market.

5 Jan. Joseph Yablonski, a former candidate for the presidency of the United Mine Workers (UMW), his wife, and his daughter are found murdered in their home.

14 Jan. The Department of Justice indicts seven firms for polluting the New York harbor.

19 Jan. Inflation reaches 6.1 percent, the highest rate since the Korean War.

28 Jan. Ford, Nissan, and Tokyo Kogyo form a joint venture to manufacture auto transmissions.

10 Feb. President Richard Nixon inaugurates a major antipollution program and improves federal park facilities.

28 Feb. The January economic indicators fall by 1.8 percent, the greatest monthly decline since the 1957 recession.

1 Mar. Westinghouse and four unions reach a contract agreement involving a 15 percent wage increase.

25 Mar. The first major postal workers' strike in American history ends after seven days.

1 Apr. Federal legislation bans cigarette advertising on radio and television, beginning 1 January 1971.

3 Apr. President Nixon signs the Water Quality Improvement Act to combat pollution and oil spills.

15 Apr. Nixon accepts a law giving federal employees 6 percent higher wages.

22 Apr. The first celebration of Earth Day takes place.

28 Apr. The Dow-Jones average falls to 724.33, the lowest level since the November 1963 assassination of President John F. Kennedy.

5 May A New Orleans grand jury indicts the Chevron Oil Company for violating pollution safeguards on ninety Gulf of Mexico oil rigs.

9 May Walter Reuther, head of the United Auto Workers (UAW), dies unexpectedly, beginning a struggle among his successors for control of the union.

1 June The Supreme Court rules 5–2 that federal judges can ban strikes that break no-strike contract clauses.

21 June Following bankruptcy, the Penn Central Railroad begins reorganization.

2 July The unemployment rate drops significantly between May and June.

31 July The House of Representatives grants President Nixon the power to control wages, prices, and rents.

4 Aug. U.S. Steel announces an 11.8 percent increase on tin mill products.

15 Sept.–
11 Nov. Four hundred thousand UAW members strike against General Motors. On 20 November the UAW and General Motors sign a new contract providing for early retirement and for substantial wage increases. On 2 December Ford signs a similar contract with the UAW.

17 Sept.	Cesar Chavez, leader of the United Farm Workers (UFW), announces a national boycott against California's lettuce growers.
2 Oct.	The Environmental Protection Agency (EPA) is created.
16 Oct.	Paul Samuelson of the Massachusetts Institute of Technology becomes the first American to win the Nobel Prize in economics.
26 Oct.	The government mandates the use of unleaded gasoline in federal vehicles.
30 Nov.	President Nixon signs legislation creating the National Railroad Passenger Corporation, a private/public company to carry passengers between larger cities. In 1971 the corporation will be renamed Amtrak.
4 Dec.	The government announces that unemployment has risen to 5.8 percent. In response, officials reduce interest rates.
11 Dec.	Following a five-month strike, Northwest Airlines grants workers a 37.5 percent wage increase.
15 Dec.	The federal government orders the recall of one million cans of tuna fish because of suspected mercury contamination.
23 Dec.	Legislation is passed granting the secretary of labor the power to set safety regulations for factories, farms, and other enterprises.
31 Dec.	President Nixon signs the National Air Quality Control Act, designed to cut air pollution 90 percent by 1975.

1971

•	The Department of the Post Office is reorganized as the semi-independent U.S. Postal Service.
7 Jan.	The Nixon administration appeals a court order prohibiting the use of DDT.
15 Jan.	The Federal Trade Commission (FTC) charges seven soft-drink companies with price-fixing.
18 Jan.	U.S. Steel accepts a court order demanding it stop dumping wastes into Lake Michigan.
22 Jan.	General Motors recalls ten thousand school buses and forty-four thousand light trucks because of faulty clutches.
6 Feb.	*Time* magazine reaches an agreement regarding job discrimination with 140 women employees.
2 Mar.	W. A. ("Tony") Boyle, the president of the United Mine Workers, is indicted for using union funds to make illegal political contributions.
3 Mar.	Following the FTC's "truth in advertising" campaign, the three largest detergent makers cancel television ads that claim their products remove all dirt stains.
8 Mar.	The Supreme Court prohibits employers from using job tests that discriminate against blacks.
29 Mar.	Ford recalls 220,000 Pintos because their engines are suspected of being susceptible to fire.
9 Apr.	Indiana passes a law restricting the amount of phosphates in laundry detergents.
5 May	The Labor Department imposes racial hiring quotas at federally sponsored construction sites in three cities.

12 May	The Civil Service Commission bans men-only and women-only designations for most federal jobs.
17 May	The government brings suit against the Wheeling-Pittsburgh Steel Corporation for polluting the Ohio and Monongahela rivers.
10 June	President Nixon ends a twenty-year trade embargo against Communist China.
1 July	The International Longshoremen's and Warehousemen's Union strikes twenty-four ports on the West Coast.
8 July	Frank Fitzsimmons is elected president of the International Brotherhood of Teamsters, Chauffeurs, Warehousemen, and Helpers of America (Teamsters Union).
20 July	The strike at American Telephone & Telegraph by 532,000 workers ends.
25 July	Thirty-five thousand workers end their twenty-six-day strike at Kennecott Copper Corporation.
2 Aug.	Congress authorizes a $250-million bailout of the Lockheed Aircraft Corporation. The Nixon administration approves the bailout on 9 September.
15 Aug.	President Nixon announces his New Economic Policy, freezing wages, prices, and rents for ninety days and initiating other broad economic controls.
1 Sept.	A precedent-setting Justice Department suit requires Florida Power and Light to build a $30-million system to clean the water it pumps into Biscayne Bay.
15 Sept.	The Department of the Interior refuses to grant two oil-drilling permits in California's Santa Barbara Channel.
1 Oct.	East and Gulf Coast longshoremen, as well as eighty thousand coal miners, go on strike. On 24 November, invoking the Taft-Hartley Act, the courts order the strike to end.
15 Oct.	Simon Kuznets of Harvard University wins the Nobel Prize in economics.
19 Oct.	In an effort to protect children from lead poisoning, the government limits the lead content of house paint.
13 Nov.	Anaconda Wire and Cable is fined two hundred thousand dollars for polluting the Hudson River.
24 Nov.	Herbert Stein replaces Paul McCracken as the chairman of the Council of Economic Advisers.
4 Dec.	General Motors recalls 6.68 million defective Chevrolet cars and trucks.
10 Dec.	President Nixon signs a $25-billion tax cut.
14 Dec.	Congress extends the Nixon administration's economic controls until April 1973.
23 Dec.	President Nixon commutes the prison term of Jimmy Hoffa, former president of the Teamsters Union.

1972

- The Dow-Jones average hits 1,000 for the first time in history.

21 Jan.	The government demands that six cigarette companies include health warnings in their advertisements.
18 Feb.	A seven-month strike against the New York Telephone Company is settled.
21 Feb.	A new contract ends the 134-day West Coast longshoremen's strike.
24 Feb.	The Department of Transportation delays by two years mandatory installation of automobile safety air bags.
9 Mar.	The House of Representatives votes to end the killing of whales and other sea mammals in U.S. waters. On 26 July the Senate passes a fifteen-year ban on the killing of ocean mammals.
29 Mar.	A Justice Department lawsuit charges twenty major aircraft manufacturers with stifling competition in research.
31 Mar.	Tony Boyle
6 May	Japanese and European steel producers promise to limit exports to the United States voluntarily for the next two years.
8 May	General Motors recalls 350,000 defective 1971 and 1972 Chevrolets.
16 May	George Shultz replaces John Connally as secretary of the treasury.
14 June	The EPA effectively bans DDT.
29 June	Ford recalls over four million 1970 and 1971 cars and trucks.
8 July	The federal government authorizes the sale of $750 million in grain to the Soviet Union.
2 Aug.	The government bans the use of livestock growth hormone (DES) in cattle feed, effective 1 January 1973.
15 Aug.	A federal court lifts an April 1970 injunction banning the construction of the Trans-Alaska Pipeline.
14 Sept.	The federal government authorizes the sale of eighteen million bushels of wheat to Communist China.
2 Oct.	The Atomic Energy Commission orders Consolidated Edison to correct severe pollution at its Indian Point plant on the Hudson River.
25 Oct.	Kenneth J. Arrow of Harvard University shares the Nobel Prize in economics with John R. Hicks of Great Britain.
27 Oct.	The Department of Labor reports that prices increased 40 percent more than wages under the Nixon administration's New Economic Policy.
1 Nov.	Standard Oil of New Jersey is renamed Exxon.
16 Nov.	Pepsico announces a deal to sell its products in the Soviet Union.
5 Dec.	A federal court postpones the August 1975 date for the installation of automobile air bags and other safety devices.
12 Dec.	The government accuses Xerox of monopolistic business practices.
22 Dec.	Arnold Miller, former UMW president, defeats Boyle

1973

- The Justice Department reveals that President Nixon's reelection committee accepted illegal campaign contributions from Gulf Oil, Goodyear Tire and Rubber, Braniff Airways, Phillips Petroleum, Minnesota Mining and Manufacturing, Ashland Oil, American Airlines, and other corporations.

4 Jan. The government approves Western Union's plan to build a domestic communications satellite system.

11 Jan. The Nixon administration ends mandatory wages and price controls, except in the food, construction, and health-care industries.

18 Jan. American Telephone and Telegraph (AT&T) pays fifteen thousand women and minority employees a total of fifteen million dollars as compensation for discriminatory practices.

13 Feb. A federal court fines the Ford Motor Company seven million dollars for improperly servicing 1973-model cars.

25 Feb. Fearing possible contamination, the United Canning Company recalls fifty thousand cans of mushrooms.

30 Mar. The government sets regulations limiting industrial emissions of asbestos, mercury, and beryllium.

2 Apr. Harold Geneen, chief executive officer of International Telephone and Telegraph (ITT), testifies before the Senate Foreign Relations subcommittee that he offered to fund the political opponents of Marxist president Salvador Allende during the 1970 Chilean elections. On 21 June the subcommittee sharply criticizes ITT for its activities.

12 Apr. Occidental Petroleum Company reaches a multibillion-dollar agreement to build a fertilizer plant in the Soviet Union.

2 May The Nixon administration announces a tightening of price controls on some six hundred large companies.

3 May A court order directs Delta Air Lines to open more positions to women and blacks.

8 May The United Rubber Workers union strikes B. F. Goodrich Company.

16 May The federal government bans the dumping of eight types of waste at sea.

31 May A four-month-old strike against the Shell Oil Company ends.

6 June The House of Representatives votes to raise the minimum hourly wage from $1.60 to $2.20. On 19 July the Senate votes to increase it to $2.00.

13 June President Nixon orders that consumer-product prices be frozen for sixty days, except for rent and unprocessed farm materials.

2 July Leading banks raise their prime lending rates to 8 percent.

17 July Following House approval, the Senate authorizes the construction of the 789-mile Trans-Alaska Pipeline.

3 Sept. George Meany, head of the American Federation of Labor and Congress of Industrial Organizations (AFL-CIO), denounces President Nixon's economic policy.

6 Sept. Former United Mine Workers president Boyle

17 Sept.   Chrysler and the autoworkers' union reach a three-year contract, with a low 5 percent wage increase in the first year.

2 Oct.   A federal court orders Detroit Edison to pay $4 million to blacks who suffered employment discrimination.

18 Oct.   Wassily Leontief of Harvard University wins the Nobel Prize in economics.

19–21 Oct.   Following the Yom Kippur War between Israel and the Arab states, some members of the Organization of Petroleum Exporting Countries (OPEC) begin an embargo of oil to the United States and other Western nations.

30 Oct.   The Justice Department accuses 541 trucking companies of discriminatory practices.

16 Nov.   President Nixon signs a bill authorizing the construction of the Trans-Alaska Pipeline.

30 Nov.   Following a decline in car sales, some twenty-five hundred Ford workers are laid off. On 28 December General Motors will lay off eighty-six thousand workers.

4 Dec.   Chrysler recalls sixty-four thousand defective 1973 and 1974 cars.

4–7 Dec.   Increasing oil shortages result in canceled airline flights and a trucker blockade of key highways in protest of high fuel costs.

22 Dec.   As a fuel-conservation and safety measure, Congress orders states to reduce interstate speed limits to 55 MPH.

1974

- David Rockefeller forms the Trilateral Commission to coordinate international economic exchanges.

- In November and December significant worker layoffs occur at Sears Roebuck, Celanese, Ford, Chrysler, General Motors, American Motors, Bethlehem Steel, Motorola, Singer Sewing Machines, Weyerhauser Lumber, and Xerox.

31 Jan.   Georgia Power and Light is ordered by the courts to pay $2.1 million in retroactive wages and benefits to black employees denied equal job opportunities.

12 Mar.   Volkswagen is fined $120,000 for violating auto-emission controls.

18 Mar.   The Arab oil-producing nations, with the exception of Libya and Syria, end their embargo of the West.

1 Apr.   Wage and price controls end in 165 industries; on 15 April they will be lifted on food retailers and wholesalers.

2 Apr.   The Soviet airline Aeroflot is granted access to Washington's Dulles Airport.

8 Apr.   President Nixon approves the extension of the minimum wage to eight million additional workers and signs an increase in the wage to $2.30 per hour.

11 Apr.   Boyle

17 Apr.   William Simon replaces George Shultz as treasury secretary.

30 Apr.   President Nixon's authority to impose wage and price controls on the American economy ends with the expiration of the 1970 Economic Wage Stabilization Act.

1975

1 June	A seven-day strike begins between the Amalgamated Clothing Workers and the men's clothing industry — the first strike between the two parties since 1927.
28 June	The Occidental Petroleum Corporation signs four twenty-year contacts with the Soviet Union.
15 July	The machinists' union strikes Trans World Airways. The strike lasts until 30 October.
9 Sept.	A 177-day strike between Dow Chemical and the United Steelworkers' union ends.
8 Oct.	President Gerald Ford announces his program to control inflation, called Whip Inflation Now (WIN). Despite a denial by President Ford, Arthur Burns, chairman of the Federal Reserve, states that a recession is under way.
26 Oct.	The 1972 Marine Protection Act, banning the dumping of hazardous wastes at sea, is extended.
29 Oct.	Federal legislation is passed banning discrimination based on gender or marital status.

- Bankruptcies set a new record of 254,484.
- Exxon Corporation replaces General Motors as the nation's wealthiest company.
- Senate and Securities and Exchange Commission investigations expose widespread illegal payoffs by U.S. businesses overseas.

1 Jan.	Following frequent fines for pollution, U.S. Steel closes ten open-hearth furnaces in Gary, Indiana.
10 Jan.	Matsushita Electric Industrial Company recalls three hundred thousand color televisions.
29 Jan.	Fearing serious defects, the government orders twenty-three nuclear reactors closed for inspection.
7 Feb.	The federal government reports January unemployment at 8.2 percent, the highest level since 1941.
18 Feb.	General Motors recalls 220,000 defective cars.
17 Mar.	The Chicago, Rock Island & Pacific Railroad declares bankruptcy.
29 Mar.	President Ford signs a $22.8-billion tax bill.
2 May	Gulf Oil admits it secretly gave $4.2 million to foreign political figures.
14 May	President Ford rejects New York City's request for federal assistance to avoid bankruptcy.
22 June	Alan Greenspan of the Council of Economic Advisers announces that "the recession, for all practical purposes, is over."
26 June	It is announced that May economic indicators have risen, the fourth consecutive increase.
18 July	The unions and railroads avert a strike by signing a settlement agreeing to a 41 percent pay increase over three years.
31 July	Former Teamsters leader Hoffa disappears.

1 Aug.   Lockheed Aircraft admits to paying $22 million in bribes to obtain foreign contracts.

3 Sept.   Some 530,000 teachers in twelve states go on strike.

7 Nov.   The Supreme Court rules unconstitutional a Utah law denying unemployment benefits to women in the third trimester of pregnancy.

27 Nov.   The Ford administration announces a five-year U.S.-Polish grain deal.

1 Dec.   In Connecticut an 154-day strike at General Dynamics ends.

1976

- Nissan beats Volkswagen as the leading foreign car importer in the United States.

- The government reports an overall improvement in air quality from 1971 to 1975, especially in the Northeast, the Great Lakes states, and urban California.

- American farmers number only 8.9 million, 4.2 percent of the total population.

2 Jan.   President Ford vetoes a bill permitting broader picketing rights by strikers at construction sites.

5 Jan.   California fines American Motors $4.2 million and bans the sale of three models of AMC cars for violating state pollution laws.

15 Jan.   Gulf Oil fires four executives for instituting a $12-million political bribery fund.

4 Feb.   The government authorizes limited U.S. landings by the supersonic Anglo-French Concorde aircraft.

8 Feb.   A National Cancer Institute study reveals that the highest U.S. cancer rates are found downwind of the chemical plants located along the New Jersey Turnpike.

13 Feb.   Following revelations regarding Lockheed's bribes to foreign officials, two top executives of the company resign.

26 Mar.   The government accuses the Encyclopaedia Britannica Company of deceptive selling and other practices.

1 Apr.   Conrail, a federally funded corporation consolidating six bankrupt northeastern railroads, begins operations.

14 Apr.   Fourth-quarter indexes suggest a strong economic recovery.

21 Apr.   The United Rubber Workers strike four tire and rubber companies.

As the last Cadillac Eldorado rolls off the assembly line, the U.S. auto industry ceases production of convertibles due to declining sales.

7 May   Allied Chemical is indicted for river dumping of wastes.

2–21 June   *Time* magazine is struck by the newspaper guild.

6 June   The Teamsters end a fourteen-week strike against Anheuser-Busch.

23 June   A grounded barge spills three hundred thousand gallons of oil in the Saint Lawrence River.

1 July The Supreme Court orders mining operators to compensate miners for black-lung disease.

25 Aug. General Motors raises its car prices an average of $344; the base sticker price for its autos is now $6,000.

2 Sept. Three senior Phillips Petroleum officials are charged with tax fraud linked to illegal political gifts.

15 Sept. American Bank and Trust Company fails, the fourth largest banking default ever.

12 Oct. Following the settlement of a Ford strike which lasted twenty-eight days, 165,000 workers return to work.

14 Oct. Milton Friedman wins the Nobel Prize in economics.

10 Dec. Chrysler recalls 208,000 cars.

15 Dec. The Liberian tanker *Argo Merchant* causes an oil spill near Nantucket, Massachusetts.

18 Dec. Over 175 U.S. companies admit bribery in excess of $300 million total since 1970.

1977

- A five-month drought threatens agriculture in the Texas panhandle.

- Sales of foreign autos reach new levels, 73 percent higher than in 1976.

- Bethlehem Steel posts the worst quarterly losses in its history.

- The United States posts the highest trade deficit in its history, $31.1 billion.

- Personal income in the United States rises 11.1 percent, the highest increase since 1973.

- Many consumers respond to high coffee prices by switching to tea.

12 Jan. The Anaconda Company, the third largest copper-mining corporation in the United States, is bought by Atlantic Richfield, the eighth largest oil company.

10 Mar. The Teamsters and the United Farm Workers settle their jurisdictional disagreements over organizing workers.

21 Mar. Secretary of Transportation Brock Adams orders U.S. automakers to install air bags in their cars, this time in the 1981 or 1982 models.

30 Apr. Mass arrests result as environmental demonstrators try to block the Seabrook, New Hampshire, nuclear-power plant construction site.

14 June Arnold Miller is reelected president of the United Mine Workers.

20 June Pumping operations begin on the 789-mile Trans-Alaska Pipeline.

30 June The government requires mandatory installation of seat belts and air bags in automobiles after 1982.

13–14 July A two-day electrical blackout strikes New York City.

1 Aug. Strikes in the iron ranges of Minnesota and Michigan halt most iron ore production.

4 Aug.   The Department of Energy is created. James Schlesinger becomes the first secretary of the department.

21 Sept.   Following criticisms of his activities with a Georgia bank, Bert Lance, director of the Office of Management and Budget and a close friend of President Jimmy Carter, resigns.

26 Sept.   Freddie Laker begins his no-frills New York-to-London Skytrain air service.

1 Oct.   Longshoremen strike thirty ports from Maine to Texas. The strike will last nearly one month.

3 Oct.   Three hundred American Airlines stewardesses who were fired for pregnancy between 1965 and 1970 receive a $2.7 million civil rights settlement.

11 Oct.   Leeway Motor Freight is ordered to pay forty-six black employees $1.8 million to compensate for discrimination.

1 Nov.   President Carter signs a law which will raise the minimum wage to $3.35 per hour by 1981.

16 Dec.   The Federal Election Commission charges the AFL-CIO with violations of campaign-spending laws.

28 Dec.   G. William Miller replaces Arthur Burns as chairman of the Federal Reserve Board.

1978

- Dean Witter and Reynolds Securities International merge to form Dean Witter Reynolds International.

- A record-breaking twelve million vehicles are recalled.

- Due to inflation, goods costing $100.00 in 1967 now cost $200.90.

- Controversy and protests over the construction of the Seabrook nuclear-power plant continue.

- The salaries and bonuses of corporate executives rise 16.7 percent.

- General Motors regains its position as the wealthiest corporation in the United States. Exxon Corporation is second.

2 Jan.   The machinists' union ends a twelve-week strike against two Lockheed plants in California.

31 Jan.   The United Farm Workers end their boycott on lettuce, table grapes, and Gallo wines.

1 Feb.   The government files suit against the Teamsters and their president, Frank Fitzsimmons, for dubious pension-fund loans.

18 Feb.   Boyle

24 Feb.   President Carter announces a tentative settlement in the eighty-one-day coal strike. A final agreement is signed on 14 March.

2 Mar.   The government fines Texaco $228,770 for safety lapses that led to the deaths of eight workers in a Port Arthur, Texas, fire.

4 Mar.   The *Chicago Daily News* ends publication.

15 Mar.   The government bans fluorocarbon aerosol sprays, which deplete the atmosphere's ozone layer.

25 Mar.   A 110-day coal miners' strike, the longest in U.S. history, ends with the signing of a new three-year contract.

17 Apr.   A new stock-trading record of 63.5 million shares is set on the New York Stock Exchange.

3 May   Alternative energy advocates declare Sun Day in order to publicize alternative energy sources.

15 June   Because of the threat that Tennessee's Tellico Dam presents to the habitat of the snail darter, an endangered species of perch, the Supreme Court orders an indefinite halt to the $100-million project.

16 Oct.   Herbert A. Simon of Carnegie-Mellon University wins the Nobel Prize in economics.

15 Dec.   McDonnell-Douglas admits that it distributed $18 million in bribes in order to gain foreign contracts.

1979

- The Islamic revolution in Iran cuts off Iranian oil and leads to widespread oil shortages and soaring energy costs.

- The government deregulates long-distance phone service.

- Toxic waste dumped by Hooker Chemicals creates a public-health crisis at Love Canal, near Buffalo, New York.

28 Mar.   A partial nuclear meltdown, followed by leaks of radioactive gas, occurs at the Three Mile Island nuclear generating station near Harrisburg, Pennsylvania.

6 May   In Washington, D.C., sixty-five thousand demonstrate against nuclear power.

9 May   California begins gasoline rationing.

18 May   A federal jury orders Kerr-McGee to pay $10.5 million to the estate of Karen Silkwood, a Kerr-McGee worker contaminated by radiation, who was killed in a mysterious 1974 auto crash.

1 June   Lockheed is fined $647,000 for secret bribes worth $2.6 million to Japanese political figures.

7 June   Independent truckers begin a strike to protest rising fuel prices and lower speed limits.

31 July   The Chrysler Corporation, the third largest automaker in the United States, requests a $1-billion federal loan to prevent bankruptcy. On 1 November the federal government guarantees a $1.5-billion loan to Chrysler.

20 Sept.   Lee Iacocca becomes the chief executive officer of Chrysler Corporation.

17 Oct.   Theodore Schultz of the University of Chicago and Arthur Lewis of Princeton University receive the Nobel Prize in economics.

22 Oct.   The government charges Sears Roebuck and Company with job discrimination.

19 Nov.   Lane Kirkland succeeds George Meany as AFL-CIO president.

27 Nov.   U.S. Steel closes thirteen plants, laying off thirteen thousand workers.

19 Dec.   The Department of Energy accuses seven major oil companies of $1 billion in overcharges from 1973 to 1976.

20 Dec.   The government files a $124.5-million suit against Occidental Petroleum for dumping hazardous wastes.

31 Dec.   In London gold reaches $524 per ounce, an increase of 132 percent in one year.

OVERVIEW

Crisis. During the 1970s business conditions and the economy began to disappoint the expectations that Americans had built up during the post–World War II years. International events — the most important being the two oil crises of 1973–1974 and 1979 — served as bookends for a decade that saw rampant inflation and slow economic growth, an unprecedented combination that led to a new term being coined, *Stagflation.* It also led to a decade-long lesson for the great institutions of the United States — the government, big business, labor unions — of their growing powerlessness to affect the economy by the means of the previous forty years.

Inflation. The effects of the Vietnam War and President Lyndon Johnson's Great Society programs on the U.S. economy came in the 1970s in the form of increasing inflation. Inflation was also exacerbated by President Richard Nixon's political unwillingness to curb government spending and his politically motivated destruction in 1971 of the Bretton Woods currency-exchange mechanism, which had helped to keep inflation in check since the aftermath of World War II. With the U.S. dollar no longer convertible to gold at a set price, inflation rose, and Nixon responded with wage and price controls.

Floundering. The increased federal involvement in the economy did not have the positive effects that most people expected. The underlying problems of the economy were not allayed and left the United States more vulnerable to the shock of the oil-price increases of 1973. President Nixon's problems with the Watergate scandal, President Gerald Ford's pardon of the former president, and President Jimmy Carter's seeming inability to grasp the realities of presidential power all helped to reinforce the public's sense of the government's inabilty to affect positively its economic life.

Bailouts. Big business also suffered during the 1970s. The Big Three automobile manufacturers — General Motors, Ford, and Chrysler — were at the mercy of changes in the oil market and consumer preferences. For the first time in memory the future of the industry appeared to be not in Detroit but in Japan. By the end of the decade Chrysler had to be propped up by government money in order to remain out of bankruptcy. Of course, the automobile industry was not alone in its troubles. The U.S. steel industry was losing its market share to European and Japanese manufacturers. There was a massive government bailout of the aviation manufacturer Lockheed Aircraft Corporation. New York City received monies from the teachers' union and, later, federal government money to stay out of bankruptcy. President Gerald Ford's earlier opposition to a bailout had inspired a classic headline in the *New York Daily News:* "FORD TO CITY: DROP DEAD."

Unions. Unions found themselves unable to protect their workers from the economic fallout. Jobs continued to be lost abroad, and wage gains were eroded by inflation. Efforts by the unions to affect government policy were either ignored or had little effect on the lives of their membership. In their ineffectiveness the unions slowly lost the goodwill of the public and were hurt badly when corruption was exposed. By the end of the decade the large labor unions were much smaller and had much less power than when the decade began.

Toward a Service Economy. Lost in the turmoil and pain of the traditional institutions in the United States was the fact that the U.S. economy was not dying but going through a painful, yet inevitable, transformation. Small companies were forming that in the years to come would radically change the landscape of the U.S. and world economy. Apple, Microsoft, Wal-Mart, and Nike all either began or grew rapidly during the 1970s, setting the stage for a new type of economy in the decade ahead. The U.S. economy became less dependent on the large manufacturing company. The vital segments of the new economy were increasingly the small service-oriented businesses. The seeds of further change were planted in the 1970s that would not bear fruit until the 1980s.

TOPICS IN THE NEWS

AIR TRANSPORTATION

Americans in the Air. Between 1971 and 1973 more than half of the U.S. population boarded scheduled airliners, and Americans were responsible for some 60 percent of the world's air traffic. By 1973 there were thirteen thousand flights a day as Americans took advantage of the convenience of air travel. The airlines made flying easy. Student discount fares allowed travelers under age twenty-one to buy tickets at half price; standby fares could be purchased at deep discounts on the basis of the availability of space at flight time; and other discounts attracted casual travelers who filled the seats left after business travelers bound to set schedules had purchased their seats at full fare.

Skyjacking. Airline hijacking became a serious problem at the beginning of the decade. Between 1930 and 1970 there had been about two hundred skyjackings, as airline hijackings were called, and over half of them occurred in the eighteen months prior to June 1970, during which ninety-six persons were killed. During eleven days in September 1970 alone there were six acts of air piracy worldwide among the eighty for the year. The situation was dire. In 1970 approximately 1.7 million passengers a year flew on international routes considered by the Federal Aviation Administration (FAA) to be at high risk for skyjackings.

The Solution. In 1971 the federal government spent $37 million on the problem, and there were still thirty-two acts of air piracy that year. On 5 January 1973 the first of two phases of an order from President Richard Nixon went into effect, requiring U. S. airlines to inspect all luggage and scan all passengers for weapons or explosives. The second phase stationed armed policemen in the boarding area for every commercial flight. These moves abruptly stopped skyjackings in the United States. Over the previous two years skyjackings had occurred at the rate of about two a month. In 1973 only one plane was pirated in the United States, and that in January. Searches at boarding gates in 1973 yielded 749 guns, 5,400 knives, and 120 explosive devices.

The CAB. Even though Americans were flying in record numbers in the 1970s, the industry faced serious problems at the beginning of the decade. The airlines

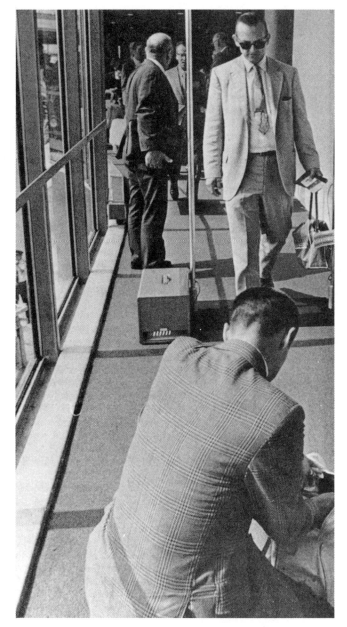

A security agent checking baggage for weapons at Kennedy Airport in New York

were suffering financially, and federal regulation prevented them from reacting promptly to market forces.

BAILING OUT LOCKHEED

In 1970 the Lockheed Aircraft Corporation faced imminent bankruptcy that would have caused the loss of an estimated sixty thousand jobs. What made the company's problem a major concern was that Lockheed was then the largest defense contractor in the United States. Caught between a disputed government contract for a military transport plane, the C5A, and a problem-laden commercial airliner, the L-1011, Lockheed was suffering severe cash flow problems. The C5A project, while over budget and hostage to the entire company's cash flow problems, did not pose the problems created by the L-1011. Lockheed's main problem was that the design for the L-1011 did not include the ability to upgrade the plane for long-range flights, thus making the plane much less desirable to foreign airlines.

By July 1970 Lockheed had received only 173 orders for the plane, far short of the 225 needed to break even. The company maintained that if the company could find the cash to stay afloat through 1972 the L-1011 project would become both profitable and cash generating, thus saving the company. Daniel J. Haughton, Lockheed chairman, approached Congress for $250 million in loan guarantees to provide the needed cash cushion.

Lockheed had support in Congress, mainly because of its importance to the military. Regardless of that importance, many in Congress hesitated to intervene in the credit markets in a situation in which the commercial banks had refused to make loans available. As William Proxmire (D–Wisc.), the chief opponent of the rescue, asserted, "You are removing a great part of the discipline of the American system." Such sentiments were widely held among a bipartisan group of senators and representatives.

The disintegrating economic situation in the United States during 1971 swayed enough votes to approve the loan guarantees by a narrow vote, 192–189 in the House of Representatives on 29 July 1971 and 49–48 in the Senate on 2 August 1971. The arguments for and against the loan guarantees foreshadowed the conflict over the Chrysler bailout at the end of the decade.

Sources: "Depression Fear Carries Loan Bill," *Aviation Week & Space Technology* (9 August 1971): 24–25;

"A Knock for Lockheed," *Newsweek* (21 June 1971): 71–72;

"Lockheed Seeks a Place to Land," *Business Week* (11 July 1970): 23–24.

The federal Civil Aeronautics Board (CAB) regulated the industry with an iron hand. Flight routes and fare schedules had to be approved by the board before they could be implemented.

Financial Strains. The problem became severe when the Arab oil embargo of 1974 increased fuel costs dramatically. Due to domestic price on fuel controls American carriers fared better than airlines in other parts of the world, but even so the fuel cost to domestic carriers increased from about eleven cents per gallon in 1973 to over twenty-three cents. Bigger jets were introduced in the early 1970s, notably the Boeing 747, the McDonnell-Douglas DC-10, and the Lockheed 747, that carried as many as five hundred passengers but cost dramatically more to fly over short distances. These planes were efficient for use on highly traveled routes, but they were so expensive to operate that they had to fly full or the airlines lost money. Airlines began complaining about overcapacity.

The Skytrain. By the late 1970s it seemed apparent that the airline industry was overregulated. In 1976 U.S. airlines lost $250 million while serving more passengers than ever before. In 1977 there was a moderate increase in profits after the CAB granted fare increases of 5 percent in 1976 and 2 percent in 1977, but discounts were limited to 15 percent during peak flying times and 20 percent on off-peak flights, and the airlines felt they needed more leeway to establish their own pricing policies. Events of 1977 brought the pricing issue to the forefront. British entrepreneur Freddie Laker announced his low-fare Skytrain service in New York. For $135 a passenger could fly to London. There was limited baggage service and no free beverage or food service. Pan American and Trans World Airlines (TWA) responded with a round-trip fare between New York and London for $280, but Laker's statement resounded: air travel was too expensive, he held, because airlines wasted money on services people were happy to do without. It was time for a democratization of air travel.

The CAB Dissolves. Lower fares increased travel dramatically, and by 1978 the industry was flourishing, largely because the CAB allowed more leeway than ever before in pricing practices. Discount fares were good for the industry, because they allowed the airlines to serve passengers more efficiently by flying full planes. The experiment in loose regulation was so successful that Congress passed a deregulation bill in the fall of 1978 that ended CAB authority over routing by 1981 and over pricing by 1983. The bill provided that a decision should be made by 1 January 1984 whether to abolish the agency altogether by 1985. The CAB petitioned to end its own existence on 1 October 1983.

Sources:
Elizabeth E. Bailey, David R. Graham, and Daniel P. Kaplan, *Deregulating the Airlines* (Cambridge, Mass.: MIT Press, 1985);

Anthony E. Brown, *The Politics of Airline Deregulation* (Knoxville: University of Tennessee Press, 1987).

An Amtrak passenger car on the New York-to-Washington route

AMTRAK

Beginnings. Amtrak, the public/private corporation formed to operate passenger rail service in the United States, went into operation on 1 May 1971. Created by the National Railroad Passenger Act of 1970, Amtrak was made necessary by the bankruptcy in June 1970 of the Penn Central system. The Penn Central had been formed in 1968 through the merger of the New York Central and Pennsylvania railroads. Since its founding in 1971 Amtrak ridership has more than doubled, though the corporation has not been able to forgo its government subsidy.

Subsidies. Subsidized by the federal government — 36 percent of its budget in 1986 — Amtrak was to provide nationwide passenger rail service. Its route system of over twenty-four thousand miles, including over twenty-six hundred miles of track that it owns, took over all noncommuter rail service in the United States. Amtrak began operation with the aging fleet of rail equipment, many without heating and air conditioning systems, inherited from the railroads. In 1975 the railway began acquiring new locomotives and passenger cars.

Limits to Profits. While Amtrak has been successful in retaining nationwide passenger rail service, there is little evidence that the system is capable of turning a profit outside the densely populated Northeast previously serviced by the Penn Central railroad.

Sources:

Michael Barone, *Our Country: The Shaping of America From Roosevelt to Reagan* (New York: Free Press, 1990);

Arthur L. Lloyd, "Amtrak," in *Railroads in the Age of Regulation*, edited by Keith L. Bryant, Jr. (New York: Bruccoli Clark Layman/Facts On File, 1988).

APPLE COMPUTER

Phone Phreaks. In spring 1970 Steven Jobs was a fifteen-year-old sophomore at Homestead High School near San Jose, California. He already had a reputation as an arrogant, intelligent "wire head" whose knowledge of electronics never quite matched his ability to talk about the subject. Jobs's genius was in impressing his visions upon people. When it came to demonstrating that vision, he turned to his friend Steve Wozniak, a true electronics wizard. While Jobs was in high school and Wozniak was at Stanford, Jobs and Wozniak conceived, Wozniak built, and Jobs sold electronic blue boxes used by "phone phreaks," as they were called, to make free long-distance telephone calls illegally. The pair made a small profit before fear of criminal prosecution inhibited their enterprise, but Jobs had seen a blurred image of the future.

Preparation. By 1975 Wozniak had graduated from Stanford and had a job as an engineer at Hewlitt-Packard designing calculators during the day, and he sharpened his engineering skills with home-hobby electronics projects at night. Jobs had dropped out of college during his first year at Reed College to concentrate on the study of Zen Buddhism and to work in the electronics department at Atari, the games manufacturer. In 1974 he left Atari to study Zen for a year in India, and on his return to California he stood out, even in the hippie culture of the time, as an unwashed, barefooted, shabbily dressed, fruit-eating, outspoken eccentric.

Altair 8800. The introduction of the Altair 8800 minicomputer kit in the January 1975 issue of *Popular Electronics* shook the small but energetic wire-head subculture. The Altair 8800 was a box with rows of switches and lights powered by an 8008 processing chip, with 256 bytes of memory, made by Intel. By flipping switches the user could input data to the processor, which responded by turning lights on and off. It was a simple machine understandable only to specialists, but to a fledgling computer culture that was able to gain access to computers only by buying expensive time-sharing on mainframes, the Altair represented an intriguing potential. To Jobs the Altair suggested the possibility that he, with Wozniak's help, could make his own computer.

Apple. The Apple Corporation — named after the Beatles' record label, the apple-harvesting gatherings at the commune with which Jobs was associated, and a staple in his fruit-based diet (and also because it came before Atari in the phone book) — was formed early in 1976 by Jobs, Wozniak, and Ron Wayne, an associate from Atari who left Apple when financial risks began to escalate. In 1976 the undercapitalized Apple had only one product, the Apple I, which was little more than a circuit-board layout designed by Wozniak and manufactured in Jobs's father's garage. Buyers had to hook the computer up to a teletype or a television for a display, and input was accomplished by flipping switches; the processor made by Motorola had eight kilobytes of memory, making it more powerful than the early Altair. The first Apple I's were not even in a case, though the Byte Shop, which had committed to a major purchase, insisted on professional packaging. An Apple I cost $250 to make and sold for $500 to suppliers. Jobs and Wozniak sold 150 of them in 1976, netting $37,500, before Jobs had a grander vision.

Apple II. Integrating the ideas of several of his associates, he imagined a complete computing unit, consisting of a keyboard for input, a central processing unit for calculation, and a video screen for display. Wozniak had the intelligence to design such a unit. Jobs had the drive and persistence to inspire the work and design the packaging. Wozniak had little interest in deals or sales: he was

The Apple II computer system, first introduced in 1977

an electronics engineer, so he willingly left business to Jobs, who, with the administrative guidance of professional managers required by new investors, managed to see the Apple II through to completion. When Wozniak's Apple II was introduced at the West Coast Computer Faire on 15 April 1977, it was the hit of the show. No other computer could match its power or its integration of components. After that success Jobs had an easier time attracting investors, and by the end of the year Wozniak had perfected an augmentation to the Apple II worthy of their attention.

Disk Drives. Minicomputers (as home computers were then called) had little access to software. Such programming tools as Basic All-purpose Symbolic Instruction Code (BASIC) were accessed in three ways: they were typed in, as on the early Apples; they were encoded onto a tape and read into the computer, as on the later Altairs; or they were encoded into a read-only-memory (ROM) chip on a circuit board. BASIC was simply a programming tool, and so the usefulness of the computer was limited to a small group of specialists. Wozniak expanded the home-computer universe enormously when he engineered a disk drive that allowed small computers to read and store large amounts of data from an outside source. The disk drive allowed users to save their work easily, and it allowed independent programmers to produce programs for the Apple. When VisiCalc, a small software producer, introduced its spreadsheet program for the Apple in January 1979 and a few months later a word-processing program called AppleWriter hit the market, they made the computer useful to non-programmers for the first time, and people bought both the computers and the programs that made them work. By late 1979 Apple had sold 50,000 computers, and both Jobs and Wozniak were millionaires. The next year sales increased to 125,000 units.

Source:
Jeffrey S. Young, *Steve Jobs: The Journey Is the Reward* (Glenview, Ill.: Scott Foresman, 1988).

AUTOMOBILE INDUSTRY IN THE 1970s

Economic Turmoil and Change. The 1970s proved to be a decade of tumultuous change for the automobile industry in the United States. Caught first in the eco-

Part of a 120-day inventory of cars that led Chrysler to close five of its six assembly plants in 1974

nomic turmoil of high interest rates, high inflation, and price control and then in the energy crises of 1973–1974 and 1979, the automobile industry bore the brunt of the changes brought upon the U.S. economy. In addition to the domestic economic situation, U.S. automakers also faced a changed international market, with more competition from foreign manufacturers.

A Poor Start. The decade started badly with a paralyzing strike by the United Auto Workers (UAW) during 1970. As a result production at the four major automakers — General Motors (GM), Ford Motor Company, Chrysler, and the American Motors Corporation (AMC) — sank by one million vehicles, 10 percent below 1969 figures. In addition to the strike, automakers were faced with a buying public that was increasingly resistant to price increases and high interest rates.

Imports. Despite a slack market, foreign carmakers sold one hundred thousand more cars in the United States during 1970 than they had in 1969. The import market share rose from 11.4 percent to 14 percent, almost all of the increase due to the increasing popularity of small, inexpensive cars such as the Volkswagen Beetle and the Toyota Corolla. Domestic makers countered with small-car models of their own, with the AMC Gremlin, Chevrolet Vega, and Ford Pinto leading the way in 1971. Another response by the Big Four U.S. automakers was to streamline their catalogue, and the

number of different models offered by the domestic manufacturers shrank in the 1971 model year from 375 to 331, the lowest number since 1962.

The Challenge of Regulation. GM struggled under a strike during part of 1971, which led to production figures that lagged for the second straight year. Labor stability returned in 1972, and domestic production rallied to more than 8.5 million vehicles, the third largest amount in industry history. The increased sales blunted the inroads of the imports, giving the industry a much-needed boost in confidence. Profits, however, were constrained somewhat by President Nixon's wage and price controls and the imposition of government regulations regarding safety features — front and rear bumpers and fire-resistant fabrics — and pollution control. GM and Ford requested price increases from the government, but these were denied by the Price Commission.

Crisis in the Industry. In late 1973 and 1974 the automobile industry experienced a serious decline because of the Arab oil embargo and the accompanying rise in inflation. The boycott, which began on 19 October 1973, caused turmoil in the world economy. Not only was the supply of gasoline greatly curtailed, causing lines at gasoline stations, but the price of petroleum went through the roof. The price of oil in December 1973 rocketed to between fourteen dollars and nineteen dollars per barrel, up from between two dollars and three dollars a year earlier. The increases presented the automobile industry its greatest challenge since the Great Depression.

Decline and Fall? Industrywide, production levels fell by almost two million vehicles, almost 22 percent. Most of the decline was traced to larger and medium-sized cars that had poor fuel economy. Production of compact and subcompact cars rose, but not as much as that of larger cars fell. As the Nixon wage and price controls ended in August 1974, inflation figures boiled upward to above 12 percent. Chrysler, faced with an inventory of cars that would last for 120 days, closed five of its six U.S. assembly plants. Automobile-production figures did not improve in 1975, falling by another 24.5 percent to a mere 6.4 million vehicles. The slump in production caused massive layoffs among autoworkers, and the unemployment rate in the auto industry reached 15.8 percent.

Downsizing. The two years of precipitous production declines, along with the shift in consumer tastes in car design, raised many problems for the domestic car industry. The industry found itself largely unable to sell its gas-guzzling large cars, which were its most profitable. Consumers, faced with rapidly increasing car and fuel prices, were demanding smaller, more economical cars that got improved gas mileage. This placed Detroit in direct competition with Japanese carmakers, which were technologically more advanced and more efficient than U.S. manufacturers. Unable to introduce immediately vehicles which had been radically redesigned to meet the desires of consumers, in 1977 U.S. carmakers instead downsized current models.

Renaissance? The strategy worked in 1977, with production increasing almost 9 percent over depressed 1976 levels. By the late 1970s production was less a concern than inflation, costs, and quality control. Automobile production was basically flat from 1977 to 1978. The inflation rate, however, rose from 7 percent in May 1978 to 11.3 percent in July 1979, a rise which was the product of both inflationary pressures still rampant in the economy and new tensions in the Middle East.

The Bell Tolls. In December 1978 the government of Iran cut off oil exports to the world. Already that year the market share for imported automobiles had risen to 18 percent, an all-time high. The ensuing rise in gasoline prices — up 52 percent from year-earlier levels in September 1979 — pushed domestic automakers seemingly to the brink of failure. By September 1979 Chrysler was insolvent and considering bankruptcy. Only a government-guaranteed loan negotiated by union officials and politicians from Michigan, and on the administrative talent of chief executive officer Lee Iaccoca, gave Chrysler the time and capital needed to plot a comeback. Ford was losing money on its domestic operations — $7 billion from 1979 to 1982 — and was kept going only on its still-profitable European markets. In 1980 even GM lost money.

In 1981 the perennial money-losing AMC was bought by Renault, the government-owned French carmaker.

To See Another Day. The 1970s changed everything for the auto industry in the United States. No longer was it the envy of the world; the Japanese now held that title. The car itself became less of a status symbol than a mode of transportation. Consumers were looking for cheaper more fuel efficient cars. After the 1970s the Detroit carmakers were faced with a decade of rebuilding lines of cars, restoring their reputation for quality, and recovering a domestic market. That they had survived such a tumultuous decade was a stunning, if not satisfactory, achievement.

Source:
George S. May, ed., *The Automobile Industry, 1920–1980* (New York: Bruccoli Clark Layman/Facts On File, 1989).

CONSUMERISM

Demanding Consumers. In 1970 one in every thirty-four households in the United States subscribed to *Consumer Reports*, and many more had access to the publication in public libraries. American consumers, people who bought goods sold in the United States, had become a demanding lot. Stirred to protest by consumer activist Ralph Nader, whose 1965 book *Unsafe at Any Speed: The Designed-in Dangers of The American Automobile* indicted General Motors in particular for producing the Corvair and the auto industry in general for indifference to the safety of their cars, Americans were becoming finicky purchasers. Because the economic fortunes of the nation depended on the reliability of American goods, the government was quick to support measures that ensured the safety and integrity of products in the marketplace.

Desire for Truth. Specifically, consumer groups wanted assurances that advertising claims were truthful, that product weights and measures were accurate, and that the goods they bought were safe. They wanted a means of voicing their concerns and their complaints, assurances that prices were fair, and protection against fraud. In 1971 Nader's Center for the Study of Responsive Law in Washington, D.C., set a fund-raising goal of one hundred thousand dollars from individuals sending in fifteen-dollar contributions. With their money he took on auto manufacturers, the aviation industry, and food producers. He set up the Office for Corporate Responsibility to encourage whistle-blowers and student watchdog groups in seven states. He announced a study of Congress for 1972.

Government Response. The government responded. President Nixon renamed a Johnson administration consumer protection agency the Office of Consumer Interests, and it handled complaints at the rate of three thousand a month. He ordered the creation of the regulatory Bureau of Product Safety, a division of the Department of Health, Education, and Welfare, with the responsibility of reducing the thirty thousand deaths and twenty

Food labeling, required by the government for some products in 1973, was adopted voluntarily by some manufacturers.

phrase "Brand X" from television advertisements because it could be misleading.

Product Labeling. In 1973 the Food and Drug Administration (FDA) required labeling on cosmetics and packaged food to inform consumers of its potentially harmful ingredients and its nutritional values. Foods making nutritional claims had to list on labels U.S. recommended daily allowances of protein and seven essential vitamins, as well as fat content and caloric value, and several manufacturers not required by the letter of the law to do so complied with the regulation.

The Primacy of Money. By the middle of the decade, the consumer movement had cooled. Disgruntled customers had by then what most people regarded as adequate opportunity to express their complaints to state and federal watchdog agencies. Still, a 1977 Harris poll showed broad support for the consumer-protection movement. By the late 1970s money had replaced safety as the primary concern of the consumer. By 1979 there were 600 million credit cards in use by the 150 million or so adults in the United States, and in 1978 there was a 19 percent increase in consumer debt. Americans were paying an astonishing 18 percent of their net income to pay consumer loans (exclusive of home mortgages). The fear at the end of the decade was that consumers had overextended themselves financially, running up debts they might never be able to repay.

Source:
Norman Isaac Silber, *Test and Protest: The Influence of Consumers Union* (New York: Holmes & Meier, 1983).

million injuries resulting from defective consumer items. Childproof caps on medicines and poisonous household goods as well as poison-control centers were early accomplishments of that agency. Even television came under scrutiny as sixty thousand parents complained about television programming for children in 1971. The Federal Communications Commission (FCC) responded with guidelines that were for the most part ignored.

Consumer Product Safety Act. On 28 October 1972 President Nixon signed the Consumer Product Safety Act, which created an independent commission to establish safeguards against unsafe household items, food, drugs, and cosmetics. The Consumer Product Safety Commission (CPSC), regarded as the most powerful independent federal agency ever created by Congress, enacted a host of regulations affecting a wide range of goods, from overly flammable mattresses to unhealthy aerosol sprays to fireworks. Federal legislation was also passed in 1972 to protect buyers of automobiles against false representations and to require disclosure of information about pharmaceutical companies and their products. The Federal Trade Commission (FTC) banned the

THE ECONOMY

Decade of Crisis. The decade of the 1970s was the most traumatic for the American economy since the Great Depression. Coming after nearly a quarter century of sustained prosperity and growth, the downturn of the 1970s hit with especially powerful force. Productivity was down, costs were up, unemployment soared, inflation was high, exports were low, imports swamped the market — nearly every economic indicator went south during the decade. The Nixon, Ford, and Carter administrations tried a variety of innovative approaches to resuscitate the economy, but most failed, and the solutions often burdened the nation with new, unintended problems. In 1972, for example, the United States sold the Soviet Union millions of tons of wheat in an effort to reduce the trade deficit; the sale, however, precipitated a 32 percent jump in food prices and much consumer anger in 1973. Although the causes of the economic decline of the 1970s are numerous and controversial, two economic problems are of primary importance: the federal deficit and trade balances.

The Federal Deficit. The growing federal deficit of the 1960s destabilized the private sector in the 1970s. The Vietnam War badly burdened the American economy. To avoid fueling opposition to the war by financing

Two thousand unemployed applying for public-service jobs in Chicago

it through unpopular taxes, the Johnson administration funded the war by borrowing and printing money, raising the national debt to an unprecedented $436 billion by 1972 and sparking runaway inflation. The manpower and material drain of the war drove prices for labor and goods higher and compromised American industrial productivity. Key American industries devoted inordinate resources to military research and development and lost some of the technical lead in consumer goods to Japanese and European competitors. Administration officials, compromising with foreign governments, traded commercial concessions for political support. The Vietnam War was a drag on the private sector and the single greatest accelerant of public spending (41.7 percent of federal outlays in 1970), but many Americans blamed the increased debt on the social welfare programs of the 1960s, enacted during a time of confidence in American prosperity. Presidents Kennedy and Johnson were sure the American economy could sustain both guns and butter — both the war in Vietnam and a host of government programs derived from the New Deal that provided unprecedented entitlements to middle-class and poor peo-

ple. They were expansive, and a huge bureaucracy of federal employees was required to administer them.

Welfare Spending. When Richard Nixon took office in 1969, his first priority was to end the war in Vietnam. After he brought the war to a close, he planned to reverse President Johnson's welfare programs, but Nixon's urban-affairs adviser, conservative Democrat Daniel Patrick Moynihan, convinced the president that the political cost would be too great. The nation had suffered through an agonizing, polarizing war, Moynihan argued. To reverse newly enacted social programs would only reignite activists whose war demonstrations had just been quieted. The president took the advice, surprising observers by expanding entitlements and offering unexpected support for such costly measures as the Job Corps and a Family Assistance Payments bill that guaranteed every American family an annual income of at least $1,600 (it was voted down by Congress). President Carter was even less willing than Nixon to cut social services, President Ford more so; but Moynihan was correct that such cuts were politically untenable. When Ford's secretary of the treasury, William Simon, suggested a more modest approach to social spending, he was widely criticized. Thus, by 1980 social spending (including Social Security and Medicare) consumed 48 percent of all federal outlays ($281 billion), defense spending, 23 percent ($134 billion). At the end of a decade of striking economic downturn, the government continued to spend money at levels appropriate to the vanished period of prosperity.

The Cost of Money. Like consumer debts, the national debt accumulates interest. In 1945 the interest on the public debt was $3.8 billion a year. In 1970 it was just under $20 billion, and by the end of the decade the interest payment alone on the national debt had grown to nearly $60 billion. During the decade a growing gulf developed between the haves and the have-nots. Wages increased, and those workers who had money to spend were so eager to buy that manufacturers were unable to keep up with the demand. As a result, prices increased at the fastest rate in history. Per-capita consumption, the amount spent by the average consumer on goods, rose from $1,830 in 1960 to $3,155 in 1970 and to $7,676 in 1980. During the same periods the average wage in all industries rose from $5,260 to $7,747 to $15,757, and unemployment went from 3.6 million people in 1960 to 3.2 million in 1970 to 6.7 million in 1980. As unemployment rose, so did the welfare rolls and the welfare expense. When the government needed more money, it minted it, with the effect of diluting the value of the money already in circulation. Between 1960 and 1970 the currency held by the public increased from about $30 billion to $49 billion. By 1980 there was a total of $115 billion in circulating currency.

Inflationary Spiral. A major effect of these circumstances was inflation — a dollar did not stretch as far in 1980 as it had in 1970, and the problem was severe. The purchasing power of one hundred 1970 dollars was

$43.40 in 1980. Although workers on average made three times more at the end of the decade as they had at the beginning, the dollars they earned were worth less than half as much as those at the beginning of the decade, largely due to increasing energy and housing costs. So confident consumers borrowed at record rates, and as the demand for loans increased, so did the interest banks charged. As the interest payments increased, the amount of money the average family had available to spend decreased, so they had to borrow more. Economists called that condition the inflationary spiral.

Imports and Exports. Traditionally, the federal government had reacted to inflation by raising interest rates to force consumers to adopt responsible budgets. But an unusual condition existed in the early 1970s. American business was faltering. Foreign producers were beginning to exploit American markets taking sales away from American businesses. Foreign goods could be imported to the United States and sold at lower prices than domestically produced goods. The electronics, automobile, and steel industries were hit particularly hard. Moreover, as the government increased the costs to American businesses of borrowing money, prices for American goods had to be raised accordingly, making them even less competitive with imports. Inflation caused the American dollar to lose its value in foreign markets, discouraging foreign investment in American businesses.

Stagflation. This combination of inflation in the economy and stagnation of business was called *stagflation*. The cure for inflation increased stagnation, and stagnation, it seemed, could only be cured by measures that resulted in out-of-control inflation. The difficulty was indicated by a perplexing statistic reported in 1970. On 15 December it was announced that the gross national product (GNP), the value of goods produced during the year in the United States, had reached a record $1 trillion; yet the real GNP, the amount adjusted for inflation, had fallen, indicating that the nation's economy was in a recession — it was faltering. There was no painless remedy.

The Nixon Plan. President Nixon responded forcefully to the inflation rates of 5.5 percent and 5.7 percent during his first two years in office. On 15 August 1971 he announced phase 1 of his economic recovery plan. It called for a ninety-day freeze on wage, price, and rent increases; the establishment of a cost-of-living council to administer the freezes and suggest further measures; a 10 percent surcharge on imports; a freeze on converting foreign-held dollars into gold; tax measures calculated to stimulate the economy; and a tightening of the federal budget. On 13 November the president enacted phase 2, which established a Pay Board and a Cost of Living Board to govern wages and prices, with the goal of reducing inflation to between 2 and 3 percent a year. Phases 3 and 4 in 1973 gradually lifted price controls. President Nixon's plan worked in the short term, but the distractions of Watergate and the inflationary effect of the 1973

Arab oil embargo combined to offset temporary gains. By middecade the nation's economic problems were as severe as ever. Double-digit inflation had returned by 1974, and basic American industries were beginning to show signs of financial instability. In 1974 Chrysler closed five of its six U.S. assembly plants, and both Ford and General Motors increased their reliance on foreign labor to make American cars. In 1976 the nation experienced the most severe recession since World War II, and the nation's leaders began referring to an impending depression.

The Carter Plan. President Jimmy Carter took office in 1977, and he was expected to pay close attention to growing anxiety among voters that financial devastation was imminent. He announced a series of voluntary programs aimed at convincing labor and industry to work together to limit inflation without burdensome regulation. But the class divide between labor and management was too great. Throughout the postwar period, management sought to increase its foreign competitiveness through automation and by moving its industrial base to low-wage labor areas abroad. While jobs expanded on average 32 percent throughout the postwar period, blue-collar jobs expanded only 19 percent — and the majority of this expansion took place in the early postwar period. By the 1970s job expansion took place primarily in the low-wage, low-skill sectors of the American economy, such as the fast-food industry. This situation was dispiriting to American workers, and productivity declined, fueling trade imbalances and the inflationary spiral. Management responded by increasing what, by the late 1970s, was termed "deindustrialization" — limiting the participation of labor in management decisions, automating the assembly line, and moving jobs overseas. United Automobile Workers president Douglas Frasier declared in 1978 that "The leaders of industry . . . have broken and discarded the fragile, unwritten compact previously existing during past periods of growth and progress." Labor rejected Carter's request to limit wage increases to 7 percent; management rejected his plea to hold price increases below 5.75 percent. On 1 November 1978 the president felt compelled to act more forcefully. In cooperation with Federal Reserve Board chairman G. William Miller he announced an increase in the federal discount rate — the rate the Federal Reserve charges for loans to banks — to a record 9.5 percent; a plan to buy $3 billion in dollars on foreign exchanges to prop up the value of the dollar abroad; and an order to sell gold to lower its price in the market and encourage investment in currency. Prudent, even noble, as Carter's plea to the American people seemed, asking them for personal sacrifice for the public good, it failed. In 1979 inflation was 11.3 percent, and in 1980 it was 13.5 percent, while unemployment increased as well. The stage was set for a new president with a new approach in 1980.

ENERGY IN THE 1970S

The Source of Change. A major source of the instability and change of the economy during the 1970s was energy. In early 1973 the United States faced shortages of electricity, gasoline, and heating oil, leading to the shutdown of factories and schools, the cancellation of some commercial airline flights, electrical brownouts, and lines at gasoline service stations. Blackouts plagued cities and industries, most spectacularly in New York City on 13–14 July 1977. High fuel prices reduced the productivity of American industry. Heavy imports of fuel harmed the U.S. balance of payments and destabilized the international monetary system.

The Embargo. On 6 October 1973 the Yom Kippur War between Israel and its Arab neighbors broke out. When the United States moved to support Israel, several of the oil-exporting nations of the Middle East cut off exports of oil on 19 October. The price of oil in December 1973 rocketed to between fourteen dollars and nineteen dollars per barrel, up from two and three dollars a year earlier. The energy problem quickly became an energy crisis. President Nixon addressed the nation on 7 November 1973 about the energy crisis and spoke about the trends that had caused the shortages:

> The average American will consume as much energy in the next seven days as most other people in the world will consume in an entire year. We have only 6 percent of the world's people in America, but we consume over 30 percent of all the energy in the world.

Causes. America's energy dependency and crisis were caused by several factors. In the 1950s and 1960s strategic and geopolitical concerns had led the government to promote the imports of fuel from overseas, especially from the Middle East. Nixon's 1971 New Economic Policy had placed price controls on the entire economy, and while other restrictions were lifted, oil remained regulated, keeping the price artificially low to consumers and increasing demand. Americans were extravagant in their use of energy; few American-made cars got better than ten miles to the gallon; homes and businesses were poorly insulated and designed. Diverse special interests had skewed portions of the government's oversight and regulation of the oil industry toward their particular interests, and passing general legislation regarding energy became a political nightmare. Accordingly, efforts to develop a consistent energy policy throughout the 1970s were diluted and diverted — and the decade would end much as it began, with the United States wastefully consuming inordinate amounts of energy, and subject, once again, to an oil crisis.

A National Policy. President Nixon, although hampered by the Watergate scandal, took steps to formulate a national energy policy. In June 1973 Nixon formed a federal Energy Policy Office, the forerunner of the Department of Energy. He asked Congress for the authority to relax environmental standards and regulate transporta-

Construction site on the Trans-Alaska Pipeline

tion schedules. Later in 1973 Congress authorized construction of the Trans-Alaska Pipeline to transport oil from well to port. William Simon was appointed to head the energy office, a position that came to be known as the "energy czar."

Simon's Actions. Simon ordered refineries to produce more heating oil than gasoline, and year-round daylight savings time was ordered to begin on 6 January 1974. He also asked motorists to drive no faster than 55 MPH and service stations to limit individual sales and operating hours.

Project Independence. Nixon also announced an ambitious program of longer-term remedies to the energy problem. Called Project Independence, the program had as its goal energy self-sufficiency for the United States by 1980. The technologies to be explored, studied, and possibly utilized in meeting the goal included fast breeder reactors, solar energy, geothermal energy, wind and hydroelectric power, coal liquefication, oil extraction, and nuclear fusion. Because of Watergate, Nixon was never able to implement his program. But Gerald Ford resubmitted the program to Congress in January 1975. Ford proposed a ten-year plan to build 200 nuclear-power plants, dig 250 new coal mines, construct 150 coal-fired power plants, erect 30 new oil refineries, and create 20 major synthetic-fuel plants. He also proposed the creation of a $100-billion synthetic and high-energy fuels program, under the supervision of Vice-president Nelson Rockefeller. Congress, balking at the cost of these programs, for the most part rejected them, but did mandate new fuel efficiency standards for American automobiles and authorized construction of the $10-billion Trans-Alaska Pipeline.

Nuclear Power. Utility companies had been well aware of the coming energy shortage during the 1960s. One of their methods to prepare for the shortfall was to construct nuclear reactors. In January 1973 there were twenty-seven functioning reactors in the United States, providing only five percent of the power generated. Fifty-five plants were under construction, and an additional seventy-eight were in the planning stages. The majority, however, would never be built. Security expenses, nuclear-waste disposal costs, and construction overruns made the return on investment in nuclear-power plants slim. Seeking to assist the nuclear industry, the Ford administration in 1974 disbanded the Atomic Energy Commission (AEC), which for twenty-eight years had overseen American nuclear development. In its place were constructed the more industry-friendly Nuclear Regulatory Commission (NRC) and the Energy Research and Development Administration (ERDA), which was empowered to develop new energy sources and market American nuclear industry abroad. The NRC streamlined the licensing and commission of reactor projects, but many of the old problems remained. Safety was a pressing issue: fires at the Indian Point 2 reactor in New York in 1971, the Zion reactor in Illinois in 1974, the Trojan reactor in Oregon in 1974, and the Brown's Ferry reactor in Alabama in 1975 underscored the potential for a catastrophic accident at nuclear plants. In 1975 the Union of Concerned Scientists presented the White House with a petition signed by two thousand scientists which called for a reduction in nuclear construction. Public opinion followed that of the scientists, and environmental groups increasingly challenged the construction of nuclear projects in the NRC and in the courts, delaying the deployment of projects and driving up the start-up costs. The 1978–1979 protests at the Seabrook nuclear power plant in New Hampshire were particularly vocal and drew national attention to the issue. Then, in the spring of 1979, an accident at the Harrisburg, Pennsylvania, Three Mile Island nuclear-power plant resulted in a partial core meltdown. Although no one was injured, the accident terrified the public and placed the future of the nuclear industry in jeopardy. Thus nuclear power was no more likely to resolve America's energy crisis in the 1980s than it had been in the 1970s.

The Carter Years. Part of the problem with the energy crisis in the 1970s was the short attention span of the public. When the oil embargo precipitated soaring prices and cutbacks in supplies, the American people complained loudly of the energy crisis. Upon the restoration of fair prices and supplies, public attention lagged. Ford's energy program in part fell victim to this apathy, and so too did Jimmy Carter's. More than his predecessors, Carter was sensitive to the U.S. energy crisis. As a former submariner in the nuclear navy, Carter was familiar with the strategic and political dangers involved in a drifting energy policy. Upon election in 1976 Carter promised an energy policy within ninety days of his inauguration, and he kept his promise. Setting former Nixon secretary of defense James Schlesinger to the task of formulating the policy, Carter introduced it to the public in April of 1977. It was a mix of programs: deregulation of oil and gas prices in place since the Nixon administration; incentives for alternative energy development, especially gasohol, a mixture of gasoline and ethyl alcohol produced from corn; and the creation of the Department of Energy. Congress and the special interests gutted much of the program, and by 1979 Carter had returned to square one, attempting to forge a new energy policy in the wake of a new energy panic impelled by the 1979 Iranian revolution.

The Effects on Business. The effects of the energy crisis and the attempts at governmental relief were myriad. The automobile industry bore the brunt of the change, being affected not only as a user of energy but also as the provider of gasoline-guzzling automobiles. Detroit lost a significant share of the domestic market to smaller, more-fuel-efficient imports in the wake of the 1973 embargo. Other manufacturers were faced with continual shortages of fuel oil, forcing many either to shut down or undergo expensive and time-consuming conversion to natural gas. Conversion called for capital expenditures, which were much more expensive given the high rates of interest from investors, concerned in part over the risk involved in oil investments and fuel-dependent industries. Risk also presented opportunities, and around the globe oil exploration expanded, particularly in Alaska, the North Sea, and Mexico. Oil companies, fearing projections that suggested inevitable depletion of their oil reserves, began to diversify their interests. Mobil Oil bought the Montgomery Ward chain of department stores, ARCO invested in copper, Exxon inaugurated an office-automation division, and Gulf Oil put in a bid for Ringling Bros. and Barnum & Bailey Circus. All told, however, the main effects of the energy crisis were higher costs, lower profitability, and sometimes, eventually, layoffs and bankruptcy.

The 1979 Shock. The 1979 Iranian revolution resulted in a de facto embargo and virulent inflationary pressures. Following soaring fuel costs, by October 1979 the inflation rate was 12.2 percent. Interest rates briefly peaked above 20 percent. World oil markets were in disarray, shortages returned to the gas stations of America, and once again the public muttered darkly about oil companies hoarding gas in tankers offshore. The resulting economic slowdown caused massive unemployment, especially in the automobile industry. Carter scrambled to meet the emergency; he decontrolled the price of gas and slapped a "windfall profits tax" on oil companies to prevent price gouging. He reactivated Nelson Rockefeller's multibillion-dollar proposal to develop synthetic fuels and fired James Schlesinger. In his farewell speech to his staff, Schlesinger warned gravely of an "energy future bleak and . . . likely to grow bleaker in the decade ahead." For Carter that dismal future had already arrived. The recession of 1979–1981 was one of the most severe since the Great Depression and contributed to Carter's defeat in the presidential election of 1980.

Source:
Michael Barone, *Our Country: The Shaping of America From Roosevelt to Reagan* (New York: Free Press, 1990).

MICROSOFT

Convergence. William Henry Gates was fifteen in 1970 and, by his own admission, the smartest kid in Seattle, Washington. He attended the progressive Lakeside School, a private high school that had a computer club. There Gates met the principal figures with whom he worked during the 1970s to form what arguably became within twenty years the most successful corporation in the world.

Lakeside Programmers Group. At Lakeside, Gates, with his friends Paul Allen and Ric Wieland, had time-sharing access to a mainframe computer. Using a programming language called BASIC, developed at Dartmouth University in the late 1950s, they could type in a set of instructions and have the machine run routines that displayed results on a teletype terminal. When he was in the eighth grade Gates and his friends wrote programs in BASIC for simple games, such as ticktacktoe, and for more useful computations, such as a conversion of a number from a base-ten system into a binary, hexadecimal, or any other base-number configuration. By the time Gates was a senior in high school, it was commonly accepted that the Lakeside Programmers Group, the school computer club, included students with remarkable ability to understand computer logic and turn it to practical uses. Gates was regarded as the best of the Lakeside programmers, followed closely by Allen and Wieland. They traded programming services to a local corporation for free time-sharing computing access, and, by the time he graduated from high school in 1973, Gates was writing class-scheduling programs for the school and serving as a consultant to private companies with computing problems, notably TRW in Canada. He had also formed his first company, Traf-O-Data, with Allen, then a sophomore at the University of Washington, to build a computer that would analyze tapes punched by traffic-counting devices.

Harvard. An 800 on his SAT in math (along with a low 700s verbal score) gained Gates admission to Harvard, where he majored in applied math. He maintained his relationship with his friends from the Lakeside Programmers Group in Seattle and took full advantage of computer access available to Harvard students and faculty to refine his BASIC routines so that his programs would be more flexible and more compact. The primary challenge was to find ways to reduce the amount of memory required to run the programs. Gates was particularly adept at devising routines that allowed the program to do more with less memory.

Bill Gates, founder of Microsoft

The Altair Inspiration. The announcement in *Popular Electronics* magazine in January 1975 of the Altair 8800, a home computer kit, excited both Gates and Allen. They had attempted unsuccessfuly to build their own small computer, and they realized the potential the Altair represented. The Altair was a basic electronics gadget. It had no video screen or keyboard. Input was accomplished by flipping a series of twenty-three switches; responses came in the flashes of thirty-two lights on the front panel. The Altair came with 256 bytes of random-access memory (RAM), enough to store only a small amount of information. But Gates and Allen saw a way to make the machine useful: they would write a version of BASIC for the machine, and then it could be used for practical computations. The conviction that computers were made useful by programs — software — was the central principle that guided their efforts.

The Program. BASIC was a simplified language that turned programmers' instructions into information the machine could understand. Using BASIC, a programmer could instruct a machine to add two numbers, for example, and BASIC turned those instructions into the electronic codes that caused the machine to perform its calculation. But each different kind of processing chip had a different set of electronic codes, and so, as the succes of the Altair inspired new computer designs, BASIC had to be adapted for each of them. Gates and Allen wrote the first and best adaptation of BASIC for the 8008 chip the Altair used, and it was the basis of their success. They sold their BASIC to the company that owned the Altair and started a new company that specialized in writing versions of BASIC and other languages for different types of computers. In 1975 they made $16,005 and were sufficiently encouraged to enter into a formal partnership.

The Company. Micro-Soft, as the company name was then written (it briefly became MicroSoft before taking its present form of Microsoft), started in an apartment in Albuquerque, New Mexico. Wieland, a senior in electrical engineering at Stanford, was enlisted to help, as were high-school students Gates trusted with the job of compiling code. Microsoft's business philosophy was that they would write programs exclusively for original equipment manufacturers (OEMs) and that they would demand a flat-fee payment in advance. In the early years Gates, Allen, and their colleagues adapted BASIC for various hardware configurations, enhancing their programs as they went along. They also provided versions of other standard programming languages such as Common Business Oriented Language (COBOL) and Formula Translation (FORTRAN) for use on the burgeoning number of small computers being introduced. In 1976 Microsoft had a profit of $22,496 on sales of $104,216. In 1977 Gates dropped out of Harvard after his junior year and moved the Microsoft office to Seattle. Microsoft earned a net income of $112,471 on sales of $381,715 that year and attracted the interest of General Electric, who engaged Gates and Allen to provide BASIC for their use. In 1978 sales totaled $1.355 million, and Microsoft made its first deal in Japan, providing software for NEC, which dominated the Japanese market.

The Challenge. By 1979 the personal computer had taken on something resembling its present configuration. Machines were being sold that had screens, keyboards, and, most important, disk drives that could be used as storage for programs and save any data the programs generated. But programs were hard to come by because each type of computer required a customized version of software tailored to its hardware configuration. As a result, unless a user knew BASIC or another programming language or was content with the limited number of programs available for his individual computer, the machine would not do much. Moreover, programmers who devised useful routines, such as VisiCalc, the first spreadsheet, or early word-processing packages, had to write their programs in several versions if they were to have a substantial audience. The environment was like an international conference held without translators.

The Vision. Gates and Allen began attacking the problem of a software operating system that would serve to translate standard programs for various combinations of keyboards, video display terminals, and central processors. To facilitate their adaptation of BASIC to various processors, they had devised a macroversion of the program that included programming for various configurations. By the end of 1979 they were marketing stand-alone BASIC, an adaptation of their master version that could, with minimal user programming, run on most standard computers. They had taken the first step toward developing an industry-standard operating system that would allow independent programmers to offer software usable on a variety of machines.

The Future. At the end of the 1970s Microsoft was recognized as the industry leader in software development, but it was still a young company in a developing industry. Microsoft was not even incorporated until 1981. The basis was laid, though, for the breakthrough that would realize Gates's dream of a computer in every home that would serve a broad range of human needs. Microsoft was ready for the alliance with IBM and the introduction of MS-DOS, a basic operating system for small computers. They were also ready to provide the expertise that would establish the primacy of software over hardware as the industry shaped itself.

Source:
Stephen Manes and Paul Andrews, *Gates: How Microsoft's Mogul Reinvented an Industry — and Made Himself the Richest Man in America* (New York: Doubleday, 1993).

MINORITIES AND WOMEN IN THE WORKPLACE

The Call for Equality. White males dominated American business before 1970 largely because of social patterns and cultural values. The domination was challenged after World War II, and slowly women and minorities began to establish a presence in American business. During World War II the war effort required women to enter the workforce in unprecedented numbers. After the war many female workers were unwilling to turn over their jobs to returning soldiers and revert to domestic roles. At the same time the incipient social upheaval of the 1950s and the outright revolution of the 1960s had provided new rights to blacks in education and in the workplace by legislation and by judicial order. Equal opportunity was a phrase that resonated throughout the post–World War II decades. To minorities the phrase offered hope; to employers it threatened stifling regulation. While equal opportunity was a concept first intended to redress racial injustice, the laws that resulted frequently applied to sexual as well as racial discrimination.

The Civil Rights Act. The key piece of legislation prohibiting racial or sexual inequity was the Civil Rights Act of 1964. It addressed discrimination on the basis of race, color, religion, national origin, and, particularly in matters of employment, gender. Among the major provision in the act was broad authority for the government to withhold funds from programs that discriminate and to bring suits against public facilities that practice discrimination. Every business in the United States that employed more than twenty-five people was ordered to provide equal rights for employment and equal opportunity for promotion. The legislation was in place in 1964; compliance took a long time.

Legislation and Judicial Action Affecting Women. In 1970 the Department of Labor issued guidelines to employers stipulating measures to avoid sexual discrimination, and the director of the Women's Bureau announced that federal sexual-discrimination guidelines would apply to companies with more than fifty employees (despite the Civil Rights Act of 1964) or companies accepting federal grants of fifty thousand dollars or more. The following year the Supreme Court held that companies could not discriminate in hiring against women with small children unless they enforced similar restrictions against men, and the Court held that pension funds must be administered without regard to the gender of the employee. In 1972 the Senate passed the Equal Rights Amendment 84–8, and the need for a constitutional statement of sexual equality was hotly debated throughout the decade as activists mobilized to promote ratification by three-fourths of the states, which was required for the amendment to be added to the U.S. Constitution. When ratification had not been achieved by 1978, the Senate extended the deadline to June 1982.

Women in the Workplace. Government statistics showed real gains in employment for women. In 1970 women made up 38 percent of the civilian workforce; in 1980, 42.5 percent of the workers were women. But they earned substantially less than men doing similar jobs. At the end of the decade, women workers as a group earned two-thirds as much money as white men and only slightly more than black men.

"Promises Made and Promises Unkept." In the annual report of the National Urban League for 1980, Director Vernon Jordan summarized the status of minority rights in the 1970s: "For black Americans, the decade of the 1970s was a time in which many of their hopes, raised by the civil rights victories of the 1960s, withered away, a time in which they saw the loss of much of the momentum that seemed to be propelling the nation along the road to true equality for all its citizens." He described "a mood of disappointment, frustration, and bitterness at promises made and promises unkept." Yet in the early 1970s other observers noted the rise of a black middle class in unprecedented proportions, and demographers pointed out that black males had made gains in management positions and in earnings.

Affirmative Action. The focus of the debate about racial discrimination during the 1970s was affirmative action — the policy of redressing injustices of the past by requiring that minorities be given preferential treatment in employment and promotion. The Equal Employment Opportunity Commission (EEOC), created by the Civil

THE STOCK MARKET IN THE 1970S

The stock market had disappointing results in the 1970s, an unsurprising development given the economic turmoil of the decade. Riven by inflation and economic downturn throughout the decade, stocks proved to be a less-than-satisfactory investment vehicle for most people. A study by the investment-banking firm Salomon Brothers ranked stocks as the worst performing investment among their list of eleven during 1969–1979.

Investment	Annual Return
Gold	19.4 percent
Chinese Ceramics	19.1 percent
Stamps	18.9 percent
Rare Books	15.7 percent
Silver	13.4 percent
Coins	12.7 percent
Paintings	12.5 percent
Diamonds	11.8 percent
Housing	9.6 percent
Bonds	5.8 percent
Stocks	3.1 percent

Source: Michael Barone, *Our Country: The Shaping of America From Roosevelt to Reagan* (New York: Free Press, 1990).

Rights Act of 1964 and given expanded authority by the Civil Rights Act of 1972, pressed for affirmative-action remedies throughout the decade, and in 1972 the Department of Labor issued statistical quotas for hiring minorities. Only companies employing over one hundred workers were subject to EEOC authority, and most nongovernment agencies were able to exempt themselves. The Supreme Court supported the notion of affirmative action in its highly publicized *Regents of the University of California* v. *Bakke* decision, in which a white student claimed that he had been a victim of discrimination by affirmative-action admission policies, but it rejected the notion of quotas. In 1979 the Court held that well-paying jobs could be reserved for minorities, and in 1980 it held that a small percentage of government contracts could be reserved for companies owned by minorities.

Blacks in the Workplace. There were some employment gains for blacks during the decade. In 1970, 76.5 percent of black males and 49.5 percent of black females participated in the civilian workforce as compared to 80 percent of white males and 42.6 percent of white females.

In 1980 those numbers had changed to 70.6 percent for black males, 48.9 percent for black females, 78.2 percent for white males, and 51.2 percent for white females. The most alarming statistic, though, was that 31.8 percent of the black civilian labor force between the ages of sixteen and twenty-four was unemployed in 1980.

Sources:

Reynolds Farley, *Blacks and Whites: Narrowing the Gap?* (Cambridge, Mass.: Harvard University Press, 1984);

Nathan Glazer, *Ethnic Dilemmas: 1964–1982* (Cambridge, Mass.: Harvard University Press, 1983);

Winifred D. Wandesee, *On the Move: American Women in the 1970s* (Boston: Twayne, 1988).

NIKE

Sports Dream. Nike was born in 1970 as the corporate incarnation of an eight-year-old sideline begun by a former track-and-field athlete bored with his work as a certified public accountant (CPA). Philip Knight had been a middle-distance runner at the University of Oregon in the late 1950s. Under the tutelage of his demanding and inspiring coach, William Bowerman, Knight once ran a 4:09 mile, but he realized that while his interests lay in track and field, he did not have the talent to participate in the sport at the national level. He went to graduate business school at Stanford, where for a class assignment he designed a plan to capitalize on his interest in sports. He knew that Japanese running shoes were both superior to and cheaper than the German Adidas shoes that dominated the American market. Knight proposed to import Japanese shoes for sale to American track-and-field athletes.

Go for It. Bored with life as a CPA, Knight decided in 1963 to try his business-school plan. He formed a company called Blue Ribbon Sports and bought Japanese Tiger shoes which he sold from the trunk of his car to runners at track meets in Oregon. His first order in 1963 was for two hundred pairs of shoes, which he stored in his father's basement and peddled at local track meets. Bowerman, Knight's former track coach, saw the need for an improved track shoe and, with a $500 investment, became a partner before the year was out. In 1965 the first Blue Ribbon Sports retail store opened in Santa Monica, California, and Bowerman was experimenting with his own designs for durable, lightweight, supportive sports shoes.

Swoosh. By 1970 Knight and Bowerman had twenty employees in a handful of stores and an East Coast distribution center; Blue Ribbon Sports had revenues of just under $300,000 and promising potential, but they needed venture capital to expand. In 1971 they sold shares to a handful of friends for $5,000 and arranged further financing in Japan, where they began manufacturing their own model of soccer shoe for import to the United States. They changed the name of the company to Nike, the name of the Greek goddess of victory, and adopted the well-known logo, called the "swoosh." From the be-ginning Nike was not just a business, it was a way of life. Employees were mostly what were called "running geeks." Encouraged by Bowerman's coachlike exhortations, they worked hard and developed an ideal of rugged quality to which they were devoted. They played with equal energy and developed a jock-club reputation in Portland.

The Prefontaine Image. At the 1972 Olympic trials University of Oregon runner Steve Prefontaine was adopted by the Nike group. His independence, which he showed by sporting the swoosh despite warnings about commercialization from Olympic officials, and his excellence as an athlete were qualities Knight and Bowerman both admired. When Prefontaine wore Nike shoes to victory in the trials, he demonstrated to the Nike bosses the importance of advertising. Sales increased because runners wanted to wear the shoes Prefontaine did. He was the first of a long line of celebrity athletes who were sponsored by Nike and who helped define Nike's corporate culture.

Endorsement. In the early years Nike made well-constructed shoes imaginatively designed for the serious athlete. Nylon uppers, waffle-shaped soles, midsole support, and lightweight materials distinguished Nike shoes. Nike was the shoe of choice for American athletes by the time of the 1976 Olympics, and celebrity athletes, such as professional tennis players Jimmy Connors and John McEnroe (who switched to Nikes because he was developing ankle trouble) became advertising spokesmen. Nike chose sports endorsers who were young, brash, outspoken, and energetic winners. In the late 1970s the company signed University of Oregon coach Dick Harter to a $2,500-a-year contract that required him to shoe his team in Nikes. It was the first of many such contracts that made Nike the shoe of choice for basketball players of the late 1970s.

The Payoff. Beginning in 1974 Nikes were manufactured in the United States as well as in the Orient, and the target market was broadened to include weekend athletes and children. By 1978 the company had aggressive manufacturing plants and aggressive marketing campaigns in Europe and South America, and it expanded its product line to include clothing. Sales were nearing $100 million by the end of the decade as Nike manufactured half the athletic shoes sold in the United States. In 1980 Nike became a publicly owned corporation, and those initial investors who had risked $5,000 in 1971 had earned $3 million. It was only the beginning.

Source:

J. B. Strasser and Lawrence Beckland, *Swoosh* (San Diego: Harcourt Brace Jovanovich, 1992).

UNIONS IN THE 1970s

Changing Labor Market. In the 1970s labor unions priced themselves out of a radically changing labor market. Too long during the decade unions continued to strike and bargain for wage increases without regard to the health of the industries whose workers they represented. In 1970 the railroad unions struck for two hours and received wage raises far above the rate of inflation without any increases in productivity. In the inflationary mid 1970s the United Auto Workers and the United Steelworkers demanded and received large increases in wages and benefits that did not recognize the severe cost pressures and profit squeezes that their respective industries were undergoing. In the recession of 1979–1981 those industries responded to those pressures by laying off hundreds of thousands of workers. Also, several major unions — the Teamsters and the United Mine Workers among them — were caught up in corruption scandals that eroded the goodwill of Americans. One sign of the declining leverage of labor unions was the average number of workers involved in work stoppages, which declined from over 1.3 million during 1973–1977 to fewer than 850,000 during 1978–1982.

Fading Power. Early in the decade unions were still seen as major players in setting economic and political policy. In 1970 an eight-week strike by the United Auto Workers crippled General Motors and helped worsen a domestic economy already slowed down by recession. Faced with Stagflation, an economic malady where growth slows but inflation worsens, President Nixon in 1971 took the radical step of freezing wages and prices. Thus the major issue for unions in 1971 was the participation by several major union leaders — George Meany of the AFL-CIO, I. W. Abel of the United Steelworkers, Floyd Smith of the Machinists, Leonard Woodcock of the United Auto Workers (UAW), and Frank Fitzsimmons of the Teamsters — in President Nixon's Pay Board. Nixon's New Economic Policy contained interventionist wage and price controls, methods which brought labor unions into the center of questions about economic policy. The Pay Board contained fifteen members, divided among government, business, and labor. Labor officials believed that they should have the majority voice on the board, it being their constituents that would have to live with the results.

Opposition. Meany ultimately refused to make wage concessions in the negotiations regarding wage and price controls and resigned from the Pay Board. Such confrontations were soon to become more commonplace between Nixon and much of organized labor. The AFL-CIO called for Nixon's resignation in 1973, ostensibly because of Watergate but with also much bitterness over stagnant wages and rampant inflation. The exception among labor regarding Nixon was the Teamsters Union. Nixon had pardoned former Teamster, president Jimmy Hoffa and counted on current president Fitzsimmons for support.

Lack of Options. As Stagflation continued, labor unions found themselves on uncertain ground. They disliked inflation, which eroded the value of the wage gains they could negotiate, but were frustrated by the tools used to fight it, which reduced employment and economic

George Meany denouncing President Richard Nixon during the 1973 AFL-CIO convention

activity. The problem was exacerbated by the growth of low-wage, low-skill, nonunion jobs, and even within unionized industries the number of enrolled workers declined. Ironically, the greatest growth for unions came among government employees, a development that would have negative effects over the next two decades.

Worsening Conditions. The oil embargo of 1973–1974 made the problem with statistics much worse. Inflation peaked above 12 percent, and unemployment reached 6.5 percent. Labor unions called for massive government spending on job training and jobless benefits, but those calls seemed to be increasingly alienating to a public that was growing more antiunion in its beliefs. Unions were seen negotiating wage hikes well above the rate of inflation and securing additional benefits — such as thirteen additional paid vacation days demanded by the UAW — that the 75 percent of the workforce not represented by unions was not able to secure.

Public Alienation. The source of the public's alienation was multifaceted. First, the economy of the United States was becoming increasingly less industrial. With more service-sector jobs not traditionally represented by skilled unions, labor found that it did not have the structure to deal with these workers. Second, many workers felt that unions were negotiating for increased wages and improved health benefits and doing nothing about the disappearing jobs in industries such as auto manufacturing and steel production. Third, corruption in major unions helped to undercut the goodwill traditionally felt between worker and union. The arrest and conviction of United Mine Workers (UMW) president W. A. ("Tony") Boyle for fraud and murder was a black eye on the entire labor movement. The disappearance and presumed murder of former Teamsters president Hoffa and later corruption charges against union officials were also damaging.

Dealing with Carter. In 1979 the unions began what seems to have been a last try to become institutionalized partners in government. On 19 November 1979 Meany stepped down as head of the AFL-CIO and was replaced by the Georgetown-educated Lane Kirkland. Earlier that year Kirkland, as chief negotiator, had reached an agreement with President Carter that institutionalized the participation of the AFL-CIO, along with the Teamsters and the UAW, in the setting of government economic and social policy in exchange for a new effort at wage restraint.

Into the 1980s. The pact proved to be a wrong turn politically, as labor became associated closely, if unfairly, with what increasingly was being seen as a failed political leader. During the 1979–1981 recession, hundreds of thousands of jobs were lost in the automobile and steel industries, and labor seemed powerless to stem the pain. As Ronald Reagan took office in 1981, the labor unions became an easy scapegoat for the economic turmoil of the 1970s. Reagan's firing of the air-traffic controllers of the PATCO union in 1981 was a public repudiation of unionism and the dead end of the many wrong turns the labor movement had taken during the 1970s.

Source:
Michael Barone, *Our Country: The Shaping of America From Roosevelt to Reagan* (New York: Free Press, 1990).

WAL-MART

New Ideas. Founded in Bentonville, Arkansas, in 1962, the Wal-Mart chain of discount stores helped revolutionize the retail industry. Disregarding the conventional wisdom of retailing, that a store must be located in an area with a population of at least one hundred thousand, Wal-Mart in the 1970s opened its stores in markets with less than twenty-five thousand potential customers. This unusual approach took advantage of the growth of small towns in the South and the concentration of larger retailers, such as K-Mart and Sears, on locating in larger cities and suburbs. As these larger markets became saturated with stores, the retailing giants began to move to the smaller markets where Wal-Mart was now preeminent. Not accustomed to the aggressive marketing and pricing strategy of Wal-Mart, the larger chains found it difficult to compete.

Ambitious Expansion. In the late 1970s Wal-Mart entered into an aggressively ambitious expansion program, planning to add 60 stores per year. In 1979 the 252-store chain had sales of $1.2 billion and earnings of $38 million. By the early 1990s Wal-Mart had displaced Sears as the number one retailer in the country. In 1992 Wal-Mart expanded into Mexico with joint efforts with Cifra, the leading Mexican retailer.

Independent of Genius. The brainchild of Sam Walton, an Arkansas retailer who learned the trade by running a chain of Ben Franklin variety stores during the 1950s, Wal-Mart was thought to be dependent on his genius, authority, and tolerance for hard work. Most commentators thought Wal-Mart's future too dependent on Walton. Yet after Walton's death in 1992, Walton's previous work in developing a management system bore fruit as Wal-Mart continued to grow.

Sources:
Harold Seneker, "A Day in the Life of Sam Walton," *Forbes* (1 December 1977): 45–47;

"Wal-Mart: A Discounter Sinks Deep Roots in Small Town, U.S.A.," *Business Week* (5 November 1979): 23–24.

HEADLINE MAKERS

W. A. ("TONY") BOYLE

1904-1985

UNITED MINE WORKERS PRESIDENT

Symbol of Corruption. As president of the United Mine Workers (UMW) from 1963 to 1972, W. A. ("Tony") Boyle came to represent the increasingly corrupt and ineffective nature of many labor unions in the United States.

Quick Rise. A longtime member of the UMW, Boyle rose quickly through the leadership ranks. In 1948 Boyle moved to Washington, D.C., to be administrative assistant to union president John L. Lewis, who took Boyle as his protégé. When Lewis retired as president in 1960, Boyle became vice-president under President Thomas Kennedy. Kennedy was old and sick when he became president, and Boyle exercised most of the power in the union. In 1963 Kennedy died, and Boyle finally became president of the UMW.

Authoritarian Style. Like Lewis before him, Boyle ran a centralized, authoritarian union, which had little patience with worker democracy or power sharing. All of the union's district leaders were chosen by Boyle and the union hierarchy, and negotiations were held with little input from the rank and file. In 1968 the union and the Consolidated Coal Company were fined $7.3 million for collusion in bargaining, a finding that led to revolt in the ranks.

Death of Yablonski. In May 1969 Joseph Yablonski, a UMW board member, announced that he was entering the race to replace Boyle as UMW president. The campaign quickly became heated, with Yablonski accusing Boyle of being "a crook and an embezzler." The results of the election showed Boyle being reelected, seventy-five thousand votes to forty-three thousand. Yablonski requested the U.S. Department of Labor to investigate the election. The government was slow to act until 5 January 1970, when Yablonski, his wife, and his daughter were found in their Clarkesville, Pennsylvania, home shot to death.

Corruption. Although Secretary of Labor George Shultz maintained that there was no known connection between the election and the murders, the Labor Department ordered that the election results be voided and that a new election be held in December 1972. In 1971 and 1972 the UMW continued to undergo legal problems. In 1971 a federal judge found that the union was liable for millions of dollars in damages in the handling of the UMW welfare fund. Boyle was ordered to resign from the fund's board of trustees. Boyle was indicted for his role in the corruption and on 31 March 1971 was found guilty of misusing funds. In June Boyle was sentenced to five years in prison and fined $130,000; afterward, he was removed as UMW president. In the new election in December 1972, Arnold Miller, an associate of Yablonski, was elected the union's president. His first act was to remove twenty union officials appointed by Boyle.

Murder Conviction. On 6 September 1973 Boyle was charged with first-degree murder for ordering the murder of Yablonski and his family. On 11 April 1974 he was found guilty and in September 1975 was sentenced to three consecutive life sentences. On 28 January 1977 the Pennsylvania Supreme Court overturned the conviction because of judicial error in the trial. Boyle was retried and convicted once again of murder in the Yablonski case. On 11 October 1979 he was sentenced to life in prison. Boyle died on 31 May 1985.

ARTHUR F. BURNS

1904-

CHAIRMAN, FEDERAL RESERVE BOARD

Government Technocrat. The 1960s and 1970s saw the rise of the government technocrat, who wielded great influence over the U.S. economy. Arthur Burns is a prime example of the species. Nonpartisan in the strictest sense, Burns served eight U.S.

presents— Dwight Eisenhower through Ronald Reagan — in various posts and became one of the most important influences in the post–World War II American economy.

Education. Burns was born in Stanislau, Austria, and immigrated as a child to Bayonne, New Jersey. An intellectually ambitious young man, Burns obtained a scholarship to Columbia University in 1921. He graduated in 1925 with both a B.A. and an M.A. in economics. He received his Ph.D. from Columbia in 1934, the same year his dissertation, *Production Trends in the United States Since 1870*, was published. In 1944 Burns returned to Columbia University as a professor. In 1948 he became the director of research at the National Bureau of Economic Research, becoming its president in 1957.

Eisenhower. In 1953 Burns became President Eisenhower's chief economic adviser, serving as the chairman of the Council of Economic Advisers. His views on taxes and spending were held in the highest regard, and he was given much credit for the 1955 economic miniboom. At the end of Eisenhower's first term in 1956, Burns resigned his official position and returned to Columbia; he continued to advise Eisenhower on an unofficial basis. During the 1960 presidential campaign, Burns was part of the "Scholars," the academics advising Republican candidate, Vice-president Richard Nixon.

Kennedy and Johnson. Burns's association with Eisenhower and Nixon did not forestall his being named as an economic adviser to President John F. Kennedy. Burns took great exception to the deliberate running of budget deficits, a tendency he saw as becoming a dangerous new economic orthodoxy. He also was an advocate of reforming the tax code, which he saw as an inefficient "legacy of the Great Depression. After Kennedy's assassination in 1963, Burns became an important adviser to President Lyndon Johnson. In 1964 he proposed an annual tax cut, a move he claimed would insure economic growth and, ironically enough in light of developments during the 1980s, increase tax revenues.

Federal Reserve. In 1968 Burns again became an adviser on economics to Nixon during the presidential campaign. In January 1969, after Nixon's victory, Burns was named to be counselor to the president, a Cabinet-level post. Burns was instrumental, along with Daniel Patrick Moynihan, in developing Nixon's almost-liberal domestic policy. That position lasted only until October, when Burns was named as chairman of the Federal Reserve System. His oversight of the money supply put Burns at the very heart of the economy. Burns's philosophy as the U.S. central banker was to control the money supply to counteract the business cycle in order to forestall both high inflation and recession.

New Economic Policy. The Nixon administration was faced with increasing inflation, a product of what many economists assert was the overheating of the economy with spending for both the Vietnam War and President Johnson's Great Society social programs. In 1970 Burns suggested wage and price controls as a means to calm inflationary pressures. Nixon at first rejected Burns's prescription, but in 1971 the president instituted a phase program of controls and currency devaluation as part of his New Economic Policy. Burns advised Nixon closely on the details of the program, continuing his advisory role even while serving as an "independent" central banker.

The Problem of Timing. Burns's performance received mixed-to-negative reviews, mainly because his theory did not take into account the timing of the moves needed to keep the economy growing. As a result, Burns kept the money supply growing robustly from 1970 to 1973, only then restraining it. The recession of 1973–1974, brought on by the oil crisis, was accompanied by double-digit inflation.

Crisis Management. The turbulent economy of the 1970s gave Burns many opportunities to carry out the crisis management activities of the central banker. Two of the most important were the 1970 bankruptcy of the Penn Central Railroad and the 1975 loan default by New York City. In both cases Burns acted quickly to provide adequate liquidity to smooth the financial system through the crisis. Burns's easy manner and mainstream ideas about economic policy and nonideological approach to government enabled him to continue serving presidents Gerald Ford and Jimmy Carter as Federal Reserve chairman. In 1978 Burns was replaced as chairman by Paul Volcker. In 1981 he was appointed by President Ronald Reagan to be ambassador to West Germany.

Source:
William Safire, *Before the Fall: An Inside View of the Pre-Watergate White House* (Garden City, N.Y.: Doubleday, 1975).

JERRY DELLA FEMINA

1936-

ADVERTISING EXECUTIVE

Iconoclast. In a business world long dominated by staid, Ivy League men in gray flannel suits, Jerry Della Femina exploded like a grenade in the late 1960s and 1970s. Not only did he propose a slogan for Panasonic, the Japanese electronic company, proclaiming, "From Those Wonderful Folks Who Gave You Pearl Harbor," but he made that campaign a financial success. (He recycled the title for his insider's book on advertising.)

Brooklyn Brash. Every bit of sassiness, iconoclasm, and aggressiveness that he had learned growing up in blue-collar Brooklyn erupted in a business long renowned for its prudence and respectability. Della Femina turned all that on its head in the name of creativity. No one else dared produce a zipper ad with a baseball catcher telling his pitcher, "Your fly is open." A campaign for Pretty Feet had as its headline, "What's the ugliest part of your body?"

On His Own. Della Femina was no less outrageous in dealing with his superiors, needling and confronting those whom he saw as blocking creativity, even as he picked up awards from advertising associations. His stance appealed to the creative side of the industry, which inevitably had disagreements with the senior executives. So Della Femina went his own way, forming an agency in 1967 that, after several rocky months, survived, throve, and ultimately became one of the biggest revenue makers of the 1970s.

Background. He grew up in the most improbable environment for an ad person: Brooklyn, in an Italian immigrant family, speaking little English until he entered grammar school. He went no further educationally, aside from a few night advertising courses at Brooklyn College. Instead, he spent seven years at odd jobs, while nurturing the dream of becoming an advertising copywriter. He submitted sample ads to an agency, which hired him in 1961, and he began climbing the ladder, moving from one agency to another and gathering acclaim in the industry for the wildly unconventional talent he displayed. He also fought constantly with his superiors, among whom one stated, "His whole life-style is to be a provocateur." This was an understatement, as Della Femina showed in an aggressive speech in 1966, which his superiors publicly disavowed in *The New York Times*. All the while, he was putting his talent on display, reaching out to the biggest names, and finally establishing an agency with several partners in September 1967.

Success. The early months were hard, and it was typical of Della Femina that he risked much of their limited capital for a showy Christmas party to project a successful image with potential clients. It paid off, as did his shrewd courting of the press through deft quotes and comments that made him popular with reporters facing deadlines. Della Femina made himself Mr. Advertising in the public mind, first with the press and then through his books, *From Those Wonderful Folks Who Gave You Pearl Harbor: Frontline Dispatches from the Advertising War* (1970) and his autobiography, *An Italian Grows in Brooklyn* (1978). Both attracted clients by seeming to tell it as it was, letting them in on the industry's unstated assumptions and conventions.

Success. The result was success, and by 1979 Della Femina, Travisano and Partners were doing $100 million in annual business and were winning awards, while Della Femina himself was leaving copywriting to younger talent while he sought new clients. His actions in the 1970s had helped transform the advertising industry, from reverence and hierarchy to amusement and openness. This corresponded to changes in American society as a whole, and it is hardly coincidental that Della Femina, an outsider to traditional structures and even to the English language, should have led the assault.

Source:
Jerry Della Femina, *From Those Wonderful Folks Who Gave You Pearl Harbor: Frontline Dispatches from the Advertising War* (New York: Simon & Schuster, 1970).

THOMAS MURPHY

1915-

EXECUTIVE, GENERAL MOTORS

Difficult Times. Thomas Aquinas Murphy was chairman and chief executive officer of General Motors (GM) from 1974 to 1980, arguably one of the most difficult times in the company's history.

Lifetime of Preparation. Beginning his career with GM in 1938, Murphy worked his way up the corporate ladder through the financial department. An accountant by training, Murphy was chosen in 1959 by then-chairman Frederick C. Donner as a possible future chairman. His subsequent positions — controller, treasurer, vice-president and group executive of the car and truck division, vice-chairman — were expected promotions for a man intended to lead the company.

Immediate Problems. When Murphy took the helm in 1974, replacing Richard Gerstenberg, GM was reeling from the Arab oil embargo of 1973 and the ensuing economic slowdown. The heart of the GM product line, the profitable big cars, were sitting unsold on dealership lots. The rising price of gasoline was generating a shift in consumer preference in favor of smaller, more fuel-efficient cars. The shift played against American manufacturers, all of whom had concentrated on larger vehicles, and benefited Japanese carmakers. Industrywide, domestic auto production fell by 22 percent in 1973 and a further 24 percent in 1974. The Big Three, GM included, were in trouble. In 1975 the unemployment rate among GM workers was 36 percent.

Smaller Cars. To combat the decline in sales and production, Murphy oversaw the introduction of smaller cars, the most important being the Chevrolet Chevette. The subcompact, an American version of a car built by German GM affiliate Opal, was not as big a seller as had been expected, but it proved to be an important stopgap product. Gerstenberg, Murphy's predecessor, had been the impetus behind the shift to smaller cars, but Murphy was able to claim the results. GM did not have the time or the capital to introduce a completely redesigned line of cars immediately, so Murphy and GM president Elliot Estes introduced the idea to downsize the GM line:

merely reduce in size and weight the existing product line.

The Iranian Crisis. By 1977 the strategy had raised GM's earnings to $800 million in the first quarter alone. The good earnings continued through much of 1979, until the Iranian oil crisis raised the prospect of even higher gasoline prices and demands by consumers for cars which were even more fuel efficient. Ford and even Chrysler responded quickly with their respective Escort and K-Cars, vehicles that GM could not match.

Bleak Future. As Murphy approached the mandatory retirement age, the future did not look as bright as recent results might have indicated. The downsizing program was reaping diminishing returns, and that called for a massive reworking of the entire GM line. The estimated cost of the redesign program was $40 billion over five years. All in all, Murphy had been a competent, if not brilliant, chairman. He was probably not the man to deal successfully with the assortment of problems that GM faced at the time, but it is doubtful that the consensus style of management at GM could have produced any other.

Source:

George S. May, "Thomas Aquinas Murphy," in *The Automobile Industry, 1920–1980*, edited by May (New York: Bruccoli Clark Layman/Facts On File, 1989).

RALPH NADER

1934-

CONSUMER ADVOCATE

True Believer. Ralph Nader is both a reformer and a visionary. His roots extended to the early-twentieth-century muckrakers, to Ida Tarbell, Upton Sinclair, and others who roused the nation against business exploitation. So he launched fact-filled thunderbolts from the 1960s onward against hazardous automobiles and natural gas pipelines, unsafe mining methods, unwholesome meat processing, and other dangers to the consumers.

David versus Goliath. Nader was a virtually monkish idealist who was single, lived ascetically, owned no property, and cared only for the truth he was uncovering. Nader's assaults fitted the temper of the Vietnam War era and the growing assumption that the country's leaders and institutions were self-centered and deceitful. Nader's *Unsafe at Any Speed: the Designed-in Dangers of the American Automobile* (1965) was a smash hit, and the thin, thirtyish man became an overnight folk hero.

Background. Nader grew up in a Lebanese immigrant family where politics was taken seriously. He went on to Princeton and Harvard Law School, where he raised doubts about the conventional argument regarding the driver's culpability in auto accidents. Could the vehicle itself be a factor? Nader continued this argument in Washington, D.C., where he found allies in Congress and in the Johnson administration who pushed through the National Traffic and Motor Vehicle Safety Act in 1967. Nader had raised a furor in 1966 by charging that General Motors had counterattacked his criticism of the Chevrolet Corvair by having private detectives harass him with investigations and sexual enticement schemes. The GM president apologized, and Nader filed a multimillion-dollar suit for damages, from which he collected $425,000 in an out-of-court settlement.

Creating an Infrastructure. Inevitably, Nader attracted followers, often young lawyers and college students who wanted to join his consumer-rights crusade and who became known as Nader's Raiders. He strengthened the crusade in 1971 by founding a network of organizations, Public Citizen, which grew out of his Washington-based Center for the Study of Responsive Law. He also established the Corporate Accountability Research Group, financing it with the money gained from GM. Finally, from 1970 onward there was the Public Interest Research Group (PIRG), which was associated with groups in twenty-six states at the community and campus level. Nader had institutionalized his movement with a variety of watchdog, lobbying, and investigative groups that probed into both corporations and the regulatory agencies that he insisted had allied themselves with the very enterprises they were supposed to supervise. By 1971 Nader stood as the sixth most popular figure in the country, according to a Harris poll, and his position with the media was unrivaled as a reliable source of news that affected everyone. Nader helped create the Environmental Protection Agency (EPA) in 1970 and the Freedom of Information Act in 1974.

Backlash. There was, however, a backlash against Nader's sustained critique of the American corporate structure as the 1970s wore on, conservatism increased, the economy declined, and Americans feared the loss of jobs more than the loss of health. His criticism had become familiar, his face yet another on television. In 1978 Congress narrowly failed to establish the Consumer Protection Agency, which he had advocated, and the automakers continued to stave off his attempts to impose inflatable air bags on their products. Nader's astringent, highly individualistic personality also cost him support, and it became easy to regard him as an uncompromising zealot.

A Deeper Commitment. Behind his concern with consumerism lay a deeper commitment, that of building structures to engage Americans deeply in political action, pulling them away from political parties per se and into the realm of independent citizenship. Being a citizen has been, to Nader, the very essence of a democracy; consumer action is simply a means to that end.

Sources:

Robert F. Buckhorn, *Nader: The People's Lawyer* (Englewood Cliffs, N.J.: Prentice-Hall, 1972);

Hays Gorey, *Nader and the Power of Everyman* (New York: Grosset & Dunlap, 1975);

Charles McCarry, *Citizen Nader* (New York: Saturday Review Press, 1972).

FRANKLIN PARSONS ("FRANK") PERDUE

1920-

FARMER, BUSINESSMAN

Chicken Recognition. When Frank Perdue took over as head of his family's chicken farm in 1952, it was a successful middle-sized local supplier of poultry to larger processing companies. But through a careful program of expansion and the use of new scientific methods, he turned Perdue Farms into one of the largest integrated processors in the United States. Through a massive advertising campaign starting in 1971, Perdue Farms also became the first marketer of fresh poultry to develop brand recognition among consumers, while Perdue, its chairman and chief executive officer, attained celebrity status as the company's chief spokesman and the star of its commercials.

Early Life and Career. Perdue's experience with chickens started in his childhood, when he assisted with the family egg business that his father, Arthur W. Perdue, had started in the early 1920s in Salisbury, Maryland. Frank was given fifty chickens to tend, and he was allowed to keep the money he earned through the sale of their eggs. He attended Salisbury State College from 1937 to 1939 but left to return to the family business. When an outbreak of leukosis at about this time destroyed much of their flock of two thousand leghorn chickens, the Perdues switched to the more disease-resistant breed of New Hampshire reds and effectively shifted their enterprise from egg to poultry production. Business improved during World War II as meat prices soared and the demand for chicken increased. Perdue Farms raised thousands of chicks to maturity using a special feed mixture and then sold them to meat-processing companies at the Delmarva broiler auction in Delaware.

Frank Takes Over. Frank Perdue became president of Perdue Farms in 1952. The company showed moderate growth until 1958, when Perdue built a new complex comprising both hatcheries and facilities for processing and storing vast amounts of feed from grain and soybeans; any excess meal or soybean oil would be sold to maximize profits. By 1967 the company's annual revenue from sales had grown from an average of $6 million when Perdue had assumed the presidency to more than $35 million. Noting that bigger profits were being made in processing than in raising and supplying poultry, Perdue expanded his company's operations by acquiring a processing plant in 1968. He also began to use computers to devise optimal feeding formulas for his chickens, and he employed geneticists and veterinarians to help develop and maintain a healthy flock.

Advertising. Even greater expansion was just around the corner, however, fueled by an enormously successful multimedia advertising campaign launched by the Scali, McCabe, Sloves agency in 1971. The television ads starred Perdue, a new advertising approach that the company's chairman originally resisted since he had no performing experience. The fact that Perdue was obviously not a professional actor, however, apparently made him a more convincing spokesperson to his audience. After a few months of the initial campaign in the New York area, a Perdue Farms survey indicated that local brand recognition had risen to 51 percent; in fact, the ad campaign pioneered brand identification in the fresh-poultry market. Perdue gradually increased his advertising budget, and the campaign spread to other major cities on the East Coast. In television ads, looking rather like a traditional New England farmer in a business suit, Perdue made such tongue-in-cheek claims as "The Perdue roaster is the master race of chickens," and "My chickens eat better than you do."

The Successful Seventies. Demand continued to grow, so in 1971 Perdue opened a second processing plant in Accomac, Virginia, followed in 1976 with an additional hatchery and a third processing plant in Lewiston, North Carolina. Although the combined production of the three plants totaled nearly two million broilers per week, Perdue opened another processing plant in Felton, Delaware, in 1977 and a plant in Georgetown, Delaware, in 1979 that specialized in processing roasters. Throughout the expansion Perdue insisted on maintaining high standards, guaranteeing consumers that every piece of poultry bearing the Perdue label had been subjected to a second inspection by company graders after it had been certified as Grade A by U.S. Department of Agriculture (USDA) inspectors. By the end of the decade the company's annual sales exceeded $150 million and by the mid 1980s would reach almost $750 million.

Continuing Success. Perdue's enterprise continued to grow throughout the 1980s. In 1981 Perdue opened an upscale fast-food restaurant in Queens, New York — specializing in chicken, of course — but he remains primarily committed to production rather than to retailing. The profitability of the business has allowed Perdue to avoid public offerings of stock, making Perdue Farms one of the largest privately owned companies in the United States.

Future. In 1991 Perdue's son Jim became chairman of Perdue Farms. Frank Perdue remained as chairman of the executive committee of the company, which in 1994 operated ten processing plants in six states and rang up $1.3 billion in sales. In addition to its operations in the United States, the company also sees opportunities for expansion in Southeast Asia.

Source:

Theresa Humphrey, "Poultry Scion Talks Turkey," *The State* (Columbia, S.C.), 11 December 1994, p. H3.

WILLIAM SIMON

1927-

ENERGY CZAR, 1973-1974; SECRETARY OF THE TREASURY, 1974-1977

A Relative Unknown. When William Simon was appointed chief of the new Federal Energy Office on 4 December 1973, he was a relatively unknown Wall Street bond trader stepping into one of the most important jobs in the country. His decisiveness and candor in allocating American energy resources during the Arab oil embargo — and during the winter of 1973–1974 — soon made him a household name. Unlike fellow Nixon administration officials, Simon made a habit of openness with the press and responsiveness to the public, which lessened, perhaps, the seeming omnipotence of the "energy czar." And while William Simon did not end the energy crisis, his level-headed administration of the emergency made him one of the most respected bureaucrats among the various governmental agencies overseeing American industry, paving the way for his appointment as secretary of the treasury in 1974.

Background. Grandson of a French-immigrant textile tycoon who lost virtually everything in the Depression, Simon's father was a New Jersey insurance broker. When Simon was eight, his mother died. He, his brother, and two sisters attended the Blair Academy and Newark Academy, where Simon earned a reputation as a popular athlete. Upon graduating he entered the army, swimming with the army team in the Pacific Olympics. Simon attended Lafayette College in Easton, Pennsylvania, after being discharged, once again becoming known more for his success as pledge master of Delta Kappa Epsilon and as a swimmer than for his academic achievements. Having married Carol Girard, a Marymount College coed, in his sophomore year, Simon abandoned plans for law school and took a job on Wall Street.

Wall Street Whiz. Simon quickly established himself as one of the savviest municipal-bond traders on Wall Street. Moving to Salomon Brothers as its chief of federal bonds and securities, Simon oversaw the tremendous expansion of the firm in the 1960s. In 1969 he became the first president of the Association of Primary Dealers in

United States government securities, and a member of the Salomon Brothers management committee. Simon's income was reportedly over $3 million a year by 1972, and he had earned a celebrated reputation in the financial community. He began to advise state and city governments on bond purchases and eventually came to the attention of George Shultz, treasury secretary in the Nixon administration. In 1972 ShultzGeorge Shultz asked him to join the government as deputy secretary of the treasury, and, putting his assets in a blind trust, Simon and his family moved to Washington.

Energy Policy. As deputy secretary of the treasury, one of Simon's responsibilities was to chair the Interagency Oil Policy Committee, and he began to study the energy problems in the United States. Before the oil embargo Americans gorged themselves on cheap energy, consuming nearly a third of the world's fuel while only having 6 percent of the world's population. The 1973 oil embargo only made a bad situation worse. The Nixon administration responded to the emergency by creating the Federal Energy Office and appointing former Colorado governor John Love as its first head. When Love resigned because of the administration's preoccupation with Watergate, Simon stepped into the job, announcing at the press conference on his appointment that "We have become a nation of great energy wastrels. We have been accustomed to an overabundance of cheap energy. That day is over. This country now faces the choice between comfort and convenience, or jobs."

Problems. As FEO chair, Simon immediately confronted a seemingly endless array of problems. Sixty different federal agencies oversaw parts of the nation's energy policy; Simon coordinated their efforts and assembled a staff of one thousand people. He prioritized energy resources to industry in order to limit the oil embargo's impact on the economy and urged citizens to lower their thermostats to 68 degrees and drive under 55 MPH in order to conserve fuel. Few appreciated his efforts. The Pentagon balked when he allocated 1.5 million barrels of military jet fuel for commercial use (they only delivered half), and the oil companies, while appreciating government incentives for resource development, took Simon's mandatory allocation program to court. The public viewed much of the energy program skeptically, convinced that the oil companies were purposely holding back supplies and driving up the price of fuel. They had reason to be suspicious: oil-company fuel inventories were nearly 9 percent higher in 1974 than they were in 1973, and Nobel Prize–winning economist Wassily Leontief, consumer advocate Ralph Nader, and ecologist Barry Commoner all charged the oil companies with price gouging. Simon responded to these suspicions by attempting to secure government statistics on private fuel inventories, and when the oil companies refused to cooperate, Simon took his difficulties to the public and assessed fines against companies that deliberately falsified their disclosures. He also set the Internal Reve-

vice on the trail of gas stations artificially increasing prices or creating shortages. He only reluctantly and temporarily regulated prices, preferring voluntary controls and the self-regulating mechanisms of the market. Such a philosophy earned him the criticism of many, especially after the oil companies posted profits during the oil shortage 46 percent higher on average than the previous year. Oilmen, testifying before Congress, argued that many of these profits were the results of overseas sales and that the figures ignored the credit squeeze investors placed on oil companies after the embargo, but many in the public remained unconvinced.

Secretary of the Treasury. Simon sidestepped the controversy over oil-company profits by developing an ambitious plan to wean the United States from its foreign imports and develop new sources of energy. He was one of the chief forces behind the Nixon administration's Project Independence, designed to develop new fuel resources for the nation. Because of Watergate, the program was neglected during the remainder of Nixon's term. Under the supervision of Vice-president Nelson Rockefeller, President Ford proposed a similar program in 1975, but it failed to pass in Congress. Ultimately, no long-term U.S. energy policy was established during the 1970s, but Simon's handling of the fuel emergency earned him (by unanimous vote in the Senate) the office of secretary of the treasury in April 1974. Continuing as secretary under Gerald Ford, Simon negotiated a grain export arrangement with the Soviet Union and advocated fiscal restraint. Stressing traditional Republican economic policies, he opposed federal loans to bail out New York City and emphasized the limits of federal economic assistance to the underprivileged. Simon left government service with the defeat of Ford in 1976, but his efforts to plan a coherent American energy policy resulted in the creation of the Energy Research and Development Administration and other energy programs important in the coming decade.

Source:
Time, 103 (21 January 1974): 22–27.

PEOPLE IN THE NEWS

On 11 May 1977 **John D. Backe,** 44, succeeded the powerful William S. Paley, 77, as chief executive officer of the Columbia Broadcasting System (CBS), a $2 billion multimedia conglomerate, as part of a long-planned change of top leadership which did not, however, prove successful; Backe was pushed out in 1980.

On 3 February 1975 **Eli M. Black,** the president and chief executive officer of the $2 billion United Brands multinational conglomerate, committed suicide in New York. The company had suffered severe losses, and the news was surfacing that it had tried to get a tax reduced by offering a bribe to the president of Honduras.

On 11 September 1975 **W. A. ("Tony") Boyle,** the head of the United Mine Workers of America, received three consecutive life terms for ordering the murder of union rival Joseph Yablonski, his wife, and his daughter, whose bodies were found on 5 January 1970.

On 22 July 1971 **Edgar M. Bronfman** took over as president and treasurer of the Distillers Corporation-Seagrams and its chief U.S. subsidiary, Joseph E. Seagram and Sons, following the death of his father, Samuel, who was the company's founder.

On 6 November 1973 **Malcolm Forbes,** publisher of the business magazine *Forbes,* landed at Gwynn Island in Chesapeake Bay after a monthlong flight in a custom-designed hot-air balloon from Coos Bay, Oregon.

In June 1978 **Henry Ford II** reorganized the top leadership of the much-troubled Ford Motor Company, essentially eliminating the ambitious Lee Iacocca, making Philip Caldwell the deputy chief executive, and appointing William Clay Ford, Henry's brother, as chairman of the executive committee.

On 1 September 1974 **Alan Greenspan** succeeded **Herbert Stein** as head of the three-member Council of Economic Advisers in the administration of President Gerald Ford.

On 26 September 1977 **Sir Frederick ("Freddie") Laker,** the British owner of Laker Airways, overcame strong opposition from the scheduled airlines to inaugurate the Skytrain, an inexpensive, no-frills, no-reservation bargain flight from New York to London and from London to Los Angeles. The Skytrain became popular among the student and backpacking set and anticipated the end of U.S. airline regulations in 1978.

On 3 May 1971 **Roger Lewis,** the former president and chief executive officer of General Dynamics, was confirmed by Congress after his appointment by President Richard Nixon as the first president of the newly formed Amtrak, previously known as the National Railroad Passenger Corporation.

On 11 September 1975 Gov. **Hugh Carey** of New York chose eminent investment banker **Felix G. Rohatyn** of Lazard Freres and Company, to be the unpaid chairman of New York City's newly created Municipal Assistance Corporation (MAC), whose purpose was to counter a possible bankruptcy of the largest and most important U.S. city.

On 30 March 1973 **Frank Stanton** retired from CBS at age sixty-five after thirty-eight years of exceptionally diligent service that carried him to the presidency but not to the position of chief executive officer that William S. Paley gripped so tightly.

DEATHS

Winthrop W. Aldrich, 88, banker, president, and board chairman of Chase Manhattan Bank; ambassador to Great Britain (1953–1957), 25 February 1974.

Stanley C. Allyn, 79, president and board chairman of National Cash Register Company, which he expanded overseas and diversified into manufacturing office machines, 31 October 1970.

John A. Barr, 70, retailer who worked his way up the ladder in Montgomery Ward for over twenty-five years, expanding the company and becoming board chairman and president (1961–1964), 16 January 1979.

Elmer H. Bobst, 93, executive in vitamins and pharmaceuticals with Warner-Lambert Pharmaceuticals, 2 August 1978.

Harold Boeschenstein, 76, executive who promoted new products using glass fibers as president and board chairman of Owens-Corning Fiberglass Company, 23 October 1972.

Ernest R. Breech, 80, president of Bendix Aviation Corporation and, after World War II, a key Ford senior executive, 3 July 1978.

Edward G. Budd, 69, president and board chairman of Philadelphia's Budd Company, one of the few remaining American locomotive and railroad-car builders, 20 May 1971.

Herbert P. Buetow, 73, president of the Minnesota Mining and Manufacturing Company (3M), famous for Scotch Tape and various abrasives, 8 January 1972.

Henry S. Burns, 71, president and chief executive officer during Shell Oil's rise as a major oil producer, 21 October 1971.

Cleo F. Craig, 85, board chairman of American Telephone and Telegraph who spent his entire career (1912–1957) moving through its ranks, 21 April 1978.

Leland Doan, 79, president and executive committee chairman of Dow Chemical Company, who was criticized during the Vietnam War for producing munitions, 4 April 1974.

Bernard C. Duffy, 72, president of Batten, Barton, Durstine, and Osborne, a prominent advertising agency that helped introduce political advertising in the United States in the 1950s, 1 September 1972.

John Dykstra, 73, General Motors executive and later a key figure at Ford Motor Company under Henry Ford II, 2 March 1972.

Cyrus Eaton, 95, Cleveland-based industrialist and financier, who won the 1960 Lenin Peace Prize for advocating good relations with the Soviet Union, 9 May 1979.

Harvey S. Firestone, 75, chief executive officer and board chairman of Firestone Tire and Rubber Corporation, who led the global expansion and diversification of the company, 1 June 1973.

Frank M. Folsom, 75, president of Radio Corporation of America (RCA) and an early promoter of television, 12 January 1970.

Benson Ford, 59, grandson of Henry Ford, vice-president of the Ford Motor Company and owner of the Detroit Lions football team, 27 July 1978.

Joseph W. Frazer, 79, automobile executive, who produced Willys-Overland's famous jeep during World War II and later joined Henry J. Kaiser to try to compete with the big auto companies, 7 August 1971.

Alfred C. Fuller, 87, founder in 1906 and leader of the Fuller Brush Company, whose door-to-door salesmen became part of American folklore, 4 December 1973.

Jean Paul Getty, 83, famous oil billionaire and patron of the Getty Art Museum in Malibu, California, 6 June 1976.

Harry F. Guggenheim, 80, scion of the wealthy and philanthropic mining family and founder-publisher of New York's *Newsday*, 22 January 1971.

Donald J. Hardenbrook, 79, executive vice-president of Union Bag–Camp Paper Corporation from 1945–1962; 1962 president of National Association of Manufacturers, 5 July 1976.

Arthur M. Hill, 80, transportation executive who helped create the Greyhound Corporation in the 1920s, 5 September 1972.

Conrad N. Hilton, 91, founder in 1946 of the Hilton Hotels Corporation, which expanded internationally to over 250 hotels, 3 January 1979.

Arthur B. Homer, 76, president and chief executive officer of Bethlehem Steel Corporation, a key force in expanding the World War II navy, 18 June 1972.

Clifford F. Hood, 83, steel company executive who had a long career with U.S. Steel subsidiaries, including president of U.S. Steel (1953–1959), 9 November 1978.

Howard R. Hughes, 70, reclusive, eccentric entrepreneur, head of Summa Corporation of Las Vegas and former moviemaker, record-setting aviator, and celebrity businessman, 5 April 1976.

George M. Humphrey, 79, president and board chairman of Cleveland's M. A. Hanna Company, a Great Lakes shipping company, and President Dwight Eisenhower's treasury secretary (1953–1957), 20 January 1970.

H. L. Hunt, 85, a secretive Texas oil billionaire, 29 November 1974.

Croil Hunter, 77, president and board chairman of Northwest Airlines, who led expansion into major domestic and international routes, 21 July 1970.

Walter J. Kohler, Jr., 71, longtime executive with posts in the Kohler Company and Republican governor of Wisconsin (1951–1957), 21 March 1976.

Roy E. Larsen, 80, president of *Time* magazine (1939–1960) after Henry Luce, who had been with the magazine from its founding in 1922 and who retired in 1979, 9 September 1979.

William P. Lear, 75, inventor and industrialist with some 150 patents in aviation, radios, and stereos; chairman of the Lear Jet Corporation, 14 May 1978.

Fowler McCormick, 74, president and board chairman of International Harvester Company, the world's largest producer of agricultural equipment, 6 January 1973.

Neil H. McElroy, 68, president and board chairman of Proctor and Gamble and Eisenhower's secretary of defense (1957–1959), 20 November 1972.

John E. McKeen, 74, president and board chairman (1949–1968) of Charles Pfizer and Company, which he helped expand, 23 February 1978.

Richard King Mellon, 70, director of Gulf Oil and the Aluminum Corporation of America (ALCOA), whose powerful financial and philanthropic family led Pittsburgh's urban renewal, 3 June 1970.

Charles G. Mortimer, 78, chief executive officer (1954–1965) of General Foods Corporation, who helped develop Birdseye frozen vegetables and Maxim coffee, 25 December 1978.

Samuel I. Newhouse, 84, publishing mogul who, starting from zero, built a huge publishing empire of newspapers, radio, television, and magazines, which his two sons inherited, 29 August 1979.

Floyd B. Odlum, 84, financier, industrialist with RKO Radio and developer of Atlas missiles with Consolidated Vultee Aircraft, 17 June 1976.

James C. Penney, 75, founder of the famous department-store chain J. C. Penney Company, which competed with Sears Roebuck in bringing wide retail choices to small-town America, 12 February 1971.

Arthur Perdue, 91, the founder of Perdue Farms, one of the largest poultry processors in the United States, 27 June 1977.

Wendell Phillips, 54, archaeologist and founder in the 1960s of Wendell Phillips Oil Company, which gained big concessions in Muscat and Oman, 4 December 1975.

William T. Piper, 88, creator of the Piper Cub, a famous lightweight plane, and other inexpensive, mass-produced small planes, 15 January 1970.

Jacob Potofsky, 84, successor to Sidney Hillman and president of the Amalgamated Clothing Workers of America (1946–1972), where he created union health and recreation centers, 5 August 1979.

Donald C. Power, 79, corporate executive, who helped merge General Telephone Corporation and Sylvania Electric Products, forming General Telephone & Electronic Corporation (GTE), where he became board chairman, 11 March 1979.

Benjamin E. Puckett, 77, president and board chairman of Allied Stores (1933–1953), whose management he decentralized, 12 February 1976.

Monroe J. Rathbone, 76, forty-four-year career executive with Standard Oil of New Jersey (now Exxon), who rose to the top as board chairman and promoted overseas expansion, 2 August 1976.

Walter P. Reuther, 62, the twenty-four-year president of the United Automobile Workers (UAW), the progressive flagship of American labor, and a strong opponent of communism, corruption, and the Vietnam War; killed in a plane crash, 9 May 1970.

Charles Revson, 68, enterpreneur of cosmetics as president of Revlon, 24 August 1975.

Edward V. Rickenbacker, 82, pioneering hero of American civil aviation as a World War I ace fighter pilot, a stunt flier, and eventually as president and board chairman of an expanding Eastern Airlines, 23 July 1973.

Lessing Rosenwald, 89, career executive and board chairman (1932–1939) of Sears Roebuck who ran the American Council for Judaism, which opposed a separate Jewish state, 25 June 1979.

Raymond Rubicam, 85, advertising executive who cofounded Young and Rubicam in 1923 and helped it become among the largest advertising agencies in revenue in the United States, 8 May 1978.

Robb H. Sagendorph, 69, founder and publisher of *Yankee* and owner of *Old Farmers's Almanac,* who raised interest in rural America, 4 July 1970.

David Sarnoff, 81, head of the National Broadcasting Corporation (NBC) and of the RCA Corporation; a pioneering figure in shaping American taste in radio and later in television, 12 December 1971.

Max L. Schuster, 72, publisher and cofounder in 1924 of Simon and Schuster, which reaped profits by shaking up the book business with mass-market titles, advertising, and paperbacks, 12 December 1970.

Andrew B. Shea, 69, president of Pan American–Grace Airways (1949–1967) and part of both its great global expansion and its decline in the 1960s due to more-flexible competitors, 15 November 1972.

Igor I. Sikorsky, 83, Russian-born aviation designer and engineer and an early helicopter innovator, 26 October 1972.

Spyros Skouras, 78, legendary Greek-born Hollywood pioneer and head of the 20th Century–Fox Corporation, 16 August 1971.

Charles E. Wilson, 85, twice president of General Electric during the 1940s and Washington war mobilization official in World War II and the Korean War, 3 January 1972.

Harry Winston, 82, gem dealer who organized Harry Winston, Inc., in 1932 and helped it become the world's largest gem dealership through astute publicity, 8 December 1978.

Philip Wrigley, 82, chewing-gum tycoon and owner of the Chicago Cubs, 12 April 1977.

Joseph Yablonski, 59, opponent of W. A. ("Tony") Boyle for the presidency of the United Mine Workers of America who was discovered murdered with his wife and daughter, 5 January 1970.

William Zeckendorf, 71, real estate developer in New York and elsewhere, creator of the site of the United Nations, and head of Webb and Knapp until its bankruptcy in 1965, 30 September 1976.

PUBLICATIONS

Stanley Aronowitz, *False Promises* (New York: McGraw-Hill, 1973);

C. Fred Bergsten, Thomas Horst, and Theodore H. Horan, *American Multinationals and American Interests* (Washington, D.C.: Brookings Institution, 1978);

Derek C. Bok and John T. Dunlap, *Labor and the American Community* (New York: Simon & Schuster, 1970);

Robert F. Buckhorn, *Nader: The People's Lawyer* (Englewood Cliffs, N.J.: Prentice-Hall, 1972);

Barry Commoner, *The Poverty of Power: Energy and the Economic Crisis* (New York: Knopf, 1976);

Congressional Quarterly, Inc., *The U.S. Economy: Challenged in the '70s* (Washington, D.C.: Congressional Quarterly, 1972);

Jerry Della Femina, *From Those Wonderful Folks Who Gave You Pearl Harbor: Frontline Dispatches from the Advertising War* (New York: Simon & Schuster, 1970).

John Kenneth Galbraith, *The Age of Uncertainty* (Boston: Houghton Mifflin, 1977);

Galbraith, *Almost Everyone's Guide to Economics* (Boston: Houghton Mifflin, 1978);

Galbraith, *Economics and the Public Purpose* (Boston: Houghton Mifflin, 1973);

Galbraith, *Money, Whence It Came, Where It Went* (Boston: Houghton Mifflin, 1973);

Hays Gorey, *Nader and the Power of Everyman* (New York: Grosset & Dunlap, 1975);

Michael Harrington, *The Twilight of Capitalism* (New York: Simon & Schuster, 1976);

Jesse Helms, *When Freemen Shall Stand* (Grand Rapids, Mich.: Zondervan, 1976);

Eliot Janeway, *You and Your Money: A Survival Guide to the Controlled Economy* (New York: McKay, 1972);

Arthur B. Laffer and Jan P. Seymour, *The Economics of the Tax Revolt: A Reader* (New York: Harcourt Brace Jovanovich, 1979);

Laffer and David Meiselman, *The Phenomenon of Worldwide Inflation* (Washington, D.C.: American Enterprise Institute, 1975);

Christopher Lasch, *The Culture of Narcissism: American Life in an Age of Diminishing Expectations* (New York: W. W. Norton, 1979);

Sar A. Levitan, *The Promise of Greatness* (Cambridge, Mass.: Harvard University Press, 1976);

Charles McCarry, *Citizen Nader* (New York: Saturday Review Press, 1972).

Roger Leroy Miller, *The New Economics of Richard Nixon: Freezes, Floats, and Fiscal Policy* (New York: Harper's Magazine Press, 1972);

Jack Newfield, *A Populist Manifesto: The Making of a New Majority* (New York: Praeger, 1972);

George A. Nikoliaeff, *Stabilizing America's Economy* (New York: H. W. Wilson, 1972);

The Politics of Planning (San Francisco: Institute for Contemporary Studies, 1976);

Robert J. Ringer, *Restoring the American Dream* (New York: Harper & Row, 1979);

William A. Simon, *A Time for Truth* (New York: Reader's Digest, 1978);

Robert Warren Stevens, *Vain Hopes, Grim Realities: The Economic Consequences of the Vietnam War* (New York: New Viewpoints, 1976);

The Urban Economy (New York: Norton, 1976);

Paul A. Volcker, *The Rediscovery of the Business Cycle* (New York: Free Press, 1978);

Business Week, periodical;

Forbes, periodical;

Fortune, periodical;

Newsweek, periodical;

Time, periodical.

EDUCATION

by HARRIET S. WILLIAMS

CONTENTS

Sidebars and tables are listed in italics.

1970

- A huge surplus of teachers exists—especially for English, French, and social studies.

8 Feb. George Wallace urges southern governors to defy integration orders at a Birmingham rally; he vows to run for president again in 1972 if President Richard Nixon "doesn't do something about the mess our schools are in."

22 Apr. The first Earth Day celebration is held to call attention to the dangers pollutants are posing to the environment; two thousand college campuses host events and over ten thousand elementary and high-school students take part.

4 May Four students are killed and eight wounded in Ohio by the National Guard at a Kent State student rally protesting the escalation of the war in Southeast Asia.

14 May During antiwar protests a student dorm at Jackson State College in Mississippi is riddled with police bullets, killing a student and a local high-school senior, both of whom are black.

25 May Secretary of the Interior Walter J. Hickel sends a letter to President Nixon warning that the administration's hard-line approach to student dissent is contributing to anarchy among U.S. students; he strongly recommends that Nixon force Vice-president Spiro Agnew to stop making hostile attacks on campus leaders.

May–June To protest the war, some colleges close in antiwar demonstrations; to honor the students killed at Kent State and Jackson State, some call off graduation ceremonies.

July Pennsylvania becomes the second state to enact legislation to legalize teacher strikes (Hawaii had been first).

- Only 300 of 892 teachers who were graduated from Sacramento State College in June have found employment.

Sept. The sixteenth annual fall survey of public elementary and secondary-school enrollments by the U.S. Office of Education (USOE) shows yearly growth of only 1.5 percent, the smallest increase since the late 1940s.

- The Saint Louis School District adopts a twelve-month schedule for elementary school and junior high; students attend nine weeks, then take three weeks off.

Dec. The White House Conference on Children is named one of ten major educational events of the year.

1971

- Sidney Marland, commissioner of USOE, calls for the abolition of the "general track" in high schools, calling it an "abomination."

- Census data shows the proportion of Americans with high-school diplomas has risen from 38 percent in the 1940s to 75 percent.

- Seven women hold superintendents' positions in the United States.

- The New York legislature passes a bill permitting a brief period of silent prayer or reflection in school.

- Blacks, who make up 11 percent of the total U.S. population, represent 7 percent of the college population.

- Ivy League colleges have a 6.7 percent decline in applications; private colleges nationwide see this trend, which is attributed partially to the economy.

- Ritalin is now prescribed for thousands of schoolchildren as an "aid to general treatment of minimal brain dysfunction," which usually manifests itself in the form of hyperkinetic activity.

- More than one million men and women have received college degrees during the calendar year; it is the first time that the USOE has ever reported degree recipients in excess of one million for a twelve-month period.

20 Apr.   The U.S. Supreme Court unanimously rules that busing to achieve racial balance is constitutional in cases in which segregation has had official sanctions and officials have offered no alternatives.

May   Federal authorities impose a strict busing plan on Austin, Texas, schools.

June   The first Indian-controlled educational institution is opened on a Navajo reservation in northeastern Arizona.

30 June   Ohio is the thirty-eighth state to ratify the Twenty-sixth Amendment to the Constitution; eighteen-year-olds now have the right to vote.

3 Aug.   President Nixon publicly repudiates the federally imposed busing plan in Texas and orders that busing be limited to the "minimum required by law."

Sept.   Philadelphia's Parkway School gets a Ford Foundation grant of $290,000; this unusual school has no school building so students attend tutorials or pursue self-directed study in businesses or other cooperating institutions in the city.

Dec.   Schools in Chicago close twelve days early for the Christmas holidays to help meet a $26 million budget deficit.

1972

- Three million eighteen- to twenty-year-olds register to vote.

- Average age of public-school teachers declines from forty to thirty-five during the decade ending in 1972.

- The National Institute for Education (NIE) is formed to "muster the power of research to solve problems."

18 Jan.   Sixteen black protesters interrupt a Stanford semiconductor course exam in a course taught by Nobel Laureate William Shockley to show their objections to Shockley's racial theories.

18 Mar.   Twenty-nine men and women draw lots and begin living together in a University of Michigan housing unit to "break down some of the barriers between the sexes."

June   The College Placement Council announces that the job market is the worst for B.A. recipients in two decades.

12–17 June   Campus Crusade for Christ stages Expo '72 in the Cotton Bowl in Dallas, hosting about seventy-five thousand students.

Sept.   The teachers' union in New York City negotiates a public-school teaching contract that breaks the twenty-thousand-dollar barrier for most qualified teachers.

19 Mar.   The Supreme Court rules 6-3 that state colleges and universities cannot expel a student for distributing material on campus that administrators find offensive.

21 Mar.   The Supreme Court rules in *Rodriguez* v. *Board of Education* that states can constitutionally finance schools through local property taxes even though funding disparities will result.

1973

4 Apr. The U.S. District Court in Atlanta orders into effect a compromise school integration plan.

5 Apr. A three-judge panel in New Jersey rules that state aid to private and parochial schools is unconstitutional.

3 Aug. Massachusetts governor Francis Sargent vetoes a bill providing for silent prayer in schools.

10 Aug. The Justice Department files suit against an Omaha, Nebraska, school district to force desegregation.

8 Sept. A Gallup poll reports only 5 percent of U.S. adults support court-ordered busing.

9 Sept. The USOE reports that about sixty thousand college and trade school students have defaulted on $55.2 million in federal-guaranteed loans.

11 Sept. Eight hundred thousand students nationwide are not back in school due to teacher strikes.

9 Oct. The Carnegie Commission on Higher Education issues the final report of a six-year study concluding that the nation's colleges and universities are in the greatest period of trauma and self-doubt in history.

13 Nov. The Department of Health, Education and Welfare (HEW) rejects college desegregation plans filed by state systems in Arkansas, Florida, Georgia, Louisiana, Mississippi, North Carolina, Oklahoma, Pennsylvania, and Virginia.

14 Dec. The New York Board of Regents orders colleges to cease permitting racial minorities to segregate themselves in on-campus housing.

1974

9 Jan. The USOE reports higher education enrollments are up 3.9 percent from 1972–1973.

17 Jan. HEW says racial discrimination still exists in Topeka, Kansas, schools, the site of the original *Brown* v. *Board of Education* suit in 1954.

21 Jan. The Supreme Court rules unanimously that a San Francisco school district must provide English-language instruction for Chinese students.

21 Mar. HEW finds the New York City school system guilty of misusing $28 million in federal funds during the years from 1965 to 1972.

8 Apr. A federal judge orders integration of Denver's seventy-thousand-student school system.

23 Apr. The Supreme Court refuses to rule on the constitutionality of law-school admissions policies giving preferential treatment to minority applicants.

June Federal judge Arthur Garrity rules that the Boston School Committee has deliberately segregated schools by race; he orders a plan exchanging students between white South Boston and black Roxbury schools.

14 Sept. White mobs in Boston greet buses carrying blacks to their schools by shouting, "Nigger, go home!" Violence ensues.

9 Oct. Massachusetts governor Francis Sargent calls out the National Guard to restore order in South Boston.

27 Dec.   Three members of the Boston School Committee are held in civil contempt of court in wake of their defiance of court-ordered busing.

1975

- The Metric Conversion Act moves the United States toward use of the metric system, causing mathematics curricula to accommodate the coming change.

5 Jan.   The Educational Testing Service reports women with doctorates are discriminated against in matters of salary and promotions in higher education.

20 Jan.   The Justice Department charges that student bodies and faculties of Mississippi's twenty-five state schools are illegally segregated.

25 Feb.   The Supreme Court rules that school-board members are liable for damages if students prove their rights were denied.

31 Mar.   The College Board reports the cost of higher education will rise 6 to 8 percent in fall 1975.

1 Aug.   Indianapolis city schools are ordered to transfer 6,533 black students to eight suburban districts.

26 Sept.   The Senate approves $36.2 billion in appropriations for HEW with the proviso it not order school busing.

7 Oct.   A $1.2 billion school-lunch bill and other child-nutrition laws are enacted over President Gerald Ford's veto.

1976

26 Jan.   Court-ordered busing in Detroit begins without incident.

24 Feb.   Judge Arthur Garrity imposes a 20 percent quota for black administrators in the Boston school system.

13 Oct.   President Ford signs a medical-education bill aimed at increasing the proportion of doctors and health professionals in deprived areas.

1977

17 Jan.   A Boston Schools Department report asserts the quality of public education has deteriorated since the start of busing.

11 Apr.   Ernest Boyer, commissioner of education, announces reorganization of HEW's Office of Education.

19 Apr.   The Supreme Court rules 5–4 that school officials can spank students without violating their constitutional rights.

11 May   The National Association of the Advancement of Colored People (NAACP) Legal Defense Fund files suit in federal court against HEW, charging abandonment of integration attempts in vocational education and programs for the handicapped in the South.

12 May   The discovery of a stick of dynamite at South Boston High, the site of most serious tensions over busing, creates a disturbance which results in the arrest of seven and injuries to seven others.

5 June   Joseph Califano, commissioner of HEW, tells the graduating class at City College in New York that the government will rely on numerical goals, not quotas, in measuring minority access to higher education.

24 Sept.   SAT scores of entering freshmen are the lowest in the fifty-one years of the test's existence.

23 Nov.   The Cleveland, Ohio, school system fails to meet its payroll.

15 Dec.   A Carnegie Foundation study recommends that higher-education curriculum reform include strengthening general educational core and eliminating electives.

1978

13 Jan.   HEW

2 Feb.   HEW rejects higher-education desegregation plans submitted by Virginia and Georgia.

21 Feb.   The Supreme Court leaves standing a U.S. Circuit Court of Appeals decision that the University of Missouri cannot refuse to recognize Gay Liberation, a student homosexual group, as an official campus organization.

21 Mar.   The Supreme Court rules 8-0 that public-school students suspended without hearings cannot collect more than one dollar in damages.

7 Apr.   New York City drops its 1977 plan of assigning teachers on the basis of race.

1 June   The House approves, 237–158, a bill to grant tuition tax credits to middle-income parents of college students.

23 June   The New York State Supreme Court rules that the state's method of financing public schools through property tax is illegal.

28 June   The Supreme Court rules in favor of Allen Bakke, who was protesting the unconstitutionality of special-admissions policies of the medical school at the University of California, Davis.

16 Sept.   The Educational Testing Service announced that the latest SAT verbal scores hold steady at 429; math scores, however, drop from 470 to 468.

1979

8 Feb.   President Jimmy Carter sends Congress his proposal for a cabinet-level Department of Education.

23 Apr.   The Supreme Court lets stand a ruling that denies an Italian-American man the right to sue a law school for rejecting his application to a special-admissions program.

11 June   The Supreme Court rules unanimously that federally funded colleges do not have to admit all handicapped applicants or make extensive modifications to accommodate them.

2 July   The Supreme Court upholds sweeping desegregation orders for two large Ohio school systems: Dayton and Columbus.

15 Aug.   The Ann Arbor, Michigan, school board approves a program to teach "Black English" to all twenty-eight teachers at Martin Luther King Elementary.

10 Sept.   Cleveland, Ohio, schools desegregate, climaxing a six-year court battle.

21 Dec.   The Chicago school board is not able to meet its payroll.

OVERVIEW

A Decade of Transformations. Activism in the 1960s may have been conducted by fewer than 5 percent of college students nationwide, but the principles of inclusion and equality of opportunity these protesters espoused became the status quo in education during the 1970s. Some schools and colleges were administered by those who believed that the success of any institution and any teacher should be measured not by the treatment of its high-achieving students, but rather by the treatment of those not achieving. They believed that society's strength is much like a chain whose ultimate value is dependent upon its weakest member. Even administrators who disagreed with this philosophy found themselves altering their positions to obtain increased federal funding often dependent upon compliance with this philosophy. Consequently, efforts to shore up opportunities for and the performance of those who had typically been shortchanged in the educational process — blacks, immigrants, the handicapped, and, to a certain extent, women — characterized education during the decade. Many of these efforts met with success: more minority students attended formerly all-white schools and later gained greater access to higher education, more nonnative speakers of English received bilingual instruction, the handicapped were granted access to programs heretofore inaccessible to them, and women broke down barriers at all levels of academia. However, achievement by public-school students as a whole suffered. According to assessment expert Paul Copperman, who analyzed national testing trends in *The Achievement Decline* (1979), a significant decline in performance as measured by standardized tests occurred in the years from 1965 to 1978. Every age group except primary students performed worse than in the prior decade, with the most significant test-score declines found among high-school students. Copperman suggests that, statistically, the decline among secondary students was the equivalent of replacing the top quarter of 1965 students with somewhat below-average 1965 students. A tug-of-war between the needs of the disadvantaged and the national need to be competitive worldwide characterized the philosophical conflicts in 1970s education.

Federal Influence on Education. Education policy in the 1970s was significantly influenced by changes that had been wrought in the prior decade. An extraordinary transformation of federal education policy was accomplished during the 1960s under successive Democratic administrations led by Presidents John Kennedy and Lyndon Johnson. In his sixth and final budget message to Congress in 1969, former schoolteacher Johnson proudly assessed these federal achievements of his Great Society: Title I of the Elementary and Secondary Education Act of 1965 (ESEA) was assisting in the education of 9 million children from low-income families; Head Start aided 716,000 preschool children, Follow Through preserved the early educational gains of 63,500 more children. Since 1964 new federal programs had been created to aid the instruction of 182,000 handicapped children. In 1970, under the Higher Education Act of 1965 (HEA), two million federally funded grants, loans, and interest subsidies for guaranteed loans would reach one out of every four college students. Also by 1970, $9 billion was earmarked for classroom, library, and laboratory construction. These significant achievements demanded an unprecedented level of federal intervention in educational policy. Previously funded and managed on the local level, education after the 1960s became more and more influenced by Washington. The 1970s were a time in which debate about the wisdom of federal control and federal financing characterized the politics of education. Spending increases had been so great that even rampant inflation followed by a recession failed to lower them. Despite serious challenges to the efficacy of many of the programs set in motion during the 1960s, lawmakers were unable or unwilling to stop the momentum toward more and more federal education programs.

Desegregation and Busing. A major political issue of 1970s education was the attempt to eliminate segregation. During the late 1960s and early 1970s great strides were made in the South, where federal rulings banning de jure segregation forced schools to accommodate minority students. The combined power of the judiciary and the threat of loss of federal funds brought the long and difficult battles in the South to a halt. A Department of Health, Education, and Welfare (HEW) report in 1974 showed that, by a wide margin, schools in the South were the most integrated in the nation. However, that same report showed that schools in the Northeast were more segregated than they had been in 1970. Outside the South separation of the races in housing patterns had created a situation of de facto segregation. In the Northeast, the Midwest, and the West many children still attended schools which were highly segregated due to the location of school-district lines. Especially in large cities, where public housing was clustered in downtown areas, minority students tended to populate inner-city schools whereas white students attended more-affluent suburban schools. Usually, these schools were administered by separate school districts. In the South, however, smaller, more rural districts were the norm. In dozens of small southern towns where there were two high schools, one for blacks and one for whites, the black high school could simply become a junior high school for both races while blacks and whites attended the formerly white high school. But in the rest of the country and in urban areas in the South, busing students across district attendance lines in order to eliminate the inherently "separate and unequal" classrooms was seen by the judiciary as the only means of facilitating desegregation. The decade was marked by unparalleled resistance on the part of many parents and politicians to this scheme. Rioting marked serious resistance to busing in Boston and Detroit, and by the decade's end many busing schemes had been abandoned.

A More Liberal Curriculum. The debate between educational traditionalists and progressives intensified during the 1970s. Traditionalists (sometimes called the back-to-basics proponents) argued that students learn best when given lots of structure, specific standards of performance, and a heavy dose of memorization of key facts and concepts. Progressives believed just as strongly that students need freedom and time to pursue questions that interest them, that sometimes structure is strictly for the convenience of the instructor and therefore hinders student learning. This debate reached a boiling point during the 1970s when more and more schools began to pursue an open or informal curriculum. With the publication of journalist and editor Charles Silberman's widely read *Crisis in the Classroom* (1970), this type of learning was introduced to the American public. It began in the primary schools, imitating the success of the impressive British infant schools in which primary children accomplished significant feats in reading and writing when allowed to work in areas of interest to them. Many professors of education taught prospective teachers about this curriculum, and many of these teachers poured into the schools, filling a national shortage of instructors that had begun in the 1960s. Soon the movement spread to high schools. A Gallup poll in 1972 showed that public approval for a nongraded curriculum (a form of free school) was at 71 percent and educators' approval rates were at 87 percent. Even college curricula underwent dramatic changes, with core requirements for degrees gradually being dropped in favor of more and more electives of interest to students.

The Conservative Backlash. By mid decade, the pendulum began to swing back toward a more traditional approach. When Harvard examined its curriculum in 1975 and Dean Henry Rosovsky suggested that a B.A. was becoming little more than a "certificate of attendance," Harvard began to reinstate core courses. Liberal educational thinker Jonathan Kozol expressed dissatisfaction with the free-school movement at the secondary level. As he put it, "If everyone is 'doing his own thing,' then why, coast-to-coast, is it the same kind of thing? Why is free choice so often the weaver's loom, tie-dye and macramé — why does organic growth turn out in every case to mean the potter's kiln? Why doesn't it ever mean a passionate and searching look into the system that makes such free schools possible?" By 1977 politicians responded to the traditionalists' concerns. As Alabama legislator Bill King explained, "Taxpayers see so much money going into education, yet producing students without basic skills. We legislators have to account for all that money." To produce just such an accounting, legislators in sixteen states instituted proficiency exams (in addition to coursework) as a bar to graduation for those who had not learned the fundamentals. The problem in defining exactly what educational skills were basic, however, remained. Many opponents of the conservative backlash despaired that all curriculum would be reduced to the minimum necessary to pass the proficiency exams.

Beyond Traditional versus Progressive. Michael A. Wallach, writing in *The Harvard Educational Review* in 1976, suggested that the significant problems in U.S. education stemmed from problems beyond the scope of the traditional versus progressive debate. He argued that either type of educational philosophy can be pursued thoughtlessly and incompetently. The traditional approach can require of the student rote memorization and parroting of authorities. These are symptoms of bad teaching, rather than necessary implications of the traditional approach. So, too, the progressive approach can be invoked as a shield for teacher lethargy and lack of planning. Calling the situation "pupil-centered," or devoted to "the whole child" can be an excuse to avoid the effort of developing and implementing a curriculum. Problems do not arise, Wallach suggested, because there are too many traditional and too few progressive schools. The problems arise because most schooling is of poor quality. Many critics agreed with Wallach that poor teaching in general was at the root of U.S. educational problems. They blamed this lack of quality control on both administrators and the teachers themselves. Students pursuing teaching degrees in the late 1960s and the 1970s came from the ranks of the lowest academic quartile, as measured by entrance exam scores such as the Scholastic Aptitude Test (SAT) and by performance in academia. Silberman, in *Crisis in the Classroom*, also indicated that lack of social status of the profession helped to bring on, as he put it, a "peculiar blight" on teaching which made the job debilitating. He listed possible causes for poor quality of teaching: an atmosphere of distrust; teaching loads providing no time for reflection, planning, or privacy; menial tasks such as patrol duty that deny professional status; an obsession with silence and lack of movement; or the inability to discuss problems or successes with colleagues. He argued that if schooling is of poor quality, it is not the teacher's fault alone. Two-thirds of parents in a Harris poll in the 1970s expressed the belief that "maintaining discipline is more important than student inquiry," thereby relegating teachers to the role of taskmaster.

Falling Enrollments. During the 1960s higher education underwent a period of continuous growth. Enrollments were up, funding was pouring in from federal sources, student attitudes were optimistic, and postgraduation opportunities abounded. The demand for students with doctorates was unprecedented, and colleges of education could not produce teachers fast enough to fill the nation's overcrowded classrooms. But the golden age of U.S. higher education ended in the 1970s, wrote Fred Hechinger in a 1976 essay called "Self Doubt in American Higher Education." The colleges at mid decade found themselves in something of a sophomore slump, as the social optimism of the 1960s turned into the economic pessimism of the 1970s. Higher education crossed a historic threshold into the unknown territory of no growth. Total enrollment at U.S. colleges rose less than 2 percent between 1972 and 1974, with minority attendance rising 11.7 percent during those years. Then, after twenty-eight consecutive years of growth, two years of decline in enrollment took place in 1975 and 1976. Many colleges were confused about their goals and purposes, as graduate programs turned out new doctorates into a job market with limited opportunities for everyone except those in the health professions. Suddenly the teaching positions from kindergarten through college were filled. In only a few years, economic and population trends undermined educational optimism and opportunity.

The "New Privatism" in Higher Education. Kenneth Keniston, editor of *Radicals and Militants: An Annotated Bibliography of Empirical Research on Campus Unrest* (1973), also pointed to a crisis in the hearts and minds of those militants who had helped to transform education in the 1960s. He called the mood the "New Privatism" — a detaching of the political and cultural aspects of the student revolt. While the political activity of the 1970s diminished and then ceased after the withdrawal of U.S. forces from Vietnam, the cultural critique of American society started in the late 1960s continued. The questioning of American public mores that began in the 1960s became, in the 1970s, private and psychological. The students admitted to college in 1973 were almost invari-

ably more cynical and self-absorbed than their older brothers and sisters. They had come to political consciousness during a period when the three Americans most admired by young people — John F. Kennedy, Robert E. Kennedy, and Martin Luther King, Jr. — all had been assassinated, when the country was involved in the most divisive war in history, and when campus protests were considered by many as the country's number one problem. Later in the decade these same students' faith in government would be shaken by the Watergate scandal. Their social and political assumptions undermined, many of these students turned inward, seeking to exercise some control over their private lives. College courses in yoga, Zen, and transcendental meditation proliferated. A great religious resurgence swept many campuses, and the Jesus movement gained many converts. Finally, the fact that college graduates of the late 1970s were entering an economy with fewer job prospects than at any time in the postwar period contributed to a sense of malaise in education.

Public Attitudes. The social disillusionment of the 1970s also penetrated the public schools. Carl Bereiter, in the essay "Schools Without Education" (1972), suggested that one could observe even among schoolchildren a "sophisticated detachment that is disastrous for the traditional school way of life. The word seems to have passed down from college to high school and now to the more with-it elementary school populations that a great deal of school work is pointless, that grades don't really tell how good you are, that school rituals are a subject for derision." Parents, responding to a 1972 Gallup poll of Public Attitudes Toward Education, mirrored their children's ambivalent feelings toward schooling. Of these respondents 64 percent disapproved of teacher tenure and only 22 percent said they would want their child to take up teaching, citing "scarce jobs" and "dangerous situations with kids running wild," as reasons. Problems in the system were numerous, and they named them (listed here in order of importance): discipline, integration, finance, teachers, facilities, and curriculum. Parents were, however, willing to shoulder some of the blame for students' poor performances; 61 percent of them claimed that children's home life was the primary reason for educational problems, whereas only 14 percent of the parents said it was the child's own fault. Because public schools not only mirror the configurations of the larger society but also contribute to maintaining them, the schools in the 1970s reflected the economic, racial, and social problems of the United States as a whole. Unfortunately, because schooling in the 1970s was marked by so much dissension, it did little to alleviate those problems.

Senate hearing, April 1978, at which Office of Management and Budget director James T. McIntyre announced President Carter's plan for a cabinet-level Department of Education

TOPICS IN THE NEWS

POLITICS AND FUNDING DURING THE NIXON-CARTER YEARS.

Questions about Great Society Programs. The decade began with some serious questioning of the unprecedented spending on education that had characterized the 1960s. President Richard Nixon's 1970 message on education reform signaled the beginning of a shift away from former president Lyndon Johnson's faith in education as a cornerstone of a Great Society. Nixon criticized some of Johnson's most highly touted compensatory education programs such as Head Start and Upward Bound. These programs, conceived to help impoverished students catch up with their middle-class peers, had made impressive gains, but testing showed those gains did not always last. President Nixon pleaded for further research into what really might work to help pull poor children up out of poverty. "We must stop congratulating ourselves for spending nearly as much money on education as does the rest of the world combined — $65 billion per year — when we are not getting as much as we should out of the dollars we spend," Nixon told Congress. Even more-liberal sources agreed that it would be wise to question the aim of spending. James Coleman, author of the 1966 federally commissioned report, *Equality of Educational Opportunity,* which criticized the impact of some anti-poverty programs, agreed with Daniel P. Moynihan, Democrat and education counselor to the president, that

the key factors in academic success remained the social backgrounds of the students themselves. "The social and economic environment of the home has more effect on what a child learns than the quality of the school he attends," commented Moynihan. Therefore, they lamented, despite some dramatic exceptions, there was growing evidence that most compensatory programs were not yet measurably improving the success of poor children in school.

The Fate of Great Society Programs. Because the Elementary and Secondary Education Act (ESEA) from its inception contained requirements for systematic evaluation of what programs worked and what programs did not, the decade was marked with the constant review of the effectiveness of federal programs in meeting the special educational needs of disadvantaged children. The results were not encouraging. In 1975, for example, a Rand educational policy study of the ESEA Title I evaluations (grants targeted for disadvantaged students) from 1965–1972 concluded that seven years and $52 million worth of evaluation efforts had produced dismal failure, an "empty ritual" that "may have done more harm than good." According to the study, the dual roots of failure were the multiple and diverse goals of such broadly aimed social-action programs and the federal system itself. In practice the U.S. Office of Education did not actually run Title I. Instead, thirty thousand local agencies administered these grants for the disadvantaged. The difficulty of overseeing these local agencies was significant. In his 1975 critique *Education in National Politics,* political scientist Norman Thomas gloomily suggested that ". . . the failure of Congress to exercise more careful and exacting oversight, and the inability of the Presidency to mount effective monitoring of the bureaucracy" had resulted in large gaps between educational objectives and actual results. Finally, the emerging suspicion that after a decade of operation, Title I and its associated compensatory educational programs had largely failed was reinforced in Julie Jeffrey's *Education for the Children of the Poor* in 1976. This book echoed established criticisms of the antipoverty war and of educational reform and refuted Johnson's view of education as "the only valid passport from poverty."

Continued Support. Despite the continued damning evaluations of Title I and plummeting SAT scores, many members of Congress, unwilling to explain to their constituents why they opposed education funding, supported the ESEA. In 1974 the House passed amendments strengthening the ESEA by a vote of 380–26, and in 1978, under the Carter administration, Congress approved a $50 billion, five-year reauthorization of the ESEA by smashing votes of 86–7 in the Senate and 350–20 in the House. At that time the Office of Education had the responsibility for pending these funds under the ESEA, with additional billions in spending on other programs such as Indian Education; Emergency School Aid (to meet problems arising from desegregation); Education for the Handicapped; Occupational, Vocational and Adult Education; Higher Education; Special Pro-

jects and Training (such as metric education, women's educational equity, and Teacher Corps); Student Loan Insurance Fund and Higher Education Facilities Loan and Insurance Fund; and Educational Activities Overseas.

Sources:

James Allan, Jr., "An Interview with James Allen," *Harvard Educational Review,* 40 (November 1970): 533;

"Delayed Impact," *Newsweek* (16 March 1970): 113;

Hugh Davis Graham, *The Uncertain Triumph: Federal Education Policy in the Kennedy and Johnson Years* (Chapel Hill: University of North Carolina Press, 1984), pp. 204–225;

Connaught Coyne Marshner, *Blackboard Tyranny* (New Rochelle, N.Y.: Arlington House, 1978).

FEDERAL EDUCATION LEGISLATION FOR THE HANDICAPPED

Equal Access for All Learners. In 1971 a state case in Pennsylvania set the stage for a dramatic change in the treatment of retarded (the term in use at the time) children's education. The state court threw out a law that had allowed school psychologists to declare some students uneducable and untrainable and provided for a free public education for the state's one hundred thousand retarded students aged six through twenty-one. At this time it was estimated that 62 percent of the intellectually and emotionally handicapped students in the United States were not receiving public education. The Vocational Rehabilitation Act of 1973 set in motion what was to become a major transformation of federal policy in public education when it mandated, "No handicapped individual shall be excluded from any program or activity receiving federal financial assistance." Since by this time every school district was receiving some funding through the ESEA, the implications were enormous for the public schools. In 1975, in order to clarify the schools' responsibilities, Public Law 94–142, better known as the Education for All Handicapped Children Act, was passed to guarantee all handicapped students a right to a free public education. This act applied to all children ages three through twenty-one who were physically handicapped, deaf, blind, mentally retarded, or emotionally disturbed. The act suggested that, when possible, these students be educated alongside nonhandicapped children.

Financial Implications of the Act. Although the states were obliged to provide this free education, the federal government provided only a modest amount of the necessary funding. A grant formula was devised in 1978 that provided states with a financial grant for each handicapped child equal to 5 percent of the national average educational expenditure per pupil per year. States also had to find, train, and hire special education teachers. Often, traditionally trained teachers with no background in special education found themselves dealing with children with special needs. Local agencies struggled to provide help in funding the extra costs of educating many children who previously had not attended public schools. Educational Turnkey Associates, a research firm, interviewed and visited eight hundred school districts in 1979 to assess the progress. During the years 1977 and 1978 most local districts reported that they had concerned themselves exclusively with federally mandated Individual Education Plans (IEPs), which had to be written for each handicapped child. Despite such efforts, 1978–1979 was proclaimed "the year of the lawyer" by district administrators who frequently found themselves in court dealing with parental challenges to placement decisions made by the schools.

Source:
Richard Van Scotter, *Public Schooling in America* (Santa Barbara, Cal.: ABC-CLIO, 1991).

FEDERAL AND STATE BILINGUAL EDUCATION POLICY

The Origins of Bilingual Education. Congress first passed the Bilingual Education Act in 1968, as Title VII of the revised ESEA, and it was renewed in 1974. In that same year the Supreme Court, in *Lau* v. *Nichols,* ruled in favor of a class-action suit brought by Chinese students, asserting that school districts serving substantial numbers of children with language deficiencies were violating the Civil Rights Act of 1964 if they did not do something special for these pupils. Similar court decisions were reached in cases featuring both Puerto Rican and Chicano plaintiffs, and in 1974 the revised Title VII provided further funding for the training of bilingual teachers. During the 1970s twenty states enacted local bilingual-education acts, a major shift in educational policy, especially since prior to 1968 many states had approved legislation requiring all public-school instruction to be conducted in English. In seven of those states teachers had formerly faced criminal penalties for conducting bilingual classes. Title VII changed all that, but because only nineteen hundred bilingual teachers were entering the field each year, and since it was estimated that twenty-four thousand bilingual teachers would be needed by the end of the 1970s, many school districts continued to struggle to provide bilingual instruction.

Controversy Over Bilingual Education. By mid decade questions began to arise about the efficacy of some bilingual education programs, especially those for Hispanic students. The United States Office of Education (USOE) reported in 1975–1976 that serious shortcomings existed in thirty-eight programs investigated by project directors. Students were staying in all-day bilingual programs long after they were able to function in English-speaking classes. These findings caused the USOE to tighten regulations for bilingual programs so that only students who were significantly limited in English were admitted. Also in 1976, a study by the American Institute for Research found that Hispanics in regular classes did about as well in general subjects as those in bilingual programs; students in bilingual programs did slightly better in math, but slightly worse in English classes. By 1979, when the program which had cost $7.5 million per

New York City public-school student from a Spanish-speaking home in his 1971 math class using Spanish-language text

year in 1968 had grown to a $150 million annual expenditure, the attacks grew significantly louder. Some claimed that extended dual-language programs threatened the "melting pot" function of the public schools. Editorial writers, including those from the *Washington Post* and the *New York Post,* criticized bilingual programs that kept students beyond the basic preparation for English-language classes.

Sources:
Alba N. Ambert, *Bilingual Education: a Sourcebook* (New York: Garland, 1985);

Hugh Davis Graham, *The Uncertain Triumph: Federal Education Policy in the Kennedy and Johnson Years* (Chapel Hill: University of North Carolina Press, 1984).

BUSING TO ACHIEVE DESEGREGATION

"With All Deliberate Speed." Busing as a means of transporting students to public schools was nothing new, with about 43 percent of the nation's schoolchildren riding buses each day in the years 1972–1973. Busing children from school to school in order to provide school districts with racial balance, however, was new. Busing for large-scale desegregation purposes was started in 1971, when the U.S. Supreme Court decided that many school districts had not complied with the 1954 *Brown* v. *Board of Education* decision and its 1955 follow-up, wherein the justices had ordered desegregation "with all deliberate speed." In the South that mandate had produced some "freedom of choice" plans under which students were technically free to choose any school in the district and hence provide racial balance; in practice, however, most students stayed where they were, and most school districts stayed segregated. By 1971, however, in *Swann* v. *Charlotte-Mecklenburg Board of Education* the Court decided that "all deliberate speed" had not been speedy enough. The school district of Charlotte, North Carolina, was ordered to bus its students across district lines to achieve desegregation. The justices reasoned that

A DESEGREGATION SUMMARY

In 1975 the National Institute of Research made public the following findings on desegregation. The spokesperson delivering the information to President Gerald Ford explained that these claims were backed up by "about 60 pounds of substantive documents":

1. Desegregation does not reduce achievement scores of whites. 2. Desegregation does slightly increase achievement scores of blacks. 3. White flight is a common phenomenon following desegregation. 4. Great differences in the severity of white flight exist from city to city; no known controls for the phenomenon have been found. 5. Some compensatory intervention can improve short-term scores of deprived children. 6. We have a growing knowledge of types of interventions and the appropriate developmental stage for those interventions. 7. People view schools as good if they contain significant numbers of middle-class students, regardless of race. 8. Within the limits of natural variations, differences in educational expenditures have little relationship to achievement.

Source: "Newsnotes," *Phi Delta Kappan,* 57 (December 1975): 289–290.

busing was warranted because the city and county in question had deliberately and knowingly taken steps in the past to frustrate the integration of their public schools.

Busing Outside the South. Although most court desegregation decisions in the 1960s were focused on the South, during the 1970s orders for busing took place all over the United States. Soon after the Charlotte case, a district court judge in Colorado ruled that even though there was no state policy of segregation, minority schools in Denver were inferior to the white schools there — by virtue of their being minority schools. Following the reasoning of *Brown,* the Colorado courts argued that separate is inherently unequal and that Denver schools must redress their racial imbalance. The Supreme Court eventually upheld this argument in *Keyes* v. *School District No. 1,* and busing was instituted in Denver. However, the next landmark case was the 1974 *Milliken* v. *Bradley* decision, in which the Supreme Court by a 5–4 vote struck down a district-court ruling which required busing between Detroit's black schools and suburban white schools. The majority reasoned that the suburban districts were not engaging in de jure segregation, and thus no interdistrict remedy was necessary. However, a year later the same Supreme Court ruled just the opposite in Delaware and mandated busing to mix white suburban

schools of New Castle County with those of Wilmington, which were 85 percent black.

More Busing, More Resistance. Throughout the decade the courts ordered compulsory busing in several cities, despite the legal difficulty of proving that segregation had resulted from de jure causes and not from de facto situations such as housing patterns. In some cities the past policies of the Federal Housing Authority and the Veterans' Administration, which had formerly encouraged segregated housing patterns, had helped create the segregated neighborhoods of the 1970s. In Louisville, Cleveland, Los Angeles, and Indianapolis, black students from the cities were bused to white suburban schools. These policies were soon followed by growing resistance by many parents to programs that attempted to go beyond merely forbidding discrimination. Proponents of busing argued that these measures were necessary to compensate blacks and other minorities for generations of segregation. Debates were long and loud, and in Boston the 1974 court-ordered busing plan was disrupted by violence and a boycott by white students. South Boston High School was eventually put under federal receivership because of neighborhood resistance to busing.

The Effects of Busing. Appraisals of the success of court-ordered busing were mixed. Sometimes even the same evaluators came up with different opinions. For example, in April 1975 James Coleman, author of the *Coleman Report,* declared that busing was a failure, claiming that enforced desegregation had pushed white kids out of city schools, actually causing more segregation. Coleman spoke again in July of 1975, revising his white flight thesis after a new analysis. Then, in a third paper in August 1975, he noted that loss of white students "proceeds at a relatively rapid rate with or without desegregation." Finally, in December 1975 he equivocated: "What is not clear now is whether desegregation itself induces increased movement of whites. . . ." Even Christopher Jencks, an educator who favored busing as a tool of economic equalization regardless of its educational merits, recognized questions about forced busing. As he put it, "If the 14th Amendment means anything, it means we must guarantee black children the right to attend desegregated schools if they want to do so, even when it involves busing blacks to schools in white neighborhoods where whites do not want them. Busing whites to schools in black neighborhoods is another story. This is not a clear or moral issue." What was clear was the cost of the plans. Two years of forced busing cost Boston about $56.6 million, and Boston residents saw a $53 annual tax increase per $1,000 of their property. In five months Detroit spent $11 million on busing, excluding police costs.

Public Opinion on Busing. Public opposition to busing was overwhelming. A Harris survey found in 1972 that 73 percent of the public was opposed to busing; only 20 percent favored it. In 1976 a Roper poll asked voters, "Suppose a candidate took stands that you agreed with on all but one of these issues. Which one issue on the list would be most likely to turn you away from him if you disagreed with his stand on the issue?" Roper found that more than any other, busing was just such a deeply felt issue: 22 percent of those polled said school busing for racial integration would be crucial for them; only 20 percent perceived inflation as vital, and only 13 percent rated abortion as so decisive an issue.

Sources:
"Coleman on the Griddle," *Time* (12 April 1976): 79;

Christopher Jencks, "Busing — The Supreme Court Goes North," *New York Times Magazine,* 19 November 1972, p. 26;

"Let's Make It Work," *Newsweek* (12 February 1973): 71;

Connaught Coyne Marshner, *Blackboard Tyranny* (New Rochelle, N.Y.: Arlington House Publishers, 1978).

THE LITERACY CRISIS

America Learns of the Problem. The debate over literacy and basic skills began in the early 1970s and heated to the boiling point by the middle of the decade. In late 1975 *Newsweek* ran a cover story on the back-to-basics movement occasioned by the fact that "nationwide, the statistics on literacy grow more appalling each year. . . . Willy-nilly, the U.S. educational system is spawning a generation of semi-literates." *Newsweek* writers attempted to define "Why Johnny Can't Write." Their opening paragraph, outlining the problem, was alarmist:

> If your children are attending college, the chances are that when they graduate they will be unable to write ordinary, expository English with any degree of structure

and lucidity. If they are in high school and planning to attend college, the chances are less than even that they will be able to write English at the minimal college level when they get there. If they are not planning to attend college, their skills in writing English may not even qualify them for secretarial or clerical work. If they are attending elementary school, they are almost certainly not being given the kind of required reading material, much less writing instruction, that might make it possible for them to eventually write comprehensible English.

The SATs Plummet. U.S. students' SAT scores spiraled to their lowest point in twelve years in 1975. Former commissioner of education Sidney Marland had taken over as head of the College Board in 1975, and his statement that he was appointing a big-name panel to "do all that we can to investigate and interpret this phenomenon to the public" made front-page headlines of newspapers all over the country. Concern about declining test scores had also been mounting outside the College Board. The National Institute of Education (NIE) held a special conference on the decline, but the researchers who met in Washington in June 1975 could not reach a consensus on what the score declines meant. Their report, which claimed that the test scores did not represent a general collapse in literacy, cast doubt about exactly what the SAT measured and whether it accurately reflected student skills. Because the SAT was the gatekeeper to all the best universities, public attention was focused on the question of whether the test takers or the test makers were to blame for the problem. There was great confusion on the part of the public as to what the SAT actually measured. The exam was defined by its creators as an aptitude test — measuring innate abilities — for which cramming would do no good. During the literacy crisis debate, however, many back-to-basics advocates heralded it as an achievement test, whose declining scores were irrefutable evidence that students were not achieving and could not write, even though test takers did not have to write an essay.

Why Did Scores Fall? Nearly everyone, from parents to researchers, suggested causes for the decline in test scores and for the possible decline in literacy. Many conservatives were convinced that schooling innovations during the 1960s and early 1970s had been at fault. Many argued that permissive education — too little reading and writing, too many soft electives, and too few required academic courses; too much politics and too little rigor — was the culprit. Even in the 1970s, however, the vast majority of public schools were still traditional in nature. Christopher Jencks, who reviewed the test-score decline in 1978, found that "secondary school students took more academic courses in 1970-1 than they had in 1960-1." There was a slight decline in the number of academic courses taken in 1972-1973, but essentially the charge that the curriculum had been watered down was not proven. Even some liberals agreed, however, that the new countercultural activism that had filtered down to high

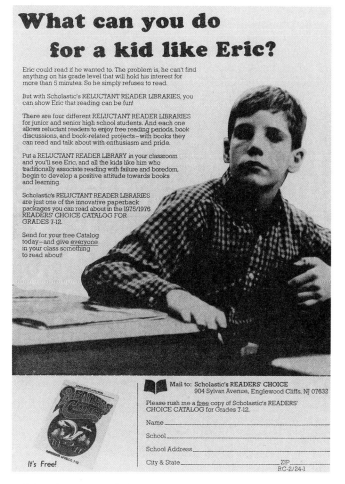

What can you do for a kid like Eric?

Eric could read if he wanted to. The problem is, he can't find anything on his grade level that will hold his interest for more than 5 minutes. So he simply refuses to read.

But with Scholastic's RELUCTANT READER LIBRARIES, you can show Eric that reading can be fun!

There are four different RELUCTANT READER LIBRARIES for junior and senior high school students. And each one allows reluctant readers to enjoy free reading periods, book discussions, and book-related projects – with books they can read and talk about with enthusiasm and pride.

Put a RELUCTANT READER LIBRARY in your classroom and you'll see Eric, and all the kids like him who traditionally associate reading with failure and boredom, begin to develop a positive attitude towards books and learning.

Scholastic's RELUCTANT READER LIBRARIES are just one of the innovative paperback packages you can read about in the 1975/1976 READERS' CHOICE CATALOG FOR GRADES 7-12.

Send for your free Catalog today – and give everyone in your class something to read about!

Mail to: Scholastic's READERS' CHOICE
904 Sylvan Avenue, Englewood Cliffs, NJ 07632

Please rush me a free copy of Scholastic's READERS' CHOICE CATALOG for Grades 7-12.

Name

School

School Address

City & State   ZIP

It's Free!   RC-2/24-1

Advertisement by Scholastic Press for materials to aid in the teaching of slow readers

schools embodied an anti-intellectualism of its own. According to Christopher Lasch, a leftist social critic, the demand for abolition of grades in academic courses masqueraded as "high pedagogical principle" but in actuality reflected a "desire for less work and a wish to avoid judgment on its quality." Others blamed the decline in test scores on too much television and an unstable family life. Most testing experts suspected that another explanation was closer to the truth: that more people from non-traditional, nonscholastic backgrounds were simply going to college in greater numbers. The SAT was therefore no longer testing an elite within society. Richard Ohmann explained it this way: "More students who used to leave school before senior year are taking the tests. . . . Young women are less excluded from education now that ten years ago; presumably this new group is less well prepared than the women who used to choose higher education. If so, the 'decline in literacy' translates partly into an increase in equality and social justice." Regardless of the cause or causes of the SAT decline, the phenomenon set off a wave of new standardized testing regimes around 1977. During that year twenty-nine states moved toward competency-based skill programs, with minimum achievement goals tested from grade to grade. Eventually

two-thirds of the states adopted such plans. Politicians and parents demanded that skills, drills, and tests fix the literacy crisis.

Sources:

Christopher Jencks, "What's Behind the Drop in Test Scores?" *Working Papers* (July–August 1978);

Christopher Lasch, *The Culture of Narcissism* (New York: Norton 1978);

Ira Shor, *Culture Wars: School and Society in the Conservative Restoration 1969–1984* (Boston: Routledge & Kegan Paul, 1986);

"Why Johnny Can't Write," *Newsweek* (8 December 1975): 58.

TEXTBOOKS UNDER FIRE

First Stirrings of Trouble. Mel and Norma Gabler, citizens of Hawkins, Texas, began a crusade for textbook censorship in 1961 when their son brought home a history text that the Gablers examined and found filled with "unpatriotic and anti-Christian teachings." From a modest beginning in an Austin school board hearing that year, the couple ignited a firestorm of national criticism of educational publishing companies. At its height in the mid 1970s this protest affected the textbook selection process throughout the United States; most of the serious debates, however, were concentrated in the twenty-two states — mostly in the South and Southwest — where textbooks had to be approved by state, rather than local, authorities.

Objections. The Gablers expressed the feelings of thousands of their supporters when they summarized their campaign as an assault on the "deviousness and danger of textbooks which are gradually but effectively directing student minds away from basic Christian values." To the Gablers, modern textbooks were too relativistic, "questioning anything fixed or absolute," and undermining "traditional, basic, biblical, exact values." Although the Gablers' opponents pointed out that children learned their values from an infinite number of sources besides textbooks, the Gablers ironically used the promotional claims of textbook publishers to reinforce their contention that textbooks had inordinate sway over the minds of young Americans. They quoted D. C. Heath, one of the larger publishers, as reportedly having said "Let me publish the textbooks of the nation and I care not who writes its songs or makes its laws," and they reasserted McGraw-Hill president Alexander Burke's contention that "public opinion is shaped by textbooks."

The Movement Grows. In 1972 a huge news flap over one chapter in Macmillan's *Search for Freedom*, a fifth-grade U.S. history text, gave the movement international coverage and assured televised publicity for the campaign. In testimony before the Texas Textbook Committee hearing, Norma Gabler objected that the book was irreligious, equating Cesar Chavez, Martin Luther King, Jr., and Mohandas Gandhi with Jesus Christ, while omitting to explain that "Benjamin Franklin once used prayer to calm a troublesome Constitutional Convention." She furthermore objected that the text devoted 6 1/2 pages to

Marilyn Monroe while it barely discussed George Washington. "Is Texas ready for Marilyn to become the mother of our country?" she asked, gaining instantaneous media attention and landing her on the front page of many U.S. newspapers.

From Textbooks to Curriculum. The Gablers' media savvy and quotability gained them thousands of new followers and forced textbook publishers into costly revisions of their books. These successes emboldened the Gablers to challenge school curricula in reading, writing, math, biology, psychology, and sociology courses. As did other proponents of "basic education," the Gablers opposed the "whole word" approach to teaching reading, preferring instead purely phonics-based instruction. They opposed writing programs that emphasized self-expression and imagination over grammatical correctness as eroding standards of language usage. They attacked "new math" out of fear that "such abstract teaching to young minds will tend to destroy the students' belief in absolutes — to believe that nothing is concrete." Finally, the Gablers and their supporters scrutinized biology, psychology, and sociology courses for objectionable discussions of homosexuality and what they considered sexually deviant behavior, succeeding in restricting candid consideration of these topics and eliminating whole sections of textbooks that addressed such issues.

West Virginian Protests. The movement inspired by the Gablers hit a peak in 1974 in West Virginia when Alice Moore, a first-term member of the Kanawha County Board of Education, challenged texts which "attacked the social values that make up civilization." After extensive media coverage, supporters of Moore protested by keeping home more than ten thousand of their children on the first day of school. The next day, thirty-five hundred miners launched a wildcat strike in sympathy with the protest movement. Exchanges of gunfire occurred around schools; cars, homes, and schools were firebombed. Eight thousand protesters marched in Charleston, the state capital, but National Education Association officials, after investigating the controversy, concluded that allowing the protesters to change textbook and curriculum guidelines would "impose upon the public schools the task of indoctrinating students to one system of cultural and religious values, inflexible and unexamined."

Liberal Criticism. The conservative scrutiny of textbooks inspired liberals, especially within academia, to conduct their own review of texts. Contrary to the Gablers, many argued that schoolbooks were biased toward conservative interests, especially in their wholehearted approval of American business and industry. Citing a study of seventeen well-known secondary texts used in Newark and New York City, historian Jean Anyon argued that "the priorities of specific groups now powerful in the U.S. industrial hierarchy are expressed by the content and structure in the social studies curricula provided by these texts."

A nun teaching in a parochial school. During the 1970s parochial-school teachers earned about 50 percent less than public-school teachers.

Outcome. Debates continued over school texts and curricula during the 1970s, but it appeared that the protest movement had made significant impact when U.S. Commissioner of Education Terrell H. Bell told the Association of American Publishers in a 1974 speech that some of their texts seemed to emphasize violence, obscenity, and moral judgments that ran counter to tradition. He called on publishers to concentrate on "good literature that will appeal to children without relying too much on blood and guts and street language for their own sake."

RELIGIOUS SCHOOLING DURING THE 1970s

Enrollment in Catholic Schools. The once-strong urban systems of parochial schools in the United States suffered a setback during the 1970s. Administrators of Catholic schools faced problems on three fronts: student enrollment, finances, and personnel. According to the United States Office of Education (USOE) figures, during the ten-year period from 1961 to 1971 public-school enrollment was up 22.5 percent while parochial school enrollment was down 8.1 percent. The National Catholic Education Association reported a steady decline in enrollments in nearly all areas of the United States from the peak enrollment years of 1965–1966. During 1970 twelve Catholic schools closed in Chicago and Detroit alone, with over fifty thousand students transferring to the public systems there. Elementary parochial schools closed nationwide at the rate of one per day in 1970–1971, and 135 Catholic high schools closed or consolidated themselves according to USOE reports. The rate of closings slowed down in 1976, and by 1978, as a result of increasing numbers of black students in urban areas entering

TRANSCENDENTAL MEDITATION IN THE PUBLIC SCHOOLS

Experiments with teaching students transcendental meditation (TM) as a way to tap into "creative intelligence" were a dramatic example of the impact of 1960s counterculture on 1970s education. As the Maharishi Mahesh Yogi, the foremost proponent of the practice, explained, "New disciples of the Science of Creative Intelligence [SCI] turn their attention inward toward subtler levels of a thought until the mind transcends the experience of the subtlest state of the thought and arrives at the source of that thought." The promise was that the attainment of higher states of consciousness, and correspondingly more profound levels of knowledge, could be within reach of anyone through the practice of transcendental meditation. Some educators and scientists agreed: the Illinois House of Representatives formally encouraged all educational institutions in that state to study the feasibility of courses in TM and SCI, and the National Institute of Mental Health awarded a grant of $121,540 to help train 120 secondary-school teachers to teach SCI in U.S. high schools. Inevitably, the practice faced resistance from those who felt the emphasis was on religion, rather than education, and the movement disappeared from most schools by the end of the decade.

Source: Paul Levine, "TM and the Science of Creative Intelligence," *Phi Delta Kappan*, 46 (December 1972): 231–235.

parochial schools for the first time, the decline eased significantly. Also, in some urban centers such as Boston, there was actually white flight into the parochial schools after school desegregation there.

Personnel Problems. During the 1970s many remaining parochial schools struggled to staff their classes. Because of an overall decline in the number of young people becoming members of religious orders, there was a far smaller pool of talent emerging from the seminaries. Moreover, many of those teachers who had entered religious service found new jobs in and out of their orders. In Chicago, for example, one thousand religious teachers in orders dropped out of the Archdiocese of Chicago parochial schools in the three-year period ending in 1971. Laymen, who replaced many seminary-trained teachers, were much quicker to protest wage inequities than those in holy orders. In New York in 1970, parochial school wages ranged from $4,600 to $8,000, compared to $6,750 to $13,750 for teachers in public schools. In that year, only settlement on a $800 raise for lay teachers averted a planned walkout of parochial school teachers in New York.

Causes. Parochial schools, although the recipients of some highly contested federal funds during the Kennedy-Johnson years, were essentially left out of much of the funding that was pouring into public schools. And even though religious schools' tuition remained modest, many parents in the cities wondered if the education were worth the cost. Catholic schools, too, suffered from the white flight that took many middle-class families out of inner-city neighborhoods into the suburbs during the 1970s. Curricular innovations in the public schools, such as the open classroom and more electives, attracted parochial students. Finally, many families were simply moving away from orthodoxy. As a Milwaukee parent and parochial-school graduate explained, "We want our children to learn that there are other good people in the world besides Catholics."

Christian Schools and Academies. Denominational schools, unlike Catholic schools, grew in enrollment during the decade, with Lutherans and Baptists nearly doubling their numbers of students. But the real story was the Christian school, a new type of institution that flourished mainly in the South and Midwest, where in many cases the church buildings themselves served as campuses. Often springing up overnight after federally enforced desegregation, these academies were not supported by one church or denomination. Most served only white families from several churches, and it was not unusual for these schools, with no accreditation whatsoever, to be staffed by volunteer teachers with few credentials, who were wedded to a Fundamentalist Christian curricula. The Tabernacle Christian School in Ohio made headlines in 1974 when its pastor-principal Levi Whisner and twelve other parents were criminally prosecuted and convicted for operating a school which lacked a state charter; the Ohio Supreme Court reversed the conviction in 1976. Eventually, an organization was formed to charter these new schools. By 1976 the American Association of Christian Schools reported 320 member schools with sixteen thousand students and another 125 affiliated schools working on achieving full membership.

Sources:
"Crisis of Confidence," *Newsweek* (2 February 1970): 76;

Connaught Coyne Marshner, *Blackboard Tyranny* (New Rochelle, N.Y.: Arlington House, 1978).

OPEN-ADMISSIONS POLICIES IN HIGHER EDUCATION

College for All? During the late 1960s and the 1970s, many colleges and universities experimented with an open-admissions policy — one that would allow any high-school graduate to matriculate. Although many state universities in the Midwest and in California had for generations accepted all applicants from within a given state, applicants generally faced stiff entrance requirements. Open admissions in the 1970s was different. The primary goal of these programs was to increase minority enrollment, to provide equity in education to that segment of the population which had been traditionally underrepresented in higher education. One of the most ambitious programs was undertaken by the City University of New York (CUNY) system, which offered free tuition, changes in grading and coursework, and remedial and compensatory services in 1970 to any secondary-school graduate who enrolled. Fully one-fourth of the thirty-five-thousand-member class of 1970 previously would not have been admitted due to academic deficiencies. Timothy Healy, CUNY vice-chancellor for academic affairs, explained the shift in policy: "The university can short-circuit the terrible rhythm of disappointment and rage that locks our inner-city youth out of careers, robs them of a stake in our city, and can create a new race of barbarians more terrible than the Goths and the Vandals." Healy promised in 1970 that the CUNY system (nine four-year campuses and eight two-year community colleges) would offer "no dilution of the educational experience. The diploma from CUNY must have integrity." This experiment and many others like it, however, offered mixed results at best.

Results. The programs did increase minority participation in higher education. At CUNY, for example, minority enrollment in 1975 reached 36.6 percent, compared to the pre-1970 average of 18.8 percent. However, after five years of experimentation with open admissions, most professors and many students deemed the plan a failure in many respects. At Manhattan Community College (MCC), for example, grade inflation had eradicated the meaning of student assessment. Prof. Barnard Bard suggested that "marks bore no relationship to performance and teachers were told to pass students along." At MCC in 1976 it was impossible to choose a valedictorian because fourteen students had perfect averages, whereas only one or two had achieved such feats before open admissions. Brooklyn high-school principal Henry Hillson complained, and many of his peers agreed, that the open-admissions policy was seriously undercutting the motivation to perform in secondary school. Another trend that researchers noted was that the students with the best high-school averages were, by 1975, the least likely to attend open-admissions schools, leaving schools such as CUNY without its traditional backbone of eager, upwardly mobile lower-middle-class students.

What Went Wrong. According to Barry Castro, a faculty member who studied the relative failure of the open-admissions program at Eugenio Maria de Hostos Community College in the south Bronx, there were several root causes. At this institution, where fewer than 15 percent of the six hundred students who entered in 1970 graduated on time, students were conscious of deficiencies in basic skills, Castro suggested, but they were frightened to face those problems. "They could dream about desirable career goals as teachers, lawyers, or doctors. However, once they actually were committed to study, their generally limited abilities to read or to do simple mathematics broke the illusions apart." Because this realization was likely to be a crushing experience, many stu-

dents used self-pacing as a convenient means of deferring it, sticking with the remedial courses as long as possible. As Bard, who participated in the plan at CUNY, explained, "Obviously, the time to get the basics is before entering, not after."

Three Faculty Approaches. Castro suggested that professors generally took one of three approaches to the problems presented by underprepared students. One group tried coercion or the imposition of traditional scholastic disciplines. These professors insisted that the students had to recognize their own deficiencies in not understanding lectures, failing tests, or writing incoherent essays — or the students could accept traditional censures in the form of no-credit reports for the courses. Since the latter was less painful, many students simply reenrolled in courses again and again, doing no better each time because they quit rather than face the difficulties. A second group of professors watered down course content and made tests easier, arguing the necessity of the need to reinforce the students with some feelings of success. However, as Castro reports, most students were fully aware that standards were being changed, and this reinforced only a further sense of failure. Castro ascribed purely political motives to a third group of faculty. Because these teachers believed that it was "impossible to teach in the context of a society in which classism and racism is [sic] so deeply rooted," their goal was to abandon teaching altogether and to work for radical social change. This group of professors created a cadre of students who would return to their own communities as activists for social change. Because none of the above approaches was particularly successful in educating students with real learning deficiencies, the notion that nothing could be done became a self-fulfilling prophecy, "an apology for irresponsibility," as Castro put it. Although many minority students did enter the world of higher education through the open-admissions policies of the 1970s, by the end of the decade many institutions began to require more-academic high school coursework for admission, and many discontinued the practice of awarding academic credit for remedial courses once students were in college.

Sources:
"An Account of the Open Admissions Experiment at CUNY," in *Education in the U.S: A Documentary History*, edited by Sol Cohen (Los Angeles: UCLA Press, 1974);

Bernard Bard, "College for All: Dream or Disaster?" *Phi Delta Kappan*, 56 (February 1975): 390–395;

Barry Castro, "Hostos: Report from a Ghetto College," *Harvard Education Review*, 44 (May 1974): 270–294.

MINORITY-ADMISSIONS POLICIES: BEFORE AND AFTER BAKKE

Minority-Admissions Policies. Many universities, graduate schools, and professional schools established special minority-admissions programs during the 1970s to assure equal opportunities to students who were either economically or educationally disadvantaged. Even in

A 1978 demonstration in front of the Supreme Court protesting the Bakke decision

schools where special-admissions policies were not made public, many admissions officers reserved the right to select students who would provide for a diverse student body. These policies were examined by the Supreme Court near the end of the decade in the *Regents of the University of California* v. *Bakke* decision, and legal guidelines were established that in many ways upheld special consideration for minority applicants.

The University of California, Davis. When a new medical school opened at the Davis campus of the University of California system in 1968, the minority population of that state was 23 percent, yet no black, Mexican-American or Native American student was admitted into the entering class (three Asian students were admitted). After 1971, however, a special-admissions program set aside sixteen seats for students who could be considered "economically or educationally disadvantaged," and a check-off box was included on the admissions form for such students to identify themselves. Although race was not a stated consideration of the program, no white student was ever admitted under the policy. The policy began to change the make-up of the medical-school class: between 1970 and 1974, of 452 students admitted, 27 were black and 39 were Mexican-American. Without the special-admissions considerations, only one black student and six Mexican-Americans would have been accepted. Each applicant was assigned a benchmark score — a composite of his or her interview, grade-point ratio from undergraduate school, grade-point ratio of science

courses, Medical Comprehensive Achievement Test scores, letters of recommendation, and personal background. Each of the above criteria was rated on a scale. Allen Bakke, a white Vietnam veteran, applied in 1973, receiving a total score of 468 of a possible 500. No general-admissions applicant with a score under 470 was accepted in 1973, however. Bakke reapplied in 1974, this time receiving a score of 549 out of a possible 600. He was not admitted, even though in both years applicants with lower scores were accepted through the special-admissions policy. Bakke sued the university, claiming he had been denied admission on the basis of race, a practice which violated Article I of the California Constitution, the Fourteenth Amendment of the U.S. Constitution, and Title VI of the Civil Rights Act of 1964.

The Bakke Decision. On 28 June 1978 the Supreme Court ruled in favor of Bakke, striking down the University of California, Davis, admissions policy. The decision affected admissions decisions nationwide. Even though Bakke was ordered admitted to Davis, the Supreme Court upheld the constitutionality of special minority admissions, maintaining that only rigid quotas for minority admissions were illegal. The University of California, Davis, violated Supreme Court guidelines with the rigid number of sixteen places set aside for minorities, with no provisions for enlarging the overall number of students accepted. In the last two years of the decade many graduate and professional schools reconfigured their admissions policy to meet the *Bakke* guidelines. For example, Rutgers School of Law reserved 30 percent of their seats in 1979 admissions for disadvantaged students, both white and black. The prevailing rule for admissions officials was no inflexible quotas and no students barred from competing solely on the basis of race. The Supreme Court decision on Bakke's case was thus not a legal command to dismantle affirmative-action programs. Instead, it presented a green light for going ahead with more carefully conceived plans to encourage diversity without creating an uneven playing field.

Source:
John Sexton, "Minority Admissions Programs After Bakke," *Harvard Educational Review*, 49 (August 1979): 313–339.

PROGRESS FOR WOMEN IN EDUCATION

Women and Education. When Harvard president Nathan Pusey realized the Vietnam draft would reduce the numbers of young men applying to graduate schools, he said, "We shall be left with the blind, the lame and the women." Although Pusey was speaking tongue-in-cheek, his comments reflected much of the reality of women's status in the field of education in 1970. At his institution there were no tenured women professors. At Yale, alumni responded positively to the administration's refusal to admit fifty more women, cheering when officials announced, "We are all for women, but Yale must produce a thousand male leaders every year." The January 1970 issue of the *American Association of University Women's*

Journal reported that a majority of the three thousand men who had responded to a survey believed that a woman's first responsibility was to be a feminine companion and mother; that women had less need to achieve in the world than men; and that the job turnover rate and sick-leave rate of women was higher than that of men. The general rule about women in education at this time was "the higher, the fewer." Although women made up 67 percent of the educational workforce, they accounted for fewer than 16 percent of administration, including 0.6 percent of superintendents. In higher education fewer than 1 percent of presidents of colleges and universities were women. However, women in education were beginning to organize for change, to combat the dearth of role models in leadership positions, and to create equity at all levels of the education community. These efforts ranged from changing elementary textbooks in order to eliminate gender bias to increasing the numbers of women faculty members in higher education. More important, the movement hoped to emphasize the necessity for a woman to be educated so as to have options in her life. As the UCLA dean of women Nola Stark suggested, "When you take a bright girl and make her 'happy' by letting her mind rot, you've got a problem."

Curricular Changes. Studies of school texts showed that sexual stereotypes start early. In most elementary basal readers (the primary literature of most schools at the time) white mommies in aprons stayed home and ironed, while daddies went off to work and then came home to solve key family crises such as lost balloons or downed kites. Women were all but absent in the curriculum of secondary and postsecondary schools. However, during the 1970s this changed dramatically. During the decade more than five thousand school-teachers wrote to the Feminist Press for information on elementary- and secondary-school course changes. By the decade's end hundreds of courses and programs in women's studies had been established in higher education. As early as 1974, 4,990 courses in women's studies were taught by 2,225 faculty members at 995 institutions of higher learning. From 1974 to 1979 the number of programs on campuses tripled, with some large programs offering from 75 to 100 courses annually.

What Is Women's Studies? The curricula in most women's studies programs, whether housed in separate departments or simply offered as adjunct courses in traditional fields, were predicated on teaching students, both men and women, to understand one or more of the following issues:

> Patriarchy in historical perspective; biological/psychological gender differences; socialization and sex roles; women in history; post-Freudian psychology and control of female sexuality; the history and function of the family; women in the workforce and the economy; laws affecting women; the history of women in social movements.

Illustration from a basal reader criticized for promoting sexual stereotypes

By the end of the decade nearly every campus offered one or more courses in which women wrote the texts, taught the courses, and offered insights into heretofore ignored perspectives on traditional subject matter.

Title IX and Other Statutes. Title IX of the Educational Amendments Act of 1972, which guaranteed equal access for women in the academic world and in athletics, was another milestone for women in education. Rep. Shirley Chisholm, in a 1979 interview, explained that Title IX was never intended to be a literal dollar-for-dollar guarantee of financial equity in women's programs and athletics, but it was intended to provide equal access to athletic participation for women. It did far more. Cindy Brown, deputy director of the Office of Civil Rights at Health, Education, and Welfare (HEW), reported on a 1978 study that had been done of ten major universities and their compliance with Title IX. Every university in the study had upgraded women's athletic programs, with the ones who had the biggest, most successful programs for men making the greatest efforts in achieving strong programs for women. In addition to Title IX, two other statutes mandated improved educational opportunities for women: the Women's Equity Act, providing funds to eliminate sexual bias and stereotyping; and an amendment to the Vocational Education

Meeting of the Wilmington, Delaware, American Federation of Teachers Local 762 in fall 1977 after the members voted to strike

Act of 1976, requiring that all federal education programs mainstream sexual equity concerns. Due in part to the organized women's movement and in part to the statutory powers of acts such as those above, by the end of the 1970s women had made significant strides in achieving more meaningful status at all levels of education.

Sources:
"An Interview on Title IX," *Harvard Educational Review,* 49 (November 1979): 504–509;

Ann Harris, "Second Sex in Academe," *American Association of University Women Bulletin,* 56 (1970): 283–284;

Florence Howe, "An Introduction: The First Decade of Women's Studies," *Harvard Educational Review,* 49 (November 1979): 489–503;

"Women Profs Fight Back," *Newsweek* (17 May 1971): 99.

TEACHER ORGANIZATIONS AND POLITICS IN THE 1970s

The NEA and the AFT. In the 1970s two of the most powerful organizations for teachers, the National Education Association (NEA) and the American Federation of Teachers (AFT), gained power and prominence as a result of the political turmoil surrounding federal funding of education. The AFT is a union affiliated with the American Federation of Labor and Congress of Industrial Organizations (AFL-CIO), which had a long history of militancy on behalf of its teacher members, most of whom were located in the Northeast. The NEA refers to itself as a professional organization, dominated by administrators, despite the fact that teachers comprised the bulk of the membership. A shift in power within the NEA occurred early in the decade when the AFT began to make inroads among the membership of the NEA, and the professional organization was moved to lobby more forcefully on behalf of its teacher-members in order to keep them in the fold. In 1973, in reaction to this shift in policy, the American Association of School Administra-

tors loosened its ties with the NEA, and other management groups did likewise; and the NEA gained a distinctly antiadministrator bias. During the 1970s the NEA became the world's largest professional organization with 1.8 million members (including members through state affiliates); the AFT had around 450,000 members. The NEA had the larger budget, about $34.5 million; the AFT, less than $10 million.

The NEA Becomes Politically Active. The NEA's Political Action Committee (NEAPAC) raised funds every other year to support candidates with similar points of view on education. In 1976 the NEA endorsed for the first time a presidential candidate, Jimmy Carter, who repaid their support by upgrading the Office of Education, formerly a part of HEW, to the Department of Education, thereby giving education cabinet-level prominence. During the decade the NEA Representative Assembly also passed resolutions that went far beyond their traditional interests in education. Whereas in the 1960s resolutions were concerned with academic freedom, censorship, integration, sex education, and teacher retirement, during the 1970s the NEA changed its focus, stating in its 1976 legislative program that:

> NEA believes that a significant part of the education process takes place outside the traditional school structure and that the NEA has a responsibility to see that the other influences experienced by students of all ages are conducive to healthy development of the individual within a just and humane society.

Expanding upon this philosophy, the NEA encouraged federal legislation providing child-care services, advocated strengthening the United Nations, urged federal welfare programs improved to "standards of human dignity," promoted changing the process of federal education appointments, won collective bargaining rights for teachers everywhere in the nation, reformed school financing so that the federal government contributes at least one-third the cost of public education, and supported reducing the federal defense budget with the reduction to be applied directly to the funding of public education. By the end of the decade the NEA's shift to a more political organization with much larger societal goals was complete, and their lobbying and political powers were at an all-time high.

Benefits for Teachers. Statistics seem to show that this political strength paid off for teachers during the 1970s. For example, even though student population numbers went down from 1971 to 1978, the number of teachers actually went up. In the 1975–1976 school year, according to NEA figures, 0.5 percent more teachers were employed than in the previous year. This higher employment happened during a year of high inflation and national unemployment. Figures published in the *Phi Delta Kappan* show the average salary for classroom teachers that year, a time of national recession, was $12,524, some 7.4 percent more than in 1974–1975. Some of these concessions could be related to collective-bargaining powers. For example, even though many states enacted strong laws against strikes by public employees, during the 1975–1976 school year there were 203 teacher strikes, of which there were 137 by NEA affiliates, and 61 by AFT affiliates. The Census Bureau, which noted that teachers were the most organized public employees in the United States, also reported that as early as 1973–1974 teachers were striking more than other state and local government employees. Teachers in unions and in powerful organizations such as the NEA transformed themselves during the 1970s from docile employees to much more active political entities.

The Union's Financial Power. Teacher organizations exerted other types of power in the 1970s. For example, in 1975 the United Federation of Teachers of New York City exercised some powerful fiscal influence: it decided to use its retirement funds to purchase $150 million worth of bonds issued by the Municipal Assistance Corporation in New York. At this time the city was in peril of defaulting, and the city fathers were quite appreciative of the financial support. Albert Shanker, later AFT president, was the leader who engineered this civic gesture. In this respect, at least, the city learned firsthand the strength of the teachers' union.

Sources:
Connaught Coyne Marshner, *Blackboard Tyranny* (New Rochelle, N.Y.: Arlington House Publishers, 1978);

Lorraine H. McDonnell, "The Internal Politics of the NEA," *Phi Delta Kappan,* 58 (October 1976): 185;

"Newsbriefs," *Phi Delta Kappan,* 57 (June 1976): 708.

BLACK EDUCATIONAL ISSUES OF THE 1970S

Institutionalizing Black Activism. Black activism on college campuses in the 1960s was widespread. Students

The first issue of a journal introduced in November 1969 to "unite black intellectuals and street radicals."

demanded a voice in admissions and in curriculum. At San Francisco State a two-month protest demanding that all blacks who applied be admitted turned violent; student takeovers at Columbia and Cornell Universities emphasized student dissatisfaction with "racist" policies; at Brandeis blacks seized the computer and telephone switchboards to protest treatment of blacks on campus. These tactics worked. By the early 1970s black students and faculty, sometimes through channels, sometimes through violence, succeeded in institutionalizing many demands that had seemed out of reach just a decade earlier. Suddenly, universities were making long-term commitments to faculty recruited for burgeoning black-studies departments or courses. This institutionalization of black studies was met with controversy and heightened emotions, but the essential aims of most programs were similar: to act as a vehicle for changing the image of Afro-Americans (the preferred term at the time), to provide blacks with a psychological identity, to foster racial understanding, and to present a systematic study of black people and their accomplishments.

Establishing a Discipline. Because so many colleges were hiring professors to set up programs for black studies, there was a great demand for teacher training. One of the first programs designed explicitly to prepare teachers was the master's program in black studies offered at Atlanta University and the associated doctoral program offered at nearby Emory University. The National Endowment for the Humanities helped significantly by providing summer institutes to train teachers. Many campuses were somewhat alarmed at the speed with which programs were instituted. At Harvard, for example, a special faculty committee on African and African-American studies labored to write policy in the interim. Their committee recommended that while "it can hardly be doubted that the study of black men in America is a legitimate and urgent academic endeavor," the program should strive to "maintain and raise academic standards and avoid experience isolation." In other words, the committee hoped that the programs would serve both black and white students, highlighting the history, literature, art, and music of blacks and simultaneously diffusing racism.

Scholarship About Black Studies. Once the field began to be established, several black scholarly journals premiered. One of the first, begun in 1970, was *The Black Scholar*. Publisher Nathan Hare, a former director of black studies at San Francisco State (one of the first institutions to create such a department), founded this journal. Its stated purpose was to "unite black intellectuals and street radicals" by "pulling the analyst out of his ebony tower and defusing the street activists' disdain for scientific analysis." This journal provided a forum for black scholarship during the decade, regardless of the theoretical orientation of the writer. However, although it promised "scholarship, not rhetoric," its first issue featured articles by many nonscholars. Among them were black radicals such as Stokely Carmichael, Bobby Seale, and Eldridge Cleaver, who "issued a call to arms for the overthrow of the machinery of the oppressive ruling class."

The Desegregation Dilemma. Many mainstream, predominantly white universities welcomed minority students and built departments of black studies or at least offered courses such as black history or the sociology of minority groups. Recruitment was so successful that by 1976 two-thirds of the eight hundred thousand black American college students were attending formerly white institutions. This shift in attendance trends left many of the country's 120 black colleges and universities in jeopardy. Ironically, many black institutions found themselves pressed to admit white students to keep federal funding of certain grants intact. Some young blacks, however, remained loyal to their historic schools. Luther Brown, a twenty-one-year-old who turned down a full Stanford scholarship to go to Howard University, explained it this way: "We can't have black leaders who have been educated with ivy league illusions about the world." Benjamin Mays, former Morehouse College president, summed up the plight of the suddenly ailing black institutions: "If America allows black colleges to die, it will be the worst kind of discrimination in history.

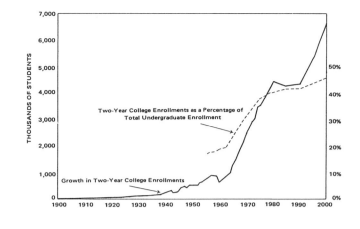

Growth in two-year college enrollments

To say that colleges born to serve Negroes are not worthy of surviving now that white colleges accept them will be a damnable act."

Sources:

"Black Colleges: The Desegregation Dilemma," *Time* (31 May 1976): 63;

"Out of the Ebony Tower," *Newsweek* (5 January 1970): 46;

Charles Valentine, "Deficit, Difference and Bi-cultural Models," *Harvard Educational Review*, 41 (May 1971): 137–157.

VOCATIONAL AND COMMUNITY COLLEGES

The Metamorphosis of Community Colleges. According to the Carnegie Commission on Higher Education, by 1975 the community-college system boasted half the total enrollment in higher education. These dramatic numbers were due primarily to the infusion of adults, who flocked to area institutions offering two-year degrees, located in major population centers, and catering to working students. Many of these students were returnees to education who had been in the workplace and who therefore had specific vocational goals in mind. The Carnegie Commission reported that one-third of the community-college students were taking vocational courses, from advertising to wildlife management.

Flexible, Community-Oriented Programs. Community colleges were able to tailor their programs to local community business and industry needs. Corning, New York, for example, boasted a special program in glassmaking, complementing the Corning glassworks nearby. An even closer tie with industry, however, was found at the General Motors Institute, the only community college designed, built, and operated by a major corporation. Located in Flint, Michigan, next to a Chevrolet plant, the college offered only two majors: electrical engineering and industrial administration, but these courses of study were augmented by numerous liberal-arts offerings in areas as diverse as black history, urban problems, and music. The 3,000-student population in 1973 included 350 black students and 111 women. After receiving a degree, 95 percent of the graduates signed on with GM for a job with starting salaries set at a healthy twelve thousand dollars. The 1973 student body president explained that there was little antiwar activism on this campus: "There's a real sense of responsibility to the company here," he said.

Minority Groups Found Community Colleges. Among the dozens of community colleges founded in the 1970s were schools located on Native American reservations. Among them were unique community schools, the Lakota Higher Education Center and Sinte Glenka College, established in 1970 on reservations in South Dakota. Less than 1 percent of the nineteen thousand Lakota (Sioux) situated on reservations had degrees. With unemployment running at over 40 percent and the average income at two thousand dollars annually, the schools were a welcome addition to their communities. Neither school had a central campus; instead, both were set up in facilities in a dozen community buildings over the five thousand square miles of reservation. Oglala Sioux director of the Lakota Center, Ray Howe, explained the endeavor: "For over 200 years the white man has promised to educate the Indian and — especially in higher education — he has failed." Funded by federal dollars and private foundations, the school set high standards. Howe noted that students who had transferred from other community colleges off the reservation with As were surprised to receive Cs at the Lakota Center. "You don't get through because you're an Indian," Howe said. "You get through because you're a student."

Sources:
"Company U," *Newsweek* (9 April 1973): 91–92;
"For Indians, By Indians," *Newsweek* (12 February 1973): 71.

THE EFFECTS OF 1960s ACTIVISM ON THE 1970s

A Decade of Ferment. The social movements, political forces, and student activism that characterized the 1960s continued, and in some cases intensified in the 1970s, profoundly affecting American education. Antiwar protests led by students continued to disrupt campus life; political activism reshaped educational curricula; the counterculture transformed student lifestyles and interests. Social preoccupations outside the university restructured life within the university. Demands for educational relevance, diversity, and democracy filtered down from the colleges to local schools. Drugs moved from campus dorm-rooms to high-school bathrooms. As James Perkins, former Cornell president explained, "The university is the canary in the coal mine. It's the most sensitive barometer of social change." The seventies were the decade when the sixties permanently altered the nature of American education.

Kent State and After. In 1970 student-led antiwar protests occurred in massive numbers and on an unprecedented scale. Although in the beginning of the year antiwar activism on college campuses had begun to wane,

Graffiti on wall of New York University building after April 1970 invasion of Cambodia

President Nixon's expansion of the Vietnam War into Cambodia resulted in outraged student protests across the nation. To many, Nixon's violation of Cambodian neutrality made a mockery of his promises to end the war in Indochina and drove thousands of moderate and conservative students and professors to take public antiwar positions. Harvard dean Ernest May, who had been identified with the faculty's conservative caucus, explained

The campus at Kent State University, where four students were killed by National Guardsmen on 4 May 1970

why so many faculty joined the ranks of student protesters: "We've been trying to work quietly for a long time, but this time the President has gone too far." After four Kent State, Ohio, and two Jackson State, Mississippi, students were killed during protests, demonstrations exploded around the country. Many colleges and universities staged formal protests at their 1970 graduations. At Oberlin, students shunned caps and gowns to protest the war; at Vassar, all graduates sported peace signs on the caps they wore to commencement. At Berkeley and a few other campuses graduation ceremonies were canceled — sometimes to mourn the dead, other times to avoid further bloodshed. Galvanized by the demonstrations, Congress forced Nixon to withdraw from Cambodia and increased pressure on him to withdraw from Vietnam altogether. When the last American troops left Indochina, in 1972, antiwar protests abated. By that time, however, political activists had moved on to new sets of issues.

New Demands. Besides the Vietnam War, student activists in the early 1970s also targeted elitism, racism, and pollution for protests. The most massive student protest in American history to date, Earth Day 1970 resulted from the organizational efforts of environmentalists, who succeeded in getting 1.5 million students to participate in the ecology-minded event. When Yale students protested unfair treatment of several Black Panthers on trial for murder in New Haven, Kingman Brewster, Yale president, told faculty he was "skeptical" about the chances of any Black Panther receiving a fair trial in the United States. Brewster's on-the-record remarks served as a model for much of the dissent that marked the decade. His assertion drew fire from Vice-president Spiro Agnew yet served to unite Yale students and faculty against the status quo and defused potentially violent protests. Similarly, college administrators became increasingly responsive to student demands for a democra-

tization of university life and for changes in traditional curriculum. Colleges around the country dropped restrictive *in loco parentis* (in the place of parents) rules, allowing students greater personal freedom and eliminating sexual and moral oversight. Colleges also allowed greater student participation in framing educational policy, reformed curriculum to make it more relevant, and improved relations with surrounding communities. As formerly radical ideas slowly seeped through universities, overt protests became superfluous. Many student activists now took their places teaching in classrooms they once boycotted. New courses and new syllabi at many institutions reflected many formerly radical notions, and underground thinkers popularized in the 1960s became objects of systematic scholastic investigation. In the first half of the decade, courses that led students to question society and government were fashionable, and through this questioning, many came to rethink the goals and structures of education itself.

A New Mood. One widespread change in higher education during the 1970s was the loosening of curricular frameworks. Students at many institutions demanded and won concessions in the number of core requirements for certain majors, and in general, most students found they had much wider choices of electives. Some former activists used these electives to indulge in courses in the supernatural. A wide variety of courses on the occult were the most popular additions to the college curriculum during this time. The fascination with the supernatural was explained by some professors as the counterculture's reaction against the rationalist scientific tradition of post-Renaissance Western thought. At the University of Washington academic credit was offered for courses in extrasensory perception (ESP), hypnotism, and yoga. Antioch College offered a five-credit course in astrology, while at the University of Wisconsin a witchcraft and astrology course boasted five hundred students. Professors at the University of California, San Francisco, noted the "huge desire" for occult studies there as a "reaction to a grossly materialistic society." Even Pepperdine, affiliated with the Church of Christ, offered a course on the supernatural with a medium as a guest lecturer, and at Oakland University a course in "ethnopsychiatry," the study of healing mental disorders through means such as witchcraft, prospered. Interest in the spiritual world was not confined to the supernatural, however. There was also an enormous rise in enrollments in traditional religion courses.

Major of the Decade. As the mood on American campuses became more spiritualistic and introspective, courses in psychology became more popular. By mid decade nearly every psychology department in the nation was inundated with students pursuing the 1970s "in" major. Nationally, enrollment in psychology graduate studies was up 114 percent over five years earlier. At UCLA psychology was the most popular major, with enrollment numbers increasing 24 percent per year. At

Michigan State University eight hundred students applied for seventy-three slots in graduate school. Many advisers saw this trend as the expression of a new attitude among college students who, after a decade of protesting social problems, now became preoccupied with the individual and his or her inner problems. In addition, many students became involved with transcendental meditation, encounter groups, and other searches for self-understanding. Students who finished psychology graduate programs were also researching different types of psychological questions from those of the 1960s. Experts in psychology tackled problems in the real world, not the lab, studying the effects on people of problems such as pollution, drugs, alcohol abuse, crime, and sexual dysfunction. The demand for psychology professors rose from twenty-five hundred in 1970 to seven thousand in 1973, and no real job glut appeared in this field until the end of the decade.

High-School Rebellion. Much of the overt rebellion common on campuses in the 1960s could be found, alive and well, in the high schools during the 1970s. Radical groups such as the Black Panthers actively recruited high-school students, and even where there was no direct recruitment, political radicalism soon spread to younger students eager to emulate the older crowd. In March 1970 Donald Reeves, age seventeen, spoke to the New York Board of Education on student demands, sounding much like university protesters of previous years: "Your solution to students organizing peacefully is repression and police. Your solution to destitute black and Puerto Rican students is to channel us into inferior occupations. There is a need for drastic revision of curriculum, social attitudes and administrative behavior. If not, within the next five years, the schools will blow up racially, blow up with drugs, and blow up politically."

The Drug Culture. One challange to authority was countercultural: drug use and abuse. Marijuana use was rampant in secondary schools, as the drug was widely available and affordable. When many administrators felt compelled to offer drug education, they had to face parental resistance to the programs as well as the fact that students sometimes were intrigued by what they learned. When David Lewis, a professor of medicine at Harvard spoke on a panel at a Boston high-school assembly, two students in the audience told him that "If drugs were worth calling off classes for a day, they are worth trying." Public opinion polls revealed that drug use in the schools was a primary worry for parents in the 1970s. Sixties activism might have left a legacy of political activism and educational democracy, but the counterculture left a legacy of chemical escapism and addiction.

Student and Teacher Rights. Although Reeves's predictions were overblown, like their older brothers and sisters, high-school students were soon protesting for greater influence within educational institutions. Demanding that the school board place real power in students' hands, New York high schoolers offered in 1970 a "student bill of rights" which would guarantee that each of New York City's ninety high schools would be governed by a board of ten students, five parents, four teachers, and a principal. Student government would be autonomous, free from administrative control, and counseling on drugs and contraception would be available without being noted in the students' records. New York officials denied the petition, but as the decade progressed, students and their teachers secured the right to speak freely in the classroom and participate in political activities, just as protesting students in the late 1960s had earned the right to challenge college administrations.

Sources:

"High School Power," *Newsweek* (9 March 1970): 63;

"High School Rebellion," in *Education in the U.S.: A Documentary History*, volume 5, edited by Sol Cohen (Los Angeles: UCLA Press, 1975): 3216–3223;

"The Kent State Aftermath: Campus Ferment," *Newsweek* (15 June 1970): 96;

"Psychology: Hot Course on Campus," *Newsweek* (21 May 1973): 105;

David Schimmel, "To Speak Out Freely: Do Teachers Have the Right?" *Phi Delta Kappan*, 54 (December 1972): 258–260;

"Voodoo U," *Newsweek* (9 April 1973): 91;

"Ethnopsychiatry" class at Oakland University, 1973

"What's Wrong with the High Schools?" *Newsweek* (16 February 1970): 65–69.

THE OPEN CLASSROOM, OPEN SCHOOLING, AND INFORMAL LEARNING

The British Open-Classroom Model. During the 1970s many early-childhood-education specialists were influenced by models found in some British infant schools (the equivalent of U.S. primary grades), particularly those in Leicestershire, England, where teachers had developed a type of open classroom in which children moved about with relative freedom. These schools were marked by little distinction between work and play, increased opportunities for children to learn from each other, and a decreased emphasis on didactic teaching. When many proponents established similar schools in this country, this philosophy of education came to be known as the "open classroom" or "informal schooling." The term implies that the activities of students will be determined, to a great extent, by their interests and needs, not by the teachers. The open-classroom approach suggests freedom of movement as well as an open philosophy that encourages students to seek answers in their own ways and to pursue individual interests. The concept replaces a front-and-center teacher and rows of desks with work areas, each devoted to different subjects. Prof. Lillian Weber of New York's City College, one of the foremost exponents of the British infant-school model, introduced the "open corridor" concept, an attempt to break away from the constricting presence of four walls and a closed door by making the corridors

and all the space in a school part of the learning environment.

The Movement Catches Hold. An axiom regarding educational trends suggests that when California catches cold the whole country sneezes. In 1971 California Superintendent of Public Instruction Wilson Riles told educators, "Don't tinker. Come up with a totally new look at early education and a whole new way of running schools and teaching in primary grades" — and the open-classroom concept got its first major toehold in U.S. education. By 1976 a wholesale reform plan to revamp early-childhood education was in its third year of operation in California. Gov. Jerry Brown was so pleased with the results that he proposed a $35 million expansion of the primary open-schools project, and the State Board of Education proposed $45.4 million to produce similar reforms in secondary schools. By the decade's end the primary curriculum in nearly every state had been influenced by the open-classroom concept, so much so that the most popular building design for new elementary schools in the 1970s was one with few or portable walls.

Results. Proponents of the open classroom argued that the concept realized the highest educational ideals. They cited dozens of examples of students who had been inspired by the freedom of the open concept to take joy in learning. As one mother of a child in an Ithaca, New York, elementary school explained, "Finally my daughter is beginning to understand that learning is something you do for yourself and not something you do for the teacher." When the Grape Street School in Watts, a deprived area of Los Angeles, changed to the open concept, an elderly man living across the street was amazed: "There used to be something bad going on in there. You'd see a black face at a window now and then — like it was saying 'Let me out of here.' Now it's tough getting kids to come home." Many teachers believed, after adjusting, that the changes were good. "I've never worked so hard, but the children are more interested in learning and the classroom is much more pleasant," said one teacher who had resisted the shift in philosophy.

Drawbacks. In many instances classes were labeled open only because the physical layout of the room was different; instruction remained exactly the same as in the closed classroom. Teachers, moreover, frequently had no voice in administrative decisions to institute open plans, a situation that often led to resistance on the part of those being forced to change. Another significant problem was the lack of in-service training for teachers who had been trained in a totally different philosophy of learning. Many experienced teachers simply did not have the time or the inclination to do the vast amounts of preparation critical for running a successful open classroom. Opponents of the open or informal concept became convinced that although there were some successes, children in general were being shortchanged in learning the basics. Many parents just did not approve of their children having the freedom to explore concepts before they had been made

Open classroom in Olathe, Kansas, 1971

to memorize information. Predictably, in some instances freedom became license, and some students, left without rigid oversight, disrupted other, more serious students. The fact that this behavior was common to traditional classrooms as well did not change the minds of those who attributed declining reading scores later in the decade directly to the open-classroom movement.

The Movement Spreads. The open-classroom idea was also the basis for a sizable reform movement in secondary schools. The nongraded high school, a concept popularized in the 1970s, was an institution in which students were allowed to work at their own pace, at their own level, to finish a somewhat negotiable curriculum. Proponents of this type of school argued that often when students are "in grades" and "assigned grades," they and their teachers become so preoccupied with the grade and with what is supposed to be learned in it that real learning takes a backseat to busy work and didacticism. One well-publicized version of this type of school was John Adams High in Portland, Oregon, which was set up and administered by seven young Harvard Ph.D. candidates. Opened in fall 1969, the school housed thirteen hundred students who traditionally would have been assigned to grades nine through eleven. These students, 25 percent of whom were black, were assigned to one of four

"Houses," where they spent the first half of each day in interdisciplinary courses in math, English, sciences, and social studies. As exemplified by the following course description, these courses also emphasized activism and "hipness": "What's Going On: a course in what can be done to change whatever it is. You pick the time and the area to study. But think in terms of social problems." During the second half of the day students were free to fill option periods as they wished; resource centers around campus were staffed by teachers willing to assist if asked. However, the students also had the option of being "free," wandering outside the building if they so desired. The students were happy: "The sense of community here is unbelievable," explained one seventeen-year-old in 1970. "No one says no."

Failed Experiments. By 1973 MIT professor Allen Graubard, who documented the progress of alternative schools such as John Adams High in his book *Free the Children*, found that most experimental secondary schools lived about eighteen months before failing or revamping their structure. The Los Angeles Community School, for example, moved from totally unstructured curriculum which got "out of hand" to a traditional structured curriculum directed toward math and reading. In Minneapolis organizers of a new secondary open school vowed to have no semblance of structure in the opening few months. Students voted that since "the school belongs to the people," they should have no janitor. Later, when rubbish piled up, they changed the policy, and in its second year, students and parents admitted that chaos mandated the establishment of rudimentary rules and a curriculum. Open-classroom reforms at the secondary level never became as widespread as those at the elementary level, and by the end of the decade only a handful of alternative schools remained. By then the term was used to define schools which tended to house students who had not succeeded at traditional institutions.

Sources:

"Best Around," *Newsweek* (16 February 1970): 68;

"Does School + Joy = Learning?" *Newsweek* (3 May 1971): 67–71;

"Easy as ECE," *Time* (19 April 1976): 78;

Neil Postman and Charles Weingartner, *The School Book* (New York: Delacorte, 1973);

"Schools with a Difference," *Newsweek* (23 April 1973): 113–116.

CURRICULAR INNOVATIONS: STEPPING FORWARD, THEN STEPPING BACK

The New Math. Although the curricular movement which came to be known as new math began in the late 1960s, the reforms did not permeate most of the school systems until the 1970s, when the big textbook companies began to publish math materials based almost exclusively on this innovation. The creators of the new-math curriculum were opposed to the view that the main object of mathematics instruction was arithmetic proficiency. The new-math approach put theory before practice, with a great deal of exposure to sophisticated concepts such as set theory, number theory, and symbolic logic. The belief was that if theory came before practice, all math reasoning would fall into place, including computation. This purely intellectual approach was touted as being more fun than memorizing the "hows" of arithmetic. In 1973 Stanford professor Edward Begle, called the "father of new math," argued that computation was a mute point anyway, since "within five years, all calculations will be done on calculators." However, the president of the National Council of Teachers of Mathematics disagreed, suggesting that "No machine has been invented to tell you when to add, subtract, multiply or divide."

Rebellion Against New Math. California schools had led the way in adapting the new-math programs, fully implementing the curriculum in 1969. However, when in 1973 the state's scores dropped 20 percent on standardized math tests, reformers met with waves of resistance from parents and many teachers. All over the state the results were the same: students with good skills when they entered the program did worse. A federal education laboratory director told of the widespread frustration: "We have people trooping in here begging, 'Please help us. Our kids can't add and the school board's mad.'" Not surprisingly, teachers all over the country reported frustrations. Many teachers were not only intellectually un-

prepared for the change but also resistant to the entire philosophy. As one principal whose staff was opposed to the curriculum explained, "It's like taking people who believed in chastity and having them teach courses in sex ed." The hurriedly concocted textbooks contributed to the problems. In San Francisco 87 percent of the math teachers reported that by the fourth year of the program they were using materials they had prepared themselves. In 1973 McGraw-Hill, one of the nation's leading textbook publishers, discontinued its new-math texts. Soon all the other companies followed, and without prepared texts the movement died rapidly.

Meter Readers. A mathematics trend that lasted the entire decade was the teaching of the metric system. In 1973 a bill was before Congress to force the United States to abandon the "archaic" English system of weights and measures in favor of the metric system. With that impetus all mathematics texts began to incorporate both systems. Innovative teachers started programs to teach children by having the children actually measure and weigh things in the classroom rather than by memorizing the tables of equivalents. California, as usual, led the national move to the metric system, declaring that by 1976 California would buy only metric texts for both science and math.

Teaching of Reading: DISTAR, Phonics, and More. One controversial beginning-reading program especially for disadvantaged children devised during the 1970s was the DISTAR plan, created by psychologist Carl Bereiter and colleagues at the University of Illinois. These researchers contended that traditional early-childhood programs are designed for middle- and upper-class children who have already mastered primary language skills; dis-

In 1976 public television made an unprecedented appearance in some of the nation's college classrooms. Students at more than three hundred colleges and universities took final exams on courses based on thirteen episodes of *The Adams Family Chronicles*, a Public Broadcasting Service series that analyzed the influence of the Massachusetts family on the founding of the United States. Although for two decades television had been used in the classroom, this exemplary series became the centerpiece of many courses, not merely an aid to instruction. At Michigan State University a professor excited about the series said, "I'm able to interest non-traditional students through it. It represents history the way no lecture could." At Bunker Hill Community College in Boston, some other nontraditional college students, police, and firemen took the course. At nearby Quincy Junior College a professor explained the interest this way: "There's a real hunger in this country for a collective past, a cherishable identity." He also revealed one of his exam questions: "Why was the working class unable to elect political leaders who would champion their cause?"

Source: "The Adams Finals," *Time* (26 April 1976): 33.

advantaged children, if they are to compete, must progress at a faster than average pace. Therefore, according to Bereiter, early school programs for these disadvantaged children should devote every moment to the development of basic language skills. His two-year reading program, DISTAR, required two hours of drill each day with an emphasis on structure — followed by rewards of hugs, raisins, and cookies for kids who had performed well. The program achieved startling test results, with one experimental group performing at the end of the year on achievement tests nearly as well as gifted children. However, the researchers were highly criticized for their rigid and narrow procedures, and opposing humanistic psychologists asked if this method were a means of "opening the door" or of "keeping the door closed permanently" for disadvantaged children.

Why Can't Johnny Write? Teachers and professors from Great Britain and from the United States gathered at the Dartmouth Conference in 1969 to ponder their differences in language instruction, especially in composition. This conference signaled the beginning of a movement to reform English education so that writing would be judged not strictly by whether or not it is correct English, but whether or not it communicates anything to an audience. During the 1970s the study of English in most U.S. schools was confined primarily to reading se-

lected great works, then answering specific factual questions about those works on objective tests. As Fred Godshalk reported in *A Survey of the Teaching of English in Secondary Schools*, commissioned by the Educational Testing Service, "too many teachers seem to think that the ultimate end of instruction in literature is knowledge of and about *Macbeth* or *Silas Marner*, rather than the processes of learning to read and write about *Macbeth* or *Silas Marner* with insight and discrimination." According to Godshalk's study, the average teacher had a load of 150 students per day, and nationwide the average amount of class time devoted to writing was about 15 percent. When writing was taught, the emphasis was almost wholly on mechanics — spelling, punctuation, grammar, sentence structure — with almost no attention to development, organization, or style. Because these mechanical points had an agreed content, and because every student was issued a text with all of the points of grammar codified, this was the content of U.S. English classes. Not surprisingly, American students were notoriously bad writers, a fact highly publicized when *Newsweek* featured the literacy crisis as its cover story in 1975. The reforms begun by those attending the Dartmouth Conference and encouraged officially by the National Council of Teachers of English made some inroads in the teaching of writing, but because most school districts were not willing to reduce teachers' huge student loads, writing still took a backseat to memorizing facts about works of literature during the seventies.

Sources:
"By the Numbers," *Time* (23 February 1976): 66;

"Math Mystique: Fear of Figuring," *Time* (14 March 1977): 36;

"Meter Readers," *Newsweek* (7 May 1973): 65;

Charles E. Silberman, *Crisis in the Classroom* (New York: Random House, 1970);

"Why Johnny Can't Add," *Newsweek* (25 June 1973): 77.

SCHOOL-FINANCING DECISIONS FROM THE COURTS

A Startling Decision. In August 1971 American public educators were startled by the California Supreme Court's decision in *Serrano* v. *Priest*, which declared that the financing of a child's public education may no longer depend on the wealth of the school district where that student lived. Instead, the court said, public schools may be funded only upon the basis of the wealth of the state as a whole. The assessed property valuation of a district was significant in public-school financing only insofar as it was part of the total state's valuation. Under *Serrano* there would be no more rich districts or poor districts. There would only be districts, entitled to fund an educational program at the same level, with the same local tax effort, as any other district. Part of the decision read, "An individual's life is surely affected more by his/her education than by his/her individual vote," and "the quality of a child's education depends upon the resources of his/her school district and ultimately upon the pocketbook of his/her parents." This reasoning was highly significant — it represented the culmination of years of hope for many school finance officers and people living in poor districts; but it confirmed the worst fears of taxpayers in rich districts who felt threatened by the need to share tax resources.

Serrano and Rodriquez. Four months later in Texas, the *Serrano* decision was applied by the U.S. District Court in San Antonio in a class-action suit filed by Demetrio Rodriquez challenging the constitutional validity of the Texas public-school-financing laws. Like California before the *Serrano* decision, Texas funded schools according to local tax receipts, and poor school districts accordingly funded poor schools. The area in which Rodriquez lived, for example, was 96 percent nonwhite and very poor. Despite one of the highest tax rates in San Antonio, the district could raise only $37 to spend toward the education of each student; with matching funds provided by the state, these children ended up with $231 per pupil per year. By contrast, the nearby wealthy, predominantly white neighborhood of Alamo Heights had a lower tax rate but was able to raise $412 for each student within its school district; when matching state and federal funds were added, Alamo Heights spent $543 per pupil per year — almost twice the funding (and twice the educational resources) available in Rodriquez's district. Rodriquez petitioned to broaden the tax base of Texas schools, to provide equal funding for all Texas students, and to even the playing field of educational competition between rich and poor. He argued that Texas school-finance laws violated the Equal Protection Clause of the Fourteenth Amendment to the Constitution. The district court agreed, but upon appeal to the Supreme Court, on 21 March 1973, the ruling was reversed, 5–4.

A Sweeping Rejection. Justice Lewis Powell, writing for the majority in the *Rodriquez* decision, rejected almost every argument offered by Rodriquez and his lawyers for equal funding of poor and rich schools. He denied a connection between poverty and poor school districts, between poor education and poverty in adulthood, between a good education and the rational exercise of democratic political processes. Powell also argued that the unequal funding of Texas schools did not result in an "absolute deprivation" of the "fundamental interest" of poor children and suggested that equal funding of public schools would be too difficult to implement. Powell denied that education was a "fundamental right" either explicitly or implicitly guaranteed to individuals by the Constitution. Therefore, if lawmakers decided to fund education in an unequal fashion, the individual had no right to petition the courts to change the law. Texas was under no obligation to provide poor children with anything other than "the basic minimal skills." In the case of education, Powell wrote, "the Equal Protection Clause does not require absolute equality."

Marshall's Dissent. Justice Thurgood Marshall, writing for the minority, noted that the reasoning in the

DOCTORS, DOCTORS, EVERYWHERE

At the beginning of the decade there was a sharp and sudden shift in academic supply and demand, and the result was the tightest job market in academe since the Depression. American universities were producing doctorates at more than three times the rate of 1960. Many men used graduate school as a means of avoiding the draft, and the baby boomers were finishing graduate programs in naturally higher numbers. In addition, dozens more institutions were granting advanced degrees. "It's terrible the number of second and third rate institutions that have gone into the Ph.D. business," complained University of California, Berkeley dean Sanford Elberg. "I blame some of this on President Johnson's idea for more 'centers of excellence,' which really meant a great leveling process in the quality of the degree." In response, Harvard and Yale agreed to cut admissions to graduate programs in 1971 by 20 percent while Berkeley (producing fifteen hundred doctorates a year by 1970) made admissions criteria more selective and limited time to complete a degree to five years. The severity of the problem is illustrated by the table below which compares doctorates registered with the Cooperative College Registry for job searches and the number of vacancies in academia in certain fields.

	Registrants	Academic Vacancies
Sociology	109	37
Physics	243	12
History	394	43
Chemistry	347	29

Source: "The Doctoral Glut," *Newsweek* (16 March 1970): 114.

Rodriquez case was opposite that found in the landmark 1954 *Brown* v. *Board of Education* decision — a case Marshall himself had argued before the Court. As in the *Brown* decision, Marshall held that while the Consitution does not explicitly guarantee the right to an education, it is nonetheless fundamental to a democracy that depends upon the rational political decisions of the citizenry. Given the degree to which education is interrelated with democracy, the courts must afford it protection. To deny children equal education is to deny them an equal voice within the democracy, and to deny them their rights guaranteed by the Fourteenth Amendment. "The Equal Protection Clause," Marshall wrote, "is not addressed to . . . minimal sufficiency." If the state provides education to children, it "must be made available to all on equal terms."

Lasting Effects. In 1973 public educators were still optimistic about the possibilities for school-finance reform. They believed that the fact that the decision was split 5–4 indicated that although the door to finance reform had been shut in that case, the door was neither slammed nor necessarily locked forever. However, there was no cause for optimism. When the *Rodriquez* decision was combined with the Nixon administration's revisions to Title I of the ESEA in 1972, the decision laid the foundation for an increasingly class-based, financially polarized school system. The state courts heard numerous school-finance cases, but because the primary source of funding remained local property taxes, there was a tendency for the "rich to get richer, and the poor to get poorer," as industry and homeowners were naturally attracted to prosperous areas with well-funded schools. The USOE commissioned a study group in the early 1970s which recommended that by 1980 the funding of public schools should be 10 percent local, 60 percent state, and 30 percent federal. Instead, at the end of the decade, the actual figures were about 40 percent local, 50 percent state, and 10 percent federal.

Sources:

William Greenbaum, "Serrano v. Priest: Implications for Educational Equality," *Harvard Educational Review,* 41 (November 1971): 501–534;

Jonathan Kozol, *Savage Inequalities: Children in America's Schools* (New York: Crown, 1991);

George Neill, "Supreme Court Ponders Momentous Texas Case," *Phi Delta Kappan,* 54 (December 1972);

Thomas Shannon, "Rodriquez: A Dream Shattered or a Call for Finance Reform?" *Phi Delta Kappan,* 54 (May 1973): 587–588.

HEADLINE MAKERS

BENJAMIN S. BLOOM

1913–

PROFESSOR OF EDUCATION, UNIVERSITY OF CHICAGO

Teaching as a Science. Bloom is perhaps best known for his *Taxonomy of Educational Objectives, Handbook I: Cognitive Domain* (1956), which had a powerful impact on attempts to reshape educational aims in the 1950s and 1960s. Bloom was a researcher whose primary interest was setting forth a hierarchical classification system for teacher objectives. He aimed to remake education into a more scientific endeavor, one in which teachers learned to organize materials and concepts into groups. Ideally, teachers could assist students in meeting clear-cut goals by having them complete objectives. Bloom defined these sets of objectives for teachers and suggested various tests to measure whether or not the desired learning had taken place at each level.

Cognitive and Affective Domains. Bloom's first handbook classifies intellectual tasks into six different levels, and he posits that learners must proceed in an orderly progression through these levels: knowledge, comprehension, application, analysis, synthesis, and evaluation. The second handbook systematically classifies types of human reactions — feeling, attitudes, and emotions — and reduces them to behavioral equivalents of such feelings. This volume, *Handbook II: Affective Domain* (written in 1964 with David Krathwold and Bertram Masia) suggests that the "affective domain" of student behaviors consists of receiving, responding, valuing, and organizing those values into a system. Bloom suggests that students have attained "mastery learning" when they have reached the top of both the cognitive and affective domains in regard to a subject.

Formative and Summative Evaluation. In 1971 Bloom extended his influence in the field of education when he published *Handbook on Formative and Summative Evaluation of Student Learning,* a monumental work that outlines precisely how educational objectives should be formulated and tested in every content area, from literature to industrial arts. The term *formative evaluation* refers to Bloom's suggestion that student learning be monitored in the intermediate stages of mastering a topic, rather than waiting for the summative evaluation that comes only at the end, when it is too late to modify instructional methods if the student is not learning appropriately. It is difficult to overestimate the influence of this handbook on teachers trained in the 1970s; it was widely used in curriculum courses for new teachers and workshops for older ones. Bloom suggests in his opening chapter, "It is hoped that students in teacher-training institutes will secure this volume early in their careers and use it frequently during their careers," and thousands of teachers did just that, starting every class period by writing the exact objective on the blackboard so that students could know exactly what they should have learned by the lesson's end. Bloom's highly organized approach to the science of teaching was welcomed by those in education who opposed the open or free concept of learning popular among many during the 1970s. This approach was as back to basics as one could get. When steadily falling test scores became a hallmark of the 1970s, Bloom's orderly classifications and objectives were seized upon as possible cures for an ailing system. Additionally, developers of early software for computer-assisted learning appropriated Bloom's taxonomy of cognitive tasks as a way of organizing programmed units of study.

Sources:

Benjamin Bloom, *Handbook on Formative and Summative Evaluation of Student Learning* (New York: McGraw-Hill, 1971);

Bloom, *Human Characteristics and School Learning* (New York: McGraw-Hill, 1976);

Bloom, ed., *Taxonomy of Educational Objectives: The Classification of Educational Goals* (New York: McKay, 1956).

JAMES COLEMAN

1926-

SOCIOLOGIST AND GOVERNMENT CONSULTANT

A Chemist Turns to Schools. Dr. James S. Coleman, a sociologist with a deep concern for a democratic, pluralistic society, had an early career as a chemical engineer with Eastman-Kodak Company in Rochester, New York, during the early 1950s. However, he became so fascinated with sociology and social problems that he decided to attend Columbia University, where he worked as a research associate with the Bureau of Applied Social Research while earning his doctorate. He first became involved in the study of schooling when, under the auspices of the United States Office of Education in 1957, he and his associates began a detailed sociological study of ten Illinois high schools. They examined both academic and social aspects of these schools, and from their research they published the research monograph, *Social Climates in High Schools* (1961), and two other academic books which were praised for their meticulous research and their objectivity.

Equality and Educational Opportunity. Under the provisions of the 1964 Civil Rights Act, the U.S. commissioner of education was instructed to conduct a study examining the extent to which racial minorities are deprived of equal educational opportunities in the nation's public schools. The commissioner chose Coleman and Ernest Q. Campbell of Vanderbilt University to design and conduct this $1.5 million study and to report the results to the president and Congress within two years. Involving some sixty thousand teachers and over six hundred thousand pupils throughout the United States, Coleman and Campbell surveyed educational opportunities available to Negroes, American Indians, Mexican-Americans, Puerto Ricans, Orientals, and disadvantaged whites. Issued in 1966, the final report, entitled Equality of Educational Opportunity, was widely known as the Coleman report.

Findings. The Coleman report indicated that de facto segregation was still widespread throughout the United States; that although predominantly nonwhite schools had somewhat poorer material resources and more crowded classes than white schools, this did not appear to be a major factor in determining academic performance of pupils; and that teachers in ghetto schools often came from deprived backgrounds and had less academic ability than teachers in more prosperous areas. According to the report, black students' dropout rates were almost twice as high as that of whites, and only about 4.6 percent of the nation's college students were black. Another significant finding was that nonwhite students in all-minority schools fell further behind their white contemporaries academically with each succeeding grade. Whereas a sixth-grade black pupil in a northeastern city was about 1.6 years behind white sixth graders, by the time he reached the twelfth grade he trailed by 3.3 years.

Influential Conclusions. The Coleman report pointed to several definite conclusions that influenced educational policy in the 1970s. For example, the report clearly suggested that increased expenditures for improved school facilities had virtually no effect on the academic achievements of pupils and that predominantly minority schools did not help children overcome the handicaps of a poor home environment. However, students from lower economic levels who were in schools with predominantly middle-class students made significant gains in educational motivation, while the middle-class students suffered no appreciable loss from the association. Coleman criticized tracking students according to ability and suggested that development of such attitudes as black pride may "have more effect on Negro achievement than any other single factor." In spring 1970 the Norfolk, Virginia, city schools announced school integration policies based "on the best social sciences data we have now available" — the Coleman report. The plan maintained a middle-class majority in each school while placing black pupils into those schools, thus maintaining an optimum educational setting as defined by Coleman's research.

Coleman and the Nixon Administration. In 1970 President Richard Nixon endorsed Coleman's conclusion that students' economic and social environments directly affect their academic achievements. Coleman acted as an adviser to Nixon in formulating a plan to give school districts in the South and North $1.5 billion during 1971 and 1972 to help alleviate the effects of racial segregation. Coleman fought to allocate the majority of the money to desegregation rather than to ineffective compensatory education programs for ghetto schools. He also criticized Nixon for stating that the administration would act only against de jure segregation and not against de facto segregation caused by housing patterns. Coleman said that racial segregation, no matter what its origin, had to be eliminated "not merely for some vague, generalized social purposes, but because desegregation is the most consistent mechanism for improving the quality of education of disadvantaged children."

PAULO FREIRE

1921-

EDUCATIONAL PHILOSOPHER

Militant Literacy. Paulo Freire came to the United States as a highly controversial educator from Latin America, best-known for his development of methodology for teaching reading to illiterate peasants. Born in Brazil, Freire was imprisoned there in 1964 when a military junta, which objected in the strongest possible terms to Freire's teaching of Brazilian peasants, seized control of the country. Upon release he was urged to leave the country, and he did so, working for five years in Chile developing adult-literacy programs. He came to the United States as a fellow of the Center for Study of Development and Social Change at Harvard, where his theories were welcomed, especially in the changing political climate of the early 1970s.

Freire's Philosophy. Freire believes that becoming literate involves far more than learning to decode the written representations of a sound system; that it is,

instead, truly an act of knowing through which a person is able to look critically at the culture which has shaped him and to move with reflection and positive action upon his world. Freire rejects the digestive concept of adult education or the belief that illiterates are undernourished, and he strongly objects to terms such as *eradication* of illiteracy. The "culture of silence" in which the oppressed live is a product, he believed, of their acceptance of someone else's definition of the world. But each man has a right to "say his own word" and "to name the world" in his own way. Through the written word one may develop a radical new consciousness of political and economic contradictions and the will to do something about them. Thus learning to read, according to Freire, is not a mere technical problem but a process of learning how to redefine one's position in the world and to take action against one's oppressors.

Freire's Influence. Freire's work exerted influence all over the world, especially among many radical critics of education. The writings he did while at Harvard include his best known work, *The Pedagogy of the Oppressed* (1972), a fully developed abstract explanation of his philosophy of literacy. This work established Freire as the voice on adult literacy among many radical theorists who had been searching for a politically relevant philosophy of education. His insistence that the pedagogy of the oppressed be forged with learners and not for learners, along with his demands that teachers open a "dialogue between equals" with their students, won over those who wanted to politicize education. Ironically, Freire's next work, *The Letters to Guinea-Bissau*, in which he attempts to put his philosophical concepts into actual practice, demonstrates that it is not always possible to dialogue with those who are culturally depressed. The letters of the title are only Freire's letters; none from oppressed peoples is included. And even though Freire goes on record as opposing primers ("Literacy education as cultural action, as I have said so often, cannot use traditional primers"), the notebooks he describes in these letters are essentially primers — complete with the advice that one should teach words "through synthesis of sound-syllabic methods, in which recognizable letters and sounds are formed into different word and syllable combinations." However, despite some operational difficulties in turning philosophy into practice, Freire was highly acclaimed during the 1970s, so much so that the United Nations Nations Education, Scientific,;and Cultural Organization Educational, Scientific, and Cultural Organization based its Experimental World Campaign for Universal Literacy upon his work.

Sources:
Paulo Freire, *The Letters to Guinea-Bissau* (New York: Seabury Press, 1978);

Freire, *The Pedagogy of the Oppressed* (New York: Herder & Herder, 1972);

Neil Postman and Charles Weingartner, *The School Book* (New York: Delacorte/Seymour Lawrence, 1973).

JOHN HOLT

1923-

SCHOOL TEACHER AND EDUCATION CRITIC

Critic of the Status Quo. John Holt rose to prominence in the 1970s as one of the nation's leading theorists on learning. His first two books, *How Children Fail* (1964) and *How Children Learn* (1967), set the tone for a great deal of the school criticism that followed in waves during the 1970s. In these books he laid bare much of what was destructive in the classroom, arguing that teachers and parents had become so habituated to teaching that rarely was there any effort made to comprehend how learning really takes place.

An Idealist and a Teacher. Holt did not begin to write until he had had many years of experience teaching young children, and his most persistent theme is that the system ignores what it knows, or should know, about how children learn. "We like to say that we send children to school to teach them to think," he explains. "What we do, all too often, is to teach them to think badly, to give up a natural and powerful way of thinking in favor of a method that does not work well for them and that we rarely use ourselves." Holt believed that traditional schooling convinced most students that "where words or symbols or abstract thought are concerned, they cannot think at all."

Holt's Influence. Holt's theories about the natural learning styles of children were extremely influential in developing teacher-training programs and in developing curricula. Essentially, he suggested that the child is curious, wanting to make sense of things, to find out how things work, and gain competence and control over himself and his environment. The child, Holt said, is patient and willing to tolerate an extraordinary amount of uncertainty, confusion, and ignorance as he waits for meaning to come to him. In talking, reading, and writing, children are able — if not hurried or made ashamed or fearful — to notice and correct most of their own mistakes, but school rarely is a place that gives the time or opportunity for this type of learning and thinking.

From Learning to Philosophy. During the 1970s Holt became disillusioned by the free-school movement which he had believed could nurture children's natural learning. In *Freedom and Beyond* (1972) he discussed his growing awareness that "it doesn't make much sense to talk of 'giving freedom' to people. The most we can do is put within reach certain choices, and remove certain coercions and constraints. Whether doing this creates for other people liberation, opportunity, or freedom — or whether it just puts them in a more painful spot than ever, is very much up to them." His other writings from the 1970s, *Escape From Childhood, Instead of Education,* and *Never Too Late,* all show more concern with critical philosophy than with bad schooling and how to deal with it, the subject which won him acclaim at the start of his career.

Sources:

John Holt, *Freedom and Beyond* (New York: Dutton, 1972);

Holt, *How Children Learn,* revised edition (New York: Delacorte/Seymour Lawrence, 1983).

CHRISTOPHER JENCKS

1936-

HARVARD CENTER FOR THE STUDY OF PUBLIC POLICY

A Voucher System. In 1970 Christopher Jencks issued a report from the HarvardHarvard Center for the Study of Public;Policy Center for the Study of Public Policy that touched off a public debate on the feasibility of a type of voucher system for education. This report, principally authored by Jencks and funded by a grant from the Office of Economic Opportunity, suggested that people be permitted to purchase, with public funds, a private education. Because this plan struck at the foundation of the public-school structure, it was vehemently opposed by many groups. Several other slightly different voucher proposals were offered about the same time, the most notably by John Coons, William Clune, and Stephen Sugarman in their book *Private Wealth and Public Education,* also published in 1970. However, Jencks's suggestions were the ones that became synonymous in the public mind with vouchers.

Debunking Myths. Jencks caused an even greater stir with the publication of *Inequality: A Reassessment of the Effect of Family and Schooling in America.* This book, the result of a three-year study funded by the Carnegie Corporation, came to conclusions that refuted one of the most pervasive U.S. beliefs: that good schooling brings good prospects for economic success. Jencks and his Harvard researchers said this premise was untrue; their data suggested that schools, no matter how good, could not do much to eliminate or even reduce the gap between rich and poor. This report is often compared to the Coleman report in that both dispute schools' ability to improve the social, economic, and intellectual status of students.

Jencks's Influence. Although his conclusions appear to be highly critical of the schools, Jencks felt strongly that schools can accomplish important goals. He argued that school can be a significant learning experience for young people, if not in terms of money and social status, then perhaps in terms of increased creativity, knowledge, enjoyment, and self-esteem. Jencks believed that if the public would recognize what schools cannot do in changing social status, they would have greater success at accomplishing more purely educational goals. Although Jencks was characterized as a liberal by members of the back-to-basics contingent, his suggestions were seized upon by conservatives who wholeheartedly embraced his voucher suggestions to advance parochial and denominational education and who used his arguments from *Inequality: A Reassessment of the Effect of Family and Schooling in America* as further evidence that funding compensatory programs in the schools was less effective than changing fundamental economic conditions in the communities surrounding the schools.

Source:

Neil Postman and Charles Weingartner, *The School Book* (New York: Delacorte/Seymour Lawrence, 1973).

JONATHAN KOZOL

1936-

TEACHER AND EDUCATION CRITIC

"Unbounded and Compensatory Rage." Jonathan Kozol, the son of a physician in the Boston suburbs, grew up in a "privileged and insulated" world. He came into contact with the less fortunate only on trips to drive his live-in maid home to Roxbury, the black section of Boston, on her day off. Years later he realized "with a wave of shame and fear" that the maid's children, brought up by their grandmother, "had been denied the childhood and happiness and care" that had been given to him by their mother. He began teaching at an elementary school in the Roxbury area in 1964, fresh from studying at Harvard and Oxford and living in Paris. In teaching fourth grade he found "a world of suffering, of hopelessness and fear." His shame turned into, as he puts it, "unbounded and compensatory rage," which propelled Kozol toward a career in writing about ghetto schools, illiteracy, and the effects on children of a segregated education. His works garnered national attention, and Kozol's career has been devoted to developing workable alternative urban schools.

National Book Award. Kozol's prominence in the world of educational criticism began in 1967, when his day-to-day account of life for teachers and students in ghetto schools was recognized as a National Book Award winner. *Death at an Early Age* and its subtitle, "The Destruction of the Hearts and Minds of Negro Children in the Boston Public Schools," is an accurate synopsis of Kozol's message. This story of his experiences in a fourth-grade compensatory program for black children describes both the physical conditions the children endured (a classroom was part of an auditorium with other classrooms conducted simultaneously) and the psychological abuse that was integral to the system (teachers regularly referred to the children as "black stuff" and worse). Kozol wrote the book after he was fired from that job for teaching a Langston Hughes poem, "The Landlord," that was not on the approved reading materials list. Kozol did, however, live in Roxbury for the next eighteen years and held other public-school teaching positions, including one at South Boston High, which the federal government placed in receivership after repeated violence rocked the school following desegregation.

A Voice of Protest. Kozol's sense of outrage grew steadily during the 1970s, and his books reflected that escalating sense of injustice. In *Free Schools* (1972) he turned his ire on those who used the free-school concept to promote an exotic and elitist lifestyle rather than to empower students to think and learn for themselves. With the publication of that book some of his old followers viewed him as a traitor to the counterculture, but Kozol felt that urban problems of black students would not be solved by allowing the children to decide on their own what to learn. Other books followed rapidly: *The Night Is Dark* and *I Am Far From Home* (both 1975), *Children of the Revolution* (1978), and *Prisoners of Silence* (1979). In *The Night Is Dark* he dedicated the last chapter to Paulo Freire, a militant literacy reformer whom Kozol met during Freire's tenure at Harvard. Motivated by Freire's reporting about a massive literacy project in Cuba after the revolution, Kozol claimed to be inspired to move from criticism to activism and to adapt Freire's methods to American education. Although Kozol's activism was not highly influential, his books were. The general public as well as professional educators studied Kozol, and many of them agreed with Kozol's basic tenet: "societal denial of the crimes by which it lives demonstrates political ineptitude and ethical betrayal, but it also tells us of that civic pride that goeth before a fall."

Sources:

Jonathan Kozol, *Epilogue to Death at An Early Age* (New York: New American Library, 1985 edition);

Kozol, *Illiterate America* (Garden City, N.Y.: Anchor/Doubleday, 1985).

SIDNEY MARLAND

1914-1992

U.S. COMMISSIONER OF EDUCATION; PRESIDENT, THE COLLEGE BOARD

Career Education. Sidney Marland, Nixon's commissioner of education from 1970 to 1973, came to be known as "the father of career education." His term began at a time of violent turmoil in U.S. education: more than four hundred campuses were on strike or disrupted after the invasion of

Cambodia in May 1970; students had been shot dead by the National Guard at Kent State in Ohio and by the police at Jackson State in Mississippi; and an army research center had been blown up on campus in Madison, Wisconsin. It was Marland's responsibility to assume federal command for U.S. schooling, and he focused attention on the element of education that could reach the widest nonradical audience — careerism. Job-training, wage-earning, the transition to adulthood, writing, and reading became the goals of the federal education bureaucracy.

Marland's Political Skills. According to his memoirs, *Career Education* (1974), Marland was given a mandate by the Nixon administration to devote "immediate attention to increasing the place of 'vocational education' . . . with no increase in the budget." The difficulties of achieving this goal with no money did not deter Marland, who quickly devised the name "career education" and planned the new program to relate "occupational aspects of human development to all levels of learning and all relevant parts of academic success." He then promoted model career-preparation programs in districts eager for a more focused curriculum and subsequently channeled federal money into those areas. His success at marketing reform was due to three things: a commanding communications strategy designed to publicize the idea; the creation of a curricular philosophy; and the creation of detailed grade-by-grade guidelines that would free school districts from having to invest in their own curriculum design. Marland's focused management style and his skill in marketing and implementing a federally devised educational plan in districts that had heretofore screamed "local control" gave him power that former commissioners had lacked.

Repudiation. Marland's premise that career education would radically improve U.S. education was not borne out by a Department of Health, Education, and Welfare study called *Work in America* (1973). Coordinated by manpower specialist James O'Toole, the report suggested that the vast oversupply of college-educated labor which existed at the time had caused the arbitrary raising of the credentials required for a job without raising the wages or the skill levels. The report also found an ineffective link between occupational education and future employment, with more than half of high schools' vocational graduates taking jobs unrelated to their training. Ironically, it was at this time that Marland left the federal position and assumed the presidency of the College Board. In 1975, when the Scholastic Aptitude Test (SAT) scores of college-bound students reached their lowest level in twelve years, Marland became a driving force in a national movement to combat the erosion of students' math and literacy skills.

Marland and the SAT. Marland knew which educational issues commanded public attention. He seized on these "hot button" problems, and media coverage always followed. For example, when he appointed a panel "to do all that we can to investigate and interpret this phenomenon (the decline in scores) to the public," his pledge appeared on front pages of newspapers across the United States. Funds for the work of the panel came from the College Board and from Educational Testing Service (ETS), the producer of the SAT and other tests administered by the College Board, both of which had a political and financial interest in the problems. Essentially, the panel identified two phases in the long score decline. The first phase, up to 1970, was identified as a demographic decline because the numbers of the test-taking group were growing so rapidly, with more people from nontraditional, nonscholastic backgrounds going on to college in greater numbers. The next phase, however, was described as a cognitive falloff, because the composition of the test-taking group had stabilized and only about 20 percent of the decline could be attributed to the nontraditional students taking the SAT. Marland's appointed panel suggested that this second phase of the drop in scores could be attributed to causes such as more electives and fewer traditional courses, less homework, too much television, unstable family life, and the political disruptions of the prior decade. It was with the identification of these factors that Marland's strongest influence was felt in the schools. Opponents of school liberalization used them as part of the intellecutal basis of a strong backlash against curriculum innovations, driving a shift toward what came to be known as the back-to-basics curriculum.

Sources:

Sidney Marland, *Career Education* (New York, 1974);

Ira Shor, *Culture Wars: School and Society in the Conservative Restoration 1969–1984* (Boston: Routledge & Kegan Paul, 1986).

CHARLES E. SILBERMAN

1925-

JOURNALIST AND EDUCATION CRITIC

Reformer. In 1970 journalist and scholar Charles Silberman published *Crisis in the Classroom*, a critique of U.S. education that seized the attention of his intended audience: "teachers and students, school board members and taxpayers, public officials and civic leaders, newspaper and magazine editors and readers, television directors and viewers, parents and children." This ambitious volume, subtitled *The Remaking of American Education*, was researched during a three-year period when Silberman was serving as director of the Carnegie Study of the Education of Educators, and it added considerable respectability to the criticisms that had been made previously by radicals and dissidents. Silberman's status as a *Fortune* editor and as an objective observer gave his inquiry weight that other critics lacked.

Findings. He begins the book with a status report on the state of U.S. education in the last third of the twentieth century: "In most large cities and a good many smaller ones the public schools are in disarray, torn apart by conflicts over integration, desegregation, decentralization, and community control. . . . In a good many placid cities, towns and suburbs, seemingly sheltered from racial conflict, schools have been closed by taxpayer revolts, teacher strikes, or student dissent. . . . Colleges and universities face equally serious, if somewhat different, problems." He points out, on the other hand, some points of pride: improvement in elementary and secondary education, enrollment of a much larger percentage of the population than ever before (more than any other society except Japan), doubling of per-pupil expenditures since the end of World War II, and a decline in the dropout rate. Despite the good news, Silberman's overall assessment of the schools he saw during his research was clearly negative: "Adults fail to appreciate what grim, joyless places most American schools are, how oppressive and petty are the rules by which they are governed, how intellectually sterile and esthetically barren the atmosphere, what an appalling lack of civility obtains on the part of teachers and principals, what contempt they unconsciously display for children as children."

Recommendations. After explaining how and why most schools — both middle-class and "slum" schools, as they were called then — had created "a generation of students who lack humane values," Silberman presented explicit recommendations for how the schools could be improved. He argued for a remaking of the elementary grades in the mold of the new English primary schools, those whose teachers and administrators shared a set of beliefs about the nature of childhood, learning, and schooling. These variously named informal, or open, schools were founded on the conviction that children learn best when learning grows out of what interests the learner, rather than what interests the teacher. Silberman did not suggest that elementary teachers abdicate their adult authority, only that they change the way they exercise it. In critiquing the secondary schools, Silberman echoed Jerome Bruner, who in 1961 suggested that education's major emphasis must be to give students an understanding of the fundamental structure of the disciplines they study. Evoking Bruner, Silberman proposed that "Whatever is introduced, let it be pursued continuously enough to give the student a sense of the power of mind that comes from a deepening of understanding." He then illustrated this precept by outlining curricular reforms in dozens of exemplary high schools. The book also critiques and suggests reforms at the college level, most notably regarding the education of teachers. Silberman criticized the "educationists" who prepared teachers for the classroom through the use of abstractions. He clearly outlined the failures in most teacher-preparation curricula; however, he failed to offer any real suggestions as to how these problems could be solved.

Silberman's Influence on Education in the 1970s. *Crisis in the Classroom* set the stage for many public debates about educational reform during the decade. Silberman reached a highly diverse audience; some observers suggested that by 1973 "almost everybody claimed to know what Silberman's book is about." Silberman's suggestions for overhauling the U.S. educational system, from kindergarten through graduate school, raised the general public's level of awareness of reform options. His criticisms and his recommendations were cited by scores of reformers during the decade.

Sources:
Neil Postman and Charles Weingartner, *The School Book* (New York: Delacorte/Seymour Lawrence, 1973);

Charles Silberman, *Crisis in the Classroom* (New York: Random House, 1970).

PEOPLE IN THE NEWS

In 1975 **Jerald Bachman,** of the University of Michigan, revealed results of a four-year study that suggested that high-school dropouts do not suffer financially or emotionally by quitting school before graduating.

Rutgers University sociologist **Peter Berger** said in a 1972 keynote address to the American Association of State Colleges and Universities that "counter culture values" among upper-middle-class students had turned some of the most prestigious universities into "vast identity workshops" where "intellectual rot" replaced a valid curriculum.

In 1972, after a Brooklyn teacher was assaulted in front of his class by the older brother of a pupil he had corrected, New York state representative **John Bingham** urged that the New York Board of Education provide every teacher with a silent electronic alarm device for protection.

In 1972 Harvard president **Derek Bok** defended special-admissions policies for minority candidates on NBC's *Meet the Press*.

In 1977 **Catherine Burke** became the first of a group of women to be named Rhodes Scholars but only after the British Parliament broke the terms of Cecil Rhodes's will that had bequeathed scholarships to males only. "I may be one of the first to go to Oxford," Burke said, "but I could also be the first one sent home."

Joe Califano, the Carter administration's secretary of HEW, said in 1977 that the two burning issues facing schools were maintaining dollars for Title I's programs for the disadvantaged and increasing dollars for college funding for the middle class.

President Jimmy Carter announced in 1977 that his daughter **Amy** would attend public schools in Washington when the family moved to the White House.

In 1973 Virginia teacher **Susan Cohen** sued her school district for forcing her to take a mandatory pregnancy leave with pay when she reached five months into her term. After losing in the lower courts, Cohen won her case on appeal, and the court declared it was "shocked at the discrimination."

John Coleman, president of all-male Quaker Haverford College, worked out a student-exchange program with all-female Bryn Mawr in 1977.

Peter Doe, an eighteen-year-old who sued the San Francisco Unified School District because he was still reading at a fifth-grade level after graduation, lost his appeal in 1976.

Superior Court judge **Michael Dugan** of Indiana ruled in 1977 that use of a ninth-grade biology text that stressed the biblical interpretation of creation violated the separation of church and state.

In 1971 Dallas school superintendent **Nolan Estes** objected to a petition to restrict corporal punishment after a child hemorrhaged from a paddling. "I will not be a superintendent in a district where principals are not allowed to spank," he said.

President Gerald Ford ordered HEW in 1976 to take another look at Title IX regulations after a federal official in Arizona ordered that a father-son banquet be changed to a parent-child banquet.

In 1979 **Bartlett Giamatti,** president of Yale, recommended a program in which Yale faculty work with elementary and secondary teachers to develop curricula for the New Haven schools.

In 1975 **Dr. Charles Glatt,** prominent national school-desegregation expert and Ohio State professor, was killed by gunmen at a Dayton, Ohio, federal building as he worked at his desk preparing a desegregation plan for the Dayton schools.

The case of **Ann** and **Dennis Graham,** who divorced in Colorado in 1976, set a precedent when a judge ruled that the value of Dennis's M.A. degree was not subject to property division.

U.S. Congresswoman **Edith Green** (D–Oregon) announced that she was leaving the House Education and Labor Committee in 1973 because of repeated presidential vetoes of educational appropriations.

When **Charles Grigg** of Florida State University sampled southern school administrators in 2,176 districts, over 75 percent reported "no noticeable difference" in white student enrollment after desegregation.

To improve the Nixon administration's understanding of campus realities, Vanderbilt University chancellor **Alexander Heard** was appointed ambassador from academia to the White House less than one week after the May 1970 shooting of four Kent State students.

Marco Hernandez became the first Puerto Rican high-school principal in New York City in 1971 (six Puerto Ricans were already elementary school principals).

University of Miami English professor **Robert Hosman** sued to have Dade County schools closed down as a "public nuisance" due to the rampant violence there in 1976.

Bodyguards were needed to protect Prof. **Arthur Jensen** at Berkeley after he refused to recant his 1969 position that IQ scores were related to race. In 1973 he published *Genetics and Education*, maintaining his thesis that poor black children need different types of education because they learn differently from middle-class children.

Harvard psychologist **Jerome Kagan** told the American Association for the Advancement of Science in 1974 that his research had convinced him that infant retardation is reversible and that cognitive development in the early years is plastic enough to permit children to make up deficits later on.

New York City College professor **Herbert Katzenstein** reported that in 1970 a survey of that school's alumni showed that black graduates were earning more than their white counterparts, $9,670 as compared to $8,050. He attributed this in part to the limited supply of black college graduates and the large numbers of corporations eager to hire a more diverse population.

In 1973 Stanford dean **William Kays** promoted engineering as a career for women in a brochure called *Consider the Possibility*. At Stanford fewer than 3 percent of engineering students were women.

Clark Kerr, chair of the Carnegie Commission on Higher Education, said college in 1973 was still a good investment, yielding ten cents per dollar spent for each year of the graduate's career.

In 1970 the *New York Review of Books* celebrated a collection of poetry of "slum children" from P.S. 61 in New York City. The collection, compiled by poet **Kenneth Koch**, was published as *Wishes, Lies, and Dreams*.

Assistant HEW secretary for education **Sidney Marland** warned that the appointment of Caspar ("Cap the Knife") Weinburger as Nixon's new secretary of HEW in 1973 would signal severe budget cutting and an attitude of "social programs be damned."

Kent State students **Jeffrey Miller, Allison Krause, William Shroeder,** and **Sandy Scheuer** were killed by the National Guard at a campus protest in Ohio in May 1970.

William Mora, Jr., a Louisiana high-school student convicted of drug possession after marijuana was found in his wallet by a gym teacher, had the conviction overturned by the Supreme Court in 1977.

In 1973 **Ralph Nader** accused the Department of Transportation of "gross neglect in failing to protect the twenty million children who ride school buses every day" and called for meaningful congressional reform of school bus standards.

Prof. **Frank Newman** of Stanford issued an HEW report in 1973 on the glut of doctorates in higher education. He discovered a surplus in education, English, history, and anthropology but found that doctorates were still needed in the health professions.

State University of New York psychology professor **Robert Nichols** suggested to an American Psychological Association assembly in 1976 that the reason for the decline in SAT scores could be genetic — ". . . intelligence has the highest heritability of all psychological traits, and those families that produce the higher-scoring children tend to produce fewer of them."

Barbara Overlands crusaded against student science-fair animal experiments in New York in 1972, claiming that of eighty-nine projects, half involved infliction of pain or lingering death for the animals.

Ellis Page of the University of Connecticut debunked an experiment done at the University of Wisconsin where researchers claimed to have raised IQ levels of disadvantaged infants by over thirty points. In his 1976 *Educational Researcher* article he cited deficiencies in research protocol such as biased selection of treatment groups, contamination of criterion tests, and failure to specify treatments.

UCLA professor **James Popham** warned a House subcommittee in 1973 that using standardized achievement tests to see how well schools are working was like "trying to measure mileage with a tablespoon." He argued that criterion-referenced tests were much better indicators of performance.

In 1973 a federal court overturned New York tenth-grade teacher **Susan Russo**'s firing for her refusal to recite the pledge of allegiance at her school; the court ruled that Russo had been coerced.

In 1973 **Albert Shanker,** of the New York chapter of the American Federation of Teachers, and **Thomas Hobart,** of the New York State Teachers Association, were chosen as copresidents when the groups merged for the first time.

In 1972 **Dr. B. F. Skinner** served as a consultant to the Dallas public schools when the Supreme Court considered *Ware* v. *Estes* a case on spanking in the public schools. The Dallas brief stated in part: "Until we reach a utopian society, we may have to use corporal punishment in all schools." The Supreme Court agreed, affirming spanking as an educational tool.

Father Paul Smith, black principal of Holy Angels Roman Catholic Elementary School in Chicago, argued in a 1973 *Newsweek* article that permissive education reflects an "Anglo-Saxon mentality of freedom. The black child of the inner city needs the tight system we have because of the chaos and disruption in the community where he lives."

Karen Stevenson, a University of North Carolina graduate, was the first black American woman to be named a Rhodes scholar in 1979.

A U.S. District Court ruled that **Jeff Tractman,** editor of Manhattan's Stuyvesant High's newspaper, could not be barred from distributing and publishing the results of a "frank and personal" questionnaire about students' sexual attitudes, experiences, and preferences.

The Educational Testing Service (ETS) sued **Max Tuchman,** operator of Tuchman Tutoring of New York, after learning that some questions on the 1978 SAT were identical to questions used in his private review courses. Tuchman, who paid fifteen thousand dollars to ETS in a settlement, had collected the questions a year earlier when acting as an SAT proctor.

In 1977 Brown University English professor **A. D. Van Nostrand** formed the Center for Research in Writing to promote his practice of teaching functional writing. Nostrand formed the center after discovering that his ivy league students could not construct sentences nor organize paragraphs.

In April 1973 New Jersey Supreme Court justice **Joseph Weintraub** found that state's school-finance scheme violated the state's constitutional provision to provide "thorough and efficient" education for all children.

In 1979 **Maharishi Mahesh Yogi**'s textbook on transcendental meditation was barred from New Jersey classrooms when a federal appeals court found that its use violated the separation of church and state.

AWARDS

NATIONAL TEACHER OF THE YEAR

1970: **Johnnie T. Dennis** — Physics and Math
Walla Walla High School, Walla Walla, Washington

1971: **Martha Stringfellow** — First Grade
Lewisville Elementary, Chester County, South Carolina

1972: **James M. Rogers** — American History and Black Studies
Durham High School, Durham, North Carolina

1973: **John A. Ensworth** — Sixth Grade
Kenwood School, Bend, Oregon

1974: **Vivian Tom** — Social Studies
Lincoln High School, Yonkers, New York

1975: **Roberta G. Heyer** — Science
Johanna Junior High School, Saint Paul, Minnesota

1976: **Ruby Murchison** — Social Studies
Washington Drive Junior High School, Fayetteville, North Carolina

1977: **Myrra L. Lee** — Social Living
Helix High School, La Mesa, California

1978: **Elaine Barbour** — Sixth Grade
Coal Creek Elementary, Montrose, Colorado

1979: **Marilyn W. Black** — Elementary Art
Bernice Ray School, Hanover, New Hampshire

DEATHS

Jacob Bronowski, professor of mathematics and sciences at Massachusetts Institute of Technology, leader in development of modern scientific humanism, 22 August 1974.

Oscar James Campbell, Jr., William Shakespeare scholar and author of the *Readers' Encyclopedia of Shakespeare,* 1 June 1970.

Horace Clayton, sociologist and author of *Black Metropolis,* a study of the place of blacks in U.S. industry, 25 January 1970.

Francis Cornell, North Carolina native who specialized in educational statistics and helped to shape the postwar educational system in West Germany, 2 July 1979.

Margaret Craighill, medical college dean and in 1943 the first woman to be commissioned directly into the Army Medical Corps, 25 July 1977.

Godfrey Dewey, son of Melvil Dewey of Dewey decimal system fame; the younger Dewey was a promoter of the phonetic spelling movement and the president of Emerson College, 20 October 1977.

Loren Eisley, anthropologist, educator, author; scientist who wrote with a poetic sensitivity, 10 July 1977.

Lloyd Fallers, American social anthropologist at the University of Chicago, 4 July 1974.

Maurice Freedman, visiting professor at Yale and Cornell, founder and managing editor of *Jewish Journal of Sociology,* 14 July 1975.

Lawrence Kimpton, chancellor of the University of Chicago and chief administrator of the metallurgy laboratory when the atomic bomb was in production there under the code name "The Manhattan Project," 2 November 1977.

Frank Laubach, crusader against illiteracy who founded the "each one teach one" method and who wrote primers for teaching in more than three hundred dialects, 11 June 1970.

Henry Noble MacCracken, foremost proponent of progressive education for women and president of Vassar for thirty-one years, 7 May 1970.

Robert MacIver, intellectual whose career influence in sociology was often compared to John Dewey's influence in philosophy, 5 June 1970.

J. F. McNeill, principal of fifty-five-hundred-student Erasmus Hall High School in Brooklyn for thirty-one years; Erasmus Hall produced more Westinghouse national science talent search scholars than any other school in the country.

Frederick Merk, scholar of American frontier history whose beloved Harvard course came to be known as "Wagon Wheels," 27 September 1977.

A. S. Neill, Scottish-born educator and founder of the Summerhill school, which attracted dozens of U.S. scholars and inspired the open classroom concept, 23 September 1973.

Hortense Powdermaker, anthropologist at Queens College and the New School for Social Research, studied Hollywood's influence on U.S. culture, 16 June 1970.

I. A. Richards, English professor at Harvard, author of many texts on literary criticism and advocate of a system called Basic English for teaching English to foreign students, 7 September 1979.

Edgar Robinson, founder of Stanford's Institute of American History, whose purpose was to upgrade the teaching of that subject in the nation's schools, 9 September 1977.

Bertrand Russell, British scholar who helped determine the direction of modern philosophy and who, although a Nobel Prize winner for literature, was deemed unfit to teach at City College, New York, 3 February 1970.

Lionel Trilling, professor emeritus at Columbia University, one of the finest American literary critics and the organizer of the Kenyon School of Letters at Indiana University, 5 November 1975.

T. Harry Williams, foremost Civil War scholar and professor at Louisiana State University who received a Pulitzer Prize for his biography of Huey Long, 6 July 1979.

Mary Clabaugh Wright, first woman full professor at Yale and scholar of Chinese history, 18 June 1970.

PUBLICATIONS

Ronald Bailey and Janet Saxe, *Teaching Black: An Evaluation of Methods and Resources* (Stanford University: Multi-Ethnic Education Resources Center, 1971);

J. Ben-David, *American Higher Education* (New York: McGraw-Hill, 1972);

Steve Bhaerman and Joel Denker, *No Particular Place to Go: The Making of a Free School* (New York: Simon & Schuster, 1972);

Caroline Bird, *The Case Against College* (New York: McKay, 1975);

J. Bremer and M. von Moschziske, *The School Without Walls* (New York: Holt, Rinehart & Winston, 1971);

Carnegie Commission on Higher Education, *Priorities for Action: Final Report* (New York: McGraw-Hill, 1972);

Ruth Dropkin and Arthur Tobeir, eds., *Roots of Open Education in America* (New York: City College Workshop Center for Open Education, 1970);

James Duggins, *Teaching Reading for Human Values in High School* (Boston: Merrill, 1972);

Paulo Freire, *Pedagogy in Process: The Letters to Guinea-Bissau* (New York: Seabury Press, 1978);

Freire, *Pedagogy of the Oppressed* (New York: Herder & Herder, 1972);

Alvin Hertzberg and Edward Stone, *Schools Are for Children: An American Approach to the Open Classroom* (New York: Schocken Books, 1971);

John Holt, *Freedom and Beyond* (New York: Dutton, 1972);

Clark Kerr, *The Uses of the University, With a Postscript — 1972* (Cambridge, Mass.: Harvard University Press, 1972);

Phyllis Klotman, ed., *Humanities Through the Black Experience* (Dubuque, Iowa: Kendall-Hunt, 1977);

Herbert Kohl, *On Teaching* (New York: Schocken Books, 1976);

Gerald Lesser, *Children and Television: Lessons from 'Sesame Street'* (New York: Random House, 1974);

Marc Libarle and Tom Seligson, *The High School Revolutionaries* (New York: Simon & Schuster, 1970);

Kate Long, *Johnny's Such a Bright Boy, What a Shame He's Retarded: In Support of Mainstreaming in the Public Schools* (Boston: Houghton Mifflin, 1977);

D. W. McNally, *Piaget, Education and Teaching* (Sussex, England: Harvester Press, 1973);

Jack Nelson and Kenneth Carlson, *Radical Ideas and the Schools* (New York: Holt, Rinehart & Winston, 1972):

Vance Packard, *The People Shapers* (Boston: Little, Brown, 1977);

Jeffrey Schrank, *Teaching Human Beings* (Boston: Beacon, 1972);

Ira Shor, *Culture Wars: School and Society in the Conservative Restoration 1969–1984* (Boston: Routledge & Kegan Paul, 1986);

Charles Silberman, *Crisis in the Classroom* (New York: Prentice-Hall, 1971);

Ronald Sobel, *CRISIS: The Taxpayer Revolt and Your Kid's Schools* (White Plains, N.Y.: Knowledge Industry Publications, 1978);

Thomas Sowell, *Black Education: Myths and Tragedies* (New York: McKay, 1973);

Laurel Tanner, *Classroom Discipline for Effective Teaching and Learning* (New York: Holt, Rinehart & Winston, 1978);

Harvey Weiner, *Any Child Can Write* (New York: McGraw-Hill, 1978);

Harry Wolcott, *Teachers Versus Technocrats* (Eugene: University of Oregon Center for Educational Policy and Management, 1977).

FASHION

by JANE GERHARD

CONTENTS

Sidebars and tables are listed in italics.

1970

- According to Rosemary McMurty, vice-president of McCall Patterns, denim blue jeans become "the youth status symbol of the world."

- The National Organization of Minority Architects (NOMA) is founded in Detroit, Michigan.

- The miniskirt continues to grow in popularity.

- The unisex T-shirt-and-jeans look becomes the uniform of choice for the college and high-school set.

- The shag haircut is the ultimate unisex hairstyle.

- The weekly haircut for men ends. Barbers complain that they are losing business as more men keep their hair long or go to salons for stylized haircuts.

- American automobile producers suffer a 10 percent decline in car sales during the 1970 model year due to new fuel-efficient foreign imports.

1971

- Hot pants, very brief shorts for women, become a fashion sensation.

- Ralph Lauren premieres his first design for women: a women's version of the classic men's cotton Oxford shirt.

- All U.S. automobile producers adjust their 1971 engines to use new low-lead or leadless gasolines in an effort to reduce pollutants from new cars.

- Chinese influence is apparent in American fashion as China rejoins the international community.

- Architects Robert Venturi and Denise Scott Brown publish *Learning From Las Vegas.*

1972

- Clogs, platform sandals, and high boots are the hot new trends in women's footware.

- "Glitter Rock," cross-dressing, and androgyny sweep major urban areas.

- Body tattoos become popular among young women after celebrities such as Cher, Joan Baez, and Grace Slick make them hip.

- American Motors introduces a new sports car, the Levi Gremlin, that has its bucket seats covered with the popular denim fabric.

- A Japanese department-store chain woos U.S. designer Bill Blass to export his menswear. Blass is quoted as saying "It's now necessary to move (fashion) towards an international basis."

- The "New York Five" architects, Michael Graves, Peter Eisenman, Richard Meier, John Hejduk, and Charles Gwathmey, publish a book of their innovative designs called *Five Architects.*

1973

- In the spirit of antifashion, the sleeveless tank top is a runaway hit in both men's and women's apparel.

- Rejecting the unisex look, Yves St. Laurent makes a decidedly feminine pantsuit high fashion for women.

- "Not being dressed to the teeth," as American designer Anne Klein puts it, becomes the first rule of fashion.

- Riding the popularity of hand-decorated jeans, Levi Strauss and Company sponsors a denim design contest that draws over ten thousand entries.

- Pioneering architectural firm Johnson and Burgee completes its first postmodern high-rise office building, the IDS Center in Minneapolis, Minnesota.

- Ralph Lauren designs the costumes for Robert Redford in the film *The Great Gatsby*.

- Interior fabrics of American cars are required by the government to meet new federal flammability standards.

- Popular 1973 automobile models bring U.S. auto manufacturers within 1 percent of realizing the "10-million-car-year."

- The American architectural firm Skidmore, Owings and Merrill completes the world's tallest building, the Sears Tower in Chicago.

- Movie hits *The Sting, The Great Gatsby,* and *Paper Moon* fuel a popular Depression-era clothing craze.

16 Oct. The Arab-dominated Organization of Petroleum Exporting Countries (OPEC) cuts the flow of oil to the United States, triggering gasoline shortages across the country.

1974

- Men turn the muscle shirt into a unique fashion statement, emphasizing the body differences between men and women.

- The bulky fisherman sweater tied with a belt becomes fall high fashion.

- The return of the curl harkens the end of the long, straight hair look for women.

- The new string bikini bathing suit becomes popular.

- In the summer the cotton espadrille sandal with rope wedge sole moves off the beach and onto city streets.

- *Architectural Forum,* one of the more avant-garde publications in the field, ceases publication with its March issue.

Nov. The Mormon Tabernacle opens in Kensington, Maryland; it is a "superb blend of church and futuristic fantasy," comments *The New York Times* critic Paul Goldberg.

1975

- Polyester and mixed-blend fabrics become popular in both men's and women's wear.

- Men's platform shoes become popular.

- Discotheques are the hottest new dance clubs, triggering a new form-fitting, more explicitly sexy look for men and women.

- Levi Strauss, with sales of more than $1 billion in 1975, claims to be the world's largest apparel maker.

1976

- The architectural firm Johnson and Burgee complete Pennzoil Place in Houston, Texas, a project designed to prove that good architecture is economically profitable for developers.

- Designer Yves St. Laurent launches his rich-peasant look for women. With its long full skirts, drawstring blouses, and vests worn with boots, this look harkens back to America's cowboy days, with a new ethnic twist.

- The newest look in women's fashion is the tabard, a sandwich-board styled garment that ties under the arms and at the waist, and is worn over pants or skirts.

- Cowl neck sweaters are popular.

- In London punk rock arrives, oriented around bands such as the Sex Pistols and the Clash; in New York City clubs such as CBGB's and Max's Kansas City host the Ramones and Blondie.

1977

- Architects at I. M. Pei and Associates complete plans for Dallas City Hall in Dallas, Texas.

- The feminine look returns to women's fashion, with longer graceful skirts, printed shawls, sundresses, and more elegant evening wear making fashion headlines.

- Fur coats become fashionable after a seven-year absence.

- The need for fuel efficiency drives the auto industry to downsize its biggest cars.

- Studio 54 opens in New York City.

- Legwarmers in patterned knits and wool become popular.

- Diane Keaton, in her starring role in the film *Annie Hall*, catapults Ralph Lauren's rumpled men's look for women to high fashion.

- The film *Saturday Night Fever*, staring John Travolta, sweeps the country and leaves a new disco look in its wake.

1978

- The new Federal Energy Act requires all automobiles to attain a mileage-per-gallon average of 18 (28.8 km), leading U.S. producers to downsize their 1978 models.

- Chrysler introduces the first domestic fifth-door hatchback on the Horizon and Omni sedans to compete against Japan's Honda Civic and Germany's Volkswagen Rabbit.

- Architects Philip Johnson and John Burgee unveil their designs for the American Telephone and Telegraph (AT&T) Building in New York City and launch postmodern architecture.

- Lead singer Johnny Rotten and the punk rock group the Sex Pistols open their first and only American tour in Atlanta.

1 June   In Washington, D.C., President Jimmy Carter officially opens the new East Wing of the National Gallery of Art, designed by architect I. M. Pei.

29 Nov.   Blue jeans manufactured by Levi Strauss and Company go on sale in East Berlin. It is the first time the denim pants are available to ordinary East German consumers using East German currency.

1979

- Architects at I. M. Pei and Associates complete the John F. Kennedy Library in Boston, Massachusetts.

- In the spring architect Michael Graves exhibits his drawings, murals, sketches, models, and photographs at the Max Protech Gallery in New York City.

- Roller disco becomes popular, and so do the satin stretch bodysuits in neon colors worn by the dancers.

- A second oil crisis grips the nation as Iranian oil is cut off by an Islamic revolution and OPEC hikes its oil prices.

OVERVIEW

Calming Down. The 1970s began where the 1960s left off: restless, critical of the status quo, questioning traditional authority and social hierarchies, and flamboyantly expressive. The social upheavals that swept the country in the mid 1960s — civil rights, women's liberation, the environmental movement, gay liberation — continued to shape the 1970s. But the 1970s were not merely a repeat of the 1960s. Political protest movements lost steam and turned instead to a focus on lifestyles and consumption. America's turn inward bequeathed to the era the sardonic title "the me decade."

Lifestyles. The focus on lifestyles reflected the desire to escape from the stream of bad news flowing from the television and the newspaper. The Vietnam War, Watergate, the oil crisis, and the recession cast doubts on the fundamental beliefs of most Americans — that American democracy worked, that hard work would lead to economic security, and that America was a benign influence on the international stage. Private life seemed to be the only refuge from the anxieties of a world in flux. "Doing your own thing," the battle cry of the 1960s, became an alternative to participating in public life.

Options. The slogan "do your own thing" elevated self-expression over traditionalism in every avenue of life. In the realm of fashion (clothing, architecture, furniture, interior design, and autos) innovation, eclecticism, and choice were the underlining values in the 1970s. American designers and architects felt free to pick and choose from a range of historical and contemporary motifs and details to create an entirely new look. As Americans became conscious of the impact of their lifestyles on the global environment and their own pocketbooks, utility became an important value. Cars became more efficient, interiors more environmental, and furniture more versatile.

Anything Goes. American women benefited enormously from the fashion innovations of the 1960s. In the wake of such fashion breakthroughs as psychedelic colors, miniskirts, and pants, American women in the 1970s had a new range of looks from which to choose. Pants were no longer controversial and came in a variety of styles and materials, from velvet hot pants to the new designer denim jeans. Women wore flowing evening pants, tailored pants with a short jacket to work, and sporty khakis on the weekends. Likewise, with the end of the hemline battles of the early 1970s, women were free to choose between the short miniskirt or the longish peasant skirt, adorned with platform sandals, Frye boots, or the espadrille. What mattered most was that each woman could create her own unique style and look.

Sportswear. If choice was the key word in women's fashion in the 1970s, then leisure was the key for menswear. Sportswear, a category of clothing that had been growing since the 1950s, exploded in the 1970s. Unstructured jackets worn over vests or sweaters emphasized that American men no longer were workaholics but lived full and satisfying lives. Rugged sportswear, once worn for hunting and fishing or for ski trips, made its way into men's weekend wear, lending an air of athleticism to the fashionable. This was the decade in which the jogging suit became the quintessential leisure wear, whether or not one jogged.

Decline of Modernism. In architecture the old modernist structures of glass and steel were giving way to a new look. Rejecting the isolation of the international high-rise, a new generation of architects designed buildings that were more sensitive to their surrounding environments. Many architects used local materials and borrowed regional features from surrounding buildings for their designs. Rejecting the elitism of modernism, popular and public vernacular became the new language of American architecture. Postmodern architecture took off at the end of the decade with the startling new look of Philip Johnson's American Telephone and Telegraph (AT&T) Building in New York City.

Interior Environments. Interior designers adopted a new guiding metaphor for their work in the 1970s. Building on the idea of shared community space made popular by the communalism of the 1960s, interior spaces were conceived as total environments where sights, sounds, furniture, and even walls were conceived of as an organic whole. Institutional spaces such as corporations and schools opted for open spaces divided by low movable walls, large plants, or furniture clusters. Glass walls or floor-to-ceiling windows became fashionable as a way to give rooms the appearance of even more open space.

Trimmed-Down Cars. American car producers in the 1970s faced challenges on two fronts: from foreign competitors and from the fuel shortages caused by the oil crises of 1973 and 1979. Together these two influences forced Detroit to rethink its most basic designs. Large American cars could remain profitable only if gas were plentiful and cheap, neither of which was true by 1974. Foreign imports were running away with the domestic market with their energy-efficient minicars. Detroit fought back and introduced a new generation of fuel-efficient compact and subcompact cars. Old favorites such as the Ford Mustang and the Chevrolet Corvette remained, however, for those who still longed for the nostalgia of the muscle car.

New Upheavals. By the end of the decade Americans slowly returned to traditionalism. Tired of political upheavals and two decades of social challenges to traditional middle-class values, Americans abandoned their emphasis on leisure and on lifestyles. Women began to dress in more feminine suits and dresses, men's unstructured look tidied up into a more preppy demeanor, and discos began to disappear. The 1970s uneasily and tentatively bridged the two very distinct and radically different decades of the 1960s and 1980s. Between the counterculture and Ronald Reagan, Americans in the 1970s faced a moment of uncertainty and political disillusionment. What they wholeheartedly embraced was the power of leisure and of self-expression to sweeten the bitter pill of change.

Gown reflecting the popularity of ethnic themes in design, circa 1971

TOPICS IN THE NEWS

WOMEN'S FASHION

Anything Goes. In the 1970s women had a new range of fashion open to them. Influenced by the women's liberation movement and the protest years of the 1960s, American women were no longer willing to follow the lead of fashion designers. Women wanted more than one look and seemed to thrive on choice. Selecting from a variety of fashions and styles suited women's new sense of fashion independence. As designer Calvin Klein explained, the new ethic in clothes was that they must work "over and over" in varying ensembles, from day to night, and from season to season. Hemlines could be either short, like the miniskirt, or long, like the peasant dress. Pants were no longer controversial. More and more women chose to wear casual no-press pants to work and luxurious velvet or satin pants for an elegant evening out. Growing interest in the Third World and Asia launched a new ethnic look for women, while concern with ecology set off an antifur backlash. With all these choices American women could design their own look, one that expressed their own unique sense of style. Choice, personality, and comfort were the fashion hallmarks of the 1970s woman.

Breaking the Rules. The 1970s also marked a breakdown of traditional categories in fashion. Until the 1970s haute couture had set fashion trends for all women. But thanks to the youth movement of the late 1960s, fashion was now created on the streets and campuses across the nation. Ordinary young Americans set the trends that fashion designers like Oscar de la Renta followed. Imitating the political slogans of 1968, Yves St. Laurent cried, "Down with the Ritz, up with the street!"

Choices. This "do your own thing" attitude in clothes emphasized a woman's personality, her independence of mind, and her spirit of experimentation. Hot pants, short shorts for women, burst into the headlines in 1971 to rival the still-popular miniskirt. Worn with high boots and a maxi coat, or platform sandals and a halter top, hot pants were popular in 1971 and 1972. Ethnic and period fashions were also big hits. Styles of the American Indian, the Tirolean peasant, the Spanish gypsy, the frontier woman, and the Victorian lady were seen throughout the fashion world. New variations on pants appeared in long and short culottes that hung like a skirt, harem pants that bloused at the ankle, and knickers worn with boots.

Day Wear. Nowhere was the line between dress and sportswear more blurred in the early 1970s than at work. Shirtdresses that fell just above or below the knee with a long-slit hemline could be worn at work or for a casual dinner out. The Saint-Tropez skirt with its spirals of cotton prints looked like vacation wear, but when combined with a vest, antique blouse, or a blazer, it became fashionable for the office. The safari-styled pantsuit with its loose drawstring jacket and sweater sets by Anne Klein were also popular work choices. Most important, women felt free to wear a range of clothes to work, from pantsuits to casual sweater sets to knee-length or midcalf-length dresses.

Fabrics and Colors. In the early years of the decade new colors and patterns multiplied. Popular patterns included stars, flowers, big arrows, zigzag argyles, and Zodiac signs. Paisley prints remained popular. There were also new fabric combinations of acetate and nylon, polyester, nylon and flax, and many variations of cotton and dacron. These fabrics held their shape and line without ironing. Sparkle and glitter were popular for evening wear. Metallics were frequently blended with wool and mohair in sweaters to add elegance and a feeling of luxury. By the end of the decade, day wear returned to more classic whites, grays, and subdued solids; evening wear turned from colors to blacks and solids.

Shoes and Cosmetics. Shoe designers fell in line with the new looks for women. Knee-high boots were the rage. The square-heel Frye boot gave this trend a western feel. Swedish clogs, linen espadrilles, and platform sandals were also big fashion hits. In cosmetics natural products took off. Cucumber lotions, herbal cleansers, vitamin E lipstick, and protein shampoos sold briskly. Spokesmen for big cosmetics firms contended that their products had

Advertisement showing the emphasis on leisure in 1970s men's fashion

always used natural ingredients and tried to capitalize on the growing interest in organic foods and gardening.

Sources:

Annalee Gold, *90 Years of Fashion* (New York: Fairchild Fashion Group, 1991);

Caroline Rennolds Milbank, *Couture: The Great Designers* (New York: Stewart, Tabori & Chang, 1985), pp. 183–186, 399–402;

Doreen Yarwood, *Fashion in the Western World: 1500–1990* (New York: Drama Book Publishers, 1992), pp. 149–165.

MENSWEAR

A Quiet Revolution. Like women, men in the 1970s benefited from the same spirit of choice and experimentation unleashed by the 1960s. The two most important innovations in the 1970s were the increase in men's leisure wear and the use of new colors and fabrics. The white shirt fell into a fashion abyss, while double-knit and stretch-knit suits became popular. Rose, purple, orange, and green became acceptable colors for men's leisure wear and regularly appeared in bright patterns on the synthetic shirts worn by men in urban centers. Wide ties in big floral prints could be seen under light-colored, wide-lapeled jackets and slightly belled and pleated pants on a typical evening out in any city in the United States. By 1977 menswear came out of its "peacock period," as one critic commented and returned to classic traditional fabrics, tailoring, and styling that would come to epitomize the look of the 1980s.

Casual Trend. Men had more choices for leisure wear in the 1970s. Throughout the decade more and more men unbuttoned their shirts and went without ties and often without jackets. Advertisers no longer showed men just at work as slave to the dollar but in holiday or weekend scenes enjoying the company of friends. This new ethic of leisure and individuality emphasized lifestyle over work, and the lifestyle of choice was fun and relaxation. In terms of fashion the most important innovation to come out of the casual trend was the unstructured jacket. Modeled after the cardigan sweater, the goal of unstructured garments was to make suits and jackets lighter and more comfortable. Sloping shoulders, low buttons, and no tapered waists gave unstructured jackets a relaxed look and fit. Sweaters and vests were popular and were often worn under loose-fitting jackets.

Leisure Spawns Fashion. By the mid 1970s the number of single men doubled in the United States from its low in the 1950s. The delaying of marriage by many men and the increase in the number of divorces created a singles culture focused around leisure activities. Increasingly, the gay liberation movement emboldened many gay designers to come out and to make their presence felt in fashion. The combination of more single men and a more visible gay subculture greatly enhanced men's fashion options. Disco dance clubs were perhaps the decade's most famous leisure image. Made popular by the 1977 movie *Saturday Night Fever*, the disco club scene spawned an entirely new leisure look for men. The disco look typically included a colorful patterned polyester shirt worn with light-colored, form-fitting, bell-bottomed pants and matching jacket. No ties were worn.

Weekend Jocks. Weekend athletics also inspired fashion. The look of the outdoor sportsman gained notoriety in such items as sturdy khaki pants, plaid hunting jackets, and flannel shirts. In 1975 the Coty American Fashion Critics awarded outdoor clothes producers L. L. Bean of Freeport, Maine; Gokey's of Saint Paul, Minnesota; and Eddie Bauer of Seattle, Washington, special citations for their contribution to menswear. Jogging suits were also a favorite weekend choice for men, whether or not they partook in the sport. Throughout the 1970s advertising images of men relaxing with friends or a special friend outnumbered those of men hard at work.

Sources:

Farid Chenoune, *A History of Men's Fashion* (Paris: Flammarion, 1993);

Annalee Gold, *90 Years of Fashion* (New York: Fairchild Fashion Group, 1991);

Caroline Rennolds Milbank, *Couture: The Great Designers* (New York: Stewart, Tabori & Chang, 1985).

HOT PANTS

"I think this hotpants craze just had to come," said Bloomingdale's veteran fashion coordinator Katie Murphy. Hot pants, she concluded, are not only about showing more of women's legs. They are about a revolution in women's clothes design. Murphy explained that not since London's Mary Quant launched the miniskirt in 1960 has the fashion world been caught so off guard. Women as well as fashion experts see hot pants as the "final crushing rebuke" to the midi and to the fashion cartel of designers that tried to drape long skirts over a resisting female population. In contrast to the designer-contrived midi, hot pants, she stated, are a "street creation." Much of the fashion establishment disliked the new fad. "We prefer not to sell hotpants but we don't have any choice," complained a New York garment maker. "We don't control ladies, they control us now."

Source: *Newsweek* (29 March 1971).

YOUTH FASHIONS

Age of Protest. The spirit of political protest did not end with the 1960s. In fact, with President Richard Nixon's expansion of the war in Vietnam in the early 1970s, young people continued to protest the war. The antiwar movement was predominantly made up of draft-age men and women who rejected the presence of American troops in what they considered to be a Vietnamese civil war. Rejecting the Nixon administration's explanation for the war, these protesters also questioned the entire value system of their parents' generation. Like the black power movement of the 1960s, the antiwar movement also spawned its own sense of alternative clothing and lifestyle.

Antifashion. Spilling over from the hippie movement of the 1960s, young Americans embraced self-expression and androgyny. United in their common rejection of the fashion industry, both men and women turned to unisex dress and hairstyles. Men and women wore faded denim jeans or army fatigues, cotton T-shirts or sleeveless tank tops, and boots. Many college-aged men and women continued to wear their hair long. The shag cut, short on top, longer on the sides and flat in back, became popular mid decade. It was one of the first haircuts to be popular with both men and women.

A New Look from Women's Liberation. Many women coming of age in the 1970s rejected the hyper-feminine ideal of their mothers' generation. The hourglass figure made famous by Christian Dior in the 1950s was considered by many women to be outdated and sexist. These women embraced the more androgynous look of slim hips and flat chests made popular by models like Twiggy. Many joined their male peers by wearing the antifashion uniform look of jeans, T-shirts, and long hair. Most important, many of these women rejected the cosmetic and beauty industries, complaining that they demeaned women. Many chose to go without makeup, lipstick, false eyelashes, or perms and celebrated "the natural look."

Born Not to Spend. Rejecting the consumerism of their parents' generation, many of the youth turned to secondhand clothing stores and army/navy outlets for their clothes instead of traditional boutiques and shops. They blended old and new looks and forged a distinct counterculture style. Wearing an antique shirt with dirty blue jeans and a beret, or an Indian tunic with army fatigues opened a range of self-designed fashion for any-one willing to play. The ecology movement also made the natural look popular among the young. Knit blends, fabrics, and polyester suits were considered establishment, whereas cottons were seen as a healthy alternative for the planet.

Sources:

Ray Browne and Marshal Fishwick, eds., *Icons of America* (New York: Popular Press, 1978);

Farid Chenoune, *A History of Men's Fashion* (Paris: Flammarion, 1993);

Barbara Ehrenreich and others, *Remaking Love: The Feminization of Sex* (New York: Anchor/Doubleday, 1987);

Annalee Gold, *90 Years of Fashion* (New York: Fairchild Fashion Group, 1991).

AMERICAN DESIGNERS

A Radical Chic. Early in the decade the unisex protest look was considered high fashion. The youth made anti-fashion fashionable by taking control of their own de-signs, and American designers followed suit. For in-stance, the androgynous look was stylized by Rudi Gernreich in his line of unisex clothing that envisioned a world without gender distinctions. American designers such as Halston rejected the vestiges of formal dressmak-ing in the spirit of innovation. His designs did without zippers, pockets, ruffles, or notched lapels.

Designer Jeans. Nothing captures the irony of "radical chic" more than designer blue jeans. In the 1960s and early 1970s blue jeans were the universal language of people under twenty-five. Dirty, ragged, and adorned with political slogans, jeans were the quintessential anti-fashion statement of a generation. Fashion moguls none-theless decided to capitalize on the jeans phenomenon. Designers such as Calvin Klein redesigned and repack-aged jeans into a haute couture item. These designer jeans had little in common with the youth culture jeans except denim. Instead of the peace symbols, globes, and women's liberation signs embroidered by protesters on their jeans, designers adorned their denim with embroi-dered logos, rhinestones, and silver studs and sold them at three and sometimes four times the cost of ordinary

Military clothing and androgynous hairstyles were popular among the young.

jeans. At Georgio's in Beverly Hills rhinestone-studded jeans sold for $100 and matching jackets for $160.

Goodbye to All That. By the mid 1970s radical chic fizzled out as did the protest movements that fueled the look. Radical chic was replaced by what was called a new American look, and that look was about leisure. A new generation of American designers took up the casual look and reinvented American fashion once again.

Sportswear. Sportswear was the most important con-tribution made by American designers in the 1970s. Sportswear originated out of men's leisure wear but soon hit women's fashions. Sportswear for men was defined by what it was not — it was everything that was not the traditional suit and tie and the world of work that that attire symbolized. This trend in men's clothing began after World War II, continued with the casual wear of the 1950s and 1960s, and culminated in the 1970s. "Weekend wear" had finally taken a more prominent position than "Sunday best" in the wardrobe. By the 1970s men's fashion was saturated with sports activities. Cross-country skiing, crewing in a sailboat race, or playing croquet were the fashion backdrops to emphasize the stylish versatility of these clothes.

Women in Menswear. Many women opted to dress in traditional men's clothes, and American designers gave them plenty of male styles from which to choose. Ralph Lauren gave them a range of choices: oversized shirts, vests, blazers, sweaters, pleated pants — a look popularized by Diane Keaton in the hit movie *Annie Hall* (1977). Sweaters, scarves, and shawls in layers were often worn under a short unstructured jacket. Women also donned the active-wear look. In 1976 designer Bill Haire offered velvet jodhpurs with a cashmere sweater, the perfect blend of men's active wear made to look soft and feminine.

What Was Popular. American designers such as Halston, Klein, and Lauren redesigned casual-dress options for women. Their collections of interchangeable separates allowed a woman to create her own look that was suitable for day and evening wear. Designers left the short miniskirt behind and introduced a line of skirts that fell to midcalf in peasant styles. When worn with boots, the look had a decidedly western feel. Comfort and simplicity were popular, and in 1978 designer Scott Barrie captured this spirit in his satin slip dress for evening wear with its elegant slit hemline. A growing interest in China inspired American designers to introduce into their offerings coolie pants, tunics, and quilted jackets in luxurious materials and colors.

Sources:
Farid Chenoune, *A History of Men's Fashion* (Paris: Flammarion, 1993);

Annalee Gold, *Ninety Years of Fashion* (New York: Fairchild Fashion Group, 1991);

Caroline Rennolds Milbank, *Couture: The Great Designers* (New York: Stewart, Tabori & Chang, 1985).

A CLEANER, MORE EFFICIENT CAR: AMERICAN AUTOMOBILES

Business as Usual. American car manufacturers in the early 1970s continued to produce the large sedans and the popular hot rod muscle cars that they had been perfecting since the 1950s and 1960s. The muscle cars — Pontiac's GTO, Ford's Mustang, and Oldsmobile's 442 — were small, modestly priced automobiles with souped-up engines that gave the driver a feeling of power and speed. The gas-guzzling muscle cars were fun but dangerous unless equipped with fully functional high-speed brakes. Detroit's large sedans — the Lincoln Continental, Cadillac, and Buick — also paid little heed to fuel efficiency. Comfortable as the traditional force in the United States automobile market, American manufacturers entered the 1970s with a sense of business — and profits — as usual.

Energy Crisis. Detroit's peace of mind was shattered, along with its business strategy, when on 16 October

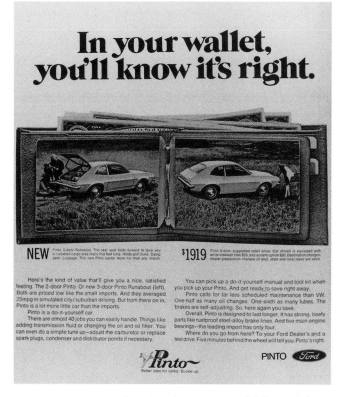

The Ford Pinto was introduced to compete with inexpensive Japanese and German subcompact models.

1973 the Arab-dominated Organization of Petroleum Exporting Countries (OPEC) cut off the flow of oil to the United States, Western Europe, and Japan in retaliation for their support of Israel in the Yom Kippur War. Within weeks the nation confronted what President Nixon called "a very stark fact: We are heading toward the most acute shortage of energy since World War II." Lasting until 18 March 1974, the energy crisis made Americans confront, for the first time, their dependence on foreign oil.

Gas Shortages. The oil crisis spawned gas shortages across the country and began to exert pressure on Detroit to make cars more fuel efficient. Suddenly Americans found themselves in long lines at gas pumps. A gas line in New Jersey stretched out to four miles. Frustrated at the pumps, drivers vented their anger on service-station attendants and on each other — fighting, stealing, and threatening violence as they waited in endless lines for a few gallons of gas. Some states closed gas stations on Sundays to discourage driving, while others introduced rationing programs. Overnight, it seemed, Americans wanted their automobiles small and energy efficient.

Government Interventions. In response to the oil embargo and gas shortages, the federal government introduced a series of new regulations on automobile production that mandated American auto manufacturers redesign their cars. New mile-per-gallon standards were set as well as new emissions standards in an effort to make American cars more fuel efficient. The oil crisis gave added weight to the growing environmental movement in the early 1970s. Consumers as well as the government were demanding cleaner cars that used less fuel and had less impact on the environment.

Imported Cars Challenge Detroit. However, American automobile producers had more to contend with than just the energy crisis in 1973 and 1974. They were also engaged in a battle against new smaller and more efficient imports gaining a foothold in the domestic car market. The Toyota Corolla subcompact, the Renault sedan, the Datsun 1200, and the Volkswagen Rabbit presented a serious challenge to Detroit in the economy-car competition. In 1977 import car sales broke all U.S. records. Nearly 1.5 million imports were sold in the January–August period, double the amount sold for the comparable period in 1976. By 1978 the Honda Civic and the diesel-engine Volkswagen Rabbit were the fastest-selling imports in the United States. Detroit needed to change that fact quickly.

New Designs. In the name of ecology, energy efficiency, and good business, Detroit introduced a variety of four-cylinder subcompact cars to fight off German and Japanese minicars. The American Motors Gremlin was the first in the fray in 1970, followed by Ford with its Pinto and Chevrolet with its Vega. U.S. automobile producers also began the long process of downsizing their formerly big and heavy classic cars. By 1977 new models of large-size Buicks, Oldsmobiles, Pontiacs, and Cadillacs had lost approximately eleven inches in length and nearly seven hundred pounds in weight.

Best-Sellers. The muscle cars of Detroit continued to hold their own against the threat of minicars and fuel efficiency. The restyled Pontiac Grand Prix and Firebird models were big sellers in 1973, along with the Ford Mustang and the Chevrolet Camaro. Yet even the leader of the pony car category, the Mustang, faced downsizing in its 1974 model. In 1976 Ford introduced the sporty yet efficient Granada that included a sports steering wheel and trimmer seats. It became one of the year's most popular models.

Source:
Peter Carroll, *It Seemed Like Nothing Happened: The Tragedy and Promise of America in the 1970s* (New York: Holt, Rinehart & Winston, 1982).

AMERICAN ARCHITECTURE: POSTMODERNISM TAKES OFF

Goodbye to Modern Architecture. American architects gained international stature in the 1950s and 1960s with their gleaming high-rise buildings of reflecting glass and steel. The generation of architects trained by Mies van der Rohe put modern architecture, the International Style as it was known, on the map. These building designs were simple, unadorned, and built with modern materials that expressed their structure. The cardinal rules of modernism were that less is more and form fol-

Houston's Pennzoil Place, designed by Philip Johnson and John Burgee

lows function. The International Style maintained that the same building could be built anywhere — New York, Lagos, or Stockholm. These buildings made no reference to history or to the cityscape around them.

Hello, Postmodernism. By the late 1960s a handful of innovative architects turned away from the cool distance of modern architectural design. Tired of glass-box monuments in the cityscape, younger architects wanted to break the rules of what they saw as a rigid and ahistorical style. They developed a new type of architecture called postmodernism. Postmodern architecture had several characteristics that distinguished it from modern architecture: historicism, an interest in the styles and adornments used in earlier eras; a fascination with everyday life and ordinary objects; a playfulness tied to the antiauthoritanism of the 1960s; and a willingness to consider buildings within their geographic and cultural context.

Philip Johnson. Oddly, the leader of the rebellious pack of young architects was none other than Philip Johnson, who earlier in his life had been an avid believer in modernist architecture. In the 1970s Johnson and his partner John Burgee gained notoriety for their unusual building designs: the IDS Center (1973) in Minneapolis and the Pennzoil Place (1976) in Houston. But it was not until Johnson and Burgee published their designs for the American Telephone and Telegraph (AT&T) Building in downtown New York in 1978 that they put postmodernism in the headlines.

The Chippendale Skyrise. The AT&T Building was provocative because it mixed classical details with contemporary structures and, in so doing, broke free of modernist esthetics. Johnson and Burgee chose to build in granite, reminiscent of the 1930s, rather than the popular glass and steel of the 1950s. Equally unusual, the upper-level facade had a row of classical Greek-styled columns. Topping it off was Johnson's crowning glory: the building had what looked like the head of an antique grandfather clock rising off its broad shoulders. Soon called the Chippendale Skyrise, in reference to eighteenth-century English furniture design, the AT&T Building was a monument to postmodern architecture.

The New York Five. With the recession of the mid 1970s, construction of buildings and the need for architects suddenly nose-dived. Young architects were hit hardest, and many turned their new ideas to designing houses for the wealthy. Five of these younger architects drew attention to themselves through their postmodern house designs. Centered in New York, they became known as the New York Five. Michael Graves, Peter Eisenman, Charles Gwathmey, Richard Meier, and John Hejduk saw architecture as an art form, and soon they became known for their elevation of design over utilitarian concerns. Peter Eisenman, for instance, built a house whose front door opened into the kitchen and a stairway ran into a blank wall. The New York Five, along with a new generation of American architects, rejected the rule of formal design. In doing so they introduced a postmodern aesthetic to home design that valued symbolism, expression, and innovation.

Venturi's Love for the Ordinary. In contrast to most modern architects, Robert Venturi and his partners did not attempt to build a coherent, unified style that could be repeated from one building to another. Rather, they sought to construct buildings that used local materials, forms, and building traditions. Like other postmodern architects, their interest in detail led them to mix and match historical forms and local traditions. More than any other architect in the 1970s, Venturi embraced the "messy vitality" of the ordinary street and strip mall. Venturi and his partners inspired both ridicule and admiration for their elevation of the ordinary to the level of art.

Wheelchair Accessibility. In 1968 the federal government passed the Architectural Barriers Act, which outlawed any architectural designs that barred wheelchair-bound and disabled citizens from gaining access to any federal or federally funded building. This legislation was strengthened in 1973 and 1974 as the country faced a new wave of disabled war veterans returning from Vietnam. These laws had important and immediate effects on American architects. Each building that used any governmental monies had to include wheelchair ramps, wider doors, new bathroom designs, lower water fountains and telephones, and easy parking. These standards were formally adopted in 1974 by the American Institute of Architects. The statement affirmed the rights of handicapped persons to "free and full development of their economic, social and personal potential through the use of man-made environments."

Sources:

Paul Goldberg, *On the Rise: Architecture and Design in a Postmodern Age* (New York: Penguin, 1983);

William Dudley Hunt, Jr., *Encyclopedia of American Architecture* (New York: McGraw-Hill, 1980);

Diane Maddex, ed., *Master Builders: A Guide to Famous American Architects* (Washington, D.C.: Preservation Press, 1985).

AMERICAN HOMES

Settling Down. Following the exuberance of the affluent and innovative 1960s, interior design in the 1970s settled down. The poor economic situation provoked moderation in home design. Rather than bizarre experimentation, people were interested in historic preservation. As a result old homes were renovated, and urban neighborhoods were reclaimed. Some homeowners combined preservation with economic moderateness by remodeling existing homes and converting stables, carriage houses, clock towers, and barns into dwellings. Eclecticism in interior design grew throughout the decade.

Opening Up Space. Open space became very popular in the 1970s. With its roots in the egalitarianism of the 1960s counterculture, interior design sought to create community by dispensing with walls as rigid space dividers. Contemporary designers of homes, offices, and schools opened up rooms to full sunlight and outside views while still accommodating the needs of the occupant. These wide-open spaces were called "interior environments." Space was no longer divided into rooms but into activity centers for eating, study, or work. Areas were separated by plants or furniture groupings.

Offices. The concept of open-space planning dominated office design in the 1970s. It provided a flexibility in the work environment, conducive to instant change and renovation. These open offices required new kinds of furniture that could be moved and combined easily. For example, fixed walls were replaced with movable screens, and free-standing storage units were mobile and could be attached to table desks or other work surfaces or put on wheels. Living plants became prominent features of modern offices and restaurants. According to a leading horticulturist, the reason for the plants' popularity was "a new understanding of the fact that people are unhappy without plants and flowers around them."

Schools. The tearing down of interior walls in schools reflected a new attitude toward school programs. Work stations and large open rooms replaced the small classroom divided by subject or grade. Carrels equipped with technical learning aids encouraged students to work at their own paces in a communal setting. Wide-open school areas also reflected a new interest in approaching learning from many different vantage points. Schools across the country embraced the new flexible attitude toward learning and the new interior learning environment.

Homes. The open-space plan, created by removing the solid barriers that enclosed each room, became increasingly popular in home design in the 1970s. Furniture arrangements emphasized flexibility and mobility. As with businesses and schools, open-room home design organized space into active and quiet areas, shared or private areas within one big environment. In June 1973 *House and Garden* writer Emilie O'Mara wrote that 1970s interiors reflected the public's urge to change: "We're constantly changing and if we deny that fact we are just deluding ourselves." People developed new tastes, new interests, and new relationships. Lifestyle and home design reflected these changes.

Furniture. Furniture for open-spaced living environments was modular and versatile. Pieces could be fit together in different shapes to fit the mood of the moment. Ottomans could become chairs with attached back bolsters and arms, and sofa pieces could be arranged in a conversation cluster or an island of seating arrangements. The popular bunk bed was redesigned to include shelving and desks that also could be redesigned into new combinations.

Designers at Home. In the 1970s fashion designers entered the lucrative market of domestic furnishings. Following a trend started by designer and perfume manufacturer Coco Chanel, U.S. and European fashion designers branched out into designing sheets, pillowcases, watches, luggage, needlepoint patterns, wallpaper, and shopping bags. Bill Blass, three-time Coty winner, turned his color and fabric expertise to bed and bath. Blass sheets and pillowcases could be coupled with quilts and towels in matching colors. Rudi Gernreich was inspired by his own 1972 fashions to make pillows and throws in geometric patterns for his home. An international company bought them on sight. Vera, the U.S. designer most widely known for her signature scarves, launched her own set of matching sheets, pillows, quilts, and shower curtains in 1970. Vera's bright bold colors against a solid white or black backdrop made her one of the period's most popular home furnishings designers.

Source:
Sherrill Whiton, *Interior Design and Decoration,* fourth edition (New York: Lippincott, 1973).

HEADLINE MAKERS

BILL BLASS

1922-

DESIGNER OF ELEGANT CLOTHES FOR WOMEN

American Casual Wear. Bill Blass is one of a handful of American designers to make casual clothes elegant and comfortable in the 1960s and 1970s. By making comfort fashionable, Blass launched what became known in fashion circles as a distinctly American look. Classic styles and tailoring emphasized the elegance and highbrow look of Blass, but his soft fabrics and exquisite materials reflected comfort and ease. Blass was especially admired for his glamorous, feminine evening clothes. His daytime fashions were considered elegant and simple and were noted for their refined cut, excellent tailoring, and for their interesting mixture of patterns and textures. As well as designing clothes for women, Blass had a line of sportswear, rainwear, *Vogue* patterns, loungewear, scarves, and men's clothing. He also designed automobiles, uniforms for American Airlines flight attendants, and even chocolates. In 1978 *Bill Blass* perfume for women was introduced.

Life. Blass was born in Fort Wayne, Indiana, in 1922. In high school he played football, worked on the school newspaper, and dabbled in art. A fascination with the fashions in *Vogue* and *Harper's Bazaar* led him to study for six months at the Parsons School of Design in New York. His first fashion job was as a sketch artist for the sportswear firm of David Crystal in 1940. When the United States entered World War II, Blass resigned and enlisted in the army. When he returned to New York in 1946, he began designing for Anna Mill and Company. In 1958 Blass became head designer when Anna Mill merged with Maurice Rentner. He eventually became vice-president, and in 1970 he became full owner. That same year Blass launched Bill Blass, Limited, to produce elegant American casuals for women. Blass has won three Coty awards and is in the Fashion Hall of Fame.

MICHAEL GRAVES

1934-

ARCHITECT

The Best of a New Generation. Michael Graves was one of the most influential architects of the last thirty years in the United States. As an educator at Princeton University, Graves influenced his students with his philosophy of architecture as a "symbolic language" that expressed not merely the need for shelter but "society's pattern of rituals." Coming of age during the heyday of modern architecture, Graves rejected the machinelike structure of the 1950s for more humanly scaled, environmentally aware, and socially conscious buildings. Like those of other postmodern architects of the 1970s, Graves's designs blend classical and modern forms in new ways.

Life. Michael Graves was born on 9 July 1934 in Indianapolis, Indiana. During childhood Graves enjoyed drawing and painting, which he claimed he turned to as a way to avoid playing the violin. His parents, who were farmers, discouraged Graves from a career in fine arts and steered him toward architecture or engineering. Graves took their advice, and in 1958 he earned his B.A. degree in architecture at the University of Cincinnati.

In Rome. In 1959 Graves completed his master's degree at Harvard University, and in 1960 he won the prestigious Prix de Rome prize. A fellowship allowed Graves to study in Rome for two years where he became fascinated by the paintings and buildings of the Renaissance and post-Renaissance periods. While in Rome Graves underwent an intellectual and artistic transformation. For him architecture was no longer simply an art form, concerned with structure and weight; instead architecture was the "human endeavor" expressed in concrete and plaster.

The Art of Architecture. When Graves returned from Rome in 1962, he took a lecture post at Princeton University. Graves gained national notoriety when he and architect Peter Eisenman designed a city extending from New York to Philadelphia. Their New Jersey Corridor

Study was shown at the Forty under Forty exhibit at the Architectural League of New York in 1966. Five of the young architects were singled out by *The New York Times* critic Paul Goldberg for special praise and were christened the "New York Five."

Works. While much of Graves's influence came from his drawings, writings, and teaching, he nonetheless built many notable buildings and houses. His most famous building is the Portland Building (1982) in Portland, Oregon. This $22.4 million, fifteen-story structure was innovative in its design while still being energy efficient and low in cost. Graves's design stirred up heated debate in the architectural world: Philip Johnson praised it, but the dean of architecture at Massachusetts Institute of Technology criticized it for being an "oversize, beribboned Christmas package." In 1983 the Portland Building won a National Honor Award for Graves.

HALSTON

1932-

DESIGNER

Casual and Sexy. As the 1971 and 1972 winner of the Coty American Fashion Critic's top award (Winnie), Halston was the premier fashion designer of the early 1970s. Halston established himself as one of the guiding forces in fashion by adapting the classical look of sportswear to the active life of American women. As one critic commented, Halston's "special brand of casual but sexy has become one of the most recognizable and individual looks in American fashion."

Life. Roy Halston Frowick was born in April 1932 in Des Moines, Iowa, the second of four children. Halston's first attempt at fashion design came in the way of a homemade red hat which "was a smash and really flattered my mother." After World War II Halston attended the University of Indiana for two years before enrolling at the Chicago Art Institute as a fine arts major. While a student he designed window displays by day and sewed hats by night on a secondhand sewing machine in his small apartment. Soon he talked the hairdresser at the Ambassador Hotel into displaying his hats. They were so well received that the twenty-one-year-old designer opened a millinery salon in the hotel. Halston stayed in the Ambassador until 1959 when he took the position of head milliner at Bergdorf's.

The Pillbox Hat. One of Halston's first customers at Bergdorf's was Jacqueline Kennedy, who needed hats to wear while accompanying her husband, John F. Kennedy, on his presidential campaign. Halston designed the celebrated beige felt pillbox that Jacqueline Kennedy wore to her husband's inauguration in 1960 and most of the other hats she wore as first lady. In recognition of his hat designs Halston received a Coty Special Award in 1962.

The "Total Look." In 1968, convinced the time was right to strike out on his own, Halston left Bergdorf's and founded Halston, Limited. By year's end he introduced a line of ready-to-wear clothes that won him another Winnie in 1969 for the "total look" he had displayed in his first solo collection. By the mid 1970s the fashion world was tired of the 1960s exotic look and embraced Halston's look of casual elegance.

The Look. Halston's designs emphasized the "casually chic look" of sweaters, soft wide-legged jersey pants, and simple, longish shirtdresses. His hallmark became the cardigan sweater loosely tied around the shoulders. Instead of doing up women to look like gypsies, peasants, or harem girls, he dressed women in tie-dyed chiffon or velvet pantsuits and slinky floor-length halter dresses. Other signature looks from Halston include the one-shouldered evening gown, tunics over pajamas, and the strapless columnar dress tied in a knot at the bustline.

Branching Out. Halston diversified his business and design interests as the decade wore on. Following the trend first set by Coco Chanel in the 1950s, Halston designed cosmetics for Max Factor, luggage for Hartman, and in the 1980s clothes for J. C. Penney. This last move was especially controversial. Bergdorf's, for instance, closed its Halston Boutique in response.

PHILIP JOHNSON

1906-

ARCHITECT

Beginnings. After fifty years spent in and around the profession, Philip Johnson is considered by some to be the dean of American architecture. His career has been varied and controversial, and his designs have always been at the leading edge of his profession.

Johnson began his career in the early 1930s as a historian and critic of architecture. As director of architecture at the newly chartered Museum of Modern Art in New York City, Johnson and critic Henry Russell Hitchcock defined what they called "the international style." They predicted that simple, unadorned modern buildings were going to be an international architecture that would reflect a global aesthetic, devoid of local and regional characteristics.

Life as a Modernist. Throughout the 1930s Johnson continued to advocate modernist architecture through museum shows, teaching, and writing. In 1936 Johnson

left his post at the Museum of Modern Art to become a practicing architect. In 1943, at the age of thirty-seven, Johnson graduated from the Graduate School of Design at Harvard University. In 1946 Johnson returned to the museum as director of its new architecture department. In this period Johnson focused his energies on house design. His most famous house from this period was the Glass House (1949), his residence in New Canaan, Connecticut, that was built entirely from glass. In the 1950s Johnson turned to building designs. He designed a new wing for the Museum of Modern Art (1950), its sculpture garden (1953), and another wing (1964). With architect Mies van der Rohe, Johnson designed the Seagram Building (1958). Johnson's building and home designs embraced the cool modernist aesthetic of simple lines and unadorned facades, with no references to the past or to the environment. Johnson left his post at the museum in 1954 to form his own firm with architect John Burgee.

Breaking Out. By the 1960s Johnson began to question the purist international style he had helped establish. "You cannot not know history," Johnson told students at Yale University who had been taught by their modernist instructors to ignore the past. Johnson started to invest his modern buildings with historical references. His design for the Museum of Pre-Columbian Art (1963) in Washington, D.C., drew inspiration from the Ottoman Empire while incorporating a glass-walled modern feel. This style of mixing the past with the present to create an entirely new look became the hallmark of postmodernism in architecture.

Postmodernism Comes of Age. Johnson continued to challenge the dominance of the "glass box" look of American high-rises throughout the 1970s. In 1978 Johnson unveiled his design for the American Telephone and Telegraph (AT&T) Building in New York. Popularly known as the Chippendale Skyrise, Johnson put postmodernism on the cultural map. Crowned with an eighteenth-century-styled highboy top, the AT&T Building stood in stark contrast to its glass and steel neighbors in Manhattan. Johnson's use of eclectic detail and an attention to the different needs of the environment was, he claimed, a sign that the American public no longer saw itself as one unified collective. As a result, one dominant look was no longer suitable for the pluralistic nation the United States had become. "Who thinks of America as a melting pot anymore?" asked Johnson in 1978. "We think of ourselves as a pluralistic society. Look at *Roots*. Our basic philosophy as a people has undergone a profound broadening. What's best for one isn't necessarily what's best for all." For Johnson, this new spirit of pluralism translated into "profound freedom" for the architect. Philip Johnson received the highest award of the American Institute of Architects, the Gold Medal, in 1978.

DONNA KARAN

1948-

FASHION DESIGNER

A Touch of Sexiness. "My clothes say woman," claimed fashion designer Donna Karan. As chief designer at Anne Klein for ten years, and later head of her own clothing line, Donna Karan defined the cutting edge of women's fashions for nearly three decades. After Anne Klein's death in 1974, Karan continued Klein's mission: to replace the flowered luncheon dresses favored by affluent suburbanites with mix-and-match separates — blouses, skirts, jackets, sweaters, pants — to create casual, elegant outfits. In the 1980s Karan softened the highly tailored male-derivative career clothes that had been the obligatory look for working women. She also added a touch of sexiness that made her a favorite with some of the country's most visible professional women, including Diane Sawyer, Barbara Walters, and Candice Bergen.

Life. Fashion figured largely in Karan's childhood. She was born on 2 October 1948 in Forest Hill, Queens, in New York City. Her mother, Helen Faske, was a model, and her father Gaby was a custom tailor. As a girl, Karan fantasized about becoming a designer. At age fourteen, she worked at a boutique and learned the basics of design: "what people looked good in and what they didn't." In 1966 Karan enrolled in Parson's School of Design in Manhattan where she met Louise Dell'Olio. The two became fast friends and pledged to work together. In 1967 Karan interned for Klein. While Klein intimidated Karan terribly, Karan nonetheless decided not to return to Parsons and took a job working full-time for Klein.

Taking the Helm. Karan was abruptly promoted to chief designer when Klein died of cancer in 1974. After six weeks of feverish activity Karan unveiled the fall 1974 collection to a stunned audience that gave her her first standing ovation. *The New York Times* fashion critic Bernadine Morris reported that Karan "had just proved that the Anne Klein fashion spirit lives." Often mistaken for Klein or for her daughter, Karan walked the fine line of continuing in Klein's legacy while establishing her own look. In 1975 Karan brought Louise Dell'Olio aboard as her associate, and together they built on Klein's sportswear legacy.

Success. In 1977 Karan and Dell'Olio were awarded their first Coty award, and in 1981 their second. In 1984 they entered the Coty Hall of Fame. As chief designer at Klein, Karan succeeded in putting her own unique touch to Klein's look. Softer, more fluid, and more sophisticated, Karan's clothes departed from Klein's neatly tailored look. "I love the freedom of body movement and modern jazz and I've always wanted to get that ease and motion into clothes." In 1984 Karan left Klein to launch her own company, Donna Karan New York.

CALVIN KLEIN

1942-

FASHION DESIGNER

Elegant Casual Wear. No one helped American fashion come into its own more than designer Calvin Klein. Storming the world of haute couture in the late 1960s, Klein reinvigorated the fashion industry at a time when it appeared to have been abandoned by a generation of antifashion youth. In 1972 Klein began creating his flexible collections of interchangeable separates that were casual and elegant. His separates offered women, and to a lesser extent men, a wide range of choice for around-the-clock wear. Known for his designer jeans, his perfumes, his underwear, and his advertisements, Klein has succeeded in reinventing himself and American fashion with each passing year.

Life. Calvin Richard Klein was born in the Bronx, New York, on 19 November 1942. As an adolescent Klein was drawn to fashion. He sewed and sketched clothes and regularly visited Loehmann's, a high-fashion discount store in the Bronx, to look at the Norman Norell samples and other high fashion. Klein graduated from the Fashion Institute of Technology in 1962 and apprenticed for designer Dan Millstein. In 1968, with backing from a childhood friend, Klein founded his own company called Calvin Klein.

Sporty Separates. In 1972 Klein turned his attention to sportswear. He launched his line of sporty separates — such as sweaters, skirts, dresses, shirts, and pants — that could be intermixed for a complete day and evening wardrobe. "I felt that the American lifestyle had changed," Klein explained. "For the most part, women today spend their time and energy working, participating in all aspects of home, community, and business. Their lives have changed and there is little time for wardrobe planning." His clothes were perfectly suited for women who wanted the look of an outfit with the easy versatility of separates.

Hall of Fame. In 1973 Klein was chosen by four hundred fashion reporters as winner of the Coty American Fashion Critics Award (Winnie). The citation commented on Klein's "innate but conformist sense of classic line . . . and his unique understanding of today's blend of casualness, luxury, and moderate price." Klein went on to win two more Winnies in 1974 and 1975, and on 25 June 1975 he was elected to the American Hall of Fame of Fashion.

RALPH LAUREN

1939-

FASHION DESIGNER

Designing the American Look. As the winner of more Coty American Fashion Critics' Awards than any other designer (three for men's clothes, three for women's), Ralph Lauren is considered by fashion observers to be the quintessential American designer of the 1970s. Lauren's designs were clean lined, adaptable, imaginative, and, at the same time, classic and contemporary. Lauren first gained attention in the late 1960s with his Polo menswear collections. In 1972 he introduced his first Ralph Lauren collection for women. "I stand for a look that is American," he explained in a 1978 interview. "It's an attitude, a sense of freedom. I believe in clothes that last, that are not dated in a season. They should look better the year after they're bought."

Life. Ralph Lauren was born Ralph Lifshitz in the Bronx, New York, on 14 October 1939, the youngest of four children. He and his siblings legally changed their name to Lauren in the mid 1950s. As a youth Lauren was interested in sports, movies, and the novels of F. Scott Fitzgerald. He first became interested in clothes when he was in the seventh grade. "My friends were the hoods wearing motorcycle jackets, but I was wearing tweed Bermudas and button down shirts." While in high school, Lauren worked part-time as a stock boy at Alexander's Department Store. He spent most of his fifty-dollar-a-week salary on clothes and would save for weeks to buy a Brooks Brothers suit.

Ties. After graduating from high school Lauren stayed on at Alexander's and took evening classes at the City College of New York. Feeling restless and bored, Lauren knew he wanted to break into the fashion world and so applied to menswear manufacturers, including Brooks Brothers. They all turned him down. "I had no portfolio and no sketches. All I had was taste." He was eventually hired by Beau Brummel Ties in 1967. Lauren's ties were made of unusual fabrics and were two inches wider than the standard three-inch width of most ties. Soon Lauren's ties were Brummel's best sellers, and he left to start his own tie company, which he named Polo, for the word's connotations of class and elegance.

Expanding to Women's Wear. Lauren's larger ties needed larger shirt collars. His larger collars led him to design suit jackets with wider lapels, all of which he designed under the Polo label in 1970. His new men's look won him his first Coty award. The next season Lauren introduced a line of women's clothes that borrowed heavily from his menswear look. The line included shirts, sweaters, skirts, blazers, slacks, suits, and coats

that were fashionable while being comfortable. "I didn't think it was necessary for a woman to dress like a vamp . . . to look attractive. Being comfortable is more important than being slinky."

Selling New Classics. Throughout the 1970s Lauren's women's collections were dominated by conservatively cut, well-tailored interchangeable separates. His 1975 line won him another Coty, and in 1977 Diane Keaton popularized Lauren's style in the movie *Annie Hall.* In 1978 Lauren introduced a western theme into his clothes. Petticoat skirts, big silver-buckled belts, and cowboy boots and hats became an instant sensation. Lauren explained that the rugged cowboy look appealed to men and women because of the confidence and independence the cowboy represents. "It's part of American culture. It's one thing France can't claim as theirs. It's ours." In May 1979 Lauren entered the Fashion Hall of Fame for his role in developing a purely American look and in establishing New York City as a rival fashion capital to Paris.

I. M. PEI

1917-

Modernist with a Flare. Architect Ioeh Ming Pei was one of a handful of American architects to have significantly affected twentieth-century architectural design. Pei's designs have often been on the leading edge of aesthetic technological and urban innovation. More than any of his contemporaries, Pei has taken modernist principles of architecture and translated them into reality.

Professional Life. Born in Canton, China, Pei attended the Massachusetts Institute of Technology and Harvard University. His principal teacher at Harvard's Graduate School of Design, Walter Gropius, liked to say that Pei was by far his most promising student. Gropius proceeded to make Pei an assistant professor in 1945 before he had finished his master's degree. In 1948 Pei left Harvard and became the director of architecture in developer William Zeckendor's firm, Webb and Knapp. Pei established his own practice in 1955 and has headed the firm I. M. Pei and Partners ever since.

Major Works. Pei designed some of the most significant structures built in the 1960s and 1970s. His National Center for Atmospheric Research (1961–1967) in Boulder, Colorado; the Dallas City Hall (1972–1977); the East Wing of the National Gallery of Art (1978) in Washington, D.C.; and the John F. Kennedy Library (1979) in Boston are the most famous of his many buildings. Pei's designs attempted to turn each urban project into an opportunity to strengthen the fabric of American cities. By creating new urban spaces, pedestrian linkages, and a sense of orderly beauty in the midst of urban chaos, Pei strived to reinvigorate and renew aging city centers.

Innovator. Pei was the first architect to have used exposed, cast-in-place, and precast concrete in modern, multistory housing. Pei's attention to detail and finish resulted in his concrete buildings looking like a polished slab of marble. He was also the most daring pioneer in the development of all-glass curtain walls, creating some of the most beautiful glass structures since the Glass Palace. Pei is perhaps best known for the East Wing of the National Gallery of Art. Shaped like a trapezoid, the East Building was constructed out of pink marble from the Tennessee quarry that provided the materials for the West Wing of the National Gallery. With his design Pei managed to update the new addition without losing coherency with the existing structure. The East Wing is considered a monument to Pei's ability to make space both active and serene.

ROBERT VENTURI

1925-

POSTMODERN ARCHITECT

Eclectic. The theories of Robert Venturi helped launch the postmodern movement in American architecture. Venturi, through his books *Complexity and Contradiction in Architecture* (1966) and *Learning from Las Vegas* (1971), did more than any other author text to advance a shift away from the simple austerity of modern architecture. More than his buildings, Venturi's writings epitomized the rejection of modernism for a more eclectic, historical, and vernacular style of architecture. His attention to everyday life, ordinary buildings, and popular designs unsettled the architectural establishment in the 1970s while inspiring a new generation of designers.

Early Life. Robert Venturi, the son of a wholesale fruit grocer, was born in 1925 in Philadelphia. From the age of four Venturi knew he wanted to be an architect. He nourished his love of architectural history at Princeton University. Venturi's studies in the history of architecture led him to appreciate the work of earlier architects rejected by the modernist movement. As the recipient of the prestigious Prix de Rome prize in 1954, Venturi spent time in Italy, where he further developed his fascination with historical styles, drawing particularly from Michelangelo and the Italian mannerists. On returning from Rome, Venturi took a position at the University of Pennsylvania. In 1964 Venturi joined with John Rauch and Denise Scott Brown to form the firm Venturi, Rauch and Scott Brown; they soon became one of the leading design firms in the United States.

Washington Plaza. In 1978 the firm unveiled its design for the Western Plaza on Pennsylvania Avenue in Washington, D.C. Heralded as the most "creative urban square proposed for any city in the United States," by *The New York Times* architecture critic, the design was called witty and stately all at once. Funded by the $5.5 million Pennsylvania Avenue Development Corporation, the plaza was to sit between Thirteenth and Fourteenth streets and have a view of the Capitol on one end and the White House on the other. In classic Venturi style, the design for the plaza was unusual. The plaza was to become a miniature walk-on map in marble and granite of the city's original design by Pierre Charles L'Enfant. The development corporation ultimately decided that Venturi's plan was too radical for Washington and so built a simpler version of his original design.

Eclectic Designs. In 1985 Venturi, Rauch and Scott Brown won the Architectural Firm Award of the American Institute of Architects. Their work has been the basis for the current eclectic attitudes of the postmodern movement and continues to challenge architectural theory and practice around the world.

MINORU YAMASAKI

1912-

ARCHITECT OF THE TWIN TOWERS OF THE WORLD TRADE CENTER

Keeping Art in Architecture. The work of architect Minoru Yamasaki was the focus of a larger controversy concerning the place of art in architecture. Detractors of Yamasaki's designs complained his buildings were too artistic and ornamental, that they existed solely as decoration. His followers, on the other hand, agreed with Yamasaki when he said that the social function of an architect is to create a work of art. Despite the controversy, Yamasaki had a considerable influence on American architecture. At a time when many modern buildings were designed as plain, sterile-looking products of the industrial age, Yamasaki designed buildings as sculpture, richly ornamental and playful or serene as the occasion demanded.

Life. Minoru Yamasaki was born in Seattle, Washington, in 1912, the son of an immigrant Japanese farmer. His uncle, an architect, fueled his interest in the profession. Determined to rise above his tenement surroundings, Yamasaki worked summers in fish canneries in Alaska to earn the tuition to attend the University of Washington's school of architecture. After graduating in 1934, Yamasaki worked in several firms in New York City and from 1943 to 1945 taught design at Columbia University. Yamasaki was able to escape internment as a Japanese-American during World War II with the help of the architects for whom he worked. Yamasaki also saved his parents from internment by sheltering them in New York City.

Major Works. Yamasaki joined several firms throughout the 1950s until he formed Minoru Yamasaki and Associates in 1959. Yamasaki has designed over eighty-five buildings. Among the most important are the Federal Science Pavilion (1961) at the World's Fair in New York, the Woodrow Wilson School of Public and International Affairs (1965) at Princeton University, and the Federal Reserve Bank (1973) in Richmond, Virginia. Yamasaki's most famous design is the twin towers of the World Trade Center (1973) in New York City.

PEOPLE IN THE NEWS

Laura Ashley, an English designer known for her floral patterns and colors, begins to influence American fashion's return to femininity in the late 1970s.

American designer **Scott Barrie** shows his simple and elegant satin slip dress in the spring of 1978. With its deep-slit hemline that showcases the wearer's legs, this dress combines the fun of the mini with the comfort and sensibility of longer skirts.

In February 1976 **Liz Claiborne** forms and soon becomes famous for her simple and affordable line of women's sportswear.

In 1978 designer **Perry Ellis** opens his new line of men's clothing, Perry Ellis Sportswear.

In 1976 former model and star of the hit television show *Charlie's Angels* **Farrah Fawcett-Majors** makes news with her feathered haircut.

In July 1975 First Lady **Betty Ford** removes historic mid-nineteenth-century wallpaper from the White House dining room. Installed by Jacqueline Kennedy, the wallpaper depicted Revolutionary War battle scenes that Ford thought were "kind of depressing."

American designer **Rudi Gernreich** somewhat cryptically declares in 1971 that "the fashion industry as we know it is dead. Today fad *equals* fashion."

American designer **Halston** incorporates his design line into Halston Enterprises in 1973, and the business becomes worth $12 million.

Designer **Holly Harp,** known for her simple yet unconventional clothes, opens her own wholesale line in 1973.

In 1974 *Newsweek* magazine declares **Lauren Hutton** Model of the Year.

In 1977 **Diane Keaton** stars in Woody Allen's *Annie Hall* dressed in clothing designed by Ralph Lauren and launches a new, slightly rumpled men's look for women.

In March 1971 Sen. Edward Kennedy's wife **Joan Kennedy** greets her dinner guests in satin hot pants, announcing the newest trend in Washington fashion.

In 1970 architect Robert Nash of Washington, D.C., becomes the first African-American to be elected president of the American Institute of Architects.

In 1975 second lady **Happy Rockefeller** oversees the redecoration of the vice-presidential mansion. Rockefeller makes news when she chooses a thirty-five-thousand-dollar designer bed, equipped with stereo lamps and telephone, for the master bedroom.

New York button manufacturer **N. G. Slater's** smiley-face button becomes a spontaneous hit, earning over $1 million in 1971.

Yves St. Laurent finally gains financial control over his famous design house in 1972 after waiting for over ten years to buy out his financial backers.

In 1971 Japanese designer **Kenzo Takada** introduces Oriental features into the fashion scene. Fuller short skirts, kimono sleeves, shawls, and draped clothing mark the growing influence of Japan on American design.

AWARDS

COTY AMERICAN FASHION CRITICS' AWARD

(The "Winnie" — to an individual selected as the leading designer of American women's fashions)

1970 — Giorgio de Sant' Angelo

    Chester Weinberg

1971 — Halston

    Betsey Johnson

1972 — John Anthony

1973 — Calvin Klein

1974 — Ralph Lauren

1975 — Carol Horn

1976 — Mary McFadden

1977 — Stephen Burrows

    Donna Karan and Louise Dell'Olio

1978 — Bill Atkinson

    Charles Suppon

1979 — Perry Ellis

RETURN AWARD

(Award to a designer whose work merits a top award for a second time)

1970 — Herbert Kasper

1971 — No Award

1972 — Halston

1973 — No Award

1974 — Calvin Klein

1975 — No Award

1976 — John Anthony

    Ralph Lauren

1977 — No Award

1978 — Mary McFadden

1979 — No Award

HALL OF FAME

("Winnie" designer chosen three separate times as the best of the year; * for Hall of Fame for Menswear)

1970 — Bill Blass

1971 — Anne Klein

1972 — Bonnie Cashin

1973 — Oscar de la Renta

1974 — Geoffrey Beene

    Halston

1975 — Piero Dimitri*

    Calvin Klein

1976 — Bill Kaiserman*

    Kasper

    Ralph Lauren*

1977 — Ralph Lauren

1979 — Mary McFadden

MENSWEAR

(Begun in 1968)

1970 — Ralph Lauren

1971 — Larry Kane

1972 — No Award

1973 — Piero Dimitri

1974 — Bill Kaiserman

1975 — Chuck Howard and Peter Wrigley

1976 — Sal Cesarani

1977 — No Award

1978 — Robert Stock

1979 — Lee Wright

SPECIAL AWARDS

(Honoring noteworthy contributions to fashion; * for Special Awards in Menswear)

1970 — Eileen Richardson and Will Richardson

Alexis Kirk

Cliff Nicolson

Marty Ruza

Bill Smith

Daniel Stenescu and Steven Brody

1971 — John Kloss

Levi Strauss

1972 — Alexander Shields*

Pinky Woman*

Dianne Beaudry*

Alan Rosanes*

Robert Margolis*

Dorothy Weatherford

1973 — Clovis Ruffin

1974 — Sal Cesarani*

Aldo Cipullo*

1975 — Nancy Knox*

1976 — Vicky Davis*

1977 — Marsha Akins*

Jeffrey Banks*

Ted Muehling

Fernando Sanchez

1978 — Danskin

Joan Halpern

Head Sports Wear*

1979 — Conrad Bell*

Barry Keiselstein-Cord*

Gil Truedson*

Joan Vass

THOMAS B. CLARKE PRIZE

(Given by the National Academy of Design for Interior Design)

1970 — Philip B. White

1971 — Charles Alson

1972 — Robert C. Baxter

1973 — William Gropper

1974 — Vincent Smith

1975 — Diana A. Marinara

1976 — Anne T. Rothe

1977 — Cornelius Ruhtenberg

1978 — Charles Reid

1979 — Selina Trieff

AMERICAN INSTITUTE OF ARCHITECTS (AIA)

AIA Gold Medal (Awarded annually to an individual for distinguished service to the architectural profession or to the institute. It is the institute's highest honor.)

1970 — R. Buckminster Fuller

1971 — Louis I. Kahn

1972 — Rietro Belluschi

1973 — No Award

1974 — No Award

1975 — No Award

1976 — No Award

1977 — Richard Joseph Neutra

1978 — Philip C. Johnson

1979 — I. M. Pei

MOTOR TREND CAR OF THE YEAR

1970 — Ford Torino

1971 — Chevrolet Vega

1972 — Citroen SM

1973 — Chevrolet Monte Carlo

1974 — Ford Mustang II

1975 — Chevrolet Monza 22 V-8

1976 — Chrysler, Dodge Aspen / Plymouth Volare

1977 — Chevrolet Caprice

1978 — Chrysler Dodge Omni / Plymouth Horizon

1979 — Buick Riviera S

MOTOR TREND IMPORT CAR OF THE YEAR

(started in 1976)

1976 — Toyota Celica Liftback

1977 — Mercedes-Benz 280E

1978 — Toyota Celica

1979 — Datsun 280ZX

DEATHS

Cristobal Banenciaga, 77, Spanish designer whose revolutionary designs in the 1950s and 1960s created a new, more relaxed look in women's clothing, 24 March 1972.

Marie-Louis Valentin Bousquet, 88, Paris editor of *Harper's Bazaar* for fifty years, 15 October 1975.

John Ely Burchard, 77, educator, architectural historian, and dean emeritus of the School of Humanities and Social Science at the Massachusetts Institute of Technology, 25 December 1975.

Gabrielle ("Coco") Chanel, 88, French designer of comfortable, fashionable women's clothes, 10 January 1971.

John Donnelly, 67, architectural sculptor who designed the facades of the New York Public Library and the Jefferson Memorial in Washington, D.C., 27 April 1970.

Charles Eames, 71, American architect and designer of formfitting chairs, 21 August 1978.

Norman Hartnell, 78, dressmaker to Queen Elizabeth II, best known for the elaborate, pearl-embroidered wedding dress for the queen's 1947 marriage to the duke of Edinburgh, 8 June 1979.

Charles James, 72, English-born dress designer known for his single one-seam or no-seam dresses that were much copied in the United States. Considered a "designer's designer," James won two Coty fashion awards, and his drawings were acquired by the Smithsonian Institute, 23 September 1978.

Louis Isadore Kahn, 73, one of the foremost architects in the United States, who established strong forms of brick and concrete as his predominant style, 17 March 1974.

Anne Klein, 51, American designer of women's wear, 19 March 1974.

Mainbocher, 85, Chicago-born designer considered to be one of the most influential designers of the twentieth century, 12 December 1976.

John Ogden Merrill, founder of Skidmore, Owings and Merrill in 1939, one of the largest and most influential American architectural firms in the world, 7 June 1975.

Louis Long, 73, star member of *The New Yorker's* original staff who covered the nightclub circuit in the 1920s and was later the fashion editor, 29 July 1974.

Rich Lorimer, 86, architect who designed the Tomb of the Unknown Soldier in Arlington, Virginia, 2 June 1978.

Richard Joseph Neutra, 78, pioneer in the development of modern architecture, 16 April 1970.

Norman Norell, 72, the American designer responsible for putting New York City in the running with Paris as a center for fashion, 25 October 1972.

Eliot F. Noyes, 66, a major industrial designer and architect whose corporate clients included International Business Machines Corporation, Westinghouse, and Mobil Corporation, 17 July 1977.

Nathan M. Orbach, 87, founder of department-store chains who built his fortune by copying Paris fashions at low prices, 19 November 1972.

Barbara ("Babe") Paley, 63, socialite and perennial on the list of best-dressed women. Known for the statement "You can't be too rich or too thin," 6 July 1978.

Russell Patterson, 82, designer who popularized the flapper look of the 1920s and who created sets and costumes for the Ziegfeld Follies, 17 March 1977.

Rose Marie Reid, 66, designer who transformed bathing suits into fashion items in the 1940s, 18 December 1978.

Clarence S. Stein, architect who, with his partner Henry Wright, pioneered community planning, 6 February 1975.

Edward Durell Stone, 76, American architect who, with Philip L. Goodwin, designed the Museum of Modern Art, 6 August 1978.

William Wilson, 70, architect and educator famous for his interest in environmentally sensitive design, 20 September 1973.

Lloyd Wright, 88, elder son of Frank Lloyd Wright and designer of the Wayfarer's Chapel in Los Angeles; known for that city's first slum clearance and urban housing project, 31 May 1978.

PUBLICATIONS

Ray Browne and Marshal Fishwick, eds., *Icons of America* (New York: Popular Press, 1978);

Sherrill Whiton, *Interior Design and Decoration*, fourth edition (New York: Lippincott, 1973);

Architectural Forum, periodical;

Architecture Record, periodical;

Art in America, periodical;

Art News, periodical;

Gentleman's Quarterly, periodical;

Glamour, periodical;

Harper's Bazaar, periodical;

Mademoiselle, periodical;

Newsweek, periodical;

Time, periodical;

Vogue, periodical.

GOVERNMENT AND POLITICS

by VICTOR BONDI

CONTENTS

Sidebars and tables are listed in italics.

1970

- Negotiations (known as the SALT talks) continue between the United States and the Soviet Union over a strategic nuclear arms limitations treaty.

- Protests against the war in Vietnam continue, reaching an especially high level in the wake of the April–May invasion of Cambodia.

6 Jan. The United States announces a heroin-control agreement with France in hopes of halting drug smuggling.

19 Jan. Federal judge G. Harrold Carswell is nominated to the Supreme Court. Citing his civil rights record, the Senate will reject the nomination.

26 Jan. President Richard M. Nixon vetoes a $19.7-billion education bill.

12 Feb. The North Vietnamese launch a spring offensive in Laos. The Nixon administration responds with a B-52 bombing campaign.

18 Feb. The antiwar radicals known as the Chicago Seven are acquitted of conspiracy to incite riots during the 1968 Democratic National Convention.

20 Feb. Henry Kissinger begins secret talks in Paris with Le Duc Tho, representative of North Vietnam, toward ending the Vietnam War.

5 Mar. A nuclear nonproliferation treaty, signed by the United States, the U.S.S.R., and forty-one other nations, goes into effect.

17 Mar. The U.S. Army announces an investigation into an alleged cover-up of a massacre of civilians at My Lai, South Vietnam, in 1968.

14 Apr. President Nixon names Adm. Thomas H. Moorer to replace Gen. Earle G. Wheeler as chairman of the U.S. Joint Chiefs of Staff.

30 Apr. President Nixon announces that U.S. and South Vietnamese troops have crossed into Cambodia in an attempt to flush out Communist sanctuaries.

4 May Members of the National Guard kill four students during an antiwar protest at Kent State University in Ohio.

15 June In *Welsh* v. *United States* the Supreme Court rules that the claim of conscientious-objector status can be argued on the basis of moral objection to war, rather than long-standing religious belief alone.

15 Sept. President Nixon orders Central Intelligence Agency (CIA) Director Richard M. Helms to disburse as much as $10 million toward undermining the newly elected Marxist government in Chile.

22 Sept. President Nixon signs a bill authorizing a nonvoting congressional representative to the House of Representatives for the District of Columbia. No District of Columbia representative had sat in the House since 1875.

26 Sept.–5 Oct. President Nixon tours Europe, visiting Rome, Belgrade, Madrid, Great Britain, and Ireland.

15 Oct. Promising "total war against organized crime," President Nixon signs the Organized Crime Control Act.

2 Dec. The Environmental Protection Agency (EPA) begins operations. William D. Ruckelshaus is the first director.

1971

- U.S. troops continue to withdraw from Vietnam. By December 140,000 American troops remain in Vietnam.

4 Jan.   Melvin H. Evans is elected the first black governor of the U.S. Virgin Islands.

9 Feb.   An earthquake in southern California kills sixty-five and causes $500 million in damage.

11 Feb.   The United States, the Soviet Union, and sixty-one other nations sign the Seabed Arms Control Treaty, banning nuclear weapons from the ocean floor.

1 Mar.   A radical activist group, the Weathermen, explode a bomb in a restroom of the U.S. Capitol. No one is injured, but the bomb causes three hundred thousand dollars in damages.

15 Mar.   In Vienna, Austria, the fourth round of the SALT talks between the United States and the Soviet Union begins.

29 Mar.   First Lt. William Calley is found guilty of murder in the 1968 massacre of Vietnamese civilians at My Lai.

7 Apr.   Chicago mayor Richard Daley wins his fifth reelection.

14–18 Apr.   A fifteen-member U.S. table-tennis team tours China.

1–3 May   Thirty thousand antiwar activists and radicals converge on Washington, D.C., with the intention of "stopping the government." Assistant Attorney General William Rehnquist announces "qualified martial law." Police arrest nearly twelve thousand. Almost all charges against the protesters will be dropped.

25 May   Murder charges against Black Panther Party leader Bobby Seale are dropped.

10 June   President Nixon drops the U.S. trade embargo with China.

13 June   *The New York Times* begins publication of the secret Defense Department study of the Vietnam War, known as the Pentagon Papers.

17 June   The United States signs a treaty restoring the island of Okinawa to Japan in 1972.

30 June   The Supreme Court sustains the right of *The New York Times* to publish the Pentagon Papers.

    •   Ratified by thirty-eight states, the Twenty-sixth Amendment to the Constitution, lowering the voting age from twenty-one to eighteen, goes into effect.

8 July   The fifth round of the SALT talks between the United States and the Soviet Union convenes in Helsinki, Finland.

15 July   The Nixon administration announces a projected May 1972 trip to China for the president. He will be the first U.S. president to visit China.

17 July   The White House organizes the infamous "plumbers unit," which investigates Daniel Ellsberg, the former Defense Department official who made the Pentagon Papers public. Over Labor Day weekend they illegally break into the office of Ellsberg's psychiatrist in an attempt to find information with which to ruin Ellsberg's reputation. They find none.

15 Aug.   President Nixon implements wage-and-price freezes and takes American currency off the gold standard.

22 Aug.   Black Power leader George Jackson is killed in San Quentin prison in California.

9–13 Sept.   A prison uprising at Attica State Correctional Facility in Attica, New York, ends when fifteen hundred state police and other law-enforcement officers stage an air-and-ground assault against the prison. Forty-three people die, including ten hostages. An inquiry subsequently discovers that all the dead had been killed by police bullets.

26 Sept. President Nixon greets Japanese emperor Hirohito at Anchorage, Alaska. It is the first trip of a Japanese emperor to the United States and the first meeting between a Japanese monarch and an American president.

30 Sept. During the SALT negotiations, the United States and the Soviet Union sign an agreement on ways to reduce the risk of accidental nuclear war.

25 Oct. With the support of the United States, members of the the United Nations vote to admit the People's Republic of China (Red China) and expel Nationalist China (Taiwan).

5 Nov. The White House announces a $136-million grain deal with the Soviet Union.

23 Dec. President Nixon grants former Teamsters leader James ("Jimmy") Hoffa a partial pardon from his thirteen-year sentence for jury tampering.

1972

5 Jan. President Nixon announces a six-year, $5.5-billion space-shuttle program.

25 Jan. President Nixon reveals that Kissinger has been secretly negotiating with the North Vietnamese in Paris.

14 Feb. President Nixon announces that he will take steps to limit the scope of court-ordered busing.

21–28 Feb. President Nixon becomes the first American president to visit China.

22 Mar. The Twenty-seventh Amendment to the Constitution, prohibiting discrimination on the basis of gender, is passed by Congress and sent to the states for ratification. By the end of 1972, twenty-two of the necessary thirty-eight states have ratified the amendment, also known as the Equal Rights Amendment.

22 Mar. The National Commission on Marijuana and Drug Abuse recommends that private possession and use of marijuana not be penalized.

7 Apr. The Federal Election Campaign Act goes into effect. The law sets limits and requires disclosures on personal contributions to political candidates.

10 Apr. The United States and 120 other nations sign a treaty banning biological weapons.

14–15 Apr. President Nixon conducts a two-day visit to Canada.

15 Apr. Responding to a spring offensive by North Vietnam, Nixon authorizes the bombing of targets in Hanoi and Haiphong.

8 May Despite the possibility that it may undermine his upcoming visit to the Soviet Union, Nixon announces the mining of Haiphong harbor.

15 May Democratic presidential candidate George C. Wallace, governor of Alabama, is shot while campaigning in Laurel, Maryland. Wallace survives the assassination attempt but is left paralyzed from the waist down.

22–30 May President Nixon becomes the first American president to visit Moscow. While in the Soviet Union he signs treaties on antiballistic missiles and other strategic weapons.

17 June Five men are arrested for breaking into the Democratic National Committee headquarters at the Watergate office complex in Washington, D.C.

19 June The Supreme Court rules that the Justice Department's claim of inherent power to wiretap without warrant is not a reasonable extension of the president's national-security authority.

19–23 June   Hurricane Agnes sweeps through the East Coast, killing hundreds and causing millions of dollars in damages.

23 June   President Nixon signs a bill providing federal money to universities and federal assistance to students.

1 July   John Mitchell, chairman of the Committee to Reelect the President, resigns, citing family problems.

14 July   Sen. George McGovern of South Dakota wins the Democratic nomination for president. Sen. Thomas F. Eagleton of Missouri is the vice-presidential nominee.

31 July   Following revelations that he had been hospitalized for depression, Senator Eagleton quits the Democratic ticket. He is replaced by former Peace Corps head Sargent Shriver.

4 Aug.   The would-be assassin of Democratic presidential candidate Wallace is sentenced to sixty-three years in prison.

12 Aug.   The last American combat troops leave Vietnam.

22 Aug.   President Nixon and Vice-president Spiro Agnew are nominated to head the 1972 Republican ticket.

29 Aug.   President Nixon announces that no administration officials were involved in the Watergate burglary.

1 Sept.   President Nixon and Japanese prime minister Kakuei Tanaka conclude three days of discussions in Hawaii.

12 Sept.   The Senate approves President Nixon's $33.5-billion revenue-sharing plan disbursing federal funds to state and local governments over a five-year period.

15 Sept.   A federal grand jury indicts former White House aides G. Gordon Liddy and E. Howard Hunt, along with the five original burglars, in the Watergate break-in case.

3 Oct.   Nixon's weapons treaties with the Soviet Union are signed into law.

8 Oct.   In a breakthrough in the Paris peace negotiations, the United States and North Vietnam initially agree to end the war. President Nguyen Van Thieu of South Vietnam, however, demands sixty-nine revisions to the agreement. Talks continue.

12–13 Oct.   Charges of institutional racism surface in the U.S. Navy after a racial brawl on the aircraft carrier *Kitty Hawk*.

27 Oct.   Citing high costs, President Nixon vetoes nine social welfare, public works, and ecology bills.

2 Nov.   Angry Native Americans seize the Bureau of Indian Affairs building in Washington, D.C., to dramatize official neglect.

7 Nov.   Richard Nixon defeats Sen. George McGovern for the presidency by 17,409,550 votes. McGovern wins electoral-college victories only in Massachusetts and the District of Columbia. The Democrats nonetheless retain their majorities in both houses of Congress.

8 Nov.   Several hundred Native Americans end their occupation of the Bureau of Indian Affairs building in Washington, D.C.

10 Nov. Chief of Naval Operations Elmo R. Zumwalt reprimands some ninety U.S. Navy officers of the *Kitty Hawk* for racism.

27–30 Nov. Nixon restructures his cabinet. Elliot Richardson replaces Melvin Laird as secretary of defense; Caspar Weinberger replaces Richardson as secretary of health, education, and welfare (HEW); James T. Lynn replaces George Romney as secretary of housing and urban development (HUD); and Peter J. Brennan is nominated to be secretary of labor.

18 Dec. Following a full collapse in the Paris peace talks, Nixon orders massive bombing raids against Hanoi and Haiphong. The campaign continues for eleven days, pausing only for Christmas.

1973

- The Watergate revelations result in continuing resignations and indictments for members of the Nixon administration. Televised hearings on the Watergate affair preoccupy Congress and the public.

2 Jan. The Democratic Caucus of the House of Representatives votes 154 to 75 to cut off funds for the Vietnam War. Two days later the Senate Democratic Caucus votes 36 to 12 to cut off funds for the war.

11 Jan. The Senate Democratic Caucus votes unanimously to establish a special committee to investigate the Watergate affair; Sen. Sam Ervin (D–North Carolina) chairs the committee.

11 Jan. The Justice Department charges President Nixon's reelection committee with eight criminal violations of the election-financing law enacted on 7 April 1972.

23 Jan. President Nixon announces that a peace settlement has been reached on Vietnam. The settlement leaves the North Vietnamese military in place in South Vietnam; retains the non-Communist government of Nguyen Van Thieu in the south; requires the United States to withdraw all forces and dismantle all installations within sixty days; demands the North Vietnamese release all American prisoners of war (POWs) within sixty days; and establishes a framework for the peaceful reunification of North and South Vietnam.

27 Jan. In Paris, Kissinger and North Vietnamese negotiator Le Duc Tho sign the cease-fire agreement on Vietnam.

30 Jan. Former Nixon campaign members James W. McCord and G. Gordon Liddy are convicted of breaking into and illegally wiretapping the Democratic party headquarters at the Watergate office complex.

12 Feb. The first American POWs released from Vietnam arrive at Clark Air Force Base in the Philippines.

14 Feb. The government announces the establishment of a commission to reconstruct and provide economic assistance for North Vietnam.

15–22 Feb. B-52s escalate air warfare over Laos in an attempt to strike at Pathet Lao positions.

28 Feb. Members of the American Indian Movement (AIM) exchange gunfire with federal agents in Wounded Knee, South Dakota. A confrontation between AIM and the government continues until 8 May.

5 Apr. The Nixon administration withdraws L. Patrick Gray from consideration as director of the Federal Bureau of Investigation (FBI).

11 Apr. The Mississippi River reaches its highest flood level in thirty years. By May the flood kills eleven people, forces the evacuation of thirty-five thousand people in nine states, and causes $500 million in damages.

16 Apr. Pentagon officials confirm continuing air raids on Communist positions in Laos.

27 Apr. William D. Ruckelshaus is named acting director of the FBI.

30 Apr. In the wake of the Watergate scandal H. R. Haldeman, White House chief of staff; John Ehrlichman, domestic policy assistant; John Dean, presidential counsel; and Richard Kleindienst, attorney general, all resign their offices. In a televised address President Nixon denies any involvement in the Watergate break-in or cover-up. Secretary of Defense Richardson becomes attorney general. James Schlesinger becomes secretary of defense. William E. Colby succeeds Schlesinger as director of the CIA.

17 May The Senate Select Committee on Presidential Campaign Activities, led by Senator Ervin, convenes public hearings to investigate the Watergate affair and other illegal activities conducted by the Committee to Reelect the President.

25 May Harvard Law School professor Archibald Cox is sworn in as Watergate special prosecutor.

29 May Los Angeles elects its first black mayor, fifty-five-year-old City Councilman Thomas Bradley.

7 June Clarence M. Kelly is nominated as director of the FBI.

13 June President Nixon orders a sixty-day freeze on consumer prices.

16–25 June Soviet Communist party chairman Leonid I. Brezhnev visits the United States. He signs accords reducing the risk of accidental nuclear war, increasing air travel, and promoting scientific exchanges between the United States and the Soviet Union.

25–29 June Former White House counsel Dean testifies before the Ervin committee, implicating himself, Haldeman, Ehrlichman, Mitchell, President Nixon, and others in the Watergate cover-up. Dean also reveals the existence of the so-called enemies list — a roster of prominent Americans and celebrities considered by the White House as administration opponents and targeted for possible harassment.

13 July During congressional testimony former White House aide Alexander Butterfield reveals the existence of taped conversations secretly recorded at the White House.

26 July After the Ervin committee, Federal Judge John J. Sirica, and Special Prosecutor Cox subpoena these tapes, the Nixon administration refuses to release them, throwing the issue to the courts.

31 July Rep. Robert F. Drinan (D-Massachusetts) introduces a resolution calling for Nixon's impeachment on four grounds: the bombing of Cambodia; the taping of conversations; the refusal to spend impounded funds; and the establishment of a "supersecret security force within the White House."

6 Aug The Justice Department reveals that Vice-president Agnew is under investigation for receiving kickbacks while serving as Baltimore County executive and governor of Maryland.

8 Aug Agnew denies the kickback charges as "false and scurrilous and malicious."

10 Oct.   Agnew resigns the vice-presidency and pleads nolo contendere (no contest) to income-tax evasion in return for the dropping of other criminal charges. He receives a three-year suspended sentence and a ten-thousand-dollar fine.

12 Oct.   Nixon nominates Rep. Gerald Ford (R–Michigan) for the vice-presidency.

20 Oct.   After Special Prosecutor Cox reproves the White House for noncompliance in the Watergate investigation, Nixon orders him fired. When both Attorney General Richardson and Deputy Attorney General Ruckelshaus refuse, Nixon dismisses them. Solicitor General Robert Bork finally fires Cox and dismisses Cox's staff of sixty attorneys, who had been investigating Watergate for over five months. Over 250,000 telegrams denounce what comes to be known as the "Saturday Night Massacre."

21 Oct.   The American Federation of Labor and Congress of Industrial Organizations (AFL-CIO) convention in Florida calls for Nixon's removal from the presidency.

23 Oct.   Eight resolutions to impeach Nixon are introduced in the House of Representatives even as Nixon begins to comply with subpoenas and turns over some of the Watergate tapes to federal judge Sirica.

25–30 Oct.   Because of fears that the Soviet Union will intervene to enforce a UN cease-fire resolution between Egypt and Syria and Israel, the Nixon administration places U.S. armed forces on worldwide military alert. A UN agreement to send a peacekeeping force to the area results in the ending of the alert.

28 Oct.   The White House announces that two of the nine subpoenaed Watergate tapes are missing.

1 Nov.   Leon A. Jaworski replaces Cox as Watergate special prosecutor. William Saxbe replaces Richardson as attorney general.

7 Nov.   Over Nixon's veto Congress passes the War Powers Act, requiring congressional approval for any commitment of U.S. forces abroad longer than sixty days.

16 Nov.   President Nixon signs a bill authorizing the Alaska pipeline.

21 Nov.   The White House reveals the existence of a mysterious 18.5-minute gap in a key Watergate tape.

27 Nov.   Nixon's personal secretary, Rose Mary Woods, testifies that she accidentally caused five minutes of the erasure; a panel of experts later concludes that the gap was deliberately created.

6 Dec.   Gerald Ford is sworn in as the new vice-president.

8 Dec.   Responding to charges of financial improprieties, Nixon releases his income-tax returns and agrees to an Internal Revenue Service audit. The audit reveals that Nixon owes $432,787.13 in back taxes.

1974

- In June President Nixon conducts tours of the Middle East, Europe, and Russia.

- Maynard Jackson is sworn in as the first black mayor of Atlanta, Georgia.

2 Jan.   President Nixon signs into law a bill that requires states to lower speed limits to 55 MPH in order to receive federal highway funds. The bill is designed to help conserve energy.

4 Jan.   William Saxbe is sworn in as attorney general.

6 Feb.	The House of Representatives grants authority to the House Judiciary Committee to investigate the Watergate affair.
7 Feb.	The United States and Panama inaugurate negotiations of a new Panama Canal treaty.
18 Mar.	The Organization of Petroleum Exporting Countries (OPEC) nations, save Libya and Syria, officially end their oil embargo against the United States.
29 Mar.	Eight former members of the Ohio National Guard are indicted by a federal grand jury for violating the civil rights of students they shot and wounded during an antiwar protest at Kent State University on 4 May 1970. Although they are acquitted, in 1979 the state of Ohio will settle a civil suit with survivors of the shooting, giving them a total of $675,000.
29 Apr.	In a nationally televised address, Nixon announces that he will release summary transcripts of the Watergate tapes on the following morning.
24 July	The Supreme Court rules, in *United States* v. *Richard M. Nixon,* that the White House has no claim to "executive privilege" in withholding the Watergate tapes from Special Prosecutor Jaworski. President Nixon turns over the tapes on 30 July and 5 August.
24 July	The House Judiciary Committee commences formal impeachment hearings against the president.
30 July	The House Judiciary Committee recommends that the House of Representatives impeach the president for three offenses: obstruction of justice, abuse of power, and contempt of Congress. Two other articles of impeachment, for secretly bombing Cambodia and for filing false tax returns, are rejected.
31 July	Former White House official John Ehrlichman is sentenced to twenty months to five years in prison for conspiracy related to his involvement in the burglary at the office of the psychiatrist of Daniel Ellsberg, who published the Pentagon Papers.
2 Aug.	Former White House counsel John Dean is sentenced to one to four years in prison for conspiracy to cover up the Watergate affair.
5 Aug	Newly released Watergate tapes demonstrate that on 23 June 1972 President Nixon ordered a cover-up of the Watergate break-in.
8 Aug.	In a televised address Richard Nixon announces his resignation from the presidency, effective at noon on 9 August. He becomes the first president to resign in American history.
9 Aug.	Gerald R. Ford is inaugurated as the thirty-eighth president of the United States.
19 Aug.	President Ford offers "earned reentry" amnesty for Vietnam War resisters.
20 Aug.	President Ford nominates former New York governor Nelson A. Rockefeller for vice-president. He is confirmed in December.
22 Aug.	The House Judiciary Committee releases its final report on the Watergate affair, detailing "clear and convincing evidence" that Richard Nixon had obstructed justice thirty-six times. The House approves the report 412–3.
4 Sept.	George Bush is named head of the U.S. liaison to China.
8 Sept.	President Ford grants Nixon "a full, free, and absolute pardon" for any crimes he might have committed while in office. In opinion polls Ford's popularity drops from 71 percent to 49 percent.

16 Sept.   Gen. Alexander M. Haig, Jr., is appointed supreme commander of North Atlantic Treaty Organization (NATO).

8 Oct.   President Ford unveils his program Whip Inflation Now (WIN) to Congress.

10 Oct.   Congress passes legislation providing for public funding of presidential primaries and elections. President Ford signs the legislation on 14 October.

17 Oct.   Ford testifies before a House subcommittee that he had no prior arrangement with Nixon to grant the former president a pardon.

5 Nov.   Democrats win in congressional elections, gaining a 61-37 majority in the Senate (with two seats held by independents) and a 291-144 majority in the House. Democrat Ella Grasso of Connecticut becomes the first woman elected governor of a U.S. state without having been preceded in office by her husband.

16–24 Nov.   President Ford conducts visits to Japan, South Korea, and the Soviet Union. Ford and Soviet party chairman Brezhnev sign a tentative agreement limiting offensive nuclear weapons.

21 Nov.   Over President Ford's veto Congress passes the Freedom of Information Act, increasing public access to government files.

26 Nov.   President Ford signs a six-year, $11.8-billion mass-transit bill.

3 Dec.   Over President Ford's veto Congress passes a bill increasing educational benefits for veterans.

6 Dec.   The Department of Labor releases figures showing that the unemployment rate reached 6.5 percent in November — the highest monthly rate since 1961.

30 Dec.   President Ford pocket vetoes a bill regulating strip-mining of coal.

1975

- Following the fall of South Vietnam, some 130,000 Indochinese refugees come to the United States.

- Exiled Soviet author Aleksandr Solzhenitsyn warns against détente with the Soviet Union.

1 Jan.   Former White House officials Haldeman, Ehrlichman, and Mitchell are all found guilty of conspiracy and obstructing justice in the Watergate affair.

8 Jan.   Three former Nixon aides, Dean, Herbert W. Kalmbach, and Jeb Stuart Magruder, are released from prison.

24 Jan.   A terrorist group seeking Puerto Rican independence bombs Fraunces Tavern in New York City, killing four and injuring fifty-three.

31 Jan.   Former Nixon aide Charles W. Colson is released from prison.

5 Feb.   Edward H. Levi is confirmed as U.S. attorney general.

7 Feb.   The Labor Department announces that the January unemployment rate is 8.2 percent — the highest rate in thirty-three years.

21 Feb.   Former White House officials Haldeman, Ehrlichman, and Mitchell are each sentenced to three years in prison for their involvement in the Watergate scandal.

27 Feb.   The Justice Department announces that former FBI director J. Edgar Hoover kept secret files on the private lives of presidents, congressmen, and other prominent public figures.

4 Mar. President Ford agrees to a sixty-day delay in increasing oil tariffs by three dollars a barrel but also vetoes a congressional effort to suspend his power to increase tariffs.

12 Mar. Former Nixon cabinet member and chief fund-raiser Maurice Stans pleads guilty to one of five counts of violating federal campaign-finance laws.

18 Mar. The government discloses that the CIA spent $250 million in a 1968 effort to salvage a Soviet submarine.

29 Mar. President Ford signs a $22.8-billion tax cut.

31 Mar. After only 22,500 of the possible 124,000 eligible participate, the clemency program for Vietnam War draft resisters and evaders ends.

23 Apr. Reacting to the most recent North Vietnamese military offensive, President Ford, in a New Orleans speech, declares the Vietnam War is "finished."

29 Apr. The last Americans leave the U.S. mission in Saigon. Gen. Duong Van Minh of the South Vietnamese army surrenders to the North Vietnamese on 30 April.

2 May The Labor Department announces an unemployment rate of 8.9 percent in April, the highest since 1941.

12–14 May The U.S. merchant ship Mayaguez is seized by Cambodian forces and charged with spying. American military forces attempt a rescue operation which kills fifteen and injures fifty, and the Mayaguez is released.

29 May President Ford vetoes a $5.3-billion job bill.

10 June The Rockefeller commission on CIA domestic activities reports that the CIA had undertaken unlawful surveillance of three hundred thousand American citizens and organizations and had supplied former president Nixon with information on his political opponents.

26 June The United States ceases economic assistance to Laos.

30 June The government extends unemployment assistance to sixty-five weeks.

30 June Exiled Soviet author Aleksandr Solzhenitsyn warns against détente with the Soviet Union.

3 July The third and final Watergate jury, serving since 1974, is dismissed.

14 July FBI Director Clarence B. Kelly confirms that the agency conducts burglaries and break-ins in national security cases. On 16 July the *Washington Post* reports that the FBI also uses break-ins during criminal investigations.

6 Aug. President Ford approves a seven-year extension of the Voting Rights Act.

27 Aug. The eight former members of the Ohio National Guard are acquitted of the federal-grand-jury charges that they violated the civil rights of students they shot during a 4 May 1970 antiwar protest at Kent State University.

31 Aug. The House Select Committee on Intelligence Activities reveals that the National Security Agency monitors almost all overseas calls to and from the United States.

17 Oct. New York City, on the verge of bankruptcy, is saved from default by the New York City Teachers Union's purchase of $150 million in municipal bonds.

20 Oct. The United States and the Soviet Union agree that the U.S.S.R. will purchase six million to eight million tons of American grain annually for the next five years.

3 Nov. President Ford shuffles members of his administration. Secretary of State Kissinger resigns as head of the National Security Council and is replaced by Brent Scowcroft; Secretary of Defense James Schlesinger is replaced by Donald Rumsfeld; CIA Director William Colby is replaced by George Bush; Secretary of Commerce Rogers Morton is replaced by Eliott Richardson. Vice-president Nelson Rockefeller announces he will not be a candidate for vice-president in 1976.

12 Nov. Supreme Court justice William O. Douglas, seventy-seven, suffering from a stroke, announces his retirement. He had sat on the bench for thirty-six years, earning a reputation as a civil libertarian. He will be replaced by Judge John Paul Stevens.

14 Nov. President Ford approves an $18-billion increase in the national-debt ceiling, raising the total national debt to $595 billion.

20 Nov. The bipartisan Senate investigation of FBI and CIA activities concludes. The Senate committee, led by Frank Church (D–Idaho), reports that both agencies illegally spied on American citizens. It further charges the CIA with plotting the assassination of foreign leaders and with maintaining stocks of illegal poisons.

5 Dec. President Ford departs China after conferring with Chinese leaders.

19 Dec. Congress refuses to authorize covert CIA actions in Angola, despite warnings that U.S. security is at stake in that country's civil war.

1976

- Rep. Carl B. Albert (D–Oklahoma) announces he will retire as Speaker of the House at the end of the current session.

30 Jan. The Supreme Court upholds the provisions of the 1974 Campaign Financing Reform Act. It also requires that members of the Federal Election Commission be appointed by the president, not Congress.

10 Feb. American officials acknowledge that the Soviet Union, in an effort to disable listening devices, had focused microwave radiation on the U.S. embassy in Moscow.

17 Feb. President Ford announces the creation of an independent board to oversee U.S. intelligence operations. He also issues an executive order forbidding domestic surveillance and harassment and outlaws the assassination of foreign leaders.

20 Mar. The government of Thailand orders a withdrawal of all American military personnel within the next four months.

23 Apr. Secretary of State Kissinger begins a twelve-day tour of African countries.

26–28 Apr. The Senate Select Committee on Intelligence issues a heavily censored report on covert intelligence operations. It urges closer congressional oversight of intelligence operations and better safeguards against violations of civil liberties.

5 May The Senate upholds President Ford's veto of a $125-million child-care bill.

28 May A test pact limiting the kiloton yields of underground nuclear tests is signed by the United States and the Soviet Union.

5 June Fourteen people are killed and $1 billion in damage is done when the Teton River dam collapses in Idaho.

16 June The United States ambassador to Lebanon, Francis E. Meloy, Jr., and an aide are assassinated in Beirut.

20 June The U.S. Navy evacuates 250 Americans from Beirut, Lebanon.

2 July The Supreme Court upholds the death penalty laws of Georgia, Florida, and Texas. It strikes down death penalties in North Carolina and Louisiana.

3–4 July The nation celebrates the two hundreth anniversary of its independence with festivals and political events around the country. The largest and most impressive festival is in New York, celebrated through a flotilla of tall ships and the music of Arthur Fiedler and the Boston Pops. After Vietnam and Watergate the celebrations serve to renew a certain amount of popular confidence in the country.

14 July The Democratic National Convention nominates former Georgia governor James Earl ("Jimmy") Carter, Jr., for the presidency. Walter Mondale, senator from Minnesota, is nominated for the vice-presidency.

1 Aug. Vietnam permits thirty-eight American citizens and their eleven Vietnamese dependents trapped in Saigon to return to the United States.

7 Aug. The United States announces a $10-billion arms sale to Iran.

18 Aug. Two American soldiers are killed in Korea when they attempt to cut down a tree blocking their view of a Korean demilitarized zone (DMZ). The attack quickly becomes a campaign issue as President Ford orders a dramatic display of military force in response. On 21 August North Korea describes the incident as regrettable but refuses to accept responsibility.

19 Aug. At the Republican National Convention Gerald Ford narrowly defeats California governor Ronald Reagan as the nominee for president. Kansas senator Robert Dole is nominated for vice-president.

27 Sept. Ford and Carter conduct the first of three presidential debates on national television. The vice-presidential candidates debate one another on 15 October.

2 Nov. Jimmy Carter defeats Gerald Ford for the presidency. The Democrats retain majorities in both houses of Congress.

6 Nov. Benjamin L. Hooks succeeds Roy Wilkins as the director of the National Association for the Advancement of Colored People (NAACP).

15 Nov. The admission of Vietnam to the United Nations is vetoed by the United States.

6 Dec. The ninetieth Congress elects Thomas P. ("Tip") O'Neill, Jr. (D–Massachusetts), as Speaker of the House.

1977

• The United States and Panama renegotiate the Panama Canal Treaty.

20 Jan. Jimmy Carter is inaugurated president of the United States. Walter Mondale takes the oath as vice-president.

21 Jan. President Carter signs an unconditional pardon for almost all Vietnam-era draft evaders.

1 Feb. Vice-president Mondale concludes a ten-day tour of Europe and Japan.

18 Feb. The *Washington Post* reports that King Hussein of Jordan has been on the CIA payroll since 1957, a charge confirmed by the government the next day.

11 Mar.   Following State Department criticism of its human-rights record, Brazil cancels its twenty-five-year-old military assistance agreement with the United States.

15 Mar.   The United States agrees to send Zaire military equipment to help it defend against Angolan aggression.

17 Mar.   In an address to the United Nations President Carter stresses human rights.

30 Mar.   The Soviet Union rejects U.S. arms limitations proposals.

9 Apr.   The United States seizes a Soviet trawler for fishing violations. The ship is released following the payment of a $250,000 fine.

12 Apr.   President Carter grants Watergate conspirator G. Gordon Liddy a commutation, making him available for parole in July.

20 Apr.   President Carter unveils a national energy policy designed to reduce energy consumption.

28 Apr.   The United States and Cuba sign agreements on fishing rights.

3 May   The United States and Vietnam begin talks on normalizing relations.

4 May   Former president Nixon begins a series of paid televised interviews with David Frost.

21 May   President Carter orders Maj. Gen. John K. Singlaub, chief of staff of U.S. forces in South Korea, home and reassigned following Singlaub's public criticism of Carter's Korean policy.

23 May   The Tax Reduction and Simplification Bill of 1977 is signed into law by President Carter.

13–14 July   A massive power failure grips New York City; thirty-seven hundred are arrested during widespread looting.

15 July   President Carter approves the admission of fifteen thousand Indochinese refugees to the United States.

20 July   Public documents reveal that from the early 1950s to the mid 1960s, the CIA conducted behavioral modification experiments on unwitting human subjects.

3 Aug.   A bill controlling strip-mining is signed into law by President Carter.

4 Aug.   The Department of Energy is created. James Schlesinger is nominated as secretary.

21 Sept.   Burt Lance resigns as director of the Office of Management and Budget. He will be succeeded by James T. McIntyre.

4 Oct.   Judge John J. Sirica reduces the prison sentences of Watergate conspirators Mitchell, Haldeman, and Ehrlichman.

5 Oct.   Two United Nations covenants on human rights are signed by President Carter.

31 Oct.   Former CIA director Richard Helms pleads no contest to two misdemeanor counts of deceiving Congress. He will be fined two thousand dollars and given a suspended two-year sentence.

1 Nov.   President Carter signs legislation raising the minimum wage to $2.30 an hour.

8 Nov.   Democrat Ed Koch is elected mayor of New York City.

21 Nov.	The National Women's Conference concludes in Houston, Texas, after framing guidelines for women's legislation.
28 Dec.	G. William Miller replaces Arthur F. Burns as the chairman of the Federal Reserve Board.
29 Dec.	President Carter begins a nine-day, 18,500-mile trip to Europe and the Middle East.

1978

- Marion Barry is elected the first black mayor of the District of Columbia.

- The United States and Colombia sign an agreement designed to interdict marijuana and cocaine shipments to the United States.

11 Jan.	The Labor Department announces that the unemployment rate for December 1977 was 6.4 percent — the lowest in three years.
13 Jan.	The United States and Japan conclude an accord designed to reduce Japan's trade surplus.
6 Feb.	New England is paralyzed by the worst blizzard (up to fifty inches of snow) in recent history.
10 Feb.	Vietnam recalls its UN ambassador after the United States accuses him of espionage.
16 Mar.	The Senate ratifies the Panama Canal Treaty, 68–32.
3 Apr.	President Carter returns from a tour of Latin America and sub-Saharan Africa. He is the first sitting president to tour sub-Saharan Africa.
6 Apr.	President Carter approves a bill making sixty-five an optional, rather than mandatory, age of retirement.
7 Apr.	President Carter defers production of the controversial neutron bomb. The nuclear weapon is designed to use enhanced radiation to kill people but leave buildings undamaged.
18 Apr.	The Senate ratifies a second Panama Canal treaty, turning control of the waterway over to Panama in 1999.
11 May	The Senate ratifies the sale of fighter aircraft to Israel, Egypt, and Saudi Arabia.
31 May	A two-day NATO summit conference in Washington concludes with the adoption of a fifteen-nation mutual-defense program.
6 June	California voters approve Proposition 13, a state constitutional amendment reducing property taxes 57 percent.
28 June	The Supreme Court rules that Allan P. Bakke, a thirty-eight-year-old white engineer, be admitted to the University of California Medical School. Claiming reverse discrimination, Bakke argued that affirmative-action programs had prevented him from being admitted. While not affirming racial quotas, the Court did uphold the constitutionality of affirmative action.
12 July	United Nations ambassador Andrew Young, in an interview published in the French newspaper *Le Matin*, claims that there are "hundreds, perhaps thousands," of political prisoners in the United States. The remarks spark demands for Young's resignation, and President Carter publicly rebukes the ambassador.
13 July	SALT talks in Geneva, Switzerland, end inconclusively.

1 Aug.	The government ends a four-year arms embargo against Turkey.
8 Aug.	President Carter signs a bill giving New York City $1.65 billion in federal long-term loan guarantees.
17 Sept.	President Carter, Prime Minister Menachem Begin of Israel, and President Anwar Sadat of Egypt end eleven days of discussions at Camp David, Maryland, by signing an accord designed to conclude a peace treaty between Egypt and Israel.
29 Sept.	In Baltimore, Maryland, a federal grand jury indicts eighteen people for corrupt practices involving the U.S. General Services Administration (GSA).
6 Oct.	The Senate votes to extend the deadline for ratification of the Equal Rights Amendment to 30 June 1982. Thirty-five states have already approved the amendment, three short of the necessary thirty-eight.
21 Oct.	Cuba releases forty-six former political prisoners and thirty-three relatives to the United States. Reports indicate that Cuban dictator Fidel Castro is prepared to release some three thousand other prisoners to the United States.
1 Nov.	President Carter modifies U.S. currency policy, increasing the value of the dollar on the Tokyo markets 5 percent and rallying the stock market.
7 Nov.	In midterm elections, despite solid gains by the Republicans, Democrats retain hold of both houses of Congress.
27 Nov.	George Moscone, the mayor of San Francisco, and Harvey Milk, a city supervisor, are assassinated by a disgruntled city employee who claims he was driven temporarily insane by junk food.
23 Dec.	SALT talks in Geneva again end inconclusively, although both sides announce agreement on most issues.
30 Dec.	The House Select Committee on Assassinations ends its two-year inquiry by concluding that the murders of President John F. Kennedy and Dr. Martin Luther King, Jr., were possibly the result of conspiracies.

1979

1 Jan.	The United States recognizes the People's Republic of China and terminates its mutual defense treaty with Taiwan.
12 Jan.	President Carter dismisses Bella Abzug from her post as cochair of the National Advisory Committee on Women. Twenty-one of the forty committee members resign in protest of the firing.
28 Jan.	Chinese deputy prime minister Deng Xiaoping arrives in the United States for a nine-day tour. It is the first American visit by a Chinese Communist official.
1 Feb.	President Carter commutes the seven-year prison sentence of Patricia Hearst, imprisoned for twenty-two months.
5 Feb.	Farmers protesting federal price supports hold a rally in Washington, D.C.
8 Feb.	The United States withdraws military and economic support from the Nicaraguan government of Anastasio Somoza Debayle in an effort to end the Nicaraguan civil war.

26 Mar. Egyptian president Anwar Sadat and Israeli prime minister Menachem Begin sign a formal peace treaty between their two nations in a ceremony held at the White House. The peace treaty, ending thirty-one years of warfare, was based upon negotiations mediated by U.S. president Jimmy Carter at Camp David in 1978.

28 Mar. A major accident at the Three Mile Island nuclear generating plant near Harrisburg, Pennsylvania, results in the evacuation of thousands. The plant manages to avoid a catastrophic core meltdown, and by 9 April the accident is fully contained.

3 Apr. Jane M. Byrne is elected the first woman mayor of Chicago.

5 Apr. President Carter announces a slow decontrol of oil prices and asks Congress for a windfall-profits tax on oil companies.

6 May More than sixty-five thousand demonstrators in Washington, D.C., protest against nuclear power.

9 May California institutes gasoline rationing in nine counties.

18 June In Vienna the SALT II accord, limiting production of nuclear weapons, is signed by President Carter and Soviet president Brezhnev.

28 June In Tokyo President Carter announces that the United States will accept fourteen thousand Indochinese refugees per month in the coming year.

29 June At the Tokyo economic conference Japan and the six major Western powers agree to limit imports of oil.

15 July Following polls showing his popularity at an all-time low of 29 percent, President Carter conducts a ten-day energy summit at Camp David. Afterward he announces a new energy program designed to lessen the American "crisis of confidence" and dependence on foreign oil. He also radically alters the composition of his cabinet.

20 July President Carter halts the withdrawal of U.S. troops from South Korea and announces that thirty-two thousand troops will remain on the Korean peninsula for at least two more years.

31 July The Chrysler Corporation, facing a record $207-million loss in the second quarter of 1979, seeks a $1-billion loan from the federal government in order to prevent bankruptcy. The third largest automaker employs 250,000 workers.

13 Aug. Mayor Frank Rizzo and other high-ranking Philadelphia officials are indicted by the Justice Department for civil rights abuses and police brutality. The charges will later be dismissed.

15 Aug. UN ambassador Young resigns following an uproar caused by his meeting with a representative of the Palestine Liberation Organization (PLO), a meeting which violated American Middle East policy.

31 Aug. The State Department confirms the presence of two thousand to three thousand Soviet combat troops in Cuba.

7 Sept. President Carter approves the $33 billion MX-missile system.

3 Oct. The Agriculture Department announces the sale of a record 25 million metric tons of grain to the Soviet Union.

22 Oct. The United States government admits the deposed shah of Iran for medical treatment at a New York hospital.

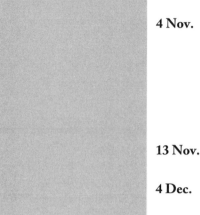

4 Nov.   In Tehran several hundred Iranian militants storm the U.S. embassy and seize the diplomatic personnel. The militants announce they will release the hostages when the United States returns the shah, who is recovering from medical treatments in a New York hospital, to Iran to stand trial. President Carter declares he will not extradite the shah; Iranian prime minister Mehdi Barzargan resigns when it becomes known that Ayatollah Ruholla Mussaui Khomeini and the Revolutionary Council had sanctioned the hostage-taking, a violation of international law.

13 Nov.   Former California governor Ronald Reagan announces his candidacy for the 1980 Republican presidential nomination.

4 Dec.   The Security Council of the United Nations unanimously approves a resolution demanding the release of American hostages held in Iran. On 15 December the World Court will also demand release of the hostages. On 31 December the UN will conditionally approve economic sanctions against Iran.

OVERVIEW

The Limits of American Power. The 1970s demonstrated, more clearly than in any other postwar decade, the limits of American power abroad. After the longest war in American history, the United States was unable to win in Vietnam and settled in 1973 for a peace treaty that functioned as little more than paper justification for a failed Asian policy. American dependence on foreign oil left the United States at the mercy of two oil shortages during the decade; the United States suffered continuing trade imbalances and witnessed a sharp decline in its domination of world markets caused by increased Japanese and European activity. There was little the United States could do to alter its oil imbalances or trade deficits. Military power was irrelevant, and economic pressure was ineffective. Similarly, efforts to acknowledge the changed status of the United States on the world stage, to conduct a less ambitious foreign policy, also failed. President Jimmy Carter's human-rights policy undermined American economic interests abroad; his friendly relations with Latin America failed to temper the endemic social turmoil south of the border. Carter's inability to halt Soviet incursions in Africa and, at the end of the decade, in Asia badly compromised his presidency. These illustrations of American impotence paled in comparison to the 1979 seizure of American diplomats by Iranian militants. No more striking symbol of the limits of American power was likely than the humiliation in Tehran, for the volatile political situation in the Middle East rendered an American military response unlikely. Thus the decade ended with the United States helplessly enduring the taunts of the Muslim theocracy (their sentiments ironically echoed by American conservatives) that the United States had become a "second-rate power."

A Thaw in the Cold War. The changed reality of American power in the world lay behind the other foreign-policy innovation of the 1970s, détente with the Soviet Union. Although Richard Nixon had been among the most zealous of the "cold warriors" in the 1950s, by the 1970s, as president, he recognized that the enormous military expenditures of both sides were bankrupting the United States and the Soviet Union. Changes within the relations of Communist nations, especially new hostilities between the Soviet Union and Red China, gave the United States the opportunity to play the interests of one superpower against the other and lessened the necessity of direct military confrontation with the Soviet Union. By 1972 Nixon and his foremost foreign-policy adviser, Henry Kissinger, had negotiated an arms-control agreement with the Soviet Union and had begun a diplomatic dialogue with China. Presidents Ford and Carter continued these initiatives, expanding the arms agreements, increasing American trade with the Communist powers, and initiating symbolic cultural exchanges, such as the 1975 joint Apollo-Soyuz spaceflight. Ultimately, however, détente unraveled as continued Soviet operations in Africa and Latin America and violations of human rights, especially of Soviet Jews, were magnified and played to political advantage by American conservatives. By 1978 Carter was calling for massive increases in American defense spending, the polarized rhetoric of the superpowers had returned, and the world settled in for another decade of the cold war.

The Crisis of Constitutional Authority. In the 1970s a long-term crisis in constitutional authority reached a critical stage. Although the Constitution provides that Congress, the most representative branch of the federal government, should be the branch most responsible for enacting legislation that affects the average American, more often than not in the postwar period key legislation was reshaped by the president or the Supreme Court. Foreign policy became the exclusive province of the president. Gone were the days when a powerful senator could take a preeminent role in the conduct of U.S. foreign policy, as had Henry Cabot Lodge after World War I. Executive authority over foreign affairs was expanded by the National Security Act of 1947, which created the National Security Agency (NSA) and Central Intelligence Agency (CIA) — fundamentally answerable to the president — and the two wars of the period — in Korea and Vietnam — were undertaken by executive fiat, without a declaration of war. Similarly, the courts became influential in domestic policy. The most important domestic-policy initiative of the postwar period was the Supreme Court's 1954 *Brown* v. *Board of Education* decision, which radically transformed American society. Similar decisions regarding women's rights and racial discrimination continued through the 1970s with *Roe* v. *Wade* (1973) and *Regents of the University of California* v. *Bakke* (1978) —

decisions whose impact on average American lives could be measured by the intense public controversy they generated.

Watergate and Congress. The legislative response to the Watergate affair illustrated the decreased authority of Congress. Although it is the only branch of the federal government constitutionally capable of removing a president, Congress consistently delayed confronting President Nixon with his illegal activities until the judiciary and the press had already exposed the scope of Nixon's actions. Had Nixon not been forced to provide taped evidence of his own misdeeds, Congress might never have acted in the matter. After Watergate editorials around the country celebrated the idea that with Nixon's resignation "the system worked." The opposite case can be equally argued: that Watergate could have occurred, that it was exposed almost solely by the judiciary and the press, and that the case rested almost wholly on the existence of the Watergate tapes constituted proof that the system was not working. By 1974 the careful balance of power so painstakingly developed by the Founding Fathers was out of kilter.

Congress Restores Its Authority. Even before Watergate, Congress had taken steps to restore the governmental balance of power. In 1973 it passed the War Powers Act, an attempt to force the executive to seek congressional authorization for military engagements. In 1973 it threatened to cut off funding for the Vietnam War, and in 1975 Congress allowed South Vietnam to fall rather than increase American military assistance. It initiated investigations into the abuse of power by the CIA and the Federal Bureau of Investigation (FBI) and as a result limited the tenure of the FBI director and strengthened congressional authority over these agencies. In an effort to increase its responsiveness to the will of the public, Congress also passed several campaign-finance-reform and ethics-in-government acts. Congress rejected two of Nixon's Supreme Court nominees, exercising the congressional oversight of the courts granted by the Constitution. Congress, not the courts, passed the Equal Rights Amendment, domestic legislation potentially as important as the *Brown* decision. The restoration of legislative authority, however, took place fundamentally at the expense of the executive. Presidential initiatives in Africa and with the Soviets were thwarted by Congress; presidential domestic reforms, especially in energy policy, suffered congressional dilution. Much of the public, accustomed to the almost-imperial authority of the president, viewed Ford and Carter as weak and Congress as obstructionist. In 1980 voters turned out a host of congressional leaders and elected Ronald Reagan in part because of his implicit promise to restore the power of the presidency.

Pluralization of Politics. In the 1970s the most significant result of the activism of the 1960s was the increased participation of African-Americans and other nonwhite groups in political life. Whereas in 1964 there were only 103 black public officials in the United States, by 1977 there were 4,311. African-Americans became mayors of some of the largest cities in the United States and increased their representation in Congress; Shirley Chisholm, an African-American woman representing part of New York City in Congress, ran for the 1972 Democratic presidential nomination; African-Americans were among President Carter's chief assistants. In a sense the civil rights movement of the 1960s took on an overtly political guise in the 1970s, as evidenced by the number of former civil rights leaders — Andrew Young, Jesse Jackson, Marion Barry — who molded African-Americans into a strong political-interest group. But African-Americans were not the only interest group transforming the character of American politics. Women, organized by the National Organization for Women (NOW), also increased their visibility, especially within the Democratic party, and pushed strongly for abortion rights and equal pay for equal work. Hispanics, Native Americans, and the handicapped figured prominently in the 1972 and 1976 Democratic National Conventions. By 1984 many of these groups backed Jackson's "rainbow coalition" within the Democratic party and were instrumental in drafting Geraldine Ferraro as the vice-presidential nominee. Republicans also diversified their politics. Women such as Phyllis Schlafly dominated the GOP's right wing, and in the 1980s President Reagan nominated women to important governmental positions, such as ambassador to the United Nations and Supreme Court justice.

Growth of the Underclass. All the political gains made by those who had historically been victims of discrimination nonetheless failed to translate into significant social and economic gains for the traditionally disadvantaged. In fact, the increased social mobility for middle-class blacks fragmented the black community and resulted in a startling growth of a new underclass. Black-family income remained, on average, 20 percent lower than that of whites, and black unemployment was double that of whites. In a decade of economic trial, nearly half of all blacks were poor or near poverty. By the end of the decade, moreover, one-third of all nonwhite families were headed by a woman, triple the number of white female-led households. Ironically, even as blacks and women were increasing their participation in politics, the underclass in the United States was also becoming increasingly nonwhite and female.

Backlash Against Big Government. In part the growth of the underclass was due to the shift in public sympathy for big government. The host of government programs developed in the 1960s to eliminate poverty, improve education, and expand the welfare system — the programs President Lyndon Johnson had termed vital to the construction of a "Great Society" — generated a political backlash that quietly gathered strength throughout the 1970s and became the foundation for Reagan's victory in the 1980 presidential election. Although broad segments of the American public, especially the white ethnic middle and working classes, had benefited from such programs, when the government focused its efforts on improving the lives of the minority poor it exposed latent racial and class resentments that were expressed in a symbolic opposition to big government. These resentments increased as the American economy, once the envy of the world, disintegrated in the 1970s. To white voters scrambling for scarce jobs, the federal government's affirmative-action programs appeared to favor nonwhite workers; federal education assistance to nonwhites appeared to improve nonwhite social mobility unfairly; busing programs threatened the social cohesion of hard-pressed urban neighborhoods. When combined with traditional racism, the economic pressures engendered by a faltering economy cracked the foundation of public goodwill upon which governmental assistance to nonwhites and the poor rested. Members of the business community, suffering from broader governmental supervision in an increasingly competitive marketplace, further undermined public confidence in big government, and conservatives, ideologically opposed to big government, steadily criticized federal programs. Ever sensitive to the mood of the electorate, politicians enlisted the support of antigovernment voters. George Wallace, the former segregationist from Alabama, first tapped into the resentment against big government during his presidential campaigns in 1968 and 1972; Nixon also pursued a "southern strategy" in his successful bids for the presidency, and as president he followed policies in employment practices, housing programs, and education designed to shore up his support among those unhappy with big government. The 1976 presidential campaign was dominated by anti-Washington rhetoric. Signs of a real shift in political sympathies were evident in the 1978 elections, especially in California, where voters passed an antitax initiative that was implicitly antigovernment. It was Reagan, however, who melded together the racial, business, and ideological impulses of the anti–big government sentiment.

Exhaustion, Cynicism, and Apathy. In the 1970s the American people not only seemed to tire of big government, they seemed to tire of all government. Public apathy toward the political process reached all-time high levels. Only about half of the eligible electorate bothered to vote in the 1976 election; the 1978 election was marked by the lowest voter participation in thirty-six years. In part the growing lack of interest in politics was a result of a broader cultural exhaustion after the turmoil of the 1960s: "me decade" people were too preoccupied with private concerns to participate in public life. But the increased apathy was also the result of a growing cynicism toward politics after Watergate. The scandal had revealed to voters not only the abuse of power by the Nixon administration but also a political culture of corruption, viciousness, and double-dealing that shocked the public. Nixon's partisans maintained he did nothing out of the ordinary, and close inspection revealed that not only Nixon but Johnson, John F. Kennedy, and congressional leaders had indeed practiced extralegal political tactics, had taken inordinate and unethical contributions from corporations and the wealthy, had abused their official powers, and had often used their offices to advance their own ends. Despite congressionally led efforts for reform, the Watergate revelations generated a corrosive cynicism among the public. A 1975 national opinion survey revealed that 69 percent of respondents felt that "over the last ten years this country's leaders have consistently lied to the people." Continued congressional misbehavior, especially the allegations of influence peddling by foreign lobbyists which was known as Koreagate, steadily undermined public confidence in government; a Harris poll in 1978 revealed only 15 percent of voters had confidence in Congress — far different from the 66 percent who gave their trust in 1966. Ironically, the more jaded the public became, the more likely the political reforms of the 1970s would fail. With fewer to hold them to standards of high political conduct, Congress once again returned to its cozy association with well-funded corporations and wealthy contributors. Although Congress outlawed large political contributions from individual donors, there was a sharp growth in the 1970s in political action committees (PACs) — associations of well-financed interest groups who continued the steady stream of funding to Congress. Whereas there had been only eighty-nine PACs in 1974, by 1979 PACs numbered thirteen hundred and influenced much of the congressional agenda. Absent a strong public interest in good government, politicians returned to the "golden rule of politics" as defined by Mark Green, director of the Public Citizen's Congress Watch: "He who has the gold, rules."

TOPICS IN THE NEWS

COLD WAR: INVOLVEMENT IN VIETNAM

An Overwhelming Problem. The Vietnam War was the single greatest political problem of the early 1970s. Supported by few allies abroad, the war undermined foreign confidence in American power. The enormous financial and manpower drain of the war compromised the military readiness of American forces in Europe, Korea, and at home. The expense of the war fueled inflation and threatened to send the nation into a recession. Domestic opposition to the war increased monthly, dividing the public and making the relationship between President Richard Nixon and Congress increasingly difficult.

The Specter of Vietnam. Nixon could not avoid the possibility that the Vietnam War might destroy his presidency. His predecessor, Lyndon Baines Johnson, had been overwhelmed by the war and refused to stand for reelection in 1968. Nixon won the election that year, but by an extremely close margin that reflected the sharp public division over Vietnam. Americans were increasingly drawn into two political camps: hawks, who saw the war as part of a larger Communist conspiracy to take over the world and who advocated all-out war (including the use of nuclear weapons) against North Vietnam; and doves, who viewed the war as a struggle for Vietnamese national independence and who favored immediate American withdrawal. In 1968 conflicts between these two camps exploded into street riots, most spectacularly in Chicago. By 1969 polls showed that a majority of Americans wanted the United States to withdraw from Vietnam; in the fall of that year massive antiwar marches swept the United States, with student protesters now joined by housewives, artisans, and businessmen. Congressional doves threatened to cut off funding for the American military in Vietnam; hawks in the Johnson administration increased extralegal wiretaps and surveillance of their political enemies. Almost no public business could be conducted until the issue of the war was settled. In a 1969 letter to Nixon, Sen. Mike Mansfield (D–Montana) made the situation clear. "The continuance of the war in Vietnam," he wrote, "in my judgment, endangers the future of this nation. Most serious are the deep divisions in our society." The Vietnam War was destroying the United States.

Chief Justice Warren Burger administering the oath of office to President Richard M. Nixon. Mrs. Nixon holds two Bibles upon which the president swears.

Nixon's Promises. Nixon had been elected in 1968 in part on his promise to "bring us together" and end the divisions between hawks and doves. To hawks he advocated a return to "law and order" and promised to end the divisive riots and street protests. To doves Nixon hinted that he had a plan to end the war and withdraw American troops from Vietnam "with honor." In fact, however, Nixon had no more of a plan for ending the war and healing domestic divisions over Vietnam than had Johnson.

Nixon's Options. Nixon considered immediate withdrawal from Vietnam impossible. Withdrawal, he felt, would lead to a political backlash from the hawks, similar to that which crippled the presidency of Harry S Truman after the fall of China to the Communists in 1949. Such a backlash would undermine Nixon's ability to draft domestic legislation and negotiate with foreign powers, especially the Soviet Union. Nixon also feared that the credibility of the United States as a world power would be compromised by immediate withdrawal. Without some face-saving peace treaty, withdrawal would appear to many allies and enemies as surrender. Like Johnson, Nixon did not want to appear to lose the war in Vietnam. Nixon therefore ruled out immediate withdrawal.

The Use of Nuclear Weapons. Nixon also considered the use of nuclear weapons in Vietnam impossible. While the United States possessed a nuclear arsenal capable of devastating North Vietnam, Nixon, like Johnson, understood that the use of nuclear weapons would only further polarize public opinion in the United States and lead to disastrous political consequences abroad, especially in Europe. The response of the Soviet Union and the People's Republic of China, both of whom considered Vietnam a client state, was, moreover, incalculable. Like Johnson, Nixon feared a retaliatory nuclear strike against an American ally, perhaps Japan. The use of nuclear weapons in Vietnam might lead to World War III.

The Odds on Victory. A conventional military victory in Vietnam was also unlikely. Immediately following his inauguration in 1969, Nixon commissioned an interdepartmental study of U.S. prospects for conventional military victory. The conclusions of the study, issued to the president as National Security Study Memorandum I, held that in the best case it would take the military 8.3 years to win the war in Vietnam; a more likely estimate was that victory would come in 13.4 years. Given the political opposition to the war that already existed, it was unlikely the public would stand for another decade of war. Victory in Vietnam appeared nearly impossible.

Vietnamization. Unable to withdraw American troops from Vietnam and equally unable to win the war, Nixon turned to an idea proposed under Johnson: the replacement of U.S. forces with South Vietnamese troops and a gradual U.S. withdrawal from Vietnam. Nixon called the program Vietnamization and hoped it would accomplish two objectives: 1) reduce the level of opposition to the war in Vietnam by returning American soldiers and ending the draft and 2) maintain foreign credibility by sustaining support for an ally and leaving South Vietnam intact. Central to this latter idea was the plan that American support would be for the non-Communist South

A SHORT HISTORY OF VIETNAMIZATION

The military inadequacies of the ARVN and unpopularity of the Thieu regime should not have been surprising to American officials. American military involvement in Vietnam had escalated precisely because of the weaknesses of the ARVN and previous South Vietnamese governments.

In the early 1960s President John F. Kennedy supported the South Vietnamese dictatorship of Ngo Dinh Diem and encouraged the ARVN to fight the Communists without American help. An unpopular Catholic in a nation of Buddhists, Diem used the ARVN as a personal guard; they performed terribly in the field. In 1963 the ARVN was routed in the battle of Ap Bac; that summer anti-Diem riots broke out around the country. Earlier, in an attempt to shore up the regime, Kennedy had increased military assistance; in fall 1963 he authorized a military coup against Diem, whose own generals murdered him on 2 November 1963; President Kennedy was assassinated three weeks later.

Kennedy's successor, Lyndon Johnson, fared no better with the Vietnamese generals who ran South Vietnam after the death of Diem. In the next year and a half over a dozen different governments formed and collapsed, as jealous generals jockeyed for power. They fought everyone except the Communists. Johnson, in an effort to rally them, initiated a bombing campaign in 1964, but the ARVN was clearly unable to protect American warplanes and crews, so Johnson authorized American troops in 1965 to protect American planes, give the ARVN time to improve its fighting posture, and restore political stability. In part it worked. The military government that came to power in 1966, led by Nguyen Van Thieu and Nguyen Cao Ky, remained in place for the remainder of the war. The intervention of hundreds of thousands of American ground troops, however, only advanced the social disintegration of Vietnam and undermined the morale of the ARVN.

With Vietnamization Richard Nixon proposed to replace American troops and support staff with the very soldiers and government whose weakness compelled direct American involvement in the first place. Vietnamization had failed before Nixon became president; it failed again during his administration.

Vietnamese government of Nguyen Van Thieu. Nixon needed Thieu's government in place when the last American troops left Vietnam so that allies and enemies of the United States would not interpret the gradual withdrawal as a military defeat. Nixon also hoped that Vietnamization would convince the North Vietnamese of U.S. sincerity in ongoing peace talks. Henry Kissinger, Nixon's National Security Adviser and chief peace negotiator, believed the policy would provide a "maximum incentive" to resolve the war. Unfortunately, aside from lessening the scale of popular opposition to the war, Vietnamization failed to accomplish any of Nixon's goals. Moreover, after briefly subsiding, antiwar protests renewed in the wake of Nixon's attempts to shore up the failed Vietnamization policy.

Difficulties of Vietnamization. The key to the failure of Vietnamization was the weakness of the American-backed Thieu regime. Corrupt, unpopular, and possessed of an enormously well-equipped army that simply refused to fight, Thieu's government was never able to rally the South Vietnamese against the Communist north. Despite modest efforts at land reform, Thieu's government remained unpopular with the peasantry; he ran unopposed for reelection as president in 1971, winning 94.3 percent of the vote, but his real political support was limited to the South Vietnamese government and Army of the Republic of Vietnam (ARVN). ARVN officers, moreover, were often more interested in advancing their personal fortunes through the sale of black-market goods than in confronting the enemy. Despite an annual American subsidy of nearly $900 million, a million-man army, and generous supplies of American arms and hardware, the ARVN performed poorly. Their February 1971 invasion of Laos to attack the supply lines of the North Vietnamese was a rout; the ARVN simply disintegrated when the North Vietnamese launched their offensive in the spring of 1972.

Vietnamization and the North Vietnamese. No one was more aware of the weaknesses of the ARVN and the Thieu regime than the North Vietnamese. Through their encounters with the ARVN they gained confidence in their military superiority; operations such as the Laotian invasion strengthened their resolve to win the war through victory rather than through negotiations. Vietnamization, moreover, actually made the North Vietnamese more reluctant to talk peace. The United States was, after all, already leaving South Vietnam. Given the weaknesses of South Vietnam once the United States left, the North Vietnamese had every confidence they would sweep to victory.

Peace Negotiations. The North Vietnamese distrusted peace negotiations. In 1954 they won a stunning military victory over the French but were forced in subsequent negotiations to accept the partition of Vietnam into northern and southern regimes — setting the stage for their conflict with the United States. The North Vietnamese were determined not to repeat this mistake. They insisted on the total withdrawal of American troops and on the ouster of Thieu. Kissinger and the Americans just as adamantly insisted on a two-track approach to negotiations: the mutual withdrawal of both American

President Nixon in spring 1970 describing his plan for a joint South Vietnamese and American invasion of Cambodia

and North Vietnamese troops from South Vietnam, followed by a postwar political settlement with Thieu remaining in place during the interim. This was, however, the type of settlement the Vietnamese had signed in 1954, and they rejected the American proposal. The Americans in turn rejected the demands of the North Vietnamese that Thieu be ousted. These two issues repeatedly deadlocked the peace talks.

The Secret Bombing of Cambodia. At the peace talks the Communists stalled and delayed while they improved their military presence in the south. The ARVN, moreover, proved ineffective in protecting U.S. troops as they withdrew and equally unable to keep control of the South Vietnamese countryside, but any escalation in the war to shore up the position of the ARVN would bring renewed antiwar protests and charges that Nixon was breaking his campaign pledge to end the war. Nixon therefore orchestrated a bombing campaign against North Vietnamese supply lines and strongholds on South Vietnam's western border — in Cambodia, a neutral country. Nixon decided against bombing North Vietnam directly because since 1968 there had been a bombing halt over North Vietnam, and Nixon did not want to give the appearance of escalating the war. He believed that bombing Cambodia would be a more effective way to limit the ability of the North Vietnamese to launch offensive operations as the Americans withdrew. He hoped that the Cambodian operation would be the military stick with which to beat the North Vietnamese to the negotiating table. There were, however, significant risks in the Cambodian campaign.

The Risks of Bombing. The greatest danger in bombing Cambodia was that the United States was extending the war into an officially neutral country. Bombing a neutral country against which the United States was not at war broke international law, and since Congress must declare war, it was quite possibly unconstitutional. Nixon believed the question of international law was unimportant, because the North Vietnamese, by operating out of Cambodia, had already violated Cambodian neutrality.

Similarly, since Johnson had conducted the war without an official declaration, Nixon discounted the constitutional question. The effect of the bombing on public opinion, however, could not easily be dismissed. Accordingly Nixon ordered the bombing be conducted in absolute secrecy. Pilots flying the missions were often not informed of their targets until they were airborne, and the military developed an elaborate dual bookkeeping system to track the missions. Even the secretary of the air force and the air force chief of staff were denied details of the bombing. With such secrecy in place, Nixon began the campaign, code-named Operation Menu, on 17 March 1969. It lasted fourteen months.

The Consequences of Operation Menu. The bombing campaign in Cambodia had three consequences, none of which Nixon anticipated. First, it proved to be impossible to keep secret, and so Nixon ordered increased surveillance and illegal wiretaps of journalists and members of his own administration. These activities set an early precedent for later abuses of presidential authority that ultimately culminated in Watergate. The bombing campaign also precipitated the disintegration of political order in Cambodia. Cambodia's ruler, Prince Norodom Sihanouk, had long attempted a delicate balancing act between the North Vietnamese and the United States. "We are a country caught between the hammer and the anvil," he said in 1967, "a country that would very much like to remain the last haven of peace in Southeast Asia." Operation Menu ended his efforts. The North Vietnamese, angered by Sihanouk's inability to halt the American bombing, began to arm the Cambodian Communists, known as the Khmer Rouge. The Cambodian military, alarmed at these developments and hoping to get increased American military assistance, overthrew Sihanouk on 18 March 1970. Gen. Lon Nol and the Cambodian army were unable, however, to establish firm control over the country, and by April Cambodia was in anarchy. Even worse for Nixon was the fact that the Cambodian bombing failed to neutralize North Vietnamese activities. Despite 3,630 B-52 sorties against Cambodia, the North Vietnamese renewed their ground assaults against South Vietnam in February 1970. Operation Menu, like Vietnamization, was a failure.

The Invasion of Cambodia. In an attempt to turn the failures of Vietnamization and Operation Menu to victory, Nixon decided to launch a joint U.S./ARVN ground invasion of Cambodia at the end of April 1970. Much of Operation Menu had been directed against the command center of the North Vietnamese (the Central Office for South Vietnam, abbreviated by the military as COSVN). Military experts assumed that just as the United States ran its war effort from a command center several acres large, the North Vietnamese must be directing their attacks from a similar complex inside Cambodia. By April 1970 it was clear that B-52 raids had failed to destroy this command center. Military officials recommended the United States attack with ground troops.

Simultaneously, the political situation in Cambodia was disintegrating. The Communist forces of the Khmer Rouge were threatening to seize the capital, Phnom Penh. Nixon decided that a dramatic ground invasion of Cambodia, fifteen thousand to twenty thousand men strong, with massive air support, would both destroy the COSVN and save Cambodia from the Communists. It did both but only temporarily. The COSVN turned out to be a series of empty huts and tunnels rather than a fortified bunker complex; the majority of the North Vietnamese withdrew rather than fight and returned after the Americans and ARVN left Cambodia. Nonetheless, the invasion turned eastern Cambodia into a battle zone. Hundreds of thousands fled west; the population of Phnom Penh doubled with refugees. The invasion temporarily relieved Lon Nol's military position, but in the long run the regime was further destabilized, and only ever-increasing amounts of American assistance kept it from collapsing. The Khmer Rouge recruited thousands of troops from among the displaced, embittered Cambodians. By the time the Americans left, two months later, the invasion had set into motion a vicious Cambodian civil war, which ended in 1975 with the victory of the Communists. The Khmer Rouge, led by doctrinaire Maoists determined to establish an agricultural utopia, murdered perhaps a million of their own people following victory. Long after Americans went home

Leonid Brezhnev and Richard Nixon celebrating the
SALT agreement

and the Vietnam War was over, the killing in Southeast
Asia continued.

COLD WAR: TRIANGULAR DIPLOMACY

Triangular Diplomacy. Richard Nixon came to the
presidency convinced that he had a historic opportunity
to restructure the international order. In 1968 the Soviet
Union achieved nuclear-missile parity with the United
States, and relations between the Soviet Union and Communist China were so bad that the two nations fought in
border clashes. The days of American military superiority
were over, and the Soviets and the Chinese were seeking
American support against each other. Nixon and Kissinger believed that international peace could be achieved by
using the United States as a power broker in conflicts
between the two Communist giants. Triangular diplomacy between the three nations would balance international power and secure world peace.

Détente and the SALT Accords. In order for triangular diplomacy to work, military competition and political
tension between the United States and the Soviet Union
had to be reduced. Nixon and Kissinger developed a
policy of détente toward the Soviet Union. The Strategic
Arms Limitation Treaty (SALT) negotiations were the
key to the policy of détente. The SALT talks, designed to
limit the scale of the nuclear-arms race, formally began in
November 1969 and continued for most of the 1970s.
The SALT discussions acknowledged a simple fact: both
sides possessed enough nuclear weapons to destroy each
other many times over, and the costs of continued nuclear
production were a strain on both economies. After numerous rounds of talks debating the types of weapons to
be reduced, as well as the means of verifying arms reductions, the United States and the Soviet Union concluded
two treaties: the Antiballistic Missile (ABM) Treaty limited the defensive nuclear weapons available to each nation and the SALT I accord limited the number of offen-

sive missiles. The White House also negotiated trade and
financial agreements with the Soviets. Together with the
SALT accords, these agreements advanced détente and
enhanced Nixon's image as a peacemaker. Nixon used
that image to his political advantage. Nixon initialed
SALT in a highly publicized visit to Moscow in May
1972 — the presidential election year.

The Opening to China. In 1963 John F. Kennedy
wanted to normalize relations with the People's Republic
of China. He failed to do so because he was afraid that
conservatives would attack him for appeasing communism. One of the conservatives he feared the most was
Nixon. For two decades Nixon had made his political
reputation as a formidable opponent of Communist
China. Now, in order to make triangular diplomacy
work, Nixon became the president who restored diplomatic relations with China. Concerned himself with criticism from the Right, Nixon's initial overtures to Chinese
officials were secret, but the Chinese responded positively, and on 10 June 1971 Nixon announced he would
drop the twenty-one-year-old embargo on American
trade with China. Kissinger, in the meantime, was secretly negotiating the terms of a state visit to Peking.
When, following these negotiations, Nixon informed the
public that he would journey to China, the news came as
a surprise. The right wing was predictably indignant,
accusing Nixon of "surrendering to international communism," but the majority of the public looked upon the
China opening favorably. There was little public objection in October when the United States reversed two
decades' worth of policy and voted to seat Communist
China in the United Nations (and acquiesced as the non-
Communist Nationalist Chinese were expelled). Public
opinion was overwhelmingly positive toward Nixon's
journey to China in February 1972. Images of the trip,
broadcast live via the latest satellite technology, awed the
American people. Beyond the images, however, the trip
accomplished little. Formal recognition by the United
States of the People's Republic of China did not occur
until 1979; the United States continued to provide military assistance to Nationalist China despite the objections of the Red Chinese. The images of Nixon in China
did advance the cause of triangular diplomacy and increased Soviet willingness to negotiate with the Americans. The most important audience for the trip, however,
was the millions of American voters waiting to cast their
ballots in the fall election.

COLD WAR: THE VIETNAM WAR ENDS

Renewed Bombing. Although by fall 1971 public protests against the Vietnam War waned, institutional opposition to the war — especially to Nixon's war program —
increased. Congress moved toward ending the war by
cutting off financial and military support. In September
the White House barely defeated a bill to end the draft
and thereby end the war. Various proposals seeking to cut

An exhibition in the U.S. Capitol Building in summer 1971 as the United States negotiated with North Vietnam for a withdrawal of American troops. The United States insisted on the release of POWs as a precondition to withdrawal; the North Vietnamese insisted on withdrawal first.

off military appropriations for Vietnam were tabled. With the 1972 presidential election on the horizon, Nixon feared that prolonging the war might jeopardize his reelection. He was just as afraid that losing South Vietnam to the Communists would also compromise his electoral chances. Yet Vietnamization did not work, and peace negotiations were stalled. Worse, from Nixon's standpoint, was the likelihood that the North Vietnamese would launch a massive military offensive in the spring of 1972. They had done so during the last presidential election year, succeeding in ruining Johnson's chances for reelection in 1968. Intelligence indicated that North Vietnamese troops were massing on the borders of South Vietnam. In 1972 a North Vietnamese military offensive might not only spoil Nixon's reelection, but, with few American combat troops left on the ground, the North Vietnamese might also win the war. Reintroducing ground troops to Vietnam was political suicide, so Nixon used the only military tool left to him (by his own Vietnamization policy) to blunt the Vietnamese offensive. In January 1972 he renewed an intensive bombing campaign against North Vietnam.

The POW Issue. Nixon and Kissinger hoped the renewed bombing would force the North Vietnamese to compromise in the peace talks. It did not. Instead, the bombings introduced a new variable to the discussions — the fate of American airmen shot down and captured by the North Vietnamese. The North Vietnamese had used the relative peace of 1971 to augment and increase their store of Russian-made surface-to-air missiles (SAMs) and other air defenses. They were effective, and Hanoi's prisons began to fill with American pilots. The United States demanded their release as a precondition to total American withdrawal; the North Vietnamese demanded that the United States withdraw before any prisoners of war (POWs) would be released. Again, the talks deadlocked.

Linkage. Nixon and Kissinger believed that one of the benefits of triangular diplomacy was that it would help end the Vietnam War. Nixon and Kissinger called this idea "linkage": the United States linked better relations with the Communist superpowers to other foreign-policy decisions, including their pressure on North Vietnam to end the war. Both the Soviet Union and China supplied arms and advisers to the North Vietnamese, but their actual influence in Hanoi was limited. When the North Vietnamese launched their military offensive in March 1972, the Soviet Union and China were in the midst of delicate negotiations with the United States. Both Communist superpowers were unable to convince Hanoi to

Henry Kissinger in Paris signing the initial cease-fire agreement with Le Duc Tho, who sits facing him

stop the offensive. Nixon and Kissinger either had to insist on linkage and break off discussions with the Soviets and the Chinese or drop linkage and pursue negotiations with the the two countries on issues unconnected to Vietnam. They dropped linkage and in so doing saved triangular diplomacy. That decision, however, left Nixon and Kissinger virtually no leverage with which to negotiate a settlement in Vietnam. Nixon compensated by increasing the air war. From May to October the United States conducted 41,500 air sorties over North Vietnam. On 8 May Nixon ordered the North Vietnamese port of Haiphong mined and approved a bombing campaign against the North Vietnamese capital of Hanoi.

A New Flexibility. The bombing campaign blunted the North Vietnamese offensive, but Hanoi retained control over large sections of South Vietnam, especially in the Mekong delta and in Quang Tri province. Its ground position was excellent; the ARVN, now suffering twenty thousand desertions per month, continued to disintegrate. Yet the bombings were punishing the North Vietnamese, and Hanoi was concerned that it was losing its Chinese and Soviet allies in their rush to engage in American détente. These factors led North Vietnamese negotiators to a new willingness to sign a peace treaty. The Nixon administration was also willing to compro-

mise. American troop withdrawals had continued, and by summer no ground combat forces remained in Vietnam. Nixon was reaping an enormous political benefit from the withdrawals; a peace treaty would be even more rewarding. Kissinger set his sights on a new goal: a peace treaty before the November election, a peace treaty certain to guarantee Nixon an enormous political victory.

The October Breakthrough. By October both North Vietnam and the United States had modified their negotiating positions. North Vietnam accepted the retention of Thieu's government in South Vietnam; the United States accepted a cease-fire in place, leaving North Vietnam in a militarily advantageous position. Both sides agreed to an exchange of prisoners and to develop a coalition government in South Vietnam — one in which the Communists would participate. On 8 October the United States agreed to halt bombing on 21 October, and the two sides set a date for the formal signing of the agreement — 31 October. On 26 October Kissinger announced to the public that "peace is at hand." Thieu, however, refused to accept a coalition government and a cease-fire. Afraid that Thieu would charge him with a sell-out if he signed the treaty and of the political consequences of such a charge, Nixon scuttled the agreement.

The Christmas Bombing. The election of 1972 passed without a resolution of the Vietnam War. Moreover, the voters sent no clear signal on Nixon's Vietnam policy: the president was reelected in a landslide, but doves won a substantial victory in the congressional elections. Nixon was certain that when Congress reconvened, further appropriations would be refused for Vietnam. He had until January 1973 to end the war on his terms. The North Vietnamese remained committed to the October accords, but getting Thieu to sign was difficult. Thieu believed the October agreement amounted to a surrender. It left hundreds of thousands of North Vietnamese troops in South Vietnam and committed Thieu to cooperate with the same Communists who for years had demanded his overthrow. To reassure Thieu, Nixon provided the ARVN with arms shipments so great that by 1973 the South Vietnamese possessed the fourth largest army in the world, the fourth largest air force, and the fifth largest navy. To demonstrate his willingness to enforce the peace (to both Thieu and the North Vietnamese), Nixon had only one option — bombing. On 17 December peace negotiations broke off. For the next eleven days the United States embarked on one of the most intensive bombing campaigns in military history. Three-fourths of all B-52 crews in the air force flew in the campaign; forty thousand tons of explosives were dropped in the vicinity of Hanoi; over sixteen hundred North Vietnamese were killed. Nixon's critics were aghast at the campaign, soon dubbed "the Christmas bombings," and Europeans were outraged. When Congress reconvened, Democratic caucuses in both houses voted to end funding for the Vietnam effort, sending the message to Thieu that a peace arranged by Congress was even less advantageous to him than a peace arranged by Nixon. Thieu gave in, and the North Vietnamese agreed to resume talks. On 27 January 1973 the United States, North Vietnam, and South Vietnam signed a peace treaty — an accord virtually identical to the pact arranged three months earlier.

An Inconclusive Peace. The Paris accord of 1973 did not bring peace to Vietnam. Nixon's critics maintained that it was not supposed to bring peace — that the treaty was a sham, a face-saving pact designed to provide Nixon with a decent interval between American withdrawal and the collapse of South Vietnam. Nixon's supporters asserted that had Nixon not become embroiled in the Watergate affair, he would have enforced the peace with American air power and supplies. Whatever the interpretation, both North and South Vietnam pressed their advantages even before the treaty was signed. Thieu's government consolidated the legal and political framework necessary to dominate a coalition government; the North Vietnamese continued their military infiltration of the south. Tensions between areas of South Vietnam held by Thieu's government and those held by the Communists remained; skirmishes and confrontations were constant. In March 1975 North Vietnam launched a direct

THE COLLAPSE OF THE ARMED FORCES

One of the most dangerous effects of Nixon's Vietnamization policy was what the June 1971 issue of the *Armed Forces Journal* called the collapse of the American military. By 1971 the easy availability of drugs in Vietnam had led to widespread drug abuse by American soldiers. The U.S. Army estimated that 35 percent of all soldiers had tried heroin; use of marijuana was nearly universal. Racial tensions in an army that was disproportionately nonwhite and poor were high, and racial confrontations often occurred. Pacifism in the military was widespread: the *Armed Forces Journal* estimated that there were 144 underground newspapers and fourteen antiwar organizations within the ranks of the military. Most important, the command structure of military authority was breaking down. Desertion rates were three times what they had been in the Korean War. Soldiers increasingly murdered their own officers, a practice known as fragging (often a fragmentation grenade was used). In a war zone it was difficult to determine murder from accidental killing, but the army itself estimated that at least 333 incidents of fragging occurred in 1971, up from 209 incidents in 1970. The policy of Vietnamization was partly to blame for the disintegration of the military because it stripped the soldier in the field of any good reason to fight: the United States was, after all, leaving Vietnam, and our allies among the South Vietnamese were reluctant to fight on their own behalf. To soldiers in Vietnam, Vietnamization was a no-win policy. American soldiers were troubled by a question that gained widespread currency among the troops after 1969: Who wants to be the last soldier to die in Vietnam?

offensive against Thieu's government. Despite their American weaponry, the ARVN disintegrated. Congress refused to appropriate emergency military aid. On 23 April Nixon's successor, Gerald Ford, conceded that the war in Vietnam was finished. On 29 April the United States embassy in Saigon was evacuated. Scenes of Americans and Vietnamese scrambling onto helicopters, of American money being set on fire, of chaos and hysteria in the embassy compound, were broadcast back to the United States. The next day the South Vietnamese surrendered. The Vietnam War was finally over.

THE GOVERNMENT AND DOMESTIC DISSENT

The Antiwar Movement. Vietnamization succeeded in neutralizing much of American antiwar opinion. As

Students at Kent State University reacting to National Guard gunfire, 30 April 1970

the troops came home, antiwar protests dissipated. By early spring 1970 the Vietnam Moratorium Committee, which organized the widespread, middle-class protests of 1969, announced that they were closing their Washington, D.C., office. Nixon, however, was highly antagonistic toward the antiwar movement. He believed it undermined the American will to win; it challenged his ability to conduct foreign policy; it threatened the same political defeats that destroyed Johnson. Nixon was therefore determined to change public opinion and crush the antiwar movement.

The Weathermen. Some elements of the antiwar movement fueled Nixon's antagonism. By 1970 small groups of extremists turned from protests to street riots and terrorist violence. In 1969 a radical splinter group known as the Weathermen, calling for revolution in the United States, organized street riots in Chicago and attacked federal buildings around the country. Believing they could wage a guerrilla war against the government, about one hundred of the Weathermen went underground. The Weathermen perpetrated several spectacular bombings, in particular destroying the army's mathematics lab center in Madison, Wisconsin, killing one person, and blowing up a part of the U.S. Capitol. Nonetheless, they had virtually no public support and were ineffective guerrillas — their most spectacular act was a 6 March 1970 explosion at their own bomb-manufacturing center

in New York City, in which three Weathermen were killed.

"Positive Polarization." Many Americans were frightened by the violence — and the violent rhetoric — of the Weathermen and other radical groups. The Nixon administration exploited this fear and sought to portray the entire antiwar movement as dominated by the Weathermen and the radicals. In dozens of speeches Vicepresident Spiro Agnew characterized the antiwar movement as pro-Communist and anti-American. He denounced academic opponents of the war and members of the press as dupes of the antiwar radicals. Aware that such rhetoric made the division between hawks and doves worse, Agnew replied that his speeches produced a "positive polarization" — one that separated those who loved the United States from those "who want to destroy it."

The Hard Hats. Despite his inaugural promise to "lower our voices" and "bring us together," President Nixon also contributed to such polarization. Echoing Agnew, Nixon argued that the majority of Americans — "the great silent majority" — supported administration policy in Vietnam. Despite such rhetoric, public-opinion polls showed that a slim majority of Americans remained opposed to the war. Nixon and Agnew's speeches, however, did succeed in uncovering class resentments created by the Vietnam War. The antiwar movement was led by middle-class Americans and privileged students often protected from the draft. Working-class Americans were not immune from the draft and served in disproportionate numbers in Vietnam. The televised spectacle of wealthy college students flouting conventional morality, defying authority, and denouncing the United States angered many blue-collar Americans. Nixon and Agnew's speeches increased their anger. In May 1970 New York construction workers attacked antiwar protesters during a demonstration, and a new political symbol was born. The hard hat came to symbolize working-class resentment of the antiwar movement. Nominally Democratic voters, the hard hats formed a new base of political support for Nixon and steeled his resolve to end the Vietnam War on his terms.

Kent State. Nixon believed his political support among the hard hats and the Vietnam hawks, as well as his gradual withdrawal of American troops, would limit criticism of his invasion of Cambodia. He was wrong. Following his 30 April 1970 announcement of the invasion, American campuses exploded with protests. Over four hundred universities and colleges shut down as a result of the protests; many schools canceled their commencement exercises. The press was highly critical. The usually supportive *Wall Street Journal* wrote that the Cambodian invasion would lead to "deeper entrapment" in Indochina. Congress was outraged and almost immediately passed legislation requiring the United States to withdraw from Cambodia. Even Nixon's own administration opposed the invasion: four members of Kissinger's staff resigned, and two hundred State Department employees signed a petition against the invasion. Most tragically, protests at Kent State University in Ohio and Jackson State University in Mississippi led to violent confrontations between authorities and protesters. Two women were killed at Jackson State; four students were killed by the National Guard at Kent State.

Reaction. The killings at Kent State cast a pall over the antiwar movement. The combination of the deaths and the strident rhetoric of the Nixon administration seemed to raise the stakes involved in antiwar protesting. Many protesters feared that they might be killed in future protests; some Americans thought that Kent State represented the beginning of a new civil war. These fears led to quieter campuses in the fall, and elements on both sides of the Vietnam issue sought to resolve the political differences dividing the country. Nixon did not. Instead, the reaction to the Cambodian invasion convinced him he needed more surveillance and control over the antiwar movement.

The Huston Plan. The federal government had monitored the antiwar movement during the Johnson administration. A variety of agencies, from naval intelligence to the Central Intelligence Agency (CIA), monitored, penetrated, and subverted the activities of antiwar protest groups, often in violation of their governmental charter. The Federal Bureau of Investigation's (FBI) Counter-In-

telligence Program (COINTELPRO) was the most effective of these groups, often employing illegal wiretaps and break-ins to gather information. After Kent State, however, Nixon was dissatisfied with these police activities. Seeking to systematize the various agencies, Nixon appointed former army intelligence specialist Tom Huston to coordinate their efforts and improve surveillance of Nixon's domestic critics. Huston proposed monitoring antiwar groups through opened mail, wiretaps, and break-ins; he suggested using the Internal Revenue Service (IRS) to harass Nixon's opponents. Despite Huston's warning that these activities were "clearly illegal," Nixon approved the plan. FBI Director J. Edgar Hoover, however, concerned over congressional investigations of illegal governmental activities, prevented the plan from being implemented, and Nixon, upon more sober reflection, agreed to drop the idea.

Illegal Activities. The Huston plan symbolized a type of siege mentality descending upon the White House. Members of the Nixon administration saw subversives and opponents everywhere. While Nixon dropped the specific program developed by Huston for domestic surveillance, he continued to use unethical and illegal means to monitor and harass his critics. Nixon used the Federal Communications Commission (FCC), responsible for licensing television stations, to try to force the networks and the press to report the news in a pro-Nixon fashion. He compiled an enemies list of prominent Americans (among whom were celebrities, such as football player Joe Namath, actress Carol Channing, and actor Steve McQueen), whom he targeted for harassment by the IRS. The Nixon administration also hired private detectives to follow political opponents and discover details of their personal lives. Such activities increased the bitterness of those who, since the 1950s, perceived Nixon as an unprincipled, immoral politician. To them, Richard Nixon more than earned the nickname of Tricky Dick.

The Calley Trial and Winter Soldier Investigations. Even with the gradual troop withdrawal, by early 1971 the Vietnam War was still the most important political issue in the United States. Increasingly, the Congress and the public questioned the conduct of the war. The trial of 1st Lt. William Calley provoked a national debate on the morality of American involvement in Vietnam. Calley faced a court-martial in 1970 for his participation in the 1968 massacre of South Vietnamese civilians in the village of My Lai. In March 1971 he was found guilty of their murders and sentenced to life imprisonment. Some sections of the public believed that the massacres were part of the normal conduct of warfare; others believed Calley was a scapegoat for widespread American brutality. After the verdict was announced, President Nixon allowed Calley to be released from the stockade, pending appeal. He also announced he would review the case. The most interesting response to the Calley trial, however, came from an antiwar group of American soldiers known as the Vietnam Veterans Against the War (VVAW).

Meeting in Detroit in a public forum they called the "Winter Soldier Investigations" (taking the term from the American Revolution's definition of a true patriot), members of the VVAW publicly testified that murder, rape, and brutality against civilians were part of the everyday conduct of the war. In April they took their case to Capitol Hill and engaged in highly publicized demonstrations against the war, demonstrations highlighted by their returning of the medals they had won in Vietnam.

The Pentagon Papers. No one person was more influenced by the debates over the morality of the war in Vietnam than former Defense Department expert Daniel Ellsberg. A Vietnam hawk and former Marine who had been a member of Kissinger's advisory staff, Ellsberg was convinced by 1970 that the war was immoral and unconscionable. In order to expose what he believed were lies about the war, in June 1971 Ellsberg passed copies of a secret 1968 Defense Department history of Vietnam to *The New York Times*. The history, known as the Pentagon Papers, caused an uproar. Many were scandalized by the extent to which the government had deceived the public about the reality of war in Vietnam. Others argued that Ellsberg had betrayed the government. Even though the Pentagon Papers said nothing about the Nixon administration, the president and his staff, concerned about breaches in governmental security and concerned that the papers would undermine public confidence in their Vietnam policy, won a court injunction to prevent *The New York Times* from publishing them. On 30 June 1971, however, the Supreme Court overturned the injunction and upheld the right of the newspaper to publish the documents.

The Plumbers Unit. President Nixon, infuriated by the Supreme Court decision in the Pentagon Papers case, responded by attacking Ellsberg. In July the Justice Department indicted Ellsberg under the Espionage Act. That same month the White House formed what it termed a "nonlegal team" to investigate Ellsberg and amass evidence to discredit him. The team, called the "plumbers unit" because it plugged governmental leaks, used illegal wiretaps to amass information on Ellsberg. On Labor Day weekend the team also burglarized the offices of Ellsberg's psychiatrist but found no compromising material. The White House, however, was so pleased with the activities of the plumbers unit that it became a permanent part of the president's staff. It was this group that would conduct the Watergate break-in in 1972. Details of the Ellsberg burglary became known after the Watergate arrests; because evidence against Ellsberg was illegally obtained, the espionage case against him was thrown out of court on 11 May 1974.

THE GOVERNMENT AND WATERGATE

A Third-Rate Burglary. At 2:00 A.M. on Saturday, 17 June 1972, four Cubans and a member of the Committee

WHO WAS "DEEP THROAT?"

As the Watergate affair increasingly preoccupied the American public, many began to speculate on the identity of one of the people responsible for exposing the scandal. "Deep Throat" (the title of a then-scandalous pornographic movie) was the pseudonym given by Bob Woodward and Carl Bernstein to a key White House official who periodically provided them with information on the scandal. Deep Throat never gave the reporters fresh information; instead, during a series of secret meetings with Woodward, he would confirm or deny allegations the reporters had already acquired. Deep Throat's input was thus crucial in keeping Woodward and Bernstein on the right track in following a convoluted story with many dead ends. After Woodward and Bernstein published their account of the scandal in *All The President's Men* (1974), many readers began to wonder about Deep Throat's actual identity, as well as his motives. Some believed Deep Throat was National Security Adviser Henry Kissinger, the one high-level administration figure untouched by the scandal. Others speculated that Deep Throat was G. Gordon Liddy, the leader of the plumbers unit, who some believed was bitter toward his superiors in the Nixon administration. The question of Deep Throat's identity was never resolved, but Woodward and Bernstein's description of him in *All The President's Men* remains intriguing: an executive-branch official with long service in the government, literate, given to drink, who "was trying to protect the office (of the presidency), to effect a change in its conduct before all was lost."

Source: Carl Bernstein and Bob Woodward, *All The President's Men* (New York: Warner, 1974).

to Reelect the President, James W. McCord, were arrested for burglarizing the offices of the Democratic National Committee, located in the Watergate office complex in Washington, D.C. The presence of McCord immediately raised suspicions of political intrigue, but on Monday, 19 June, the president's spokesman, Ron Ziegler, characterized the break-in as nothing more than a "third-rate burglary" and dismissed its importance. The burglary would lead to the first resignation of a president in American history and expose to the public a dark underside of politics they scarcely knew existed. Public cynicism about politics after Watergate would not only affect Nixon but the presidencies of Gerald Ford and Jimmy Carter.

Background to Watergate. The motives and orders for the Watergate break-in have yet to be established; until scholars gain access to Nixon's personal papers and tapes, who ordered the break-in and why the break-in took place will remain unclear. It is known that the Nixon administration had already engaged in illegal harassment and surveillance of its political opponents; that the Nixon administration often preferred operating covertly to conducting policy publicly; and that Nixon, in early 1972 (when the Watergate affair was set in motion), was unsure of his prospects for reelection. Against this backdrop members of the Committee to Reelect the President (Nixon abbreviated it as CRP; almost everyone else, including his own staff, abbreviated it as CREEP) hatched plots to wiretap both Democratic presidential nominee George McGovern and Democratic National Committee chairman Lawrence O'Brien (whose office was located at Watergate). Both buggings failed; the Watergate arrest was for the second CREEP break-in at O'Brien's office, an attempt to replace a defective listening device. It is also known that six days following the arrests President Nixon directed his staff to thwart an FBI investigation of the case and cover up the connections between the burglars and CREEP. This order was the first of many attempts by the most powerful law-enforcement official in the United States to obstruct justice.

Woodward, Bernstein, and Sirica. President Nixon ordered a cover-up because he feared that an investigation into the Watergate break-in would expose the numerous illegal activities of his administration. During the election Democrats who charged that Watergate represented wider political illegalities were dismissed as partisan, and the break-in had no effect on Nixon's campaign victory. The story would have died were it not for the criminal trial of the Watergate burglars and for two intrepid reporters from the *Washington Post,* Bob Woodward and Carl Bernstein. Woodward and Bernstein dug into the case; together with the federal judge overseeing the criminal trial, John J. Sirica, they kept the pressure on the White House for an explanation of the break-in and of McCord's connections to CREEP.

Damage Control. The White House sought desperately to isolate McCord, to suggest to the public that he or his superiors in CREEP ordered the break-in without the president's knowledge. CREEP immediately disavowed McCord (even as it secretly paid his legal fees). Files were destroyed; hush money was offered to the principals involved. The evidence was nonetheless unmistakable that someone high up in the administration authorized the Watergate break-in. One by one, connections between the burglars and their superiors in CREEP were disclosed; one by one, connections between members of CREEP and the White House staff were revealed. Members of Nixon's staff moved to protect themselves from criminal prosecution. Resignations became commonplace. CREEP chairman John Mitchell and CREEP treasurer Hugh Sloan left in the fall of 1972; White House chief of staff H. R. Haldeman, domestic-policy assistant John Ehrlichman, presidential counsel

Sen. Sam Ervin chairing a meeting of the Senate Select Committee on Watergate, 1973

John Dean, and Attorney General Richard Kleindienst left on 30 April 1973. McCord informed Sirica that members of the Nixon administration had perjured themselves during his criminal trial. No one in the conspiracy was willing to take the blame for the crime, and eventually the questions Woodward and Bernstein sought to answer were how much did the president know, and when did he know it? The Democrats and the Congress also wanted to know the answer to these questions. On 7 February 1973 the Senate voted seventy to zero to establish a seven-man committee, headed by Sen. Sam Ervin (D–North Carolina), to probe the Watergate case. Immediately following his second inauguration, after one of the greatest electoral victories in American history, Nixon was fighting for his political life.

Startling Revelations. The criminal trial of the Watergate burglars, Woodward and Bernstein's reporting, and the investigations of the Ervin committee kept the American people transfixed in 1973. In May a special prosecutor, Archibald Cox, authorized by the Justice Department to study Watergate without interference from the White House, also began investigations. These sources brought forth startling revelations: a "dirty tricks" campaign against the Democrats; campaign-finance violations; the burglary of the office of Ellsberg's psychia-

President Nixon's secretary, Rose Mary Woods, demonstrating how she might have inadvertently erased tapes of the president's conversations, November 1973

trist; the enemies list; an attempt to forge documents and discredit former president Kennedy; the use of government funds to improve Nixon's private houses; Nixon's wiretap of his own brother, Donald; and improprieties with Nixon's income-tax returns. The Ervin committee's televised hearings climaxed in the stunning testimony of White House counsel Dean, which implicated the president in the Watergate cover-up. Even more damaging was the public testimony of White House aide Alexander Butterfield on 16 July. He revealed the existence of a secret recording system installed in the White House. Unbelievably, presidential decisions regarding Watergate were recorded on tape.

The Struggle for the Tapes. Ervin, Cox, and Sirica immediately pressed the White House to release the Watergate tapes to them. Nixon rejected their requests. He claimed the tapes were private property; he asserted that the tapes contained material that might compromise national security; he argued that he had a right to withhold them under the dubious constitutional claim of executive privilege — an idea that the president could decide for himself how much he might cooperate with other branches of the government. Nixon's rationalizations were a public-relations disaster. The press charged the president with stonewalling access to the truth of the Watergate affair. Nixon's popularity plummeted twenty-eight points in the polls, to below 40 percent. When the Ervin committee offered to review the tapes privately,

Nixon still refused; when Cox and Sirica subpoenaed seven of the tapes, Nixon nonetheless withheld them, challenging their authority to investigate the White House.

The Saturday Night Massacre. On 12 October the U.S. District Court of Appeals ordered Nixon to turn over the subpoenaed Watergate tapes to Cox and Sirica. Instead Nixon proposed releasing prepared transcripts of the tapes. The decision infuriated Special Prosecutor Cox, who attacked the administration for noncompliance. Nixon responded by ordering Cox to be fired, but Attorney General Richardson, who had promised the Senate in his confirmation hearing that he would not interfere with the special prosecutor, refused. Nixon then fired Richardson and ordered Deputy Attorney General William Ruckelshaus to fire Cox. Ruckelshaus also refused, and Nixon fired Ruckelshaus. Nixon finally persuaded Solicitor General Robert Bork to dismiss Cox. The FBI then moved in and sealed off the offices of the three terminated men from their staff. The public was outraged, and the press termed the firings the "Saturday Night Massacre." Calls for Nixon's impeachment echoed in Congress. Nixon's popularity rating dropped to an unprecedented low of 22 percent. Even worse for Nixon was the fact that the negative public response ensured that the new attorney general and new special prosecutor could not appear to be even slightly favorable to the administration. These new officials — Attorney General

William Saxbe (former senator from Ohio) and Special Prosecutor Leon Jaworski, a Houston lawyer — pursued the Watergate investigation as zealously as had Richardson and Cox.

The White House Transcripts. By the end of October Nixon still had not complied with court orders for the tapes. In fact, he announced that two of the subpoenaed tapes did not even exist. Critics charged Nixon with destroying the tapes. The charges became more plausible after he revealed that another of the subpoenaed tapes had a mysterious 18.5-minute gap in it. Nixon's secretary, Rose Mary Woods, claimed she had accidentally erased part of the tape, but the explanation satisfied few and confirmed the suspicions of those afraid that Nixon would doctor the tapes in his possession. In an effort to turn the tide of public opinion, on 29 April 1974 Nixon released a 1,308-page edited transcript of the Watergate tapes. He maintained that the transcripts proved that he did not know about the Watergate cover-up until 21 March 1973. Nixon hoped the publication of the transcripts would restore public confidence in his candor; instead, the transcripts, with "expletive deleted" peppered across the pages, embarrassed the president and made him the object of ridicule.

Prosecutions. Indictments and convictions for criminal wrongdoing further eroded the president's public support. McCord and G. Gordon Liddy, his superior at CREEP, were convicted of the Watergate break-in in January 1973. In June and July 1974 White House aides Charles Colson and Ehrlichman were found guilty of conspiracy and perjury in the Ellsberg break-in. CREEP official Dwight Chapin was sent to prison for his role in covering up the dirty-tricks campaign. White House counsel Dean was found guilty of conspiracy and began to cooperate with prosecutors. CREEP officials Mitchell and Maurice Stans were placed on trial for campaign-financing violations. Vice-president Agnew, who so often made law and order the theme of his speeches, was investigated by the Justice Department for criminal charges unrelated to Watergate. On 10 October 1973 Agnew resigned the vice-presidency and pleaded no contest to one count of income-tax evasion. In return for the plea the Justice Department dropped other counts of bribery and extortion associated with Agnew's tenure as governor of Maryland. Finally, on 1 March 1974 Special Prosecutor Jaworski secured from a federal grand jury indictments for obstruction of justice against seven Nixon aides — including Mitchell, Colson, Haldeman, and Ehrlichman. The grand jury found Nixon to be an "unindicted co-conspirator" because Jaworski doubted that a sitting president was subject to criminal indictment by a grand jury. Under the Constitution only Congress could indict a president for criminal wrongdoing, a process known as impeachment. During the impeachment process the House of Representatives determines whether an indictment is justified, and then the chief justice of the Supreme Court presides over a trial, with the Senate acting as jury. If the president is found guilty of high crimes or misdemeanors, he can be removed from office.

"ONE DAY IN OCTOBER"

For almost a week President Nixon and Watergate Special Prosecutor Archibald Cox had been at loggerheads. The issue was a 12 October 1973 federal court directive demanding that the president turn over the Watergate tapes for inspection by federal judge John J. Sirica and Special Prosecutor Cox. Nixon refused to comply with the order, citing executive privilege and insisting the tapes were his personal property — a position the federal court had invalidated. Nixon offered to turn over transcripts of the tapes, with their authenticity certified by Mississippi senator John Stennis. Attorney General Elliot Richardson suggested a panel of political leaders verify the transcripts in sworn affidavits. Nixon dismissed the proposal and on 18 October added that once he had delivered the transcripts of the tapes, he would refuse any further requests for Watergate materials. It was all too much for Cox. In a press conference on the morning of 20 October, Cox attacked the administration for stonewalling. Cox's statements infuriated Nixon, and he ordered Richardson to fire Cox. In a PBS interview years after the event, Richardson described his confrontation with Nixon over the Cox firing:

"And he said, 'Do you realize, Elliot, that (Soviet President) Brezhnev may conclude that I am losing control of my own administration?'

"But I said, 'Mr. President, I am committed to the independence of the special prosecutor. For me to have acquiesced in his being fired would be a total betrayal of that commitment.'

"He said, 'I'm sorry that you choose to prefer your purely personal commitments to the national interest.'

"Mustering all my self-control, I said — in as level a voice as I could, 'Mr. President, it would appear that we have a different assessment of the national interest.'"

Cox's reflections on the resignations and firings — characterized by the press as the "Saturday Night Massacre" — were more blunt. Alluding to the 1963 film *Seven Days in May,* wherein a megalomaniac tries to seize control of the U.S. government, Cox told *Time* magazine after he was fired, "Perhaps it wasn't *Seven Days in May,* but it was *One Day in October.*"

Source: *Time,* 102 (29 October 1973): pp. 12–19.

Richard M. Nixon leaving Washington on 9 August 1974, the morning after he resigned as president of the United States

United States v. Richard Nixon. With impeachment on the horizon, Judge Sirica turned over Watergate evidence to the House Judiciary Committee, impaneled to draw up articles of impeachment upon which the full House would vote. With meticulous care and the assistance of politically independent attorney John Doar, chairman Peter Rodino (D–New Jersey) sifted through the evidence. Rodino and Doar believed that a conversation Nixon had with Haldeman on 23 June 1972 would reveal whether or not the president had obstructed justice. As had Jaworski, they subpoenaed Nixon for the tape of that conversation and of others, but he refused to cooperate, again citing executive privilege and the already-published White House transcripts. It was left to the Supreme Court to decide the merit of Nixon's claim. On 24 July 1974, in *United States* v. *Richard M. Nixon,* they unanimously upheld the constitutionality of executive privilege but denied that it applied to the Watergate tapes; they ordered Nixon to turn over the tapes — including the 23 June tape — to Jaworski. Then, on 30 July, the House Judiciary Committee recommended to

the full House that it vote to impeach the president for three offenses: obstruction of justice, abuse of power, and contempt of Congress.

Resignation. With the Supreme Court ruling against him and the House about to vote on his impeachment, Nixon was trapped. On 5 August transcripts of the 23 June conversation became available to the public. It was the smoking gun Nixon's supporters feared, proving that the president had ordered a cover-up. His defenders were stunned, and leading Republicans went to the White House to report that Nixon had lost all congressional support. On 8 August 1974 in a televised address, Nixon resigned the presidency, effective at noon the following day. Vice-president Gerald R. Ford, who had assumed the office after Agnew resigned, became the thirty-eighth president of the United States.

Reaction. At his inaugural President Ford announced an end to "our long national nightmare," but Watergate and its effect on American political life did not easily disappear. Nixon had repeatedly charged that the crimes of his administration were no different than the activities of previous (Democratic) presidencies. Investigators and historians substantiated the charges: Kennedy and Johnson had also made secret tapes, profited from their offices, and engaged in dirty political tricks. Along with Watergate, such revelations induced a new public cynicism toward politics, a cynicism reflected in increasing voter apathy. More directly, character became the foremost issue in presidential politics. In 1976 voters found in Jimmy Carter a politician whose honesty and integrity seemed unassailable. They could have found the same qualities in President Ford, a man noted for his decency, but for one act of Ford's presidency: on 8 September 1974, to spare Nixon the indignity of undergoing a criminal prosecution for obstruction of justice, Ford granted Nixon a "full, free and absolute pardon." Within a week Ford's popularity fell from 71 percent to 49 percent — the largest single drop in polling history. Ford never recovered. Like the seventy Nixon administration members found guilty and punished for criminal activities, Ford's association with Nixon was nothing if not destructive.

THE MISERIES OF THE AMERICAN ECONOMY

A Disintegrating Economy. The constant context for American politics in the 1970s was the disintegration of the economy. Since the end of World War II the American economy had been the most dynamic in the world, growing more or less continuously at a rate between 3 and 4 percent and enjoying huge trade surpluses as the economies of Europe and Asia recovered from the devastation of World War II. By the 1970s, however, the period of prosperity was at an end. A host of economic problems arrived simultaneously. Foreign competition had begun to seize large parts of the U.S. domestic market; in 1971

Service station owner protesting against gas shortages caused by the Arab oil embargo

the United States posted its first trade deficit in eighty years. Johnson's attempt to finance the Vietnam War by borrowing and printing money created large governmental deficits and sparked runaway inflation. The consumer dollar was worth less; households found they could not pay their bills. The increasing automation of industry and the relocation of manufacturing overseas threw thousands out of work. Nixon and his successors Ford and Carter attempted to deal with these issues while simultaneously resolving three difficult economic problems with real political consequences: inflation, unemployment, and energy shortages.

Inflation and Unemployment. Inflation was one of the worst of the nation's economic problems. In the 1970s prices skyrocketed (the cost of living increased 15 percent from 1970 to 1971 alone) and seemed out of control. Nixon attempted to control inflation through a three-phase program of governmental regulation of prices and wages, which worked temporarily, but when Nixon abandoned the regulations, inflation soared once more, reaching 12 percent by 1974. Inheriting this situation, Ford attempted voluntary regulation of inflation and launched a highly publicized Whip Inflation Now campaign (symbolized by buttons stamped with WIN across them). When the WIN campaign failed, the Ford administration raised interest rates and restricted federal spending. By 1976 Ford's efforts had lowered inflation to

5 percent, but the nation plunged into its worst recession since the 1930s, and unemployment rose to nearly 9 percent. Carter, more aware of the political dangers of high unemployment, made it, not inflation, the object of concentration during his presidency. To combat unemployment, Carter increased public funding and cut federal taxes. Unemployment fell to slightly above 5 percent in 1978, but, predictably, inflation rose once more, to over 10 percent annually. With Carter's tax cuts, the federal deficit had reached $60 billion by the end of his term.

The Arab Oil Embargo. An even more vexing economic and political problem for the Nixon, Ford, and Carter presidencies was the energy crisis. Like its Western allies and Japan, the United States had become increasingly dependent on cheap Middle Eastern oil and gasoline. Whereas the West demanded 19 million barrels of oil a day in 1960, by 1972 44 million barrels a day were being consumed. The oil-producing nations, taking advantage of the growing dependency of the United States and other Western nations, established the Organization of Petroleum Exporting Countries (OPEC) to fix prices. In 1970 the OPEC nations, led by Libya, began to demand a greater share of the oil profits of Western companies located on their soil; that meant higher oil prices for consumers and placed pressure on the American economy. From 1970 to 1973 the price of crude oil doubled. Then, during the October 1973 Arab-Israeli war, the

Arab states of OPEC initiated an embargo against Israel's Western allies, including the United States. Although the embargo only amounted to 9 percent of the world's total daily oil production, prices soared as distributors, businesses, and consumers hoarded oil and gasoline. The non-Arab states of OPEC took advantage of the embargo to raise their prices. Retail gasoline prices jumped 40 percent, and around the country long lines of automobiles queued up to get the precious fuel. On 18 March 1974, in response to improved peace negotiations between Israel and her Arab neighbors, the Arab states ended their embargo.

Many Americans had responded to the oil shortage by abandoning their larger, gas-guzzling automobiles for fuel-efficient, foreign-manufactured subcompacts — leading to huge layoffs in Detroit and increasing America's trade deficit. To most Americans the embargo demonstrated a heretofore unsuspected economic vulnerability. Nixon would have had to deal with the political consequences of that shock had he not already been embroiled in the Watergate scandal. Ford, however, had no such luxury. OPEC prices continued to rise, but Ford was unable to initiate any new energy policy. An ambitious program to achieve independence from foreign oil inherited from Nixon failed to pass Congress, and the best Ford could do for an energy policy was to continue construction on the Alaskan pipeline and set higher fuel-efficiency standards for automobiles — achievements that did little to advance his political fortunes in 1976.

The Second Oil Crisis. Carter proved more adept at energy policy than Ford, but his political inepititude turned his triumph into failure. Skillful negotiations in 1977 and 1978 with Iran and the politically moderate Arab states, especially Saudi Arabia, restored low prices. Carter also sought to promote energy conservation and domestic oil production, but his program for weaning the United States from foreign oil was whittled down to virtually nothing by Congress. The lack of an energy policy proved costly. In 1979 Iran, in the midst of political turmoil, ceased all oil exports. The remaining OPEC nations raised prices and precipitated a second oil panic. Once again customers hoarded oil, especially large oil companies concerned lest a fundamentalist Islamic revolution sweep through the Middle East as it had in Iran. The gasoline lines returned. Carter's public-approval rating plummeted to 26 percent; he canceled a scheduled energy address and retreated to Camp David for ten days of discussions with economists and political experts. He emerged with good proposals: oil-price decontrol coupled with a windfall-profits tax and a crash program to develop synthetic fuels. But the speech in which he proposed these programs — admonishing Americans to conserve energy, placing the oil problems in the context of a "crisis of confidence" and the country's larger economic decline — was a disaster. It was not what Americans in gasoline lines sweltering through the summer wanted to hear. Carter followed the "malaise" speech by restructur-

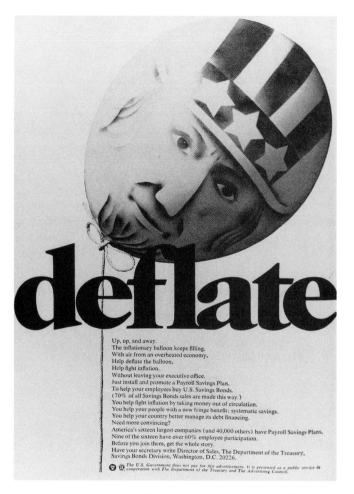

Cooperative stop inflation advertisement by the U.S Department of the Treasury and the Advertising Council, fall 1971

ing his entire cabinet and firing five advisers. He thought it would renew the confidence of the American people in his government, but it was widely interpreted as an expression of his incompetence to govern. And it did not end the energy crisis. Oddly enough, the same economic and political forces that created the oil panic in the first place fractured OPEC, and in the next year there was actually an oil surplus. It was all too late for Carter, who was facing Ronald Reagan in a presidential campaign by fall 1980. When Reagan asked the American people to consider whether they were better off in 1980 than they were when Carter took office, millions of them, remembering the summer of 1979 spent waiting for gasoline, concluded they were not. Carter lost the election.

NATIONAL POLITICS: ELECTION 1970

Law and Order. President Nixon set the theme for Republican candidates campaigning in the congressional elections of 1970: law and order. After the civil disruptions following May's invasion of Cambodia, law and order was a topic of intense interest to many voters. Extending the themes he had used in speeches earlier in the year, Nixon used the stump as an opportunity to

House	91st Congress	92nd Congress	Gain/Loss
Democrats	243	255	+12
Republicans	192	180	-12

Senate	91st Congress	92nd Congress	Gain/Loss
Democrats	58	55	-3
Republicans	42	45	+3

Governors	1968	1970	Gain/Loss
Democrats	19	29	+10
Republicans	31	21	-10

denounce antiwar protesters and to portray them as a threat to public order. Angling for a Republican majority in the Senate, Nixon also put Vice-president Spiro Agnew on the campaign, armed with incendiary speeches on "crime in the streets" and the "the rising tide of terrorism and crime." Republicans embellished these themes with speeches denouncing pornography, marijuana, and forced busing to achieve integration. Republicans charged the Democrats with permissiveness, with tolerating obscenity, immorality, and anti-Americanism. Democrats countered by charging that the Republicans were mounting a campaign of fear. Much of the electorate, however, was indeed afraid that personal security and old-fashioned values were being eroded.

Stagflation and "Nixonomics." Rather than focus on social issues, Democrats campaigning in 1970 focused on the economy. An unprecedented combination of nearly 6 percent unemployment and 6 percent inflation led experts to coin a new word, *stagflation* (a combination of stagnation and inflation), to describe the miseries of the American economy. Voters implicitly grasped the meaning of the new term. Their real income and buying power were being undermined, and the country was slipping into recession. The Nixon administration, led by Treasury Secretary David Kennedy, did little to combat the slide, preferring to concentrate on a balanced budget. Democratic National Committee chairman O'Brien called this approach "Nixonomics," and many Democratic candidates campaigned for more-active management of the economy. When, in early October, the majority Democratic Senate passed a series of Nixonian anticrime bills, Democrats were less vulnerable to the charge that they were soft on crime. The poor economy remained, however, hurting the credibility of President Nixon and his Republican supporters.

Economics over Social Issues. On election day the Democrats defeated the Republicans. Democrats increased their majority in the House of Representatives by twelve seats. The Republicans did better in the Senate, gaining three seats, but the Democrats remained the majority. More important, the Democrats gained ten governorships and increased their 1968 margin of victory by 4.5 million votes.

NATIONAL POLITICS: REPUBLICAN PRIMARIES AND CONVENTION 1972

1972 Republican Primaries. In the spring of 1971, distressed over his low approval ratings in the polls, President Nixon feared he would not be renominated. In the spring primaries of 1972, however, his only challengers were Rep. Paul N. McCloskey of California, who campaigned on an antiwar platform, and Rep. John M. Ashbrook of Ohio, seeking to steer the president toward a more conservative foreign policy. Nixon coasted to victory over both men. The only question remaining among Republicans was Nixon's choice for vice-president. Nixon himself hinted that Vice-president Agnew might be dumped in favor of former Democrat John Connally of Texas. Connally had no real support among Republicans, however, and Agnew was retained.

An Enormous War Chest. Nixon had spent $36.5 million in the 1968 campaign, much of that money raised through generous contributions by the rich. Congress, concerned over undue political influence on the part of the wealthy, revamped federal election laws in early 1972, requiring candidates to identify their contributors and expenditures. Stans, CREEP's chief fund-raiser, made unexpected use of the law. He pointed out to potential contributors (many of whom were angling for federal contracts) that their names would become public knowledge after 7 April 1972, when the law went into effect. Between the passage of the law at the beginning of March and 7 April, Stans raised over $20 million for CREEP. He ultimately amassed $60 million, much of which, according to Nixon's critics, was raised unethically, if not illegally. They maintained that Nixon traded contributions for favors: in 1971 the dairy industry had pledged $2 million to the Nixon campaign; afterward the administration reversed an earlier decision and increased the federal price support for milk. International Telephone and Telegraph (ITT), facing antitrust violations that same spring, contributed $400,000 to the Republicans, and the antitrust suit was settled. Stans reportedly threatened businessmen with investigation by the Environmental Protection Agency (EPA) unless they made contributions, and he set up a Mexican money-laundering operation in order that donations could not be traced by American authorities. Stans ultimately pleaded guilty to campaign-finance violations in 1975.

A Scripted Convention. In August the Republicans convened in Miami to ratify President Nixon as the party's nominee. With the outcome never in doubt, the White House used the convention as a televised promotion for Nixon. The traditional workings of the convention — debate over the platform, debate over the candidates — were carefully crafted to maximize the public image of the president. Speeches of delegates were written by the White House in advance, and floor managers cued delegates to respond to specific lines — certain speeches even contained pauses so that the delegates could express "spontaneous" enthusiasm. Access to the convention was tightly controlled, and the press was kept on a short leash. The convention introduced the themes of the fall campaign: the Democrats were the party of extremism and discord, the Republicans the party of sobriety and conciliation. President Nixon was presented as "the great helmsman" — statesmanlike and above the pettiness of political campaigning. The strategy worked. Following the convention, polls showed Nixon with a 64 to 30 percent lead over Democratic nominee George McGovern.

Sources:

Stephen Ambrose, *Nixon* (New York: Simon & Schuster, 1989);

Carl Bernstein and Bob Woodward, *All The President's Men* (New York: Warner, 1974);

Jonathan Schell, *The Time of Illusion* (New York: Vintage, 1976).

NATIONAL POLITICS: DEMOCRATIC PRIMARIES AND CONVENTION 1972

Democratic Primaries. As the primary season began, the two front-runners for the nomination were both conservatives: George Wallace, governor of Alabama, and Edmund Muskie, senator from Maine. Wallace had made his national reputation in the early 1960s as a prosegregationist. By 1972 his position had modified somewhat, and he campaigned on an anticrime, antibusing, populist platform that had immediate appeal for millions of conservative, blue-collar Democrats. Muskie's reputation was that of a statesmanlike, prudent politician. The favorite of Democratic party bosses, Muskie did not possess the natural constituency of Wallace but did carry considerable financial and organizational clout.

Dirty Tricks. Unknown to the Democrats, President Nixon's campaign utilized illegal and unethical tactics to defeat them. Led by Donald Segretti and Chapin, CREEP developed a dirty-tricks campaign to undermine the Democrats. They spent four hundred thousand dollars during the 1970 Democratic gubernatorial primary in Alabama in an attempt to defeat Wallace. Nixon also had Wallace investigated by the IRS in an attempt to derail his candidacy. CREEP monitored Muskie's private conversations and leaked them to the press. They attempted to wiretap Sen. George McGovern and Democratic National Committee chairman O'Brien. CREEP hired twenty-eight people in seventeen states to forge letters using Democratic candidates' letterheads, produce phony letters to newspapers, leak false statements, concoct rumors, cancel and switch appearances, and make incendi-

ary phone calls in the middle of the night to supporters. The dirty tricks did not, by themselves, defeat any of the Democratic candidates. They did, however, create an atmosphere of discord among the Democrats and disconcert the candidates. CREEP sharply increased the normal pressures and competition of campaigning.

Muskie Defeated. The dirty-tricks campaign was especially effective against Muskie. Nixon feared the Maine senator might well beat him. National polls in the previous year often indicated voter support for Muskie; CREEP did their best to defeat him in the Democratic primaries so that Nixon would face a less formidable challenger in the general election. Muskie was expected to win in New Hampshire, a state next to his own, and he did, but not by an impressive margin. CREEP had circulated rumors concerning Muskie and disparaging remarks about Americans of French-Canadian descent (a large number of whom lived in New Hampshire). The rumors were published in the conservative Manchester newspaper *Union Leader*, along with an unflattering article about Muskie's wife. Muskie, angered by the articles, attacked the editor of the *Union Leader* on national television and appeared to cry, undermining his statesmanlike reputation. In the next primary, in Florida, CREEP stepped up its anti-Muskie activities. It circulated leaflets with racial and sexual slurs about the other Democratic candidates and attributed the leaflets to the Muskie campaign; it stole Muskie's mail, planted spies among his staffers, and made and canceled appointments for Muskie. The disruptions worked and embittered relations among the

Democratic candidates. Muskie lost Florida, then Wisconsin, Pennsylvania, and Massachusetts. By the end of April he withdrew from further primaries.

Wallace Shot Down. With Muskie out of the running, Wallace seemed more and more formidable. He won the Florida, Tennessee, and North Carolina primaries and finished second in Wisconsin, Indiana, and Pennsylvania. He completely eclipsed Sen. Henry Jackson of Washington, running on similar defense issues but with a different social agenda. Jackson soon dropped out of the race. The liberal wing of the Democratic party was troubled by Wallace's surprising popularity and sought to block the possibility that he would become the Democratic standard-bearer in the fall. His candidacy also troubled President Nixon. Nixon was counting on many of the same Democratic, blue-collar voters to endorse Wallace. Should liberal Democrats block Wallace's nomination, Nixon feared that Wallace would run as a third-party candidate in the fall and steal the votes of conservative Democrats from him. The fears of liberal Democrats and conservative Republicans, however, went unrealized. On 15 May in Laurel, Maryland, Wallace was shot by a would-be assassin. Doctors saved his life, but Wallace was left unable to walk, and his campaign was destroyed.

The Liberal Democrats. With the withdrawal of the conservatives, liberal Democrats moved to the forefront of the primaries. One candidate, former Republican mayor of New York, John Lindsey, had little organizational support within the Democratic party and faded after a poor showing in the Florida primary. Another liberal, Hubert H. Humphrey, the 1968 presidential nominee, carried considerable organizational support, but he was burdened with already having lost to Nixon and inspired little enthusiasm among voters. The most surprising liberal candidate was McGovern, senator from South Dakota. Running almost exclusively on his opposition to the war in Vietnam, McGovern had come in second in New Hampshire. Leaving Florida to Muskie and Wallace, McGovern concentrated his forces in Wisconsin and built an energetic organization populated with young volunteers. Not only did they deliver Wisconsin to McGovern, but the candidate himself proved remarkably popular among blue-collar workers there — people most experts thought would vote for Wallace or Humphrey. McGovern repeated his Wisconsin performance 25 April in Massachusetts, gaining 52 percent of the vote. He also proved shrewd at gaining the votes of convention delegates in nonprimary states. By April the contest was between McGovern and Humphrey.

New Politics versus the Old Guard. From the Ohio to the California primaries, McGovern and Humphrey engaged in the type of intraparty antagonism impossible to heal at the convention. The bloodletting divided and weakened the Democrats, making them an easy mark for Nixon. The issues were fundamentally cultural and generational. McGovern's base of support was among young people and liberals. He banked on

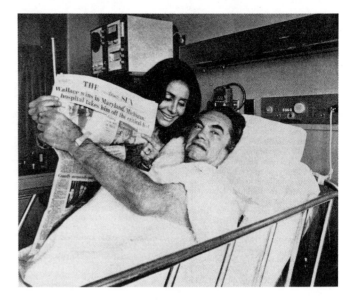

Lurleen and George Wallace in his hospital room two days after an attempted assassination during the Alabama governor's presidential campaign

the voters brought into the system by the Twenty-sixth Amendment, passed a year earlier, which lowered the voting age to eighteen. In 1972 Americans between the ages of fourteen and twenty-four constituted 20 percent of the population; 25 million of them were eligible to vote. McGovern promised this group not only an end to the war in Vietnam but what he termed a "new politics" — one more responsive to the needs of minorities and women, pacific in foreign policy, and activist on domestic issues. Humphrey found his core constituency among a much different group. He appealed to what remained of the New Deal Democratic coalition: labor unions; urban politicians; and elderly, black, and Jewish voters. Humphrey's core constituency was a generation (or two) removed from the young, and the young derided them as the old guard, the Democrats responsible for Vietnam. Humphrey's supporters similarly viewed McGovern's backers as radicals, anarchists, and hippies out to destroy traditional values. Polarized by these attitudes, Democrats split their votes for the remainder of the primary season: in Ohio Humphrey narrowly defeated McGovern, but in Nebraska McGovern won, 41 percent to 35 percent; in California McGovern won by a slim margin, 44.3 percent to 39.2 percent. The divisiveness of these primary elections set the stage for a volatile national convention.

A Divided Convention. In 1968 the Democrats had also been divided over Vietnam, divided between doves and hawks, the young and the old. There the old guard had triumphed, and their candidate, Humphrey, won the nomination. To placate young Democrats, however, in 1969 the party initiated a reform of its organizational structure, revamping the convention-delegate selection process to open it to new participation. The leader of the reform commission was McGovern. His reforms brought

McGovern for President headquarters in Washington, D.C., 1972

new blood to the party, and at the 1972 convention women and minorities were represented as never before. The old guard was shut out of the platform process, and McGovern got the nomination. Some of the old guard, embittered, bolted the party to join Democrats for halfheartedly for McGovern in the general election. Senator McGovern, who wanted to unify a United States badly divided by Vietnam, could not even bring unity to his own party.

Sources:

Hunter S. Thompson, *Fear and Loathing: On the Campaign Trail '72* (New York: Warner, 1973);

Theodore H. White, *The Making of the President, 1972* (New York: Atheneum, 1973).

NATIONAL POLITICS: ELECTION 1972

Outmaneuvered on Peace. McGovern entered the fall 1972 campaign with little political ammunition to attack the president. To McGovern Vietnam remained the most important issue. He had a record of introducing antiwar legislation, characterized Vietnam as "the wound in American life that will not heal," and often portrayed the war as a symptom of a larger moral failure in the United States. The majority of the voters did not see the war that way. By the fall of 1972 Nixon had succeeded in removing all combat ground troops from Vietnam, and the air campaign against the Vietnamese inspired little moral indignation. As a peace candidate, moreover, McGovern was no match for Nixon. Nixon had journeyed to Moscow and Peking, he had drafted the SALT accords, and he had stopped American boys from dying in Vietnam.

Outmaneuvered on Defense. McGovern ardently maintained that the Vietnam War had made the United States a dangerous, militarist power. He proposed a detailed plan to slash the Pentagon budget 37 percent, to $54.8 billion, and turn the savings over to social spending. Nixon countered this proposal by arguing the McGovern plan left the United States open to aggression. He touted his own SALT discussions and détente with China and the Soviet Union as a more prudent approach to lowered defense spending. Nixon argued that it was important to maintain a military sufficient to negotiate with foreign powers from a position of strength. Local politicians and union leaders, from the shipbuilding areas of the Northeast to the aircraft manufacturing centers of the Northwest, agreed with Nixon; so, too, did the majority of voters.

Outmaneuvered on Domestic Policy. McGovern introduced a host of innovative social and economic programs during the 1972 stump — too innovative, it turned out, for the American voter. He proposed tax reforms that would have closed loopholes for the rich and would have exempted the poor. He proposed capping inheri-

House	92nd Congress	93rd Congress	Gain/Loss
Democrats	255	243	-12
Republicans	180	192	+12

Senate	92nd Congress	93rd Congress	Gain/Loss
Democrats	55	57	+2
Republicans	45	43	-2

Governors	1970	1972	Gain/Loss
Democrats	29	31	+2
Republicans	21	19	-2

tances at five hundred thousand dollars, an idea designed to democratize opportunity but interpreted by many voters as the repudiation of opportunity itself. Most damaging to the McGovern campaign was his proposal to guarantee every American one thousand dollars a year, regardless of his or her need. Despite the fact that welfare assistance in the United States often totaled more per person per year than McGovern's proposal, and despite the fact that Nixon had proposed something similar to Congress in 1971, McGovern's guaranteed-income proposal was widely ridiculed — especially by the White House — as a giveaway.

Nixon's Credibility. The sole issue on which Nixon remained vulnerable was Vietnam — not for his policies but for his promises. In 1968 Nixon had promised to end the war, and in his first term he repeated the promise, often indicating that he would rather serve one term than see the war drag on. McGovern repeatedly emphasized that the war continued, and that Nixon had, in fact, widened the war into Cambodia and Laos. Nixon, already burdened with his Tricky Dick reputation, appeared to be a man the public could not count on to keep his promises.

The Eagleton Affair. In contrast to Nixon, McGovern appeared to be a man of unimpeachable honesty and sincerity. McGovern's character was his chief asset during the primaries, but by the general election McGovern had squandered this advantage. McGovern lost his reputation for honesty, and his hope of winning the election, when he selected Sen. Thomas Eagleton of Missouri for his running mate. The decision had been made at the last minute at the Miami convention, without any real background check, in the hope that Eagleton would bring Catholic and labor votes to the ticket. He brought disas-

ter instead. Ten days after he accepted the vice-presidential slot, reports surfaced that Eagleton had been hospitalized and had received electric-shock treatments for depression. The reports were true and a crippling blow to the campaign. The majority of Americans could not accept a potential president with a history of nervous exhaustion, and Eagleton became a liability. McGovern, however, was slow to drop Eagleton and was comfortable with Eagleton from the ticket. He announced first that he solidly supported Eagleton and was comfortable with Eagleton and was comfortable with Eagleton's mental condition. Then, bowing to considerable public pressure, McGovern replaced Eagleton with former Peace Corps head Sargent Shriver. McGovern's vacillations over Eagleton destroyed the public perception of him as a politician who was decisive, honest, loyal, and sincere — someone who would not go to any lengths to get elected. It was a no-win situation: had Eagleton remained, the election would be lost; with Eagleton gone, McGovern appeared to be caving in to politics as usual. His reputation was compromised. Eagleton's departure stripped McGovern of the only real possibility he had of beating Nixon.

Culture and Character. With McGovern out-maneuvered on most of the substantial issues, the fall campaign was dominated by rhetoric concerning personal character. McGovern attempted to connect Nixon to the Watergate affair, arguing that it reflected his duplicity. The cover-up, however, was temporarily successful, and an uninterested public dismissed McGovern's charges as partisan. Nixon was more effective in characterizing McGovern as extremist. With a huge lead in the polls, the president's strategy was to stay above the fray and appear presidential. Republican party regulars such as Nelson Rockefeller and Ronald Reagan, however, consistently portrayed McGovern as the candidate of "acid, abortion and amnesty" — tying him to the radical politics and counterculture of the 1960s.

A Nixon Landslide. The public, exhausted by the war in Vietnam, by the divisions left unhealed, and by the radicalism of 1960s, decisively repudiated McGovern. Nixon won by a huge landslide, 60.7 percent of the popular vote and every state in the electoral college except Massachusetts and the District of Columbia. The youth vote, upon which the McGovern campaign had focused so much strategy, never materialized. For Nixon, however, the election was a hollow victory. Voter turnout was low, about half of the eligible electorate, and while the Republicans won twelve seats in the House, the Democrats added two seats in the Senate and retained their majority in both houses. Many Republicans blamed Nixon for the weak showing of the GOP; he had hardly campaigned for other candidates and had earmarked only $1 million of his $60 million war chest to other Republican candidates. Nixon's short coattails would come back to haunt him: in 1973, when the Watergate story finally broke, Nixon would find he had little political cover in Congress.

House	93rd Congress	94th Congress	Gain/ Loss
Democrats	243	291	+48
Republicans	192	144	-48

Senate	93rd Congress	94th Congress	Gain/ Loss
Democrats	57	61	+4
Republicans	43	38	-5
Independents	0	1	+1

Governors	1972	1974	Gain/ Loss
Democrats	31	36	+5
Republicans	19	13	-6
Independents	0	1	+1

NATIONAL POLITICS: ELECTION 1974

The Lingering Presence of Watergate. Watergate was the biggest presidential story of the year, and it had a deep impact on the congressional elections of 1974. Voters were disenchanted with politics generally and disgusted with the drift in policy (inflation, unemployment, and consumer shortages were unaddressed problems) that occurred as the nation pursued Watergate. Only 38 percent of the electorate participated, and they punished conservative Republicans. Republicans lost forty-eight seats in the House, and two GOP senators lost their seats — one to Gary Hart, manager of McGovern's 1972 presidential campaign. Every incumbent Democratic senator was reelected, and moderate Republicans increased their ranks in Congress. Democrats won twenty-seven of the thirty-five races for governor, overturning Republican rule in ten states.

New Faces. The anti-incumbent sentiment of voters was best expressed in Maine, where independent James B. Longley defeated the gubernatorial candidates of both parties. Elsewhere, new political figures emerged who would go on to national reputations. In California Edmund G. ("Jerry") Brown, Jr., son of former governor Pat Brown, succeeded the retiring Ronald Reagan as governor. In Massachusetts Michael S. Dukakis defeated Republican incumbent Francis S. Sargent for governor. Dale Bumpers of Arkansas and John Glenn of Ohio took seats on the Democratic side of the Senate aisle. Six new women menbers were elected to the House, raising the total to eighteen; every black representative was reelected, plus a new member from Tennessee, raising the total to seventeen. Ella T. Grasso became governor of Connecticut, the first woman so elected whose husband did not precede her in that post.

NATIONAL POLITICS: REPUBLICAN PRIMARIES AND CONVENTION 1976

Ford's Shaky Incumbency. In 1974, when he began his presidency, Gerald Ford expressed little interest in running for the office in his own right. Convinced that a caretaker president was virtually powerless, he quickly changed his mind and by the summer of 1975 had declared his candidacy in the next year's election. Ford had little record on which to run. His chief asset, his personal integrity, had been compromised with his pardon of Nixon. His effectiveness as a policy maker was undermined by a Democratic Congress, insisting on reasserting its constitutional power after Watergate. In foreign affairs Ford had overseen the collapse of South Vietnam, in domestic affairs the collapse of the economy. Ford was an unusually vulnerable incumbent, by no means certain of his party's nomination.

Challenge from the Right. The foremost challenge to Ford's nomination came from GOP conservatives. Even before Ford's presidency, they felt marginalized within the Republican party. They disapproved of Nixon's détente with the Soviet Union and China and were shocked by the fall of South Vietnam; they abhorred governmental regulation of business and environmental legislation; they deplored the social-welfare programs of the Democrats. Ford intensified their ire when, to balance the Nixon pardon, he offered a limited amnesty to Vietnam War draft evaders. Against the wishes of conservatives, Ford also increased the national debt in a futile effort to restore economic prosperity, and he selected Nelson Rockefeller — long the leader of liberal Republicans — to be his vice-president. Since Barry Goldwater's failed 1964 campaign for the presidency, GOP conservatives had been promoting a former actor turned politician, Ronald Reagan, as their champion. In 1976 they rallied behind him in an effort to dump Ford from the head of the Republican ticket.

Ford as Underdog. Ford's strengths as Nixon's replacement — his disarming candor and his capacity to project the image that he was "just one of us" — proved to be weaknesses in a campaign against Reagan. Seasoned, telegenic, a master of the media, former California governor Reagan made Ford appear bumbling by contrast, an appearance made worse by Ford's penchant for minor mishaps — bumping his head against doors, falling down on skis, tripping on carpets and runways. The real strength of Reagan's candidacy, however, was his willingness to run against Washington, to offer himself as the champion of the common man, whose interests, he maintained, the federal government had neglected. "Our nation's capital has become the seat of a buddy system that functions for its own benefit," Reagan said, an-

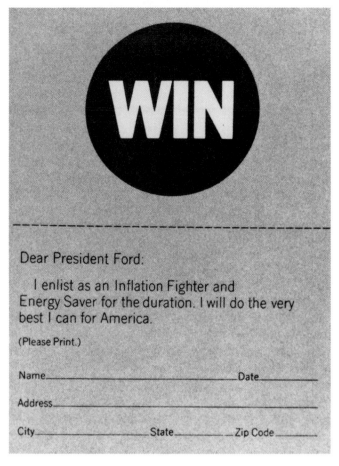

Solicitation for President Ford's "Whip Inflation Now"
program, 1974

best served by deploying U.S. troops. These incidents, magnified by Ford for political advantage, made inroads into Reagan's lead. Ford also used the immense prestige of his office and his ability to dispense presidential favors to increase his stature with voters and delegates to the Republican convention. Ford's strategy worked. In the first three primaries, New Hampshire, Florida, and Illinois, he scored narrow victories over Reagan. Still, Reagan was a formidable opponent, and in states with open primaries, where conservative Democratic voters could cross party lines and vote for Republicans, Reagan won. By the end of the primary season, neither candidate had amassed a sufficient number of Republican delegates to be nominated for president.

A Divided Convention. At the Republican convention in Kansas City, Ford's control over the party organization gave him a slight advantage. Reagan defeated his own nomination, however, in a last-ditch effort to extend the base of his political support. Less than a month before the convention, Reagan announced his selection of a vice-presidential candidate: Richard Schweiker, senator from Pennsylvania and one of the most liberal members of the Republican party. The Reagan organization thought that Schweiker would gain them support among uncommitted northeastern delegates; instead, he lost them the support of conservative southerners. To many conservatives Schweiker was unacceptable, and Reagan, by selecting him, appeared less a man of principle than another untrustworthy politician. Ford won the nomination and tried to unify the party by abandoning Rockefeller and enlisting conservative senator Robert Dole of Kansas as his running mate. The selection seemed to satisfy the disappointed supporters of Reagan, but Ford nonetheless entered the general election with the half-hearted support of his own party — against a unified Democratic party and an enthusiastic candidate, James Earl ("Jimmy") Carter, Jr.

NATIONAL POLITICS: DEMOCRATIC PRIMARIES AND CONVENTION 1976

A Party in Search of Itself. As the 1976 political season opened, the Democratic party seemed to be suffering from an identity crisis. The polarization of the liberal and conservative wings of the party remained; the air of defeat in 1972 lingered. Liberals looked unenthusiastically to Humphrey or Massachusetts senator Edward M. Kennedy for leadership; conservatives, equally glum, turned toward Wallace. These venerable party leaders appeared exhausted: Wallace still struggled to regain the vitality stolen from him by the assassination attempt in 1972, and Humphrey, tired of perennial candidacy, declined to run. Kennedy, young and able, carrying the glamorous name of his brothers, was the potential front-runner. As he had in 1972, however, Kennedy also declined to run. He cited family problems; but there was also the likely prospect of an attempt on his life and the lingering scan-

nouncing his candidacy, "increasingly insensitive to the needs of the American worker who supports it with his taxes." Reagan proposed major tax cuts and gutting the social-welfare programs of the Great Society. He was also sharply critical of Ford and Henry Kissinger's foreign policy, maintaining that détente with the Soviet Union led the United States to become a "second-best power." Coming after Watergate and the defeat in Vietnam, Reagan's antistatist, somewhat-belligerent rhetoric resonated with Republican voters. Before the first primary Ford trailed in public-opinion polls 32 percent to Reagan's 40 percent. Ford was the president, but he was also the underdog for the 1976 Republican presidential nomination.

Dead Heat in the Primaries. Ford's only hope in the election was to portray Reagan as a right-wing ideologue, a reckless political outsider certain to be defeated by the Democrats in the fall; by contrast he pictured himself as sober, responsible, and presidential. Ford seized upon several of Reagan's notorious gaffes to construct his portrait of Reagan. Reagan suggested that he could save the federal government $90 billion by returning federal dollars to the states; he hinted that Social Security funds should be invested in the stock market; he asserted that American interests in Panama and Rhodesia might be

Presidential nominee Jimmy Carter with his family at the 1976 Democratic National Convention

dal associated with a 1969 automobile accident at Chappaquiddick Island, Massachusetts, which had claimed the life of a young woman, Mary Jo Kopechne. The field was wide open for a new standard-bearer to assert himself.

An Unlikely Prospect. Carter was by far the longshot among prospective Democratic candidates. A peanut farmer who attended the Naval Academy and became a nuclear engineer, Carter's only political experience was a brief stint as a Georgia state senator and one term as Georgia's governor. Most of the other candidates seemed more qualified: Sen. Henry M. Jackson of Washington had spent thirty-five years in Congress and had been a candidate for president in 1972; former Sen. Fred R. Harris of Oklahoma had a good following for his version of midwestern populism; Sen. Birch E. Bayh, Jr.

The Representative of the New South. In 1976 Carter's anonymity turned out to be an asset. After Watergate, voter discontent with politics was high. Carter, with greater credibility than the others, presented himself as the Washington outsider, ready to represent the middle class and return honesty to government. Wallace had introduced that image to Democratic politics, but he carried the taint of segregation, and his health remained an issue. Wallace nonetheless ran, and the beneficiary of his effort was Carter. Carter presented himself as a candidate of the "New South" — one as committed as Wallace to southern values and blue-collar populism but liberal on race and less committed to revolutionizing American politics than reforming it. Wallace excoriated "pointy-headed bureaucrats" in Washington; Carter simply urged a paring of governmental agencies. Wallace was dead-set opposed to busing; Carter favored voluntary desegregation but pledged to uphold court orders. Carter thus sold himself to conservatives as a Wallace capable of winning a general election; to liberals he presented himself as an alternative to the much-feared Wallace. Carter reinforced his ideological ambiguity by stressing his personal

character rather than programs. "I will never lie to you," he promised voters. With his earnest character, his down-home conviviality, and solid moral background (he was a Baptist Sunday school teacher), Carter seemed the perfect representative of a new honesty in politics.

Primary Victories. Carter also mounted a highly organized, personal campaign. His entire family joined him on the stump; troops of enthusiastic Georgians, nicknamed the "Peanut Brigade," rang doorbells for him in primary states. Carter also made terrific use of the media; after Nixon, Carter's openness with the press earned him sympathetic coverage. His organization, his cultivation of the media, and his ideological ambiguity worked. In New Hampshire he presented himself as a conservative and won 30 percent of the ballot, while four liberal candidates split the remainder, the nearest winning only 24 percent of the vote. In Florida, two weeks later, Carter ran as a liberal version of Wallace and beat the Alabaman by 3.7 percent of ballots cast. In Illinois he crushed Wallace by twenty percentage points; in North Carolina he prevailed by almost nineteen points, and the Wallace candidacy was over. Rep. Morris Udall of Arizona, Carter's closest remaining competition on the left, fell to him in Wisconsin. Senator Jackson, Carter's closest competition on the right, was defeated in Pennsylvania. By May polls showed Carter outranking not only the remaining Democrats but also leading President Ford. Carter romped through the remaining southern primaries, but last-minute challenges by Idaho senator Frank Church and California governor Brown set Carter back in the west. Nonetheless, Carter continued to accumulate delegate votes even in states where he lost. By June the opposition to him had crumbled, and Carter entered the convention with the backing of almost all of his former opponents.

A United Convention. With the nomination in the bag, Carter turned the 1976 Democratic convention into an exercise in coalition building. Carter used the search for a vice-presidential candidate, which McGovern had so spectacularly botched, as an opportunity to solicit opinion and flatter every interest group within the party. Sen. Walter Mondale of Minnesota, a liberal with strong labor support, got the nod. Platform differences were papered over, and the convention, anticipating the general election, stressed Carter's character rather than the issues. Following his acceptance speech, Carter's former opponents joined him on the convention podium. The display gave the appearance of unity, but the fissures that split the party in 1968 and 1972 remained. The Democrats were not ideologically reunified, but they did share the desire to put a Democrat — the dark horse candidate from Georgia — in the White House.

NATIONAL POLITICS: ELECTION 1976

Candidates and Character. The 1976 presidential election, a contest between a moderate Democrat and a

House	94th Congress	95th Congress	Gain/Loss
Democrats	291	292	+1
Republicans	144	143	-1

Senate	94th Congress	95th Congress	Gain/Loss
Democrats	61	61	0
Republicans	38	38	0
Independents	1	1	0

Governors	1974	1976	Gain/Loss
Democrats	36	37	+1
Republicans	13	12	-1
Independents	1	1	0

moderate Republican, was not fought over issues. On the controversial topics of the day — busing, abortion, nuclear power, the Equal Rights Amendment — Carter and Ford held virtually identical moderate positions. They were also financially equal. A federal campaign-reform law capped expenditures at $21.8 million. The decisive issue was the character and competence of the candidates. Watergate, in a sense, made the election: whichever politician could demonstrate to the public that he was less political than the other would win. In that contest Carter held the advantage. He could honestly claim to be more a Washington outsider than Ford, and he had not pardoned Richard Nixon. In the general election Ford would be on the defensive. Because of that, Ford agreed to debate Carter on three occasions, the first presidential debates since 1960. They would be the high point of the election.

Gaffes. Despite Carter's advantage over Ford, his public support was weak. As both conservative and liberal, Carter did not strongly appeal to either group. As the election drew near, Carter's large lead over Ford declined. Like the president he was vulnerable to mistakes and gaffes. In an interview with *Playboy* magazine Carter confessed that, although he was a practicing Christian, he often "looked on a lot of women with lust." Carter was attempting to make a point about Christian humility, but given the forum, the lust quote generated the attention. It suggested that Carter was not as pure as he seemed to be and impugned his credibility. An attempt to link Ford to Nixon and to dredge up the pardon issue was also damaging. The voters wanted to move beyond Watergate, and

Carter quickly dropped the tactic. However, Ford's mistakes were more spectacular. After Secretary of Agriculture Earl Butz was overheard telling racist jokes, Ford waited an inordinately long time before he requested Butz's resignation, appearing racially insensitive. More important, in the second debate Ford maintained that "there is no Soviet domination of Eastern Europe and there never will be under a Ford administration." The assertion, intended to reassert longtime U.S. policy that Soviet domination in Eastern Europe was not recognized or accepted, merely seemed to fly in the face of geopolitical realities and once more focused attention on Ford's competence.

The Carter Victory. On election day only 54.4 percent of the electorate bothered to vote, a reflection of the growing cynicism toward politics. They chose Carter, but narrowly. Carter outpolled Ford 40.8 million to 39.1 million popular votes. Carter won by less than 60 electoral college votes. In the end Carter's deliberately vague campaign appealed to a spectrum of voters, especially blacks, but not very deeply. In Congress Democrats maintained a majority, 61 to 38 in the Senate (1 independent) and 292 to 143 in the House — ratios of party strength virtually identical to the previous Congress. Seeing little difference between the Democrats and Republicans at all levels, the voters seemed content to leave things as they were.

NATIONAL POLITICS: ELECTION 1978

Continued Apathy. Continued apathy (the lowest voter participation since 1942) characterized the elections of 1978 at the national level. There was virtually no change in the division of party strength in Congress. The Republicans picked up sixteen seats in the House, but the majority of these gains were in districts that had been Republican before 1974, when voter backlash against Watergate elected Democrats in traditionally Republican areas. Senatorial races reflected the growing conservatism of those who bothered to vote. Although the Republicans only gained three seats in the Senate, five incumbent liberal Democrats were defeated. Republicans gained the Minnesota seat once held by archliberal Humphrey, and in Mississippi Republican Thad Cochran defeated Democrat Maurice Dantin for the spot once held by Democrat James Eastland. Cochran was the first Republican to represent Mississippi since Reconstruction. Despite these victories voters also selected Democrats who would become forces in the Senate in the 1980s: Paul Tsongas in Massachusetts, Bill Bradley in New Jersey, and David Boren in Oklahoma. These victories, however, did not offset the growing independence of congressional Democrats. In the Ninety-sixth Congress, half of all House Democrats had been elected since 1974, and party voting was at its lowest level in thirty-six years.

House	95th Congress	96th Congress	Gain/Loss
Democrats	292	276	-16
Republicans	143	159	+16

Senate	95th Congress	96th Congress	Gain/Loss
Democrats	61	58	-3
Republicans	38	41	+3
Independents	1	1	0

Governors	1976	1978	Gain/Loss
Democrats	37	32	-5
Republicans	12	18	+6
Independents	1	0	-1

State Races. At the state level Republicans won the election of 1978. Future Democratic president Bill Clinton was elected to his first term as governor of Arkansas (and the youngest governor in the nation), and Democrat Hugh Carey won a second term as governor of New York, but the remaining significant gains were Republican. The GOP won 298 new seats in state legislatures and gained six governorships. More important, in California conservative Republicans led a popular tax revolt — the most significant political development of the season. Proposition 13, a ballot initiative, was approved by California voters on 6 June. It cut property taxes 57 percent and placed a ceiling of 2 percent per year on tax increases. Because of a $5-billion surplus in the state treasury, the effect of Proposition 13 on social services was not immediately felt, but the political tactic behind the initiative — to attack popular social services by cutting unpopular taxation — was successfully imitated in various states and anticipated the method Reagan would use as president to limit the rise in social spending.

THE NEW CONSERVATISM AND THE FATE OF THE GREAT SOCIETY

The Great Society and Its Opponents. Except for the Vietnam War, no other political issue left over from the 1960s was as controversial as the Great Society. The New Deal and the liberal social legislation that followed World War II had elevated millions of working-class Americans into the ranks of the middle class. In the 1960s politicians such as Johnson, Humphrey, and Mc-Govern attempted to use similar government-sponsored programs (often called the Great Society for what they were trying to achieve) to elevate the living conditions of a new group of poor Americans. In the 1960s perhaps 20 percent of Americans remained in poverty. Through educational and legal assistance, through job-training programs and expanded welfare benefits, supporters of the Great Society hoped to bring poor people into the middle class. Even though the Great Society benefited poor whites, to many middle-class white Americans it appeared the government was devoting select attention to racial minorities. Conservative politicians such as Goldwater and Reagan asserted that this was not the proper function for a government of all the people. They agreed with the liberals that America should be a land of equal opportunity for all; they disagreed with the liberals as to the extent of inequality in society. They also disagreed about the role of government in redressing that inequality.

The Great Society and the Decline of the Middle Class. Public support for the Great Society dissolved as inflation, unemployment, and other economic woes of the 1970s struck the middle class. These economic troubles undermined the goodwill upon which so much of the Great Society rested. In times of prosperity the middle class could afford attempts to eliminate poverty; during an economic downturn the middle class did all it could to stay out of poverty itself. Conservative politicians used this economic pressure to political advantage. Ignoring revenue losses caused by subsidies and tax breaks given to big businesses, they argued that the government could not afford the Great Society. They also maintained that the Great Society unfairly rewarded the poor at the very time when the middle class saw little reward for their work. This argument had enormous political impact. In the 1970s conservative politicians found the Great Society useful as a scapegoat for the nation's economic miseries.

Busing and the Great Society. No aspect of the Great Society generated more controversy than the attempt by the federal government to desegregate American schools. Despite fifteen years of court orders to desegregate American schools, by 1970 the majority of schools remained segregated. The problem fundamentally stemmed from the segregated living patterns of Americans: white schools remained predominantly white because neighborhoods tended to be predominantly white; the same was true of nonwhite schools. Some school districts developed elaborate busing programs, transporting black and white students out of their neighborhoods and across town. In many places federal courts ordered school districts to initiate busing. In 1974, when the courts ordered schools in Boston, Massachusetts, to begin busing black students into a predominantly white neighborhood, riots broke out. Simple racism was a factor in such disturbances, as it was in opposition to busing generally. But to many busing opponents, such programs also compromised the integrity of the neighborhood and violated the tradition of locally run schools. Bostonians in the working-class Irish neighborhood of Southie, where the black students were bused, pointed out that the federal courts had ordered poor blacks bused into their neighborhoods rather than into the suburban neighborhoods of more affluent whites. They believed they were being used as guinea pigs in social experimentation. Politicians such as Wallace expressed their anger, castigating so-called "limousine liberals" (liberals who expected other people to enact their principles) and calling for an end to busing.

Affirmative Action. Many voters similarly resented affirmative-action programs. Taking note of historical patterns of racial discrimination, these programs required by law that businesses, public-service occupations, unions, and universities hire specific percentages of nonwhites. Many whites argued that affirmative action put them at a disadvantage when competing with nonwhites for regulated positions. In 1970, for example, 30 percent of all construction workers were occasionally unemployed, one third of those for more than four months. Under that kind of economic pressure, white construction workers became infuriated when the government forced construction companies and unions to meet hiring quotas of nonwhites. Politicians, notably Reagan and Wallace, tapped into this anger and argued that affirmative action was unfair. The federal courts were ambiguous on the matter: in the 1978 *Regents of the University of California* v. *Bakke* decision the Supreme Court ruled that while affirmative action was legal, setting quotas to achieve it was not.

Nixon and the Great Society. Nixon was also ambivalent about the Great Society. On one hand, he hoped to use governmental programs to redress social inequalities: he assigned funds for urban renewal and attempted an overhaul of the welfare system designed to guarantee the poorest Americans a minimum income. On the other hand, Nixon realized the political capital to be made by opposing the Great Society: he slashed Great Society programs, he attempted to abolish the Great Society's administrative agency, the Office of Economic Opportunity, and he went so far as to impound funds Congress had appropriated for social welfare — an act of questionable constitutionality. More dramatically, Nixon refused to enforce court-ordered desegregation, again on questionable constitutional grounds, and repeatedly voiced his opposition to busing. Nixon also blamed the Great Society for being a source of economic woe. These techniques worked, and in 1972 Nixon garnered much of his landslide from those Americans disgruntled with the Great Society.

Reagan and the Great Society. Presidents Ford and Carter failed to take political advantage of a growing backlash against the Great Society among working-class and middle-class white voters. With conservative political figures leading the drumbeat of criticism against the

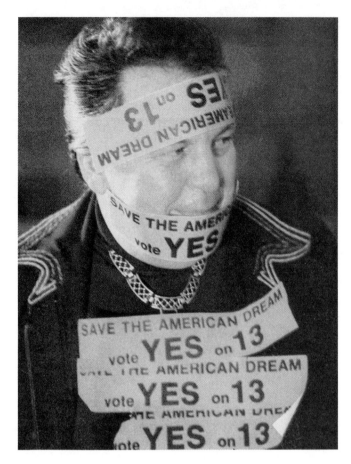

A supporter of the California referendum to roll back state taxes, 1976

Great Society, many voters blamed it for the economic dislocations of the 1970s. Carter, a moderate liberal, remained committed to the objectives of the Great Society, but, like Ford, he found himself trimming back its budget in an effort to control federal spending. Reagan, who outflanked both men on this issue, had a far simpler solution: abandon the Great Society altogether. On the strength of this position, as well as on a somewhat belligerent posture in foreign policy, Reagan led the neoconservative movement, the most significant political insurgency of the 1970s.

Proposition 13. Reagan represented conservatives who, since the days of Herbert Hoover, had argued that social programs create dependent individuals and undermine private-sector initiative. They were opposed to government spending for Social Security, Medicare, libraries, parks, and schools — programs that had the support of the majority of voters. On one hand, Reagan's anti–Great Society rhetoric had whittled away some of the support for these programs; on the other hand, conservatives attacked social spending by concealing their opposition to it in the form of a tax revolt. Led by Howard Jarvis, a retired California businessman, Republican conservatives attacked social programs by cutting off their tax funding. Downplaying their philosophical opposition to social spending, they argued that taxation was too high and government too inefficient. Cutting taxes, they argued, would force government to act more efficiently, but conservatives also understood that, with less revenue, government would be forced to cut the social programs they opposed. The tactic worked. In 1978 in California voters passed the ballot initiative Proposition 13, which cut California property taxes by 57 percent. Several states followed with proposals of their own, and in Congress a bill to cut taxes by one-third was introduced by Rep. Jack Kemp (R–New York) and Sen. William Roth (R–Delaware). Carter was forced to compromise the revenue act of 1978 and cut taxes for the wealthiest 2 percent of Americans. Many bills failed, including Kemp-Roth, but the tax revolt symbolized the first surfacing of growing conservative political strength.

The New Conservative Coalition. Since the New Deal, American politics had been dominated by a coalition of southern conservatives, northern liberals, blue-collar ethnic voters, and blacks, all uneasy cohorts within the Democratic party. In the 1970s the New Deal coalition fragmented, and a new conservative coalition, located in the Republican party, was born. It would come to dominate politics in the 1980s. The new conservative coalition drew strength from three sources: traditional conservatives, who backed Reagan throughout the 1970s and pushed Proposition 13; a new, politically active group of religious fundamentalists, especially evangelical Christians; and a small group of disenchanted former liberals and radicals known as neoconservatives, who formed the intellectual backbone of the conservative coalition.

Evangelicals and Neoconservatives. Unlike traditional conservatives, both the new religious Right and the neoconservatives formed in reaction to the 1960s. The evangelical Christians who organized the bulk of the new religious Right were led by ministers such as Jerry Falwell, a Virginia televangelist who created the conservative group Moral Majority in 1979. Shocked by the counterculture of the 1960s and the cultural permissiveness it inspired, wedded to Old Testament axioms of behavior, and stunned by the Supreme Court's 1973 *Roe* v. *Wade* decision legalizing abortion, Falwell and preachers like him used sophisticated advertising techniques and television ministries to turn his Christian congregations toward social activism. Increasingly, the religious Right was less concerned with personal salvation than with opposition to the Equal Rights Amendment, pornography, gay and women's liberation, humanistic school textbooks, and the candidacies of liberal Democrats. Similar concerns animated the more academic neoconservatives. Angered by the countercultural threat to the status quo, neoconservatives launched a broad repudiation, in the pages of journals such as *Commentary* and *National Review*, of liberal political and economic positions they had formerly embraced. They turned on the Great Society, demanded it be dismantled, and provided the intellectual justification for a new economic philosophy, "supply-side

Moral Majority leader Jerry Falwell and Phyllis Schlafly, head of the STOP ERA campaign, at an I Love America rally

economics," that sought to promote growth by providing tax breaks for the well-heeled. The fiscal and social proposals of conservatives, the religious Right, and the neoconservatives offered certainty during a decade when traditional political certainties — prosperity, equality of opportunity, America's preeminent place in the world — disappeared.

The End of the Great Society. The Great Society was the chief victim of such uncertainty. After the tax revolts and conservative victories of the 1978 elections, even liberal Democrats shifted to the Right, and Carter focused on balancing the federal budget by slashing the social programs of the Great Society. His actions anticipated those of Reagan in the 1980s — a shift of budget priorities from social spending to defense and the creation of massive federal deficits to be paid off by eliminating social programs. Sen. Edward Kennedy, an unabashed supporter of the Great Society, criticized Carter's turn to the Right. "The administration's budget," he complained, "asks the poor, the black, the sick, the young, the cities and the unemployed to bear a disproportionate share of the billions of dollars of reductions in Federal spending." Kennedy's complaints were in vain. The growing conservativism of Carter's agenda after 1978 anticipated the policies that would end the Great Society in the 1980s.

THE RETURN OF THE COLD WAR

Nixon Repudiated. As Nixon resigned the presidency in 1974, Kissinger told him that his foreign-policy achievements would assure him a positive place in history. The achievements seemed substantial: détente with the Soviet Union; the opening to China; withdrawal from Vietnam; a brokered peace in the Middle East. Already, however, Nixon's foreign policy had come under considerable fire, and by the end of the 1970s his policies appeared repudiated. Southeast Asia fell to communism, and détente with the Soviet Union was abandoned. Triangular diplomacy was dead, and the Cold War returned.

Attack from the Right. Members of Nixon's own party were the first to repudiate his foreign policy. Conservative Republicans, sensitive to defense issues and concerned with the country's standing among the world powers, were deeply shaken by the fall of South Vietnam to the Communists. Postwar reductions in defense spending increased their fear that the military posture of the United States was declining. The Soviet Union's continued violation of the civil liberties of Soviet dissidents, as well as their hostility toward the migration of Soviet Jews to Israel, convinced conservatives that the Soviets could not be trusted and that détente was a failure. By 1976 their criticism of Nixon's foreign policy became a campaign issue for Reagan, who was challenging Nixon's successor, Ford, for the Republican presidential nomination. Reagan seized upon symbolic issues, such as a proposed treaty turning the Panama Canal over to Panamanian ownership, as examples of the decline of American power. Although Reagan lost the nomination, and Ford lost the election, Republican criticism of foreign policy continued during the presidency of Carter$ICarter, Jimmy[Carter].

The Restoration of Congressional Authority. During the presidencies of Ford and Carter, Congress exercised a role in foreign policy it had not taken during Nixon's administration. Smarting from the inordinate power amassed by the executive branch during the Vietnam War, Congress reasserted its constitutional prerogative to help frame foreign policy. Hoping to assure that no president could again slowly escalate a war, as was done in Vietnam, in 1973 Congress passed the War Powers Act. The act required a president to get congressional authorization for any deployment of troops after a military operation has continued over ninety days. In 1975, exhausted by the interminable conflict in Southeast Asia, Congress refused to grant emergency military assistance to South Vietnam. Congress also launched a broad investigation into the operations of the Central Intelligence Agency (CIA) — an important foreign-policy bureau of the executive branch. Their investigations revealed widespread and sensational abuses of power — attempted assassinations of foreign leaders, illegal domestic activities such as wiretapping and mail surveillance. The investigations prompted renewed congressional oversight of CIA activities.

Human Rights under Carter. President Ford attempted to reassure conservatives that American power was sound, but even his May 1975 military retaliation against the Cambodian Communists who seized an American trawler, the *Mayaguez*, failed to convince them. President Carter tried a different approach. Casting the United States as the moral leader of the world, CarterCarter, Jimmy[Carter] placed human rights at the

U.S. TRADE, 1970-1979	
(In billions of dollars)	
1970	+2.7
1971	-2.0
1972	-6.4
1973	+1.3
1974	-4.51
1975	+9.1
1976	+8.3
1977	-29.2
1978	-31.1
1979	-27.6

Source: Statistical Abstract of the United States (Washington: U.S. Government Printing Office).

center of his foreign policy. Establishing a Bureau of Human Affairs at the State Department, Carter rejected Nixon and Kissinger's realpolitik approach to foreign policy and insisted that governments dealing with the United States respect basic human liberties. Initially, the policy satisfied both conservatives, who sought to punish the Soviet Union for violating the civil liberties of prominent dissidents such as physicist Andrey Sakharov, and idealists, who hoped the United States might force a change in the authoritarian policies of some developing nations. Eventually, however, human rights proved to be a difficult basis for foreign policy. Conflicts over human rights nearly scuttled disarmament talks between the United States and the Soviet Union. American negotiators were forced to choose between a foreign policy based upon the Soviet Union's treatment of its own citizens or one based upon reducing the possibility of nuclear confrontation between the two superpowers. It chose to reduce tension, the only politically tenable move. Similar choices confronted Carter in Africa, Asia, and Latin America. Eventually, the administration downplayed its human rights policy, but not before it became a permanent part of international relations, in the coming decade a more and more important component of world affairs.

Departures in Latin America. By 1976 relations between the United States and the Third World were at an all-time low. The war in Vietnam, American participation in the 1973 overthrow of Chilean president Salvador Allende, and the continuing refusal of Washington to consider the problems of Palestinian Arabs in Israel all contributed to anti-American sentiment in the Third World. Carter, the first president who spoke Spanish, set out to change the reputation of the United States in the Third World. Shortly after his inauguration he became the first president to visit sub-Saharan Africa and appointed black clergyman and civil rights activist Andrew Young as ambassador to the United Nations. Against heavy conservative opposition he secured Senate ratification of a treaty turning the Panama Canal over to Panamanian control by 1999. Most important, Carter gave limited support to the 1979 Sandinista revolution in Nicaragua, breaking a seventy-year record of American backing for authoritarian Latin American regimes. These initiatives had the effect of improving U.S. esteem, especially in the United Nations, but the forced resignation of Ambassador Young in 1979 (for unauthorized discussions with the Palestinians) and the resumption of American military aid to authoritarian regimes in Central America in 1980 signaled a return to strained relations with the Third World.

Peace in the Middle East. In the Middle East Carter expanded upon the peace initiatives begun by Kissinger. By 1978 President Anwar as-Sadat of Egypt and Prime Minister Menachem Begin of Israel had begun dramatic efforts to move their two nations toward peace, but discussions had stalled. Carter seized the moment and invited the two heads of state to the presidential retreat at Camp David, Maryland, in an effort to break the deadlock. After weeks of negotiations the leaders emerged with a "Framework for Peace in the Middle East." This agreement, commonly called the Camp David accords, was enacted in March 1979. Although much of the agreement was ambiguous and left crucial problems unresolved, the accords ended thirty years of war between Israel and Egypt and established a precedent for peace in the region.

Revolution in the Middle East. Carter's negotiating skills were less successful with the other Middle Eastern problem that developed at the end of the 1970s — a fundamentalist Islamic revolution which swept through the Middle East and resulted in the overthrow of the American-backed government in Iran. When Iranian nationalist Mohammad Mossadegh nationalized Western petrochemical interests in the early 1950s, the United States and Britain fomented a coup and replaced Mossadegh with the self-proclaimed heir to the Persian throne, Mohammad Reza Pahlavi, the shah of Iran. The shah, educated in the West, not only proved more acceptable than Mossadegh to petrochemical interests but became the chief ally in the Persian Gulf region. The shah purchased billions of dollars' worth of American arms and committed his country to a crash program in modernization — a program which by the 1970s had generated a political and cultural backlash led by Islamic

CARTER'S PURGE

Heads rolled. Following a politically disastrous summer filled with oil shortages, energy summits, and falling poll numbers, at the end of July 1979 President Jimmy Carter did the unexpected. He dished out blame, requesting the resignations of thirty-four Cabinet officers and top aides and firing those he deemed disloyal or ineffective. Gone were Secretary of Health, Education, and Welfare Joseph A. Califano, Jr.; Secretary of the Treasury Michael Blumenthal; Secretary of Energy James Schlesinger; Secretary of Transportation Brock Adams; and Attorney General Griffin Bell. The purge was sudden and heavy-handed. Newly elevated Chief of Staff Hamilton Jordan submitted a probing and humiliating thirty-question evaluation form to facilitate subcabinet ousters. The suddenness of the mass firing was reminiscent of the 1972 mass resignation of Richard Nixon's staff — a comparison Carter officials were loath to embrace, although public reaction to both the purges was similar. Gold surged on the international markets, passing three hundred dollars an ounce for the first time in history. Congress reacted with alarm and indignation. The target audience for the purge, however, was not Congress but the American people. Carter and his top aides hoped the resolute firing of the cabinet would restore confidence in Carter's leadership. Instead, once more, Carter was perceived as vacillating and inconsistent. In the end the affair was summed up best by an anonymous White House official: "We've burned down the house to roast the pig."

Source: *Time*, 114 (30 July 1979): pp. 10–16.

fundamentalists. In an effort to contain this backlash, the shah resorted to increasingly authoritarian measures but only succeeded in alienating his countrymen to the point of revolution. In 1979 he was overthrown and forced into exile, and a Muslim theocracy, led by the Ayatolla Ruholla Khomeini, assumed power. The U.S. embassy in the Iranian capital, Tehran, warned Carter that admitting the shah into the United States would precipitate a crisis with the new Iranian government, but the shah, ill with cancer, was admitted to a New York hospital on 23 October. A few days later, a mob of Iranian militants seized the U.S. embassy in Tehran, detained fifty-three members of the consulate as hostages, and demanded the extradition of the shah to Iran in return for the release of the hostages. President Carter refused to be blackmailed into extraditing the shah, who died of cancer in Panama the following year. Because the hostage taking violated diplomatic convention and international law, Carter was able to rally world opinion against Iran and impose an economic embargo. But he was unable to win release of the hostages, and a rescue attempt failed. Although popular opinion at first rallied behind Carter, as the crisis dragged on without resolution (lasting 444 days) many Americans concluded Carter was inept and irresolute. They demanded a military response, but Carter refused, afraid of jeopardizing the lives of the hostages and of inflaming the political instability in the Middle East. Coming after the 1979 oil crisis, the hostage taking fatally undermined Carter's presidency and became a major factor in his electoral defeat in 1980.

The Return of the Cold War. Carter's troubles with Iran were compounded by increasing Soviet-American rancor. At the beginning of his presidency Carter sought to continue the lessening of tensions begun by Nixon and Ford. SALT negotiations continued, and the SALT II treaty, placing ceilings on the development of strategic weapons, was signed by Carter and Soviet premier Leonid Brezhnev in 1979; triangular diplomacy also continued, and the United States formally recognized the People's Republic of China that same year. Initially, moreover, Carter adopted a conciliatory posture toward the Soviets, canceling production of the B-1 bomber and withholding approval of the new neutron bomb. These actions increased conservative criticism of Carter's foreign policy. They argued that continued Soviet suppression of dissenters and of Jews wishing to emigrate proved that the Soviets were untrustworthy; they pointed toward increasing Soviet intervention in Africa and urged that détente be scrapped. To appease conservatives, Carter endorsed increasing military expenditures even as he pursued détente. By 1979 he approved construction of the Trident submarine, authorized development of a new nuclear-powered aircraft carrier and the mobile MX missile, announced the deployment of strategic and cruise missiles in Europe, and required young American males to register for a potential draft. This aggressive stance became permanent policy following the Soviet invasion of Afghanistan at the end of December 1979. Some American policy makers suggested that the Soviets were attempting to prevent the type of fundamentalist Islamic revolution sweeping Iran from seizing power in another country bordering the Soviet Union; others ominously hinted that the Soviet Union was seeking to exploit the confusion in the area by pushing toward the Persian Gulf in order to seize Western oil and establish a Soviet warm-water port. Carter sided with those who believed the Soviets were driving toward the gulf. He withdrew SALT

"A DISORDERLY HILL"

For decades Congress had been a forum for party politics. Powerful party politicians, like Sam Rayburn or Lyndon Johnson, made national reputations for themselves by strong-arming congressmen and senators to vote the party line. In the 1970s that changed. As more and more voters registered independent or crossed party lines, congressional candidates relied less and less on the Democratic or Republican party to get elected, and they kept their independent perspective if they won. The Ninety-fifth Congress (1977—1979) was particularly independent. Disgusted with Watergate, voters turned dozens of incumbents out of office in 1974; twenty-six representatives and eight senators—a modern record—retired in 1976; 43 percent of representatives in the House were newcomers in 1978. These new members of both houses were young and outspoken, refusing to defer to the party system, congressional seniority, or the president. The new members of Congress made a virtue of their independence, arguing that they were more responsive to the needs of the constituents and diverse in their interests. Veterans of the hill, however, often criticized such individualism. Typical was the observation of Rep. John Anderson, Republican from Illinois: "A huge majority (in Congress) has to be under some type of discipline to be effective. If everybody says he is king of the hill, then it's going to be a disorderly hill."

Source: *Time*, 111 (28 January 1978): 8–16.

II from the Senate, embargoed grain sales to the Soviet Union, canceled U.S. participation in the 1980 Olympics in Moscow, announced that the Persian Gulf area was a vital American interest to be defended by military force, and issued a presidential directive making possible a first-strike nuclear attack on the Soviet Union. Détente was finished. Carter, who began his presidency with a shift in foreign policy away from superpower confrontation, ended his term in office by returning the United States to the Cold War.

HEADLINE MAKERS

EDMUND G. ("JERRY") BROWN, JR.

1938-

GOVERNOR OF CALIFORNIA, 1974-1982

Governor Moonbeam. A charismatic and controversial figure during the 1970s, Jerry Brown fused old-fashioned liberalism to an assimilated counterculture and offered some of the more unconventional departures in American politics during the 1970s. First elected California governor in 1974, Brown rode a wave of voter disgust with "politics as usual" into office; from there he used his position to advocate unusual politics. He urged Americans to "lower their expectations" and live sparingly; as governor he eliminated elaborate ceremonies and sought to simplify official language. He expressed the traditional liberal concern with the rights of minorities (especially migrant workers), but he attacked bureaucracy, high taxes, and elitist education. He inaugurated programs to utilize California's geothermal, solar, and wind power. His vocal opinions, willingness to argue abstractions (fluent in Latin and Greek, he had a predilection for the theologies of Jesuits and Zen Buddhists), propensity to propose odd programs (a state of California space academy, never passed), and unorthodox lifestyle (he was often accompanied in public by pop singer Linda Ronstadt) earned him the somewhat humorous nickname of Governor Moonbeam.

Electoral Reformer. The only son of former California governor Edmund G. ("Pat") Brown, Jerry Brown was born in San Francisco on 7 April 1938. Originally planning to become a Jesuit priest, Brown abandoned the seminary and graduated from Berkeley in 1961. He went on to Yale Law School, graduating in 1964, and set up a law practice in Los Angeles. In the late 1960s he began to be politically active, organizing migrant workers and antiwar groups. In 1970 he was elected secretary of state of California and used the office, traditionally limited in scope, to initiate highly publi-

cized suits for campaign-contribution violations against corporations such as Standard Oil and International Telephone and Telegraph. Brown's suits won him the acclaim of voters, and in 1974, without much help from his father's political allies, he won the gubernatorial race.

An Unorthodox Governor. As governor of California, Brown adopted some standard liberal positions, such as vetoing the death penalty (overridden), favoring the right to choose abortion, strengthening environmental regulation and conservation, and protecting the rights of migrant workers. He simultaneously made significant departures from traditional liberalism, such as favoring right-to-die legislation, urging an equal-wage law for California state employees, and adopting a heavy law-and-order stance. More important, his willingness to refuse the trappings of his office — canceling a raise for himself, refusing to ride in limousines, failing to occupy the governor's mansion — proved popular with voters, and by the 1976 presidential election Brown's California approval rating stood near 80 percent. Brown attempted to cash in on this popularity with a last-minute run at the Democratic presidential nomination, but he started too late, after Jimmy Carter

JAMES EARL ("JIMMY") CARTER, JR.

1924-

PRESIDENT OF THE UNITED STATES, 1977-1981

Between Past and Present. Perhaps the most representative figure of the decade, James Earl Carter, Jr. (he preferred to be called "Jimmy"), symbolized a new type of American politician, one who fused the traditional values of small-town America to the new global realities of the 1970s. "We must adjust to changing times and still hold to unchanging principles," he said in his inaugural address. The difficulties in accommodating old values to new realities, however, led to an often-uncertain and vacillating presidency. Ultimately Carter, like the nation itself, would choose to return to traditional values — even if they contradicted the facts of the modern global setting of the United States.

Small-Town Background. Jimmy Carter was born in Plains, Georgia, on 1 October 1924. His family had lived in southwest Georgia for generations. Carter grew up in a home steeped in traditions of hard work, temperance, fair dealing, and compassion for others. His father prospered as a farmer and grocer, even during the Depression. Eventually Carter would also become a successful peanut farmer and wholesaler, but as a boy he set his sights on a naval career. He entered Annapolis in 1943, graduating too late to see service in World War II but in time to begin service in the newly born nuclear-submarine fleet. From his service Carter became a detail-minded and disciplined problem solver and put these traits to work when he took over his father's business in 1953. His success in agriculture led to his involvement in public life. He ran for the Georgia state Senate in 1962 and was defeated. Suspecting vote fraud in the election, he challenged the balloting in court and among the Democratic party hierarchy; he won, and in 1964 he aided a voting-reform law through the state house. His tenacity resurfaced following his 1966 defeat by Lester Maddox for governor of Georgia. He immediately began running for governor in 1970, giving over eighteen hundred speeches and campaigning endlessly. He finally won the office of governor in 1970, and the triumph set the stage for his national ambitions.

Progressive Traditionalist. Carter's movement into national politics seemed natural for a man of his talents and abilities. His tenacity and discipline drove him from virtual obscurity to national attention before his four-year term as governor expired. His fiscal conservatism linked him to traditional southern Democrats, but his racial moderation and support among poor blacks marked him as a visible representative of the "New South" — one coming to terms with the new desegregated regional order. Notwithstanding these characteristics, it was Carter's personal earnestness and morality — rooted in a complex mix of academic theology and evangelical Christianity — that generated the most interest from voters. After Richard Nixon, Carter seemed reassuring; his liberal stance on issues of race, public assistance, and the environment gave him the appearance of personal flexibility, especially when compared to the fixity of politicians such as George Wallace, Ronald Reagan, and Gerald Ford. Carter cultivated this ambiguous image. As a national political figure he was often noncommittal on divisive public issues like busing and abortion. Carter's opponents often accused him of duplicity, but Carter's tendency to elude easy political categorization (he called his approach "enlightened conservatism") was characteristic. As president he would also pursue policies that ranged from traditional to progressive.

From Innovation to Conservatism. During Carter's years as president he moved from innovation to traditionalism; like the public, he seemed to tire of liberal reform and moved toward conservatism. He began his tenure with a host of symbolic departures from political tradition. He chose to walk rather than ride in a limousine during the inaugural parade, demonstrating his willingness to turn the presidency away from the imperial mode of the Nixon years. As he had campaigned as a governmental outsider, he pressed for wide reforms in the governing process: the White House staff was cut by a third; cabinet officers were required to drive their own cars to work; ethics regulations regarding the relationship of government officials and big business were tightened. He canceled nineteen pork barrels (government projects), struggled to develop a new national energy policy, and placed expensive Pentagon weapon developments on hold. He promised new departures in foreign policy, especially an emphasis on human rights and an improved relationship with developing nations. On his first day in office he offered a "full, complete, and unconditional pardon" to Vietnam War draft resisters. Carter offered these innovations as a corrective to the distortions of the democratic process that had come with the country's imperial position in the postwar world and as techniques to deal with its new, less powerful, less dominating position in world affairs. As welcome as these overtures were in some quarters, however, many Americans reacted with hostility. Conservatives led the criticism of Carter's foreign and domestic policy. Barry Goldwater, for example, called the Vietnam amnesty, "the most disgraceful thing a president has ever done." Carter's reputation was further compromised by rumors that members of his staff acted inappropriately on social occasions. Questions were raised regarding drug use among Carter's staff and financial improprieties by associates and members of his family. At times Carter seemed unable to direct his unusually independent subordinates or influence the Democratic Congress to pass his legislation. In 1978 conservatives parlayed their criticism of Carter into victory in the congressional elections. Sensing the mood in the electorate, Carter shifted toward a more conservative approach, but he still could not withstand the challenge of Reagan and the new Right. They offered traditionalism unalloyed by Carter's ambiguities. In 1980 Carter lost his campaign for reelection.

Citizen Carter. Throughout the 1980s Carter acted as a hands-on philanthropist, sponsoring housing for the poor and promoting world peace. Following the 1992 election of fellow Democrat Bill Clinton to the presidency, Carter assumed the role of elder statesman and experienced diplomat. In 1994 he aided the Clinton administration by negotiating with a volatile and threatening North Korea. It was a remarkable political comeback. When Carter left the presidency he was reviled by many as incompetent and weak, and he was intensely disliked by many citizens. By the 1990s, however, many Americans had changed their opinion of Carter. In retrospect many believed he had governed according to an ethical standard far higher than subsequent presidents; his intelligence and honesty once more became prized. Like Ford, Carter set the highest standard of personal conduct in a period of American history characterized by political dishonesty.

Source:

James Wooten, *Dasher: The Roots and Rising of Jimmy Carter* (New York: Summit Books, 1978).

FRANK CHURCH

1924-1984

SENATOR FROM IDAHO

A Steady Investigator. In a decade filled with congressional investigations, those conducted by Idaho senator Frank Church produced some of the most sensational and scandalous revelations. In 1973, as chairman of the Senate Foreign Relations Committee's subcommittee on multinational corporations, Church exposed the bribery of foreign officials by American companies and revealed the attempt by International Telephone and Telegraph to finance opposition to Marxist candidate Salvador Allende in the Chilean presidential elections of 1970. In 1975, as chairman of the Senate Select Committee to Study Government Operations With Respect to Intelligence Activities, he uncovered widespread abuses of power and illegal surveillance activities by the CIA, FBI, and NSA. Church's activities inspired reevaluations by the House of Representatives of the assassinations of John F. Kennedy and Martin Luther King, Jr., that later concluded that there were possible conspiracies in both killings. Church's investigations brought to light some of the most subterranean activities of the U.S. government.

Background. The grandson of an Idaho pioneer, Frank Church was born in Boise on 25 July 1924. His talent as an orator earned him a scholarship to Stanford University, but he interrupted his college career for service as an intelligence officer in World War II. After the war he finished his degree and enrolled in Harvard Law School in 1947, only to have his education once more halted by a bout with cancer, diagnosed as terminal. X-ray treatments and surgery saved his life, however, and he finished his law school education at Stanford, taking up practice in Boise. Although defeated in a 1952 bid for the state legislature, Church beat incumbent Sen. Herman Welker in 1956 and continued to be reelected. Church was an unusual senator from the normally conservative and Republican state. An unabashed liberal Democrat, Church favored civil rights, social welfare, health insur-

ance, education reform, and the minimum wage. He balanced his support for environmental legislation and conservation (opposed by Idaho's mining and timber interests) with continued support and delivery of water projects to Idaho, including the Bruces Eddy dam and the Snake River reservoir.

Vietnam War Opponent. Church first rose to national attention as an early opponent of American involvement in the Vietnam War. As early as 1963 he urged the government not to alienate developing nations by supporting unpopular dictators, as the United States was doing by supporting Ngo Dinh Diem in South Vietnam. In 1965 Church called for direct negotiations with the Vietnamese Communists; in 1966 he was among fifteen Democratic senators who sent a letter to President Johnson opposing the war. Following the invasion of Cambodia in 1970, Church, along with Sen. John S. Cooper (R–Kentucky), proposed a bill which would have prohibited funds for American troops in Cambodia and forced their withdrawal. Later, Church would introduce other proposals, all defeated, with the same object in mind — ending the war by cutting off its funding. Apprehensive about the increasing power of the president to conduct foreign policy without consulting Congress, Church was also instrumental in paring military appropriations and in passing the 1973 War Powers Act, designed to limit the ability of future presidents to engage the military in long-term combat without a congressional declaration of war.

Intelligence Investigations. Church's leadership of Senate committees investigating intelligence operations was an extension of his efforts to reassert constitutional limitations on the power of the presidency. His inquiries uncovered fantastic abuses of power: plots to assassinate foreign leaders, such as Fidel Castro of Cuba and Patrice Lumumba of the Congo; active participation in military coups against leaders such as Salvador Allende, Raphael Trujillo, and Ngo Dinh Diem; the hiring of mafia hit men to assassinate foreign leaders; domestic surveillance of Martin Luther King, Jr., Adlai Stevenson, and Supreme Court justice William O. Douglas; routine violations of basic rights of privacy via wiretapping, illegal inspection of mail, and interception of cables; harassment of political dissidents by the IRS; the stockpiling of biological weapons and other poisons; secret experiments with LSD and other drugs on unwitting subjects. To correct such abuses, the Church committee recommended a renewed role for Congress in foreign affairs and closer oversight by Congress of intelligence activities. Church parlayed his visibility into a last-minute run for the 1976 Democratic presidential nomination, too late to do any real damage to Jimmy Carter's prospects for nomination. He endorsed the Georgia governor, and after Carter was elected president, Church became one of his key Senate backers, crucial in helping pass the Panama Canal Treaty. In 1980 Church was defeated for reelection by conservatives who had targeted his seat in the Senate. He died of cancer in 1984.

Source:
Loch K. Johnson, *A Season of Inquiry: The Senate Intelligence Investigation* (Lexington: University of Kentucky Press, 1985).

SHIRLEY CHISHOLM

1924-

REPRESENTATIVE FROM NEW YORK

"Fighting Shirley Chisholm." The first African-American woman ever to sit in the U.S. Congress, "Fighting Shirley Chisholm," as she liked to be called, established herself as a vocal defender of women and the poor. Articulate and energetic, she gained national recognition for her efforts, and in 1972 she launched a failed campaign for the Democratic nomination for president.

Life and Background. Born in Brooklyn, New York, on 30 November 1924, Shirley Anita St. Hill grew up on the farm of her maternal grandmother in Barbados. At age eleven she returned to Brooklyn with her parents and graduated cum laude from Brooklyn College. She went on to earn a master's degree from Columbia University and in 1949 married Conrad Chisholm, a New York City government official. She gained valuable governmental experience as director of New York's child-care centers, and in 1964 she won election to the New York State Assembly. In 1968 she defeated Republican representative James Farmer for the congressional seat from Brooklyn's Bedford-Stuyvesant district.

Candidate Chisholm. As a congresswoman Chisholm quickly established herself as a independent-minded activist. She snubbed party leaders by rejecting freshman appointments to House subcommittees dealing with timber and agriculture because she represented a constituency of urban laborers. She was an outspoken critic of the Vietnam War and of racial discrimination. Although her 1972 campaign for the presidency was a longshot (her best showing in the primaries, in Florida, gained only 4 percent of the vote), Chisholm proved popular among women and the poor, and she achieved her goal of keeping the presidential campaign from becoming an exclusively "white, male decision." Returning to Congress, Shirley Chisholm once more took up the banner of reform. "I am, was, and always will be a catalyst for change."

Source:
Shirley Chisholm, *Unbought and Unbossed* (Boston: Houghton Mifflin, 1970).

SAMUEL J. ERVIN, JR.

1896-1985

CHAIRMAN OF THE WATERGATE COMMITTEE; SENATOR FROM NORTH CAROLINA

A Watergate Celebrity. One of the most colorful figures to emerge from the Watergate affair, Sen. Sam Ervin (D–North Carolina) became nationally acclaimed for his deft management of the Senate Select Committee to Investigate Presidential Campaign Practices (commonly referred to as the Watergate committee or the Ervin committee). His leadership, visible to millions daily during the televised Watergate proceedings, seemed to exemplify the best in American politics: fairness, honesty, a passion for truth, and a reverence for the Constitution. By the end of summer 1973, he had become an American folk hero, and "Uncle Sam" fan clubs, complete with T-shirts and buttons featuring Ervin, appeared around the country.

Reluctant Politician. The son of a Morganton, North Carolina, lawyer, Ervin grew up memorizing the King James Bible, Shakespeare, and the Constitution; to his father, descendant of Scots-Presbyterian stock, such an education was essential in a democracy. Sam Ervin followed his father into law, graduating from the University of North Carolina in 1917. In the army during World War I, he was awarded the Purple Heart, Silver Star, and Distinguished Service Cross. Following the war, Ervin attended Harvard Law School, graduating in 1922. He married Margaret Bruce Bell in 1924 and, like his father, settled down to practice law in Morganton. Ervin served three terms in the North Carolina state assembly (once helping to defeat a bill to ban the teaching of evolution), but his aspirations were judicial, not political. He became Burke County judge in 1935 and a justice on the North Carolina Supreme Court in 1948. In 1946 he served a brief term as a representative to Congress, a spot he assumed following the death of his brother, who had been elected to the office. In 1954 Ervin again assumed political office following the death of a sitting official — in this case the U.S. senator Clyde R. Hoey. Ever reluctant to campaign, but enormously popular with his constituents, Ervin remained in the Senate, acquiring a reputation as a foe of what he believed to be a governmentally-imposed civil rights movement.

Partisan of Due Process. Ervin's sound but unspectacular record as a senator changed with the election of Richard Nixon to the presidency in 1968. As chairman of the Constitutional Rights Subcommittee, Ervin found himself as the Senate's chief opponent to several Nixonian programs designed to increase the police powers of the federal government. He opposed Nixon's attempt to reactivate the Subversive Activities Control Board and attacked Nixon's effort to impound funds earmarked by Congress for programs Nixon opposed. Nixon's 1970 anticrime bill, granting the police sweeping powers to investigate and prosecute suspects, earned Ervin's scorn. He denounced the bill as a "blueprint for a police state" and called it "a garbage pail of the most repressive, nearsighted, intolerant, unfair and vindictive legislation that the Senate has ever been presented."

Ervin versus the President's Men. Ervin's opposition to Nixon's expansion of police powers was based on his deeply felt antipathy toward coercive government and his belief in the inalienable rights of the individual. Like Nixon, Ervin was a hawk on Vietnam and did not look sympathetically on protesters in the streets. Nonetheless, to Ervin the capacity of government in a computer age to undermine personal freedom was great, and he increasingly felt compelled to take a visible stance against potential abuses of power, even if, as many in the Nixon administration argued, they were undertaken to restore order. To millions of the television viewers watching the Watergate hearings, Ervin's insistence that the means of governmental power must be commensurate with the end of democracy and that the Constitution must be obeyed in spirit and letter placed the ethics of the young, ambitious, and unprincipled Nixon administration officials who appeared before his committee in sharp and unfavorable relief. To many Americans Ervin became the guardian of Jeffersonian democracy, the embodiment of a national principle Ervin articulated in 1971: "No one man and no one executive department should have the absolute power to order government spying on how people use their right of free speech. This is what we mean by a government of laws and not of men." Ervin retired from the Senate in 1975; he died in 1985 at the age of 88.

Source:
Paul R. Clancy, *Just a Country Lawyer: A Biography of Senator Sam Ervin* (Bloomington: Indiana University Press, 1974).

GERALD R. FORD, JR.

1913-

PRESIDENT OF THE UNITED STATES, 1974-1977

The Accidental President. When Gerald Ford became president on 9 August 1974, a unique and perhaps unimaginable series of circumstances brought him to the office. In the wake of the Kennedy assassination, the Twenty-fifth Amendment to the Constitution was ratified in 1967, changing the constitutional order of presidential succession. Prior to the amendment, the office of vice-president stood vacant if, as in the case of Lyndon Johnson, the vice-president became president. The Twenty-fifth Amendment allowed the president to appoint, with the approval of Congress, a new vice-president. The amendment was passed with the death or disability of the president or vice-president in mind; few imagined that the first use of the law would be to replace a vice-president under criminal indictment — especially if that vice-president were Spiro Agnew, renowned for his tough law-and-order speeches. Nonetheless, in 1973, facing prison terms for racketeering and bribery, Agnew resigned the vice-presidency in return for the dismissal of most criminal charges. When Richard Nixon nominated Ford to replace Agnew under the Twenty-fifth Amendment, even fewer imagined that Nixon, who won one of the greatest electoral victories in American history in 1972, would also be forced from office for criminal misdeeds. Yet in 1974 Nixon resigned, and Gerald Ford became the thirty-eighth president of the United States, the only man to become president without being elected to the office of president or vice-president.

Life and Background. Ford's background and life made him the quintessential midwestern American president. Born in Omaha, Nebraska, on 14 July 1913, Ford's parents divorced when he was an infant, and his mother resettled in Grand Rapids, Michigan, marrying Gerald R. Ford, a paint and varnish salesman. Given the name of his adoptive and beloved stepfather, Ford grew up in a household animated by honesty and hard work — values that would become crucial to Ford's reputation as a politician. He was an excellent athlete, in 1934 voted the most valuable player for the University of Michigan football team. Graduating the next year, Ford went on to Yale Law School, supporting himself by working as an assistant football coach. Returning to Grand Rapids just before World War II, Ford opened a law practice but quit to enlist in the navy, in which he served as an officer for forty-seven months. Following the war he returned to Grand Rapids and married Elizabeth ("Betty") Bloomer, a professional dancer and model. He began his political career in 1948, winning election to the House as representative for Michigan's fifth district. In Congress he earned a reputation as a hard worker with a spotless personal record and moderately conservative politics. Declining the 1964 vice-presidential slot, he served on the Warren Commission investigating the assassination of John F. Kennedy, and in 1965 he replaced Charles A. Halleck as House minority leader. Ford was chairman of the Republican National Convention when Nixon was nominated for president in 1968.

Accession to the Presidency. Ford's 1973 nomination for the vice-presidency came as a surprise to him, as he was contemplating retirement from public life. In his years in Congress, however, he had earned bipartisan respect and trust and was a shoo-in for the nomination. As vice-president he shepherded that trust by keeping himself at a distance from Watergate. Upon becoming president he quickly demonstrated the personal traits that earned him such respect and trust in Congress to a public unfamiliar with him. His disarming modesty — "I am a

Ford, not a Lincoln," he said in his first speech as president — and his common bearing restored a degree of public confidence in the presidency lost with Watergate. That confidence evaporated when Ford pardoned Nixon on 8 September 1974 for any crimes he might have committed. The pardon was so widely considered to be part of a secret deal between Ford and Nixon that Ford would have to testify before a congressional subcommittee to dispel the rumors. It would not help. Almost overnight Ford's approval rating dropped twenty-two points, and public disapproval of the pardon was later considered by many to be the cause of Ford's defeat in the election of 1976.

896 Days. As president, Ford's brief period in office— 896 days — was too short for any major initiatives, but he acted firmly to build upon the positive achievements of the Nixon administration. He extended détente with the Soviets and courted peace with the Chinese Communists; he made an effort to wean the United States from its dependency on foreign oil. Like Nixon, Ford was sorely challenged by runaway inflation, economic stagnation, and unemployment. Unlike Nixon, Ford returned to traditional Republican solutions, especially spending cuts and higher interest rates, which reduced inflation but sparked the worst recession since the Great Depression. By 1976 the recession had bottomed out, and the economy was rebounding, but it was too late for Ford to gain any real political benefit from the recovery.

Solid Service. None of Ford's policies as president are as important as the character he brought to the office. Ford was steady, solid, and trustworthy. He restored amicable relations between the executive office and the legislature after the combativeness of the Watergate period. Many Americans joined incoming president Jimmy Carter, who, during his inaugural address, thanked Ford for moving the country beyond Watergate. "For myself and for our nation," Carter said, "I want to thank my predecessor for all he has done to heal our land."

Sources:
James Cannon, *Time and Chance: Gerald Ford's Appointment with History* (New York: HarperCollins, 1994);

Time, 102 (22 October 1973): 15–18.

HENRY KISSINGER

1923-

NATIONAL SECURITY ADVISER, 1969-1975; SECRETARY OF STATE, 1973-1976

A Flamboyant Figure. Widely acknowledged as the most influential foreign-policy figure in the 1970s, Henry Kissinger's career in diplomacy was marked by surprising initiatives, sudden announcements, and secret negotiations. His high visibility made him a celebrity; before he married Nancy Maginnes in 1974 he had a reputation as a playboy, followed by both the press and the paparazzi. His flamboyance often led to tensions between him and the two presidents he served, but his presence provided vital continuity between the Nixon and Ford administrations.

A Scholarly Background. Born in Fürth, Germany, on 27 May 1923, Kissinger and his parents fled the Nazis and immigrated to New York City in 1938. He earned his bachelor's, master's, and doctorate degrees from Harvard and stayed on there as a political scientist and member of the Center for International Affairs. An early book, *Nuclear Weapons and Foreign Policy* (1958), earned him a national reputation on defense issues and foreign policy. A devotee of balance-of-power theories, Kissinger was one of the first to argue that nuclear weapons made large-scale warfare between great nation-states obsolete. He held that the United States could best demonstrate its power not through direct confrontation with the Soviet Union, but through credible displays of conventional military power in Third World theaters of action. Kissinger maintained that a realpolitik, not moralistic, approach to foreign affairs would best serve American interests, and he developed sophisticated methods of conflict resolution and negotiation.

Association with Nixon. Originally associated with New York governor Nelson Rockefeller, in 1968 Kissinger joined Richard Nixon's presidential campaign as a foreign-policy consultant. Following the election, Nixon appointed him National Security Adviser. It was to Kissinger, not Secretary of State William Rogers, that Nixon turned for foreign policy. The two developed a complex, difficult relationship, but they shared many qualities: a flair for the dramatic, contempt for others, a mania for secrecy. Together they framed the major policy initiatives of Nixon's first term: the Cambodian bombing and invasion, the SALT accords, the opening to China, the Vietnam peace (for which Kissinger won a Nobel Prize). They developed a grudging admiration for one another that became increasingly important as Watergate crippled Nixon's presidency. In the final days of Nixon's administration Kissinger became Nixon's confidant and sounding board, easing him out of the office. As the only high administration figure untainted by Watergate, he was also a key link to the incoming Ford administration.

Shuttle Diplomacy. At the end of Nixon's tenure and under Ford, Kissinger increasingly focused his attentions on the Middle East. His highly personal approach to negotiations was designed to increase confidence on all sides of the Arab-Israeli dispute and resulted in his shuttling by air from capital to capital. By October 1974 Kissinger had traveled 130,000 miles on eight Middle Eastern trips and had succeeded in creating a viable framework for peace. Cease-fires and troop disengagements were accepted, diplomatic relations between the United States and Egypt were restored for the first time since 1967, and Palestinian demands for autonomy were debated. Kissinger's personal approach to diplomacy, however, generated friction with Congress, reasserting its foreign-policy role in the wake of the Vietnam War, and by 1975 Kissinger was embroiled in controversies over détente with the Soviet Union, the Cypriot civil war, and the Panama Canal Treaty. To deflect criticism of Kissinger, Ford eased him out of his dual role as both secretary of state and national security adviser and made him only secretary of state.

Place in History. After Ford's defeat in 1976, Kissinger returned to private life, acting as a high-powered consultant to multinational corporations. He routinely appeared on television as a commentator on political affairs. His achievements in office seemed repudiated by the foreign policies of the next two presidential administrations. Kissinger nonetheless seems secure in history as one of the first American political figures who recognized the limits of American power and sought to build a realistic and secure foreign policy around those limitations.

Sources:
Walter Issacson, *Kissinger* (New York: Simon & Schuster, 1992);

Marvin Kalb and Bernard Kalb, *Kissinger* (Boston: Little, Brown, 1974).

GEORGE MCGOVERN

1922-

DEMOCRATIC CANDIDATE FOR PRESIDENT, 1972

Small-Town Background. The 1972 Democratic nominee for president, George McGovern, distinguished himself through his calls for a new morality in politics and through his sincerity and integrity. These qualities derived from his South Dakota youth. Son of a coal miner turned Methodist preacher, McGovern had grown up with a strong family life in the small town of Mitchell, an agricultural community. Educated at Dakota Wesleyan, McGovern served in World War II as a B-24 pilot, winning the Distinguished Service Flying Cross. After the war he earned a doctorate in American history at Northwestern and returned to South Dakota determined to break the hold the Republican party had on the state's politics. Elected to the House of Representatives in 1957, he was the author and director of John F. Kennedy's Food for Peace program. Moving to the Senate in 1962, he became an early opponent of the Vietnam War, his attacks all the more successful because of his reputation for honesty.

The Youth Candidate. McGovern called the Vietnam War "a moral and political disaster — a terrible cancer eating away the soul of the nation." That perspective made McGovern the inheritor of Eugene McCarthy's 1968 political crusade against the war, and in 1972 many of the same student volunteers who aided McCarthy backed McGovern — this time with the added clout of the Twenty-sixth Amendment, which lowered the voting age to eighteen. McGovern tailored his 1972 campaign to this core group: he condemned the government as the servant of militarists and big business; he proposed a guaranteed minimum income for all Americans; he favored an amnesty for Vietnam War resisters; he was for integration, busing, and an end to criminal penalties for marijuana possession. These ideas generated enthusiasm among his followers but failed to resonate with the larger population. With the war in Vietnam winding down, McGovern's antiwar stance seemed incidental; as McGovern cast about for a wider constituency and for broader issues, his reputation for honesty and sincerity became tarnished. He lost the 1972 election by one of the largest margins in U.S. history, winning only the electoral votes of Massachusetts and Washington, D.C.

Impact on American Politics. Even with his defeat, McGovern's impact on American politics was substantial. His emphasis on personal character and morality became central to presidential politics. In the wake of Watergate McGovern's campaign speeches about Nixon's questionable character seemed wise and insightful to a disappointed electorate. And the next presidential election would be won by a Democratic candidate from a small-town, agricultural background, who echoed McGovern's call for morality and honesty in politics: James Earl ("Jimmy") Carter, Jr.

Sources:
Robert Sam Anson, *McGovern: A Biography* (New York: Holt, Rinehart & Winston, 1972);

George McGovern, *Grassroots* (New York: Random House, 1977).

RICHARD M. NIXON

1913-1994

PRESIDENT OF THE UNITED STATES, 1969-1974

Nixon and His Enemies. As Richard Nixon resigned the presidency in 1974, he left the public with a bit of advice. Speaking to his staff, Nixon said, "Always give your best, never get discouraged, never be petty; always remember, others may hate you, but those who hate you don't win unless you hate them — and then you destroy yourself." Ironically, Nixon's downfall was partially precipitated by his own pettiness, by his tendency to despise and hate his own enemies. At times, Nixon seemed to go out of his way to create enemies.

A Humble Background. A certain amount of Nixon's antagonistic character perhaps stemmed from his difficult upbringing. Born in 1913 in Yorba Linda, California, he was raised there and in the nearby agricultural community of Whittier. His father was a hardworking converted

Quaker who failed with a citrus grove and then worked tirelessly to eke out a living as a small grocer and gas-station manager. Frank Nixon nurtured a burning anger toward his wife and her family, good Quakers who believed that Hannah Milhous had married beneath her. She passed her social ambitions on to her son, especially after two of her brothers died; Hannah Nixon believed that Richard tried hard to compensate for the loss. He indeed worked as hard as three men, establishing a good academic record; Ivy League schools offered him admissions interviews. Nixon, needed by his family at home, attended nearby Whittier College instead, and he proved himself as sensitive to social slights as his father: when an elite fraternity turned him down, Nixon organized his own fraternity and was elected student-body president. His drive and ambition distinguished him at Duke Law School, but lacking an elite pedigree, Nixon failed to get a job with any of the prestigious East Coast law firms he solicited. Disappointed, Nixon returned to Whittier; married a young schoolteacher, Pat Ryan; enlisted in the navy during World War II; and returned home after the war with political ambitions.

The Forgotten Man and the Eastern Establishment. From the beginning of his political career in 1946, Nixon harnessed his disappointments and resentments for electoral advantage. He portrayed himself as the champion of the common man, humble, hardworking, patriotic, somewhat contemptuous of the elitist and the flamboyant. Nixon also proved to have a real instinct to go for the jugular: although he knew little about communism, he used the emerging anti-Communist hysteria to political advantage and insinuated that his political opponents were Communist sympathizers. He became a national political star when he insisted that a former State Department official, Alger Hiss, was a Soviet spy. Hiss, the product of an Ivy League education and member of the East Coast establishment which had slighted Nixon years before, was precisely the type of political figure Nixon instinctively disliked. Nixon hounded him mercilessly and contributed to Hiss's conviction on a perjury charge. The Hiss affair and Nixon's incessant red-baiting earned him the enmity of many, but right-wing Republican conservatives loved him and succeeded in making him Eisenhower's vice-president.

Hard Work versus Kennedy. As vice-president Nixon distinguished himself in two ways: hard work, especially in foreign affairs, and relentless, partisan attacks against the Democratic opposition, especially two-time presidential candidate Adlai Stevenson, the type of mannered intellectual Nixon always disdained. Nixon gained real visibility and experience as vice-president, and he was easily the front-runner in the 1960 presidential campaign. John F. Kennedy's victory over him was a crushing blow for various deep-seated reasons. Kennedy represented much that Nixon resented: glamour, wealth, good education, an ease with people for which Nixon always strived but never achieved. Kennedy's senatorial record was mediocre; he had a reputation as a playboy and dilettante. Nixon had worked tirelessly to improve himself, to build experience and a strong record; to him Kennedy's victory was a triumph of style over substance. He blamed television and the press, which he felt had slighted him. He harbored a deep suspicion of the outcome, the narrowest victory in American history. Nixon speculated that Kennedy and Democratic politicians had stolen the election from him; he vowed to use whatever means, legal or illegal, to win in the future. One more defeat, however, was ahead. He lost a 1962 California gubernatorial run against Democrat Pat Brown, blamed the press, and lashed out against them in an angry "last" postelection press conference. His political career seemed over.

A Remarkable Comeback. Following the 1962 campaign, Nixon briefly tried private law. Politics, however, was in his blood, and he soon returned to grassroots fund-raising, endlessly touring the Republican speaking circuit and building support for a 1968 run for the presidency. He made a remarkable comeback and won his party's nomination. In the general election against Democrat Hubert Humphrey, he waged a strong law-and-order campaign, part of a broader strategy of wooing disaffected blue-collar Democrats. After watching an early lead disintegrate, he won, but by a slim margin. Nevertheless, by age fifty-five Nixon had achieved the office he had so ardently sought — but in a nation badly divided by the war in Vietnam and by cultural and generational conflict, a nation unlikely to be easily reunified.

Confrontation. In victory Nixon promised the American people to "bring us together," but conciliation was not part of his character. Confrontation suited Nixon. As president he was determined to silence dissent, crush his opponents, and settle old scores. Harboring resentments against the East Coast elite, Nixon sought to purge them from their positions in government, and he forbade his staff to hire Ivy Leaguers. In speeches he and Vice-president Spiro Agnew excoriated intellectuals as "nattering nabobs of negativism"; he sought to humble the press and threatened unfriendly television executives with loss of their Federal Communications Commission licenses. There was not enough power, even in the White House, to get done what he wanted. He reorganized the executive branch several times, concentrating power among an exclusive inner circle; when the FBI and other government agencies were unable to attack dissent as effectively as he liked, Nixon organized his own extralegal operations against the antiwar movement and political opponents. He developed lists of enemies and established a hierarchy of punishments to use against them. He believed the nation was gravely imperiled by the radicalism stemming from the Vietnam War protests and the counterculture; to him that peril sanctioned virtually any presidential operation. A siege mentality gripped Nixon and his inner circle, and they began to view the future of the nation as dependent upon Nixon's personal leadership. In the 1972 presidential election they sought absolute victory — not simply the defeat of Democrat George McGovern but his total humiliation. Nixon and his circle got what they wanted, but by using a host of illegal and unethical techniques that were revealed during the Watergate scandals. Nixon's ruthlessness and his unprincipled willingness to destroy and humiliate his opponents became public knowledge with the publication of the Watergate transcripts, and these revelations disgusted the American people. When he resigned the presidency in 1974, he was, without a doubt, one of the most reviled figures in the United States.

Another Remarkable Comeback. Nixon suffered the greatest humiliation in U.S. history: he was the first president to resign the office. The defeat was doubly crushing for Nixon because he destroyed himself. He could have easily won the 1972 election without the skulduggery; his own paranoid need to protect himself with secret tapes gave his enemies the tools to undermine him. Had Nixon been slightly less ruthless with his opponents, they might have been less ruthless with him. Despite a career in politics championing the common man, Nixon's own distrust of the American people prevented him from being frank with them, and this need for secrecy, more than any other characteristic, was the most damaging aspect of the Watergate affair. Remarkably, for the remainder of his life Nixon worked at regaining the confidence of the public. He orchestrated another amazing political comeback and by the end of the 1980s earned a reputation as an elder statesman. When he died in 1994, his funeral was an informal state occasion, attended by the current president, former presidents, and diplomats from around the world. It was a tribute to a man who once remarked that all he wanted for his life was one more triumph than defeat.

Sources:

Stephen E. Ambrose, *Nixon*, 3 volumes (New York: Simon & Schuster, 1987–1991);

Garry Wills, *Nixon Agonistes: The Crisis of the Self-Made Man* (Boston: Houghton Mifflin, 1970);

Wills, "Nixon In Heaven," *Esquire*, 122 (July 1994): 39–43.

GEORGE C. WALLACE, JR.

1919-

GOVERNOR OF ALABAMA; PRESIDENTIAL CANDIDATE

Fashioning a Conservative Electorate. Earlier than any other political figure, George Wallace recognized the ideological shift in American voters — especially blue-collar Democrats — that would eventually vault Ronald Reagan to the presidency in 1980. A gritty southern populist,

Wallace tapped into the resentments of an electorate sick of the cultural revolutions of the 1960s, opposed to governmental power, and determined to reassert old-fashioned verities in a volatile age. Every winning presidential candidate from 1968 to 1984 built upon the conservative electorate Wallace first fashioned as his own; Wallace's inability to use this voting base to become president in his own right exemplifies the limits of his political abilities.

Standing in the University Doorway. Born in Clio, Alabama, on 25 August 1919, Wallace received a law degree from the University of Alabama and then joined the military. After World War II he began a political career that took him from assistant attorney general of Alabama (1946–1947) to governor of Alabama (1963–1967, 1970–1978, 1983–1987). He achieved national prominence in 1963, when he stood in the entrance to the University of Alabama and defied President John F. Kennedy's order to integrate the school. He quickly became known as an opponent of federal power and of liberalism. In 1968, running as an independent candidate for president, Wallace received 13 percent of the popular vote and won electoral victories in several southern states. After a promising start his 1972 presidential run was destroyed by a nearly fatal assassination attempt, which left him confined to a wheelchair. His postshooting health, combined with Jimmy Carter's deft courtship of Wallace's constituency, led to his defeat in the Democratic primaries of 1976.

A Conservative Populist. Wallace's presidential runs were repeatedly undermined by his fire-eating rhetoric and his segregationist past. Northern Democrats and liberals remained deeply opposed to him, but his supporters, especially in the South, saw him as a champion of the common man, a politician principled enough to speak bluntly. In the 1970s Wallace introduced several conservative populist themes to American politics, themes which less-divisive candidates would use to their benefit. A former Golden Gloves boxer, the pugnacious Wallace attacked the liberal, eastern elite as snobbish and authoritarian and dismissed intellectuals as "over-educated Ivory-tower folks." He was an ardent hawk on the Vietnam War and portrayed doves as unpatriotic and immoral. He was one of the earliest politicians to mobilize fundamentalist Christian support and earned votes in the North and South through his opposition to court-enforced busing. For all his cultural conservatism, however, he was an economic liberal of the New Deal stripe, committed to Social Security, public health care, and a safe workplace. Wallace presented the perfect combination of political ideas for disaffected blue-collar Democrats. Carter realized this and in 1976 presented his candidacy to blue-collar Democrats as a moderate version of Wallace. The Republicans seized even more upon Wallace's constituency. By 1980 Reagan fashioned a political program which echoed all of Wallace's rhetorical themes even as it abandoned his economic populism — a synthesis that dominated American politics in the 1980s.

Sources:

Jody Carlson, *George C. Wallace and the Politics of Powerlessness* (New Brunswick, N.J.: Transaction, 1981);

Marshall Frady, *Wallace* (New York: New American Library, 1968).

ANDREW JACKSON YOUNG, JR.

1932-

AMBASSADOR TO THE UNITED NATIONS, 1977-1979

A New Symbol. Upon Andrew Young's 1976 nomination to become U.S. ambassador to the United Nations, syndicated columnist Mary McGrory wrote that the "symbolism of a black American speaking for this country to all the nations of the world will not be lost," and Young became the symbol of the Carter administration's effort to transform U.S. foreign policy. He repaired strained relations between the United States and the Third World and drew attention to human-rights abuses around the globe. Traditionalists critical of such foreign-policy shifts also focused on Young. Their opposition to him, combined with Young's tendency for off-the-cuff remarks and undiplomatic language, forced him from office in 1979.

Civil Rights Leader. A lifetime of advocacy for social justice and morality in government made Young the perfect symbol of the Carter administration's commitment to human rights in foreign policy. The son of a New Orleans dentist and a schoolteacher, Young grew up in a predominantely Irish and Italian neighborhood, where he developed a lifelong commitment to integration. Young had initially followed in his father's footsteps, but at Howard University he abandoned dentistry and became a clergyman. At Hartford Theological Seminary he was first exposed to the works of Indian nationalist Mohandas K. Gandhi and became convinced that nonviolence was the best means to achieve integration in the United States. Receiving his divinity degree in 1955, Young went south to participate in the developing civil rights movement, spearheading voter-registration efforts. Hired by the National Council of Churches in 1959, he led outreach programs to New York City's impoverished youth. His efforts brought him to the attention of Martin Luther King, Jr.'s, Southern Christian Leadership Conference (SCLC). By 1964 Young had become the executive director of the SCLC and one of King's closest aides, helping King coordinate the breakthrough Birmingham desegregation battle. Following King's 1968 assassination, Young moved toward the leadership of the SCLC and, with Ralph Abernathy, led the 1968 Poor People's Campaign for social and economic justice.

Association with Carter. In the early 1970s Young turned to politics. Although defeated in his run for Congress in 1970, he became the first black elected to the House of Representatives from Atlanta, Georgia, in 1972 and was reelected twice. He distinguished himself in Congress as an advocate for poor people, championing liberal causes, such as the minimum wage, day care, and national health care, as well as establishing himself as an opponent of increased military expenditures. His insistence on higher moral standards in government brought him to the attention of the like-minded governor of Georgia, Jimmy Carter, and in 1976 Young led a voter-registration drive that resulted in perhaps three million votes for Carter's presidential effort. In return Carter made Young U.S. ambassador to the United Nations.

A Controversial Ambassador. Young established himself as one of the most outspoken international representatives of the United States, advocating U.S. recognition of Communist Vietnam and economic sanctions against the authoritarian white-minority regimes in South Africa and Rhodesia. He considered human rights one of the most pressing problems in international diplomacy. He pushed U.S. assistance to Africa and Latin America, building American goodwill in those areas. His intemperate remarks concerning racism in Great Britain, the Soviet Union, and Sweden, however, drew fire; a charge that there were political prisoners in the United States earned Young the scorn of many. In August 1979 Young held unauthorized meetings with members of the Palestine Liberation Organization (PLO) — a violation of official Middle Eastern policy. His critics seized upon the meeting and demanded that Young be fired. President Carter reluctantly accepted Young's resignation on 15 August. Despite his short tenure as UN ambassador, Young's insistence that governments around the world guarantee the human rights of their citizens was a lasting contribution to international affairs and established a moral basis for U.S. diplomacy in the future.

Source:

Carl Gardner, *Andrew Young: A Biography* (New York: Drake, 1978).

PEOPLE IN THE NEWS

On January 1975 after four and a half years underground, radical Weatherman **Jane Alpert** surrendered herself to police. Alpert received a twenty-seven-month sentence.

On 11 August 1970 the Reverend **Daniel J. Berrigan,** one of a group of peace activists known as the Catonsville Nine convicted of burning draft records in Catonsville, Maryland, in 1968, was seized by the FBI. Berrigan had been a fugitive for four months.

On 12 January 1971 antiwar activist, the Reverend **Philip F. Berrigan,** already imprisoned for burning draft cards, was indicted along with six others for conspiring to kidnap National Security Adviser Henry Kissinger and bomb the heating systems of federal buildings in Washington, D.C. The subsequent "Harrisburg Seven" trial ended in a hung jury. On 5 September 1972 the Justice Department dropped all charges.

On 4 October 1976, in the midst of President Gerald Ford's election campaign, Secretary of Agriculture **Earl Butz** resigned following his "gross indiscretion" of racist jokes and remarks.

In 1977 **Robert C. Byrd** (D–West Virginia) became Senate majority leader. Byrd, a bluegrass fiddler and former member of the Ku Klux Klan, soon moderated some of his established conservatism and earned a reputation as a technician, deftly moving legislation through Congress.

On 29 March 1971 1st Lt. **William L. Calley, Jr.,** was convicted of premeditated murder in the 1968 massacre of twenty-eight South Vietnamese civilians at My Lai. On 20 August he is sentenced to life in prison, a sentence which was reduced on appeal to twenty years imprisonment. He was paroled by the army on 8 November 1974.

On 8 April 1970 Judge **G. Harrold Carswell** of Georgia was rejected by the Senate for nomination to the Supreme Court. President Nixon, who had placed Carswell's name in nomination, responded by chastising the Senate for an act of "regional discrimination."

In November 1975 presidential aspirant Ronald Reagan was attacked by twenty-year-old college dropout **Michael Lance Carvin.** Having assaulted Reagan with a plastic gun, Carvin was arrested and turned over to authorities for psychiatric care.

On 13 October 1970 black activist and former UCLA instructor **Angela Davis** was arrested in New York and charged with kidnapping, murder, and conspiracy in connection with an 7 August shootout in a San Rafael, California, courtroom. She was acquitted of all charges on 4 June 1972.

Thirteen-term Michigan Democrat **Charles Diggs** was censured in 1979 by the House for padding his payroll and taking public funds for personal use. Diggs had been reelected in 1978 despite accusations of corruption and became the first congressman since 1921 to be censured by the House.

Former representative **Joshua Eilberg** (D–Pennsylvania) pleaded guilty in 1979 to conflict of interest in a kickback scheme.

On 5 September 1978 Representative **Daniel Flood** (D–Pennsylvania) was indicted by a federal grand jury for kickbacks and conflict of interest. The case ended in mistrial in 1979. Flood retired from the House in 1980.

Lynette ("Squeaky") Fromme, 26, attempted to assassinate President Ford in 1975. A member of the infamous Manson family, which had been responsible for a California murder spree in 1969, Fromme was sentenced to life in prison.

On 1 September 1974 **Alan Greenspan** succeeded Herbert Stein as chairman of the Council of Economic Advisers. A controversial appointment, critics feared that Greenspan and his adherence to Ayn Rand's semi-philosophical "objectivist" economics would unduly influence President Ford.

On 16 September 1974 President Ford nominated White House Chief of Staff Gen. **Alexander M. Haig, Jr.,** to head North Atlantic Treaty Organization (NATO) forces in Europe. During the last days of the Nixon administration, Haig was a stabilizing influence in the White House, in effect, according to some, "running the country." Although the nomination was controversial, Haig

Rep. **Richard Hanna** (D–California) was sentenced to prison in 1977 for taking $200,000 in bribes from South Korean lobbyist Tongsun Park.

On 25 May 1976 Rep. **Wayne Hays** (D–Ohio) acknowledged a personal relationship with his secretary, Elizabeth Ray, but denied that the fourteen-thousand-dollar-per-year salary she earned was for sexual favors. Ray had made the charge, adding "I can't type. I can't file; I can't even answer the phone." Hays responded by arguing that Ray had "emotional and psychological problems."

On 5 March 1975 the Senate confirmed **Carla A. Hills** as secretary of Housing and Urban Development. She was the third woman in U.S. history to serve in a cabinet-level post.

On 6 August 1975 **Alger Hiss,** former State Department official convicted of perjury in a sensational spy trial twenty-five years earlier, was reinstated to the Massachusetts bar.

On 24 July 1974 Rep. **Barbara Jordan** (D–Texas) earned national acclaim for her speech during the House Judiciary Committee's debate over the impeachment of President Nixon. The first black woman elected to Congress from the Deep South, Jordan began her address by remarking that she, as an African-American woman, was originally left out of the "We the People," compact of the Constitution. She went on to remark that the strength of the Constitution is its capacity for amendment. "My faith in the Constitution is whole, it is complete, it is total," she concluded, "and I am not going to sit here and be an idle spectator to the diminution, the subversion, the destruction of the Constitution." She voted to recommend to the House that they impeach Nixon on three counts, as did the majority of the committee.

In winter 1978 White House aide **Hamilton Jordan** became a nearly constant subject for Washington's tabloid press. First came reports of Jordan's sexual overtures toward the Egyptian ambassador's wife; then separation from his wife of seven years; then reports that he spat a drink down the dress of a woman in Sarsfield's, a suburban bar. The final report so incensed the White House that Press Secretary Jody Powell issued an eight-thousand-word, thirty-three-page denial of the Sarsfield's incident, including a deposition from the bartender. Despite the gossip, in August 1979 Jordan became President Carter's chief of staff.

On 21 September 1977 Carter presidential adviser **Burt Lance** resigned as director of the Office of Management and Budget. Lance was criticized for his "unsound and unsafe" practices as head of a Georgia bank, as well as suffering from charges that he had peddled influence for Arab banking interests.

On 10 December 1974 Arkansas Democrat **Wilbur D. Mills** resigned his post as House Ways and Means chairman. Mills had been linked to several well-publicized incidents with stripper Fanne Foxe, "The Argentine Firecracker."

In 1975 **Sara Jane Moore,** a middle-aged housewife and social activist obsessed with Patty Hearst, attempted to assassinate President Ford in San Francisco. At her trial Moore declared that "any government (that) uses assassination . . . must expect that tool to be turned back against itself." She was sentenced to life in prison.

In February 1970 a memorandum drafted for President Nixon by his adviser **Daniel Patrick Moynihan** was leaked to the press and ignited a firestorm of protest. The memorandum, which recommended to Nixon that he allow race relations in the United States to lapse into a period of "benign neglect," was denounced by liberals and black activists.

On 20 October 1976 the Justice Department announced an investigation of South Korean businessman **Tongsun Park,** a South Korean lobbyist. Park was suspected of making cash contributions of $500,000 to $1 million annually to influence congressional legislation. The scandal associated with Park became known as Koreagate. He was acquitted, but the IRS nonetheless sought $4.5 million in back taxes from him.

In September 1971 Gov. **Nelson Rockefeller** of New York refused to negotiate with Attica State Prison inmates who have taken over the facility and seized hostages to protest conditions within the prison. Rockefeller ordered the prison stormed by state police. The facility was retaken, but forty-three people were killed, including ten hostages. A subsequent investigative commission revealed that all were killed by police bullets.

On 30 July 1974 **Peter W. Rodino, Jr.,** chairman of the House Judiciary Committee, submitted to the full House his committee's recommendation that it impeach President Nixon for three counts of "high crimes and misdemeanors." Although Nixon's resignation on 8 August rendered the vote academic, on 20 August the House approved the report 412–3 — a measure of what would have happened on an impeachment vote had Nixon not resigned.

On 19 January 1977 President Ford granted a pardon to **Tokyo Rose** (Iva Toguri D'Aquino). She had been convicted of treason because of her broadcasts from Japan during World War II designed to demoralize U.S. troops

On 29 July 1976 Rep. **Robert L. F. Sikes,** Democrat of Florida, was reprimanded by the House of Representatives by a vote of 381–3 for financial misconduct.

DEATHS

Rudolf Abel, 68, spy who oversaw Soviet intelligence in New York during the 1950s; he was swapped for a captured American spy pilot in 1962, 15 November 1961.

Creighton W. Abrams, 59, U.S. commander in Vietnam (1968–1972), former army chief of staff, 4 September 1974.

Dean Acheson, 78, presidential adviser and secretary of state under Harry S Truman, 12 October 1971.

Saul Alinsky, 63, social organizer and self-styled radical; his books include *Reveille for Radicals* (1946) and *Rules for Radicals* (1971), 12 June 1972.

Adolf A. Berle, Jr., 76, influential member of Franklin Roosevelt's Brain Trust, later a prominent Latin American diplomat, 17 February 1971.

Hugo L. Black, 85, Supreme Court justice (1937–1971), known as a champion of civil liberties, 23 September 1971.

Charles E. Bohlen, 69, career diplomat and expert on the Soviet Union, 1 January 1974.

Earl Browder, 82, head of the Communist party of the United States (1930–1945), 27 June 1973.

Ralph Bunche, 67, ambassador to the United Nations (1957–1971), winner of the 1950 Nobel Peace Prize, 9 December 1971.

Prescott Bush, 77, Republican senator from Connecticut (1952–1963), father of President George Bush, 8 October 1972.

James F. Byrnes, 92, Democratic representative of South Carolina (1911–1925), U.S. senator (1930–1941) associate justice of the Supreme Court (1941–1942), secretary of state (1945–1947), governor of South Carolina (1951–1955), 9 April 1972.

Chou En-Lai, 78, Chinese statesman; since 1949 premier of the People's Republic of China, 8 January 1976.

Lucius D. Clay, 80, U.S. Army general, administrator of postwar Germany, he coordinated the Berlin airlift, 17 April 1978.

Charles E. Coughlin, 88, conservative, anti-Semitic radio priest popular during the Great Depression, 27 October 1979.

Richard J. Daley, 74, Democratic representative and senator of Illinois (1936–1946) and controversial mayor of Chicago (1955–1976), 20 December 1976.

Vera Micheles Dean, 69, author and foreign-policy expert, editor and research director of the Foreign Policy Association (1931–1961), 11 October 1972.

Thomas E. Dewey, 68, governor of New York (1942–1955), twice GOP candidate for president, 16 March 1971.

Martin Dies, 71, first chairman of the House Un-American Activities Committee (1938–1945), 14 November 1972.

Merle Fainsod, 64, U.S.-Soviet scholar, director of the Russian Research Center at Harvard (1959–1964), 10 February 1972.

Herbert Feis, 78, scholar and adviser to the State Department (1931–1943) and War Department (1943–1947), 2 March 1972.

Leslie R. Groves, 73, U.S. Army officer, director of the Manhattan Project, which constructed the world's first atomic bomb, 13 July 1970.

Ernest Gruening, 87, Democratic senator from Alaska (1959–1969), instrumental in achieving Alaskan statehood, early critic of the Vietnam War, 26 June 1974.

Fannie Lou Hamer, 60, civil rights leader, organizer of the Mississippi Freedom Democratic party, 14 March 1977.

Alvin H. Hansen, 87, U.S. economist instrumental in the creation of the Social Security system and the New Deal, 6 June 1975.

John Marshall Harlan, 72, Supreme Court justice (1955–1971) noted for the conservative nature of his opinions, 29 December 1971.

Thomas C. Hart, 94, commander of the Pacific Fleet at Pearl Harbor when it was bombed by the Japanese, 4 July 1971.

J. Edgar Hoover, 77, director of the Federal Bureau of Investigation since 1924, 2 May 1972.

Hubert Horatio Humphrey, mayor of Minneapolis (1945–1948), Democratic senator from Minnesota (1949–1965, 1970–1977), four-time presidential aspirant, vice-president under Lyndon Johnson (1965–1969), 13 January 1978.

Daniel James, Jr., 58, first black general in the United States, 25 February 1978.

Lyndon Baines Johnson, 64, thirty-sixth president of the United States (1963–1968), 22 January 1973.

Dorothy Kenyon, 83, women's rights leader and New York municipal-court judge, 12 February 1972.

Thomas C. Kinkaid, 84, commander of U.S. naval forces in the Pacific during World War II, 17 November 1972.

William F. Knowland, 65, publisher of the *Oakland Tribune,* influential Republican senator from California (1945–1959), majority leader (1953–1954); minority leader (1955–1958); 23 February 1974.

Frederick J. Libby, 95, clergyman and peace activist, since 1921 executive secretary of the National Council for the Prevention of War, 26 June 1970.

Anthony C. McAuliffe, 77, acting commander of the 101st Airborne Division during the Battle of the Bulge whose famous "Nuts!" response to a German surrender demand emboldened U.S. forces, 11 August 1975.

John L. McClellan, 81, Democratic senator of Arkansas (1942–1977), influential champion of military appropriations, influential foe of civil rights legislation, 28 November 1977.

Martha Mitchell, 56, outspoken wife of former attorney general John Mitchell, she provided information on the Watergate scandal, 31 May 1976.

Raymond Moley, 88, former member of Franklin Roosevelt

Joseph M. Montoya, 62, Democratic senator of New Mexico (1965–1977), opponent of the Vietnam War, known for his defense of Native Americans and the poor, 5 June 1978.

Wayne L. Morse, 73, senator from Oregon (Republican, 1944–1953; liberal, 1953–1956; Democrat, 1956–1968), one of two senators who voted against the 1964 Tonkin Gulf Resolution, which gave congressional endorsement to the Vietnam War, 22 July 1974.

Karl E. Mundt, 74, Republican senator from South Dakota (1948–1973), staunch anti-Communist during the McCarthy years, 16 August 1974.

Audie Murphy, 46, during World War II the soldier most decorated by the United States, 28 May 1971.

Gerald P. Nye, 78, Republican senator from North Dakota (1925–1944) whose Depression-era hearings on the causes of World War I did much to animate isolationism, 17 July 1971.

Adam Clayton Powell, Jr., 63, Baptist minister and flamboyant congressman from New York (1945–1970), 4 April 1972.

Arthur W. Radford, 77, naval officer, chairman of the Joint Chiefs of Staff under Eisenhower (1953–1957), 17 August 1973.

A. Philip Randolph, 90, pathbreaking labor and civil rights leader, responsible for the 1963 March on Washington, 16 May 1979.

Jeannette Rankin, 92, Republican congresswoman from Montana (1917–1919, 1941–1943), first woman elected to Congress, only member of Congress to vote against U.S. entry into both world wars, 18 May 1973.

Edward V. Rickenbacker, 82, World War I air ace, 23 July 1973.

Nelson A. Rockefeller, 70, governor of New York (1959–1973), presidential aspirant, vice-president under Gerald Ford, 26 January 1979.

Nellie T. Ross, 101, first woman elected governor of a state (Wyoming, 1925–1927), 19 December 1977.

Richard Rovere, 64, political writer; his publications include *Senator Joe McCarthy* (1959), 23 November 1979.

Richard B. Russell, 73, long-standing leader of the Senate, Democrat of Georgia, 21 January 1971.

Gerald L. K. Smith, 78, anti-Catholic and anti-Semitic founder of the National Christian Crusade, 15 April 1976.

Carl A. Spaats, 83, first chief of staff of the U.S. Air Force, 14 July 1974.

Arthur B. Spingarn, 93, president of the National Association for the Advancement of Colored People (NAACP) (1940–1965), 1 December 1971.

Stephen Gill Spottswood, 77, chairman since 1961 of the NAACP, 1 December 1974.

Harold Raynsford Stark, 91, chief of naval operations at the time of the bombing of Pearl Harbor, 20 August 1972.

Lewis L. Strauss, 78, former head of the Atomic Energy Commission (1953–1958), 22 January 1974.

Arthur E. Summerfield, 73, leading Republican, managed Eisenhower's two presidential campaigns, 26 April 1972.

J. Parnell Thomas, 75, Republican representative from New Jersey (1937–1950), chairman of the House Committee on Un-American Activities (1947–1950), prominent anti-Communist until his 1950 imprisonment for padding his congressional payroll, 19 November 1970.

Llewellyn E. Thompson, Jr., 67, diplomat, ambassador to the Soviet Union under Eisenhower, 6 February 1972.

Harry S Truman, 88, thirty-third president of the United States (1945–1952), 26 December 1972.

Rexford Guy Tugwell, 88, leading figure in Franklin Roosevelt's Brain Trust, 21 July 1979.

John Paul Vann, 47, counterinsurgency expert, leading critic of the conduct of operations in Vietnam; he resigned in protest from the U.S. Army in 1963, 9 June 1972.

Earl Warren, 83, governor of California (1943–1954), 1948 GOP vice-presidential candidate, chief justice of the United States (1953–1968), 9 July 1974.

Burton K. Wheeler, 92, Democratic senator from Montana (1923–1947), key Senate figure during the New Deal, 6 January 1975.

Earle Wheeler, 67, chairman of the Joint Chiefs of Staff (1964–1970), 18 December 1975.

Charles Evans Whittaker, 72, associate justice of the Supreme Court (1957–1962), 26 November 1973.

Whitney M. Young, Jr., 49, since 1961 head of the National Urban League, 11 March 1971.

Abraham Zapruder, 66, Dallas businessman whose home movies of the assassination of John F. Kennedy were used by the Warren Commission, 30 August 1970.

PUBLICATIONS

Carl Bernstein and Bob Woodward, *All The President's Men* (New York: Warner, 1974);

Bernstein and Woodward, *The Final Days* (New York: Avon, 1976);

John Dean, *Blind Ambition: The White House Years* (London: W. H. Allen, 1976);

H. R. Haldeman, *The Ends of Power* (New York: New York Times Books, 1978);

Marvin Kalb and Bernard Kalb, *Kissinger* (Boston: Little, Brown, 1974);

Henry Kissinger, *White House Years* (Boston: Little, Brown, 1977);

J. Anthony Lukas, *Nightmare: The Underside of the Nixon Years* (New York: Viking, 1976);

Bruce Mazlish, *Kissinger: The European Mind in American Policy* (New York: Basic Books, 1976);

Richard Nixon, *RN: The Memoirs of Richard Nixon* (New York: Grosset & Dunlap, 1978);

John Osborne, *The White House Watch: The Ford Years* (Washington, D.C.: New Republic, 1977);

Richard Reeves, *A Ford, Not a Lincoln* (New York: Harcourt Brace Jovanovich, 1975);

William Safire, *Before the Fall: An Inside View of the Pre-Watergate White House* (Garden City, N.Y.: Doubleday, 1975);

Robert Scheer, *America After Nixon: The Age of Multinationals* (New York: McGraw-Hill, 1974);

Jonathan Schell, *The Time of Illusion* (New York: Knopf, 1976);

Martin Schram, *Running for President, 1976: The Carter Campaign* (New York: Stein & Day, 1977);

Peter Steinfels, *The Neoconservatives: The Men Who Are Changing America's Politics* (New York: Simon & Schuster, 1979);

Kandy Stroud, *How Jimmy Won: The Victory Campaign from Plains to the White House* (New York: Morrow, 1977);

Tad Szulc, *The Illusion of Peace: Foreign Policy in the Nixon Years* (New York: Viking, 1978);

Hunter S. Thompson, *Fear and Loathing: On The Campaign Trail '72* (New York: Time Warner, 1973);

Thompson, *The Great Shark Hunt* (New York: Simon & Schuster, 1979);

Theodore H. White, *Breach of Faith: The Fall of Richard Nixon* (New York: Antheneum, 1975);

White, *The Making of the President, 1972* (New York: Atheneum, 1973);

Garry Wills, *Nixon Agonistes: The Crisis of the Self-Made Man* (Boston: Houghton Mifflin, 1970);

Jules Witcover, *Marathon: The Pursuit of the Presidency, 1972–1976* (New York: Viking, 1977);

Witcover, *White Knight: The Rise of Spiro Agnew* (New York: Random House, 1972);

James Wooten, *Dasher: The Roots and the Rising of Jimmy Carter* (New York: Summit Books, 1978).

Abortion reform rally in Saint Louis, 1970

LAW AND JUSTICE

by SUSAN STERETT

CONTENTS

Sidebars and tables are listed in italics.

1970

19 Jan. President Richard Nixon nominates G. Harrold Carswell for Supreme Court justice. On 8 April the Senate cites Carswell's weak on civil rights record in rejecting the nomination.

18 Feb. The trial of the Chicago Seven ends with an acquittal of all seven defendants on charges that they conspired to cause a riot at the 1968 Democratic National Convention. Five defendants are eventually convicted of individually crossing state lines with intent to cause a riot. In 1972 these convictions are overturned because of prejudicial conduct by the trial judge.

23 Mar. The Supreme Court decides that people receiving Aid to Families with Dependent Children are entitled to a hearing before their benefits are cut off.

12 May The Senate unanimously approves the nomination of Harry A. Blackmun for the Supreme Court.

15 May The Supreme Court decides by a five to three vote that men who object to military service for moral reasons are entitled to draft exemptions as conscientious objectors.

7 Aug. Armed black revolutionary Jonathan Jackson frees convicts James McClain and William Christmas from McClain's trial for stabbing a prison guard. The three take five hostages — the trial judge, the prosecutor, and three women jurors. When they are stopped at a roadblock, they shoot the judge and then are killed by police gunfire. Black activist and UCLA philosophy professor Angela Davis is charged with providing Jackson with the weapons, but she is acquitted.

15 Oct. President Nixon signs the Organized Crime Control Act of 1970. The act gives police and prosecutors several new powers. The most controversial of those powers are the Racketeer-Influenced and Corrupt Organizations (RICO) provisions, which enable prosecutors to confiscate organized crime money invested in legitimate businesses.

31 Dec. President Nixon signs the Clean Air Act, setting a six-year deadline for the automobile industry to make a pollution-free vehicle and setting air quality standards for ten major pollutants.

1971

30 Jan. Gov. Ronald Reagan of California, who has long objected to the work of California Rural Legal Assistance, tries to block the program by vetoing its funding. The debate leads to a reconsideration of how legal aid attorneys are financed and organized.

24 Feb. The Supreme Court holds five to four that the statement of a defendant can be used in court to contradict his testimony, even if the defendant had not been read his rights beforehand.

8 Mar. The Supreme Court decides that if a hiring practice discriminates against minorities or white women the business must show that the practice is necessary for the business.

29 Mar. A military court finds Lt. William Calley guilty of the murder of at least twenty-two civilians and sentences him to life imprisonment at hard labor for his role in the My Lai massacre. Calley's platoon killed over one hundred women, children, and old men in My Lai even though there were no enemy soldiers present.

24 May   Trial judge Harold Mulvey declares a mistrial in the murder trial of two members of the Black Panther party, a radical black nationalist group. Bobby Seale and Erika Huggins are charged with ordering the torture and murder of a suspected informer, but the jury declares itself hopelessly deadlocked. On 25 May Mulvey dismisses all charges against Seale and Huggins because the massive pretrial publicity makes it impossible for them to receive a fair trial.

13 June   *The New York Times* begins to publish the Pentagon Papers, excerpts from a Department of Defense study of U.S. policy regarding Vietnam.

21 June   The Supreme Court decides by a six-to-three vote that juveniles do not have a constitutional right to a jury trial.

30 June   The Supreme Court decides that the government cannot prohibit publication of the Pentagon Papers by *The New York Times.*

1 July   The Office of Economic Opportunity makes public a report on California Rural Legal Assistance. The report says that Governor Reagan's charges against the legal services group are "unfounded" and "irresponsible."

21 Aug.   George Jackson, an inmate at San Quentin prison, is killed along with two other inmates and three prison guards in an apparent escape attempt. Jackson, a black activist, is one of the "Soledad Brothers" accused of killing a prison guard at Soledad prison. Jackson's family and attorneys accuse prison officials of murdering Jackson.

9 Sept.   Prisoners riot in the Attica prison in New York State. After four days Gov. Nelson Rockefeller orders the state police to retake the prison by force. Police gunfire kills ten hostages and twenty-nine inmates in the attack.

17 Sept.   Justice Hugo Black retires from the Supreme Court.

23 Sept.   Justice John Marshall Harlan retires from the Supreme Court.

6 Dec.   Lewis Powell is confirmed by the Senate in his appointment to the Supreme Court.

10 Dec.   William Rehnquist is confirmed in his appointment to the Supreme Court.

1972

- Oregon becomes the first state to decriminalize the possession of small amounts of marijuana.

22 Mar.   The Senate passes the Equal Rights Amendment by a vote of eighty-four to eight, sending it to the states to consider.

12 June   The Supreme Court holds that a defendant is entitled to an attorney whenever a jail sentence is a possible penalty for the crime of which the defendant is accused.

17 June   Police arrest five men for breaking into the Democratic National Committee's headquarters at the Watergate Hotel. Three of the men have ties to President Nixon's reelection campaign.

29 June   The Supreme Court in *Furman* v. *Georgia* holds the death penalty unconstitutional unless administered equally and in specific circumstances that the state must list ahead of time.

2 Nov.   The Commission on Inquiry into the Black Panthers and Law Enforcement in Illinois issues a report condemning the Illinois state attorney's handling of a 1969 Chicago raid of the Black Panthers, calling the use of guns unnecessary.

1973

20 Jan. The Supreme Court in *Roe* v. *Wade* and *Doe* v. *Bolton* holds by a vote of six to three that women's interest in privacy means that states cannot prohibit abortion in the first trimester of pregnancy.

1 Feb. The District of Columbia Court of Appeals tells the Environmental Protection Agency that it cannot give seventeen states a two-year extension to comply with the 1970 Clean Air Act.

21 June The Supreme Court decides that a roving border patrol cannot conduct searches of cars without a warrant or probable cause.

21 June The Supreme Court hands down new standards for judging obscenity cases. States may prohibit sexual material only if the materials are patently offensive to community standards and do not have "serious literary, artistic, political or scientific value."

20 Oct. Acting Attorney General Robert H. Bork fires the Watergate special prosecutor, Archibald Cox. Attorney General Elliot Richardson and Deputy Attorney General William Ruckelshaus resign rather than fire Cox.

1974

• Rubin ("Hurricane") Carter publishes his autobiography, *The Sixteenth Round: From Number One Contender to Number 45472.*

5 Feb. Patricia Hearst is kidnapped from her Berkeley, California, home by the Symbionese Liberation Army (SLA). In April she joins the SLA in their robbery of the Hibernia Bank in San Francisco.

24 July The Supreme Court unanimously rules that President Nixon must turn over tapes requested by the special prosecutor. The Court holds that President Nixon does not have unlimited "executive privilege" as he claims.

9 Aug. President Nixon resigns, and Vice-president Gerald R. Ford becomes president.

8 Sept. President Ford pardons former president Nixon.

13 Nov. Karen Silkwood, who claimed to have evidence about serious lapses in quality control at the Kerr/McGee nuclear fuel plant, is killed in a car accident on her way to a meeting with a *New York Times* reporter. No evidence is found.

1975

• Bob Dylan releases his song "Hurricane," proclaiming the innocence of Rubin ("Hurricane") Carter.

22 Jan. The Supreme Court decides that before suspending students from school, officials must grant students informal hearings.

26 June A standoff between federal government officials and the American Indian Movement (AIM) at the Pine Ridge Sioux Indian Reservation in South Dakota erupts into a shoot-out. One AIM member and two FBI agents are killed.

20 Oct. The Supreme Court holds that school administrators may hit students to punish them, even if parents object.

12 Nov. Justice William O. Douglas retires from the Supreme Court after serving a record-setting thirty-six-year term.

18 Nov.   Eldridge Cleaver, onetime minister of information for the Black Panther party, returns to the United States and is immediately arrested by the FBI. Cleaver fled the country in 1968 to avoid trial on attempted murder charges, stemming from a shoot-out between Oakland police and the Black Panthers. Cleaver is never tried. In December 1979 he pleads guilty to a charge of assault and is sentenced to community service and probation.

17 Dec.   The Senate unanimously confirms the appointment of John Paul Stevens to the Supreme Court.

1976

20 Mar.   Patricia Hearst is convicted of bank robbery for her participation in the robbery of the Hibernia Bank with the Symbionese Liberation Army. She serves two years in prison before President Jimmy Carter commutes her sentence.

2 July   The Supreme Court, overturning *Furman* v. *Georgia*, holds in *Gregg* v. *Georgia* that the death penalty does not violate the Eighth or Fourteenth amendments.

15 July   Frank Edward Ray, a school-bus driver, and the children on his school bus are kidnapped and held underground in Chowchilla, California, for sixteen hours.

7 Dec.   The Supreme Court rules by a vote of six to three in *Gilbert* v. *General Electric* that it is not sex discrimination for companies to provide disability insurance that covers some men-only disabilities but not pregnancy.

22 Dec.   Rubin ("Hurricane") Carter is again convicted in a retrial on a murder charge. In 1985 the verdict of this trial is overturned because the reviewing judge finds that the prosecution case was based on racism.

31 Dec.   The California Supreme Court decides that when people who are living together separate, a partner could be entitled to payment like alimony — "palimony."

1977

17 Jan.   Gary Gilmore, convicted of murder in Utah, is the first person in ten years to be executed under the death penalty.

18 Apr.   Leonard Peltier, an AIM activist, is convicted of the murder of two FBI agents at the Pine Ridge Sioux Reservation in June 1975.

19 Apr.   The Supreme Court decides by a five-to-four vote that corporal punishment of students is not "cruel and unusual punishment" and is therefore not prohibited by the Eighth Amendment.

20 June   The Supreme Court upholds by a vote of six to three the authority of the states to refuse to pay for poor women's abortions unless a physician says that it is medically necessary.

29 June   The Supreme Court by a vote of six to three overturns a school desegregation order for the city of Omaha, saying that the lower courts have to look more closely at the effect of segregation on schoolchildren.

21 Sept.   Bert Lance resigns as the director of the Office of Management and Budget with "regret and sorrow" after accusations of financial misdealings.

3 Dec.   The FBI issues a report calling wife battering the country's least reported crime. The women's movement calls for more public attention and more police effort in response to this crime.

1978

10 Apr.   A federal grand jury indicts former FBI acting director L. Patrick Gray and two former high-ranking FBI officials, Edward Miller and Mark Felt. Unable to obtain search warrants, the FBI officials ordered FBI agents to break into the homes of friends and relatives of fugitive members of the radical Weatherman group in 1972 and 1973.

24 Apr.   The Supreme Court lets stand the lower court's conviction of Patricia Hearst for armed robbery.

31 May   The Supreme Court decides that newspapers can be searched and their reporting and photographs used in the investigation of a crime.

3 July   The Supreme Court decides that universities may take race into account in admissions to try to diversify the student body but may not have strict numerical quotas.

26 Oct.   President Carter signs an ethics-in-government law provoked largely by Watergate; it provides for the appointment of special prosecutors.

27 Nov.   Mayor George Moscone and Supervisor Harvey Milk of San Francisco are murdered by Dan White in part for their support of rights for gay men.

1979

5 Mar.   The Supreme Court rules six to three that it is unconstitutional sex discrimination for state laws to require divorcing husbands to pay alimony.

21 May   Dan White, a former city supervisor, is convicted of voluntary manslaughter in the killing of George Moscone and Harvey Milk in San Francisco.

23 May   A federal grand jury charges Bert Lance, former director of the Office of Management and Budget under President Carter, with conspiracy to file false statements and mislead government regulatory agencies.

27 June   The Supreme Court okays a voluntary affirmative action plan to increase the proportion of black employees holding skilled positions at an aluminum and chemical plant.

2 July   The Supreme Court rules that a state may require parental consent for a minor's abortion. However, the state must provide the option of having a judge decide if the minor does not want to tell her parents or cannot.

2 July   The Supreme Court holds by a vote of five to four that members of the public have no constitutional right to attend trials. A court can close trials if pretrial publicity would hurt a defendant's chances of a fair trial.

6 Sept.   President Jimmy Carter, citing humane considerations, frees four Puerto Rican nationalists who committed acts of political terrorism in the 1950s. Carter commutes the sentence of Oscar Collazo, who tried to assassinate President Harry S Truman in 1950. He also grants clemency to Lolita Lebron, Irving Flores Rodriguez, and Rafael Cancel-Miranda who shot and wounded five U.S. congressmen in 1954.

26 Nov.   The Supreme Court agrees to hear challenges to the Hyde amendment, addressing whether Medicaid can exclude payment for abortions.

OVERVIEW

Society and the Law. Law, courts, and lawyers played increasing roles in the central social and political conflicts of the 1970s. Concerns about rising crime rates, the rights of the accused, and the death penalty were key social issues. Growing prison populations and prison riots raised difficult questions about prison conditions and the use of stricter sentencing to respond to rising crime rates. Debates about school busing and school desegregation were carried on in courtrooms and in the streets. The Supreme Court established a woman's right to abortion and changed the course of national politics. Legal disputes over the president's executive privilege and custody of the White House tapes played a pivotal role in the Watergate crisis. And environmental groups and business firms fought out the battles of environmental policy in courtrooms across the country.

Crime in the 1970s. Public concern about crime remained high, constantly near the top of the list of the most important issues. Crime statistics showed increased rates in the early 1970s, a leveling off during the middle years, and an increase again at the end of the decade. In the major cities crime declined somewhat, particularly crimes against property. In smaller cities and towns it rose slightly. Despite variability in different areas, people's fears seemed to increase across the country. Americans who could afford it increased their use of alarms and watchdogs. They also supported more spending on police and prisons.

Law and Order. Conservatives such as Richard Nixon and Spiro Agnew argued that the rise in crime was a result of the decline of family responsibility and growing social permissiveness, particularly with regard to sexual behavior and drug use. Sexually oriented movies and magazines became more available, even in small towns and rural areas. Fewer couples felt that marriage was a prerequisite for living together. More children were born outside of marriage and in single-parent families. Divorce rates climbed. Much of the public and many officials condoned marijuana use, and several states decriminalized its possession. Conservatives campaigned to reestablish family responsibility and respect for the law. While they achieved some of their policy goals, crime rates,

births by unwed mothers, and drug use came down slowly, if at all.

Nixon and the Supreme Court. In his 1968 campaign Nixon told Americans that the Supreme Court had overstepped its constitutional role. He criticized the Warren Court's expansion of the rights of accused criminals and its use of busing to desegregate public schools. He pledged to appoint Supreme Court justices who would reverse the liberal decisions of the Warren Court. Nixon's appointments did move the Supreme Court in a more conservative direction. The Court backtracked somewhat on the rights of accused criminals, but not as much as Nixon wanted. The court also limited the application of school-desegregation orders, particularly in northern cities. However, the court also established a woman's right to an abortion and expanded protections against employment discrimination. Nixon's desire for a "constitutional counter-revolution" against the Warren Court's judicial activism would have to wait until the 1980s and President Ronald Reagan and George Bush's appointments to the Court.

Ethics in Government. Nixon's law-and-order stance was undermined by the behavior of his own administration. The Watergate affair, the Nixon administration's "enemies list," and the illegal searches and wiretapping revealed what many Americans saw as governmental contempt for the law. "Koreagate," a scandal involving bribes from Korean lobbyists, subjected leading congressmen to similar criticisms. As a result, government officials were subject to much closer scrutiny of their adherence to law. The public carefully monitored financial investments of Carter administration members and their use of power in office.

The Environmental Decade. Public support for stronger environmental laws blossomed in the 1970s. Congress enacted new statutes to achieve cleaner air and water and to increase the consideration of the environment in governmental decision making. These issues often ended up in the courts. However, courts often had difficulty sorting out priorities between environmental protection and the economic interests of polluting firms.

Equality for Women. The woman's rights movement grew out of the earlier civil rights movement. Constitutional questions provided the material for much of the movement. The Supreme Court considered whether distinguishing between men and women was analogous to distinguishing among people by race and thus almost always unconstitutional. The Court concluded that states might sometimes have reasons for distinguishing between men and women. But they had to have good reasons.

Equal Rights Amendment. While the Court was struggling with determining the conditions under which the law could discriminate according to gender, the country was considering a constitutional amendment that would have made those distinctions much harder. The Equal Rights Amendment fell three states short of ratification in 1982. It would have prohibited states from abridging rights on the basis of sex.

Abortion. Some women in the women's movement saw men's and women's different responsibilities in childbearing as important for women's equality. Some argued for a constitutional right to choose to have an abortion. In 1973 in *Roe* v. *Wade* and *Doe* v. *Bolton* the Supreme Court upheld a woman's right to choose an abortion during the first trimester of pregnancy. This decision, alongside the movement for the Equal Rights Amendment, threatened many women who were concerned that these rights made women's roles in the home less important. They opposed access to abortion and the Equal Rights Amendment.

Equal Protection of the Laws. Equality for women was just one area of equality that Americans debated. The Court's interpretations of the Fourteenth Amendment, which guarantees equal protection, inspired discussions about racial inequality in education and employment. Court decisions expanded some of the protections for racial minorities. However, they also began to take account of many white Americans' fears that such laws discriminated against them. The federal courts' affirmative-action decisions, in particular, struggled to draw the line between adequate protection for minorities and claims by white males that they were being wrongly deprived of opportunities.

Divorce. Divorce touched more families than ever before. Between 1964 and 1974 the divorce rate doubled. While Americans became more willing to dissolve marriages, they also showed concern for what divorce meant for families. Movies such as *Kramer vs. Kramer* (1979) linked divorce with the women's movement by showing women leaving their marriages to find happiness. In reality, many women and children were financially dependent on their husbands and fathers. The lack of enforcement of child-support laws would emerge as an issue in the 1980s.

Unresolved Issues. Law and courts became more involved in these issues, but that did not usually mean that conflict over the issues was resolved. Most of these issues remained important and difficult. The increased political strength of the religious Right and the judicial appointments of the Reagan and Bush administrations also resulted in a continued shift toward decisions that were more conservative, finally overturning some of the more liberal decisions of the 1960s and early 1970s.

TOPICS IN THE NEWS

ABORTION: ROE V. WADE

Meet Jane Roe. In late 1969 Norma McCorvey, twenty-one and single, found herself with an unwanted pregnancy. She worked as a waitress in a bar; previously she had worked with a traveling circus selling tickets. She already had a five-year-old daughter for whom she could not afford to care. McCorvey's mother had taken custody of her daughter. She had little money and nowhere to go. McCorvey's father was unable to provide for both Norma and her future child. She did not think she was in any condition to care for another child. She wanted an abortion. In Texas she could have one only if her life was endangered by a pregnancy, which it was not.

Coffee and Weddington. McCorvey met Linda Coffee, a young attorney concerned about feminist issues. Coffee spoke on women's rights around Dallas, where she lived. She was active in the Women's Equity Action League, an organization that worked for equal employment opportunity for women. One of five women in the 1965 first-year law-school class at the University of Texas, Coffee had found it difficult to find a job despite her stellar law-school record. She believed that equality was not possible for women until they had control over their fertility. She joined up with Sarah Weddington, a law-school classmate. They wanted to challenge Texas's abortion statutes in court as unconstitutional. Once they met McCorvey, they knew they had found a case. McCorvey agreed to be a plaintiff. Sarah Weddington and Linda Coffee warned her that the decision would not come fast enough to allow her actually to have an abortion; she would almost certainly have to agree to give birth. She did. In addition, McCorvey was concerned about publicity. She agreed to be a plaintiff only if the lawsuit did not use her name. Norma McCorvey became Jane Roe, and her lawsuit became *Roe* v. *Wade*. Henry Wade was the Texas district attorney arguing in favor of abortion laws.

Precedents. The Supreme Court had decided cases that provided some reason to think that it might be willing to rule against antiabortion statutes such as that found in Texas. In 1968 the Court held in *Griswold* v. *Connecticut* that a state could not prohibit the sale of contraceptives to married people. This decision held that

THE DECISION TO HAVE A BABY COULD SOON BE BETWEEN YOU, YOUR HUSBAND AND YOUR SENATOR.

Pro-choice Planned Parenthood advertisement

the Constitution recognized a right to privacy. In 1971 in *Eisenstadt* v. *Baird* the Supreme Court extended that right to unmarried people. Those cases had not been exceptionally controversial among the broad public, and the stage was set for a more sweeping ruling regarding reproduction and the right to privacy.

The Decision. When the Supreme Court agreed to hear *Roe* v. *Wade* many organizations wrote papers for the Court, called amicus curiae or friend-of-the-court briefs, arguing for a decision on one side or the other. Such briefs are routinely submitted for important Supreme Court cases. Most organizations writing to the Court supported holding antiabortion statutes unconstitutional. On 21 January 1973 the Supreme Court handed down decisions in *Roe* v. *Wade* and *Doe* v. *Bolton,* a challenge to a slightly different antiabortion law in Georgia. The Court held that in the first trimester of pregnancy the state cannot prohibit a woman in consultation with her doctor from getting an abortion. It allowed greater regulation of abortion in the second trimester and strong regulations in the final trimester.

The Prolife Movement Emerges. The campaign to

The yard in D block at Attica prison on 12 September 1971 after rioting prisoners were subdued by law-enforcement officers

challenge the laws prohibiting abortion did not receive much media attention before *Roe* v. *Wade* and *Doe* v. *Bolton.* Many supporters of abortion restrictions were shocked by the decisions establishing a right to abortion. Many grassroots antiabortion, or prolife, groups organized in response to the decisions. The prolife movement obtained new restrictions on abortion in state legislatures. Several states enacted laws requiring consent from the parents of minors, the spouse, or the prospective father before an abortion could be performed. In *Planned Parenthood* v. *Danforth* (1976) the Supreme Court struck down these consent provisions as too restrictive of a woman's right to an abortion. Several states also imposed restrictions on public funding for abortions. Pennsylvania and Connecticut strongly limited Medicaid funding for abortions. Saint Louis barred city-owned hospitals, where most poor residents received their medical care, from performing abortions. Financial restrictions were upheld by the Supreme Court in *Beal* v. *Doe* (1977), *Maher* v. *Roe* (1977), and *Poelker* v. *Doe*(1977). The Supreme Court said that the *Roe* v. *Wade* decision prevented states from restricting abortions, but that it did not require that states pay for them.

Continued Controversy. The 1973 *Roe* v. *Wade* decision guaranteed a woman's right to an abortion. It also set off a series of legislative and legal contests about the exact terms of that right. Prolife advocates won many legislative and some legal battles over the regulation of abortion during the 1970s. These political and legal struggles con-

tinued to be a defining element of the politics of the 1980s and 1990s.

Sources:
Marian Faux, *Roe v. Wade* (New York: Macmillan, 1988);

Kristin Luker, *Abortion and the Politics of Motherhood* (Berkeley & Los Angeles: University of California Press, 1984).

Norma McCorvey, *I Am Roe* (New York: HarperCollins, 1994).

THE ATTICA RIOT AND THE RIGHTS OF PRISONERS

The Attica Riot. On 9 September 1971 inmates began a riot and takeover at the Attica State Correctional Facility in New York. The takeover ended four days later when law enforcement officers stormed the prison. Forty-three people were killed: ten prison guards who were being held as hostages and thirty-three inmates. The Attica riot captured the attention of the nation, directing interest to prison conditions and the rights of prisoners.

Background. The riot at Attica came after a summer of tension and unrest at the prison. The prison was overcrowded, housing 2,250 men in a facility considered safe for 1,600. Racial tensions were also high. The prison had no black guards and only one Puerto Rican guard, yet the inmates were 54 percent black and 9 percent Puerto Rican. Tensions at the prison grew after inmate George Jackson was shot to death at San Quentin prison in California. Inmates assumed that he had been murdered because he was a black radical. On 9 September minor disciplinary actions against two fighting inmates erupted quickly into a full-scale riot involving more than a thousand inmates. Fifty prison guards were taken as hostages. Most were beaten by angry inmates. Several seriously injured hostages were released, and one hostage died as a result of his injuries.

Demands. The inmates quickly organized a negotiating team to put together demands for the prison administration. Their initial demands included complete amnesty for participants in the riot, federal intervention, and the organization of an independent negotiating committee made up of public figures sympathetic to the prisoners' conditions to ensure that the prison officials kept their promises. State officials refused to offer amnesty, particularly after the hostage guard died. They did organize the negotiating team requested by the inmates. The negotiations focused on amnesty and prison conditions. The prison administration agreed to twenty-eight of the inmates' requests, including an end to the censorship of reading materials, a right to be active politically, a more nutritious diet, an expansion of library programs, more recreational opportunities, and true religious freedom. Officials refused a complete amnesty from criminal prosecution for the riot and the removal of the prison superintendent. Negotiations stalled at this point. State officials then presented an ultimatum to the inmates: either accept the offer or have the prison retaken by force. The inmates refused to accept.

Storming the Yard. New York governor Nelson Rockefeller then ordered state police, sheriffs' deputies, and correctional officers to launch an attack on the area of the prison controlled by inmates. They fired tear gas into the cell blocks; officers fired rifles and shotguns into the prison yard from roofs and other high points. The attack lasted ten minutes. Initial reports stated that nine hostages had their throats slashed by inmates and that twenty-eight inmates were killed in the attack. Later investigations made clear that inmates had not killed any hostages during the attack. Instead, ten hostages had been killed by gunshots from the police and prison guards retaking the prison yard. Twenty-nine inmates were killed in the attack; three others had been killed by other inmates before the attack.

The Aftermath. New York State officials were heavily criticized as the cause of the hostages' deaths became known. They were criticized for their attack and for the prison conditions that had led to the riot in the first place. Attica came to symbolize the dangerous conditions of many prisons and the often-petty restrictions on prisoners' religious and political freedoms. The Attica riot provoked several efforts to reform prison conditions across the United States. Those reform efforts often failed because of budget constraints and escalating prison populations, which increased prison overcrowding. Prison populations grew 88 percent from 1970 to 1981, while new prison building lagged behind. Prison conditions and overcrowding were considered more of a prob-

Year	No. of law schools	Law school admissions	Bar admissions
1970	146	86,028	17,922
1971	147	95,943	20,510
1972	149	105,245	25,086
1973	151	114,800	30,707
1974	154	116,517	33,358
1975	164	122,542	34,930
1976	163	125,010	35,741
1977	168	126,085	37,302
1978	168	126,937	39,086
1979	169	126,915	42,756

NUMBER OF LAW SCHOOLS AND BAR ADMISSIONS

lem at the end of the 1970s than they were at the time of the Attica riot.

The Constitutional Rights of Prisoners. The 1970s also brought a growing concern for the constitutional rights of prisoners. The general principle was stated by the Supreme Court in *Wolff* v. *McConnell* (1974): "Lawful imprisonment necessarily makes unavailable many rights and privileges of the ordinary citizen.... But though his rights may be diminished by the needs and exigencies of the institutional environment, a prisoner is not wholly stripped of constitutional protections when he is imprisoned for crime. There is no iron curtain drawn between the Constitution and the prisons of this country." In *Wolff* v. *McConnell* the Court guaranteed prisoners a hearing before they could be denied time off for good behavior. Prisoners were also guaranteed a hearing in initial parole decisions, but not when the prisoner was being transferred from one prison to another. Prisoners were guaranteed the right to marriage. They were denied any right to be interviewed by members of the press.

Local Challenges. District courts also heard several challenges to prison conditions. Prisoners challenged overcrowding, poor medical care, solitary confinement, and inadequate food and sanitation as violations of the constitutional prohibition of cruel and unusual punishment. District courts in Arkansas, Alabama, and Ohio ordered prison officials to correct some problems, particularly overcrowding and poor medical care. However, by the early 1980s the Supreme Court had restricted the reach of the cruel and unusual punishment clause. The Court ordered district courts to defer to the decisions of prison officials. Prison conditions were no longer a constitutional issue.

Source:
Tom Wicker, *A Time to Die* (New York: Quadrangle, 1975).

THE CHANGING LEGAL PROFESSION

An Increase in Lawyers. The legal profession underwent major changes in the 1970s. The number of lawyers almost doubled between 1970 and 1980, from 278,000 to 525,000. The number of lawyers relative to the population also increased. In 1970 the United States had one lawyer for every 572 people. In 1980 there was one lawyer for every 418 people, a bigger change than in any other ten-year period. The biggest jump in enrollment in law schools and admission to the bar occurred between 1970 and 1972.

Expansion of Firms. Long-term changes in the practice continued. The percentage of lawyers who practiced by themselves declined from 36.6 percent to 33.2 percent. Overall, the number of lawyers who worked in private law firms declined from 72.7 percent of all lawyers to 68.3 percent. The number of associates, or beginning lawyers, in law firms increased. Overall government employment stayed about the same, and there was a substantial increase in lawyers who worked for local government, from 2.4 percent to 5.6 percent.

Earnings. The substantial increase in the number of lawyers and the number of law-school graduates entering practice kept the average lawyer's earnings down. Measured in constant 1979 dollars, lawyers and judges earned an average of $39,000 in 1969 and only $36,700 in 1979. Earnings varied by the type of practice. Attorneys in firms saw dramatic increases in their earnings. Partners' earnings went from $59,800 in 1971 to $82,900 in 1979. Attorneys practicing on their own went from earning on average about $25,100 in 1971 to about $31,900 in 1979.

Background. The 1970s saw an expansion in the number of women in law schools. In 1970 women made up 8.9 percent of the full-time students in law schools approved by the American Bar Association (ABA). In 1980 women constituted 34.3 percent of the students. However, they did not make up as great a part of the profession once they graduated. In 1970 women were about 5 percent of all lawyers; in 1980 they were about 8 percent. People of color, incorporating black, Hispanic-American, Puerto Rican, Asian/Pacific Islander and American Indian, similarly increased their representation in law schools. Those groups made up about 20 percent of the American population. In the 1969–1970 school year they made up 4.3 percent of the student body in ABA-approved law schools. In 1979–1980 they were 8.1 percent of the student body. The increase has not been as rapid since then.

Source:
Richard L. Abel, *American Lawyers* (New York: Oxford University Press, 1989).

CRIME AND PUBLIC OPINION

A Political Issue. Public concern about crime grew in the late 1960s. In 1968 Richard Nixon and George Wallace made crime a major part of their campaigns for the presidency. This concern about crime continued in the 1970s. Public-opinion surveys repeatedly listed it as one of the top public priorities.

An Increase in Crime Rates. Rates for many crimes did increase in the late 1960s and early 1970s. According to the FBI, the rate of violent crimes increased from 364 per 100,000 population in 1970 to 581 in 1980, an increase of 60 percent from 1970 to 1980. The rates for property crimes went from 3,621 in 1970 to 5,319 in 1980, an increase of 47 percent from 1970 to 1980. The increases in crime rates during the 1970s occurred mostly in the first four years and the last two years of the decade. Many experts blamed part of the increase in crime on the increased leniency of the criminal justice system and criticized the new rights granted criminal defendants by the Supreme Court. Some authorities pointed to the continuing high levels of poverty in many areas, particularly in the central cities, where crime rates were highest. Finally, many pointed to what they saw as the decline of important social institutions, particularly community and the family among black and other minority groups, and increased permissiveness toward drug use, welfare, and sexual behavior. One reaction to the increasing crime rates was increasing imprisonment of convicted criminals. More convicted criminals were sentenced to time in prison, judges sentenced them to longer terms, and parole boards were more reluctant to release inmates from prison on parole. Federal and state prison populations grew from 196,000 in 1970 to 369,000 in 1981. It is not clear, however, that increasing imprisonment had the desired effect of reducing crime rates.

Decriminalization? Even as they got tougher on violent offenders, Americans began to rethink their attitude toward drug crimes. The use of marijuana, in particular, was common among young people and seemed to have few ill effects for society. Even first ladies Betty Ford and Rosalyn Carter admitted that their children probably tried marijuana. Rather than impose criminal penalties for marijuana, in 1973 Oregon decided to impose a fine. Seven other states soon followed Oregon's example, but the decriminalization movement faded as the government in the 1980s reasserted the necessity of a "war on drugs."

Rethinking Domestic Violence. The women's movement also redefined the boundary between social convention and criminal behavior. Domestic violence, especially wife beating and child abuse, often went unnoticed by the public. An unspoken tolerance for these acts and fear, guilt, and shame on the part of the victims often kept domestic violence from public attention. In 1976 the FBI noted that many crimes of this nature went unreported; they added that because victims often felt afraid and ashamed, rape also was underreported. As battered-women's shelters opened in the mid 1970s, however, the public became less likely to blame the victim of domestic violence or rape and increasingly subjected the perpetrators to criminal prosecution.

Source:
David M. O'Brien, *Constitutional Law and Politics,* volume 1 (New York: Norton, 1991).

THE DEATH PENALTY

The Death Penalty in the 1960s. In 1970 thirty-nine states allowed the death penalty for some crimes. Six states had abolished the death penalty in the 1960s, and about 40 percent of the people who were asked in public-opinion surveys said that the death penalty should be abolished. States were executing few inmates, largely because death-penalty opponents were mounting a legal campaign to obtain stays of execution in every case. During the 1960s about forty persons a year were sentenced to death, but only a few were executed. No one was executed in the years from 1968 to 1971.

Challenges. The legal campaign against the death penalty was led by the National Association for the Advancement of Colored People (NAACP) Legal Defense and Education Fund (LDF) and the American Civil Liberties Union (ACLU). The LDF had long been concerned with the death penalty because it was more often imposed on blacks than on white people who had committed the same crime. The LDF mounted a campaign to challenge the constitutionality of the death penalty precisely because it did not provide "equal protection of the laws," as required by the Fourteenth Amendment. In

Isadore Hodges, one of thirteen Tennessee convicts spared the electric chair by the 1972 Supreme Court decision in *Furman* v. *Georgia*

denying equality, the LDF argued, the death penalty became cruel and unusual punishment, prohibited by the Eighth Amendment.

Furman v. Georgia. The LDF brought challenges to several states' death penalty statutes. The Supreme Court decided four of those cases in *Furman* v. *Georgia* (1972). In a close decision five justices held that the death penalty, as then administered, was an unconstitutional violation of the prohibition against cruel and unusual punishment. Only two justices held that the death penalty was unconstitutional in all circumstances. The other three justices cited the arbitrary criteria for the sentence. They compared the "wanton" and "freak[ish] manner" in which the death penalty was imposed with being struck by lightning. Four justices disagreed with the decision, arguing that the Court was legislating its own preferences rather than interpreting the Constitution.

Rethinking the Law. Thirty-five states enacted new death-penalty laws in the three years after the *Furman* v. *Georgia* decision. These laws were designed to limit the arbitrariness of the death penalty. The Supreme Court considered these new laws in *Gregg* v. *Georgia* (1975). The LDF once again led the argument against the death penalty. They argued that, even under the new laws, the penalty was imposed arbitrarily and that its imposition continued to discriminate against blacks. They also argued that the death penalty was never deserved for any crime and that crime prevention could better be addressed through effective policing.

Democracy and Rights. The dilemma for the Court was between individual rights and the democratic will. The Court was concerned that in this contentious issue thirty-five state legislatures had tried hard to enact constitutional death penalty statutes after *Furman* v. *Georgia*, showing that they supported the death penalty. In a democracy, many justices believed, those decisions deserved some respect from the Court. On the other hand, the point of a constitution is to say that there are some things legislative majorities cannot take away from the citizens, such as their right to free speech.

The Gregg v. Georgia Decision. On 2 July 1976 the Supreme Court decided that it could not take the power to decide from legislatures. They noted the difficulty of telling whether the death penalty deterred any crimes at all. For the seven-member majority the divisiveness and uncertainty of the issue meant legislatures should decide it. They argued that as long as the state specified conditions for the death penalty — Georgia listed ten aggravating circumstances, including, for example, murder committed during the commission of a felony — legislatures could demand its imposition.

After Gregg v. Georgia. In 1977 almost six hundred prisoners were under a death sentence, and the number increased for the rest of the decade. However, states did not execute many people in those years. Attorneys for those inmates continued to pursue every legal avenue of appeal. While Americans supported the death penalty, they were actually reluctant to execute prisoners.

Source:
Lee Epstein and Joseph F. Kobylka, *The Supreme Court and Legal Change* (Chapel Hill: University of North Carolina Press, 1992).

THE DUE-PROCESS REVOLUTION

The Case of Esther Lett. Esther Lett received Aid to Families with Dependent Children (AFDC), government assistance that went largely to single-parent families in which the adult in the family did not have a job. In 1967 the state of New York cut off her assistance, claiming that she had worked without informing them. That violated the rules. But Lett had not worked in violation of the rules. She should not have been cut off from payments. She could ask for a hearing to challenge the decision, but in the meantime she and her children had to find whatever charity they could. Neighbors gave them food. Some of it was spoiled, and Lett and her children ended up in the hospital from food poisoning. Afterward she sued the welfare agency, and it reinvestigated her case and reinstated her.

Brutal Need and the AFDC Recipient. Legal-services attorneys who worked in the New York Mobilization for Youth (MFY) program were looking for ways to make the law work for the poor. They argued that because the people on AFDC needed the money so badly — because they were in "brutal need" of assistance — government agencies should not be able to cut off benefits without first providing a hearing. MFY attorneys put Lett's case together with twelve others and sued. The due-process clause of the Fifth and Fourteenth Amendments says that no one shall "be deprived of life, liberty or property without due process of law." But what process is due? The attorneys argued that due process required that people be given hearings with a chance to present evidence before officials cut their welfare benefits off.

Some Kind of a Hearing. The Supreme Court agreed with the MFY attorneys in *Goldberg* v. *Kelly* (1970). The Court held that the receipt of welfare payments was a property right granted by the government, like a license to sell liquor or a defense contract. Therefore the government must grant the recipient a hearing before terminating that right. The court cited the "brutal need" of recipients in holding that the hearing must come *before* the benefits are cut off, since terminating the benefits before the hearing may "deprive an *eligible* recipient of the very means by which to live while he waits." That case became the basis for others, heralding a due process revolution. The Supreme Court, however, worried about the administrative burden it might be imposing on agencies and in later cases tried to make the hearings more flexible. In *Goss* v. *Lopez* (1975) the Court decided that before being suspended from school for more than three days a student should be able to present his or her side to a school administrator. However, the Court emphasized that that hearing could be informal, just an administrator talking with the student. In *Mathews* v. *Eldridge* (1976) the Court decided that people on disability payments could ask for hearings after the benefits were cut off. The Court emphasized that only some kind of hearing must be involved and that the exact requirements depended on the situation.

Precedent and Application. The Supreme Court uses the ruling from cases in many different settings. A case about hearings in AFDC is useful to help decide a case about hearings in other government programs. In this way in the 1970s courts and attorneys brought thinking about due process from Lett to school students.

Source:
Martha Davis, *Brutal Need* (New Haven: Yale University Press, 1994).

Water pollution control official sampling the water in Lake Michigan in compliance with the Water Pollution Control Act of 1972

EMPLOYMENT OPPORTUNITY: JOB REQUIREMENTS AND DISCRIMINATION

Low Wages, No Transfer. The Dan River Steam Station, owned by the Duke Power Company, had ninety-five employees. Fourteen were black. Employees could work in one of five areas: labor, coal handling, operations, maintenance, and laboratories and testing. The highest wages in the labor section were lower than the lowest wages in any other area. It was generally not possible to transfer between areas. All the black employees were in labor, with no hope of moving up.

The Civil Rights Act and Employment Opportunity. The Civil Rights Act of 1964 prohibited racial discrimination in employment. Duke Power could no longer officially discriminate. In September 1965 Duke Power instituted two tests—the Wonderlic Personnel Test and the Bennett Mechanical Comprehensive Test. If an employee passed the tests, he could transfer between sections. Black employees seldom passed the tests and therefore could not transfer to better jobs. They sued Duke Power with the help of the NAACP Legal Defense and Education Fund. They maintained that the tests did not measure the employee's ability to do a job and that they resulted in black employees being passed over for better

jobs. Duke Power itself could not show that those who did well on the tests performed better in their new positions. The black employees argued that the test violated the new Civil Rights Act.

Griggs v. Duke Power. The Supreme Court decided the issue in *Griggs* v. *Duke Power* (1971). They held that if a test were given as a prerequisite for a job, the employer would have to show that the requirement actually measured a skill related to the job. The Court said that it was not necessary for the employee to show that the employer *intended* to discriminate by using a test, only that the job exam had the effect of discriminating. The Court placed the burden of showing that obligatory tests helped select better workers squarely on the employer. Many traditional job requirements could not be shown to help employers pick employees who could do a better job, including some of the federal government's own civil service examinations; they had to be dropped.

Source:
Griggs v. *Duke Power*, 401 U.S. 424 (1971).

ENVIRONMENTAL LAW

New Laws and New Roles for the Courts. Debate over environmental protection grew markedly during the

1970s, and much of the struggle occurred in the courts. Congress passed several statutes that gave courts a central role in environmental enforcement. The National Environmental Policy Act of 1970 (NEPA) required the federal government to write an environmental impact statement for all "federal projects with a significant environmental impact." Opponents of a project could go to court to challenge the adequacy of the impact statement. The Clean Air Act amendments of 1970 required the Environmental Protection Agency (EPA) to set health-based standards for local air quality. Areas whose air quality did not meet those standards had to develop plans for meeting them. The Water Pollution Control Act amendments of 1972 imposed similar requirements for water pollution. Standards could be challenged by environmental groups or by companies required to reduce their pollution. As a result, courts became a principal battleground in the struggle over environmental regulation. During the 1970s there were 855 federal lawsuits involving NEPA, 233 involving clean air, and 508 involving clean water.

Environmental Impact Statements and Nuclear Power. The NEPA requirement for environmental impact statements was used extensively to oppose the licensing of nuclear power plants. Environmental groups such as the National Resources Defense Council or the Sierra Club sued the Atomic Energy Commission (AEC), which was responsible for licensing the plants. They claimed that the AEC had not taken adequate consideration of the safety and efficiency of the plants. District courts, located in the area that would be affected by the plant, often upheld the concerns of the environmental groups. The nuclear plant owners then appealed and usually won final approval. In the *Vermont Yankee* case, the Supreme Court said that the NEPA was a procedural law and could not be used to impose environmental standards on nuclear power plants. The builders of nuclear power plants won the legal issue, but the environmental groups won the war. By the end of the decade builders had mostly given up plans to build more nuclear power plants because the delay and expense of fighting the lawsuits often made them too expensive.

Local Air and Tall Smokestacks. The EPA and the courts also had to deal with questions about how localities avoided meeting the local air-quality standards. One subterfuge was to build tall smokestacks that would reduce the effect of a major pollution source such as a power plant. The tall stacks dispersed the pollution over a much larger area and thus reduced its impact on the local area. Environmentalists complained that this shifted the burden of the pollution to this broader area and sued the EPA to prevent it from approving plans that allowed tall smokestacks. Power companies sued the EPA to allow them to build the smokestacks. Because of these suits the courts rather than the EPA decided the regulations for allowing the use of tall smokestacks, and they placed strong restrictions on the use of smokestacks to disperse air pollution out of the local area.

Antifeminists demonstrating at the November 1977 National Women's Conference in Houston

Water Pollution and Effluent Standards. The EPA was also often caught in the middle of competing lawsuits in their regulation of water pollution. Environmentalists sued for vigorous EPA enforcement of pollution standards regardless of mitigating considerations. Firms having trouble meeting the water-pollution standards sued, claiming that the law only required them to make the "best practicable treatment" and that it was too expensive to eliminate their pollution totally. The courts reviewed the EPA's decisions about "best practicable treatment," sometimes siding with the environmental groups and sometimes with the polluter. The EPA could not develop consistent national standards for its enforcement of water-pollution laws because it could not anticipate how courts would evaluate those standards. On the other hand, environmental groups and polluters were both guaranteed a hearing where they could make their arguments about whether the EPA's restrictions should be made stronger or more lenient.

The Continuing Role of Courts. Courts continue to be at the center of environmental regulation. The environmental and economic interests involved are so important that neither side is willing to give up its ability to challenge regulatory decisions in court. No other issue better illustrates how the structure of American administrative law guarantees that courts are often placed in the position of deciding difficult conflicts in public policy.

Sources:
R. Shep Melnick, *Regulation and the Courts* (Washington, D.C.: Brookings Institution, 1983);

Lettie Wenner, *The Environmental Decade in Court* (Bloomington: Indiana University Press, 1982).

THE EQUAL RIGHTS AMENDMENT

The Amendment. Debate over ratification of the Equal Rights Amendment provided one of the key political struggles of the 1970s. Congress passed the Equal

Rights Amendment in 1972. However, before it could become part of the Constitution, it had to be ratified by three-fourths (thirty-eight) of the states. The text of the amendment was simple:

1. Equality of rights under the law shall not be denied or abridged by the United States or by any State on account of sex.

2. The Congress shall have the power to enforce, by appropriate legislation, the provisions of this article.

3. This amendment shall take effect two years after the date of ratification.

Quick Support in 1972. Congress first considered an equal rights amendment in 1923, and the proposal came up regularly after that. Proponents never overcame the opposition of social reformers and labor unions concerned about how the ERA would affect labor legislation protecting women and children. By 1972 organized labor dropped its objections, and in March of that year Congress passed the ERA. The only contentious issue was whether the amendment should explicitly exclude women from the military draft. ERA proponents objected to any special treatment and managed to defeat the provision. Many states were eager to ratify the ERA. Twenty-five minutes after it passed Congress, both houses of the Hawaii legislature voted unanimously for the amendment. By early 1973 twenty-five of the required thirty-eight states had ratified it.

Slowing Down. Ratification slowed after that, however. Ten more states ratified the amendment by the end of 1977, leaving the amendment only three states short of adoption. Proponents were able to get Congress to extend the original 1979 deadline for ratification to 1982. However, no state ratified it after 1977, and three states rescinded their ratification (although it was not clear that they could legally do this). In 1982 the amendment died.

What Happened? The Equal Rights Amendment always had support from a majority of Americans, both men and women. However, ratifying a constitutional amendment requires more than majority support. It requires that proponents secure majority support in each of three-fourths of the states. An amendment must have extraordinarily broad support and little concerted opposition. Opponents of the ERA were able to emphasize several key issues that stopped ratification. These issues were most important in conservative southern states. Many Americans feared changes in the roles of men and women, especially in families. Phyllis Schlafly, a politically active conservative woman, organized the STOP ERA campaign based on these concerns. Opponents convinced people that the ERA would bring radical changes to their lives: an end to husbands' obligations to support their wives and families, single-sex bathrooms, the drafting of women into the military. These claims about the effects of the ERA were exaggerated, but they struck a responsive chord among Americans concerned about families and the changing roles of men and women in

society. They were enough to generate concerted opposition in the conservative southern states that had not yet ratified the ERA.

Public Opinion and the ERA. A substantial majority of Americans favored the ERA during the whole time the states were considering ratification. However, saying they supported the ERA meant that they agreed in principle to equality, not that they supported changing the traditional roles of men and women. For example, a 1977 poll revealed that 66 percent of Americans who supported the ERA also believed that a preschool child would suffer if the child's mother worked. Sixty-two percent said that if there are a limited number of jobs, a married woman should not be employed if her husband is able to support her. Fifty-five percent believed that it is more important for a wife to support her husband's career than to have one herself.

Waiting for Changes in State Legislatures. Recognizing the importance and difficulty of winning in all regions, few proponents of the ERA supported working on the amendment again. They argued instead that it was more important to work on election of women to state legislatures. State legislatures are responsible for many policies that affect women, such as family and divorce law, welfare, and equal employment. They felt that electing women to the legislatures would accomplish more than would enacting an Equal Rights Amendment.

Source:
Jane J. Mansbridge, *Why We Lost the ERA* (Chicago: University of Chicago Press, 1986).

EQUALITY BEFORE THE LAW: MEN AND WOMEN

Military Husbands and Wives. The Equal Rights Amendment was not ratified, but even as the states considered it, the Supreme Court was contemplating the extent to which the law could treat men and women differently. Sharron Frontiero, a lieutenant in the United States Air Force, challenged the military's benefits rules. Military wives were automatically extended health and medical benefits. But when Frontiero asked for those benefits for her husband, she was turned down. Frontiero claimed that the policy discriminated against women, violating the Fourteenth Amendment's guarantee of "equal protection of the laws."

Gross, Stereotyped Distinctions. In *Frontiero* v. *Richardson* (1973), the Supreme Court decided that the military policy violated the equal protection clause. The Court said that the government had to have a good reason to treat men and women differently because of their sex. It was not enough to assume that husbands support their wives, but that wives do not support their husbands. As Justice William Brennan put it, "Our statute books gradually became laden with gross, stereotyped distinctions between the sexes." Such distinctions could no longer be the basis of policy and law.

Beer, the Draft, and Statutory Rape. The *Frontiero* v. *Richardson* decision opened up a series of questions about when governments could treat men and women differently. The decision said that the government could discriminate between men and women, but that it had to have strong reasons to do so. The question then became how strong the reasons had to be. The Court struck down an Oklahoma law in *Craig* v. *Boren* (1976) that allowed women under twenty-one but not young men to buy 3.2 percent alcohol beer. Later decisions allowed state employers to give preferences to military veterans even though that benefited more men than women, affirmed male-only draft registration and restricted statutory rape laws to men.

Source:
David M. O'Brien, *Constitutional Law and Politics,* volume 2 (New York: Norton, 1991).

LEGAL SERVICES

The Great Society and Legal Assistance. The Office of Economic Opportunity began to fund lawyers for poor people in 1965. While legal-aid programs already existed in many cities, they were poorly funded and often unable to meet requests for help. The federally funded legal-services programs were designed to coordinate the provision of legal aid and to help the poor by working for social change through law. They also represented the poor in their ordinary legal troubles, such as conflict with landlords or family problems. The efforts of legal service attorneys to benefit the poor were extremely controversial. Congress regularly considered cutting back the cases that the attorneys could take.

The California Story. California legal-services attorneys, particularly the California Rural Legal Assistance (CRLA) program, brought many of the lawsuits that expanded legal protections for poor people. The CRLA also tried to work with farmworkers for better conditions in agricultural labor. They worked extensively with Cesar Chavez, a leading organizer of the United Farmworkers' Organization. Organizing for agricultural laborers was extremely controversial because of the political power of California farm owners. The CRLA was therefore the target of much criticism. The CRLA was successful in challenging cuts to public medical care in California and in challenging the use of alien farm laborers in California. In 1970 Gov. Ronald Reagan vetoed appropriation of $1.8 million to the CRLA from the federal government because he objected to the program. He charged it with misuse of funds.

Response. In response to Governor Reagan's complaints President Richard Nixon appointed a commission to investigate the CRLA in January of 1971. In June the Office of Economic Opportunity made the report public, calling Governor Reagan's charges "unfounded, without merit, unfair and irresponsible." Under pressure from President Nixon, Governor Reagan reinstated the CRLA's funds. But the face-off had received national

President Nixon on 29 April 1974 in a televised address in which he announced that he would release edited versions of the sixty-four Watergate tapes requested by Special Prosecutor Leon Jaworski

attention and provided the pretext for congressional attempts to reorganize the Legal Services Program.

Limits on Work. In 1974 Congress and President Nixon enacted limits on what legal-services attorneys could do. They could no longer represent undocumented workers, which specifically impacted California Rural Legal Assistance. Nor could they be involved in any school desegregation or abortion cases. They also could not organize low-income people or participate in demonstrations.

Politics and Organization. Congress also reorganized the Legal Services Program into the Legal Services Corporation (LSC). Sponsored in part by the American Bar Association, the reorganization was an attempt to insulate legal assistance from the dismantling of antipoverty programs that President Nixon began in the 1970s. The reorganization also gained support from those who wanted to limit the work of legal-services attorneys. They halted funding designed to meet poor communities' needs. Instead, the LSC distributed legal aid money on a per capita basis. Legal-services programs now subsidized routine legal services for poor people rather than seeking to act as a source of social change.

Source:
Mark Kessler, *Legal Services for the Poor* (Westport, Conn.: Greenwood Press, 1987).

THE OTHER SIDE OF LAW AND ORDER: NIXON AND THE CONSTRAINTS OF LAW

The Example of Watergate. President Nixon's emphasis on law and order often clashed with the way the Nixon administration operated. The administration often acted as if it were not subject to the limits of constitutional and statutory restrictions, particularly in its political-campaign activities. The conduct of the Watergate affair and cover-up provides the clearest example of this attitude. The Watergate affair started with the arrest of Nixon campaign operatives for attempting to burglarize the Democratic National Committee headquarters. Several officials, including Nixon, then became involved in an illegal cover-up. Their actions included destroying evidence, paying the Watergate burglars to keep silent, and refusing to obey court orders to provide evidence. The cover-up conspiracy failed only when one of the convicted burglars revealed the payoffs and prosecutors were able to persuade White House officials to cooperate. White House and campaign officials were convicted and served time in prison for their actions. Nixon himself would have stood trial if President Gerald Ford had not pardoned him.

Political Enemies and Security Targets. After the Watergate affair was revealed, it became clear that the Nixon administration's conduct was typical of its approach to politics. Presidential operatives connected to the White House or the reelection campaign undertook many illegal activities against those they considered political enemies. They broke into the office of former Pentagon official Daniel Ellsberg's psychiatrist hoping to find embarrassing information after Ellsberg helped release the secret Department of Defense study of the Vietnam War, commonly referred to as the Pentagon Papers. They constructed an "enemies list" and then directed the FBI, IRS, and other federal agencies to target those individuals and groups for harrassment. They approved the "Huston plan," which authorized the CIA, FBI, and Department of Defense to commit burglaries and other illegal acts against persons identified as "internal security targets." They organized a group of aides called the Plumbers to probe and plug leaks of government and political information to the press. These and other illegal actions by the Nixon administration and reelection campaign made it clear that they believed that they should be free from the provisions of the criminal law that they argued should be strictly applied to others.

Executive Privilege. Nixon's resistance to the Watergate investigations also raised important constitutional questions about the relative powers of the presidency,

"A LOT OF MEDIOCRE JUDGES"

Criticism of Judge Harrold Carswell's nomination did not rest only on his civil rights record. Many lawyers believed that he was a mediocre judge. In response Sen. Roman Hruska of Nebraska argued, "Even if he is mediocre, there are a lot of mediocre judges and people and lawyers. They are entitled to a little representation, aren't they, and a little chance? We can't have all Brandeises, Cardozos and Frankfurters and stuff like that there."

Source: Alpheus Thomas Mason, *The Supreme Court from Taft to Burger* (Baton Rouge: Louisiana State University Press, 1979).

Congress, and the courts. Most important was the issue of executive privilege. The issue came up in the fight over tape recordings that Nixon regularly made of his meetings in the White House. Archibald Cox, the special prosecutor appointed to investigate the Watergate cover-up, requested those tapes. He wanted to know what White House officials knew of Watergate and whether they discussed a cover-up. President Nixon refused to turn over the tapes. He argued that to do their jobs all presidents need to conduct free and open exchanges with aides and staff in an environment protected from public scrutiny; thus it would be against the public interest to produce the tapes. President Nixon claimed that all presidents have an "executive privilege," meaning that they do not have to comply with requests for information from Congress or the courts.

United States v. Nixon. The Supreme Court finally addressed the question of executive privilege in *United States* v. *Nixon* on 24 July 1974. The Court faced a dilemma. Certainly free and open discussion between the president and his aides was desirable. But if that meant presidents never had to comply with court orders, the Court would be agreeing that the president was completely above the law. That approach was not compatible with a constitutional system. The Supreme Court unanimously decided that President Nixon had to turn over the tapes. However, they also agreed that there was some limited form of executive privilege. They restricted executive privilege to national security considerations.

Aftermath. The Supreme Court decision marked the end of Nixon's resistance. He turned over the tapes as ordered. The House of Representatives Judiciary Committee soon approved three articles of impeachment. On 9 August 1974 President Nixon resigned, and Vice-president Gerald R. Ford became president. The Watergate affair raised questions about the role of the president in American democracy. Americans since have been concerned about abuses of power in the presidency. The legacy of Watergate includes the creation of special

The Burger Court: seated: Potter Stewart, William O. Douglas, Warren E. Burger, William J. Brennan, Jr., and Byron R. White; standing: Lewis F. Powell, Jr., Thurgood Marshall, Harry A. Blackmun, and William H. Rehnquist

prosecutors, who have been used several times to investigate possible wrongdoing.

Sources:

Philip B. Kurland, *Watergate and the Constitution* (Chicago: University of Chicago Press, 1978);

David M. O'Brien, *Constitutional Law and Politics,* volume 1 (New York: Norton, 1991).

THE SUPREME COURT AND PUBLIC POLICY: THE SUPREME COURT OF THE 1970S

The Warren Court and Judicial Activism. As Richard Nixon ran for president in 1968, he promised the American people he would restructure the Supreme Court. Reflecting the attitudes of many conservatives, Nixon opposed the judicial activism of the Warren Court, which, since the 1954 *Brown* v. *Board of Education* decision, had used the court system to end racial discrimination in education, employment, and politics. The Warren Court also expanded the scope of individual liberties, especially the rights of the accused, and eliminated restrictions on free speech and publications. The Warren Court was dominated by liberals such as William O. Douglas, Abe Fortas, William Brennan, and Thurgood Marshall — men who believed in using their constitutional authority to expand civil liberties and redress social inequality. Nixon had a different perspective on the Court. He promised to appoint only "strict constructionists," men who favored a narrow interpretation of the Constitution

and who would return the Supreme Court to its traditional conservatism. Nixon soon had the opportunity to keep his promise. He replaced retiring Chief Justice Earl Warren with Warren Burger soon after taking office in 1969. He appointed three other justices in 1970 and 1971. Initially, however, he had difficulty getting his nominees confirmed.

Failed Nominations. After the appointment of Burger, President Nixon wanted to appoint a southerner to the Court. His first nominee to replace Justice Abe Fortas, Judge Clement F. Haynsworth, Jr., was rejected in June of 1969 because of questions about his ability and concerns about his civil rights record. The president then nominated G. Harrold Carswell, who had been a Federal District Court judge for seven years in Tallahassee, Florida, and a United States Court of Appeals judge for six months. However, Carswell met with substantial opposition. In 1948 Carswell had declared his "firm, vigorous belief in the principles of White Supremacy." He said he no longer believed in that. However, he had also worked to change a Tallahassee golf course from public to private to avoid desegregation. Judge Carswell was rejected by a vote in the Senate of fifty-one to forty-five. Nixon complained that the Senate was discriminating against his nominees because they were from the South.

Congress, the Court, and Politics. In return for the opposition to the president's nominees, some of the president's allies in Congress moved to impeach Justice

Douglas in 1970. He was, they believed, simply too liberal. Responding to the observation that Justice Douglas had done nothing for which he could be impeached, Congressman Gerald Ford argued that an official could be impeached for "whatever a majority of the House of Representatives considers impeachment to be at a given moment in history." Without charges of substance, the impeachment effort failed.

An Experienced Candidate. President Nixon temporarily abandoned his search for a southerner and appointed a friend of Chief Justice Burger's, Harry A. Blackmun. In addition to an early career as an attorney in Minnesota, Blackmun had been a judge on the United States Court of Appeals for eleven years. He was quickly confirmed.

A Southern Appointment. President Nixon was able to appoint two justices when Justices Hugo L. Black and John Marshall Harlan retired late in 1971. He nominated Lewis F. Powell, Jr., who had had a long career as an attorney in Richmond, Virginia. He had also been the president of the American Bar Association. The Black Caucus in Congress opposed him because he had served on the antidesegregation Richmond school board and the Virginia Board of Education. However, Powell was approved with just one dissenting vote.

An Assistant Attorney General. Next President Nixon appointed William Rehnquist, an assistant attorney general for the president. Rehnquist also aroused some opposition. As a law clerk for Justice Jackson he had written a memo expressing doubt about the wisdom of holding segregation unconstitutional in *Brown* v. *Board of Education.* Furthermore, he seemed to have been involved in suppressing the turnout of black voters when he worked in Arizona. Other positions that seemed to oppose civil liberties led the American Civil Liberties Union for the first time to oppose a nomination. Nonetheless, Rehnquist was approved by the Senate by a vote of sixty-eight to twenty-six.

The Longest-Serving Justice Retires. Justice Douglas retired in November 1975 after he had a stroke. President Ford nominated John Paul Stevens, a federal appeals court judge. With that appointment the Nixon and Ford administrations had appointed a majority of the Supreme Court.

The Burger Court: A Balance Between Liberals and Conservatives. The Burger Court departed from the liberal trend of the Warren Court, but the justices' views were split enough that the Court did not really reverse that trend. Justices Brennan and Marshall formed the liberal wing of the Court. Justice Rehnquist and Chief Justice Burger made up the conservative wing. Justices Stevens, Blackmun, Byron White, Potter Stewart, and Powell made up the middle. It was these five justices whose votes generally decided the issues. The balance on the Court often meant that the Court would not stake out broad new constitutional principles as did both the

Warren Court of the 1960s and the Rehnquist Court of the late 1980s and 1990s. It also meant that individual justices could find themselves in a powerful position as the swing vote in a particular case. For instance, Justice Powell was the swing vote in the affirmative-action case of *Regents of the University of California* v. *Bakke* (1978). His opinion therefore stated the law that came out of the case. He decided that universities could try to diversify their student body by race but that they could not set numerical quotas for race-based admissions.

Consolidating a Conservative Court. The appointments of the 1970s meant that the justices most likely to retire were the longer-serving, more-liberal justices. This paved the way for the Reagan and Bush appointments of the 1980s, which brought more conservatives to the Court and resulted in the conservative Rehnquist Court.

Source:
Alpheus Thomas Mason, *The Supreme Court from Taft to Burger* (Baton Rouge: Louisiana State University Press, 1979).

PADDLING IN SCHOOLS

Slow to Respond. Another due-process issue involved corporal punishment in school. James Ingraham was a student at Drew Junior High School in Dade County, Florida, in the fall of 1970. On 6 October 1970 Ingraham did not leave the stage in the school auditorium as quickly as his teacher expected when the teacher asked. Ingraham was sent to the principal's office for a paddling. He protested his innocence and refused to submit to the punishment. Two assistant principals held him over a table while the principal hit him twenty times with a paddle. Ingraham went to the hospital and was out of school for two weeks as a result.

Cruel and Unusual? Many students at Drew had similar stories. The principals continued to beat the children after their parents objected. The parents decided to sue. They claimed that the school discipline violated the Eighth Amendment of the United States Constitution, which prohibits cruel and unusual punishment. They also claimed that the paddling violated the due process clause of the Fourteenth Amendment because the students did not get some kind of hearing to determine whether they had violated the rules.

Decision. The Supreme Court announced its decision in the case on 19 April 1977. The Court decided with a five-to-four vote that the schools could paddle children. The Court also decided that requiring hearings would disrupt the school atmosphere and the value of the immediacy of discipline.

Limiting the Due-Process Revolution. In allowing corporal punishment the Supreme Court was in accord with what many Americans believed. Eighty percent of school districts allowed corporal punishment, though its use was on the decline. And many Americans thought it was a good idea. Because of that support, the Supreme

Demonstration in South Boston protesting the forced busing of about one-fifth of the public-school students in the area

Court decided that the full due-process revolution would not reach to the schools.

Source:
Ingraham v. *Wright*, 430 U.S. 651 (1977).

THE RIGHTS OF THE ACCUSED

The Supreme Court Rethinks Rights. One of the key targets of critics of the Supreme Court was the rights granted to accused criminals. President Nixon looked to eliminate or reduce those rights in appointing Warren Burger as chief justice to replace Earl Warren. However, the Burger Court did not revoke the rights granted by the Warren Court. Nor did it eliminate the exclusionary rule, which prohibited illegally obtained evidence from being used in trying the accused. The Court's changes were much more limited. For example, the Court decided that even if an accused person had not been read his Miranda rights, a statement he made could be used to counter his in-court testimony. That was a retreat from the principle that only if one's rights had been read to him could the evidence be used in courts. But the Court had not completely overturned the requirement that the police read an accused person his or her rights. The votes in these cases were divided, and changes in the law moved slowly.

Continuity. Sometimes the different sides in the Court agreed on an extension of the rights of the accused.

For example, the Court decided unanimously in 1972 in *Argersinger* v. *Hamlin* that anyone accused of a crime for which he could be put in prison was entitled to an attorney. That decision was based on the Warren Court's decision in 1963, *Gideon* v. *Wainwright*. It increased the number of accused criminals who were entitled to have the government provide them with an attorney.

Wiretapping. The Supreme Court also had to consider the constitutionality of wiretaps and the requirement of a warrant before a search. In 1972 the Nixon administration argued that when it claimed national security it did not need to get a warrant. The Supreme Court ruled against the administration, concerned that officials would always claim national security. But the Court decided that search warrants were not always required. For example, pen registers, which record the phone numbers dialed from a phone, did not require a warrant. In addressing new technology the Court in some circumstances gave extended authority to the police. In the other areas of criminal procedure, however, the Court moved only slightly away from the innovations of the Warren Court.

SCHOOL DESEGREGATION

Desegregation in the 1970s. By 1972 black children

and white children in the South were going to school together. Much of the resistance to desegregation evident in the late 1950s and 1960s had been resolved in the South. The Department of Justice's efforts at enforcement, alongside the threat of cutting off federal funds under the 1964 Education Act, had effectively desegregated many southern schools. When desegregation moved north, however, circumstances changed. In 1970 the Department of Health, Education, and Welfare pursued fifteen desegregation cases; in 1973 it pursued one.

Moving Schoolchildren. In 1971 the Supreme Court decided *Swann* v. *Charlotte-Mecklenburg.* It held that the Constitution required school districts to dismantle systems that had long been segregated. The Court specifically held that this might mean changing attendance zones and putting children on school buses for the purpose of school desegregation. While courts ordered busing to desegregate schools, President Nixon opposed it. He intended to appoint justices to the Supreme Court who would not pursue desegregation. The Department of Justice under him also stopped pursuing desegregation cases. Congress considered forbidding courts from ordering busing for the purposes of integration. Nonetheless, the district courts continued to hear such cases.

Boston. In Boston federal judge Arthur Garrity ordered a program of busing to desegregate the school system. Garrity supervised the busing program because the Boston school board, historically unresponsive to the needs of Boston's black community, refused to comply with the court order. African-American students were bused to South Boston High School, located in the white ethnic community of South Boston, less than two miles from Roxbury. White residents of South Boston were overwhelmingly opposed to the busing program. To them it violated the tradition of local control of schools and threatened the historic pattern of segregated housing in Boston. Their protests were loud and often unruly; fights between whites and blacks at South Boston High School were common. In the face of such opposition many African-American parents became uneasy about desegregation. They were concerned with the toll such hostility would take on their children and were afraid that the violence would harm their children's education. In an attempt to resolve the crisis Judge Garrity worked out a compromise that emphasized black school board participation and the hiring of black teachers. But whites remained hostile to desegregation and transferred their children from the public school system to Boston's private schools, whose high cost limited black participation. The protests faded, and Boston's schools became more segregated than ever.

Urban/Suburban Segregation. In other cities white families were moving to the suburbs. In 1974 the Supreme Court decided *Milliken* v. *Bradley,* a desegregation case concerning Detroit. About 70 percent of the schoolchildren in the Detroit public schools in the 1970s

"A DIFFERENT CONCLUSION"

The trial judge in the *Swann* v. *Charlotte-Mecklenburg* case that established busing as a remedy for past school segregation, Federal District Judge James B. McMillan, said,

I grew up . . . accepting the segregated life which was the way of America for its first 300 years. . . . I hoped that we would be forever saved from the folly of transporting children from one school to another for the purpose of maintaining a racial balance of students in each school. . . . I first said, "What's wrong in Charlotte?" . . . I set the case for hearing reluctantly. I heard it reluctantly, at first unbelievingly. After . . . I began to deal in terms of facts and information instead of in terms of my natural-born raising, I began to realize . . . that something should be done. . . . I have had to spend some thousands of hours studying the subject . . . and have been brought by pressure of information to a different conclusion . . . Charlotte — and I suspect that is true of most cities — is segregated by Government action. We need to be reminded, also, as I did remind myself in 1969, that the issue is one of constitutional law, not politics; and constitutional rights should not be swept away by temporary majorities.

Source: Jennifer Hochschild, *The New American Dilemma* (New Haven: Yale University Press, 1984).

were black, and the proportion was increasing. If children were to be mixed by race it would have to happen across town boundaries. However, in *Milliken* v. *Bradley* the Supreme Court made it harder for federal district courts to require busing across town lines. That would hold true for many other cities too. Most of the mixing of children that was going to happen happened before 1974.

How Mixed Are the Schools? In the South in 1968, 19 percent of black children attended mixed schools where more than half of the students were minority students. By 1980, 42.9 percent did. In the Northeast, by contrast, in 1968, 33.2 percent of black children attended mixed schools. In 1980, 20 percent did. Many white children moved to the suburbs where fewer blacks and other minorities lived and the government made less of an effort to desegregate schools. Even as schools in the South were desegregated, schools in the Northeast became more segregated, not less.

Source:
Jennifer Hochschild, *The New American Dilemma* (New Haven: Yale University Press, 1984).

HEADLINE MAKERS

ALLAN BAKKE

1940-

MEDICAL STUDENT AND LITIGANT

From Engineer to Doctor. Allan Bakke was a symbol of the white backlash to civil rights and affirmative action programs. Son of a Minneapolis mailman and a teacher, Bakke originally was graduated from the University of Minnesota with a degree in engineering. To complete his obligations to NROTC, Bakke served four years in the marines, including a tour in Vietnam. He later maintained his experience in the war caused his interests to turn from engineering to medicine, but upon his return to America, he received a master's degree from Stanford, and became an engineer at the NASA Ames Research Center, south of San Francisco. At Ames, Bakke designed experimental equipment to test the effects of weightlessness and radiation on animals. The work furthered his interests in medicine, and working full-time, he enrolled in a full schedule of premed courses, and volunteered at a local hospital. In 1972 he applied for admission to eleven medical schools in the country, including the nearby, state-subsidized University of California, Davis. Despite high test scores (above the ninetieth percentile in three of four Medical College Admission Test categories), Bakke was rejected by all eleven schools.

Reserved Places. Bakke's first choice of medical schools, the University of California, Davis, had opened in 1968 with the expressed purpose of improving the physician care available to rural upstate California. Davis also initiated a minority recruitment program in 1970. Out of the 100 spaces available in its entering medical school class, Davis set aside sixteen of the positions for "economically or educationally disadvantaged" candidates. While Bakke's admissions scores were lower than those in the general admit pool, they were better than some of the scores of candidates in the reserved pool. He

believed his rejection was therefore unconstitutional, as the minority set-aside quotas violated the "equal protection of the laws" clause of the Fourteenth Amendment and placed him at a disadvantage in the admissions competition. In 1973, he reapplied to Davis, and threatened to sue the university for discrimination. His letter drew the attention of a sympathetic dean, Peter C. Storandt, who responded by suggesting that, should Bakke again be rejected for admission, he sue. Agreeing with Bakke that the minority recruitment program discriminated against whites, Storandt explained, "It seemed to me that Davis faculty were of the conviction that 'disadvantaged' means 'membership in a minority race.' " Storandt even passed Bakke the names of several lawyers. In 1974, when Bakke was again rejected for admission, he sued the University of California, Davis for discrimination.

The Supreme Court. While the Yolo County Superior Court Judge F. Leslie Manker agreed with Bakke that the University of California, Davis's admissions quotas were unfair, he refused to order Bakke's admission, arguing that Bakke had failed to prove he would have been admitted had the minority recruitment program not existed. Both sides appealed the decision to the California Supreme Court, who voided the minority recruitment program as unconstitutional. The Board of Regents of the University of California then debated appealing the decision to the Supreme Court of the United States. Liberal members of the board, afraid that the conservative Supreme Court would issue a sweeping decision invalidating affirmative action programs nationwide, were opposed to filing an appeal. However, conservatives succeeded in pressing the case in Washington. In July 1978 the Supreme Court decided the case. It ruled that while the University of California could take race into account to compensate for discrimination and to diversify its student body, it could not set aside a specific number of places for students of color. Affirmative action plans were held to be constitutional and Allan Bakke was admitted to the University of California.

Graduation. Bakke began classes in the fall of 1978. He was married and had three children, so his life was different from that of most of the students, and he found adjusting to classes difficult. A reserved man, he refused to discuss the case with reporters, and his low-key approach to his celebrity defused any animosity his fellow students might have had toward him. As Hector Flores, one of his classmates, explained, "Allan Bakke is more of a symbol. For us to levy any personal attack on him would be detrimental. He's not the issue." Bakke was graduated in 1982, and received an internship at the Mayo Clinic in his native Minnesota.

Sources:

David M. O'Brien, *Constitutional Law and Politics*, volume 1 (New York: Norton, 1991);

Timothy J. O'Neill, *Bakke & The Politics of Equality: Friends and Foes in the Classroom of Litigation* (Middletown, Conn.; Wesleyan University Press, 1985);

Time (10 July 1978): 8–16.

WARREN BURGER

1907-

CHIEF JUSTICE OF THE SUPREME COURT

Nixon's Judicial Counterrevolution. President Richard Nixon wanted to change the direction of the U.S. Supreme Court when he appointed Warren Burger as chief justice in 1969. For the previous sixteen years the chief justice had been Earl Warren. Warren presided over an era of unprecedented judicial activity. The Court asserted constitutional limits on national and state governments in the areas of racial segregation, criminal justice, and legislative representation. In 1968 fearing that Richard Nixon — whom Warren detested — would be elected president, Warren resigned in 1968 so that Lyndon Johnson could select his replacement. However, when Johnson's choice, Abe Fortas, withdrew from the nomination because of questionable financial dealings, Nixon got his chance.

Nixon Chooses Burger. Nixon chose little-known federal appeals court judge Warren Burger. Burger's judicial record reflected Nixon's concerns in two important ways. First, Burger argued for "strict constructionism," where courts would "apply the law" and not use the Constitution to legislate social policy. He thought that courts should interfere less with the actions of school districts and police departments. Second, Burger felt strongly that courts focused too much on protecting the rights of criminal defendants and that they ignored the importance of punishing criminals. He was especially opposed to the exclusionary rule, which did not allow prosecutors to use evidence that was not properly obtained. He did not think that criminals should go free if their confessions were obtained without a sufficient warning about their rights or if evidence had been seized from their car or home without a proper warrant. Nixon agreed strongly with this position. He felt that the Warren Court's expansion of the rights of criminal defendants contributed to the decline in law and order that plagued America at the beginning of his term.

The Burger Record. Burger's term as chief justice reflected Nixon's reaction to the Warren Court, but it also demonstrated the continuity of judicial decision making. While the Burger Court did backtrack on some of the decisions of the Warren Court, in some areas of law they continued the trend of the earlier court. In criminal procedure they did not overturn the exclusionary rule, but they did create more flexibility for police in the application of the search and seizure and interrogation rules. They established the use of busing to achieve school desegregation and then imposed increasing limits on how busing could be used. They recognized a woman's right to abortion and liberalized procedures for showing racial discrimination in employment. Overall, it is more accurate to characterize the Burger Court as gradually limiting the trends of the Warren Court rather than simply reacting to the Warren Court or creating, as Nixon wanted, a constitutional counterrevolution. Fundamental changes in Supreme Court doctrine did not come until later in the next decade with the appointment of consistently conservative justices by President Ronald Reagan.

The Chief Justice as Administrator. Rather than leading the reaction to the Warren Court, Burger concerned himself primarily with the administration of justice. He believed that the courts were too busy, particularly with claims that he did not believe deserved the attention of the federal courts. He continually tried to find a way to streamline court cases. He made many public speeches about the problems of court delay and the overuse of courts. In 1974 he supported the creation of a new court to screen applications to the Supreme Court, but that innovation failed to attract the necessary support. Undeterred, Chief Justice Burger continued to pursue his concerns about burdens on the federal courts.

Burger and the Supreme Court in Transition. Burger served as chief justice until his surprise resignation at the end of the 1986 term. By this time the Supreme Court had begun to take a more conservative turn. Reagan had nominated conservative justices Sandra Day O'Connor and Antonin Scalia to fill his first two vacancies on the Court. He also nominated sitting justice William Rehnquist to replace Burger as chief justice. It was not until these changes took place that Nixon's vision of a constitutional counterrevolution began to take place. The Burger Court did not mark any radical changes from the Warren Court. Instead it served as a transition between the liberal Warren Court and the conservative Rehnquist Court.

Sources:

Charles Lamb and Stephen Halpern, eds., *The Burger Court: Political and Judicial Profiles* (Chicago: University of Illinois Press, 1991);

David O'Brien, *Storm Center: The Supreme Court in American Politics* (New York: Norton, 1986).

WILLIAM CALLEY

1943-

ARMY OFFICER

My Lai and the Vietnam War. The trial of Lt. William Calley for the murder of unarmed Vietnamese civilians in My Lai raised many difficult issues for the American people over the conduct of the Vietnam War. The massacre was cited by many as a war crime and genocide, demonstrating the immorality of the American war effort. Others defended Calley, saying that he was a soldier doing his duty in a brutal war. They said that it was unfair to punish Calley without also punishing the whole army as well as the society that had placed him in Vietnam and taught him to kill.

The My Lai Massacre. On 16 March 1968 Lieutenant Calley led his platoon into My Lai, South Vietnam, along with two other platoons of Charlie Company. They had expected to meet heavy Vietcong resistance, but they reached the village without a challenge. Finding only women, children, and old men in the village, they nonetheless went in shooting. They rounded up other villagers, herded them into a ditch, and shot them with automatic weapons. Calley's platoon was responsible for over one hundred deaths. Many young women and girls were raped and assaulted. Calley participated directly in the massacre, shooting some villagers himself and ordering his soldiers to shoot others. There was no evidence that the villagers put up any armed resistance.

The Emerging Scandal and Cover-up. No reports of the massacre at My Lai became public until the following year when returning Vietnam veterans and news reporters began to piece together reports from Vietnamese refugees and American soldiers who had seen or heard of the killings. As the story came out, both the horror of the massacre and the broad scale of the army cover-up shocked the American people. The army formally charged Calley with the murder of civilians in September 1969. Calley's immediate superior, Capt. Ernest Medina, was also charged, as were six enlisted men in Calley's platoon. In addition, fourteen army officers, including two generals, were charged with violating army regulations in covering up the My Lai incident.

The Court-Martial. Calley's court martial trial started in November 1970. The trial revealed the horror of American soldiers killing defenseless Vietnamese civilians. While he disagreed with some details, Calley did not deny that he shot civilians and ordered his soldiers to do so. He explained, "I was ordered to go in there and destroy the enemy. That was my job on that day. That was the mission I was given. I did not sit down and think in terms of men, women, and children. They were all classified the same, and that was the classification we dealt with, just as enemy soldiers." The court martial jury, made up of six army combat veterans, convicted Calley of the premeditated murder of at least twenty-two civilians. The jury sentenced Calley to life imprisonment at hard labor, choosing against imposing the death penalty. Calley was the only officer or enlisted man convicted at court martial for the massacre at My Lai. Six enlisted men were tried, but none was convicted, largely because they were responding to Lieutenant Calley's orders at My Lai. Charges were dropped against Calley's superior, Captain Medina, for his role. Several officers, including the two generals, were demoted and reprimanded for their roles in covering up the massacre.

Support for Calley. There was an immediate uproar in support of Calley. The White House reported receiving more than one hundred thousand letters and telegrams, the great majority in support of Calley. American Legion officials objected to Calley being punished for doing his duty. A spokesman for the Vietnam Veterans Against the War said, "We are all of us in this country guilty for having allowed the war to go on. We only want this country to realize that it cannot try a Calley for something which generals and presidents and our way of life encourage him to do. And if you try him, then at the same time you must try all those generals and presidents and soldiers who have part of this responsibility."

Aftermath. President Nixon ordered Calley released from the military stockade and placed under house arrest while his conviction was being appealed. He served three years under house arrest before a federal court overturned his conviction in 1974. The Supreme Court refused to review the case when it came to them in 1976, effectively ending Calley's prosecution.

Sources:
Michael Bilton, *Four Hours in My Lai* (New York: Viking, 1992);
Seymour Hersh, *Cover-Up* (New York: Random House, 1972).

LEON JAWORSKI

1905-1982

SPECIAL PROSECUTOR IN THE WATERGATE CASE

An Independent Prosecutor. When in November 1973 the Nixon administration appointed Leon Jaworski special prosecutor in the Watergate case, many suspected that he was a Nixon crony, bent on obstructing the legal issues in the case and absolving the Nixon administration of wrongdoing. Nixon had already fired the previous Watergate special prosecutor, Harvard law professor Archibald Cox, precisely because of his insistence on pursuit of the truth in the case no matter which administration officials — including the president — were hurt. Jaworski, moreover, seemed comfortable with those whose political conduct may have left them vulnerable to scandal. He successfully defended Lyndon Johnson against vote-rigging charges following the congressional elections of 1948; won another electoral case for Johnson in 1960; and was associated by many with fellow Texan John Connally, whose close ties to Nixon were well known. Yet Jaworski kept Cox's staff, continued his investigation of corruption in the Nixon administration, and subpoenaed the White House for Watergate tapes and documents — evidence that ultimately brought down the Nixon presidency. Leon Jaworski was every bit as high-minded and unbiased in pursuing the truth as had been Cox.

Background and Career. Like Cox, Jaworski was an achiever whose hard work and intelligence brought him wealth and influence. Son of a Polish father and Austrian mother who immigrated to Waco, Texas, Jaworski grew up poor but earned a reputation as an outstanding student. He graduated from high school at fifteen and went on to Baylor University, where he supplemented his scholarship by correcting papers for seventeen cents an hour. At sixteen he was admitted to the Baylor University Law School; at eighteen he graduated first in his class, and he became the youngest person admitted to the Texas bar in 1924. Jaworski returned to Waco and began his law career representing bootleggers and moonshiners. He lost a sensational case against a black client accused of murdering a white couple in 1929, but at a time when lynching was still common in Texas, Jaworski's defense gained him statewide attention and a position with the Houston firm of Fulbright, Cooker, Freeman and Bates. By age twenty-nine he was a full partner and the confidant of some of Texas's most powerful and influential businessmen. Jaworski served as a colonel in the army during World War II and henceforth would be nicknamed "Colonel" by friends and subordinates. After the war he became chief of the war crimes trial section of the Judge Advocate General's Corps, later recounting his experiences prosecuting Nazi criminals in a memoir, *Fifteen Years After* (1961). Returning to the United States, he renewed his law practice in Houston, becoming a senior partner in the Fulbright firm in 1946.

Democratic Counsel. During the 1950s and 1960s Jaworski extended his contacts among Texan business and political interests, becoming a close associate of Lyndon Johnson and an influential figure in the Democratic party. From 1962 to 1965 he worked for Archibald Cox and Robert Kennedy, pressing contempt charges against Mississippi governor Ross Barnett for his failure to comply with school desegregation orders. Later he served on the Warren Commission, investigating the assassination of John Kennedy, and on President Johnson's crime and violence commissions. By the 1970s Jaworski had also built his law firm into one of the largest in the country. It

was famous for its egalitarianism — his was the first law firm in the Houston area to hire Jews, blacks, and women. From July 1971 to July 1972 Jaworski served as president of the American Bar Association, notable, given his future role, for his concern over "errant lawyers," who possessed "vanishing respect for law."

Special Prosecutor. Especially after the firing of Cox, Jaworski understood the politically tenuous nature of his job as special prosecutor. His position required that he collect evidence in the Watergate case, present it to grand juries, and prosecute wrongdoing, but not appear partisan or vindictive. Jaworski's judicious temperament and patient amassing of evidence insulated him from any partisan charges. To demonstrate his independence from the White House which appointed him, Jaworski retained Cox's staff of lawyers and broadened the scope of their investigations to include not only events connected to the Watergate break-in and cover-up but also illegal contributions to the Nixon reelection campaign. Ultimately, like Cox, Jaworski found himself at odds with the Nixon administration over the Watergate tapes, which Jaworski sought to review for evidence but which Nixon refused to surrender. As had Cox, Jaworski rejected the Nixon administration's claims to "executive privilege" and compromise proposals wherein the White House would provide transcripts of the tapes instead of the tapes themselves. In the spring of 1974 he subpoenaed the administration for sixty-four tapes, but the White House refused to comply. Jaworski took his case to the Supreme Court. On 24 July 1974 the Supreme Court ruled, eight to zero, that Nixon must turn over the tapes, including the famous 23 June 1972 "smoking gun" tape, which proved that Nixon personally ordered his subordinates to obstruct justice. Sixteen days later Nixon became the first president in American history to resign the office.

Prosecuting Nixon. Jaworski had not taken the job as special prosecutor in order to bring down Nixon. On the contrary, he consistently operated with deference to and respect for the president, suggesting, for example, a compromise regarding the delivery of Watergate tapes, which Nixon rejected. He also refused to expand his powers beyond their limits, failing, while Nixon was still a sitting president, to indict Nixon for obstruction of justice, because he believed it to be beyond his power. Jaworski believed that it was a constitutional requirement that Congress prosecute the president. With Nixon's resignation, that dilemma was resolved, and Jaworski moved to prosecute Nixon as he had his fellow Watergate conspirators. President Ford's pardon of Nixon ended his efforts. On 25 October 1974 Jaworski returned to Houston. Under the third special Watergate prosecutor, Henry S. Ruth, Jr., White House officials John Mitchell, John Ehrlichman, H. R. Haldeman, and Robert Mardian were found guilty of conspiracy to obstruct justice. Judge John Sirica sentenced Mitchell, Haldeman, and Ehrlichman to two and a half to eight years in prison; Mardian was sentenced to ten months to three years. Twenty-seven corporate executives and lawyers were found guilty of campaign violations, but only three received prison sentences. Jaworski had not taken an active role in these prosecutions. His importance was symbolic: stepping into the role of special prosecutor after its independence had been called into question, Jaworski proved that the special prosecutor's office could be both impartial and rigorous — setting the stage for more extensive investigations by special prosecutors in the future.

Source:
James Doyle, *Not Above the Law: The Battles of Watergate Prosecutors Cox and Jaworski* (New York: Morrow, 1977).

MICHELLE MARVIN

1931-

PALIMONY LITIGANT

Palimony. Michelle Marvin was a Las Vegas dancer and a supper-club singer. In 1964 she met the actor Lee Marvin on the set of the movie *Ship of Fools,* and she moved in with him shortly after that. When they split up in the early 1970s, she claimed she had cooked and cleaned for him and taken care of him after he had been drinking. She said he told her "What I have is yours and what you have is mine." California had laws requiring that married people split the assets of their marriage; although the Marvins were not formally married, Michelle believed she was entitled to money from him. Lee Marvin disagreed. Their dispute went to the California Supreme Court.

Palimony. The California Supreme Court held in 1976 that Lee Marvin and Michelle Marvin had an implied contract, of a type that was legally recognized. Although Michelle Marvin was not married to her live-in partner, she was entitled to a financial settlement (called palimony by the press) after their split for the same reason a married woman might be eligible for alimony. Aware that they were setting precedent, the court held that a trial court would always have to evaluate the particular situation in palimony suits. It would have to check, for example, whether a couple had mixed money and property or perhaps identified themselves as "Mr. and Mrs." With this decision Michelle Marvin took her case back to a trial court.

Outcome. The trial judge had treated the case as most divorces were then being treated. Judges were reluctant to award long-term alimony in divorces, even where a wife had been a homemaker for a long time and would find it difficult to find a job. The trial judge decided that Michelle Marvin was not entitled to one-half of Lee Marvin's assets but that she did deserve the equivalent of two years' salary. Michelle Marvin received a judgment of $104,000, thus establishing an important legal precedent.

JOHN J. SIRICA

1905-

FEDERAL JUDGE

Man of the Year. *Time* magazine's Man of the Year in 1973, John J. Sirica was a model of integrity as the presiding federal court judge during the Watergate case. He exposed the truth behind the various deceits of the Nixon administration, flushed malefactors from cover, and insisted that the president act according to the law he was sworn to obey. His zeal in pursuing the case made him the object of some criticism, but without Sirica's dogged persistence Watergate might never have been exposed.

Fighting for Success. Sirica's determination to get at the truth in the Watergate case was characteristic of a man whose life was spent overcoming adversity. Son of an Italian immigrant stricken with tuberculosis, Sirica followed his father (a barber) and the rest of his family on their travels through the South and the West — Florida, Louisiana, California — seeking a healthy climate. The constant in their lives was poverty: Sirica supplemented his father's income by waxing cars and selling newspapers. He nonetheless managed to graduate from Columbia Preparatory School and, after several false starts, in 1926 finally graduated from Georgetown Law School. Although an unimposing man physically (standing five feet six inches tall), Sirica worked his way through college as a boxing coach and sparring partner; his lifelong friend, boxing champion Jack Dempsey, was his best man when he wed, in 1952.

"Maximum John." A Republican, Sirica's first law position was as a prosecutor on the staff of the U.S. Attorney General in Washington under President Herbert Hoover. The Roosevelt years were a lean time for Sirica, who was struggling with a private law practice. His activism in Republican politics, however, resulted in his appointment to the federal bench by President Dwight Eisenhower in 1957. Sirica gained the nickname "Maximum John" by being a favorite of prosecutors, especially hard when sentencing white-collar criminals. His quick temper and combativeness and his tendency to ignore legal nuances resulted in many of his decisions being overturned on appeal and brought him constant criticism from civil libertarians.

Hunt for the Truth. Ironically, Sirica's tendency to stretch the law for the sake of justice was precisely what made him such an effective participant in the Watergate case. Called to preside over the original case charging seven men with the break-in of the Democratic National Committee headquarters at the Watergate complex, Sirica consistently refused to accept the evasions and excuses of the Watergate burglars. The Nixon administration originally proposed that the seven-man burglary team operated independently of the White House; Sirica rejected the notion outright. During testimony in the case, when burglar Bernard Barker maintained he did not know who paid his expenses, Sirica snapped, "Well, I'm sorry, but I don't believe you." He jailed *Los Angeles Times* newsman John Lawrence for contempt of court when he refused to turn over Watergate-related evidence (a decision reversed on appeal). Most important, he imposed stiff sentences for five of the Watergate burglars — thirty-five to forty years each — but made the sentences "provisional" upon their cooperation in getting to the heart of the Watergate affair. With burglar James McCord, such tactics eventually elicited the confession that testimony in the Watergate case had been perjured and that political pressure had been applied to the defendants from the White House. McCord's confession broke the Watergate case but brought protests from civil libertarians that Sirica was acting in a biased fashion. Such accusations brought a typically blunt response from Sirica: "I don't think we should sit up here like nincompoops," he said. "The function of a trial court is to search for the truth."

Sources:
J. Anthony Lukas, *Nightmare: The Underside of the Nixon Years* (New York: Viking, 1976);

Time, 103 (7 January 1974): 8–20.

SARAH WEDDINGTON

1946-

WOMAN LAWYER AND ABORTION RIGHTS ACTIVIST

Roe v. Wade. When the Supreme Court ruled on 22 January 1973 that state abortion laws must be changed to allow women the choice of legal, safe abortion, no one was more surprised than Sarah Weddington. A longtime Texas advocate for woman's rights, Weddington, along with her associate Linda Coffee, had never tried a case before *Roe*. When they won their class-action suit against the State of Texas, the Texas Attorney General appealed the case to the Supreme Court. The case was virtually unprecedented, and some observers believed the novelty of the issue, as well as Weddington's inexperience, were behind the Court's unusual request to hear arguments in the case twice. Weddington nonetheless convinced the Court of the merit of her case, and *Roe* v. *Wade* became the most sweeping — and controversial — Supreme Court decision since *Brown* v. *Board of Education* (1954). In her first court case, Sarah Weddington had succeeded in altering one of the fundamental laws of the United States.

Background. Sarah Weddington's background was instrumental in her success. From her father, a Methodist preacher, she gained a high moral consciousness and an utter conviction in the rectitude of her cause; from her mother, an educator, she gained the discipline and tenacity to consider a law case from every angle. Despite her father's itinerant ministry in central Texas, Weddington excelled at school, skipping two grades and graduating from McMurry College in Abilene (a small Methodist church school) at age nineteen. In 1967 she and Linda Coffee were two of only five female graduates of the University of Texas Law School — and the only two intending to go on to practice law. Despite outstanding academic records, both women were rejected for employment by large Texas firms. Coffee turned to a small firm specializing in bankruptcy law; Weddington worked on the American Bar Association's project to standarize legal ethics. Both women became increasingly involved in feminist projects. Convinced that reproductive choice was essential to a woman's rights, they began to seek a woman for whom they could file a class-action suit challenging Texas' abortion laws. When they met an out-of-luck, out-of-work, pregnant former carnival barker named Norma McCorvey in 1969, they found their woman, dubbed "Jane Roe" for the purposes of anonymity.

Aftermath. Following the success of *Roe* v. *Wade* Linda Coffee returned to Texas to practice business law, but the case catapulted Sarah Weddington into a seat in the Texas state legislature, where she served from 1973 to 1977. Weddington then served a year as general counsel, or main lawyer, for the Department of Agriculture under President Jimmy Carter. She agreed to serve under him despite his opposition to public funding for abortions. In 1978 Weddington became Carter's assistant on woman's issues. Following Carter's defeat in 1980, she remained in Washington as a lobbyist for the state of Texas, still active on woman's issues and fighting to maintain abortion rights in the face of conservative efforts to rescind them. In 1981 she testified against a Senate bill to ban abortions, arguing that the proposal "blatantly disregards the integrity of the constitutional process, the separation of powers, the religious liberty of our citizens, the will of the people, the sound practice of medicine and the desperate needs of women facing problem pregnancies." The bill was tabled. In 1986 Weddington returned to Austin to practice law.

Sources:
Marian Faux, *Roe v. Wade* (New York: Macmillan, 1988);

Norma McCorvey, *I Am Roe* (New York: HarperCollins, 1994).

PEOPLE IN THE NEWS

In 1978 **David Berkowitz** pleaded guilty to six murders and seven attempted murders in what had become known as the "Son of Sam" case in New York City. Berkowitz terrorized the New York City area for over a year with a series of random shootings of people in parked cars with a .44-caliber pistol. He identified himself as the Son of Sam. He later explained that he adopted the name because the "demons" in his neighbor Sam Carr's dog "made him do it." Berkowitz originally pleaded insanity but was found competent to stand trial. He was sentenced to twenty-five years to life for each of the murders.

In 1976 **Don Bolles**, a reporter for the *Arizona Republic* newspaper, was killed when a bomb exploded in his car. Bolles had written a series of articles exposing organized crime's involvement in land fraud. Three men were convicted of Bolles's murder. The three men were connected with **Kemper Marley, Sr.**, an Arizona liquor wholesaler who was reportedly angered by Bolles's articles and thought they had cost him a seat on the Arizona Racing Commission. Marley was not charged in Bolles's murder.

In 1976 **Rubin ("Hurricane") Carter**, a former prize-fighter, was retried for murders he insisted he did not commit. His insistence on his innocence drew many supporters. He was convicted in two separate trials but was finally released in 1985 as having been wrongly convicted. The judge ruled that his conviction was based "on an appeal to racism rather than reason." He had served eighteen years in prison.

In 1971 **D. B. Cooper** hijacked an airplane and escaped by parachuting out the rear entrance with two hundred thousand dollars. He was never found.

On 12 July 1979 reputed Mafia leader **Carmine Galante** was gunned down in an Italian restaurant in Brooklyn by three men wearing ski masks and carrying shotguns and automatic weapons. Galante was reported to be the head of the two-hundred-member Bonano family in New York City. Police speculated that he was killed because he pushed too hard to be "boss of all bosses" of the New York Mafia.

On 7 April 1972 Mafia boss **Joseph ("Crazy Joey") Gallo**

was murdered in a clam house in New York City's Little Italy as he celebrated his forty-third birthday. Gallo's killing was believed to be linked to an assassination attempt on rival mob leader **Joseph Columbo** the previous year.

On 17 January 1977 **Gary Gilmore** became the first person subjected to the death penalty in the United States in ten years. Many appeals were made on his behalf up to the moment of his execution. He objected to all of them, insisting he wanted to die.

In 1977 **David Hall** and **Patrick Kearney** turned themselves in for having committed the "trash bag" murders in southern California. Their eight victims were left in trash bags.

In 1979 a judge on the California Court of Appeals, **Paul Halvonik**, was arrested for possession of marijuana.

On 30 July 1975 **Jimmy Hoffa**, former Teamsters Union boss, disappeared. In the middle of a struggle to regain power in the Teamsters, Hoffa had arranged to meet his friend and reputed Mafia chief **Anthony ("Tony Jack") Giacolone**. Hoffa was never found. Police officials speculate that he was killed by Mafia figures because they did not want him to challenge their control over the Teamsters and its billion-dollar pension fund.

On 21 August 1971 **George Jackson**, a prisoner and black activist, was killed along with five others in an escape attempt from San Quentin prison in California; they became known as the "San Quentin Six."

In August 1970 four people died in a shoot-out in the San Rafael, California, Superior Court. They were **J. D. McClain**, a black activist who was on trial for murder; **Judge H. J. Haley**, the presiding judge; **J. Jackson**, who had come into the court to try to free McClain; and **W. A. Christmas**, who was a defense witness.

In 1973 **George Metesky**, the "mad bomber" of the New York City area in the 1950s, was released after seventeen years in a mental hospital.

In June of 1977 **James Earl Ray**, convicted of murdering Dr. Martin Luther King, Jr., escaped from prison in

Bushy Mountain, Tennessee. He was captured fifty-four hours later.

In 1977 **James** and **Richard Schoenfeld** and **Frederick Woods IV** were tried and convicted for kidnapping a school bus full of children in Chowchilla, California.

In 1977 Illinois governor **James Thompson** granted clemency to **Patricia Dorkey Evans**, convicted in 1975 of killing her husband after he had physically abused her for years.

On 21 May 1979 **Dan White** was convicted of voluntary manslaughter in the shooting deaths of the mayor and a supervisor of San Francisco, both supporters of rights for gay men. He had been charged with first-degree murder but argued that his addiction to junk food impaired his judgment. Three thousand people demonstrated against the leniency of the verdict.

DEATHS

Barbara N. Armstrong, 85, first woman law professor in the United States, 18 January 1976.

Alexander M. Bickel, constitutional-law scholar at Yale University, 7 November 1974.

Hugo L. Black, 85, associate justice of the Supreme Court (1937–1971), 25 September 1971.

Leo Brewster, 76, United States District Court judge who supervised and decided the school-desegregation case in Fort Worth, Texas, 27 November 1976.

James F. Byrnes, 93, associate justice of the Supreme Court (1941–1942), 8 April 1972.

Tom C. Clark, 78, associate justice on the Supreme Court (1949–1967), 13 June 1977.

Ben C. Connally, 65, federal district court judge who presided over Houston's school-desegregation case, 2 December 1975.

Clifford J. Durr, 76, lawyer in the New Deal and in the Truman administration until he objected to loyalty oaths; active in civil rights in Montgomery, Alabama, 12 May 1975.

Morris L. Ernst, 87, lawyer who successfully defended James Joyce's *Ulysses* against charges of obscenity, 22 May 1976.

Lon L. Fuller, 75, leading legal scholar of contracts and jurisprudence, 8 April 1978.

Carlo Gambino, 74, organized-crime leader, 15 October 1976.

Murray I. Gurfein, 72, United States Court of Appeals judge who upheld the right of *The New York Times* to publish the Pentagon Papers in 1971 despite the objection of the Nixon administration, 16 December 1979.

John Marshall Harlan, 72, associate justice on the Supreme Court (1955–1971), 29 December 1971.

Philip A. Hart, 64, senator from Michigan who worked on school desegregation, gun control, and environmental legislation, 25 December 1976.

William H. Hastie, 71, civil rights activist and first African-American appointed to United States Court of Appeals, 14 April 1976.

John Edgar Hoover, 77, director of the Federal Bureau of Investigation since 1924, 2 May 1972.

Orrin G. Judd, 69, United States District Court judge who presided over a landmark constitutional challenge to the conditions in a school for the retarded, 7 July 1976.

Stanley D. Levison, 67, lawyer and adviser to Martin Luther King, Jr., and participant in the Southern Christian Leadership Conference, 12 September 1979.

Richard P. Loving, who successfully challenged Virginia's laws against interracial marriage, including his own, 30 June 1975.

Thomas C. Matthews, Jr., 48, lawyer who unsuccessfully challenged the constitutionality of the Hatch Act, which restricted the political activity of federal civil servants, 13 November 1979.

Shad Polier, 70, civil rights lawyer who participated in the landmark Scottsboro case, in which nine African-American men were wrongly accused of rape, 30 June 1976.

Edith Spurlock Sampson, 76, first African-American woman elected to the judiciary in Illinois, 8 October 1979.

J. T. Scopes, 70, teacher tried in 1925 for teaching evolution, which the state of Tennessee prohibited, 22 October 1970.

Abraham Unger, 76, lawyer who in the 1930s and 1940s defended Communist clients, 16 July 1975.

Herbert Walker, 77, judge who sentenced Sirhan B. Sirhan (who killed Robert Kennedy) and nineteen other men to die in the gas chamber, 20 November 1976.

Earl Warren, 83, chief justice of the United States (1953–1969), 10 July 1974.

Ruth Whitehead Whaley, 76, first black woman to practice law actively in New York State, 23 December 1977.

Charles E. Whittaker, 72, associate justice of the Supreme Court (1957–1962), 26 November 1973.

Abraham Lincoln Wirin, 77, first full-time lawyer for the American Civil Liberties Union, 4 February 1978.

PUBLICATIONS

Shana Alexander, *Anyone's Daughter* (New York: Viking, 1979);

Carl Bernstein and Robert Woodward, *All the President's Men* (New York: Simon & Schuster, 1974);

Bernstein and Woodward, *The Final Days* (New York: Simon & Schuster, 1976);

Charles Black, Jr., *Capital Punishment: The Inevitability of Caprice and Mistake* (New York: Norton, 1974);

Rubin Carter, *The Sixteenth Round: From Number One Contender to Number 45472* (New York: Viking, 1974);

Seymour Hersh, *Cover-Up* (New York: Random House, 1972);

Philip B. Kurland, *Watergate and the Constitution* (Chicago: University of Chicago Press, 1978);

Norman Mailer, *The Executioner's Song* (Boston: Little, Brown, 1979);

R. Shep Melnick, *Regulation and the Courts: The Case of the Clean Air Act* (Washington, D. C.: Brookings Institution, 1983);

National Staff of Environmental Action, *Earth Day — The Beginning: A Guide for Survival* (New York: Arno, 1970);

Tom Wicker, *A Time to Die* (New York: Quadrangle, 1975);

J. Harvie Wilkinson III, *From Brown to Bakke: The Supreme Court and School Integration, 1954–1978* (New York: Oxford University Press, 1979);

ABA Journal, periodical;

American Lawyer, periodical;

National Law Journal, periodical;

New York Times, periodical.

California Superior Court Judge Harold J. Haley being held hostage outside his San Rafael courtroom by James D. McClain, left, and an associate. Both men holding Haley and the judge were killed.

LIFESTYLES AND SOCIAL TRENDS

by VICTOR BONDI and PETER C. HOLLORAN

CONTENTS

Sidebars and tables are listed in italics.

1970

- Ralph Nader's citizens' lobbying group, nicknamed "Nader's Raiders," petitions the government for consumer protection.

- Common Cause, a citizens' group lobbying for political reform, is formed.

- For the first time in American history, a majority of Americans live in suburbs.

- The Weathermen, a terrorist guerrilla organization, explode a bomb at the Army Math Research Center at the University of Wisconsin — Madison, killing a graduate student.

- At Stanford University student protesters set fire to the behavioral-studies building and destroy the lifetime collection of notes, files, and manuscripts of M. N. Scrinivas, a visiting Indian scholar.

- The governor of Ohio calls out the National Guard to end a six-hour battle between student protesters and police on the campus of Kent State University. Four students are killed, thirteen injured, and six hundred arrested in the affair.

- Police touch off a riot in the barrio of East Los Angeles, resulting in the death of prominent Hispanic journalist Ruben Salazar and inspiring the growing Chicano consciousness movement.

29 Aug. A parade of ten thousand women in New York celebrates the fiftieth anniversary of the passage of the Nineteenth Amendment; the women demand abortion reform, day care, and equal opportunity.

1971

- The Twenty-sixth Amendment to the Constitution, lowering the voting age from twenty-one to eighteen, is ratified.

- In *Reed* v. *Reed* the U.S. Supreme Court bans gender discrimination.

- The hot-pants fad begins in New York City boutiques.

- In Chicago the Reverend Jesse Jackson forms People United to Save Humanity (PUSH).

- The Italian American Civil Rights League of New York sponsors Unity Day.

1972

- Congress approves the Equal Right Amendment (ERA) and sends it to the states to be ratified.

- *Ms.* magazine begins publication.

- The number of women in the workplace increases to thirty-four million.

- Protesting Native Americans march in Washington, D.C.

- *Life* magazine ceases publication.

- Congress passes the Ethnic Heritage Studies Act "to legitimatize ethnicity and pluralism in America."

1973

- The American Psychiatric Association rules that homosexuality is not a mental disorder.

- Phyllis Schlafly organizes the Stop ERA lobby.

- Maynard Jackson is elected the first black mayor of Atlanta; Thomas Bradley is elected the first black mayor of Los Angeles; Coleman Young becomes the first black mayor of Detroit.

- The Organization of Petroleum Exporting Countries' (OPEC) oil embargo leads Americans to lower their thermostats, cease Sunday drives, and cancel airline trips, all in an effort to save fuel.

- The Census Bureau reports that interracial marriages increased 63 percent during the 1960s.

- Little League Baseball teams in New Jersey accept the first female players in the league.

- Federal agencies accept *Ms.* in place of *Miss* or *Mrs.*

- Inspired by the Bruce Lee film *Enter the Dragon,* a martial arts craze sweeps U.S. urban centers.

29 Jan. The first female commercial pilot is hired.

1974

- Maternity leave for teachers is approved by the U.S. Supreme Court.

- First Lady Betty Ford publicly discusses her breast-cancer mastectomy.

- A fad known as "streaking," where people sprint naked through public thoroughfares and ceremonies, sweeps the country.

4 Feb. In Berkeley, California, nineteen-year-old newspaper heiress Patricia Hearst is kidnapped by the Symbionese Liberation Army.

22 Feb. The editor of the *Atlanta Constitution,* J. Reginald Murphy, is found unharmed after seven hundred thousand dollars is paid to his kidnappers, the self-proclaimed American Revolutionary Army.

4 May Expo '74, a world's fair with an environmental theme, opens in Spokane, Washington.

30 June Mrs. Martin Luther King, Sr., mother of the civil rights leader, is murdered by a gunman in Ebenezer Baptist Church in Atlanta.

3 Oct. Frank Robinson becomes the manager of the Cleveland Indians, making him the first black manager of a major-league baseball team.

1975

- The first personal computer for home use is introduced by retailers.

- Violent antibusing riots rock Louisville and Boston.

- General Motors recalls 220,000 defective cars.

- The disco-music fad emerges from the gay and Latino underground of many American cities.

- Twenty million mood rings — a type of jewelry that changes color with body temperature — are sold in the United States.

- The pet rock, an elaborately packaged stone, becomes a popular holiday gift.

24 Jan. A New York City landmark, Fraunces Tavern, is bombed, killing four and injuring fifty-three.

4 Feb. Menominee Indian activists agree to end a takeover of a Roman Catholic noviate in Gresham, Wisconsin, in return for the deed to what they argue is their property.

2 July The United Nations–sponsored International Women's Year Conference, meeting in Mexico City, ends.

18 Sept. Patricia Hearst is arrested by the FBI, ending a nineteen-month search.

29 Dec. At New York's LaGuardia Airport, a bomb explodes, killing eleven and injuring seventy-five.

31 Dec. Higher U.S. postal rates are imposed.

1976

- Punk fashions from London arrive in U.S. shops.

- The National Aeronautics and Space Administration (NASA) accepts its first female astronaut trainees.

- Barbara Walters becomes the first newscaster to be offered $1 million to broadcast the nightly news.

20 Mar. Patricia Hearst is found guilty of taking part in a 1974 bank robbery and is sentenced to seven years in prison.

24 May The first transatlantic flights of the supersonic Concorde aircraft begin.

2 June Don Bolles, an investigative reporter for the *Arizona Republic,* is critically injured when his car explodes in Phoenix. He dies on 13 June, and his investigation of political influence in land deals will never be concluded.

4 July The United States celebrates the two hundreth anniversary of the Declaration of Independence.

9 July The National Institute on Drug Abuse reports that Valium is the nation's most prescribed drug.

27 Aug. Transsexual Renee Richards, formerly Richard Raskind, an eye surgeon, is barred from competing in the women's tennis competition at the U.S. Open after she refuses a chromosome test.

11 Sept. Croatian terrorists explode a bomb in New York, killing one and wounding three. They hijack an aircraft the next day but surrender in Paris.

18 Sept. The Reverend Sun Myung Moon presides over a God Bless America rally in Washington, D.C. Fifty thousand followers of Moon attend.

1977

- The Apple II, the first personal computer with color graphics, is introduced for home use.

- The State Department urges an emergency admission of ten thousand Indochinese boat people.

- Congress bans fluorocarbon aerosol spray cans.

- Twenty-five million CB radios are in use by motorists.

8 Feb.   Larry Flynt, publisher of the magazine *Hustler*, is convicted of obscenity in Cincinnati.

10 Aug.   In New York police arrest David Berkowitz, age twenty-four, as the suspect in the "Son of Sam" serial murder case.

23 Aug.   The first successful man-powered aircraft, the seventy-seven-pound *Gossamer Condor*, is flown in Shafter, California.

1978

- Epson introduces the dot-matrix printer for personal computers.

- In Washington, D.C., sixty-five thousand women march in support of the Equal Rights Amendment.

- An Ohio court rules that girls may play on Little League Baseball teams.

- The world's first test-tube baby is born in England.

- Larry Flynt is gunned down and critically wounded after testifying at his own obscenity trial.

- Construction of a nuclear-power plant in Seabrook, New Hampshire, is suspended due to public opposition.

- Following a traveling museum exhibit of Egyptian antiquities, a King Tut craze sweeps the nation.

11 May   The first female general in the Marine Corps, Margaret A. Brewer, is appointed.

28 June   The Supreme Court decision in the *Regents of the University of California* v. *Bakke* case limits the scope of affirmative action.

6 Oct.   At the University of Chicago the first female president of a coed university, Hannah H. Gray, is inaugurated.

18 Nov.   Authorities discover the mass suicides and murders of over nine hundred members of Jim Jones's Peoples Temple cult in Guyana.

27 Nov.   George Moscone, mayor of San Francisco, and Harvey Milk, city supervisor, are killed by Dan White, a disgruntled former supervisor.

1979

- Over 14.5 million Americans identify themselves as Hispanic.

- Jerry Falwell organizes the conservative Moral Majority lobby.

- The Sony Walkman portable personal radio is introduced.

- A palimony lawsuit against movie actor Lee Marvin is filed.

- One hundred thousand march in Washington, D.C., in support of gay liberation.

11 Jan.   U.S. surgeon general Julius B. Richmond labels cigarette smoking the "single most important environmental factor contributing to early death."

3 Apr.   Jane Byrne is elected mayor of Chicago by the largest majority since 1901.

OVERVIEW

1960s Legacy. The decade of the 1970s was in many ways a continuation of the late 1960s. The liberals and radicals of the 1960s inspired the social-justice crusades or liberation movements of the 1970s. There was new freedom for women, homosexuals, Native Americans, Chicanos, the elderly, the handicapped, and other minorities.

Assassinations. This decade, however, also reflected the dashed hopes and widespread political disillusionment that followed. Assassinations (John F. Kennedy, Malcolm X, Martin Luther King, Jr., Robert F. Kennedy), campus unrest and urban riots, the resignation of President Richard Nixon, and American participation in the Vietnam War all contributed to the unease of the decade.

Baby Boomers. The seventy-five million baby boomers who grew up in the 1950s and 1960s were maturing in the 1970s. They had educations, jobs, careers, freedom, and independence. What they did with these things and the choices they made in their leisure time are as important as indicators of American society as how they voted. Their huge numbers made an enormous impact on everything in the culture, and their tastes and fads became national trends. As they matured from children to adults, they had an important influence on every aspect of American society.

Economic Decline. The 1960s were a period of economic growth so remarkable as to be dubbed the "age of affluence," but by the 1970s serious economic problems developed. By the end of the decade Americans had faced three recessions, double-digit inflation and double-digit unemployment, the first imposition of peacetime wage and price controls, the collapse of the manufacturing sector, two oil embargoes, and 20 percent mortgage and credit-card interest rates. In the face of such an uncertain future, many Americans abandoned their former liberal or radical politics and social views. A conservative backlash appeared, and the New Right offered baby boomers traditional values and born-again Christianity which many found appealing. Others turned to trendy self-improvement, human growth potential, and new psychotherapy movements.

Diminished Expectations. These and other changes in the lifestyles and social trends in the United States in the 1970s are evidence that the seventies were both an end and a beginning. The decade marks the close of the age of affluence and the beginning of a new period in American and world history, one characterized by limitations on resources and power; one less optimistic about the ability of the United States to reshape the world. How Americans experienced the 1970s at home can be deciphered in the contrasting words of two presidents. In 1961 John F. Kennedy said Americans would "pay any price, bear any burden, meet any hardship, support any friend, oppose any foe to assure the survival and the success of liberty." In 1971 Richard M. Nixon said that "Americans cannot — and will not — conceive all the plans, design all the programs, execute all the decisions, and undertake all the defenses of the free nations of the world." This change marked an inward turn in the American mind and spirit that is a hallmark of the 1970s.

New Consumerism. Social critics feared this turn inward would result in political passivity and cultural narcissism. As the antiwar movement wound down and political radicalism faded, Americans in the 1970s began to enjoy the freedom and pleasures the counterculture offered. For many young Americans the counterculture became a part of everyday life, and the lifestyle of the hippies was assimilated into mainstream society. Illegal drugs became fashionable, regarded as no more dangerous than the alcohol or cigarettes so popular in the 1940s and 1950s. More traditionally, Americans also enjoyed new consumer products, stereos, color television, electronic gadgets, and air-conditioning.

Radicalism Tamed. Popular music anticipated the decade's mood swing. Bob Dylan, Joan Baez, Arlo Guthrie, and other protest singers mellowed, and the Beatles broke up. After the revolutionary gestures of the early 1970s, movement heavies continued New Left politics, but in small, quiet, local community organizations rather than through apocalyptic violence. Public service and the helping professions attracted many of the best and brightest radicals, while others found careers and wealth as hip capitalists. By 1979 even the hippie-Yippie guru Jerry Rubin was working on Wall Street.

Sun Belt. Other social trends included a major population shift to the Sun Belt states in the Southwest and West Coast. This meant increasing numbers of families moved more often and further from home. Ethnic consciousness, which had faded after World War II, became fashionable again. Feminism, perhaps the most important consequence of the 1960s, was seen as less radical and more acceptable, although it remained the focus of continuing controversy in the culture.

Feminism and the Future. Feminism remained the most controversial aspect of 1970s culture because it, more than any other ism inherited from the 1960s, carried within it the most radical implications of that decade of upheaval. The New Left and the student movements of the 1960s demanded participatory democracy and a change in the status quo; feminists in the 1970s offered "the politics of empathy" and tried to create a less confrontational, more nurturing society. Black activists challenged racial discrimination and elite rule; feminists attacked sexual subordination and male dominance. The counterculture proposed a less repressive, more tolerant society; feminists worked to build a more open, inclusive community. There were few American institutions or traditional norms left unchallenged. Feminists demanded access to male-dominated businesses and universities; made inroads into politics at the local, state, and national levels; transformed the character of the American family and in so doing transformed their husbands and children; became doctors, lawyers, teachers, priests, scientists, writers, plumbers, dockworkers, pilots, stockbrokers, and sports heroes. Feminists questioned fundamental assumptions regarding sexuality and the human body and began experiments with alternative family structures, work discipline, pedagogy, and self-expression. The impact of feminism was such that it became the focus of opposition by traditionalists uncomfortable with the changed environment of the 1970s. From their battles with feminists over the Equal Rights Amendment and abortion, some conservatives extrapolated that feminism was responsible for many ills and miseries which seemed to have little connection with the feminist movement. Feminism was blamed for permissiveness and the creation of a poor workforce who undermined American productivity in the global market; gender anomie and passivity, which resulted in Soviet advances against American geopolitical positions; coddling and sentimentality toward the downtrodden and oppressed, which resulted in the creation of a dependent underclass and a rise in crime. The irony of the 1970s was that the more successful feminism was in changing the character of American society, the more its opponents could charge it was changing the United States for the worse. However tenuous the causal connections to social ills, because feminism was the most influential social movement of the decade, it became an easy target and rallying mark for those uncertain and uncomfortable with the pace of historical change. Feminism accordingly became as indispensable to its opponents as to its supporters; and as cultural and political transformations continued into the 1980s and 1990s, feminism remained at the center of the debate over how — and how fast — the country should change.

ASSIMILATION OF THE COUNTERCULTURE

A Chasm of Misunderstanding. Counterculture was the youth culture of the 1960s, which continued to flourish in the 1970s. As the term implied, it was a culture that developed against the established culture. Young people rejected capitalism, competition, social conventions, and the work ethic of their parents. They embraced communitarianism, cooperation, toleration, and "doing your own thing." In contrast to the heterosexual monogamy of their parents, young people championed sexual experimentation; in place of the three-martini lunch, young people had marijuana picnics. For those embracing the counterculture, sex, drugs, and rock 'n' roll took precedence over hard work, sobriety, and suburbia. Uncounted numbers of adolescents left home or school in the early 1970s to enjoy the hippie life in Boston, New York's Greenwich Village, San Francisco's Haight-Ashbury, or in rural communes. By the mid 1970s, however, the countercultural energies of these centers were spent; the publicity and media attention on the counterculture had nonetheless diffused aspects of it to every American town, city, and suburb. While Theodore Rozak, Charles Reich, and Herbert Marcuse argued that the counterculture was a form of philosophical romanticism, destined to alter radically the character of technological capitalism, much of the counterculture was simply adolescent rebellion and indulgent mischievousness. As the counterculture became more widely disseminated, its playfulness and rebelliousness became more important than its philosophical foundations. It remained consistently the province of the young, the distinguishing feature between age groups, and the most obvious cause of the famous generation gap. Even President Nixon, in his 1969 inaugural address, acknowledged cultural divisions among Americans, noting that "old and young across the nation shout across a chasm of misunderstanding." As the 1970s progressed, that chasm got deeper and wider.

Diminishing Possibilities. Part of the growing distance between young and old in the 1970s was due to the downturn in the American economy. The counterculture was born during a period of economic prosperity, when the traditional work discipline and personal mores of

1974 insurance company advertisement addressing the increase in drug use among adolescents

Americans could be liberalized with apparently little social cost. The 1970s were different, an era of diminishing opportunity, characterized by inflation, unemployment, rising national debt, pollution, and widespread fear for the future. Faced with these realities, middle-class college students and working-class teenagers were attracted to the counterculture for less romantic, and more overtly rebellious, reasons. Some aspects of the counterculture became more defiantly antisocial, and some countercultural rebels became more alienated from the mainstream.

Drug Abuse. Drug abuse was the most obvious symptom of the pathological turn the counterculture took in the 1970s. In the 1960s young people often experimented with drugs — especially psilocybin mushrooms, mescaline, and LSD — as part of a broader search for spirituality and meaning in life. In the 1970s drug users turned to amphetamines, cocaine, opiates, and heroin, rejecting meaning altogether and reflecting a deep dispiritedness. The countercultural centers of the 1960s were superseded in most urban centers by drug ghettos and "needle parks" where addicts replaced hippies. Organized crime became the main supplier of illegal drugs, replacing the associations of countercultural hippies who supplied drugs in the 1960s. Especially for members of the working class, drugs in the 1970s became a permanent ticket to dependency and poverty, rather than a means toward transcendent spirituality. Drug addiction and sales became serious medical and law-enforcement problems in the late 1970s and were closely connected to an increase in urban crime rates. By the end of the decade half of all crimes were committed by young people between the ages of ten and seventeen, many of whom were addicted to drugs.

Drug Use. While parts of U.S. urban centers disintegrated around increasing hard-drug abuse, the counterculture brought milder drugs to suburbs and small towns and made them a permanent feature of American life. Marijuana was the most commonly used recreational drug, and using it was less a revolutionary or radical statement than it had been in the 1950s or 1960s. Instead it became a normal experience. A survey in 1975 by the National Institute on Drug Abuse found that 45 percent of high-school seniors reported they had used some illegal drugs in the past year. This figure increased to 54 percent by 1979. Among the population eighteen to twenty-five years of age in 1979, the number who reported illicit drug use was 69.9 percent. Eleven percent of teens reported they smoked marijuana every day; two-thirds reported they smoked the drug at least three times a week. While most Americans dropped casual drug use as they matured, toward the end of the decade some former hippies shared their habits with their own teenagers. The culture seemed generally more tolerant of drug use, and drugs were commonly featured in pop music, movies, and television.

Hippie Capitalism. The counterculture's impact on the 1970s was not limited to drugs. One reason so many viewed soft-drug use as acceptable to mainstream Americans is that much of the rest of the counterculture became mainstream. Countercultural rock music, psychedelic fashions, hypnotic art, water beds, and black lights were integrated into the already-flourishing consumer culture of suburban America. "Head shops," selling drug paraphernalia, black-light posters, psychedelic fashions, and gag gifts, opened in nearly every American city. The rock-music industry, earning over $2 billion a year, became one of the biggest businesses of the decade, and rock impresarios such as Bill Graham and David Geffen set the standard for a new type of hip entrepreneur, bringing long hair and open-collared polyester suits into the formerly stodgy boardroom. Alternative medicine, therapeutic massage, and the growing computer-software industry provided livelihoods for hippie capitalists. The success of Peter Fonda's 1969 film *Easy Rider* led Hollywood to make a host of imitative, antiestablishment films appealing to a countercultural audience. Upstart, formerly underground, magazines such as *Rolling Stone* rev-

STUDIO 54

Studio 54 was a Manhattan discotheque at the center of the New York City social scene for most of the 1970s. Steve Rubell opened this dance club in a run-down warehouse, designing it to appeal to the hip and trendy "beautiful people" bored by ordinary discotheques. Studio 54 admitted only a select few each night. Large crowds of wanna-bes stood in line for hours for a chance to be admitted or to see movie stars, famous athletes, or political celebrities coming and going. The club was the focus of drug investigations in 1979 after President Jimmy Carter's chief aide, Hamilton Jordan, was reported to have sampled cocaine there. Insiders claimed celebrity customers commonly snorted and purchased cocaine in the nightclub.

When the disco craze faded by decade's end, Lubell became disenchanted with the celebrity life and later served a prison sentence for tax evasion. By 1988 he had invested $125 million in the refurbished Royalton Hotel, which *Vanity Fair* called the best-designed hotel in New York. Although Studio 54 continued to attract the curious in the 1980s, its glamorous heyday had passed. Lubell, Studio 54's puckish ringmaster, died suddenly on 25 July 1989, and his once-hot disco closed soon after.

olutionized staid journalism. Television shows such as *The Partridge Family* and *The Brady Bunch* fused traditional family values to counterculture fashions and sensibilities. Men stopped cutting their hair and bought suits with bell-bottom pants; women's fashions emphasized open, unrepressed sexuality. As mainstream culture embraced some aspects of the counterculture, countercultural rebels joined the mainstream. Student radicals became college professors, black activists became authors, feminists became politicians, and antiwar protesters became lawyers and stockbrokers. Most communes failed, and their inhabitants moved to more traditional family structures in the suburbs. Although the decade ended with a political shift to the right, American culture and lifestyle at the end of the 1970s was a firm mix of traditional consumerism and countercultural innovation — a synthesis which would become the constant target of conservative wrath in the 1980s.

Sources:

George Beschner and Alfred S. Friedman, *Teen Drug Use* (Lexington, Mass.: Lexington Books, 1986);

Jo Freeman, ed., *Social Movements of the Sixties and Seventies* (New York: Longman, 1983);

Charles Perry, *The Haight-Ashbury: A History* (New York: Random House, 1984);

ORGANIC FOOD

Organic food was a 1970s fad that became a staple of mainstream American culture by the end of the decade. Farming practices that exclude synthetic pesticides, fertilizers, feed additives, and growth regulators in preference for biological pest control, animal manure, and crop rotation promised enlightened consumers better, safer, and more-natural food products. Adele Davis, a biochemist and nutrition expert, was a popular advocate of eating right, and her five books on food were best-sellers, especially *Let's Eat Right to Keep Fit* (1970) and *You Can Get Well* (1972). Her suggestions for proper cooking of natural foods and use of vitamin supplements found an enthusiastic public. By the mid 1970s many supermarkets stocked natural foods for the educated customers interested in healthy diets and dietary cures for illness. Community and home gardeners took pride in organic, natural vegetables, and a weekly home garden show, *Jim Crockett's Victory Garden*, was an unexpected hit on PBS.

The national concern for the environment and nature reflected a widespread obsession with tofu, brown rice, lentils, sprouts, and whole-grain bread. Chemical preservatives, food additives, sugar, salt, and white flour were avoided by the health-conscious, and *natural, biodegradable*, and *organic* became buzzwords for consumers. New Age politics began on a foundation of eating natural, organic food in the 1970s, a minority viewpoint that would have an important impact on mainstream American culture by the 1990s.

Tom Wolfe, *The Electric Kool-Aid Acid Test* (New York: Farrar, Straus & Giroux, 1968).

BACK TO NATURE

New Age Environmentalism. The back to the earth movement was one aspect of a New Age Movement that was predicated on the belief that people were able to attain an increased level of awareness by communing with nature. On 24 February 1977 the prestigious Rand Corporation described the shift of one million people from urban centers to rural areas in 1970–1975 as one of the most important trends in recent American history. Later events proved this claim was somewhat exaggerated, but this back-to-the-earth movement was no mere fad. The hippies celebrated nature, saw Native Americans as a spiritual people close to Mother Nature and God, and rejected the urban capitalist industrial society. Millions of hippies, and countless other would-be or weekend hippie wanna-bes, flocked to the countryside. Abandoned farms in New England or upstate New York became hippie communes, as did isolated sites in the Northwest and Southwest. Any inexpensive, remote rural locations (with convenient access to highways for trips to the city) could become a New Age farm.

Organic Food. Many New Age farmers, however, were city or suburban college dropouts or liberal-arts graduates with no experience or training in agriculture. Most communal farms failed or became vacation retreats for affluent hippies, but some were successful. Educated newcomers read books, government manuals, and Agricultural Extension Service bulletins to learn how to farm the land. As part of the back-to-the-earth movement, organic farming was obligatory, and the market for organic produce was expanding. Consumers preferred natural foods without additives and preservatives, and some rural communes produced organic farm products and natural handicrafts for hip city boutiques.

New Rural Blood. The rural population, declining since the nineteenth century and surpassed by the urban population in 1920, increased for the first time in 1970–1975. New blood revived many dying farm communities, providing alternatives to the family farm and agribusiness as well as to enthusiastic young residents with new ideas, attitudes, and energy.

Sources:

Bennett M. Berger, *The Survival of a Counterculture* (Berkeley: University of California Press, 1981);

Raymond Mungo, *Total Loss Farm: A Year in the Life* (New York: Dutton, 1970).

CHANGING SEXUAL MORALITY

Sexual Revolution. The so-called sexual revolution was considered by many to be the most shocking social trend in the 1970s. The sexual revolution, an outgrowth of the counterculture, cast aside traditional sexual restraints and began a decade of alternative eroticism, experimentation, and promiscuity. In part facilitated by the development of the birth-control pill and other contraceptives, Americans in the 1970s broke many sexual taboos. Interracial dating, open homosexuality, communal living, casual nudity, and dirty language all seemed to indicate a profound change in sexual behavior. Sexual activity among the young especially increased. Surveys during the 1970s reported that by age nineteen, four-fifths of all males and two-thirds of all females had had sex. Fashion designers promoted a new sensuality, producing miniskirts, hot pants, halter tops, and formfitting clothes designed to accentuate women's sexuality. Abandoning the censorious production code, Hollywood used nudity and eroticism to attract audiences (and, all too often, to cover shortcomings in screenplays). Hard-core pornography annually earned $4 billion. Graphic suggestion and profanity became a staple of rock music and popular novels. Public schools offered sexual education courses for adolescents. Most of these developments took place without the hand-wringing and guilt that had formerly characterized American attitudes toward sex.

Pornography. The growing visibility of pornography in the 1970s was one sign that sexual attitudes were changing. Nudity and sex had been used by countercultural artists in the late 1960s to challenge social convention. Artists in the 1970s continued to use such techniques, often tying graphic sex to larger statements about the human condition. Films such as Bernardo Bertolucci's *Last Tango in Paris* (1973) tied explicit sex to themes of human loneliness and madness. Erica Jong's 1973 novel *Fear of Flying* described uninhibited sexuality as a feminist act. Most pornography, however, was not nearly so high-minded, being for the most part voyeuristic displays of acrobatic intercourse with little or no plot. Much film pornography was shown in adult-movie theaters and peep shows in seedy urban districts such as New York's Times Square, Boston's Combat Zone, or San Francisco's North Beach. Often closely associated with prostitution and organized crime, the pornography business nonetheless became increasingly acceptable. In the 1970s pornographic films such as *Deep Throat* and *Behind the Green Door* were genuine hits, and their stars, Linda Lovelace, Harry Reems, and Marilyn Chambers, achieved celebrity status. Established men's magazines such as Hugh Hefner's *Playboy* were forced by the popularity of more-explicit competitors such as *Penthouse* and *Hustler* to become more graphic. Even women became consumers of pornography. Eroticized romance novels with titles such as *Royal Bondage* and *Sweet Savage Love* sold twenty million copies a year, primarily to women. A female-oriented magazine filled with pictures of naked men, *Playgirl*, began publishing in 1973. Sexual liberation, which in the 1960s was supposed to lead to greater self-expression and transcendence, became, in the 1970s, a coarse consumer business.

Sex Manuals. The growth of pornography was connected to increased middle-class sexual exploration and adventurism. Sexual manuals such as *The Joy of Sex, Everything You Always Wanted to Know about Sex But were Afraid to Ask* and *The Sensuous Man* provided frank and explicit advice concerning a host of sexual activities, in a tone that presented sex as a healthy human pleasure. These best-sellers were popular with millions of American couples, especially those living together before or in place of marriage. A small minority of American couples also experimented with traditional, heterosexual marriage, sometimes introducing extra partners into their relationships, sometimes experimenting with same-sex partners. Open marriage and wife swapping were practiced occasionally in 1970s suburbia, often after consulting the popular sex manuals. Given the decade's mania for self-help, seeking instruction on sex in these users' manuals often seemed a trendy solution to sexual problems.

Critics. Critics of the sexual revolution ranged from conservatives to clergymen to public-health officials to

---

DEEP THROAT

Deep Throat, starring Linda Lovelace and Harry Reems, was the most popular pornographic movie of the 1970s. The New York Criminal Court ruled this 1972 movie to be indisputably obscene on 1 March 1973, and the film producer, nine distributors, and actor Harry Reems were convicted of interstate distribution of obscene material in a Memphis federal court on 30 April 1976. Despite these legal problems, *Deep Throat* became an X-rated adult-film classic. Linda (Marchiano) Lovelace was the star of a milder sequel, *Deep Throat Part II*, in 1974, but she claimed to be the victim of sexual abuse in her 1986 autobiography, *Out of Bondage*. This movie entered American political lore when *Washington Post* reporters investigating the Watergate scandal dubbed their secret White House news source "Deep Throat."

Source: Linda Lovelace and Mike McGrady, *Out of Bondage* (Secaucus, N.J.: Stuart, 1986).

---

feminists. Although the National Commission on Obscenity and Pornography reported in 1970 that there was no connection between pornography and crime, delinquency, or sexual deviation, President Nixon rejected their findings, condemning the report as "morally bankrupt." Like Nixon, conservatives argued that sexual promiscuity was part of a larger decline in society. Sexual promiscuity, they argued, was immoral and dangerous, ultimately compromising social discipline. Some linked the new sexual freedom to rising divorce rates, to an epidemic of sexually transmitted diseases, and even to the failure of the United States to win the war in Vietnam. Clergymen often echoed the concerns of conservatives, condemning the new sexual toleration and guiltless attitudes toward premarital sex and single motherhood. Public-health officials sometimes shared these concerns, pointing to increased incidence of teenage pregnancy. Despite the wider availability of birth control and abortion, teenage pregnancies reached one million per year; about 87 percent of these teenagers kept their children. While many of these critics blamed feminism for such problems, some feminists were themselves deeply troubled by the new sexual adventurism and the growth of pornography. Feminist writers such as Judith Rossner, in her novel *Looking for Mr. Goodbar* (1975), objected that one-night stands and the singles scene were predatory, consumerist, and meaningless. Lesbian feminists such as Andrea Dworkin protested that pornography objectified women and acted as a catalyst for male dehumanization of women, wife battering, and rape. As Susan Brownmiller argued in her 1975 study *Against Our Will: Men, Women and Rape*, "Pornography, like rape, is a male invention, designed to dehumanize women, to reduce the

Feminist Susan Brownmiller in 1970 just after she organized a nine-hour protest at the offices of John Mack Carter, the editor of *Ladies' Home Journal*. He agreed to publish a supplement written entirely by women.

female to an object of sexual access, not to free sensuality from moralistic or parental inhibition." All the critics of the liberalization of sex in the 1970s saw the phenomenon as emptying sexuality of its mystery, joy, and intimacy.

Revolution? Aside from the growth of sex as a consumer item and the increase in premarital sex and teenage pregnancies, the long-term consequences of the sexual revolution remained unclear. Most Americans continued to practice monogamous heterosexuality, usually within marriage. Sexual explorers of the 1970s generally settled down to monogamous relationships in the 1980s. Even Tony Manero, the barhopping sexual buccaneer portrayed by John Travolta in *Saturday Night Fever* (1977), ended the film disgusted with the meaninglessness of the New York singles scene. Kinsey Institute researchers revealed in a 1989 report that the sexual revolution had not been as common as the media and its critics believed. The researchers could find no revolution in American attitudes toward sexuality, and they noted that many groups remained hostile to sexual permissiveness, especially Fundamentalists and pious Christians, those with less education and less sexual experience before marriage, rural people, and those from restrictive backgrounds. Relegated to the background during the sexual consumerism of the 1970s, such groups became outspoken in the 1980s, continuing the debate over the limits of legitimate sexual activity begun in the 1960s.

Sources:
Albert D. Klassen, Colin J. Williams, and others, *Sex and Morality in the U.S.* (Middletown, Conn.: Wesleyan University Press, 1989);

Christopher Lasch, *The Culture of Narcissism: American Life in an Age of Diminishing Expectations* (New York: Norton, 1979);

Rex Weiner and Deanne Stillman, *Woodstock Census: The Nationwide Survey of the Sixties Generation* (New York: Viking, 1979).

THE ENERGY CRISIS

Energy Crisis. The energy crisis came to public attention when an oil embargo by the Arab-controlled Organization of Petroleum Exporting Countries (OPEC) was imposed from October 1973 to March 1974 to protest U.S. military support of Israel. This was an important shift in world economics and politics, and it caused President Nixon to impose emergency energy-conservation measures. He ordered thermostats lowered to sixty-eight degrees, reduced air travel and highway speed limits, halted coal-to-oil conversions, licensed more nuclear power plants, relaxed environmental regulations, and approved daylight savings time in winter. Carpools and public transportation increased as gas stations closed or limited sales. Business and school schedules were shortened to conserve fuel.

Alternatives. The energy crisis pointed to Americans' lavish consumption of oil. With only 6 percent of the world population, the United States annually consumed 30 percent of the world's energy, increasingly in foreign oil. One result of the energy crisis was to draw attention to environmental issues and to alternative forms of energy (wind and solar power) and transportation (bicycles, walking, and public transportation). A more popular response to the gas shortage was to buy smaller, fuel-efficient automobiles such as the General Motors Vega as well as imported cars such as Germany's Volkswagen and Japan's Toyota. Due to this shift, in 1973 American

COMPACT CARS

Compact cars became popular as a result of the energy crisis and the end of the postwar economic boom. The Arab oil embargo in 1973, organized by the Organization of Petroleum Exporting Countries (OPEC), caused severe oil and gasoline shortages in the United States. Oil prices increased 350 percent in 1973; for the first time gas cost more than one dollar per gallon. Although the OPEC embargo ended early in 1974, multinational oil companies earned record profits (70 percent in 1973 and 40 percent in 1974), and inflation and unemployment also increased. Simultaneously, the auto industry suffered a recession; General Motors laid off 6 percent of its workers.

Consumers refused to purchase gas-guzzling cars and turned to small, fuel-efficient foreign cars from Germany, Sweden, and Japan. Ford, Chrysler, and General Motors closed large-car plants and retooled to manufacture smaller compact cars. By 1974 compact-car sales surpassed those of standard large cars, and imported cars were increasingly popular. Volkswagen, Toyota, Saab, and Volvo automobiles were considered not only more economical and efficient but superior to downsized Detroit products such as the American Motors Gremlin or the Ford Pinto. General Motors's recall of five hundred thousand Chevy Vegas in July 1972 shook consumer confidence. In 1974 Volkswagen replaced its popular three-thousand-dollar Beetle with the more comfortable VW Golf to maintain its appeal to American drivers. By 1976 the customized van was a popular American alternative to compact foreign or domestic automobiles.

Sources: James J. Flink, *The Car Culture* (Cambridge, Mass.: MIT Press, 1975);

Hays Gorey, *Nader and the Power of Everyman* (New York: Grosset & Dunlap, 1975).

car sales declined by eleven million and in 1974 by seven million more.

Sources:
Donald R. Kelley, ed., *The Energy Crisis: An International Perspective* (New York: Praeger, 1977);

Tad Szulc, *The Energy Crisis* (New York: Watts, 1978).

ENVIRONMENTALISM

Environmentalism. Environmentalism was a new concern for the ecology of the human habitat, a social trend derived from the space program, the energy crisis, scientific warnings about pollution and a future shortage of natural resources, the counterculture's back-to-the-

earth movement; and the new interests in health, nature, Asian religion, and human-potential movements.

Response. Congress reacted to new public pressures, and in 1970 President Nixon signed the National Environmental Policy Act, which required government agencies to assess the environmental impact of public projects and to protect endangered species. Nixon also signed the Clean Air Act (1970), the Clean Water Act (1972), and the Pesticide Control Act (1972). The first Earth Day, on 22 April 1970, was a national teach-in on pollution and ecological problems on fifteen hundred college and ten thousand high-school campuses. But to many Americans the environmentalists seemed to be making the 1970s the doomsday decade.

Impact. In 1971 Barry Commoner published an influential book, *The Closing Circle*, warning that environmental pollution may be an irreversible process and that the human economy must be compatible with the human ecology. An accident in March 1975 at one of the world's largest nuclear reactors at Brown's Ferry, Alabama, gave credence to the activist's fears. As more Americans became concerned about environmental issues, local and state groups lobbied legislators for protective laws. In response Oregon passed the first state bottle-recycling law in 1972. Environmentalists took advantage of the energy crisis in 1973 to advocate alternative, safe, clean energy (solar, wind, geothermal) and lobbied Congress for tax incentives and research funds to end U.S. dependence on oil and coal. Ordinary citizens saw environmentalism as a sensible, low-cost, moral step.

Ozone and Activism. Although fluorocarbons in aerosol spray cans were said to harm the ozone layer in the atmosphere in 1975, federal agencies did not ban the use of fluorocarbons until 1977. Delays like this led to a loss of confidence in scientific and governmental authority, and membership in environmental organizations (Sierra Club, Audubon Society, Greenpeace, Appalachian Mountain Club) rose dramatically as public awareness sharpened.

Sources:
Barry Commoner, *The Closing Circle: Nature, Man and Technology* (New York: Knopf, 1971);

Kirkpatrick Sale, *The Green Revolution: The American Environmental Movement, 1962–1992* (New York: Hill & Wang, 1993).

ETHNIC CONSCIOUSNESS

Pride. Ethnic pride reappeared in the 1970s in a wave of group consciousness and group identification among members of virtually all ethnic and racial groups. While ethnic and racial pride had always been quietly present in American life, even becoming an intellectual vogue in the early part of this century, since World War I ethnic consciousness had been subsumed to Anglo-Saxon culture and the melting-pot tradition. Stimulated by the success of the Black Power movement and by conservative political appeals to white ethnic voters, pride in one's own roots became popular.

Black Pride. The second phase of the civil rights movement of the 1960s, focused on black nationalism and militance, spawned the soul culture of the 1970s. Rejecting white standards of beauty, art, and culture, blacks reclaimed their African heritage. The Afro or "natural" hairstyle rejected conking and other methods of making African-American hair straight like that of whites. Women adopted West African cotton print dresses and scarves, and dashikis were popular.

Media Visibility. Network television responded to growing black pride with sitcoms such as *Sanford and Son* (1972–1977), *Good Times* (1974–1979), and *The Jeffersons* (1975–1984). Featuring African-Americans as the primary actors, these programs portrayed blacks positively and were popular with black and white audiences alike. Aimed at a more distinctly African-American audience, "blaxploitation" films such as *Sweet Sweetback's Baadasssss Song* (1971), *Shaft* (1971), *Superfly* (1972), *Blacula* (1972), and *Cleopatra Jones* (1973) gained wide popularity in urban theaters. Although these films featured black stars and were often directed by respected African-American artists such as Melvin Van Peebles, Gordon Parks, Sr., and Gordon Parks, Jr., the National Association for the Advancement of Colored People (NAACP) and film critics condemned most of these movies for excessive violence, foul language, sexism, and the glorification of drugs.

Roots. Black Americans found new reasons to be proud of their ethnic and racial origins when *Roots,* a best-selling 1976 book by Alex Haley, became the basis for the most popular television miniseries ever broadcast. For eight consecutive nights in January 1977, 130 million Americans tuned in to ABC to watch the story of Haley's West African ancestors: the boy Kunta Kinte came to Virginia as a slave in 1750 and became the progenitor of the Tennessee family that produced Haley. Although historians and genealogists questioned the accuracy or possibility of tracing a slave ancestor to an African village, Haley's tale enthralled readers and viewers of every ethnic background.

Native Americans. Like African-Americans, Native Americans adopted a new ethnic pride as a result of the civil rights movements of the 1960s. At the beginning of the decade, four out of ten Native Americans were unemployed, and nine out of ten lived in substandard housing. Indians suffered a greater incidence of alcoholism, tuberculosis, and suicide than any other ethnic group. Since the 1880s Indian tribes were confined to federal reservations, which received few benefits of modern life (roads, electricity, water and sewer systems) or economic development.

AIM. The American Indian Movement (AIM), a militant Native American group organized on the model of the Black Panthers, responded to the plight of Indians by

American Indian Movement guard manning a roadblock at Wounded Knee

occupying Alcatraz Island in San Francisco Bay. For eighteen months AIM protested Indian living conditions and treaty violations by the U.S. government. In 1972 AIM occupied the Bureau of Indian Affairs in Washington. When the Interior Department responded by increasing police at the Pine Ridge Reservation at Wounded Knee, South Dakota (site of a massacre by the U.S. Army in 1890), tensions escalated into a seventy-one-day armed standoff. Russell Means and Dennis Banks, leaders of AIM, criticized Indian leaders negotiating a conciliatory end to the siege as "Uncle Tomahawks" or "Apples" (red outside, white inside). Support by the Congressional Black Caucus, Gloria Steinem, Angela Davis, Marlon Brando, and *New York Times* columnist Tom Wicker, however, won favorable publicity for the case and led to its peaceful conclusion.

Treaty Rights. AIM's militance sparked a decade's worth of change for Native Americans. Indian pride surged, and many Americans with distant or no Indian ancestry began to identify themselves as Native Americans. By 1990 the census found 1.7 million Americans identifying themselves as Native American, up from 800,000 in 1970 — an impossible surge, given levels of natural increase. Native Americans used this new attitude to secure the Indian Self-Determination Act of 1974, giving Indians the right to control federal and educational aid on their reservations. Indians also challenged the legality of treaties with the U.S. government in court. The Eskimos, Aleuts, and other native Alaskans won $1 billion in 1971 for outstanding land claims. In 1980 the Lakota won a judgment of $107 million for lands illegally seized by the government. Native American pride resulted in Native American progress.

Hispanics. Hispanic-Americans also promoted ethnic pride and social reform. Although *Hispanic-American*

Joseph Colombo, Sr., reputed boss of the Mafia's Bonanno family, holding umbrella, during picketing of FBI headquarters in New York City to protest defamation of Italians

suggests citizens of Spanish descent, fewer than 250,000 Spaniards immigrated to the United States between 1820 and 1975. The majority of Hispanic-Americans came from Puerto Rico, Cuba, Mexico, or other Latin American countries and became the fastest growing immigrant group in the United States during the 1970s. Hispanics concentrated in southwestern states and cities, such as California, Arizona, New Mexico, and Texas, which Hispanic militants called "Aztlan" — the "conquered territories" won by the U.S. government in the Mexican War (1846–1848). Hispanics eventually established huge minority communities in Los Angeles, Denver, Santa Fe — even in eastern cities such as Miami and New York — and became nearly half the population of San Antonio and the majority of citizens in El Paso. Many Hispanics were undocumented workers who moved north after the Mexican economy declined in the mid 1960s. Often treated with contempt by their employers, working low-paying, menial jobs, Hispanic males earned only 71 percent of white male income in the 1970s; Hispanic women, 86 percent.

Brown Power. In the early 1970s riots between young Hispanics and the police in East Los Angeles brought media attention to the problems of Hispanic-Americans. Like blacks and American Indians, Hispanics began to organize for better treatment and higher wages. The "brown power" movement was led by militants such as the Brown Berets, who sought to provide meals to pre-schools and courses in Chicano studies; Cesar Chavez and the United Farm Workers, who sought to organize agricultural and migrant labor; and La Raza Unida, a political group located in the Southwest and East Los Angeles. Spanish-language newspapers, such as *La Raza,* and Hispanic television stations, such as KMEX in Los Angeles, cultivated ethnic consciousness. Chicanos developed their own slang, including the Hispanic equivalent of Uncle Tom: "Tio Taco." Hispanic-Americans became a political force in southwestern states and sparked a Chicano renaissance in the arts. Chicano women — Chicanas — such as Angela de Hoyos articulated both ethnic pride and feminist consciousness. Luis Valdez's 1978 theater production *Zoot Suit* affirmed Chicano identity and set attendance records in Los Angeles. Even network television recognized the emergence of Hispanic ethnic pride with a breakthrough sitcom on life in the East Los Angeles barrio, *Chico and the Man* (1974–1978). It was an instant hit until the featured player, a young Puerto Rican stand-up comic, Freddie Prinze, committed suicide in 1977.

Italians. White ethnic groups also discovered their

roots in the 1970s. The Italian-American Historical Association began in 1966 to study the contributions of Italian-Americans in the United States. In 1970 the Italian-American Civil Rights League was founded to combat the belief that an Italian-American crime syndicate existed. This group opposed the defamation of Italian-Americans and picketed organizations (including the FBI) they felt were guilty of discrimination. New York City Italian-Americans were also organized by an unlikely leader, crime boss Joseph Colombo, who died in a gang shooting at an Italian-American pride rally. A more conventional Italian-American leader, Ella Grasso, was elected governor of Connecticut in 1974, the first woman in U.S. history to win that post who was not the wife of a former governor.

Irish. Irish-Americans also demonstrated ethnic solidarity. Catholic demands for self-determination in Northern Ireland led to chronic violence with the Irish Protestants of Ulster and the British army. Irish-Americans responded to the strife in Northern Ireland with sympathy, an outpouring of funds, and the creation of an Irish-American lobby in Congress. Led by Senators Edward Kennedy and Daniel Patrick Moynihan, as well as by Speaker of the House Thomas P. ("Tip") O'Neill, political and economic pressure was brought to bear on the Irish and British governments to find peaceful solutions to the Irish troubles.

Ethnic Roots. Almost every ethnic group in the United States celebrated its ethnic background with neighborhood parades, political organizations, and artistic and cultural productions. Asian-Americans, such as Maxine Hong Kingston in her book *The Woman Warrior,* often expressed ambivalence about strong assimilationist tendencies within their communities — communities where Japanese-Americans and Chinese-Americans made way for new emigrants from Korea, the Philippines, and, especially after the fall of Vietnam in 1975, Indochina. American Jews were energized by the 1978 television miniseries *Holocaust,* in much the same way as were blacks with *Roots.* What was soon being called the "Roots phenomenon" in fact swept through every ethnic group. Libraries, archives, and schools were overwhelmed with demands for information and technical assistance, as amateur genealogists pored over books, records, photograph albums, and scrapbooks in an attempt to trace their family trees. Membership in local historical societies mushroomed, and history and ethnic-studies courses in schools, colleges, and adult-education centers experienced new popularity.

Sources:

Alex Haley, *Roots* (Garden City, N.Y.: Doubleday, 1976);

David Hey, *The Oxford Guide to Family History* (New York: Oxford University Press, 1993);

Joan W. Moore and Harry Pachon, *Hispanics in the United States* (Englewood Cliffs, N. J.: Prentice-Hall, 1985);

Michael Novak, *The Rise of the Unmeltable Ethnics: Politics and Culture in the Seventies* (New York: Macmillan, 1972);

Orlando Patterson, *Ethnic Chauvinism* (New York: Stein & Day, 1977).

FAMILY LIFE

Change. Family life changed considerably in this decade. In 1960 married couples with children comprised 44.2 percent of American households; by 1980 this had dropped to 30.9 percent. The number of men living alone rose from 4.3 to 8.6 percent, and women living alone from 8.7 to 14 percent. The percentage of the population who never married also increased from 17.3 to 22.5. The median age at first marriage increased, as did the divorce rate, the number of births to unmarried mothers, and the number of adults in unmarried-couple households.

Explanations. Although the explanations for the increase in divorce vary, many experts believe that because the courts accepted mental cruelty as grounds for divorce and tended to award custody of children to their mothers, divorce and remarriage became more acceptable to and for women. Greater employment opportunities and economic independence for women also contributed to the increased divorce rate. Also, no-fault divorce laws passed by many states in the 1970s permitted couples with irreconcilable differences or incompatible relationships to end their marriages quickly and inexpensively on nonadversarial grounds.

Empty Nest Syndrome. American birth and fertility rates, which increased dramatically in the 1950s and declined rapidly in the 1960s and early 1970s, were fairly steady by 1975. Perhaps the most significant change in family life was the trend for young adults to leave their parents' home after age eighteen. As the number of adolescents attending college (often living away from home) increased in the 1970s, fewer graduates returned home after college. The empty-nest syndrome referred to parents of college-age children who had no children living at home. With children away at college or living in their own apartments, middle-aged parents often felt a sense of loss. Some mothers reentered the labor force after decades of child rearing and housekeeping; others returned to college or worked in nonprofit community organizations.

Blended Families. Birth control and a lower birth rate also affected families, as did the number of working women. Average family size declined from 3.67 members in 1960 to 3.29 members in 1980. Increasing divorce rates also produced more "blended" families, as divorced parents remarried spouses with children. This social trend was represented in the popular but unrealistic television series *The Brady Bunch* (1969–1974), featuring a widow with three daughters happily married to a widower with three sons.

The Louds. Network television sitcoms like *The Partridge Family* (ABC) and *My Three Sons* (CBS) also reflected these changes in the American family. But in 1973 many viewers were shocked by a PBS documentary,

Disney World opened on a forty-four-square-mile site near Orlando, Florida, in 1971. Building on the enormous success of the Disneyland amusement park opened in Anaheim, California, in 1955, Walt Disney designed this Florida amusement park in 1964, but it was not completed until after his death. The thirty-thousand-acre site quickly became one of the world's most popular vacation resorts.

In 1965 Walt Disney also broke ground for the adjacent Experimental Prototype Community of Tomorrow (EPCOT Center), which opened in 1982. Together, Walt Disney World and the EPCOT Center feature many unique technological wonders and have attracted 500 million visitors by 1994. The Walt Disney World Resort combines the glitter of Hollywood with the magic of Disney and has changed forever the image, nature, and scope of amusement theme parks in the United States.

Source: Marc Eliot, *Walt Disney: Hollywood's Dark Prince* (New York: Birch Lane Press, 1993).

An American Family, depicting an affluent California household. The Loud family unexpectedly disintegrated on camera as the parents divorced and their son announced he was gay. Although they later appeared on talk shows claiming to be a "typical" American family, the Louds exemplified what many felt to be a new and serious social trend — the decline of the family.

Causes. Experts differ in explaining why the family changed in the 1970s. One theory is that the "crisis of the family" is no crisis at all but merely a convenient way to explain the paradox of poverty amid prosperity. Historically, Americans have blamed socioeconomic problems on changes in the family rather than grapple with economic imbalance or injustice in the social structure. Others see the decline of social welfare programs, shrinking union membership rates, declining employment opportunities for young workers, decreasing real wages for men, and increased labor participation by women as the economic causes of family social disruption and discontent. Finally, the anger, cynicism, selfishness, consumerism, extreme individualism, and erosion of civic-mindedness can be seen as a source of family and community malaise in the 1970s.

Source:
Stephanie Coontz, *The Way We Never Were* (New York: Basic Books, 1992);

Pat Loud and Nora Johnson, *Pat Loud: A Woman's Story* (New York: Bantam, 1974).

HOUSING

Costs. Housing costs in the United States increased rapidly in the 1970s. The median-priced single-family home in 1970 cost $23,000 at an average interest rate of 8.5 percent, which represented 17 percent of the home owner's income. By 1979 the same house cost $55,700 at 10.9 percent interest, or 25 percent of the owner's income. This trend continued in the next decade, contributing to inflation, urban decay, and the problem of homelessness.

Size. The affluent society of the 1960s, measured by a gross national product (GNP) increase of 4 percent annually, created new consumer demands for larger housing units. The average family home in the 1950s had 800 square feet, but this doubled by 1970, when 1.5 million new housing starts occurred. Related to this suburbanization of the United States was federal funding of highway construction, which grew from $429 million in 1950 to $4.6 billion in 1970.

Suburbs. Modern roads meant easy access to the cities for suburbanites, so adults could work in urban centers and live in bedroom communities. In this new world made by the automobile, three of four suburbanites drove to work each day. By 1970 about 40 percent of Americans lived in suburbs, and each census recorded a further decline in both urban and rural population. These new suburbs were not merely bedroom communities; they had schools, churches, office parks, industrial parks, and sprawling shopping malls for suburban residents.

Quality. But suburbs were a different kind of America by the 1970s, overwhelmingly white and affluent. Blacks made up 11 percent of the nation's population in 1970 but only 4.7 percent of suburban residents. Suburbs also were aging, as children left home for college or work. Maturing suburban children found urban housing after high school or college, rather than living with their parents until marriage. By age twenty-one increasing numbers moved into apartments or, after 1975, condominiums. Also, more of the 7.4 million college students in 1970 abandoned dormitories for off-campus housing.

White Flight. Suburbanization was associated with the white flight phenomenon, as millions of urban residents moved out of cities to avoid the growing black urban population, school busing for racial integration, city crime, congestion, traffic, and high taxes. The proportion of adults over twenty-five who completed college doubled between 1950 and 1973, and the average college graduate earned almost 60 percent more than the high-school graduate in lifetime earnings. This resulted in the rapid growth of suburbs as affluent white-collar and professional workers moved from urban to suburban communities.

Housing Crisis. All these factors created a housing crisis to which builders responded only slowly. In mid-decade new construction was supplemented by the more economical and rapid renovation of existing urban housing units. Rehabilitated urban apartment buildings with exposed brick walls and beams became trendy, but the suburban population (37.6 percent) continued to grow, exceeding urban (31.4 percent) and rural residents (31 percent) for the first time in 1970. Banks and the Veterans Administration provided the credit, making suburban housing possible for millions of Americans, many of whom moved to the suburban communities developing around Sun Belt cities such as Los Angeles, San Diego, Phoenix, Tucson, Miami, Houston, and Dallas.

Sources:
Kenneth T. Jackson, *The Crabgrass Frontier: The Suburbanization of the United States* (New York: Oxford University Press, 1985);

Landon Y. Jones, *Great Expectations: America and the Baby Boom Generation* (New York: Coward, McCann & Geoghegan, 1980);

Gwendolyn Wright, *Building the Dream: A Social History of Housing in America* (Cambridge, Mass.: MIT Press, 1983).

GAY LIBERATION

Stonewall. Gay liberation was an important social-justice movement precipitated by the spirit of the 1960s. In June 1970 more than five thousand gay men and women marched in Greenwich Village to celebrate the first anniversary of the Stonewall riot, a violent clash between New York City police and gay people at the Stonewall bar on Christopher Street. Each year in a growing number of cities, the Stonewall marchers called for "Gay Power" and "Gay Liberation," and their politics and consciousness transformed a small reform movement into a grassroots gay liberation crusade. Hundreds of gay rights organizations in American cities demanded legal reform, access to public services, and an end to discrimination. By 1973 the American Psychiatric Association removed homosexuality from its list of mental disorders in response to lobbying by gay liberation groups who charged that psychiatry provided the underpinnings for many antihomosexual practices. The National Association of Social Workers, the American Sociological Association, other academic organizations, and several states took similar action by 1975.

Politics. The success of the gay liberation and gay rights movement prompted gay candidates to run for public office. In Massachusetts Gerry Studds, a gay Democrat from Cape Cod, Massachusetts, was elected to Congress in 1973. Elaine Noble was the first openly homosexual woman to be elected to the Massachusetts legislature in 1974. Barney Frank, a gay man who served effectively in the administration of Boston mayor Kevin White and in the Massachusetts legislature, would be elected as a Democrat to Congress in 1980. Other gay candidates campaigned or were elected to office in California, Missouri, Minnesota, and Florida. The election of openly or covertly homosexual candidates marked a new mood of tolerance and acceptance in the United States.

Harvey Milk. In San Francisco Harvey Milk, a prominent gay activist, was elected to the Board of Supervisors in 1977 and served ably until November 1978, when Milk

Scene outside city hall in San Francisco as the bodies of Harvey Milk and George Moscone are removed

and Mayor George Moscone were shot and killed in city hall by Dan White, a former policeman who also served on the Board of Supervisors. When White received a lenient prison sentence based on the so-called "Twinkie defense" (eating junk food had impaired his mental capacity), San Francisco City Hall was rocked by demonstrations and violence. In 1984 *The Times of Harvey Milk* won an Oscar for best documentary film.

Anita Bryant. Energized by these political changes, the gay and lesbian movement in the late 1970s emphasized two major issues — the repeal of sodomy laws and passage of antidiscrimination legislation. It proved very difficult to organize factionalized homosexual communities around legislative issues, though. Gay activism was only slowly emerging outside of a few large cities. However, gay liberation advocates did rally in response to an anti–gay rights crusade. Begun in 1978 in Dade County, Florida, and led by the evangelist singer Anita Bryant, the antigay crusade persuaded Dade County voters to repeal a civil rights law prohibiting discrimination on the basis of sexual orientation. Within a year Bryant's Save Our Children organization and evangelical groups, including the Reverend Jerry Falwell, repealed similar laws in Minnesota, Kansas, and Oklahoma and attempted to do so in Oregon and California. Perhaps in reaction to the economic recession of the late 1970s, these conservative critics of homosexuality, dubbed the New Right or neoconservatives, made a concerted effort to assert their moral and religious views in legislative bodies on all levels. Nevertheless, gay rights advocates won the support of liberal and moderate voters.

Results. Increased personal tolerance for sexual experimentation during the 1960s and 1970s is referred to as the sexual revolution. Although some sexual inhibitions loosened, homosexuals and lesbians did not find widespread public acceptance. Colleges, for example, relaxed in loco parentis rules for heterosexuals long before they tolerated gay men and women. Gay pride marches and legal protection from discrimination were to come slowly in the mid 1970s. The problems gay high-school students faced were only slowly addressed, although New York

City soon opened the Harvey Milk School for gay and lesbian high-school students.

THE ME DECADE

Me Decade. The term *me decade* was coined by novelist Tom Wolfe in *New York* magazine in August 1976, describing the new American preoccupation with self-awareness and the collective retreat from history, community, and human reciprocity. The term seemed to describe the age so aptly that it quickly became commonly associated with the 1970s. Compared to the 1960s, Americans in the 1970s were self-absorbed and passive. Americans turned from street theater to self-therapy, from political activism to psychological analysis. Everyone, it seemed, had an analyst, adviser, guru, genie, prophet, priest, or spirit. In the 1970s the only way many Americans could relate to one another was as members of a national therapy group.

Self-fulfillment. Much of what the term *me decade* actually described was merely a stylistic change in American preoccupations. Whereas the 1960s had been preoccupied with questions of social and political justice, the 1970s were concerned with self-fulfillment and personal happiness. Unable to solve social problems, many self-absorbed Americans focused on personal fulfillment through health food, diets, hot tubs, and physical exercise. Specialized sportswear appeared in stores by the mid 1970s, and young Americans took up kung fu, aikido, yoga, tennis, jogging, massage, camping, hiking, skiing, and dancing as a means toward self-fulfillment. Californians, including many film and television celebrities, pioneered these trendy pastimes, and Woody Allen satirized the health food and fitness craze in his Oscar-winning comedy *Annie Hall* (1977). Nevertheless, most Americans followed as these fads migrated from the West Coast to the East. Slogans like "do your own thing" and "cool out" reflected the attitude of the time.

Cults and Gurus. More significantly, the me decade reflected a sense of spiritual crisis. Because the counterculture of the 1960s had rejected traditional religion as meaningless and corrupt, when Americans turned to spiritual matters in the 1970s, they often looked east. Typical of the time was radical activist Rennie Davis. One of the Chicago Eight, accused and acquitted of inciting riots at the 1968 Democratic National Convention, in 1973 Davis became a proponent of the fifteen-year-old Indian guru Maharaj Ji, who promised "perfection" on earth by 1976. Richard Alpert, who along with Timothy Leary had been an advocate of LSD and other psychedelic drugs in the 1960s, changed his name to Ram Dass in the 1970s and championed Hindu mysticism. Alan Watts, an English writer and Episcopal priest, became the foremost exponent of Zen Buddhism in the late 1960s and early 1970s before his death in 1975. In dozens of books, articles, campus lectures, and radio and television programs, he offered new hope to the disillusioned. His

Concerned parents protesting the recruiting practices of Sun Myung Moon and his Unification Church.

concept of inner peace and release from the guilt and restrictions of Judeo-Christian culture earned him an enthusiastic following. Indian mystic Maharishi Mahesh Yogi also gained a wide countercultural audience. He introduced a mantra-chanting system called transcendental meditation (TM) to Americans. Popular with many as a means for achieving a relaxed physical and mental state, relieving anxiety or stress, and enhancing morale and productivity, TM was even adopted by some colleges and corporations. Disciples of the Swami A. C. Bhaktivedanta also became familiar to Americans. Commonly called Hare Krishna for a mantra they chanted, the cotton-robed Krishna were most often visible on street corners or in airports, where they enthusiastically solicited funds for their practice.

The Therapy Business. Krishna were not the only cultists seeking donations in the 1970s. Therapy became big business, and a host of therapeutic and quasi-religious cults developed which, usually for steep fees, promised peace of mind to their members. Most of these therapies fused aspects of the counterculture, Eastern religions, and Western psychology. Primal-scream therapy, humanistic psychology, Silva mind control, Rolfing, and Scientology promised transcendence and beatitude. Perhaps the most interesting of these therapeutic businesses was Erhard Seminar Training, or EST. EST was introduced in San Francisco by former encyclopedia salesman Werner Erhard in 1971. Promising increased confidence, energy, and happiness, EST was a complex mix of modern advertising hype and authoritarian humiliation. For two hundred dollars interested parties were "processed" by two weekend-long seminars where they were kept from eating, urinating, sleeping, and moving, all the while subjected to long meditations and harangues concerning their worthlessness. Graduates claimed to gain a new, efficient, positive outlook on life; EST earned $6 million annually by 1976.

Moonies. Before the vogue for EST faded, it claimed to have processed over 160,000 people. Even more suc-

Influenced by Bruce Lee's 1973 martial-arts film *Enter the Dragon*, many Americans in the 1970s became obsessed with kung fu and Asian martial arts. What it all meant was difficult to discern. Was the kung fu craze an unconscious acknowledgment of the American defeat in Vietnam and an attempt to master new skills in order to beat the Asians at their game? Was it because so many of the skills featured the subtle use of force, was it yet another passive/aggressive skill cultivated during the me decade? Was it simply another exotic form of violence imported by a nation obsessed with violence? Was it a reflection of rising crime rates? Or a ghetto revenge fantasy? Whatever it meant, it was popular: almost every American city and suburb boasted a storefront gym wherein karate, kung fu, judo, jujitsu, aikido, or some other form of Asian fighting was taught. Movies featured Bruce Lee, Tom Laughlin (*Billy Jack*), and Chuck Norris in kick-boxing epics. Television aired the weekly western *Kung Fu*, in which David Carradine, as Kwai Chang Caine, wandered the Old West chopping bad guys in the neck and dispensing Buddhist wisdom. "Kung Fu Fighting" was a number-one gold hit for Carl Douglas in October 1974. Even Miss Piggy of the Muppets and Elvis Presley were renowned for their air-chopping skills. Although the craze for martial arts gradually died down, it remained a permanent feature of American pop culture into the 1980s and 1990s.

cessful was the Unification Church. A fusion of Asian philosophy, Christianity, and capitalist apologia, the Unification Church was created by a South Korean Presbyterian minister, the Reverend Sun Myung Moon. Moon claimed to be the new messiah who would unite all world religions and reinterpret the Bible. His missionaries were in the United States by 1960 but did not attract widespread attention until Moon transferred his headquarters to New York and preached to twenty thousand people at Madison Square Garden in September 1974. Thereafter young Moonies were increasingly visible proselytizing on street corners, like the Krishna working the airports selling flowers for the organization. Moon used the church's funds to establish profitable businesses, including a fishing fleet in Massachusetts and the *Washington Times* newspaper. By the end of the decade, however, the Unification Church became the object of substantial criticism. Many attacked the controversial rite of "blessing": mass weddings of as many as sixty-five hundred couples, wherein Moon preselected the marriage partners, who sometimes were meeting for the first time. Parents of Moonies protested that the church brainwashed their children; some hired deprogrammers to kidnap their children from the church's communal living centers and return them to their families. Reports of financial scandals and illegal political contributions also raised alarm, but Moon's connections to prominent businessmen and conservative politicians protected him from the more-disabling criticisms. In the 1980s and 1990s the cult continued to grow, and Moon's secular investments, such as the *Washington Times*, seemed almost respectable, especially to those unaware of the connection to Moon.

The Occult and Parapsychology. A corollary to the rise of cults was the growth of occultism in the United States. Popular culture reflected an increasing interest in satanism and witchcraft. Films with occult themes such as *The Exorcist* (1974) and *The Omen* (1976) were box-office successes. Americans of all stripes dabbled with the I Ching, tarot cards, astrology, and other forms of prophecy. Paperback books on mysticism, such as those by Carlos Castaneda, or on the Bermuda Triangle, the lost island of Atlantis, and unidentified flying objects (UFOs) were common. Similarly, many Americans were interested in parapsychology and speculated on the character of things such as extrasensory perception (ESP), telekinesis, and out-of-body experiences. Apollo astronaut Edgar Mitchell conducted ESP experiments during spaceflight. And, despite the fact that both scientists and magicians dismissed him as a fraud, many Americans were convinced that Uri Geller, an Israeli psychic, could bend forks and stop watches using the power of his mind.

Alarm. Such preoccupations, as well as the popularity of therapeutic businesses and religious cults, began to alarm many Americans. Following the mass suicide and murder of over nine hundred members of Jim Jones's cult in 1978, the public subjected cults to increasing scrutiny. Reverend Moon was denied a charter by the New York Board of Regents for his Unification Theological Seminary, and the Internal Revenue Service (IRS) began an investigation into Moon's finances. Leftist activists, in particular, viewed me-decade attitudes and organizations negatively. Michael Rossman, a 1960s radical, argued in *New Age Blues* (1979) that me-decade self-absorption was draining away progressive political activism. He believed consciousness had become a growth industry. New Left historian Christopher Lasch criticized the me decade more substantially in *The Culture of Narcissism* (1979). Placing the decade's social preoccupations in a broad philosophical and historical context, Lasch argued that Western liberalism and consumer capitalism had combined to form a personality type which Lasch termed *the narcissist*. In contrast to the acquisitive instincts and work ethic of the early capitalist, the narcissist possesses a new "ethic of leisure, hedonism and self-fulfillment." The narcissist lives for immediate personal gratification, unconnected to tradition or history. He or she has no connection to the past and no expectation for the future but lives in a perpetual present, wherein the fundamental object is to feel good. Such a personality type is, for Lasch, the ultimate expression of consumerist obsolescence — an individual for whom his or her own experiences and personal reflections are disposable items. Such a person, argued Lasch, has no sense of self other than as a self purchased from the consumer culture. "... All of modern capitalism," wrote Lasch, "continually tries to create new demands and new discontents that can be assuaged only by the consumption of commodities." The growth in cults and therapies were symptoms of the extent to which capitalism had made mystic experience and spirituality commodities for sale. Lasch's argument implied, in a sense, that "I shop, therefore I am," had replaced "I think, therefore I am," as an axiomatic expression of Western consciousness.

Assimilation. Lasch's analysis of the me decade reflected the awareness of many of the New Left that the political essence of the counterculture — its emphasis on decentralized power, participatory democracy, and attack on multinational capitalism — was being abandoned even as the form of the counterculture — its liberated sexuality, rebellious style, and cultural innovations — were being assimilated into the mainstream. In the 1970s radical departures in music, film, and lifestyle were incorporated into new, hip, consumable items, even as radicalism in politics was abandoned. Similarly, many countercultural rebels resolved their spiritual dilemma in the 1970s not by turning to Eastern religions but by embracing old-fashioned, resurgent American evangelicalism. "Jesus freaks," who in the early 1970s attended Broadway plays like *Godspell* and *Jesus Christ Superstar* and who listened to "God-rock" pop hits such as "My Sweet Lord," "Put Your Hand in the Hand," "Spirit in the Sky," and "You Light Up My Life,"You Light Up My Life,"

ended the decade by joining Fundamentalist and Evangelical churches and political movements such as Jerry Falwell's Moral Majority. The case of 1960s radical Eldridge Cleaver is perhaps more typical and long-lasting than that of Davis or Alpert. Cleaver, minister of information for the Black Panther Party, returned to the United States from a politically imposed exile only to undergo a curious conversion from born-again Christianity to the Unification Church to Mormonism — which had only begun accepting black members in 1978. Cleaver, a militant who wanted to overthrow "white Amerikkka" in the 1960s, then ran unsuccessfully for public office — as a conservative Republican. Ironically, the counterculture that seemed so threatening to the establishment in the 1960s became the liberal consumerism and resurgent conservatism of the 1970s and led to a reinforcing of status quo in the 1980s.

Sources:

Eileen Barker, *The Making of a Moonie: Choice or Brainwashing?* (New York: Oxford University Press, 1984);

Christopher Edwards, *Crazy for God* (Englewood Cliffs, N.J.: Prentice-Hall, 1979);

Christopher Lasch, *The Culture of Narcissism* (New York: Norton, 1979);

Michael Rossman, *New Age Blues* (New York: Dutton, 1979);

D. T. Suzuki, *An Introduction to Zen Buddhism* (New York: Grove, 1991);

Alan Watts, *This is It* (New York: Pantheon, 1960).

NEOCONSERVATISM

New Right. Neoconservatism was the most influential and distinctive social trend to emerge in the 1970s, drawing its leaders from former leftists and liberal Democrats disillusioned with the political changes and popular democracy of the 1960s. Neoconservatives, called by wits "liberals mugged by reality," railed against radicalism disguised as liberalism and defended elitism. Unlike earlier conservative Republican leaders, such as Sen. Barry M. Goldwater and President Richard M. Nixon, the most prominent neoconservatives tended to be prolific intellectual writers, such as Daniel Patrick Moynihan, Daniel Bell, Irving Kristol, Norman Podhoretz, Jeanne Kirkpatrick, and William Bennett.

Moynihan. Moynihan was the most prominent of the neoconservative spokesmen and has served as Democratic U.S. senator from New York after 1977. Before entering politics he was a professor of government at Harvard University and made a national reputation as an adviser to Presidents John Kennedy, Lyndon Johnson, Nixon, and Gerald Ford, as well as serving as ambassador to India (1973–1975) and ambassador to the United Nations (1975–1976).

Benign Neglect. This liberal Democrat became a neoconservative hero when he wrote a memo in 1970 to President Nixon suggesting a period of "benign neglect" for race issues, which led to enormous controversy when it was leaked to *The New York Times*. His essays and

Jimmy Swaggart, televangelist and host of a television program syndicated to over two hundred stations in the late 1970s

books revealed his increasing doubts about the liberal agenda, especially *Beyond the Melting Pot* (1963), *Maximum Feasible Misunderstanding* (1969), and *Coping: On the Practice of Government* (1974).

Bell. Another former liberal Harvard professor who joined the neoconservative cause is Daniel Bell, whose book *The End of Ideology* (1960) exerted wide influence in the 1960s. Originally a socialist radical, Bell moved away from leftist views in the 1950s. He developed a gloomy assessment of modern political economy in *The Coming of Post-Industrial Society* (1973) and *The Cultural Contradictions of Capitalism* (1976), wherein he argued that the consumerism necessary to sustain modern capitalism undermined the work discipline necessary for its continued advancement.

A New Ideology. Bell and Irving Kristol, who collaborated in writing *Capitalism Today* in 1971, were trenchant social critics attempting to form a neoconservative ideology. They tried to explain and to change the persistently liberal American society by linking socioeconomic policy to explicit moral values. Like all political ideologies, neoconservatism arose in reaction to challenges to authority and institutional hierarchy. Neoconservatives were dissatisfied and even bitter about the turbulent so-

cial reforms of the 1960s, which they viewed as having destroyed refined moral values by advancing an insipid egalitarianism.

Rethinking the Great Society. The election of Nixon as president in 1968 gave neoconservatives such as *Commentary* editor Kristol a powerful ally in resisting social revolution of the 1960s. Kristol was one of the first intellectuals to embrace the neoconservative label disparagingly applied by leftist Michael Harrington to academics who questioned the new politics of the late 1960s. As a New York University professor with ties to the Central Intelligence Agency, Kristol supported the Nixon administration's crackdown on domestic protest and terrorism in 1971. Writing for *Fortune* and *The Wall Street Journal* and in newspaper and television interviews, Kristol warned of social disaster as the young ignored traditional values and embraced hedonism, drugs, and radicalism. These lucid jeremiads impressed conservatives in both the Republican and Democratic parties and provided an easy scapegoat for economic problems in the 1970s. Kristol, along with Nathan Glazer, launched the first academic critique of the Great Society's social programs of the 1960s. Arguing that the programs were inefficient and elitist, while still endorsing the welfare state, they urged the dismantling of the Great Society programs.

The "New Class." Criticism of the New Left and the counterculture was common, but in the 1970s the prestigious New York literary figure Norman Podhoretz, also an editor of *Commentary,* began a more systematic attack. He had criticized Kennedy's New Frontier and Johnson's Great Society, and *Commentary* now turned on the women's movement, Ralph Nader, environmentalists, the Black Panthers, the Chicago Seven, and the "new politics" presidential campaigns of Sen. Eugene McCarthy and Sen. George McGovern. Central to such critiques was the idea that a "new class" of professional social engineers, bureaucrats, media figures, and therapists was draining the life from American society. Postulating a kind of social parasitism, neoconservatives argued that the new class undermined society in three ways: it fostered an adversarial culture which compromised established norms and traditions; it created a permanent dependent class in society among the poor, the maladjusted, and others needing social and economic assistance; and it became a drag upon the nation's economic productivity, absorbing, in the inflated estimate of neoconservative Michael Novak, 35 percent of the nation's gross national product. Conservatives such as *National Review* editor William F. Buckley, Jr., were surprised but pleased to find these eloquent new allies from the old Left.

Business Conservatives. Stagflation, the combination of inflation and rising unemployment, in the 1970s prompted many other writers, such as Nathan Glazer, Bennett, and Kirkpatrick, to reject Democratic Party politics, liberalism, and popular democracy as solutions for American social, economic, and political issues. In a world of scarce or more-costly energy and raw materials and a slower rate of economic growth, neoconservatives objected to rising taxes, increasing government regulations, and expanding public expenditures which drained investment capital from the private sector. Many proponents of these positions were not actually neoconservatives but long-standing conservative businessmen located in the right wing of the Republican Party. Businessmen such as Henry Salvatori, Holmes Tuttle, and Taft Schreiber, established think tanks such as the American Enterprise Institute and the Heritage Foundation, sponsored academics such as Milton Friedman and George Gilder, and financed political candidates, such as Goldwater. An unlikely spokesman for their views was Ronald Reagan, a movie actor who supported Goldwater for president in 1964. Reagan rode the neoconservative tide to win two four-year terms as governor of California (1967–1975) and election as president in 1980 and 1984.

Kirkpatrick. Two younger neoconservatives who achieved prominence in the 1970s were Jeanne Kirkpatrick and William Bennett. Kirkpatrick was a liberal Democrat and professor of political science at Georgetown University (1967–1981). Her human rights views became neoconservative policy in 1979 when she stressed

CONSUMER PROTECTION

Consumer protection became an important social trend by the early 1970s. Ralph Nader, a Washington, D.C., lawyer in the Department of Labor, became interested in the safety of American automobiles in 1958 while a student at Harvard Law School. In 1965 he left government service and published a best-selling book, *Unsafe at Any Speed,* which was critical of automobile industry designs and standards. Nader was especially concerned with the safety of the Chevrolet Corvair, a popular compact car with a rear engine, which was reputed to be unsafe at high speeds.

By the 1970s Nader had expanded the scope of his concerns. Nader's campaign for safe, reliable products — cars, food, natural gas — aroused much national interest. He won greater attention in 1970 when General Motors (GM) settled a lawsuit for $425,000 and the president of GM apologized publicly for using GM detectives harass Nader and to violate his privacy.

Nader assembled "Nader's Raiders" — a group of talented young volunteers who researched a wide variety of health and safety issues and used class-action lawsuits to inform the public, educate legislators, and influence government agencies about consumer issues. Nader's Raiders were responsible for passage of the 1966 National Traffic and Motor Vehicle Safety Act, the 1967 Wholesale Meat Act, the 1968 National Gas Pipeline Safety Act, the 1968 Wholesale Poultry Products Act, the 1969 Federal Coal Mine Health and Safety Act, and the 1971 reorganization of the Interstate Commerce Commission.

Ralph Nader's work inspired a multitude of federal, state, and local groups who sought to protect consumers. These advocates distrusted government regulatory agencies, which often seemed to be mere lobbies for industries. Most states reacted to this new public concern in product safety with consumer protection laws. Some states passed "lemon laws" mandating refunds for defective used cars. The consumer-protection movement was characteristic of the frustration and disillusionment many Americans felt with governmental oversight and business ethics during the decade.

Sources: Hays Gorey, *Nader and the Power of Everyman* (New York: Grosset & Dunlap, 1975);

Thomas Whiteside, *The Investigation of Ralph Nader: General Motors vs. One Determined Man* (New York: Arbor House, 1972).

the difference between right-wing authoritarian regimes friendly to U.S. interests and totalitarian Communist re-

The Gray Panthers was a lobby founded by Margaret E. ("Maggie") Kuhn to save the elderly, an expanding population. Life expectancy in the United States rose to 69.5 years for white men and 77.2 for white women. The American population over 65 years of age increased 20 percent in the decade, and 12 million people joined the American Association of Retired Persons. In response to sit-ins and picket lines by the Gray Panthers lobby and public concern that the Social Security Administration would be bankrupt, Congress passed laws to end age discrimination and to increase the age of mandatory retirement from 65 to 70 in 1978.

gimes. She also wrote about the problem of naiveté in President Jimmy Carter's foreign policy, attracting much Republican support, and later served as ambassador to the United Nations (1981–1985).

Bennett. William Bennett was a philosophy and law professor at the University of Texas and Boston University and president (1976–1981) of the National Humanities Center, a scholarly research institute in North Carolina. He earned his neoconservative reputation as a critic of liberal education programs and by advocating a return to a classical humanities curriculum in public schools. The back-to-basics approach to schools proved very attractive to neoconservative critics of recent liberal educational reforms. Bennett later served as chairman of the National Endowment for the Humanities (1982–1985), as secretary of education (1985–1988), and as director of the Federal Office of Drug Control Policy (1989–1990).

The New Right. Neoconservatism, however, did not focus only on politics and economics; in many ways it was a cultural movement extremely critical of the countercultural changes in lifestyle, sexual standards, and family life. With only loose ties to the major political parties and profound concerns about contemporary social trends, the neoconservatives found powerful allies in the Fundamentalist Protestant churches which became politically active in the 1970s. Promoted by popular television evangelists and organized by the Moral Majority, the New Religious Right opposed the liberal influences and secularism it found inimical to American values. Like neoconservatives, Fundamentalists reacted against the turmoil of the 1960s. Often called born-again Christians, they reflected one aspect of the spiritual quest of many Americans in the era. Protestant churches, especially in the South and West, enjoyed increased membership after the 1960s. In a 1970 Gallup poll only 4 percent said that religion was influential in their lives, but by 1976, 44 percent not only acknowledged the importance of religion in their lives, but 65 percent had more confidence in the church than in any other institution. Fundamentalist and Evangelical sects preached an inspirational Christian faith that not only attracted many rural and suburban white conservatives but also many former hippies.

Evangelicals. Ruth Carter Stapelton, President Carter's sister, won a large Evangelical following in her North Carolina church. *The Gift of Inner Healing,* her popular 1976 book, did much to publicize the born-again Christian movement. Southern Baptists were especially interested in charismatic preaching, the gift of tongues, and faith healing by the power of the Holy Ghost. President Carter, who taught a Sunday school class in his Plains, Georgia, hometown, spoke publicly of his pride in being born-again.

Televangelists. Television evangelists such as Jimmy Swaggart, Oral Roberts, Jim Bakker, Billy Graham, and Jerry Falwell had an estimated audience of twenty-four million weekly viewers who contributed millions each year to their crusades. Pat Robertson founded the Christian Broadcasting Network in 1960, and from 1968 to 1986 he was the host of *The 700 Club,* a popular conservative television talk show. Jerry Falwell broadcast his televangelist program on three hundred stations by 1971, attributing the breakdown of sexual standards and family values to a larger moral decline. Millions of Americans responded to this religious awakening, and President Carter won two-thirds of the born-again votes in 1976.

Moral Majority. In 1979 Jerry Falwell organized the Moral Majority to press for laws reflecting conservative Christian values and to oppose abortion, homosexuality, pornography, and the Equal Rights Amendment. Four million Moral Majority members advocated prayer in schools, teaching biblical creationism, and increased military budgets. This special-interest lobby exerted great influence on neoconservatives and the Republican Party.

Sources:
Gabriel J. Fackre, *The Religious Right and Christian Faith* (Grand Rapids, Mich.: Eerdmans, 1982);
Peter Steinfels, *The Neo-Conservatives* (New York: Simon & Schuster, 1979).

TERRORISM

Clandestine Warfare. Terrorism, which became a major international issue in the 1970s, refers to acts or threats of violence intended to intimidate political opponents or to publicize grievances. Modern terrorists use murder, bombing, airplane hijacking, kidnapping of hostages, and assassination to force the media, public opinion, and governments to address their demands. Groups most often accused of clandestine warfare or terrorism in the 1970s included the Irish Republican Army's Provisional Wing (IRA Provos), the Palestine Liberation Organization (PLO), the Red Brigades in Italy, and the Baader-Meinhof gang in Germany.

Black September. The most notorious terrorist action of the decade was when Black September, a PLO terrorist group, killed Israeli Olympic athletes in Munich in September 1972. Despite this widely condemned act, by 1974 the United Nations and several Arab states recognized the PLO as the government of the Palestinian people.

Amin. In 1977 Ugandan dictator Idi Amin held hostage two hundred Americans living in his country, leading President Carter to plan a military invasion. Amin was persuaded to release the hostages. Terrorism came to the United States two weeks later. A small group of Hanafi Muslims held 130 people at gunpoint in three Washington, D.C., buildings. Federal officials ended the siege peacefully in three days.

Skyjacking. Commercial flights were often subject to skyjackings by terrorists, and metal detectors and other security measures became common in American airports after a group of Black Panthers seized a plane in Florida in July 1972 and took it to Algeria with $1 million in ransom. The kidnapping of Patty Hearst in California in 1974 by the Symbionese Liberation Army (SLA), an American terrorist gang, proved that this revolutionary and/or criminal tactic was not only a problem abroad.

Student Violence. As early as 1969 President Nixon had focused attention on domestic disorder, urban riots and campus unrest, directing Attorney General John Mitchell and Federal Bureau of Investigation Director J. Edgar Hoover to wage counterintelligence campaigns against radicals and domestic terrorists such as the Weathermen and the Black Panther Party. Although student radicalism was overestimated as a public-safety threat, the expanding war in Vietnam; the assassinations of Martin Luther King, Jr., and Robert Kennedy; and the televised violence between Chicago police and three thousand demonstrators at the 1968 Chicago Democratic National Convention created public fear. Conservative Americans and the emerging neoconservative lobby demanded law-and-order measures to curb the militant student protesters who could infect young Americans with terrorism like that seen in Japan, Italy, France, Germany, Mexico, and South Korea.

The Chicago Seven. The 1969 federal trial of the Chicago Seven for conspiracy to incite a riot proved Nixon's determination to suppress the radical leaders of the antiwar movement. President Nixon said, "It is not too strong a statement to declare that this is the way civilizations begin to die." The absurd nature of the trial aroused much sympathy for the defendants, especially when two Black Panther leaders, Fred Hampton and Mark Clark, were killed by the Chicago police while sleeping. On 20 February 1970 Tom Hayden, one of the defendants in the Chicago trial, was sentenced to five years in prison for his role in the demonstrations, precipitating campus marches and riots across the country, but

Black Power activists outside the dormitory at Jackson State College, Jackson, Mississippi, where two blacks were killed during demonstrations on 15 May 1970

ultimately the Chicago Seven were effectively acquitted of all charges.

Kent State. Nixon's invasion of Cambodia in May 1970 led to more demonstrations at one-third of the nation's colleges, from Yale to Stanford. The overreaction of state and federal government to college students' protests became clear on 4 May 1970, when the Ohio National Guard killed four peaceful Kent State University students at a campus protest rally, and a similar incident occurred eleven days later in Mississippi at Jackson State University. These tragedies coincided with the collapse of the Students for a Democratic Society (SDS) and the formation of a splinter group of terrorist guerrillas, the Weathermen. Taking their name from a line in a Bob Dylan song, the Weathermen used the paramilitary tactics of Che Guevara to effect more than 250 bombings and to resist what they saw as government oppression.

Wiretaps. By 1970 many New Left groups were infiltrated by the FBI and other law enforcement agencies, who collected information, planted rumors, stole mail, and even incited illegal actions for which the militants could be arrested. When *The New York Times* reported the Cambodian bombing, Nixon and his national security adviser, Henry Kissinger, ordered the FBI to wiretap the telephones of White House staff members and journalists suspected of leaking information to aid the militant protesters.

Iranian Hostages. More-serious terrorist activities faced the United States in 1979 when the shah of Iran's government was overthrown by Iranian revolutionaries led by the Ayatollah Ruholla Khomeini. President Carter was faced with the kidnapping and torture of fifty-two American citizens in Tehran for more than a year. Carter refused Khomeini's demands that the United States return the shah for trial and that the United States apologize for aiding the shah's regime. This terrorist crisis contributed to Carter's defeat in the 1980 election by

Symbionese Liberation Army hideout where six SLA members were killed by a Los Angeles SWAT team on the afternoon of 17 May 1974

Ronald Reagan and was only resolved when Carter left office.

WOMEN'S LIBERATION

Cigarettes and Liberation. One of the most popular advertising campaigns of the early 1970s was that of Virginia Slims cigarettes. The cigarette was thinner than most, but beyond that, hardly remarkable. The ad campaign, however, was an eye grabber. Magazines and billboards displayed slender, apparently self-assertive models in the latest fashions clutching the cigarette. The ad copy said, "You've Come a Long Way, Baby." Sometimes featuring an insert photograph of women in turn-of-the-century dress being punished for smoking by police, ministers, or other authority figures, the ad successfully tied cigarette smoking to the burgeoning women's liberation movement. Emphasizing the fact that at one time it was thought unladylike to smoke, the ad implied that to continue smoking Virginia Slims was an act of rebellion against women's traditional roles. Hugely successful as an ad campaign, the caption "You've Come a Long Way, Baby" also embodied for many the triumph of the women's movement and feminism in the 1970s.

New Roles. The women's liberation movement shattered many established traditions of female subordination in American life and opened up a host of heretofore closed occupations to women. Feminism revolutionized women's and men's sense of their gender roles and transformed literary theory, art, and social analysis. Women's liberation was to the 1970s what the civil rights movement was to the early 1960s — the most significant social movement in the United States. Like the civil rights movement, feminism was controversial and never wanted for opponents; like the civil rights movement, the political and social effects of feminism were widespread and deep reaching. Because the women's movement was so powerful, not only did it rectify a host of injustices in American life, but it also raised important questions which remain unresolved. The Virginia Slims ad campaign, for example, demonstrated the difficulty feminism faced transforming deeply held gender assumptions. As perhaps the most visible everyday reminder of the women's movement, some feminists applauded the ad campaign as reinforcing their conviction that a liberated woman need follow no established social rule save that set by her own conscience. Many feminists, however, were troubled that the antiestablishment women's movement could be so easily appropriated for crassly commercial ends. Many more feminists were troubled that the women in the ad copy were uniformly beautiful and young, unlike the majority of women feminists were attempting to liberate. The ad campaign seemed to many to be the sexist expression of an antisexist philosophy.

Such problematic advances, however, were typical of the women's movement in the 1970s. Women had come a long way; they had a long way yet to go.

Equal Pay. By the 1970s women's liberationists were active on a variety of fronts. Reform of divorce and rape laws, improvement of the health-care system, and promotion of day care were important goals. One of feminism's most significant demands was for equal pay for equal work. Increasing numbers of young women, rejecting the role of suburban housewife, were entering the factory and office. Their mothers followed them into the workplace, pressured by the economic downturn of the decade, which forced many families to seek both male and female sources of income. Neither the young activists nor their mothers were paid as well as men, on average earning 57 percent of male wages. Women were further shortchanged by labor laws passed at the turn of the century that prevented women from working overtime; moreover, like African-Americans, women usually were forced to work the lowest-paid, most menial jobs. Women activists sought to change the conditions in the workplace by appealing to the equal-protection clause of the Fourteenth Amendment. A female lawyer for the American Civil Liberties Union (ACLU), Ruth Bader Ginsburg, hoped to repeat the success the civil rights movement had in challenging inequality in the courts. She won two workplace cases before the Supreme Court, *Reed* v. *Reed* (1971), and *Frontiero* v. *Richardson* (1973), both of which confirmed that it was illegal to deny women economic equality with men. The federal government reinforced these claims of job equality. Title VII of the Civil Rights Act of 1964 made job discrimination against women illegal, but the federal agency set up to enforce this law, the Equal Employment Opportunity Commission (EEOC), failed to act on behalf of women for most of the 1960s. In 1970, under a new set of administrators, the EEOC filed suit against American Telephone and Telegraph (AT&T), and won the company's agreement to set up an affirmative-action program. By 1973 the EEOC had filed 147 more suits, and occupational barriers against women began to fall. AT&T hired women to climb up telephone poles and string wire and employed men to sit at desks and operate telephones. The military academies began to admit women, and the Ivy League universities went coed. Even Las Vegas hired female blackjack dealers. By 1974 only Nevada retained laws limiting overtime work for women. Congress passed a host of legislation reinforcing the prohibition on sex discrimination; women even succeeded in gaining a tax deduction for child care in families with both parents working (a similar proposal to establish a national system of day care was vetoed by President Richard Nixon). Much of the progress, however, was more apparent than real. In 1979 women's wages remained an average of 57 percent of men's, and many professional women complained that high-paying, high-prestige jobs were still denied them. To feminists it was clear that the

In 1903, while walking her dog, Collette McNitt stepped into the hedge to smoke a cigarette. Her dog stepped in to prove once again that dog is *man's* best friend.

You've come a long way, baby.

VIRGINIA SLIMS

Slimmer than the fat cigarettes men smoke.

Fashions: Michel Hrniak for R.E.F.

16 mg. "tar," 0.9 mg. nicotine av. per cigarette, FTC Report Dec.'76

Warning: The Surgeon General Has Determined That Cigarette Smoking Is Dangerous to Your Health.

1977 advertisement

laws on the books were not sufficient. Many sought a new law, in the form of an equal rights amendment to the Constitution.

ERA. The Equal Rights Amendment (ERA) had first been proposed to Congress in 1923. Resubmitted in a new form, prohibiting discrimination on account of gender, it overwhelmingly passed Congress in March 1973 and was quickly ratified by thirty states. Thereafter the ratification process stalled, several states short of the required three-fourths majority. Part of the problem with passage was that many laws already passed at the state and federal level prohibited discrimination, and the ERA seemed superfluous. The major objection to the ERA, however, was that the amendment was so vague and open-ended as to lead to sweeping changes in American social life. Middle- and working-class women particularly feared the ERA would lead to a loss of alimony in divorce cases, the drafting of women into the military, and the creation of unisex bathrooms. These fears were seized upon and amplified by a female conservative, Phyllis Schlafly, who organized the National Committee to Stop ERA in 1972. Schlafly, a longtime activist in the right wing of the Republican Party, was fundamentally opposed to the ERA on ideological grounds. A militant anti-Communist and opponent of big government, Schlafly feared the ERA would give the government the power to intervene radically in American family life and restructure established customs and laws regarding marriage, divorce, child custody, and adoption. Schlafly pointed out that because the ERA affected only state and federal governments, it would not change discrimination by private employers. She also suggested to state legislators that the amendment would transfer state power to the federal government. Such arguments were persuasive, but Stop ERA's real power lay in grassroots organization and in enlisting the fears of many Americans that the pace of social change was proceeding too quickly. Schlafly's organization included local groups such as WWWW (Women Who Want to be Women) and HOW (Happiness of Womanhood), who flooded state capitols with telegrams, phone calls, and homemade breads and pies, and who protested at rallies behind placards reading "Preserve us from a congressional jam; Vote against the ERA sham." Such efforts resulted in several states rescinding their approval of the ERA. In 1979 the ratification period expired. Congress passed a three-year extension, but not a single new state approved the amendment. By 1982 the ERA was dead.

Conservatives and Abortion. The ERA defeat was symptomatic of a growing conservatism among Americans, both men and women. Sown by economic frustration and harvested by conservative politicians, animosity toward feminists and their social agenda was a staple of the 1970s. Hostility toward women's reproductive rights was particularly pronounced. In the landmark 1973 *Roe* v. *Wade* case, the Supreme Court decided that women, as part of their constitutional right to privacy, may choose to abort a pregnancy in the first trimester. The decision invalidated many state laws that punished abortion — even as a result of rape, incest, or (rarely) because of the threat to the mother's life — as a criminal offense. Although abortion had been legal in most of the United States until after the Civil War, the *Roe* decision seemed to many to be a radical break with the past and was immediately denounced by religious groups, especially Catholics, Mormons, and Fundamentalist Protestants. Such groups argued that human life begins at conception and that abortion is murder. Many conservative Americans also feared that safe, legal abortions would lead to widespread promiscuity, undermining family cohesion and creating social chaos.

Feminists and Abortion. Feminists, by contrast, celebrated the *Roe* decision. For many feminists abortion rights were axiomatic. As Lucina Cisler put it in her essay in the feminist anthology *Sisterhood is Powerful* (1970), "Without the full capacity to limit her own reproduction, a woman's other 'freedoms' are tantalizing mockeries that cannot be exercised." For feminists such as Cisler, pregnancy was a trap, whereby men kept women in the home, out of the wider world, and away from self-fulfillment. Cisler noted that in 1970, 40 percent of states still had laws preventing the use of contraception, even by married couples — proof that pregnancy was being used to oppress women. Cisler argued that whatever the law,

THE JOBS THAT WOMEN HOLD

	Number of Women Workers—	Proportion of Jobs Held by Women		Number of Women Workers—	Proportion of Jobs Held by Women
Secretaries	2,922,000	99%	Social workers	195,000	55%
Receptionists	423,000	97%	Office managers	132,000	42%
Typists	980,000	96%	Real-estate agents	128,000	37%
Child-care workers	341,000	96%	Cleaning-service workers	680,000	33%
Nurses, dietitians	879,000	96%	Restaurant workers	160,000	32%
Hairdressers, cosmetologists	354,000	91%	Writers, artists, entertainers	284,000	32%
Bank tellers	252,000	88%	College teachers	130,000	28%
Bookkeepers	1,393,000	88%	Accountants	155,000	22%
Cashiers	864,000	87%	Bank, financial officers	81,000	19%
Health-service workers	1,310,000	87%	Sales managers	90,000	16%
File clerks	231,000	85%	Physicians and dentists	58,000	9%
Librarians	125,000	83%	Science technicians	75,000	9%
Counter clerks (nonfood)	243,000	74%	Policemen, firemen	65,000	5–6%
Office-machine operators	480,000	71%	Lawyers	12,000	4%
School-teachers	1,988,000	70%	Engineers	9,000	Less than 1%
Health technicians	220,000	70%	Construction craftsmen	20,000	Less than 1%
Food-service workers	2,277,000	70%			
Retail clerks	1,600,000	69%			

Source: U. S. Dept. of Labor unpublished survey

1974 U.S. Department of Labor chart

women wanted the right to control when, and by whom, they became pregnant. Despite the prohibition on abortion before *Roe*, Cisler estimated that one in every four births in the United States was aborted, and of these abortions 85 percent were performed on married women, who usually already had children and sought to limit the size of their families. Because abortion was illegal before *Roe*, the operation was performed in a variety of ways: wealthy women flew abroad to have safe abortions in foreign hospitals; doctors would sometimes use legal loopholes to perform the operations; illegal clinics operated in major cities, so long as there were bribable police; poorer women patronized "back-alley" abortionists, who often were not doctors, or tried folk remedies on themselves, often inducing severe illness and sometimes death. Cisler estimated that five hundred to one thousand abortion deaths occurred every year; of these, the majority (79 percent of New York City's abortion deaths) were among poor, nonwhite women. For feminists, given the new contraceptive and abortion technologies of the 1960s and 1970s, such deaths were inexcusable. Such deaths reemphasized the narrow scope of female life options in a society that seemed determined to force women to adopt narrowly defined, biologically based gender roles. "Thus the real question," Cisler wrote, "is not, 'How can we justify abortion?' but, 'How can we justify compulsory childbearing?'"

Unresolved Questions. Many feminists supported *Roe* and access to abortion because they felt it was central to a new role for women in American society. Few feminists argued that abortion was a positive good, but they insisted that women had the intellectual capacity — and emotional compassion — to determine for themselves

NOW demonstration at the 1976 Republican convention

whether or not to terminate a pregnancy. They called their position pro-choice, and in *Roe* the Supreme Court substantially agreed with their outlook. The Supreme Court, however, was ahead of many Americans. Although the majority of respondents in public-opinion polls favored a reform of the strictest abortion laws (but not all of them), many Americans uncomfortable with the changing role of women in American society seized upon the abortion issue as a means of expressing their discontent. Often they tied their opposition to abortion to wider protests against the changing character of the times. Pro-life for such people often meant more than the defense of the unborn. It meant an attempt to affirm "natural" limits and boundaries — to the family, the community, and the state. Fundamentalist opponents of abortion routinely condemned not only the abortion procedure, but feminists, liberals, relativism, secular humanism, and any philosophy advanced without reference to absolutes. Conservative politicians and televangelists quickly realized the centrality of the abortion issue in the minds of these Americans and used opposition to abortion to construct a tremendous political coalition, one which would seize Congress in 1978 and the presidency in 1980. Ironically, abortion came to hold as central a place in the social philosophy of conservatives as it did in the political theory of feminists.

Success. Although conservatives mounted the kind of grassroots campaign against abortion they used against the ERA, they had less success. The Hyde Amendment, passed by Congress in 1976, outlawed the use of Medicaid funding to provide abortions; beyond this, however, conservatives proved ineffectual — especially in their general opposition to feminism. In fact, the 1970s were a decade filled with female firsts and women's achievements. In 1972 women increased their representation in state legislatures by an unprecedented 28 percent. Although Shirley Chisholm, an African-American woman, unsuccessfully challenged male candidates for the Democratic nomination for president that year, Americans sent record numbers of women to Congress, including Pat Schroeder, Elizabeth Holtzman, and Barbara Jordan — women who would become political forces in the 1970s. President Nixon appointed the first two women generals in May 1970, and the FBI hired its first female agent in 1972. Women also flooded into the professions. The proportion of women entering law schools increased 500 percent; 40 percent of those entering classes in medical schools were women; and 25 percent of doctorates earned went to women. Women became increasingly visible in the media, especially as journalists. Female publishers such as Katharine Graham of the *Washington Post* and Helen Gurley Brown of *Cosmopolitan* were widely admired. *Ms.*, a new feminist magazine begun in 1972 by the articulate journalist Gloria Steinem, sold 250,000 copies of its first issue in eight days. A television sitcom focusing on the character of an independent, female television news producer, *The Mary Tyler Moore Show*, was one of the highest-rated programs of the decade. Movies with feminist themes, such as *Julia* (1977), *The Turning Point* (1977), *Kramer vs. Kramer* (1979), and *Norma Rae* (1979), were box-office successes. Even female athletes, heretofore eclipsed by their male counterparts, gained the public's attention. Women ran in the Boston Marathon for the first time on 17 April 1972. In a nationally televised challenge, 1939 Wimbledon champion Bobby Riggs boasted he could still beat decades-younger women's tennis star Billie Jean King. On 20 September 1973 King whipped Riggs in straight sets, gaining new admiration and respect for women athletes.

Impact. The real impact of feminism took place at the local level, reshaping the intimate conduct of American life. Like its conservative opposition, women's liberation was also a grassroots movement, and in localities across the nation women established badly needed women's health clinics, rape-crisis centers, and battered-women's shelters. Colleges and universities created women's studies programs. In small communities throughout the United States, women demanded new respect from men, access to better-paying jobs, and an end to sexism in everyday life. More secure with their sexuality and less likely to be pressured into compulsory childbirth, women experimented with premarital and casual sex. Women across the country demanded that men set aside their male chauvinism and belief in male superiority. Women increasingly voiced criticisms of sexism in language and manners. They demanded male help with housework and child care. Feminism also promised to reshape public attitudes toward masculinity as well as to liberate femininity. With the help of celebrity friends, actress Marlo Thomas made a children's record, *Free to Be You and Me*, which inverted traditional gender roles and encouraged female athleticism and male sensitivity. That pro football star Roosevelt Grier could sing to boys, "It's all right to cry / Crying gets the sad out of you," was a sign that gender roles in the United States were changing.

Intellectual Revolution. Women's liberation inspired the emergence of a sophisticated feminist social theory that promised to further the restructuring of gender roles in the United States. Inverting the radical political theory of the 1960s, feminist intellectuals and academics argued that systematic male domination, which they termed patriarchy, was responsible for many social ills. Patriarchy was manifest not only in sexism but in irresponsible individualism, sterile science, dehumanizing technology, and punitive capitalism — all of which were the result of masculine rationality. Feminists sought to make the world a more empathic, intuitive, and compassionate place. Borrowing an axiom from the New Left, feminists maintained that "the personal is political." A revolution in gender roles and personal relationships would accordingly result in a revolution in the productive apparatus of mod-

DAY CARE

Day care became an important social trend in the 1970s as both the number of single parents and working women with young children dramatically increased. The percentage of children in preschool programs rose from 27 percent in 1966 to 55 percent by 1986, or approximately five million American children. Most of these nursery schools, Montessori schools, and day-care centers were private schools or nonprofit community and cooperative agencies, although proprietary and franchise day-care services became popular. Preschool programs operated on the concept of play as a form of education, alternating structured activities directed by a teacher with supervised play. Besides caring for children while parents were working, day care was a bridge between the family and society, preparing children to enter elementary school.

Children from low-income families were eligible for the Head Start program begun in 1965 with 3,300 centers serving more than 550,000 children. It grew throughout the 1970s to a national year-round program for 500,000 youngsters funded by the U.S. Department of Health and Human Services. It provided educational services to the children and parents, as well as medical, nutritional, and social services. The growth of child development as an academic discipline introduced new concepts concerning the maturation, intelligence, and health of children and provided great impetus for the day-care and preschool movement.

Recognizing that as many as 70 percent of the mothers of school-age children work outside the home, the women's movement was vocal in its demands for universal child-care services. By the 1970s most child-welfare specialists and educators joined in lobbying for greater access to these important social services for all children. Congress responded by increased funding for Head Start and other educational programs.

ern society. More radically, some feminists suggested that patriarchy operated best by hiding its domination in the guise of a "natural" world order. They maintained that traditionally accepted social arrangements — the family, childrearing by women, heterosexuality — were masks for male domination. Such feminists argued that gender was constructed by a set of social and historical relations that privileged men. By the end of the decade, feminist artists such as Judy Chicago, Cindy Sherman, and Jenny

Holzer were giving expression to such intellectual formulation in sculpture, photography, and verse and challenging established conventions in art and society.

Divisions. The rigor and insight of feminist social theory made it the most effective vehicle for maintaining 1960s radicalism in the 1970s. The incompatibility of such theoretical formulations with the established order of society led to divisions and political fragmentation among feminists. Younger, more militant feminists such as Robin Morgan sought a full-scale overthrow of society; older feminists, such as Betty Friedan, were more interested in achievable social reform. Other feminists were divided over the radical argument that any relationship with men is by definition oppressive. Lesbian feminists suggested that heterosexual feminists were not true feminists. "It is the primacy of women's relations to women," wrote one lesbian feminist, "which is at the heart of women's liberation and the basis of cultural revolution." Radical lesbians such as Andrea Dworkin argued that, given contemporary social and sexual values, heterosexual intercourse was rape and campaigned against pornography, erotica, and offensive speech which they felt were part of a culture of violence against women. Such arguments, especially as they became more fixed in the 1980s, mirrored those of male critics of the women's liberation movement who believed that biology is destiny.

Feminism and the Working Class. Conservatives sometimes used such lesbian arguments to discredit feminism among more moderate women and men, but the women's liberation movement as a whole divided naturally — and sharply — over the issue of class. Many older American women hardly felt oppressed by their marriages. For them domesticity was a positive good, and they feared that feminism would corrode the bond of family. Furthermore, many feminist leaders came from privileged backgrounds and limited their critique of society to its limits on opportunities for women of their class. For working-class Americans feminism did not promise access to the boardroom, the university chair, or the legislature, but to dreary factory or clerical work at low wages. Against such a prospect domestic life seemed indeed blissful. Schlafly, sensitive to such fears, was often able to mobilize female support more effectively than left-leaning feminists. Her success forced many feminists to reexamine the implicit elitism of their approach. By the end of the decade, moreover, the concrete results of women's liberation forced many feminists to reconsider their movement soberly.

The Feminization of Poverty. The class divisions among feminists were most obvious when considering two issues — child care and divorce. Upper-class feminists discussed child care but rarely marshaled their forces to push for increased day care facilities nationally. Wealthy Americans had the economic resources to provide for child supervision in a two-income family, and feminists pursuing professional careers often were uncon-

NINE TO FIVE

Nine to Five was a new union formed by Karen Nussbaum in Boston in 1973. She saw her fellow office workers and secretaries were overworked, were underpaid, and seldom had the respect male employees enjoyed. Her first victory was to organize the librarians at Brandeis University, the first time professional librarians in the United States joined a labor union.

By 1975 Nine to Five affiliated with the Service Employees International Union (SEIU) as Local 925 and spread rapidly to other cities. The introduction of computers in the workplace changed the role of many office workers, presenting new health and safety concerns. Nine to Five was quick to recognize these work issues and offered white-collar office staffers militant union representation. Although union membership had dropped to twenty million by 1970, 54 percent of American women now worked outside the home, and these thirty-two million women in the labor force attracted the interest of new labor leaders. In 1970 the National Organization of Women (NOW) pointed out that women earned only 63 percent of men's incomes. This, and other issues identified by the women's movement, did much to raise the consciousness of female workers and drove many to join unions. The plight of female office workers was the basis for the popular movie comedy *9 to 5* (1980), starring Jane Fonda, Dolly Parton, and Lily Tomlin. A television sitcom was later based on the story of three savvy secretaries who inadvertently find an opportunity to take revenge on their sexist, domineering boss. But the problems working women encountered remained troubling to business, social, and government leaders.

Source: Ellen Cassedy and Karen Nussbaum, *9 to 5: The Working Woman's Guide to Office Survival* (New York: Penguin, 1983).

cerned with child-care issues. After President Nixon vetoed day-care legislation in 1972, women's liberation at the national level abandoned the issue, although ad hoc efforts at the local level continued to be pursued. The need for quality day care, medical assistance, and maternity leave became acute as working-class male income declined and women were forced to take jobs (usually low-skill, low-paying) outside the home. By 1976 one-half of all American mothers were employed. Without a systematic nationwide system of maternity leave and child care, women often found themselves simultaneously struggling to raise children, maintain a household, and hold a job. Similarly, divorce reform that benefited wealthy women proved disastrous to the poor. In the

Smoking was a social habit that declined drastically in the 1970s. In 1976 the U.S. Public Health Service reported that 52 percent of American men and 31 percent of women had smoked cigarettes in 1964, but only 39 percent of the men and 29 percent of the women did so in 1975. Public attitudes toward all tobacco products had turned increasingly negative. More nonsmokers complained it was annoying or unhealthy to be near cigarette smokers, and by 1973 thirty states responded with laws banning smoking in certain public places. Businesses also prohibited or limited smoking to reduce housekeeping costs, improve productivity, and promote employee health.

Since 1954 public-health experts had warned Americans of the dangers of smoking — to smokers as well as to those around them — and despite counterclaims by the tobacco industry, most Americans gradually agreed that it was a problem. In 1971 Congress banned cigarette commercials on radio and television, and many magazines and newspapers eliminated cigarette ads. In 1972 tobacco companies agreed to include health warnings in cigarette ads and introduced "safer" cigarettes lower in tar and nicotine. Commercial clinics, such as Smokenders and Smoke Watchers, offered programs to help nicotine addicts quit.

The antismoking trend continued to gain support in 1979 when U.S. Surgeon General Julius B. Richmond released a report (on the fifteenth anniversary of the 1964 surgeon general's report on smoking) expanding earlier warnings about the health risks of smoking. Antismoking lobbies also had much success in local and state campaigns to ban smoking in restaurants, bars, hotels, and public transportation. Nevertheless, cigarette sales increased each year since 1971, reaching a peak in 1976. For many Americans, smoking remained a sophisticated social habit.

early 1970s feminists sought liberalized divorce legislation — including the quick, no-fault divorce — in order to increase the life options available to unhappy women. Successful in passing such legislation, feminists watched in amazement as men took advantage of the laws, gaining quick divorces and freeing themselves from alimony payments to former wives, leaving often unprepared women to forage for jobs in an increasingly competitive marketplace. Divorce rates climbed 82 percent during the decade. Usually saddled with the task of supporting children and able to work only in low-paying jobs, divorced women swelled the ranks of the poor. By the 1980s, 60 percent of poor families were headed by women, and the compound pressures of raising a family, low wages, and cutbacks in social services made their situation even more dismal. By the end of the decade Betty Friedan conceded that NOW's support of liberalized divorce legislation — without provisions for job training and child support — had been a "trap." Such realizations forced feminists to reconsider women's liberation as a movement directed towards limited goals for a limited elite of Americans. Some feminists returned to the broader social agenda of the late 1960s, which supplied the initial impetus for women's liberation. Historian Barbara Eherenreich called for a return to basics: ". . . that nothing short of equality will do *and* that in a society marred by injustice and cruelty, equality will never be good enough . . . is still the best idea . . . that women have ever had."

Sources:

Peter Carroll, *It Seemed Like Nothing Happened: The Tragedy and Promise of America in the 1970s* (New York: Holt, Rinehart & Winston, 1982);

Barbara Ehrenreich, *The Worst Years of Our Lives: Irreverent Notes from a Decade of Greed* (New York: Random House, 1990);

Robin Morgan, ed., *Sisterhood is Powerful: An Anthology of Writings from the Women's Liberation Movement* (New York: Vintage, 1990);

John T. Noonan, *A Private Choice: Abortion in the Seventies* (New York: Free Press, 1972);

Rosalind Rosenberg, *Divided Lives: American Women in the Twentieth Century* (New York: Hill & Wang, 1992).

HEADLINE MAKERS

BELLA ABZUG

1920-

CONGRESSWOMAN

Flamboyant Advocate. Bella Abzug made news in the 1970s as a vocal and flamboyant advocate for equal rights for women. Born in New York City in 1920, Bella Savitsky Abzug was the daughter of Russian-Jewish immigrants. She attended Bronx public schools, and, after graduating from Hunter College and Columbia University Law School, she was admitted to the New York bar in 1947. In the 1950s and 1960s she was a leader in the anti-McCarthy and civil rights movement and served as a labor and American Civil Liberties Union lawyer.

Elevation to Congress. By the mid 1960s she lobbied for nuclear disarmament and was a vigorous critic of the Vietnam War policies of Presidents Lyndon Johnson and Richard Nixon. Her leadership roles in the women's liberation movement and in the new Democratic coalition led to her serving in Congress from 1971–1976.

First Jewish Congresswomen. Defeating a seven-term regular Democrat in 1970 in her first political campaign, Bella Abzug was one of only twelve women in the House and the first Jewish woman to be elected to Congress. In the House Abzug was well-known for her large hats, colorful personality, and fierce determination to act and talk as forcefully as her male colleagues. She attracted much media attention, as well as much criticism from congressional conservatives unaccustomed to liberated women in the House.

Challenging Seniority. Disregarding the quiet role adopted by most freshman members of Congress, Abzug challenged the House seniority system and assumed a leadership role in the antiwar and women's rights movements. Her campaign against the selective service system and demands for national day-care centers and the Equal Rights Amendment won her national support. Losing a campaign for the United States Senate in 1976 and another campaign for the House in 1978, Abzug became cochair of the President's National Advisory Committee on Women (1977–1979). Abzug pressured the government to fund the 1978 Houston Women's Conference, a nationwide convention organized to explore the problems of working women and working mothers. When, following the conference, Abzug's committee issued a report critical of the Carter administration's fiscal priorities, which they felt hurt working women, and demanded a firm administration commitment to the ERA, Abzug was fired. Carter staffers attempted to make political hay of the event by portraying Abzug as an extremist and reaffirming Carter's centrism. The tactic failed, and many women dropped their support for Carter in the 1980 election. Abzug wryly noted the error. Carter's staff, she said, "had as much information on the women's movement as they had on Iran."

Sources:
Bella Abzug and Mel Ziegler, *Bella: Ms. Abzug Goes to Washington* (New York: Saturday Review Press, 1972);

Abzug and Mim Kleber, *Gender Gap: Bella Abzug's Guide to Political Power for American Women* (Boston: Houghton Mifflin, 1984);

Zillah R. Eisenstein, *The Radical Future of Liberal Feminism* (New York: Longman, 1981).

CESAR CHAVEZ

1927-1993

LABOR ORGANIZER

United Farm Workers. Cesar Chavez was the most effective labor leader of the 1970s, rising from poverty as a Hispanic migrant worker in Arizona to international celebrity as the leader of the United Farm Workers Union. In 1962 Chavez left his job as director of the Community Service Organization in California to establish the National Farm Workers Association. His success with Hispanic and Filipino farm pickers led to the formation of the United Farm Workers (UFW) in 1966.

Democratic Support. Supported by Sen. Robert F. Kennedy, United Auto Workers president Walter Reuther, and other prominent liberals, Chavez adroitly used church meetings, sit-ins, picket lines, consumer boycotts, and media propaganda to win a bitter strike against twenty-six California table-grape growers. The growers signed a contract with the UFW in July 1970, and in 1972 he negotiated a contract with the agribusiness giant Minute Maid in Florida.

Nonviolence. Chavez promoted social change by nonviolent tactics at a time when protest violence was becoming endemic, thereby earning public admiration. He also organized workers and supporters across ethnic, class, gender, and racial lines while the country became more segregated and stratified. In 1970 his chief assistant, Dolores Huerta, was elected vice-president of the UFW, demonstrating that the UFW could also overcome sexist barriers under the charismatic leadership of Chavez.

A Moral Example. His self-imposed poverty (he was paid only five dollars a day like all UFW organizers), humility, courage, and insight inspired respect and admiration. His popularity and prestige transcended the southwestern Chicano community, and more than 14.5 million Hispanic-Americans in 1979 looked to Chavez for leadership and moral example.

Sources:
Peter Matthiessen, *Sal Si Puedes: Cesar Chavez and the New American Revolution* (New York: Random House, 1969);

Ronald B. Taylor, *Chavez and the Farm Workers* (Boston: Beacon, 1975).

JULIA CHILD

1912-

COOK

A Cultural Icon. Julia Child taught millions of Americans to enjoy French cuisine with her popular cookbook, *Mastering the Art of French Cooking* (1961), and a second volume published in 1970. Her Public Broadcasting System (PBS) program, *The French Chef,* began in 1963 on Boston's WGBH station and was quickly syndicated and endlessly rebroadcast. By the mid 1970s Julia Child was a popular-culture icon, an imposing (over six feet tall) WASP Francophile matron bustling expertly around a studio kitchen. Her next book, *From Julia Child's Kitchen* (1975), reflected her celebrity status and witty persona.

She won an Emmy in 1966 and many honors from culinary organizations at home and abroad.

Secret Agent Cook. Julia Child was, however, a cook with a difference. Born in Pasadena and educated at Smith College, she was an Office of Strategic Services (OSS) agent, with assignments that took her all over the world. In Paris she was one of the first American women to attend the Cordon Bleu culinary school. Not content with a domestic life when she settled in Cambridge, Massachusetts, in the 1950s, Child brought her gastronomic skills from the home to television. At a time when increasing numbers of educated, affluent feminists rejected the traditional domestic role, Julia Child made fine cooking chic. With peerless showmanship and affable sophistication, she proved the modern woman (and man) could be professional at work and at home.

Sources:
Simone Beck, Louisette Bertholle, and Julia Child, *Mastering the Art of French Cooking* (New York: Knopf, 1961);

Julia Child, *From Julia Child's Kitchen* (New York: Knopf, 1975).

ARTHUR FIEDLER

1894-1979

CONDUCTOR

Classical Popularizer. Arthur Fiedler was responsible to an extraordinary degree for the popularity of classical music by the 1970s. Born in Boston on 17 December 1894, he studied music with his father and at the Royal Academy of Music in Berlin. He was a pianist, second violinist, and violist with the Boston Symphony Orchestra from 1915 to 1930. In 1924 he formed the Boston Sinfonietta, a chamber orchestra drawn from the Boston Symphony Orchestra staff. In 1929 he demonstrated his genius for broadening the classical-music audience by founding the Esplanade Concerts, a free summer concert series on the banks of the Charles River.

New Audiences. By 1930 Fiedler was the conductor of the renamed Boston Pops Orchestra, staffed by Boston Symphony musicians, which attracted thousands of new listeners. Lovers of classical music resisted this popularization at first, but the charming (and sometimes crusty) Fiedler won over his critics. He had proved that new concert audiences for classical music could be won by public outreach.

Unparalleled Showmanship. For fifty years the white-maned, mustachioed Boston Pops maestro led the world's most successful concert and recording orchestra. His unparalleled showmanship and knack for public tastes brought Broadway, Hollywood, radio, and television stars to the Pops stage. Like sports, classical music had changed by the 1970s to entertain a mass audience.

Fiedler presented most major recording stars, mixing classical selections with show tunes and film scores. When he died in Brookline, Massachusetts, on 10 July 1979, the American public acceptance of classical music was no longer a fad but an established fact.

Sources:
Johanna Fiedler, *Arthur Fiedler: Papa, the Pops and Me* (Garden City: Doubleday, 1994);

James R. Holland, *Mr. Pops* (Barre, Mass.: Barre Publishers, 1972).

PATRICIA HEARST

1953-

HEIRESS, KIDNAPING VICTIM

Kidnapped. Patricia Hearst became an American celebrity, victim, and criminal in February 1974 when she was kidnapped by a leftist terrorist group, the Symbionese Liberation Army (SLA). This obscure Oakland, California, revolutionary group held her for a $2-million ransom. Patricia was the granddaughter of William Randolph Hearst, the wealthy California newspaper publisher, but during months of harsh captivity she was allegedly brainwashed and renamed "Tania." To obtain her release, her parents donated millions of dollars worth of food to the poor, but the giveaway became a fiasco and did not result in her release.

Urban Guerrilla. When Hearst was filmed in April 1974 assisting the SLA in a San Francisco bank robbery, the kidnapping victim was transformed in the public mind into another spoiled, rich college student whose unconventional lifestyle led to crime as a self-confessed "urban guerrilla" and "radical feminist." Patty was captured a year later during a police shoot-out. She was convicted of bank robbery in a sensational California trial in January 1976. On 24 September she was sent to prison for seven years, but President Carter commuted her sentence on 29 January 1979.

Public Skepticism. This was a major news story, but with a bizarre twist. The victim received little sympathy because the public was disgusted with assassins, radicals, and revolutionaries. The naive college student who became a gun-toting bank robber found little understanding or forgiveness. The story did not end when she was released from prison. Public fascination with the abduction of the newspaper heiress was stimulated by a 1975 biography, her own memoirs published in 1982, and a movie, *Patty Hearst,* in 1988.

Sources:
Patricia Campbell Hearst and Alvin Moscow, *Every Secret Thing* (Garden City, N.Y.: Doubleday, 1982);

Don West, *Patty/Tania* (New York: Pyramid, 1975).

ABBIE HOFFMAN

1936-1989

SOCIAL ACTIVIST

Revolutionary Hedonism. Abbie Hoffman was a countercultural leader whose commitment to radical politics spanned the civil rights, antiwar, and environmentalist movements. When the Student Nonviolent Coordinating Committee expelled all whites in 1964, Hoffman moved into the hippie movement, seeing the counterculture as an arena for political change. He pioneered the idea that experimental use of sex, drugs, clothing, and communal living were revolutionary activities.

Street Theater. Hoffman, who was born in a middle-class Jewish family in Worcester, Massachusetts, and graduated from Brandeis University, was influenced by both Marshall McLuhan and Herbert Marcuse. His political career demonstrated his dramatic flair in using the media to promote himself as well as his unconventional Marxism. The generation gap, not class conflict, sparked his social and political revolution. With fellow hippie-radical spokesman Jerry Rubin he created the Yippies — the Youth International Party, which pioneered the use of street theater as a means of political protest. They made the 1968 Democratic National Convention a showcase for antiwar politics, parading a pig, "Pigasus," through the streets as a potential presidential nominee and calling for the legalization of drugs, free sex, and the abolition of work.

Outlaw. After a sensational trial for conspiracy to incite a riot during the Democratic convention in Chicago, Hoffman was acquitted in 1973. He was disillusioned by the dissipation of the intellectual fervor and political intensity of the 1960s but refused to market his celebrity. In New York City he was arrested for selling cocaine, went underground for eight years, and taunted the FBI like an outlaw hero. The movement's underground permitted him to create a new identity as a community organizer, Barry Freed, in upstate New York. In 1980 he negotiated a settlement of his legal problems with the police and joined the talk-show circuit after a brief prison term.

Suicide. But the 1980s were not fertile ground for a 1960s hippie media star, and after a lackluster campaign against the conservative policies of President Ronald Reagan, Hoffman suffered manic-depressive episodes and committed suicide in 1989 in a New Jersey motel.

Sources:
Abbie Hoffman and Daniel Simon, eds., *The Best of Abbie Hoffman* (New York: Four Walls Eight Windows, 1989);

Jack Hoffman and Simon, *Run, Run, Run: The Lives of Abbie Hoffman* (New York: Putnam, 1994).

PHYLLIS SCHLAFLY

1924-

ANTIFEMINIST

Backlash. Phyllis Schlafly represented the conservative and traditional American women in the 1970s who feared and rejected the liberal women's liberation movement. Dubbed the "Gloria Steinem of the Right," this Illinois activist organized the Stop ERA lobby in 1972. She argued that social changes were a threat to the family and traditional sex roles.

Congressional Candidate. Born in Saint Louis in 1924, Schlafly was educated at Washington University and Radcliffe College, worked briefly as a congressional aide, and married a wealthy Illinois lawyer in 1949. Although a self-described housewife and mother of six, she ran for Congress three times, wrote and published several books on conservative issues, worked as a radio commentator, and was editor of the *Phyllis Schlafly Newsletter*. As a campaigner for Joseph McCarthy and Barry Goldwater, she adopted an early and consistent anti-Communist position, and she even criticized President Nixon and Secretary of State Henry Kissinger for their conciliatory détente policy with the Soviet Union.

Stop ERA. Strongly influenced by her Catholic family and conservative husband, Schlafly was an effective conservative Republican spokesperson in the 1970s. By organizing and operating the Stop ERA lobby as well as the Eagle Forum, she aroused enough opposition to prevent ratification of the Equal Rights Amendment to the Constitution. When Congress approved the amendment in 1972, it seemed to be very popular. But Schlafly's campaign, more than anything else, convinced voters and legislators it was a threat to American values. After the defeat of the ERA, Schlafly's Eagle Forum waged a national campaign against the women's liberation movement, whose leaders she called "femlib fanatics."

Sources:
Carol Felsenthal, *The Sweetheart of the Silent Majority: The Biography of Phyllis Schlafly* (Garden City, N.Y.: Doubleday, 1981);

Phyllis Schlafly, *The Power of the Positive Woman* (New York: Harcourt Brace Jovanovich, 1977).

BENJAMIN SPOCK

1903-

PEDIATRICIAN, AUTHOR

Baby Boom Influence. Benjamin Spock exerted enormous influence on the baby-boom generation (people born in 1946–1965) who came of age in the 1970s. Dr. Spock was a pediatrician, author, and social reformer who published *The Common Sense Book of Baby and Child Care* (1946), an immediate best-seller and quickly one of the most influential books in postwar America. Retitled and republished as *Baby and Child Care* (1968, 1976, and 1985), it was an ideal guide for a country preoccupied with children and just the kind of gentle, warm, and thoughtful expert advice young parents needed in the baby-boom years. In contrast to prevailing child-rearing customs and advice, Spock emphasized affectionate and loving parenting, which was dubbed by his critics as permissiveness.

Against Vietnam. Reassuring parents that "You know more than you think you know," Dr. Spock became a household name as maternity hospitals and diaper services gave copies of the paperback to new parents. His articles and columns in the *Ladies' Home Journal* and *Redbook* magazines continued to popularize his sensitive, sensible notions of childhood and family life. In 1963 he was a public critic of the war in Vietnam, and in 1967 he retired as a professor of child development to work with the National Committee for a Sane Nuclear Policy. In 1968 Spock was convicted of conspiracy to violate the selective service laws. The conviction was reversed by the U.S. Court of Appeals, making Dr. Spock an elderly hero to the young and anathema to their conservative parents.

Critics of Permissiveness. A wide range of social problems in the 1970s — drug abuse, sexual promiscuity, juvenile delinquency, and even the hippie movement — were attributed by such conservatives to Dr. Spock's permissiveness. Parents who took Spock's advice to raise children gently and indulgently were blamed for social and moral decay. He responded to his critics by frequent television and newspaper interviews, and in 1976 he revised his best-seller to eliminate outdated sexism and to include fathers, baby-sitters and day-care services. Dr. Spock remains an influential spokesman for modern child rearing today.

Source:
Benjamin Spock and Mary Morgan, *Spock on Spock: A Memoir of Growing Up with the Century* (New York: Pantheon, 1989).

PEOPLE IN THE NEWS

On 19 July 1977 **Anita Bryant** was retained as a spokesperson for the Florida Citrus Commission despite her outspoken antigay opinions and activities.

On 22 February 1970 **Ellsworth Bunker, Henry Cabot Lodge, Red Skelton, Anita Bryant,** and **Kate Smith** were awarded the Freedom Foundation Award for "furthering American values."

On 4 June 1972 former University of California at San Diego philosophy professor **Angela Davis** was acquitted of charges that she helped to murder Judge Harold Haley in a August 1970 kidnapping attempt. The kidnapping of Judge Haley was executed in order to publicize the cause of the "Soledad Brothers," three Soledad prison inmates charged in the murder of another inmate.

Lee Elder became the first black golfer to qualify for the Masters golf tournament by winning the Monsanto Open on 21 April 1974.

First Lady **Betty Ford** underwent a radical mastectomy to combat breast cancer on 28 September 1974. On 5 March 1978 she was released from Long Beach (California) Naval Hospital for treatment of addiction to alcohol and painkillers.

On 6 June 1973 **George F. Getty II,** the oldest son of billionaire **J. Paul Getty,** died of an overdose of barbituates and alcohol.

Antiwar activists **Tom Hayden** and **Jane Fonda** were married on 20 January 1973.

On 3 November 1970 former American Football League quarterback **Jack Kemp** won a New York congressional seat.

On 30 March 1974 **Henry Kissinger** married **Nancy Maginnes.**

On 10 January 1970 book dealer **Hans Kraus** donated an original Amerigo Vespucci letter dated 1504 to the Library of Congress.

On 21 May 1970 **Robin Lee** made landfall at Long Beach, California, to become the youngest person to sail solo around the world.

Sportswriter **Melissa Ludtke** won a court case on 25 September 1978 with a ruling that she could not be denied access by the management of the New York Yankees to the baseball team's locker room after a game solely because of her sex.

Sex researchers **William Masters** and **Virginia Johnson** were married on 7 January 1971.

In a speech on 13 August 1972 to the American Bar Association, Supreme Court associate justice **Lewis Powell** said that new social mores were destroying religion and the free-enterprise system.

Singer **Elvis Presley** died on 16 August 1977 and became an even more important pop culture icon. Two days later, two female mourners were killed when a drunk driver plowed into a crowd outside Presley's Graceland mansion in Memphis Tennessee.

Sally Priesand was ordained as the first female rabbi in the United States on 3 June 1972.

On 13 October 1970 **Charles Reich**'s *The Greening of America* was published. The book is an indictment of technology and endorsement of the 1960s youth culture.

On 15 January 1970 **Diana Ross** made her last appearance with the **Supremes.**

On 29 July 1970 **Alvin Toffler**'s *Future Shock* was published. The book calls for drastic and radical changes in educational and social policies to meet the challenge of the future.

Deaths

Saul Alinsky, 63, social organizer, 12 June 1972.

Charles Atlas, 79, bodybuilder, 24 December 1972.

Dr. Eric Berne, 60, psychiatrist and author of *Games People Play* (1964), 15 July 1970.

Margaret Bourke-White, 67, photojournalist with *Life* magazine, 27 August 1971.

Al Capp, 70, cartoonist, creator of "Lil' Abner," 5 November 1979.

Roberto Clemente, 38, baseball player and philanthropist, 31 December 1972.

Marie Dionne, 35, one of the Dionne quintuplets, 28 May 1970.

Virginia O'Hanlon Douglas, 80, famous for having written the letter to the *New York Sun* that brought the famous editorial reply, "Yes, Virginia, there is a Santa Claus," 13 May 1971.

Mamie Doud Eisenhower, 82, wife of President Dwight D. Eisenhower, 14 November 1979.

Duke Ellington, 75, composer and bandleader, 24 May 1974.

Walker Evans, 71, photographer whose most famous work was *Let Us Now Praise Famous Men* (1941), a collaboration with James Agee, 10 April 1975.

Arthur Fiedler, 84, conductor of the Boston Pops Orchestra, 10 July 1979.

Erle Stanley Gardner, 80, lawyer and author of the Perry Mason mystery series, 11 March 1970.

Euell Gibbons, 64, naturalist, 29 December 1975.

Dr. Haim Ginott, 51, child pyschologist who wrote the best-seller *Between Parent and Child*, 4 November 1973.

Samuel Goldwyn, 91, movie producer and phenomenologist, 31 January 1974.

Paul Goodman, 60, social critic and author of *Growing Up Absurd* (1960), 2 August 1972.

Dr. Alan F. Guttmaker, 75, pioneer in the birth-control movement, 18 March 1974.

Betty Grable, 56, film star and pin-up girl, 2 July 1973.

Harry F. Guggenheim, 80, publisher, philanthropist, and horseman, 22 January 1971.

Jimi Hendrix, 27, rock muscician, 18 September 1970.

Dr. Edith B. Jackson, 82, originator of rooming-in care for newborn infants and their mothers and a leader in child-care and preventive psychiatry, 5 June 1977.

Jim Jones, 47, leader of the Peoples Temple cult that committed mass suicide in Guyana, 18 November 1978.

Janis Joplin, 27, rock musician, 4 October 1970.

Arthur Kallet, 69, publisher of *Consumer Reports*, 24 February 1972.

Emmett Kelly, 80, circus clown, 28 March 1979.

Walt Kelly, 59, cartoonist, creator of "Pogo," 18 October 1973.

Joseph Wood Krutch, 76, naturalist and conservationist, 22 May 1970.

Bruce Lee, 33, actor and martial artist, 20 July 1973.

Charles Lindbergh, 72, aviator, 26 August 1974.

Charles Lochridge, 65, bridge champion, 11 November 1970.

Alma Lutz, 83, lifelong activist for women's rights, including suffrage and the Equal Rights Amendment, 31 August 1973.

Groucho Marx, 86, actor and comedian, 17 July 1977.

Margaret Mead, 76, anthropologist, author of *Coming of Age in Samoa* (1928), 15 November 1978.

Emma Guffey Miller, 95, activist in the movement for suffrage for women and in the struggle for the Equal Rights Amendment from the 1930s through the 1960s, 24 February 1970.

Martha Mitchell, 56, wife of U.S. attorney general John Mitchell, 31 May 1976.

Jim Morrison, 27, rock musician, 3 July 1971.

Elijah Muhammad, 72, leader of the Nation of Islam, 25 February 1975.

John Mulholland, 71, magician, 25 February 1970.

Gardner Murphy, 83, psychologist, pioneer scientist in the field of parapsychology, and director of research at the Menninger Foundation (1952–1968), 19 March 1979;

Ozzie Nelson, 68, television actor, star of *The Adventures of Ozzie and Harriet,* 3 June 1975.

Louella Parsons, 91, movie columnist, 9 December 1972.

Alice Paul, 93, activist for woman suffrage and for the Equal Rights Amendment, 9 July 1977.

Dr. Marion Hill Preminger, 58, film actress who became a disciple of Dr. Albert Schweitzer, served in the Congo (1950–1965), and lectured to raise funds for hospitals and other philanthropies, 15 April 1972.

Elvis Presley, 42, singer, 16 August 1977.

Eddie Rickenbacker, 82, race-car driver, World War I flying ace, and airline executive, 23 July 1973.

Jackie Robinson, 53, first black baseball player in the Major Leagues, 24 October 1972.

Norman Rockwell, 84, artist and illustrator known for his covers drawn for the *Saturday Evening Post,* 9 November 1978.

Rose Schneiderman, 90, activist for woman suffrage and in the Women's Trade Union League, 12 August 1972.

John Thomas Scopes, 70, defendent in the 1925 Scopes "monkey trial," 21 October 1971.

Dr. Samuel H. Sheppard, 46, osteopath who was freed in the second trial for his wife's murder; the case was the inspiration for the television show *The Fugitive,* 6 April 1970.

G. L. K. Smith, 78, rabble-rouser, 15 April 1976.

Ed Sullivan, 73, television impresario and newspaper columnist, 13 October 1974.

Jacqueline Sussann, 53, author of *Valley of the Dolls,* 21 September 1974.

Harold Stirling Vanderbilt, 75, financier and yachtsman, 4 July 1970.

Alan Watts, 58, booster of Zen Buddhism, 16 November 1973.

John Wayne, 72, actor, 11 June 1979.

Walter Winchell, 74, newspaper columnist, 20 February 1972.

Chic Young, 72, cartoonist, creator of "Blondie," 14 March 1973.

M. Whitney Young, Jr., 49, civil rights activist, 11 March 1971.

PUBLICATIONS

Simone de Beauvoir, *The Second Sex: The Classic Manifesto of the Liberated Woman* (New York: Vintage, 1974);

Susan Brownmiller, *Against Our Will: Men, Women and Rape* (New York: Simon & Schuster, 1975);

Julia Child, *From Julia Child's Kitchen* (New York: Knopf, 1975);

Alex Comfort, ed., *The Joy of Sex: A Gourmet Guide to Lovemaking* (New York: Crown, 1972);

Barry Commoner, *The Closing Circle: Nature, Man and Technology* (New York: Knopf, 1971);

Andrea Dworkin, *Our Blood: Prophecies and Discourses on Sexual Politics* (New York: Putnam, 1976);

Christopher Edwards, *Crazy for God* (Englewood Cliffs, N.J.: Prentice-Hall, 1979);

Barbara Ehrenreich and Deidre English, *For Her Own Good: 150 Years of the Experts' Advice to Women* (Garden City, N.Y.: Doubleday, 1978);

Zillah R. Eisenstein, *Capitalist Patriarchy and the Case for Socialist Feminism* (New York: Monthly Review, 1979);

Gloria Emerson, *Winners and Losers: Battles, Retreats,*

Gains, Loses, and Ruins from a Long War (New York: Random House, 1976);

Sara Evans, *Personal Politics: The Roots of Women's Liberation in the Civil Rights Movement and the New Left* (New York: Vintage, 1979);

Vivian Gornick and Barbara K. Moran, *Women in Sexist Society: Studies in Power and Powerlessness* (New York: Basic Books, 1971);

Jeffrey Greenfield, *No Peace, No Place: Excavations Along the Generational Fault Line* (Garden City, N.Y.: Doubleday, 1973);

Germaine Greer, *The Female Eunuch* (New York: Bantam, 1972);

David Halberstam, *The Powers That Be* (New York: Dell, 1979);

Alex Haley, *Roots* (Garden City, N.Y.: Doubleday, 1976);

Michael Herr, *Dispatches* (New York: Knopf, 1977);

James R. Holland, *Mr. Pops* (Barre, Mass.: Barre Publishers, 1972);

George Jackson, *Soledad Brother: The Prison Letters of George Jackson* (New York: Coward-McCann, 1970);

Erica Jong, *Fear of Flying* (New York: Holt, Rinehart & Winston, 1974);

Michael Korda, *Male Chauvinism: How It Works* (New York: Random House, 1973);

Christopher Lasch, *The Culture of Narcissism: American Life in an Age of Diminishing Expectations* (New York: Norton, 1979);

Pat Loud and Nora Johnson, *Pat Loud: A Woman's Story* (New York: Bantam, 1974);

Norman Mailer, *The Prisoner of Sex* (Boston: Little, Brown, 1971);

William H. Masters and Virginia E. Johnson, *Human Sexual Inadequacy* (Boston: Little, Brown, 1970);

Kate Millet, *Flying* (New York: Knopf, 1974);

Marabel Morgan, *The Total Woman* (New York: Pocket Books, 1975);

Robin Morgan, ed., *Sisterhood is Powerful: An Anthology of Writings from the Women's Liberation Movement* (New York: Vintage, 1970);

Raymond Mungo, *Total Loss Farm: A Year in the Life* (New York: Dutton, 1970);

John T. Noonan, *A Private Choice: Abortion in the Seventies* (New York: Free Press, 1972);

Michael Novak, *The Rise of Unmeltable Ethnics: Politics and Culture in the Seventies* (New York: Macmillan, 1972);

Our Bodies, Ourselves: A Book by and for Women (Boston: Boston Women's Health Book Collective, 1971);

Orlando Patterson, *Ethnic Chauvinism* (New York: Stein & Day, 1977);

Charles A. Reich, *The Greening of America* (New York: Bantam, 1971);

Michael Rossman, *New Age Blues* (New York: Dutton, 1979);

Jerry Rubin, *We Are Everywhere* (New York: Harper & Row, 1971);

Phyllis Schlafly, *The Power of the Positive Woman* (New York: Harcourt Brace Jovanovich, 1977);

Philip Slater, *The Pursuit of Loneliness* (Boston: Beacon, 1970);

Valerie Solanas, *S.C.U.M. (Society for Cutting Up Men) Manifesto* (New York: Olympia, 1971);

Rex Weiner and Deanne Stillman, *Woodstock Census: The Nationwide Survey of the Sixties Generation* (New York: Viking, 1979);

Don West, *Patty/Tania* (New York: Pyramid, 1975).

MEDIA

by DARREN HARRIS-FAIN

CONTENTS

Sidebars and tables are listed in italics.

1970

- President Richard M. Nixon signs the Failing Newspaper Act (later renamed the Newspaper Preservation Act) into law. The act, overturning a U.S. Supreme Court decision from the previous year, allows local newspapers to share production facilities provided that one of the papers is in financial trouble and that the agreement does not deter competition.

- The Harris Corporation of Cleveland introduces the first computer editing terminal for newspapers; its first customers include the Gannett group.

- The Postal Reorganization Act raises second-class rates and eliminates a relaxed scale for periodicals, resulting in the failure or size reduction of several magazines.

- *Negro Digest* is renamed *Black World.*

- An article in *Playboy* calls underground comics "obscene, anarchistic, sophomoric, subversive and apocalyptic."

- *National Lampoon* first appears.

- *Smithsonian* magazine is founded; within the decade its circulation expands from around 160,000 to nearly 2,000,000.

1 Jan.	Robert Sarnoff is named RCA's chairman of the board.
26 Jan.	Atlanta entrepreneur Ted Turner purchases a small independent television station. WTCG (later renamed WTBS) becomes a superstation valued at more than $40 million by 1978.
26 Jan.	National Football League commissioner Pete Rozelle announces a four-year, $142 million contract with the three major television networks.
Mar.	The Federal Communications Commission outlaws the common ownership of radio and television stations in the same market.
May	The first issue of *Essence* magazine, directed at black women, appears on newsstands.
May	The Federal Communications Commission, hoping to bolster local programming on public affairs, enacts the Prime Time Access Rule, which limits prime-time programming by networks to three hours a night.
2 May	Mississippi educational television bans *Sesame Street* for its racial content. The State Commission for Educational TV reverses the decision on 24 May.
31 July	Television newsman Chet Huntley retires from NBC.
19 Sept.	*The Mary Tyler Moore Show,* a sitcom about an independent single woman, debuts on CBS.
21 Sept.	*Monday Night Football* premieres on ABC.
5 Oct.	National Educational Television (NET) is superseded by the Public Broadcasting System (PBS).

1971

- CBS debuts the controversial sitcom *All in the Family,* featuring a bigoted, white, blue-collar protagonist, Archie Bunker.

- *The New York Times* acquires *Family Circle* magazine.

Jan.   Marvel Comics' Captain America teams with the Falcon, a black superhero.

2 Jan.   The 1969 Public Health Cigarette Smoking Act, which bans cigarette advertising on television and radio, goes into effect.

29 Apr.   The *Amsterdam News,* the black newspaper with the largest U.S. circulation, is sold to a group of black investors for $2 million.

6 June   *The Ed Sullivan Show,* which debuted on CBS as *Toast of the Town* in 1948, is canceled.

26 July   *Apollo 15* sends the first color pictures from space via television.

4 Sept.   ABC cancels *The Lawrence Welk Show,* but it soon goes into syndication, with new shows being produced until 1982.

13 Oct.   At the urging of NBC, the World Series offers its first night game so that the series can be shown during prime time.

16 Oct.   *Look* magazine ceases publication after thirty-four years in business.

1972

- In *Branzburg* v. *Hayes* the U.S. Supreme Court rules that journalists do not have special immunity from testifying before grand juries, even if to do so threatens their relationships with their sources.

- One billion people watch the Olympics, held in Munich, via satellite television broadcasts.

- The National Association of Broadcasters bans hosts of children's shows from making sales pitches to children on behalf of sponsors. The resulting drop in sponsorship leads to the cancellation of many local children's programs and an increased emphasis on cartoons for those that survive.

- The business magazine *Money* is founded.

Feb.   The Federal Communications Commission places limits on CATV, which by this time refers more to cable than "community antenna television," in one hundred markets in America. Stations are required to offer channels for public access as well as to schools and governments.

Spring   The first videotape film rentals are available from Sears.

30 Apr.   *Arthur Godfrey Time,* on CBS Radio for twenty-seven years, goes off the air.

1 May   *The Tonight Show* moves from New York to Los Angeles.

8 Nov.   HBO premieres on cable television. Its first subscribers are 365 Pennsylvanians.

Dec.   *Life* magazine ceases publication after thirty-six years.

1973

- In *Miami Herald Publishing Company* v. *Tornillo,* based on a case in which a political candidate sued a newspaper for not publishing his responses to critical editorials, the U.S. Supreme Court rules that newspapers are not required to provide access to citizens.

- In two decisions the U.S. Supreme Court declares that broadcasters are under no obligation to sell time for editorial advertisements, provided that networks do not violate the FCC's Fairness Doctrine, which requires broadcasters to allow ample treatment of controversial topics and to provide those with opposing viewpoints the opportunity to express their ideas.

- *Playgirl* magazine is founded.

- *Evergreen Review,* an experimental literary journal begun in 1957, publishes its last issue.

15 Oct.   The *Tomorrow* show, hosted by Tom Snyder, premieres on NBC.

3 Dec.   The Federal Communications Commission says that NBC violated its Fairness Doctrine in a September 1972 documentary on pension funds.

1974

Mar.   *Nova* premieres on PBS.

4 Mar.   *People,* a weekly featuring stories on "the stars, the important doers, the comers, and . . . ordinary men and women caught up in extraordinary situations," publishes its first issue. It quickly becomes one of the most successful magazines of the decade.

4 Mar.   The U.S. Supreme Court rules that cable television providers do not violate U.S. copyright laws by picking up long-distance television signals and offering them to paid customers.

16 Mar.   *Editor and Publisher* announces that U.S. daily newspapers increased their total circulation by six hundred thousand in 1973.

Aug.   Marvel Comics begins *Savage Sword of Conan,* a black-and-white magazine that does not have to carry the Comics Code Authority seal and thus can address a more adult audience.

30 Nov.   Ridder Publications and Knight Newspapers combine to create a thirty-six-newspaper conglomerate in sixteen states.

1975

- Bert and Ernie, two of Jim Henson's muppets from PBS's *Sesame Street,* become exhibits at the Smithsonian Institution in Washington, D.C.

- Sony introduces its Betamax videocassette recorder.

1 Sept.   *Gunsmoke,* which premiered in 1955, goes off the air.

29 Sept.   WGPR-TV, a black station in Detroit, begins operations.

30 Sept.   HBO becomes a national cable network via satellite.

11 Oct.   *Saturday Night Live* debuts on NBC.

Nov.   DC Comics and Marvel Comics publish their first joint venture, an adaptation of *The Wizard of Oz.* The following year they publish *Superman vs. the Amazing Spider-Man.*

1976

- More than one hundred children from ages four to six are asked which they prefer — "television or daddy?" Forty-five percent respond that they prefer television.

- Chicago educational station WTTW hires film critics Gene Siskel and Roger Ebert, from rival newspapers, to review new movies for a show called *Sneak Previews.*

Jan. Marvel Comics publishes the first issue of *Howard the Duck,* a satiric comic that quickly becomes a campus sensation.

5 Jan. *The Robert MacNeil Report,* an in-depth news program, appears on PBS across the country after a trial run on the East Coast beginning 20 October 1975. Later in 1976 it becomes *The MacNeil-Lehrer Report.*

10 July Showtime debuts on cable television.

Sept. President Gerald Ford signs into law the Sunshine Act, which reduces the permissibility of most closed-door meetings in more than fifty government agencies. The act goes into effect 12 March 1977.

3 Nov. *Good Morning America* premieres on ABC.

1977

- Warner Cable Corporation establishes QUBE, an interactive multichannel cable system, in Columbus, Ohio.

- ABC becomes the highest-rated network for the first time, thanks to popular shows such as *Charlie's Angels, Happy Days, The Six Million Dollar Man,* and the phenomenally successful miniseries *Roots.*

- National Lampoon, Inc., publishes the first issues of *Heavy Metal,* which reprints European adult comics.

7 Feb. The Federal Trade Commission prohibits television advertising for Spider-Man vitamins directly to children.

Spring *Isaac Asimov's Science Fiction Magazine* appears for the first time.

5 Mar. President Jimmy Carter holds a national call-in interview show on radio.

Apr. The Christian Broadcasting Network (CBN) makes its debut.

Sept. The cable-television USA Network debuts.

10 Oct. *The Dick Cavett Show* premieres on PBS.

30 Nov. Eric Sevareid retires after thirty-eight years with CBS.

1978

- Led by Knight-Ridder and Gannett, 167 newspaper groups own more than 60 percent of the 1,753 daily newspapers published in the United States and enjoy 72 percent of newspaper circulation.

- The Library of Congress announces a future archive for radio and television to "preserve the broadcasting heritage of the American people."

- Jim Davis's comic strip "Garfield" first appears in newspapers.

- *Dallas* premieres on CBS.

1 Jan.   The new Copyright Act, passed in 1976, goes into effect. New broadcast regulations allow programs to be copyrighted and for CATV systems to acquire secondary rights for programs they receive on the air and send to subscribers.

20 Jan.   Fred Silverman becomes chief executive officer at NBC.

6 Mar.   Larry Flynt, owner of the pornographic magazine *Hustler,* is shot and critically wounded in Lawrenceville, Georgia, while in the state for an obscenity trial.

3 July   The U.S. Supreme Court rules that the Federal Communications Commission can ban language that is not obscene by legal standards. The court thus overturns a 1977 Court of Appeals decision against the FCC's ability to censor programming in response to a 1973 complaint over a public-radio broadcast of George Carlin's comedy routine about the "seven dirty words you can never say on television."

25 Sept.   A suit by *Sports Illustrated* reporter Melissa Ludtke is resolved by U.S. District Court judge Constance Baker Motley, who rules that baseball teams cannot keep a female sportswriter out of the locker room following a game.

Oct.   *Omni* magazine, combining science articles with science fiction and fantasy, appears on the newsstands.

14, 21 Oct.   In a two-part special, "Rescue from Gilligan's Island," the seven characters from the 1964–1967 television show are finally rescued, only to be marooned on the same island at the end.

Nov.   A giant Kermit the Frog balloon debuts in the Macy's Thanksgiving Parade in New York.

1979

- In the first network broadcast using fiber-optic technology, CBS employs a fiber-optic link of nearly six miles to connect Tampa Stadium with its downtown studio; from there an NFL game is broadcast to twenty cities.

Mar.   The U.S. House of Representatives establishes the Cable Satellite Public Affairs Network (C-SPAN) and allows television cameras into the chambers.

Apr.   Nickelodeon makes its debut on cable television.

Aug.   In response to a suit filed by Lone Ranger Television, Inc., the Los Angeles Superior Court forbids actor Clayton Moore to wear the Lone Ranger mask in public appearances. Moore appeals the decision, in the meantime donning large, dark sunglasses as part of his costume.

25 Sept.   ABC offers the winning bid, $225 million, to broadcast the 1984 Summer Olympics. Rights for the previous games were acquired by NBC for $87 million.

OVERVIEW

The Worst of Times, the Best of Times. After the social and cultural upheavals of the 1960s, the 1970s in general seemed a less exciting decade. In the media, however, things were definitely exciting, particularly as the concerns of the preceding decade affected everyday practice in newspapers, magazines, radio, and television. The media helped to uncover military abuses during the Vietnam War and exposed a corrupt presidential administration; magazines promoted social reforms with a vigor they had lacked for several years; and even television adopted a more socially responsible standpoint. The United States as a whole may have seemed to linger in a cultural and political malaise during the 1970s, but the media were more active than ever.

Relevance. Because of the political malaise of the decade, many social problems were addressed in the media and entertainment rather than in more practical arenas. Much of the entertainment media was simply commercial, but even popular situation comedies and television dramas addressed social issues. Norman Lear's situation comedies, particularly *All in the Family*, dealt with controversial issues television usually avoided, such as race relations, feminism, sexuality, and abortion. Likewise, *M*A*S*H* mixed the humor of the sitcom with the horror of a war drama. A new wave of minority comedies, such as *Sanford and Son, Good Times, Chico and the Man*, and *The Jeffersons*, employed stereotypes occasionally — in fact, actor John Amos left *Good Times* in 1976 over a dispute with producer Lear about how the character of J. J. revived traditional caricatures of blacks — but such shows changed the nature of American television. On Saturday mornings kids could learn about the dangers of drugs and of strangers from a wide range of characters. Television was not alone in such matters: comic books violated their own content codes to promote antidrug messages, while new magazines such as *Ms.* and *Mother Jones* devoted themselves to progressive causes.

Escape from Hard Times. While the media entertained viewers, listeners, and readers, the serious issues kept piling up. The 1970s were depressing in many respects: Americans witnessed the fall of a president, defeat in Vietnam, recessions and energy crises, and fellow Americans held hostage. Given such a context, many Americans sought escapism instead of relevance. Programs with nostalgic themes, suggesting more innocent and less troubled times, were popular. Shows such as *Laverne and Shirley* and the show from which it was a spin-off, the tellingly titled *Happy Days*, painted a glowing portrait of a 1950s devoid of red-baiting or Cold War fears; *Little House on the Prairie* took Americans back to seemingly heroic pioneer days; and *The Waltons* even made the Depression look appealing. In an era of economic downturn, these shows emphasized family instead of prosperity — even if one's "family" was to be found at the workplace, as in *The Mary Tyler Moore Show* or *Barney Miller*.

Television Reigns. During the 1970s television, popular since its introduction in the late 1940s, dominated the media. Several television genres, such as the sitcom and the detective show, were especially popular, and many of them were critically acclaimed. Television also continued to threaten the viability of motion pictures, which were forced to go where television could not go and increasingly depended upon large doses of sex, violence, and expensive special effects. Not that television respected its established limitations: as the decade progressed the medium included more sex, violence, and high-tech wizardry than ever before. Television was also aided by improvements in technology that reached even more people. Advances in satellite technology and cable allowed the television news media direct coverage of international events, while the increased availability of color television sets made the medium even more popular than before.

The Splintering of the Market. Another technique that assisted television in its domination of the media during the 1970s was an increased emphasis on targeting more-specific markets. Children could be watching a program directed at their age group in one room while parents watched an adult program in another room. The popularity of cable television, which began to blossom in the late 1970s and burgeoned during the 1980s, carried this trend even further. This target-audience approach was not limited to television, however. Radio stations and magazines continued to cater to more narrowly defined audiences, while newspapers added features and whole sections designed to appeal to specific interests. Older, general-interest magazines such as *Look* and *Life* fell by the wayside, overshadowed by special-interest periodicals such as the restructured *Cosmopolitan*.

The Restructuring of Radio. In the 1970s radio changed less than television or print media, but it changed nonetheless. Most radios in 1970 carried only one band, AM or FM. AM was more popular and more commercial: in 1970, 95 percent of American households owned an AM radio, in contrast to the 74 percent of homes owning an FM radio. That year there were more than four thousand commercial AM stations and only about two thousand commercial FM stations. AM signals carried farther than FM, but FM signals were clearer and could be broadcast in stereo. FM accordingly catered originally to those who sought high-fidelity broadcasts. Classical-music stations dominated the band, but beginning in the 1970s more and more FM stations adopted a format known as album-oriented rock (AOR), which originally meant that they played entire albums uninterrupted by commercials or talk and later came to mean any format playing songs from albums rather than individually released singles. In addition, FM in general tended to be more alternative — influenced in large part by college radio stations of the late 1960s and early 1970s — and led the way in the assimilation of alternative culture into the mainstream during the decade. By the end of the 1970s the disparity between the popularity of AM and FM was nearly reversed, with FM stations, which adopted popular music as their mainstay, practically dominating the radio market.

Going Conservative. The so-called counterculture was not the only cultural movement to take advantage of new media technology and approaches; the growing conservative movement also made use of it. Christian broadcasting made use of cable and satellite television, extending influence beyond the South. Christian broadcasters also seized hold of less profitable, older technologies. Many conservatives bought AM radio stations or ultrahigh frequency (UHF) television channels. As the newspaper and magazine businesses restructured, conservatives gained news organs for their political and social perspectives. For instance, the *Washington Times* was bought by conservative Rev. Sun Myung Moon. Whereas the counterculture was assimilated by mainstream media and made to serve preestablished commercial purposes, conservatives took a less commercial, more ideological approach to the media business. After 1978 conservatives would become increasingly influential in American politics, contributing significantly to the 1980 conservative electoral victory.

TOPICS IN THE NEWS

THE MEDIA AND VIETNAM

The Living-Room War. By the 1970s popular support for the Vietnam War had diminished in the United States. As the war became increasingly unpopular with many Americans, the media presented it in a negative light. Prior to the 1968 Tet offensive the media had generally supported the government's position on Vietnam; the majority of the public approved of the war, and the media reported on it favorably. The Tet offensive, however, belied in dramatic fashion government optimism over the war and suggested that the conflict was unwinnable. Even CBS newscaster Walter Cronkite, "the most trusted man in America," spoke out against the claims of politicians and the military, saying the war would result in either a stalemate or defeat. An apocryphal story has President Lyndon B. Johnson telling an aide, "Well, if I've lost Cronkite, I've lost middle America." An increasingly critical approach to the war by tele-vision helped Americans take more seriously the critiques appearing in other media. Michael Herr had been writing critical, incisive articles on the war for *Esquire* since 1967. *Harper's* magazine had published Norman Mailer's "The Steps of the Pentagon" in its March 1968 issue; the magazine later published Seymour M. Hersh's long article "My Lai: The First Detailed Account of the Vietnam Massacre" in its May 1970 issue. Protests were increasingly frequent, and those in which students were killed at Kent State University in Ohio and Jackson State University in Mississippi in 1970 heightened already-strained tensions between the government and much of the public. Television news brought protests and the war itself into people's living rooms. Still, many people, including those in the media, had confidence that the government was trying to do the right thing in Vietnam, and reporters sometimes continued to paint a rosy picture of U.S. military intervention there.

Americans' television exposure to the war was a powerful stimulus to antiwar sentiment.

Storm and Stress. The Nixon administration, following a strategy begun during the Johnson years, suggested that journalists who challenged the government's presentation of the war were in essence aiding the enemy. In November 1969 President Nixon made a widely viewed prime-time television speech suggesting that the "great silent majority" of Americans supported the war and that the media were undermining the war effort. "North Vietnam cannot defeat or humiliate the United States," Nixon concluded. "Only Americans can do that." Vicepresident Spiro Agnew went even further, accusing the media of fomenting negative feelings about the war and waging a personal war against the president and his administration. At a regional Republican gathering broadcast by all three networks, Agnew claimed, "Perhaps the place to start looking for a credibility gap is not in the offices of government in Washington but in the studios of the networks in New York." Agnew lambasted news commentators as "nattering nabobs of negativism." He often reminded his audiences that television was licensed by the government through the Federal Communications Commission (FCC), implicitly threatening the autonomy of the medium if it went too far. It did not take long for the implications of such veiled threats to be realized, and networks backed off from negative commentary or posted disclaimers distancing themselves from the views

of their commentators. Also, CBS dropped its "instant analysis" of addresses by the president. (The network restored the practice during the last days of the Nixon presidency.) In addition, in June 1970 the Office of Telecommunications Policy (OTP), a White House advisory agency, was founded, with Clay Whitehead as its director. The OTP sought to promote positive media coverage for the Nixon administration and to question indirectly the media's accuracy. After Nixon's resignation the OTP was eliminated.

Losing Middle America. Official censure, if not censorship, could do little to deter the media as more information about atrocities and cover-ups became available. In addition to critical stories in the press, about which the government could do little, CBS attracted government criticism with its 23 February 1971 documentary "The Selling of the Pentagon," which alleged that the military was wasting large amounts of tax money promoting its role in the war. On 17 April the House Special Subcommittee on Investigations asked CBS to provide "all notes, film, sound tape recordings, scripts, names and addresses of all persons appearing in the telecast, and a statement of all disbursements of money made in connection with the program." CBS refused, citing the First Amendment.

The Pentagon Papers. Positive portraits of U.S. involvement in Vietnam were also undermined by the publication of excerpts from a secret 3,000-page Pentagon study, "History of the U.S. Decision-making Process on Vietnam Policy" — better known as the Pentagon Papers. *The New York Times* managed to get a stolen copy of the papers in March 1971 from former Department of Defense official Daniel Ellsberg. They began printing a series of excerpts from the papers on 13 June. Nixon asked Attorney General John Mitchell to halt publication on the grounds that it threatened national security. When the newspaper refused, the government asked the federal district court in New York to step in. Judge Murray Gurfein issued a temporary restraining order on 15 June, but four days later he said that he would not make it permanent. The temporary restraining order was overturned on 23 June by the federal court of appeals in New York. By this time the *Washington Post* had begun excerpting the Pentagon Papers as well. Government attempts to stop publication failed in the courts. On 25 June the U.S. Supreme Court issued a temporary restraining order while it heard arguments. The newspapers claimed that the government could not prove that publication of the Pentagon Papers threatened national security. The Court agreed.

Americans Go Home. In the 1970s the bias of the media shifted: the government was treated critically, while antiwar protests were covered with a degree of sympathy, especially when students were killed in protests. Following Nixon's 1969 policy of Vietnamization, turning more of the war effort over to the South Vietnamese, it became increasingly obvious that South Vietnam was fighting a losing battle. Despite the efforts of the South Vietnamese government and U.S. officials to restrict media access to the battlefield, the media continued to capture news of the war as it happened, including both the 1973 withdrawal of the last U.S. troops from Vietnam and the fall of South Vietnam to the Communist North two years later. Before long, however, Vietnam seemed to vanish from the American consciousness as the nation turned its attention to a domestic concern — Watergate.

Sources:

Harry Castleman and Walter J. Podrazik, *Watching TV: Four Decades of American Television* (New York: McGraw-Hill, 1982);

Daniel C. Hallin, *The "Uncensored War": The Media and Vietnam* (New York & Oxford: Oxford University Press, 1986);

Robert V. Hudson, *Mass Media: A Chronological Encyclopedia of Television, Radio, Motion Pictures, Magazines, Newspapers, and Books in the United States* (New York: Garland, 1987);

Doug James, *Cronkite: His Life and Times* (Brentwood, Tenn.: J. M. Press, 1991);

Clarence R. Wyatt, *Paper Soldiers: The American Press and the Vietnam War* (New York & London: Norton, 1993).

THE MEDIA AND WATERGATE

A Third-Rate Burglary. The 17 June 1972 break-in at the Democratic National Committee headquarters at the

Senator Sam Ervin and chief counsel Sam Dash during a televised portion of the 1973 Watergate hearings. Networks rotated coverage to minimize disruption of their daily programming and to protect advertising earnings.

Watergate office and apartment complex in Washington, D.C., made few headlines at first. Over the next few years the implications of the failed burglary came to dominate the newspapers, as it did the media in general. The *Washington Post* in particular revealed information about the case that led to the resignation of President Nixon and prison terms for several members of his staff. Nixon had used the media effectively for most of his political career: for instance, his 1972 visits to China, the Soviet Union, and Poland were all televised, bolstering his image as a skillful statesman capable of easing Cold War tensions. With Watergate such skills failed, and the media helped lead to his downfall.

All the President's Men. The five men who were caught bugging the Watergate complex had ties with the Committee to Reelect the President (CREEP). The Nixon administration nonetheless denied any connection with the burglary on the Democratic headquarters, and Nixon easily won reelection in 1972. Media scrutiny became more intense due to investigative newspaper stories by Bob Woodward and Carl Bernstein of the *Washington Post,* who eventually revealed a cover-up to hide White House involvement. Woodward and Bernstein's reports earned their newspaper a 1973 Pulitzer Prize. The story was difficult to piece together. For one thing, Nixon's advisers viewed the press as an enemy out to get the president and were on the defensive against anything that might impugn him. In addition, Vice-president Spiro Agnew waged his own private war against the media in the late 1960s, setting up an adversarial relationship between the administration and journalists who were growing increasingly skeptical about the role of the United States in the Vietnam War. Sources were scared and reluctant to talk, and *Washington Post* editor Ben Bradlee insisted that information be verified, leading Woodward and Bernstein to use questionable ethical methods, the most memorable of which was a disputed anonymous source called "Deep Throat." They kept at the story, however, establishing bit by bit the connections between the burglary and the White House. They were later rewarded for their diligence, both professionally and commercially, with their best-selling book on their search, *All the President's Men* (1974). In April 1973 Nixon's aides testified before a congressional committee on the Watergate affair, quickly leading to the resignations of top White House staff members. The following month *The New York Times* joined the fray, reporting on Republican "dirty tricks" during the 1972 presidential campaign. Even as several of his aides were implicated in a series of finger-pointing testimonies, however, Nixon denied any wrongdoing.

Live from Congress. The Senate was not convinced, and it held hearings beginning in 1973. These hearings were carried on live television and helped to increase the amount of television news coverage of the Watergate investigations. On 25 June former White House counsel John Dean testified before the Senate, claiming that Nixon participated in the attempted cover-up and that he had warned the chief executive of "a cancer growing on the Presidency." The following month Alexander P. Butterfield, a Nixon aide, revealed the existence of a taping system at the White House, prompting the Senate committee to requisition tapes of White House meetings. Nixon resisted, instead turning over 1,308 pages of edited transcripts in April 1974. He was forced in a July decision by the U.S. Supreme Court to relinquish all the tapes. All of these deliberations were related in detail by the media, as were Nixon's televised statements in which he proclaimed his innocence. Broadcast excerpts of White House transcripts and tape recordings, along with a best-selling transcript of the tapes in book form, nevertheless painted an increasingly dark picture of goings-on in the Oval Office and swayed public opinion against the president. Following the televised July 1974 impeachment hearings in the House of Representatives, in August Nixon released the "smoking gun" tape revealing his knowledge of the burglary and cover-up. Three days later, on 8 August, he announced his resignation. Gerald Ford, his vice-president following the resignation of Spiro Agnew for tax fraud, was sworn in as president the following day and pardoned Nixon for his crimes one month later.

Television Resignation. Just as television had brought the death and funeral of President John F. Kennedy into the homes of Americans in 1963, so with Watergate Americans experienced President Nixon's fall with immediacy. Stations canceled regularly scheduled programming in order to broadcast important hearings. And when Nixon resigned, he did so live on national television. Even though news stories subsided after the resignation, Watergate remained a popular and profitable subject as a flood of memoirs and analyses appeared for

the remainder of the decade. Nixon's death and the twentieth anniversary of his resignation brought a renewal of interest in Watergate in 1994.

Sources:

Robert V. Hudson, *Mass Media: A Chronological Encyclopedia of Television, Radio, Motion Pictures, Magazines, Newspapers, and Books in the United States* (New York: Garland, 1987);

Michael Schudson, *Watergate in American Memory: How We Remember, Forget, and Reconstruct the Past* (New York: Basic Books, 1992);

Bob Woodward and Carl Bernstein, *All the President's Men* (New York: Simon & Schuster, 1974);

Woodward and Bernstein, *The Final Days* (New York: Simon & Schuster, 1976).

PUBLIC TELEVISION AND RADIO

A Slow Start. Public television and public radio first received extensive federal support in the late 1960s. This funding served to unify poorly funded local programming under the respective banners of the Public Broadcasting System (PBS) and National Public Radio (NPR). In 1967 the Carnegie Commission released *Public Television: A Program for Action,* upon which President Lyndon B. Johnson drew to encourage a national public broadcasting system. The resulting Public Broadcasting Act in November 1967 provided the foundation for the Corporation for Public Broadcasting (CPB), which would serve to provide financial support for educational television. Support for public radio was also included, though some critics worried that its inclusion would weaken the program's chance of success since public radio stations would need a great deal of money. In addition, some critics feared that public radio and television would be used for government propaganda. Supporters outweighed detractors, however, and the programs began. Both public television and radio got off to a slow start due to limitations in funding during the late 1960s because of the Vietnam War. In the 1970s each proved itself viable with programming that was both critically acclaimed and popular with the public. Its success meant that the networks needed rely less on outside support, though organizations such as the Ford Foundation had been essential to its early survival.

Success. A key element in PBS's gradual success was the phenomenal appeal of *Sesame Street,* which was first broadcast in November 1969, eight months after the CPB was established. The colorful, fast-paced show was a radical departure from most shows on earlier public television. Though aimed to help urban preschool-age children be better prepared when they entered school, even school-age children fell in love with the program, and adults took notice of the noncommercial network. While PBS seldom presented a challenge to commercial television in terms of ratings, programs such as *Masterpiece Theater,* which presented the highly acclaimed series-within-a-series *Upstairs, Downstairs,* won Emmy awards and found loyal viewers throughout the decade.

Scene from the popular PBS series *Upstairs, Downstairs,* a British television saga imported for American audiences

Threat. Despite such early successes and a dramatic increase in the number of public television and radio stations, the existence of public television was challenged in 1972 by President Nixon's veto of an important appropriations measure, which forced the system to reconsider its means of support and to lay off many employees. Public television, according to the Nixon administration, should concentrate on local programming and should be more decentralized, from PBS's perspective, a step backwards. As files made public in 1979 revealed, the Nixon administration also tried to control who served on the CPB board in order to bias it toward the administration. Ironically, interest in public television was renewed by its extensive coverage of the Watergate hearings. However, the inconsistency of government support forced PBS to rely increasingly on semiannual fund-raising appeals and corporate sponsorship. Such pitches were difficult but successful: by 1974 funding had risen to such levels that the Ford Foundation could announce a significant reduction in its support of educational television.

Quality News and No Commercials. The rationale behind NPR, founded in 1970, was the same as with public television: to bring local noncommercial stations together with common programming. Programs funded by the CPB were started in April 1971. The following month NPR's popular *All Things Considered* made its debut. The late-afternoon show was soon praised for its in-depth coverage of news and cultural affairs. Its companion, *Morning Edition,* made its debut in 1979. The fact that NPR broadcasts, like those of public television,

were not interrupted by commercials helped, although viewers and listeners have had to suffer through seasonal fund-raising drives to supplement governmental and foundational support. Never a real threat to commercial broadcasting, public radio and television nonetheless found their respective audience niches during the 1970s.

Sources:

Erik Barnouw, *Tube of Plenty: The Evolution of American Television,* revised edition (New York & Oxford: Oxford University Press, 1990);

Mary Collins, *National Public Radio: The Cast of Characters* (Washington, D.C.: Seven Locks Press, 1993);

Robert V. Hudson, *Mass Media: A Chronological Encyclopedia of Television, Radio, Motion Pictures, Magazines, Newspapers, and Books in the United States* (New York: Garland, 1987);

Roselle Kovitz, *The History of Public Broadcasting* (Washington, D.C.: Current Newspaper, 1987).

RADICALS AND REACTIONARIES: THE MEDIA ASSIMILATION OF THE COUNTERCULTURE

From Fringe to Mainstream. American media, like most aspects of American culture in the 1970s, was dramatically affected by the social changes of the 1960s. While American culture proved fundamentally resistant to many aspects of 1960s radicalism — rejecting, for example, Black Power, Maoism, and revolutionary violence, or only partially accepting aspects of feminism and civil rights — the media almost wholly assimilated the countercultural preoccupations of the 1960s. Self-expression, sexual liberation, recreational drug use, and

In 1970 Howard Hughes was one of the richest men in America. A recluse for many years, he was as noteworthy for his reputed eccentricity as for his wealth. Little wonder, then, that the announcement of a Hughes autobiography by *Life* magazine and the publishing firm of McGraw-Hill on 7 December 1971 drew a great deal of publicity. The autobiography, as told to author Clifford Irving, was to be published on 7 March 1972, with portions to appear beforehand in *Life.*

Irving was not well known at the end of 1971, but early in the following year he became famous. Claiming to have based the book on many hours of secret meetings conducted "throughout the Western Hemisphere," Irving was at first treated with caution, since previous efforts by others to get to Hughes had been frustrated by legal threats and his own obdurately kept privacy. Hughes did not immediately say anything about the book, but his attorneys attempted to halt publication. By this time, however, the public was anxious for its arrival, taking Hughes's silence as confirmation of its validity. Hughes did respond a month later, speaking to seven Los Angeles journalists from a hotel in the Bahamas after their initial questions confirmed to them that they were speaking to him and not an impostor. He said, "I don't know Irving. I never saw him." The televised event was Hughes's first interview since 1958.

This did not settle the matter. Experts on Hughes who examined the manuscript Irving had given to McGraw-Hill asserted it to be genuine, both in appearance and content. Other evidence seemed to support the book's authenticity. McGraw-Hill had written more than $500,000 in checks for Irving to deliver to Hughes; these were signed and deposited in a Swiss bank account by "H. R. Hughes." Also, lie-detector tests conducted on Irving failed to prove any wrongdoing. The fact that Hughes had come forward to deny any involvement with his supposed autobiography led to intense scrutiny of the case by government investigators in the United States and Switzerland, by American journalists, and by Hughes's hired detectives.

Investigators soon learned that "H. R. Hughes," who withdrew the money from the Swiss bank account not long after it was deposited, was actually "Helga R. Hughes," who was actually Edith Irving, wife of Clifford Irving. Moreover, detectives found the details of Irving's supposed meetings with Hughes to be contradictory or impossible when checked. Still, the manuscript and its faithfulness to what was known about Hughes gave skeptics pause. Frank McCullough of *Time,* for instance, had last interviewed Hughes in person; when he examined Irving's manuscript, he found previously unpublished details that only he and Hughes could know and thus took the manuscript as genuine.

It was not, as soon became evident. A reporter named James Phelan had worked with a former Hughes aide, Noah Dietrich, on an abandoned book about the billionaire. Hughes had told Dietrich about the McCullough interview, among other things, and this information found its way into their abandoned manuscript — which, unknown to Phelan, had been given to a friend of Dietrich's, who passed it along to Irving. That accounted for the seeming truthfulness of Irving's account. Irving had forged Hughes's handwriting based on a copy of a letter published in the 21 December 1970 issue of *Newsweek.* McGraw-Hill finally admitted that they had been taken by Irving, his wife, and their assistant Richard Suskind — all of whom were convicted of fraud as a result. Irving himself served a year and a half in jail.

Source: Morris P. Colden and David A. Plott, "Literary Cons: Hoaxes, Frauds, and Plagiarism in American Literature," in *American Literary Almanac: From 1608 to the Present — An Original Compendium of Facts and Anecdotes about Literary Life in the United States of America,* edited by Karen L. Rood (New York & Oxford: Facts on File, 1988), pp. 192–194.

rock music — major characteristics of the so-called counterculture — all found a place in 1970s media. Magazines, radio, and television had, to some extent, been instrumental in creating the counterculture by publicizing the preoccupations of countercultural centers such as San Francisco, or that of countercultural events such as Woodstock, to the rest of the country. The radical implications of the counterculture (*sexual revolution,* for example, originally referred to the political upheaval that would follow the establishment of expressive, guilt-free sexual practices) were quickly obscured by the media, which focused on the sensational gloss of the counterculture. The counterculture's insurrectionary "sex, drugs, and rock 'n' roll" went mainstream. Sexual liberation was co-opted by magazines searching for a more thoroughly eroticized image; drugs lost their rebellious character and became part of pop music's emphasis on partying; rock music became a multibillion-dollar business and spectacle, outgrossing film and television. The media organs of a rebellious, subversive counterculture in the 1960s, moreover, pioneered new expressive techniques that transformed the established media in the 1970s. Underground comics somewhat liberalized commercial comic books; libertine and youthful, art-house films demanded a new explicitness from Hollywood; *Rolling Stone* pioneered a new, impressionistic pop-culture journalism; and FM radio shattered the narrow formats of AM radio stations. Some powerhouse media institutions, unable to grapple with such challenges, died. Both *Life* and *Look* magazines ceased publishing during the decade, and veteran newscaster Chet Huntley retired. As the old guard receded, a younger generation stepped in to take its place, bringing to the media an infusion of fresh ideas and approaches.

FM Radio. Perhaps the best example of media's assimilation of the counterculture was the growth of FM radio. In the 1960s FM (frequency modulation, for the type of radio signal) had constituted the backwaters of the radio dial. Although capable of high-fidelity broadcasts, FM was limited in range, and thus commercial advertisers favored AM (amplitude modulation) radio. By the end of the 1960s AM stations were winning the competition for advertising dollars by formatting their broadcasts to feature restrictive Top 40 playlists with songs less than three minutes long (and with their playing speed often slightly increased), and by promoting hyperkinetic drive-time disc jockeys to grab the listener's attention. FM, by contrast, was an oasis of countercultural bliss. Many stations featured classical music and jazz broadcasts aimed at a limited audience. FM rock stations usually featured more laid-back disc jockeys, who, especially at night, provided countercultural observations between record cuts. Increasingly geared to the college audience, FM rock radio adapted to the students' taste for long-playing, progressive, experimental rock. As recording technologies improved, FM turned to such high-fidelity rock records as Pink Floyd's *The Dark Side of the Moon* (1973) or Led Zeppelin's untitled album, commonly called "*ZoSo*" (1972) and made stars of these bands. Advertisers, recognizing the potential of the new FM market niche, began to patronize FM stations. And FM stations, recognizing their new commercial potential, began to format their playlists after Top 40 radio (albeit with a slightly more expansive notion of the Top 40) and hire "air personalities" to introduce records. The music became blander and less rebellious. Metromedia radio abandoned the cooler-than-cool FM disc jockey altogether and tied their nationwide chain of FM radio stations together via an entirely automated, Top 40 playlist. By the end of the decade countercultural FM radio was dead, aside from a few college-owned FM stations with limited broadcasting range. Ironically, as FM radio became more profitable and more homogeneous, AM radio diversified its format, becoming the site of radio innovation in the 1980s.

Front cover for the first issue of *Ms.*, distributed as an insert to *New York* magazine

New Journalism. In the 1970s print journalism also assimilated the counterculture in a fashion similar to that of FM radio. Disgusted with the conservatism of mainstream media, young radicals in the 1960s began their own underground newspapers and magazines, which featured a mix of highly impressionistic reporting on political issues and discussions of drugs, sex, and rock music. Even mainstream journalists such as Tom Wolfe and Joan Didion adopted the new style of reporting, extended in the process into a form called New Journalism, in magazines such as *Esquire, Playboy,* and *The New Yorker*. San Francisco–based *Rolling Stone* was by far the most influential of the underground magazines of the late 1960s and featured a crop of writers — including Hunter S. Thompson and Lester Bangs — who set even the New Journalism on its ear as they pursued a style of drug-induced exposition sometimes called gonzo journalism. In format and style *Rolling Stone* was the most successful magazine of the decade and profoundly influenced the rest of American publishing, especially after it became a multimillion-dollar enterprise and relocated to New York. Both print journalism and television focused increasing attention on popular culture, entertainment, and social trends. By the end of the decade *Rolling Stone* was the establishment, capable of soliciting interviews from prominent public figures and promoting nationwide fads. Its antagonistic response to punk rock, lukewarm acceptance of disco, and promotion of the fitness craze and the Carter presidency all marked it as a bastion of the baby-boom counterculture grown respectable and assimilated.

Television. As America's electronic mirror, television quickly seized upon the counterculture. Afraid of losing younger viewers, staid networks and Hollywood production companies cautiously embraced aspects of the counterculture. Since the radical implications of the counterculture, however, were anathema to television advertisers, media corporations, and most television viewers, television used the counterculture as a whetstone against which to sharpen traditional values. Typical of this process was *The Partridge Family*, a television program that featured a family whose members, dressed in hip clothes, were a rock band with everyday problems. Similarly, *The Brady Bunch* featured with-it parents who taught their children — also dressed in hip clothes — traditional family values. *The Mod Squad* starred three apparently countercultural figures — a white male activist, a female hippie, and a tough male black militant — who on weekly episodes went to work for the establishment as undercover cops. Sonny and Cher, the pop singing duo from the 1960s who appeared to be advocates of the counterculture, hosted a popular variety show whose blandness (they named their infant daughter, an occasional star on the show, Chastity) was offset only by Cher's Las Vegas–showgirl outfits. Antonio Fargas, a black character actor who was featured as a pimp and a junkie in many early 1970s blaxploitation films, ended the 1970s essentially reprising his character on television's police drama *Starsky and Hutch*. On television, however, his junkie/pimp character was toned down. Still preening and street-smart, "Huggy Bear" was no longer a marginally rebellious, outlaw figure but a cool restaurateur who cooperated with white cops.

A Newsroom of One's Own. Feminism was one of the most important movements of the 1960s to impact media in the 1970s. Feminism in the media began in 1970 when author Susan Brownmiller led a protest demanding both a female editor in chief and a day-care center at the offices of *Ladies' Home Journal*. Gloria Steinem's magazine *Ms.*, founded in 1972, and *New Woman*, established the previous year, offered feminist perspectives on American politics and culture. Helen Gurley Brown's *Cosmopolitan* adopted a feminist perspective, and even general-interest magazines, such as *Time* and *Newsweek*, offered stories on the women's movement. In 1975 *Time* named ten women as its Man of the Year. Newscaster Barbara Walters became the first reporter to earn $1 million per year for her telecasts, and *Washington Post* publisher Katherine Graham became one of the most respected members of the fourth estate. Even *Playboy*, setting itself apart from more explicit competitors, purported to champion the feminist cause. Other magazines, such as *Play-*

THE TOP TEN TELEVISION SHOWS, 1973-1974*	
All in the Family (CBS)	31.2 percent of homes with television
The Waltons (CBS)	27.9
Sanford and Son (NBC)	27.6
M*A*S*H (CBS)	25.8
Hawaii Five-O (CBS)	23.7
Sonny & Cher (CBS)	23.4
Maude (CBS)	23.3
Kojak (CBS)	23.3
The Mary Tyler Moore Show (CBS), 23.2	
Cannon (CBS)	23.0

* Nielsen averages through 8 May 1974 as reported in *Variety*

Source: Erik Barnouw, *Tube of Plenty: The Evolution of American Television*, revised edition (New York & Oxford: Oxford University Press, 1990).

girl, founded in 1973, catered to a new feminine market for erotic media, as did novels such as Erica Jong's *Fear of Flying* (1973).

Advertisements. As erotica discovered a new female market, so did advertisers. Feminism was reflected in advertisements of products such as Virginia Slims cigarettes ("You've Come a Long Way, Baby," read the captions) and Enjoli cologne, whose television ads proclaimed, "I can bring home the bacon / fry it up in a pan / and never, never, never let you forget you're a man! 'Cause I'm a woman. . . ." Irish Spring soap had a woman acknowledging that the soap was intended for men: "Manly, yes, but I like it too," she intoned. The independent woman of the Charlie cologne ads not only signs her own checks but also asks men to dance. Tiparillo cigars suggested that the liberated woman smokes Tiparillos, and the liberated man offers them to her. Liquid Paper proposed itself as a tool of the liberated secretary.

Superwomen. Television programmers suggested to girls that having muscles and superpowers was perfectly valid for women. Saturday-morning television introduced a superheroine named Isis on *The Shazam Isis Hour* in 1975, and she received her own program, *The Secrets of*

AND NOW FOR SOMETHING COMPLETELY DIFFERENT

American television during the 1970s was more diverse than at any previous point in its history. In their efforts to reach as many markets as possible, network executives promoted shows aimed at target audiences, resulting in a wide viewing spectrum ranging from children's shows to youth-oriented fare to adult situation comedies and dramas that tackled previously taboo subjects. Nothing, however, could prepare Americans for the latest British invasion when *Monty Python's Flying Circus* came to public television beginning in 1974.

Monty Python, a group of six talented and inventive comedians, offered — as a common lead-in on their 1969–1974 British television show promised — "something completely different." Even the antics of the later *Saturday Night Live* comedians seemed sane by comparison. *Monty Python's Flying Circus* featured skits by Graham Chapman, John Cleese, Terry Gilliam, Eric Idle, Terry Jones, and Michael Palin on dead parrots, the Department of Funny Walks, boxes of chocolates with nasty surprise centers, and other inspired silliness. While the comedy of Monty Python was often distinctly British, capable of being simultaneously intellectual and ribald, it scored a hit with many in the United States.

Their success in England and the United States led the troupe to expand into movies, beginning with *And Now for Something Completely Different* (1972), with skits based on the television show, and continuing with *Monty Python and the Holy Grail* (1974) and *The Life of Brian* (1979). The group disbanded in the early 1980s, though its members have often appeared in other members' independent projects.

Source: *The Complete Monty Python's Flying Circus: All the Words*, 2 volumes (New York: Pantheon, 1989).

Isis, two years later. One segment of *The Krofft Supershow* featured Electro Woman and Dyna Girl. On prime-time television Lynda Carter revealed amazing powers (and a fair amount of skin) as Wonder Woman (who, in original comic book form, appeared on the cover of the July 1972 issue of *Ms.*). As the Bionic Woman, Lindsay Wagner could run faster and hit harder than any man — except for the Six-Million-Dollar Man, of course. In the comics themselves, a new character named Ms. Marvel was introduced in 1977 by Marvel Comics; "This female fights back!" readers were promised.

Stereotypes or Role Models? Wonder Woman and the Bionic Woman were not the only feminist characters on television. *The Mary Tyler Moore Show, Maude, Rhoda, Alice,* and *Phyllis* all featured strong, independent women characters. The popular blaxploitation films — which often featured quasi-feminist leads, as in *Coffy* (1973) and *Foxy Brown* (1974) — spurred ABC to launch a weekly series in 1974, *Get Christie Love!*, starring Teresa Graves as a black woman who karate-chopped the bad guys while purring, "You're under arrest, sugar." The dual message — both feminist and sexist — of shows such as *Get Christie Love!* was more fully expressed in the phenomenally successful *Charlie's Angels*, which debuted in 1976. In *Charlie's Angels* three women detectives mastered evildoers on weekly episodes — clad usually in bikinis, tight-fitting sweaters, or other revealing clothing. While the *Charlie's Angels* characters were resourceful and independent, they were also fashion-conscious and glamorous. The program, along with *Three's Company* and *The Dukes of Hazzard*, provided the basis for the phrase *jiggle TV*. Feminists of the day worried that programs such as *Charlie's Angels* and advertisements such as those of Virginia Slims represented a step backward for the women's movement. As author Pagan Kennedy puts it, "We who grew up in the . . . late seventies learned that women could be powerful, but only if they dressed the part."

New Faces. Ambiguous messages were also characteristic of the growing multicultural character of American television and other media. The racial and ethnic pride of the late 1960s and early 1970s was reflected in many shows, from prime-time sitcoms to children's shows, offering multiracial, ethnic, and all-black casts. Variety shows and sitcoms such as *The Flip Wilson Show, That's My Mamma, What's Happening!!, Good Times, The Jeffersons,* and *Sanford and Son* featured black casts, often in realistic urban settings; *The Tony Orlando and Dawn Show, Chico and the Man,* and *Welcome Back, Kotter* featured ethnic characters of all descriptions, usually played for laughs. White ethnics were featured in dramas, especially detective shows, including *Kojak, Baretta, Columbo,* and *Starsky and Hutch*. And of course Archie Bunker, of *All in the Family*, made the white, working-class everyman a television star. The problem with such ethnic visibility was that it often portrayed stereotypes that bordered on the bigoted. By 1978 *Time* protested against the absence of strong black fathers on television, and in 1980 *Ebony* dismissed almost all black characterizations on television as implicitly racist. While the miniseries *Roots* (1977), a story of a African-American family, was told with intelligence and sympathy, it was the exception. In the 1970s television expanded its repertory of ethnic characters, but only enough to include the clichés.

Coming Out. Homosexuals were even less successful in being portrayed positively in the media. Like feminism and multiculturalism, gay liberation was an extension of the 1960s counterculture. *The Advocate*, a magazine established in 1967 for gay and lesbian readers, continued to survive and even prosper through the 1970s, but, apart from its objective discussions about gays and lesbians, most images of homosexuality in the media were closeted and capable of passing for straight. The most notorious example was *Three's Company,* a sitcom about two women sharing an apartment with a man who pretends to the homophobic landlord that he is gay; why such a landlord would tolerate a homosexual tenant, but not heterosexual tenants living together, is left unaddressed. A more respectful approach (but still played for laughs) could be found on ABC's *Soap,* which featured Billy Crystal as one of the first openly gay characters on network television. The Village People, titans of the disco boom (enormously indebted to the gay subculture) sang campy gay songs ("Macho Man," "Y.M.C.A.," "In the Navy") whose coded messages went right over the heads of middle America. The antidisco backlash on radio during 1978–1979 was in part due to the fact that straight, white suburbanites finally got the joke. The most common image of the homosexual in the media during the late 1970s was the stereotype of the sexually obsessed pedophile promoted by antigay activists such as orange-juice spokeswoman Anita Bryant. Denouncing homosexual "recruitment" in the public schools and the "unnaturalness" of homosexuality, Bryant and her political pressure group, Save Our Children, succeeded in rescinding civil rights ordinances protecting gays in Miami and other communities. Ironically, homosexuals were pioneering both the consumerist sexuality (one reason disco was such a hit) and alternative family structures. By the time Bryant denounced them, homosexuals had begun to enter the mainstream.

Nostalgia. Gays were not the only American group experimenting with alternative family structures. The counterculture had championed communal relationships, and, as the divorce rate climbed in the 1970s, more and more Americans considered alternative family structures. Popular television sitcoms featured single mothers (*The Partridge Family, What's Happening!!, One Day at a Time*), divorcées (*Alice*), and implausible families (*The Brady Bunch,* a marriage between a widower with three boys and a widow with three girls; *Mork and Mindy,* an earth girl and alien man). Archie Bunker, of *All in the Family,* began the 1970s in a traditional household, but by the end of the decade (with the rest of the characters either dead or moved to California) was forced to find his family at *Archie's Place,* a bar he ran. The ensemble comedy, such as *Taxi* and *WKRP in Cincinnati,* constructed de facto families in the absence of real ones. Television, ever the agent of fantasy, also responded to the breakdown in the postwar family by returning to imagined ages of stability and tradition, and nostalgia television was born. *Happy Days,* itself an indirect spin-off of the hugely successful nostalgia film *American Graffiti* (1973), created a timeless world of the 1950s, where even the delinquents, such as Fonzie, had a heart of gold. *Laverne and Shirley,* and *The Sha Na Na Show* existed in some strange crossbreed 1950s–1970s world where doo-wop and blow-dried hair coexisted. *Little House on the Prairie* returned

Americans to the rugged family values of the pioneer days; *The Waltons* managed to make the Great Depression seem cozy. Nostalgia television, part of a national mania for a roseate past also expressed in movies and novels, was symptomatic of a deep loss of cultural center and a desire to avoid confronting the present. These trends would coalesce in the development of a conservative culture at the end of the decade.

Conservative Culture. Conservative culture affirmed what the counterculture denied: absolutes, tradition, sexual denial, hierarchy, and mainline religion. Ironically, conservative culture developed because of the success the counterculture had in transforming the cultural landscape. As women and ethnic groups, for example, gained a more certain definition of self, and as advertisers refined ever-narrower demographic groups, conservatives, especially southerners associated with evangelical and fundamentalist denominations, also sharpened their communal identity. Organized by political leaders such as Phyllis Schlafly, Anita Bryant, and Jerry Falwell, such conservatives moved into media institutions abandoned by the counterculture. AM radio stations, for example, were purchased inexpensively during the 1970s by evangelical groups who reformatted the stations for religious programming and right-wing talk shows. UHF television stations, and later cable television, both less profitable than mainstream channels, became the basis of a broad-based Christian broadcasting empire during the 1970s. Specialized magazines, such as *Commentary* and the *National Review,* appealing to the sense of disenfranchisement felt by many conservatives, lambasted the "liberal" bent of mainstream media. Most important, conservatives developed innovative communication techniques, such as direct-mail solicitation, which swelled their numbers, and found ready advertisers, such as Coors beer and Wal-Mart department stores, to support their programming. By the end of the 1970s the insurrectionary culture in America was no longer that of the 1960s radical but that of the 1980s conservative. The success liberal media had in assimilating the counterculture had created its own counter with the rise of conservatism.

Sources:

Mike Benton, *The Comic Book in America: An Illustrated History* (Dallas: Taylor, 1989);

Marcia Cohen, *The Sisterhood: The True Story of the Women Who Changed the World* (New York: Simon & Schuster, 1988);

Gary Grossman, *Saturday Morning TV* (New York: Dell, 1981);

Amy Janello and Brennon Jones, *The American Magazine* (New York: Abrams, 1991);

Pagan Kennedy, *Platforms: A Microwaved Cultural Chronicle of the 1970s* (New York: St. Martin's Press, 1994);

Suzanne Levine and Harriet Lyons, and others, *The Decade of Women: A* Ms. *History of the Seventies in Words and Pictures* (New York: Paragon, 1980).

ROOTS AND THE BIRTH OF THE MINISERIES

Roots. One of the biggest media successes of the 1970s was the television miniseries. Such shows, essentially made-for-television movies influenced by the British "limited series," extended over more than two nights and attracted millions of viewers. One of the first popular miniseries, ABC's *Rich Man, Poor Man* (1976), showed that such programming could work. No miniseries was more successful, however, than *Roots.*

Breaking Records. Broadcast in January 1977 over eight successive nights, the twelve-hour *Roots* was based on the nonfiction book by Alex Haley in which he traces his family history from its African origins through years of slavery and emancipation. Featuring an impressive cast (including John Amos, Ed Asner, Maya Angelou, Chuck Connors, Louis Gossett, Jr., Lorne Greene, O. J. Simpson, Cicely Tyson, Leslie Uggams, Ben Vereen, and newcomer LeVar Burton) and a vast historical sweep, *Roots* captivated an estimated 130 million viewers, with some episodes breaking viewer records. Ordinary people and even members of Congress changed their schedules for a week in order not to miss the next installment. In all the excitement *Roots* quietly broke new ground in American television by briefly showing bare-breasted women, the first time a prime-time network other than PBS offered frontal nudity. A fourteen-hour sequel, *Roots: The Next Generations,* which aired in February 1979 and starred James Earl Jones as Haley, was also successful.

The Sincerest Form of Flattery. Other networks soon followed suit with a host of imitations of varying quality. NBC showed its acclaimed four-part miniseries *Holocaust* in April the following year. The network claimed that 120 million people watched the show in whole or in part. Both *Holocaust* and *Roots* achieved further successes with syndication around the world. *Roots* also had a significant cultural impact in driving Haley's book to the best-seller lists and spurring an unprecedented interest in genealogy.

Sources:

Erik Barnouw, *Tube of Plenty: The Evolution of American Television,* revised edition (New York & Oxford: Oxford University Press, 1990);

Andrew J. Edelstein and Kevin McDonough, *The Seventies: From Hot Pants to Hot Tubs* (New York: Dutton, 1990);

J. Fred MacDonald, *Blacks and White TV: African Americans in Television since 1948,* second edition (Chicago: Nelson-Hall, 1992);

Vincent Terrace, *Television, 1970–1980* (San Diego: A. S. Barnes /London: Tantivy, 1981).

SATURDAY-MORNING TELEVISION

Animation Rules. Saturday-morning television had been devoted to children's programming almost since the introduction of the medium, but the nature of the programming changed gradually over the decades. By the 1970s Saturday-morning television was virtually dominated by animated shows, many of them revivals of older features such as the Warner Bros. cartoons featuring

Cicely Tyson and Maya Angelou in the scene depicting the birth of Kunta Kinte, the main character of *Roots,* a twelve-hour miniseries broadcast broadcast on eight consecutive nights by ABC in January 1977

Bugs Bunny, Daffy Duck, and other characters. One of the most popular new characters, the Pink Panther (premiered 1969), was created by Blake Edwards and featured music by Henry Mancini.

Cartoon Relevance. PBS's *Sesame Street* proved that education and entertainment were compatible in children's television. On the commercial networks some producers attempted to follow suit with socially conscious cartoons. In 1973, for instance, ABC introduced *Schoolhouse Rock,* a series of animated shorts on grammar, mathematics, and history. One of the most successful efforts was CBS's *Fat Albert and the Cosby Kids,* introduced in 1972 and featuring Bill Cosby as a host who reinforced the moral at the end of each story. It set an industry trend in seeking input from educators and psychologists on each show's content. In general, children's programming during the 1970s became more sensitive to the social concerns of the decade. One area that resisted this trend was television violence, which increased in children's television during the decade just as it did in adult television, causing children's advocates to worry about the medium's potential for harm.

Live-Action's Last Stand. Live-action series, which constituted the bulk of Saturday-morning programming in earlier decades, held only a small percentage of the programs available. Superheroes appeared in the flesh, for instance, in shows such as *Shazam!,* *The Secrets of Isis,* and *Electro Woman and Dyna Girl.* One of the most popular of the live-action shows was Sid and Marty Krofft's *Land of the Lost,* about a family that finds itself in a strange prehistoric land after a rafting mishap.

Characters from the CBS Saturday-morning cartoon series *Fat Albert and the Cosby Kids,* created by Bill Cosby to provide palatable moral lessons for children

The Limits of Marketing. Saturday-morning television for children was also noteworthy during the 1970s for the reforms that were made in how products were pitched to young audiences. Advertisers had capitalized on children's programming since the early days of television, but they became especially aggressive in the 1960s. Responding to pressure from advertisers, the National Association of Broadcasters (NAB) set aside sixteen minutes of every hour for advertising on Saturdays, as opposed to the nine and a half minutes per hour found in prime time. Consumer groups such as Action for Children's Television (ACT) forced the NAB to drop this figure to twelve minutes in 1973 and to nine and a half minutes in 1976. Reformers also succeeded in banning television hosts or characters from selling products to kids. Furthermore, a 1974 statement issued by the FCC declared that television stations must include children's programming, part of which must be educational. Television deregulation under the Reagan administration lessened the impact of these reforms during the next decade, but the Children's Television Act of 1990 once again limited commercial time on children's shows and mandated that shows contain some amount of educational and informational material.

Sources:
Les Brown, *Les Brown's Encyclopedia of Television,* third edition (Detroit & London: Gale, 1992);

Gary H. Grossman, *Saturday Morning TV* (New York: Dell, 1981).

SEX AND THE MEDIA

Men's Magazines. Hugh Hefner's *Playboy,* founded in 1953, had dominated men's magazines featuring female nudity since the first years of its existence. By the 1970s the rise of hard-core porn, both in movies and in maga-zines, and the growth of new magazines such as *Gallery, Oui,* and *Hustler* posed a brief threat to its market position. The biggest challenge came from Bob Guccione's *Penthouse,* which began publishing in the United States in 1969.

The Porn Wars. *Penthouse* was less sophisticated than *Playboy* but more sophisticated than *Hustler.* And while *Penthouse* did not take its photography of genitalia to the extremes that *Hustler* did, it was more daring than *Playboy,* both in explicitness and in pictorials, and therefore posed a commercial threat to Hefner's magazine. Thus the porn wars began. *Playboy* did little to change its image, but it did begin offering fuller views of its famous Playmates.

Obscene or Just Offensive? Less acceptable to the public was the proliferation of pornographic movies during the decade. Local communities protested: in February 1973 a court in Tennessee indicted the producers of the movie *Deep Throat* on obscenity charges. In addition, a New York judge a month later declared the movie to be "irredeemably obscene." These court cases hinged on the question of whether erotic material or pornography was by definition essentially obscene or whether obscenity was relative and dependent upon community standards. Most observers argued that obscenity was a matter of community opinion, but throughout the decade verdicts were delivered based on the argument that such material was fundamentally obscene, as in the 1977 judgment against *Hustler* publisher Larry Flynt.

Sex, American Style. Despite such judgments erotic material extended into every medium of American culture. Indeed, during the 1970s the erotic/pornographic novel entered the publishing mainstream with books such as Erica Jong's *Fear of Flying* (1973), Jacqueline Susann's *Once Is Not Enough* (1973), and a new breed of romance novels sometimes described as "bodice rippers." Even pornographic movies such as *Behind the Green Door* and *Deep Throat* were shown in many theaters, and Bernardo Bertolucci's *Last Tango in Paris* (1973), starring Marlon Brando, combined explicit erotic content with art-film aesthetics. Television was naturally far tamer in its use of sex, but it did use sex in a manner far more suggestive than it had before, prompting concerned citizens and lawmakers to criticize the amount of sex (along with violence) on the small screen. Their protests were usually in vain.

Sources:
John D'Emilio and Estelle B. Freedman, *Intimate Matters: A History of Sexuality in America* (New York: Harper & Row, 1988);

Robert V. Hudson, *Mass Media: A Chronological Encyclopedia of Television, Radio, Motion Pictures, Magazines, Newspapers, and Books in the United States* (New York: Garland, 1987);

Amy Janello and Brennon Jones, *The American Magazine* (New York: Abrams, 1991).

THE RISE AND FALL OF FAMILY TIME

In April 1974 the National Association of Broadcasters (NAB), responding to public criticism of sex and violence on television and the threat of government intervention, established a two-hour slot in prime time set aside for family-oriented programs. At the urging of FCC chairman Richard Wiley and CBS representative Arthur Taylor, the NAB adopted a "family viewing policy" that set aside two hours in the prime-time schedule during which "entertainment programming inappropriate for viewing by a general family audience should not be broadcast."

While well-intentioned, the measure did not reduce the amount of sex and violence on the screen — it merely prompted networks to rearrange scheduling so that certain shows appeared at times other than "family time" or the "family hour," as the slot came to be known. Nonetheless, the creators of television programs were outraged by what they saw as a limitation of their freedom. One lawsuit challenging the policy was filed by the Writers Guild of America; another was filed by writer-producer Norman Lear, whose *All in the Family* clearly did not fit the family-time template and was moved from eight to nine o'clock. Another writer-producer, Larry Gelbart, was especially vocal in testifying on behalf of the Writers Guild, relating how CBS tried to pressure him to cut or revise the type of script material that had made *M*A*S*H* a favorite with audiences and critics alike. In court in 1976 family time was declared to be a violation of the First Amendment and was scrapped.

Sources: Erik Barnouw, *Tube of Plenty: The Evolution of American Television,* revised edition (New York & Oxford: Oxford University Press, 1990);

Geoffrey Cowan, *See No Evil: The Backstage Battle over Sex and Violence on Television* (New York: Simon & Schuster, 1978).

TO MARKET, TO MARKET: COMIC BOOKS IN THE BEST OF TIMES, THE WORST OF TIMES

The End of the Silver Age. The 1960s was a flourishing decade for comic books in the United States, its so-called silver age. Begun by DC Comics in the late 1950s, the silver age of comics was spurred by the impressive successes in the 1960s of Marvel Comics, which revolutionized the medium by introducing characters with realistic personal problems in story lines that continued from issue to issue. But by the end of the decade interest in superheroes, which had driven the silver age, was declining, and it was not obvious what would take its place in the market. For comic books the early 1970s represented the end of one era, and the late 1970s ushered in a comic-book renaissance that continued into the 1980s.

A New Direction. Besides the fact that there was a glut of superheroes during the 1960s, it was hard for many to take such characters seriously after the success of ABC's *Batman* (1966–1969), whose campy treatment of the character made the superhero appear comic rather than dramatic. After following suit in its own Batman comics, DC reversed direction in the early 1970s thanks to the work of two young creators, writer Denny O'Neil and artist Neal Adams. The team was assigned to DC's *Green Lantern* (which also featured the character Green Arrow). They quickly began addressing contemporary issues such as drug abuse, prejudice, and ecology, ushering in a new wave of relevance to comics. Marvel soon engaged such topics, leading to a noteworthy showdown between comics publishers and their self-imposed production code in 1971. Both *Green Lantern* issues 85 and 86 (September–November) and Marvel's *The Amazing Spider-Man* issues 95–97 (April–June) addressed the heretofore forbidden issue of drug abuse. These comics came into conflict with the Comics Code Authority for portraying drug use and its effects despite the fact that the writers came down heavily against drugs. The code was established by the comics industry in the mid 1950s in response to intense criticism about the contents of the magazines, and one thing that the code prohibited was any depiction of drug use. *Green Lantern* received the Comics Code Authority "stamp," but *The Amazing Spider-Man* was published without it, the first time a mainstream comic defied the authority of the code. As a result the code was modified so that such topics could be addressed. At the same time the code was revised to allow for more violence and the freer use of horror elements. The year 1972 witnessed a rebirth of the horror comic; the best example was DC's *Swamp Thing* by Len Wein and Berni Wrightson.

Changes in the Market. Perhaps the most significant development in the comic-book industry during the 1970s had to do not with content but with commerce. The best-selling titles of the major publishers — Archie, Charlton, DC, Gold Key, Harvey, and Marvel — routinely sold hundreds of thousands of copies per issue. There was little competition, however, and by 1974 these six publishers were the only ones left in the industry. A new company, Atlas/Seaboard, was started in 1975, but it folded by the end of the year. This domination would be short-lived. In 1977 *Cerebus the Aardvark,* begun by Canadian writer and artist Dave Sim as a parody of the successful Conan comics of the 1970s, became the first regularly published comic book to be published and distributed independently. It paved the way for an explosion of independent comics companies in the late 1970s and the 1980s. Such comics were rarely available on newsstands and in drug stores — until this period the most popular places to buy comics — but they could often be

THE SHOCKING TRUTH ABOUT DRUGS!

Cover for the *Green Lantern* 85 (September 1971), which defied the Comics Code Authority restriction on depicting drug use but nonetheless received its approval

found in shops specializing in comics. Such shops constituted another major shift in the comics market. While they made comics more available, they also had the effect of promoting comics collecting, which drove up prices for back issues considerably.

Things to Come. Two other novelties in comic books were introduced in the late 1970s that would have a considerable influence on the market in the years to come. The first "graphic novel" — a book-length comic published in book form — appeared in 1978 with *Empire,* written by science-fiction author Samuel R. Delany and illustrated by Howard Chaykin. Published by Berkley, the graphic novel appeared in bookstores as well as with more traditional comics. The second new idea, the comic-book miniseries, may have taken its inspiration from the phenomenally successful television miniseries *Roots* and from Marvel's adaptation of the enormously successful 1977 film *Star Wars.* DC was first with the three-issue *World of Krypton* in 1979; many others soon followed. During the 1980s and early 1990s many comics would be published in separate issues as a miniseries and then published in book form as a graphic novel, allowing companies nearly to double their profits for a single comic.

Sources:

Mike Benton, *The Comic Book in America: An Illustrated History,* revised edition (Dallas: Taylor, 1993);

Will Jacobs and Gerald Jones, *The Comic Book Heroes from the Silver Age to the Present* (New York: Crown, 1985).

HEADLINE MAKERS

CARL BERNSTEIN AND BOB WOODWARD

1944- ; 1943-

NEWSPAPER JOURNALISTS

From Newspaper Reporters to Media Stars. Between the 1972 Watergate break-in and the 1974 resignation of President Richard M. Nixon, two reporters for the *Washington Post,* Bob Woodward and Carl Bernstein, were acclaimed for their investigative journalism. As a result of their exposure of the Watergate affair, they became subjects of media attention themselves, and their success spurred a revival of investigative reporting in the United States. As Ben Bradlee, their editor, observed in 1975, "They're part of American folklore now. Everybody knows their names." Their book *All the President's Men* (1974) was a best-seller and became the basis for a well-known film two years later in which they were portrayed, respectively, by Robert Redford and Dustin Hoffman.

Different Backgrounds. Bob Woodward grew up the son of a lawyer in conservative Wheaton, Illinois, and attended Yale University on a Naval ROTC scholarship. The son of liberal Jewish parents, Carl Bernstein grew up in the greater Washington, D.C., area and began working after high school as a copyboy for the *Washington Star.* During the 1960s Bernstein worked his way up to reporter, beginning work for the *Washington Post* in 1966, while Woodward completed his education at Yale, served on an aircraft carrier after graduation, and worked in communications at the Pentagon. In 1970 Woodward started working as a reporter for the *Montgomery County*

Sentinel of Rockville, Maryland. He was hired by the *Washington Post* a year later.

"Woodstein." Woodward, unlike the volatile Bernstein, soon earned the confidence of executive editor Bradlee, who assigned Woodward to help on the story about the 17 June 1972 break-in at the Democratic Party headquarters at the Watergate complex. Bernstein was also working on the story, and they were mentioned, with six other reporters, at the end of the first Watergate story, written by Alfred Lewis, that appeared in the *Washington Post* on 18 June. The following day their first joint story was published, beginning a long series of collaborative investigative reporting in which they tenaciously tracked down sources and worked seven days a week, twelve to eighteen hours a day, to build an obscure story into a national obsession. Bit by bit, "Woodstein" (as the team became known at the newspaper), with the assistance of city editor Barry Sussman, linked the burglary to members of the Committee to Reelect the President (CREEP), revealing in the process that the organization had received approval from White House officials. In 1972 Woodward and Bernstein were among the recipients of the prestigious George Polk Memorial Award for outstanding achievements in journalism. They also won the Pulitzer Prize.

Fame and Fortune. The pair worked on writing *All the President's Men* in the latter half of 1973. They received a $55,000 advance from Simon & Schuster, $25,000 for a serialization in *Playboy* in May and June 1974, and $30,000 from the Book-of-the-Month Club. Released exactly two years after the Watergate break-in, it remained on *The New York Times* best-seller list for fifteen weeks. Avon Books paid $1 million for paperback rights, the most paid for a nonfiction paperback book at the time. While a popular and critical success, some critics have argued that the book took creative license with the actual events. Others believe the critically acclaimed and commercially successful movie went even further. In 1974 Robert Redford's production company paid nearly half a million dollars for the film rights to *All the President's Men,* which featured Jason Robards as Bradlee, Hal Holbrook as Woodward's anonymous source "Deep

Throat," Dustin Hoffman as Bernstein, and Redford as Woodward.

Separate Ways. The two reporters wrote a less successful 1976 book on Nixon's fall, *The Final Days,* whose title accurately describes their own professional relationship. Bernstein resigned from the *Washington Post* in 1976 to write books and freelance articles for periodicals such as *Rolling Stone;* he also worked for ABC from 1979 to 1983. Woodward also worked on books but remained at the newspaper, becoming assistant managing editor of the metro section in 1979. Woodward aided Bernstein in the latter's book about his youth, called *Loyalties* (1989).

Sources:

Adrian Havill, *Deep Truth: The Lives of Bob Woodward and Carl Bernstein* (New York: Birch Lane Press, 1993);

Carl Bernstein and Bob Woodward, *All the President's Men* (New York: Simon & Schuster, 1974).

HELEN GURLEY BROWN

1922-

MAGAZINE EDITOR AND WRITER

A Model for Women. During the 1970s there were several examples in the media of the independent, liberated woman, including Mary Tyler Moore, Gloria Steinem, and Helen Gurley Brown. Having worked her way up from humble beginnings to become editor in chief of a major magazine, Brown exemplified a combination of ambition, intelligence, and open sensuality that her magazine, *Cosmopolitan,* mirrored. Without being ideological in intent, *Cosmopolitan* injected its own brand of feminism into American culture thanks to Brown. Every year between 1976 and 1981 the *World Almanac* included her as one of the twenty-five most influential women in the country. In 1988 she was inducted into the Publishers' Hall of Fame.

Starting at the Bottom. Helen Gurley was born in Green Forest, Arkansas. After attending a business college she worked as a secretary for several entertainment companies. In 1948 she joined Foote, Cone, and Belding, an advertising agency, and worked her way up to copywriter. By 1959, when she married movie producer David Brown, she was a successful advertising copywriter but wanted something more. In 1962 she completed her first book, *Sex and the Single Girl,* which became an instant best-seller. Based on her own experiences as a working woman, the book championed career women and argued that women could still be attractive after thirty — at a time when American women were expected to marry young and tie their identities to their husbands.

Cosmopolitan. After working as a newspaper columnist, in 1965 Brown became editor in chief of *Cosmopolitan,* one of America's oldest magazines (it was founded as a general-interest magazine in 1886) which had been commercially successful until the early 1960s. With no prior magazine experience, Brown single-handedly redefined the image of the magazine, directing it toward "Cosmo girls" — envisioned as independent, youthful (if not young) women with careers outside the home who were interested in fashion, current events, and great sex. The Cosmo girl, in other words, was a counterpart to the target reader of Hugh Hefner's *Playboy.* (However, apart from a famous nude spread of Burt Reynolds, *Cosmopolitan* did not typically include nude pictorial features.) Under Brown's guidance the magazine exemplified one version of contemporary feminism but stood in contrast to Steinem's more intellectual *Ms.,* founded in 1972, which was more concerned with political change than beauty tips and sex. The magazine prospered despite the claims of some feminists that the image of the Cosmo girl, taken to the nth degree with the beautiful women on each cover, played to male fantasies and that the magazine's celebration of physical attractiveness was detrimental to women. By 1990, when Brown celebrated her twenty-fifth anniversary with the periodical, *Cosmopolitan* was being distributed to seventy countries.

Feminist Backlash. During the 1970s hard-line feminists proved the magazine's toughest critics. Many feminists were uncomfortable, for instance, with Brown's suggestion that a woman's attractiveness could help her succeed in business. In 1970 feminist activists, including literary critic Kate Millett, staged a sit-in at the *Cosmopolitan* offices. Some feminists were bothered that the magazine did not use its large circulation to promote more explicitly feminist ideas, while others considered its articles on finding men a slap in the face to the women's movement. Brown took the objections in stride, later arguing that "a feminist believes in equality for men and women" and that "a woman should be free to develop every facet of her life and talent without interference." However, she added, "I also think a feminist should accept it if a woman doesn't want to realize her potential." True to the laissez-faire spirit of her magazine, Brown opposed the consciousness-raising efforts of more militant feminists. While still not accepted by many feminists, *Cosmopolitan* nevertheless gained the respect of such activists as Betty Friedan and Steinem by the 1980s.

Sources:

Lucille Falkof, *Helen Gurley Brown: The Queen of "Cosmopolitan"* (Ada, Okla.: Garrett Educational Corporation, 1992);

Amy Janello and Brennon Jones, *The American Magazine* (New York: Abrams, 1991).

JIM HENSON

1936-1990

MUPPETEER, DIRECTOR, AND PRODUCER

Gentle Genius. During the 1970s Jim Henson was hailed as one of the most creative entertainers working in television. PBS's *Sesame Street,* begun in 1969, was an enormous success, in no small part due to Henson's puppet characters, the Muppets. *The Muppet Show* (1976–1981), a program featuring characters Henson had made famous on *Sesame Street,* along with new characters, was the most successful syndicated television program of the decade. A gentle, soft-spoken, hardworking man with a keen sense of humor, Henson expressed himself best through his Muppets, particularly Kermit the Frog and Rowlf the Dog.

An Early Start. Just out of high school, Henson got his first job in television in 1954, working as a puppeteer on a local television show in Maryland. His second show, *Sam and Friends,* lasted from 1955 to 1961. During this period Henson introduced a new technique in television puppetry: instead of televising a traditional puppet theater, as had been done in the past, he and his fellow performers watched their puppets on television monitors as they performed, thus creating a greater sense of immediacy. He also used camera tricks to do new stunts. In early television commercials featuring Henson's Muppets, he introduced the first full-body Muppet, the La Choy dragon — a precursor to his famous full-body Muppet Big Bird.

Becoming Established. In 1959 Henson introduced his most famous creation, Kermit (not yet a frog), made from his mother's old coat and halves of a ping-pong ball. This and other Henson creations that followed combined puppetry with the movable limbs of some kinds of marionettes, hence the name *Muppets.* By the early 1960s the Muppets were appearing on the *Today* morning program and *The Tonight Show,* and Rowlf the Dog was a regular on *The Jimmy Dean Show* (1963–1966), which gave Henson practice in playing his Muppets against live performers. While working in television, he made a short film called *Timepiece* (1965) that was nominated for an Academy Award. However, he was best known in television.

The Big Break. In 1969 Henson's Muppets were featured on a new educational program called *Sesame Street,* produced by the Children's Television Workshop for public television. Though the show offered an entertaining mix of animation and live characters from the beginning, Henson's Muppets were likely the driving force behind the show's popularity. During the 1970s his creations — including Kermit the Frog, Bert and Ernie, Big Bird, the Cookie Monster, and Oscar the Grouch — became household names among American children as well as those in the other countries to which *Sesame Street* spread. Henson's most frequent collaborator, Frank Oz, was responsible for creating the personalities of several of the characters. The use of humor on the show that both children and adults could appreciate proved crucial in Henson's next venture.

Ready for Prime Time. Interested in reaching a larger audience, Henson made *The Muppet Valentine Special* in 1974. Like the future *Muppet Show,* it featured one guest star (Mia Farrow) interacting with Muppets on an elevated set that allowed for greater character action than a conventional puppet theater, an innovation Henson perfected on *Sesame Street.* In 1975 his Muppets appeared as guests on television programs and in specials. A new set of Henson creations appeared regularly during the first season of *Saturday Night Live* (1975–1976). But Henson wanted his own show. In March 1975 a pilot, jokingly called *The Muppet Show: Sex and Violence,* was broadcast, but it lacked two things that helped the later show's success: a human guest star and Kermit the Frog as host. ABC, which broadcast the pilot, decided not to pick it up as a series. CBS passed as well. It was finally supported by ITC, an American branch of the British Associated Communications Corporation, as a syndicated show to be sold for the 7:30–8:00 P.M. time slot newly opened to local stations by the Federal Communications Commission. *The Muppet Show* was produced in England, and by its second season it had become a hit in the United States. The weekly program was a variety show about a variety show run by Muppets, with a different human guest star each week. In 1978 *The Muppet Show* won its first Emmy award; before it left the air, after its fifth season, it won two more. By this time the program was being broadcast in more than one hundred countries.

Later Ventures. Henson expanded his horizons once again in 1979 with *The Muppet Movie,* which he produced, based on the characters from the show. During the 1980s he was involved in other films, some featuring his Muppets, others utilizing his increasingly sophisticated puppetry. He remained active in television with new shows such as *Fraggle Rock, Muppet Babies,* and *The Jim Henson Hour.* He also marketed his Muppets through various publishing, recording, and licensing ventures. By 1989 Henson's empire was worth $150 million, the amount Disney reportedly offered to purchase it. Before the deal was finalized Henson unexpectedly died of acute pneumonia at age fifty-three. His son Brian inherited his father's mantle and completed a different deal with Disney that maintained the autonomy of Jim Henson Productions.

Source:
Christopher Finch, *Jim Henson: The Works — The Art, the Magic, the Imagination* (New York: Random House, 1993).

NORMAN LEAR

1922-

TELEVISION PRODUCER

Television Innovator. Before the 1970s American television comedies were mostly formulaic shows that presented a largely idealized portrait of middle-class life. One example is the popular program *The Brady Bunch*, which ran from 1969 to 1974. Even during the turbulent 1960s, situation comedies failed to reflect what life was like for most American families. During the 1970s, however, many creators in the media sought to introduce a greater degree of relevance into their work. One of the most prominent — and controversial — to do so in television was Norman Lear. His many successes during the 1970s changed the nature of much American television comedy.

Finding a Niche. Lear began his television career in the mid 1950s as a comedy writer. In 1959 he formed a production company, Tandem, with director Bud Yorkin. They produced theater films during the 1960s; achieving little success, they turned their efforts toward television in 1970 with *All in the Family*, the program with which Lear is most often associated. Lear wrote the script for the pilot episodes, in which he set the pattern for the series (at first called "Those Were the Days") by using references to contemporary issues and previously forbidden language. ABC rejected the pilots in 1969, but in 1970 CBS bought the series as a midseason replacement.

America's Most Likable Bigot. *All in the Family* premiered in January 1971. Based on the British comedy *Till Death Do Us Part*, Lear's show went boldly where no U.S. television show had gone before: into a more realistic yet satiric portrait of a working-class family who argued over such contemporary topics as racism, sexism, sexual issues, and pacifism. The nominal head of the family, based on Lear's own father, was world-class bigot Archie Bunker (played by Carroll O'Connor). His loudmouthed, ultra-conservative views were countered by his not-too-bright but good-hearted wife Edith (Jean Stapleton); their activist daughter Gloria (Sally Struthers); and Gloria's liberal husband Mike (Rob Reiner). What made these clashes so shocking for many was the language Archie used to express his ideas. For instance, Archie referred to blacks as "jungle bunnies" who lived on welfare and craved fried chicken and ribs. While Lear obviously intended Archie to appear as wrongheaded, with his arguments countered by the rest of his family, many women and minority viewers nonetheless found his declamations offensive. Moreover, while Archie was portrayed as narrow-minded, he was also funny and even likable to many viewers, which some critics believed counteracted the show's liberal intent. At any rate *All in the Family* got

people talking, which is to Lear's credit. The program, though it got off to a slow start, was successful and enjoyed a long run. Struthers and Reiner left in 1978, and Stapleton's character last appeared during the 1979–1980 season, when the show was renamed *Archie's Place*. The program broadcast its last new episode in 1983. As an ironic touch, Lear's short-lived program *704 Hauser* (1994) featured a black character living in Archie's old house.

Good Intentions. The success of *All in the Family* prompted Lear and Yorkin to create similar shows. These included *Sanford and Son* (1972–1977), about a cantankerous black junk man and his liberal son, and *Maude* (1972–1978), a spin-off from *All in the Family* about Archie's liberal cousin (played by Beatrice Arthur). One episode of the show was particularly controversial: the fortyish Maude announced that she was pregnant and going to have an abortion. Other Lear spin-offs included the black-cast sitcoms *The Jeffersons* (1975–1985) and *Good Times* (1974–1979). In 1974 he helped create another production company, TAT, this time with Jerry Perenchio. Through TAT Lear scored another considerable success with *Mary Hartman, Mary Hartman* (1976–1977), a syndicated send-up of soap operas that starred Louise Lasser as a demented homemaker surrounded by an equally demented set of characters.

Bad Results. While Lear was the most successful television producer of the 1970s, he was by no means immune to failures, which increased in number during the 1980s and early 1990s. His business enterprises of the 1980s also enjoyed mixed results. Lear achieved more success with the organization People for the American Way, which he helped to found in the early 1980s to counter the efforts of the religious Right to influence American media and politics.

Sources:

Richard P. Adler, *All in the Family: A Critical Appraisal* (New York: Praeger, 1979);

Geoffrey Cowan, *See No Evil: The Backstage Battle over Sex and Violence on Television* (New York: Simon & Schuster, 1979);

Donna McCrohan, *Archie & Edith, Mike & Gloria Revisited: A Retrospective Appreciation of All in the Family* (New York: Workman, 1987).

MARY TYLER MOORE

1937-

TELEVISION ACTRESS

The New Woman. In many ways the 1970s was the decade of the television sitcom. While programs such as *All in the Family* and *M*A*S*H* revolutionized the form, many viewers and critics believed that *The Mary Tyler Moore Show* (1970–1977) perfected it. As the clean-cut heart of the show, Moore's character, Mary Richards, exemplified a new image for American women: intelligent and professional yet personable, looking for love but not tying her self-image to a prospective husband and family. As *TV Guide* put it in 1973, "Thirty-three, unmarried and unworried — Mary is the liberated woman's ideal." Rather than preaching, the show used an effective blend of humor and everyday life to depict the lives of a career woman and her friends.

Building a Show. In the 1960s Moore played Laura Petrie on *The Dick Van Dyke Show* and had appeared in a few movies; by 1970 she was ready to have her own show. She worked with her husband, Grant Tinker, who was then a television producer, and writers Allan Burns and James L. Brooks. The result was a sitcom with its center of focus being Mary Richards, an assistant news producer for a television station in Minneapolis. The show's creators originally intended to make the single Mary divorced, but CBS was afraid of losing viewers. (Moore herself filed for divorce from Tinker in 1980.) She was supported by an effective ensemble cast. It included Valerie Harper as Rhoda Morgenstern, Mary's best friend; Ed Asner as Lou Grant, Mary's gruff but supportive boss; Cloris Leachman as Phyllis Lindstrom, Mary's strong-willed landlady; Ted Knight as Ted Baxter, a self-absorbed news anchorman; Gavin MacLeod as the wisecracking Murray Slaughter, a news writer and a frustrated creative writer; Georgia Engel as Georgette Franklin, a good-hearted dumb blonde introduced in the third season; and Betty White as the wacky, sex-starved co-worker Sue Ann Nivens, introduced in the fourth season.

Success. Such a diverse cast of characters allowed the writers to pursue a wide range of topics, from relationships and marriage to career fulfillment to weight loss. In addition to such subjects, to which viewers could easily relate, *The Mary Tyler Moore Show* succeeded because of its realism. Characters had problems that could not be resolved in the space of thirty minutes; characters had sex lives, about which they worried and were occasionally obsessed; and, as in many other sitcoms after it, characters found a second family in the world of work. Success came easily to the Saturday-night show, which by 1971 had become so popular that, as a writer for *The New York Times Magazine* noted, "Mary is so In . . . it has become fashionable to drift into the den at a party or even to go home at 9 on Saturday because you simply must not miss this program." By the decision of its creators the program ended in 1977 while still at the top of its form.

Later Efforts. In the late 1970s Moore attempted two comedy-variety programs, *Mary* and *The Mary Tyler Moore Hour*. Neither won over audiences or network executives, but the success of *The Mary Tyler Moore Show* enabled MTM Productions, Moore's production company with Tinker, to gain a foothold as one of the most prosperous of such companies in television thanks to programs such as *Rhoda, Lou Grant* (both spin-offs of *The Mary Tyler Moore Show*), and *The Bob Newhart Show.*

(Tinker left MTM in 1981, when he became president of NBC.) Moore won an Emmy for her performance in the television movie *First, You Cry* (1978), about television journalist Betty Rollin's bout with breast cancer and surgery. During the 1980s and 1990s Moore appeared in several other made-for-television movies as well as theatrical films. In 1994 she was inducted into the Comedy Hall of Fame.

Sources:

Robert S. Alley and Irby B. Brown, *Love Is All Around: The Making of "The Mary Tyler Moore Show"* (New York: Delta, 1989);

Jason Bonderoff, *Mary Tyler Moore* (New York: St. Martin's Press, 1986);

Andrew J. Edelstein and Kevin McDonough, *The Seventies: From Hot Pants to Hot Tubs* (New York: Dutton, 1990).

GLORIA STEINEM

1934-

MAGAZINE WRITER AND EDITOR

From Writer to Editor. Gloria Steinem entered the 1970s as an admired magazine writer and ended the decade as one of the most respected and influential magazine editors of the decade. Her involvement with *Ms.*, which she helped to found in 1972 and which she edited for the next fifteen years, placed her at the forefront of the growing feminist movement in the United States.

The Path to Feminism. Steinem was born in Toledo, Ohio. She attended Smith College, where she was Phi Beta Kappa, and she also studied in India. During the 1960s she worked as a freelance journalist. Her 1963 breakthrough article in *Show*, about her undercover experience as a Playboy Bunny, led to assignments for high-profile magazines such as *Cosmopolitan* and *Vogue*. While a supporter of the civil rights movement, for most of the 1960s Steinem was not an active feminist. In 1968 she began writing columns on politics for *New York* magazine, which she helped Clay Felker to establish. The following year she surprised her readers and colleagues with positive articles on abortion rights and feminism.

The Founding of an Institution. The backlash against her feminist articles only propelled Steinem further into the women's movement. In 1971 she worked with Bella Abzug, Shirley Chisholm, and Betty Friedan to create the National Women's Political Caucus, which would promote feminist issues and encourage women to run for political office. Steinem also became interested in creating a magazine by and for women that would address their concerns. *Ms.* first appeared as a thirty-page supplement in the 20 December 1971 issue of *New York*. The following month it appeared as a magazine in its own right and was greeted with phenomenal sales. With former *Look* editor Patricia Carbine as publisher and

Steinem as editor in chief and frequent contributor, *Ms.* became one of the most successful and most discussed magazines of the decade and beyond.

Public Image. Steinem's impact on American feminism extended beyond the magazine. Her articulateness and (despite feminists' fight against the objectification of women based on appearance) her attractiveness won several supporters who might otherwise have objected to the often-controversial notions she espoused. A classical liberal feminist, she promoted equal rights and equal pay for women, claiming that the full liberation of women from conventional roles would liberate men as well. In Steinem the American public found a nonthreatening, even congenial, proponent of a set of ideas that some segments of the public resisted.

Books. Steinem's 1983 essay collection *Outrageous Acts and Everyday Rebellions* was a best-seller; it contains twenty years of her work, including her recollection of her developing feminism. She also wrote a biography of Marilyn Monroe in 1986. She left *Ms.* in 1987 when the magazine was sold to an Australian company; three years later it regained its independence. Since then Steinem has continued to write on feminism and self-esteem.

Source:
Mark Hoff, *Gloria Steinem: The Women's Movement* (Brookfield, Conn.: New Directions/Millbrook Press, 1991).

GARRY TRUDEAU

1948-

CARTOONIST

A Remarkable Achievement. Garry Trudeau was the most notable — and often the most controversial — cartoonist of the 1970s. His comic strip, "Doonesbury," simultaneously poked fun at and commented on the various sacred cows of American life. As President Gerald Ford remarked in a 1975 speech to the Radio and Television Correspondents Association, "There are only three major vehicles to keep us informed as to what is going on in Washington: the electronic media, the print media and *Doonesbury* . . . not necessarily in that order." Trudeau's was the first comic strip ever to receive the Pulitzer Prize.

From Yale to the United States. Born in New York, Trudeau attended Yale University, where he got his start in the late 1960s drawing for the student newspaper a comic strip, "Bull Tales," that held campus administrators up to scrutiny and ridicule. He started graduate school, but the new Universal Press Syndicate, created by James Andrews and John McMeel, offered him a contract to pen a new cartoon expanding on his established characters. His retooled strip, renamed for its most prominent character, debuted in nearly thirty newspapers, including the *Washington Post,* in 1970.

Success. "Doonesbury" soon became widely known and widely syndicated. Though some newspapers dropped it due to Trudeau's no-holds-barred lampoons of contemporary politics (in particular his satiric treatment of U.S. involvement in the Vietnam War) and culture, which some readers failed to find either humorous or enlightening, other newspapers kept the strip or picked it up because their readers demanded it. By the time Trudeau received the Pulitzer Prize in 1975, "Doonesbury" appeared in more than four hundred newspapers and had an estimated forty million readers. Much in demand as a speaker on college campuses and as a contributor to magazines such as *Rolling Stone* and *Harper's,* Trudeau nonetheless managed to keep a low profile. However, he did travel with the press corps during President Ford's 1975 visit to China. He also insisted that his characters not be used in merchandising or advertising.

Older but Still Sharp. While "Doonesbury" still remains controversial — with newspapers sometimes moving it to the editorial page, occasionally dropping selected segments, and with subscribers periodically threatening to cancel — in 1994 the strip appeared in approximately nine hundred newspapers across the United States. Trudeau has also published book collections of "Doonesbury" cartoons since the early 1970s. Though still an intensely private man, he has eased gradually into the public eye since his 1980 marriage to television journalist Jane Pauley.

Sources:
Ron Goulart, ed., *The Encyclopedia of American Comics* (New York & Oxford: Facts on File, 1990);
"New Look on the Funny Pages," *Newsweek* (5 March 1973): 76–77.

TED TURNER

1938-

TELEVISION EXECUTIVE

Cable Visionary. More than any other figure in American television, Ted Turner saw the potential inherent in cable television in its early days and developed that potential into a communications empire. The local successes the confident, flamboyant Turner enjoyed in cable during the 1970s foreshadowed his international successes in the next decade. He also gained media attention in 1977 as captain of the winning ship, *Courageous,* in the America's Cup. In addition to being called "the Mouth of the South," Turner has since been called Captain Courageous or, sometimes, Captain Outrageous.

Small Beginnings. Following the suicide of his father in 1960, Turner became the head of his family's billboard company in Atlanta, but only after going into debt to save the business from changing hands. During the next ten years he turned the company into a prosperous advertising firm called Turner Communications Group (TCG). In 1970 TCG bought an independent Atlanta UHF station, which it renamed WTCG. An early proponent of cable, Turner turned to the comparatively new technology to have his station (later renamed WTBS) carried throughout the South.

Superstation. By the mid 1970s Turner was wealthy enough to purchase the Atlanta Braves baseball team and to own a considerable portion of the Atlanta Hawks basketball team. In 1976 he began supplementing WTBS's twenty-four-hour lineup of television and movie repeats with an increased amount of sporting events. Late in 1976 the station began sending its signal via satellite to cable stations across the country. By the end of the 1970s Turner's innovative superstation was one of the best-known cable networks in America, reaching three million viewers in addition to cable subscribers in six southern states.

CNN and Beyond. For all the gambles that paid off during the decade, the 1970s proved a mere stepping-stone to Turner's greater achievements, such as the twenty-four-hour Cable News Network (CNN), which began broadcasting in 1980, and Turner Network Television (TNT), which began in 1986; both made him a billionaire. In 1986 he purchased M-G-M/United Artists, along with its film library, and earned the scorn of many film buffs by colorizing old black-and-white movies. In 1991 he purchased Hanna-Barbera, providing material for his new Cartoon Channel. That same year he was *Time* magazine's Man of the Year, and in 1992 he again grabbed headlines by marrying actress Jane Fonda after a two-year relationship.

Sources:
Porter Bibb, *It Ain't As Easy As It Looks: Ted Turner's Amazing Story* (New York: Crown, 1993);

Christian Williams, *Lead, Follow or Get Out of the Way: The Story of Ted Turner* (New York: Times Books, 1981).

PEOPLE IN THE NEWS

Between 1977 and 1981 **Steve Allen** impressed viewers and critics with his PBS series *Meeting of the Minds,* which he wrote and hosted. The show offered round-table talks between historical figures, such as Benjamin Franklin and Cleopatra, played by actors.

1st Lt. William L. Calley gave a series of interviews with *Esquire* in 1970. The following year he was convicted of murder for having ordered the 1968 massacre of civilians in My Lai, Vietnam.

Chapters of **Truman Capote's** projected novel "Answered Prayers" appeared in *Esquire* in 1975 and 1976. Capote drew on friends' confidences and took revenge on enemies, thinking no one would know the real identities of his characters. He nonetheless became unpopular in literary and social circles as a result of the *Esquire* excerpts.

President **Jimmy Carter** was interviewed by *Playboy* in 1976, leading many of his fellow evangelicals to criticize him for consenting to talk with a magazine specializing in nude photographs.

During the first season of ABC's *Charlie's Angels,* actress **Farrah Fawcett-Majors** noted, "When the show was No. 3, I figured it was our acting. When it got to be No. 1, I decided it could only be because none of us wears a bra."

Through the PBS program *Evening at Pops,* conductor **Arthur Fiedler** made the Boston Pops Orchestra the best-known pops orchestra in the United States from the show's premiere in 1970 to his death in 1979. **John Williams** took up Fiedler's baton in 1980.

The year 1973 was good to **Bob Fosse:** in addition to an Academy Award for directing *Cabaret* and two Antoinette Perry (Tony) Awards for directing and choreographing *Pippin,* he won three Emmy Awards for producing, directing, and choreographing a television special on Liza Minnelli called *Liza with a Z.*

David Frost interviewed former president **Richard M. Nixon** in 1977 in five hour-long shows; Nixon received one million dollars.

In 1974 *Washington Post* publisher **Katharine Graham** became the first woman to be asked to join the Associated Press board.

Willie Morris, editor of *Harper's* magazine, lost his job due to negative fallout from the March 1971 issue, which published **Norman Mailer**'s critique of feminism, "Prisoner of Sex." Nonetheless, that issue of the magazine set a single-issue sales record for the publication up to that time.

On 23 February 1976 **Daniel Schorr** severed his relationship with CBS News under pressure after twenty-three years of service after he had leaked information about a secret document from the House of Representatives and passed it on for publication in the *Village Voice*. He later became a news commentator for National Public Radio.

On 6 April 1973 a Los Angeles court awarded **Tom** and **Dick Smothers** $776,300 in damages from CBS, which had canceled their successful but controversial show in April 1969 after the comedy duo publicly argued with the network over its efforts to limit the satiric content of *The Smothers Brothers Comedy Hour,* first broadcast in 1967. The network claimed the pair failed to fulfill the requirements of their contract, but the press agreed with the Smothers Brothers that censorship was the real reason for the cancellation.

In April 1976 **Barbara Walters** received a five-year, $5-million contract from ABC, making her the first female anchor of a network television news program and the highest-paid journalist in history.

AWARDS

EMMY AWARDS

1970

Outstanding Dramatic Series: *Marcus Welby, M.D.* (ABC)

Outstanding Comedy Series: *My World and Welcome to It* (NBC)

Outstanding Variety Series: *The David Frost Show* (syndicated)

1971

Outstanding Dramatic Series: "The Senator" segment of *The Bold Ones* (NBC)

Outstanding Comedy Series: *All in the Family* (CBS)

Outstanding Variety Series — Musical: *The Flip Wilson Show* (NBC)

Outstanding Variety Series — Talk: *The David Frost Show* (syndicated)

1972

Outstanding Dramatic Series: *Elizabeth R* on *Masterpiece Theater* (PBS)

Outstanding Comedy Series: *All in the Family* (CBS)

Outstanding Variety Series — Musical: *The Carol Burnett Show* (CBS)

Outstanding Variety Series — Talk: *The Dick Cavett Show* (ABC)

1973

Outstanding Dramatic Series: *The Waltons* (CBS)

Outstanding Comedy Series: *All in the Family* (CBS)

Outstanding Variety Series: *The Julie Andrews Hour* (ABC)

1974

Outstanding Dramatic Series: *Upstairs, Downstairs* on *Masterpiece Theater* (PBS)

Outstanding Comedy Series: *M*A*S*H* (CBS)

Outstanding Variety Series: *The Carol Burnett Show* (CBS)

1975

Outstanding Dramatic Series: *Upstairs, Downstairs* on *Masterpiece Theater* (PBS)

Outstanding Comedy Series: *The Mary Tyler Moore Show* (CBS)

Outstanding Variety Series: *The Carol Burnett Show* (CBS)

1976

Outstanding Dramatic Series: *Police Story* (NBC)

Outstanding Comedy Series: *The Mary Tyler Moore Show* (CBS)

Outstanding Variety Series: *NBC's Saturday Night Live* (NBC)

1977

Outstanding Dramatic Series: *Upstairs, Downstairs* on *Masterpiece Theater* (PBS)

Outstanding Comedy Series: *The Mary Tyler Moore Show* (CBS)

Outstanding Variety Series: *Van Dyke and Company* (NBC)

1978

Outstanding Dramatic Series: *The Rockford Files* (NBC)

Outstanding Comedy Series: *All in the Family* (CBS)

Outstanding Variety Series: *The Muppet Show* (syndicated)

1979

Outstanding Dramatic Series: *Lou Grant* (CBS)

Outstanding Comedy Series: *Taxi* (ABC)

Outstanding Variety Program: *Steve & Eydie Celebrate Irving Berlin* (NBC)

PULITZER PRIZES FOR JOURNALISM

1970

Public Service: *Newsday*

National Reporting: William J. Eaton, *Chicago Daily News*

International Reporting: Seymour M. Hersh, Dispatch News Service

Local Reporting: Thomas Fitzpatrick, *Chicago Sun-Times*

Editorial Writing: Philip L. Geyelin, *Washington Post*

Editorial Cartoons: Thomas F. Darcy, *Newsday*

1971

Public Service: *Winston-Salem* (N.C.) *Journal & Sentinel*

National Reporting: Lucinda Franks and Thomas Powers, United Press International

International Reporting: Jimmie Lee Hoagland, *Washington Post*

Local Reporting: *Akron* (Ohio) *Beacon Journal*

Editorial Writing: Horace G. Davis, Jr., *Gainesville* (Fla.) *Sun*

Editorial Cartoons: Paul Conrad, *Los Angeles Times*

1972

Public Service: *The New York Times*

National Reporting: Jack Anderson, United Feature Syndicate

International Reporting: Peter R. Kann, *Wall Street Journal*

Local Reporting: Richard Cooper and John Machacek, *Rochester* (N.Y.) *Times-Union*

Editorial Writing: John Strohmeyer, *Bethlehem* (Pa.) *Globe-Times*

Editorial Cartoons: Jeffrey K. MacNelly, *Richmond* (Va.) *News-Leader*

1973

Public Service: *Washington Post*

National Reporting: Robert Boyd and Clark Hoyt, Knight Newspapers

International Reporting: Max Frankel, *The New York Times*

Local Reporting: *Chicago Tribune*

Editorial Writing: Roger B. Linscott, *Berkshire Eagle* (Pittsfield, Mass.)

Editorial Cartoons: No award

1974

Public Service: *Newsday*

National Reporting: James R. Polk, *Washington* (D.C.) *Star-News*, and Jack White, *Providence* (R.I.) *Journal-Bulletin*

International Reporting: Hedrick Smith, *The New York Times*

Local Reporting: Hugh F. Hough and Arthur M. Petacque, *Chicago Sun-Times*

Editorial Writing: F. Gilman Spencer, *Trenton* (N.J.) *Trentonian*

Editorial Cartoons: Paul Szep, *Boston Globe*

1975

Public Service: *Boston Globe*

National Reporting: Donald L. Bartlett and James B. Steele, *Philadelphia Inquirer*

International Reporting: William Mullen and Ovie Carter, *Chicago Tribune*

Local Reporting: *Xenia* (Ohio) *Daily Gazette*

Editorial Writing: John D. Maurice, *Charleston* (W.Va.) *Daily Mail*

Editorial Cartoons: Garry Trudeau, Universal Press Syndicate

1976

Public Service: *Anchorage Daily News*

National Reporting: James Risser, *Des Moines Register*

International Reporting: Sydney H. Schanberg, *The New York Times*

Local Reporting: Gene Miller, *Miami Herald*

Editorial Writing: Philip Kerby, *Los Angeles Times*

Editorial Cartoons: Tony Auth, *Philadelphia Inquirer*

1977

Public Service: *Lufkin* (Tex.) *News*

National Reporting: Walter Mears, Associated Press

International Reporting: No award

Local Reporting: Margo Huston, *Milwaukee Journal*

Editorial Writing: Warren L. Lerude, Foster Church, and Norman F. Cardoza, *Reno Evening Gazette and Nevada State Journal*

Editorial Cartoons: Paul Szep, *Boston Globe*

1978

Public Service: *Philadelphia Inquirer*

National Reporting: Gaylord D. Shaw, *Los Angeles Times*

International Reporting: Henry Kamm, *The New York Times*

Local Reporting: Richard Whitt, *Louisville* (Ky.) *Courier-Journal*

Editorial Writing: Meg Greenfield, *Washington Post*

Editorial Cartoons: Jeffrey K. MacNelly, *Richmond* (Va.) *News-Leader*

1979

Public Service: *Point Reyes* (Cal.) *Light*

National Reporting: James Risser, *Des Moines Register*

International Reporting: Richard Ben Cramer, *Philadelphia Inquirer*

Local Reporting: *San Diego Evening Tribune*

Editorial Writing: Edwin M. Yoder, *Washington* (D.C.) *Star*

Editorial Cartoons: Herbert L. Block, *Washington Post*

DEATHS

Bud Abbott, 78, of the comedy team Abbott and Costello, 24 April 1974.

Carl W. Ackerman, 80, former dean of the Columbia School of Journalism, 9 October 1970.

David Akeman, 57, television and country-music stage comedian known as Stringbean, 11 November 1973.

Eben Alexander, 79, former managing editor of *Time* magazine, 30 October 1978.

Stewart Alsop, 60, political columnist, 26 May 1974.

Edward Anthony, 76, former publisher of *Collier's* magazine, 17 August 1971.

John J. Anthony, 68, radio advisor, 16 July 1970.

Hamilton Fish Armstrong, 80, founder of *Foreign Affairs* magazine, 24 April 1973.

George Baker, 59, creator of comic character Sad Sack, 9 May 1975.

John Banner, 63, television actor, 28 January 1973.

Perry Barlow, cartoonist for *The New Yorker,* 26 December 1977.

Herbert A. Bell, 79, radio pioneer, 30 January 1970.

Jack Benny, 80, radio and television comedian, 20 December 1974.

Walter Berndt, 79, cartoonist, 13 August 1979.

Carl Betz, 56, television actor, 18 January 1978.

Bruce Bliven, 87, former editor of the *New Republic,* 27 May 1977.

Dan Blocker, 43, best known as Hoss on the long-running television program *Bonanza,* 13 May 1972.

Margaret Bourke-White, 67, respected photojournalist, 27 August 1971.

Heloise Bowles, 58, wrote successful "Hints from Heloise" syndicated newspaper column, 28 December 1977.

William Boyd, 74, movie and television actor, 12 September 1972.

Hal Boyle, 63, Pulitzer Prize–winning journalist, 2 April 1974.

Martin Michael Branner, 81, creator of the "Winnie Winkle" comic strip, 19 May 1970.

Dave Breger, 61, cartoonist who coined the term *GI Joe,* 16 January 1970.

Geraldine Brooks, 52, stage, film, and television actress, 19 June 1977.

Edgar Buchanan, 76, movie and television actor, 4 April 1979.

Sebastian Cabot, 59, television actor, 23 August 1977.

John W. Campbell, Jr., 61, influential editor of *Analog* (formerly *Astounding Science Fiction*), 11 July 1971.

Al Capp, 70, creator of the "L'il Abner" comic strip, 5 November 1979.

Hodding Carter, Jr., 65, Mississippi newspaper editor who won the Pulitzer Prize for his antisegregation editorials, 4 April 1972.

Bennett A. Cerf, 73, founding partner of Random House and panelist on television's *What's My Line?,* 27 August 1971.

Norman Chandler, 74, former publisher of the *Los Angeles Times,* 20 October 1973.

Lee J. Cobb, 64, stage, film, and television actor, 11 February 1976.

Robert Considine, 68, journalist and radio and television commentator, 25 September 1975.

Charles J. Correll, 82, played Andy on radio's *Amos 'n' Andy,* 26 September 1972.

Rev. Charles Coughlin, 88, controversial religious radio commentator and celebrated anti-Communist preacher, 27 October 1979.

Louis Cowan, 66, former president of CBS-TV, 18 November 1976.

James M. Cox, 71, newspaper and broadcasting executive, 27 October 1974.

Wally Cox, 48, television actor, 15 February 1973.

Bob Crane, 49, star of television's *Hogan's Heroes,* 29 June 1978.

Roy Crane, 75, cartoonist who created Captain Easy and other characters, 7 July 1977.

Jay Hanna ("Dizzy") Dean, 63, former pitcher and baseball announcer, 17 July 1974.

Virginia O'Hanlon Douglas, 81, whose 1897 letter to the *New York Sun* prompted the response, "Yes, Virginia, there is a Santa Claus," 13 May 1971.

Alan Dunn, 73, cartoonist for *The New Yorker,* 20 May 1974.

Beatrice Fairfax (Marion C. McCarroll), 84, wrote syndicated "Advice to the Lovelorn" column, 4 August 1977.

Philo T. Farnsworth, 64, television technology pioneer, 11 March 1971.

Roger K. Fawcett, 69, magazine and book publisher, 3 October 1979.

Janet ("Genet") Flanner, 86, author and frequent contributor to *The New Yorker,* 7 November 1978.

Doris Fleeson, 69, newspaper columnist, 1 August 1970.

Max Fleischer, 89, creator of the comic and cartoon character Popeye, 11 September 1972.

Joe Flynn, 49, film and television actor, 18 July 1974.

Edward H. ("Senator") Ford, 83, vaudeville and radio comedian, 27 January 1970.

William Gallagher, 52, Pulitzer Prize–winning photographer, 28 September 1975.

Will Geer, 76, television actor, 22 April 1978.

Bruce Geller, 47, television writer and producer, 21 May 1978.

Arnold Gingrich, 72, founder and former editor of *Esquire,* 9 July 1976.

Ralph J. Gleason, 58, journalist, cofounder and editor of *Rolling Stone* magazine, 3 June 1975.

Rube Goldberg, 87, cartoonist whose humorously impractical inventions bear his name, 7 December 1970.

Jane Grant, 80, instrumental with first husband Harold Ross in founding of *The New Yorker,* 16 March 1972.

Ben Grauer, 68, radio reporter, 31 May 1977.

William H. Grimes, 79, former editor of the *Wall Street Journal,* 14 January 1972.

Harry F. Guggenheim, 80, founder of *Newsday,* 22 January 1971.

Jean Hagen, 54, movie and television actress, 29 August 1977.

Phillippe Halsman, 73, Latvian-born photographer who created more than one hundred covers for *Life*, 25 June 1979.

Gabriel Heatter, 81, radio broadcaster, 30 March 1972.

Ben Hibbs, 73, former editor of the *Saturday Evening Post*, 29 March 1975.

Al Hodge, 66, actor who played the Green Hornet on radio and Captain Video on television, 19 March 1979.

Eric Hodgins, 71, author and former publisher of *Fortune* magazine, 7 January 1971.

William Hopper, 55, television actor, 6 March 1970.

Palmer Hoyt, 82, editor and publisher of the *Denver Post* (1946–1971), 25 June 1979.

Chet Huntley, 62, television newscaster and coanchor with David Brinkley of the NBC evening news, 20 March 1974.

Crocker Johnson, 68, creator of the comic strip "Barnaby," 11 July 1975.

Earl J. Johnson, 73, longtime editor with United Press International, 3 January 1974.

Mary Anissa Jones, 18, television actress, 28 August 1976.

Victor O. Jones, 64, former executive editor of the *Boston Globe*, 21 April 1970.

Emmett Kelly, 80, famous clown, 28 March 1979.

Stephen E. Kelly, 58, magazine publisher, 6 April 1978.

Walt Kelly, 60, creator of the acclaimed comic strip "Pogo," 18 October 1973.

Walter Kiernan, 75, newspaper, radio, and television commentator, 8 January 1978.

Freda Kirchwey, 82, former editor and publisher of *The Nation*, 3 January 1976.

Arthur Krock, 87, journalist, 12 April 1974.

David Lawrence, 84, founder and editor of *U.S. News and World Report*, 11 February 1973.

Oscar Levant, 72, pianist and sardonic film, radio, and television personality, 14 August 1972.

Walter Lippmann, 85, prominent political journalist and columnist, 14 December 1974.

Guy Lombardo, 75, bandleader famous for New Year's Eve broadcasts, 5 November 1977.

Jim Lucas, 56, Pulitzer Prize–winning journalist, 21 July 1970.

Ted Mack, host of television's *Original Amateur Hour*, 12 July 1976.

Hal March, 49, actor and television emcee, 19 January 1970.

Lester Markel, 83, longtime Sunday editor of *The New York Times*, 23 October 1977.

Frank V. Martinek, 75, creator of comic-strip character Don Winslow, 22 February 1971.

Groucho Marx, 86, stage and film comedian with the Marx Brothers, host of television's *You Bet Your Life*, 20 August 1977.

Mary Margaret McBride, 76, radio talk-show host, 7 April 1976.

George B. ("The Real") McCoy, 72, radio personality, 22 December 1976.

Frank McGee, 52, television host of NBC's *Today*, 17 April 1974.

Paul McGrath, 74, radio actor, 13 April 1978.

Benjamin M. McKelway, 80, former editor of the *Washington* (D.C.) *Star* and president of the Associated Press, 30 August 1976.

Sal Mineo, 37, stage, film, and television actor, 12 February 1976.

Bob Montana, 54, creator of Archie comic books, 4 January 1975.

Claudia Morgan, 62, actress who played Nora Charles on the radio program *The Thin Man*, 17 September 1974.

Jane Morgan, 91, vaudeville, radio, and television actress, 2 January 1972.

Morris, 17, finicky cat of well-known television commercials, 7 July 1978.

Bret Morrison, 66, actor who played the Shadow on the radio during the 1930s and 1940s, 25 September 1978.

Malcolm Muir, 93, book and magazine publisher, 30 January 1979.

Joe Musial, 72, cartoonist and comic-book artist, 6 June 1977.

Ozzie Nelson, radio and television star of *The Adventures of Ozzie and Harriet*, 3 June 1975.

Samuel I. Newhouse, 84, newspaper, magazine, and broadcasting magnate, 29 August 1979.

Virginia Payne, 66, actress who played Ma Perkins on radio, 10 February 1977.

Mary Petty, 77, cartoonist for *The New Yorker*, 6 March 1976.

Ed Platt, 58, television actor, 20 March 1974.

Clilan Powell, 83, former editor and publisher of the *New York Amsterdam News*, 22 September 1977.

Freddie Prinze, 22, television actor and comedian, 29 January 1977.

Joe Pyne, 44, television talk-show host, 23 March 1970.

Alan Reed, 69, actor who provided the voice of Fred on *The Flintstones,* 14 June 1977.

Carol Reed, 44, television personality, 4 June 1970.

Helen Rogers Reid, 87, former publisher of the *New York Herald Tribune,* 27 July 1970.

Norman Rockwell, 84, popular artist who created many covers for the *Saturday Evening Post,* 8 November 1978.

Rufus C. Rose, 70, creator of the television marionette Howdy Doody, 29 May 1975.

Irene Ryan, 70, actress who played Granny on *The Beverly Hillbillies,* 26 April 1973.

Robb Sagendorph, 69, publisher of the *Old Farmer's Almanac,* 4 July 1970.

David Sarnoff, 80, radio and television pioneer, former head of RCA and NBC, 12 December 1971.

Carl M. Saunders, 83, Pulitzer Prize–winning editor for the 1949 editorial suggesting a national day of prayer, 2 October 1974.

Gilbert Seldes, 77, author and critic, 29 September 1970.

Rod Serling, 50, Emmy Award–winning television writer and host of *The Twilight Zone,* 28 June 1975.

Archbishop Fulton J. Sheen, 84, author known for the 1950s television program *Life Is Worth Living,* 9 December 1979.

Merriman Smith, 57, newspaper journalist, 13 April 1970.

Otto Soglow, 74, cartoonist, 3 April 1975.

Jack Soo, 63, television actor, 11 January 1979.

George H. Soule, Jr., 82, editor of the *New Republic* (1924–1947), 14 April 1970.

Robert G. Spivak, 55, syndicated columnist, 25 June 1970.

Inger Stevens, 35, television actress, 30 April 1970.

Ed Sullivan, 73, host of the long-lived television variety program *The Ed Sullivan Show,* 13 October 1974.

Frank Sutton, 51, television actor who played Sergeant Carter on *Gomer Pyle, USMC,* 28 June 1974.

James Swinnerton, 98, newspaper cartoonist, 5 September 1974.

Paul H. Terry, 84, creator of Mighty Mouse, Heckle and Jeckle, and other animated characters, 25 October 1971.

William Todman, 63, television game-show producer, 29 July 1979.

George W. Trendle, 87, radio producer, 10 May 1972.

Lionel Trilling, 70, professor and literary critic, 5 November 1975.

Vivian Vance, 68, television actress, 17 August 1979.

Amy Vanderbilt, 66, etiquette columnist, 27 December 1974.

Jimmy Wallington, 64, radio announcer, 21 December 1972.

Edmund Wilson, 77, man of letters, 12 June 1972.

Walter Winchell, 74, distinctive radio broadcaster and gossip columnist, 20 February 1972.

Frederick E. Woltman, 65, Pulitzer Prize–winning reporter, 5 March 1970.

Ruth Cornwall Woodman, 75, radio writer, 2 April 1970.

Carlton G. Young, 64, radio actor, 11 July 1971.

Chic Young, 72, creator of the comic strip "Blondie," 14 March 1972.

PUBLICATIONS

Elliot Anderson and Mary Kinzie, eds., *The Little Magazine in America: A Modern Documentary History* (Yonkers, N.Y.: Pushcart Press, 1978);

Robert Campbell, *The Golden Years of Broadcasting: A Celebration of the First 50 Years of Radio and TV on NBC* (New York: Scribners, 1976);

Geoffrey Cowan, *See No Evil: The Backstage Battle over Sex and Violence on Television* (New York: Simon & Schuster, 1979);

Timothy Crouse, *The Boys on the Bus* (New York: Random House, 1972);

Les Daniels, *Comix: A History of Comic Books in America* (New York: Crown, 1971);

Harlan Ellison, *The Glass Teat: Essays of Opinion on Television* (New York: Ace, 1970);

Ellison, *The Other Glass Teat: Further Essays on Opinion on Television* (New York: Pyramid, 1975);

George N. Gordon, *The Communications Revolution: A History of Mass Media in the United States* (New York: Hastings House, 1977);

Jeff Greenfield, *Television: The First Fifty Years* (New York: Abrams, 1977);

Ernest C. Hynds, *American Newspapers in the 1970s* (New York: Hastings House, 1975);

Gerald S. Lesser, *Children and Television: Lessons from Sesame Street* (New York: Random House, 1974);

Dick Lupoff and Don Thompson, eds., *All in Color for a Dime* (New Rochelle, N.Y.: Arlington House, 1970);

David T. MacFarland, *The Development of the Top 40 Radio Format* (New York: Arno, 1979);

Kevin McAuliffe, *The Great American Newspaper* (New York: Scribners, 1978);

Robert Metz, *CBS: Reflections in a Bloodshot Eye* (New York: Playboy Press, 1975);

James Monaco, *Media Culture: Television, Radio, Records, Books, Magazines, Newspapers, Movies* (New York: Dell, 1978);

James Steranko, *The Steranko History of Comics,* 2 volumes (Reading, Pa.: Supergraphics, 1970, 1972);

Marie Winn, *The Plug-In Drug* (New York: Viking, 1977);

Tom Wolfe and E. W. Johnson, eds., *The New Journalism* (New York: Harper & Row, 1973);

Broadcasting, periodical;

Editor and Publisher, periodical;

Television Age, periodical;

TV Guide, periodical.

William Frazee, press chief for the *Washington Post,* after the Supreme Court approves publication of the Pentagon Papers, 1 July 1971

MEDICINE
AND
HEALTH

by JOAN LAXSON

CONTENTS

Sidebars and tables are listed in italics.

1970

- Congress passes the Occupational Safety and Health Act.

- Hospital-care costs in the United States reach an average of $81 per patient per day, with average patient costs of $664.28 per stay.

- The first nerve transplant is performed.

- The first synthesis of an artificial gene is accomplished.

- The Food and Drug Administration (FDA) warns that birth-control pills may produce blood clots.

1 July The most liberal abortion law in the United States goes into effect in the state of New York.

23 July The nutritional content of U.S. breakfast cereals comes under fire before the Senate Commerce Committee.

28 Oct. The FDA orders the makers of baby food to label the nutritional value of their products.

15 Dec. The FDA announces that, at a minimum, nearly one million cans of tuna fish have been removed from the market as a precaution because tests indicated mercury contamination.

23 Dec. The FDA announces that excessive amounts of mercury have been found in 89 percent of samples of frozen swordfish tested, and nearly all brands sold in the United States have been removed from the market.

30 Dec. Congress passes the Poison Prevention Packaging Act, requiring manufacturers of potentially dangerous products to put safety tops on their containers so children will not be able to open them. The law takes effect in 1972.

1971

- The diamond-bladed scalpel is introduced in surgery.

- The first heart and lung transplants are performed.

- Britain's Royal College of Physicians reports that cigarette smoking has become a cause of death comparable to the great epidemic diseases of typhoid and cholera in the nineteenth century.

- Cigarette advertising on U.S. radio and television is banned.

- Researchers at the Anderson Tumor Institute in Texas isolate the cold-sore herpes virus from the lymph cell–cancer known as Burkitt's lymphoma.

Jan. The human growth hormone is synthesized at the University of California at Berkeley.

18 Mar. Soft contact lenses win FDA approval.

Nov. U.S. physicians receive an FDA warning against administering diethylstilbestrol (DES) to pregnant women because of the increased risk of vaginal cancer in their daughters.

24 Dec. President Richard Nixon signs into law the National Cancer Act, authorizing appropriations of $1.5 billion per year to combat the national second leading cause of death.

1972

- The National Academy of Sciences suggests that air pollution probably explains the tendency of city dwellers to suffer twice the rural rate of cancer.

10 Jan. The Surgeon General's Report on smoking warns that nonsmokers exposed to cigarette smoke may suffer health hazards.

10 Mar. The FDA orders the lowering of lead content in all household paints, toys, and other articles to no more than .5 percent after 31 December, and to no more than .06 percent after 31 December 1973. Fifty thousand to one hundred thousand children a year require treatment for lead poisoning.

14 Mar. The Department of Agriculture reports that 1.25 million chickens were destroyed in Maine after high polychlorinated biphenyls (PCBs) were found in some of them. Contaminated feed was believed to be the source.

17 Mar. The FDA publishes proposed limits on the use of PCBs. After sixty days these chemicals could not be used in plants producing food, animal feed, or food packaging and would be banned from recycled paper. The chemicals were implicated in skin irritations, liver damage, and birth defects.

26 May A patient undergoing a skin graft in New York City is anesthetized by acupuncture.

8 Dec. The FDA reports that antibiotic overuse results in tens of thousands of unnecessary deaths in the United States each year. Overuse leads to the development of immune strains of bacteria and causes a major wave of hospital blood poisoning from superinfections.

13 Dec. The FDA announces a proposal to restrict the amounts of vitamins A and D sold in over-the-counter products. Overdoses could retard children's growth, cause liver and spleen enlargement, or increase calcium deposits, leading to hypertension and kidney failure.

1973

- The American Psychiatric Association removes homosexuality from its list of mental illnesses, redefining it as a "sexual orientation disturbance."

- The birth rate slips below the 2.1 child-per-woman ratio required for the natural replacement of the population and remains about 1.8 for the remainder of the decade.

- The Boston Women's Health Collective publishes *Our Bodies, Ourselves,* which becomes an immensely popular book directed at women's health issues and needs.

- Congress passes the HMO Act, regulating Health Maintenance Organizations.

8 Jan. The American Hospital Association releases a twelve-point patients' bill of rights intended to "contribute to more effective patient care and greater satisfaction for the patient, his physician, and the hospital organization."

22 Jan. The U.S. Supreme Court's *Roe* v. *Wade* decision provides women with a Constitutional guarantee of abortion rights.

9 Mar. Scientists at the Medical College of Wisconsin report substantial concentrations of carbon monoxide in the blood of Americans living in metropolitan areas, especially among cigarette smokers.

11 Mar. The FDA recalls all products containing mushrooms from a mushroom company in Ohio because the botulism toxin was found in one lot of cans on retail shelves.

5 Apr. The Center for Disease Control reports that forty-seven Americans were stricken with botulism over the past two years, ten of whom died.

20 Apr. The state of Nevada sets up a state-licensing system for acupuncture therapists.

1974

- The computerized axial tomography (CAT) scanner gains wide use.

- Dentists are warned about exposing patients to excessive radiation through too-frequent use of dental X rays.

- The Manufacturing Chemists Association releases evidence showing vinyl chloride, a plastic used in bottling, is linked to human cancer.

- The National Academy of Sciences urges a temporary ban on recombinant DNA experiments.

- U.S. insurance companies raise rates on malpractice policies, forcing physicians' fees and hospital rates to rise.

Jan.–June A smallpox epidemic takes thirty thousand lives in India.

Feb. The contamination of chicken feed by the pesticides aldrin and dieldrin force the killing of thousands of chickens in Mississippi.

6 Feb. President Nixon describes national health insurance as "an idea whose time has come in America."

June The Heimlich maneuver is introduced as first aid for choking.

12 Aug. President Gerald Ford asks Congress for passage of national health insurance.

1975

- A Cornell University study claims two to four million needless operations a year cause some twelve thousand deaths. One-third of all hysterectomies and tonsilectomies are probably unnecessary.

- Lyme disease is identified in Lyme, Connecticut.

- Mexican authorities spray marijuana fields with the herbicide paraquat in a $35-million U.S.-funded program to wipe out the drug.

- Versions of antibodies produced by the body are first manufactured in the laboratory.

- The first U.S. strike by doctors is carried out in New York City hospitals.

8 Jan. National Cancer Institute scientists announce the first human cancer virus ever isolated in an uncontaminated state. The newly found virus was obtained from a sixty-one-year-old woman suffering from acute myelogenous leukemia.

May California doctors organize a month-long strike to protest rising insurance costs and slowdowns in health care.

1 July Major malpractice insurance companies announce a tripling of doctors' premiums and a general cancellation of malpractice policies.

5 July   Researchers report that infants who died from sudden infant death syndrome or crib death show an abnormally low concentration of the enzyme PEPCK. The syndrome claims ten thousand lives annually.

28 Aug.   The FDA proposes to end the use of polyvinyl chloride for food packaging because of a potential cancer risk.

1976

- President Ford withdraws the administration's plan for national health insurance, saying it would make inflation worse.

- The General Accounting Office of Congress reports a startling program of sterilization of thousands of Native American women without their consent by the Indian Health Service.

- Karen Ann Quinlan's parents win a court fight to turn off the respirator keeping their comatose daughter alive.

- An outbreak of Legionnaires' disease occurs at the Philadelphia convention of the American Legion. Twenty-nine die.

- A swine-flu epidemic threatens the United States. Millions are vaccinated, but the warning turns out to be a false alarm.

- The FDA approves the use of inderal, a beta-blocker effective in treating high blood pressure.

- Perrier water is introduced to U.S. markets and gains in popularity as fitness-minded Americans switch from alcoholic beverages.

- A viral cause of multiple sclerosis is discovered.

23 June   The National Institutes of Health end the voluntary moratorium on recombinant DNA research but ban certain forms of genetic experimentation and tightly regulate others.

28 Aug.   A bacterial gene is constructed in the lab and implanted in a living cell where it functions normally, a breakthrough in genetic engineering.

16 Sept.   The Hyde Amendment clears Congress and bars use of federal funds for abortions "except where the life of the mother would be endangered if the fetus were brought to term."

13 Nov.   The World Health Organization (WHO) reports that Asia is free of smallpox for the first time in history.

1977

- The baby-food industry agrees to remove extra salt and sugar from its products.

- The National Center for Health Statistics announces death rates caused by strokes and cardiovascular disease declined significantly in the 1970s. Between 1969 and 1977 the death rate from heart disease declined 19.2 percent for men, 24.1 percent for women.

- Lung cancer deaths among U.S. women (14.9 per 100,000, up from 1.5 per 100,000 in 1930) surpass the number of colorectal-cancer deaths (14.3 per 100,000) and begin to approach the number of breast-cancer deaths.

- Balloon angioplasty is developed for reopening diseased arteries.

- U.S. scientists identify the previously unknown bacterium responsible for Legionnaires' disease.

- The U.S. Department of Agriculture attempts to reduce the amount of nitrates used by meat processors following reports that crisply fried bacon contains carcinogens.

- Saccharin intake comes under fire from the FDA, pointing out a potential link with bladder cancer.

- A life-threatening viral infection — herpes encephalitis — is successfully treated with a drug for the first time.

- President Jimmy Carter tries to contain hospital costs, but while his program passes the Senate, it dies in the House.

23 May   The first recombinant DNA product — human insulin — is produced.

2 July   The first magnetic resonance imaging (MRI) scanner is tested.

23 Aug.   A revolutionary new ulcer-treating drug, Tagamet (cimetidine), developed in Britain, wins FDA approval.

26 Oct.   The world's last known case of smallpox is reported in Somalia. Two years later the disease will be considered eradicated.

1978

- The Supreme Court rules against the legality of fixed racial quotas to assure the entry of a minimum number of minority students each year into the University of California Davis, medical school. It orders the admission of Allan Bakke, a white student denied admission despite higher grades than some successful minority applicants.

- A study of occupational health commissioned by the Department of Health, Education, and Welfare (HEW) concludes that at least 20 percent of all cancers in the United States "may be work related."

11 Jan.   The HEW secretary calls cigarette smoking "slow-motion suicide."

13 Jan.   The FDA requires blood intended for transfusions be labeled as coming from a paid donor or a volunteer donor. Blood from paid donors and commercial blood banks was found to cause hepatitis three to ten times more often than blood from volunteer donors.

17 Feb.   The FDA issues the first federal mandatory safety performance standard for equipment producing ultrasonic radiation used in physical-therapy treatments.

15 May   The U.S. Department of Agriculture issues regulations calling for a reduction in the use of nitrates in curing bacon. Sodium nitrate was found to produce lymph cancer in laboratory rats.

16 May   A Washington University scientific research team reports the possibility that panfrying hamburgers might increase the risk of cancer. The concern was with the heat, not the meat itself.

11 July   Estimates presented by experts before a House subcommittee suggest that mothers X-rayed needlessly during pregnancy produce seventy children a year who could be expected to develop cancer.

25 July   The world's first test-tube baby is born in London.

1979

- The escalating cost of Medicare-funded kidney dialysis treatment raises questions about how much the nation can afford without slighting other health needs.

20 Jan.   Officials of the Venereal Disease Control Division of the National Center for Disease Control report the antibiotic tetracycline in pill form is as effective as penicillin injections in treating gonorrhea.

11 Feb.   The Commerce Department reports that the output of U.S. cigarette manufacturers continues to increase despite cancer warnings.

19 Mar.   The American Heart Association says moderate consumption of alcoholic beverages may protect against death from heart disease.

25 June   The large-scale use of antibiotics in animal feeds makes bacteria more resistant to drugs and causes a growing risk to human health according to the Office of Technology Assessment, a research arm of Congress.

10 Sept.   A panel of doctors and former Valium users tells a Senate Human Resources health subcommittee that the drug, the most widely prescribed tranquilizer in the United States, is potentially addictive, even in moderate doses.

14 Sept.   A panel of national experts warns that women who took estrogen after menopause may have increased their risk of developing uterine cancer by as much as eight times. The group urges that the hormone be used in the smallest possible dose for the shortest possible time.

Oct.   Demonstrations by marijuana smokers in Washington, D.C. force the government to cut off support for the paraquat program after the Centers for Disease Control warns that cannabis tainted with paraquat may cause irreversible lung damage.

18 Nov.   The Centers for Disease Control reports that the incidence of gonorrhea has leveled off, but syphilis, a far more serious venereal disease, is on the increase.

OVERVIEW

A Crisis of Confidence. A crisis of confidence in the health-care-delivery system in the United States began and ended the decade of the 1970s. Although American medical science made spectacular advances and improvements in the overall American death rate and the infant and maternal mortality rates leveled off, the United States still lagged behind many other nations in these measures of health care. By the 1970s the medical and health industries became second only to the military industry in size and cost. Many inequalities in Americans' access to health care still existed. In March and April of 1971 hearings before the Subcommittee on Health of the Committee on Labor and Public Welfare of the U.S. Senate summarized five major problems in the health-care system:

1. maldistribution and shortage of health manpower;

2. inequality in health care and inequality in access to health care, including financing;

3. rising costs;

4. too little attention paid to keeping people well;

5. lack of coordination in the health-care system, resulting in waste and duplication.

A Shortage of Health Providers. By the beginning of the decade about 275,000 doctors in the United States were actually giving patient care, and there were many concerns about their distribution. Most concentrated in urban areas, and their increasing tendency to specialize made the shortage of physicians even more severe because specialists also concentrated in cities. A shortage no longer existed by the end of the decade because of expanding enrollments in medical schools and increases in the number of medical schools. By 1979, 399,000 physicians were actively giving patient care, but the number of specialists as opposed to primary-care physicians (family doctors) still remained an issue. Nurses increased in number from 700,000 to 1,075,000 over the decade.

Inequality in Health Care. In American society a person's state of health and chances of getting good medical care depended a lot on who that person was, how much money that person had, and where that person lived. The problems of poverty and ill health tended to be closely linked. Often, too, they were compounded by geography. Some rural areas had no care at all. Many American families had no health insurance protection, public or private, and many more had limited coverage.

Costs. Rising health-care costs were of great concern to American citizens and government officials. Financing of medical care in the United States was largely through a fee-for-service system partly covered by private health insurance, but in 1978 one in five families had no health insurance, and almost one in four were not covered for out-of-hospital costs. In 1970 Americans spent an average of $312 each for medical care, but by 1979 this more than doubled to $825 for each American. In 1969 a baby was delivered at Manhattan's New York Hospital-Cornell Medical Center for $350 in hospital bills, not including the obstetrician's fee. But by 1979 the same delivery in the same hospital cost twenty-eight hundred dollars — thirteen hundred dollars of which went to the hospital alone. In 1969 Massachusetts General Hospital in Boston charged $80 a day for a semiprivate room, but by 1979 costs rose to $189 a day. Total payments to doctors and hospitals averaged over $3,300 for a family of four during that same year. In 1979 half of all doctors made $65,000 or more a year. The highest paid specialists were hospital-based pathologists and radiologists whose median incomes in 1975 were $138,000 and $122,000 respectively. The median income for American families in general was $19,684 in 1979.

Prevention. The United States separated the practice of preventive medicine from curative medicine. Many who analyzed medicine and health in the 1970s saw this as part of the fragmentation of the medical system and an example of its lack of coordination. Before antibiotics and other drugs became commonplace, prevention was important because there were no cures. But following the introduction of such drugs, public health in the United States was given a secondary status, thus contributing to increased costs because a cure is nearly always more expensive than prevention. In some cases prevention may be the cure. The Framingham, Massachusetts, heart study showed half of all persons who died suddenly from heart attacks had no previous evidence of that disease detectable by doctors. The authors of the study concluded that the only way to reduce premature death from heart attack would be prevention of the underlying disease itself. Some experts thought this goal required major changes in the American lifestyle, not a typical emphasis of curative medicine in the 1970s.

System versus Nonsystem. The lack of coordination in the system and the expensive duplication of technology and services were also causes for concern. By 1979 health care in the United States was a vast conglomeration of large systems such as hospitals, the pharmaceutical, health insurance companies, and physicians and other health-care workers industry, Medicare and Medicaid (the government-sponsored health insurance programs for the elderly and poor). This vast system was uncoordinated and decentralized. All of its parts were conditioned to buy the best without worrying about cost, reflecting the American philosophy that nothing is too expensive where one's health was concerned.

Health Issues. Many health problems from previous decades existed in the 1970s. Diseases of the heart and arteries, including arteriosclerosis and hypertension, were still major concerns, as were cancer, mental health problems, and trauma-related injuries. During the early 1970s the shortage and expense of gasoline caused a temporary decline in automotive deaths and injuries. In a historic resolution of a fiercely controversial issue, the Supreme Court ruled in 1973 that the decision to have an abortion lies with a woman and her doctor during the first three months of pregnancy. Changing social customs caused a rise in the incidence of some venereal diseases such as syphilis; and addiction to narcotics and other drug abuse including alcoholism alarmed health-care workers, politicians, and the public. Epidemic diseases such as swine flu continued to be unpredictable threats, and new diseases such as the 1976 outbreak of Legionnaires' disease made their first appearances. The dread disease eventually to be known as acquired immune deficiency syndrome (AIDS) made its first documented appearance in the United States in 1978 when isolated cases of the disease now known as AIDS began to occur, although AIDS was not identified or given a name until several years later.

Technology and Science. The application of chemistry and physics continued to contribute to medical advances, as did the application of engineering. The computer contributed to several branches of medicine and created a virtual revolution in some areas of roentgenology such as computerized axial tomography (CAT) scanners and magnetic resonance imaging (MRI).

The Practice of Medicine. Most doctors practiced medicine privately in their own offices, with only 12 percent in group practices at the beginning of the decade.

Patient visits to doctors changed during the 1970s, with patient visits per doctor dropping from an average of 132.5 to 116.6 a week. This decline was due both to the increased number of physicians and to a declining use of physicians' services. Twenty-five percent of these physicians said they wanted to see more patients. The decade saw a real increase in prepaid, group health plans called health maintenance organizations (HMOs). From 1972 to 1979 the number of these plans increased from 133 to 225, with more than eight million subscribers. HMOs provided a wide range of medical benefits, including doctors' services and hospitalization, to subscribers and their families for a single prearranged monthly fee — regardless of how much medical care they actually used. This marked a big change from the old fee-for-service arrangement, in which a patient paid for each separate doctor's visit and service. The crisis in medical economics brought about the growth of these HMOs during the 1970s.

A Time of Change. During the 1970s scientific knowledge and technology continued to contribute to medicine and health, and the spread of specialty boards in all branches of medicine enriched the nation with highly qualified specialists, widely, if unequally, distributed. New or revised forms of medical practice became increasingly common: group practice, professional corporations, prepayment insurance plans, and HMOs. The American population was widely influenced by all the media and continued to be intensely interested in health. In medicine, as in most other spheres of activity, the participation and power of the government grew, including its participation in the sensitive issue of abortion. In 1974 President Richard M. Nixon described national health insurance as "an idea whose time has come in America," but cynics suggested this observation was intended merely as a distraction from his Watergate problems.

Sources:

Barbara J. Culliton, "Health Care Economics: The High Cost of Getting Well," *Scientific American,* 222 (April 1970): 883–885;

Stanley R. Garfield, "The Delivery of Medical Care," *Scientific American,* 222 (April 1970): 15–22;

"Health Costs: What Limit?," *Time* (28 May 1979): 60–68;

Saul Jarcho, M.D., and Gene Brown, eds., *Medicine and Health Care* (New York: The New York Times/Arno Press, 1977);

Jean Mayer, *Health* (New York: Van Nostrand, 1974);

Paul Starr, *The Social Transformation of American Medicine* (New York: Basic Books, 1982);

Statistical Abstracts of the U. S. (Washington, D.C.: U.S. Department of Commerce, Bureau of the Census, 1980);

Statistical Abstracts of the U. S. (Washington, D.C.: U.S. Department of Commerce, Bureau of the Census, 1981).

Demonstration in New York City urging liberalization of abortion laws

TOPICS IN THE NEWS

THE ABORTION CONTROVERSY

Roe v. Wade. On 22 January 1973 the Supreme Court of the United States handed down its ruling making abortion legal throughout the country. In a historic decision, *Roe* v. *Wade*, the Court drafted a new set of nationwide guidelines resulting in broadly liberalized abortion laws in the United States. Before the Supreme Court's decision, laws varied from state to state. Some states prohibited all abortions except those to save a mother's life. Others permitted abortions when a doctor found in "his best clinical judgment" that continued pregnancy would threaten the woman's life or health; if the fetus would be likely to be born defective; or if the pregnancy was the result of rape. The Supreme Court emphasized that this medical judgment should include all relevant factors: physical, emotional, psychological, familial, and the woman's age.

Limitations. The Court did not grant women unrestricted access to abortions. The decision to have an abortion during the first three months was to be made privately between the woman and her doctor, because during this period fewer women died from abortions than from normal childbirth. From this three-month period until the last ten weeks of pregnancy, the Court decreed, a state may regulate the abortion procedure by licensing and regulating abortion providers. Since the fetus is viable during the last ten weeks, the Court allowed any state to prohibit abortion during this period, if it wished, except where it might be necessary to preserve the life or health of the mother.

The Impact of Roe v. Wade. As legal abortions reduced the medical risks of the procedure, the number of recorded abortions rose; in 1974 nearly one million abortions were performed. Women between the ages of twenty and twenty-four had half of all abortions. The availability of abortions, combined with improvements in medical technology allowing evaluations of the chromosomal state of the unborn child, aided in reducing deformed fetuses. However, with this came the public's expectation of the "right" to have perfect children, and malpractice suits and insurance costs soared for obstetricians.

Sources:

Peter N. Carroll, *It Seemed Like Nothing Happened: The Tragedy and Promise of America in the 1970s* (New York: Holt, Rinehart & Winston, 1982);

Carol Emmens, *The Abortion Controversy* (New York: Julian Messner, 1987);

"High Court Rules Abortions Legal the First 3 Months," in *Medicine and Health Care*, edited by Saul Jarcho, M.D., and Gene Brown (New York: The New York Times/Arno Press, 1977), pp. 384–385.

ACUPUNCTURE

A Visit to China. In September 1971 Dr. Paul Dudley White of Massachusetts General Hospital, and Dr. E. Grey Dimond of the University of Missouri Medical School, along with their wives, were invited to the Peoples' Republic of China by the China Medical Association. When the western physicians expressed an interest in acupuncture, they were invited to witness several surgical procedures using this traditional form of Chinese medicine. Acupuncture involves the placement of needles at strategic points on the body as an anesthetic or to treat acute or chronic conditions. While acupuncture had been practiced for years among Chinese Americans, it was not until President Richard Nixon visited China in 1972 that this different means of treatment was publicized to other Americans.

How Does It Work? Dr. John W. C. Fox, a Brooklyn anesthesiologist, hypothesized that it worked on the "gate control" technique. According to his idea, sensations passing along peripheral neural fibers must pass through a "gate" in the spinal cord before they are transmitted to the brain. Pain is transmitted along relatively thin fibers and tends to keep the gate open. Acupuncture needles placed in these fibers override the pain sensation by producing a vibratory stimulus that closes the gate and blocks the transmission of pain to the brain. The traditional Chinese explanation is that vital forces pass through meridians or pathways throughout the body. The needles, when manipulated in precise ways, cause changes to take place within the meridians, and if this procedure is done correctly, the process restores the desired balance of heat and cold, or yin and yang, and the pain is anesthetized. "The classical balance between *yin*

Treatment diagram from a Peking institute of medicine showing acupuncture points

and *yang* is very poetic," said Dr. Fox, "but acupuncture can be explained in terms the Western scientists will accept."

Curiosity and Crackdown. After U.S. scientists brought back glowing reports of acupuncture's use in mainland China, acupuncture practices in the nation's Chinatowns were swamped with non-Chinese Americans wanting treatment. It did not take long for concern to be expressed about unlicensed practitioners. In the United States Chinese acupuncturists practiced without interference for years, although they were unlicensed by state medical boards. Many held medical degrees from Chinese institutions, but bad publicity from unscrupulous practitioners threatened their livelihoods. Various states set up systems for state licensing to regulate acupuncture. The Internal Revenue Service ruled that it was a deductible medical expense for income tax purposes — a sign the practice had gained mainstream recognition.

A Medical Fad. By the end of the decade at least one-quarter of the world's population used acupuncture for analgesia and treatment. It was incorporated to some degree in medical practice and training in many other countries, and in the People's Republic of China it was a routine part of the national health-care system. Its advocates maintained it could be used as an anesthetic in such procedures as open-heart surgery; and it effectively treated conditions such as the common cold, infectious hepatitis, acute appendicitis, toothache, schizophrenia, and migraines. Acupuncture therapists claimed it could even help someone quit smoking, but by 1979 the procedure was all but ignored in the United States.

Acupuncture and American Medical Values. Most Americans dismissed acupuncture because it fit poorly into the value system of American medicine. Acupuncture is an ancient and foreign tradition, a procedure at odds with the American concept of modern, scientifically based medicine. The procedure lacks the technological mystique of the white-coated scientist using complicated instruments to effect cures. There was, moreover, no major advocate of the procedure in the United States demanding clinical trials and laboratory experiments for the practice; and the commercial potential of acupuncture seemed unattractive to the medical industry. However, acupuncture has continued to exist quietly on the medical fringe, used by a small number of adherents as an alternative to Western medicine.

Sources:

"Acupuncture Crackdown," *Time* (18 September 1972): 55;

"Acupuncture U.S. Style," *Newsweek* (12 June 1972): 74;

E. Grey Dimond, M.D., "Acupuncture Anesthesia: Western Medicine and Chinese Traditional Medicine," *Saturday Evening Post* (Summer 1972): 70+;

Richard A. Kurtz and H. Paul Chalfant, *The Sociology of Medicine and Illness* (Boston: Allyn & Bacon, 1984).

Karen Ann Quinlan in 1972

THE CASE OF KAREN ANN QUINLAN

A Dangerous Cocktail. In an early hour of the morning of 15 April 1975, Julia and Joseph Quinlan of Landing, New Jersey, received the call every parent dreads. The nurse in the intensive-care unit at Newton Memorial Hospital called to tell them that their twenty-one-year-old adopted daughter, Karen, had been brought to the emergency room. That night Karen had been at a friend's birthday party, where she drank gin and tonics and swallowed tranquilizers. After she came home her roommates checked on her, and when they discovered she was not breathing, they called the police.

Coma. By the time her parents saw her, she had lapsed into a coma. The doctors believed her brain damage was caused by a lack of oxygen, and the damage was irreversible, but they were unsure of the exact reason she stopped breathing. They placed her on a respirator, but within days of her admission she began to assume a fetal position. Her family hoped she would come out of the coma, but as they saw the brain damage progressing, they realized there was no hope. Her father concluded, "I'm sure that with the mechanism [the respirator] she could continue in the state she's in, but that's not really living. She's just a vegetable."

The Right to Die. Within a few weeks Karen's parents came to believe it was pointless and even cruel, to attempt to keep her alive indefinitely using the respirator. Her father signed a release to have her taken off the respirator so she would be allowed to die "with grace and dignity," but her doctors refused to turn off the machine. Physicians swear to "do no harm" when they ritually take the Hippocratic Oath; and in 1975 questions of the legal definition of death and of patients' rights meant that the Quinlans' request would not be granted. Joseph Quinlan appealed to the court to be appointed Karen's legal guardian to authorize the decision to disconnect the respirator.

What is Death? By the time of Karen Quinlan's dilemma, the medical profession faced problems of its own. New medical technology could keep patients alive who previously would have died. The traditional legal definition of death — the stopping of all vital bodily functions including breathing and a beating heart — was complicated by the fact that as long as a patient is supported by an artificial respirator, doctors cannot tell if the heart is beating naturally. Only a few months before Karen lapsed into a coma, the American Medical Association (AMA) adopted a resolution urging that physicians, not legislators, decide when death occurs. The AMA included "permanent and irreversible cessation of function of the brain" as a criteria to broaden the medical definition of death which in the past was determined in most cases by the heart ceasing to beat. Karen's case opened a host of complex legal and moral dilemmas. Has anyone the legal right to terminate care and condemn a patient to certain death? If so, who? By what criteria? The courts were faced with making the decision for the first time because medical technology had outstripped the law.

The Decision to Stop Treatment. Decisions to turn off respirators and stop other kinds of treatment are not simple decisions. Initially, a lower court denied Joseph Quinlan's request, but a year after Karen became comatose, the New Jersey Supreme Court rejected the lower court's decision, and in a landmark legal victory ruled that her father could be her guardian. It authorized him to decide to disconnect the life-support system with the agreement of the hospital's ethics committee. Ironically, when Karen Ann Quinlan was finally taken off the respirator over a year after entering into her coma, she breathed on her own, and the physicians in charge of the case ruled that she would continue to receive appropriate nutrients and antibiotics to fight infections. She remained comatose, breathing on her own and fed through a nasogastric tube, for the rest of her life, dying of pneumonia on 11 June 1985, at the age of thirty one.

Sources:
B. D. Colen, *Karen Ann Quinlan. Dying in the Age of Eternal Life* (New York: Nash, 1976);

Saul Jarcho, M.D., and Gene Brown, eds., *Medicine and Health Care* (New York: The New York Times/Arno Press, 1977).

DEINSTITUTIONALIZING THE MENTALLY ILL

The Rediscovery of Community. The effort to deinstitutionalize the mentally ill was one example of the continuing extension of civil rights from the 1960s. Traditionally, the mentally ill were isolated in large state-run institutions and were often kept calm with heavy doses of drugs. Because of a growing trend emphasizing care at home and in the community, by the mid 1970s many mental institutions had released half or more of their inmates. This shift received strong encouragement from advocates of community psychiatry, who argued state hospitals reinforced disability and isolation, while local services and halfway houses could help return the mentally ill to normal roles in society.

Costs and Civil Rights. The growing use of tranquilizers to treat patients on an outpatient basis also caused a movement away from mental hospitals. New Social Security regulations provided greater aid to states to support the aged in nursing homes instead of mental institutions. Taxpayers were increasingly reluctant to pay for facilities and personnel needed to treat the growing numbers of persons diagnosed as mentally ill. In the 1970s there was a growing impetus to protect the civil rights of the mentally ill, largely because of reports of bad conditions in mental institutions. Facilities were overcrowded, and investigators labeled some as snake pits. Those arguing for

---

THE MOST NEGLECTED DISEASE

In 1974 *Family Health* magazine reported the leading untreated illness in the United States was not cancer, heart disease, or diabetes, but depression. Government reports estimated twenty million adults suffered serious depressive symptoms each year; but according to Dr. Nathan S. Kline, director of the Rockland State Research Center at Orangeburg, New York, few family physicians treated it because they were unable to identify the true signs of depression. In particular, symptoms of anhedonia — a total absence of any feeling of pleasure — were often overlooked. Dr. Kline urged the establishment of on-the-job-training programs for family doctors with an initial consultation from a psychiatrist.

Source: "News from the World of Medicine," *Reader's Digest* (Pleasantville, New York, January 1975): 117.

---

the deinstitutionalization of the mentally ill said patients' lives in institutions were so regulated that they had little opportunity to make their own choices or to function effectively in the outside world. Critics argued that life in a mental hospital was not always a dehumanizing and oppressive experience. They claimed that the kind of patients being sent out into the community were chronic schizophrenics — persons out of touch with reality who need a structured environment. As former patients made their way into scattered local programs, others criticized the lack of continuity in patient care and feared that they might suffer relapses, creating a danger to themselves and others.

Facilities. Community-based facilities differed widely in quality and type. Some were halfway houses operating on shoestring budgets in low-income areas. Large centers provided day-care activities for patients who lived at home but could not yet handle everyday activities on their own. The federal government indicated its support by establishing community support systems (CSS) to help the 1.5–2 million mentally disabled who were not sick enough to be hospitalized but not well enough to care for themselves. The CSS contracts were an enormous undertaking.

Controversy Arises. Deinstitutionalization had mixed results and generated its own controversies. The president of the American Federation of State, County, and Municipal Employees charged that " 'deinstitutionalization,' a lofty idea, has become something very ugly." A director of psychiatric services at a California hospital said that "sheer chaos" resulted from the shift to community programs because of lack of funding. Home owners and businessmen complained that the existence of halfway houses in their communities threatened their lives and livelihoods because of inadequate facilities and supervisory staff; and horror stories of crimes committed by former mental patients made their way into the media.

Acceptance with Reservations. Specialists, politicians, and the public developed, with reservations, an acceptance of community-based mental-health care. Ultimately some attitudes changed, as more people began to see the mentally ill as human, as people who need help in living on their own, rather than being locked up in an institution.

Sources:

"Emptying the Mental Wards: New Treatment Stirs a Controversy," *U.S. News and World Report* (24 February 1975): 71–73;

Constance Holden, "New Attempt to Help the Deinstitutionalized," *Science* (2 December 1977): 903;

Paul Starr, *The Social Transformation of American Medicine* (New York: Basic Books, 1982).

THE ECONOMICS OF HEALTH CARE

A Crisis of Cost. "You always used to think in this country that there would be bad times followed by good times," said a Chicago housewife. "Now, maybe it's bad times followed by hard times followed by harder times." As the economy of the 1970s declined dollars bought less, and unemployment and inflation reached double digits. Medical care was expensive, and its cost rose at a rate far exceeding the general rise in the cost of living. By 1979 the total cost of medical care reached $212.2 billion or 9.1 percent of the gross national product (GNP), up from $74.9 billion (7.6 percent of the GNP) in 1970, an increase of nearly 20 percent. For individuals personal income was not adequate for financing medical care, except for those who remained relatively healthy and had enormous wealth. One in five families had no health insurance at all, and almost one in four was not covered for out-of-hospital costs. Many families were ruined by staggering medical bills, especially in cases of catastrophic illness. In 1970 a survey found that 75 percent of American heads of families agreed that there was a crisis in health care in the United States. It was understood that this was a crisis of money.

Physicians' Fees and Health Insurance. Why had health-care costs risen so rapidly, and why did they not seem to follow basic economic laws? Doctors' fees appeared to be free from the law of supply and demand. When patients paid bills out of their own pockets, doctors' fees could not rise higher than the patient could afford to pay. When Congress passed legislation establishing Medicare for the elderly and Medicaid for the poor in 1965, many people were brought into the health-care system for the first time. Doctors and hospitals found a sudden increase in work demands, and they raised their fees. Although providing health care was an important humanitarian act for many millions of people, Congress failed to introduce cost-control measures, and costs soared.

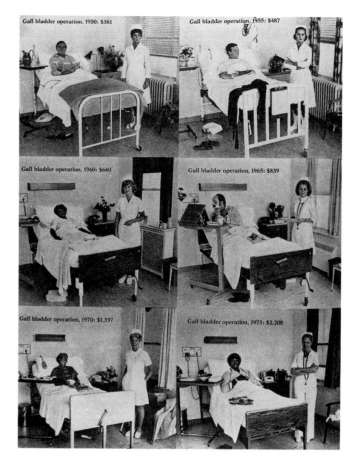

1976 Blue Cross/Blue Shield ad showing rise in costs for gallbladder surgery

Income and Fees. Before the 1970s the American Medical Association influenced the supply of physicians in the country by controlling the number of medical schools and the admissions of medical students. There was no longer a shortage of physicians by 1979 because medical schools increased in number and enrollments expanded. Yet even with the increase in numbers of physicians, their fees continued to rise dramatically. In 1977 doctors's fees rose 9.3 percent, or 50 percent more than other consumer prices. With fewer paying patients to go around, some physicians were thought to set a target income and raise their fees to attain it.

Debt. Medicine in the United States was practiced primarily by specialists with higher fees than those of primary care physicians. It cost a great deal of money to go to medical school, and by the time a new doctor graduated, he or she was in debt. This contributed to physician specialization because specialists could make a higher income. The lack of a comprehensive system of health care, coupled with the emphasis on specialities, meant that patients often went from one specialized physician to another at great expense — an expense that was covered by insurance payments for about 80 percent of the population.

Technology. The American love affair with high technology and the competitive nature of American business also contributed to high costs. Medical technology often required a number of personnel to operate it. Health-care providers and hospitals often purchased the equipment for its prestige value, and the competition and lack of cooperation often meant expensive duplication of resources. Physicians increasingly used the hospital with all its technical equipment in addition to their office practices. In fact, many procedures were only covered by health insurance if they were done in the hospital. With the high cost of hospital procedures, increased use of technology meant skyrocketing expenses.

Malpractice Suits. The civil rights struggle of the 1960s spun off a new health-rights movement concerned with rights in health care. Instead of marching through the streets, advocates marched through the courts. The new health-rights movement challenged the traditional distribution of power and expertise, and the ties between doctor and patient were weakened. This resulted in a progressive increase in the number and size of malpractice claims brought against doctors and medical facilities during the 1970s, with two very expensive effects: a marked increase in malpractice insurance premiums and the practice of defensive medicine on the part of doctors who ordered many tests and procedures regardless of cost, knowing it would be covered by insurance, and further driving up the cost of health insurance.

A Seller's Market. Consumers seemed even more powerless in purchasing medical care than in most other sectors of the economy. A patient told he needed bypass heart surgery was often more emotional than rational about his needs, and he might not have sufficient information or control when deciding on the use of services. Some economists concluded it was not the purchaser of medical services who was the consumer, as in nonmedical markets, but the physician, who also had a financial interest in the services to be purchased. In January 1970 the editors of *Fortune,* in a special issue on medical care, declared that American medicine stood "on the brink of chaos." "Whether poor or not," the editors stated, "most Americans are badly served by the obsolete, over-strained medical system that has grown up around them helter-skelter . . . the time has come for radical change."

Government Concerns. The rapidly rising costs concerned the government as well as the ordinary American. "We face a massive crisis in this area," President Nixon told a press conference on assuming office. "Unless action is taken within the next two or three years . . . we will have a breakdown in our medical system." In the early 1970s, unlike later in the decade, the sense of crisis in health care was accompanied by considerable discussion about the possibilities for successful reform in the form of national health insurance, government regulation, or new forms of medical-care delivery systems such as health maintenance organizations.

Sources:
"Doctors' Fees — Free from the Law of Supply and Demand," *Science* (7 April 1978): 30;

HOW MUCH DID DOCTORS MAKE?

In 1975 the average physician made $47,520 from his or her solo practice, but there was much variation based on speciality. The median family income for the average American family was $14,816 for the same year.

General Practitioners	$38,560
Internists	$53,670
General surgeons	$53,700
Obstetricians-gynecologists	$57,500
Pediatricians	$43,460
Psychiatrists	$39,460 (in 1974)
Family practitioners	$48,160
Orthopedic surgeons	$62,410 (in 1974)
Dentists	$30,200 (in 1974)

Source: *Statistical Abstracts of the United States* (Washington, D.C., U.S. Bureau of the Census, 1977): 102 and 443.

Paul J. Feldstein, *Health Care Economics* (New York: John Wiley & Sons, 1979);

"Health Costs: What Limit?," *Time* (28 May 1979): 60–68;

Richard A. Kurtz and H. Paul Chalfant, *The Sociology of Medicine and Illness* (Boston: Allyn & Bacon, 1984);

Paul Starr, *The Social Transformation of American Medicine* (New York: Basic Books, 1982);

Statistical Abstracts of the United States (Washington, D.C.: U.S. Department of Commerce, Bureau of the Census, 1980);

Andrew C. Twaddle and Richard M. Hessler, *A Sociology of Health* (New York: Macmillan, 1987).

THE FITNESS CRAZE

Aerobics to Yoga. From "exercises you can do in your car" to "exercises you can do lying down," Americans in the 1970s would do anything to improve their health, cure a bad back, flatten a stomach, or handle their anxieties. Aerobics, dancing, isometrics, stretching, jogging, walking, bicycling, swimming, yoga — Americans increasingly worked out. By 1977 a record 87.5 million U.S. adults over the age of eighteen claimed to participate in athletic activities. The most visible sign of the fitness boom were some eight million joggers who trotted along big-city park paths and suburban byways. Popular marathons attracted thousands of participants; and Sen. William Proxmire, a five-mile-a-day runner, claimed, "It's a super feeling, like being immortal." "A good run," said a woman jogger in New York City, "makes you feel sort of holy."

Big Business. Unlike traditional sports, the new athletics minimized the importance of competition. Aerobic dancing, home-conditioning equipment, and enrollment in health spas fueled a $2-billion-a-year supply industry. The movement's bible was said to be Dallas physician Kenneth H. Cooper's *Aerobics,* first published in 1968. Jim Fixx's *The Complete Book of Running* topped the national best-seller lists for months. A more controversial book co-authored by Lawrence E. Morehouse and Leonard Gross, which sold 2.5 million copies in two years, suggested that you could achieve *Total Fitness in Thirty Minutes a Week;* but the President's Council on Fitness and Sports maintained that at least thirty minutes a day was required to become fit.

A Social Event. After tennis star Billie Jean King defeated Bobby Riggs in 1973, the fitness craze became more popular with women, and they started to play tennis in large numbers. The coed sports scene transformed fitness activity from a solitary to a social event. In many large cities the health club or jogging track replaced the singles bar as a place to meet someone. "I've met some really good-looking boys on the track," reported a sophomore jogger at University of California, Los Angeles. Jeff Darman, president of the Washington-based Road Runners of America, said that jogging dates were "a very normal thing, since running is an easy way to get to know someone. . . ." Joining the fitness movement became a trend, but most of those working out belonged to the middle and upper classes.

Medical Benefits. The medical profession approved the exercise craze, believing it not only made people feel better but might actually prolong their lives. Exercise increases the strength of the heart muscle and its ability to pump blood. It reduces heart rate and blood pressure and alters the composition of body tissues by increasing the proportion of muscle and decreasing the proportion of fat. Physicians warned that, since 10 to 15 percent of Americans had coronary heart trouble, everyone over thirty-five who began exercising should first have a medical checkup; and that exercisers needed to know that some kinds of exercise were better than others. Experts also concluded that exercise does as much for the psyche as it does for the heart. William Morgan, a University of Wisconsin psychologist, found chronically depressed people who exercised regularly showed a gradual reduction of their symptoms. "They had an increased estimation of their physical selves," said Morgan, "and anything they did felt better."

THE COST OF AN OFFICE VISIT

If you visited a physician in 1975, an average visit would cost you $21.16 and a follow-up visit averaged $13.08. But costs varied considerably by specialty.

All specialties (including others not shown separately)	Initial	Follow-up
General practice	$13.10	$9.29
Internal medicine	$26.11	$13.56
Surgery	$20.81	$12.22
Pediatrics	$16.18	$11.07
Obstetrics-gynecology	$23.57	$13.73
Psychiatry (1974)	$41.39	(Not available)

Source: *Statistical Abstracts of the United States* (Washington, D.C., U.S. Bureau of the Census, 1978): 106.

The Craze Peaks. By the end of the decade the jogging craze and other fitness fads slowed down. Twenty-three percent of the general public said that nothing could get them involved in physical activity.

Sources:
Peter N. Carroll, *It Seemed Like Nothing Happened: The Tragedy and Promise of America in the 1970s* (New York: Holt, Rinehart & Winston, 1982);

Matt Clark and Mariana Gosnell, "How It Helps — and Hurts," *Newsweek* (23 May 1977): 82–83;

"Fitness Findings," *Reader's Digest* (June 1979): 10;

Harry F. Waters, Lisa Whitman, Ann Ray Martin, and Dewey Gram, "Keeping Fit: America Tries to Shape Up," *Newsweek* (23 May 1977): 78–79+.

HEALTH MAINTENANCE ORGANIZATIONS

Prepaid Group Practice. Americans became more familiar with health maintenance organizations, or HMOs, during the 1970s. HMOs were first regarded as a radical fringe movement in American medicine, but the crisis in medical economics brought about a change in perception. An HMO is a prepaid group practice in which a person, or his or her employer, pays a monthly premium for comprehensive health care services. HMOs try to keep costs down by avoiding hospitalization and by emphasizing preventive services. Physicians work in HMOs on salary rather than for specific fees. Members receive doctors' services, laboratory tests, X rays, and perhaps prescription drugs and other health needs at little or no additional cost. Hospital coverage is also provided. There are some disadvantages to HMOs. Patients might be treated by whoever is on duty (especially nights or weekends) rather than their doctor of choice, and patients have to use the physicians that are available within the organization. Nevertheless, HMOs attracted much attention in the United States because of their potential for cost control.

Health Insurance. HMOs got their start in the debates over health care during the Depression. Before World War II health insurance emerged for some as an employment benefit. Blue Cross and Blue Shield, commonly referred to as the "Blues," rose during the Depression to provide insurance for hospital care. After World War II commercial insurance companies increased their roles in the health care system, on the model of the "Blues."

The Kaiser-Permanente Plan. Though overshadowed by the huge expansion of the Blues and commercial insurance after the war, direct-service prepayment plans developed into a new kind of corporate medical organization. War industrialist Henry J. Kaiser arranged medical services for his employees by providing comprehensive health services to workers in his shipyards and steel mills on the West Coast. Kaiser believed he could reorganize medical care to provide millions of Americans with prepaid and comprehensive services at prices they could afford. Ten years after the war the Kaiser-Permanente health plan had a growing network of hospitals and clinics and half a million people enrolled.

HMOs. By the early 1970s some government officials called for comprehensive programs of medical care through a single, federally operated health-insurance system. Some officials from the Department of Health, Education, and Welfare (HEW) met with a Minneapolis physician, Paul M. Ellwood, Jr., who argued that any financing system should reward health maintenance and prepayment for comprehensive care could be modelled on the Kaiser-Permanente plan. It was at that meeting on 5 February 1970 that Dr. Ellwood first suggested calling these comprehensive health-care corporations health maintenance organizations.

The Government's Role. At first the federal government seemed enthusiastic about the ability of HMOs to cut health care costs. On 18 February 1971 President Nixon announced a "new national health strategy." The president called on Congress to establish planning grants and loan guarantees for new HMOs. The Health Maintenance Organization Act of 1973 provided federal financial assistance and regulations to HMOs as well as assistance with legal matters. It also hampered them by putting them at a competitive disadvantage. For example, one set of provisions required HMOs to charge all subscribers the same community rate and to allow open enrollment of individuals, regardless of health, for at least thirty days once a year. The insurance companies in competition with HMOs did not have these requirements. The 1973 law threatened to make HMOs the most heavily regulated part of the entire health-care industry and less competitive with existing health insurance than they were before. The immediate impact of the law was damaging. Because of the contradictory requirements of federal legislation, the built-in risk in starting new business organizations, and the lack of motivation in the industry to initiate HMOs or to cooperate with them, the development of HMOs in the mid 1970s was slower than its promoters had hoped. The number of HMOs and their enrollment rapidly increased after this, but less than 9 percent of the population was enrolled in HMOs by the end of the 1970s. This suggested that substantial growth of this system of health-care delivery might still lie in the future.

Sources:

William C. Cockerham, *Medical Sociology* (Englewood Cliffs, N. J.: Prentice-Hall, 1989);

"A Group-Health Plan That Has Come of Age," *U.S. News and World Report* (8 October 1979): 79;

"Health Costs: What Limit?," *Time* (28 May 1979): 60–68;

Paul Starr, *The Social Transformation of American Medicine* (New York: Basic Books, 1982).

LEGIONNAIRES' DISEASE AND THE SCIENCE OF EPIDEMIOLOGY

The Disease Detectives. When an epidemic breaks out, the immediate question for medical professionals is how to control the outbreak. Often public health officials known as epidemiologists collect evidence helping to break the chain of transmission and, in the case of several new diseases that arose during the 1970s, identify the cause of the epidemic. Known as the disease detectives, epidemiologists begin by asking questions: Who are the victims? What sets them apart from those who are not sick? Where do they live? Where were they when they became ill? What were they doing? What did they eat and drink?

A Killer Disease. The "who" and the "where" in August 1976 were the people who had attended a Pennsylvania American Legion convention in Philadelphia. Twenty-nine people died of an unidentified, flulike disease, and others were hospitalized with pneumonialike symptoms of high fever, chest pains, and lung congestion. All of them had either been among the ten thousand conventioneers or could be linked to the convention site. About one out of every five people who caught the disease died.

Detectives at Work. Researchers from the Centers for Disease Control (CDC) in Atlanta, Georgia, were called in to investigate the puzzling outbreak. The CDC is a federal governmental agency that does research on health problems and works to prevent and control the spread of disease. Tracking down the Philadelphia killer became

Dr. Donald Fraser, chief of the Council for Disease Control team investigating the Legionnaires' disease outbreak in Philadelphia

LYME DISEASE

Puzzling Symptoms. Polly Murray was alarmed. One by one her family developed a strange combination of shared symptoms: rashes, headaches, pain and stiffness in their joints. "By the summer of 1975 my husband and two of the children were on crutches. Meanwhile I kept hearing about other people, most of them children, with the same symptoms." So she contacted state health authorities. At the same time, Yale University rheumatologist Allen Steere received a phone call about a mysterious outbreak of arthritis around Lyme, Connecticut. Many children were affected, and since juvenile arthritis was rare and was not known to be infectious, Steere was almost certain he was looking at a new disease. Unlike Legionnaires' disease, this new disease was debilitating but not normally fatal.

What Was It? Using epidemiological techniques, Steere found that all of the victims including Polly Murray and her family lived near wooded areas and first noticed their symptoms in summer or fall. Warm weather is insect time, and woods are a perfect breeding ground. Many patients mentioned an unusual bull's-eye rash that appeared weeks before their symptoms began. It was similar to a rash reported in Europe, thought to be caused by a tick bite.

Ixodes dammini. Researchers collected ticks, and in 1979 a medical entomologist Andrew Spielman described the suspect tick as a new species, *Ixodes dammini*. In a two-year life cycle tick larvae hatch in late summer and take a blood meal from white-footed mice. The next spring the tick nymphs feed sometimes from humans, but more often from white-tailed deer. The deer themselves do not become ill, but in the previous few decades deer populations had greatly increased in number, and so, therefore, had the ticks. Two years later scientists discovered that *I. dammini* was infected with a corkscrew-shaped bacterium called a spirochete, and the search for a vaccine began. One means of controlling the disease was to place insecticide-soaked cotton in the woods where white-footed mice took it home to line their nests. The insecticide killed the ticks but did not harm the mice. By the end of the decade antibiotic treatment was the only weapon against the disease. It had spread throughout the United States, and the infection continued to frighten much of the country each summer.

Source:
Peter Jaret, "The Disease Detectives," *National Geographic* (January 1991): 114–140.

NEW TECHNOLOGIES IN MEDICINE

The Technological Revolution in Medicine. New developments in science and technology continued to change the face of medicine throughout the decade. The Korean and Vietnam wars both contributed new types of military technology which later found peacetime use in medicine. Advanced computers appeared in the early

one of the biggest and most intensive medical investigations of all time. The epidemiologists were unable to find any single factor appearing in every case other than attendance or presence at one convention hotel. They did find a typical pattern: a small number of people falling ill at the outbreak, more toward the middle, then a decline in new illnesses. When an epidemic follows this pattern, the epidemiologists know there is probably a common cause. All those who became sick were probably exposed at the same time and in the same place.

The Mystery Solved. The disease subsequently spread to nineteen states. Researchers determined that it was caused by a previously unidentified bacterium. A breakthrough for the disease detectives came in 1978 when the bacterium, named *Legionella pneumophila,* was isolated in water taken from a cooling tower in a Bloomington, Indiana, hotel after three people died and eighteen others were struck. Of the twenty-one people involved, nineteen had spent at least one night at the hotel. The source of the bacterium was finally traced to the air-conditioning systems of hotels. The mystery of the killer disease was solved, and further outbreaks could then be controlled.

Source:
Melvin Berger, *Disease Detectives* (New York: Crowell, 1978).

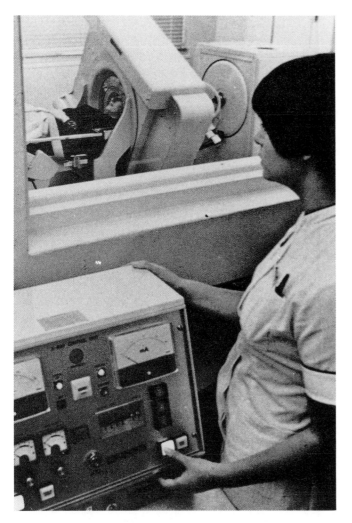

Technician overseeing computerized axial tomography brain scan. Patient can be viewed through a window that shields the technician from X rays.

tefiore Hospital and Medical Center in New York City. "There was always the chance of jabbing it into some vital area. Now you can see where the head, heart, and umbilical cord are."

Computerized Axial Tomography. An imaging device closely related to ultrasound, computerized axial tomography (CAT) scanner takes many X rays and combines them to provide a cross-sectional picture — tomograms — of the patient's body. Computers then put the millions of bits of information together to form a picture on the computer screen. Instead of an uncomfortable experience such as pneumoencephalography (where a patient with a suspected brain tumor has to undergo diagnosis by having air injected into his brain), a CAT scan can provide a clear picture inside the body. A patient is placed on a special couch or gantry and then slowly moved by conveyor belt into a hatch in a huge machine. Beams of X rays rotate and change angles, collecting and storing new sets of data. A radiologist peers at a computer console to read and interpret the data. Diagnosis is made in a short period of time with little discomfort to the patient.

Magnetic Resonance Imagery. A physicist's tool — nuclear magnetic resonance (NMR) or magnetic resonance imagery (MRI) — can detect differences between healthy tissues and some kinds of cancerous tissues. In 1977 its designer, Dr. Raymond Damadian, hoped it could also treat cancer. Damadian, a medical doctor with degrees in math and physics, designed his scanner to make the body's natural elements give off radio signals to tell what is going on in the chemical world inside the tissues. "The beauty is," he said, "that the technique is non-invasive. You don't need surgery or X-rays. . . ."

Microsurgery. High-powered microscopes capable of magnifying nerves and blood vessels up to forty times, scissors with tiny blades, miniature forceps, and surgical thread so thin it was nearly invisible to the naked eye are used to reattach severed limbs in feats rarely possible before the 1970s. A better understanding of the complicated structure of nerves also aids in surgery. The replacement of a severed thumb by a big toe, with its attached blood vessels, nerves, and tendons, is done so carefully and thoroughly that the toe-become-thumb has enough feeling to function. Another important use of microsurgery is in stroke-prevention surgery, where one artery in the brain can be hooked to another nearby, thus bypassing an obstruction cutting off the flow of blood. If this is done before irreversible brain damage occurs, it can reduce the toll from strokes.

Hopes and Fears. Despite all the promises of biotechnology, the new instruments caused concerns. Dr. Ivan L. Bennett, Jr., provost of the School of Medicine at New York University, cautioned, "Medical technologies are neither perfect nor risk-free." Many in the medical community felt ultrasound was being alarmingly overused, especially for fetal monitoring where misinterpretation

1960s. By the early 1970s bioengineering, the wedding of medicine and physics, began to appear in medical schools. Controversies arose about the benefits and costs. Critics feared the dehumanizing aspects of bioengineering technologies and worried about hidden medical dangers. Hospitals vied for prestigious equipment, and expensive duplication of machines drove costs up.

Ultrasound. Medicine borrowed sonar technology from the military and used it to identify body organs and problems without surgery. This sonar technology, called ultrasound, could detect gallstones and prostate-gland malfunctions and had many other uses. Its most widespread use was in obstetrics, where it was used to monitor almost half of all pregnancies and deliveries by 1979. It also made amniocentesis much safer. In this procedure a hollow needle is inserted into the amniotic cavity surrounding the fetus, and fluid is drawn off to aid in the detection of genetic abnormalities. "A few years ago, before ultrasound, we used to have to stick the needle in without knowing exactly where," said Dr. Heidi Weissman, a radiologist and ultrasound specialist at Monof data sometimes led to unnecessary cesarean sections. Some viewed the new technologies as dehumanizing. Before the availability of all the new equipment, intensive-care units were relatively quiet, calm places. With the new technology patients surrounded by bright lights and beeping machines occasionally developed "ICU psychosis," where they stopped reacting and retreated into their own worlds. Given the expense of the new equipment, concerns were voiced about even greater geographic imbalance in availability of treatment, particularly in rural areas. The overall price tag of the new technology also stirred debate. Dr. Seymour Perry, the acting head of HEW's National Center for Health-Care Technology, commented, "Americans have long had a love affair with technology. . . . Our aim should be to make sure that medical technology is our servant and never becomes our master."

Sources:

Laurence Cherry, "Medical Technology: The New Revolution," *New York Times Magazine*, 5 August 1979, pp. 12–16+;

Susan Renner-Smith, "Damadian's Supermagnet: How He Hopes To Use It To Detect Cancer," *Popular Science* (December 1977): 76–79+.

Nursing in Transition

Upgrading of Education. In the 1970s the most important trend in nursing was autonomy. Nurses struggled to take on more decision-making responsibilities than they had in the past. The upgrading of nursing education symbolized this trend as nurses entered the profession with at least a college-level degree in nursing. The traditional hospital school, offering a two-year, posthigh-school training program and diploma, was being phased out. Many nurses additionally received a master's or doctorate degree.

A Profession in Turmoil. America's 1.4 million nurses in 1979 made up the largest group of health care professionals in the country. But shortages on hospital nursing staffs and high turnover rates caused hospitals to close some of their floors. Low pay, long hours, and overwork led to strikes and slowdowns by nurses in many cities. Within the profession itself there was an identity problem. Traditionally, nurses followed doctors' orders, but the woman's rights movement spurred on the development of a new, more active kind of nurse — the nurse-practitioner.

New Specialties for Nurses. The nurse-practitioner was the first of many professional changes. Nurse-practitioners provide primary care to patients in areas with a doctor shortage. Their skills emphasize preventive medicine and early detection of disease. Thirty-eight states amended laws to allow nurse-practitioners to diagnose, prescribe drugs, and perform other duties that were formerly prohibited. Increasingly, nurse-midwives delivered babies. At first these midwives faced much opposition from physicians, but they gradually gained some acceptance. In 1965 the University of Colorado's School

of Nursing set up a program to train nurses as pediatric assistants. By the end of the 1970s more than two hundred programs spent nine months to two years training some fifteen thousand nurse-practitioners in specialties including family, community, geriatric, pediatric, and maternity practice.

Supernurses or Semidoctors? Although the women's movement influenced the rapid development of nurse practitioners, health experts thought the rise of the supernurse was largely brought about by urgent medical need. But problems arose both within the profession and between nurses and physicians as nurses struggled to define their new identity. A major source of friction was the wide gap in pay between doctors and nurses. In 1977 the average income for nurses ranged from $9,072 in Rhode Island to $14,216 in California — compared with an average income of $65,000 for doctors. Many nurses felt frustrated by the lack of income and the lack of professional opportunity. Some nurses said that physicians regarded them as competitors and saw the use of nurse-practitioners as an economic threat. In Atlanta nurse-practitioners competed directly with doctors for patients in the same neighborhood. In other cases, a growing number of doctors set up joint practices with nurses; and nurse-practitioner positions were common in HMOs. As health officials saw it, the doctor/nurse relationship was slowly changing from hierarchical to collaborative practice — with benefits on both sides.

Sources:

Matt Clark, Frank Maier, Phyllis Malamud, and Evert Clark, "Supernurses; Nurse Practitioners," *Newsweek* (5 December 1977): 64;

"For 'New Nurse': Bigger Role in Health Care," *U.S. News and World Report* (14 January 1980): 59–61.

Nutritionists and the Battle Over Sugared Cereals

Nutrition Activists. In the early 1970s, sugared breakfast cereals came under fire from several different quarters. Health care professionals attacked the poor nutritional value of the cereals. Reflecting their concerns, Sen. George McGovern issued a report arguing that "Too much fat, too much sugar or salt . . . are linked directly to heart disease, cancer, obesity and stroke, among other killer diseases. Six of ten leading causes of death in the United States have been linked to our diets." McGovern and physicians were concerned that a diet of sugared cereal established poor eating habits in Americans. Other critics of the breakfast cereal industry complained to the Federal Trade Commission that cereal companies were engaging in monopolistic practices and inflating prices, especially through the use of commercials aimed at children. Hunger concultant Robert Burnett Choate, Jr., linked these criticisms of the cereal companies in his testimony before Congress on 23 July 1970. Choate argued that forty of the top sixty dry cereals had empty calories. Cereal manufacturers countered by adding vitamins and other nutrients but continued to promote their

BIG KIDS

American children, both white and black, ranked among the biggest in the world in 1973, according to U.S. Public Health Service data on children ages six to eleven. White American children were in the top group — both in height and weight — compared to European children. A steady increase occurred over the past ninety years, with children 10 percent taller and 15 percent to 30 percent heavier, on the average.

At age six boys were slightly taller and heavier, but by age eleven the girls caught up and were larger.

Boys of both races were the same height, but white boys were slightly heavier than their black peers.

Black girls were taller than white girls their age. Although they weighed slightly less until age eleven, black girls then became heavier than white girls.

Comparing urban to rural areas found no significant difference of height or weight among children of otherwise similar socioeconomic backgrounds.

The socioeconomic status of the parents did seem to affect the height and weight of the children. The higher the family income, the taller and heavier the children tended to be. Likewise, the better educated the parents, the taller and heavier were the children.

Source: *Journal of the American Medical Association* (4 June 1973): 1336.

heavily sweetened products to children via advertisements with cuddly bears and adorable tigers during weekend-morning "kidvid." As the passion for physical fitness led to a reassessment of American eating habits, these breakfast cereals became the subject of conflict between nutrition activists and food manufacturers.

Consumer Objections. Consumer activists made presweetened cereals the major target for regulation for several reasons: the prime consumers were children, whose lifetime eating habits were in the process of being formed; sugared cereals were often eaten as snacks — eating them without milk made them more likely to stick to the teeth and lead to tooth decay — and sweetened cereals were overpriced as well as oversweetened. The Boston-based Action for Children's Television (ACT) and the Center for Science in the Public Interest (CSPI) also petitioned the FTC to regulate advertising on children's television programs — a threat to the television and advertising industries as drastic as Congress's 1970 ban on cigarette commercials.

Food Manufacturers Fight Back. The cereal companies, which spent more than $600 million annually for commercials aimed at children, fought the critics by becoming increasingly aggressive. The Kellogg Company took out newspaper ads to rebut health charges and voluntarily instituted some reforms. Most advertisers began to display their products on tables alongside juice, milk, and other wholesome foods and added vocal disclaimers such as "a good part of a good breakfast." ACT retorted, "It's almost worse than having no disclaimer there at all." On 15 November 1977 companies staged a media blitz to convince the public that the only way to convince children to eat enough nutrients was to sugarcoat everything. An unrepentant industry continued to feed the debate when it announced the creation of yet another entry into the sugar wars — a cold cereal called Cookie Crisp, which was 45 percent sugar, came in chocolate or vanilla, looked like tiny cookies, and could "change your bowl into a cookie jar!"

Sources:

Peter N. Carroll, *It Seemed Like Nothing Happened. The Tragedy and Promise of America in the 1970s* (New York: Holt, Rinehart & Winston, 1982);

Constance Holden, "Battle Heats Up Over Sugared Cereals," *Science* (2 December 1977): 902–903;

H. F. Waters and J. D. Copeland, "Sugar in the Morning . . . ," *Newsweek* (30 January 1978): 91.

THE SWINE FLU SCARE

Fears of a Major Pandemic. When in February 1976 swine flu was first identified as the agent responsible for a small outbreak of respiratory disease among recruits at Fort Dix, New Jersey, there was ample cause for concern. *Hsw* 1 *N* 1, the swine flu virus, was the cause of the pandemic of 1918, which killed twenty million people worldwide and five hundred thousand in the United States. Since the late 1920s the strain could be found only in pigs; no human being under age fifty could have built up antibodies to it. This meant that what might (or might not) be a virulent human flu virus had acquired a new outer coat of antigenic proteins that might (or might not) make it very contagious to humans. The federal government's Centers for Disease Control recommended a major effort to produce a vaccine against the new strain.

President Ford's Decision. In March President Gerald Ford announced an unprecedented nationwide campaign to inoculate every American against swine flu. Congress appropriated $135 million to finance the effort, and after a variety of delays and concerns about proper dosages, it got under way on 1 October.

Guillain-Barré Syndrome. In the first ten days of the program, more than one million people were vaccinated. Then, first in Pittsburgh and later elsewhere, came reports of deaths following vaccinations. A final tragedy came in December. A rare paralytic disease called Guillain-Barré syndrome was reported in a few people who had been vaccinated. It was never clear whether the

Joe brought it home from the office. He gave it to Betty . . .

In California, Betty's mother gave it to her best friend, Dotty. But Dotty had a heart condition and she died.

. . . and one of his kids, and to Betty's mother. But Betty's mother went back to California the next day.

GET A SHOT OF PROTECTION. THE SWINE FLU SHOT.

A 1976 public service announcement urging Americans to protect themselves against swine flu. Congress appropriated $15 million to finance the vaccination campaign.

syndrome was related to the swine flu vaccine, but it was clear that the program had to be suspended. The mass-immunization program ended on 16 December and was not resumed. The epidemic never occurred.

"The Swine Flu Fiasco." In February 1977 Joseph Califano, the new secretary of Health, Education, and Welfare, commissioned a review of what had become known as "the swine flu fiasco." It was clear that a mass epidemic was cause for concern. But hindsight suggested that a better option was not considered soon enough:

stockpiling a vaccine and waiting for evidence of a significant spread of the virus before proceeding to mass immunization. Not enough attention had been paid to preparing the public for such foreseeable incidents as the Pittsburgh deaths or reacting to the appearance of a side effect such as the Guillain-Barré syndrome. The authors of the review, Richard E. Neustadt of Harvard University's John F. Kennedy School of Government, and Harvey V. Fineberg, M.D. of the Harvard School of Public Health, examined the administrative and technical difficulties that arise whenever science and public policy come

Editorial cartoon from the Denver *Rocky Mountain News* criticizing the Tuskegee Syphilic Study in which four hundred syphilitic patients went untreated for forty years

together and concluded, "[in 1976] in the absence of *manifest* danger, all-out action was a mistake."

Source:
"Swine Flu Affair; Neustadt-Fineberg Report," *Scientific American* (January 1979): 80+.

THE TUSKEGEE SYPHILIS STUDY

Shocking Revelations. Perhaps the most shocking medical story of 1972 was the tale of the medical experiments in Tuskegee, Alabama. For forty years the U.S. Public Health Service conducted a study in which four hundred African-American syphilis victims unknowingly served as the subjects of a medical experiment. Even though penicillin, a cure for syphilis, became available in 1943, the study subjects were never treated for the disease. Instead the study used the corpses of the subjects to determine the effects of disease on the human body. The officials of the health service who began the study were long retired by 1972; but their successors expressed serious doubts about the morality of the investigation. The experiment raised important new ethical questions for the medical profession.

New Regulations. Under examination by the press, the Public Health Service was not able to locate a formal protocol for the experiment. Later it was learned that one had never existed. Procedure simply evolved. Public and political outrage led to a national review of federal guidelines on human experimentation, and the result was a complete reworking of HEW regulations on human experimentation.

The Survivors. For the men in the Tuskegee study, the changes were all too late. Beginning in April 1973 the Centers for Disease Control found the few survivors, and the government promised to provide and pay for their medical expenses for the rest of their lives. In 1975 the government extended treatment to their wives who had contracted syphilis and their children with congenital syphilis, many of whom had syphilis directly attributable to the government's failure to treat the men. But more than any other experiment in American history, the Tuskegee study convinced legislators and bureaucrats alike that tough new regulations had to be adopted if human subjects of medical experiments were to be protected.

Sources:
Saul Jarcho, M.D., and Gene Brown, eds., *Medicine and Health Care* (New York: The New York Times/Arno Press, 1977), p. 383;

James H. Jones, *Bad Blood* (New York: Free Press, 1981).

WHO WORKED IN HEALTH CARE?

A Typical Medical Student/Physician. By 1979 a record 63,800 students were enrolled in medical schools.

The first-year medical student was typically a white male between the ages of twenty-one and twenty-three. (Men accounted for 74.7 percent of the medical student body.) He came from an upper- or upper-middle-class family and was likely to have a parent or close relative who was a physician. He had at least a bachelor's degree with a 3.4 (on a 4.0 scale) premedical grade point average. Most likely his undergraduate college major was in biology, chemistry, zoology, premedicine, or psychology. While women made up 25.3 percent of medical students by the end of the decade (an increase of almost 16 percent), they remained a mere 10 percent of practicing physicians. In 1979–1980, 5.7 percent of the students enrolled in medical school were African-Americans, a considerable increase over ten or twenty years before. U.S. medical schools reported fewer admissions of students from lower- and middle-income families as medical education costs increased dramatically. Borrowing for their education often led students to choose specialized and areas of practice to help them pay off their debts, and this contributed to the decline in relatively lower-paid family and general practitioners.

Women in Health Care. In the mid 1970s women made up 75 percent of the workforce in the health industry, but they were found in the less well paying part of that workforce and were the followers rather than the leaders of the profession. In 1975 only 7 percent of practicing physicians were women; only 2 percent of the nurses were men. Women physicians were less well paid than their male counterparts (an estimated twenty-seven thousand dollars per year versus forty-eight thousand dollars). Most women in the health labor force had incomes ranging around five thousand dollars. Women M.D.'s tended to be concentrated among pediatricians and psychiatrists. Women professors were scarce in the medical schools, department chairs even scarcer. The number of women and minorities in the profession increased slowly during the 1970s. But the question of their influence and role remained unanswered, including whether a sharp increase in women practitioners would actually make any difference to medicine from the patient's perspective.

MALPRACTICE INSURANCE PREMIUMS IN 1975

In addition to their other expenses for setting up an office, physicians had to pay for malpractice insurance. In 1975 the median cost for all M.D.'s was $1,900, but by 1979 the median cost had risen to $3,300. These costs varied a great deal by specialty.

	1975	1979
General practitioners	$1,300	$2,210
Family practitioners	$1,200	$2,300
Internists	$900	$1,900
General surgeons	$4,000	$7,190
Obstetricians-gynecologists	$4,900	$8,050
Pediatricians	$800	$1,710

Source: *Statistical Abstracts of the United States* (Washington, D.C., U.S. Bureau of the Census) 1978: 107; 1981: 108.

Sources:
William C. Cockerham, *Medical Sociology* (Englewood Cliffs, N. J.: Prentice-Hall, 1989);

Richard A. Kurtz and H. Paul Chalfant, *The Sociology of Medicine and Illness* (Boston: Allyn & Bacon, 1984);

New York Times, 30 September 1979, p. 24;

New York Times, 12 October 1979, p. 18;

New York Times, 2 December 1979, p. 72;

George A. Silver, M.D., "Women in Medicine," *Nation* (21 June 1975): 741–742;

Paul Starr, *The Social Transformation of American Medicine* (New York: Basic Books, 1982).

HEADLINE MAKERS

BARUCH S. BLUMBERG

1925-

VIROLOGIST

Virologist. The 1976 Nobel Prize for medicine or physiology was awarded jointly to American virologists Dr. Baruch S. Blumberg and Dr. D. Carleton Gajdusek for their discoveries concerning mechanisms involved in the origin and spread of infectious diseases. Dr. Blumberg's identification of a chemical marker in the blood showing the presence of hepatitis B paved the way for an experimental anti–hepatitis B vaccine for this most severe and often fatal form of the liver inflammation known as viral hepatitis.

Medical Anthropologist. Dr. Blumberg's interest in how and why people of different racial, ethnic, and family backgrounds react differently to disease in terms of resistance and susceptibility took him around the world. "In a lot of these places," he said, "I would be the only outsider except for some anthropologist. So, naturally, I got interested in anthropology and such questions as how social behaviors influence susceptibility to disease. I've always been interested in human variation, and I suppose if I hadn't made the discoveries regarding hepatitis I'd be working on that."

A Chance Discovery. Sometimes major medical discoveries are the results of happenstance. Dr. Blumberg did not start off looking for the hepatitis virus, but during his early studies he found that a New York patient's blood serums formed antibodies when mixed with an antigen from an Australian aborigine. Blumberg then tested the unusual New York blood sample against thousands of other samples, trying to find out why this reaction occurred. Finally he discovered a high correlation between the antigen and hepatitis.

Protecting the Blood Supply. The first major practical result of his discovery was the development of a blood test for screening out hepatitis B virus carriers from among prospective blood donors. In 1971 the American Association of Blood Banks ordered all of its members to use the hepatitis test. Consequently, the incidence of hepatitis after transfusions decreased by about 25 percent. Hepatitis is one of the major infectious diseases found throughout the world, and hepatitis B is the more dangerous form. Carriers can be without symptoms but capable of infecting others, and it can lead to liver disease and death.

People and Intuition. Dr. Blumberg won numerous awards for his work, but his chief interest remained in people. He held the posts of professor of medicine and medical anthropology at the University of Pennsylvania, adjunct professor of anthropology at Temple University, and associate director of the Institute for Cancer Research in Philadelphia. "You can't get too far away from people and diseases," he said, "if you're going to understand people and the diseases they get." In his view, intuition is as important as reason. "Science is not as scientific as most people think it is," he explained. "Direct, cold logic is not the only method scientists use. Individual intuition and style are very important."

Source:
J. L. Melnick, "1976 Nobel Prize for Physiology or Medicine," *Science* (26 November 1976): 927.

GERALDINE CANNON

1935-

WOMAN'S RIGHTS ACTIVIST

A Would-Be Physician. Geraldine Cannon wanted to be a doctor. But when this young grandmother applied to the University of Chicago and Northwestern University medical schools in 1974 at the age of thirty-nine, she was told that anyone over the age of thirty had little chance of being admitted. This struck her as unfair to women, who are more likely than men to interrupt their educations to raise a family. Cannon, then a senior at Trinity College in Illinois, complained to the Department of Health, Education, and Welfare (HEW).

Bureaucracy. Her complaint vanished into HEW's bureaucracy. Frustrated, she took her case to federal courts and the lower courts, but they told her only HEW could enforce the section of the civil rights laws, Title IX, that bans sex discrimination against students and applicants to educational institutions receiving federal funds. Finally, in May 1979 the U.S. Supreme Court ruled six to three that individuals could bring sex discrimination suits against schools and colleges through the courts.

A Breakthrough for Woman's Rights. Women's groups applauded the decision, and so did White House special assistant Sarah Weddington, who argued it was better to have individuals able to bring their cases to court than to have to rely on HEW, which was hopelessly backlogged with discrimination complaints. This decision of the high court made people aware of their rights to bring suit under Title VI (race discrimination) and Title IX (sex discrimination).

A Nurse Instead. But the period of five years it took Geraldine Cannon to get legal action was too long for her to wait. By the time the Supreme Court ruled on her discrimination complaint, she had completed nursing training and was a surgical nurse at Skokie Valley Community Hospital in Illinois.

Source:
"Getting In," *Time* (28 May 1979): 57.

KENNETH C. EDELIN

1937-

ABORTION DOCTOR

The Case. Dr. Kenneth C. Edelin was found guilty of manslaughter in Boston on 15 February 1975. He was accused of the death of a male fetus after a legal abortion he performed at the Boston City Hospital on 3 October 1973. The prosecution charged that Dr. Edelin killed the fetus by depriving it of life-sustaining oxygen while it was still in the womb. The prosecution argued that the fetus was old enough to be viable. However, viability was questionable because the gestational age was somewhere between eighteen and twenty-four weeks. The defense maintained that Dr. Edelin could not have committed manslaughter because the fetus was not a person and therefore no person ever existed. Furthermore, the defense maintained, the law had never given rights to the unborn. The fetus never lived and therefore could not have been killed. Dr. Edelin was sentenced to one year's probation and continued to practice at Boston City Hospital.

Legal Issues. The Supreme Court decision *Roe* v. *Wade* (1973) prevented states from interfering with a woman's right to an elective abortion. In his charge to the jury the judge said that *Roe* v. *Wade* protected Dr. Edelin from criminal conduct for having performed the abortion. But because Massachusetts had not taken legislative action to regulate abortion in the second trimester of pregnancy, in Dr. Edelin's case the laws concerning manslaughter and definitions of a person and fetus were "inextricably intertwined."

Impact. The verdict added fuel to the fiery controversy over abortion and made obstetricians much more cautious about performing abortions during the second trimester of pregnancy. The verdict was widely regarded as a victory for anti-abortion and "right-to-life" groups. After his conviction, doctors in many hospitals refused to perform abortions in the middle stages of pregnancy for fear they too might be prosecuted.

Epilogue. Nearly two years later the Massachusetts Supreme Court overturned Dr. Edelin's lower-court conviction by ruling that a doctor commits manslaughter only if he ends the life of a fetus that is definitely alive outside of a woman's body. In April 1979, four years after his trial, Dr. Edelin was named chairman of the obstetrics and gynecology department at Boston University's School of Medicine.

Sources:
"Abortion Conviction of Boston Doctor Upset," *New York Times*, 18 December 1976, pp. 1;

Saul Jarcho, M.D., and Gene Brown, eds., *Medicine and Health Care* (New York: The New York Times/Arno Press, 1977), pp. 388–389.

DONALD A. HENDERSON

1928-

DIRECTOR OF THE WORLD HEALTH ORGANIZATION PROGRAM TO ERADICATE SMALLPOX

A Rare Award. In 1976 the United Nations (UN) World Health Organization (WHO) in Geneva received the rarely given Albert Lasker Public Health Service Award for "the imminent eradication of smallpox — the first and only disease ever to be eradicated from the earth." When Dr. Donald A. Henderson, the director of the organization's global smallpox eradication program, accepted the award for the UN agency, he said that only two known smallpox cases existed — in Somalia. Final confirmation of eradication requiredatleasttwoyearsofsearchineveryinfectedarea in the world. A few years later the world became free of this dread disease.

A Global Eradication Program. Henderson was born in Ohio, graduated from the University of Rochester Medical School, and joined HEW's disease-control center, where he worked to control such diseases as measles and smallpox. When President Lyndon B. Johnson decided to offer assistance in smallpox eradication to eighteen countries of western and central Africa in 1965, Henderson was designated the program's director. Six months later WHO asked him to come to Geneva to organize an intensified global eradication program. The goal was to stamp out smallpox in ten years.

A Dread Disease. Smallpox was one of the most terrible diseases known to humankind. Caused by a virus, it led to a high fever and aching pain, and ultimately to disfiguring scabs. Of those infected with the most virulent strain of the disease, 20 to 30 percent died. Those who survived were scarred and sometimes blinded. There was no treatment for the disease, but vaccines, first discovered by Englishman Edward Jenner in 1796, provided some preventive measures. Unfortunately, even when 95 percent of a population was vaccinated, an outbreak continued to spread.

An Enormous Task. The task seemed enormous when Henderson began. But the nature of the disease itself provided the WHO team with the hope of success. The smallpox virus passed from one person to another through face-to-face contact from tiny droplets expelled from the mouth and nose. No animal or insect host was known, and the disease was rarely transmitted via clothing or bedding. A victim usually infected no more than five others, and the disease spread slowly and left its evidence in scarred survivors.

Surveillance Containment. Once enough vaccine was available, reporting techniques had been improved, and outbreaks had been tracked down, Henderson's teams initiated massive vaccination programs. But the most effective approach was a second strategy, called surveillance containment. "Fire-fighting" teams discovered outbreaks, isolated patients, and vaccinated entire villages. By hunting for the source of infection, they found other outbreaks and contained them — breaking, one by one, the chains of transmission. After 1979 Henderson could announce that smallpox no longer was a threat to humanity. But the virus was not extinct. Samples of the organism continued to survive in a few laboratories throughout the world.

Sources:

Donald A. Henderson, M.D., "The Eradication of Smallpox," *Scientific American* (October 1976): 25–33;

Henderson, "Smallpox — Epitaph for a Killer?," *National Geographic* (December 1978): 796–805;

"Scientist, 2 Doctors, and WHO Agency Win Lasker Awards," *New York Times,* 18 November 1976, p. 30.

HEINZ KOHUT

1913-1981

CREATOR OF SELF-PSYCHOLOGY

A Challenge to Freud. According to Sigmund Freud, the Oedipus complex — a boy's aggressive impulse against the adult father and love for the mother, accompanied by castration fear — is the central conflict in a child's development. Nonresolution of this complex could lead to neurotic behavior in the adult. Heinz Kohut, the creator of a new body of analytic theory called self-psychology, focused instead on the narcissist — the person whose vital mental health dimension of self-love has gone amiss. His new explanations and treatment of the narcissist's problems bypassed the Oedipus stage and caused conflicts in the psychoanalytic community.

Formative Years. As the German son of a Jewish father and Roman Catholic mother during the Hitler era, Kohut was forced to flee Vienna under Nazi racial laws. He traveled first to Britain, then to the United States, where he became a leading practitioner and teacher of Freudian theory. Kohut believed it was the disruption of his life in Germany and Austria and the challenge to his love of Germanic culture that made him "alert to the problems of the fragmented personality and how it tries to cure itself."

A New Treatment. Self-psychology was a new method of treating this fragmented, narcissistic personality. Kohut's first book, *The Analysis of the Self* (1971), contradicted orthodox psychoanalysis which held that the narcissistic character disorder was resistant to psychoanalytic treatment. Traditional psychoanalysts believed that the inability of the narcissist to form attachments to others originated in an infant's preverbal relationships with his parents. Since these interactions occurred before a child could talk, psychoanalysts thought they were inaccessible to a talking cure. Kohut felt that narcissistic disorders derived from a failure in parental empathy instead of an unresolved Oedipus complex. Patient and analyst could, therefore, explore together what happened in the patient's early childhood to reach a new understanding of his flawed early parental relationship. The patient then could become more able to regulate his own self-esteem.

A Bold Challenge. Kohut's second book, *The Restoration of the Self* (1977), was an even-bolder challenge to Freud's ideas and led to his alienation from the analytic establishment. Before he challenged orthodox theory Kohut recalled, "I was Mr. Psychoanalysis. In every room I entered there were smiles. Now, everybody looks away. I've rocked the boat." In Kohut's new treatment there was less struggle with the patient than in traditional analysis.

Critics felt that some struggles were necessary and that Kohut avoided them. They accused him of neglecting the angry, aggressive dimension of personality disorders.

Growing Interest. Even with all the controversy, interest in Kohut's work grew. Many from the psychoanalytic community agreed that narcissism was at the frontier of psychiatry. Traditional psychoanalysis consisting of long-term expensive treatment was being challenged by the growing popularity of other shorter, less arduous, and less expensive treatments of emotional disorders, many of which derived from Kohut. The 1979 meeting of the American Psychological Association in New York was crammed with hundreds of analysts trying to get a view of Kohut, and conferences on self-psychology in other cities attracted large crowds. Kohut, the analyst of narcissism, had become a celebrity.

Source:
Susan Quinn, "Oedipus vs. Narcissus," *New York Times Magazine,* 9 November 1980, pp. 120+.

ELISABETH KÜBLER-ROSS

1926-

A Societal Taboo on Discussion of Death. When Swiss-born psychiatrist Dr. Elisabeth Kübler-Ross published her 1969 best-selling book, *On Death and Dying,* most people in the United States, including those in the medical profession, were reluctant to confront death openly. Kübler-Ross found that medical professionals typically abandoned the dying patient. They dropped in occasionally to see how things were going but spent as little time as possible with the terminally ill. Even for physicians, death was a taboo subject.

The Five Stages of Dying. In her series of conversations with dying patients, Dr. Kübler-Ross identified five main stages through which terminally ill patients pass. The first stage is *Denial,* the "not me" phase when the patient is unwilling or unable to accept the fact of imminent death. *Anger,* the "why me?" stage, sets in when symptoms make further denial impossible. The "why now?" stage or *Bargaining,* is when the patient tries hard to delay the inevitable. He might become an extremely good patient, or donate body parts to science. Then the patient sinks into depression, or *Grieving,* when he realizes that he must indeed say good-bye to everything and everyone he loves. The final stage is *Acceptance,* when the patient is ready to let go. While other researchers were unable to repeat her findings and concluded that not all dying patients follow the same progression, almost all investigators found in most cases at least one or two of Dr. Kübler-Ross's stages.

Side Effects. At the beginning Dr. Kübler-Ross's high professional standing helped to focus public and scientific attention on her and her work. Many who attended her seminars and workshops asked her for advice in handling specific problems, and she trained both the medical and lay communities in the art of helping people die. The concept of stages had an enormous impact on health-care providers, especially nurses. Instead of doing little to aid patients in their struggle to come to terms with death, nurses now aim at bringing the patient to the stage of acceptance. The zeal with which some nurses pursue this goal, however, has led to charges that some nurses bully patients to die by the stages.

Growing Skepticism. Much of Dr. Kübler-Ross's later research was directed toward proving the existence of life after death. Her publication *To Live Until We Say Goodbye* (1979) was both praised as a "celebration of life" and criticized as "prettifying" the real situation. It also included a description of Shanti Nilaya (Home of Peace in Sanskrit), Dr. Kübler-Ross's teaching and healing center in California. She founded this center in the late 1970s as the first of what she hoped would be a worldwide network of similar retreats in which she could expound her theories of survival of the spirit after death in the form of a living entity. Because of the direction that her new research took, she met with growing skepticism from the medical community. However, the public continued to approve of her methods of caring for the dying.

Sources:
Derek Gill, *Quest: The Life of Elisabeth Kübler-Ross* (New York: Harper & Row, 1980);

D. Goleman, "The Child Will Always be There. Real Love Doesn't Die," *Psychology Today* (September 1976): 48+;

K. G. Jackovich, "Sex, Visitors from the Grave, Psychic Healing: Kübler-Ross is a Public Storm Center Again," *People* (29 October 1979): 28+.

W. DELANO MERIWETHER

1943-

HEMATOLOGIST AND PHYSICIAN-ATHLETE

Medical Researcher. Dr. W. Delano Meriwether, the director of the federal government's 1976 ambitious and controversial swine flu immunization program, was the first African-American student to integrate Duke University's School of Medicine in Durham, North Carolina. He developed an interest in medical research and decided to become a hematologist. Hematology is the study of the anatomy, physiology, pathology, and therapeutics of blood. Dr. Meriwether's studies centered on leukemia and sickle-cell anemia. After graduation he became affiliated with the National Institutes of Health, where he worked with young leukemia patients.

Sports Hero. In 1970, in an effort to take his mind off the depressing aspects of the tragic situation of the leukemia victims he treated, he took up running in the evenings on a high-school track. At the age of twenty-seven, without any previous training in track or any other organized sport, he won two National Amateur Athletic Union sprinting championships. He became a legend for his unorthodox but winning running form (poor starts out of the block compensated for by incredible bursts of speed), his odd track costume (snug gold swimming trunks, a white hospital shirt, and gold and white suspenders), and his low-key manner. In his successes he symbolized the fantasies of many armchair athletes and physical-fitness buffs.

Director of the Swine Flu Immunization Program. Dr. Meriwether became one of the most appealing sports heroes in the United States after his stunning upset victory at his first track meet, where he defeated two record-holding sprinters in the 60-yard dash with a time of 6.0 seconds, just .1 second off the world indoor record. Although injuries kept him out of the 1972 and 1976 Olympics, Dr. Meriwether continued to compete in track and to practice medicine. In 1973 his professional career took him to Washington, D.C., where he served as a special assistant at HEW. In addition to articles about him in *Sports Illustrated*, he was in the news in 1976 as the director of the federal government's swine flu immunization program.

Sources:

R. H. Boyle, "Champion of the Armchair Athletes," *Sports Illustrated* (22 February 1971): 20+;

H. Johnson, "Dr. W. Delano Meriwether: Boss of the Swine Flu Immunization Program," *Ebony* (December 1976): 55+;

S. Treadwell, "Hey, I Can Beat Those Guys," *Sports Illustrated* (18 January 1971): 14+;

"World's Fastest M.D.," *Ebony* (February 1972): 59+.

ELWOOD L. SCHMIDT

1931-

PHYSICIAN

A Doctor Shortage. In the rich Permian Basin oil fields of southeastern New Mexico stands the Jal General Hospital, built in 1961. By 1971 it had fifteen double rooms, an emergency room, and two operating rooms, and it served a community of almost forty-five hundred people. The only doctor in town and the only physician responsible for the hospital staff of twenty-six was a forty-year-old general practitioner (G.P.) named Elwood L. Schmidt.

A General Practitioner's Day. On a typical day Dr. Schmidt was likely to treat patients for duodenal ulcers, upper respiratory infections, possible heart attacks, acute bronchitis, anxiety states, morning sickness, infected knees, temporomandibular arthritis, rashes, gallstones, coughs, and high blood pressure. He might have to perform appendectomies and cesarean sections. Dr. Schmidt admitted, "I like the variety. I don't think I could stand the sameness of the specialties ... On the other hand, I know my limitations — in surgery, anyway ... I know when to refer, or defer, and knock on wood ... — I've never had any serious trouble. I've never even had a malpractice suit."

A Problem of Distribution of Physicians. Dr. Schmidt illustrated the problem of physician maldistribution when he commented, "I was practicing in Slaton, Texas, up near Lubbock, and Slaton was over-doctored. It was full of doctors and I had so little to do I was bored to death, and when the Jal Chamber of Commerce advertised ... I jumped at the chance. And now look at me!" He continued, "I haven't had a day off in four months. Solo practice has its satisfactions, but this is just a little too solo."

G.P.'s — A Vanishing Breed? "I'm not really complaining," he asserted. "I only mean that I'd like to be able to count on a day off every now and then. I truly enjoy my practice. I like taking care of Jal. I like being a G.P. ... I think I'm a good family doctor. I think I do my job. But, you know, I sometimes wonder who ... is going to take my place? Another G.P.? Not likely — we're a vanishing breed of cat ... ," said Dr. Schmidt, echoing the increasing problem of the shortage of general practitioners compared to specialists.

Sources:

Berton Roueché, "The Doctor Who Goes It Alone ... Grumbles ... and Loves It," *Today's Health* (May 1972): 48–53+;

"Solo," *New Yorker* (1 January 1972): 30.

LEWIS THOMAS

1913-

PHYSICIAN-AUTHOR

Notes of a Biology Watcher. Dr. Lewis Thomas became known to the lay community in 1971 when he began writing, in language accessible to the nonscientific world, a series of essays for the *New England Journal of Medicine* that he called "Notes of a Biology Watcher." These essays were spotted by Viking Press, and in 1974 twenty-nine of his essays appeared in *The Lives of a Cell; Notes of a Biology Watcher*. His work received national attention and critical acceptance, and he was awarded a National Book Award in the arts and letters category in 1975. In 1983 he followed his earlier success with *The Youngest Science: Notes of a Medicine-Watcher*.

Renaissance Man. In 1973 Dr. Thomas began heading one of the world's major institutions in the field of cancer research as president and chief executive officer of the Memorial Sloan-Kettering Cancer Center in New York City. In trying to find a candidate for the job, the trustees looked for a man of Thomas's broad vision and scientific knowledge, rather than a cancer specialist or a professional administrator. Prior to this appointment, Dr. Thomas's medical interests lay in the area of research and new knowledge, and he researched infectious diseases, rheumatic fever, and rheumatic heart disease. He also chaired the Narcotics Advisory Committee of the New York City Health Research Council and was professor and chairman of the pathology departments at Yale University and the New Haven Medical Center. After years of research in experimental pathology, the location of this appointment gave him access to the Marine Biological Laboratory at Woods Hole, Massachusetts, where he began investigating the intricate relationships of defense mechanisms in humans and animals. His house on Cape Cod gave him pleasant weekends to study sea life and gather material for some of the essays that were to make up the book *The Lives of a Cell*.

A Look at Ourselves. Dr. Thomas's philosophy of humankind's place in the universe is best stated in his opening lines of the title essay in *The Lives of a Cell*. "We are told," he writes, "that the trouble with Modern Man is that he has been trying to detach himself from nature. . . . Man comes on as a stupendous lethal force, and the earth is pictured as something delicate, like rising bubbles at the surface of a country pond, or flights of fragile birds. But it is an illusion to think that there is anything fragile about the life of the earth; surely this is the toughest membrane imaginable in the universe, opaque to probability, impermeable to death. We are the delicate part, transient and vulnerable as cilia." His renaissance-man curiosity continued to provide him with material for his thought-provoking essays.

Source:
"Boswell of Organelles," *Newsweek* (24 June 1974): 89.

ROSALYN SUSSMAN YALOW

1921-

NOBEL PRIZE-WINNING MEDICAL PHYSICIST

The Second Woman Winner in Medicine. In 1977 Rosalyn S. Yalow became the second woman ever to win the Nobel Prize for medicine. She was honored for her development of radioimmunoassay (RIA), an application of nuclear physics in clinical medicine. Her technique made it possible for scientists to use radio-isotopic tracers to measure the concentration of hundreds of pharmacological and biological substances in the blood and other fluids of the human body. Dr. Yalow first invented the technique in 1959 to measure the amount of insulin in the blood of adult diabetics.

A Woman Pioneer. After World War II the Veterans Administration (VA) began a research program to explore the use of radioactive substances in the diagnosis and treatment of diseases. One of the hospitals chosen for the nuclear-medicine project was the VA hospital in the Bronx, which hired Dr. Yalow as a consultant in nuclear physics in 1947, two years after she became the second woman to receive a Ph.D. in physics from the University of Illinois. In collaboration with Dr. Solomon A. Berson, her associate from 1950 until his death in 1972, Dr. Yalow explored the uses of radioactive iodine and developed a revolutionary method of RIA.

Nuclear Medicine. RIA is a laboratory procedure that uses radioisotopes and immunologic methods to measure substances in the blood or other body fluids. In the past these substances had been difficult or impossible to measure, either because they were present in small quantities or because their chemical properties were too similar to those of other substances. Following their groundbreaking work on insulin retention in adult diabetics, Dr. Yalow and Dr. Berson applied RIA to the study of other hormones, and the use of RIA was extended into virtually all medical specialties.

More Recognition. In 1976 Dr. Yalow became the first woman ever to win the Albert Lasker Prize for Basic Medical Research. As only the second woman to win a Nobel Prize for medicine, she called for women to believe in themselves and match their aspirations with "the competence, courage and determination to succeed." Dr. Yalow added in her acceptance speech in Stockholm, "we must feel a personal responsibility to ease the path for those who come after us. The world cannot afford the loss of the talents of half its people if we are to solve the many problems that beset us."

Source:
Elizabeth Stone, "A Mme. Curie from the Bronx," *New York Times Magazine*, 9 April 1978, pp. 29+.

PEOPLE IN THE NEWS

On 21 September 1970 two physicians, **Werner A. Bleyer** and **Robert T. Brekenridge,** advised mothers to avoid taking aspirin in the latter stages of pregnancy to avoid developing bleeding problems in their babies.

Health, Education, and Welfare secretary **Joseph A. Califano** attacked the tobacco industry on 11 January 1978 with his statement that cigarette smoking is "slow-motion suicide." But **President Jimmy Carter** undercut Califano's anti-smoking campaign during his visit to North Carolina by pledging government support of efforts to make cigarettes "even safer than they are."

Dr. Morris E. Chafetz, director of the National Institute on Alcohol Abuse and Alcoholism, reported on 18 February 1972 that alcoholism was the nation's greatest drug problem, with as many as nine million Americans affected.

On 23 July 1970 U.S. breakfast cereals came under fire from hunger consultant **Robert Burnett Choate, Jr.,** who testified before a Senate committee that forty of the top sixty dry cereals had little nutritional content, with the worst advertised to children on television.

Full-scale testing of the swine flu vaccine to be used in the largest, most intensive U.S. immunization program began 21 April 1976, when **Dr. Theodore Cooper,** assistant secretary of Health, Education, and Welfare, administered the first shot to **Dr. Harry M. Meyer, Jr.,** director of the Food and Drug Administration's Bureau of Biologics.

Raymond V. Damadian, a medical researcher from Brooklyn, New York, tested his first magnetic resonance imaging (MRI) scanner in 1977. His diagnostic tool came to be widely used to detect cancer and other abnormalities without exposing patients to X-ray radiation.

Brother physicians **Herbert** and **Irving Dardik** successfully used veins from umbilical cords as substitutes for clogged and dysfunctional arteries in the legs of adult patients on 18 September 1975.

On 24 March 1975 **Dr. Isaac Djerassi,** a Pennsylvania physician, reported the development of a drug therapy that could significantly improve the survival chances of children suffering from osteogenic sarcoma, a highly lethal bone cancer.

Dr. Eugene Gangerosa reported on 13 April 1975 that a simple oral treatment for dehydration could wipe out the mortality caused by cholera, infantile diarrhea, and other disorders.

In 1973 comedian **Bob Hope** was given a Citation to a Layman for Distinguished Service Award from the American Medical Association.

A test to determine sickle-cell anemia from sampling the amniotic fluid was developed on 4 November 1978 by **Dr. Yuet Wai Kan,** a professor of medicine at the University of California Medical Center in San Francisco.

Nobel Prize laureate **Har Gobind Khorana** and other Massachusetts Institute of Technology researchers reported on 28 August 1976 that his team had provided a breakthrough in genetic engineering by successfully constructing a bacterial gene and implanting it in a living cell where it functioned normally.

Drs. Terry King and **Noel Mills** announced on 17 April 1975 the development of a new technique for closing a hole in the wall between the heart's upper chambers without the use of open-heart surgery

Drs. Harold Kolansky and **William T. Moore,** two psychoanalysts from Philadelphia, reported on 18 April 1971 that regular smoking of marijuana by "normal" youths could cause them to suffer serious psychological disturbances.

On 26 January 1976 **Drs. Louis E. Kopolow** and **Frank M. Ochberg** of the National Institute of Mental Health blamed the economic recession and accompanying inflation for a marked increase in admissions to mental health facilities.

On 29 March 1971 **Dr. Saul Krugman,** head of the New York University Medical Center research team, announced preliminary results in an experiment in immunization against serum hepatitis, a highly infectious and sometimes fatal liver disease.

In 1979 newspaper columnist **Ann Landers** was given a Citation to a Layman for Distinguished Service from the American Medical Association.

Dr. Timothy F. Leary, the controversial LSD researcher and promoter, was released on parole from San Diego's Metropolitan Correctional Center on 7 June 1976 after serving six years of his ten-year narcotic conviction.

On 24 March 1972 **Dr. Arthur S. Leonard,** head of the University of Minnesota's pediatric surgery division at the school of medicine, reported that he and his associates had developed a simple test that could detect the presence of neuroblastoma — a killer of young children — when it was at a stage curable by surgery.

Dr. Robert I. Levy of the National Heart, Lung and Blood Institute, a division of the National Institutes of Health, reported on 23 February 1979 that the number of deaths caused by strokes and the incidence of new episodes of strokes had declined dramatically since 1972.

On 6 January 1971 **Dr. Choh Hao Li,** professor of biochemistry at the University of California Medical Center in San Francisco, synthesized the hormone responsible for growth in the human body. He was assisted by **Donald H. Yamashiro,** a research biochemist.

Saint Louis sex researchers **Dr. William H. Masters,** and **Virginia E. Johnson** on 23 April 1979 reported treating fifty-four homosexual men and thirteen lesbian women who wanted to function as heterosexuals, using a combination of sex therapy and psychotherapy. About 35 percent failed to achieve a long-standing reversal of their homosexuality. Masters and Johnson said their study convinced them that homosexuality is a form of "learned behavior" for most individuals, rather than a physical or emotional illness or a genetic disorder.

Dr. James S. McKenzie-Pollock, medical director of the American Social Health Association, on 13 July 1970 reported on a dramatic rise in infectious syphilis, reversing a ten-year trend of decline in the incidence of the disease.

On 10 June 1975, **Drs. Thomas Milhorat** and **James McClenathan** reported a new development in treating hydrocephalus, a brain disorder in children. Their new device shunted excess brain fluid to the heart and had a coil to lengthen the shunt as the child grew, thus reducing the necessity for dangerous repeated operations to replace shunts.

University of Louisville Medical School physician **Dr. Condict Moore** reported his finding on 25 October 1971 that smokers who continue to smoke after successful cancer treatment face a much greater risk of developing another malignancy than do smokers who stop after treatment for cancer.

Dr. Karl Z. Morgan, a physics professor at the Georgia Institute of Technology, charged on 27 March 1974 that Americans were receiving harmful overdoses of radiation from diagnostic X rays.

Dr. Buford Nichols of the Baylor College of Medicine reported on 5 January 1979 that women who breast-feed their infants are less likely to develop breast cancer than those who do not.

Nevada governor **Mike O'Callaghan** signed a bill on 20 April 1973 that set up a system for state licensing of acupuncture.

On 18 November 1970 **Dr. Linus Pauling,** Nobel Prize–winning scientist, said that the common cold or flu could be warded off and treated with relatively large doses of ascorbic acid, or vitamin C.

Dr. Donald Pinkel, a leading leukemia researcher from Saint Jude Children's Research Hospital in Memphis, disclosed in a report of 26 April 1971 that certain combinations of drug and radiation therapy were making inroads against acute lymphocytic leukemia, a killer of more young American children than any other disease.

A research team in Texas including **Drs. Elizabeth S. Priori, Leon Dmochowski, Brooks Meyers,** and **J. R. Wilbur** announced on 2 July 1971 that it isolated a cancer virus from cells taken from a cancer patient. Specialists saw the development as a significant new lead in the search for human cancer viruses.

On 20 January 1973 **Dr. David L. Rosenhan,** a Stanford University psychologist, reported on a three-year experiment to determine whether personnel at mental hospitals could tell the sane from the insane. His conclusion was that they could not.

The longest-surviving recipient of a transplanted heart, **Louis B. Russell,** died at the age of forty-nine on 27 November 1974, after having received his new heart in 1968.

Two medical professors, **Drs. Kenneth Ryan** and **John Morris,** testified before a House Commerce subcommittee on 9 May 1977 that hysterectomies — many of them unnecessary — were performed more often than tonsillectomies.

Dr. Albert B. Sabin, developer of the polio vaccine bearing his name, told the National Academy of Sciences in Washington, D.C., on 24 April 1973 that common herpes viruses are factors in nine kinds of cancer. But Sabin said he had not learned what mechanism turns these common viruses into cancer-causing agents.

Stanford University cardiologist **Dr. John Speer Schroeder** reported on 6 May 1979 that 70 percent of heart transplant recipients lived at least a year after the operation, making the surgery an effective way to extend the lives of up to seventy-five thousand heart patients each year.

Haskell Shanks, age sixty-three, who was living with a mechanical heart pump affixed to his heart's aorta, died of unrelated kidney failure on 14 November 1971. The device had been implanted in Shanks's heart on 11 August. He lived longer with the pump than any other recipient of such a device.

On 3 December 1976 the discovery of the first biochemical test for chronic alcoholism was reported by **Drs. Spencer Shaw, Charles S. Lieber,** and **Barry Stimmel** of the Bronx Veterans Administration Hospital.

U.S. surgeon general **Jesse L. Steinfeld** asserted on 10 January 1972 that persons who do not smoke cigarettes face some of the same health hazards of smoking that imperil smokers.

On 23 May 1974 the scientific review committee at the Memorial Sloan-Kettering Cancer Center in New York City concluded that **Dr. William T. Summerlin** deliberately falsified research involving skin grafting experiments with white mice.

On 1 June 1976 **Dr. William Trager** of Rockefeller University in New York City cultured the most lethal form of the malaria parasite, a key step toward development of a malaria vaccine.

In 1979 **William C. Triplett** and **Richard B. A. Morrow** patented a monitoring system that detects when a hospital patient is about to get out of bed or when he raises his head, thus alerting hospital staff to potential accidents.

A 1979 study coordinated by Harvard University psychologist **Dr. George E. Vaillant** indicated that men who are happy with their jobs, marriages, and leisure time enjoy longer, healthier lives.

On 3 May 1976 **Dr. Andrew Weiland** was one of a team of surgeons at Johns Hopkins that replaced a cancerous portion of a boy's thighbone with a part of his lower leg bone in order to reconstruct his leg.

On 10 August 1977 physicians **Richard Whitley** and **Charles Alford** of the University of Alabama Medical Center in Birmingham conducted the first successful clinical trial of a drug, adenine arabinoside (ara-A), to treat a life-threatening viral infection — herpes encephalitis (a brain inflammation).

Dr. Roger J. Williams, a nutritionist and biochemist at the University of Texas, reported on 21 October 1970 that a series of his laboratory experiments had led him to believe that the ordinary white bread most Americans ate every day was "nutritionally far below" what it could be.

On 25 March 1974 **Dr. Ernst L. Wynder** said that a low-fat, low-cholesterol diet might protect against cancer of the colon and rectum, the second largest cause of cancer deaths in the United States.

Dr. InBae Yoon announced on 10 February 1975 a new surgical technique for female sterilization which could be performed in ten to fifteen minutes under a local anesthetic.

AWARGS

NOBEL PRIZE WINNERS FOR MEDICINE OR PHYSIOLOGY

1970

Julius Axelrod (United States), **Ulf von Euler** (Sweden), and **Bernard Katz** (Great Britain, born in Germany) for their discoveries of humoral transmitters in the nerve terminals and the mechanism for their storage, release, and inactivation.

1971

Earl W. Sutherland, Jr., (United States), for his discoveries concerning the mechanisms or actions of hormones.

1972

Gerald M. Edelman (United States) and **Rodney R. Porter** (Great Britain) for their work in immunology on the chemical structure of antibodies.

1973

Karl von Frisch (Austria), **Konrad Lorenz** (Austria), and **Niko Tinbergen** (Great Britain, born in the Netherlands) for their discoveries of the organization and elicitation of individual and social behavioral patterns in animals, including those with genetic foundations.

1974

Albert Clause (United States, born in Luxembourg), **Christian Rene de Duve** (Belgium, born in England), and **George E. Palade** (United States, born in Romania) for their founding of cell-biology science and work on the structural and functional organization of the cell.

1975

David Baltimore (United States), **Renato Dulbecco** (United States, born in Italy), and **Howard M. Temin** (United States) for their discoveries which provided scientists with a blueprint of the interaction between tumor viruses and the genetic material of the cell.

1976

Baruch S. Blumberg (United States) and **D. Carleton Gajdusek** (United States) for their findings of new mechanisms for the origin and dissemination of infectious diseases, including the identification of a new class of human diseases caused by unique infectious agents.

1977

Roger Guillemin (United States, born in France) and **Andrew V. Schalley** (United States, born in Poland) for their discoveries of the peptide hormone production of the brain; and **Rosalyn S. Yalow** (United States) for the development of radioimmunoassays of peptide hormones.

1978

Werner Arber (Switzerland), **Daniel Nathans** (United States), and **Hamilton O. Smith** (United States) for the discovery of restriction enzymes and their application to molecular genetics.

1979

Allan Cormack (United States, born in South Africa) and **Godfrey Hounsfield** (Great Britain) for the development of computer-assisted tomography.

AMERICAN MEDICAL ASSOCIATION DISTINGUISHED SERVICE AWARD RECIPIENTS

The AMA Distinguished Service Award honors a member of the association for general meritorious service.

1970

Henry L. Bockus, Philadelphia, Pennsylvania

1971

George R. Herrmann, Galveston, Texas

1972

Milton Helpern, New York, New York

1973

George Hoyt Whipple, Rochester, New York

1974

William Fouts House, Los Angeles, California

1975

William R. Willard, Moundville, Alabama

1976

Claude E. Welch, Boston, Massachusetts

1977

Franz J. Ingelfinger, Boston, Massachusetts

1978

William P. Longmire, Jr., Los Angeles, California

1979

William A. Sodeman, Sr., Toledo, Ohio

ALBERT LASKER AWARDS

The Albert Lasker Awards are given in honor of medical research of a pioneering nature.

Basic Research Awards

1970

Earl W. Sutherland for his discovery of a regulator of body chemistry called cyclic AMP.

1971

Seymour Benzer, **Sydney Brenner** (Great Britain), and **Charles Yanofsky**, whose decoding of genetic material helped explain the nature of genetic mutations.

1972

No award

1973

No award

1974

Ludwick Gross, who contributed to knowledge of leukemia- and cancer-causing viruses in mammals; **Howard E. Skipper** for research in the chemotherapy of cancer; **Sol Spiegelman** for research in molecular biology; and **Howard M. Temin** for his work on the biology of RNA-containing cancer viruses.

1975

Roger C. L. Guillemin for discovering several hormones, including somatostatin, and **Andrew V. Schalley** for discovering luteinizing hormone-releasing hormone; **Frank Dixon** and **Henry G. Kunkel** for discoveries that help explain immunological disorders that may underlie chronic kidney, heart, and joint diseases.

1976

Rosalyn S. Yalow, for her role in developing with the late **Dr. Solomon A. Berson**, radioimmunoassay techniques that measure changes between normal and disease states.

1977

K. Sune D. Berstrom (Sweden), Bengt Samuelsson (Sweden), and Dr. John R. Vane (Great Britain) for discoveries and other pioneering research concerning prostaglandins.

1978

Hans W. Kosterlitz (Great Britain), John Hughes (Great Britain), and Solomon H. Snyder for chemical discoveries affecting pain control.

1979

Walter Gilbert and Frederick Sanger (Great Britain) for major contributions made to the understanding of the chemistry of heredity; Roger W. Sperry for studies in the functioning of the human brain.

CLINICAL RESEARCH AWARDS

1970

Robert A. Good for discovering the mysteries of immunology and using the findings to cure fatal diseases.

1971

Edward D. Freis for his work in hypertensive disease and his findings that moderate cases of high blood pressure could be treated with drugs, reducing strokes and heart failure.

1972

Vincent T. DeVita, Jr., Emil Frei III, Emil J. Freireich, James F. Holland, Donald Pinkel, Paul Carbone, Min Chiu Li, Roy Hertz, Edmund Klein, Eugene J. Van Scott, Denis Burkitt (Great Britain), Joseph H. Burchenal, John L. Ziegler (Uganda), V. Anomah Ngu (United Republic of Cameroon), Isaac Djerassi, and C. Gordon Zubrod, all of whom pioneered in the use of drugs to combat cancers.

1973

William Bennett Kouwenhausen, for developing techniques of external heart massage; Paul M. Zoll whose research led to the development of the pacemaker.

1974

Prof. John Charnley for perfection of the operation that involves replacement with artificial materials of the hip socket and the top of the thighbone.

1975

Engineer Godfrey N. Hounsfield (Great Britain) for his invention of computer-assisted tomography, a computerized X-ray device used in brain scanning, with William Oldendorf, who conceived of scanning the brain with X rays a decade before Hounsfield independently developed the scanner.

1976

Raymond P. Ahlquist and James W. Black (Great Britain) for independent research that led to the development of drugs called beta-blockers and the drug propanolol (also called inderal), which prevents irregular heartbeats and lowers blood pressure.

1977

Inge G. Edler (Sweden) and C. Hellmuth Hertz (Sweden) for pioneering work in applying ultrasound vibrations to diagnose heart disorders and other serious illnesses.

1978

Michael Heidelberger for immunochemistry research leading to vaccines made from polysaccharides; Robert Austrian for the development of a vaccine against the pneumococci bacterium; Emil Gotschlich for the development of a vaccine against meningitis.

1979

No award

SPECIAL AWARDS

1972

C. Gordon Zubrod, Special Award for his administrative leadership in creating "an effective national cancer chemotherapy program."

1973

Sen. Warren G. Magnuson, Public Service Award for crucial legislative leadership guaranteeing that major types of cancer will be conquered in his lifetime.

1975

Jules Stein, Public Service Award for his support of research that has led to the development of several techniques to prevent blindness. Karl H. Beyer, James M. Sprague, John E. Baer, and Frederick C. Novello, Special Public Health Award for creating a new class of drugs — thiazide diuretics — to control high blood pressure and swelling associated with heart disease.

1976

World Health Organization, Public Service Award for historic achievement in the eradication of smallpox.

1978

Elliot L. Richardson and Theodore Cooper, Public Service Award for initiating the National High Blood Pressure Education Program.

1979

Sir John Wilson (Great Britain), Public Service Award for important contributions to the worldwide campaign against blindness.

MCALPINE MEDAL

The Mental Health Association began giving the McAlpine Medal in 1972 for outstanding research in the causes and prevention of mental illness.

1972

Seymour Kety, biochemical research in schizophrenia

1973

Robert Coles

1974

Erik H. Erikson, psychoanalysis and human development

1975

Alexander Leighton, social psychiatry

1976

William E. Bunney, biochemistry of depression

1977

Lyman Winn and **Margaret Singer,** work on schizophrenia

1978

Neal E. Miller

1979

Daniel X. Freedman

PASSANO FOUNDATION AWARDS

Passano Foundation Awards honor distinguished work done in the United States in medical research. Originally one award was endowed. Beginning in 1974 there were two awards, a Senior Award and a Junior Award.

1970

Paul Charles Zamecnik, Massachusetts General Hospital, Boston

1971

Stephen W. Kuffler, Harvard Medical School, Boston, Massachusetts

1972

Kimishige Ishizaka, Johns Hopkins University School of Medicine, Baltimore, Maryland

1973

Roger W. Sperry, California Institute of Technology, Pasadena

SENIOR AWARDS

1974

Seymour S. Cohen, University of Colorado School of Medicine, Denver

1975

Henry G. Kunkel, Rockefeller University, New York

1976

Roger Guillemin, Salk Institute, San Diego, California

1977

Curt P. Richter, Johns Hopkins University School of Medicine, Baltimore, Maryland

1978

Michael S. Brown and **Joseph L. Goldstein,** University of Texas Health Center, Dallas

1979

Donald F. Steiner, University of Chicago, Illinois

JUNIOR AWARDS

1974

Baruch S. Blumberg, Institute for Cancer Research, Fox Chase, Philadelphia, Pennsylvania

1975

Joan Argetsinger Steitz, Yale University, New Haven, Connecticut

1976

Robert A. Bradshaw, University of Washington School of Medicine, Seattle

1977

Eric A. Jaffee, Cornell University Medical College, Ithaca, New York

1978

Robert J. Lefkowitz, Duke University, Durham, North Carolina

1979

Richard Axel, Columbia University, New York

NURSING AWARDS

The **Anna Fillmore Award** recognizes contributions in the development and administration of community health services on a local, state, or national level.

1977

Eva M. Reese

1979

Virgina Coker Phillips

The **Lucile Petry Leone Award** is given every two years to an outstanding nurse-teacher with no more than seven years of teaching experience in the last ten years.

1971

Ada Sue Hinshaw

1973

Rhoda B. Epstein

1975

Lillian Gatlin Stokes

1977

Gail Elaine Wiscarz Stuart

1979

Christine A. Tanner

The **National League for Nursing Distinguished Service Award** honors an individual, group, or team for outstanding leadership and service.

1971

Mary C. Rockefeller

Alabama League for Nursing

1973

Ruth Sleeper

1975

Anna M. Fillmore

1977

Lulu Wolf Hassenplug

1979

Lillian S. Brunner

The **Mary Adelaide Nutting Award** is given every two years to honor outstanding leadership and achievement in nursing education or nursing service.

1971

Jessie M. Scott

W. K. Kellogg Foundation

1973

Lucile Petry Leone

Ester Lucile Brown

1975

Jo Eleanor Elliott

Mary Kelly Mullane

1977

Virginia Henderson

1979

Rena E. Boyle

The **Linda Richards Award** honors an individual actively engaged in nursing whose contribution is unique, of a pioneering nature, or of such excellence as to merit national recognition.

1971

No award

1973

Hildegard Peplau

Mabel Keaton Staupers

1975

Rosemary Wood

1977

M. Lucille Kinlein

1979

Loretta C. Ford

DEATHS

Dr. Lucie Adelsberger, 75, medical researcher and immunologist who discovered a link between red blood cell changes as an incipient cancer warning; imprisoned in Auschwitz by the Nazis, she reported her ordeal in her best-seller *A Report of the Facts,* 2 November 1971.

Dr. Walter Clement Alvarez, 93, a Mayo Clinic specialist (1926–1951) who became a widely syndicated writer on health subjects after his retirement, 18 June 1978.

Dr. Virginia Apgar, 65, developer of the Apgar Score, a test to determine quickly the health of a newborn infant, 7 August 1974.

Dr. Walter Sydney Atkinson, 86, prominent Canadian-born ophthalmologist and eye surgeon who presided over various professional organizations, 6 January 1978.

Dr. Pearce Bailey, 73, neurologist, author, and the first director of the National Institute of Neurological and Communicative Disorders and Stroke at the National Institutes of Health, 23 June 1976.

Dr. Henry K. Beecher, 72, helped make anesthesiology a specialized field of medicine, 25 July 1976.

Dr. Charles Best, 79, physician and codiscoverer of insulin treatment for diabetes, 31 March 1978.

Dr. Grete L. Bibring, 78, a protégé and later associate of Sigmund Freud who in the 1930s helped Freud found the Vienna Psychoanalytic Institute, 10 August 1977.

Dr. Arthur Hendley Blakemore, 73, surgeon and medical teacher, known for his pioneering work in vascular surgery, 8 October 1970.

Dr. William Brady, 91, writer of a syndicated medical column for fifty-eight years, 25 February 1972.

Paul R. Brukholder, 69, the first man to isolate azeserine, a drug used to combat leukemia, 11 August 1972.

Dr. Isadore E. Buff, 65, leader in the battle to obtain black-lung benefits for coal miners, 14 March 1974.

Dr. Ezra P. Casman, 66, bacteriologist who received the U.S. distinguished service award for his discovery of the principal organisms responsible for food poisoning, 16 October 1970.

Richard Chamberlain, 60, pioneer in nuclear medicine and in the use of radioactive substances for therapy and diagnosis, 5 December 1975.

William D. Coolidge, 101, inventor of the X-ray tube, 3 February 1975.

Dr. George C. Cotzias, 58, developer of L-Dopa therapy for Parkinson's disease, 13 June 1977.

Dr. Lyman C. Craig, 68, revolutionizer of techniques for purifying drugs, penicillins, proteins, and hormones, 7 July 1974.

Dr. Leo Davidoff, 73, a founder of the Albert Einstein College of Medicine; he helped establish the department of neurosurgery and served as its chairman until 1966, 23 December 1975.

Theodosius Dobzhansky, 75, geneticist, 19 December 1975.

Dr. Lester R. Dragstedt, 81, who performed the first successful surgical separation of Siamese twins in 1955; he is credited with the development of the vagotomy operation for duodenal ulcers, 16 July 1975.

Dr. Rolla E. Dyer, 84, director of the National Institutes of Health (1942–1950), expert on diseases caused by rickettsia, awarded 1948 Albert Lasker Award, 2 June 1971.

Dr. Herbert McLean Evans, 88, discoverer of vitamin E in 1922, head of the Institute of Experimental Biology at Berkeley, 6 March 1971.

Dr. Howard D. Fabing, 62, former president of the American Academy of Neurology and of the Society of Biological Psychiatry and a pioneer in the research of hallucinogenic drugs such as LSD, 29 July 1970.

Dr. Sidney Farber, 69, pioneer in children's cancer research and 1966 winner of the Albert Lasker Award for clinical research, 30 March 1973.

Dr. Morris Fishbein, 87, former editor of the *Journal of the American Medical Association* (1924–1949) and controversial figure whose outspoken opinions caused the AMA to force him into retirement, 27 September 1976.

Aime J. Forand, 76, Medicare advocate who served twenty-two years in the House of Representatives (D–Rhode Island), 18 January 1972.

Dr. Herbert G. Fowler, 58, genetic psychiatrist who studied the inheritance patterns of mental illness in American Indians, 2 January 1977.

Rose N. Franzblau, 77, psychologist, advice columnist; her syndicated column, "Human Relations," appeared in newspapers across the country daily from 1951 to 1976, 2 September 1979.

Dr. Frank Fremont-Smith, 78, mental-health leader, 27 February 1974.

Dr. Maurice Fremont-Smith, 88, popularizer of the Pap smear test for cervical cancer, 4 May 1979.

Ralph Waldo Gerard, 73, who contributed to a general understanding of the brain and nervous system; he tied schizophrenia to body chemistry, 17 February 1974.

Dr. John H. Gibbon, Jr., 69, who performed the first successful open-heart operation, 5 February 1973.

Dr. Haim Ginott, 51, child psychologist who wrote the best-seller *Between Parent and Child,* 4 November 1973.

Dr. Harry Goldblatt, 86, pioneer blood researcher who in 1934 performed a classic experiment that established that alteration in the blood flow to the kidneys plays an important role in high blood pressure, 6 January 1977.

Dr. Alan F. Guttmaker, 75, pioneer in the birth-control movement, 18 March 1974.

Heinz Hartmann, 75, Vienna-born psychoanalyst and author (*Psychoanalysis and Moral Values*), 17 May 1970.

Dr. Victor G. Heiser, 99, author (*American Doctor's Odyssey*) and pioneer in mass treatment of lepers, 27 February 1972.

Joseph Hoffman, 65, physicist who helped develop the atom bomb during the Manhattan Project at Los Alamos, New Mexico (1944–1946) and director of cancer research at Roswell Park Memorial Institute in Buffalo, 8 December 1974.

Dr. David M. Hume, 55, who helped develop the technique of human organ transplants; he died in a plane crash in California, 19 May 1973.

Blanche Ittleson, 99, mental-health pioneer, 16 August 1975.

Dr. Andrew Ivy, 84, cancer researcher who at one time promoted the anticancer drug krebiozen; indicted in 1965 on federal charges in connection with krebiozen, he was later acquitted, 7 February 1978.

Dr. Edith B. Jackson, 82, the originator of rooming-in care for newborn infants and their mothers and a leader in childcare and preventive psychiatry, 5 June 1977.

Dr. Louis N. Katz, 75, a pioneer in arteriosclerosis research and a past president of the American Heart Association, 2 April 1973.

Dr. Edward C. Kendall, 86, winner of the 1950 Nobel Prize for medicine and physiology for work with cortisone, 4 May 1972.

Dr. John H. Knowles, 52, president of the Rockefeller Foundation since 1972 and director of Massachusetts General Hospital (1962–1971), becoming controversial as an outspoken critic of high medical fees and unnecessary surgery, 6 March 1979.

Dr. Lawrence Kolb, 91, pioneer in medical treatment of narcotics addicts; he helped create the National Institute of Mental Health, 17 November 1972.

Dr. Chauncey D. Leake, 81, writer on the relation of science to ethics and the humanities; he was credited with introducing diviny ether into the practice of anesthesiology in 1930, 11 January 1978.

Dr. David M. Levy, 84, child psychiatrist who coined the term *sibling rivalry* and introduced the diagnostic Rorschach test for personality traits to the United States after a trip to Switzerland in 1926, 1 March 1977.

Eli Lilly, 91, former president and chairman of Eli Lilly and Company, the drug company founded by his grandfather; in 1937 he founded Lilly Endowment Incorporated, a philanthropic fund which donated over $250 million to charity, 24 January 1977.

Dr. Erich Lindeman, 74, psychiatrist and social scientist who applied sociology to psychiatric problems; he was named director of the country's first community health center (1948), 16 November 1974.

Dr. Clarence Cook Little, 83, leading geneticist and cancer researcher who founded (1929) and directed (until 1956) the Roscoe B. Jackson Memorial Laboratory for cancer research, 22 December 1971.

Dr. Charles LeRoy Lowman, 97, a leading orthopedic surgeon who founded the Orthopaedic Hospital in Los Angeles (1909); he was awarded a 1974 Medal of Freedom for his work with handicapped children in Mexico and the United States, 17 April 1977.

Dr. David Marine, 96, pathologist who discovered the iodine treatment for goiter and other thyroid disorders, 26 November 1979.

Abby Rockefeller Mauze, 72, a leading philanthropist and board member of the Memorial Sloan-Kettering Cancer Center in New York and one of its chief benefactors, 27 May 1976.

Dr. Edward McCormick, 83, president of the American Medical Association (1953–1954) who appealed to the association to draw up a schedule of fees for physicians, 7 January 1975.

Hiram Houston Merrit, 78, pioneer neurologist and co-developer of the antiepilepsy drug dilantin, 9 January 1979.

Dr. Karl Meyer, 89, noted veterinarian and viral scientist credited with finding a remedy when a deadly form of food poisoning was crippling the canning industry, 27 April 1974.

Dr. Harry Willis Miller, 97, surgeon, nutritionist, and medical missionary popularly known as the China doctor; he developed the process of extracting milk from soybeans and founded twenty Seventh Day Adventist church hospitals throughout the Far East, 1 January 1977.

Dr. Jacob Haskell Milstone, 64, professor at Yale University School of Medicine who was credited with major discoveries in the field of blood coagulation, 27 January 1977.

Gardner Murphy, 83, psychologist, pioneer scientist in the field of parapsychology and director of research at the Menninger Foundation (1952–1968), 19 March 1979.

Dr. Dwight Murray, 86, former president of the AMA (1956) and critic of socialized medicine, 7 October 1974.

Dr. Carl Muschenheim, 72, lung specialist who helped develop a drug treatment for tuberculosis that reduced the U.S. death rate from the disease by almost 70 percent, 27 April 1977.

Dr. Dorothy Klenke Nash, 77, a Pittsburgh neurosurgeon who reportedly was the only woman neurosurgeon in the United States from 1928 to 1960, 5 March 1976.

Dr. William D. ("Shorty") Paul, 77, inventor of buffered aspirin, 19 December 1977.

Dr. Lyndon Peer, 78, pioneer plastic surgeon who helped found the nation's first medical society devoted to the field; he developed a method of ear reconstruction based on the body's natural healing process, 8 October 1977.

Dr. Frederick S. Perls, 76, founder of the Gestalt school of psychotherapy, 14 March 1970.

Jerry Pettis, 58, member of the House of Representatives, (R–California) since 1966; he developed a successful system of tapes of medical findings for doctors to use in their cars (1953), 14 February 1975.

Dr. Robert Allan Phillips, 70, U.S. Navy physician and public-health leader who led the fight against cholera, 20 September 1976.

Dr. Robert F. Pitts, 68, physiologist whose research in kidney function and disease led to medical therapies, including the use of diuretic drugs, 6 June 1977.

Dr. Clilan B. Powell, 83, former editor and publisher (1935–1971) of the *New York Amsterdam News*; he was the first black appointed to the New York State Athletic Commission and the first black physician to specialize in X rays, 22 September 1977.

Dr. Marion Hill Preminger, 58, film actress who became a disciple of Dr. Albert Schweitzer, served in the Congo (1950–1965), and lectured to raise funds for hospitals and other philanthropies, 15 April 1972.

Dr. Armand J. Quick, 83, developer in 1932 of the prothrombin time test, also known as the Quick test, which was used in regulating the dosage of blood-thinning drugs and in diagnosing liver diseases, 26 January 1978.

Dr. Isador S. Ravdin, 77, one of the leading surgeons and cancer specialists in the United States and a member of the team that treated President Dwight D. Eisenhower, 27 August 1972.

Dr. Dickinson W. Richards, 77, Columbia University physician who shared the Nobel Prize for medicine in 1956 for heart research, 23 February 1973.

Dr. Sandor Rodo, 82, Hungarian-born physician who became one of Freud's first disciples and leader of the psychoanalytic movement; he fled Germany for the United States during the Nazi era and helped establish the first school of psychoanalysis at Columbia University, 14 May 1972.

Dr. May E. Romm, 86, psychiatrist who served as technical adviser for several motion pictures and former president of the Los Angeles and Southern California Psychoanalytic societies, 15 October 1977.

Theodor Rosebury, 72, bacteriologist, specialist in venereal disease, and writer whose most popular book was *Microbes and Morals*, 25 November 1976.

Dr. Peyton Rous, 90, winner of the 1966 Nobel Prize for medicine, 16 February 1970.

Dr. John Scudder, 76, pioneer of blood storage who helped set up blood banks in the United States and abroad; in 1959 he advocated the controversial "race to race" policy in blood transfusions which he said might prevent the creation of blood disease, 6 December 1976.

Dr. Samuel H. Sheppard, 46, osteopath who was freed in the second trial for his first wife's murder; the case was the inspiration for the television show *The Fugitive,* 6 April 1970.

Dr. Fred L. Soper, 83, director emeritus of the Pan American Health Organization; his work in the control of yellow fever, malaria, and typhus spanned three continents and nearly four decades, 9 February 1977.

Dr. Mal Stevens, 79, orthopedic surgeon and football coach at Yale, 6 December 1979.

Dr. Alfred H. Sturtevant, 78, geneticist, 5 April 1970.

Kanematsu Sugiura, 89, Japanese-born research scientist and pioneer in the development of chemotherapy in the treatment of cancer, 21 October 1979.

Dr. Earl W. Sutherland, Jr., 58, winner of the 1971 Nobel Prize for medicine and physiology for research on hormones, 9 March 1974.

Mary Switzer, 71, administrator of the Social and Rehabilitation Service of the Department of Health, Education, and Welfare (1967–1970) she directed sweeping changes in programs for the disabled, 16 October 1971.

Edward L. Tatum, 65, cowinner of the 1958 Nobel Prize for medicine for his pioneering genetics studies with microorganisms, 5 November 1975.

Dr. Max Theiler, 73, winner of the 1951 Nobel Prize for medicine and the virologist who developed the vaccine for yellow fever, 11 August 1972.

Dr. Georg von Bekesy, 73, winner of the 1961 Nobel Prize for medicine for human ear research, 13 June 1972.

Dr. Selman A. Waksman, 85, winner of the 1952 Nobel Prize for medicine, principal discoverer of streptomycin, and coiner of the word *antibiotic*, 16 August 1973.

Dr. Alexander S. Weiner, 70, codiscoverer of the Rh blood factor, 6 November 1976.

Dr. George Hoyt Whipple, 97, pathologist and cowinner of the 1934 Nobel Prize for medicine for his discovery that pernicious anemia could be controlled with a liver diet, 1 February 1976.

Dr. Paul Dudley White, 87, heart specialist and international authority on heart disease who advocated exercise as prevention and therapy; he treated President Eisenhower after his first heart attack, 31 October 1973.

Dr. Edward Wiss, 81, a student and early associate of Freud who founded the Italian Psychoanalytic Society in 1931, 15 December 1970.

Dr. William Barry Wood, Jr., 60, Harvard athlete who achieved prominence in the medical world as a bacteriologist, physician, researcher, and teacher; he was vice-president of (1955), 9 March 1971.

PUBLICATIONS

James Lee Anderson, *The West Point Fitness and Diet Book* (New York: Rawson, 1977);

Earl R. Babbie, *Science and Morality in Medicine. A Survey of Medical Educators* (Berkeley: University of California Press, 1970);

Samuel J. Barr and Dan Abelow, *A Woman's Choice* (New York: Rawson, 1977);

H. S. Becker, B. Geer, and S. J. Miller, "Medical Education," in *Handbook of Medical Sociology*, edited by H. Freeman, S. Levine, and L. Reeder (Englewood Cliffs, N.J.: Prentice-Hall, 1972);

Melvin Berger, *Disease Detectives* (New York: Crowell, 1978);

Boston Women's Health Collective, *Our Bodies, Ourselves* (New York: Simon & Schuster, 1973);

Baruch Brody, *Abortion and the Sanctity of Human Life: A Philosophical View* (Cambridge, Mass.: MIT Press, 1975);

E. Richard Brown, *Rockefeller Medicine Men: Medicine and Capitalism in America* (Berkeley: University of California Press, 1979);

John J. Burt, *Personal Health Behavior in Today's Society* (Philadelphia: W. B. Saunders, 1972);

Daniel Callahan, *Abortion: Law, Choice and Morality* (New York: Macmillan, 1970);

Rita Ricardo Campbell, *Economics of Health and Public Policy* (Washington, D.C.: American Enterprise Institute for Public Policy Research, 1971);

Center for Information on America, Guide to Prepaid Group Health Care Programs (Oak Park, Cal.: The Center, 1976);

B. D. Colen, *Karen Ann Quinlan. Dying in the Age of Eternal Life* (New York: Nash, 1976);

Adelle Davis, *Let's Have Healthy Children,* expanded edition (New York: Harcourt Brace Jovanovich, 1972);

Barbara Deckard, *The Women's Movement* (New York: Harper & Row, 1975);

Marc Duke, *Acupuncture* (New York: Pyramid House, 1972);

Elizabeth W. Etheridge, *The Butterfly Caste. A Social History of Pellagra in the South* (Westport, Conn.: Greenwood Press, 1972);

Joseph L. Falkson, *HMOs and the Politics of Health System Reform* (Chicago: American Hospital Association, 1980);

Paul J. Feldstein, *Health Care Economics* (New York: John Wiley & Sons, 1979);

James F. Fixx, *The Complete Book of Running* (New York: Random House, 1977);

Linda Bird Francke, *The Ambivalence of Abortion* (New York: Random House, 1978);

Eliot Freidson, *Doctoring Together: A Study of Professional Social Control* (New York: Elsevier, 1975);

Richard L. Ganz, ed., *Thou Shalt Not Kill* (New York: Arlington House, 1978);

Linda Gordon, *Woman's Body, Woman's Right* (New York: Grossman, 1976);

Gerald Grob, ed., *Mental Illness and Social Policy: The American Experience* (New York: Arno, 1973);

Saul Jarcho, M.D., and Gene Brown, eds., *Medicine and Health Care* (New York: The New York Times/Arno Press, 1977);

James H. Jones, *Bad Blood* (New York: Free Press, 1981);

Alan Klass, *There's Gold in Them Thar Pills: An Inquiry into the Medical-Industrial Complex* (New York: Penguin, 1975);

E. Russel Kodet and Bradford Angier, *The Home Medical Handbook* (New York: Association Press, 1970);

Helen Kruger, *Other Healers, Other Cures: A Guide to Alternative Medicine* (Indianapolis: Bobbs-Merrill, 1974);

Charles T. Kuntzleman, *The Complete Book of Walking* (New York: Simon & Schuster, 1978);

Kenneth M. Ludmerer, *Genetics and American Society* (Baltimore: Johns Hopkins University Press, 1972);

Yoshio Manaka, *The Layman's Guide to Acupuncture* (New York: Weatherhill, 1972);

Felix Mann, *Acupuncture: the Ancient Chinese Art of Healing and How It Works Scientifically* (New York: Vintage, 1973);

Helen E. Marshall, *Mary Adelaide Nutting: Pioneer of Modern Nursing* (Baltimore: Johns Hopkins University Press, 1972);

B. Martin, "Physician Manpower, 1972," in *'73 Profile of Medical Practice,* edited by S. Vahovich (Chicago: American Medical Association, 1973);

William S. Middleton, *Values in Modern Medicine* (Madison: University of Wisconsin Press, 1972);

Lawrence E. Morehouse and Leonard Gross, *Total Fitness in 30 Minutes a Week* (New York: Simon & Schuster, 1975);

Robin Morgan, ed., *Sisterhood Is Powerful* (New York: Random House, 1970);

Richard E. Neustadt and Harvey V. Fineberg, *The Swine Flu Affair: Decision-Making on a Slippery Disease* (Washington, D.C.: Department of Health, Education, and Welfare, 1978);

John T. Noonan, ed., *The Morality of Abortion: Legal and Historical Perspectives* (Cambridge, Mass.: Harvard University Press, 1970);

John R. Paul, *A History of Poliomyelitis* (New Haven: Yale University Press, 1972);

Joseph and Julia Quinlan, *Karen Ann: The Quinlans Tell Their Story* (Garden City, N.Y.: Doubleday, 1977);

Charles E. Rosenberg, ed., *Medicine and Society in America* (New York: Arno, 1972);

Jeffrey Rubin, *Economics, Mental Health, and the Law* (Lexington, Mass., D.C. Heath, 1978);

Lauren R. Sass, *Abortion: Freedom of Choice and Right to Life* (New York: Facts on File, 1978);

Leong T. Tan, Margaret Y.-C. Tan, and Ilza Veith, *Acupuncture Therapy; Current Chinese Practice* (Philadelphia, Pa.: Temple University Press, 1973);

The Way Things Work: Book of the Body (New York: Simon & Schuster, 1979);

Leonard Tushnet, M.D., *The Medicine Men. The Myth of Quality Medical Care in America Today* (New York: St. Martin's Press, 1972);

S. Vahovich, *Profile of Medical Practice* (Chicago: American Medical Association, 1973);

James C. Whorton, *Before Silent Spring. Pesticides and Public Health in Pre-DDT America* (Princeton, N.J.: Princeton University Press, 1976);

Greer Williams, *Kaiser-Permanente Health Plan: Why It Works* (Oakland, Cal.: Henry J. Kaiser Foundation, 1971);

Health;

Health Facts, begun in 1976;

"Medical Sciences," column in occasional issues of *Science News;*

Network News, begun in 1976;

"News from the World of Medicine," monthly feature in the *Readers' Digest;*

A. E. Nourse, "Family Doctor," monthly feature of *Good Housekeeping;*

Prevention;

Science News Letter, annual report on medicine;

C. SerVaas, "Medical Mailbox," weekly report in the *Saturday Evening Post;*

Today's Health, absorbed by *Family Health* in 1976;

B. Yuncker, "Keep Up with Medicine," monthly feature in *Good Housekeeping;*

D. R. Zimmerman, "Medicine Today," monthly feature in *Ladies' Home Journal.*

1978 Public Service announcement by the President's Council on Physical Fitness and Sports

RELIGION

by JOHN SCOTT WILSON

CONTENTS

Sidebars and tables are listed in italics.

1970

17 Jan. The Right Reverend John M. Burgess is installed as bishop of the Massachusetts diocese. He is the first black presiding bishop in the Episcopal church.

2 Feb. Sister Anita Caspany, president of the Immaculate Heart of Mary religious order in Los Angeles, announces that 315 of the 400 members of the order will end their religious ties and set up a lay community to continue their work.

6 Feb. The Orthodox church in the Soviet Union grants autonomy to the United States Russian Orthodox Greek Catholic church over the protests of the Ecumenical patriarch in Istanbul. The new 800,000-member, autocephalous denomination takes the name the Orthodox Church in America.

23 Feb. Archbishop James J. Byrrie of Dubuque names Mrs. Cornell Deery of Eagle Grove, Iowa, and Mary Sandman of New Vienna, Iowa, as the first laywomen in the United States permitted to distribute the Eucharist in the absence of regular priests.

20 Apr. The General Conference of the United Methodist Church accepts a statement characterizing the war in Vietnam as a "fiasco" and urges accelerated talks to end the conflict.

16 June The *New English Bible,* the work of a group of British religious and literary scholars, is published.

29 June The Lutheran Church in America agrees to the ordination of women, the first Lutheran denomination to permit this.

2 July The twentieth biennial meeting of the Clergy-Laity Congress of the Greek Orthodox church agrees to allow the use of the vernacular in liturgies, when approved by the local bishop.

30 Sept. The *New American Bible* is published, the first Roman Catholic translation from the original texts into English.

24 Oct. The American Lutheran Church approves the ordination of women.

25 Oct. Three hundred members of the First Baptist Church of Birmingham, Alabama, including the pastor, split from the church when the congregation refuses to approve the membership of a black woman and her daughter. They organize a new congregation.

1971

2 Feb. To protest the system of apartheid the General Assembly of the Episcopal church petitions General Motors Corporation to end manufacturing in South Africa.

2 Nov. A synod of bishops, meeting in Vatican City, reaffirms celibacy for Roman Catholic religious orders.

21 Dec. The New York Federation of Catholic Teachers votes to end their twenty-nine-day strike against schools run by the New York archdiocese and accept the terms offered by the archdiocese. This is the first major strike against a parochial school system in the United States.

1972

27 Jan. The black and white United Methodist Church conferences in South Carolina agree to merge.

1973

22 Mar.	The Supreme Court overturns a ninety-three-year-old Massachusetts law banning the sale of birth control devices to the unmarried.
22 May	The General Assembly of the United Presbyterian church asks for a total, immediate withdrawal of American forces from Vietnam.

8 Jan.	The Society of Jesus announces that it will close two of its five training institutes because of declining applications. Woodstock College in New York and the Saint Louis School of Divinity will stop taking Jesuit students.
2 Feb.	Pope Paul VI nominates the Most Reverend Luis Aponte Martinez, archbishop of Puerto Rico, to the College of Cardinals. He is the first Puerto Rican to be named cardinal.
6 Apr.	Delegates of the eight Protestant denominations engaged in the Consultation on Church Union (COCU) vote to postpone indefinitely the study of plans for a merger called the Church of Christ Uniting.

1974

3 Mar.	A commission of U.S. Roman Catholic and Lutheran theologians declares that the issue of papal primacy need not be an obstacle to the reconciliation of the two denominations, divided since the Reformation.
8 Apr.	Rev. C. Shelby Rooks is named the first black president of the predominantly white Chicago Theological Seminary.
16 June	Rev. Dr. Lawrence Bottoms is elected as the first black moderator of the Presbyterian church (U.S.).
29 July	Four bishops of the Episcopal church defy church law by ordaining eleven women into the priesthood.

1975

•	The United Church of Christ endorses ending all discrimination "relating to sexual or affectional preference."
Jan.	Volume one of *The Torah: A Modern Commentary* is published by the Union of American Hebrew Congregations (Reform).
17 Jan.	A joint session of the Pacific Association of Reform Rabbis and the Western States Region of the Rabbinical Assembly (Conservative) asks the government of Israel to allow Reform and Conservative rabbis to perform ceremonies for "life-cycle occasions" in the Jewish state.
12 Feb.	The National Council of Catholic Bishops approves a "New American Sunday Missal."
14 Sept.	Pope Paul VI canonizes Mother Elizabeth Ann Bayley Seton. She is the first saint born in the United States.
11 Oct.	The Central Conference of American Rabbis (Reform) issues a new prayer book, *The Gates of Prayer: the New Union Prayer Book.* It incorporates a gender-neutral vocabulary.

1976

16 Sept.   The General Convention of the Episcopal church approves the ordination of women. Six years earlier the House of Bishops of the convention had rejected a similar motion.

4 Dec.   The Association of Evangelical Lutheran Churches is formed from moderates leaving the Lutheran Church-Missouri Synod.

1977

19 Jan.   Pope Paul VI canonizes Bishop John N. Newman, the first American male saint.

25 Oct.   The Orthodox Church in America elects its first American-born prelate, Bishop Theodosius of Baltimore.

1978

9 June   Spencer W. Kimball, president of the Church of Jesus Christ of Latter-day Saints (Mormons), signs a letter admitting black men to the Mormon priesthood. Women are still excluded.

7 Dec.   Eleven high-ranking members of the Church of Scientology are convicted for conspiring to infiltrate the Justice Department and the Internal Revenue Service in order to monitor government investigations of the church. They are given four- and five-year sentences.

1979

12 Sept.   The Triennial Convention of the Episcopal church approves a new *Prayerbook* to replace the 1928 revision.

1-7 Oct.   Pope John Paul II visits the United States. He is the first pope to meet a U.S. president at the White House.

OVERVIEW

Decline of the Mainline Churches. The decline of membership and influence of Mainline Protestant denominations continued in the 1970s. Conservatives charged that these denominations had lost their fire, and consequently their membership, to more committed groups. Perhaps more people left the Mainline organizations for new modes of worship or because organized religion had lost its relevance to them.

Cultural Pressures. The Mainline churches struggled over accommodating the cultural changes that had begun in midcentury. Their leaders and many of their members had become outspoken opponents of the American involvement in the Vietnam War. Their influence was more significant in forcing the Nixon administration to the diplomatic bargaining table than were the strident and often violent actions of the organized antiwar movement. In spite of their traditional Republican Party roots, people in these denominations became the most effective opponents of President Richard Nixon in the ongoing Watergate scandal. This political action offended conservatives and seemed to distract them from more spiritual matters.

The Challenge of feminism. These denominations also wrestled with the implications of the growing feminist movement. Some denominations, such as the Disciples of Christ, the United Methodist church, and the leading Presbyterian churches, had admitted women to the ministry in the past. Now the Lutheran churches and the Episcopal church wrestled over the question of the ordination of females. Most accepted the practice before the decade was over.

Sex. While few Protestant denominations had reservations about the use of birth control, each struggled to come to grips with the new, relaxed standards of sexual morality, including premarital sex and abortion. They also began the long-term discussion of homosexuality and the legitimacy of the ordination of practicing homosexuals.

The Rise of Evangelicals. The number of conservative Protestants, increasingly called Evangelicals but including traditional Evangelicals, Fundamentalists, and Pentecostalists, grew rapidly in the decade. Their denominations and organizations acquired new self-confidence and assurance as the groups reflected the growing economic, social, and political influence of their members. The public became familiar with the phrase *born-again* in the presidential election of 1976 when Jimmy Carter, a Georgia peanut farmer and businessman, as well as a Southern Baptist, introduced conversion theology to the general public. *Newsweek* celebrated 1976 as the "Year of the Evangelical." As the membership of these conservative denominations grew, they began to move aggressively into the public arena, particularly over social and cultural questions such as abortion, gay rights, and the Equal Rights Amendment. In the long run President Carter would be the target of their anger.

Television Ministries. Part of the newfound confidence of these Evangelicals came from the growing popularity of television ministries that used the now-established and burgeoning medium of cable television. Pat Robertson's Christian Broadcasting Network (CBN) was the largest religious system, but other televangelists, as they were called, attracted large audiences and became subjects of public discussion before the decade was over. Jim and Tammy Bakker, with their PTL ministry; Jimmy Swaggart; and Jerry Falwell were celebrities in a celebrity-conscious society.

Change and Tradition in Catholicism. The Roman Catholic community continued to adjust to the forces of change unleashed by the Second Vatican Council of 1963–1965. Priests and nuns continued to leave their orders, and lay people became more assertive in religious affairs. The clearest evidence of this new assertiveness was the growing number of Catholics who used birth control. Although Pope John Paul II, the first Polish pope and the first non-Italian pope in centuries, attempted to reassert the leadership of the clergy in sexual issues, his popularity in the United States did not change the behavior of his U.S. followers.

Yom Kippur War. The Jewish community increasingly identified itself with the Jewish state of Israel after the Arab-Israel war of 1967. That identification intensified when the frontline Arab states launched a surprise attack on Israel on Yom Kippur, the holiest day of the Jewish calendar, in 1973. The Israeli forces were nearly overwhelmed until massive amounts of American military equipment replaced that destroyed by the Arabs. American Jews were disappointed by what they considered the failure of liberal Protestants and Catholics to support the leading democratic state in the Middle East, but they willingly accepted the support of Evangelicals who saw the Jewish state as a confirmation of biblical prophecy that Jesus was returning soon.

Cults and Nontraditional Religions. Members of the three traditional religious communities were concerned about the growth of new religious groups in the nation. While many observers were tolerant of religions brought from Asia by immigrants allowed under the revised immigration rules of 1965, some of these imports seemed to target young Americans and often seemed to take their converts not only from their traditional faiths but even from their old communities and families. In the course of the decade there was much talk of cults and brainwashing, and people calling themselves deprogrammers offered their services to parents who hoped to reclaim their children from some religious quest that seemed bizarre to those in familiar faiths. This fear of cults climaxed with the mass suicides and murders in Guyana in 1978 when Jim Jones led or forced nearly a thousand of his followers into what he called "revolutionary suicide."

Politics of Religion. By the end of the decade some conservative voters had fused their religious and political views into partisan political activism to stop the rush of cultural change and promote the political advancement of their economic and political views. The most famous of these movements was Jerry Falwell's Moral Majority, which aimed at reasserting what he believed were America's traditional social values in a secular culture that was dominated by government and that seemed open to sexual immorality. If the United States were to be strong in world affairs, the Moral Majority asserted, it needed to be strong in the moral values which had made the country great. Evangelicals, who had left politics after the collapse of Prohibition in the 1930s, returned to the political arena to "save America's soul."

TOPICS IN THE NEWS

ABORTION

Abortion as a Political Issue. The issue of relaxing laws restricting medical abortions was one of the many reforms raised in the seething climate of the 1960s. For some years efforts had been made to ease the restraint on abortion so that women would have access to safe medical termination of their pregnancies. Sexual reformers were joined during the decade by other groups, among them the new women's advocacy groups, such as the National Organization for Women (NOW), which advocated the repeal of abortion laws at its second annual convention in November 1967. These groups demanded modification if not repeal of the various states' laws prohibiting the termination of pregnancy in order to increase women's freedom. Other groups concerned with the world's exploding population, such as Zero Population Growth, saw access to abortion a part of their larger goals. By 1969 there was sufficient interest to create a national organization, the National Association for the Repeal of Abortion Laws (NARAL).

Local Emphasis. People associated with NARAL assumed they would have to achieve their goals at the state level and quickly made progress by drawing on the support of religious liberals, both individuals and denominations. In 1970 both the Lutheran Church in America and the American Lutheran church gave qualified approval to abortion, and the United Methodist Board of Church and Society was particularly active in the push for reform. By organizing local activists, abortion reformers had eased access to legal, medical abortions in four states, including New York, and campaigns were active in other states, despite vigorous resistance.

Roe v. Wade. The reformers seemed to have achieved an unexpected, complete victory when on 22 January 1973 the Supreme Court, in *Roe* v. *Wade,* ruled that an inherent right to privacy exists within the Constitution and that this right prohibited the states' interference in the medical relation between a woman and her physician in the first trimester of her pregnancy. States could regulate abortion in the later stages of pregnancy, as the fetus became viable outside the womb.

Catholic Reaction. The *Roe* decision sent shock waves through some religious groups. The Roman Catholic church, which had been working against relaxing anti-abortion laws, found the ruling abhorrent. The National Council of Catholic Bishops quickly issued a pastoral

In a 1973 issue of the Catholic periodical *America*, Timothy E. O'Connell wrote:

"Roman Catholics's parent-immigrants believed that the political order could be implicitly trusted, that it would not let them down. . . .We were naive. We were foolish. Indeed, we were unfair to the civil order. For in our childish faith we expected that order to do more than it was able. We expected it to mediate in an infallible way the will of God for our lives. . . . We expected the government to guarantee a comfortable meld of 'Christian' and 'American.' That it just can't do. . . . if the Supreme Court has not killed Catholic civil religious, it has at least struck it a serious blow."

Source: *America*, 128 (2 June 1973): 517.

warning that those people either undergoing or performing abortion would place themselves in a state of excommunication. The bishops charged the *Roe* decision was "wrong and contrary to the fundamental principles of morality. . . . The Supreme Court has certainly overstepped itself in making law rather than interpreting it." The National Council of Catholic Bishops then turned the National Right to Life Committee into a membership organization which became the largest and most visible of the antiabortion groups, with over eighteen hundred affiliates and an estimated eleven million members by the end of the decade.

Conservative Opposition. Not all its members were Catholics, of course. Conservative Protestants also had reservations about the end of legal restraints on abortion. The evangelical *Christianity Today* charged that the "majority of the Supreme Court has explicitly rejected Christian moral teaching" and "clearly decided for paganism, and against Christianity." Religious conservatives formed organizations that sought to overturn or modify the *Roe* decision, which seemed a part of the growing secularization of American society and its rejection of traditional moral and biblical values.

Life versus Choice. The antiabortion movement referred to itself as pro-life, attempting to target its opponents as advocates of death. Those who supported women's right to abortion insisted that they were not necessarily in favor of abortion but of the right of a woman to choose for herself whether she would bear a child. These advocates called themselves pro-choice.

The Hyde Amendment. The struggle between the groups was intense. In spite of general support for the right to an abortion, the antiabortion movement was able to target its energies at legislative bodies and achieved a significant success in 1976 when Congress adopted the so-called Hyde amendment to the Medicaid appropriation, which forbade using federal funds to pay for abortion except when the mother's life was in danger. Abortion foes pressured individual states to take similar steps to refuse to pay for abortions except for therapeutic reasons. In 1980 the Supreme Court upheld the Hyde amendment.

Moral Values of the Nation. The antiabortion movement brought together a variety of attitudes besides the belief that human life was engendered at the moment of conception. Social conservatives saw abortion as more evidence of the collapse of the nation's moral values in that it offered women an additional way to ignore their sexual responsibility. This seemed another manifestation of the feminist movement. These conservatives linked abortion, gay rights, and feminism as part of a general effort to overturn the natural, God-given order of sexual relations.

The New Religious Right. These intensifying conservative concerns about social and cultural issues led to the political coalition of the late 1970s called the New Religious Right. Its most famous organization, Jerry Falwell's Moral Majority, was organized in 1979. While the New Religious Right drew its original energy from conservative Protestants, its leaders hoped to bring Roman Catholics into alignment in time.

Sources:

David J. Garrow, *Liberty and Sexuality: The Right to Privacy and the Making of* Roe v. Wade (New York: Macmillan, 1994);

Faye D. Ginsburg, *Contested Lives: The Abortion Debate in an American Community* (Berkeley: University of California Press, 1989);

Ted G. Jelen and Marthe A. Chandler, eds., *Abortion Politics in the United States and Canada: Studies in Public Opinion* (Westport, Conn.: Praeger, 1994);

Michele McKeegan, *Abortion Politics: Mutiny in the Ranks of the Right* (New York: Free Press, 1992);

Suzanne Staggenborg, *The Pro-Choice Movement: Organization and Activism in the Abortion Conflict* (New York: Oxford University Press, 1991).

CULTS

New Religions. In the open cultural climate of the 1960s and 1970s a variety of religions new to, or previously unnoticed in, the United States attracted attention from the press and the general public. Some of these organizations engaged their converts in beliefs and activities that seemed strange by traditional American standards, occupied all their time, and frequently tried to break their ties with their families. The detractors of these groups labeled them "cults" and warned of the danger, particularly to the young.

Hare Krishna. Some of these groups came from India, such as the International Movement for Krishna Consciousness, which incorporated itself in the United States in 1966. The organization attracted increasing numbers of young people, who were called Hare Krishnas by out-

Maharaj Ji, fifteen-year-old guru of the Divine Life Mission

siders due to their chanting public worship. In cities with large numbers of hippies, passersby encountered Hare Krishnas, dressed in saffron robes and with strange haircuts, performing on the streets. Even more startling were the Hare Krishnas soliciting contributions in airport terminals and other public places. People suspected the leaders benefited from the money the young people raised.

Divine Light Mission. Another group with an Eastern-inspired background was the Divine Light Mission, which followed the teachings of the teenage Maharaj Ji, who attracted a large following in his personal mission to the United States in the early 1970s. He moved his world headquarters to Denver, Colorado, where about a thousand young people filled the group's communes. In 1973 the Divine Light Mission rented the Houston Astrodome for a meeting called "Millennium '73," in which Rennie Davis, one of those charged with disrupting the 1968 Democratic National Convention in Chicago, was a chief participant. The Houston rally was not as successful as anticipated, even though it brought in Maharaj Ji's followers from around the world. The movement gradually declined after Maharaj Ji married his secretary, over his mother's protests, and his family in India severed their connections with him.

TM. Another popular Indian guru was Maharishi Mahesh Yogi, who taught transcendental meditation. In the early 1970s large numbers of people, an estimated ten thousand a month by middecade, went to one of the 350 training centers, where they were each given a personal mantra, a word which they used for engaging in meditation. Initially there were questions whether TM, as it was sometimes called, was a religion or a drug-free means of attaining an altered consciousness. Inspired in part by TM, physicians and psychologists began investigating the psychic value of meditation. In 1974 the Yogi bought Parsons College in Fairfield, Iowa, and named it Maharishi International University. When the Maharishi Mahesh Yogi's followers began to claim that they were able to levitate and that their meditation could alter world affairs, the movement went into a decline, although meditation continued to gain in popularity.

The Unification Church. Among the most widely publicized and criticized of the new religions was the Unification church, founded and headed by the Reverend Sun Myung Moon in South Korea. As early as 1959 three of Moon's followers came to the United States to proselytize the series of revelations about Christianity that Moon called the Divine Principle. These revelations urged the unification of the Christian churches, presumably under Moon.

Vigorous Growth. Although Moon came to the United States for brief visits in 1965 and 1969, it was only when he came for an extended stay in 1971 that his church began its vigorous and controversial growth as it directed its attention toward college campuses and other centers where young people congregated.

Emphasis on the Young. The success of the Unification church in recruiting young people and the commitment of the new converts to the organization, often breaking their ties with their families, triggered widespread apprehension. In most cities "Moonies," as they were called, were seen selling roses or otherwise attempting to raise money for the church. Charges were made that converts were lured into the church by deceptive means and then brainwashed with Moon's teachings. Ted Patrick, who organized the Citizens' Freedom Foundation, attracted attention with his claims that he was able to deprogram converts who had been brainwashed.

Politics of Moon. The Unification church also acquired notoriety through its political and financial activities. The Unification church was militantly anti-Communist and aligned itself with conservative politics. During the Watergate crisis the church held mass demonstrations in Washington in support of President Nixon, and Moon took out advertisements saying that "at this moment God has chosen Richard Nixon to be President of the United States." More surreptitious political activity, including Moon's alleged ties to the South Korean intelligence forces, led to inconclusive congressional investigations.

Money Questions. The lavish spending of the Unification church for public and patriotic rallies, the purchase

THE COMET COMES!

by Moses David

··CHAOS REIGNS!

Cover of the pamphlet by Moses David warning of doomsday
when the comet Kohoutek would collide with the earth
on about 31 January 1974

nine hundred of the *Mo Letters* were published, delivering doctrines that departed increasingly from mainstream Christianity. The appearance of Children of God groups in various countries and some of the organization's tactics aroused intense local opposition from time to time, but the organization still functioned at the end of the decade.

Scientology. Another group that aroused concern due to its cultlike qualities was the Church of Scientology, founded by the science-fiction writer L. Ron Hubbard and based on his book *Dianetics: The Modern Science of Mental Health* (1950). By the 1960s Hubbard abandoned his science-fiction writing to concentrate on developing his ideas, which he now insisted was a new faith he called Scientology. His many detractors insisted that he took this guise to avoid government interference and taxation. He too left the United States for Britain and continued to develop the tenets of his faith. In 1977 the Federal Bureau of Investigation (FBI) conducted a raid on the Scientology office in Washington, D.C., to uncover evidence that the church had attempted to infiltrate the FBI and other investigative agencies. The participants in the plan were tried and convicted in federal court.

Sources:

Steve Allen, *Beloved Son: A Story of the Jesus Cults* (Indianapolis: Bobbs-Merrill, 1982);

David G. Bromley and Anson D. Shupe, Jr., *"Moonies" in America: Cult, Church, and Crusade* (Beverly Hills, Cal.: Sage Publications, 1979);

Mack Calanter, *Cults: Faith, Healing, and Coercion* (New York: Oxford University Press, 1989);

Ronald B. Flowers, *Religion in Strange Times: The 1960s and 1970s* (Macon, Ga.: Mercer University Press, 1984);

John R. Hall, *Gone From the Promised Land: Jonestown in American Cultural History* (New Brunswick, N.J.: Transaction, 1987);

Ruth Wangerin, *The Children of God: A Make-Believe Revolution?* (Westport, Conn.: Bergin & Garvey, 1994).

ECUMENICISM

Consultation on Church Union. The 1970s opened with high hopes for closer relationships between various religious groups. The most obvious evidence was the developing plans for a merger of nine of the leading Mainline Protestant denominations in the Consultation on Church Union (COCU). Here representatives from the African Methodist Episcopal, the African Methodist Zion, and the Central Methodist Episcopal churches; the Christian church, or Disciples of Christ; the Episcopal church; the Presbyterian Church in the U.S.; the United Church of Christ; the United Methodist church; and the United Presbyterian church worked on a structure that would permit the creation of a denomination with about twenty-three million members. Observers found it interesting that the COCU denominations had lost nearly two million members since the project began a decade earlier.

Plan of Union. In 1971 COCU sent its Plan of Union, a document on how to create what would be called "The Church of Christ Uniting" to its member groups and immediately encountered opposition on the basis of gov-

of expensive property, and Moon's expensive living costs aroused concern about the source of his funds. It was bad if those funds were from South Korean political groups, even worse if they were from the exploitation of his young American converts. In 1978 the New York Board of Regents refused to grant a charter to Moon's Unification Theological Seminary in Barrytown, New York, partly because of academic standards, partly because of financial questions, but also because of "deceptive claims." The Internal Revenue Service began an investigation into Moon's finances by the end of the decade.

Moses David. A group that started as a Christian mission to young people in the California counterculture in the late 1960s took on cultlike qualities when David Berg, the founder of Teens for Christ, began to see himself as the Messiah, and he changed his name to Moses David. While the group's name changed several times, it was best known as the Children of God. Berg and his followers established a variety of communes on the West Coast and in Texas. Berg himself went to Britain, and his movement began proselytizing around the world. Berg communicated with his followers in letters, called the *Mo Letters,* that spelled out the terms of his developing set of beliefs for his followers. In the course of the decade over

"WHAT OUGHT THE CHURCH TO BE"

In a 1972 issue of *Christian Century*, churchman Douglas M. Campbell reacted to plans for a united church:

"COCU leaves large numbers of Christians unsatisfied because it fails to deal with the true point of conflict in American Protestantism; namely, what ought the church to be and do? The Plan of Union [for the Church of Christ Uniting] is the work of middle-aged churchmen who have achieved status in the several communions. Essentially, it offers 'more of the same,' only bigger . . . the Plan of Union sent to the churches . . . calls for a structure more bureaucratic and more centralized than that of any of the participating denominations . . . just when the demand for decentralization of vast ecclesiastical institutions is becoming more articulate, the plan proposes increased nationalization."

Source: Douglas M. Campbell, "COCU and the Future," *Christian Century*, 89 (16 August 1972): 820–822.

Jews and Catholics. The Vatican also worked out new details on its relations with Jews, now that the old anti-Semitic charge that the Jews were responsible for the execution of Jesus had been expressly repudiated at the Second Vatican Council. The "Guidelines and Suggestions for Implementing the Councillor Declaration 'Nostre Aetate' [In Our Time]" referred to the "spiritual bonds and historical links" between Christians and Jews. It explicitly condemned anti-Semitism and recommended an extended interfaith dialogue.

Bridges for the Future. In March 1979 representatives of various Protestant denominations met with theologians from the Roman Catholic and Orthodox churches at the Southern Baptist Theological Seminary in Louisville, Kentucky, where they agreed to a document outlining their common understanding of the sacrament of baptism. New bridges were being built for the future.

Sources:
David M. Campbell, "COCU and the Future: Is the Consultation Dead?," *Christian Century*, 89 (16 August 1972): 820–822;

"The Disuniting Church," *Time*, 99 (5 June 1972): 57–58;

"Ecumenicism and COCU," *America*, 126 (24 June 1972): 643–644;

John A. Mackay, "Thoughts of Unity," *Christianity Today*, 16 (14 April 1972): 10–12.

ernance, tradition, and theology. When the United Presbyterian church left the organization the enterprise collapsed, and in April 1973 delegates of the eight remaining denominations voted to postpone indefinitely the study of merger at the top and instead supported interchurch cooperation at the local level.

Presbyterian Reunion. The ecumenical surge had not crested, however. The United Presbyterian church and the Presbyterian Church in the U.S. (southern) voted once again to consider reunion. This movement gave some reason for optimism as conservatives in the southern church dropped out to align with other conservative denominations or to form an alternative southern Presbyterian church. These conservatives feared that what they considered a growing liberalism in their church home would lead to a merger with the unacceptably liberal northern church. The new southern denomination called itself the Presbyterian Church in America.

Catholic Openings. But interchurch cooperation strengthened across old, bitter divisions. The Roman Catholic church proved open to cooperation with other religious groups after the Second Vatican Conference in the 1960s. In 1970 new guidelines for marriages between Roman Catholics and other Christians erased some of the old reasons for tensions between the Roman Catholic church and other denominations. While non-Catholic spouses would be reminded that a child should be reared in the church, the non-Catholic partner would not be required to pledge that action.

CHURCHES AND HOMOSEXUALITY

Protesting Discrimination. In the 1970s homosexuals, now identifying themselves as gays and lesbians, began to demand an end to the discrimination they encountered because of their sexual orientation and activities. They achieved some public success in large, tolerant cities like New York City and San Francisco but encountered opposition in other places. In 1977 Anita Bryant, a former Miss Oklahoma and well-known singing star, led a successful effort to keep Dade County, Florida, from adopting laws to bar discrimination based on sexual orientation. Bryant, the most visible member of the antigay organization Save Our Children, based much of her argument against nondiscrimination laws on religious grounds and received most of her support from other religious conservatives. While she won this war and the ordinance failed to pass, she ultimately lost her position as a spokesperson for the Florida Citrus Commission, which preferred not to work with a "controversial" public figure.

Religious Response. As the demand for gay rights intensified, homosexual members of various religious groups, such as the Episcopal Integrity and the Roman Catholic Dignity, organized to influence their denominations. Pressed by these groups and the current of the times, denominations wrestled first with the issue of homosexuality itself and then with the question of whether gay and lesbian people should be ordained.

Ambivalence. The terms of the debate were set by the National Council of Churches in 1975, when its governing board voted overwhelmingly to support equal rights

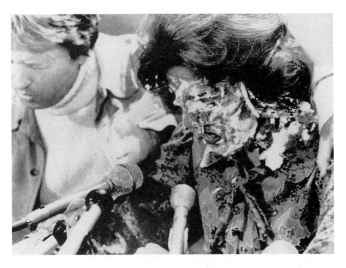

Anita Bryant after being hit with a pie by a homosexual at a press conference

for homosexuals but discouraged their participation in the ministry. The same year the General Assembly of the United Presbyterian Church agreed that homosexuality was not condemned by Scripture but refused to recognize the Presbyterian Gay Caucus. When a commission established to review ordination recommended that gays and lesbians be ordained, the General Assembly rejected the recommendation, except in the case of celibate homosexuals. The Southern Baptist Convention flatly refused ordination to homosexuals. The Episcopal church was sharply divided when Bishop Paul Moore, Jr., of New York ordained an avowed lesbian in 1977. Later that year the Episcopal bishops condemned homosexual activity and opposed ordination as counter to Scripture but did not take action against Moore. In 1978 Rabbi Abraham B. Hecht, president of the Rabbinical Alliance of America, which represented Orthodox rabbis, announced an "all-out campaign against gay rights." He contended that while homosexuality should not be illegal, the state should not legitimize perversion.

Reaction. While many homosexuals remained in their congregations and continued their loyalty to their denominations, others left their home churches to join or establish other congregations. The Metropolitan Community Church, a ministry to gays and lesbians, was founded in Los Angeles in 1968 by the Reverend Troy Perry. The Metropolitan Community Church quickly found other gays and lesbians who felt rejected by their churches for their orientation and behavior and established Community Churches in other major cities. This denomination, calling itself the Universal Fellowship of Metropolitan Community Churches (UFMCC), acquired an estimated twenty thousand members by the end of the decade. Many of its ministers were men and women ordained in other denominations who now found a home in an ecumenical communion of Christians united by their belief that Jesus loved them. The

UFMCC would later apply, unsuccessfully, for admission to the National Council of Churches.

THE PEOPLES TEMPLE

The Jonestown Massacre. On 18 November 1978 James Warren ("Jim") Jones, founder and head of the Peoples Temple, ordered the assassination of California congressman Leo Ryan and the mass suicide of nearly a thousand of his followers in the colony he had established in the jungles of Guyana, the Promised Land. Jones himself died in the catastrophe. The events in Jonestown, as reporters called the enclave, stunned the world and deepened the fear of cults that was already rampant in the United States.

Beginnings. Jim Jones was born in Indiana in 1931. He went into the Pentecostal ministry as a youth, establishing a congregation in Indianapolis that took the name Peoples Temple in 1955. In time Jones affiliated both himself and his congregation with the Mainline denomination the Disciples of Christ. From the beginning Jones maintained a biracial congregation.

Apocalyptic Visions. In the early 1960s Jones became increasingly concerned about the nuclear threat and left Indianapolis for about two years, visiting Hawaii, Guyana, and finally Brazil before he returned to his congregation in Indiana and began to shift his beliefs from his original Christian base. In 1965 he sent the first of his followers to Mendocino County in northern California, incorporating the Peoples Temple there in 1966. He listed eighty-six followers at that time. When Jones moved himself and his family to the city of Ukiah, on the Russian River, the Peoples Temple began to expand. He opened branches in San Francisco and Los Angeles and converted middle-class whites, as well as elderly black followers.

San Francisco. In 1970 he opened his temple on Geary Street in San Francisco and concentrated his efforts there. In California Jones presented his ministry as a part of the Christian spectrum, only revealing his increasingly radical political and religious tenets to those he fully trusted. From the beginning of his California enterprise, Jones recognized the political influence he and his loyal followers could wield. Through volunteer work, clever public relations, and effective voting, the Peoples Temple became a force, first in the Republican Party in Mendocino County and then in Democratic politics in San Francisco. Jones and his lieutenants also organized his followers for fund-raising, for health care of the elderly, and other enterprises. Jones left millions of dollars after his death, and critics debate over whether he exploited his followers financially.

Jones's Popularity. By 1976 Jones was well known in San Francisco. Many admired his opposition to racism and his left-wing political views. He helped organize Jimmy Carter's presidential campaign in 1976 and was

Death scene at the Peoples Temple, Jonestown, Guyana, 18 November 1978

appointed to the city's Public Housing Authority. The following year he was invited to sit at the head table at the annual banquet of Religion in American Life.

Darker Shadows. Jones was expanding his darker side during this time, however. His political and social ideas were becoming increasingly radical as he moved to "apostolic socialism" and identified himself to his followers as a Communist. He left Christian tenets to tell his followers he was God. He also began to toy with the idea of a mass suicide of his followers — what he called "revolutionary suicide," death as a demonstration of radical will. He had also decided to move his flock to the South American nation of Guyana, where the Socialist politics and isolation were comfortable to him. In 1976 he leased the land he had chosen there for his colony, the Promised Land, and sent an early group of his followers to prepare for Jones and the others.

Defectors. By 1976 there were several defectors from the Peoples Temple, including Grace Stoen, whose husband had signed a document in 1972 saying that Jones was the father of Grace's child. While Tim Stoen was still working for Jones, Grace began to demand access to her child. In 1976 the boy was taken to Guyana, and Jones himself soon followed.

New West Exposé. Jones's publicity and flamboyant actions aroused curiosity as rumors circulated around San Francisco about the minister, the Peoples Temple, and its members. In 1977 *New West,* a magazine recently purchased by Rupert Murdock, scheduled a story about Jones based on material from former followers. Jones's loyalists generated publicity for the story when they first attempted to block the exposé and then tried to discredit the information it contained, but Jones was already in his refuge in Guyana by the time the story broke.

Concern over Guyana. The stories about the Peoples Temple, along with reports of strange actions by other groups labeled cults, led families of members of the temple to organize a Concerned Parents group to try to retrieve their relatives from Guyana. Jones's alleged son John Victor Stoen was one of the chief targets; Tim Stoen left the cult and joined the boy's mother in pressing for his return.

Government Investigation. The federal government was increasingly concerned with the actions of the Peoples Temple in Guyana as stories of gunrunning to Jonestown and unexplained bank transactions circulated. Jones by this time was ill, addicted to drugs, and possibly demented. He still ruled his colony, however, and in 1978 he began to excite his followers so isolated from the rest of the world with stories of impending disaster. He began to call for "white nights," during which the inhabitants of the Promised Land would practice suicide.

Death of Ryan. In November 1978 Congressman Leo Ryan of California came to Guyana to see for himself the conditions of Jonestown. When the congressman left, he took with him others who wanted to leave the colony. His plane was attacked, and Ryan and others were killed. Back at Jonestown Jones carried out the final performance of his "white nights," revolutionary suicide. When investigators arrived at the colony, they found the bodies of Jones and 913 of his followers, people who had swallowed Kool-Aid laced with cyanide or who had been shot by Jones's loyalists.

Sources:

Marc Galanter, *Cults: Faith, Healing, and Coercion* (New York: Oxford University Press, 1989);

John R. Hall, *Gone From the Promised Land: Jonestown in American Cultural History* (New Brunswick, N.J.: Transaction, 1987);

George Klineman, Sherman Butler, and David Conn, *The Cult That Died: The Tragedy of Jim Jones and the Peoples Temple* (New York: Putnam, 1980).

POLITICS AND RELIGION

Traditional Involvement. At the beginning of the 1970s religious leaders active in politics came mostly from the Left. Mainline Protestant ministers and Roman Catholic priests opposed the war in Vietnam and supported government action to alleviate the problems of race and poverty at home. The scandal of Watergate and Richard Nixon's political disgrace tainted even the respected Billy Graham, who had openly supported his old friend's election bids and had performed religious services in the White House, as well as invited the president to his crusades and Billy Graham Day in Charlotte, North Carolina. Although Graham had distanced himself from Nixon after 1973, he insisted after the Watergate revelations that he was deeply troubled by his failure to know the darker aspects of Nixon's personality and actions. Apparently Nixon's use of foul language in private was most disturbing to Graham.

Rise of the Conservatives. By the end of the decade religious liberals seemed weak, and activists came from the Right as conservative Protestants and Mormons, with support from the Roman Catholic hierarchy, organized to overturn the Supreme Court's abortion decision in *Roe V. Wade*, oppose the ratification of the Equal Rights Amendment (ERA), and inhibit the growth of the gay rights movement. Some, mostly Protestants, continued this culture war to demand an end to sex education in the schools and require the teaching of what they called "Creation Science" in the schools to balance the teaching of evolution.

Jimmy Carter. The shift of political activism from Left to Right, from Mainline religious liberals to religious and cultural conservatives, became apparent in the election of 1976, when the former Georgia governor Jimmy Carter won the Democratic nomination for the presidency and then the election. Observers were astonished when Carter, a Southern Baptist, identified himself as born-again, meaning that he had not only accepted

The president of the American Unification church, Neil Salonen, and his wife demonstrate in Washington during the Watergate investigation

Jesus as his Savior but had also had an experience that convinced him that Jesus had accepted his conversion.

Admission of Adultery. It was easy for urban elites to dismiss Carter's candidacy as well as his religion at the beginning of the campaign. When Carter said in an interview published in *Playboy* magazine that he had committed adultery because he had looked at women with lust in his heart, many were astounded. That Carter had a sister who was a prominent faith healer was equally bemusing. Carter's election and the revelation that 40 percent of Americans identified themselves as born-again Christians forced many Americans, especially Northeastern urbanites and members of Mainline churches, to reconsider their understanding of the nation and its culture.

Carter's Seeming Contradictions. Despite Carter's religious convictions, the president's support for the ERA and his failure to oppose abortion, check the onslaught of pornography, or repress the increasingly assertive homosexual community offended cultural conservatives. Foreign-policy conservatives were offended by Carter's interjection of human-rights issues into a world dominated by the Cold War, his unwillingness to share their view of the

"I was terribly disappointed in those [Watergate] tapes. Not only disappointed, but just *overwhelmingly* sickened by them. Oh, the language. I'd never heard him use those words. I didn't even know he *knew* them. . . . I went too far when I did things to help him [Nixon] politically. I should have limited myself to the moral and spiritual situation in the country."

Source: Charles Hirshberg, "The Eternal Crusader," *Life,* 9 (November 1994): 114, 116.

enormity of the Soviet threat until the U.S.S.R. invaded Afghanistan in 1979, and his failure to free the hostages seized by Iranian radicals.

Religious Round Table. The sharp political and cultural divisions of the nation and the chaotic economic situation created by the costs of the Vietnam War and the oil crises of 1973 and 1979 created a situation for a possible alignment of political and religious conservatives. In 1976 Paul Weyrich organized the Christian Voice, a self-proclaimed conservative body that rated politicians on the religious value of their political actions. In 1979 other religious conservatives created other political action groups, including the Religious Round Table, made up of a variety of conservative religious leaders. The most vigorous and best known of the religious-political groups was Jerry Falwell's Moral Majority, organized in 1979 to voice right-wing views during the upcoming presidential election. The Moral Majority aimed to bring together those people who were pro-life, pro-traditional family, pro-moral, and pro-American, which was defined as supporting a strong national defense and full support for the Jewish state of Israel. A part of the group's constituency was those people whose cars bore the bumper sticker reading "God Spoke It. The Bible Declares It. I Believe It. That Settles It." As Ronald Reagan readied himself for the presidential election of 1980, he found allies in the evangelical religious communities who were socially and culturally distant from the traditional Republican base. His political success in the presidential campaign of 1980 depended on bringing these groups together into a new political coalition.

Sources:

Charles Colson, *Born Again* (Old Tappan, N.J.: Chosen Books, 1976);

Robert C. Liebman and Robert Wuthnow, eds., *The New Christian Right: Mobilization and Legitimation* (New York: Aldine, 1983);

Anson Shupe and William A. Stacey, *Born Again Politics and the Moral Majority: What Social Surveys Really Show* (New York: Edwin Mellen Press, 1982);

Corwin E. Smidt, *Contemporary Evangelical Political Involvement: An Analysis and Assessment* (Lanham, Md.: University Press of America, 1989);

Garry Wills, "Born Again Politics," *New York Times Magazine,* 1 August 1976, pp. 8–9.

POPE JOHN PAUL II VISITS THE UNITED STATES

A New Pope. On 1 October 1979 Pope John Paul II arrived in Boston on the first leg of his first trip to the United States. Pope John Paul II had been elevated to the chair of Saint Peter the previous October after the sudden death of Pope John Paul I, whose thirty-four-day reign was the shortest in modern history. The new pope, formerly Cardinal Karol Woytyla, archbishop of Krakow, Poland, was the first non-Italian pope since 1522 elevated to the papacy.

The Pope's Message. American Catholics received John Paul II with great excitement at his stops in Boston, New York City, Philadelphia, Des Moines, Chicago, and Washington, D.C. In New York the pope spoke to the United Nations, endorsing support from industrial countries for the less-developed nations of the world which struggled to provide for their people. He also spoke out vigorously for human rights: "All human beings in every nation and country should be able to enjoy effectively their full rights under any political regime or system." On the Middle East he insisted that the Palestinian question would have to be addressed before peace could be achieved.

Conservative Views. While the pope's political and economic views were generally liberal, he also used his time in the United States to reiterate his conservative views on sexuality and the nature of the priesthood. In Boston he urged young people to abandon selfishness for sacrifice and to give up the self-indulgence of sex, drugs, and entertainment for true love and its demands. At a convocation of 350 bishops in Philadelphia John Paul II reasserted the tenets of *Humanae Vita,* which opposed the use of artificial birth control. He also demanded Catholics reject abortion, divorce, homosexual practices, and nonmarital sex. On the issue of the ordination of female priests, he insisted on maintaining the tradition of the male priesthood. John Paul II also reasserted his stand insisting on the celibacy of priests, even though more and more priests in the United States were leaving their orders for marriage and family.

The Capital City. In Washington, D.C., John Paul II visited for three hours with President Jimmy Carter at the White House, the first pope to visit that building. He also celebrated a mass for thirty-five hundred women religious at the Shrine of the Immaculate Conception, where he encouraged women to recognize the holiness of their calling. He was taken aback when Sister Theresa Kane, president of the Leadership of Women Religious, confronted him with the assertion that all priestly offices should be open to all persons of the church. Only a few of the women at the service openly protested the limitations on their religious calling.

Message Recognized? When Pope John Paul II left the United States 7 October he had met with rapturous crowds, including hundreds of thousands of fellow Poles in Chicago and an estimated 350,000 people who poured into mostly Protestant Iowa when he visited a small church near Des Moines. The pope and the American bishops hoped to focus on the religious message John Paul II brought to the United States, but ribbons, banners, flags, and T-shirts with such slogans as "I Got a Peep at the Pope" which sold as souvenirs to his audiences exemplified the carnival-like excitement.

Limited Influence. In spite of the pope's charm and the hopes of Catholic conservatives, there is little evidence that John Paul II's visit changed the behavior or ideas of laymen about private sexual behavior or even the possibility of women priests. The Second Vatican Council had unleashed the independent thinking of an increasingly well educated laity in America, who were fully adapted to the culture of the late twentieth century. They loved John Paul II the man but rejected the parts of his message that did not fit their perceptions of life and faith, a pattern that would continue though the first Polish pope's reign.

RELIGION AND THE POPULAR ARTS

The Christian Arts. With the growth of the Pentecostal and Evangelical movements a new segment of commercial entertainment appeared. In 1979 people could order directly from the *Born Again Christian Catalogue* or learn the latest in the music world from *Contemporary Christian Music.* New Christian music carved out a body of listeners that overlapped but did not cover those who listened to traditional gospel music. Christian artists like Bill Gaither won not only the commercial industry's Grammy Award year after year but also the Gospel Music Association's Dove Award. Maranantha! Music, established in 1972 in Costa Mesa, California, developed a small empire in providing products for the expanding number of Christian-music buyers.

Fiction. There were Christian romance novels for women interested in that genre of fiction, which was popular in the decade. The religious publishing house, Thomas Nelson, joined like-minded publishers with a line called "Promise Romance" that not only reassured readers of the possibility of true love and happiness but also of God's redeeming love for them. Some of the romantic novels were of respectable quality, such as Shirley Nelson's *The Last Year of the War* (1978) or Janette Oke's *Love Comes Softly* (1979).

Commercial Appeal. The commercial world also recognized the potential of religious themes. The youth culture of the 1960s merged with the story of Jesus in two popular musicals in the early 1970s. In 1971 Stephen Schwartz wrote *Godspell,* based on the Gospel of Matthew. The simple music and the affecting story made this a success not only on the professional stage but for youth groups from various churches. More commercial was *Jesus Christ Superstar* (1971) featuring music composed by Andrew Lloyd Webber, which had a successful run in London and on Broadway. Both productions were made into films and released two years later with modest box-office success.

Television. A more successful film was the six-and-a-half-hour production of *Jesus of Nazareth,* directed by Franco Zeffirelli for NBC television. Before the film was shown, Fundamentalists protested its portrayal of Jesus as an ordinary man, and General Motors withdrew its sponsorship. But critics and an estimated ninety million viewers responded enthusiastically to the miniseries when it was broadcast in 1977.

Controversy. Conservative Christians were even more offended by the film *Life of Brian* (1979), made by the satiric British group Monty Python. This account of a Jewish man whose life paralleled Jesus' was criticized by the New York archdiocese as well as Jewish groups such as the Union of Orthodox Rabbis in the United States and Canada and the Rabbinical Alliance. Protesters secured a brief injunction against showing the movie in Valdosta, Georgia, and one large theater chain cut its showings of the film, especially in the South.

Biographical Film. Two interesting biographies of religious figures were filmed during the decade. In 1972 Marjoe Gortner starred in *Marjoe,* an Academy Award–winning documentary of his life as a child evangelist. This exposé of fakery in the Evangelical circuit attracted attention and confirmed the prejudices of many people about the revival movement. Less successful was a film version of Charles Colson's widely read autobiography *Born Again* (1978). This account of a Watergate conspirator's fall from power and imprisonment attracted only a limited audience. Watergate was too close for many to concern themselves with the conversion and reform of those men who brought disgrace on the presidency.

Satan. Far more people came to see a film that dealt with the devil's work in the world. Inspired by the 1968 success of *Rosemary's Baby,* in which a coven of witches in New York conspires to have a young woman impregnated by Satan, moviemakers were attracted to the themes of demonic possession and the appearance of the Antichrist. William Peter Blatty won an Academy Award for the

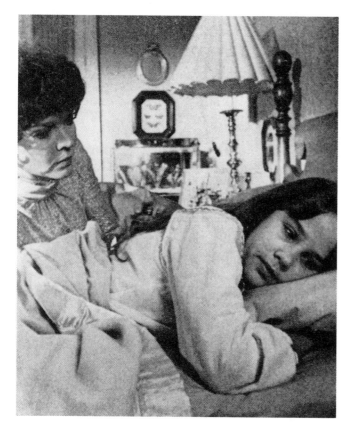

Ellen Burstyn and Linda Blair in *The Exorcist*

1973 screenplay of his best-selling novel *The Exorcist*. Audiences were horrified by the special effects and intrigued by the account of the devil's possession of a young girl, played by Linda Blair. Four years later a turgid sequel, *Exorcist 2: The Heretic*, was released, but it was only modestly successful. The second sequel, *Exorcist 3* (1990), had even less success at the box office.

The Antichrist. In 1976 Gregory Peck starred in a film relating the childhood of the Antichrist. *The Omen* was given an R rating for its violence. Two years later a sequel, *Damien — Omen II*, was released. While it still had high production values, this and the 1981 sequel, *The Final Conflict*, followed predictable paths, relating stories of evil personified.

World Out of Control. The success of these films was linked to people's deepening sense of the world's being out of control, as seen in the increase of inexplicable violence, such as the Manson family murders of 1969. The trial of Charles Manson and his followers for the deaths of Sharon Tate, the pregnant wife of Roman Polanski (who directed *Rosemary's Baby*), and her friends in 1971 attracted a nation that struggled to comprehend their actions. When the U.S. Supreme Court overturned the death penalty as it stood in 1972, the death sentences of the Manson family were reduced to life imprisonment, reinforcing a sense that old values no longer applied. The mass suicide of Jim Jones and his Peoples Temple followers at the end of the decade at their retreat in Guyana,

South America, was for many a confirmation that even religion had become somehow perverted.

Apocalypse. Cultural confusions and personal tensions contributed to the growing sense that the end of the world was at hand, as reflected in the popularity of Hal Lindsey's apocalyptic book *The Late, Great Planet Earth* (1970). Inspired by the Israeli capture of Jerusalem in the 1967 war, Lindsey worked out most of the ideas of his book in the sermons he gave to students for the parachurch organization the Campus Crusade for Christ. Lindsey's study of the signs of the times forecasting Jesus' Second Coming sold more than ten million copies during the decade after its publication. Many Christians were convinced that the Jews' return to Jerusalem and the creation of the European Common Market fulfilled biblical prophecies prefiguring the Apocalypse.

Sources:

Paul Boyer, *When Time Shall Be No More: Prophesy Belief in Modern American Culture* (Cambridge, Mass.: Belknap Press of Harvard University Press, 1992);

Don Hustad, *Jubilate! Church Music in the Evangelical Tradition* (Carol Stream, Ill.: Hope, 1981);

James T. Richardson, Joel Best, and David G. Bromley, eds., *The Satanism Scare* (New York: De Gruyter, 1991);

Jules Victor Schwerin, *Go Tell It: Mahalia Jackson, Queen of Gospel* (New York: Oxford University Press, 1992).

THE SUPREME COURT AND RELIGION

Taxes and the Church. The Court continued to wrestle with religious issues during the decade. In 1970 the Court upheld the right of New York State to grant tax exemptions for church property used for religious purposes. This had national application since all fifty states and the District of Columbia gave such exemptions. It was estimated that this affected over seventy billion dollars worth of property in the nation.

Rights of Religious Belief. Issues in education continued to appear before the Court. In 1971 the Court upheld a decision of the Wisconsin Supreme Court which struck down a state law requiring Amish families to send their children to schools until they were sixteen. The Court ruled that the Amish were exempt from that law after their children completed the eighth grade. The three-hundred-year history of the educational practices of that group demonstrated that limited education was a religious tenet.

Evolution. The Court also grappled with the issue of public schools and the teaching of evolution. For a hundred years they had resisted scientific challenges to the biblical account of creation on the grounds that the Bible was infallible in all its parts and that if one part were wrong, the entire faith would be challenged. In 1974 the Court let stand a decision dismissing an action brought by parents in Houston to stop public schools from using textbooks that taught evolution but ignored the biblical creation story. The following year the Court let stand a district court ruling that a Tennessee law requiring text-

Cover for a Florida telephone book promoting Christian businesses

books to include various theories of creation, including the biblical story, violated both the First Amendment to the Constitution and the Tennessee state constitution.

TELEVANGELISM

The Great Commission. Christians from the beginning were committed to using all means to carry out the Great Commission of Jesus, to go to all the world and preach the gospel. When electronic communication systems were developed in the twentieth century, preachers used the radio and then television to broadcast their good news. While Charles Fuller's *Old Time Gospel Hour* did not make the transition from radio to television, such successors as Billy Graham quickly recognized the potential of the new medium. The pattern set by Graham and Bishop Fulton J. Sheen in the 1950s dominated religion on television for nearly twenty years.

Governmental Incentive. In the 1960s evangelists began to adapt to the potential of television. When the Federal Communications Commission ruled that stations did not have to provide free time for community service, including religion, television companies began to sell their religious time to anyone who wanted it. Buyers turned out to be primarily conservatives and Pentecostalists; most were men, although Kathryn Kuhlman had a successful ministry until her death in 1976. These evan-

gelists began to recognize that television ministries were more effective if they employed the entertainment aspects of the medium.

Oral Roberts. In 1969 Oral Roberts modified what had essentially been a film of his services and adopted the trappings of show business with religious overtones. He became the most popular minister on television. An estimated twenty-five million people saw his Thanksgiving show in 1975, and by 1979 he was appearing on as many as 170 stations. He also became a talk-show guest on commercial television, a show-business celebrity.

Pat Robertson. The potential of television was also recognized early by Marion ("Pat") Robertson, who carried out God's message to him and purchased a failing UHF station in Virginia Beach, Virginia. He began full-time religious broadcasting in 1961 and later in the decade created the Christian Broadcasting Network (CBN), buying time for his programs on other stations and tying them together in a network system. In the 1970s Robertson was joined by other religious networks, including Paul Crouch's Trinity Broadcast Network and Jim Bakker's inspirational PTL Network. These networks not only provided airtime for their owners but also rented time to other evangelists.

Expansion. As more and more homes were tied into community cable systems, which could carry more than the usual three or four local broadcast channels, the religious networks expanded their reach and audiences could watch religious programs all the time. At the end of the decade CBN and then PTL leased satellite time and were able to reach their national audiences simultaneously rather than through the use of delayed film as in the past. As these television ministries grew, they also expanded into other parts of the world with their broadcasts. By 1977 television ministries including those of Bakker, Robertson, and Robert Schuller had acquired formidable audiences, although those audiences were never as large as claimed by the various ministers. In 1979 Jerry Falwell claimed he had as many as 20 million viewers, but more-cautious observers estimated he had only 1.5 million in his audience then.

Fund-raising. The television ministries required enormous sums, not only for equipment and production costs, but also for the purchase of broadcast time. The only way these costs could be met was by constant appeals for financial support from their viewers. Following Oral Roberts's example they used computers which generated personalized mass mailings that kept the ministries in regular contact with their viewers. But this equipment too was expensive to buy and use, so more funds were needed. The frantic appeals for funds aroused scrutiny from critics who wondered why more money was always needed and where the funds actually went. While Sinclair Lewis's *Elmer Gantry* (1927) was in the past, Marjoe Gortner's evangelical fakery was a part of the decade.

Rising Concern. As the television ministries grew, so

did their incomes, and secular and Mainline denominations expressed their concern about these independent ministries' constant pleas for money and overall lack of accountability. In 1977 the state of Minnesota forced the Billy Graham Evangelical Association to open its books for the first time since the early 1950s. While Graham was able to give a clear accounting for the money given to his ministry, the growing questions about accountability led him to help create the Evangelical Council for Financial Responsibility, an organization that reassured contributors that their money was used as claimed, in 1978. Not all ministries joined the council, but this did not seem to affect contributors until the spectacular scandals in the following decade.

Sources:

David Edwin Harrell, Jr., *Oral Roberts: An American Life* (Bloomington: Indiana University Press, 1985);

Harrell, *Pat Robertson: A Personal, Religious, and Political Portrait* (San Francisco: Harper & Row, 1987);

Peter G. Horsfield, *Religious Television: The American Experience* (New York: Longman, 1984);

Larry Martz with Ginny Carroll, *Ministry of Greed: The Inside Story of the Televangelists and Their Holy Wars* (New York: Weidenfeld & Nicolson, 1988).

WAR IN VIETNAM

In February 1972 the Ecumenical Witness of Protestants, Eastern Orthodox, Roman Catholics, and Jews in Kansas City, Kansas, called for an immediate end to the war, arguing that the Nixon administration's policy of turning the war over to the South Vietnamese was immoral. They declared that the policy of Vietnamization is "fundamentally immoral because it forces Asian people to be our [American] proxy army, dying in our places for our supposed interests. . . . The present Administration's Vietnamization policy looks toward not a negotiated political settlement but an eventual military victory. We will continue to provide the weaponry and air power, the massive technological support, the advisers and the money. Asians will provide the casualties."

Source: "Ecumenical Witness: Withdraw Now!," *Christian Century*, 89 (22 February 1972): 81.

VIETNAM

Declining Concern? As 1970 began, public concern about the long American involvement in the Vietnam War seemed to decline as the Nixon administration withdrew ground troops, announced future troop reductions, and escalated the air war, with a resulting decline in American casualties. This had not been true the previous autumn when religious leaders, mostly Roman Catholic and Mainline Protestant, were prominent in the great, peaceful demonstrations in October and November 1969 called the Vietnam Moratorium. Crowds, large and small, clerical and lay, met in cities and communities around the country in the most extensive protest in the nation's history to express their disappointment with the new administration's failure to end the war more quickly. At this time Middle America seemed to be speaking about what liberals considered a moral and political issue.

Nixon's Response. In response to the moratorium President Nixon appealed to another part of the middle class, what he called the "silent majority," the great mass of Americans who did their work, worshiped their God, and supported their nation. He effectively contrasted these people with the war's opponents by suggesting that those who did not support his efforts to end the war aligned themselves with the radical young whose violent and vocal protests offended people more than did the war itself.

Support and Opposition. The Reverend Carl McIntire, who had based his life on opposing the Mainline Protestant denominations in the National and World Councils of Churches, attempted to tie himself to Nixon's appeal to Middle America when he led an esti-

mated ten thousand to fifteen thousand prowar demonstrators in a march in Washington just before Easter 1970. McIntire insisted there were at least fifty thousand people at the demonstration. The marchers carried flags both American and Confederate, Bibles, and signs supporting the war and demanding prayer in public schools. McIntire's histrionics drew more press coverage that the seventy-day protest led by Clergy and Laity Concerned About Vietnam that also ended that Easter.

Cambodia and Kent State. In May 1970 the American military incursion into Cambodia and the Ohio National Guard's killing of four students at Kent State University brought a dramatic series of protests as many colleges and universities, religious as well as secular, were closed by outraged students. Once again Washington became a center of protest, but this time not from radical youth, but middle-aged, middle-class people, including clergy from around the nation, who lobbied and petitioned their representatives to reduce the U.S. involvement in Vietnam.

Response of the Churches. Revulsion against the war was strong in the Mainline Protestant denominations. The Executive Council of the Episcopal church called for the total withdrawal from Vietnam and an end of the war. Later that year, however, the House of Deputies at the denomination's convention refused to endorse that extreme position. The lay delegates to the General Assembly of the United Presbyterian church removed a strong condemnation of the Cambodian incursion from a resolution regarding the war but did call for an American withdrawal. The clergy seemed far ahead of their parishioners on the war issue.

Pastoral Issued. As the American involvement in the

war tapered off, with a resulting decline in American casualties, protests against the war also declined. But concern remained in religious circles. In May 1972 Cardinal Terrance Cooke, archbishop of New York and military vicar of the armed forces, issued a pastoral calling for a "speedy end" to the war by greater use of the United Nations. While there was an upsurge of revulsion in liberal religious circles about the massive bombing of North Vietnam in December 1972, and while some religious leaders bitterly condemned Nixon's policy of mass destruction, the peace accords of January 1973 brought an end to the American participation in the conflict and offered an opportunity for ending some of the divisions at home.

War over Meaning. That hope was an illusion. The fight among Americans about the war and its meaning continued long after the prisoners of war and the troops returned home, however. Debate over the implications of the long struggle paralleled debates over the question of amnesty for those who opposed or dodged the draft or deserted from the military. As those debates went on they affected the religious and political landscapes. Political conservatives found themselves aligned with religious conservatives in criticizing the liberal leaders and bureaucrats of the Mainline denominations. The decade's divisions over foreign and domestic politics and moral and cultural issues split Protestants, Catholics, and Jews into liberal and conservative camps and fueled the political divisions of the last part of the century

Source:

Mitchell K. Hall, *Because of Their Faith: CALCAV and Religious Opposition to the Vietnam War* (New York: Columbia University Press, 1990).

WOMEN'S ORDINATION

feminism. The rebirth of feminism was one of the crucial movements of the 1970s. Women demanded and received admission into the professional world, and ratification of the ERA, which would outlaw discrimination on the basis of sex, became one of the most hotly debated issues of the decade. In this context there was an inevitable attempt to advance the position of women in religious groups, including the right of women to ordination to the highest priestly office. Liberal groups, including Reformed Jews, who ordained their first woman rabbi in 1972, had relatively little difficulty in permitting women to exercise their highest spiritual office. Some Protestant denominations had long ordained women to the ministry, and other Mainline Protestant denominations extended that right in the latter half of the century. In 1970 both the American Lutheran church and the Lutheran Church in America authorized women's ordination.

Schism over Ordination. Religious conservatives saw this acceptance of women in the pulpits as clear evidence of the general liberalism of the Mainline denominations and equated it with a decline in traditional religious beliefs. Women's ordination seemed an explicit rejection of

Bishop James M. Allen (right) in Philadelphia, ordaining eleven women as ministers in the Episcopal church, 29 July 1974

Paul's admonition to women to keep silent in the churches (1 Cor. 14:34). This violation of tradition led to the creation of splinter groups, such as the Presbyterian Church in America, which found the ordination of women one of the prime reasons for leaving the Southern Presbyterian church. Conservatives in the Lutheran Church-Missouri Synod saw women's ordination as one of several reasons to stay aloof from close connection to other Lutheran churches. The struggle over women's ordination was most bitter in those churches that centered their worship on the celebration of the Eucharist rather than the sermon. Here Communion was a miraculous repetition of Jesus' sacrifice of himself for his followers rather than a commemoration of the Last Supper. In these churches priests could be ordained only by bishops, who traced their authority back to the original church, where Jesus' disciples were all males. Breaking the centuries-long tradition was not only a repudiation of history but a reevaluation of the nature of the Mass itself.

Triennial Convention. The most spectacular struggle took place in the Episcopal church. In 1970 the denomination's Triennial Convention rejected ordination of women even though more than 50 percent of the denomination was female and the official organization Episcopal Women had voted that the church approve their ordination. Instead, women were seated as delegates in the House of Deputies for the first time, and deaconesses were given the same status as deacons (a step below the priesthood) in the church. When the House of

Bishops blocked women's ordination at the next triennial meeting, some bishop proponents decided to act unilaterally. In July 1974 four bishops ordained eleven deaconesses as priestesses. Others ordinations followed in spite of suspension of these new priestesses by various bishops and the difficulty these women priests had in finding a place to carry out their ministries. In 1976, responding to growing demands for change, the Triennial Convention finally approved women's ordination. Following the pattern in other denominations, various Episcopal parishes around the nation began to leave the church to establish new structures faithful to their understanding of the nature of the all-male priesthood, the tradition of the Anglican church, and the old Book of Common Prayer.

Catholic Refusal. The Roman Catholic church refused to consider women's ordination, even though a coalition of women's religious groups organized to support that change and a liberal organization of priests, Priest for Equality, endorsed their ordination. When Pope John Paul II came to the United States in 1979 and addressed an audience of women religious at the Shrine of the Immaculate Conception in Washington, D.C., he was stunned when Sister Theresa Kane, president of the Leadership Conference of Women Religious, confronted him by saying, "The church must respond by providing the possibility of women as persons being included in all ministries of our church." He quickly recovered himself and did not change his position on the issue that the priesthood was reserved for males.

Mormon Change. In 1978 Spenser Kimball, president of the Church of Jesus Christ of Latter-day Saints, announced that women could give prayers in all services open to them. The highest services in the church were still restricted to men, however.

Source:
Jacqueline S. Field-Bibb, *Women Toward Priesthood: Ministerial Politics and Feminist Praxis* (New York: Cambridge University Press, 1991).

THE YOM KIPPUR WAR, 1973

Day of Atonement. On 6 October 1973 Egypt and Syria launched a surprise attack against the Jewish state of Israel. It was Yom Kippur, the Day of Atonement, the holiest day of the Jewish year. The war was brief, but it was hard fought in its early stages when the combined forces of Egypt and Syria, armed with Soviet weapons, nearly overwhelmed the Israeli forces. It was only with the resupply of Israeli weapons by the United States and the U.S. warning to the Soviet Union to stay out of the conflict that Israeli forces rallied and the Arab states were defeated.

The Oil Weapon. In response to the support for Israel from the United States and other Western European powers, the Organization of Petroleum Exporting Countries (OPEC), dominated by the Arab states, employed the "oil weapon," an embargo on the export of oil from the Middle East to those nations they deemed sympathetic to Israel. The result was a sharp decline in the availability of oil and a corresponding increase in prices of oil and related products. Gasoline soared in price and heating fuel was not only expensive but scarce. Americans faced new inflation as well as lower temperatures in their homes and workplaces and lower driving speeds on their highways.

Response by U.S. Jews. All Americans were inconvenienced by the results of the conflict, but U.S. Jews were emotionally overwhelmed by the war. Since 1967 they had increasingly identified themselves with the existence of the Jewish state. The near destruction of Israel at this time once again triggered nightmares of the Holocaust. That the attack took place on the holy day of Yom Kippur only added insult to the threat of the extinction of the Jewish state. As in the Six-Day War in 1967 there was an outpouring of financial and political support for Israel from the Jewish community. They also looked for support from other Americans.

Christian Ambivalence. The U.S. Christian community was divided in its response, to the consternation of many Jews. While the National Council of Catholic Bishops quickly expressed its support of the right of Israel to exist and urged negotiations for peace, the bishops did not condemn the Arabs' violation of the cease-fire they had signed in 1967. Nor did the bishops condemn the obvious Arab aggression and the Arab unwillingness to recognize Israel's legitimacy. In the midst of the conflict the executive committee of the National Council of Churches did ask for an end to the fighting, but it also asked the outside powers, meaning the Soviet Union and the United States, to refrain from sending more arms into the region. As Jewish observers to the executive committee's meeting remarked, this overlooked the Arabs' surprise attack and ignored the fact that the Soviets had already supplied the arms which were now being used against Israel. Without immediate U.S. military supplies Israel would fall.

Evenhanded Controversy. This same call for peace and negotiation without recognizing and condemning Arab aggression was evident in several of the Mainline Protestant denominations, such as the Disciples of Christ, the United Church of Christ, and some of their agencies. While they supported the existence of Israel, as expressed in United Nations Resolution 242, they also asked that attention be paid to the issues of the Palestinians and did not condemn the Egyptian-Syrian violation of the cease-fire those nations had signed six years earlier. The more liberal Protestant denominations frequently expressed their concern about Palestinian refugees and access of all religious communities to Jerusalem; according to some U.S. Jews, the liberal protestants seemed to ignore the threats to Israel's very existence.

Conservative Support. American Jews took comfort from the many religious leaders, regional religious councils, and Christian publications, Protestant and Catholic, black and white, who not only expressed strong support for Israel but criticized the Arab role in the war and insisted the Arabs were responsible for the oil crisis that followed. Some of that support came from the more conservative Evangelical groups and individuals who now aligned themselves openly with the Jewish state and its control of Jerusalem. The First Baptist Church of Dallas, Texas, headed by the conservative Reverend W. A. Criswell, took out a full-page newspaper advertisement encouraging Christians to support Israel through their letters and contributions to the Jewish Welfare Federation.

Commitment and Reconsideration. The Yom Kippur War solidified U.S. Jews' identification with Israel and strengthened their commitment to and work for the existence of the Jewish state. Their intensified commitment to Israel also caused many Jews to reconsider their allies. While they continued to share social goals with liberal Protestants, Jews questioned whether these Protestants fully understood the meaning of Israel to Jews. This became most evident in the growing distance between Jews and the black community. Previously the two groups had been allied in the civil rights struggle, but now some blacks displayed anti-Semitism, as exemplified by the prominent Rev. Jesse Jackson openly embracing Yasser Arafat, who was pledged to the destruction of Israel. Social and religious conservatives, however, championed not only Israel but also supported Jewish control of Jerusalem. Jews were forced to ask themselves, who were their real friends?

Source:
Judith Hershcopf Banki, *Christian Responses to the Yom Kippur War: Implications for Christian-Jewish Relations* (New York: Jewish Committee, n.d.).

HEADLINE MAKERS

HERBERT W. ARMSTRONG

1892-1986

FOUNDER OF WORLDWIDE CHURCH OF GOD; RADIO AND TELEVISION PERSONALITY

Worldwide Church of God. Herbert W. Armstrong founded the Worldwide Church of God in Oregon in 1931. This church, which celebrated the Sabbath on Saturday, grew in large part by Armstrong's effective use of radio. In 1935 he began to call his program *The World Tomorrow,* a name which he carried over into his television broadcasts. In 1947 he opened his Ambassador College in Pasadena, California, which became the headquarters for his faith. Armstrong's broadcasts and his publication, *Plain Truth,* concentrated on presenting his explanation of biblical mysteries. In time he abandoned the concept of the Trinity and declared himself God's Chosen Apostle, warning his listeners that the end of the world was approaching.

His ministry attracted a devoted following who accepted the severe strictures of their faith and eagerly supported their church financially.

Family Controversy. The Worldwide Church of God was shaken by a series of crises in the 1970s. Armstrong himself violated the rules he had given to his followers when he married his previously divorced secretary after the death of his first wife. For years he had forbidden both divorce and marriage to divorced persons to his followers. In time he divorced this second wife. He also finally broke with his presumed successor, his son, Garner Ted Armstrong. The father had expelled his son three times earlier in the decade for allegations of sexual improprieties but each time had reinstated him. In 1978 Garner Ted Armstrong was excommunicated, ending the expectations that the younger man would succeed to his father's position.

Diversion of Funds. In the resulting conflict charges were made that the senior Armstrong and his chief assistant were conspiring to divert church funds to their personal accounts. In 1979 the state of California placed the ministry and Ambassador College in temporary receivership. When the two church leaders easily posted a two-million-dollar bond and promised a public audit of church finances, the receivership was lifted, and Armstrong was returned to power in his church and college. The scandals, which foreshadowed the televangelists' scandals of the 1980s, disrupted the ministry for a time, but Armstrong rallied to revive his following, and the church survived his death in 1986.

Sources:

Herbert W. Armstrong, *Autobiography of Herbert W. Armstrong* (Pasadena, Cal.: Worldwide Church of God, 1967);

Stanley R. Rader, *Against the Gates of Hell* (New York: Everest House, 1980).

JIM AND TAMMY BAKKER

1940- ; 1942-

TELEVANGELIST TEAM; FOUNDERS OF THE PTL NETWORK

Beginnings. In 1965 Jim and Tammy Bakker, two young, itinerant evangelists, joined station WYAH in Virginia, Beach, Virginia with a Christian puppet show. It quickly attracted a devoted local audience and also became one of the most successful syndicated programs for Pat Robertson's developing Christian Broadcasting Network (CBN). A year later Jim Bakker was allowed to broadcast the Christian talk show of which he had always dreamed, with a format based on the popular *The Tonight Show*. *The 700 Club,* as Bakker called it, became the prototype of the developing television ministry. Both the puppet show and *The 700 Club* were crucial in bringing new stations into the CBN system. It was also on *The 700 Club* that Bakker learned how effective his pleas for funds could be. When he weepingly asked his viewers to send in money to keep CBN on the air during an early fund-raising campaign, the station was flooded with pledges. Bakker would make financial crises a regular part of his ministry when he later set up on his own.

California. In 1972 Jim and Tammy Bakker left CBN and moved to California, where Jim helped to put together another religious broadcasting system, the Trinity Broadcast Network. There he introduced his talk show with a new name, the *PTL Club.* Originally the initials stood for "Praise The Lord," but to soften the charismatic implications of that phrase the initials were sometimes said to mean "People That Love." In time Bakker's critics would say they stood for "Pass The Loot."

PTL Network. In 1974 the Bakkers moved to Charlotte, North Carolina, where they set up a new broadcasting system, which they called the PTL Network. PTL quickly syndicated the Bakkers' show, which attracted larger and larger audiences. PTL became one of the leading religious television networks, and the Bakkers became religious celebrities. By 1975 contributions to PTL amounted to over five million dollars, and the amount was rising. Bakker insisted his was the world's fastest-growing ministry.

PTL's Message. The PTL Club reflected the developing nature of Pentecostalism in America. The production costs were high, requiring lavish sets, expensive clothing, and large numbers of volunteers to take pledges and talk with people who called into the program with their issues. Jim Bakker's engaging personality and Tammy's trademark heavy makeup, often spoiled by her tears, earned them devoted followers. Bakker softened the restrictive qualities of early Pentecostalism and suggested that God wanted his followers to be successful and live well. Certainly he and Tammy exemplified this in their own lives.

Competition. Bakker and Robertson seemed to be in competition during the late 1970s. Bakker insisted PTL was larger than CBN because he had more stations in his network, but CBN covered larger markets. PTL quickly followed CBN in leasing access to satellite broadcasting, making simultaneous broadcasting possible, and both expanded their physical facilities with funds generated from viewer donations.

Downfall. But before the end of the decade Bakker began to lay the basis for the financial scandal that would eventually bring down his empire. In 1978 he broke ground for a complex outside Charlotte, in neighboring South Carolina, that became Heritage USA. Bakker wanted this planned community of condominiums, shops, and meeting halls to serve as a combination resort, retreat, and retirement village for Christians. The project quickly drained the contributions that flowed to the ministry. Bakker's pleas for money to avert one financial catastrophe or another became commonplace on his program.

Prison. By 1979 the Bakkers' lavish lifestyle, extravagant projects, financial problems, and suspect pleas for funds to send to missions in Korea and Brazil attracted the attention of *The Charlotte Observer*, which began a long-term investigation of PTL. At the same time the Federal Communications Commission also started an inconclusive investigation into the financial activities of the ministry. The investigation culminated in Jim Bakker's conviction in 1988 of overselling timeshares at Heritage USA.

Sources:

Jim Bakker, *Move That Mountain* (Charlotte, N.C.: PTL Network, 1975);

Larry Martz with Ginny Carroll, *Ministry of Greed: The Inside Story of the Televangelists and Their Holy Wars* (New York: Weidenfeld & Nicolson, 1988);

Charles E. Shepard, *Forgiven: The Rise and Fall of Jim Bakker and the PTL Ministry* (New York: Atlantic Monthly Press, 1989).

BILL BRIGHT

1921-

NONDENOMINATIONAL MINISTER; FOUNDER OF THE CAMPUS CRUSADE FOR CHRIST

Targeting Youth. In 1951 Bill Bright founded the Campus Crusade for Christ, a nondenominational ministry that targeted the salvation of high-school and college students. His "Four Spiritual Laws," which spelled out his basic belief that salvation comes from the acceptance of Jesus as Lord and Savior, were effective evangelizing tools. The laws were

- God loves you and has a plan for your life.

- Sin separates us from God.

- Jesus is the only provision for man's sin.

- We must individually receive Christ as our Savior.

Vietnam. The Campus Crusade for Christ attracted increasing numbers of young people, although some observers noticed that Bright's workers had a minister's exemption from the draft in the turbulent days of the Vietnam War and wondered if that accounted for the young men who joined his program.

Explos. In the 1970s Bright set as his target the carrying of the word of Jesus to the entire world, and he staged a series of what he called "Explos" to bring young people together to stimulate the advance of Christianity. Explo '72 was in Dallas and attracted an estimated eighty thousand participants. Explo '74 in South Korea attracted an estimated three hundred thousand young people from around the world.

Source:
Richard Quebedeaux, *I Found It: The Story of Bill Bright and the Campus Crusade* (San Francisco: Harper & Row, 1979).

BILLY GRAHAM

1918-

EVANGELIST

Political Ties. Billy Graham expanded his influence in the course of the 1970s after the embarrassment of his close association with the failed presidency of Richard Nixon. Graham had a long friendship with Nixon. In contrast to his hesitation in 1960, Graham endorsed Nixon in the 1968 and 1972 presidential races. Nixon even half offered the vice-presidential nomination to the evangelist in 1968, an offer easily declined in jest.

Graham and Nixon. Graham's esteem for the new president was obvious in his frequent presence at White House prayer breakfasts and other quasi-religious events. In May 1970 Graham invited the president to join his crusade in Knoxville, Tennessee, where the president spoke to a huge audience at the University of Tennessee football stadium, the first university campus Nixon had visited since the student turmoil which followed the Kent State shootings earlier that month. In spite of the sympathetic crowd in this Republican area of the country, there were protesters, whose behavior was effectively used by Nixon to gain the crowd's support. The Supreme Court refused to review a case of one of the protesters, who had been punished for breaking a state law prohibiting the disturbance of a religious event.

Billy Graham Day. The following year Nixon flew to Charlotte, North Carolina, Graham's hometown, for the city's celebration of Billy Graham Day. The police carefully monitored the people going to the meeting where the president would appear, checking and frisking those who looked suspicious, including many who simply wanted to share in the religious celebration. While a small group of people were offended by what they saw as an alliance among local politicians, the Graham organization, and Nixon, most people in the area continued their respect for both leaders. The city of Charlotte named a highway for Graham.

Sorrow over Watergate. The Watergate scandal, which began unraveling in 1973, deeply upset Graham. He believed that Nixon had been distancing himself, and as the press reported more and more sordid stories, he thought he understood why. Graham managed to offend both Nixon's supporters and enemies with his refusal to defend the president forcefully and his attempts to urge higher moral standards at all levels. The greatest blow to Graham, he would say for the rest of his life, was the revelation of the bitterness and vulgarity of the private life of Nixon. The preacher insisted that he had never known the president to speak as was revealed on the White House tapes made of private conversations: "What comes through these tapes is not the man I have known for many years." Graham's critics noted he seemed more concerned about Nixon's vulgarity than the president's criminal actions.

World Evangelization Conference. Graham was a moving force in organizing the great 1974 Lausanne International Congress on World Evangelization in Switzerland. While some of the other organizers saw the congress as an alternative to the increasing radicalism they saw in the World Council of Churches, Graham insisted that the Lausanne congress aimed at carrying the word of Jesus to all parts of the world and to bring together those people whose commitment and energy would bring this about.

World Crusades. Throughout the 1970s Graham himself continued his schedule of crusades around the world. In Seoul, Korea, his five-day crusade climaxed with an audience of over a million people, the largest in his career. In 1974 he spent the weeks after the Lausanne congress in Brazil. The following year he was in Taiwan. While Graham himself was the center of adulation, his work depended in large part on the efforts of his associates in the Billy Graham Evangelical Association. But for the American people he himself was consistently rated one of the most popular and respected men in the nation.

Sources:

Marshall Frady, *Billy Graham: A Parable of American Righteousness* (Boston: Little, Brown, 1979);

William C. Martin, *A Prophet with Honor: The Billy Graham Story* (New York: Morrow, 1991);

John Pollock, *Billy Graham: Evangelist to the World* (San Francisco: Harper & Row, 1979).

ANDREW MORAN GREELEY

1928-

ROMAN CATHOLIC PRIEST; SOCIOLOGIST; AUTHOR

Education and Writings. Andrew Moran Greeley was born in Chicago and educated in Catholic schools and Mundelein College. He was ordained in 1954 and assigned to a prosperous suburban Chicago parish, an experience that became the basis for his *The Church and the Suburbs* (1959). He was permitted to do graduate work at the University of Chicago and completed his Ph.D. in 1961, a study that led to *The Education of American Catholics* (1966), which attracted attention with evidence that American Catholics were becoming the best educated of American ethnic groups.

Sociological Studies. After his degree Greeley affiliated with the National Opinion Research Center (NORC), focusing on analyzing the social implications of religion and ethnicity. In 1965 he was released from parish duties and permitted to devote himself to academic and scholarly work. In 1970 the Ford Foundation funded the Center for the Study of American Pluralism, associated with the NORC, which became the base of his scholarly work in sociology.

Theories Attract Attention. Greeley's work attracted increasing attention in the 1970s, particularly his study of *Catholic Schools in a Declining Church* (1976), which asserted that parochial education was one of the most effective means of developing loyalty to the church, this at a time when bishops were slowing their commitment to building more schools. More sensational was the revelation in his research that the reason for the decline in recent Catholic commitment was not bewil-

derment by the rush of change that followed the Second VaticanCouncil but the refusal of the American laity to accept the church's teachings of sexuality and birth control, as stated in *Humanae Vita* (1968). His studies said that only 15 percent of American Catholics accepted the rule against artificial birth control, a sharp drop for the more than half who accepted the church's teachings in this area in 1963. Paralleling this drop in acceptance of teachings on sexuality was a drop in the acceptance of papal authority and a decline in Catholic practices. The impact of *Humanae Vita* was also evident in the clergy, where 80 percent of the priests would not enforce the strictures against birth control. *Time* magazine paid particular notice to his work. These conclusions were confirmed in *American Catholics: A Social Portrait* (1977).

Controversial Claims. Greeley then turned his attention to the use and effect of symbols in religion, paying attention to the Virgin in a study, *The Mary Myth: On the Femininity of God* (1977). That with his reports on church politics of the election of Pope John Paul II made him one of the most famous and controversial Catholic writers. In 1990 he took a professorship at the University of Arizona, where he would spend half his years teaching and in parish work.

Popular Fiction. At the end of the 1970s Greeley turned to expressing his views in poetry and fiction. He published two modestly successful novels before the end of the decade and before reaching the vast readership he attained with his fiction in the 1980s, when novels like *Cardinal Sins* (1981) sold millions of copies and attracted a band of devoted readers and admirers. Greeley felt that his fiction was a more effective way to communicate his ideas than the scholarly works he had written earlier and turned his efforts increasingly to more creative forms of writing.

Sources:

Andrew M. Greeley, *Confessions of a Parish Priest: An Autobiography* (New York: Simon & Schuster, 1986);

Ingrid H. Shafer, *Eros and the Womanliness of God: Andrew Greeley's Romances of Renewal* (Chicago: Loyola University Press, 1991).

BILLY JAMES HARGIS

1925-

RIGHT-WING CHRISTIAN MINISTER

Right-Wing Christianity. Billy James Hargis attracted public attention in the 1960s with his Christian Anti-Communist Crusade ministry, located in Tulsa, Oklahoma. This right-wing political and religious group focused on the threat of Communist subversion in the United States and Communist influence in Mainline Protestant denominations.

American Christian College. In 1970 Hargis organized the American Christian College in Tulsa to teach "anti-Communist, patriotic Americanism." The following year he organized Americans for Life, one of the growing number of antiAbortion groups hoping to block the liberalization of Abortion laws. Hargis's thriving ministry erupted in scandal in 1974 when several of the students at his college, male and female, accused him of sexual improprieties. In spite of Hargis's resignation from the college presidency, the American Christian College closed in 1977. Meanwhile Hargis himself returned to the revival circuit, opening the Billy James Hargis Evangelistic Association in 1975, but he had passed the peak of his influence.

JESSE JACKSON

1941-

BAPTIST MINISTER AND CIVIL RIGHTS LEADER

Links with King. The Reverend Jesse Jackson came a long way very quickly from his beginnings as an illegitimate child in Greenville, South Carolina. His charm, drive, intelligence, and athletic ability led him into a football scholarship at North Carolina A & T University in Greensboro, where he became a leader in desegregation activities. His desire to become a Baptist minister led him to Chicago. Jackson first attracted national attention when he led a delegation from the Chicago Theological Seminary, where he was a student, to join demonstrations in Selma, Alabama, in 1965 organized by Dr. Martin Luther King, Jr. Impressed by the young man's ability, King gave Jackson a job organizing black preachers in Chicago for the Southern Christian Leadership Conference (SCLC). When King moved his campaign north to Chicago in 1966, Jackson moved even closer to the center of the SCLC. He was placed in charge of Operation Breadbasket, which placed economic pressures on businesses to hire black workers. Jackson's highly publicized selective boycotts secured some work for black Chicagoans, and deposits in black-controlled banks sharply increased. He was becoming a public figure at an early age. His commitment to change in the South led him back to the South.

King's Death. Jackson was in Memphis with King in April 1968 to help focus attention on the city's striking sanitation workers. King's close associates were dismayed when Jackson appeared on network television the evening of King's assassination to claim he had been with King at the time of his death.

Suspension. Still working with the SCLC, Jackson had found the spotlight, and he attempted to focus it on his work with Operation Breadbasket. He staged Black Expo '70 in 1970 and repeated this celebration of black-

ness and black business the following year. When the SCLC discovered Jackson had incorporated Black Expo under his own name, he was suspended from the organization.

Operation PUSH. Jackson then formed his own organization, Operation PUSH (People United to Save Humanity), taking with him most of his staff from the SCLC and local support from his previous work. PUSH aimed to secure jobs for the unemployed, organize people not making a living wage, and support minority-owned businesses. Jackson now took on larger businesses, such as Coca-Cola, Seven-Up, and Burger King, which signed agreements to hire more blacks and work more closely with black businesses.

Radio. Observers believed that the center of Jackson's power at this time was his Saturday radio broadcast from 9:00 A.M. to 12:00 P.M. Thousands tuned in to hear him lead his followers in his widely acclaimed chant:

> I am — Somebody!
>
> I may be poor, but I am — Somebody!
>
> I may be on welfare, but I am — Somebody!
>
> I may be uneducated, but I am — Somebody!
>
> I may be in jail, but I am — Somebody!
>
> I am — Somebody!

Visibility. Young, handsome, charismatic, and attention seeking, Jackson acquired a national reputation, appearing on talk shows and news programs. He was the topic of cover stories in *Playboy, Penthouse,* and *Time.* By middecade he was probably the most visible black leader in the United States.

PUSH for Excellence. In 1975 Jackson began a self-help program for young people in the increasingly black urban slums of the nation. Like many self-help preachers, Jackson believed that opportunities were now open to young blacks if they were willing and prepared to take them. He assured his young audiences, "No one will save us for us but us." Instead of simply blaming white society for their problems, Jackson claimed that blacks must recognize that hard work, self-discipline, delayed gratification, and persistence were essential for success. The target of PUSH for Excellence (PUSH/Excel), as he called his program, was young people, but he hoped to muster the strengths of the black community, its schools, its families, and its churches to give young people the support they needed.

Government Aid. As Jackson took his message around the country, city after city organized local programs. In 1977, with the encouragement of former vice-president Hubert Humphrey, the Department of Health, Education, and Welfare began awarding PUSH/Excel millions of dollars, and by 1979 twenty-two programs had been established.

Embracing Arafat. But in September 1979 Jackson attracted significant criticism and negative publicity when he went to the Middle East and a photograph of him embracing Yasser Arafat of the Palestine Liberation Organization appeared in American papers. The already-serious tension between the black and Jewish communities heated up, and Jackson became a target of anger. In many locations his PUSH/Excel program lost local support and went into decline, but his career continued as he sought to lead the black community, as well as advance his own fame in the coming decades. The issue was whether he could lead blacks more effectively as a preacher or as a politician.

Sources:

Ernest R. House, *Jesse Jackson and the Politics of Charisma: The Rise and Fall of the PUSH/Excel Program* (Boulder, Colo., & London: Westview Press, 1988);

Gary Wills, *Under God: Religion and American Politics* (New York: Simon & Schuster, 1990).

MEIR KAHANE

1932-1990

JEWISH RABBI; MILITANT JEWISH ACTIVIST

Beginnings. Martin David Kahane was born in Brooklyn, the son of a distinguished Hassidic family. His father, a rabbi of an Orthodox synagogue, was an ardent Zionist, working actively to support the Jews in Palestine before the creation of Israel. Meir, as he would later call himself, grew up with both his politics and religion intertwined. In 1946 he joined Betar, a quasi-military, international youth movement which aimed at protecting Jewish people from their enemies. Clearly this involvement was the source of Kahane's cofounding of the Jewish Defense League several years later.

Education. Kahane was educated in Talmud schools but graduated from a public high school in Brooklyn. He attended Brooklyn College and took a law degree from New York University, but he never took the state bar examination. He married, had four children, and served in the late 1950s as rabbi of the Howard Beach Jewish Center, where he generated opposition from the adults by his inculcating what they considered extreme religious and ethnic ideas in their children.

Political Activities. In the 1960s Kahane entered a period of life that he never made clear, but apparently he became an FBI informant, infiltrating and reporting on various groups including the right-wing John Birch Society. As the U.S. became more deeply involved in the war in Vietnam, he attempted to organize prowar support on college campuses. Kahane also began writing for the conservative *Jewish Press,* an Orthodox publication that became his major avenue to his followers in the Orthodox community.

Jewish Defense League. In 1968 Kahane was one of the three founders of the Jewish Defense League (JDL). The JDL, created in the euphoria that followed the Six-Day War of 1967, was designed to assert Jewish pride and power in the racial politics of New York City. Tension was increasing between militant blacks, who were adopting an openly anti-Semitic rhetoric, and the large population of older Jews left in declining neighborhoods as people fled the city for the suburbs. The JDL played on the memories of the Holocaust with its slogan "Never Again" and to the pride in the Israeli success in the Six-Day War with the slogan "Every Jew a .22."

Publicity. While the JDL seemed to promise to protect these weak and elderly Jews from the presumed threat of young, black toughs, its highly publicized actions, often violent, heightened tension in the city during the great school strike of 1968–1969. In one of the periodic attempts to improve school performance, small, local boards were created to control neighborhood schools. In some black districts these boards reassigned teachers and principals, sometimes in violation of established procedures. The teachers union, with a large Jewish membership, responded with a strike and demonstrations. The JDL was the self-protector of union members and attracted some followers from that group.

Anti-Soviet Demonstrations. By 1969 and 1972 Kahane, whose charismatic personality and lust for publicity made him the central figure of the JDL, turned his attention to international politics when he focused on the plight of Jews who were being denied permission to leave the Soviet Union. The JDL demonstrated at Soviet agencies in New York City, occupying offices, harassing Soviet officials, and exploding bombs which damaged Soviet property. These highly publicized anti-Soviet actions attracted the attention of politicians in Washington as well as New York. The plight of Soviet Jews became an American political issue and a cause for tension between the United States and the Soviet Union.

Further Militant Actions. In 1971 Kahane was arrested and pleaded guilty in federal court for conspiring to manufacture firebombs. He was given a sentence of four years probation and was prohibited from having any firearms or contact with people or groups with arms. That year Kahane left the United States for Israel, where he established a branch of the JDL. His penchant for violence and publicity continued. He was tried three times in Israel for his agitation against Arabs but did not serve a prison sentence. In 1975 his probation in the United States was revoked, and he served a year for violation of the terms of his probation as he continued his campaign of violence against Communists and Arabs.

Campaign for Israeli Parliament. Observers, whether friends or critics, had trouble deciphering Kahane's intentions from the contradictions of his remarks and actions in these early years in Israel. Instead of joining either the conservative party of Menachem Begin or one of the religious parties, Kahane organized his own political party, Kach

Theories. In *The Jewish Idea* (1974) he articulated his beliefs that the Arab presence polluted the essence and spirit of Judaism and that their expulsion was necessary for the redemption of the Jewish people. He asserted that the history of the Jews revealed the working of a divine pledge through time which would culminate with the return of the Messiah. This would mean the annexation of the Occupied Territories, which he called Judea and Samaria, and the construction of a new temple on the site of King David's original structure.

Increasing Controversy. As Kahane's racism became more strident, he continued to offend the governments of both Israel and the United States. Israel for a time held up his passport, keeping him from his periodic trips to the United States, and the U.S. later attempted to revoke his passport when he was finally elected to the Knesset. He also had difficulty with the American leadership of the JDL, who became concerned with new revelations of Kahane's womanizing. They believed publicity about such affairs would demolish an organization which had carefully preached morality and ethics. In spite of his opposition, Kahane managed to maintain his control of the JDL and Kach

Source:
Robert I. Friedman, *The False Prophet: Rabbi Meir Kahane, From FBI Informant to Knesset Member* (Brooklyn: Lawrence Hill, 1990).

TIM AND BEVERLY LA HAYE

1926- ; 1926-

RELIGIOUS RIGHT-WING ACTIVIST TEAM

Christian Heritage College. Tim and Beverly La Haye married in 1950 while students at the Bob Jones College, the Fundamentalist school in Greenville, South Carolina. Unable to continue at the college because of their marriage, they then began a Baptist mission, moving in time to California, where they created a television program, *The La Hayes on Family Life,* that ran for three years. In 1965 Tim La Haye opened the Christian High School of San Diego, which expanded to the Christian Heritage College in 1970. He remained president of the school until 1976.

Sexual Manual for Christians. In 1972 the La Hayes expanded their television program into their *Family Life Seminars,* a ministry designed to revitalize Christian marriages. In 1976 the Christian publishing company Zondervan published their *Act of Marriage,* a sexual manual for Christians. Some observers believed this explicit book

was an important signal of the lessening of conservative Christians' concern over sexual pleasure.

Creation Science. Tim La Haye was also a founder of the Institution for Creation Research, which insisted that biblical accounts of creation could be studied scientifically. He sought to include what he called creation science in the public-school curriculum, to be taught along with evolution. La Haye insisted his opponents not only were secularists but also practiced a new religion that he called secular humanism, adding a catchphrase to the decade.

Concerned Women for America. In 1979 Beverly La Haye organized Concerned Women for America, a major group of the New Religious Right, opposing ERA, Abortion, and gay rights and supportive of prayer in schools. Tim La Haye was one of the organizers of the Moral Majority, the political-action wing of the Christian Right. The La Hayes demonstrated the shift of conservative Protestants from religion and cultural issues to explicit political issues that would become a critical part of life in the coming decades.

Sources:
Michele McKeegan, *Abortion Politics: Mutiny in the Ranks of the Right* (New York: Free Press, 1992);

Corwin E. Smidt, *Contemporary Evangelical Political Involvement: An Analysis and Assessment* (Lanham, Md.: University Press of America, 1989).

ORAL ROBERTS

1918-

TELEVANGELIST; FOUNDER OF ORAL ROBERTS UNIVERSITY

Public Notice. In the early 1970s Oral Roberts attained a newfound acceptance and celebrity, symbolized in part by his induction into the Oklahoma Hall of Fame in 1972. His television program, *Oral Roberts and You,* took on the trappings of regular television entertainment to widen its appeal and consistently attracted the largest audiences for regular religious programming for most of the decade of the 1970s. Roberts became a frequent guest on talk shows and other commercial television programs. As the nation's most famous charismatic preacher, he had become a part of the celebrity culture, having dinner with Billy Graham and President Jimmy Carter in the White House.

Oral Roberts University. Part of Roberts's acceptance came from the success of Oral Roberts University in Tulsa. Roberts continued to serve as president of the University, but about half the expenses of the institution came from contributions to the Oral Roberts Evangelical Association, which operated his ministry. By the end of the decade there were about four thousand students enrolled in its various programs, and many fans followed the success of the ORU Titans basketball team. In middecade the University instituted graduate programs in business, theology, nursing, and education, and Roberts announced that schools of law, dentistry, and medicine would soon be added.

Family Misfortunes. But family misfortunes accumulated in the last years of the decade. His older daughter and her husband were killed in an airplane accident in 1977. Richard, his older son and mainstay in the ministry, was divorced two years later, and his younger son's life was spiraling downward toward an ultimate suicide.

Basketball Scandals. In addition to his children's tribulations, Oral Roberts University attracted widespread criticism as the decade wore on. The basketball successes of the ORU Titans declined after their high point in 1974. Critics questioned the school's efforts to restore the team's faded glory, particularly the coaches' extravagant salaries, and in 1979 the National Collegiate Athletic Association announced penalties for the Titans for recent rule violations.

Conversations with God. More bitter questions came from Roberts's decision to add a hospital and medical complex to ORU. In 1977 he announced that God had spoken to him and demanded he add a City of Faith, a medical complex that would contain a hospital with 777 beds, a sixty-story clinic, and a twenty-story research center. Derisive questions were raised about Roberts's direct conversations with God. More serious questions were raised by local hospitals in Tulsa about the politics of Roberts's efforts to secure a certificate of need for the new medical facility. While people in Tulsa agreed that a medical school would be useful for the city, many community leaders insisted that already there was a surplus of hospital beds in the area and that a new hospital would drain patients from the hospitals already operating, leading to their financial difficulties. In spite of the protests ground was broken on a scaled-back version of Roberts's City of Faith, and he and his political allies pushed through an acceptance of his plans. Even as work on the City of Faith went forward, Roberts found himself engulfed in new controversy when he announced that he had talked with Jesus and that he was nine hundred feet tall. By the time comedians had finished with that episode, Roberts announced that God would call him home if his followers did not send an immediate five million dollars for his ministry. The respect he had carefully acquired after playing down his charismatic tendencies washed away in the years that followed. Even the City of Faith was forced into closing by the 1990s.

Source:
David Edwin Harrell, Jr., *Oral Roberts: An American Life* (Bloomington: Indiana University Press, 1985).

PAT ROBERTSON

1930-

TELEVANGELIST; FOUNDER OF THE CHRISTIAN BROADCASTING NETWORK

Background. In 1960 Marion ("Pat") Robertson, son of a U.S. senator from Virginia and graduate of Yale Law School, purchased a UHF television station in Virginia Beach, Virginia. He had gone through a religious experience that led him to the New York Theological Seminary and showed him how, as he explained, he was ready to carry out God's order to begin a religious television ministry. His original audience was small. Not only did the signals of UHF stations have a limited range, only recently had television manufacturers been forced to make sets that could receive their signals. Robertson struggled in his early years. At a low point he asked for seven hundred listeners to join his ministry by contributing ten dollars a month to keep his station on the air. The response of what he called his "faith partners" was astounding, and the Christian Broadcasting Network (CBN) was underway.

The 700 Club. By the 1970s CBN and *The 700 Club*, hosted by Jim Bakker in its early years, began to spread by syndication across the country. Initially Robertson bought time on other UHF stations in the nation's major cities, and by the end of the decade his 120 channels covered most of the major markets. He quickly recognized the potential of the cable systems, which were growing in most urban markets. These companies needed more than local channels to attract customers and were often willing to rent cheaply or even give away time for their excess channels.

Satellite. Robertson also moved quickly when satellite technology became available for commercial use. His satellite was the first to lease satellite space to link his stations by direct broadcast. He also made money by permitting other programmers to rent time from his system.

CBN University. CBN's growth was stunning, and as contributions poured into the ministry Robertson decided to expand his range from broadcasting to education. In 1978 he opened CBN University, now Regents University, in Virginia.

New Religious Right. Robertson, like many conservative Evangelicals, expressed growing concern about what he saw as the moral decay of the nation. By the end of the 1970s he was ready to join others in the New Religious Right to enter politics and change those government policies he believed encouraged the decline of faith and values.

Sources:

Dick Dabnesy, "God's Own Network: The TV Kingdom of Pat Robertson," *Harpers*, 261 (August 1980): 33–52;

Janice Peck, *The Gods of Televangelism* (Cresskill, N.J.: Hampton Press, 1993);

Richard Quebedeaux, *The Worldly Evangelicals* (San Francisco: Harper & Row, 1978);

Pat Robertson, *Shout It from the Housetops* (South Plainfield, N.J.: Bridge, 1977).

ROBERT SCHULLER

1926-

REFORM MINISTER; TELEVANGELIST

Move to California. In 1955 Robert Schuller, who was ordained in the Reformed Church of America, moved to Garden Grove, California, to establish a church in this fast-growing region of southern California. His resources were modest, so he rented one of the ubiquitous drive-in movie theaters for his Sunday services and advertised for an audience, "Come as you are in your family car." His success was stunning in this booming suburb that had few established churches. In 1961 he opened his new building for the Garden Grove Community Church, which had a conventional sanctuary but still provided for his drive-in members. (He carefully omitted his congregation's affiliation with the Reformed Church of America to avoid sectarian confusion.)

Hour of Power. The Garden Grove Community Church was one of the fastest-growing congregations in the nation, and Schuller organized the Robert Schuller Institute for Successful Church Growth, which gave population seminars to train others in the techniques he found successful. In 1970 he began his television ministry with his *Hour of Power* and quickly expanded to over 150 stations.

Positive Thinking. Schuller attracted one of the larger television audiences during the 1970s but also aroused concern in Evangelical circles, where questions were raised about his theology, which sometimes seemed as optimistic as that of his Pentecostal peers. In many ways Schuller continued the "positive thinking" line of his fellow Reform minister Norman Vincent Peale. Schuller urged his listeners to cast out negative thoughts and focus on "possibility thinking."

Crystal Cathedral. By the end of the decade Schuller's ministry began the construction of one of the more famous buildings of the decade, a glass-sided sanctuary designed by famous architect Philip Johnson. The Crystal Cathedral had become a tourist attraction even before it opened for worship.

Sources:

Robert Schuller, *Peace of Mind with Possibility Thinking* (Garden City, N.Y.: Doubleday, 1977);

Dennis N. Voskuil, *Mountains into Gold Mines: Robert Schuller and the Gospel of Success* (Grand Rapids, Mich.: Eerdmans, 1983).

PEOPLE IN THE NEWS

On 29 May 1973 **Rev. Philip Berrigan** and **Sr. Elizabeth McAlister** revealed that they had married in 1969.

On 16 June 1974 the **Reverend Dr. Lawrence W. Bottoms** was elected the first black moderator of the Presbyterian Church in the U.S. Blacks made up about 1 percent of the nine hundred thousand members of the largely southern denomination.

On 16 November 1977 the Florida Citrus Commission renewed its contract with singer **Anita Bryant** despite her antigay activity in Miami.

On 7 December 1972 **Rev. W. Sterling Cary** of the United Church of Christ was elected the first African-American president of the National Council of Churches.

On 14 August 1977 **Rev. William Sloane Coffin** was named senior minister of Riverside Church in New York. He had resigned the previous year from his position as chaplain of Yale University.

On 6 May 1973 **Rennie Davis,** who had been tried as one of the Chicago Seven for his activities in riots during the Democratic National Convention in Chicago in 1968, announced he was now a follower of **Maharaj Ji,** the fifteen-year-old Indian guru.

On 5 December 1976 **Bishop Carroll T. Dozier** of Memphis granted a mass absolution to about fourteen thousand divorced, remarried, and estranged Roman Catholics of his diocese.

On 10 April 1970 **Fr. James E. Groppi** resigned as pastor of Saint Boniface parish in Minneapolis. He said it was time to appoint a black priest for the parish. Father Groppi attracted national attention for his demonstrations against housing discrimination a few years earlier.

On 23 June 1973 **Margaret A. Haywood,** a superior court judge in the District of Columbia, was elected moderator of the United Church of Christ's biennial synod. She was the first black woman to hold such a high position in a biracial denomination.

On 18 April 1975 the self-proclaimed **Rev. Marvin Horan** and an associate were convicted for a school-bus bombing that climaxed a series of protests over "un-Christian" textbooks in Kanawha County, West Virginia. A federal district judge ruled that while the textbooks might offend some people, the books did not violate the principles of separation of church and state.

On 5 March 1973 **Most Rev. Joseph Lawson Howze** was installed as the auxiliary bishop of the Mississippi diocese of the Roman Catholic church. He was the third black bishop in the American church's history.

On 5 December 1979 **Sonia Johnson,** head of Mormons for the ERA, was excommunicated from her church for "spreading false doctrine." She charged that she was expelled because her work for the ERA had become an embarrassment to the church.

On 20 August 1972 **Sehia Kalif** of Michigan was elected president of the Federation of Islamic Associations in the United States and Canada. She was the first woman to head the federation, which then represented two million Muslims in North America.

On 17 June 1975 **Jeb Stuart Magruder,** who had completed his prison sentence for his part in the Watergate scandal, was named vice-president for administration and communications of Young Life.

On 2 February 1973 Pope Paul VI nominated the **Most Reverend Timothy Manning,** archbishop of Los Angeles; the **Most Reverend Humberto S. Medeiros,** archbishop of Boston; and the **Most Reverend Luis Aponte Martinez,** archbishop of San Juan, Puerto Rico, as cardinals of the church. Archbishop Aponte would be the first Puerto Rican cardinal.

On 1 January **Jacqueline Means** became the first American woman ordained an Episcopal priestess.

On 18 September 1976 over fifty thousand people attended a "God Bless America" rally conducted by **Rev. Sun Myung Moon,** head of the Unification church, in Washington, D.C.

On 26 February 1975 **Wallace D. Muhammad** was declared the leader of the Nation of Islam, replacing his father, **Elijah Muhammad,** who died the day before. In June the new imam opened the former black-separatist group by asking whites to become followers of Islam and join his organization.

On 2 March 1979 federal appeals court dismissed a suit by **Madalyn Murray O'Hair** to remove the slogan "In God We Trust" from the national currency.

On 3 June 1972 **Sally J. Priesand,** 25, became the first woman rabbi ordained in the United States. She studied at the Hebrew Union College — Jewish Institute of Religion, the Reform Judaism seminary in Cincinnati.

On 13 October 1973 **Claire Randall** was elected general secretary (chief executive officer) of the National Council of Churches, the first woman to hold that position.

On 10 September 1979 **Rabbi Moses Teitelbaum** was selected to replace his recently deceased uncle as the leader of the Satmar Hasidim, with headquarters in New York.

On 20 January 1974 **Dr. John H. Tiejen** was suspended as president of Concordia Seminary in Saint Louis. He was charged by the president of the Lutheran Church-Missouri Synod, with administrative malfeasance and advocating false doctrines. Dr. Tiejen's suspension was the culmination of a long struggle between the conservative president of the denomination and what he considered the liberal teachings of the denomination's leading seminary. Following Dr. Tietjen's suspension most of the 520 students went on strike and ultimately formed a Seminary in Exile.

DEATHS

Henry J. Cadbury, 90, founder of the American Friends Service Committee in 1917, 7 October 1973.

Father Charles E. Caughlin, 88, radio priest and founder of Social Justice; in the early 1930s the most popular religious and political speaker on radio; later opposed the New Deal; ordered to cease his radio ministry when he became involved in anti-Semitic activities before World War II, 27 October 1979.

Cardinal Richard Cushing, 75, former archbishop of Boston; considered a liberal in his time and known for his support of the Kennedy family, 2 November 1970.

Maurice N. Eisnedrath, 71, spiritual leader of Reformed Judaism, noted for his social activism, 9 November 1973.

Rev. Leonard Feeny, 80, Roman Catholic priest who was excommunicated in 1953 for continuing to assert there was no salvation outside the Catholic church (the expulsion was rescinded in 1972), 31 January 1978.

Joseph Roswell Flowers, 82, a founder of the Assemblies of God in 1914; served as foreign-missions secretary and then general secretary and treasurer of the denomination, 23 July 1970.

Mordeh Friedman, 80, former president of the Union of Hassidic Rabbis, 2 March 1971.

Nelson Glueck, 70, a leader of Reformed Judaism and biblical archeologist. In 1934 he identified the site of King Solomon's mines, 12 February 1971.

Rose Halprin, 82, two-time president of the Zionist women's organization Hadassah, 8 January 1978.

Will Herberg, 75, Jewish theologian who attracted attention with his study of religion in the United States, *Protestant, Catholic, Jew: An Essay in American Religious Sociology* (1955), 27 March 1977.

Rabbi Abraham Joshua Herschel, 65, theologian at Jewish Theological Seminary in New York. His books included *God in Search of Man* and *A Philosophy of Judaism* (1955), 23 December 1972.

Mahalia Jackson, 60, gospel singer, 27 January 1972.

Father James G. Keller, 76, founder of the Christophers, which made famous its motto "better to light one little candle than curse the darkness," 7 February 1977.

Kathryn Kuhlman, television spiritual healer, 20 February 1976.

Rev. Dr. Mary Ely Lyman, 87, professor of religion at Union Theological Seminary, 9 January 1975.

Cardinal James McIntyre, 93, archbishop of Los Angeles (1948–1970), 16 July 1979.

Elijah Muhammad, 77, leader of the Nation of Islam for forty-one years, 25 February 1975.

Rev. Reinhold Neibuhr, 78, theologian at Union Seminary in New York and political activist, 1 June 1971.

Bishop Fulton J. Sheen, 88, archbishop of Rochester, New York; moved easily from radio to television and in the 1950s attracted one of the largest television audiences in the nation, 9 December 1979.

Rabbi Joel Teitelbaum, 93, head of the ultraorthodox Satmar Hassids; an anti-Zionist, arguing that only the Messiah could create a Jewish state, 19 August 1979.

Clara Ward, 48, leader of the Clara Ward Gospel Singers, 16 January 1973.

Ethel Waters, 80, long active in show business; starred as a blues singer, actress, and gospel singer in the last years of her life, 1 September 1977.

Alan Watts, 58, poet and popularizer of Zen Buddhism in midcentury, 16 November 1973.

PUBLICATIONS

Jim Bakker, *Move That Mountain* (Charlotte, N.C.: PTL Network, 1975);

David G. Bromley and Anson D. Shupe, Jr., *"Moonies" in America: Cult, Church, and Crusade* (Beverly Hills, Cal.: Sage Publications, 1979);

Charles Colson, *Born Again* (Old Tappan, N.J.: Chosen Books, 1976);

Marshall Frady, *Billy Graham: A Parable of American Righteousness* (Boston: Little, Brown, 1979);

Paul Goodman, *New Reformation: Notes of a Neolithic Conservative* (New York: Random House, 1979);

Andrew Greeley, *The American Catholic: A Social Portrait* (New York: Basic Books, 1977);

John Pollock, *Billy Graham: Evangelist to the World* (San Francisco: Harper & Row, 1979);

Richard Quebedeaux, *I Found It: The Story of Bill Bright and the Campus Crusade* (San Francisco: Harper & Row, 1979);

Quebedeaux, *The Worldly Evangelicals* (San Francisco: Harper & Row, 1978);

Pat Robertson, *Shout It from the Housetops* (South Plainfield, N.J.: Bridge, 1977);

Robert Schuller, *Peace of Mind with Possibility Thinking* (Garden City, N.Y.: Doubleday, 1977);

The Worldly Evangelicals (San Francisco: Harper & Row, 1978);

America, periodical;

Catholic Reporter, periodical;

Christian Century, periodical;

Christianity Today, periodical;

Soujourners, periodical.

CHAPTER TWELVE

SCIENCE AND TECHNOLOGY

by LAURA BRIGGS

CONTENTS

Sidebars and tables are listed in italics.

1970

- The floppy disk is introduced for storing computer information.

- Large reflecting telescopes are completed at Kitt Peak, Arizona, and Mauna Kea, Hawaii.

- The enzyme reverse transcriptase is isolated, proving that information from RNA can be transcribed onto DNA. Previously it was believed that only the opposite was possible.

- The first enzyme (restriction enzyme) that breaks DNA at a specific site, making recombinant DNA possible, is isolated.

21 Jan. The Boeing 747, the first jumbo jet, is put into commercial service.

11 Apr. The *Apollo 13* mission is begun. Two days later an oxygen leak and fire disable the spacecraft, and the astronauts barely make it home safely.

22 Apr. The first Earth Day is celebrated.

31 Dec. President Richard Nixon signs the National Air Quality Control Act, designed to reduce automobile pollution by 90 percent by 1975.

1971

- Direct telephone dialing begins between parts of the United States and Europe on a regular basis.

- The first computer chip (microprocessor) is introduced by Intel.

- Texas Instruments introduces the first pocket calculator, weighing 2.5 pounds and costing around $150.

- Various restriction enzymes are developed by Daniel Nathans and Hamilton Smith.

31 Jan. The *Apollo 14* mission is launched; it returns 9 February with 98 pounds of Moon rocks.

9 Feb. An earthquake with a magnitude of 6.5 on the Richter scale hits San Fernando, California, killing sixty-two people.

8 May Mars probe *Mariner 8* is launched. It suffers engine failure, falls back to Earth, and comes down north of Puerto Rico.

30 May The second Mars probe, *Mariner 9,* is launched. On 13 November it enters orbit around Mars, sending back pictures of astonishing clarity.

26 July The *Apollo 15* mission is begun. It includes a ride around the Moon's surface in the Lunar Rover.

1972

- The California State Board of Education demands that textbooks give equal weight to creationism as a type of evolutionary theory.

- The large particle accelerator at Fermi National Accelerator Laboratory in Batavia, Illinois, begins operation.

- The first recombinant DNA molecules are generated at Stanford University.

22 Mar. The *Pioneer 10* space probe is launched to explore the outer planets; on 13 June 1983 it becomes the first human-created object to leave the solar system.

16 Apr. The *Apollo 16* mission, the fifth Moon landing, is launched.

14 June Following warnings that DDT is interfering with the reproduction of birds and is potentially toxic to humans, the Environmental Protection Agency (EPA) announces a ban on most uses of the pesticide, beginning 31 December.

7 Dec. *Apollo 17,* the last manned lunar landing, is launched.

1973

- A calf is produced from a frozen embryo.

- The push-through tab is introduced in soft drink and beer cans.

- Foreign DNA is successfully transferred into *E. coli,* creating potential for insertion of any gene into bacteria.

- Scientists first express concern to the public that genetic engineering might produce new and dangerous microorganisms.

5 Apr. *Pioneer 11* is launched. It becomes the first human-made object to fly by Saturn in 1979.

25 May The first Skylab mission is launched. A three-man crew conducts experiments for twenty-eight days in this space station orbiting the earth.

29 July The second Skylab mission is launched. It lasts fifty-nine days.

3 Nov. The *Mariner 10* probe is launched to collect data from Mercury.

16 Nov. The third Skylab crew is launched. This mission lasts eighty-four days and gathers medical information on the extended spaceflight.

1974

- Scientists warn that chlorofluorocarbons used as propellants in spray cans may be destroying the ozone layer of the Earth's atmosphere.

- The subatomic J/psi particle is first observed.

- The thirteenth known moon of Jupiter is seen.

- Hewlett Packard introduces a programmable pocket calculator.

18 July Scientists at the Asilomar conference call for a halt to genetic engineering research until its implications are better understood.

24 Nov. A three-million-year-old humanlike skeleton is found in Ethiopia and named Lucy.

1975

- A fourteenth moon of Jupiter is observed.

- The first personal computer, the Altair 8800, is introduced in kit form.

15 July In a gesture of cooperation across superpower borders, the American-Soviet *Apollo-Soyuz* orbiting space station project is launched.

Aug. A new subatomic particle, the tau lepton, or tauon, is discovered.

20 Aug. *Viking 1* is launched. It begins sending pictures from Mars in June 1976.

9 Sept. *Viking 2* probe is sent. It sends data from Mars from 1976 to 1980.

1976

- The French-English supersonic jet Concorde begins regular passenger service.

- Astronomers find that Pluto's surface is at least partially frozen methane.

- Aboard an airborne observatory, astronomers first see rings around Uranus when it passes in front of a star.

- Genentech, the first company devoted to creating products through genetic engineering, is founded in San Francisco, California.

23 June   Reflecting rising public concern, the National Institutes of Health issues guidelines prohibiting many categories of recombinant DNA experiments.

12 Sept.   The *Viking 2* lander extends its arm and scoops up a sample of Martian soil, which it feeds to a miniature lander on the spacecraft.

13 Sept.   The U.S. National Academy of Sciences says that chlorofluorocarbons (CFCs), especially those in aerosol cans, endanger the ozone layer.

1977

- Deep-sea "chimneys" are found near the Galapagos Islands, where warm water allows bacteria, giant clams, and tube worms to survive beyond the reach of sunlight.

- The Apple II, the first successful personal computer, is introduced.

- A full sequence of bases in a viral DNA is identified for the first time.

20 Aug. and 5 Sept.   Space probes *Voyager 1* and *Voyager 2* are launched on a journey to Jupiter and the outer planets.

1978

- Lois Gibbs of the Love Canal Homeowners Association demonstrates that residents' health is being seriously affected by a nearby toxic-waste dump.

- U.S. medical personnel remove the inhabitants of Bikini Atoll in the Pacific when it is shown that earlier testing of the hydrogen bomb had rendered the island unsafe for habitation.

- Apple releases the first disk drive for use with personal computers.

- The Nobel Prize for medicine is awarded for work making genetic engineering possible.

- Production of the first human hormone through recombinant DNA begins.

15 Mar.   CFCs are banned as spray propellants.

20 May and 8 Aug.   Two Pioneer space probes are launched toward Venus.

22 June   Astronomers find a moon they name Charon orbiting Pluto.

1979

- VisiCalc introduces a spreadsheet program for personal computers, allowing users who know nothing about programming to use a business application for computers for the first time.

- The National Institutes of Health relaxes its guidelines on genetic engineering.

- An Antarctic meteorite (believed to be uncontaminated by Earth) is found to contain traces of amino acids.

- Evidence from deep-seabed cores shows that there are no fossils for a period of about one hundred thousand years about sixty-five million years ago.

- Microbial fossils from Western Australia are found to be $3,500 \times 10^6$ years old.

Mar.   Information from *Voyager 1* is used to identify a ring around Jupiter.

28 Mar. Partial meltdown begins in the reactor at Unit 2 of Three Mile Island nuclear power plant in Harrisburg, Pennsylvania.

11 July Skylab falls into the atmosphere, breaking up over Australia and the Indian Ocean.

OVERVIEW

Meeting Ground. The decade of the 1970s was a meeting ground for two opposing attitudes about science and technology: optimism that science could bring progress and prosperity and radical mistrust of its power to change life for the better. In the 1950s there had been a general public consensus that science advanced the power of the United States and made domestic life in the newly constructed suburbs easier. In the 1960s, however, many Americans questioned the uses of U.S. power, especially during the Vietnam War, and they viewed the domestic ease facilitated by technology as corruptive to spiritual values and as destructive to the environment. In the 1970s these two attitudes toward science often clashed and combined, making the debate over the progress of science often as important as the progress with science.

An Era of Debate. In the 1970s the tendency to question authority spread among a wider segment of the population. Ordinary people who disagreed with the directions science took asked questions and argued with the experts. Scientists, industrialists, and governmental bureaucrats — the "experts" — were no longer simply trusted to make all the decisions about the use and development of science. Overt protest of scientific and technological priorities was no longer unusual. In the controversy over genetic engineering, most Americans felt it was perfectly appropriate for them to have opinions about basic research issues. This boldness would have been unthinkable two decades earlier. Fundamentalists and evangelical Christians, who had abandoned their opposition to the teaching of evolution in the middle third of the twentieth century, began again to argue that evolutionary science could be questioned. The presence of toxic waste and pesticides in the soil and water became subjects of concern and opposition in small communities across the country. The daily news was full of controversy over what scientists and engineers should do. At the same time, U.S. society refused to give up its hopefulness and awe at the wonders accomplished by science.

Optimism. Perhaps the best symbol of American faith in science was the excitement about the exploration of space. The space program, especially the manned moon flights early in the decade, seemed to symbolize the strength of the United States and its unlimited technical and scientific capabilities. A measure of its popularity is the extent to which product marketing tried to associate itself with astronauts. Tang, a popular orange-flavored drink, was "the breakfast of astronauts." Food Sticks, a sweet, chewy snack, and Actifed, a nasal decongestant and antihistamine, were advertised as having been taken on Apollo flights. The Volkswagen Beetle, a type of automobile, compared itself to a lunar module.

Understanding. The faith in scientific progress typical of the 1950s was evident in the public response to new technologies that brought the world closer together. People would understand each other better through faster air travel and better telephones. Personal computers could give everybody unlimited access to information that previously had been limited to large corporations. Even the distance between species narrowed as primatologists taught apes and chimpanzees to use human languages so they could tell us how the world looked from their perspective.

The Vietnam Syndrome. Yet the realization that progress could bring destruction as well as cooperation also grew. By 1970 a majority of Americans opposed the U.S. war in Vietnam and wanted a withdrawal of troops. Science and technology symbolized the horror of war to its opponents. The sounds of the Huey helicopter and machine-gun fire became the audio signatures of the war, replayed endlessly on the evening news. American planes rained fire and poison on Vietnam. Napalm, Agent Orange, and white phosphorus chemical technology destroyed crops, forests, and mangrove swamps and burned combatants and civilians alike. The surreal mathematics of the Pentagon's daily body counts — which, when added up, would have every Vietnamese man, woman, and child dead more than once — seemed a further example of out-of-control science and technology.

Asking for the Moon. Even the Apollo space program could be criticized as serving elite goals and contributing to the uneven distribution of national resources. Democrats, seeking to recapture the White House in 1972, promised to scale back space exploration and redirect the funds to education, the war on poverty, and other social programs. Entertainer and social critic Gil Scott Heron contrasted the deprivation of black life in the ghetto with the extravagance of putting "Whitey on the moon." The National Aeronautics and Space Administration (NASA) was particularly irritating to the black community because it had the worst record of any government agency for hiring black Americans for any position — never mind as astronauts.

Scientists and Engineers. The science professions were affected by the same social trends as the rest of society. Many were horrified by the Vietnam War. Nobel Prize–winning geneticist James Watson noted that scientists concerned over the military exploitation of their work were altering the direction of their research. At the 1972 meeting of the American Association for the Advancement of Science, one member threw a tomato at former vice-president Hubert Humphrey to protest the war, an unheard-of breach of decorum. But some of the same people who questioned the profession's ability to do harm believed in its capacity to do good. Physicists, who had been shaken decades earlier by their role in creating weapons of mass destruction, searched enthusiastically for particles smaller than the atom, the fundamental building blocks of matter. Astronomers looked for signs of life in the solar system. Chemists and engineers sought ways to undo the damage of pollution.

Decade's End. There was no clear resolution to the debates begun in the 1970s. Some things were halted as a result of public outcry. DDT, Agent Orange, and some aerosol sprays, believed to be damaging to humans and the environment, were banned. The era of rapid building of new nuclear power plants in the United States ended as a result of the Three Mile Island accident (and, later, the Soviet Chernobyl disaster), though this was not yet clear in 1980. The program to put humans in space was suspended and started up again with a slightly more modest budget. Genetic engineering research moved from academic centers to industry, where it shielded itself from public and regulatory scrutiny. A project to map the purpose of all human genes began, quietly and uncontroversially funded by the government at a level rivaling the Apollo program. Some scientists and lay people felt all the debate had been harmful and tried to avoid it. Others were more suspicious than ever before.

TOPICS IN THE NEWS

ACTIVISM FOR THE ENVIRONMENT

A Decade of Growing Activism. The 1970s were a time of rapidly growing consciousness about the importance of protecting the environment. Not since the decade after 1910 had ecology seemed so significant to such a broad group of people, including students, scientists, politicians, people in business, and the most ordinary of citizens. Of course, these groups did not always find themselves on the same side. When housewife and mother Lois Gibbs formed the Love Canal Homeowners Association to investigate and publicize the fact that a toxic-waste dump in her community was causing residents to have a high rate of illness, businessmen were hardly thrilled. Yet the words of President Nixon, a supporter of business interests, suggest how widespread the consensus on environmental issues was in 1970. He said, "A major goal for the next ten years for this country must be to restore the cleanliness of the air, the water, the broader problem of population congestion, transport and the like."

Earth Day. One measure of the unanimity about environmental problems was the national celebration of Earth Day on 22 April 1970. Millions of Americans participated in demonstrations, teach-ins, and community cleanup projects for the environment. The observance, coordinated by a group in Washington that included congressional designees in honorary positions, was modeled after the anti–Vietnam War demonstrations of 1969. Intended to galvanize public sentiment for environmental issues, it was celebrated in a variety of ways. In New York tens of thousands marched down Fifth Avenue. In Boston a small group was arrested at Logan Airport protesting noise pollution and the development of supersonic jets. Students in Minneapolis and Chicago gained entrance to stockholders' meetings of major polluters, including General Electric and Commonwealth Edison, to demand changes in policy and priorities. There was at least one sign that not everybody saw environmental issues in the same way: Secretary of the Interior Walter Hickel used the occasion to announce the approval of the proposed Alaskan oil pipeline, which

This land is your land.

And it's going to take a big push to clean it up. Everybody's needed if the 1974 Keep America Beautiful Day campaign is to get the litter off the ground, promote recycling programs, plant trees and shrubs, and clean up waterways, beaches, parks.

On April 27, the Boy Scouts and Girl Scouts with individual and corporate volunteers will dedicate the day to highlighting what must be a year-long effort. Join them. Won't you please volunteer your support, time, supplies, skills.

Write or call: Keep America Beautiful, Inc. 99 Park Avenue / New York, N.Y. 10016 (212) 682-4564

Keep America Beautiful Day. April 27, 1974.

Advertisement for Keep America Beautiful Day, the successor to Earth Day

environmental groups had opposed in the belief that it would destroy the unique habitat of the tundra and disturb migratory patterns of many animals.

Reducing Chemicals. The presence of artificially synthesized chemicals in food and the environment became the focus of numerous skirmishes between citizens and industry. Toxic-waste sites, the pesticide DDT, and chlorofluorocarbons (CFCs) in aerosol cans became rallying causes for those who believed the environment needed protection from big business and big science. When federal regulators, over the objection of pesticide companies, banned DDT in 1972 as dangerous to humans and wildlife, many found in this action a symbol of the need for strong oversight of irresponsible science and industry. Johnny Carson spoke for many when he said on *The Tonight Show* in May 1977, "I say we should trust science. Remember science has given us DDT ... DDT has worked so well we don't have to use it anymore, because it's working everywhere, in the rivers, in our food, and in our lungs."

CFCs. Another chemical compound, CFCs, could be found in nearly every household, not only in aerosol cans, but also in styrofoam, foam mattresses, air conditioners, and refrigerators. Some scientists — beginning with Sherwood Rowland and Mario Molina in 1973 — argued

that CFCs were depleting the ozone layer of the upper atmosphere, exposing life on earth to ever-increasing amounts of ultraviolet radiation from the sun. Excess ultraviolet would result in higher human skin cancer rates, lower crop yields, and a cooling effect on the global climate. Following these warnings, chemical companies, notably DuPont, insisted that if CFCs were dangerous, they would cease production immediately to protect the environment. Then they did nothing for five years and lobbied Congress to postpone efforts to restrict the chemicals, calling for more studies. To some this seemed like responsible business practice; to others, stalling. Finally, in 1978, the FDA stepped in, banning CFCs in aerosol products.

Ecofeminism. Some participants in the woman's rights movement felt that there was also a connection between what they saw as men's oppression of women and human domination of nature. They believed that the idea that women were somehow closer to nature might be part of why and how men exploited both. Susan Griffin's 1978 book, *Woman and Nature,* was an important statement of the movement that began to call itself ecofeminism. In this prose poem Griffin blends together mistreatment of women and nature by the rapacious male: "He says she cannot continue without him. He says she must have what he gives her. He says also that he protects her from predators. That he gives her chlordan, parathion, Malathion, chlorophenol. . . ."

Sources:
Susan Griffin, *Woman and Nature* (New York: Harper, 1978);

Gill Kirkup and Laurie Smith Keller, *Inventing Women: Science, Technology, and Gender* (Cambridge, Mass.: Polity Press, 1992);

"Worried Scientists," *Time* (12 January 1970): 29.

AGENT ORANGE

Defoliant. Another chemical at the center of controversy was Agent Orange. Agent Orange was a defoliant used extensively in the U.S. war in Vietnam to deny ground cover and food to North Vietnamese guerrillas by destroying forests and crops. Named for the orange stripe painted on fifty-five-gallon barrels for identification, it was developed by the army in the 1950s as an alternative to biological weapons. It was a combination of two herbicides — 2,4-D (n-butyl-2,4, dichlorophenoxyacetate) and 2, 4, 5-T (n-butyl-2,4,5-trichlorophenoxyacetate) — and was tremendously effective. By 1970, 11.2 million gallons had been dropped by airborne C-123 cargo planes, destroying the plant life of 4.5 million acres. In addition to the areas officially targeted, fruit trees, mangrove swamps, and crops were also destroyed by leaky spray nozzles, wind drift, and vaporization from the heat. The cumulative effect crippled the Vietnamese economy and did substantial damage to the environment. In 1971, following criticism from the National Academy of Sciences, international organizations, and the American public, the military agreed to halt the herbicide campaign.

Contaminated school playground in Niagara Falls, New York, 1978

Vietnam Vets. In the spring of 1978 Paul Reutershan shocked the audience of the *Today* show, saying, "I died in Vietnam, but I didn't even know it." Reutershan had flown almost daily missions through clouds of Agent Orange as a member of the 20th Engineering Brigade during the war. He believed it responsible for the cancer from which he ultimately died nine months later. Many Vietnam veterans suffered health problems when they returned home, but the Veterans Administration (VA) said they were not caused by Agent Orange. Perhaps, the VA suggested, the psychological impact of fighting an unpopular war had made veterans ill. The herbicide, they believed, could cause skin rashes, but nothing more. At issue was the extent of dioxin contamination of Agent Orange. Dioxin, a by-product of Agent Orange, is an extremely toxic chemical, believed to cause birth defects, cancer, and nerve damage. While dioxin was present in all samples of Agent Orange tested, federal chemists and health officials believed it existed in quantities too small to be harmful. Despite lawsuits, the Department of Defense never agreed that Agent Orange could have damaged the health of veterans.

Sources:

Neil Sheehan, *A Bright Shining Lie: John Paul Vann and America in Vietnam* (New York: Random House, 1988);

Fred Wilcox, *Waiting for an Army to Die: The Tragedy of Agent Orange* (New York: Random House, 1983).

APOLLO AND SKYLAB PROGRAMS

Moon Walks and Moon Rocks. After millions watched the first Moon walks in 1969 with amazement and the near-fatal *Apollo 13* accident with anxiety, lunar landings began occurring with such regularity and precision they became almost commonplace. In 1971 and 1972 there were two landings a year, each nearly a carbon copy of the other. With the Command Module orbiting overhead, the crew landed a Lunar Excursion Module (or LEM, but constantly being renamed: Eagle, Falcon, Challenger) on the Moon's surface. Each landing was a memorable moment for the public-relations specialists. The *Apollo 14* mission included Alan Shepard lightheartedly hitting a golf ball on the Moon. On the *Apollo 15* landing David Scott demonstrated the effects of zero atmosphere by dropping a hammer and a feather at the same time. Astronaut James Irwin kept the camera rolling as both struck the Moon's surface at the same time. Each mission brought back bigger bags of Moon rocks, generating tremendous public excitement and enabling scientists to learn more about the composition of the Moon. The metallic composition of the lunar surface turned out to be significantly different from Earth's, encouraging fresh speculation about the origins of the two bodies.

Cars in Space. A nation obsessed with cars could hardly expect its proud representatives to arrive in space

Particle accelerator, one of the largest atom smashers in the world, at Fermi National Accelerator Laboratory in Batavia, Illinois

without one. Beginning with the *Apollo 15* mission, the crews tooled around in a Lunar Rover, sort of a jeep with a big umbrella in front. Wrote astronaut Michael Collins, "The battery-powered Rover was an ingenious machine. Even its birth amazed me. The astronaut pulled a lanyard on the side of the Lunar Module, and, like a newborn giraffe, the Rover plopped to the ground and unfolded. It could do about 11 mph, downhill."

The Race to Beat the Soviet Union. The force driving this passion for space travel was, of course, the Cold War. Ever since the Soviet *Sputnik I* had beaten the Americans into space in 1957, the "race for space" was on. Each side was concerned about the potential military advantage the other might gain through superiority in space. Early in the 1970s it seemed the U.S. advantage was in Moon landings, and the Soviets excelled in extended stays in space.

Space Stations. The Cold War context made cooperation between Americans and Soviets in space doubly remarkable. The first U.S. space station, Skylab, began orbiting the Earth in May 1973 as still another competitive U.S. effort. It was designed for astronomical observa-

tion and to study the effects of weightlessness, with an eye toward the possibility of a permanent human presence in space. Over the next several months nine astronauts in three crews and separate missions spent twenty-eight, fifty-nine, and eighty-four days in space. Now Americans were setting the space endurance records. But then the Cold War abated somewhat. In the summer of 1975 a joint space station was constructed by docking Apollo and Soyuz modules. Soyuz, the Soviet equivalent of the Apollo program, had been designed as the precursor to a program that would launch inhabited Earth-orbiting space stations and perhaps, in the distant future, lead to colonization of the Moon or Mars. After the successful docking of the two nations' spacecrafts, Soviet president Leonid Brezhnev sent a hopeful message that read, "One can say that the Soyuz/Apollo is a forerunner of future international orbital stations." It was the final Apollo mission.

Sources:
Michael Collins, *Liftoff: The Story of America's Adventure in Space* (New York: Grove, 1988);

Alexander Hellemans and Bryan Bunch, *The Timetable of Science* (New York: Simon & Schuster, 1988);

Alan Shepard on the Moon during the *Apollo 14* mission

Phil Patton, *Made in USA: The Secret Histories of the Things That Made America* (New York: Penguin, 1992);

SALYUT: Soviet Steps Toward Permanent Human Presence in Space — A Technological Memorandum (Washington, D.C.: U.S. Congress, Office of Technology Assessment, December 1983).

DISASTERS IN SPACE

Apollo 13. Unlucky number 13 was the Apollo mission that never landed on the Moon and barely made it back to Earth. NASA had had one previous disaster: in 1967 three astronauts died in a fire on the launchpad. But the *Apollo 13* accident in 1970 was unprecedented for the American space program. Three men in space, with the eyes of the world upon them, suddenly heard a loud bang and watched as their oxygen tanks suddenly emptied. "OK, Houston, we've had a problem," they reported to the command center in a masterpiece of understatement. They still had the Lunar Module, though, and used it as a lifeboat on the long, cold trip home. The temperature was lowered to 38° F to conserve oxygen and electricity.

Even so, the astronauts barely made it back to Earth ahead of the failure of their oxygen.

The Soyuz Mission. The following year tragedy did strike Soviet cosmonauts. Following a record-setting twenty-four-day stay in a space station, the cosmonauts separated their ship, *Soyuz 11*, and began landing procedures. Braking rockets fired as the ship reentered Earth's atmosphere. After that, ground controllers lost contact with the ship. The parachute system functioned normally, and soft-landing engines were fired. But when the ground crew went to pick them up, they opened the hatch and found all three cosmonauts dead. An investigation found that thirty minutes before landing, the hatch had opened slightly, due to a combination of human error and mechanical failure. Their air supply was sucked out into space, suffocating them.

Skylab Falls. While the Apollo and Soyuz accidents may have made people more solemn about the risks of space flight, the falling of the Skylab space station made

NASA the butt of jokes. Apollo could be said to have turned out safely. Cold War fervor made the Soyuz deaths appear to be evidence of Soviet incompetence. But the announcement in June 1979 (only months after the Three Mile Island accident) that the $2.6 billion Skylab was in a decaying orbit and that the equipment previously designed to boost it higher had failed generated bad press for NASA. Even Congress joined in the ridicule of NASA. "Whereas, everything that goes up must come down," began a proposed resolution from an Oregon representative, "it is the sense of the Congress that Skylab should not be permitted to fall in Oregon, where it might mar the natural beauty." Despite the odds, Skylab did not fall into one of the world's oceans, as NASA officials had hoped it would. Instead, it landed in sparsely populated Western Australia. Fortunately, no one was injured.

Questioning Priorities. These accidents tarnished NASA's reputation. They provided ammunition for the naysayers and doubters who felt the billions spent on the space program would be better used on Earth. A major theme of the Democratic Party effort to defeat Nixon in 1972 was that science funding should be redirected from the space program and the Vietnam War to health, education, poverty, crime, and drug control improvements. Even the National Academy of Sciences criticized the space program from time to time for being wasteful and expensive. The Space Shuttle, designed as a reusable craft that could orbit the Earth for up to thirty days, was slated to be ready for use by late in the decade but was plagued by technical problems and NASA funding cuts. From the end of the Apollo program in 1975 until the first shuttle launch in 1981, it seemed that the era of human space flight was petering out.

Source:
Michael Collins, *Liftoff: The Story of America's Adventure in Space* (New York: Grove, 1988).

EXPLORATION BEYOND THE MOON

Probes. Space research carried out in the second half of the decade while the shuttle was delayed and budgets were cut was done mainly by space probes. Probes, with no need for life support, could go further and endure harsher conditions than spaceflight involving humans. The various probe programs of the 1970s (all with romantic names: Mariner, Voyager, Viking, Pioneer) sent back information about the five nearest planets: Mercury, Venus, Mars, Jupiter, and Saturn. Uranus and Neptune would be reached in the next decade.

Martians. Some of the earliest and most eagerly awaited photos came from Mars. In the 1960s three of the Mariner probes had successfully flown by Mars and returned with pictures. But NASA hit the jackpot with *Mariner 9* in January 1972: unlike previous space probes, this one orbited the planet. After a week of blinding dust storms, Mariner suddenly began sending back stunningly clear photos — 7,329 of them. They were discouraging to

those who hoped for suggestions of life on Mars; they showed that the long, canyonlike rills astronomers had observed were not "canals, nor were the seasonal dark bands" vegetation. Yet *Mariner 9* mapped the whole surface of Mars before contact was lost, unexpectedly finding volcanoes and giving scientists detailed information about the topography of the planet. Two Viking probes, launched in 1975, found a way to see Mars from an even closer perspective: each carried a landing craft with its own photographic gear and a small biological laboratory. These produced panoramic shots of the pock-marked, rocky Martian surface, which were relayed by the still-orbiting Viking craft. The landers also ran tests on soil samples in an unsuccessful attempt to find signs of life. The Viking orbiters continued sending back aerial views of the planet, even after the landers ceased transmitting. One, *Viking 2*, continued sending photos until 1980.

Voyagers. The other richly successful space probe of the decade was *Voyager 2*, launched on 20 August 1977, the first human-made object to leave the solar system (in 1989, after twelve years of flight). It carried with it greetings, in virtually every human language, as well as the call of the humpback whale to whoever might find it. Due to an unusual alignment of planets, it was able to pass the four large outer planets before leaving the solar system. In its flight by Jupiter and Saturn, Voyager had the company of its twin, *Voyager 1*, traveling somewhat behind it. Both found the Jovian moons covered with ice, and Saturn's rings, composed of thousands of small rings, infinitely more complex than imagined. The photos, the first detailed glimpses of the outer planets, captivated the public and thrilled scientists, who were able to study Jovian weather patterns and the composition of Saturn's rings for the first time.

THE COMPACT DISC

Ever since the phonograph was developed in 1877, recordings have been made by the vibrations of a needle on a groove. Eventually, the groove and the needle wear out, and the sound quality deteriorates.

In 1972 optoelectronics made the development of the compact disk, or CD, practical. Lasers could convert sound into microscopic traces on the surface of a disk. Other lasers could detect them and convert them back into sound. The recordings came out stunningly clear, more information could be packed in than before, and there was almost no wear. The first commercially successful audio CDs were introduced in Japan and Europe in 1982 and in the United States the following year.

FIBER OPTICS

Improving Telephones. Beginning in the mid 1960s researchers began to explore the possibilities of fiber-optic technology. By the beginning of the 1970s it was apparent that fiber optics had tremendous potential to improve the clarity and speed of telephone signals. A single hair-thin optical fiber could carry as many messages as a thick copper-wire cable containing 512 wires. Unlike copper wires, the glass fiber is unaffected by motors, electrical generators, power lines, or lightning storms — common causes of static on the line.

How It Works. The thin, extremely pure glass of an optical fiber, surrounded by a reflective casing, can bend light. This makes it possible to use light, specifically light generated by lasers, in place of electricity. Light can be carried faster, more cheaply, and more efficiently than electrical signals. Sounds are converted into a pattern of light, transmitted, received at the other end, then converted back into sound.

Putting It to Use. One of the first uses of fiber optics was in 1977 in Chicago. There two offices of Bell Telephone and a third for customers were successfully connected by light-carrying glass fibers. In 1978 the phones at Disney World were linked through fiber optics, and Disney also used them for video transmission, lighting, and alarm systems. They also built an intriguing two-way video-speaker arrangement, like a phone with a picture, for use at their EPCOT Center. Fiber optics have made possible fax technology, laser printers, high-quality copy machines, new medical tools that allow surgeons to see inside a patient using a tiny incision, and the rapid modem links between computers.

GENETIC ENGINEERING

Frankenstein and the Miracle. Perhaps more than any other issue, genetic engineering or recombinant DNA captures both the hopefulness and the unease that characterized feelings about science in the 1970s. It held out the hope of fantastic health benefits, promising to make drugs easy to synthesize and diseases treatable. Yet it also threatened the specter of Frankenstein: artificial life escaping from the lab and unleashing new diseases on the world. In 1974 scientists concerned about such a scenario called a halt to genetic engineering work. By the end of the decade environmental activists and much of the general public were deeply worried by these experiments, but most biologists were convinced they could control it. Entrepreneurial companies like Genentech, formed in 1976, were looking for ways to exploit the commercial potential of genetic engineering. The U.S. government, after first imposing strict guidelines on recombinant DNA research, ultimately relaxed restrictions.

The Idea. DNA, or deoxyribonucleic acid, is one of the most basic building blocks of life, found in every organism. DNA molecules are composed of chains of

Warning posted on the laboratory door of DNA researchers

meaningful information, commonly referred to as genes, encoded by combinations of four amino acids. Each gene produces a different effect in a cell: telling it to grow bone, for example. In 1972 microbiologists found that they could take a fragment of DNA from one organism and splice it together with DNA from another. This allowed them to do two kinds of experiments. First, they were able to tell what genes did by implanting them in a different kind of cell. If, for example, a genetically modified bacterium suddenly began producing a human hormone, then researchers would know that they had found the DNA segment that coded for that hormone. Similarly, researchers and commercial labs were interested in whether hormones such as insulin, commonly used by diabetics, could be produced easily and cheaply using simple organisms as manufacturers.

The Technique. The technique developed steadily over the decade. The first landmark was to develop a tool that would cut DNA. Since DNA is far too small for even the steadiest hand to slice with a mechanical tool without smashing it, the technique developed in 1970 to cut it was the use of a restriction enzyme, a protein that would fragment the DNA at a specific site. DNA is a double molecule, two chains joined together and wound into a double helix. Some restriction enzymes cut both sides, but at slightly different sites, leaving the end of one hanging off. Since each of the four amino acid bases can be mated to only one of the other four, a strip beginning with the same sequence of bases as the one just separated would be sticky; it would tend to attach itself to the DNA fragment. The enzyme ligase (from the Latin *ligare*, to tie) helps make these sticky fragments attach themselves firmly. The result is recombinant DNA, a kind of DNA not found in nature: part belonging to one organism, part to another. The recombinant DNA is placed in a host cell, usually a bacterium.

Controversy. Scientists first became concerned about the impact of these procedures in 1973 when researcher Paul Berg proposed experiments that involved using bacteria commonly found in humans, *E. coli*, to carry a virus that caused cancer tumors. The experiment was canceled, but scientists who discussed it at two important meetings that year felt it symbolized the dangerous potential recombinant DNA possessed. Following the decision to halt most further research in this area or conduct it under the most stringent guidelines, the press exploded with a discussion of its dangers and potential benefits. Laypeople and environmental activists, such as Friends of the Earth, participated in a public debate that would have been unimaginable two decades earlier about the direction scientific research ought to pursue. When the government relaxed its genetic engineering guidelines in 1979, persuaded by biologists' arguments that the lab strains of *E. coli* used in genetic research were so weakened that they could never survive in the wild to carry deadly genetic material, Friends of the Earth filed suit. They succeeded in delaying implementation of the new guidelines, insisting that federal regulators were required to conduct an environmental-impact study on the effect of creating new, unpredictable organisms. Some scientists, like geneticist James Watson, one of the early opponents of genetic engineering, grew bitter about the unprecedented public oversight of scientific priorities. Some activists, on the other hand, initially encouraged by signs of social concern by scientists over the impact of new technologies, felt betrayed by the ultimate refusal of the scientific community and regulators to listen to their concerns. In the 1980s biotechnology became a rapidly growing industry, and the federal government quietly began funding gene research on a scale matched only by the Apollo project.

Sources:
William Bains, *Genetic Engineering for Almost Everybody* (New York: Pelican, 1987);

Jeremy Rifkin and Nicanor Perlas, *Algeny* (New York: Penguin, 1983);

James Watson and John Tooze, *The DNA Story: A Documentary History of Gene Cloning* (San Francisco: W. H. Freeman, 1981).

INVENTING THE PERSONAL COMPUTER

Computer Lib. Despite the pin-striped reputation personal computers acquired from their rapid expansion into the business market in the 1980s, they began their existence with solidly countercultural credentials. An important early manifesto was Theodore Nelson's 1974 book, *Computer Lib/Dream Machines*. Nelson believed personal computers would free individuals from the big corporate computers, giving them access to their own computing power. Small, easy to use, and affordable, microcomputers would be available to all, with free software, community access, and "liberated information."

The Chip. The computers of the early 1960s were mammoth affairs, requiring entire rooms to house them, and so expensive that only large organizations and the government could afford them. Later, minicomputers were produced, more attractive to businesses and researchers in size and cost. The breakthrough that made the personal microcomputer possible came in 1971, when Theodore Hoff of Intel created the microprocessing chip. Much of the power of the bulky mainframe had been converted into a chip that could be held in the palm of the hand.

Kits. In keeping with its underground beginnings, the first microcomputers sold were kits. Featured on the cover of *Popular Electronics*, the kit was marketed by Altair for electronics amateurs beginning in January 1975. Meanwhile, the young technowizard Steve Jobs had sold his Volkswagen microbus to finance the development of a personal computer, which he watched his friend Stephen Wozniak build in his garage. In 1977 he introduced the Apple II, a line of personal computers upon which they would build a multibillion-dollar company. In the next two years Jobs and his entrepreneurial associates developed the essential tools for the explosion of personal computer use in the 1980s: a disk-drive system and a graphics and spreadsheet program, VisiCalc, that made it possible to use the machine for sophisticated applications without knowing computer programming.

Sources:
Alexander Hellemans and Bryan Bunch, *The Timetable of Science* (New York: Simon & Schuster, 1988);

Phil Patton, *Made in USA: The Secret Histories of the Things That Made America* (New York: Penguin, 1992).

JUMBO JET

Boeing 747. For those bound closer to the earth, the introduction of the Boeing 747 was treated as a revolution in air travel. The *Christian Science Monitor* greeted its first commercial flight on 21 January 1970 with the kind of words usually reserved for things spiritual. "As the world's physical and mental problems mount," the paper intoned, "so does the need for men to recognize the universality of their brotherhood and the oneness of their basic interests." *The New York Times* was not far behind: "The 747 will make it possible for more and more people to discover what their neighbors are like on the other side of the world."

Air Bus. What was the big deal? The 747 was huge by the standards of the day. It could carry as many as 490 people, while the next largest commercial plane, the Boe-

Joseph Sutter, chief engineer of the first wide-bodied airplane, the Boeing 747

ing 707, could accommodate only 132. The press called it an "air bus." Despite its size, the innovative use of a titanium body made it light enough to go great distances. It had a tremendous range, capable of going forty-six hundred nautical miles without refueling. These two features made it an ideal plane for transcontinental flights.

Safety. The sheer number of passengers on board such a plane raised the specter of air disasters on a scale unheard of before. Boeing had made safety its chief priority in the development of the 747. The opening pages of the design manual *Design Objectives and Criteria* said, "Safety is the prime design objective of the 747 Design Program; it shall be given first priority in all design decisions." The company swore the plane was safe, and its later record proved them right. Still, there were some terrible tragedies. On 27 March 1977 more than 570 people died when two 747s crashed into each other on the runway of a Canary Islands airport, the worst aviation disaster to date.

Breaking the Bank. By the end of the decade millions of people had traveled in 747s. Initially, though, it was not at all clear that the plane would be a success. It seemed impractical: no airport in the world had terminals that could accommodate its bulk, and everyone knew that

the future was in supersonics. Both Boeing and Pan Am, which invested heavily in its development, nearly went broke trying to build it. The team fashioning the 747 at Boeing, led by Joseph Sutter, became known as "Sutter's Runaways" as they consumed the company's money at a rate of $5 million a day. Boeing went on to prosper, but Pan Am declared bankruptcy in the 1980s. The company was principally a victim of harsh economic times and difficulties with leadership, but its investment in the 747 proved a liability.

Supersonics. If the building of the 747 had harsh consequences for some in the industry, it was a bigger success than the Supersonic Transport (SST). Despite federal spending of hundreds of millions of dollars for research and development, the American SST program never got off the ground. Supersonics — planes that can travel faster than the speed of sound — produce a sonic boom as they take off. The idea that this earth-shaking noise would become an everyday occurrence aroused public antipathy, and scientists warned that nitrogen emissions from the high-flying planes would deplete the ozone layer. As a result of the controversy, in March 1971 the Senate canceled funds for the program, effectively halting it. When the French and British governments announced in 1976 that their version of the SST, the

Dr. Donald Johanson with the fossil remains of Lucy, the 3–3.5 million-year-old skeleton he and an international team of archaeologists discovered in Afar, Ethiopia, in 1974

Concorde, was ready for passenger service, a lawsuit by environmental group Friends of the Earth held off its arrival for seventeen months. Though finally permitted to land in the United States, passenger service on the Concorde never proved profitable, and in 1979 the French and British governments canceled their development program as well, though existing Concordes continue to fly.

Source:
Clive Irving, *Wide-Body: The Triumph of the 747* (New York: Morrow, 1993).

LOOKING FOR HUMAN ORIGINS

Lucy and the Search for Earliest Man. In the early 1970s, if you had asked most Americans who the reigning king of "early man" studies was, they almost certainly would have said Richard Leakey, or perhaps his father, Louis Leakey. Both were made famous by *National Geographic* television specials celebrating their discoveries of fossil remains of large-brained tool users in East Africa. But much of that changed in 1974, when a team led by American Don Johanson and Frenchman Maurice Taieb reported that they had found a three-million-year-old hominid (humanlike) skeleton in Afar, Ethiopia. The fossil was older and more complete than any hominid ever found before. The shape of the pelvis showed it to be female, while the knee joint and thigh revealed that she walked upright. She was surprisingly short, less than four feet tall. Whimsically, the English members of the team named her Lucy, for the Beatles' song "Lucy in the Sky

with Diamonds." Her Swahili name was more respectful: Denkanesh, meaning "you are wonderful."

Debates. Initially Johanson argued that her upright stature and humanlike features made Lucy a member of the genus *Homo,* placing her in the same classification as modern humans and Leakey's more modern fossils. After considerable debate, anthropologists assigned her to the genus *Australopithecus.* The assignment meant that both Leakey and Johanson could now claim they had found the remains of the earliest man. However, Leakey believed *Australopithecus* was a branch of the evolutionary tree that had died out, while Johanson thought it was an ancestor of modern humans. Further discoveries intensified the disagreement between the two men. In 1975 Johanson's team found a large group of 3.7-million-year-old hominid fossils together, representing at least thirteen individuals, including an infant and several juveniles. They became known as the "first family." Taken together, along with a skull found in Tanzania by Mary Leakey, Richard's mother, Johanson and his collaborators argued that they had found a new species, and they called it *Australopithecus afarensis.*

Man the Hunter. If it seems strange that the star specimen of early man should be female, it is. Yet in the 1960s and 1970s, as interest in questions of human evolution increased sharply, so, too, did the conviction that males were the engine of the train of human evolution. Men hunt, the argument went, and hunting requires tools, intelligence, and an erect stature. Women stayed home with the babies. Thus it was men's activities that

WHEN FIRST I SIGHTED LUCY

It was November 24, 1974, and the sun stood scorchingly overhead. I had intended to devote this Sunday morning to bringing my field notes up-to-date. But Tom had persuaded me to relocate a spot where we had collected fossil animal bones the year before. We spent some time surveying, gathered up what bones we found, and started back toward the Land-Rover. As we walked, I glanced over my shoulder — and there on the ground I saw a fragment of an arm bone.

My pulse was quickening. Although the bone was very small, it lacked the characteristic bony flange of a monkey. Suddenly I found myself saying, "It's hominid!"

Something else caught my eye. "Do you suppose it belongs with those skull fragments?" It was high noon that memorable day when the realization struck us both that we might have found a skeleton. An extraordinary skeleton.

We looked up the slope. There incredibly, lay a multitude of bone fragments — a nearly complete lower jaw, a thigh bone, arm bones, ribs, vertebrae, and more! The searing heat was forgotten. Tom and I yelled, hugged each other, and danced, mad as any Englishmen in the midday sun.

Source: Donald C. Johanson, "Ethiopia Yields First 'Family' of Early Man," *National Geographic*, 150 (December 1976): 790–811.

---

caused human evolution. Lucy, with her personable name (and one of the few early fossils to have any identifiable sex-specific characteristics), may have marked the beginning of the end of the view that the important qualities of early man were male.

Woman the Gatherer. In 1971 Sally Linton published a paper called *Woman the Gatherer*. Linton, and other female anthropologists after her, suggested that what we know from studying primates and subsistence societies is that hunting is relatively unimportant. It supplies a relatively small portion of the food for a community. Rather, it is the generally female activity of gathering plants, roots, and berries and sharing them with their offspring that is the significant feature of food accumulation. Thus she thought the first tools were probably containers for carrying infants and the material gathered. Few champions of the "man the hunter" thesis took notice of Linton's paper at the time, but by the end of the decade her arguments had gained a secure foothold in beliefs about human evolution. Among other things, it was difficult to find ways that the earliest tools found — simple choppers and hand axes — could have been used for hunting.

While there was little agreement over a more important role for women in the process, most accepted that gathering and other women's work were significant in early human survival.

Sources:

Linda Marie Fedigan, "The Changing Role of Women in Models of Human Evolution," *Annual Review of Anthropology*, 15 (1986): 25–66;

Donna Haraway, *Primate Visions: Gender, Race, and Nature in the World of Modern Science* (New York: Routledge, 1989);

Donald C. Johanson, "Ethiopia Yields First 'Family' of Early Man," *National Geographic*, 150 (December 1976): 790–811;

"Puzzling Out Man's Ascent," *Time* (2 November 1977): 64–78;

John Reader, *Missing Links: The Hunt for Earliest Man* (New York: Penguin, 1988).

LOOKING TO THE BIBLE

The Challenge. In the 1970s mainstream science was once again challenged by creationists. Advocates of creationism, almost exclusively evangelical and fundamentalist Christians, as were the earlier critics of evolution, believed that the biblical version of the beginning of time in the Book of Genesis ruled out the possibility of evolution. In the strict creationist account, popularized in John Whitcomb and Henry Morris's *The Genesis Flood* in 1961, the earth had been formed about ten thousand years ago, and God created all plants, animals, and humans in the following six days. Humans and dinosaurs had coexisted. Fossils were the result of the mass deaths in the biblical flood. Carbon-14 dating, by which scientists had established the antiquity of many fossils, could be explained away by a vapor cloud that had covered the earth during the flood and prevented radioactivity from reaching the earth.

Skirmish in California. Initially *The Genesis Flood* had no impact outside extremely conservative Christian circles, and even there it was controversial. But creationism burst into public consciousness in 1972, when the California Board of Education accepted the arguments of a handful of fundamentalist Christian parents that creationism should be taught alongside theories of evolution. The parents believed that to do less was to engage in religious prejudice against fundamentalists. After all, the rest of the curriculum encouraged children to weigh alternative arguments and decide which one was best, so why not science? California was a particularly important place for such a victory. As it had the largest school system in the country, the state had a significant impact on textbook publishers.

The Battle Goes National. Most scientists in the half century since the 1920s had simply regarded creationism as a crackpot theory like the flat earth and had not been willing even to dignify it with a response. In 1972 evolutionists finally roused themselves to refute creationism. Both the National Academy of Sciences and the American Association for the Advancement of Science issued statements denouncing it. Momentum continued to build. In 1978 a young law student, Wendell Bird, proposed a new strategy for writing laws supporting the teaching of creationism. Creationism, he argued, was a scientific doctrine, not a religion. Teaching it, then, did not violate the freedom-of-religion clause of the Constitution (as many evolutionists argued), but not teaching it violated the rights of creationist students. This approach resulted in the immediate passage of bills in Louisiana and Arkansas, and twenty other states considered similar legislation. Not until the mid 1980s, following many court cases over creationism and the public schools, did the enthusiasm for creationism die down.

Source:
Ron Numbers, *The Creationists: The Evolution of Scientific Creationism* (New York: Knopf, 1992).

NUCLEAR POWER

Utilities Go Nuclear. In 1954 the government authorized private ownership of nuclear reactors as part of President Dwight D. Eisenhower's Atoms for Peace initiative, paving the way for utility companies to build nuclear power plants. By the mid 1960s many had "gone nuclear," though the cost of building reactors had proved far more than the early hopes that they could provide power for pennies a day. There was some public opposition to the plants — after all, most Americans' sole experience with the power of the atom was the devastating bombing of Hiroshima and Nagasaki in 1945. In California residents demanded the cancellation of the planned Bodega Bay reactor, sited on a geological fault, after an earthquake disrupted construction. Inhabitants of New York City resisted the siting of a plant in that densely populated area.

Energy Independence. Nevertheless, most people liked the idea of building atomic energy plants. The country was using increasing amounts of electric energy, and nuclear power promised to be cheaper and cleaner than burning fossil fuels, which created air pollution. Moreover, nuclear power had the aura of a neat, high-tech solution to complicated problems that people had come to expect from science and business. When an oil embargo by countries in the Middle East in 1973–1974 created shortages and high prices, atomic energy seemed to offer a way for the nation to achieve energy independence. Support for nuclear power was high, and its opponents were ridiculed. The antinuclear movement carried forward the traditions of the anti–Vietnam War movement and demonstrated against power plants, most visibly at the proposed site of Seabrook Station in New Hampshire, with what seemed ludicrously inadequate tools: sit-ins, civil disobedience, celebrity concerts, and rallies. To many, protesters' fear of radiation made them appear to be nature-loving cowards, and their opposition to nuclear power seemed to be vaguely un-American. One writer caricatured them as "vegetarians in leather jackets who drive imported cars to Seabrook listening to

MELTDOWN

A meltdown is the out-of-control melting of a superheated reactor core, which would become so hot that nothing could contain it. Experts differ on what would happen next. One early theory was that the core would fall through the earth and just keep going, "all the way to China." This scenario was later pushed aside, though not before it spawned a nuclear disaster movie starring Jane Fonda called *The China Syndrome* (1979). Now, some believe that it would simply wind up encased in volcanic glass about one hundred feet below the ground, sealed safely. Others disagree, suggesting that the breach of the containment dome would release fantastic amounts of radioactivity into the surrounding area, killing thousands, perhaps hundreds of thousands. One thing is clear: Unit 2 of the Three Mile Island nuclear power plant came perilously close to a full-scale disaster. The Presidential Commission report suggests that if the reactor had remained uncovered another twenty minutes, it would have melted down.

the Grateful Dead on their Japanese tape decks amid a marijuana haze."

Three Mile Island. At 4:00 A.M. on 28 March 1979 a mechanical failure of the cooling system at the Three Mile Island plant, near Harrisburg, Pennsylvania, was compounded by operator error. Technicians in the control room of the Unit 2 reactor, misunderstanding the nature of the problem, shut off all water to the reactor. With no water cooling it, the reactor became extremely hot — in excess of five thousand degrees — and began to melt. Within hours there was enough radiation in the containment dome to kill a person in minutes, and some radiation began leaking into the environment. It was another two days before the public learned how serious the accident was and officials began talking about a meltdown. Pregnant women and small children were evacuated. Ironically, the worst danger of a meltdown passed before the evacuation order was given — by then the reactor was underwater again. Nine days later the core had cooled sufficiently so that public officials felt safe in encouraging nearby residents to return to their homes; but the reactor was still hot even a year later.

The Aftermath. While there were no apparent injuries at Three Mile Island, it dealt the nuclear power industry a blow that sent it sharply into decline. In April 1979 a Gallup poll found that 66 percent of the nation believed nuclear power to be unsafe. Although that number declined to 50 percent nine months later, the accident cre-

RACE AND BIOLOGY

After fifteen years of civil rights struggle to assure black Americans of the full rights of citizenship and four decades of work by scientists to dismantle the notion of a biological basis for racial difference, Nobel Prize–winning physicist William Shockley became a controversial figure in the 1970s when he argued that black Americans were genetically endowed with inferior intelligence. He was rebuffed by the National Academy of Sciences in 1970, when it refused to conduct a study along these lines. Shockley was increasingly unpopular on U.S. campuses by late 1973, when he was prevented from fulfilling speaking engagements by students who protested that he was a racist and a Fascist. In 1974 anthropologist Peggy Sanday offered a study many believed discredited Shockley's views, arguing that IQ differences were "exclusively a matter of environment."

fore switching to research in particle physics, the place quickly acquired the nickname of Fermilab. The purpose of the accelerator is to push electrons extremely rapidly, breaking them into smaller parts, such as quarks. Physicists share time on accelerators, and during the period in which they use it, they try to design experiments that will tell them about the small particles produced.

Discovery. With Fermilab joining the accelerators at Stanford and the smaller one at the University of California at Berkeley, American physicists (including the many German-Jewish expatriate physicists who had fled the Nazis) began in the 1970s to have the resources to do a lot of research. New knowledge about fundamental particles was produced in the United States at a startling rate. In the 1970s high-energy particle physicists found the high-energy particle physicists found the tauon (1974), the J/psi particle, proving the existence of charm (1974), and the gluon (1979).

Sources:

Alexander Hellemans and Bryan Bunch, *The Timetable of Science* (New York: Simon & Schuster, 1988);

Carrol W. Pursell, Jr., ed., *Technology in America: A History of Individuals and Ideas,* second edition (Cambridge, Mass.: MIT Press, 1990);

Sharon Traweek, *Beamtimes and Lifetimes: The World of High Energy Physicists* (Cambridge, Mass.: Harvard University Press, 1988).

ated an enduring pessimism about the industry. In 1980 environmental crusader Ralph Nader noted the changed climate of debate. "When I first began speaking against nuclear power," he said, "the audiences would ask me how I could prove that nuclear reactors were badly designed and poorly run. Now the audiences accept these problems without question and ask what alternatives we have to nuclear power."

Sources:

Carrol W. Pursell, Jr., ed., *Technology in America: A History of Individuals and Ideas,* second edition (Cambridge, Mass.: MIT Press, 1990);

Mark Stephens, *Three Mile Island: The Hour-by-Hour Account of What Really Happened* (New York: Random House, 1980).

PARTICLE PHYSICS

High-Energy Particle Physics. Following World War II tremendous amounts of federal funding became available for atom-smashing physics because of its association with weapons research. This largesse was extended to high-energy particle research throughout the 1970s, despite the fact that this work had no discernible military applications and almost all high-energy physicists had refused to do secret research or work on weapons. Particle physicists were the doves of physics, preferring to search for the smallest (or "fundamental") particles of matter rather than develop weapons. Generous funding had allowed them to build the million-dollar equipment required to find such particles.

Fermilab. In 1972 the large accelerator at the Fermi National Accelerator Laboratory in Batavia, Illinois, near Chicago, began operation. Named for the Nobel Prize–winning physicist Enrico Fermi, who laid the groundwork for both nuclear energy and weapons research be-

TOXIC WASTE AT LOVE CANAL

Storing Industrial Wastes. In the 1930s and 1940s corporations and citizens did not worry too much about what happened to the chemicals left over from industrial processes. While regulations existed, enforcement was haphazard or nonexistent. Corporations such as Hooker Company in Niagara Falls, New York, which made pesticides, plastics, and other chemicals, mostly just sealed them in fifty-five-gallon metal drums and left them someplace nearby. For Hooker one convenient place was Love Canal, a never-finished part of a Great Lakes canal system begun in the late nineteenth century. While children played and swam nearby, Hooker dumped more than twenty-one thousand tons of chemicals into Love Canal, then filled it in with dirt. In 1953 they gave the covered-over lot to the town for an elementary school and a playground.

Early Warnings. As young families built homes near the elementary school, many noticed that their basements leaked. Some thought they noticed chemical smells and strange colors in water that leaked in. Few knew much about the history of chemical dumping. A dramatic sign that something was amiss came in 1974, when one family's backyard pool rose two feet out of the ground. When they removed it blue, yellow, and purple chemicals suddenly rushed in where the pool had been. By 1977, after several years of unusually heavy rain and snowfall, the former canal was turning into a marsh, and chemicals were noticeably seeping into surrounding soil and streams. The city explored means of dealing with it, but the cost was prohibitively high, and the project became entangled in red tape. While some nearby residents were concerned, it became difficult for them to move as their homes became increasingly worthless. Who would buy a house next to a toxic dump?

Love Canal Homeowners Association. Finally, in 1978 the results of state, local, and federal testing of the air and water in Love Canal basements — testing done after repeated requests from residents — became public. State Health Commissioner Dr. Robert Whalen announced in August that Love Canal was a "great and imminent peril to the health of the public" and urged pregnant women and children under two to leave the homes that abutted one end of the canal. There, studies had found conclusive evidence of an abnormally high rate of miscarriages and birth defects. The announcement left homeowners angry, frightened, and frustrated. Many quickly drew the conclusion that adults and older children in the area, and of neighboring streets, might also be in danger. "Do I let my three-year old stay?" asked one. They organized the Love Canal Homeowners Association to pressure officials to buy their homes and elected as president Lois Gibbs, a twenty-seven-year-old housewife who lived two blocks away from the canal. Gibbs turned out to have a tremendous talent for organizing residents and keeping the issue in the news.

Disaster. Shortly after the formation of the association, President Jimmy Carter proclaimed the area a federal disaster area, freeing up funds for residents of the south end of the canal to relocate. However, this still left those in surrounding areas unable to move, despite growing evidence of high rates of cancer and other illnesses. Local activists began systematically testing substances in their homes, streams, and soil, gradually accumulating a long list of chemicals, including C-56 (a pesticide believed to be carcinogenic), benzene, toluene, and even PCBs (a highly toxic substance). Gibbs undertook a systematic health survey of residents outside the evacuation area and turned up high rates of kidney and bladder troubles, birth defects, miscarriages, and nervous disorders. After six months the state agreed to pay for pregnant women and those with small children to be relocated, yet it forced them to return to Love Canal when the children grew older. Unsatisfied, residents continued to sign petitions, write letters, and hold demonstrations. Then in 1980 the state confirmed what some had long suspected: that among the chemicals at Love Canal was

OTHER SOURCES OF ENERGY

Solar energy attracted considerable interest in the 1970s among the "back to nature" crowd, though industry thought it impractical and little research was funded. It developed into a popular hobby, and photovoltaic cells began appearing on rooftops as enterprising homeowners found they could heat their homes and run their electricity completely or partially without fossil fuels or utility companies. Though it never developed into a widespread or commercially successful venture, getting "off the grid" became a rallying cry among some and a manifesto for personal energy independence. Wood stoves, too, found a thriving market.

Cars proved more difficult: photovoltaic cells just do not receive or store as much energy as most people are accustomed to having in a car. Still, design proposals for solar-powered cars turned up regularly on the evening news, particularly during the energy crisis of 1973–1974. John Reuyl, president of Energy Self-Reliance, designed a solar-powered house/car arrangement. The vehicle offered a sixty-mile range, a top speed a good deal faster than the legal limit, superior acceleration, and a gasoline engine for backup. Another alternative was to replace gasoline with alcohol-based fuels, or with gasohol.

dioxin, one of the most acutely toxic substances ever created. When this news was released, the state finally agreed to buy the nearby homes. After two years of anxiety and activism, homeowners there were finally permitted to leave. Whether this was the end of the saga remains uncertain. A decade later the government put these houses on the market again, and a new community of homeowners moved in amid controversy about whether the site was still unsafely contaminated with toxic waste.

Sources:

Michael Brown, *Laying Waste: The Poisoning of America by Toxic Chemicals* (New York: Pocket Books, 1981);

Donald McNeil, "Upstate Waste Site May Endanger Lives," *New York Times*, 2 August 1978, p. 1.

HEADLINE MAKERS

ROBERT BALLARD

1942-

GEOLOGIST, OCEAN EXPLORER, ENGINEER

Galápagos Hydrothermal Expedition. In 1977 Robert Ballard and the team of geologists and chemists of the Galápagos Hydrothermal Expedition were taking pictures of the ocean bottom off the coast of South America when they found something completely unexpected. Well below the reach of sunlight at the mouth of a volcanolike structure, an area certain to be too hot and too remote to support life — they found a thriving community of crabs, eels, and tube worms. The excursion had set out to learn more about geological activity in the deep sea, evidence that might prove that the earth's crust is composed of massive plates. Yet when they developed their pictures, scientists learned that they had made an even greater discovery: somehow life can be sustained at pressures of 3,650 pounds per square inch and in the complete absence of photosynthesizing plants.

Return. Naturally biologists were eager to examine the area where geologists had mapped five separate colonies blooming with life. Ballard returned with them, accompanied by a *National Geographic* camera crew. Taking pictures around the clock, Ballard and the crew found and studied these diverse, improbable colonies deep beneath the sea. They produced the television special *Dive to the Edge of Creation.* It focused on theories that bacteria, living at the edge of these deep ocean vents that were spewing sulfur-rich water into the surrounding ocean, must be feeding on sulfites. The bacteria, in turn, provided a food source for larger animals. This, they suggested, might have been how life on earth began.

Fascination with Technology. Though he earned his Ph.D. from the University of Rhode Island based on marine geography research, Ballard was also fascinated by the technology making deep ocean dives possible. Back in 1972 Ballard had first proposed using manned, deepwater diving equipment to study plate tectonics. While this suggestion was met with skepticism, Ballard returned to his laboratory at Woods Hole Oceanographic Institute and participated in the development of the navy's *Alvin* submersible, which could dive to depths previously inaccessible. In 1974, as chief scientist on a joint French-American research venture, Ballard studied the earthquakes and volcanic lava flows of the Cayman Ridge south of Cuba, believed to be another area where tectonic plates come together. Another new development, the *Angus* camera sled, made the Galápagos photography possible. Later, in 1985, Ballard tried out another new device he developed: the *Jason-Argo,* an unmanned deep-sea research system equipped with strobe lights, computer-enhanced cameras, sonar, and a self-propelling robot with a mechanical arm for collecting samples. Together with the *Angus,* the new system performed brilliantly: it found the long-sought *Titanic,* missing since it was wrecked in 1912.

Source:
David L. Clark, "Life in the Warm Depths Off Galápagos," *Oceans,* 12 (November–December 1979): 42–45.

VIRGINIA E. JOHNSON

1925-

SEX RESEARCHER

Sexual Revolution. In the 1970s Virginia Johnson and her partner William Masters were a focal point for debate about what contemporaries called the sexual revolution. They published a study of sexual dysfunction, *Human Sexual Inadequacy,* in 1970 and ran seminars and therapy groups to treat or prevent sexual problems. They also contributed regularly to *Redbook* magazine. They discussed such issues as women's liberation, "swinging" (married couples exchanging sexual partners), impotence, premature ejaculation, and situational orgasmic dysfunction. Reviews were uneven. They were accused of fostering infidelity by some critics. Germaine Greer, in her book *The Female Eunuch* (1970), criticized them for promoting "standard, low agitation, cool-out monogamy." If that were not confusing enough, another critic accused them of "creating the end of sex." Johnson herself insisted that the couple (who married in 1971 after more than a decade of scientific collaboration) was conservative. "It's a coincidence that our field is the subject of dirty jokes," she told a reporter.

Response. Masters and Johnson created a sensation with the publication in 1966 of their book *Human Sexual Response.* Though the first scientific study of human reactions to sexual stimulation might be expected to be interesting reading, the book itself was exhaustively detailed and rather dry. The pair used sophisticated electronics, including electrocardiograph, electroencephalograph, and color motion-picture cameras to monitor the increase and decrease in the response of certain organs, particularly the sexual organs, to stimulation. Masters and Johnson were eager to be thought of as scientists. Initially the book was advertised only in medical journals, and their publisher, Little, Brown, promised to fill orders only from medical book outlets. Their intentions were quickly overwhelmed by the public interest in the book, which made the huge, expensive volume an overnight best-seller.

Collaboration. Johnson became involved with this work in 1957. After two failed marriages (one, to Missouri politician George Johnson, lasted two days) Virginia Johnson was looking for a job that would allow her to go back to college for an undergraduate degree in sociology. She applied for, and got, a job at Washington University helping Masters screen volunteers for his study of female sexual response. Over the years she became a research assistant and later a research instructor. She also continued her studies. In 1964, before their research was published, she was forced to make a choice: either complete her doctorate or become a research associate at the Reproductive Biology Research Foundation. She chose the foundation, and in 1973 she became its codirector.

ARNO PENZIAS

1933-

ASTROPHYSICIST

Big Bang. In 1978 Arno Penzias and his colleague Robert W. Wilson shared the Nobel Prize for physics for their detection in 1965 of microwave background radiation, a discovery that proved that the universe had been created in a big bang of exploding matter. This discovery settled an argument among scientists. Opponents of the big bang theory argued for a steady-state theory that said the universe had always existed in its present form, with new matter created spontaneously as it expands. If all the matter in the universe had been generated in a single big bang, scientists argued, energy traces from that explosion should still be detectable in the universe. Penzias and Wilson claimed to have found it.

Immigrant Childhood. Penzias was not always confident about his abilities as a researcher and scholar. He has referred to his graduate thesis at Columbia as "dreadful" and described his memories of being an undergraduate attending the tuition-free City College of New York in these terms: "I had a feeling at that time of not being terribly good — of being a barely adequate physicist." His family immigrated to the United States when he was six, expelled from Germany when the Nazis began systematically deporting Jews without German citizenship (Penzias's father was Polish). Arno Penzias began calling himself Allen, though his accent still marked him as an outsider. Not until he attended Brooklyn Technical High School did he begin to make friends.

Defective Antenna. After a stint in the military Penzias took a job at American Telephone and Telegraph's Bell Labs. There he and Wilson worked together on an antenna designed to pick up radio signals from NASA's *Echo* balloon. To test it they pointed it at an area in space where no radio waves were expected. To their dismay, they began picking up unexpected noise. They spent a year trying to correct the problem, taking the antenna apart, smoothing its surfaces, checking connections, and reassembling it. They even dislodged a pair of pigeons who had made their home there, meticulously cleaning pigeon droppings. No matter what they did, the noise persisted. Penzias related that it was "like cigar smoke in a room with no cigar." Then Penzias learned that a team of astronomers led by P. J. E. Peebles at Princeton was predicting that the energy from a big bang explosion would have slowed from light waves to radio waves, at a frequency close to the annoying sounds his equipment was picking up. In 1965 he and Wilson put Peebles's theory together with their observations in an article in *Astrophysical Journal.* As *The New York Times* put it, their observation set in motion a "surge of cosmological discovery." Further measurements by other scientists sounded the death knell for the steady-state theory.

E(DWARD) O(SBORNE) WILSON

1929-

BIOLOGIST

Genetics as Destiny. E. O. Wilson's 1975 book *Sociobiology* vigorously contested the firm boundary between biology, on the one hand, and culture on the other. He proposed that traits like altruism and aggression, believed since the 1930s to be exclusively learned behaviors, were in fact the result of genetic predisposition. He extended the field of population biology and evolutionary theory to argue that many social behaviors, including human ones, are the result of a biological impulse lodged in one's genes. For example, even the altruistic sacrifice of one life for another increases the chances that genes from one's species will survive. Wilson writes that "In a Darwinist sense, the organism does not live for itself. Its primary function is not even to reproduce other organisms; it reproduces genes and serves as their temporary carrier." He popularized these views in his 1978 Pulitzer Prize–winning book, *On Human Nature*.

Ants. Educated at the University of Alabama and Harvard, Wilson's training was in entomology, the study of insects. He received his Ph.D. for exhaustive study of the ant genus *Lasius*. Most of his books have focused on entomology, including *The Insect Societies* (1971) and *The Insects* (1977). However, he also has done research on population ecology. In 1969 Wilson worked with D. S. Simberloff to study insect populations on a Florida island. They began by spraying the island with pesticides to remove all insect life, then observed that the same species returned, and in the same proportions in which they had originally occupied the island. From this they concluded that a given ecosystem could only sustain a fixed number of species.

Controversy. Wilson's work founded a new discipline, sociobiology. Sociobiology has given rise to controversial propositions, such as the adaptive features of rape. Rape can be seen as an aggressive means of furthering the survival of the male's genes. Unsurprisingly, the idea that rape and other undesirable human behaviors are natural has been vigorously disputed. Although Wilson has tried to reassure critics that he believes only about 10 percent of human behaviors are biologically determined, his students have gone farther. Wilson has been picketed, and at his home institution of Harvard the Committee Against Racism has called sociobiology "dangerously racist." The notion of biology as determinative of human behavior recalls late-nineteenth- and early-twentieth-century notions of a biological basis of racial inferiority and social Darwinism, a set of doctrines that proposes that the poor are poor because their inadequate genetic endowment dooms them to failure in the struggle for the survival of the fittest.

PEOPLE IN THE NEWS

J. M. Adovasio and his students began the excavation of Meadowcroft, west of Pittsburgh, Pennsylvania, in June 1970. It was subsequently shown to have been inhabited by humans as early as nineteen thousand years ago — eight thousand years earlier than other known North American sites.

Independently **David Baltimore** and **Howard Martin Temin** found an enzyme called reverse transcriptase, which makes possible the transcription of RNA onto DNA. Previously it was thought that genetic information only moved one way, from DNA to RNA. They shared the Nobel Prize in 1975 for this discovery.

In 1973 **Charles H. Bennett** showed how to build a computer without the components known to cause energy loss.

In April 1978 **David Botstein, Ronald Davis,** and **Mak Skolnick** proposed that DNA sequencing can be used to identify genetic diseases in utero, paving the way for fetal genetic screening.

In 1974 **Samuel Chao Chung Ting** and **Burton Richter,** working independently, each produced a subatomic particle that contained a new fundamental particle. Called the J/psi particle, the discovery, which had been predicted by the theory of charm, was made possible by the massive new particle accelerators. They shared the Nobel Prize for this work in 1976.

James W. Christy and **Robert S. Harrington** found in 1978 that the planet Pluto has a satellite. The satellite, named Charon, is believed to be half the size of Pluto itself.

Herbert W. Boyer and **Stanley H. Cohen** carried out the first genetic engineering experiment, with *E. coli,* E. coli, in 1973.

French oceanographer **Jacques Cousteau** brought vivid images of marine environments to millions of U.S.

viewers in the 1970s through the ABC series *The Undersea World of Jacques Cousteau.*

Albert Victor Crewe, a British-born American physicist, invented the scanning electron microscope in 1970, enhancing research on small particles.

Researchers in Boulder, Colorado, led by **Kenneth M. Evenson,** calculated a figure for the speed of light much more precise than any previously obtained. Working with a chain of lasers in 1972, they found the speed of light to be 186,282.3959 miles per second.

David Geiger invented what was to become a new kind of sports arena in 1970: the air-supported, teflon-coated fabric dome. Built like a giant balloon, with air pressure inside 20 percent higher than outside, the Pontiac Silverdome near Detroit was constructed by Geiger for a fraction of the cost of similar concrete structures.

Martin F. Gellert and coworkers identified gyrase as the enzyme responsible for the coiled state of most DNA in cells in 1976.

In 1970 physicists **John W. Gofman** and **Arthur R. Tamplin** challenged the Atomic Energy Commission (AEC), arguing that "safe radiation release standards for nuclear power plants were too high and would cause thirty-two thousand cancer deaths a year. Despite mounting pressure throughout the decade from congressional and United Nations committees and labor and citizen groups, the AEC refused to change its guidelines, though it compromised by offering new operating procedures to reduce radiation leakage.

Har Gobind Korana and his research team at the University of Wisconsin developed the first synthetic gene in 1970. In 1976 they announced that they were able to place such a DNA segment into a plant, where it functioned normally.

Marine biologist **Sylvia Earle Mead** led a team of five women aquanauts, who did extended underwater research for two weeks without surfacing in July 1970. The work was part of the ongoing Tektite II project, which studied marine life and explored how long people could live underwater.

In 1977 **Ann Moore** patented the Snugli, a cloth carrier that holds a small child close to the chest. Moore borrowed the idea from women she had seen using a similar device while she was with the Peace Corps in Africa.

In 1970 **Daniel Nathans** and **Hamilton Othanel Smith** found the first restriction enzyme, which can cut a DNA strand so it can be reassembled differently, making the work of genetic engineering possible. In 1978 they won the Nobel Prize for medicine for this work, sharing the prize with Werner Arber of Switzerland.

In 1979 the Gillette Corporation bought the Liquid Paper Company from entrepreneur **Bette Nesmith** for $47.5 million plus royalties. Nesmith had invented the quick-drying typing correction fluid while working as a secretary. In the 1950s she had offered it to IBM, who refused.

Martin L. Perl found in 1974 that when two subatomic particles, the electron and the positron, are smashed together, they create a larger particle. This was named the tau electron or tauon.

Research chemist **Marguerite Shue-Wen Chang** won the Federal Women's Award in 1973 for outstanding government service, including the invention of the device that triggers underground nuclear test explosives.

Nicholas Wirth developed PASCAL, a popular computer language, in 1972.

Physicist **Chien-Shiung Wu** won the U.S. National Medal of Science in 1976 for her experimental work disproving the theory of conservation of parity, revolutionizing particle physics.

AWARDS

NOBEL PRIZES

1970

No award.

1971

Earl W. Sutherland, Jr., wins the Nobel Prize for physiology or medicine for work on the action of hormones.

1972

Christian Boehmer Anfinsen, Stanford Moore, and William H. Stein, all of the United States, share the Nobel Prize for chemistry for "fundamental contributions to enzyme chemistry."

John Bardeen, Leon N. Cooper, and John R. Schrieffer win the Nobel Prize for physics for the development of the theory of superconductivity.

1973

Norwegian-American physicist Ivar Glaever, Leo Esaki of Japan, and Brian Josephson of England win the Nobel Prize for physics for their work in tunneling in superconductors and semiconductors.

1974

Paul J. Flory wins the Nobel Prize for chemistry for his studies of long-chain molecules.

1975

L. James Rainwater of the United States and Ben Mottelson and Aage Bohr of Denmark win the Nobel Prize for physics for work toward understanding of the atomic nucleus that paved the way for nuclear fusion.

1976

Burton Richter and Samuel C. C. Ting of the United States win the Nobel Prize for physics for the parallel identification of a new class of subatomic particles, psi, or J.

1977

Philip Warren Anderson and John Hasbrouck Van Vleck of the United States, and Sir Nevill Francis Mott of England share the Nobel Prize for physics — Mott and Anderson for research on amorphous semiconductors, Van Vleck for work on the magnetic properties of atoms.

1978

Arno Penzias and Robert Wilson of the United States and Pyotr L. Kapitsa of the Soviet Union share the Nobel Prize for physics, the Americans for their discovery of microwave background, providing support for the big bang theory, and Kapitsa for work in low-temperature physics.

1979

English-American chemist Herbert C. Brown and German George Wittig win the Nobel Prize for chemistry for work on the introduction of compounds of boron and phosphorus in the synthesis of organic substances.

Steven Weinberg and Sheldon Glashow of the United States and Abdus Salam of Pakistan win the Nobel Prize for physics for establishing a link between electromagnetism and the weak force of radioactive decay.

DEATHS

Georg von Békésy, 83, Hungarian-born American physicist who won the Nobel Prize for physiology or medicine for discoveries on stimulation within the cochlea of the ear, 13 June 1972.

Vannevar Bush, 84, electrical engineer who invented the differential analyzer, 28 June 1974.

William David Coolidge, 101, physical chemist who invented ductile tungsten, which was essential in the development of the modern incandescent lamp bulb and the X-ray tube, 3 February 1975.

Theodosius Dobzhansky, 75, Russian-American geneticist who contributed to the synthetic theory of evolution, 18 December 1975.

Vincent Du Vigneaud, 77, biochemist who won the Nobel Prize for research on pituitary hormones, 11 December 1978.

John Ray Dunning, 67, physicist whose experiments in nuclear fission helped lay the groundwork for development of the atomic bomb, 25 August 1975.

William Maurice Ewing, 67, geophysicist who established bases of plate tectonics and made early photographs and seismic studies of the ocean floor, 4 May 1974.

Kurt Gödel, 71, Austrian-American mathematician who showed that the logic of any sufficiently complex logical mathematic system contains propositions that cannot be proved or disproved from within that system, 24 January 1978.

Marie Goeppert-Mayer, 65, physicist who helped develop the atomic bomb and won the Nobel Prize for physics for the shell theory, her analysis of atomic structure, 20 February 1972.

Peter Carl Goldmark, 71, physicist who developed the long-playing (LP) record and the first practical color television technology, 7 December 1977.

Samuel Abraham Goudsmit, 77, Dutch-born American physicist who discovered electron spin, 4 December 1978.

Bruce Charles Heezen, 53, oceanographer and geologist, and the first to suggest that some features of the ocean floor could be accounted for by continental drift, 21 June 1977.

Edward Calvin Kendall, 86, biochemist and winner of the Nobel Prize for physiology or medicine for isolating thyroxin and cortisone, 4 May 1972.

Gerard Peter Kuiper, 68, Dutch-born American astronomer who discovered moons of Neptune and Uranus and directed the Ranger space project, 23 December 1973.

Charles A. Lindbergh, 72, aviator who completed first nonstop transatlantic solo flight from New York to Paris, 26 August 1974.

Donald Howard Menzel, 75, astronomer who studied coronas of stars, planets, and nebulae and developed new theories of the structure of sunspots and solar flares, 14 December 1976.

Erwin Wilhelm Mueller, 65, physicist who developed new microscopes and studied atomic structure, 17 May 1977.

Hortense Powdermaker, 73, anthropologist who did fieldwork in Africa and the U.S. South and also studied the Hollywood film industry, 15 June 1970.

Ida Cohen Rosenthal, 87, inventor of cupped, multisize brassieres and founder of the Maiden Form Brassiere Company, 28 March 1973.

Francis Peyton Rous, 90, physician who won the Nobel Prize for medicine for his discovery that viruses can cause cancer, 16 February 1970.

Blanche Stuart Scott, 84, pioneering aviator, 12 January 1970.

Harlow Shapley, 86, astronomer who calculated the size and shape of the Milky Way galaxy and located Earth's sun at its outer edge, 20 October 1972.

Philip Edward Smith, 86, endocrinologist, 8 December 1970.

Wendell Meredith Stanley, 66, biochemist who discovered that viruses are nucleoproteins and was awarded the Nobel Prize for chemistry for preparing enzymes and virus proteins in pure form, 15 June 1971.

Earl Wilbur Sutherland, Jr., 58, physician and pharmacologist who was awarded the Nobel Prize for physiology or medicine for research on hormonal control of human metabolism, 9 March 1974.

Edward Lawrie Tatum, 63, biochemist who was awarded the Nobel Prize for chemistry for showing how genes control chemical reactions and in 1909 discovering transduction, 5 November 1975.

Wernher Magnus Maximilian von Braun, 62, German-American rocket engineer who played a major role in developing the German V-2 and American Explorer I and Saturn rockets, 16 June 1977.

George Hoyt Whipple, 97, physician who was awarded the Nobel Prize for physiology or medicine for the use of liver to treat pernicious anemia, 1 February 1976.

Robert Burns Woodward, 62, chemist who was awarded the Nobel Prize for chemistry for synthesizing chlorophyll and other organic compounds, 8 July 1979.

PUBLICATIONS

Enzo Angelucci, *Airplanes from the Dawn of Flight to the Present Day* (New York: McGraw-Hill, 1973);

Daniel Behrman, *Solar Energy: The Awakening Science* (Boston: Little, Brown, 1976);

Joseph Ben-David, *The Scientist's Role in Society* (Englewood Cliffs, N. J.: Prentice-Hall, 1971);

Donald J. Bennet, *The Elements of Nuclear Power* (New York: Wiley, 1973);

J. Boyne and Donald Lopez, eds., *The Jet Age: Forty Years of Jet Aviation* (Washington, D.C.: National Air and Space Museum, Smithsonian Institute Press, 1979);

Michael Brown, *Laying Waste: The Poisoning of America by Toxic Chemicals* (New York: Washington Square Press, 1979);

Federal Interagency Committee on Recombinant DNA Research, *Report of the Federal Interagency Committee on Recombinant DNA Research* (Washington, D.C.: Federal Interagency Committee on Recombinant DNA Research, 1977);

Joseph Fletcher, *The Ethics of Genetic Control: Ending Reproductive Roulette* (Garden City, N.Y.: Anchor/ Doubleday, 1974);

Susan Griffin, *Woman and Nature* (New York: Harper & Row, 1978);

Laurence Karp, *Genetic Engineering: Threat or Promise?* (Chicago: Nelson-Hall, 1976);

Richard Leakey, *Origins* (New York: Dutton, 1977);

Arthur Levine, *The Future of the U.S. Space Program* (New York: Praeger, 1975);

Sally Linton/Slocum, "Woman the Gatherer: Male Bias in Anthropology," in *Women in Perspective: A Guide for Cross Cultural Studies,* edited by Sue-Ellen Jacobs (Urbana: University of Illinois Press, 1975), pp. 9–21;

Henry L. Morris, ed., *Scientific Creationism* (San Diego: Creation-Life Publishers, 1974);

Sheldon Novick, *The Electric War: The Fight Over Nuclear Power* (San Francisco: Sierra Club Books, 1976);

Paul Ramsey, *Fabricated Man: The Ethics of Genetic Control* (New Haven, Conn.: Yale University Press, 1970);

Robert Sansom, *The New American Dream Machine: Toward a Simpler Lifestyle in an Environmental Age* (Garden City, N.Y.: Anchor/Doubleday, 1976);

Fred H. Schmidt, *The Fight Over Nuclear Power: The Energy Controversy* (San Francisco: Albion, 1976);

Mark Stephens, *Three Mile Island: The Hour-by-Hour Account of What Really Happened* (New York: Random House, 1980);

L. B. Taylor, *For All Mankind: America's Space Programs of the 1970s and Beyond* (New York: Dutton, 1974);

U.S. Congress, Committee on Veterans' Affairs, *Oversight Hearing to Receive Testimony on Agent Orange: Hearing Before the Subcommittee on Medical Facilities and Benefits* (Washington, D.C.: Government Printing Office, 1980);

U.S. Environmental Protection Agency, *Don't Leave it All to the Experts: The Citizen's Role in Environmental Protection* (Washington, D.C.: Government Printing Office, 1972);

Thomas Whiteside, *The Pendulum and the Toxic Cloud: The Course of Dioxin Contamination* (New Haven, Conn.: Yale University Press, 1979);

Edward O. Wilson, *Sociobiology: The New Synthesis* (Cambridge, Mass.: Harvard University Press, 1975);

Tom Wolfe, *The Right Stuff* (New York: Farrar, Straus & Giroux, 1979);

Astronautics and Aeronautics, periodical;

Astrophysical Journal, periodical;

Civil Jet Development and Progress Report, periodical;

Ecologist, periodical;

"Environment," weekly column in *Time*;

Gene, periodical;

National Geographic, periodical;

Oceans, periodical;

Physics Today, periodical;

Popular Mechanics, periodical;

Recombinant DNA Technical Bulletin, begun in 1977, published by U.S. Department of Health, Education, and Welfare.

SPORTS

by DENNIS LYNCH

CONTENTS

Sidebars and tables are listed in italics.

1970

11 Jan.　Billy Casper wins the Los Angeles Open golf tournament and becomes the second pro golfer (Arnold Palmer was the first) to earn $1 million in his career. By the end of the season Jack Nicklaus would surpass his earnings total.

11 Jan.　In an upset the Kansas City Chiefs win the Super Bowl over the Minnesota Vikings, 23–7.

26 Jan.　National Football League (NFL) commissioner Pete Rozelle announces a four-year, $142-million contract with the three major television networks to broadcast professional football games.

16 Feb.　Joe Frazier wins the undisputed heavyweight boxing championship, knocking out Jimmy Ellis in the fifth round.

19 Feb.　Detroit Tigers pitcher Denny McLain receives the first of his two suspensions from baseball, this one for consorting with gamblers. He is suspended again on 9 September for carrying a gun.

14 Mar.　Kansas University wins the National Collegiate Athletic Association (NCAA) indoor track-and-field championship.

21 Mar.　UCLA defeats Jacksonville University 80–69 to win the NCAA basketball championship.

Apr.　The American League (AL) baseball team the Seattle Pilots moves to Milwaukee and becomes the Brewers.

5 Apr.　Russian Boris Spassky defeats Bobby Fischer for the world chess championship.

13 Apr.　Billy Casper wins the Masters golf tournament in Augusta, Georgia.

8 May　The New York Knickerbockers defeat the Los Angeles Lakers four games to three to win the National Basketball Association (NBA) championship.

10 May　The Boston Bruins win the Stanley Cup over the Saint Louis Blues in four games, ending the first National Hockey League (NHL) playoff since 1918 that included no Canadian teams.

30 May　Al Unser wins the Indianapolis 500 with an average speed of 155.749 MPH and a purse of $271,697.

20 June　The University of California wins the NCAA outdoor track-and-field championship but is later disqualified for using an ineligible runner.

5 July　Donna Caponi wins the U.S. Women's Open golf title for the second consecutive year.

16 July　The opening game is played at Three Rivers Stadium, the new home of the Pittsburgh Pirates baseball team; the Pirates lose to the Cincinnati Reds, 3–2.

3 Aug.　NFL players end a four-day strike for increased pension benefits.

12 Aug.　In a case brought by Philadelphia Phillies outfielder Curt Flood, federal court judge Ben Cooper rules that a 1922 Supreme Court decision finding that organized baseball does not violate antitrust laws is still binding. The Major League Baseball Players Association announces that it will take the case to the Supreme Court.

16 Aug.　Dave Stockton wins the Professional Golfers Association (PGA) championship.

31 Aug.　The United States wins the Davis Cup, defeating West Germany, 5–0.

7 Sept. Thirty-nine-year-old jockey Willie Shoemaker sets a new world record with 6,033 wins.

15 Oct. The Baltimore Orioles win the World Series in five games over the Cincinnati Reds.

26 Oct. Muhammad Ali knocks out Jerry Quarry in three rounds in his first fight since his license to box was revoked in 1967.

21 Nov. Thirty-five thoroughbreds are killed in a Cherry Hill, New Jersey, stable fire.

1971

1 Jan. The University of Nebraska finishes an unbeaten season and earns the Associated Press's (AP) vote as best collegiate football team of the year by winning the Orange Bowl 17–12 over Louisiana State University.

17 Jan. The Baltimore Colts defeat the Dallas Cowboys 16–13 in Super Bowl V.

9 Feb. Satchell Paige is elected to the Baseball Hall of Fame.

28 Feb. Jack Nicklaus becomes the first golfer to win the PGA championship twice.

8 Mar. Joe Frazier wins a fifteen-round unanimous decision over Muhammad Ali to retain the heavyweight boxing championship. Each boxer is guaranteed $2.5 million.

27 Mar. UCLA wins its seventh NCAA basketball title in eight years, defeating Villanova University, 68–62.

7 Apr. New York City opens the nation's first off-track betting stations.

10 Apr. Charles Coody wins the Masters golf tournament.

17 Apr. The U.S. table-tennis team completes a week-long goodwill tour of China.

27 Apr. Professional baseball player Curt Flood, who tested baseball's reserve clause, announces his retirement.

30 Apr. The Milwaukee Bucks win the NBA championship in four games over the Baltimore Bullets.

1 May Cannonero II is the fourth field horse in history to win the Kentucky Derby.

7 May The American Basketball Association (ABA) and the National Basketball League (NBL) seek congressional approval to merge.

16 May Marty Liquori, world-record holder in the mile, meets Jim Ryun, former world-record holder in several distance events, in the "Dream Mile" at the King Games in Philadelphia. Liquori won in three minutes fifty-six seconds; Ryun was one stride back.

18 May The Montreal Canadiens defeat the Chicago Blackhawks four games to three in the Stanley Cup hockey championship.

30 May Willie Mays scores his National League record 1,950th run.

21 June	Lee Trevino defeats Jack Nicklaus in the U.S. Open golf championship.
24 June	The National Basketball Association commissioner announces that the league will no longer require four years of college for eligibility to play in the NBA.
28 June	The Supreme Court rules that the Justice Department erred in denying Muhammad Ali an exemption from the draft as a conscientious objector.
July	The International Lawn Tennis Association announces that as of 1 January 1972 contract professional tennis players will be banned from tournaments it sponsors, including Wimbledon and Forest Hills.
10 July	Lee Trevino wins the British Open golf tournament. He is the fourth golfer in history to win the U.S. Open and the British Open in the same year. (Bobby Jones in 1930, Gene Sarazen in 1932, and Ben Hogan in 1953 are the others.)
25 July	Arnold Palmer wins the $250,000 Westchester Classic golf tournament, his third win of the year.
31 July	Vince Lombardi and Jim Brown are among inductees in the Pro Football Hall of Fame.
26 Aug.	The New York Giants football team relocates from New York to New Jersey, where they play at the seventy-five-thousand-seat Meadowlands Stadium.
29 Aug.	Hank Aaron becomes the first National League baseball player to drive in one hundred runs in eleven straight seasons.
9 Sept.	All-time professional hockey scoring leader Gordie Howe retires from the Detroit Red Wings, ending a twenty-five-year career.
15 Sept.	Billie Jean King and Stan Smith win the U.S. Open tennis singles championships.
17 Oct.	The Pittsburgh Pirates win the World Series in seven games over the Baltimore Orioles.
26 Oct.	Bobby Fischer beats Tigran Petrosian in a chess match to determine a challenger for the world championship against Boris Spassky.
30 Oct.	Cornell University football running back Ed Marinaro sets an NCAA record of 4,132 career yards after gaining 272 yards against Columbia University.
9 Nov.	The NHL announces new franchises in Atlanta and Los Angeles.
14 Nov.	Golfers Jack Nicklaus and Lee Trevino team to win the World Cup for the United States.
6 Dec.	Winning the Disney World golf tournament, Jack Nicklaus brings his season's earnings to a record $244,490.

1972

1 Jan.	The University of Nebraska football team clinches a national championship after winning its twenty-third consecutive game, defeating the University of Alabama in the Orange Bowl, 38–6.
16 Jan.	The Dallas Cowboys win the Super Bowl, defeating the Miami Dolphins, 24–3.

19 Jan. Golfer Lee Trevino, winner of six tournaments in 1971, is named male athlete of the year by the Associated Press.

30 Jan. Wilt Chamberlain, center for the Los Angeles Lakers, sets a career record for rebounds with 21,734.

3 Feb. The Winter Olympics open in Sapporo, Japan.

10 Feb. Ann Henning sets an Olympic record, winning the gold medal in the women's 500-meter speed skating.

11 Feb. Barbara Cochran wins the only U.S. gold medal in skiing, the women's special slalom.

13 Feb. Closing ceremonies for the Winter Olympics are held.

23 Feb. Villanova University basketball team is reprimanded by the NCAA after it is learned that the 1971 team's All-American guard, Howard Porter, had signed a professional contract in 1970. Similar action is taken against Western Kentucky two weeks later when it is learned that its center, Jim McDaniels, had also signed a pro contract in 1970.

6 Mar. Jack Nicklaus becomes golf's career-earnings leader after winning the Doral Open, bringing his earnings to $1,427,200.

25 Mar. UCLA wins its sixth consecutive NCAA championship basketball title with an 81–76 win over Florida State University.

5 Apr. University of Kentucky basketball coach Adolph Rupp is forced by mandatory retirement rules to leave the team, having won 879 games, more than any basketball coach in history.

17 Apr. The opening of the professional baseball season is delayed as the players begin a thirteen-day strike over the amount of the owners' contributions to the players' pension fund.

30 Apr. The first Boston Marathon to allow female runners is held.

7 May The Los Angeles Lakers win the NBA championship over the New York Knicks in five games.

7 May The People's Republic of China table-tennis team ends its nineteen-day exhibition tour of the United States.

11 May The Boston Bruins win the Stanley Cup championship over the New York Rangers in six games.

27 May Mark Donahue wins the Indianapolis 500.

13 June Bobby Byrne testifies before a congressional committee that he had drugged hundreds of racehorses in attempts to fix races.

19 June The Supreme Court reaffirms the exemption of professional baseball from antitrust laws.

2 July Susie Maxwell Berning wins the U. S. Women's Open golf championship.

7 July Billie Jean King wins the Wimbledon women's tennis championship.

9 July   Stan Smith wins the Wimbledon men's tennis championship.

13 July   Owners of the Baltimore Colts and Los Angeles Raiders trade entire teams with one another.

6 Aug.   U.S. Olympic trials in Chicago conclude. During the meet American swimmers break eleven world records.

22 Aug.   The XX Olympic Games open in Munich.

1 Sept.   Bobby Fischer wins the world chess championship in the twenty-first of a scheduled twenty-four games. He is the first American to hold the title.

4 Sept.   Swimmer Mark Spitz wins his seventh gold medal, one for each event in which he competed.

5 Sept.   The Olympic Games are suspended for two days after Arab commandos kill two Israeli athletes and kidnap nine others.

10 Sept.   The Olympic Games close. The U.S. team wins thirty-three gold medals among its ninety-four total, second only to the Soviet Union, with ninety-nine medals, including fifty gold.

10 Sept.   Avery Brundage retires as president of the International Olympic Committee.

18 Sept.   Art Williams is the first black umpire in major-league baseball.

15 Oct.   Stan Smith leads the United States tennis team to its fifth consecutive Davis Cup championship.

22 Oct.   The Oakland Athletics win the World Series over the Cincinnati Reds in seven games.

1973

1 Jan.   The University of Southern California football team beats Ohio State in the Rose Bowl 45–23 to earn the designation as the top team in the nation.

14 Jan.   The Miami Dolphins win the Super Bowl and are the the first professional football team to complete a season undefeated.

20 Jan.   Pole-vaulter Steve Smith sets an indoor world record with a vault of seventeen feet, eleven inches.

22 Jan.   George Foreman knocks out Joe Frazier in the second round to become the new heavyweight boxing champion.

18 Feb.   Richard Petty wins the Daytona 500 stock-car race with an average speed of 157.2 MPH.

25 Feb.   Baseball owners and players reach a three-year agreement to submit salary disputes to binding arbitration.

4 Mar.   Eighteen-year-old Chris Evert wins her first professional tennis title, in the S&H Green Stamp tournament.

5 Mar.   NBA players sign a three-year collective bargaining agreement that stipulates a twenty-thousand-dollar minimum salary for the 1973–1974 season.

31 Mar. Ken Norton defeats Muhammad Ali in a twelve-round split decision.

22 Apr. Chris Evert wins the Saint Petersburg Open tennis tournament, her fifth straight professional win.

5 May Secretariat wins the Kentucky Derby.

10 May The New York Knicks defeat the Los Angeles Lakers four games to one to win the NBA championship.

10 May The Montreal Canadiens defeat the Chicago Blackhawks four games to two to win the Stanley Cup hockey championship.

15 May Nolan Ryan of the California Angels pitches a no-hit game against the Kansas City Royals.

19 May Secretariat wins the Preakness.

30 May Gordon Johncock wins the Indianapolis 500.

9 June Secretariat wins the Belmont Stakes and is the first horse since 1948 to win horse racing's Triple Crown.

18 June Forty-five-year-old Gordie Howe signs a four-year, $1-million contract with the Houston Astros in the World Hockey Association.

7 July Billie Jean King defeats Chris Evert in an all-American final in the Wimbledon women's singles tennis championship.

15 July Nolan Ryan pitches his second no-hitter of the year, becoming the first professional pitcher in twenty-one years to do so.

24 July Los Angeles Rams star receiver Lance Rentzel is suspended from professional football for possession of marijuana.

1 Aug. The New York Nets of the ABA pay $4 million for the contract of Julius Erving.

12 Aug. Jack Nicklaus wins the PGA tournament by four strokes.

19 Aug. Chris Evert wins the U.S. Clay Court tennis championship.

2 Sept. Detroit Tigers manager Billy Martin is suspended by the American League, then fired, for instructing his pitchers to throw illegal spitballs.

21 Sept. Billie Jean King defeats Bobby Riggs in a highly publicized tennis match billed as the Battle of the Sexes.

26 Sept. Wilt Chamberlain signs a $1.8-million contract to serve as player-coach for the San Diego Conquistadors in the ABA.

21 Oct. The Oakland Athletics win the World Series in seven games over the New York Mets.

28 Oct. Secretariat runs, and wins, the last race of his career.

11 Dec. Houston Astros baseball star Cesar Cedeno is jailed in the Dominican Republic for involuntary manslaughter.

16 Dec. After a two-hundred-yard day against the New York Jets, Buffalo Bills running back O. J. Simpson becomes the first player to gain over two thousand yards.

31 Dec. Notre Dame defeats the University of Alabama football team 24–23 in the Sugar Bowl and is named national champion.

1974

13 Jan.	The Miami Dolphins win the Super Bowl for the second year in a row, defeating the Minnesota Vikings, 24–7.
28 Jan.	Muhammad Ali wins a unanimous twelve-round decision over Joe Frazier.
30 Jan.	The ABA files a $600-million antitrust suit against the NBA.
17 Feb.	Richard Petty wins his fifth Daytona 500 stock-car race.
7 Mar.	The NBA grants a franchise for $6.1 million to a New Orleans business group.
24 Mar.	North Carolina State University wins the NCAA basketball championship over Marquette University, 76–64.
8 Apr.	Hank Aaron of the Atlanta Braves hits his 715th career home run, breaking Babe Ruth's record.
24 Apr.	The NFL awards a franchise to a Tampa Bay business group.
25 Apr.	The NFL announces major rule changes, including a sudden-death play-off to settle ties and moving the goal posts from the goal line to the back line.
3 May	UCLA basketball star center Bill Walton signs a five-year, $2.5-million contract with the Portland Trail Blazers.
12 May	The Boston Celtics win the NBA championship in seven games over the Milwaukee Bucks.
19 May	The Philadelphia Flyers win the Stanley Cup hockey championship in six games over the Boston Bruins.
26 May	George Foreman retains the heavyweight boxing championship by knocking out Ken Norton in the second round.
26 May	Johnny Rutherford wins the Indianapolis 500.
1 June	Two gamblers in New York City are convicted of conspiracy and bribery in attempts to fix harness races.
4 June	The NFL awards a franchise to a Seattle business group for $16 million.
12 June	Little League Baseball announces that girls will be allowed to play on teams.
12 June	The NHL announces new franchises in Denver and Seattle.
19 June	Kansas City Royals pitcher Jim Busby throws a no-hitter against the Milwaukee Brewers.
30 June	Tom Watson wins his first professional golf tournament, the forty-thousand-dollar Western Open.
1 July	NFL players begin a seven-week strike for free-agency rights.
18 July	Saint Louis Cardinals pitcher Bob Gibson strikes out his three-thousandth batter, a National League record.
12 Aug.	California Angels pitcher Nolan Ryan strikes out nineteen Boston Red Sox players in nine innings, a major-league record.
8 Sept.	Daredevil Evel Knievel fails in his attempt to rocket across Snake River Canyon in Idaho.
10 Sept.	Saint Louis Cardinals Lou Brock steals his 105th base, setting a major-league baseball record. Brock steals ten more bases before the season ends.

16 Sept.   Light heavyweight boxing champion Bob Foster retires, having defended his championship fourteen times.

29 Sept.   California Angels pitcher Nolan Ryan pitches his third no-hitter, defeating the Minnesota Twins.

1 Oct.   All-time scoring leader Wilt Chamberlain announces his retirement from professional basketball.

3 Oct.   Frank Robinson is named manager of the Cleveland Indians and becomes the first black manager in major-league baseball.

17 Oct.   The Oakland Athletics win their third World Series in a row, defeating the Los Angeles Dodgers in five games.

30 Oct.   Muhammad Ali knocks out George Foreman in the eighth round to regain the heavyweight boxing championship.

27 Nov.   New York Yankees owner George Steinbrenner is banned from baseball for two years after he is found guilty of making illegal campaign contributions to Richard Nixon and others.

Dec.   Ara Parseghian announces his retirement as football coach at Notre Dame University.

20 Dec.   A federal court judge rules that the NFL contract and reserve system is illegal.

1975

1 Jan.   The University of Southern California defeats Ohio State in the Rose Bowl 18–17 to earn a contested designation as the nation's best college football team.

12 Jan.   The Pittsburgh Steelers win the Super Bowl, defeating the Minnesota Vikings, 16–6.

8 Feb.   Bill Russell is elected to the Basketball Hall of Fame.

16 Feb.   Jimmy Connors is the first player to win three straight national indoor tennis tournaments.

31 Mar.   UCLA defeats the University of Kentucky 92–85 to win the NCAA basketball championship. Having coached his team to national championships in ten of the past twelve seasons, John Wooden retires as coach.

3 Apr.   Bobby Fischer is stripped of his world championship chess title for refusing to defend it in the required time.

5 Apr.   Chris Evert wins the forty-thousand-dollar Virginia Slims tennis tournament, claiming the largest purse ever offered for a women's tennis match.

13 Apr.   Jack Nicklaus wins the forty-thousand-dollar Masters golf tournament.

26 Apr.   Jimmy Connors wins five hundred thousand dollars in a tennis challenge match against John Newcomb.

30 Apr.   Former postmaster general Lawrence O'Brien is named commissioner of the NBA.

1 May   In a game against the Detroit Tigers, Hank Aaron of the Milwaukee Brewers breaks Babe Ruth's record of 2,209 RBIs.

25 May   The Golden State Warriors win the NBA championship in four games over the Washington Bullets.

25 May   Bobby Unser wins the Indianapolis 500 when a storm causes flooding, ending the race after 435 miles.

31 May   The Philadelphia 76ers sign high-school basketball player Daryl Dawkins to a $1-million contract; Dawkins is the first high-school player to be signed by an NBA team.

1 June   California Angels pitcher Nolan Ryan matches Sandy Koufax's record of four no-hitters in a career with a win against the Baltimore Orioles.

3 June   The New York Cosmos professional soccer team signs Pele to a three-year, $7-million contract, making him the highest-paid athlete in the world.

14 June   Chris Evert wins the French Open tennis tournament singles championship for the second year in a row.

5 July   Arthur Ashe defeats Jimmy Connors to win the Wimbledon men's singles championship.

7 July   The unbeaten filly Ruffian breaks down at Belmont Park during a match race with Foolish Pleasure and is destroyed.

10 Aug.   Jack Nicklaus wins his fourth PGA Championship.

6 Sept.   Chris Evert wins the U.S. Open women's tennis championship.

22 Oct.   The Cincinnati Reds win the World Series over the Boston Red Sox in seven games.

6 Nov.   Detroit Red Wing Dan Maloney is charged with assault for behavior during a hockey game with the Toronto Maple Leafs.

9 Nov.   A. J. Foyt wins his fifty-fourth career Championship Trail automobile race, the Phoenix 150, wrapping up the U.S. Auto Club championship.

2 Dec.   Ohio State running back Archie Griffin is the first football player ever to win the Heisman Trophy twice. He ends his college career with a record 5,177 yards rushing.

10 Dec.   A syndicate headed by Bill Veeck buys the Chicago White Sox baseball team for $9.75 million.

30 Dec.   A federal court judge rules that the free-agency rules of the NFL violate anti-trust laws.

1976

18 Jan.   The Pittsburgh Steelers defeat the Dallas Cowboys 21–17 to win the Super Bowl.

4 Feb.   The Winter Olympics open in Innsbruck, Austria.

15 Feb.   The Winter Olympics end. Speed skaters Peter Mueller and Sheila Young and figure skater Dorothy Hamill win the only gold medals among the ten total medals won by Americans.

29 Mar.   Indiana University defeats the University of Michigan 86–68 to complete the season unbeaten and win the NCAA basketball championship.

11 Apr. Ray Floyd wins the Masters golf tournament by eight strokes with a record-equaling 271 total score.

16 May The Montreal Canadiens beat the Philadelphia Flyers in four games to win the Stanley Cup hockey championship.

29 May Earl Bell of Arkansas State University sets a world pole-vault record of 18 feet, 7 1/4 inches.

30 May Johnny Rutherford wins the Indianapolis 500 for the second time in three years. The race was stopped after 102 laps (355 miles) due to heavy rain.

6 June The Boston Celtics with their thirteenth NBA championship, defeating the Phoenix Suns in six games.

17 June The NBA accepts four of the six teams in the ABA in a merger recommended by a federal judge to settle antitrust litigation.

17 July The Summer Olympics open in Montreal.

1 Aug. The XXI Olympiad ends. The United States is third in medals after the Soviet Union and East Germany, winning thirty-four gold among its ninety-four total medals.

27 Aug. Dr. Renee Richards, a transsexual, is barred from competition in the U.S. Open tennis tournament.

11 Sept. Chris Evert wins the U.S. Open women's tennis singles championship, her second grand-slam championship win of the year.

12 Sept. Jimmy Connors defeats Bjorn Borg to win the U.S. Open men's tennis singles.

16 Oct. Ove Johansson of Abilene Christian College kicks a sixty-nine-yard field goal, the longest ever in competition, including professional football.

21 Oct. The Cincinnati Reds defeat the New York Yankees in four games to win the World Series.

24 Oct. Bill Rodgers wins the first citywide New York Marathon in two hours, ten minutes, ten seconds.

1977

1 Jan. The University of Pittsburgh defeats the University of Georgia in the Sugar Bowl 27–3 and is subsequently named the national champion college football team by the Associated Press.

9 Jan. The Oakland Raiders defeat the Minnesota Vikings 32–14 in Super Bowl XI.

1 Mar. The NFL players and owners sign a five-year contract.

27 Mar. Chris Evert wins her fourth Virginia Slims tennis tournament.

28 Mar. Marquette University defeats the University of North Carolina 67–59 to win the NCAA basketball championship.

10 Apr. Tom Watson wins the Masters golf tournament.

25 Apr. The strike by NBA referees ends.

14 May The Montreal Canadiens win the Stanley Cup hockey championship in four games over the Boston Bruins.

23 May Forty-nine-year-old Gordie Howe and his two sons sign a multimillion-dollar contract with the World Hockey Association New England Whalers.

29 May A. J. Foyt wins his record fourth Indianapolis 500.

5 June The Portland Trail Blazers beat the Philadelphia 76ers in six games to win the NBA championship.

11 June Seattle Slew wins the Triple Crown. He is the tenth Triple Crown winner and the first undefeated winner.

14 Aug. Lanny Wadkins wins the PGA tournament.

29 Aug. Lou Brock of the Saint Louis Cardinals breaks the stolen-bases record previously held by Ty Cobb.

7 Sept. Fourteen-year-old Tracy Austin, the youngest player ever to advance to the quarterfinals of the U.S. Open tennis tournament, is defeated.

10 Sept. Chris Evert wins her third straight U.S. Open women's tennis championship.

29 Sept. An estimated seventy million television viewers, the largest audience in history for a boxing match, watch Muhammad Ali win a unanimous decision over Earnie Shavers.

18 Oct. The New York Yankees win the World Series, defeating the Los Angeles Dodgers in six games.

26 Oct. The NFL signs an agreement with the three major networks for rights to televise NFL games in exchange for $576 million to $656 million.

7 Dec. Gordie Howe scores his one-thousandth career hockey goal, setting a record.

10 Dec. Seventeen-year-old jockey Steve Cauthen earns $6 million in horse racing purses during the year, a record.

31 Dec. Vitas Gerulaitis wins the Australian Open men's singles tennis championship.

1978

2 Jan. Notre Dame, with quarterback Joe Montana, defeats the previously unbeaten University of Texas 38-10 in the Cotton Bowl and is subsequently named national collegiate football champions.

15 Jan. The Dallas Cowboys defeat the Denver Broncos 27–10 in Super Bowl XII.

24 Jan. Joe Namath retires as a professional football player.

15 Feb. Leon Spinks wins a split decision against Muhammad Ali to become heavyweight champion of the world.

27 Mar. The University of Kentucky wins the NCAA basketball championship, defeating Duke University 94–88.

9 Apr. The National Hockey League season ends with twelve of the league's eighteen teams qualifying for the championship playoffs.

6 May Affirmed, ridden by eighteen-year-old Steve Cauthen, wins the Kentucky Derby.

20 May Affirmed, with Cauthen up, wins the Preakness.

25 May The Montreal Canadiens win the Stanley Cup hockey championship over the Boston Bruins in six games.

28 May	Al Unser wins the Indianapolis 500.
29 May	John McEnroe of Stanford University wins the NCAA men's singles tennis championship.
7 June	The Washington Bullets win the NBA championship in seven games over the Seattle SuperSonics.
10 June	Affirmed, with Cauthen as jockey, wins the Belmont Stakes and becomes the eleventh racehorse to win the Triple Crown.
18 June	First-year professional golfer Nancy Lopez breaks the Ladies Professional Golfers Association (LPGA) record for consecutive wins and accumulates record earnings for a rookie of $153,336.
15 July	Jack Nicklaus wins his third British Open golf tournament.
10 Sept.	Chris Evert and Jimmy Connors win singles championships at the U.S. Open tennis tournament.
15 Sept.	Muhammad Ali becomes the first man ever to win the heavyweight boxing championship three times, defeating Leon Spinks in a fifteen-round decision. Reportedly the televised fight is viewed in more homes than any sporting event ever before.
17 Oct.	The New York Yankees win the World Series in six games over the Los Angeles Dodgers.
5 Dec.	Pete Rose, a free agent in the professional baseball draft, signs a $3.2-million contract with the Philadelphia Phillies, making him baseball's highest-paid player.
29 Dec.	Clemson University defeats Ohio State in the Gator Bowl. Ohio State coach Woody Hayes is fired after punching a Clemson player on the sideline after the player had intercepted an Ohio State pass.

1979

1 Jan.	The University of Alabama defeats Penn State in the Sugar Bowl 14–7 and is named collegiate football champion by the Associated Press.
21 Jan.	The Pittsburgh Steelers win their third Super Bowl in a row, a record.
22 Mar.	The NHL and the World Hockey League merge.
26 Mar.	Michigan State University wins the NCAA basketball championship over Indiana State University, 75–64.
18 May	Professional-baseball umpires settle a three-month strike.
21 May	The Montreal Canadiens win the Stanley Cup hockey championship over the New York Rangers in five games.
27 May	Rick Mears, in his second season of major track racing, wins the Indianapolis 500.
1 June	The Seattle SuperSonics win the NBA championship in five games over the Washington Bullets.

9 Sept.   Tracy Austin and John McEnroe win the singles championships at the U. S. Open tennis tournament.

25 Sept.   ABC bids $225 million, winning the rights to televise the 1984 Olympics in Los Angeles.

17 Oct.   The Pittsburgh Pirates win the World Series over the Baltimore Orioles in four games.

19 Nov.   Pitcher Nolan Ryan signs a $4.5 million four-year contract with the Houston Astros.

30 Nov.   Sugar Ray Leonard wins the World Boxing Council welterweight championship in a fifteen-round TKO over Wilfredo Benitez.

16 Dec.   Led by the play of John McEnroe and Vitas Gerulaitis, the United States wins the Davis Cup tennis championship 5–0 over Italy.

OVERVIEW

Big Business. Sports in the 1970s was very big business. Television had reshaped the sports industry in the decade before, and now the businessmen went to work to exploit their market. Football, baseball, basketball, boxing, auto racing, golf, and tennis were where the sports entertainment money was, and by the end of the 1970s top athletes demanded as much as a million dollars a year to perform. But their earning capacity did not come without a fight.

Free Agency. Traditionally in team sports athletes had been considered property whose value lay with a team owner or manager who could market their skills. Baseball, football, and basketball players belonged to the teams that drafted them, and players could be traded at the owners' discretion. As the stakes increased in the 1960s players began to agitate for some freedom. They realized they were not property, they were commodities, and they should have the right to market themselves to team owners at auctions to realize their highest value. Before 1970 only a handful of athletes made over $100,000 a year. By the end of the decade hundreds did, and the stars made much more because the marketplace for athletes had been opened to the highest bidder. Baseball player Pete Rose took advantage of free agency to get a contract that reportedly paid him $1 million a year in 1979. The average salary for players in the National Basketball Association (NBA) was $109,000 by mid decade and 50 percent more by the end of the 1970s.

Earnings. Individual athletes prospered as well. Bjorn Borg made $1.5 million as the best male tennis player in the world in 1978, and Jack Nicklaus set record earnings figures every year, making over $300,000 annually by mid decade. Muhammad Ali, the most recognizable sports figure in the world, earned $2.5 million for his title fight against Joe Frazier in 1971 and his purse doubled when he regained the championship against George Foreman in 1975.

Television. Team owners faced business pressures similar to those of managers in other industries. Athletes unionized and went on strike when their demands were not addressed. Fans expected to be entertained and refused to pay for substandard performances. Television brought huge infusions of capital — $656 million to pro-

fessional football in 1978 — but the networks expected concessions for their money. They expected an increase in the number of games teams played in a season, they dictated play-offs among the best teams to maximize the potential television audience, and they exacted subtle rule changes to accommodate the demands of television. The National Football League (NFL), for example, increased its season from fourteen to sixteen games, and major league baseball introduced a lengthy play-off calculated to spread the excitement of the World Series throughout the middle of September and well into October. The sports entertainment business was highly competitive, and only the strong survived — athletes as well as team organizations. The World Hockey League (WHL) succumbed to National Hockey League (NHL) domination, and the American Basketball Association (ABA) merged with the NBA. Baseball's Seattle Pilots and Washington Senators could not earn enough to stay afloat with mediocre teams, so their franchises were moved to more lucrative locations.

Women. Women were neglected by the major sports. Five-foot nine-inch UCLA all-American basketball player Ann Myer was offered a $50,000 contract with the Indiana Pacers in the NBA in 1979, but she was dropped from the team before the season began and signed with the less-heralded Women's Basketball League. Title IX of the Civil Rights Act of 1972 guaranteed women equal educational opportunities, and that was construed to mean equal opportunity to participate in major college sports. Activists insisted that the law required universities receiving federal funds to spend equal amounts on men's and women's athletic teams, and that notion was considered no less revolutionary in the 1970s than *Brown* v. *Board of Education* had been to segregationists in the 1950s. Women fared better in individual sports than in team sports. Billie Jean King, Chris Evert, Tracy Austin, and Evonne Goolagong were marketable, and they knew it. In 1972 King received $10,000 for winning the U.S. Open tennis championship while the male winner, Ilie Nastase, got $25,000. She agitated for parity in purses, and in 1973 she got it. That year, when she prevailed over promoter and former Wimbledon champion Bobby Riggs in a winner-take-all, for-television tennis match billed as a battle between the sexes with a purse of

$100,000, heat exhaustion kept her from the U.S. Open title; but winner Margaret Court received $25,000, the same as the male champion, John Newcombe. Women golfers were less attractive to viewers than female athletes in other sports, but still their purses increased to about one-third those of male golfers. The advent of the Colgate–Dinah Shore Winners Circle tournament brought women's golf to television, where the money is, and the purse was $250,000, comparable to major men's tournaments. But there was only one Dinah Shore tournament each year. Among the boldest moves by a woman into a male domain was by Janet Gutherie, a thirty-eight-year-old physicist who passed her rookie test and was licensed to drive in the Indianapolis 500 auto race. It was 1977 before she got a car good enough to qualify. That year she came in eighteenth among the starting field of thirty-three cars.

Blacks. Frank Robinson became baseball's first black manager in 1974, thirty years after Jackie Robinson had become the first black player, but Robinson was an exception; front offices in baseball as well as football were overwhelmingly white. Blacks had better luck in basketball management, but the owners were all white. Even though Hank Aaron brought the Atlanta Braves two-seasons' worth of feature publicity, tying Babe Ruth's record at the end of the 1973 season and beating it at the beginning of the next, he felt that racism kept the team from offering him a managerial position at his retirement, and he went to the Milwaukee Brewers to finish his career with the promise of a front-office job after he retired. Black star players achieved spectacular salaries, though, and their exposure to as many as seventy million television viewers during key sporting events convinced most of the public and most of the owners that they deserved at least as much compensation as whites. Social equality follows economic equality, and the basis was laid in the 1970s for color-blind athletics, but the achievement of that goal remained a distant promise.

TOPICS IN THE NEWS

BASEBALL

The McClain Metaphor. Baseball was struggling in 1970. It had lost its innocence long ago, but now it was faced with disgrace. Public scandals, labor disputes, greed, arrogance, dissolution, and hucksterism characterized the nation's game. It took more and more spectacular plays every year to draw the fans' attentions from the pages of the tabloids to the field. At the beginning of the decade the character of the entire game seemed to be symbolized by the misfortunes of the blustery Detroit Tigers pitcher Denny McClain. He had won thirty-one games in 1968 — the first pitcher since Dizzy Dean in 1934 to win over thirty — and he had twenty-four wins in 1969. He was at the top of the game, and then he self-destructed. First he was suspended from baseball for two months for his involvement with professional bookmakers. He turned from insufferable braggart to self-pitying apologist overnight, explaining that his association with gamblers had resulted from financial misfortunes and that he had been taken advantage of by unscrupulous men. When he returned contritely to the mound, he had lost his brilliance, and he was too thin-skinned to take the criticism of sports reporters. He was suspended from the team for a week by manager Mayo Smith when he angrily threw ice water on two sports reporters. He floundered after his second return, winning fourteen of twenty-eight games before he was finally suspended again, for carrying a gun in violation of the commissioner's probation set after the first suspension. Two years later McClain was pitching in the minor leagues. The image of baseball suffered similar disgrace.

Financial Woes. In the 1970s baseball owners had to defend their business practices in court. After he was traded from the Saint Louis Cardinals to the Philadelphia Phillies against his will, Curt Flood challenged baseball's reserve clause, which defined players as property. It was a challenge that cost Flood his career and baseball its reputation, and the case dragged on throughout the decade, finally reaching the Supreme Court. The baseball umpires went on strike for more money just before the playoffs began, and the Seattle Pilots declared bankruptcy, claiming to have lost $1 million in the past year with no profits in sight.

1970. On the field the Cincinnati Reds and the Baltimore Orioles reminded fans what the game was about. The Reds fought a close battle with the Chicago Cubs for the National League pennant and won behind the solid play of Johnny Bench, Pete Rose, Lee May, Tony Perez,

Homemade poster in Oakland after the World Series in the year of the handlebar mustache

began openly questioning the wisdom of exempting professional baseball from antitrust laws. Fans expressed their dissatisfaction with the state of the game by staying at home. By midseason, attendance had fallen to distressing lows, and observers speculated that lack of excitement on the field was only part of the reason; fans were fed up with the off-field image of baseball. Oakland pitcher Vida Blue provided some interest when he won his first ten games of the season, but Blue cooled in the second half of the season and ended with a respectable twenty-four wins, well short of record-threatening excitement. In the American League Baltimore dominated, winning its division by twelve games, and beat Oakland in three straight to win the pennant. The Giants survived an end-of-season charge by the Dodgers to win their division but faltered in the play-offs against Pittsburgh. In the series Pittsburgh prevailed in seven games after losing the first two. Pirate hitter Roberto Clemente hit .414.

1972. Gil Hodges, a star from the glory days of baseball and the manager who had led the amazing Mets to their first World Series win, died during spring training for the 1972 season. The players were on strike at the time, demanding that the owners contribute more to the players' pension funds. More than eighty games were canceled during the strike before the owners gave in, and still there was no peace. Too many business issues remained unresolved, free agency chief among them. As the leagues struggled to institute new rules intended to resolve the issue, matters only became more complicated, and it was at times necessary for courts to issue orders before it was clear which players would take the field in major league games. Despite Blue's holdout through much of the season in a contract dispute, the Oakland Athletics dominated the American League. Twenty-game winner Jim ("Catfish") Hunter, ace reliever Rollie Fingers, hitters Reggie Jackson and Joe Rudi, and base stealer Bert Campaneris joined manager Dick Williams in an unusual display of familylike unity to win the World Series over the Cincinnati Reds in seven games. The handlebar mustaches, sported by half the A's, were a throwback to baseball's simpler days and provided a temporary nostalgic illusion for the fans.

Roberto Clemente. The year 1972 ended with a tragedy that immortalized a hero and brought fans together, if briefly, to mourn him. On the last day of the season, Pittsburgh Pirate star Clemente got his three thousandth career hit. Two-and-one-half months later, when Nicaragua was rocked by a devastating earthquake, Clemente mounted a relief drive and was on his way to oversee distribution of the money and goods he had collected when his small aircraft crashed into the Pacific Ocean. The governor of his native Puerto Rico declared a three-day period of grieving for him, and baseball players and owners put aside their greed, all too briefly, to reflect on the charitable model Clemente had provided.

Free Agents. But the greed returned quickly enough. In 1972 the Supreme Court ruled that the agreement to

and Bobby Tolan. The Orioles brought solid defense to the series. Pitchers Mike Cuellar, Dave McNally, and Jim Palmer — all twenty-game winners — had support in the field and at bat from Boog Powell, Frank Robinson, and the superb fielding of Brooks Robinson. The Orioles won in five games in a series that brought particular joy to Oriole fans, who had expected a series victory a year earlier.

Bad Business. Better profit potential was the reason given for moving the Washington Senators to Dallas, where they became the Texas Rangers. The move underscored the fact that baseball was business, pure and simple. In an overview of the 1971 season, Bill Braddock of *The New York Times* wrote that "Washington, the nation's capital, wound up the year without a baseball team but with more men in position to alter the structure of the game than any city with a ball club." The Supreme Court agreed to review the Curt Flood case, and people

exempt major league baseball from antitrust laws was legal, and Curt Flood lost his challenge to the reserve clause. But player-rights negotiator Marvin Miller had already begun a more effective means of subverting the hated clause. He began chipping away, little by little. First he crafted an agreement in 1973 between owners and players by which they would agree to arbitration to settle salary disputes. Then he got the owners to agree that players with ten years in the major leagues and five with the same team could veto a trade involving them that they did not like. Finally, in 1975, he found a loophole in the reserve clause. An arbitrator upheld the players' association's contention that if a player worked for a year without a contract, he could declare himself a free agent and market his services to the highest bidder. Twenty-four players took advantage of the ruling in 1976. As the American League added teams in Seattle and Toronto, twelve of the new free agents signed contracts for more than $1 million. Baseball had entered a new era.

Onerous Owners. Team owners garnered as much publicity as the players. George Steinbrenner, the meddling owner of the New York Yankees, was suspended in 1974. Charlie Finley of the Oakland Athletics was reprimanded and overruled by Commissioner Bowie Kuhn in 1976 when he tried to sell Blue, Rudi, and Fingers, the heart of his team, for $3.5 million. Ted Turner, the flamboyant owner of the Atlanta Braves, was suspended in 1977 when he tried to evade the free-agent rule; and, failing to learn by example, San Diego Padres owner Ray Kroc was fined $100,000 for the same offense in 1979. Meanwhile, the American League, in an attempt to inject more excitement into the game, instituted a designated hitter rule so that a pitcher's turn at bat could be taken by a pinch hitter. The change seemed to work.

Fiery A's. In 1973 the New York Mets added some excitement to the game by rallying to win a National-League pennant, motivating players and fans with the slogan "You Gotta Believe." Belief was not quite enough to win the World Series against the more talented A's, however. Reggie Jackson hit .310, including a key home run in the last game, and Rudi hit .333 as the A's narrowly won the Series in seven games. Oakland owner Charles O. Finley drew a fine and a reprimand from Commissioner Kuhn when he fired second baseman Mike Andrews for making two errors in the second game of the series, which Oakland lost in twelve innings. When the hapless player was ordered back onto the team, fans cheered his return. After the season manager Dick Williams had had enough of Finley. Finley left the Athletics and was replaced by Al Dark, who led the talent-packed A's to their third straight World Series title. In 1974 the A's beat the youthful Los Angeles Dodgers in five games, ending a season that had reached its high point in the performances of veterans: Hank Aaron of the Atlanta Braves broke Babe Ruth's career home-run record of 714; Saint Louis Cardinal Bob Gibson struck out

By 1969 both the American and National leagues had expanded to twelve teams. The owners had by that time a clear sense of the importance of television to the future of their sport, and they were aware of the additional television audience that postseason play — restricted to the World Series until then — attracted. So they instituted a playoff season. Each league was divided into two divisions, and the division winners played one another in a five-game series to determine the pennant winner.

Revenues aside, it was not a perfect system, as the New York Mets proved in 1973 by becoming arguably the worst team in history to almost win the World Series. The Mets ended the season in a near three-way tie in the weak National League Eastern division, and only clinched the title on the last regular-season game. But the Mets had seventeen fewer wins than the National League Western division winner, the Cincinnati Reds. Relying on strong pitching, the Mets managed to get through the playoffs to meet the Oakland Athletics in the World Series. That was the year Charles O. Finley fired his second baseman for making two errors in the second game, dampening his team's spirits. The Mets took the series to seven games and lost the final game 4–3 when Reggie Jackson and Bert Campaneris hit the A's first home runs of the series. The Mets finished the season having won only 50.9 percent of their games.

his three thousandth batter, and Cardinal Lou Brock stole a record 118 bases.

Sox vs. Reds. Baseball seemed to have worked out its business difficulties by 1975 — as far as the fans were concerned, at least. Over seventy million fans watched the World Series on television. It was an exciting match between the Boston Red Sox and the Cincinnati Reds in which the overmatched Red Sox scratched out victories when they needed them most. The sixth game at Fenway Park was a baseball classic. It went twelve innings before Carleton Fisk hit a home run to win the game 7–6. The seventh game seemed a continuation of the sixth, as the gritty Red Sox broke out on top, scoring three runs in the third. The Reds scored two in the sixth and another in the seventh to set up the dramatic last inning. The teams were tied 3–3 going into the ninth. Joe Morgan of the Reds drove in the winning run with a blooping single, and the Red Sox were unable to answer.

Money Can't Buy Happiness. The Cincinnati Reds

were the first National League team in fifty-four years to win back-to-back World Series titles. Johnny Bench's two home runs in the final game were the highlight of the 1976 series. The Reds won in a four-game sweep against the New York Yankees, but the Yankees had returned to prominence, to the dismay of fans both in and outside of New York who hated owner George Steinbrenner. They considered it outrageous in 1977 that the Yankees had a team payroll of $3.5 million and that eleven players had annual salaries of over $100,000. They were the best team money could buy, as critics claimed, and they were good enough to win three straight pennants and two straight World Series before egotism did them in.

The Prize. In 1977 the Yankees beat their former cross-town rivals, the Dodgers, in six games. The win did not come without a struggle, but most of the difficulty was in off-the-field bickering. Contentious manager Billy Martin fought with Steinbrenner, with star slugger Reggie Jackson (bought from the Oakland Athletics) and with anyone else who dared to cross him. He claimed he deserved the Nobel Peace Prize for holding the team together; some wags suggested that a jail sentence for inciting to riot might be more appropriate. Nonetheless, the Yankees were New York, and the city gave their world champions a ticker-tape parade after the last game of the series.

Yankee Perils and Rose's Lament. At midseason in 1978 the Yankees were fourteen games behind the Red Sox in the American League East. Then Martin suspended Reggie Jackson for bunting when he was instructed to hit away. Jackson retaliated by defaming his manager in the newspapers, and Martin answered similarly. Steinbrenner called them both liars and fired Martin, whose replacement, Bob Lemon, led the team to a pennant. The Dodgers won the National League race again and promptly established a two-game advantage in the series. At that point the Yankees quit fighting and began playing. They were the first team in World Series history to win four straight games after losing the first two. The baseball year was like a soap opera. The other highlight was the hitting streak of Cincinnati Red Pete Rose, who set a National League record of hits in forty-four consecutive games and set his sights on one of the most respected records in the game, Joe DiMaggio's 1941 major league mark of hits in fifty-six consecutive games. After he failed to hit in his forty-fifth straight game, against Atlanta pitchers Larry McWilliams and Gene Garber, Rose whined that they "pitched me like it was the seventh game of the World Series." But he got his reward. He became the first baseball player in history to sign a contract for $1 million a season when he took advantage of the free-agent ruling to sign with the Philadelphia Phillies in 1979.

Pops. The Yankees finally self-destructed in 1979, finishing fourth in the American League East. That year, the series focused on a more inspiring group, the Pittsburgh Pirates, who won a hard-fought seven-game series

Julius Erving, star of the ABA, in 1973

against the Baltimore Orioles. Led by thirty-eight-year-old Willie Stargell, called "Pops" by his younger teammates, the Pirates came back from a three-games-to-one deficit to win the series. Stargell hit .400 during the series, with a home run in the seventh game. He won every most-valuable-player award available to him.

PROFESSIONAL BASKETBALL

The Big Men. The battles between Wilt Chamberlain and Bill Russell of the 1960s had popularized and revolutionized professional basketball. Every time the two big men — Chamberlain of the Philadelphia Warriors and Los Angeles Lakers and Russell of the Boston Celtics — met on court, a momentous clash of opposing styles of play and personalities occurred. Wilt ("the Stilt") Chamberlain was the scoring wonder, Russell the defensive specialist. Chamberlain scowled as if he had homicidal intentions; Russell played an unselfish game seemingly without emotion. As Chamberlain wound down his career in the early 1970s, however, and Russell left the game, a void was created, and no team or player seemed able to fill it.

Profits. Nevertheless, as public interest in professional basketball waned, the sport seemed to be in good shape financially — at least as far as the sport's athletes were concerned. Professional basketball's 240 players averaged $158,000 a year in salaries by the end of the decade. At the end of the 1960s salaries had averaged $43,000. The NBA had survived competition offered up by the ABA, which folded in 1976, and had a lucrative $74 million television contract with CBS, paying about an average of $800,000 a year to each team in the league. Television ratings had slipped badly by 1980, however, and game attendance fell as ticket prices remained high — as much as $12.50.

Explanations. College basketball, conversely, was soaring in popularity. Various explanations — other than high ticket prices — were offered for declining interest in pro basketball. Some believed that white fans' interest in pro basketball declined as the number of black athletes entering the pro ranks dramatically increased during the 1970s. By the end of the decade 75 percent of professional basketball players were African-American. An executive within the Dallas ABA franchise during the 1970s used this explanation for poor attendance to justify removing four of ten blacks on the team's eleven-man roster: "Whites in Dallas are simply not interested in paying to see an all-black team, and the black population alone cannot support us." Others blamed changes in the game's rules — which put a premium on a "run and gun" style of play and took away from one-on-one duels fought inside the key.

Street Ball. Most critics of pro basketball, however, focused on the lack of a team concept within the NBA. In a 1980 issue of *Basketball Digest* Earl Monroe reflected on the last decade of basketball and concluded that the "demise of team play" was brought about by team front offices more concerned with marketing superstars than winning championships: "They started showcasing guys. Every team has a guy who is the designated superstar. The star has to play more minutes and have a big game because he is the show. Basketball should be the show." A street ball style of play had come to dominate the NBA, with emphasis placed on a player's offensive flair within the key and his ability to dunk.

Doctor J. Attention paid to a player's "hang time" — how long he could stay in the air around the basket — had much to do with the presence of Julius Erving, who in 1971 was drafted by the ABA's Virginia Squires. He was signed before he had completed his senior year at the University of Massachusetts — the signing of undergraduates having become a trademark of the ABA by the early 1970s. Known as "Doctor J," Erving in 1973 moved to the New York Nets, where his high-flying act around the rim thrilled metropolitan audiences and gained him exposure in a major media center. Leading the Nets to their

Flower child Bill Walton, dominating center for the Portland Trail Blazers, in 1973

first ABA title and heading up the league with a 27.4-point scoring average, Erving was soon the troubled league's biggest superstar, lending much-needed credibility to the league. Doctor J's ability to defy gravity left audiences shaking their heads in disbelief. His dunks and delicate finger-roll shots often started with a leap from the foul line. After the merger of the ABA and NBA Doctor J. moved on to the Philadelphia 76ers, becoming part of one of the most talented teams of the 1970s. Considered to have been the most gifted pro basketball player of his generation, Erving combined unprecedented grace, strength, court presence, imagination, and intelligence in creating a new style of offensive play that would be emulated by other guards and small forwards — and later further perfected by the Chicago Bulls' Michael Jordan.

Merger. On 17 June 1976 the ABA folded, having reached an agreement with the NBA in which four ABA franchises — New York, Denver, Indiana, and San Antonio — would be moved to the senior league. Despite its high-profile signings of legitimate stars such as Doctor J., Artis Gilmore, and Moses Malone (a dominating, big man drafted out of high school), the failure of the ABA had seemed to most observers by the early 1970s to be inevitable. By 1976 league franchises in San Diego and Utah had failed, bringing the number of ABA teams down to seven. The ABA's talent pool and the dash and style of its play — best represented by the league's official red, white, and blue ball — were attractive to the NBA. Other aspects of ABA play, such as the three-point field goal, were also adopted by the NBA.

Big-City Ball. The success of major-market teams such as the New York Knicks, the Los Angeles Lakers, and the Boston Celtics gave important vitality to the NBA during the league's lean years. The Knicks were the NBA's most popular team during the early 1970s, and their gutty victory in the 1970 and 1973 NBA championships thrilled fans. The Knicks teams of this era featured an odd mix of players and playing styles. Willis Reed, at six feet, ten inches, was considered a "small" big man at center, yet he had a wonderful range of motion and was able to hit the outside shot. Princeton all-American and Rhodes scholar Bill Bradley slashed through the lane, while Dave DeBusschere and Dick Barnett looked for the big rebound. The Knicks' playmaker was Walt Frazier, a guard who could shoot, pass, play brilliant defense, and run the offense with a kind of silky grace that at the time was unmatched in the league. No group of players during the decade blended as well, and as a team their play was often inspirational. In one of basketball's most stirring moments, Reed hobbled onto the court in the decisive seventh game of the NBA championship series against the Milwaukee Bucks. He had hurt his leg badly in the fifth game, and most observers were convinced that he was lost for the rest of the series. Reed's surprise entrance rallied the Knicks, and they went on to beat what many thought to be a far superior Milwaukee Bucks club led by superstars Kareem Abdul-Jabbar and Oscar Robertson. In 1973 Jerry Lucas joined the Knicks, and the team returned to the championship, beating the Lakers in seven games.

Champions. Many observers believed that during the 1970s they were witnessing the onset of parity among NBA teams. When the Rick Barry–led Golden State Warriors swept the Washington Bullets to take the championship in 1975, it marked an unprecedented sixth year in a row that no team had repeated as NBA champion. Insiders felt that the lack of a dynasty was at least partly responsible for decreasing fan interest: there was simply no dominating team that other clubs could gun for, and no one team that evoked love and hate of fans nationwide. Basketball's once domineering Celtics took the 1976 title in an exhausting series with the Phoenix Suns that included a triple-overtime game — the 128–126 Boston victory — that was, up until that time, the longest ever played in the NBA finals. The next three seasons, however, were won by the Bill Walton–led Portland Trail Blazers, the Washington Bullets with their "million-dollar bench," and the Seattle Super Sonics.

Magic and Bird. Just when professional basketball seemed to hit rock bottom in terms of popularity and cash flow, along came Earvin ("Magic") Johnson and Larry Bird. During the 1980s these two players would revitalize professional basketball, and — as had Chamberlain and Russell — raise the sport to a new level.

BOXING

The Champ. During the 1970s the sport of boxing was Muhammad Ali, and Ali was boxing. At the beginning of the decade, on 20 June 1970, Ali's five-year jail sentence for his refusal to join the army was reversed, and in September of that year his boxing license was restored. Ali came back from his three-year exile having been stripped of his heavyweight championship but loudly proclaiming himself "The People's Champion." It was no idle boast: Ali's extraordinary popularity cut across racial lines. Many whites saw in Ali the reincarnation of Joe Louis, the great heavyweight champion who during his reign seemed to move easily and comfortably among white fans. Yet unlike Louis, Ali brought to his public-relations campaign an eloquence rarely seen among athletes practicing such a brutish sport. His desire to speak out on issues of race did not seem to pose a threat to the white community, for Ali attached wit to everything he did both in and out of the ring; many whites simply tuned out the controversial Ali and chose to instead tune in Ali the funnyman — his ring predictions issued in rhyme and his constant clowning with sportscaster Howard Cosell. To African-Americans, however, Ali was a leader and a spokesman. He preached a Black Muslim message of revolutionary change within the African-American community, and he became a kind of unofficial statesman representing the interests of the American black community during his visits to African and Muslim countries. As he had in the late 1960s, he loudly denounced the Vietnam War and publicly questioned why a disproportionate number of ghetto blacks were carrying the burden of fighting the war. Surrounding Ali was not only the sound of fans applauding his skill but also the shrill voices of students, Black Muslims, and white bigots demonstrating in favor of or against the pronouncements of Ali. No other high-profile athlete addressed the social controversies and politics of his era in such an outspoken fashion as did Ali.

Stars. In the ring Ali returned the heavyweight division to lofty heights, remaking it boxing's premier weight division. The heavyweight division was deep in talent and, with Ali in one corner, put on some of boxing's most memorable fights: "The Fight of the Century," "The Rumble in the Jungle," "The Thrilla in Manila." Black athletes continued to dominate the division, with the likes of Joe Frazier, Ken Norton, and George Foreman. The white boxing fan's "Great White Hope" during the early part of the decade was Jerry Quarry. In Ali's 26 October 1970 return to the ring, however, Ali knocked out Quarry in the third round. He bloodied the face of the Great White Hope again in a 1972 Las Vegas bout.

The Fight. In 1971 Ali got his title shot against reigning heavyweight champion "Smokin'" Joe Frazier of Phil-

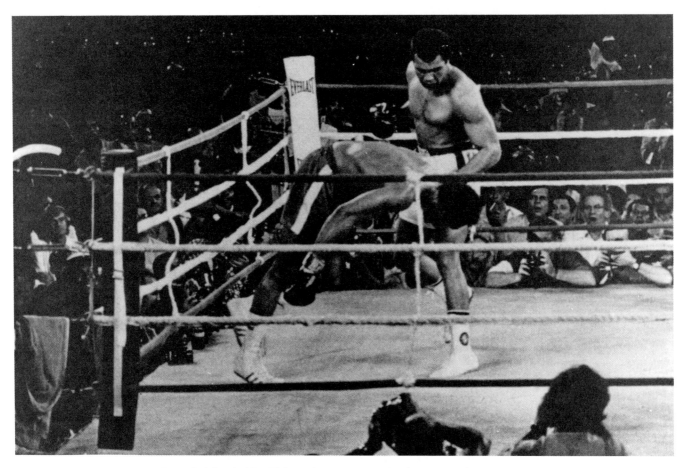

Round eight of "The Fight," after Muhammad Ali threw the final punch

adelphia. Frazier, unlike the dancing and jabbing Ali, came straight at his often-taller opponents with devastating punching power and a furious determination to fight toe-to-toe. The prefight hoopla was extraordinary, and both fighters were guaranteed an unprecedented $2.5 million each to face off in what was being billed as "The Fight of the Century." It took place in New York's Madison Square Garden on 8 March, and from the first round on the fight met nearly everyone's expectations. Through much of the fifteen-round bout Ali used his superior mobility to evade Frazier. In the eleventh round, however, Frazier caught up to Ali and took control of the fight; in the final round Frazier floored Ali — the first time in Ali's career he had been knocked down. Frazier won the fight in a unanimous decision, but both fighters, having taken severe beatings, ended up in the hospital.

Foreman. Coached and advised by Joe Louis and Archie Moore and trained by former featherweight great Sandy Saddler, George Foreman in 1973 challenged Frazier for the championship. Foreman was the strongest, most devastating puncher of his era, and he was also a popular challenger. Middle America remembered Foreman as the fighter who during the 1968 Olympics in Mexico City waved a small American flag inside the ring. Unlike Ali, Foreman went punch-for-punch against Frazier in the January 1973 bout fought in Kingston,

Jamaica, and knocked the champion down six times before the fight was stopped in the second round. Two months later, on 31 March, Ken Norton beat Ali, breaking his jaw and taking a twelve-round decision. The heavyweight division had become a rumble in which two of the best the sport had ever seen — Ali and Frazier — had been reduced to challengers. The two men met once again in a 28 January 1974 bout held in Madison Square Garden, Ali dancing, jabbing, and outpointing Frazier to win "The Fight II" in twelve rounds.

Rumble in the Jungle. Once again the number one challenger, Ali in January 1974 met champ George Foreman in a title fight held in Kinshasa, Zaire. Called "The Rumble in the Jungle," the fight guaranteed Ali a career-high payday of $5,450,000. Yet sportswriters prior to the fight had begun to question whether Ali had the will — and the jaw — to stand up to Foreman's punching power. Few believed that this time around Ali could back up his bravado, and fans wondered whether perhaps this would be a career-ending fight. Through most of the fight Ali stayed on the ropes, covering up as Foreman unloaded with heavy hitting. Ali's strategy, which he called the "ropadope," was to wait on the ropes until Foreman had turned punch-weary and then go on the attack. In the eighth round Ali emerged from the ropadope cover-up and flattened Foreman with a long right. This fight more than any other established Ali as "The Greatest," for it erased all doubt concerning Ali's punching power and his ability to stand up under heavy hitting.

Three-Time Champ. On 30 September 1975 Ali faced Frazier for the third time in what was called "The Thrilla in Manila." Ali took the fight to Frazier in this memorable bout, and in the fourteenth round Frazier's corner ended the fight. Ali had taken on the appearance of being invincible, and his superman image was furthered by his seeming desire to take on and beat all comers. From 1976 to 1977 Ali defended his belt a grueling eight times in nineteen months. By 1978, however, these bouts — many of which were televised by ABC-TV and commentator Howard Cosell — were beginning to wear on Ali. In February 1978 Leon Spinks upset Ali in a fifteen-round decision. Ali, however, reclaimed his crown eight months later by outpointing Spinks, winning the championship an unprecedented three times. Ali retired afterward, but in 1980 he launched another comeback that proved unsuccessful — and unpopular among boxing fans who preferred to remember Ali in his heyday, rather than the overweight, punch-drunk fighter he had become.

Leonard. With Ali out of the picture, heavyweight boxing in America lost much of its allure. Attention once again was focused on lighter-weight classes. Welterweight Sugar Ray Leonard had created a sensation with his gold-medal performance at the 1976 Olympics in Montreal, and by the end of the decade fight fans were anticipating a matchup between him and Panama's Roberto Duran, in 1980 considered to be, pound-for-pound, boxing's greatest. The Leonard-Duran wars of the 1980s kept interest in boxing alive, while an up-and-comer in the middleweight division, Marvin Hagler, was emerging as U.S. boxing's new hope. Many of the sport's fans, however, were gradually being alienated as network-television coverage of boxing decreased and more and more of the great fights were being shown on closed-circuit and cable television.

COLLEGE BASKETBALL

Rebound. At the beginning of the decade, few fans held their breath over what team would be crowned champion of college basketball. Many fans — and even a few sportswriters — complained that the winning ways of the John Wooden–coached UCLA Bruins had robbed the season and the NCAA championship tournament of any drama. But Wooden eventually retired and the Bruins' level of play returned to earth. Great teams led by brilliant and colorful — if not slightly deranged — coaches emerged in the Midwest, and in 1979 two superstars faced off against each other in the NCAA finals, giving birth to the media-hyped carnival atmosphere that has made the tournament one of the greatest events in American sports. Larry Bird and Earvin ("Magic") John-

son in the next decade went on to become pro basketball's saviors, but they left behind a college game that had achieved new heights in popularity.

The Bruins. UCLA had become the New York Yankees of college basketball. They had won the NCAA championship an astounding five times in the previous decade — in 1964, 1965, 1967, 1968, and 1969. It seemed that the Bruins always had a big-play man to lead them, and when Lew Alcindor left for the pro ranks, all-American forward Sidney Wicks stepped forward along with brilliant six-foot-one-inch playmaker Henry Bibby to fill the void. As were the great Yankees dynasty teams of the 1950s, the UCLA Bruins were simply expected to win — which they did with awesome efficiency. The Bruins' bench was crowded with top-notch basketball talent, and as the players themselves began to assume that they would win on virtually every outing, controversies arose over playing time and which players would get to take direct part in the victory. Indeed, if UCLA had one problem during its dynasty years, it was that winning — and the high expectations that they seemed to meet with ease — at times created a morale problem. After graduation former Bruin Lynn Shackelford said that winning the championships they were expected to win "took a lot out of the actual accomplishment. I think that was one reason for our businesslike manner on the court. We were only doing what we'd been expected to do."

Challenges. In the 1970 NCAA tournament finals, UCLA routed the Jacksonville Dolphins, 80–69. The Bruins' fourth championship in a row, however, was especially significant given that the tournament's final four featured three other very strong teams — Jacksonville, Saint Bonaventure, and New Mexico State. Jacksonville had the enormously talented seven-foot-two-inch Artis Gilmore, and Saint Bonaventure was led by the Buffalo, six-foot-eleven-inch, 265-pound Bob Lanier. During the 1960s UCLA's detractors had liked to point out that college basketball had too few quality opponents that could even stay a single half on the same court with the star-studded Bruins. In the early 1970s, however, college basketball was expanding in talent, as many schools began to realize that their basketball programs could potentially be greater cash cows than their football programs, which had become more and more expensive to fund. As such, schools in once-powerful basketball regions such as the East were stepping up their recruiting efforts.

East vs. West. In the 1971 NCAA finals the Bruins received a scare from the Wildcats of Villanova University. Led by Jack Kraft, basketball's coach of the year, the Wildcats from Philadelphia carried the hopes of a region into the finals. As Villanova's Hank Siemiontkowski explained, "The whole East Coast will go up in flames if we win." And in the last thirty seconds of the game it looked as if fire departments were ready to go on alert, with the two teams trading baskets in the Bruins' first uncomfortably close final in years. UCLA prevailed, however, 68-62. After the tournament, old questions about the eligibility of Villanova star and tournament MVP Howard Porter resurfaced. He and Western Kentucky's Jim McDaniels had signed ABA contracts prior to the end of the season, and the NCAA "vacated" Villanova and Western Kentucky from the tournament's final standings. East Coast basketball had served notice to the West, however, and the venue for the tournament's final four had the look and feel of a big-time event. The Astrodome offered much greater seating capacity than did virtually any other site, and over 63,000 fans packed the dome for both the semifinal games. But the raised court in the middle of the Astrodome's vastness created for the players problems of depth perception when shooting as well as the danger of tumbling off the side of the court. Of the raised court and the great distance between the stands and the players one reporter commented, "the spectators at ground level needed periscopes, while the spectators in the stands needed telescopes."

Walton. As Joe Ireland of Loyola University liked to put it, the NCAA tournament had become the "UCLA Invitational." Yet, prior to the 1972 season many sportswriters were picking teams from the East and Midwest to bring to an end the Bruins' reign over college basketball. Many of UCLA's big players had graduated. But early in the season the Bruins were already proving the depth of their recruitments, and, as it had happened on previous Bruin teams, a megastar emerged. Bill Walton, a freckle-faced, curly-red-haired, six-foot-eleven-inch sophomore with tendinitis in both knees became the dominant big man in college basketball. Walton was a reluctant hero, however. He resented being called a superstar and was easily irked by reporters' questions that focused on his play rather than the play of the entire team. On the basketball floor, opposing teams often intentionally fouled Walton in order to move him out of the key; when Walton complained, players, coaches, officials, sportswriters, and fans labeled him a crybaby.

Off-Court. More than any other college athlete of the early 1970s, Walton was closely identified with the campus counterculture. A politically involved student, Walton loudly protested the government's mining of Haiphong Harbor, took part in many peace marches and sit-ins, and in one highly publicized incident stretched out on Wilshire Boulevard to demonstrate against the Vietnam War. Once arrested for demonstrating, Walton was forced to pay a $50 fine and was put on two-year, conditional probation by the university — a sentence that relieved many Bruin fans who, perhaps unrealistically, worried that their star player would be expelled. Walton was also sensitive to issues of race and took offense any time he detected in a reporter's question the suggestion that he was basketball's "Great White Hope." He often claimed that materialism — and the lure of a lucrative pro contract — meant nothing to him, and he wondered

Sidney Wicks (center), UCLA star, in the 1971 NCAA finals

out loud if organized athletics would ever be put in its proper place by a sports-obsessed American society.

Memphis State. Bill Walton and the Bruins won the championship over Florida State in 1972 — with Walton also taking player of the year honors — and again over Memphis State in 1973. The Memphis State Tigers were an extraordinary team in 1973, as much for what they signified away from the court as for how well they played on it. In 1970 Gene Bartow had come to Memphis State and found a locker room divided by racial strife, a problem that reflected severed race relations on the campus and in the surrounding southern community — the scene of the murder of Dr. Martin Luther King, Jr., in 1968. Under Bartow, however, the Tigers, black and white, came together as a team and began having success. Memphis reporters, leaders in the city's black and white communities, and Memphis mayor Wyeth Chandler all began to notice an easing of race relations that came with the success of the Tigers. As the Tigers made their run for a national title, Chandler commented on the broader implications of Tiger success: "This team has unified the city like it's never been unified before.... Black and white, rich and poor, young and old are caught up in its success. Memphis is a better city now, thanks to the Memphis State team."

The Streak. During the 1973 season the Bruins beat Notre Dame to win their sixty-first consecutive game, surpassing the record set by the Bill Russell–led University of San Francisco teams. In 1974 the Notre Dame Fighting Irish ended UCLA's streak at eighty-eight games. In the following weeks, UCLA succumbed to a few weaker teams and finally seemed ready to be toppled. The defending champs regrouped, however, and charged into the NCAA tournament semifinals, played for the first time in the South at Greensboro, North Carolina. Their opponents, North Carolina State, could practically claim home court. Although the other semifinal game between Marquette University and Kansas brought together the number one and number two teams in the polls, UCLA versus N.C. State was the premier matchup. Brilliantly coached by Norm Sloan, the N.C. State Wolfpack squeaked ahead of the Bruins in the game's second overtime and in front of a wild partisan crowd ended the UCLA dynasty. The Wolfpack went on to beat Marquette in the finals, but the big story was what UCLA had failed to do.

Wooden's Last Shot. UCLA returned to the semifinals in 1975, but the season had been dominated on the court by Bobby Knight's number one Indiana Hoosiers and off the court by rumors that Wooden was close to retirement. The morning of UCLA's semifinal game against Louisville, Los Angeles papers confirmed that Wooden was stepping down at the end of the season. Wanting to go out a winner, Wooden drove his team to an overtime victory over the Cardinals, then to a close-fought 92–85 championship-game victory over the Kentucky Wildcats. The Bruins had won their eighth championship of the decade — a total of twelve over the past fourteen seasons — but they had lost Wooden and their prominent position at the top of college basketball.

Indiana. Prior to the 1976 season, many were picking UCLA — now coached by Gene Bartow — to repeat as champions. A few insiders had different ideas, however. Among the minority was Marquette's feisty head coach, Al McGuire, who picked equally as feisty head coach Bobby Knight and his Indiana Hoosiers to go all the way: "Indiana has the best team with the best players and the best coach." Knight's growing reputation as a brilliant tactician and motivator was turning the heads of other coaches in college basketball. His reputation as an ill-tempered bad boy who closed team practices to gawking alums, abused his players verbally, stalked officials along the sidelines, and splintered chairs against scorers' tables was also turning the heads of many in the basketball world.

Perfect Hoosiers. In 1971 Knight had come to Indiana University from West Point — having coached the cadets into the nation's top twenty — and brought with him a style of basketball that emphasized tenacious defense. Soon IU fans were won over by Knight and his brand of coaching, as the Hoosiers in his first season finished with a 17–8 record and posted a third-place finish in the Big Ten. Improvement at IU under Knight was extraordinarily rapid, and in 1975 the Hoosiers were undefeated before losing to Kentucky in the NCAA regional final — a loss that many blamed on an injury to star forward Scott May. The 1976 Hoosier squad was once again led by May and by the brilliant play of point guard Quinn Buckner. The Hoosiers in that year went on to a perfect 32–0, beating fellow Big Ten member Michigan in the NCAA finals. Both the good and bad sides of Knight's legendary reputation would continue to grow, and he would go on to coach other championship Hoosier teams. But the perfect 1976 Hoosiers remain as one of the greatest college basketball teams of all time.

Marquette. Coach McGuire and his Marquette squad won the NCAA title in 1977 over Dean Smith's North Carolina Tar Heels and their four-corners offense. A time-killing tactic that involved passing the ball from one corner of half-court to the next in an effort to hold the ball and frustrate the opponent, the four corners in many ways reflected the brilliant tactical mind of Smith and the highly disciplined, methodical style of basketball he instilled in his players. Although close friends with Smith, McGuire was very much Smith's antithesis. McGuire was an alumnus of fabled coach Frank McGuire's Saint John's program and a product of New York street-style basketball. He considered himself Irish-tough and streetwise, and it was an image that his players came to respect: on more than one occasion McGuire physically confronted an out-of-line player. Yet, despite McGuire's emphasis on disciplined ballhandling and methodically run offenses, the Marquette Warriors and their coach had the reputation for being a group of free spirits, and the biggest free spirit among them, star guard Butch Lee, was a favorite of McGuire. In the final game against the Tar Heels, McGuire turned the Tar Heels four-corners to his advantage, taking away Smith's backdoor plays and running his own version of the four-corners offense. McGuire retired after the 1977 season, having capped a twenty-year coaching career with an NCAA championship.

The Wildcats. The Kentucky Wildcats, coached by Joe Hall, met preseason expectations by holding on to the number-one spot in the polls through most of the year and then winning the 1978 NCAA championship. Hall's reaction to winning the championship was one of relief. He had followed the late Adolph Rupp as Kentucky's head coach and as such had the shadow of a legend and the fans' memory of four Rupp-coached NCAA championship teams looming over him. Prior to the start of the NCAA final game against Bill Foster's Duke University Blue Devils, UK fans paraded around the court with a bedsheet that read, "Win one for Rupp!" Upon seeing the sign a Kentucky fan in the stands yelled what was almost certainly Hall's sentiment: "To hell with Rupp! Win one for Joe Hall!" The win exorcised the ghost of Rupp, and the program had thus become exclusively Hall's.

Magic and Bird. At the end of the decade college

Fans preparing for the 1971 Thanksgiving Day football game between Oklahoma and Nebraska, who won the game and the national championship

basketball and its showcase event, the NCAA championship tournament, had reached new heights in popularity. By 1977 the tournament's championship game was averaging over forty-two million television viewers, and in 1979 overall fan attendance during the season surpassed thirty million. In 1959 only twenty-two college basketball teams played in arenas with a seating capacity of ten thousand or more. During the 1970s major arena-construction projects were under way at all collegiate levels, and more than one hundred teams played half their games in ten-thousand-seat arenas. In 1979 two star college players emerged, raising the excitement that had already surrounded college basketball to a fever pitch. Larry Bird was a six-foot-nine-inch forward with phenomenal shooting, passing, and rebounding skills. From French Lick, Indiana, Bird powered the little-known Indiana State Sycamores to a number one ranking. Compounding all the excitement raised by his brilliant play was the inescapable fact that Bird was white, and in a sport dominated by talented players who happened to be black, many pointed to Bird as the next Great White Hope. Meanwhile, Michigan State's six-foot-eight-inch Earvin ("Magic") Johnson of Lansing, Michigan, was stunning fans with unbelievable displays of passing, shooting, and rebounding. His assists were something like art, and he took a special thrill out of feeding perfectly lobbed passes to teammate Greg ("Special K") Kelser, who would catch the pass above the rim and spectacularly slam it through the hoop.

Showdown. A nation eagerly awaited the showdown between the two players, as the Indiana State Sycamores and the Michigan State Spartans steadily made their way past the competition in the NCAA tournament toward a meeting in the championship game. Once in the finals, however, the Spartans proved to be too deep with talent for the mismatched Sycamores and scored an easy victory. Nevertheless, the Final Four had become a big-time event, as well as a national showcase for the talents of Johnson and Bird. Kids watching the two players on television became instant fans of basketball and the all-around game, which held ballhandling and passing to be equally as important as shooting. The era of the big man was coming to an end, and taking his place were small forwards and passing guards. Bird and Johnson took their act to the pros — Bird signing with the Boston Celtics, Johnson leaving college in his sophomore year to play with the Los Angeles Lakers — each in the next decade having legendary careers while raising the popularity of pro basketball to new levels.

COLLEGE FOOTBALL

A Saturday Tradition Returns. By middecade, college football fans were filling campus stadiums in record numbers. With the end of the Vietnam War and the onset of an economic recession, football — along with fraternities and sororities — regained popularity among students seeking a return to the traditional collegiate lifestyle. The millions who sat in the bleachers on Saturday afternoons or watched on television had much to root for. During the 1970s college football stood for innovation and high scoring — and many of the game's new fans were indeed former Sunday armchair quarterbacks who had grown bored with stodgy, defense-minded NFL teams and their two-back offenses and who were looking to the campuses for an alternative brand of football.

Power Backs. The college game, which throve on trickery and deceit, featured four-back offenses and aerial attacks led by such great passing quarterbacks as Art Schlichter of Ohio State, Joe Theismann of Notre Dame, and Jim Plunkett of Stanford. The decade also saw some of college football's greatest running backs. In the West, Southern California's Anthony Davis, Charles White, and Ricky Bell followed in the wake of 1960s Southern California superstar O. J. Simpson. Big Eight speedsters Johnny Rodgers of Nebraska and Billy Sims of Oklahoma provided the excitement in the school's option backfields. Earl Campbell of Texas gained considerable fame — and a Heisman Trophy — with an up-the-middle power style of ball carrying. And Tony Dorsett of Pittsburgh set fifteen collegiate rushing records in leading the Panthers to the college national title in 1976. Pitt became the first team from the East to win the number one ranking since the 1959 Syracuse squad. The Pitt Panthers' national title signaled the revitalization of East Coast football as a power to be reckoned with.

The Big Vine. Teams that had dominated college football during the previous decade, however, remained on top during the 1970s. West Coast leader Southern California, the top Big Ten schools Michigan and Ohio State, Big Eight powerhouses Nebraska and Oklahoma, Southwest Conference perennial leader Texas, fabled coach Paul ("Bear") Bryant's Southeastern Conference power Alabama, and legendary programs at Penn State and Notre Dame all regularly occupied spots in the top rankings. A 16 September 1979 article in *The New York Times* argued that these schools, "the Gang of Nine," had had an alarmingly disproportionate number of appearances in the rankings — and television was to blame. "The Big Nine had 136 coast-to-coast [television] appearances," declared *The New York Times*, "or approximately 48 percent of the total." Whether networks covering collegiate football, such as ABC, were justified in concentrating their attentions on a handful of schools is debatable, but the popularity of the Big Nine was undeniable.

The article in *The New York Times* nevertheless did point out the indisputable fact that for most of the 139 major college football teams during the 1970s the distribution of television revenues — approximately $250,000 per television appearance during the late 1970s — greatly influenced recruiting patterns and helped determine the success of teams and their conferences. As costs for funding football programs rose dramatically (one study during the mid 1970s reported that it cost approximately three hundred dollars just to suit up one college football player), many schools discontinued football altogether, while others adopted an eleven-game season. With teams and conferences becoming increasingly dependent on

University of Southern California running back Anthony Davis scoring a touchdown against Ohio State in the 1973 Rose Bowl. USC won 42–17.

television revenue, traditional postseason bowl matchups took on new importance. Even the ultratraditional Big Ten, which in the past had never allowed more than one of its teams to enter a postseason game, began to let its runner-up teams participate in bowls in search of additional television revenues for the conference.

Violations. Because of television, big-time college football became a big-money game, and as the stakes increased so did the temptation to cheat. The Oklahoma Sooners, for instance — once considered a model NCAA football program — received probation and were prohibited from making television appearances for having forged a high-school transcript. By the end of the decade nearly one hundred athletes at about two dozen schools had been implicated in transcript scandals. In 1976 the once-high-riding Spartans of Michigan State received what were at the time some of the stiffest penalties for recruiting violations ever meted out by the NCAA. The three-year probation, the loss of eligibility by twenty-seven members of the team, and the firing of one assistant coach soon led to the resignation of head coach Denny Stolz. Sportswriters and social critics across the country were decrying the disturbing trends in college-football recruiting and had begun to question, as did one end-of-the-decade *Sports Illustrated* editorial, whether "there are enough quality athletes to be found who can fill arenas and stadiums and also are capable of making the grade in the classroom. Without cheating, that is." Ques-

The coach of the decade, Alabama's Paul ("Bear") Bryant, before the 1979 Sugar Bowl, which his team won to cap an unbeaten season

tionable recruiting practices, of course, were not relegated to the transcript forgers. As one southwestern coach explained it in the 26 January 1976 issue of *The New York Times,* he liked to recruit high-school players from New York because "we send them across the border into Mexico to shack up for a few days. Every one of those kids signs on the dotted line when he gets back."

Rule Bending. For many athletic directors overseeing big-time athletic programs, aggressive recruiting practices had in the words of Michigan athletic director Don Canham, become a "necessary evil." Rule bending among overzealous recruiters, however, was not the only consequence of college teams scrambling for glory, as well as for television and gate receipts. Athletic directors and university presidents became increasingly tolerant of the poor behavior displayed by some coaches — as long as those coaches continued to win. In 1971 ABC cameras captured Ohio State's ill-tempered and militaristic head coach Woody Hayes ripping up sideline markers in a fit of rage. When asked for his response to the episode, Canham said he would buy the opposing coach all the sideline markers he could possibly rip up, adding "When Ohio State comes to Michigan, who do you think our fans come to see — the players? No sir, they come to see Woody Hayes. He's worth an extra 30,000 tickets. The

men take their children down to the field and point him out. I've seen it."

Reform. Through most of the 1970s Hayes continued to build upon his reputation for being abusive toward game officials, sportswriters, and even his own players; but his winning record and cultish following insulated him from job-threatening criticism. After the Buckeyes' appearance against Clemson in the 1978 Gator Bowl, however, Ohio State officials were forced to act. During that game Clemson's Charlie Bauman had intercepted a pass and run out of bounds along the Ohio State sidelines. In college football's most infamous televised scene, a frustrated and angered Hayes punched Bauman. Hayes lost his job as a result. Arizona State's Frank Kush was similarly forced to resign as head coach when it was reported that he had hit one of his own players during practice. The forced resignations indicated that college football was coming to an end of a coaching trend identified by a Vince Lombardian emphasis on unquestioned discipline and loyalty and further shaped by an intense pressure to succeed. Issues of liability in an already-violent game became prominent in the thinking of university officials; and as recruiting wars intensified, players were being treated like prizes not to be mishandled. For better or worse, college athletes therefore began to have more of a voice in how they were to be coached — and in how their programs should be run.

PROFESSIONAL FOOTBALL

America's Game. As had the Green Bay Packers in the previous decade, the Pittsburgh Steelers in the 1970s dominated professional football, winning four Super Bowls between 1975 and 1980. The Steelers were not the only glamour team during the decade. The Dallas Cowboys, Miami Dolphins, Minnesota Vikings, and Oakland Raiders each inspired either intense love or hate in football fans from coast to coast. Pro football by the end of the decade had indeed become America's game. Results from a 1978 Harris sports survey showed that football enjoyed a 70 percent following among American sports fans — compared to 54 percent for baseball. More than a quarter of the fans surveyed named football as their favorite sport; 16 percent named baseball. Record numbers of American families viewed Super Bowls VI through XIV on their televisions, making the glitzy, heavily hyped championship between the American and National Football Conferences one of the most-watched sporting events of all time.

Football Everywhere. As the game and its fans moved from icy fields and rickety bleachers to ultramodern domed stadiums carpeted with artificial turf, football more than any other professionally played major sport came to reflect the high-paced, high-tech society in which it was played. Highbrow Sunday-afternoon television programming of the fifties and early sixties gradually gave way to hours of football coverage to entertain the millions of fans. At the beginning of the decade the sport became a big hit in prime-time television thanks to ABC's *Monday Night Football;* and as football became a mainstay in the family living room both afternoon and night, politicians, businessmen, and even housewives adopted the language of the sport to serve as a metaphor for the way Americans conducted both commerce and family life: to get along one had to be "a team player" who was "willing to take the ball and run with it." The decade saw more and more pro football stars use their newfound commercial appeal to peddle everything from sunglasses to panty hose, and in so doing to convert many more American fans into consumers. On Sunday afternoons and Monday nights during the season it seemed as if all of America was watching pro football. Even a president of the United States, Richard Nixon, admitted he was a pro football addict. And he was not above using the influence of the Oval Office to live out an armchair quarterback's fantasy; a Miami fan, Nixon told Miami coach Don Shula prior to Super Bowl VI, "I think you can hit [wide receiver Paul] Warfield on that down-and-in pattern." Warfield did catch four passes in a 24–3 Super Bowl loss to Dallas.

Merger. Enormous change in the sport took place at the beginning of the decade. The merger between the

Miami Dolphins fullback Larry Csonka in the 1974 Superbowl

NFL and AFL was finalized for the 1970 season — four years after the two leagues had reached an agreement. In structuring and balancing two new conferences within a single league, three former NFL teams — the Baltimore Colts, the Cleveland Browns, and Pittsburgh — were joined with former AFL clubs to create the American Football Conference; the rest of the old NFL teams became the National Football Conference, and the two conferences composed the National Football League. Both the newly created AFC and NFC consisted of three divisions — Eastern, Central, and Western. The old AFL clubs brought to the NFL a new sense of style, a lot of swagger, and some innovation: three things badly lacking in the stale and stodgy senior league.

AFC. By 1970 it had become a league rule that all player jerseys must have the wearer's name appearing on the back, a fashion that had its beginnings in the AFL. The AFL also brought to the merger a fresh cast of characters that included the highly penalized, outlaw-branded Oakland Raiders and the New York Jets quarterback Joe Namath. "Broadway Joe," as he was called, was the prototypical modern megastar. He parlayed his golden arm, rebel reputation, and good looks into successful commercial endorsements and celebrity status. He also had the audacity to guarantee a Jets victory over the NFL's Colts and aging star Johnny Unitas in the third Super Bowl. In backing up his talk, Broadway Joe gave the AFL new legitimacy in the eyes of many once-die-hard NFL fans, while simultaneously recreating himself as a living sports legend. When Hank Stramm and his innovative brand of offensive and defensive football helped win the Super Bowl for the AFL's Kansas City Chiefs in 1969, the junior league successfully served notice to rival NFL teams that they could do much more than compete on an equal footing with more established

Drugs had a dual meaning in professional and world-class sports. There were the drugs players took for performance, and there were the drugs they took for fun. Both were in plentiful supply and constant demand during the 1970s. For performance, the players in the muscle sports took steroids in massive doses, despite the unpleasant side effects. One observer described the steroid takers as big men with small balls. Because irritability was a side effect of heavy steroid use, domestic violence became a major problem among athletes. In 1976 testing was initiated at the Olympics to identify and disqualify athletes taking steroids, and by 1979 plans were completed to test Olympic competitors for some two hundred types of drugs at a cost of about $1 million for the winter games and $3-4 million for the summer games.

For pain athletes took various numbing agents to enable them to compete, and the press praised their courage. Analyst Robert Yeager notes that Evonne Goolagong won the Virginia Slims tennis tournament with the help of procaine injections that helped her compete despite "severe blisters, a damaged arch, and bursitis at the base of her Achilles' tendon." In the National Football League it was common for hurt players to leave the field, receive a painkilling injection on the sidelines, and return to action.

In 1973 the San Diego Chargers took a novel ap-proach to drug use on their team: they hired a team psychiatrist to administer mood-altering chemicals to help the team perform better. Team psychiatrist Arnold Mandell explained "there was no way to discuss or manipulate the psychological aspects of pro football without grappling with the pervasive, systematic use of mood-altering drugs." So he wrote prescriptions for the players, "so that they wouldn't go to Tijuana and get the bad stuff." This development coming in the year after the NFL had endured a congressional investigation into drug abuse among players was too much for commissioner Pete Rozelle to endure. He fined the general manager of the Chargers and eight players a total of $40,000 and placed the team on probation. It was widely acknowledged that the penalty had little more than a cosmetic effect.

Three NFL players and one former star were arrested for drug trafficking before the decade was out — Shelby Jordon of the Boston Patriots in 1976, Randy Crowder and Don Reese of the Miami Dolphins in 1977, and Bob Hayes, former world-record holder in the one-hundred-yard dash and star running back for the Dallas Cowboys in 1979. He was sentenced to five years in prison in 1980.

Sources: David Harris, The League: The Rise and Decline of the NFL (New York: Bantam, 1986);

Phyllis E. Lehmann, "Psyching out the Athletes' Medicine Chest," *Sciquest*, 52 (November 1979): 6-11;

Robert C. Yeager, *Seasons of Shame: The New Violence in Sports* (New York: McGraw-Hill, 1979).

clubs. And indeed during the 1970s the AFC dominated the NFL.

Super Hype. At the beginning of the decade, NFL commissioner Pete Rozelle and the team owners searched for ways to capitalize on football's growing popularity. With major league baseball attendance — and even fan interest in the World Series — on the decline, the NFL worked on glamorizing the image of the Super Bowl, hoping that it would replace the Series as America's most important sporting event. The 1966 AFL-NFL championship game had been a box-office disaster, attracting only 63,035 fans to the Los Angeles Memorial Coliseum. In 1967 the AFL and NFL began calling the championship game the Super Bowl, and for the 1971 game between Dallas and Baltimore the league affixed a Roman numeral to Super Bowl and billed the extravaganza as something even bigger than sport. Super Bowl V — a title which sounded more appropriate for gladiatorial opera than a championship game — was watched on television by more than sixty million viewers; pregame through postgame coverage of the event lasted nearly six hours — the game itself lasting only three. A capacity crowd filled Miami's Orange Bowl and was treated to a halftime extravaganza featuring Anita Bryant. The game proved less than super, however. Although its final score was decided on a last-second field goal, the game was hardly an exhibition of either football skill or artistry. Sportswriters dubbed Super Bowl V the Blooper Bowl and took turns at pinpricking its inflated image created by glitzy self-promotion. Larry Merchant offered a wry summary of Super Bowl V: "It featured a total of XII fumbles and interceptions and XIV penalties (for CLXIV yards)."

The 1,000-Yard Club. During the 1972 season a record ten backs broke the 1,000-yard barrier for rushing in a single season. It was not what NFL officials had originally hoped for. In fact, the season had opened with rule changes designed to discourage rush-oriented offenses. The space between the two lines of hash marks was narrowed by three yards in an attempt to neutralize the increasingly popular zone defenses and open up the passing game. However, as defensive coordinators scrambled for new ways to defend receivers, running backs continued to ramble through the lines for big gains. This was a brand of football the average fan found boring — and one which NFL officials thought would become less common after having merged with the AFL and the young league's wide-open, go-for-broke offensive style. But a new generation of running backs had entered pro football by the beginning of the decade and as a group brought greater speed, agility, and power to the rushing game. Miami tore their way to a Super Bowl victory and a 17–0 record — the NFL's one and only perfect season — behind the slashing running attack of Eugene ("Mercury") Morris and the brute strength of Larry Csonka, a man who literally ran over defensemen and was feared by even the most fearsome of linebackers. Morris and Csonka became the first teammates to gain 1,000 yards each in a single season.

Juice. The league's leading rusher for the 1972 season, however, was O. J. Simpson with 1,251 yards. Having begun his pro career with the Buffalo Bills in 1969, the former Heisman Trophy winner from the University of Southern California underwhelmed fans in his first three seasons, gaining a total of only 1,927 yards while laboring behind the Bills' weak offensive line. But in 1972 Lou Sabin became the Bills' new head coach and immediately began assembling an offensive line that would create gaping holes in the defense for his primary running back. By the 1973 season the Bills' offensive line had become known as the Electric Company, the power source behind the brilliant running of O. J. Simpson, who was being called "the Juice." In that year, Simpson cut, stutter-stepped, and sprinted for 2,003 yards, breaking Jim Brown's single season rushing record of 1,863 yards. In 1976 Simpson set a single-game record of 273 yards rushing against the Detroit Lions on Thanksgiving Day. Simpson spent the last two seasons of his career in San Francisco and retired in 1979 as the second leading rusher of all time behind Jim Brown. Although Simpson never played on a championship team during his pro career, his brilliant style of running made him football's most dominant player during the decade. For a new generation of running backs he was one of the most watched and most emulated ball carriers. For a new generation of fans Simpson was the most recognized. His good looks and charisma made him the perfect Madison Avenue pitchman for a multitude of products, including sunglasses and rental cars.

The Building of a Dynasty. During the early 1970s, most fans and sportswriters figured that they were witnessing in the Don Shula–coached Miami Dolphins the beginning of a football dynasty that would rule over the pro ranks for a decade. The team's three straight appearances in the Super Bowl from 1972 to 1974 — and back-to-back victories in 1973 and 1974 — seemed evidence enough that they were unstoppable, at least in their own conference. Elsewhere in the AFC, however, a team that for nearly four decades had labored at or near the bottom

of the pro standings had begun to show signs of turning its fortunes around. The Pittsburgh Steelers had in 1969 named Chuck Noll as their head coach, and in Noll's first season the team compiled a miserable 1-13 record. But Noll had the faith of Steelers owner Art Rooney — a man adored by players, staff, and fans alike — and, perhaps more important, a bag full of high draft picks. Through the draft Noll pursued such talents as Terry Bradshaw (the first player drafted in 1970), Mean Joe Green, Mel Blount, Jack Ham — and a relatively obscure Penn State running back, Franco Harris.

Franco's Army. Rooney lobbied hard for the Harris pick in the 1972 draft, despite opposition from his own front office. Rooney recognized in Harris a depth of character that would mean more to a team than talent alone. Harris's mixed African-American and Italian ancestry also served to unite fans from diverse ethnic neighborhoods in Pittsburgh. Calling themselves Franco's Italian Army, fanatic fans of Harris had much to cheer about. During these building years, Harris's number was called often in the Steelers' offensive schemes — the Steelers still several years away from having a potent passing attack — and in his rookie year he posted phenomenal numbers, rushing for 100 yards in six straight games.

Mean Joe Green. Noll's most important draft pick, however, was his first one made as Steelers head coach. Taken as the fourth overall choice in the 1969 draft, Joe Green was an unheralded defensive lineman from North Texas State. In his rookie season, despite playing for a 1–13 team, Green was named the league's Defensive Player of the Year, an honor he would capture again in 1972 and 1974. Green was the new generation's prototypical defensive lineman; he was big and strong, but, more significant, he was fast. He attacked quarterbacks with a speed and ferocity more often attributed to outside rushers rather than defensive lineman. Called "Mean Joe," he also had a reputation for being a nasty player, especially if an opposing offensive lineman made him mad. Around Mean Joe Green the Steelers built their heralded "steel curtain" defense with such players as tackle Ernie Holmes and defensive ends Dwight White and L. C. Greenwood.

The Immaculate Reception. A miraculous play in a 23 December 1972 AFC divisional play-off game between Pittsburgh and the Oakland Raiders first brought the reconstituted Steelers to the attention of fans nationwide. In the fourth quarter the Raiders appeared to have the game, which was played in Pittsburgh, wrapped up. The Raiders had played their new quarterback, Kenny Stabler, in the second half, and Stabler, who earned the nickname "the Snake," had scrambled for a touchdown to go ahead of the Steelers 7–6 with one minute and thirteen seconds remaining. When the clock showed twenty-two seconds remaining in the game, Steelers quarterback Terry Bradshaw and his offense had the ball on their own forty-yard line on fourth-and-ten. In the final play of the game Bradshaw passed, and the ball, Steelers running back John ("Frenchy") Fuqua, and Raiders safety Jack Tatum collided at the thirty-five-yard line. The ball ricocheted back to Harris, who in full sprint caught the ball and ran in to the end zone for what delirious Steelers fans thought was a winning touchdown. As Raiders coach John Madden and Tatum loudly complained to officials that the ball had bounced off Fuqua into Harris's hands (until 1978 an illegal play), referees conferred with NFL supervisors in the press box. But nobody, including cameramen, seemed to have had a clear view showing whether the ball had bounced off Tatum or Fuqua. Finally, the referee signaled a touchdown, and Three Rivers Stadium and the city of Pittsburgh went wild. Steelers radio announcer Myron Cope called Harris's catch the Immaculate Reception. Oakland players and coaches had other words to describe the play. "It hit Frenchy and he knows it," Tatum insisted. Fuqua has never publicly said whether or not Tatum was right.

Miraculous Playoffs. Later on the same day of the Immaculate Reception, another remarkable play-off game was played. After being pummeled by the San Francisco 49ers for three quarters, the Dallas Cowboys pulled quarterback Craig Morton and replaced him with Roger Staubach, who had been nursing a separated shoulder through most of the season. Within a span of two minutes — the time left in the game — Staubach, with the help of an onside kick recovered by Mel Renfro, rallied the Cowboys, scoring fourteen points to go ahead of the 49ers 30–28 and win the game. Of the stunning come-from-behind victory Jerry Magee of the *San Diego Union* wrote that it was "the most miraculous playoff finish staged in the NFL in the last three hours."

Super Bowl X. In their frequent trips to the Super Bowl, the Steelers twice met Dallas, who had a couple of victories of their own in the big game — Super Bowls VI (over Miami) and XII (over Denver). By Super Bowl X — the first meeting between the Steelers and Cowboys — the big game had the reputation for being a super bore, in which one hapless team such as four-time loser the Minnesota Vikings got trounced in an undramatic fashion. Expectations for a Pittsburgh-Dallas matchup were high, however, and both teams swaggered into Super Bowl X, played in Miami's Orange Bowl on 18 January 1976. The Steelers were the defending league champions, having crushed Minnesota the year before; and Dallas was the first wild-card team to reach a Super Bowl. Both teams had big-play offenses and star-studded defenses. The game did not disappoint fans, as the lead changed hands and Roger Staubach — whose reputation for leading comebacks had by now become legend — in the end led Dallas in a last-minute drive to overcome a four-point deficit. Steelers fans across the country let out a collective sigh of relief when Staubach's "Hail Mary" pass was intercepted in the end zone, clinching a 21–17 victory for Pittsburgh. More memorable than the close score, however, was the astounding play of Pittsburgh's wide receiver Lynn Swann, whose graceful, diving catch

Pittsburgh receiver Lynn Swann in Super Bowl X, the second of Pittsburgh's four Super Bowl wins

over Dallas cornerback Mark Washington assured him the game's MVP award.

America's Team. Super Bowl XIII served as an end-of-the-decade sequel to Super Bowl X, as once again Dallas and Pittsburgh met in the Orange Bowl and provided fans with thrills in a spectacularly played and agonizingly close contest. For Dallas fans the 35–31 Cowboys loss seemed especially tragic, for veteran Cowboys tight end Jackie Smith dropped a perfectly thrown touchdown pass in the end zone, and in so doing all but ended Dallas's hopes for a come-from-behind win. Dallas's failed onside kick iced the victory for Pittsburgh. The 21 January 1979 game was a fitting end to a successful ten years for the NFL, which saw the finalization of the merger between two leagues — and as a consequence the end of a costly bidding war — changes in the game (such as moving the uprights to the back line of the end zone, designed to open up the field for offenses), and the beginning of another dynasty. The Steelers would go on to win the Super Bowl again in 1980, and Dallas would continue to enjoy success until 1982, when a thrilling loss to San Francisco in the NFC championship game signaled the beginning of the Cowboys' decline. By the end of the 1970s, however, Dallas had become known as America's team — fans rightly expected them to win — and football had become America's game.

GOLF

Everyman's Game. In the 1970s the game of golf at all levels — from the professional to the amateur ranks — had never been healthier. Americans in 1971 watched on television as astronaut Alan B. Shepard sent a six-iron shot sailing in the moon's thin atmosphere; millions shared an enthusiasm for the sport with Shepard. In the previous decade Arnold Palmer in swashbuckling, go-for-broke style had popularized the game and had opened country-club gates to legions of middle-class fans. Although he played a sport perceived by many Americans to be snobbish, Palmer was seen as an everyman on the golf course, his untrained-looking swing wildly hooking the ball into the woods then slashing it back into play. "The King," as he was called by his fans, sweated and chain-smoked his way through a round with a determined walk and stare. As millions of Americans headed out to the public links to emulate their new hero Palmer, a pudgy-faced, long-hitting Ohioan named Jack Nicklaus began challenging Palmer's rule. By the 1970s "the Golden Bear" was seemingly winning everything in sight and had claimed all four major titles. Nicklaus was Palmer's successor — just as Palmer had succeeded Ben Hogan. But as the decade progressed many became convinced that Nicklaus had surpassed all of his predecessors and had become golf's greatest player ever.

A Mass Sport. More and more public courses were being built in the 1970s, and important equipment changes were keeping pace with the golfing boom. In 1968 Spalding had begun selling a Surlyn-covered two-piece ball, the Top-Flite. The new ball flew farther and was more durable. Although many in the pro ranks shunned the new ball because it was difficult to impart spin on the hard cover, thus making it harder to control, the two-piece, hard-covered ball meant more distance and lower cost for the average golfer. Golf clubs also became less expensive during the decade. Mass-produced, investment-cast clubs came into the market, and many new companies sought to cash in on inexpensive club making. As a result middle-class Americans could afford equipment once reserved for the upper class. Expanded television coverage of men's and women's PGA Tour events also helped in bringing greater attention to golf during the decade. Some of the difficulties and expenses of golf coverage were solved with the addition of handheld cameras and on-course commentators following groups of players.

The PGA Tour. Television and a broader fan base meant big money for the American PGA Tour during the 1970s. By the end of the decade, total tour purse money exceeded $10 million, and the beginnings of a Senior

Jack Nicklaus and Lee Trevino after their 1971 World Cup win

PGA Tour — extraordinarily popular and lucrative in the 1980s — could be found in the Liberty Mutual Legends of Golf tournament played at Onion Creek in Austin, Texas, an event which debuted in 1978. An expanded tour schedule, more television coverage, and larger purses — due largely to the PGA having aggressively courted corporate sponsors — fit the vision of Deane Beman, the once-great amateur golfer who became the tour's commissioner in 1974. Beman's critics snidely suggested that his goal was to assure the tour journeyman that, like Nicklaus and Palmer, he too could become a millionaire playing golf. Indeed, the efforts Beman made to fatten tour purses meant that pro golf could provide a fine living for men other than the game's elite. The days spent on the road grinding from one event to the next were, for the average tour pro, coming to an end and would be replaced by first-class air travel and decent hotels.

The Women's Tour. In 1973 Kathy Whitworth, the leading money winner of the LPGA Tour during much of the late 1960s and early 1970s, led pro women in year's earnings with $87,000. In that year Jack Nicklaus led the men's tour with $320,000. Fewer events, less television coverage and fan support, and fewer corporate sponsors meant that the LPGA Tour players lagged well behind their male counterparts in wealth and recognition. The LPGA, however, had no shortage of talent. Great and charismatic players such as JoAnne Carner, Donna Caponi Young, Sandra Haynie, and Judy Rankin dueled week after week for prize money that was a fraction of the purses for which the men played. In 1976 Rankin became the first woman golfer to win more than $100,000 in one year, and by the end of the decade purses for women's events were averaging over $100,000. The LPGA was beginning to profit from increased corporate sponsorship and television coverage — and the patronage of Dinah Shore. In 1972 the popular entertainer became involved with one of the tour's major tournaments, which became known as the Colgate–Dinah Shore Winners Circle. Shore soon became addicted to the game of golf, and her association with the tournament — and her play in the tournament's celebrity pro-am event — meant expanded coverage by NBC, greater corporate interest, and, most important, greater fan interest in women's golf. Shore succeeded in doing for the LPGA what Bing Crosby and his association with the Pebble Beach tour stop had done for PGA popularity.

The LPGA's Superstar. In 1978 junior golfing sensation Nancy Lopez burst onto the LPGA Tour and became what women's golf most needed — the game's greatest star since Mildred ("Babe") Zaharias. Her unusual swing, endearing smile and personality, and winning ways attracted millions to women's golf, as she dominated the tour in her rookie year with nine victories — including the LPGA championship, which she won by six strokes — and a record single-season total of $189,813 in prize money. In one remarkable stretch during that 1978 campaign, Lopez won five consecutive times, stunning the sports world. She took Player of the Year honors for 1978, as well as Rookie of the Year — a feat unheard-of until then. She repeated as Player of the Year in 1979, having won eight more tournaments. In that year she also won her second Vare Trophy, awarded to the player with the lowest scoring average. Lopez's dominating presence on the golf course further revolutionized golf during the next decade, as purses became richer and fans and the media began to pay greater attention to the LPGA Tour.

Merry Mex. Although Palmer and his municipal-course swing were being overshadowed by Nicklaus, with his cool demeanor and mechanical efficiency during the 1970s, golf fans had other everymen to follow, most notably Lee Trevino. Known to fans as the "Merry Mex," Trevino was born in Dallas, Texas, where he eked out a living as a $30-a-week assistant pro at a driving range hustling bets on the side. A great storyteller, Trevino claims to have beaten opponents in money games using a Coke bottle. Trevino exploded onto the big-time golfing scene in the late 1960s, winning the 1968 U. S. Open and becoming a permanent fixture at or near the top of the tour money list through much of the 1970s. He replaced Palmer in golf's Big Three, joining Nicklaus and South Africa's Gary Player, when in 1971 Trevino pulled off a phenomenal triple, winning the U.S., Canadian, and British Opens in a space of four weeks. Although the Merry Mex and his constant chatter were big hits with the gallery and television audiences, Trevino was beginning to give the Golden Bear fits by often squeaking ahead of Nicklaus in the final round. Such was the case in the 1974 PGA Championship, and in that year Trevino also captured the Vardon Trophy, awarded to the PGA Tour player with the lowest scoring average.

Blacks. Despite the presence of such tradition-defying players as Palmer and Trevino and the game's increased affordability and popularity among the middle class, professional golf largely remained lily-white in its racial attitudes, as many of the tour's venues remained discriminatory in their policies. Nevertheless, the 1970s saw the

Avery Brundage (right) handing over the gavel of office to incoming International Olympic Committee president Lord Killanin (left). The mayor of Lausanne is between them.

continuing success of Charles Sifford, whose emergence on the PGA Tour in the late 1950s helped overturn the tour's "all-white" rule in 1960. In 1975 Sifford won the PGA Seniors title, capping off a career in which he won over $340,000. The tour's first nationally prominent black star, however, was Robert Lee Elder. A product of the black United Golf Association tour, Elder qualified for PGA Tour play for the 1968 season, and in that year faced off against Nicklaus in a thrilling televised sudden-death play-off at the American Golf Classic. Elder lost on the fifth hole, but the play-off had placed him in the national limelight. He captured his first PGA title in 1974 at the Monsanto Open. He won twice in 1978, and in 1979 at the age of forty-five he became the first black to play for America's Ryder Cup team. Both Sifford and Elder became fixtures on the Senior Tour during the 1980s.

Young Talent. Throughout the decade young, talented players challenged Nicklaus's primacy on the golf course, and in the act of doing so some even became superstars, such as Tom Weiskopf, Texans Ben Crenshaw and Tom Kite, and Californian Johnny Miller, who shot an incredible 63 on the lightning-fast greens of Pittsburgh's Oakmont Country Club to win the 1973 U.S. Open. In 1974 Miller had one of professional golf's greatest years, winning eight tournaments. By 1976, however, Miller's star was fading, and Nicklaus remained on top of the heap. The Golden Bear had won a record fifth Masters in 1975, and in 1978 he won another British Open, giving him at least three victories in all four majors. In 1980 he won his fourth U.S. Open at famed Baltusrol, shooting a record 272 for seventy-two holes.

Watson. One player emerged in the late 1970s whom many felt would succeed Nicklaus as golf's greatest. Tom Watson, a midwesterner with a Huck Finn face, served notice to the golfing world in 1975, when he won the British Open at Carnoustie and finished in the top ten in the other three majors that year. In one of the finest

The 1972 U.S. Olympic basketball team celebrating their apparent victory at one of the conclusions of play. Though time had expired, officials ordered the last shot replayed twice, after which the Soviets prevailed.

head-to-head golfing contests ever witnessed, Watson outplayed Nicklaus in the fourth round to win the 1977 British Open. The contest played over the links layout in Turnberry, Scotland, was soon being called "The Duel in the Sun" and served as a preview of other spectacular Watson-Nicklaus duels in which the play of the two men would rise well above that of the rest of the field. From 1977 to 1979 Watson owned the Vardon Trophy and Player of the Year honors, and his best year, 1980, was yet to come.

THE OLYMPICS: 1972

Amateurism. The retirement of Avery Brundage as president of the International Olympic Committee at the end of the 1972 Olympics marked the beginning of the end of pretense about the games being restricted to amateur athletes. Star athletes had challenged the rule in the Olympics of the 1960s, and by 1972 it was clear that Western athletes enjoyed a level of support that approached the Eastern system of state support. The new president, Lord Killanin of Ireland, announced immediately that his first priority would be to reconsider the definition of amateurism as it related to the qualification of athletes for the games.

The Winter Games. The Winter Olympics were held in Sapporo, Japan, from 3 to 13 February. There were 1,015 men and 212 women from thirty-seven nations competing. A hint of controversy arose when Austrian skier Karl Schranz was banned from competition for flagrant commercialism. Although he encouraged his team to compete, they did not fare as well as expected. Americans won three gold medals, including a surprise win by Barbara Cochran in the slalom. American women won two other gold medals in speed skating. Sixteen-year-old world-record-holder Anne Henning won the 500-meter competition, despite a near collision with a Canadian skater who was disqualified for obstruction. Dianne Holum won the 1500 meters and took the silver medal in the 3000 to add to her silver and bronze medals won in the 1968 Olympics. No American man won a gold medal at the Winter Olympics. The United States won a total of eight medals, placing sixth among nations after the Soviet Union, with eight golds and sixteen total medals, East Germany, Norway, Switzerland, and the Netherlands.

The XX Olympiad. The summer games were held in

Munich. The West German government spent $265 million to offer a hospitable setting and discourage comparison to the XX Olympiad with the last held in Germany, the 1936 Berlin games conducted under the watchful eye of Adolf Hitler. The Munich Olympics drew a record number of athletes, 5,848 men and 1,299 women, from a record 122 nations, to compete between 26 August and 10 September. There was controversy before the games opened about the participation of the integrated team from Rhodesia, which planned to compete as a British colony. The threats of black African nations to withdraw convinced the International Olympic Committee to ban Rhodesia just prior to the opening of competition.

American Misfortune. For Americans the XX Olympiad was marred by bad luck and horrible memories. Only the swimmers performed according to expectations, and they were magnificent. The track-and-field competitions were a nightmare. In the men's 100-meter sprint, Eddie Hart was considered the only challenger to Soviet favorite Valery Borozov, though Hart's teammate Rey Robinson had equaled Hart's 9.9 seconds in the Olympic trials. Both Americans won their heats in the first round, which began at 11:09 A.M. on 31 August and advanced to the quarterfinals scheduled for 4:15 that afternoon. Their coach, though, had an eighteen-month old preliminary schedule that showed their heats beginning at 7 P.M. Hart, Robinson, and Robert Taylor, the other American qualifier, were strolling back to the Olympic stadium at 4:15 when they stopped by ABC headquarters and saw the heats they were scheduled for on a live-feed transmission. Taylor's heat was the last to be run, and ABC technicians got him to the track just in time to take the blocks. He finished second to Borzov but qualified for the next round. Taylor went on to take the silver medal; his teammates were disqualified. Hart ran the anchor for the 4 x 100-meter relay team that won the gold medal in world-record time. Other gold medals in track and field went to Vince Matthews in the 400 meters, Dave Wottle in the 800 meters, Frank Shorter in the marathon, and Rod Milburn in the 110-meter hurdles.

Spitz and the Swimming Team. The U.S. swimmers dominated the competition. The men's and the women's team won nine gold medals each and set a total of twelve world records. The star of the team was Mark Spitz. He won seven gold medals, in four individual and three team events, and he or his team set a world record to match each of the medals. The women swimmers set six world records in winning their nine gold medals, paced by Keena Rothhammer, Melissa Belote, and Karen Moe.

Foul Play. Outside the swimming pavilion the U.S. team had a rough time. The gymnasts were shut out of gold medal contention, as was the boxing team. When boxer Reggie Jones lost a decision against a thoroughly beaten-up Russian opponent, there was nearly a riot in the audience. In the heavyweight wrestling competition, 412-pound Chris Taylor wrestled his 231-pound Ukrainian opponent Aleksandr Medved to a draw but lost the

WHO'S RUDE?

Dwight Stones was the best high jumper in America during the 1970s but he was never at his best in Olympic competition. He was expected to take a gold medal in 1972 in Munich, but he could manage only a bronze. The Montreal games in 1976 were his last chance at the Olympic record books. But Stones let his tongue beat him.

The Canadians were sensitive about accommodations in Montreal, and with good cause. The various Olympic venues cost them $1.5 billion and revenues were not nearly high enough to cover the cost. When the games began, the roof on the stadium where track and field events were held was not finished, and if it rained, the field got wet. So when Stones, now a world record holder in the high jump, complained that his performance might be affected should it rain, matters were bad enough. But when he went on to accuse the French Canadians of rudeness in not planning better for his arrival, the Olympic hosts exploded. Stones was excoriated in local newspapers, and the mere mention of his name at the games was enough to cause booing and hissing. When nationalistic Americans took offense, there were even fistfights. Every time Stones took the field for competition, the unfinished Olympic stadium erupted with shouts of disapproval. Stones's appearance on the second day of the competition in an "I Love French Canadians" t-shirt did not help. Officials made him take it off, and when he had a Nike shirt underneath, they made him take that off too. Then it rained.

Stones finished fourth in the high jump, slogging through a wet approach to his jumps. The Canadians felt it was better than he deserved but good enough to claim cosmic retribution.

match when the referee deducted a point from Taylor for passivity. The Ukrainian won the gold medal; Taylor, who won all the rest of his matches, got a silver; and the referee was dismissed from the Olympics for his bad decision. The U.S. men's basketball team had won sixty-two straight games going into the finals against the Soviets. The game was apparently over, with the Americans ahead 50–49, when there was a dispute about the time. Three times the Soviets were given the ball for the final shot of the game, and after the second time, three seconds were added to the game clock. The Soviets scored, finally, and were awarded the game. The American team refused to accept their silver medals, and American coach

Hank Iba filed a formal protest. His pocket was picked while he was registering his complaint.

Tragedy. The defining moment of the 1972 Games occurred on the morning of 5 September when eight Arab terrorists broke into the Israeli compound, murdered two athletes, and kidnapped nine others. The Arabs, members of the terrorist organization Black September, demanded the release of two hundred Arab guerrillas held in Israeli prisons. After the terrorists had moved to a Munich airport, they were stormed by an Israeli antiterrorist team, and all nine of the hostages were killed along with five of the terrorists. Three of the Arabs were captured. It was later acknowledged that the rescue operation was approved by Golda Meir, premier of Israel; Willy Brandt, chancellor of West Germany; and Avery Brundage, president of the International Olympic Committee. The games were suspended for thirty-four hours, and a memorial was held for the slain athletes in the main stadium.

Medal Count. At the conclusion of the games the Soviet total of ninety-nine medals, including fifty gold, and the American team's second-place total of ninety-three medals, of which thirty-three were gold, seemed to have diminished significance.

THE OLYMPICS: 1976

Innsbruck. The 1976 Winter Olympics were held at Innsbruck, Austria, in the Tyrolean Alps, from 4 to 15 February. For Americans, all of the winning opportunities came on the ice. Figure skater Dorothy Hamill upset the reigning world champion Dianne de Leeuw to win the gold medal in figure skating. Her coach, Carlo Fassi, had the unusual distinction of also coaching the winner of the men's gold medal in figure skating, John Curry from Great Britain. Peter Mueller won the gold in the 1000-meter speed skating, and Sheila Young set an Olympic record in winning the gold in the 500 meters. Young, who also won a silver in the 1500 meters and a bronze in the 1000 meters accounted for nearly a third of the ten medals won by the United States team.

Boycotts. The Summer Olympics held in Montreal, Canada, began with the political controversy that had come to be identified with the games in the postwar period. This time the New Zealand team was the center of attention. New Zealand had sent a rugby team to play in South Africa, and the black African nations wanted that country banned from Olympic competition as a result. Tanzania led the black African protesters, and they were joined by Iraq and Guyana. Taiwan boycotted because the Canadians insisted that they not call themselves the Republic of China. By the time the games were declared in progress on 17 July, thirty-two nations had for some reason announced a boycott, leaving eighty-eight nations to compete with teams that included 4,834 men and 1,251 women.

Black September terrorist on the balcony of the Israeli living quarters on 5 September 1976

Costs. Security at the 1976 games was heavy. It was estimated that over $15,000 was spent on security for each of the visiting athletes, a total of about $100 million. The city of Montreal and the province of Quebec had to construct most of the facilities for the games. The total cost was some $1.5 billion, and the Canadians were left with a deficit of about $1 billion at the end of the games.

Disappointment. The U.S. team's overall performance was disappointing. Only two women won individual gold medals, Luann Ryon in archery and Jennifer Chandler in springboard diving. The U.S. women's swimming team won the 400-meter freestyle relay but no other gold medals, a stark contrast to the splendid showing in the 1972 games. U.S. men won only six gold medals in the track-and-field competition, but that included the decathlon win by Bruce Jenner, which was particularly satisfying. Edwin Moses in the 400-meter relay, Arnie Robinson in the long jump, and Mac Wilkins in the discus accounted for the other individual golds.

Gold. The Americans were buoyed by the outstanding

performance of the men's swimming team, which won twelve gold medals, plus the gold in the springboard diving competition. Backstroker John Nabor broke the world record twice on his way to a win in the 100-meter race, and in the 200 meters he set a world record again and was the first ever to break the two-minute barrier. He won two more gold medals in team relay events.

Boxing. The media stars on the American team were the boxers. Coming off a very disappointing performance in 1972, the American boxers felt they had something to prove. They were cocky and well-coached; moreover, they included the most talented class of amateurs in many years. By the end of the competition the Americans had won five of the eleven events, and they did so with unusual style. Eighteen-year-old Leo Randolph, who won unexpectedly in the flyweight division, called his victory the best thing that had happened to him since he became a Christian. Twenty-year-old Howard Davis vowed to win the gold for his mother, who died two days before the Olympic competition began; Davis disposed of two of his five opponents in first-round knockouts. Personable light welterweight Sugar Ray Leonard tucked a photo of his girlfriend and their two-year-old son in his sock before dancing his way to a series of popular one-sided wins. The Spinks brothers, Michael and Leon, cheered one another to middleweight and light heavyweight medals. The members of the 1976 boxing team dominated professional boxing during the 1980s.

Team Standings. The team competition ended as it usually did, with the Soviets winning most medals overall (125 total, 47 gold) and the United States second in total medals (94 total, 34 gold); the East Germans won 90 total medals and 40 gold. The Americans took considerable satisfaction in regaining the men's basketball championship but were denied the pleasure of beating the Soviets in the finals. The U.S. team beat the Yugoslavs 95–74.

PROFESSIONAL HOCKEY

Parity. As it had through much of the previous decade, the National Hockey League (NHL) during the 1970s suffered from shrinking attendance, yet the league continued its aggressive program of expansion begun in the late 1960s, when the NHL doubled in size from six teams to twelve. By 1975 the league had grown to eighteen teams, and NHL owners and officials were predicting even further expansion. As the game moved from the snowbelt to exotic places such as Los Angeles, Atlanta, and Kansas City, many sportswriters and longtime hockey fans feared that the quality of play would diminish. With each team added the talent became more thinly spread across the league. The magic word among NHL officials, however, was parity — a word soon echoed in other professional sports circles. The NHL looked forward to the day when each of its teams was a legitimate

Stanley Cup contender, and, hence, when each of its teams was a viable moneymaker.

WHA. At the beginning of the decade, however, the NHL's state of affairs appeared dismal to the league's numbers crunchers. Far from introducing parity to the NHL, the expansion clubs were whipping boys at the hands of the established clubs. Furthermore, the venerable league found itself faced off with a competing organization when in July 1971 two California entrepreneurs, Dennis Murphy and Gary Davidson, helped create the World Hockey Association (WHA). Murphy and Davidson had been involved in the American Basketball Association — the National Basketball Association's upstart rival — and were savvy sports promoters.

Signings. The WHA was soon signing NHL players willing to defect. In June 1972 the new league landed its first superstar when the Winnipeg Jets paid Bobby Hull a $1 million bonus to sign a ten-year contract worth $2.75 million. Hull's contract marked the beginning of bidding wars between the two leagues, and as players' salaries rose the financial hardships were more severely felt by many teams from both the NHL and WHA. Nevertheless, the WHA continued in its high-profile pursuit of big-name players. In 1973 the WHA's Houston Aeros signed forty-six-year-old hockey legend Gordie Howe and his two teenage sons, Mark and Marty, in what many disgruntled NHL fans dismissed as nothing more than a glitzy publicity stunt. The signings attracted the fans' attention, however, and the Aeros went on to win the WHL championship trophy, the Avco Cup (named for a finance company), twice.

Merger. As early as 1973 owners and officials representing the rival leagues had been holding secret meetings to discuss a merger. But a deal between the NHL and WHA was not reached until 1979, when the WHA agreed to discontinue operations. By that year the WHA had dwindled from a league high of fourteen teams in 1974–1975 — when fan interest in the new league was at its peak — to eight, and expatriated NHL players had begun to drift back to their former league in search of job security. For the 1979–1980 season the NHL expanded to twenty-one teams when it added four former WHA franchises: the Edmonton Oilers, the Hartford (formerly New England) Whalers, the Quebec Nordiques, and the Winnipeg Jets.

The Big Bad Bruins. During the early and mid 1960s, the Boston Bruins had been a basement team. At the beginning of the decade the Big Bad Bruins, as they were affectionately called by their fans, were residing at the top of the NHL standings and along with teams such as the New York Rangers represented a youth movement in hockey. The Bruins of the early and mid 1970s were indeed big and bad, as their rugged, blue-collar style of hockey emphasized hard checking punctuated by the whippy slap-shot attack of superstars Phil Esposito and

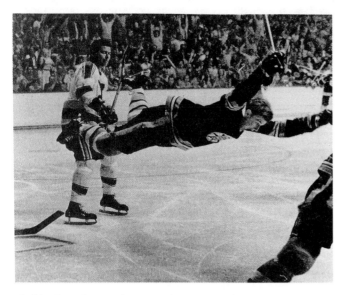

Bobby Orr after scoring the overtime goal that won the Stanley Cup for the Boston Bruins against the Saint Louis Blues

Bobby Orr, the brilliant defenseman whose aggressive style of play revolutionized his position.

Lunch Pail Gang. Bruins coach Harry Sinden was once told, "You don't have a team; you have a gang." Indeed, the Bruins during this period brought to mind baseball's Gas House Gang — the Saint Louis Cardinals of the 1930s — for their color, swagger, and talent. They won the Stanley Cup in 1970 and 1972 — and reached the finals in 1971 and 1974 — before one of hockey's most stunning trades ended the era of the Big Bad Bruins. In 1975 Esposito was sent to the New York Rangers in exchange for three younger players. At the beginning of the 1975–1976 season Orr had undergone knee surgery, and the great defenseman's career was suddenly in doubt. The Big Bad Bruins, however, were soon replaced by an equally colorful cast of characters, known as the Bruins' Lunch Pail Athletic Club. The Lunch Pail Gang reasserted the Bruins' blue-collar image and the organization's place among hockey's elite teams when Boston returned to the Stanley Cup finals in 1979.

The Broad Street Bullies. By the end of the 1972–1973 season the Philadelphia Flyers seemed to be emerging as the team that would turn the dreams of proexpansion NHL officials into reality. In their successful drive to become the first expansion team to win a Stanley Cup, however, the Flyers, alias the Broad Street Bullies, became the living nightmare of most NHLers, as the Bullies' bloody-knuckled style of hockey, based on Flyers coach Fred Shero's creed, "If you can't beat 'em in the alley, you can't beat 'em on the ice," terrorized the league. Former Buffalo and Vancouver defenseman Mike Robitaille once tried to sum up the feelings of dread shared by hockey players visiting the Spectrum, the Flyers' home ice located on Broad Street in South Philadelphia's dour industrial section: "Whenever I walked through that big, black door leading into the visiting locker room . . . I thought I was walking through the gates of hell."

Philadelphia Flu. Upon arriving in the City of Brotherly Love, key players on visiting teams were suddenly struck down with mysterious illnesses, which collectively and commonly became known as the Philadelphia Flu. The Bullies' list of exploits during the decade read like a motorcycle gang's rap sheet, as the team racked up penalty minutes for rowdiness on the ice and court appearances for creating mayhem off it; more than once Flyers charged into the stands to brawl with heckling fans. Out on the ice the Bullies were charged with an astounding 1,750 penalty minutes, a record 600 of which were earned by Bullies enforcer Dave ("The Hammer") Schultz. In a postgame interview Flyers defenseman Andre ("Moose") Dupont, with cigarette and beer in hand, summed up what had become a typical day at work for the Broad Street Bullies: "It was a good day for us. We didn't go to jail, we beat up their chicken forwards, we scored goals, and we won. Now, the Moose drinks beer."

Popularity. The Flyers' reign over the NHL with their 1974 and 1975 Stanley Cup victories was not solely the product of their thuggery. Flyers captain Bobby Clarke, a diabetic with a choirboy's face, was a prolific goal scorer, a brilliant passer of the puck, and one of the finest centers in the league. Rick MacLeish's breakaway speed was another potent offensive weapon, and Flyers goalie Bernie Parent was at the heart of one of the stingiest defenses in professional hockey. To many NHL insiders the Flyers' flawless execution of Shero's system was more intimidating than their back-checking and flailing fists. Yet to compete with the Broad Street Bullies many NHL teams felt that they had to adopt their questionable tactics. Furthermore, the fighting seemed to attract new fans to the sport, for there was little doubt that the Broad Street Bullies, although despised by opposing teams, sold seats. The role of the enforcer became a common part of hockey during the 1970s, and key opposing players became the targets of on-the-ice muggings. As a result players were facing off in the courtroom.

Bullying The Soviets. Among sportswriters and critics there seemed to be little doubt that the classic style of hockey, which emphasized speed and finesse, had been replaced by something more akin to professional wrestling. Nowhere was this better illustrated than in the 1976 exhibition game between the Flyers and the Soviet Red Army team. The Soviets were simply the greatest practitioners of the classic European style. But the Bullies, uninterested in the Soviets' speed and deft puck handling, simply beat them up and chased them off the ice. The Red Army coach only returned his team to the ice after officials threatened to withold payment from the Soviets.

A New Era. Just when many were writing off hockey as spectacle rather than sport, the Montreal Canadiens reemerged as the class act of the NHL. Lacking the size and brawn of the Broad Street Bullies, the Canadiens nevertheless went on a streak of four straight Stanley Cup wins, beginning in 1976. Montreal hockey emphasized speed and the brilliant offensive play of Guy Lafleur. Gradually, other NHL teams such as the New York Islanders were trading and drafting for speed rather than size. The return to the classical style of hockey was furthered by the 1979 merger of the two leagues and the introduction of former WHA scoring star Wayne Gretzky to the NHL. In 1978 at the age of seventeen, Gretzky had signed with the WHA Indianapolis Racers, and when the Racers organization went broke in the following year, his contract was purchased by the Edmonton Oilers. When the Oilers became an NHL team following the merger, many felt that the teenage phenomenon would prove too small to compete. In his first season he scored fifty-one goals and had eighty-six assists, and in so doing ushered in a new era for hockey.

Playful Muhammed Ali, adjusting the hairpiece of ABC announcer Howard Cosell during a 1972 broadcast

SPORTS AND TELEVISION

The "Big Daddy." The business of sports television boomed during the 1970s. At the beginning of the decade ABC, CBS, and NBC televised a combined 787 hours of sports yearly. By 1979 that figure had increased by 72 percent, as sports telecasting hours totaled 1,356. In the 1950s ABC had ranked a weak third among the three major televison networks; in the 1970s ABC achieved dominance that was largely due to the phenomenal viewer numbers generated by the network's glitzy sports coverage. *The New York Times* called television in the 1970s the "big daddy" of sports. Certainly during the decade big-daddy television paid out billions to professional and college sports in order to acquire broadcasting rights — and certainly made much more in return. That professional and big-time college athletics partly owed their continued survival to television had become clear. Yet it had also become clear by the late 1970s that the modern era of American sports had been in large part the creation of the broadcasting industry.

Arledge. In 1960 Roone Arledge, one of ABC's young and ambitious producers, sent to his superiors a remarkable memo outlining his vision of the future of televised sports. The game on the field, Arledge prophesied, would no longer be covered passively. Rather, the roving camera eye, cutting-edge production technology, and animated commentary would combine to add "human drama" to the game. Arledge proclaimed, "WE ARE GOING TO ADD SHOW BUSINESS TO SPORTS!" Soon after, Arledge created *Wide World of Sports* and fulfilled his own prophecy. Segments of *Wide World of Sports* opened with Jim McKay's voice promising that the show would deliver "The Thrill of Victory, The Agony of Defeat." Once-obscure sporting events, such as demolition derbies held in America's backwater towns during the 1960s and 1970s, were captured on videotape, edited, and spiced up with dubbed-over commentary to deliver the "human

drama" Arledge had promised. In 1970 Arledge brought his finely honed production skills to the NFL. *Monday Night Football* caused an immediate sensation, and it had become clear that sports as show business had made an indelible mark on American culture. By the mid 1970s ABC's rival networks had introduced their versions of *Wide World of Sports,* and the business of shaping games and their participants into the stuff of high drama — or, at the very least, entertaining spectacle — had forever altered how sports in the United States would be played — and watched.

Prime Time. By the end of the 1960s NFL czar Pete Rozelle had successfully presided over the merger of his league with the AFL, the annexing of Sunday-afternoon television, and the creation of the Super Bowl as the sport world's ultimate media event. Yet as the NFL entered a new decade Rozelle still had one dream unfulfilled: he longed for the day when professional football would become a part of prime-time television. He pitched his idea to executives at NBC and CBS. Although the two networks had begun to reap the financial rewards of covering professional football, their programmers gave sports a low priority, and the idea was not enthusiastically received. Rozelle next went to ABC, where he was able to attract the interest of sports-division head Arledge but not that of the network's key executives. Rozelle, however, soon threatened to sell his prime-time package to the Hughes Sports Network — which would feed its programming through ABC stations — and as a result ABC reluctantly launched *Monday Night Football* with a game featuring the New York Jets and the Cleveland Browns on 21 September 1970.

Curing the Monday-Night Blues. *Monday Night Football* gave Arledge the opportunity once again to put to work his production philosophy of sports as show business and, more important, to place his product in direct competition with the slick and glittery sitcoms, teledramas, and variety shows that filled prime-time programming slots. *Monday Night Football* promised state-of-the-art coverage. Twelve cameras were used to focus on individual player matchups, provide replay images of the action from different angles, capture sideline reactions, and pan the stands for local color. Just as important were the three commentators, former Cowboys quarterback Don Meredith, New York lawyer-turned-broadcaster Howard Cosell, and veteran announcer Keith Jackson. In the second year of *Monday Night Football* Jackson was replaced by former Giants star and experienced play-by-play man Frank Gifford.

The Meredith-Cosell-Gifford combination proved to be irresistible television. Cosell's long-winded and boorish manner — and grating delivery — were complemented by Dandy Don Meredith's good-ol'-boy commentary. Gifford provided the balance between his two colleagues as straight play-by-play man and soft-spoken sex symbol. It soon became clear to television researchers that *Monday Night Football* did have sex appeal, as the all-important female viewers tuned in in unexpected numbers. In its first season the show had captured nearly a third of the Monday-night audience. Restaurants, bars, and movie theaters experienced a significant decline in Monday-night business, as did prostitution, according to the nation's vice squads. *Monday Night Football* went on to become the third longest running prime-time series in television history, trailing only *Walt Disney* and *60 Minutes*.

"Trashsport." The huge success of *Wide World of Sports* and *Monday Night Football* convinced network heads of the immense entertainment value in sports programming. In 1972 ABC lost its NBA contract to CBS, and Arledge had to scramble to fill the vacant weekend time slots and the appetite of the American sports junkie. Synthetic sporting events, called "trashsports" by their critics, were created to meet the demand, and *The Superstars* was born. The idea for the show had originated with Dick Button, an Olympic figure-skating gold medalist who had dreamed up a format pitting participants from a variety of sports in order to establish who was the best all-around athlete. As such, 350-pound linebackers squared off against horse-racing jockeys in made-for-television events such as bicycling, rowing, tug-of-war, weightlifting, and negotiating an obstacle course.

Imitation. The instant success of *The Superstars* spawned *The Women Superstars* and *The World Superstars*. At CBS programming executives attempted to cash in on the widely watched 1973 battle of the sexes tennis match between Bobby Riggs and Billie Jean King by airing *The Challenge of the Sexes* and *Celebrity Challenge of the Sexes*. A highly successful prime-time venture, *Celebrity Challenge* featured teams composed of stars from the three major networks with color commentary by Howard Cosell. For one of its segments *Celebrity Challenge* drew a staggering 49 percent of the television audience — most of whom tuned in to watch Bill Cosby play tennis against

---

DUD STUD?

Secretariat was the greatest racehorse of all time. He set a record in the Kentucky Derby that was never broken, and he won the Belmont Stakes by 31 lengths. When "Super Red," as he was called, retired from racing in 1973, he was considered to have begun a period in which his real earning potential would be realized — as a stud. Mrs. Penney Tweedy, Secretariat's owner, formed a syndicate to invest in her horse's post-retirement fortune. Twenty-eight syndicate members paid $190,000 each — a total of over $6 million — to share in the profits from Secretariat's breeding. Then they watched anxiously as the great horse met his first mate.

It turned out that Secretariat took better to a fast track than to a fast mare. He was a reluctant suitor at first, and when he did manage to breed, there was an indication of some foreign matter in his semen. The Syndicate ordered the appropriate tests, and received the comforting answer. "Super Red" was OK; he simply needed a period of adjustment to his new role, after which he performed admirably.

---

television sex symbol Farrah Fawcett-Majors. The proliferation of trashsport continued up until the early 1980s, when even the most devoted couch potatoes had come to reject the various made-for-television sports formats. At the height of the 1970s synthetic-sports craze, ABC veteran broadcaster Kurt Gowdy wryly warned that by the way sports television was going, "we'll see Secretariat racing a Wyoming antelope."

ESPN. In 1979 only about 50 percent of the country had access to cable television. Nevertheless, in that year a cable company launched the Entertainment and Sports Programming Network (ESPN). Backed by the combined interest of the NCAA and Getty Oil and with one major advertiser, Anheuser-Busch, in its pocket, the all-sports channel began airing on 7 September. Initially, ESPN set out to televise those college sports that lacked coverage. During its first night on the air, ESPN offered three hours of slow-pitch softball and a taped college soccer match. In the following year ESPN expanded its telecast to twenty-four hours a day, seven days a week, and introduced America's sports junkies to Australian-rules football. By that time, it had become clear to media watchers that cable television was exploding and that ESPN telecasts would become competitive with the sports programming of the major commercial networks.

Tennis

The Open Era. The year 1968 signaled the beginning of a revolution for those athletes who sought to make a living playing a sport known for its snobbish appeal and starchy white-flannel image. In that year tennis's "open era" began, and professionals could compete with amateurs for the sport's most coveted titles. Tennis was free to enter the new decade unabashedly commercial, casting off its "shamateur" label earned during the previous era in which the game's spokesmen hypocritically held up tennis as pure amateur sport while paying off players under the table.

The "In" Sport. During the 1970s the tennis revolution took to the streets, as tennis became the "in" sport in the United States and certainly the nation's growth sport. The country's middle class embraced tennis as theirs and spent millions on equipment and clothing. By the end of the decade it was estimated that more than a quarter of the country's population — and a nearly equal number of blacks and whites — played tennis at least four times a year; approximately 160,000 tennis courts had been built, with an extraordinary 5,000 more expected for each coming year. In 1978 the nation's premier tennis tournament, the U.S. Open, was moved from tony, exclusive Forest Hills to a public park, the recently built National Tennis Center in Flushing Meadows, Queens, New York. The change of venues ordered by United States Tennis Association (USTA) president and oil millionaire W. E. "Slew" Hester reflected what professional tennis in America had become: glitzy, fast-paced, big-money entertainment with mass appeal.

An American Revolution. In less than ten years the U.S. Open had moved from the patrician grass and clay surfaces of Forest Hills to hard courts — like the asphalt surface played on by the vast majority of the American public and the surface with which the rest of the world had come to associate tennis in the United States. While in other parts of the world the game continued to stand still — and Wimbledon, tennis's "lawn court championship," with its insistence on all-white shirts, shorts, and balls, remained the game's monument to tradition — tennis in the United States was a whirlwind of social and technological change. Television-friendly yellow balls replaced white ones; splashy pastels became a part of tennis fashion; metal and graphite replaced wood in rackets built to be stronger, larger, and more powerful; and tournament prize money for the winners jumped from the thousands to the hundreds of thousands of dollars.

Renee Richards. During the decade the sport also rebelled against its socially conservative image. Professional women tennis players such as Billie Jean King were at the forefront of the women's lib movement as they worked to establish their own organizations and circuits — and fought for and won increased prize purses. Tennis also found itself embroiled in gender-bending experimentation and controversy when in 1976 the for-

mer Dr. Richard Raskind, an ophthalmologist and one-time captain of Yale's tennis team, entered the women's professional tennis circuit as Dr. Renee Richards, professional sports' first transsexual. Fearing that Richards might possess an unfair advantage in strength, endurance, and speed — fears that proved to be unfounded — many women players opposed her acceptance on the circuit. She was denied entrance to the 1976 U.S. Open. But she was admitted in 1977 after having successfully sued for entry in a highly publicized court case.

Circuits. In the first years of the so-called open era, competition among pro tennis organizations greatly contributed to the increase in the number of events and stunning growth in prize money. Implementation by the International Tennis Federation (ITF) of a points system, the Grand Prix, in 1970 created a method for establishing the world's best player, heightening the drama of tour events and thereby attracting new fans to the tournament gates. World Championship Tennis (WCT), a professional tour bankrolled by Texas oilman Lamar Hunt, had by 1970 successfully contracted many of the big-name players. The WCT announced for 1971 a "million-dollar" circuit leading to a nationally televised final played in Dallas and worth $50,000 to the winner. As a result more American stars such as Arthur Ashe hopped onto the WCT bandwagon, lured by the tour's promise of guaranteed big money. To keep players from defecting, the ITF began increasing the prize money at its events; players became the objects of hot bidding wars. But the high profile enjoyed by tennis, the steady increase in purses, and the phenomenal growth in number of fans and active participants in the sport during the 1970s were mostly due to television.

Laver and Rosewall. Two televised matches in the early 1970s were largely responsible for the tennis boom in the United States — and for tennis's transformation into a major American spectator sport. In 1972 two of

Jimmy Connors and his fiancée Chris Evert, winners of singles titles at Wimbledon in 1974

tennis's most dominant players, Aussies Rod Laver and Ken Rosewall, met in Dallas for the WCT Championship finals. The match was played late on a Mother's Day afternoon and was televised nationally by CBS. As the two players traded sets and sweated out superbly played points, the match entered the dinner hour and the size of its television audience had swelled to nearly 52 million. The network preempted its regular evening shows in order to stick with the three-hour-and-forty-five-minute tennis marathon; and Americans and their families, many of whom had never so much as touched a tennis racket, sat glued to their televisions as the match entered the decisive, fifth-set tiebreaker. Rosewall, then in the last years of his brilliant career, upset the exhausted Laver, and the next day millions of Americans flocked to sporting-goods stores to purchase their first rackets.

Connors and Evert. King might have brought to the sport a women's libber's edge and sense of social import, but Jimmy Connors and Chris Evert, the decade's king and queen of American tennis, brought youth, brash attitude, and even a little romance. Engaged to be married, Connors and Evert each became Wimbledon singles champions in 1974. By the fall of that year the couple had broken up, but the love affair each had begun with fans furthered the American tennis boom — and sustained America's newly found prominence in a sport that had been dominated by the Aussies. Unlike his former fiancée, Connors was subject to temper tantrums on the court. His relations with fellow players was often chilly, and his boycott of the Davis Cup did not make him the darling of the U.S. tennis establishment. But his fiery brand of competition endeared him to many. He was a new breed of player whose two-handed backhand, metal racket, and bold and arrogant attitude constantly challenged tennis convention. Evert also was breaking new ground. In 1976, in only her third season on the tour, she became the first woman to earn $1 million in prize money. She simply dominated the tour, winning twelve

of seventeen tournaments in 1976, including Wimbledon. Her stoic demeanor, intense look of concentration, and baseline style punctuated by her two-handed backhand were emulated by high-school players. Her presence in women's tennis was responsible for the cultivation of future champions, most notably Tracy Austin. In 1977, at the age of fourteen, Austin reached the U.S. Open quarterfinals; in 1979 she beat Evert in straight sets to win the tournament.

Fortune. At decade's end many — such as Neil Amdur in his January 1979 *World Tennis* article, "Has the Tennis Boom Lost its Bloom?" — were wondering if American interest in the sport had peaked. Tournament attendance figures and the numbers of Americans taking up the sport continued to remain high, but recreational interest in sports such as racquetball seemed to be greater. Furthermore, many feared that the glut of tennis programming on television was overkill, as the same matches were often shown repeatedly. Connors and his American successor John McEnroe were also displaying an ugly side to competitive tennis, and temper tantrums were becoming more frequent at junior tennis events as well. Critics such as former great Jack Kramer warned that the sport was becoming too fast-paced, too rich, and consequently too obnoxious for even the most spectacle-loving American sports fans to stomach. At the end of decade Kramer was sounding a warning: "The game is headed for a great depression unless we solve the problems."

VIOLENCE AND COMPETITION

An American Mirror. Sports in the United States has always served to reflect the best and worst the culture has to offer. The big-money wheeling and dealing of professional sports and the increased professionalization of amateur athletics since the end of World War II were, after all, reflective of an American society that was maturing in its new role as a political and economic world power. During the 1970s, however, the image of Americans mirrored by their participation in and obsession with sports was far from pretty — indeed, had never before been more disturbing. The frightening rise of violence at all levels of American sport during the decade seemed to be not only tolerated but also embraced.

Institutionalized Violence. The country's failed military intervention in Vietnam; domestic social ills, such as the decay of America's cities and the sharp increase in crime; and a loss of faith in the American government brought on by the Watergate scandal contributed to an atmosphere of cynicism. American institutions of business, family, and government were being questioned and attacked — and in the institution of American sport, in the way in which Americans played and competed, could be seen the ugliness of the social transformation. Fan violence poured out of the stands and onto the field. In major professional sports the acceptance of the "enforcer" — or designated thug — by athletes, fans, and sportswriters meant the birth and celebration of the sports antihero: the guy willing to break the game's rules and codes of behavior in order to win. By the mid 1970s many social critics and those sports fans horrified by the spectacle of institutionalized violence began questioning the value of "anything-goes" competition to a healthy American culture.

Bullies. By 1974 professional hockey's Philadelphia Flyers and the image of their Broad Street Bullies dominated the sport, and key Bullies enforcer Dave ("the Hammer") Schultz — a defenseman with little skating or stick-handling ability who possessed a devastating uppercut — had a cult following among hockey fans. To catch up with the pugilistic Flyers and an emerging trend in hockey, other once-lousy teams such as the Pittsburgh Penguins made desperate trades late in the 1973–1974 season to replace players who had speed and finesse with intimidators and brawlers. Star scorers soon became the frequent victims of unprovoked attacks by the enforcers, who were usually much larger. Hockey commissioner Clarence Campbell publicly decried the violence and the disturbing new "era of brawling. . . and intimidation" that the Flyers had inaugurated. Privately, however, Campbell recognized the encouraging economics of Broad Street Bullies hockey, as the Flyers were not only Philly's hottest ticket but had also become a boon to box-office sales when on the road. "What really bothers Campbell," *Sports Illustrated* reported in its 3 June 1974 issue, "is the game-delaying sweater pulling and the like . . . 'I'm not concerned when two guys fight,' Campbell says. 'I'm only concerned when they won't *stop* fighting.' "

Brawl Game. Baseball, the country's other major non-contact sport, had had its share of bench-clearing brawls during its history, and intimidation had certainly always been a significant part of the game as pitchers were taught to throw the high-and-inside fastball to shake a batter's confidence. By middecade, however, baseball reporters were taking note of an alarmingly violent trend taking place in the bleachers. Baseball fans bore a close resemblance to Europe's soccer hooligans as one rowdy bleacher incident after another was reported. Ten-cent-beer night on 4 June 1974 in Cleveland's Stadium turned into a riot when rowdy fans jumped onto the outfield and assaulted Texas Ranger right fielder Jeff Burroughs. Many other incidents in which ballplayers on the field were being physically attacked by the fans made it clear that professional athletes were no longer held in the same regard that they once were by fans. Just as the 1970s were a time during which professional sports entered into its modern era, so too was it a time when fans came to judge athletes as big-money businessmen with more loyalty to the dollar than to a team or town. The 1974 article in *Sports Illustrated* "Take Me Out to the Brawl Game" summed up the dilemma of fan cynicism and the violence it bred: "The ball park was once a place to escape the pressures and violence of life outside. Now, it seems, there is no escape."

THE RULES OF THE KNIFE FIGHT

Two incidents in the violent domain of professional sports during the 1970s proved too brutal even for bloodthirsty fans. Kermit Washington of the Los Angeles Lakers had a reputation to maintain after he was featured in the October 1977 *Sports Illustrated* article "The Enforcers," which noted his intimidating style of play. On 9 December in a game between the Lakers and the Houston Rockets, a fight broke out, with Washington in the middle of the melee. When mild-mannered Houston team captain Rudy Tomjonovich rushed in to break it up, he was met with a right hand that would have done a heavyweight boxing champion proud. Tomjonovich's injury, his subsequent lawsuit against Washington stated, included fractures of the nose, jaw, and skull; facial lacerations and a brain concussion; loss of blood and leakage of spinal fluid from the brain cavity. His injuries required surgery, and Tomjonovich was unable to play the rest of the season. Washington explained that the blow "was an honest, unfortunate mistake." Nonetheless, the league suspended him for sixty days and fined him $10,000 (twice the fine it had levied the week before against Kareem Abdul-Jabbar, who broke his hand hitting Milwaukee Bucks center Kent Benson).

Defensive back Jack Tatum of the NFL Oakland Raiders was named to the 1976 list of the ten meanest players in football. In a game with the New England Patriots he proved his claim to the honor. On 12 August 1978 Oakland was being embarrassed by the play of twenty-six-year-old wide receiver Darryl Stingley. He had caught two successive passes for forty yards, and the Patriots were threatening to score. On the last play of his career, Stingley ran a crossing route in which he went straight down the field and then cut across the middle. As the pass was delivered to him at Oakland's twelve-yard line and Stingley was concentrating on the ball, Tatum rushed in from the blind side and delivered a blow that brought Oakland fans to their feet with appreciation. Stingley hit the ground and stayed there, the fourth and fifth vertebrae in his neck fractured and his spinal cord damaged. He was permanently paralyzed—with a brutal tackle that was legal, by the rules of football. "You hate to see anybody get hurt," Tatum explained, "but I was just doing my job."

Source: Robert C. Yeager, *Seasons of Shame: The New Violence in Sports* (New York: McGraw-Hill, 1979).

Dave ("Hammer") Schultz, pinned to the wall

Assessments. In 1970 self-described "Super Hippie" Dave Smith held what he called the World's Peace Pentathlon — swimming, parachuting, running, skydiving, and trail-biking — in order to make "a six-hour statement on the absurdity of competition." At the end of the decade books such as Robert C. Yeager's *Seasons of Shame: The New Violence in Sports* (1979) and Don Atyeo's *Blood & Guts: Violence in Sports* (1979) were attacking the attitudes among athletes and coaches and the blood lust among fans that seemed to stem from misguided notions of competition. The controversy over the role filled by competitive sports in American society had been partly fueled by President Gerald Ford's 1974 article, "In Defense of the Competitive Urge," which ran in *Sports Illustrated*. Asserting that the "competitive urge is deep-rooted in the American character," Ford questioned the intestinal fortitude of the new generation of Americans — those who would question the value of competition — and wondered if they were merely "adjusting to the times" or if they had been "spoiled by them." Further arguing that "There is much to be said for Ping-Pong diplomacy," Ford summarized the importance of competitive sports to the well-being of an entire nation: "a sports triumph can be as uplifting to a nation's spirit as, well, a battlefield victory."

HEADLINE MAKERS

MUHAMMAD ALI

1942-

HEAVYWEIGHT CHAMPION BOXER

The Greatest. Muhammad Ali called himself "the Greatest." While sports historians may argue whether he was a greater boxer than Joe Louis, Rocky Marciano, or Jack Dempsey, none could dispute that he was the most publicized sports personality of the 1970s and, indeed, of the century. In the six-year period beginning September 1970 Ali won more than $26 million in fight purses, and he fought all comers at the remarkable rate for a heavyweight of four to six times a year; he met twenty-two opponents in those six years. But Ali's fame did not stem only from his boxing prowess. The ring was simply his stage. Ali was a celebrity because he was the most articulate and attractive black man of his time who could demand the world's attention, and he took that opportunity to address issues more profound than who was the best boxer of the era. He was a role model for his race; he was a paragon of athletic prowess; he was a man of unshakable principle; he was a martyr to a cause who was defeated and rose up again to triumph over his enemies; and he was a talented entertainer whose attractiveness could not be suppressed.

The "Louisville Lip." Eighteen-year-old Muhammad Ali, named Cassius Clay then, won the gold medal in the light heavyweight division of boxing at the 1960 Olympics in Rome and promptly turned pro. He was known as the "Louisville Lip" for his brash prefight predictions, and he was ridiculed for his arrogance. Reporters smirked at his confident braggadocio, and Clay fed them stories by predicting — in rhyme — the rounds in which he would knock out his opponents. Between 29 October 1960, when he won a six-round decision over Tunney Hunsacker, and 18 June 1963, when he fought his last tune-up fight before taking on fearsome champion Sonny Liston, Clay fought nineteen times, winning every match, sixteen by knockout. Clay was thought too young and too light to beat champion Sonny Liston; fight reporters even speculated about his sanity before the fight because of his near-hysterical bravado. But at fight time Clay quit talking and soundly outboxed the champion before knocking him out in the seventh round.

Champion. Then, as if to prove he had taken leave of his senses, the new champion seemed to throw away a lucrative career by announcing that he was forsaking his slave name Cassius Clay for the Muslim name Muhammad Ali. He took a Muslim bride and prepared for a rematch against Liston. This time Liston fell in one, and Ali assumed the air of invincibility. He announced his opposition to the draft and declared that he would not serve in the military if called, meanwhile defending his title nine times (seven by knockout). In April 1967, when antiwar protests were at their peak and the U.S. government could no longer abide a heavyweight champion who claimed to be a conscientious objector, Ali was challenged on his beliefs. He refused induction into the armed services and was charged with draft evasion. His license to box — and thus his livelihood — was taken from him. He was stripped of his title.

Defeat. In September 1970 the U.S. Supreme Court ruled that the lower court had denied Ali's exemption on faulty grounds, and he was exonerated. His license to box was restored, and the former champion, now a rusty twenty-eight, began another campaign for the heavyweight title. He knocked out highly regarded Jerry Quarry in three and the big Oscar Bonavena in fifteen before taking on Joe Frazier for the championship. The fight was considered one of the best in modern times, worthy of its record purse — both fighters were guaranteed $2.5 million. Ali was slighly behind on points when Frazier hit him with a devastating left hook in the fifteenth round and knocked Ali to the canvas. He got up, but the fight was lost — Ali's first defeat in the ring.

Norton and Frazier. Ali was back in the ring again in four months, and he fought six times in 1972, knocking out the best opponents available to him and preaching the word of Elijah Muhammad, his spiritual leader, in between. He lost again to Ken Norton in 1973 in a remarkably courageous bout. Ali's jaw was broken in the second round when he was hit with his mouth open, taunting his opponent; yet, Ali fought ten more rounds to a split-decision loss. He beat Norton in a rematch and then in January 1974 took on Frazier again, winning a twelve-round decision against the former champion, who had just lost his title to knockout artist George Foreman. Now Ali, considered past his prime at thirty-three, had won the right to fight Foreman for the championship and become the second man ever to regain the title.

"The Fight." Observers feared for Ali's safety on 30 October 1974 against the hard-hitting Foreman, especially when he adopted the strategy of letting Foreman punch himself out. But Ali's trainer, the sage Angelo Dundee, had loosened the ropes so his fighter could rock back against them to absorb Foreman's blows. By the eighth round, the exhausted Foreman had thrown every punch he had. Ali danced to the offensive and knocked the champion out. The new champ had made history in a contest that was thereafter referred to simply as "The Fight," and he had at least one great fight left in him.

"The Thrilla in Manila." On 30 September 1975 Ali and Frazier met again in Manila. Ali prevailed in the early rounds, Frazier in the middle, then Ali took control again. At the beginning of the fifteenth round Frazier was too exhausted to answer the bell. Ali retained the championship. He had by that time earned over $31 million in the ring.

Coda. Ali said that boxing would die when he retired because no one could fill his shoes. He brought more than pugilistic ability to his sport; he infused boxing with spirit and character and purpose. He was a true world champion, because he embodied qualities that inspired universal admiration. He fought on for another decade, losing and then regaining the title again, but fans understood that he was playing out the coda to a heroic career.

Source:
Muhammad Ali, *The Greatest: My Own Story* (New York: Random House, 1975).

JAMES F. FIXX
1932-1984
POPULARIZER OF RUNNING

A Best-seller. James F. Fixx was a soft, self-indulgent, 220-pound magazine editor in 1969 when he received the call to exercise. He found that his "roly-poly" tennis game suffered because he had trouble getting to the net, so he took up running to improve his conditioning. That decision changed his life. Fixx fell victim to the obsession with conditioning that only runners can understand. He responded with the dedication of an athlete and the perception of a journalist. The result was the bible of runners in

the late 1970s, *The Complete Book of Running*. It sold 993,000 copies in hardback and topped *The New York Times* nonfiction best-seller list for eleven weeks in 1978.

A Runner's Passion. Fixx's father suffered his first heart attack at thirty-six and died at forty-three. The author was aware of the genetic character of heart disease and the positive cardiovascular effects of aerobic exercise, but his passion for running had no single cause. Running provided what he described as an array of benefits, from weight control to an improved sex life. He was convincing enough to reassure, if not convince, a generation of joggers that they were on the right track. By the end of the 1970s one hundred thousand Americans were finishing marathons each year, and it was estimated that nine million people ran at least one hundred days a year. Fixx deserved some of the credit.

As He Liked It. Fixx himself progressed from an end-of-the-pack finisher in the Greenwich, Connecticut, Memorial Day five-mile run to an eight-time Boston Marathoner whose best time was three hours, sixteen minutes. He lost seventy pounds during the 1970s and gave up smoking. But he was unable to overcome his father's genes. In 1984, after having ignored chest pains for some weeks, Fixx fell dead of a heart attack near the end of a training run. Confirmed slugabouts cited his death as ironic proof that the claims of jogging's health benefits were wildly exaggerated, but runners knew that not only had Fixx improved and extended his life, he died as he would have preferred.

Legacy. In 1994 *Sports Illustrated* named Fixx one of the most influential sports figures of the past forty years, declaring "He gave us back our bodies — to improve, to enjoy, to fret over."

Sources:
"James Fixx, Running, Forty for the Ages," *Sports Illustrated* (19 September 1994): 30;

Anna Quindlen, "A Successful Writer on the Right Track," *New York Times*, 4 January 1978.

BILLIE JEAN KING
1943-
CHAMPION OF WOMEN'S TENNIS

Billie Jean King transformed women's tennis into a professional sport. When she won her first Wimbledon singles title in 1966, the prize was a gift certificate for clothes. King's response was to begin a campaign, along with leading men's tennis players, to demand prize money at all U.S. Lawn Tennis Association tournaments. Five years later she was the first woman to earn $100,000 in a year as a professional tennis player. Rod Laver, the leading money winner on the men's tour, won $290,000 that year, suggesting the next inequity King challenged.

In 1972 she complained loudly when she received only $10,000 for winning the U.S. Open, while male champion Ilie Nastase received $25,000. The women deserved parity, she argued, and they got it. Margaret Court won the U.S. Open in the first year of parity, as least partly because King was exhausted by September, when the tournament took place.

King had just experienced what may have been the most publicized event in American tennis history — a challenge match against self-described male chauvinist pig Bobby Riggs. The match was pure made-for-television promotion — $100,000, winner-take-all. Riggs arrived courtside wearing a crown — he was king of the pigs — and waving an oversized model of a Sugar Daddy candy stick. King was carried in by male porters. He gave her roses, and she accepted with good humor. The tennis stunk. Riggs had had some tour experience, but he was, as he admitted, over-the-hill at age fifty-five. He lost in three straight sets, and she won the goodwill of the American public, over forty million of whom had watched the match on television.

In 1973 King was instrumental in forming the Women's Tennis Association (WTA), a union established to lobby for women's rights on the professional tour. It was a time of strong women players, Chris Evert chief among them. Evert helped improve the marketability of women's tennis in America, and King saw to it that the opportunity was exploited. The Virginia Slims Championship was the first all-women tournament, and the prize money was sufficient to attract the best. King and her husband founded the magazine *womenSport* to redress inadequate attention paid to women's athletics in the major sports journals, and they used their magazine to lobby for changes in sports rules.

As the 1970s wore on, King gradually made the transition from athlete to sports diplomat. She was still ranked by the WTA in 1981, and she managed to progress to the semifinals at Wimbledon that year, but it was the end of her playing days. She had won thirty-nine Grand Slam titles — including the singles, doubles, and mixed doubles at Wimbledon in 1973 — and her athletic record was unmatched. She turned to work as a coach, an organizer, and an inspiration to young athletes. A highly publicized lesbian palimony suit in 1981 threatened her reputation briefly, but King's candid confrontation of the issue turned a character assault into another victory, as she not only won in court but also preserved her integrity amid the publicity squall.

In 1994 *Sports Illustrated* ranked Billie Jean King fifth among the most important sports figures of the preceding forty years. "Not only is she among the greatest women tennis players ever, she is credited with furthering the cause of all female athletes and making tennis more popular," the citation stated.

Source:
Billie Jean King with Frank Deford, *Billie Jean* (New York: Viking, 1982).

JACK NICKLAUS

1940-

PROFESSIONAL GOLFER

Player of the Century. For most of the past thirty years Jack Nicklaus has been considered golf's greatest. His longevity has proved equal to Arnold Palmer's, and only Ben Hogan and Bobby Jones can be considered players in Nicklaus's league. But in numbers of major tournaments won, Nicklaus stands alone with twenty victories — a remarkable figure that does not include major titles won on the Senior Tour. He has won seventy times on the PGA Tour and has fifty-eight second-place and thirty-six third-place finishes. Nicklaus has finished top PGA Tour money winner and held the tour's low-scoring average eight times. He was named the PGA's Player of the Year in 1967, 1972, 1973, 1975, and 1976, and *Golf* magazine in 1988 celebrated American golf's centennial by naming Nicklaus the "Player of the Century."

Upstart. Nicklaus began playing golf at the age of ten in his hometown of Columbus, Ohio. He shot a fifty-one for the first nine holes he ever played. At the age of thirteen he broke seventy and held a three handicap. By then his hero had become the great Jones, who won the 1926 U.S. Open at Nicklaus's home course, the Scioto Country Club. Tutored by club pro Jack Grout, Nicklaus early on realized his potential for tournament play, dominating local and national junior golf events and going on to capture two U.S. Amateur Championships (1959 and 1961). Indeed, by the time he turned pro in November 1961 he had established himself as the country's greatest amateur golfer while simultaneously giving the professionals a scare as runner-up to Arnold Palmer by only two strokes in the 1960 U.S. Open and as a fourth-place finisher in the 1961 U.S. Open.

Intensity. In 1962, at the Oakmont Country Club outside of Pittsburgh, Nicklaus beat Arnold Palmer in a play-off to win the U.S. Open. Palmer's millions of die-hard fans — and the huge throng of gallery members, called Arnie's Army, that followed their hero from tee to green — were crushed by their hero's loss, and the Nicklaus victory went down as one of the most unpopular the world of golf had ever known. The two men could not have been more different in appearance and temperament. Palmer was a handsome, dashing figure whose powerful, lunging swing often knocked his ball into troublesome spots well off the fairway. Nicklaus was round-faced and pudgy — his girth and blond hair giving rise to his nickname, the Golden Bear — and his well-oiled, smoothly tempoed swing rarely failed him. Palmer wore his emotions on his sleeve, often grimacing and chain-smoking his way through a particularly tough round. Nicklaus was often expressionless on the course, and although he also smoked — at one time as much as two packs a day — he never lit up on the golf course. In explaining his ability to abstain from a nerve-soothing addiction while playing a nerve-racking game, Nicklaus simply stated, "I don't think about it." Nicklaus's mind, even more than his great natural talent and long-ball swing, was the key to his phenomenal success. He rarely made a poor tactical decision in a tournament; he had an unflappable ego, never second-guessing himself — and his powers of concentration were intense.

Masters Tournaments. In 1963 Nicklaus won the Masters and the PGA. He ran away with the 1965 Masters, winning by nine strokes in what Jones called "the greatest performance in golf history." Nicklaus shattered Hogan's seemingly insurmountable Masters record of 274 by three strokes. Nicklaus successfully defended his Masters title the following year and won his first British Open, becoming one of only four golfers to win all four majors (the others are Gene Sarazen, Hogan, and Gary Player). At the 1967 U.S. Open Nicklaus pulled away from Palmer in the final round to win by four strokes, signaling to even the most obstinate among Arnie's Army that the Golden Bear had forever robbed the king of his throne.

The New Bear. The beginning of the new decade saw a leaner, more fashionable Bear. Nicklaus dropped weight and let his golden hair grow prior to the 1970 season. He adopted more colorful golf course attire, adding color and flair to an image that had suffered from fat jokes and the general perception that Nicklaus was boring and mechanical. When it came to winning consistently, however, Nicklaus was every bit a machine. Between 1970 and 1975 he won seven more majors — the only victories "that count," he liked to say. His 1973 PGA title put him one ahead of Jones's thirteen major victories, and his 1975 Masters was his fifth win in Augusta, Georgia, and was proclaimed by observers and sportswriters to have been one of the most thrilling golf victories of all time. On Augusta's sixteenth hole the last day of the tournament, Nicklaus sank a forty-foot putt to take a one-stroke lead and held on the last two holes — winning by one over Tom Weiskopf and two over Johnny Miller.

Idol. In 1977 Nicklaus was involved in a thrilling duel with Tom Watson, America's new star, at the British Open. He lost what sportswriters later called the "Duel in the Sun" but returned in 1978 to claim the British title as his. With the emergence of players such as Watson, however, Nicklaus's victories seemed less easy to come by with each passing year, and by the end of the decade, many in the golfing world believed that Nicklaus's dominance — at least when it came to the majors — had

ended. In 1979 Nicklaus had his worst season to date, having gone winless and finishing seventy-first on the money list. His length off the tee and the long flight and high trajectory of his iron shots had once given him a huge advantage over the rest of the field — and had revolutionized the game. But there was a new generation of golfers who hit the ball as high and as far as their idol could. Nicklaus decided to go back to the drawing board, looking to improve his biggest weakness — the short game — and turn it into a strength. In 1980 he returned to top form, winning the U.S. Open and PGA. He continued to rack up significant wins on the PGA Tour during the 1980s, and at the 1986 Masters he scored perhaps golf's most emotion-stirring victory. He had by then become the game's elder statesman and had gone from being golf's villain — the fat kid who beat Arnie — to being one of the most popular athletes the world of sports had ever known.

CATHY RIGBY

1952-

AMERICAN GYMNAST

Cameo. Cathy Rigby was designated America's finest gymnast and a contender for a gold medal at the 1972 Olympic Games by the media. She was pretty, pixie-ish, talented, and hard working; just as important, she was good copy. Born with collapsed lungs, a chronic sufferer of bronchitis and pneumonia when she was a child, Rigby overcame her physical disabilities with pure grit. She began gymnastics at the age of eleven after she impressed her father with her skills on a trampoline and worked hard to be the best gymnast in the United States.

Olympian. In 1963 Mr. Rigby took his daughter to coach Bud Marquette, whose Southern California Acro Team (SCAT) is considered one of the finest gymnastics teams in the nation. "In two months, she was better than girls who had been training for two years," Marquette recalled. "She never fooled around." By 1968 she was performing at the Olympic level, but only by American standards. At the 1968 Olympics in Mexico City, the United States team finished sixth, and Rigby led the team, finishing sixteenth overall. "In 1968 it was all fun and games," Rigby commented. When she returned home, she got down to work.

A Silver Medal. In the four years after the 1968 Games, Rigby trained eight hours a day, seven days a week. In 1970 she was the first American woman ever the win a medal in international gymnastics competition when she took the silver at the World Games in Ljubljana, Yugoslavia. Four feet, eleven inches tall and weighing in at between eighty-nine and ninety-three pounds, the attractive Rigby was pleasant to watch as she bounced energetically through her routines. She became a media favorite as publicity for the 1972 Olympic Games in Munich mounted.

Setback. In the Olympic trials, Rigby fell during her dismount from the high bar. Her spotter was able to break her fall, but the judges were obligated to make major deductions from her score. The next day during her floor exercise routine, she twisted her ankle while landing after a flip and had to withdraw from competition with one day remaining. Roxanne Pierce won the trials, two-time Olympian Linda Metheny was second, and Kim Chace was third; Rigby was not among the first six. But the Olympic Gymnastics Committee felt she deserved a place on the team and they exercised their prerogative to elect her.

1972 Games. In Munich, Rigby led the women's gymnastic team to a fourth-place finish in the all-around competition, and she herself placed tenth in the overall standings, which was dominated by Soviet star Olga Korbut. Rigby returned home the most celebrated tenth-place finisher on the entire American team and retired from competition. She was frequently seen on television endorsing products or providing color commentary for gymnastic events. She married and tried to overcome the effects of ten years of grueling training. Her weight had been critical to her performance, and she developed bulimia, which she overcame and spoke publicly about in an effort to help other sufferers.

Peter Pan. In 1974, faced with pressure to return to training for the 1976 Olympics, she embarked instead on a theatrical career, adapting her acrobatic talent to the stage in the role of Peter Pan, which she played for six years. "Flying is such a joy," she explained. "You just want to hoot."

Sources:

Mark Goodman, "Cathy Rigby, Flying High," *People* (6 May 1991): 107;

Anita Verschoth, "Sugar and Spice—and Iron," *Sports Illustrated* (21 August 1972): 23–27.

O. J. SIMPSON

1947-

RUNNING BACK, BUFFALO BILLS

The Best. Weeb Ewbank, one of pro football's greatest head coaches, once said of Orenthal James Simpson, "The problem isn't to tackle O. J., it's to catch him." As the most dominant running back of the 1970s, O. J. Simpson combined the strength and durability of Jim Brown and the phenomenal cutting ability of Gale Sayers in forging a new style of running that would be emulated by the next generation of football players. His extraordinary peripheral vision allowed him to seek out and pick holes in the defensive line quickly, as well as to avoid tacklers. He cut and stutter-stepped his way through defenses, then relied on bursts of speed to outrace pursuers. In this way Simpson turned losses into four-yard gains — and the four-yarder into the occasional forty-yard breakaway dash. Of his elusive style Simpson once said, "I run like a coward." To many, however, "the Juice" was an American hero, a charismatic team player who generously shared the credit for his rushing success with his offensive line, "the Electric Company," and in so doing symbolized the best in professional sports.

Rags to Riches. Part of Simpson's appeal with sports fans was his rags-to-riches story. He was born 7 July 1947 to James and Eunice Simpson and was raised in Potrero Hill, then a predominantly black housing project neighborhood in San Francisco, California. By the time he had turned five years old, his parents had separated, and he was being raised mostly by his mother. Simpson attended Galileo High School in San Francisco's North Beach section and went out for the football, baseball, and track teams. He soon gave up track and field to concentrate on football, having made the varsity team in his sophomore year. Simpson displayed talent on the field, but off it he struggled with poor grades and often exhibited less-than-stellar behavior. Once after spending a night in custody at the Youth Guidance Center, Simpson was introduced to Willie Mays, the star outfielder for the San Francisco Giants who often volunteered his services to youth projects. Later describing the visit with Mays as a turning point in his life, Simpson was taken to his hero's house, where he received a glimpse of Mays's rich lifestyle earned playing baseball. The great ballplayer lectured Simpson on staying out of trouble and on the importance of appreciating one's fans.

USC. Simpson was setting junior-college football records at City College of San Francisco in 1966 while the University of Southern California football team was struggling. He came to USC to run track and play football. He ran the 100-yard dash in 9.4 seconds and the 40-yard dash, so important in football, in 4.5 seconds in full playing gear. In 1967 he was a member of the USC 440 relay team that set a world record. Simpson played only two years at USC, but they were enough for him to attain stardom. He ran for 3,123 yards and set a Pac-10 career average of 164.4 per game. He was an all-American in both 1967 and 1968; he was second in Heisman Trophy voting in 1967 and won the Heisman in 1968; with Marcus Allen he holds the USC record for most points (138) and most touchdowns (23) in a single season. Largely on the strength of Simpson's ability, USC won the national football championship in 1967, and they retired his number, 32.

Pro Career. By the time he was drafted by the lowly Buffalo Bills in 1969, O. J. Simpson was a national celebrity. He played on losing teams for most of his pro career —

in six of his eleven years as a professional player his team won three or fewer games — and that made his accomplishment all the more spectacular. He was the leading rusher in professional football during the decade with 10,539 yards, 25 percent more than Franco Harris of the mighty Pittsburgh Steelers, who was second. In 1978 Simpson announced that he wanted to play where it is warm, and he set another record when he signed with the San Francisco 49ers. Now he was the highest paid professional football player — $806,668 per year, $356,668 per year more than Walter Payton, the second highest paid.

Simpson had a history of knee injuries, and in 1979 knee surgery ended his football career. But he had all the makings of a media star. After football he worked as a sports announcer, a movie actor, and a commercial endorser. His career came to an abrupt halt in 1994, when he was accused of murdering his estranged wife, Nicole Simpson, precipitating the most frenzied media event in the history of American jurisprudence.

MARK SPITZ

1950-

WINNER OF SEVEN OLYMPIC GOLD MEDALS

Winning. Mark Spitz was a precocious swimmer. At the age of ten he held seventeen national age-group swimming records and practiced ninety minutes a day. He was encouraged by his father, a steel-company executive, who impressed one message upon him relentlessly: "Swimming isn't everything, winning is."

Early Disappointment. Mark Spitz was seventeen in 1967 when he set his first world record, 4:10.6 in the 400-meter freestyle, and he was widely regarded to be as talented as his Santa Clara swimming teammate Don Schollander, who had won four gold medals at the 1964 Olympics. Spitz went to the 1968 Olympics in Mexico City with lofty expectations, and he came away disappointed. He had qualified for three individual events and

three relays, but he won only two gold medals, both in relay events. "I had the worst meet of my life," he told a reporter. So he worked harder. In the next four years before the 1972 Olympics, he set twenty-two more world records, and by that time he had set thirty-five U.S. records in swimming events.

"Doc" Counsilman. In 1969 Spitz enrolled as a pre-dental student at Indiana University, which was a traditional powerhouse in swimming and diving. He came under the tutelage of Jim ("Doc") Counsilman at Indiana and began what the swimming community considered to be a comeback at the age of nineteen. In 1971 Spitz was named World Swimmer of the Year by *Swimming World* and the amateur athlete of the year by the American Athletic Union. At the Olympic trials in August 1972 he set a world record in the 200-meter butterfly and qualified for four individual meets as well as three relay teams.

Seven Golds. At the 1972 Olympics Spitz was stunning. He not only won every event in which he competed, he set world records in each of them, twice establishing his world marks at the rate of two per day. He won his record-setting seventh gold medal of the Olympics in the 400-meter medley relay on 4 September. Early the next morning Arab terrorists broke into the Israeli athletes' housing unit, killing two and kidnapping nine others. Later that day the nine hostages were killed in a shootout with an Israeli antiterrorist squad. Spitz, a Jew, was ushered from the Olympic site under heavy security and returned home for fear that his life was in danger.

The Aftermath. After the Olympics Spitz was one of the most recognizable men in America. His good looks (he was compared to Omar Sharif) and the enormous popularity of a poster on which he wore his seven gold medals made him a celebrity. In 1973 Spitz married Suzy Weiner and gave up dental school for a contract with the William Morris Agency, who handled his public appearances. He had had his fill of swimming — for the time being, at least. In 1990 he toyed with the idea of training for the 1992 Olympics, but his time had past, and he gave it up.

Source:
Kenny Moore, "Bionic Man," *Sports Illustrated* (23 October 1989): 80ff.

PEOPLE IN THE NEWS

Kareem Abdul-Jabbar was named most valuable player in the National Basketball Association five times during the 1970s, in 1971, 1972, 1974, 1976, and 1977. He was also named MVP in 1980.

Mario Andretti won the World Drivers' Championship in 1978; he was only the second American to do so.

Earl Anthony won the Professional Bowlers Association championship three years in a row, beginning in 1973.

Swimmer Shirley Babashoff won eight medals (two gold and six silver) in the 1972 and 1976 Olympics.

George Blanda scored his record 2,002nd point as a professional football player in 1975.

Geoff Bodine won fifty-five NASCAR modified stock-car races in 1978.

Bobby Bond of the San Francisco Giants set a season record of 180 strikeouts in 1970.

Wilt Chamberlain had a .727 field-goal average (426 of 586) for the Los Angeles Lakers basketball team in 1972.

Ben Crenshaw of the University of Texas won three consecutive NCAA golf championships beginning in 1971.

Tom Ferguson won six consecutive All-Around Cowboy titles at the Rodeo World Championships, beginning in 1974.

In 1972 Michael Finneran was the first diver ever to be given a perfect score of 10 by all seven judges during the U.S. Olympic Trials.

Bill Fricker with *Intrepid* in 1971, Ted Hood with *Courageous* in 1974, and Ted Turner with *Courageous* in 1977 won America's Cup sailing championships.

University of Southern Mississippi punter Ray Guy set an NCAA career record average of 44.7 yards per kick between 1970 and 1972.

Larry Kenson of the San Antonio Spurs basketball team had a record eleven steals on 26 December 1976 against the Kansas City Kings.

In 1979 Billie Jean King won her twentieth Wimbledon title, of which four had been in singles, ten in doubles, and four in mixed doubles.

In 1976 Ronald Owen Laird won his sixty-fifth national walking title.

University of Minnesota running back Kent Litzmann carried the ball a record fifty-seven times on 12 November 1977 against the University of Illinois.

The Los Angeles Lakers beat the Golden State Warriors 162–99, the greatest winning margin in the history of the National Basketball Association.

In 1970 Pete Maravich of Louisiana State University scored a record 1,381 points during the basketball season, bringing his career total to 3,667 points.

Kitty O'Neil set a record for terminal velocity of a dragster in 1977 — 392.4 MPH.

Chicago Bear Walter Payton rushed for 275 yards in a football game against the Minnesota Vikings on 20 November 1977.

Richard Petty won four of his record seven Daytona 500 stock-car races during the 1970s, in 1971, 1973, 1974, and 1979.

Walter Poenisch, Sr., swam from Cuba to Duck Key, Florida, in 34 hours, 15 minutes, arriving on 13 July 1978.

Dave Ponza, who had a 112 season average, bowled a perfect 300 game in 1978.

Golden Richards of Brigham Young University and Cliff Branch of the University of Colorado returned four punts for touchdowns during the 1971 NCAA football season.

Frank Robinson of the Baltimore Orioles hit two grand-slam home runs on 26 June 1970.

Bill Rodgers won every New York City Marathon from 1976 to 1979.

Mark Roth won eight Professional Bowlers Association titles in 1978.

Both Tom Seaver (in 1975) and Jim Palmer (in 1976) won their third Cy Young award for outstanding pitching.

Rick Swenson won the Iditarod Trail dogsled race in 1977 and 1979.

The Tampa Bay Buccaneers football team lost a record twenty-six straight games in 1976 and 1977.

Chris Taylor, the heaviest wrestler in Olympic history at six feet, five inches, and 420 pounds, won a bronze medal in the 1972 Olympics.

Cecil Turner of the Chicago Bears returned four kickoffs for touchdowns during the 1970 football season.

The sixty-three-game winning streak of the United States Olympic basketball team was ended by the Soviet Union in the finals of the 1972 Olympics.

The University of Southern California won its eleventh NCAA Division I baseball championship in 1978.

Al Unser won the Indianapolis 500 three times during the 1970s, in 1970, 1971, and 1978. In 1987 he tied A. J. Foyt's record four career wins.

Both Kenny Walker of the University of Kentucky (11 for 11 in 1976) and Marvin Barnes of Providence College (10 for 10 in 1973) had perfect single-game field-goal records during NCAA basketball tournaments.

Bill Walton of UCLA had the highest percentage of successful field-goal attempts during the NCAA basketball tournament. Between 1972 and 1974 he scored a record 109 times in 159 attempts.

Sharon Weber won the world amateur surfing championship in 1970 and 1972.

Peter J. Westbrook won the U.S. saber fencing championship in 1974, 1975, and 1979, beginning an eight-year championship run.

John Wilcox rolled three perfect games in professional bowling competition in 1979.

Cynthia Woodhead set a U.S. national record in the 200-meter freestyle of 1:58.23.

AWARDS

1970

Major League Baseball World Series — Baltimore Orioles (American League), 4 vs. Cincinnati Reds (National League), 1

Super Bowl V — Baltimore Colts, 16 vs. Dallas Cowboys, 13

Heisman Trophy, Collegiate Football — Jim Plunkett (Stanford)

National Basketball Association Championship — New York Knicks, 4 vs. Los Angeles Lakers, 3

National Collegiate Athletic Association Basketball — UCLA, 80 vs. University of Jacksonville, 69

National Hockey League Stanley Cup — Boston Bruins, 4 vs. Saint Louis Blues, 0

Kentucky Derby, Horse Racing — Dust Commander (Mike Manganello, jockey)

American Basketball Association Championship — Indiana Pacers, 4 vs. Los Angeles Stars, 2

Masters Golf Tournament — Billy Casper

U.S. Open Tennis Tournament — Ken Rosewall; Margaret Court

Athletes of the Year — George Blanda (Football) and Chi Cheng (Track and Field)

1971

Major League Baseball World Series — Pittsburgh Pirates (National League), 4 vs. Baltimore Orioles (American League), 3

Super Bowl VI — Dallas Cowboys, 24 vs. Miami Dolphins, 3

Heisman Trophy, Collegiate Football — Pat Sullivan (Auburn)

National Basketball Association Championship — Milwaukee Bucks, 4 vs. Baltimore Bullets, 0

National Collegiate Athletic Association Basketball — UCLA, 68 vs. Villanova, 62

National Hockey League Stanley Cup — Montreal Canadiens, 4 vs. Chicago Blackhawks, 3

Kentucky Derby, Horse Racing — Canonero (Gustava Avila, jockey)

American Basketball Association Championship — Utah Stars, 4 vs. Kentucky Colonels, 3

Masters Golf Tournament — Charles Coody

U.S. Open Tennis Tournament — Stan Smith; Billie Jean King

Athletes of the Year — Evonne Goolagong (Tennis) and Lee Trevino (Golf)

1972

Major League Baseball World Series — Oakland Athletics (American League), 4 vs. Cincinnati Reds (National League), 3

Super Bowl VII — Miami Dolphins, 14 vs. Washington Redskins, 7

Heisman Trophy, Collegiate Football — Johnny Rodgers (Nebraska)

National Basketball Association Championship — Los Angeles Lakers, 4 vs. New York Knicks, 1

National Collegiate Athletic Association Basketball — UCLA, 81 vs. Florida State, 7

National Hockey League Stanley Cup — Boston Bruins, 4 vs. New York Rangers, 2

Kentucky Derby, Horse Racing — Riva Ridge (Ron Turcotte, jockey)

American Basketball Association Championship — Indiana Pacers, 4 vs. New York Nets, 2

Masters Golf Tournament — Jack Nicklaus

U.S. Open Tennis Tournament — Ilia Nastase; Billie Jean King

Athletes of the Year — Mark Spitz (Swimming) and Olga Korbut (Gymnastics)

1973

Major League Baseball World Series — Oakland Athletics (American League), 4 vs. New York Mets (National League), 3

Super Bowl VIII — Miami Dolphins, 24 vs. Minnesota Vikings, 7

Heisman Trophy, Collegiate Football — John Cappelletti (Penn State)

National Basketball Association Championship — New York Knicks, 4 vs. Los Angeles Lakers, 1

National Collegiate Athletic Association Basketball — UCLA, 87 vs. Memphis State, 66

National Hockey League Stanley Cup — Montreal Canadiens, 4 vs. Chicago Blackhawks, 2

Kentucky Derby, Horse Racing — Secretariat (Ron Turcotte, jockey)

American Basketball Association Championship — Indiana Pacers, 4 vs. Kentucky Colonels, 3

Masters Golf Tournament — Tommy Aaron

U.S. Open Tennis Tournament — John Newcombe; Margaret Court

Athletes of the Year — O. J. Simpson (Football) and Billie Jean King (Tennis)

1974

Major League Baseball World Series — Oakland Athletics (American League), 4 vs. Los Angeles Dodgers (National League), 1

Super Bowl IX — Pittsburgh Steelers, 16 vs. Minnesota Vikings, 6

Heisman Trophy, Collegiate Football — Archie Griffin (Ohio State)

National Basketball Association Championship — Boston Celtics, 4 vs. Milwaukee Bucks, 3

National Collegiate Athletic Association Basketball — North Carolina State, 76 vs. Marquette, 64

National Hockey League Stanley Cup — Philadelphia Flyers, 4 vs. Boston Bruins, 2

Kentucky Derby, Horse Racing — Cannonade (Angel Cordero, jockey)

American Basketball Association Championship — New York Nets, 4 vs. Utah Stars, 1

Masters Golf Tournament — Gary Player

U.S. Open Tennis Tournament — Jimmy Connors; Billie Jean King

Athletes of the Year — Muhammad Ali (Boxing) and Chris Evert (Tennis)

1975

Major League Baseball World Series — Cincinnati Reds (National League), 4 vs. Boston Red Sox (American League), 3

Super Bowl X — Pittsburgh Steelers, 21 vs. Dallas Cowboys, 17

Heisman Trophy, Collegiate Football — Archie Griffin (Ohio State)

National Basketball Association Championship — Golden State Warriors, 4 vs. Washington Bullets, 0

National Collegiate Athletic Association Basketball — UCLA, 92 vs. Kentucky, 85

National Hockey League Stanley Cup — Philadelphia Flyers, 4 vs. Buffalo Sabres, 2

Kentucky Derby, Horse Racing — Foolish Pleasure (Jacinto Vasquez, jockey)

American Basketball Association Championship — Kentucky Colonels, 4 vs. Indiana Pacers, 1

Masters Golf Tournament — Jack Nicklaus

U.S. National Tennis Tournament — Manuel Ovantes; Chris Evert

Athletes of the Year — Fred Lynn (Baseball) and Chris Evert (Tennis)

1976

Major League Baseball World Series — Cincinnati Reds (National League), 4 vs. New York Yankees (American League), 0

Super Bowl XI — Oakland Raiders, 32 vs. Minnesota Vikings, 14

Heisman Trophy, Collegiate Football — Tony Dorsett (Pittsburgh)

National Basketball Association Championship — Boston Celtics, 4 vs. Phoenix Suns, 2

National Collegiate Athletic Association Basketball — Indiana, 86 vs. Michigan, 68

National Hockey League Stanley Cup — Montreal Canadiens, 4 vs. Philadelphia Flyers, 0

Kentucky Derby, Horse Racing — Bold Forbes (Angel Cordero, jockey)

American Basketball Association Championship — New York Nets, 4 vs. Denver Rockets, 2

Masters Golf Tournament — Raymond Floyd

U.S. National Tennis Tournament — Jimmy Connors; Chris Evert

Athletes of the Year — Bruce Jenner (Track and Field) and Nadia Comaneci (Gymnastics)

1977

Major League Baseball World Series — Los Angeles Dodgers, (National League), 4 vs. New York Yankees (American League), 2

Super Bowl XII — Dallas Cowboys, 27 vs. Denver Broncos, 10

Heisman Trophy, Collegiate Football — Earl Campbell (Texas)

National Basketball Association Championship — Portland Trail Blazers, 4 vs. Philadelphia 76ers, 2

National Collegiate Athletic Association Basketball — Marquette, 67 vs. North Carolina, 59

National Hockey League Stanley Cup — Montreal Canadiens, 4 vs. Boston Bruins, 0

Kentucky Derby, Horse Racing — Seattle Slew (Jean Chuguet, jockey)

Masters Golf Tournament — Tom Watson

U.S. National Tennis Tournament — Guillermo Vilas; Chris Evert

Athletes of the Year — Steve Cauthen (Horse Racing) and Chris Evert (Tennis)

1978

Major League Baseball World Series — New York Yankees (American League), 4 vs. Los Angeles Dodgers (National League), 2

Super Bowl XIII — Pittsburgh Steelers, 35 vs. Dallas Cowboys, 31

Heisman Trophy, Collegiate Football — Billy Sims (Oklahoma)

National Basketball Association Championship — Washington Bullets, 4 vs. Seattle Supersonics, 3

National Collegiate Athletic Association Basketball — Kentucky, 94 vs. Duke, 88

National Hockey League Stanley Cup — Montreal Canadiens, 4 vs. Boston Bruins, 2

Kentucky Derby, Horse Racing — Affirmed (Steve Cauthen, jockey)

Masters Golf Tournament — Gary Player

U.S. National Tennis Tournament — Jimmy Connors; Chris Evert

Athletes of the Year — Ron Guidry (Baseball) and Nancy Lopez (Golf)

1979

Major League Baseball World Series — Pittsburgh Pirates (National League), 4 vs. Baltimore Orioles (American League), 2

Super Bowl XIV — Pittsburgh Steelers, 31 vs. Los Angeles Rams, 19

Heisman Trophy, Collegiate Football — Charles White (Southern California)

National Basketball Association Championship — Seattle Super Sonics, 4 vs. Washington Bullets, 1

National Collegiate Athletic Association Basketball — Michigan State, 75 vs. Indiana, 64

National Hockey League Stanley Cup — Montreal Canadiens, 4 vs. New York Rangers, 1

Kentucky Derby, Horse Racing — Spectacular Bid (Ronnie Franklin, jockey)

Masters Golf Tournament — Frank U. ("Fuzzy") Zoeller

U.S. National Tennis Tournament — John McEnroe; Tracy Austin

Athletes of the Year — Willie Stargell (Baseball) and Tracy Austin (Tennis)

DEATHS

Stanley Benham, 57, U.S. bobsled champion in the early 1950s, 22 April 1970.

Moe Berg, 70, major league baseball catcher from 1924 to 1939 and reputed spy, 29 May 1972.

Lyman Bostick, 28, professional baseball player for the Minnesota Twins and the California Angels, 23 September 1978.

Ezzard Charles, 53, heavyweight boxing champion (1949–1951), 28 May 1975.

Paul Christman, 61, professional football player in the 1950s and later television sports announcer, 2 March 1970.

Fred Corcoran, 72, helped found the Ladies Professional Golf Association in 1950, 23 June 1977.

Alvin Crowder, 73, major league baseball pitcher (1926–1936), 3 April 1972.

Arthur Daley, 69, Pulitzer Prize–winning sports columnist for *The New York Times,* 3 January 1974.

Dizzy Dean, 63, Saint Louis Cardinals pitcher in the 1930s; won thirty games in 1934, 17 July 1974.

E. A. Diddle, 74, Western Kentucky basketball coach for forty-three years, 2 January 1970.

Charles Evans, 89, first winner of the U.S. Open and U.S. Amateur golf championships in the same year in 1916, 6 November 1979.

Daniel Ferris, 87, official of the Amateur Athletic Union from 1907 until his death, 2 May 1977.

Nat Fleischer, 84, boxing expert and founder of *Ring* magazine, 25 June 1972.

Nelson Fox, 48, professional baseball player for the Chicago White Sox (1950–1965), 1 December 1975.

Ford Frick, 83, president of the National League in baseball (1934–1951) and commissioner of major league baseball (1951–1965), 8 April 1978.

Frank Frisch, 75, professional baseball player in the 1920s and 1930s, manager of the Saint Louis Cardinals "Gashouse Gang," member of the Baseball Hall of Fame, 12 March 1973.

Warren Giles, 82, president of the National League in baseball (1951–1969), 7 February 1979.

Gabby Hartnett, 72, major league baseball catcher and manager, member of the Baseball Hall of Fame, 20 December 1972.

Charles Hughes, 28, football player for the Detroit Lions who died during a game, 24 October 1971.

Tony Hulman, 76, owner of the Indianapolis Motor Speedway, where he became the voice who announced before the start of the Indianapolis 500, "Gentlemen, start your engines," 27 October 1977.

Jack Hurley, 74, boxing promoter, 16 November 1972.

Walter Kennedy, 64, commissioner of the National Basketball Association (1963–1975), 26 June 1977.

Elmer Layden, 70, one of the "Four Horsemen" of the 1924 University of Notre Dame football team, coach and athletic director at Notre Dame (1934–1940), first commissioner of the National Football League (1941–1946), 30 June 1973.

Frank Leahy, 65, University of Notre Dame football coach (1941–1954), during which period his team lost only eleven games; later *Chicago Daily News* columnist, 21 June 1973.

Charles ("Sonny") Liston, 38?, heavyweight boxing champion (1962–1964), 28 December 1972.

Eddie Machen, 40, heavyweight boxer of the 1950s and 1960s, 7 August 1972.

Chick Meehan, college football coach at Syracuse University and Manhattan College (1920–1937), 9 November 1972.

John J. Murphy, 62, pitcher for the New York Yankees in the 1930s, general manager of the New York Mets from 1967, 14 January 1970.

Ernest Nevers, 72, professional football player in the 1920s and 1930s and professional baseball pitcher (1926–1928), 3 May 1976.

Walter O'Malley, 75, owner of the Los Angeles Dodgers baseball team, 1957–1979, 9 August 1979.

Joan Whitney Payson, 72, owner of Greentree Racing

Stable and owner of the New York Mets, 4 October 1975.

Lou Perini, 68, owner of the Boston Braves baseball team, 16 April 1972.

Brian Piccolo, 26, Chicago Bears halfback, 16 June 1970.

Daniel F. Reeves, 58, owner of the Los Angeles Rams football team, 15 April 1971.

Clifford Roberts, 84, cofounder and chairman from 1934 to 1976 of the Masters golf tournament, 19 September 1977.

Jackie Robinson, 53, first black man to play major league baseball, 24 October 1972.

Carroll Rosenblum, 72, owner of the Baltimore Colts professional football team from 1953 to 1971, when he traded the team for the Los Angeles Rams, 2 April 1979.

Adolph Rupp, 76, head coach of the University of Kentucky basketball team (1930–1972) whose teams won a record 879 games during his tenure, 10 December 1977.

Elizabeth Ryan, 86, winner of 659 tennis tournaments during her career that extended from 1914 to 1934, 6 July 1979.

George Harold Sisler, 80, Saint Louis Browns batting champion in the 1920s, member of the Baseball Hall of Fame, 26 March 1973.

Casey Stengel, 85, baseball manager who led the New York Yankees to ten American League pennants and seven World Series championships (1949–1960) and who was the first manager of the New York Mets in 1961, 29 September 1975.

Daniel Reid Topping, 61, part owner of the New York Yankees baseball team (1945–1964), 18 May 1974.

Paul Howard ("Dizzy") Trout, 56, Detroit Tigers pitcher (1939–1952), 16 March 1972.

Harold ("Pie") Traynor, 72, baseball player for the Pittsburgh Pirates during 1920s and 1930s, named the greatest third baseman in baseball history in 1966, 16 March 1972.

Gene Tunney, 80, heavyweight boxing champion (1926–1928), 7 November 1978.

Garfield Arthur Wood, 91, speedboat racer of the 1930s, 19 June 1971.

PUBLICATIONS

Yuri Brokhin, *The Big Red Machine: The Rise and Fall of Soviet Olympic Champions* (New York: Random House, 1978);

Heywood Hale Broun, *Tumultuous Merriment* (New York: R. Marek, 1979);

Jimmy Cannon, *Nobody Asked Me, But . . . : the World of Jimmy Cannon* (New York: Holt, Rinehart & Winston, 1978);

John Charles Daly, ed. *Pro Sports — Should Government Intervene?: A Round Table Held on February 22, 1977, and Sponsored by the American Enterprise Institute for Public Policy Research, Washington, D.C.* (Washington, D.C.: The Institute, 1977);

Parnell Donahue, *Sports Doc: Medical Advice, Diet, Fitness Tips, and other Essential Hints for Young Athletes* (New York: Knopf, 1979);

Paul Gardner, *Nice Guys Finish Last: Sport and American Life* (New York: Universe Books, 1975);

Government and the Sports Business: papers prepared for a conference of experts, with an introduction and summary (Washington, D.C.: Brookings Institution, 1974);

Isao Hirata, *The Doctor and the Athlete*, second edition (Philadelphia: Lippincott, 1974);

Jerome Holtzman, *No Cheering in the Press Box* (New York: Holt, Rinehart & Winston 1974);

Individual Sports for Women, fifth edition (Philadelphia: Saunders, 1971);

Jerry Izenberg, *How Many Miles to Camelot? The All-American Sport Myth* (New York: Holt, Rinehart & Winston, 1972);

Donald G. Jones, *Sports Ethics in America: A Bibliography, 1970–1990* (New York: Greenwood Press, 1992);

Don Kowet, *The Rich Who Own Sports* (New York: Random House, 1977);

Robert Lipsyte, *Sportsworld: An American Dreamland*

(New York: Quadrangle/New York Times Books, 1975);

John A. Lucas, *Saga of American Sport* (Philadelphia: Lea & Febiger, 1978);

Richard A. Magill, Michael J. Smoll, and Frank L. Ash, eds., *Children in Sport: A Contemporary Anthology* (Champaign, Ill.: Human Kinetics Publishers, 1978);

Rainer Martens, ed., *Joy and Sadness in Children's Sports* (Champaign, Ill.: Human Kinetics Publishers, 1978);

Peter C. McIntosh, *Fair Play: Ethics in Sport and Education* (London: Heinemann, 1979);

James A. Michener, *Sports in America* (New York: Random House, 1976);

Gabe Mirkin, *The Sports Medicine Book* (Boston: Little, Brown, 1978);

Patsy Neal, *Coaching Girls and Women: Psychological Perspectives* (Boston: Allyn & Bacon, 1975);

Craig T. Norback, *The New American Guide to Athletics, Sports & Recreation* (New York: New American Library, 1979);

Michael Novak, *The Joy of Sports: End Zones, Bases, Baskets, Balls, and the Consecration of the American Spirit* (New York: Basic Books, 1976);

Grigori Raiport, *Red Gold: Peak Performance Techniques of the Russian and East German Olympic Victors* (Los Angeles: Tarcher, 1988);

Allan J. Ryan, *Sports Medicine* (New York: Academic Press, 1974);

Jack Scott, *The Athletic Revolution* (New York: Free Press, 1971);

George Sheehan, *Encyclopedia of Athletic Medicine* (Mountain View, Cal.: World, 1972);

Uriel Simri, *1925 — A Historical Analysis of the Role of Women in the Modern Olympic Games* (Netanya, Israel: Wingate Institute for Physical Education and Sport, 1977);

Betty Mary Spears, *History of Sport and Physical Activity in the United States* (Dubuque, Iowa: Wm. C. Brown, 1978);

Peter N. Sperryn, *Sport and Medicine* (London & Boston: Butterworth, 1983);

Steven I. Subotnick, *The Running Foot Doctor* (Mountain View, Calif.: World Publications, 1977);

Jerry R. Thomas, *Youth Sports Guide for Coaches and Parents* (Washington: Manufactures Life Insurance, 1977);

William A. Thompson, *Modern Sports Officiating: A Practical Guide,* second edition (Dubuque, Iowa: Wm. C. Brown, 1979);

Wells Twombly, *200 Years of Sport in America: A Pageant of a Nation at Play* (New York: McGraw-Hill, 1976);

Maryhelen Vannier, *1915 — Individual and Team Sports for Girls and Women,* third edition (Philadelphia: Saunders, 1976);

J. G. P. Williams, *Sports Medicine,* second edition, edited by Williams and Sperryn; foreword by Lord Porritt (London: Edward Arnold, 1976);

Women and Sport: From Myth to Reality (Philadelphia: Lea & Febiger, 1978);

Women's Athletics: Coping with Controversy (Washington, D.C.: American Association for Health, Physical Education, and Recreation, 1974);

Sport, periodical;

Sports Illustrated, periodical;

womenSport, periodical.

GENERAL REFERENCES

GENERAL

John Morton Blum, *Years of Discord: American Politics and Society, 1961–1974* (New York: Norton, 1991);

Peter N. Carroll, *It Seemed Like Nothing Happened: The Tragedy and Promise of America in the 1970s* (New York: Holt, Rinehart & Winston, 1982);

William H. Chafe, *The Unfinished Journey: America Since World War II* (New York: Oxford University Press, 1986);

Chronicle of the 20th Century (Mount Kisco, N.Y.: Chronicle Publications, 1987);

Current Biography Yearbook (New York: Wilson, [various years]);

John Patrick Diggins, *The Proud Decades* (New York: Norton, 1988);

Barbara Ehrenreich and others, *Remaking Love: The Feminization of Sex* (New York: Anchor/Doubleday, 1987);

Encyclopaedia Britannica Book of the Year (Chicago: Encyclopaedia Britannica, 1971–1980);

Steve Fraser and Gary Gerstle, eds., *The Rise and Fall of the New Deal Order, 1930–1980* (Princeton: Princeton University Press, 1989);

Paul Johnson, *Modern Times: From the Twenties to the Nineties,* revised edition (New York: HarperCollins, 1991);

Gerald McConnell, *Thirty Years of Award Winners* (New York: Hastings House, 1981);

Kim McQuaid, *The Anxious Years: America in the Vietnam-Watergate Era* (New York: Basic Books, 1989);

Edward P. Morgan, *The '60s Experience: Hard Lessons about Modern America* (Philadelphia: Temple, 1991);

Oxford Analytica, *America in Perspective: Major Trends in the United States through the 1990s* (Boston: Houghton Mifflin, 1986);

Thomas Parker and Douglas Nelson, *Day by Day: The Seventies,* 2 volumes (New York: Facts On File, 1988);

Michael Downey Rice, *Prentice-Hall Dictionary of Business, Finance, and Law* (Englewood Cliffs, N.J.: Prentice-Hall, 1983);

Statistical Abstract of the United States (Washington, D.C.: U.S. Department of Commerce, various dates);

Time Lines on File (New York: Facts On File, 1988);

James Trager, *The People's Chronology,* revised edition (New York: Holt, 1992);

Claire Walter, *Winners: The Blue Ribbon Encyclopedia of Awards* (New York: Facts On File, 1982);

Theodore H. White, *America in Search of Itself: The Making of the President, 1956–1980* (New York: Warner, 1982);

Leigh Carol Yuster and others, eds., *Ulrich's International Periodicals Directory: A Classified Guide to Current Periodicals, Foreign and Domestic, 1986–1987,* twenty-fifth edition, volume 2 (New York & London: R. R. Bowker, 1986);

Howard Zinn, *The Twentieth Century: A People's History* (New York: Harper & Row, 1984).

ARTS

John Beardsley and Jane Livingston, *Hispanic Art in the United States* (New York: Abbeville Press, 1987);

Gerald M. Berkowitz, *New Broadways: Theater Across America 1950–1980* (Totowa, N.J.: Rowman & Littlefield, 1982);

Donald Boyle, *Blacks in American Films and Television: An Encyclopedia* (New York: Garland, 1988);

Fred Bronson, *The Billboard Book of Number One Hits* (New York: Billboard Publications, 1988);

Richard Burbank, *Twentieth Century Music: Orchestral, Chamber, Operatic & Dance Music 1900–1980* (New York: Facts On File, 1984);

Helen Krich Chinay and Linda Walsh Jenkins, *Women in American Theater* (New York: Crown, 1981);

Mary Clarke and Clement Crisp, *The History of Dance* (New York: Crown, 1981);

Jean-Luc Daval, *Photography: History of an Art* (New York: Rizzoli International Publications, 1982);

Stanley Green, *Broadway Musicals: Show by Show* (Milwaukee: Hal Leonard Books, 1985);

Otis L. Guernsey, Jr., *Broadway: Song and Story* (New York: Dodd, Mead, 1985);

Charles Hall, *A Twentieth Century Musical Chronicle: Events 1900–1988* (New York: Greenwood Press, 1989);

Leslie Halliwell, *The Filmgoer's Companion* (New York: Scribners, 1980);

Molly Haskell, *From Reverence to Rape: The Treatment of Women in the Movies* (Chicago: University of Chicago Press, 1987);

Errol Hill, ed., *The Theater of Black Americans* (New York: Applause Theater, 1980);

Ted Hoffman, ed., *Famous American Plays of the 1970s* (New York: Dell, 1981);

Pauline Kael, *When the Lights Go Down* (New York: Holt, Rinehart & Winston, 1980);

Frederick R. Karl, *American Fictions 1940–1980: A Comprehensive History and Critical Evaluation* (New York: Harper & Row, 1983);

Paul Kingsbury and Alan Axelrod, eds., *Country: The Music and the Musicians* (New York: Abbeville Press, 1988);

Leonard S. Klein, ed., *Latin American Literature in the 20th Century: A Guide* (New York: Ungar, 1986);

Robert Phillip Kolker, *A Cinema of Loneliness: Penn, Kubrick, Coppola, Scorcese, Altman* (New York: Oxford University Press, 1980);

Richard A. Long and Eugenia W. Colliers, eds., *Afro-American Writing: An Anthology of Prose and Poetry* (University Park: Pennsylvania State University Press, 1985);

Edward Lucie-Smith, *Race, Sex, and Gender in Contemporary Art* (New York: Abrams, 1989);

Jim Miller, ed., *The Rolling Stone Illustrated History of Rock and Roll* (New York: Knopf, 1980);

Ethan Mordden, *The American Theatre* (New York: Oxford University Press, 1981);

Norm N. Nite, *Rock On Almanac: The First Four Decades of Rock 'n' Roll* (New York: Harper & Row, 1989);

Catherine Rainwater and William J. Scheik, eds., *Contemporary American Women Writers: Narrative Strategies* (Lexington: University Press of Kentucky, 1985);

Arlene Raven, *Crossing Over: Feminism and Art of Social Concern* (Ann Arbor, Mich.: UMI Research Press, 1988);

Robert V. Rozelle, Alvia Wardlaw, and Maureen A. Mc-

Kenna, eds., *Black Art: The African Impulse in African-American Art* (New York: Abrams, 1989);

Peter Selz, *Art in Our Times: A Pictorial History 1890–1980* (New York: Abrams, 1981);

David P. Szatmary, *Rockin' in Time: A Social History of Rock and Roll* (Englewood Cliffs, N.J.: Prentice-Hall, 1987);

David Thomson, *Overexposures: The Crisis in American Filmmaking* (New York: Morrow, 1981);

Joel Whitburn, *The Billboard Book of Top 40 Hits* (New York: Billboard Publications, 1985).

BUSINESS AND THE ECONOMY

Daniel Bell, *The Coming of Post-Industrial Society* (New York: Basic Books, 1973);

John Brooks, *The Autobiography of American Business* (Garden City, N.Y.: Doubleday, 1974);

Keith L. Bryant, Jr., and Henry C. Dethloff, *A History of American Business* (Englewood Cliffs, N.J.: Prentice-Hall, 1983);

Bryant, ed., *Encyclopedia of American Business History and Biography: Railroads in the Age of Regulation, 1900–1980* (Columbia, S.C.: Bruccoli Clark Layman / New York: Facts On File, 1988);

John M. Dobson, *A History of American Enterprise* (Englewood Cliffs, N.J.: Prentice-Hall, 1988);

Hays Gorey, *Nader and the Power of Everyman* (New York: Grosset & Dunlap, 1975);

James R. Green, *The World of the Worker: Labor in Twentieth-Century America* (New York: Hill & Wang, 1980);

Donald R. Kelley, ed., *The Energy Crisis: An International Perspective* (New York: Praeger, 1977);

William M. Leary, ed., *Encyclopedia of American Business History and Biography: The Airline Industry* (Columbia, S.C.: Bruccoli Clark Layman / New York: Facts On File, 1992);

Amory B. Lovins and L. Hunter Lovins, *Brittle Power: Energy Strategy for National Security* (Andover, Mass.: Brick House, 1982);

George S. May, ed., *Encyclopedia of American Business History and Biography: The Automobile Industry, 1920–1980* (Columbia, S.C.: Bruccoli Clark Layman / New York: Facts On File, 1989);

Glenn Porter, ed., *Encyclopedia of American Economic History: Studies of the Principal Movements and Ideas,* 3 volumes (New York: Scribners, 1980);

Joseph C. Pusateri, *A History of American Business* (Arlington Heights, Ill.: Harlan Davidson, 1984);

Sidney Ratner, James H. Soltow, and Richard Sylla, *The*

Evolution of the American Economy (New York: Basic Books, 1979);

Archie Robinson, *George Meany and His Times: A Biography* (New York: Simon & Schuster, 1981);

Graham Robinson, *Pictorial History of the Automobile* (New York: W. H. Smith, 1987);

Robert Scheer, *America After Nixon: The Age of Multinationals* (New York: McGraw-Hill, 1974);

E. F. Schumacher, *Small Is Beautiful* (New York: Harper & Row, 1973);

Larry E. Schweikart, ed., *Encyclopedia of American Business History and Biography: Banking and Finance, 1913–1989* (Columbia, S.C.: Bruccoli Clark Layman / New York: Facts On File, 1990);

Bruce Seely, ed., *Encyclopedia of American Business History and Biography: Iron and Steel in the Twentieth Century* (Columbia, S.C.: Bruccoli Clark Layman / New York: Facts On File, 1993);

Tad Szulc, *The Energy Crisis* (New York: Watts, 1978);

Thomas Whiteside, *The Investigation of Ralph Nader: General Motors vs. One Determined Man* (New York: Arbor House, 1972);

Daniel Yergin, *The Prize: The Epic Quest for Oil, Money, and Power* (New York: Simon & Schuster, 1991).

EDUCATION

Alba N. Ambert, *Bilingual Education: A Sourcebook* (New York: Garland, 1985);

J. Ben-David, *American Higher Education* (New York: McGraw-Hill, 1972);

Sol Cohen, ed., *Education in the U.S.: A Documentary History* (Los Angeles: UCLA Press, 1974);

Hugh Davis Graham, *The Uncertain Triumph: Federal Education Policy in the Kennedy and Johnson Years* (Chapel Hill: University of North Carolina Press, 1984);

Phyllis Klotman, ed., *Humanities Through the Black Experience* (Dubuque, Iowa: Kendall-Hunt, 1977);

Mary and Herbert Knapp, *One Potato, Two Potato . . . The Secret Education of American Children* (New York: Norton, 1976);

Jonathan Kozol, *Illiterate America* (Garden City, N.Y.: Anchor/Doubleday, 1985);

Kozol, *Savage Inequalities: Children in America's Schools* (New York: Crown, 1991);

Connaught Coyne Marshner, *Blackboard Tyranny* (New Rochelle, N.Y.: Arlington House, 1978);

D. W. McNally, *Piaget, Education and Teaching* (Sussex, U.K.: Harvester Press, 1973);

Jack Nelson and Kenneth Carlson, *Radical Ideas and the Schools* (New York: Holt, Rinehart & Winston, 1972);

Vance Packard, *The People Shapers* (Boston: Little, Brown, 1977);

Neil Postman and Charles Weingartner, *The School Book* (New York: Delacorte, 1973);

Ira Shor, *Culture Wars: School and Society in the Conservative Restoration, 1969–1984* (Boston: Routledge & Kegan Paul, 1986);

Joseph Turow, *Entertainment, Education, and the Hard Sell: Three Decades of Network Children's Television* (New York: Praeger, 1981);

Richard Van Scotter, *Public Schooling in America* (Santa Barbara, Cal.: ABC-CLIO, 1991);

Harry Wolcott, *Teachers Versus Technocrats* (Eugene: University of Oregon Center for Educational Policy and Management, 1977).

FASHION

Michael Batterberry, *Mirror, Mirror: A Social History of Fashion* (New York: Holt, Rinehart & Winston, 1977);

Curtis F. Brown, *Star-Spangled Kitsch* (New York: Universe Books, 1975);

Ray Browne and Marshal Fishwick, eds., *Icons of America* (New York: Popular Press, 1978);

Farid Chenoune, *A History of Men's Fashion* (Paris: Flammarion, 1993);

The Encyclopedia of Fashion (New York: Abrams, 1986);

Annalee Gold, *90 Years of Fashion* (New York: Fairchild Fashion Group, 1991);

Paul Goldberg, *On the Rise: Architecture and Design in a Postmodern Age* (New York: Penguin, 1983);

Georgina Howell, *In Vogue: Six Decades of Fashion* (London: Allen Lane, 1975);

William Dudley Hunt, Jr., *Encyclopedia of American Architecture* (New York: McGraw-Hill, 1980);

Udo Kultermann, *Architecture in the 20th Century* (New York: Reinhold, 1993);

Diane Maddex, ed., *Master Builders: A Guide to Famous American Architects* (Washington, D.C.: Preservation Press, 1985);

Caroline Rennolds Milbank, *Couture: The Great Designers* (New York: Stewart, Tabori & Chang, 1985);

Jane Mulvagh, *"Vogue" History of 20th Century Fashion* (New York: Viking, 1988);

John Peacock, *20th Century Fashion: The Complete Sourcebook* (New York: Thames & Hudson, 1993);

Anne Stegemeyer, *Who's Who in Fashion* (New York: Fairchild, 1988);

Sherrill Whiton, *Interior Design and Decoration*, fourth edition (New York: Lippincott, 1973);

Elizabeth Wilson, *Adorned in Dreams: Fashion and Modernity* (Berkeley: University of California Press, 1987);

Tom Wolfe, *From Bauhaus to Our House* (New York: Farrar, Straus & Giroux, 1981);

Doreen Yarwood, *Fashion in the Western World: 1500–1990* (New York: Drama Book Publishers, 1992).

GOVERNMENT AND POLITICS

Stephen Ambrose, *Nixon*, 3 volumes (New York: Simon & Schuster, 1987–1991);

Michael Barone, *Our Country: The Shaping of America from Roosevelt to Reagan* (New York: Free Press, 1990);

David Bennett, *The Party of Fear: From Nativist Movements to the New Right in American History* (Chapel Hill: University of North Carolina Press, 1988);

Fawn M. Brodie, *Richard Nixon: The Shaping of His Character* (New York: Norton, 1981);

James Cannon, *Time and Chance: Gerald Ford's Appointment with History* (New York: HarperCollins, 1994);

William H. Chafe, *The Unfinished Journey: America Since World War II,* second edition (New York: Oxford University Press, 1991);

Rowland Evans and Robert Novak, *Nixon in the White House* (New York: Random House, 1971);

Benjamin Frankel, ed., *The Cold War, 1945–1991: Leaders and Other Important Figures in the United States and Western Europe* (Detroit: Gale, 1992);

Ernest B. Furguson, *Hard Right: The Rise of Jesse Helms* (New York: Norton, 1986);

James William Gibson, *The Perfect War: The War We Couldn't Lose and How We Did* (New York: Vintage, 1986);

Betty Glad, *Jimmy Carter: In Search of the Great White House* (New York: Norton, 1980);

George C. Herring, *America's Longest War: The United States and Vietnam, 1950–1975* (New York: Random House, 1986);

Jerome Himmelstein, *To the Right: The Transformation of American Conservatism* (Berkeley: University of California Press, 1990);

Joan Hoff, *Nixon Reconsidered* (New York: Basic Books, 1994);

Walter Issacson, *Kissinger* (New York: Simon & Schuster, 1992);

Haynes Johnson, *In the Absence of Power: Governing America* (New York: Viking, 1980);

Loch K. Johnson, *A Season of Inquiry: The Senate Intelligence Investigation* (Lexington: University Press of Kentucky, 1985);

Stanley Karnow, *Vietnam: A History* (New York: Viking, 1984);

Stanley Kutler, *The Wars of Watergate* (New York: Knopf, 1990);

John Lukacs, *Outgrowing Democracy: A History of the United States in the Twentieth Century* (Garden City, N.Y.: Doubleday, 1984);

Lukacs, *Passing of the Modern Age* (New York: Harper & Row, 1970);

J. Anthony Lukas, *Nightmare: The Underside of the Nixon Years* (New York: Viking, 1976);

George Donelson Moss, *Vietnam: An American Ordeal* (Englewood Cliffs, N.J.: Prentice-Hall, 1994);

William A. Rusher, *The Rise of the Right* (New York: Morrow, 1984);

Michael Schudson, *Watergate in American Memory* (New York: Basic Books, 1992);

Neil Sheehan, *A Bright Shining Lie: John Paul Vann and America in Vietnam* (New York: Random House, 1988);

Tad Szulc, *The Illusion of Peace: Foreign Policy in the Nixon Years* (New York: Viking, 1978);

Theodore White, *Breach of Faith: The Fall of Richard Nixon* (New York: Atheneum, 1975);

Tom Wicker, *One of Us: Richard Nixon and the American Dream* (New York: Random House, 1991);

Marilyn B. Young, *The Vietnam Wars, 1945–1990* (New York: Harper, 1991).

LAW

Richard Abel, *American Lawyers* (New York: Oxford University Press, 1989);

Michael Bilton, *Four Hours in My Lai* (New York: Viking, 1992);

David P. Currie, *The Constitution in the Supreme Court: The Second Century* (Chicago: University of Chicago Press, 1990);

Martha Davis, *Brutal Need* (New Haven: Yale University Press, 1994);

James Doyle, *Not Above the Law: The Battles of Watergate Prosecutors Cox and Jaworski* (New York: Morrow, 1977);

Lee Epstein and Joseph F. Kobylka, *The Supreme Court and Legal Change* (Chapel Hill: University of North Carolina Press, 1992);

Marian Faux, *Roe v. Wade* (New York: Macmillan, 1988);

Seymour Hersh, *Cover-Up* (New York: Random House, 1972);

Jennifer Hochschild, *The New American Dilemma* (New Haven: Yale University Press, 1984);

Mark Kessler, *Legal Service for the Poor* (Greenwood, Conn.: Greenwood Press, 1987);

Philip B. Kurland, *Watergate and the Constitution* (Chicago: University of Chicago Press, 1978);

Charles Lamb and Stephen Halpen, eds., *The Burger Court: Political and Judicial Profiles* (Chicago: University of Illinois Press, 1991);

Kristin Luker, *Abortion and the Politics of Motherhood* (Berkeley: University of California Press, 1984);

Alpheus Thomas Mason, *The Supreme Court from Taft to Burger* (Baton Rouge: Louisiana State University Press, 1979);

Norma McCorvey, *I Am Roe* (New York: HarperCollins, 1994);

R. Shep Melnick, *Regulation and the Courts* (Washington, D.C.: Brookings Institution, 1983);

David M. O'Brien, *Constitutional Law and Politics*, 2 volumes (New York: Norton, 1991);

O'Brien, *Storm Center: The Supreme Court in American Politics* (New York: Norton, 1986);

Timothy J. O'Neill, *Bakke & The Politics of Equality: Friends and Foes in the Classroom of Litigation* (Middletown, Conn.: Wesleyan University Press, 1985);

Robert Shnayerson, *The Illustrated History of the Supreme Court of the United States* (New York: Abrams, 1986);

Lettie Wenner, *The Environmental Decade in Court* (Bloomington: Indiana University Press, 1982);

Tom Wicker, *A Time to Die* (New York: Quadrangle, 1975).

LIFESTYLES AND SOCIAL TRENDS

Beth L. Bailey, *From Front Porch to Back Seat: Courtship in Twentieth-Century America* (Baltimore: Johns Hopkins University Press, 1988);

Eileen Barker, *The Making of a Moonie: Choice or Brainwashing?* (New York: Oxford University Press, 1984);

Bennett M. Berger, *The Survival of a Counterculture* (Berkeley & Los Angeles: University of California Press, 1981);

George Beschner and Alfred S. Friedman, *Teen Drug Use* (Lexington, Mass.: Lexington Books, 1986);

Stephanie Coontz, *The Way We Never Were: American Families and the Nostalgia Trap* (New York: Basic Books, 1992);

The Culture of Consumption: Critical Essays in American History, 1880–1980 (New York: Pantheon, 1983);

Andrew J. Edelstein and Kevin McDonough, *The Seventies: From Hot Pants to Hot Tubs* (New York: Dutton, 1990);

Barbara Ehrenreich, *The Worst Years of Our Lives: Irreverent Notes from a Decade of Greed* (New York: Holt, Rinehart & Winston, 1982);

Carol Felsenthal, *The Sweetheart of the Silent Majority: The Biography of Phyllis Schlafly* (Garden City, N.Y.: Doubleday, 1981);

Johanna Fiedler, *Arthur Fiedler: Papa, the Pops and Me* (Garden City, N.Y.: Doubleday, 1994);

James J. Flink, *The Car Culture* (Cambridge, Mass.: MIT Press, 1975);

Jo Freeman, ed., *Social Movements of the Sixties and Seventies* (New York: Longman, 1983);

David Hey, *The Oxford Guide to Family History* (New York: Oxford University Press, 1993);

Joan Hoff-Wilson, *Rights of Passage: The Past and Future of the ERA* (Bloomington: Indiana University Press, 1986);

Kenneth T. Jackson, *The Crabgrass Frontier: The Suburbanization of the United States* (New York: Oxford University Press, 1985);

Elizabeth Janeway, *Cross Sections from a Decade of Change* (New York: Morrow, 1982);

Landon Y. Jones, *Great Expectations: America and the Baby Boom Generation* (New York: Coward, McCann & Geoghegan, 1980);

Pagan Kennedy, *Platforms: A Microwaved Cultural Chronicle of the 1970s* (New York: St. Martin's Press, 1994);

Albert D. Klassen, Colin J. Williams, and others, *Sex and Morality in the U.S.* (Middletown, Conn.: Wesleyan University Press, 1989);

William Kowinski, *The Malling of America: An Inside Look at the Great Consumer Paradise* (New York: Morrow, 1985);

Bart Landry, *The New Black Middle Class* (Berkeley: University of California Press, 1987);

Mark Long, *The World of CB Radio* (Summertown, Tenn.: Book Publishing, 1987);

Richard Maltby, *Passing Parade: A History of Popular Culture in the Twentieth Century* (New York: Oxford University Press, 1989);

Jane J. Mansbridge, *Why We Lost the ERA* (Chicago: University of Chicago Press, 1986);

Joan Moore and Harry Pachon, *Hispanics in the United States* (Englewood Cliffs, N.J.: Prentice-Hall, 1985);

H. Wayne Morgan, *Drugs in America: A Social History, 1800–1980* (Syracuse, N.Y.: Syracuse University Press, 1981);

100 Years of the Automobile (Los Angeles: Petersen, 1985);

Charles Perry, *The Haight-Ashbury: A History* (New York: Random House, 1984);

Charles A. Reich, *The Greening of America: How the Youth Revolution Is Trying to Make America Livable* (New York: Random House, 1970);

Rosalind Rosenberg, *Divided Lives: American Women in the Twentieth Century* (New York: Hill & Wang, 1992);

Ellen K. Rothman, *Hands and Hearts: A History of Courtship in America* (New York: Basic Books, 1984);

Mary P. Ryan, *Womanhood in America: From Colonial Times to the Present* (Danbury, Conn.: Franklin Watts, 1977);

Kirkpatrick Sale, *The Green Revolution: The American Environmental Movement, 1962–1992* (New York: Hill & Wang, 1993);

Peter L. Skolnik, *Fads: America's Crazes, Fevers, and Fancies from the 1890s to the 1970s* (New York: Crowell, 1978);

Arthur Stein, *Seeds of the Seventies: Values, Work, Commitment in Post-Vietnam America* (Hanover, N.H.: University Press of New England, 1985);

Peter Steinfels, *The Neoconservatives* (New York: Touchstone, 1979);

D. T. Suzuki, *An Introduction to Zen Buddhism* (New York: Grove, 1991);

Ronald B. Taylor, *Chavez and the Farm Workers* (Boston: Beacon, 1975);

Lenore J. Weitzman, *The Divorce Revolution* (New York: Free Press, 1985);

Tom Wolfe, *The Purple Decades: A Reader* (New York: Farrar, Straus & Giroux, 1982);

Gwendolyn Wright, *Building the Dream: A Social History of Housing in America* (Cambridge, Mass.: MIT Press, 1983).

MEDIA

Erik Barnouw, *Tube of Plenty*, second edition (New York: Oxford University Press, 1990);

Mike Benton, *The Comic Book in America: An Illustrated History* (Dallas: Taylor, 1989);

Tim Brooks, *The Complete Directory to Prime Time TV Stars: 1946–Present* (New York: Ballantine, 1987);

Harry Castleman and Walter J. Podrazik, *Watching TV: Four Decades of American Television* (New York: McGraw-Hill, 1982);

Marcia Cohen, *The Sisterhood: The True Story of the Women Who Changed the World* (New York: Simon & Schuster, 1988);

John Dunning, *Tune in Yesterday: The Ultimate Encyclopedia of Old-Time Radio 1925–1976* (Englewood Cliffs, N.J.: Prentice-Hall, 1976);

Gary Grossman, *Saturday Morning TV* (New York: Dell, 1981);

Amy Janello and Brennon Jones, *The American Magazine* (New York: Abrams, 1991);

Suzanne Levine, Harriet Lyons, and others, *The Decade of Women: A* Ms. *History of the Seventies in Words and Pictures* (New York: Paragon, 1980);

Laurence W. Lichty and Malachi Topping, *American Broadcasting: A Source Book on the History of Radio and Television* (New York: Hastings House, 1975);

Alexander McNeil, *Total Television: A Comprehensive Guide to Programming from 1948–1980* (New York: Penguin, 1980);

James Robert Parish, *Actors' Television Credits: 1950–1972* (Metuchen, N.J.: Scarecrow Press, 1973);

Jeb Perry, *Universal Television: The Studio and Its Programs, 1950–1980* (Metuchen, N.J.: Scarecrow Press, 1983);

Gloria Steinem, *Outrageous Acts and Everyday Rebellions* (New York: Holt, Rinehart & Winston, 1983);

Christopher Sterling, ed., *Broadcasting and Mass Media: A Survey Bibliography* (Philadelphia: Temple University Press, 1974);

Sterling, ed., *The History of Broadcasting: Radio to Television,* 32 volumes (New York: New York Times/Arno, 1972);

Sterling, ed., *Telecommunications,* 34 volumes (New York: New York Times/Arno, 1974);

Vincent Terrace, *The Complete Encyclopedia of Television Programs: 1947–1979,* second edition (New York: Barnes, 1980);

Antoon J. van Zuilen, *The Life Cycle of Magazines: A Historical Study of the Decline and Fall of the General Interest Mass Audience Magazine in the United States During the Period 1946–1972* (Uithoorn, Netherlands: Graduate Press, 1977).

MEDICINE AND HEALTH

James Lee Anderson, *The West Point Fitness and Diet Book* (New York: Rawson, 1977);

Earl R. Babbie, *Science and Morality in Medicine: A Survey of Medical Educators* (Berkeley: University of California Press, 1970).

Samuel J. Barr and Dan Abelow, *A Woman's Choice* (New York: Rawson, 1977);

Melvin Berger, *Disease Detectives* (New York: Crowell, 1978);

Boston Women's Health Collective, *Our Bodies, Ourselves* (New York: Simon & Schuster, 1973);

Baruch Brody, *Abortion and the Sanctity of Human Life: A Philosophical View* (Cambridge, Mass.: MIT Press, 1975);

E. Richard Brown, *Rockefeller Medicine Men: Medicine and Capitalism in America* (Berkeley: University of California Press, 1979);

John J. Burt, *Personal Health Behavior in Today's Society* (Philadelphia: W. B. Saunders, 1972);

Daniel Callahan: *Abortion: Law, Choice and Morality* (New York: Macmillan, 1970);

The Cambridge World History of Human Disease (New York: Cambridge University Press, 1993);

Rick J. Carlson, *The End of Medicine* (New York: Wiley, 1975);

Frederic Fox Cartwright, *Disease and History* (New York: Crowell, 1972);

James H. Cassedy, *Medicine in America: A Short History* (Baltimore: Johns Hopkins University Press, 1991);

William C. Cockerham, *Medical Sociology* (Englewood Cliffs, N.J.: Prentice-Hall, 1989);

B. D. Colen, *Karen Ann Quinlan: Dying in the Age of Eternal Life* (New York: Nash, 1976);

Companion Encyclopedia of the History of Medicine (London: Routledge, 1993);

John Patrick Dolan, *Health and Society: A Documentary History of Medicine* (New York: Seabury, 1978);

Martin Duke, *The Development of Medical Techniques and Treatments: From Leeches to Heart Surgery* (Madison, Conn.: International Universities Press, 1991);

Carol Emmens, *The Abortion Controversy* (New York: Messner, 1987);

Paul J. Feldstein, *Health Care Economics* (New York: John Wiley & Sons, 1979);

H. Freeman, S. Levine, and L. Reeder, eds., *Handbook of Medical Sociology* (Englewood Cliffs, N.J.: Prentice-Hall, 1972);

Derek Gill, *Quest: The Life of Elisabeth Kübler-Ross* (New York: Harper & Row, 1980);

Saul Jarcho and Gene Brown, eds., *Medicine and Health Care* (New York: New York Times/Arno, 1977);

James H. Jones, *Bad Blood* (New York: Free Press, 1981);

Richard A. Kurtz and H. Paul Chalfant, *The Sociology of Medicine and Illness* (Boston: Allyn & Bacon, 1984);

Albert S. Lyons, *Medicine: An Illustrated History* (New York: Abrams, 1978);

Jean Mayer, *Health* (New York: Van Nostrand, 1974);

William A. Nolen, *A Surgeon's World* (New York: Random House, 1972);

Sherwin B. Nuland, *Doctors: The Biography of Medicine* (New York: Knopf, 1988);

Stanley Joel Reiser, *Medicine and the Reign of Technology* (New York: Cambridge University Press, 1978);

Jeffrey Rubin, *Economics, Mental Health, and the Law* (Lexington, Mass.: D. C. Heath, 1978);

Lauren R. Sass, *Abortion: Freedom of Choice and Right to Life* (New York: Facts On File, 1978);

Paul Starr, *The Social Transformation of American Medicine* (New York: Basic Books, 1982);

Rosemary Stevens, *American Medicine and the Public Interest* (New Haven: Yale University Press, 1971);

Andrew C. Twaddle and Richard M. Hessler, *A Sociology of Health* (New York: Macmillan, 1987);

Elliot S. Valenstein, *Great and Desperate Cures* (New York: Basic Books, 1986).

RELIGION

Steve Allen, *Beloved Son: A Story of the Jesus Cults* (Indianapolis: Bobbs-Merrill, 1982);

Nancy T. Ammerman, *Bible Believers: Fundamentalists in the Modern World* (New Brunswick, N.J.: Rutgers University Press, 1987);

Michael Baignet and Richard Leigh, *The Dead Sea Scrolls Deception* (New York: Summit, 1991);

Judith Hershcopf Banki, *Christian Responses to the Yom Kippur War: Implications for Christian-Jewish Relation* (New York: Jewish Committee, n.d.);

Bernham P. Beckwith, *The Decline of U.S. Religious Faith, 1912–1984* (Palo Alto, Cal.: B. P. Beckwith, 1985);

Robert N. Bellah and Frederick E. Greenspahn, eds., *Uncivil Religion: Irreligious Hostility in America* (New York: Crossroads, 1987);

Paul Boyer, *When Time Shall Be No More: Prophesy Belief in Modern American Culture* (Cambridge: Belknap Press, 1992);

David G. Bromley and Anson D. Shupe, Jr., *"Moonies" in America: Cult, Church, and Crusade* (Beverly Hills, Cal.: Sage Publications, 1979);

Charles C. Brown, *Niebuhr and His Age: Reinhold Niebuhr's Prophetic Role in the Twentieth Century* (Philadelphia: Trinity Press International, 1992);

Mark Calanter, *Cults: Faith, Healing, and Coercion* (New York: Oxford University Press, 1989);

Jackson W. Carroll, *Beyond Establishment: Protestant Identity in a Post-Protestant Age* (Louisville, Ky.: Westminster/John Knox, 1993);

Harvey Cox, *Turning East: The Promise and Peril of the New Orientalism* (New York: Simon & Schuster, 1977);

Jay P. Dolan, *The American Catholic Experience* (Garden City, N.Y.: Doubleday, 1985);

John L. Eighmy, *Churches in Cultural Captivity: A History of the Social Attitudes of Southern Baptists* (Knoxville: University of Tennessee Press, 1987);

Robert S. Ellwood, *The Sixties Spiritual Awakening: American Religion Moving from Modern to Post Modern* (New Brunswick, N.J.: Rutgers University Press, 1994);

Gabriel J. Fackre, *The Religious Right and Christian Faith* (Grand Rapids, Mich.: Eerdmans, 1982);

Jacqueline S. Field-Bibb, *Women Toward Priesthood: Ministerial Politics and Feminist Praxis* (New York: Cambridge University Press, 1991);

Ronald B. Flowers, *Religion in Strange Times: The 1960s and 1970s* (Macon, Ga.: Mercer University Press, 1984);

Marshall Frady, *Billy Graham: A Parable of American Righteousness* (Boston: Little, Brown, 1979);

Robert I. Friedman, *The False Prophet: Rabbi Meir Kahane, From FBI Informant to Knesset Member* (Brooklyn: Lawrence Hill, 1990);

Marc Galanter, *Cults: Faith, Healing, and Coercion* (New York: Oxford University Press, 1989);

David J. Garrow, *Liberty and Sexuality: The Right to Privacy and the Making of* Roe *v.* Wade (New York: Macmillan, 1994);

Langdon B. Gilkey, *Catholicism Confronts Modernism: A Protestant View* (New York: Seabury, 1975);

Faye D. Ginsburg, *Contested Lives: The Abortion Debate in an American Community* (Berkeley: University of California Press, 1989);

Andrew M. Greeley, *The American Catholic: A Social Portrait* (New York: Basic Books, 1977);

John R. Hall, *Gone from the Promised Land: Jonestown in American Cultural History* (New Brunswick, N.J.: Transaction, 1987);

Mitchell K. Hall, *Because of Their Faith: CALCAV and Religious Opposition to the Vietnam War* (New York: Columbia University Press, 1990);

David Edwin Harrell, Jr., *Oral Roberts: An American Life* (Bloomington: Indiana University Press, 1985);

Peter G. Horsfield, *Religious Television: The American Experience* (New York: Longman, 1984);

Ernest R. House, *Jesse Jackson and the Politics of Charisma: The Rise and Fall of the PUSH/Excel Program* (Boulder & London: Westview Press, 1988);

James Davison Hunter, *American Evangelicalism: Conservative Religion and the Quandary of Modernity* (New Brunswick, N.J.: Rutgers University Press, 1983);

Ted G. Jelen and Marthe A. Chandler, eds., *Abortion Politics in the United States and Canada* (Westport, Conn.: Praeger, 1994);

Donald G. Jones and Russell E. Richey, eds., *American Civil Religion* (San Francisco: Mellen Research University Press, 1990);

George Klineman and Sherman Butler, *The Cult That Died: The Tragedy of Jim Jones and the Peoples Temple* (New York: Putnam, 1980);

Robert C. Liebman and Robert Wuthnow, eds., *The New Christian Right: Mobilization and Legitimation* (New York: Aldine, 1983);

William C. Martin, *A Prophet with Honor: The Billy Graham Story* (New York: Morrow, 1991);

Martin Marty, *Pilgrims in Their Own Land: 500 Years of Religion in America* (Boston: Houghton Mifflin, 1984);

Larry Martz and Ginny Carroll, *Ministry of Greed: The Inside Story of the Televangelists and Their Holy War* (New York: Weidenfeld & Nicolson, 1988);

Michele McKeegan, *Abortion Politics: Mutiny in the Ranks of the Right* (New York: Free Press, 1992);

Janice Peck, *The Gods of Televangelism* (Cresskill, N.J.: Hampton Press, 1993);

John Pollock, *Billy Graham: Evangelist to the World* (San Francisco: Harper & Row, 1979);

Richard Quebedeaux, *I Found It: The Story of Bill Bright and the Campus Crusade* (San Francisco: Harper & Row, 1979);

Quebedeaux, *The Worldly Evangelicals* (San Francisco: Harper & Row, 1978);

Stanley R. Rader, *Against the Gates of Hell* (New York: Everest House, 1980);

James T. Richardson, Joel Best, and David G. Bromley, eds., *The Satanism Scare* (New York: Aldine de Gruyter, 1991);

Peter Rowley, *New Gods in America* (New York: McKay, 1971);

Jules Victor Schwerin, *Go Tell It On the Mountain: Mahalia Jackson, Queen of Gospel* (New York: Oxford University Press, 1992);

Ingrid H. Shafer, *Eros and the Womanliness of God: Andrew Greeley's Romance of Renewal* (Chicago: Loyola University Press, 1991);

Edward S. Shapiro, *A Time for Healing: American Jewry since 1945* (Baltimore: Johns Hopkins University Press, 1992);

Charles E. Shepard, *Forgiven: The Rise and Fall of Jim Bakker and the PTL Ministry* (New York: Atlantic Monthly Press, 1989);

Anson Shupe and William A. Stacey, *Born Again Politics*

and the Moral Majority: What Social Surveys Really Show (New York: Edwin Mellen Press, 1982);

Corwin E. Smidt, *Contemporary Evangelical Political Involvement: An Analysis and Assessment* (Lanham, Md.: University Press of America, 1989);

Suzanne Staggenborg, *The Pro-Choice Movement: Organization and Activism in the Abortion Conflict* (New York: Oxford University Press, 1991);

Dennis N. Voskuil, *Mountains into Gold Mines: Robert Schuller and the Gospel of Success* (Grand Rapids, Mich.: Eerdmans, 1983);

Ruth Wangerin, *The Children of God: A Make-Believe Revolution?* (Westport, Conn.: Bergin & Garvey, 1994);

Garry Wills, *Under God: Religion and American Politics* (New York: Simon & Schuster, 1990);

Irving I. Zaretsky and Mark P. Leone, eds., *Religious Movements in Contemporary America* (Princeton: Princeton University Press, 1974).

SCIENCE AND TECHNOLOGY

Gary M. Abshire, ed., *The Impact of Computers on Society and Ethics: A Bibliography* (Morristown, N.J.: Creative Computing, 1980);

William Bains, *Genetic Engineering for Almost Everybody* (New York: Pelican, 1987);

Jack Belzer, Albert G. Holzman, and Allen Kent, eds., *Encyclopedia of Computer Science and Technology,* 16 volumes (New York: Marcel Dekker, 1975–1981);

Michael Brown, *Laying Waste: The Poisoning of America by Toxic Chemicals* (New York: Pocket Books, 1981);

Michael Collins, *Liftoff: The Story of America's Adventure in Space* (New York: Grove, 1988);

Herman H. Goldstein, *The Computer from Pascal to von Neumann* (Princeton: Princeton University Press, 1972);

Donna Haraway, *Primate Visions: Gender, Race, and Nature in the World of Modern Science* (New York: Routledge, 1989);

J. Haugelan, *Artificial Intelligence: The Very Idea* (Cambridge, Mass.: MIT Press, 1985);

Alexander Hellemans and Bryan Bunch, *The Timetable of Science* (New York: Simon & Schuster, 1988);

Clive Irving, *Wide-Body: The Triumph of the 747* (New York: Morrow, 1993);

Gill Kirkup and Laurie Smith Keller, *Inventing Women: Science, Technology, and Gender* (Cambridge, Mass.: Polity Press, 1992);

McGraw-Hill Encyclopedia of Science and Technology, fourth edition, 14 volumes (New York: McGraw-Hill, 1977);

N. Metropolis, ed., *A History of Computing in the Twentieth Century* (New York: Academic Press, 1980);

Sy Montgomery, *Walking with the Great Apes: Jane Goodall, Dian Fossey, Biruté Galdikas* (Boston: Houghton Mifflin, 1991);

Ron Numbers, *The Creationists: The Evolution of Scientific Creationism* (New York: Knopf, 1992);

Phil Patton, *Made in the USA: The Secret Histories of Things That Made America* (New York: Simon & Schuster, 1988);

Carrol W. Pursell, Jr., ed., *Technology in America: A History of Individuals and Ideas,* second edition (Cambridge, Mass.: MIT Press, 1990);

John Reader, *Missing Links: The Hunt for Earliest Man* (New York: Penguin, 1988);

Jeremy Rifkin and Nicanor Perlas, *Algeny* (New York: Penguin, 1983);

Cass Schichtle, *The National Space Program from the Fifties to the Eighties* (Washington, D.C.: GPO, 1983);

Science & Technology Desk Reference, edited by Carnegie Library of Pittsburgh, Science and Technology Department (Detroit: Gale, 1993);

Mark Stephens, *Three Mile Island: The Hour-by-Hour Account of What Really Happened* (New York: Random House, 1980);

Sharon Traweek, *Beamtimes and Lifetimes: The World of High Energy Physicists* (Cambridge, Mass.: Harvard University Press, 1988);

James Watson and John Tooze, *The DNA Story: A Documentary History of Gene Cloning* (San Francisco: W. H. Freeman, 1981);

Fred Wilcox, *Waiting for an Army to Die: The Tragedy of Agent Orange* (New York: Random House, 1983).

SPORTS

Charles C. Alexander, *Our Game: An American Baseball History* (New York: Holt, 1991);

Arthur R. Ashe, Jr., *A Hard Road to Glory: A History of the African-American Athlete Since 1946* (New York: Warner, 1988);

William J. Baker and John M. Carrol, eds., *Sports in Modern America* (Saint Louis: River City Publishers, 1981);

Jim Benagh, *Incredible Olympic Feats* (New York: McGraw-Hill, 1976);

Edwin H. Cady, *The Big Game: College Sports and American Life* (Knoxville: University of Tennessee Press, 1978);

Erich Camper, *Encyclopedia of the Olympic Games* (New York: McGraw-Hill, 1972);

James B. Dworkin, *Owners Versus Players: Baseball and Collective Bargaining* (Boston: Auburn House, 1981);

Ellen W. Gerber, Jan Feshlin, Pearl Berlin, and Waneen Wyrick, *The American Woman in Sport* (Reading, Mass.: Addison-Wesley, 1974);

Elliott J. Gorn, *The Manly Art* (Ithaca, N.Y.: Cornell University Press, 1986);

Peter J. Graham and Horst Ueberhorst, eds., *The Modern Olympic Games* (Cornwall, N.Y.: Leisure Press, 1976);

Allen Guttman, *A Whole New Ball Game: An Interpretation of American Sports* (Chapel Hill: University of North Carolina Press, 1988);

Dorothy V. Harris, ed., *Women and Sport* (State College: Pennsylvania State University Press, 1972);

Robert J. Higgs, *Sports: A Reference Guide* (Westport, Conn.: Greenwood Press, 1982);

Neil D. Isaacs, *All the Moves: A History of College Basketball* (Philadelphia: Lippincott, 1975);

Bill James, *The Bill James Historical Baseball Abstract* (New York: Villard Books, 1986);

William O. Johnson, *All That Glitters Is Not Gold* (New York: Putnam, 1972);

Ivan N. Kaye, *Good Clean Violence: A History of College Football* (Philadelphia: Lippincott, 1973);

Lee Lowenfish, *The Imperfect Diamond: A History of Baseball's Labor Wars* (New York: Da Capo, 1991);

Richard D. Mandel, *Sport: A Cultural History* (New York: Columbia University Press, 1984);

Robert Mechicoff and Steven Estes, *A History and Philosophy of Sport and Physical Education* (Dubuque, Iowa: William C. Brown, 1993);

James A. Michener, *Sports in America* (New York: Random House, 1976);

Benjamin G. Rader, *American Sports: From the Age of Folk Games to the Age of Spectators* (Englewood Cliffs, N.J.: Prentice-Hall, 1983);

Steven A. Riess, ed., *The American Sporting Experience* (West Point, N.Y.: Leisure Press, 1984);

Leverett T. Smith, Jr., *The American Dream and the National Game* (Bowling Green, Ohio: Bowling Green University Popular Press, 1975);

Betty Spears and Richard A. Swanson, *History of Sport and Physical Education,* third edition (Dubuque, Iowa: William C. Brown, 1983);

Jules Tygel, *Baseball's Great Experiment* (New York: Oxford University Press, 1983);

David Q. Voigt, *America Through Baseball* (Chicago: Nelson-Hall, 1976).

CONTRIBUTORS

ARTS

JIM ZRIMSEK
Chicago, Illinois

BUSINESS

JAMES W. HIPP
Bruccoli Clark Layman

and

LEONARD BUSHKOFF
Boston, Massachusetts

EDUCATION

HARRIET WILLIAMS
University of South Carolina

FASHION

JANE GERHARD
Brown University

GOVERNMENT

VICTOR BONDI
University of Massachusetts — Boston

MEDIA

DARREN HARRIS-FAIN
Bruccoli Clark Layman

MEDICINE

JOAN LAXSON
Boston, Massachusetts

LAW

SUSAN STERETT
University of Denver

LIFESTYLES

VICTOR BONDI
University of Massachusetts — Boston
PETER C. HOLLORAN
Pine Manor College

RELIGION

JOHN SCOTT WILSON
University of South Carolina

SCIENCE AND TECHNOLOGY

LAURA BRIGGS
Brown University

SPORTS

DENNIS LYNCH
Texas A&M University

INDEX OF PHOTOGRAPHS

INDEX

and Bernstein), 31, 62, 246, 369, 380

"All the Young Dudes" (Mott the Hoople), 69

"All Things Considered" (NPR), 370

Allen, Woody, 81–82, 386

Allen, Irwin, 28, 30, 64

Allen, Marcus, 547

Allen, Paul, 130–131

Allen, Woody, 29, 31, 34–36, 40, 58–59, 62–63, 66, 210

Allende Gossens, Salvador, 4–6, 8–9, 110, 266, 270

Allied Chemical, 113

Allied Stores, 144

The Allman Brothers, 40, 69, 78

Allman, Duane, 69, 96

Allyn, Stanley C., 143

Allyson, June, 57

"Alone Again Naturally" (O'Sullivan), 28

Alpert, Herb, 36

Alpert, Jane, 278

Alpert, Richard, 337

Alson, Charles, 212

Alsop, Stewart, 389

Altair, 122, 130–131

Altair 8800, 473

Alternating Current (Paz), 8

Alther, Lisa, 53

Altman, Robert, 26–27, 31, 57–58, 61, 63

Aluminum Corporation of America (ALCOA), 144

Alunni, Corrado, 21

Alvarez, Dr. Walter Clement, 432

Alvin submersible, 491

Amadeus (Shaffer), 22

Amalgamated Clothing Workers of America, 112, 144

Amarcord (Fellini), 10

The Amazing Spider-Man (Marvel Comics), 378

Ambassador College, 459–460

Ambassador Hotel, 205

Amdur, Neil, 540

Amerasinghe, H. S., 17

"America" (song), 88

America (the band), 28, 31

American Academy and Institute of Arts and Letters, 86, 92

American Academy of Neurology, 432

American Airlines, 110, 115, 204

American Association for the Advancement, 487

American Association for the Advancement of Science, 187, 477

American Association of Blood Banks, 419

American Association of Christian Schools, 164

American Association of Retired Persons, 342

American Association of School Administrators, 168

American Association of State Colleges and Universities, 186

American Association of University Women's Journal, 167

American Ballet Theater (ABT), 33, 38, 45–46, 49

American Bank and Trust Company, 114

American Bar Association (ABA), 297, 303, 306, 312, 314

American Basketball Association, 512

American Broadcasting Company (ABC), 360–361, 363–364, 374–376, 378, 381–383, 386–387

American Buffalo, 39, 51, 87, 92

American Christian College, 463

American Civil Liberties Union (ACLU), 298, 306, 317, 345

American Council for Judaism, 145

American Doctor's Odyssey (Heiser), 433

American Federation of Labor and Congress of Industrial Organizations (AFL-CIO), 168, 222

American Federation of State, County, and Municipal Employees, 407

American Federation of Teachers (AFT), 168–169, 187

American Football Conference, 526

American Football League, 355

American Friends Service Committee, 469

American Golf Classic, 531

American Graffiti, 29, 38, 57, 61, 63–66, 83, 375

American Hall of Fame of Fashion, 207

American Heart Association (AHA), 401, 433

American Hospital Association (AHA), 397

American Hot Wax, 48, 65

An American in Paris, 98

American Indian Movement (AIM), 220, 288–289, 332

American Institute for Research, 159

American Institute of Architects (AIA), 203, 206, 209–210, 212

American Legion, 311, 399

American Lutheran Church, 444, 457

American Medical Association (AMA), 406, 408, 425–426, 428, 432, 434

American Motors Corporation (AMC), 111, 113, 123–124, 192

American Music Awards, 31, 89

"American Pie" (McLean), 28, 38

American Psychiatric Association (APA), 320, 336, 397

American Psychological Association (APA), 187, 422

American Social Health Association (ASHA), 426

American Sociological Association, 336

American Telephone and Telegraph (AT&T), 108, 110, 143, 194, 196, 202–203, 206, 345

"American Top 40", 26

"American Woman" (Guess Who), 26, 69

American Zoetrope Studio, 82, 84

Amin, Hafizullah, 22, 24

Amin, Idi, 5, 14, 18–19, 23, 343

Amnesty International, 19

Amoco Cadiz, 20

Amos, John, 376

Amos 'n' Andy, 390

Amsterdam News, 361

Amtrak, 107, 121, 143

An American Family, 334

Anaconda Wire and Cable, 108, 114

Analog, 390

The Analysis of the Self (Kohut), 421

Anchorage Daily News, 389

. . . And Justice for All, 63, 87

And Now for Something Completely Different, 28, 66, 374

Anderson, Eddie ("Rochester"), 96

Anderson, Laurie, 38, 44–45, 75, 79, 91, 267, 388

Anderson, Leroy, 97

Anderson, Lindsay, 8

Anderson, Philip Warren, 495

Anderson, William, 97

Anderson Tumor Institute, 396

Andersonville (Kantor), 98

de Andrea, John, 44

Andrea True Connection, 32, 73

Andreotti, Giulio, 17
Andretti, Mario, 549
Andrews, James, 385
Andrews, Julie, 36, 57
Andrews, Mike, 515
The Andromeda Strain, 65
The Andy Williams Show, 70
Anesthesiology, 432–433
Anfinsen, Christian Boehmer, 495
Angelou, Maya, 37, 376
"Angie" (Rolling Stones), 29
Angioplasty, 399
Angle of Repose, 93
Angus camera sled, 491
Anhedonia, 80
Anheuser-Busch, 113
Anka, Paul, 30
Ann-Margret, 27, 31
Anna Fillmore Award, 430
Anna Mill and Company, 205
Annie, 34, 39, 52, 95
Annie Hall, 34, 58, 62, 80, 95, 194,
    201, 208, 210, 337
Another Woman (movie), 81
Answered Prayers (Capote), 52, 386
Anthony, Earl, 549
Anthony, Edward, 389
Anthony, John, 211
Anti–big government, 235
Antiballistic Missile (ABM) Treaty,
    240
Antidisco backlash, 74
Antigovernment, 235
Antioch College, 172
Antitax initiative, 235
Antiwar movement, 236, 245, 253
Antoinette Perry Awards (Tonys),
    94
Anyon, Jean, 163
Apgar Score, 432
Apgar, Dr. Virginia, 432
Apocalypse Now, 36, 62, 63, 65, 67,
    83, 88
Apollo 10, 68
Apollo 13, 472, 480–481
Apollo 14, 472, 481
Apollo 15, 361, 472, 481
Apollo 16, 473
Apollo 17, 473
Apollo space program, 481
Apollo/Soyuz spaceflight, 13, 233,
    473
Appalachian Mountain Club, 331
Appendicitis, 406, 423
Applause (musical), 94
Apple Computer, 118, 122, 323,
    474, 484

Apple resulted in a partial core, 122
Arab League, 22
Arab-African conference, Cairo, 18
Arab-controlled Organization of
    Petroleum Countries (OPEC),
    330
Arab-Israeli War, 1967, 4–5, 14
Arafat, Yasser, 459, 464
Arber, Dr. Werner, 428, 494
Archie Bunker's Place, 375, 383
Archie Publishers, 378
The Archies, 71
Architectural Barriers Act, 203
Architectural Firm Award, 209
Architectural Forum, 193
Architectural League of New York,
    205
ARCO, 129
Argento, Dominick, 94
Argersinger v. *Hamlin*, 307
Argo Merchant (tanker ship), 114
Arizona Republic, 315, 323
Arizona State University (football
    team), 525
Arledge, Roone, 537
Armatrading, Joan, 38, 68
Armed Forces Journal, 243
Armstrong, Barbara N., 316
Armstrong, Garner Ted, 459
Armstrong, Herbert W., 459–460
Armstrong, Louis, 27, 96
Armstrong, William, 91, 389
Army Medical Corps, 189
Army of the Republic of Vietnam
    (ARVN), 237–239, 242–243
Arrow, Kenneth J., 109
Art Institute, Chicago, 36
Arthur, Beatrice, 383
Arthur Godfrey Time, 361
Arthur, Jean, 57
The Artist's Father (Cézanne), 26
as-Sadat, Anwar, 266
Ashbery, John, 93
Ashbrook, John M., 253
Ashby, Hal, 29, 35, 62
Ashe, Arthur, 508
Ashland Oil, 110
Ashley, Laura, 210
Asia Society, 35
Asilomar conference, 473
Asimov, Isaac, 39
Asner, Ed, 376, 384
Assemblies of God, 469
Associated Press, 387, 389, 391
Association of American Publishers,
    163

Association of Country Entertainers
    (ACE), 41, 79
Association of Primary Dealers, 141
Astounding Science Fiction, 390
Aswan High Dam, 4
At Long Last Love, 65
"At Seventeen" (Ian), 38, 68
Atari, 122
Atkins, Chet, 77
Atkinson, Bill, 211
Atkinson, Dr. Walter Sydney, 432
Atlanta Braves, 386, 513
Atlanta Constitution,, 322
Atlanta Hawks, 386
Atlanta University, 170
Atlantic Richfield, 114
Atlas, Charles, 356
Atlas/Seaboard, 378
Atomic Energy Commission
    (AEC), 109, 129, 281, 301, 494
Atoms for Peace, 488
Attica State Correctional Facility,
    217, 279, 287, 295–296
Attie, Dottie, 42
Atyeo, Don, 542
Auchincloss, Louis, 28, 34–35
Auden, W. H., 97
Audrey Rose, 64
Audubon Society, 331
August 1914 (Solzhenitsyn), 6
Austin, Gene, 97
Austin, Tracy, 510, 512, 540, 552
Australopithecus., 486
Austrian, Dr. Robert, 429
Auth, Tony, 389
*The Autobiography of Miss Jane Pitt-
    man* (Gaines), 27, 52
Autumn of the Patriarch (García
    Márquez), 13, 53
Avalanche, 64
Avco Cup, 535
Avila, Gustava, 550
Awards, 387
    Best actor, 82, 86
    Best Actress, 80, 84
    Best Adaptation Score, 91
    Best Director, 80–83
    Best Female R&B Vocal Perfor-
    mance, 89
    Best Inspirational Performance,
    89
    Best musical, 88
    Best Original Score, 91
    Best Original Song, 91
    Best Picture, 80–83
    Best Screenplay, 81–84
    Best Song, 89

Axel, Dr. Richard, 430
Axelrod, Dr. Julius, 427
Aycock, Alice, 42
B-52, 243
The B-52s, 76, 220
B.F. Goodrich Company, 110
Baader-Meinhof gang, 342
Babashoff, Shirley, 549
Babbitt, Milton, 88
Baby and Child Care, 354
"Baby Don't Get Hooked on Me" (Davis), 28
Bacall, Lauren, 94
Bach, Richard, 26
Bachman Turner Overdrive (BTO), 68–69
Bachman, Jerald, 186
Bachman, Randy, 69
Bachman-Turner Overdrive, 30
"Back Stabbers" (O'Jays), 28, 72
Backe, John D., 142
"Bad Bad Leroy Brown" (Croce), 29
"Bad Blood" (Sedaka), 31
"Bad Girls" (Summer), 36, 74, 89
"Bad Time" (Grand Funk Railroad), 31
Baddeley, Angela, 96
Badlands, 29, 62
Badura, Michael, 44
Baer, Dr. John E., 429
Baez, Joan, 67, 192, 324
Bagaza, Jean-Baptiste, 17
Bailey, Dr. Pearce, 432
Baker, Don, 66
Baker, George, 389
Baker, Josephine, 97
"Baker Street" (Rafferty), 35
Baker's Dozen, 48
Bakhtiar, Shahpur, 21
Bakke v. *University of California*, 132, 152, 166, 229, 309–310, 400
Bakker, Jim, 342, 455, 460, 466
Bakker, Jim and Tammy, 443
Bakr, Ahmad Hassan al-, 23
Balaban, Barney, 96
Balanchine, George, 26, 45–46, 49
Baldwin, Faith, 97
Baldwin, James, 28, 30, 52
"Ball of Confusion" (The Temptation), 72
"Ballad of the Green Berets" (Sadler), 77, 79
Ballard, Florence, 96
Ballard, Robert, 491
"Ballroom Blitz" (Sweet), 31
Baltimore Bullets, 501, 550
Baltimore Colts, 501, 504, 526, 550

Baltimore Orioles, 512–513, 550, 552
Baltimore, Dr. David, 428, 493
Bambara, Toni Cade, 85
Bananas, 66, 80
Bancroft, Anne, 34, 57
The Band, 77
"Band on the Run" (Wings), 30
Banenciaga, Cristobal, 213
Bangs, Lester, 372
Banks, Dennis, 332
Banks, Jeffrey, 212
Banner, John, 389
Barbarella (movie), 58, 83
Barbirolli, John, 96
Barbour, Elaine, 188
Bard, Barnard, 165
Bardeen, John, 495
Bardot, Brigitte, 57
Baretta, 374
Barker, Bernard, 314
Barlow, Perry, 390
"Barnaby" (Johnson), 391
Barnes, Marvin, 550
Barnett, Dick, 518
Barnett, Ross, 312
Barney Miller, 365
Barr, John A., 143
Barrie, Scott, 201, 210
Barry, Marion, 229, 234
Barry, Rick, 518
Barth, John, 52
Barthelme, Donald, 30, 52
Bartlett, Donald L., 389
Bartow, Gene, 521–522
Baryshnikov, Mikhail, 34, 38, 45–46, 49
Barzargan, Mehdi, 232
Baseball, 364, 513
BASIC (programming language), 122, 130–131
The Basic Training of Pavlo Hummel, 39, 51, 86, 94
Basketball Digest, 517
Bates, Alan, 94
Batman, 378
Batten, Barton, Durstine, and Osborne, 143
Battle of the Bulge, 281
Bauman, Charlie, 525
Baxter, Robert C., 212
Baxter, Ted, 384
Bay City Rollers, 32
Bayh, Jr., Birch E., 260
Baylor College of Medicine, 426
Beal v. *Doe*, 295

"Beat on the Brat" (The Ramones), 75
Beatlemania, 34
The Beatles, 26, 34, 43, 48, 66–67, 72, 92, 122
Beatty, Warren, 27, 31, 35, 63, 66
Beau Brummel Ties, 208
Beaudry, Dianne, 212
Beck, Jeff, 40
Beckley, Bill, 45
Bedford, Brian, 94
The Bee Gees, 27, 31–32, 35–36, 40, 48, 73
Beecher, Dr. Henry K., 432
Beene, Geoffrey, 211
Beethoven, Ludwig von, 43
Begin, Menachem, 18–19, 21, 230–231, 266
The Beginnings of a Complex (Aycock), 42
Begle, Edward, 176
Begley, Ed, 96
Behind the Green Door, 66, 329, 377
Behrman, S. N., 96
Being There (Kosinski), 26, 62
Bekesy, Dr. Georg von, 435
Belafonte, Harry, 56
Bell Labs, 492
Bell, Conrad, 212
Bell, Daniel, 340
Bell, Earl, 509
Bell, Ricky, 524
Bell, Terrell H., 163
Bell, Thom, 73, 266, 390
Bellamy Brothers, 32
The Bellarosa Connection (Bellow), 82
The Belle of Amherst, 94
Bellote, Pete, 89
Bellow, Saul, 81–82, 92, 93
Bellow, Saul, 26, 31, 33, 39, 52–53
Belluschi, Rietro, 212
Belmont Stakes, 538
Belote, Melissa, 533
Beloved (Morrison), 86
Belushi, John, 35, 66
Beman, Deane, 530
Ben Franklin variety stores, 135
Ben-Hur, 98
Bench, Johnny, 513, 516
Benchley, Peter, 30, 54
A Bend in the River (Naipaul), 21
Bendix Aviation Corporation, 143
Benham, Stanley, 553
Benitez, Wilfredo, 512
Benjamin, Richard, 26, 59
Bennett, Charles H., 493

Chandler, Jennifer, 534
Chandler, Norman, 390
Chanel, Coco, 204, 206, 213
Channing, Carol, 245
Chao Chung Ting, Samuel, 493
Chapin, Dwight, 249
Chapin, Harry, 30, 68, 70
Chapin, James, 97
Chaplin, Charlie, 80, 97
Chapman, Graham, 374
Chariots of the Gods (Von Daniken), 39
Charles, Ezzard, 553
Charles, Ray, 73, 391
Charles Pfizer and Company, 144
Charleston (W.Va.) *Daily Mail*, 389
A Charlie Brown Christmas, 98
Charlie Daniels Band, 69
Charlie's Angels, 71, 210, 363, 374, 386
Charlotte Observer, 460
Charlton Publishers, 378
Charm, 489, 493
Charnley, Prof. John, 429
Charon, 474, 493
Charter 77, 18
Chase, Ilka, 97
Chase Manhattan Bank, 143
Chavez, Cesar, 107, 162, 333, 351
Chaykin, Howard, 379
Cheever, John, 29, 34–35, 39, 52–53, 93
Cheng, Chi, 550
Cher, 27, 29–30, 71, 192, 373
Chernobyl, 477
Chevalier, Maurice, 97
Chevrolet, 108
Chevrolet Corvair, 139
Chevrolet Vega, 123
Chevron Oil Company, 106
The Chi-Lites, 28, 73
Chic, 36, 40, 74
Chicago, 50, 85
Chicago (the band), 32, 69
Chicago Art Institute, 205
Chicago Blackhawks, 501, 505, 550–551
Chicago Cubs, 513
Chicago Daily News, 388
Chicago, Judy, 38, 41–42, 348
Chicago Seven, 216, 286, 341, 343
Chicago Sun-Times, 388
Chicago Symphony, 27
Chicago Theological Seminary, 463
Chicago Tribune, 388–389
Chicago, Rock Island & Pacific Railroad, 112

Chico and the Man, 374
Child, Julia, 352
Child's Play (play), 94
Child-care bill, 226
Children of God, 447
Children of the Revolution (Kozol), 183
Children's Television Act of 1990, 377
Children's Television Workshop, 382
Childress, Alice, 29, 53
China Medical Association, 405
The China Syndrome, 36, 58, 63, 84, 488
Chinatown, 30, 63
Chirundu (Mpthalhele), 21
Chisholm, Conrad, 271
Chisholm, Shirley, 167, 234, 271, 347, 384
Chlorofluorocarbons, 474, 479
Choate, Robert Burnett, Jr., 414, 425
The Choirboys (Wambaugh), 31
Cholera, 396, 425, 434
Chopin, Frédéric, 92
A Chorus Line (play), 38–39, 45, 47, 49–51, 93–94
Chou En-lai, 16
Christa (Sandys), 42
Christian Anti-Communist Crusade, 462
Christian Broadcasting Network (CBN), 342, 363, 443, 455, 460, 466
Christian Democratic Party, Italy, 20
Christian Heritage College, 465
Christian High School of San Diego, 465
Christian Voice, 452
Christianity, 68, 156, 162–164, 183, 269, 276, 375
Christianity Today (magazine), 445
Christie, Agatha, 97
Christie, Julie, 27, 31, 35, 57–58
Christman, Paul, 553
Christmas, W. A., 315
Christmas, William, 286
Christo, 42–43
Christy, James W., 493
Chrysler Corporation, 111, 114, 116, 118, 123–124, 127, 139, 194, 231, 331
Chujoy, Anatole, 46
Church, Frank, 226, 260, 270, 389
Church, Frederick Edwin, 36

Church of Christ, 172
Church of Jesus, 458
Church of Scientology, 447
Churchill, Caryl, 22
Cifra, 135
Cimino, Michael, 35, 64
Cincinnati Reds, 501, 504, 508–509, 513–515, 550–552
Cipullo, Aldo, 212
Cisler, Lucina, 346
Citation to a Layman for Distinguished Service Award, 425–426
Citizens Band (CB) radio, 79
Citrine, Charlie, 82
City College of New York, 152, 174, 187, 189, 208
City Complex One (Heizer), 42
City University of New York (CUNY), 165
Civil Aeronautics Board (CAB), 120
Civil rights, 161, 196, 216, 223, 225, 231, 234, 270–271, 277, 280–281, 286, 292, 300, 304–305, 309, 316, 370, 375, 384, 407, 409, 420
Civil Rights Act of 1964, 131–132, 159, 166, 180, 300
Civil Service Commission, 108
Claiborne, Liz, 210
Clapton, Eric, 30, 40, 66, 71
Clark Air Force Base, 220
Clark, Brian, 22
Clark, Dick, 31
Clark, Joe, 23–24
Clark, Mark, 343
Clark, Tom. C., 316
Clarke, Bobby, 536
The Clash, 40, 67, 75–76, 194
Claudine, 30, 56
Clause, Dr. Albert, 428
Clavell, James, 53
Clay, Cassius, 543
Clay, Lucius D., 280
Clayburgh, Jill, 28, 35, 38, 58
Clayton, Horace, 189
Clean Air Act, 1970, 286, 288, 301
Clean Water Act, 331
Cleaver, Eldridge, 170, 289, 339
Cleese, John, 374
Clemente, Roberto, 356, 514
Clemson University (football team), 525
Cleopatra, 386
Cleopatra Jones, 54, 332
Clergy and Laity Concerned About Vietnam, 456

Cleveland Browns, 526, 537
Cleveland Indians, 322
Cliburn, Van, 33
Cliff, Jimmy, 29, 76
Cline, Patsy, 77
Clinton, George, 73, 262
A Clockwork Orange, 27, 60–61
Close Encounters of the Third Kind, 34
Close Encounters of the Third Kind (movie), 34–35, 54, 61, 63
"Close to You" (Carpenters), 26
Close, Chuck, 43
The Closing Circle (Commoner), 331
"Cloud Nine" (The Temptations), 22, 72
The Clowns (Fellini), 5
Clune, William, 182
Coal Creek Elementary, 188
Coal Miner's Daughter, 79
Cobb, Lee J., 97, 390
Cobb, Ty, 510
Coca-Cola, 463
Cocaine, 87
Cochran, Barbara, 503, 532
Cochran, Thad, 261
Cocker, Joe, 69
Cockpit (Kosinski), 31
Coffee, Linda, 294, 314
Coffin, William Sloane, 467
Coffy, 54–55, 374
Coggan, F. Donald, 10
Cohen, Dr. Seymour S., 430
Cohen, Leonard, 67
Cohen, Stanley H., 493
Cohen, Susan, 186
Colburn, Donald L., 93
Colby, William E., 221, 226
Cold War, 233, 265, 267, 368
"Cold warriors," 233
Cole, Jack, 85
Coleman, Dr. James S., 157, 160, 180–181
Coleman, John, 186
Coles, Robert, 430
Colgate–Dinah Shore Winners Circle, 513, 531
Colgrass, Michael, 93
Collazo, Oscar, 291
Collected Poems (Wright), 93
Collected Stories (Stafford), 93
College basketball, 520
College Board, 151, 161, 184
College football, 523
College Placement Council, 149
Collier's magazine, 389
Collins, Judy, 67

Collins, Michael, 481
Colombo, Joseph, 334
Colson, Charles W., 224, 249, 453
Colter, Jessi, 78
Columbia, 95, 367
Columbia Broadcasting System (CBS), 50, 142–143, 360–361, 363, 366, 367, 376–377, 382–383, 387, 390
Columbia Records, 79
Columbia School of Journalism, 389
Columbia University, 137, 169, 180, 189, 209, 271, 430, 434
Columbo, 374
Columbo, Joseph, 315
Coma, 65
Comaneci, Nadia, 552
Come Back Little Sheba, 98
Comedy Hall of Fame, 384
Comes a Horseman, 84
Comic books, 378
Comics Code Authority, 362, 378
Coming Home, 35, 58–59, 62–63, 65, 84, 87, 95
The Coming of Post-Industrial Society (Bell), 340
Commentary, 264, 375
Commercialization, 76
Committee to Reelect the President (CREEP), 219, 221, 246–247, 249, 253–254, 368, 380
The Commodores, 35
Common Cause, 320
Commoner, Barry, 141, 331
The Common Sense Book of Baby and Child Care (Spock), 354
Communism, 92, 237, 239, 240, 243, 265, 233, 270, 275
Communist Party, Cambodia, 19
Communist Party, China, 11, 23
Communist Party, East Germany, 5
Communist Party, Italy, 14
Community support systems (CSS), 407
Company, 39, 49, 88, 94, 95
The Complete Book of Running (Fixx), 410, 544
Complexity and Contradiction in Architecture (Venturi), 209
Computerized axial tomography (CAT) scanner, 398, 403, 413, 428–429
Computers in medicine, 413
"Conan comics," 378
"Concept" groups, 76
Concerned Women for America, 465

Concert for Bangladesh, 27
Concorde, 24, 113, 323, 474, 485
The Concorde: Airport '79, 64
Concordia Seminary, 468
Condon, Eddie, 97
Condon, Richard, 34
Cone, Honey, 72
Conference of Nonaligned Nations, 9
Conference on Security and Cooperation in Europe, 9
Congress Party, India, 7, 18
Congressional Black Caucus, 332
Congressional misbehavior, 235
Conklin, Chester, 97
Connally, Ben C., 316
Connally, John, 109, 253
Connors, Chuck, 376
Connors, Jimmy, 133, 507–509, 511, 540, 551–552
Conrad, Joseph, 65
Conrad, Paul, 388
Conrail, 113
Conscientious objector, 216
Conservative culture, 375
Conservative Party, Great Britain, 4, 11, 13, 23
Conservatives, 233, 240, 260, 264–265
Consider the Possibility (Kays), 187
Considine, Robert, 390
Consolidated Coal Company, 136
Consolidated Edison, 109
Consolidated Vultee Aircraft, 144
Constitution, 217–218, 234, 271–272, 279
Constitutional Authority, 233
Constitutional Convention, 162
Constitutional Rights Subcommittee, 271
Consul's File (Theroux), 34
Consultation on Church Union (COCU), 447
Consumer Product Safety Act, 125
Consumer Product Safety Commission (CPSC), 125
Consumer Protection Agency, 139
Consumer Reports, 124
Consumer shortages, 258
Conti, Bill, 34
Conti, Tom, 94
The Conversation, 30, 61–63, 84
Conversation in the Cathedral (Vargas Llosa), 13
"Convoy" (McCall), 32, 79
Cooder, Ry, 36
Coody, Charles, 501, 551

Executive Council of the Episcopal Church, 456

"Executive privilege," 288, 292, 304, 312

Exile, 35

Exile on Main Street (Rolling Stones), 67

The Exorcist, 27, 29, 39–40, 53, 61, 64–65, 67

Explo '72, 461

Explo '74, 461

Expo '70, 3

Expo '74, 322

Extended plays (EPs), 76

Exxon Corporation, 109, 112, 115, 129, 145

The Eye of the Storm (White), 10

Fabing, Dr. Howard D., 432

Failing Newspaper Act, 360

Fainsod, Merle, 280

Fairfax, Beatrice (Marion C. McCarroll), 390

Fairness Doctrine (FCC), 362

Faisal, King (Saudi Arabia), 14

Faith, Percy, 97

Falcon, 481

Falcon (Marvel Comics), 361

Falconer (Cheever), 34, 53

Fallers, Lloyd, 189

Falwell, Jerry, 264, 324, 336, 339, 342, 375, 443–445, 452, 455

"Fame" (Bowie), 31

"Family Affair" (Sly and the Family Stone), 27

The Family Arsenal (Theroux), 32

Family Assistance Payments, 126

Family Circle, 360

Family Plot (movie), 32

"Family viewing policy," 378

The Fan Club (Wallace), 30

Fantasy, 364

Farber, Dr. Sidney, 432

Fargas, Antonio, 373

Fargo, Donna, 28, 78

Farmer, James, 271

Farnsworth, Philo T., 390

Farrell, James T., 97

Farrow, Mia, 30, 82, 382

Fashion Hall of Fame, 205, 208

Fashion Institute of Technology, 207

Faske, Helen, 207

Fassbinder, Rainer Werner, 22

Fassi, Carlo, 534

Fat Albert and the Cosby Kids (CBS), 376, 377

Fawcett, Roger K. , 390

Fawcett-Majors, Farrah, 32, 210, 386, 538

Fear of Flying (Jong), 29, 52, 329, 373, 377

Federal Aviation Administration, 119

Federal Bureau of Investigation (FBI), 60, 220–221, 225–226, 234, 245, 247, 270, 275, 278, 281, 288–290, 297–298, 304, 316, 447

Federal Coal Mine Health and Safety Act, 341

Federal Communications Commission (FCC), 125, 245, 275, 360–362, 364, 367, 377–378, 382, 455, 460

Federal Election Campaign Act, 218

Federal Election Commission, 115, 226

Federal Energy Act, 194

Federal Energy Office (FEO), 141

Federal Housing Authority, 160

Federal Reserve Bank, 210

Federal Reserve Board, 112, 115, 127, 136–137, 229

Federal Science Pavilion, 210

Federal Trade Commission (FTC), 107, 125, 363, 414, 415

Federal Women's Award, 494

Federation of Islamic Associations, 468

"Feel Like Makin' Love" (Flack), 30

Feis, Herbert, 280

Felt, Mark, 290

Femina, Jerry Della, 137

Feminism, 325, 370, 373–374, 381, 384–385, 387, 443, 445, 457

Feminists, 84, 374, 381, 384–385

Fenny, Rev. Leonard, 469

Ferguson, Tom, 549

Fermi National Accelerator Laboratory, 472, 489

Ferraro, Geraldine, 234

Ferren, John, 97

Ferris, Daniel, 553

Ferry, Bryan, 75

Fiber-optic, 364, 482

Fiddler on the Roof, 28

Fiedler, Arthur, 32, 43, 97, 227, 352, 356, 386

Field, Betty, 98

Field, Sally, 34, 36, 96

Fields, Dorothy, 27, 98

Fifteen Years After (Jaworski), 312

Fifth Amendment, 299

"A Fifth of Beethoven," 74

Fifth of July, 50

"50 Ways to Leave Your Lover" (Simon), 32

Filas for Sale (Searles), 42

Fillmore, Anna M., 431

The Final Days (Woodward), 381

Finch, Peter, 32, 96, 97

Find Your Way Home, 95

Fine Arts Museum, San Francisco, 35

Fineberg, Dr. Harvey V., 416

Finely, Charles O., 515

Fingers, Rollie, 514

"Fingertips Pt. 2" (Wonder), 89

Finian's Rainbow (movie), 82

Finley, Charles O., 515

Finneran, Michael, 549

"Fire" (Ohio Players), 31, 73

Firestone, Harvey S., 143

Firestone Tire and Rubber Corporation, 143

First Amendment, 60, 378

First Baptist Church of Dallas, 459

"The First Time Ever I Saw Your" "Face" (Flack), 28

First, You Cry, 384

Fischer, Bobby, 7, 500, 502, 504, 507

Fishbein, Dr. Morris, 432

Fisher, Carrie, 34

Fisk, Carleton, 515

Fitzgerald, F. Scott, 208

Fitzpatrick, Thomas, 388

Fitzsimmons, Frank, 108, 115, 134

Five Architects (Gwathemy), 192

Five Easy Pieces (movie), 26, 63

Fixx, James F., 410, 544

Flack, Roberta, 28–30, 70, 73

Flanner, Janet ("Genet"), 390

"Flashlight" (Parliament), 73

Fleeson, Doris, 390

Fleetwood Mac, 31, 34, 40, 70–71

Fleischer, Nat, 553

Fleischer, Van Humboldt, 82, 390

Fletcher, Louise, 31, 95

The Flip Wilson Show, 87, 374, 387

Flood, Curt, 500–501, 513–515

Flood, Daniel, 278

Flores, Hector, 310

Florida Citrus Commission, 448, 467

Florida Power and Light, 108

Florida State University, 186

Florida State University (basketball team), 503, 551

407, 409–410, 414, 423, 427, 429, 435

"Heart Like a Wheel" (Ronstadt), 78

Heart of Darkness (Conrad), 65

"Heart of Glass" (Blondie), 36, 76

"Heart of Gold" (Young), 28

Heart transplants, 396, 426

Heath, Edward, 4, 11

Heatter, Gabriel, 391

Heaven Can Wait, 35, 63, 66

Heaven's Gate, 63

Heavy Metal (National Lampoon, Inc.), 363

Hebrew Union College, 468

Hechinger, Fred, 156

Hecht, Abraham B., 449

Heckle and Jeckle (Terry), 392

Hedda, 57

Hee Haw, 78

Heezen, Bruce Charles, 496

Heflin, Van, 98

Hefner, Hugh, 329, 377, 381

Heidelberger, Dr. Michael, 429

Heimlich maneuver, 398

Heinlein, Robert A., 39

Heiser, Dr. Victor G., 433

Heizer, Michael, 42

Hejduk, John, 192

Helix High School, 188

Heller, Joseph, 30, 52

Hellman, Lillian, 58–59, 84, 91

Hello, Dolly!, 64

Helms, Richard M., 216, 228

Helpern, Dr. Milton, 428

Hematology, 422

Hemingway, Ernest, 98

Henderson, Dr. Donald A., 420–421

Henderson the Rain King (Bellow), 81

Henderson, Virginia, 431

Hendrix, Jimi, 26, 40, 66–67, 71, 98, 356

Henley, Don, 70

Henning, Ann, 503

Henning, Anne, 532

Henry V, 33

Henson, Jim, 382

Hepatitis, 400, 406, 419, 425

Hepburn, Audrey, 57

Hepburn, Katharine, 57

Herberg, Will, 469

Herbert, Frank, 39

"Here You Come Again" (Parton), 79

Heresies, 42

Heritage Foundation, 341

Heritage USA, 460

Hernandez, Marco, 187

A Hero Ain't Nothin' But a Sandwich (Childress), 29, 52

A Hero Ain't Nothin' But a Sandwich (movie), 56

Heron, Gil Scott, 476

Herpes, 396, 400, 426, 427

Herr, Michael, 366

Herrman, Bernard, 98

Herrmann, Dr. George R., 428

Herschel, Rabbi Abraham Joshua, 469

Hersh, Seymour M., 366, 388

Hertz, Dr. Hellmuth, 429

Hertz, Dr. Roy, 429

Herzog (Bellow), 81

Herzog, Werner, 13

Hester, W. E. ("Slew"), 539

Heston, Charlton, 30, 64–65

Hewlett Packard, 473

"Hey Big Spender" (number), 85

Heyer, Roberta G., 188

Hibbs, Ben, 391

Hickel, Walter J., 148, 479

Hicks, John R., 109

"High School" (MC5), 69

High Windows (Larkin), 10

Higher Education Act (HEA), 154

"Higher Ground" (Wonder), 90

Hill, Arthur M., 144

Hillbilly Central Studio (Glaser), 78

Hillery, Patrick J., 17

Hilliard, John, 44

Hills, Carla A., 279

Hills, Denis, 14

Hillson, Henry, 165

Hilton, Conrad N., 144

Hilton Hotels Corporation, 144

Hinshaw, Ada Sue, 430

"Hints from Heloise" (Bowles), 390

Hippocratic Oath, 406

Hiroshima, 488

Hispanics, 234

Hiss, Alger, 275, 279

Hit!, 87

Hitchcock, Alfred, 32, 98

Hitchcock, Henry Russell, 206

Hitler, Adolf, 421

Hoagland, Jimmie Lee, 388

Hobart, Thomas, 187

Hodge, Al, 391

Hodges, Gil, 514

Hodges, Isadore, 298

Hodgins, Eric, 391

Hoey, Clyde R., 271

Hoff, Theodore, 484

Hoffa, Jimmy, 108, 112, 134–135, 218, 315

Hoffman, Abbie, 353

Hoffman, Dustin, 26, 30, 32, 36, 59, 62, 86–87, 95, 380

Hoffman, Joseph, 433

Hogan's Heroes, 390

Hogan, Ben, 502, 545–546

Holbrook, Hal, 380

Holden, William, 32

Holiday, Billie, 56, 64

Holland, Dr. James F., 429

Hollywood, 98–99

Holocaust, 376

Holt, John, 173, 182

Holtzman, Elizabeth, 347

Holum, Dianne, 532

Holy Angels Roman Catholic Elementary School, 188

Holzer, Jenny, 348

Home Box Office (HBO), 361–362

Homer, Arthur B., 144

Honecker, Erich, 5

Honeysuckle Rose, 79

Honky Tonk Heroes (Jennings), 78

The Honorary Consul (Greene), 10

The Honourable Schoolboy (le Carré), 17

Hood, Clifford F., 144

Hooker Chemicals, 116

Hooker Company, 489

Hooks, Benjamin L., 227

Hooper, 66

Hoover, Herbert, 313

Hoover, J. Edgar, 245, 263, 281, 316, 343

Hope, Bob, 425

Hopper, William, 391

Horan, Marvin, 468

Horn, Carol, 211

Hornblow, Arthur, 98

Horowitz, Vladimir, 33

"A Horse With No Name" (America), 28

Horses (Smith), 67, 75

Horton, Edward Everett, 98

Hosman, Robert, 187

The Hospital, 27, 63

The Hot Baltimore, Fifth of July, 51

Hot Chocolate, 73

"Hot Stuff" (Summer), 36, 89

"Hotel California" (Eagles), 34, 70–71

Hotter Than July (Wonder), 90

Hough, Hugh F., 388

Hounsfield, Godfrey N., 428, 429

In the Heat of the Night (movie), 57
"In the Navy" (The Village People), 73, 375
In the Night (ballet), 92
Indian Health Service, 399
Indian-Pakistani War, 6, 9
Indian Point 2 (nuclear reactor), 129
The Indian Wants the Bronx, 87
Indiana Pacers, 512, 550–551
Indiana University, 189
Indiana University (basketball team), 508, 511, 522, 523, 552
Indianapolis 500, 513
Indianapolis Racers, 537
Individual Education Plans (IEPs), 159
Inequality: A Reassessment of the Effect of Family and Schooling in America, 182, 183
Inflation, 251–253, 258, 262
The Informer, 97
Inge, William, 98
Ingelfinger, Dr. Franz J., 428
Ingraham, James, 306
Innaurato, Albert, 50
Innervisions (Wonder), 72, 90
The Innocent (Visconti), 21
Instead of Education (Holt), 182
Institute for Cancer Research, 419, 430
Institute of Experimental Biology at Berkeley, 432
Intel, 472, 484
Inter-American literature prize, 91
Interagency Oil Policy Committee, 141
Interest groups, 235
Interiors (movie), 35, 58, 62, 80–81
Internal Revenue Service (IRS), 222, 245, 254, 270, 279, 304, 405, 447
International Business Machines Corporation, 213
International Dance Council, 29
International Harvester Company, 144
International Longshoremen's Union, 108
International Monetary Fund, 20
International Movement for Krishna Consciousness, 445–446
International Olympic Committee, 533
International Reporting (Pulitzer Prize), 110, 253, 270, 388–389
International Tennis Federation (ITF), 539

International Whaling Commission, 23
International Women's Year, 1975, 13
International Women's Year Conference, 323
Interstate Commerce Commission, 341
Into the Woods, 89
Invisible Cities (Calvino), 6
Iran, 116, 124, 129, 139
Iranian militants, 233
Iraq Petroleum Company, 7
Ireland, Joe, 521
Irish Republican Army, 8, 17, 23
Irish Republican Army's Provisional Wing (IRA Provos), 342
Irish Spring soap, 373
Irving, Clifford, 371
Irving, John, 35, 54
Irwin, James, 481
Isaac Asimov's Science Fiction Magazine, 363
Ishizaka, Dr. Kimishige, 430
Isis, 373
The Island (Benchley), 54, 94
"Island Girl" (John), 31
Israel, 128
Italian American Civil Rights League, 82, 320, 333
Italian Psychoanalytic Society, 435
ITC, 382
"It's Too Late" (King), 27
Ittleson, Blanche, 433
Ivy, Dr. Andrew, 433
Ixodes dammini, 412
J. C. Penney, 206
J. C. Penney Company, 144
J/psi, 473, 489
J/psi particle, 493
"Jackie Blue" (Ozark Mountain Daredevils), 31
Jacks, Terry, 30
Jackson, Dr. Edith B., 433
The Jackson Five, 26, 70, 76, 84, 90, 96, 217, 222, 234, 255, 260
Jackson, George, 287, 295, 315
Jackson, Glenda, 38, 57–58
Jackson, J., 315
Jackson, Jesse, 320, 459, 463–464
Jackson, Jonathan, 286
Jackson, Justice, 306
Jackson, Keith, 538
Jackson, Mahalia, 98, 469
Jackson, Maynard, 322
Jackson, Michael, 36, 48, 72, 75, 83, 89, 95, 217, 222, 234, 255, 260

Jackson, Mississippi, 184
Jackson, Reggie, 514–516
Jackson State University (Mississippi), 148, 172, 184, 245
Jackson State University Vietnam protests, 366
Jacksonville University (basketball team), 500
Jaffee, Dr. Eric A., 430
Jagger, Mick, 66
Jal Chamber of Commerce, 423
Jal General Hospital, 423
"Jalousie" (Boston Pops), 43
James Bond films, 57
James, Charles, 213
James, Jr., Daniel, 281
Janata Party, India, 18
Japanese Kabuki theater, 88
Japanese Red Army, 14
Jarvis, Howard, 264
Jaworski, Leon A., 222–223, 249–250, 303, 311–313
Jaws (Benchley), 30–31, 39–40, 53, 61, 63–64, 66
Jean Chuguet, 552
Jeff Lorber Fusion, 69
Jeffers, Lance, 52
The Jefferson Airplane, 68
Jefferson Memorial, 213
The Jeffersons, 365, 374, 383
Jeffrey, Julie, 158
Jencks, Christopher, 160–161, 182–183
Jenner, Bruce, 534, 552
Jenner, Edward, 421
Jennings, Waylon, 41, 78–79
Jensen, Arthur, 187
Jerry Lucas, 518
Jesus, 444, 448–449, 451, 453–455, 457–458, 461, 466
Jesus Christ Superstar, 27, 48, 68, 339
"Jesus Is Just Alright" (Doobie Brothers), 68
Jethro Tull, 68
Jewish Defense League (JDL), 464–465
Jewish Journal of Sociology (Freedman), 189
Jewish Theological Seminary, 469
Jewish Welfare Federation, 459
"Jiggle TV," 374
Jim Crockett's Victory Garden,, 328
The Jim Henson Hour (Henson), 382
Jim Henson Productions (Henson), 382
The Jimmy Dean Show, 382
"Jive Talkin'" (Bee Gees), 31, 48, 73

Kent State University, 26, 148, 171–172, 184, 187, 216, 223, 225, 245, 320, 343, 366, 456, 461
Kent, Rockwell, 98
Kenton, Stan, 98
Kentucky Colonels, 551
Kentucky Derby, 538
Kenwood School, 188
Kenyon, Dorothy, 281
Kerby, Philip, 389
Kermit the Frog (Henson), 364, 382
Kerouac, Jack, 52
Kerr, Clark, 187
Kerr, Deborah, 57
Kerr, John, 15
Kerr-McGee nuclear fuel plant, 116, 288
Kety, Dr. Seymour, 430
Keyes v. *School District No. 1*, 160
Khalid, King (Saudi Arabia), 14
Khmer Rouge, 14, 22, 239
Khomeini, Ayatollah Ruhollah, 22–23, 232, 266, 343
Khorana, Har Gobind, 425
The Kids Are Alright, 48
Kiernan, Walter, 391
Killanin, Lord, 532
The Killer Angels (Shaara), 93
"Killer Queen" (Queen), 31
"Killing Me Softly" (Flack), 29
Kimball, Spenser, 458
Kimpton, Lawrence, 189
Kinflicks (Alther), 53
King, Carole, 27, 38, 67, 91, 155–156, 230, 270, 277
The King and I, 88
King Charlemagne, 85
King Crimson, 68
King David, 465
The King and I , 99
"King of the Road" (song), 78
King Tut, 34, 45, 324
King, Billie Jean, 348, 410, 502–503, 505, 512, 538–539, 544, 549, 551
King, Dr. Terry, 425
King, Martin Luther, Jr., 162, 270, 315–316, 343, 463
King, Mrs. Martin Luther, Sr, 322
King, Stephen, 39, 53
Kinkaid, Thomas C., 281
The Kinks, 66
Kinlein, M. Lucille, 431
Kinte, Kunta, 376
Kipnis, Alexander, 98
Kirchwey, Freda, 391
Kirk, Alexis, 212

Kirkland, Gelsey, 46, 49
Kirkland, Lane, 116, 135
Kirkpatrick, Jeanne, 339, 341
Kirkwood, James, 93
Kirov Ballet, 46
Kiss, 68–69
Kiss Me Kate (movie), 84
Kiss of the Spider Woman (Puig), 16
"Kiss You All Over" (Exile), 35
Kissinger, Henry, 216, 218, 220, 226, 233, 238, 240–242, 245–246, 259, 265–266, 273–274, 278, 343, 354–355
Kite, Tom, 531
Kitty Hawk, 219–220
Kleban, Edward, 93
Klein, Anne, 193, 207, 211, 213
Klein, Calvin, 197, 200–201, 207, 211
Klein, Dr. Edmund, 429
Kleindienst, Richard, 221, 247
Kline, Dr. Nathan S., 407
Kloss, John, 212
Klute (movie), 27, 58, 85, 95
The Knack, 36, 76
Knesset, 465
Knievel, Evel, 506
Knight, Bobby, 522
Knight, Gladys, 29, 72
Knight, Jean, 72
Knight Newspapers, 388
Knight, Philip, 133
Knight, Ted, 384
Knight-Ridder and Gannett, 363
"Knock on Wood" (Stewart), 74
Knowland, William F., 281
Knowles, Christopher, 50
Knowles, Dr. John H., 433
Knox, Nancy, 212
Knuckles (Hare), 10
Koch, Ed, 228
Koch, Kenneth, 187
Kohler Company, 144
Kohler, Walter J. Jr., 144
Kohut, Heinz, 421–422
Kojak (CBS), 373–374
Kolansky, Dr. Harold, 425
Kolb, Dr. Lawrence, 433
Kool and the Gang, 73
Kopechne, Mary Jo, 260
Kopolow, Dr. Louis E., 425
Korbut, Olga, 547, 551
Koreagate, 235, 292
Korean War, 106, 145, 239, 243, 412
Kosinski, Jerzy, 26, 29, 31, 34, 36, 53

Kosterlitz, Dr. Hans W., 429
Kotto, Yaphet, 87
Koufax, Sandy, 508
Kouwenhausen, Dr. William Bennett, 429
Kovic, Ron, 87
Kozol, Jonathan, 155, 183
Kraft, Jack, 520
Kramer vs. Kramer (movie), 35, 59, 61–62, 87, 95, 293, 348
Kramer, Jack, 540
Krantz, Judith, 35, 39, 54
Krathwold, David, 179
Kraus, Hans, 355
Krause, Allison, 187
Krebiozen, 433
Kristofferson, Kris, 30, 32, 78–79
Kristol, Irving, 339, 340
Krock, Arthur, 391
Krofft, Sid, 376
The Krofft Supershow, 373
Krugman, Dr. Saul, 425
Krupa, Gene, 98
Krutch, Joseph Wood, 356
Ku Klux Klan, 278
Kübler-Ross, Dr. Elisabeth, 422
Kubrick, Stanley, 27, 31, 59–61
Kuffler, Dr. Stephen W., 430
"The Kugelmass Episode" (short story), 81
Kuhlman, Kathryn, 455, 469
Kuhn, Margaret E., 342
Kuiper, Gerard Peter, 496
Kumin, Maxine K., 93
Kundera, Milan, 21
Kung Fu, 29, 338
"Kung Fu Fighting" (Douglas), 30–31
Kunkel, Dr. Henry G., 428, 430
Kush, Frank, 525
Kuznets, Simon, 108
Kwanza organization, 87
L. L. Bean, 199
La Boheme (opera), 34
La Choy dragon (Henson), 382
"La Cote Basque" (Capote), 52
La Grande Jatte (Seurat), 88
La Haye, Tim and Beverly, 465
La Prensa, 20
La Raza Unida, 333
Labelle, 31
Labor Party, Israel, 11, 18
Labor unions, 149, 169
Labour Party, Australia, 11
Labour Party, Great Britain, 11–12, 23
Lacombe, Lucien (Malle), 10

Lieber, Dr. Charles S., 427

Life (magazine), 22, 361, 366, 371–372, 391, 453

Life and Times of Josef Stalin, 50

Life Is Worth Living (Sheen), 392

The Life of Brian, 374

Lifshitz, Ralph, 208

Ligase, 483

Lightfoot, Gordon, 30, 32

Likud Party, Israel, 18

"Lil Abner" (Capp), 390

Lilly Endowment Incorporated, 433

Lilly, Eli, 433

limousine liberals, 263

Lincoln Center, 33

Lincoln High School, 188

Lincoln, Abraham, 32

Linda Richards Award, 431

Lindbergh, Charles A., 356, 496

Lindeman, Dr. Erich, 433

Linden, Hal, 94

Lindsay, John, 60, 255

Lindsey, Hal, 454

Linscott, Roger B., 388

Linton, Sally, 487

Lippmann, Walter, 391

Lipstick, 58

Liquid Paper, 373, 494

Liquori, Marty, 501

"Listen to What the Man Said" (Wings), 31

Liston, Charles ("Sonny"), 543, 553

Little, Cleavon, 30, 87, 94, 365

Little Big Man, 26, 60–62

Little House on the Prairie, 375

Little League Baseball, 324

Little Me (show), 84

A Little Night Music, 29, 39, 49, 88, 94

Little Stevie Wonder: The Twelve-Year-Old Genius, 89

Little, Brown, 92

Little, Dr. Clarence Cook, 433

Litzmann, Kent, 549

"Live and Let Die" (Wings), 29

"Live from Lincoln Center" (telecast), 33

Live in Concert, 57

Live-action series, 376

The Lives of a Cell: Notes of a Biology Watcher (Thomas), 423, 424

"Living for the City" (Wonder), 73, 90

Liza with a Z, 85, 386

Llosa, Mario Vargas, 53

Lloyd, Harold, 99

Loaded (Velvet Underground), 67

Local Reporting (Pulitzer Prize), 388–389

Lochridge, Charles, 356

Lockheed Aircraft Corporation, 108, 113, 115–116, 118, 120

"The Loco-Motion" (Grand Funk Railroad), 30

Lodge, Henry Cabot, 233, 355

Loehmann's, 207

Logan's Run, 32, 39, 64

Loggins and Messina, 70

Lombardi, Vince, 502

Lombardo, Guy, 99, 391

Lon Nol, 3, 9, 239

London Symphony Orchestra, 30

Lone Ranger Television, Inc., 364

"The Long and Winding Road" (Beatles), 26

The Long Goodbye, 65

The Long Run (Eagles), 70

Long, Huey, 189

Long, Louis, 213

The Longest Yard, 66

Longmire, Dr. William P., Jr., 428

Look (magazine), 361, 366, 372, 384

Looking for Mr. Goodbar (Rossner), 52, 58–59, 329

Looking Glass, 28

Loose Change (Davidson), 34, 53

López Arellano, Oswaldo, 14

Lopez, Nancy, 511, 531, 552

Lopez, Vincent, 99

The Lord of the Rings (Tolkein), 39

"Lord's Prayer" (Mead), 68

Loren, Sophia, 57

Lorenz, Dr. Konrad, 427

Lorimer, Rich, 213

Los Angeles Community School, 175

Los Angeles County Museum of Art, 32–33

Los Angeles Dodgers, 507, 510–511, 551–552

Los Angeles Lakers, 500, 503, 505, 518, 523, 541, 549–551

Los Angeles Psychoanalytic society, 434

Los Angeles Raiders, 504

Los Angeles Rams, 552

Los Angeles Stars, 550

Los Angeles Superior Court, 364

Los Angeles Symphony Orchestra, 98

Los Angeles Times, 314, 388–390

Lou Grant, 384, 388

Loudon, Dorothy, 94

Louis Harris poll, 156

Louis, Joe, 518, 519, 543

Louisiana State University, 189

Louisiana State University (football team), 501

Louisville (Ky.) *Courier-Journal*, 389

Love and Death, 31, 66, 80

Love Canal, 489

Love Canal Homeowners Association, 474, 478, 490

"Love Hangover" (Ross), 32

Love in the Ruins (Walker), 27

"Love Is in Control (Finger on the Trigger)" (Summer), 89

"Love Machine Pt. 1" (The Miracles), 73

"Love Rollercoaster" (The Ohio Players), 73

"Love Song" (Murray), 78

Love Story (movie), 26, 39, 54, 61, 65, 67

"Love Theme from *A Star Is Born* (Evergreen)" (Streisand), 34, 71

"Love to Love You Baby" (Summer), 74, 90, 31

"Love Train" (O'Jays), 29, 73

"Love Will Keep Us Together" (Captain and Tenille), 31

"The Love You Save" (Jackson Five), 72, 26

Love, John, 141

Lovelace, Linda, 60, 65, 329

"Lovin' You" (Ripperton), 31

Loving, Richard P., 316

Lowe, Nick, 75

Lowell, Robert, 99

Lowman, Dr. Charles LeRoy, 433

Loyalties (Bernstein), 381

Loyola University (basketball team), 521

LPGA Tour, 530–531

LSD, 270

Lucas, George, 29, 34, 40, 64, 82–83, 391

Luce, Henry, 144

Lucile Petry Leone Award, 430

"Luckenback, Texas" (Jennings), 79

Lucky Lady (movie), 65

Lucy, 473, 486–487

Ludlum, Robert, 39

Ludtke, Melissa, 355, 364

Ludwig, Jack, 81

Lufkin (Tex.) *News*, 389

Lukas, Paul, 99

Lule, Yusufu, 23

Lumet, Sidney, 31, 32, 62, 86

Luna 16, 4

Lunar Module, 481

Marx, Zeppo, 99
Marxist, 216
Mary Adelaide Nutting Award, 431
Mary Hartman, Mary Hartman (Lear), 383
The Mary Tyler Moore Hour, 384
The Mary Tyler Moore Show, 360, 373–374, 383–384, 388
Marymount College, 141
M*A*S*H, 26, 61, 65, 373, 378, 388
Masia, Bertram, 179
Mason, Marsha, 34
Massachusetts General Hospital, 107, 175, 189, 205, 208, 213, 402, 405, 425, 430, 433
Massachusetts Institute of Technology (MIT), 107, 175, 189, 205, 208, 213, 425
Massachusetts Supreme Court, 420
Masterpiece Theater (PBS), 369, 387–388
Masters Golf Tournament, 546
Masters, Dr. William H., 355, 426, 491
Mathews v. *Eldridge*, 299
Matsushita Electric Industrial Company, 112
Matthews, Thomas C., Jr., 316
Matthews, Vince, 533
Mattson, Henry, 99
Maude, 373–374, 383
Maurice, John D., 4, 389
Mauze, Abby Rockafeller, 433
Max Factor, 206
Max Protech Gallery, 195
Max's Kansas City, 75, 194
May, Elaine, 59
May, Ernest, 171
May, Lee, 513
May, Scott, 522
Mayaguez, 14, 225, 265
Mayfield, Curtis, 28–29, 72
Mayo Clinic, 432
Mays, Benjamin, 170
Mays, Willie, 501, 547
Mazursky, Paul, 62
MC5, 69, 75, 76
McAlister, Elizabeth, 467
McAlpine Medal, 429
McAuliffe, Anthony C., 281
McBride, Mary Margaret, 391
McCabe and Mrs. Miller, 27, 58, 61, 63
McCall Patterns, 192
McCall, C. W., 32
McCarthy, Joseph, 92, 274, 281
McCarthy, Eugene, 341

McCarthy, Mary, 27
McCartney, Linda, 27
McCartney, Paul, 27, 29–32, 35, 48, 71, 90, 92
McClain, Denny, 513
McClain, J. D., 315
McClain, James, 286
McClellan, John L., 281
McClenathan, Dr. James, 426
McCloskey, Paul N., 253
McCord, James W., 220, 246–247, 249, 314
McCormick, Dr. Edward, 433
McCormick, Fowler, 144
McCorvey, Norma, 294, 314
McCoy, Van, 31, 73, 391
McCracken, Paul, 108
McCrae, George, 30
McCullough, Colleen, 39, 53
McCullough, Frank, 371
McDaniels, Jim, 503, 521
McDonnell-Douglas, 116
McElroy, Neil H., 144
McEnroe, John, 133, 511–512, 540, 552
McFadden, Mary, 211
McGee, Frank, 391
McGinley, Phyllis, 99
McGovern, George, 219, 247, 254–258, 260, 262, 274, 276, 341, 414
McGovern, Maureen, 29
McGrath, Paul, 391
McGraw, Ali, 26
McGraw-Hill, Inc., 162, 176, 371
McGrory, Mary, 277
McGuire, Al, 522
McGuire, Frank, 522
McIntire, Carl, 456
McIntyre, James T., 157, 228, 469
McKay, Jim, 537
McKechnie, Donna, 47, 94
McKeen, John E., 144
McKelway, Benjamin M., 391
McKenney, Ruth, 99
McKenzie-Pollock, Dr. James S., 426
McLain, Denny, 500
McLaren, Malcolm, 75
McLean, Don, 28, 38
McLuhan, Marshall, 353
McMahon, Frank, 95
McMeel, John, 385
McMillan, James B., 308
McMurtry, Larry, 31
McMurty, Rosemary, 192
McNally, Dave, 514
McNally, Terence, 50

McNeill, J. F., 189
McPherson, James Alan, 34, 37, 52, 93
McQueen, Steve, 30, 245
McWilliams, Larry, 516
"Me and Bobby McGee" (Joplin), 27
"Me and Mrs. Jones" (Paul), 28, 73
Mead, Margaret, 356
Mead, Sister Janet, 68
Mead, Sylvia Earle, 494
Meadowcroft, Pennsylvania, 493
Mean Streets (movie), 29, 62–63, 65
Means, Jacqueline, 468
Means, Russell, 332
Meany, George, 110, 116, 134–135
Mears, Rick, 511
Mears, Walter, 389
Measles, 421
Meat Loaf, 55
Meatballs (movie), 66
Meco, 34
Medal of Freedom, 32, 91, 433
Medeiros, Humberto S., 468
Medicaid, 291, 403, 408, 445
Medical College of Wisconsin, 397
Medical Comprehensive Achievement Test (MCAT), 166
Medicare, 126, 401, 403, 408, 433
Medina, Ernest, 311
Medved, Aleksandr, 533
Meehan, Chick, 553
Meet the Press, 186
Meeting of the Minds (Allen), 386
Meier, Richard, 192
Meir, Golda, 11, 534
Melanie, 26–27
Mellon, Paul, 26, 91
Mellon, Richard King, 144
Meloy, Francis E., 227
Memorial Sloan-Kettering Cancer Center, 423, 427, 433
Memphis State University (basketball team), 521, 551
Meningitis, 429
Menninger Foundation, 434
Menominee Indians, 323
Menotti, Gian Carlo, 33
Mental health, 164, 403, 407–408, 421–422, 425–426, 429, 433
Mental Health Association, 429
Menzel, Donald Howard, 496
Mercer, Johnny, 99
Mercury, 473, 482
"Mercy Mercy Me", 68
Meredith, Don, 538
Meridian (Walker), 32, 52

National Book Critics Circle Award, 53, 86
National Broadcasting Company (NBC), 145, 360–362, 364, 384, 392, 453
  evening news, 391
National Bureau of Economic Research, 137
National cable network, 362
National Cancer Act, 396
National Cancer Institute, 113, 398
National Cash Register Company, 143
National Catholic Education Association, 163
National Center for Atmospheric Research, 208
National Center for Disease Control, 401
National Center for Health Statistics, 399
National Christian Crusade, 281
National Collegiate Athletic Association, 466
National Commission on Marijuana and Drug Abuse, 218
National Committee for a Sane Nuclear Policy, 354
National Council for the Prevention of War, 281
National Council of Catholic Bishops, 444–445, 458
National Council of Churches, 277, 448–449, 458, 467–468
National Council of Teachers of Mathematics, 176
National Council of Teachers of English, 177
National Day of Prayer, 392
National Education Association (NEA), 163, 168–169
National Education Association Political Action Committee (NEAPAC), 168
National Education Association Representative Assembly, 168
National Educational Television (NET), 360
National Endowment for the Arts, 26, 33, 45–46
National Endowment for the Humanities, 170
National Environmental Policy Act of 1970 (NEPA), 301, 331
National Football Conference, 526
National Football League (NFL), 360, 364, 512, 527

National Front, Iran, 21
National Gallery of Art, 26, 33, 35, 91, 195, 208–209
National Geographic, 486, 491
National Heart, Lung and Blood Institute, 426
National High Blood Pressure Education Program, 429
National Hockey League, 512, 535
National Honor Award, 205
National Humanities Center, 342
National Institute for Education (NIE), 149
National Institute of Arts and Letters, 93
National Institute of Education (NIE), 161
National Institute of Mental Health, 164, 425, 433
National Institute of Neurological Communicative Disorders and Stroke, 432
National Institute of Research, 160
National Institute on Alcohol Abuse and Alcoholism, 425
National Institute on Drug Abuse, 323, 327
National Institutes of Health, 399, 422, 426, 432, 474–475
National Lampoon, 360
National Lampoon's Animal House, 35 48, 61, 66
National Lampoon, Inc., 363
National League for Nursing Distinguished Service Award, 431
National Opinion Research Center (NORC), 462
National Organization for Women (NOW), 234, 349–350, 444
National Organization of Minority Architects (NOMA), 192
National Palace, Managua, Nicaragua, 21
National Public Radio (NPR), 369, 370, 387
National Railroad Passenger Act of 1970, 121
National Railroad Passenger Corporation, 107
National Reporting (Pulitzer Prize), 388–389
National Resources Defense Council, 301
National Review, 264, 341, 375
National Right to Life Committee, 445
National Security Act of 1947, 233

National Security Adviser, 273, 278
National Security Agency (NSA), 225, 233, 270
National Security Study Memorandum I, 237
National Society of Film Critics, 80
National Traffic and Motor Vehicle Safety Act, 139, 341
National Urban League, 132, 282
National Women's Conference, 1977, 229, 301
National Women's Political Caucus, 384
Native Americans, 234
Naval ROTC scholarship, 380
Nazareth, 70
Nazi Party, 62, 421, 432, 434
Nazism, 85
NBA, 512, 517
NBC's Saturday Night, 388
Neal, Patricia, 57
Negro Digest, 360
Negro Ensemble Company, 51
Neibuhr, Rev. Reinhold, 469
Neill, A. S., 189
Nelson, Ozzie, 99, 357
Nelson, Theodore, 484
Nelson, Willie, 41, 78–79, 391
Nemerov, Howard, 93
Neptune, 482
The Neptune Factor (movie), 65
Neruda, Pablo, 6, 99
Nesmith, Bette, 494
Network (movie), 32, 58, 62, 95, 97
Neuroblastoma, 426
Neustadt, Richard E., 416
Neutra, Richard Joseph, 212–213
Never Too Late (Holt), 182
Nevers, Ernest, 553
New Age Blues, 338
New Deal, 262, 264, 276, 281, 316
New Democracy Party, Greece, 13
New Economic Policy (Nixon), 108–109, 128, 134, 137
New England Journal of Medicine, 423
New England Patriots, 541
New Frontier, 341
New Girl in Town (show), 85
New Haven Medical Center, 424
New Jersey Corridor Study, 205
New Jersey Supreme Court, 188, 407
New Jersey Turnpike, 113
New Jewel Movement, Grenada, 22
"New Journalism," 372
New Left, 324, 340

New math, 163, 176

New Mexico State University (basketball team), 520

"New politics," 255

New Religious Right, 342, 445

New Republic, 390, 392

New Right, 324

New School for Social Research, 189

New wave music, 75–77

New Woman, 373

New York Daily News, 118, 372

New York Actors' Studio, 86

New York Amsterdam News, 391, 434

New York Board of Education, 173, 186

New York Board of Regents, 150, 447

New York City Ballet, 26, 44, 92

New York City Federal Plaza, 43

New York City Health Research Council Narcotics Advisory Committee, 424

New York City Opera, 92

New York City Teachers Union, 225

New York Cosmos, 508

The New York Dolls, 40, 69

New York Drama Critics Circle Award, 51–52, 88, 92

New York Film Critics Circle, 80

New York Five, 192, 203, 205

New York Giants, 502

New York Herald Tribune, 392

New York Hospital-Cornell Medical Center, 402

New York Jets, 526, 537

New York Knicks, 500, 503, 505, 518, 550–551

New York magazine, 52, 384

New York Metropolitan Opera House Orchestra, 28

New York Mets, 505, 515, 551

New York Nets, 517, 551–552

New York Philharmonic, 30, 33, 91, 98

The New York Post, 159

New York Public Library, 213

New York Rangers, 503, 511, 551–552

New York Review of Books, 187

New York Shakespeare Festival, 33, 39, 47, 51

New York Shakespeare Public Theater, 51

New York State Assembly, 271

New York State Athletic Commission, 434

New York State Supreme Court, 152

New York State Teachers Association, 187

New York Stock Exchange, 116

New York Sun, 390

New York Telephone Company, 109

New York Theological Seminary, 466

The New York Times, 29, 34, 81, 193, 205, 207, 209, 246, 287–288, 316, 360, 368 –369, 380, 388–389, 391

The New York Times Magazine, 384

New York University, 413, 425, 464

New York Yankees, 509–511, 516, 552

New York, New York (movie), 34, 62–63, 65

New Yorker, 213, 372, 390–391

Newark Academy, 141

Newberry Medal for Children's Literature, 91

Newcombe, John, 513, 551

Newhouse, Samuel I., 144, 391

Newman, Alfred E., 99

Newman, Barnett, 99

Newman, Frank, 187

Newman, Paul, 29–30

Newman, Randy, 67

Newport Jazz Festival, 34

Newsday, 388, 390

Newspaper, 363

Newspaper Preservation Act, 360

Newsweek, 32, 46, 81, 87, 161, 188, 210, 371, 373

Newton Memorial Hospital, 406

Newton-John, Olivia, 30–31, 35, 41, 70, 79

Ngu, Dr. V. Anomah, 429

Nichols, Dr. Buford, 426

Nichols, Mike, 26–27, 34, 59–60

Nichols, Robert, 187

Nicholson, Jack, 26–27, 29–31, 63, 82, 86, 95

Nickelodeon, 364

Nicklaus, Jack, 500–503, 505, 507–508, 511–512, 530–531, 545–546, 551

Nicks, Stevie, 70

Nicolson, Cliff, 212

Nielsen ratings, 33, 373

"The Night Chicago Died" (Paper Lace), 30

Night and Day (Stoppard), 19

"Night Fever" (Bee Gees), 35, 48

The Night Is Dark (Kozol), 183

Night of the Lepus (movie), 65

"The Night the Lights Went Out in Georgia" (Lawrence), 29

Nike, 118, 133

Nilsson, 28

Nimeiri, Jafaar Mohammad, 6

Nin, Anaïs, 99

Nine to Five, 349

Nineteenth Amendment, 320

Nissan, 106, 113

Nivens, Sue Ann, 384

Nixon, Richard M., 10, 77, 106–111, 118–119, 123–129, 134, 137, 141–143, 148–149, 157, 171–172, 179, 181, 183–184, 187, 199, 201, 216–225, 228, 233–258, 260–261, 263, 265–267, 269, 271–276, 278–279, 286–288, 292, 297, 303–308, 310–313, 316, 324, 326, 329, 331, 339, 343, 345, 349, 351, 354, 360, 367–370, 380–381, 387, 396, 398, 403, 405, 409, 411, 443, 446, 451, 456–457, 461, 472, 478, 507, 526

"Nixonomics," 253

"No future" (The Sex Pistols), 75

No Man's Land (Pinter), 13

"No More Tears (Enough Is Enough)" (Summer), 36, 89

No Name in the Street (Baldwin), 28

No No Nanette (musical), 94

No Place to Be Somebody (play), 51, 93

"No Wave," 76

Nobel laureate, 149, 425

Nobel Peace Prize, 6, 12, 19, 280

Nobel Prize for literature, 6, 33, 35, 53, 82, 86, 91 189

Nobel Prize for medicine or physiology, 419, 424, 427, 433–435

Nobel Prize for science, 426

Noble, Elaine, 336

Noll, Chuck, 528

Norell, Norman, 207, 213

Norma Rae (movie), 36, 58, 95, 348

Norman, Marsha, 51

Norris, Chuck, 338

North Atlantic Treaty Organization (NATO), 12, 16, 224, 229, 278

North by Northwest, 99

North Carolina A & T University, 463

Razaf, Andy, 99
Readers' Encyclopedia of Shakespeare
    (Campbell), 189
Reagan, Ronald, 41, 79, 135, 137,
    227, 232, 234–235, 252, 257,
    259, 262–265, 269, 276, 278,
    286–287, 292–293, 303, 306,
    310, 341, 343, 353, 452
"Reason to Believe" (Stewart), 27
Recording Industry Association of
    America, 33
Red Brigades, 20–21, 342
Red, Hot and Blue, 98
Red River, 98
Redbook, 491
Redding, Otis, 71
Reddy, Helen, 28–30, 38, 68, 70
Reford, Robert, 29–30, 32, 66, 193,
    380
Redgrave, Vanessa, 34, 57, 83–84
Redhead (show), 84
Reed College, 122
Reed v. *Reed*, 320, 345
Reed, Carol, 99
Reed, Lou, 69, 75–76, 84, 392
Reed, Willis, 518
Reems, Harry, 65, 329
Rees, Merlyn, 16
Reese, Don, 527
Reese, Eva M., 430
Reeves, Daniel F., 554
Reeves, Donald, 173
Reformed Church of America, 467
Refried Beans for Instants (Ander-
    son), 45
Regal Club, 72
Regents of the University of California
    v. *Bakke*, 166, 306, 324
Regents University, 466
Reggae, 75
Regiment of Women (Berger), 29
Rehnquist Court, 306, 310
Rehnquist, William H., 217, 287,
    305, 306, 310
Reich, Charles, 326, 355
Reich, Steve, 75
Reid, Charles, 212
Reid, Helen Rogers, 392
Reid, Rose Marie, 213
Reiner, Rob, 383
Religious Round Table, 452
The Remaking of American Education
    (Silberman), 184
Rembrandt, 91
Rembrandt's Hat (Malamud), 29
Remick, Lee, 32
Renaissance period, 205

Renault, 124
Renfro, Mel, 529
Rentner, Maurice, 205
Rentzel, Lance, 505
A Report of the Facts (Adelsberger),
    432
Reproductive Biology Research
    Foundation, 492
Republican National Convention,
    227, 272
Republican Party, 234, 257–258,
    262, 280
"Rescue from Gilligan's Island," 364
The Residents, 76
"Respect Yourself" (Staple Singers),
    72
The Restoration of the Self (Kohut),
    421
"Reunited" (Peaches and Herb), 36
Reutershan, Paul, 480
Reuther, Walter P., 106, 145
Reuyl, John, 490
Revlon, 145
Revolution (movie), 87
Revolutionary Command Council,
    Iraq, 23
Revolutionary Council, 232
Revolutionary Council, Afghani-
    stan, 22
Revolutionary War, 210
Revson, Charles, 145
Reynaldo and Clara (movie), 48
Reynolds, Burt, 28, 34, 59, 66, 381
"Rhiannon" (Fleetwood Mac), 31
"Rhinestone Cowboy" (Campbell),
    31
Rhoda, 374, 384
Rhodes, Cecil, 186
Rhodes Scholars, 186, 188
Rice, Tim, 27, 36
Rich, Charlie, 29, 41, 78
"Rich Girl" (Hall and Oates), 34
Rich Man, Poor Man (Shaw), 26, 39,
    54, 376
Richard Hell and the Voidoids, 75
Richard Pryor Live (movie), 87
Richard Pryor's Live and Smokin'
    (movie), 57
Richards, Dr. Dickinson W., 434
Richards, Golden, 549
Richards, I. A., 189
Richards, Mary, 384
Richards, Renee, 323, 509, 539
Richardson, Eileen, 211
Richardson, Elliot, 220–222, 226,
    248–249, 288
Richardson, Elliot L., 429

Richardson, Tony, 59
Richardson, Will, 211
Richmond (Va.) *News-Leader*, 388,
    389
Richmond, Julius B., 324, 350
Richter, Burton, 493, 495
Richter, Dr. Curt P., 430
Rickenbacker, Edward V., 145, 281
Rickenbacker, Eddie, 357
Ridder Publications and Knight
    Newspaper, 362
"Riders on the Storm" (Doors), 27
Rigby, Cathy, 546
Riggs, Bobby, 348, 410, 505, 512,
    538, 545
Riles, Wilson, 174
"Ring My Bell" (Ward), 36, 74
Ringgold, Faith, 42
Ringling Brothers and Barnum and
    Bailey Circus, 98, 129
Ripperton, Minnie, 31, 99
"Rise" (Alpert), 36
Risser, James, 389
Ritalin, 149
Ritter, Tex, 99
Ritter, Thelma, 99
The Ritz (play), 50
Riva Ridge, 551
The River Niger (play), 51, 94
Rizzo, Frank, 231
RKO Radio, 144
RNA, 472, 493
Road Runners of America, 410
Robards, Jason, 34, 380
The Robber Bridegroom (play), 94
Robbins, Harold, 27, 39, 53
Robbins, Jerome, 31, 46, 49, 84, 92
The Robert MacNeil Report (PBS),
    363
Robert Schuller Institute for Suc-
    cessful Church Growth, 467
Roberts Oral, 342, 455, 465–466
Roberts, Clifford, 554
Robertson, Oscar, 518
Robertson, Pat, 443, 455, 460, 466
Robeson, Paul, 99
Robinson, Arnie, 534
Robinson, Brooks, 514
Robinson, Edgar, 189
Robinson, Edward G., 99
Robinson, Frank, 322, 507, 513–
    514, 549
Robinson, Jackie, 357, 513, 554
Robinson, Rey, 533
Robinson, Smokey, 26, 72
Robinson, Vicki Sue, 32, 73
Rochester (N.Y.) *Times-Union*, 388

"Rock 'n Me" (Steve Miller Band), 32

Rock 'n' roll, 74–75, 77

Rock 'n' Roll High School (movie), 36, 48, 76

"Rock and Roll Part 2" (Glitter), 68

Rock of the Westies (John), 32

"Rock the Boat" (Hues Corporation), 30–31, 73

"Rock Your Baby" (McCrae), 30–31, 73

Rockefeller commission, 225

Rockefeller, David, 111

Rockefeller Foundation, 433

Rockefeller, Happy, 210

Rockefeller, John D. III, 35

Rockefeller, Mary C., 431

Rockefeller, Nelson, 128–129, 142, 223, 226, 257, 273, 279, 281, 287, 296

Rockefeller University, 427, 430

Rockettes, 35

The Rockford Files (NBC), 388

Rockland State Research Center, 407

Rockwell, Norman, 99, 357, 392

Rocky (movie), 32, 59, 61, 66, 95

The Rocky Horror Picture Show (movie), 31–32, 55

The Rocky Horror Show (rock opera), 55

Rocky Mountain News, 417

Rodgers, Bill, 509, 549

Rodgers, Johnny, 524, 551

Rodgers, Richard, 35, 92, 99

Rodino, Peter, 250, 279

Rodo, Dr. Sandor, 434

Rodriguez, Irving Flores, 291

Rodriguez Lara, Guillermo, 15

Rodriguez v. *Board of Education*, 149

Rodriquez, Demetrio, 178–179

Roe v. *Wade*, 233, 264, 288, 293–295, 314, 346, 397, 404–405, 420

"Roe, Jane", 294, 314

Roeg, Nicholas, 15

Rogers, James M., 188

Rogers, William, 273

Rohatyn, Felix G., 143

Role Models, 374

Rolfing, 337

Rollercoaster (movie), 64

Rollin, Betty, 384

Rolling Stone, 327, 371–372, 381, 385, 390

The Rolling Stones, 27, 29, 35, 67–68, 71, 74, 89–90

Rollins, Walter, 99

Rolls-Royce, 5

Roman Catholic church, 443–445, 448, 451–452, 456–458, 462, 468–469

Roman Catholic Dignity, 448

Romero, Carlos Humberto, 23–24

Romm, Dr. May E., 434

Romney, George T., 220

Ronstadt, Linda, 31, 40–41, 70, 78

Room at the Top, 98

A Room with a View (Forster), 97

Rooney, Art, 528

Roosevelt, Franklin, 280, 282, 313

's Brain Trust transcripts, and these revelations disgusted the American people. When he resigned the presidency in 1974, 281

Roosevelt Roads naval base, 24

Roosevelt, Franklin D., 313

Roots (Haley), 34, 37, 54, 87, 91, 332, 363, 374, 376, 379

Roots: The Next Generations (Haley), 376

Roper poll, 160–161

Rorem, Ned, 93

Rorschach test, 433

Rosanes, Alan, 212

Roscoe B. Jackson Memorial Laboratory for cancer research, 433

The Rose, 48, 94, 392

Rose A (Steir), 42

"Rose Garden" (song), 78

Rose, Pete, 511–513, 516

Rosebury, Theodor, 434

Rosenblum, Carroll, 554

Rosenhan, Dr. David L., 426

Rosenthal, Ida Cohen, 496

Rosenwald, Lessing, 145

Rosewall, Ken, 540, 550

Rosovsky, Henry, 155

Ross, Diana, 26, 28–29, 32, 56, 64, 73, 92, 281, 355, 390

Ross, Diane, 31

Ross, Donna, 70

Ross, Herbert, 34

Rossellini, Roberto, 99

Rossman, Michael, 338

Rossner, Judith, 31, 39, 52, 329

Roswell Park Memorial Institute, 433

Roth, Mark, 549

Roth, Philip, 36, 52–53, 92

Roth, William, 264

Rothe, Anne T., 212

Rothhammer, Keena, 533

Rothko, Mark, 99

The Rothschilds (musical), 94

Rotten, Johnny, 35, 75–77, 195

Roundtree, Richard, 27, 54

Rous, Francis Peyton, 496

Rous, Dr. Peyton, 434

Rovere, Richard, 281

Rowland, Sherwood, 479

Rowlands, Gena, 57

Rowlf the Dog (Henson), 382

Roxy Music, 69, 75

Roxy Theater, 55

Royal Academy of Music, 352

Royal Bondage, 329

Royal Opera House, 91

Royalton Hotel, 327

Royce, Rose, 34, 34

Rozak, Theodore, 326

Rozelle, Pete, 360, 500, 527, 537

RSO, 48

Rubens, Peter Paul, 20

Rubicam, Raymond, 145

Rubin, Jerry, 324, 353

Rubinstein, Arthur, 32, 35

Rubyfruit Jungle (Brown), 53

Ruckelshaus, William D., 216, 221–222, 248, 288

Rudd, Paul, 33

Rudi, Joe, 514

Rudy Vallee Show, 87

Ruffian, 508

Ruffin, Clovis, 212

Ruhtenberg, Cornelius, 212

Rumble Fish, 83

Rumours (Fleetwood Mac), 34, 70–71

Rumsfeld, Donald, 226

"Runaway Child Running Wild" (The Temptations), 72

Runaway Horses (Mishima), 3

Running Fence (Christo), 43

Rupp, Adolph, 503, 522, 554

Russell, Nipsey, 87, 281

Russell, Bertrand, 189

Russell, Bill, 507, 516, 522

Russell, Jean, 57

Russell, Ken, 31

Russell, Louis B., 426

Russell, Rosalind, 99

Russian Research Center at Harvard, 280

Russo, Susan, 187

Rust Never Sleeps, 48

Rutgers University, 166, 186

Ruth, Babe, 507, 513, 515

Ruth, Henry S., Jr., 312

Rutherford, Johnny, 506, 509

Rutherford, Margaret, 99

Ruza, Marty, 212

Ryan, Cornelius, 30
Ryan, Dr. Kenneth, 426
Ryan, Elizabeth, 554
Ryan, Leo, 449–451
Ryan, Nolan, 505–508, 512
Ryan, Pat, 275, 392
Ryan, Robert, 99
Ryder Cup, 531
Ryon, Luann, 534
Ryun, Jim, 501
Saab, 331
Saar, Bettye, 42
Sabin, Dr. Albert B., 426
Sabin, Lou, 528
Saccharin, 400
Sacramento State College, 148
Sad Sack (Baker), 389
Sadat, Anwar, 4, 19, 21, 230–231
The Saddest Story (Mizener), 28
Saddler, Sandy, 519
Sadler, Barry, 77
Sagendorph, Robb H., 145, 392
Saint Bonaventure University (basketball team), 520
Saint Jack (Theroux), 29
Saint John's University (basketball team), 522
Saint Jude Children's Research Hospital, 426
Saint Louis Blues, 500, 550
Saint Louis Cardinals, 513
Saint Louis School District, 148
Saint Louis Symphony, 98
Saint Patrick's Cathedral, 26, 92
Saint-Tropez skirt, 198
Salam, Abdus, 495
Salazar, Antonio, 4
Salazar, Ruben, 320
Salinger, J. D., 52
Salisbury State College, 140
Salk Institute, 430
Salomon Brothers, 141
Salonen, Neil, 451
Salvatori, Henry, 341
Sam and Friends (Henson), 382
Same Time Next Year, 94
Sampson, Edith Spurlock, 317
Samuelson, Paul, 107
Samuelsson, Dr. Bengt, 429
San Carlo Opera Company, 98
San Diego Chargers, 527
San Diego Conquistadors, 505
San Diego Evening Tribune, 389
San Diego's Metropolitan Correctional Center, 426
San Francisco 49ers, 529
San Francisco Ballet, 46

San Francisco State University, 169–170
San Francisco Unified School District, 186
"San Quentin Six", 315
Sanchez, Fernando, 212
Sanday, Peggy, 489
Sanders, George, 99
Sandinista National Liberation Front, 20–21, 23
Sandys, Edwina, 42
Sanford and Son, 87, 332, 373–374, 383
Sang, Samantha, 48
Sanger, Dr. Frederick, 429
Santana, 69
Sarandon, Susan, 31
Sarazen, Gene, 502, 546
Sargent, Francis S., 258
Sargent, Francis, 150
Sarnoff, Robert, 360, 392
Sarnoff, David, 145
Saroyan, William, 26
Sarsfield's, 279
Satellite, 362
Satmar Hasidim, 468
Satmar Hassids, 469
Sato, Eisaku, 12
Saturday Evening Post, 391–392
"Saturday Night" (Bay City Rollers), 32, 88
Saturday Night Fever, 34, 38, 48, 61, 65, 73, 194, 199, 330
Saturday Night Live, 66, 87, 362, 374, 382
Saturday Night Massacre, 222, 248–249
Saturn, 482
Saunders, Carl M., 392
Savage Sword of Conan (Marvel Comics), 362
Save Our Children, 336, 375, 448
Save the Tiger (movie), 63, 95
Sawyer, Diane, 207
Saxbe, William, 222, 249
Sayer, Leo, 70
Sayers, Gale, 547
Scali, McCabe, 140
Scarecrow, 66
Scarface, 87
Scenes from a Marriage (Bergman), 8
Scent of a Woman, 87
Schalley, Dr. Andrew V., 428
Schanberg, Sydney H., 389
Schapiro, Miriam, 42
Scharansky, Anatoly B., 20
Scheider, Roy, 31, 36

Scheuer, Sandy, 187
Schippers, Thomas, 99
Schizophrenia, 406–407, 430, 433
Schlafly, Phyllis, 234, 264, 302, 320, 345, 354, 375
Schlesinger, James, 115, 129, 221, 226, 228, 266
Schlichter, Art, 524
Schlondorff, Volker, 22
Schmidt, Dr. Elwood L., 423
Schmidt, Helmut, 11, 17
Schneider, Rolf, 21
Schoenfeld, James, 316
Schoenfeld, Richard, 316
Scholastic Aptitude Test (SAT), 152, 155, 158, 161–162, 184, 187–188
Scholastic Press, 162
The School for Wives, 94
"School's Out" (Cooper), 68
Schoolhouse Rock, 376
"Schools Without Education" (Bareiter), 156
Schorr, Daniel, 387
Schreiber, Taft, 341
Schrieffer, John R., 495
Schroeder, Dr. John Speer, 426
Schroeder, Pat, 347
Schuller, Robert, 455, 467
Schultz, Dave, 536, 541
Schultz, Michael, 31–32, 57, 87
Schultz, Theodore, 116
Schuster, Max, 99
Schuster, Max L., 145
Schwantner, Joseph, 94
Schwartz, Stephen, 453
Schweiker, Richard, 259
Schweitzer, Dr. Albert, 434
Science fiction, 364
Science of Creative Intelligence (SCI), 164
Scientology, 337
Scopes, J. T., 317
Scopes, John Thomas, 357
Scorcese, Martin, 29–30, 32, 34, 62–63, 65, 98
Scott, George C., 86–87, 95
Scott Brown, Denise, 192, 209
Scott, Blanche Stuart, 496
Scott, David, 481
Scott, George C., 26–27, 63
Scott, Jessie M., 431
Scott, Paul, 13
Scotto, Renata, 34
Scowcroft, Brent, 226
Scrinivas, M. N., 320
Scruples (Krantz), 35, 54

Swine-flu, 399

Swinnerton, James, 392

Swissair, 3

Switzer, Mary, 435

Sylvania Electric Products, 144

Symbionese Liberation Army (SLA), 288–289, 343, 353

A Symphony for Three Orchestras (Elliott), 91

Symphony No. 1 (Menotti), 33

Synchronisms No. 6 (Davidovsky), 94

Syphilis, 401, 403, 417, 426

Szep, Paul, 389,

T-Rex, 69

Tabernacle Christian School, 164

Table-tennis, 217

Taft-Hartley Act, 108

Tagamet, 400

Taieb, Maurice, 486

Takada, Kenzo, 210

"Take Me Home, Country Roads" (Denver), 78

Take the Money and Run (movie), 80

The Takeover (Spark), 16

"Takin' Care of Business" (Bachman Turner Overdrive), 30, 69

The Taking of Miss Janie (play), 50

Talent 52 (show), 84

Talking Book (Wonder), 72

The Talking Heads, 40, 76

Tampa Bay Buccaneers, 550

Tamplin, Arthur R., 494

Tanaka, Kakuei, 13, 17, 219

Tandem (Lear), 383

Tandy, Jessica, 94

Tang, 476

Tanner, Christine A., 431

Tapestry (King), 38, 67, 92

Tar Baby (Morrison), 86

Taraki, Nur Mohammad, 20

Tarbell, Ida, 139

Tass, 35

A Taste of Honey, 35, 74

TAT (Lear), 383

Tate, Sharon, 454

Tatum, Dr. Edward L., 435

Tatum, Edward Lawrie, 497

Tatum, Jack, 529, 541

Tau lepton, 473

Tauon, 473, 489, 494

Tax Reduction and Simplification Bill of 1977, 228

Taxi, 375, 388

Taxi Driver (movie), 32, 62–63, 65, 98

Taxonomy of Educational Objectives,

Handbook I: Cognitive Domain (Bloom), 179

Taxonomy of Educational Objectives, Handbook II: Affective Domain (Bloom), 179

Taylor, Chris, 533, 550

Taylor, James, 40, 70–71, 92, 378

Taylor, Johnnie, 32–33

Taylor, Paul, 46–48

Taylor, Robert, 533

Tchaikovsky, Pyotr Ilich, 43

Teamsters, 134

Teamsters Union, 108, 112–115, 134–135, 315

"Tears of a Clown" (Smokey Robinson and the Miracles), 26, 72

Teenage Jesus and the Jerks, 76

Teens for Christ, 447

Teitelbaum, Rabbi Joel, 469

Teitelbaum, Rabbi Moses, 468

Tektite II project, 494

Televangelists, 264

Television, 76, 274, 363–364, 367, 370, 373–377

Television (the band), 40

Television (punk rock group), 76

Tellico Dam, 116

Temin, Dr. Howard M., 428, 493

Temple University, 419

The Temptations, 27–28, 72

10 (movie), 36

10cc, 31

Ten Days That Shook the World (movie), 82

The Tenants (Malamud), 27

Tennis, 539

The Terminal Man (Crichton), 28

Terms of Endearment (McMurtry), 31

Terra Nostra (Fuentes), 53

The Terror (movie), 82

terrorism, 3–4, 7–11, 15, 17–18, 20, 24

Terry, Paul H., 392

test-tube baby, 21

Tet Offensive, 366

Teton River dam, 226

Tetracycline, 401

Texaco, 115

The Texas Chainsaw Massacre (movie), 65

Texas Instruments, 472

Texas Rangers, 541

Texas Southern University, 85

Texas Textbook Committee, 162

Texas, University of, 294, 314

"Thank God I'm a Country Boy" (Denver), 31, 78

Thank God It's Friday (movie), 48, 74, 89

"Thank You (Falettin' Me Be Mice Elf Agin)" (Sly and the Family Stone), 26

Tharp, Twyla, 38, 45–46, 48–49

That's Entertainment (movie), 65

That's Entertainment, Part 2 (movie), 65

That's My Mamma, 374

"That's the Way (I Like It)" KC and the Sunshine Band, 31

"That's the Way I Always Heard" "It Should Be" (Simon), 38, 68

Thatcher, Margaret, 13, 23

The 1969 Public Health Cigarette Smoking Act, 361

The Brady Bunch, 327, 334

The Challenge of the Sexes, 538

The China Syndrome (movie), 488

The Closing Circle, 331

The Coming of Post-Industrial Society, 340

The Common Sense Book of Baby and Child Care, 354

The Complete Book of Running, Fixx, 544

The Cultural Contradictions of Capitalism, 340

The End of Ideology, 340

The French Chef, 352

The Gift of Inner Healing, 342

The Hyde Amendment, 445

The Jeffersons, 332

The Joy of Sex, 329

The Mary Tyler Moore Show, 347

THE OLYMPICS: 1972, 532

THE OLYMPICS: 1976, 534

The Partridge Family, 26, 327, 334

The Ramones, 67

The Sensuous Man, 329

The Superstars, 538

The Times of Harvey Milk, 336

The Turning Point, 348

The Undersea World of Jacques Cousteau, 494

The Weathermen, 320

The Women Superstars, 538

Theiler, Dr. Max, 435

Theismann, Joe, 524

Them (Oates), 91

"Theme from Mahogany" (Ross), 32, 73

"Theme from Shaft" (Hayes), 27

"Theme from *SWAT*" (song), 74

Truman, Harry S, 237, 280, 282, 291, 316

Trumbo, Dalton, 92, 99

Truth, Sojourner, 41

TRW, 130

Tsongas, Paul, 262

Tuberculosis, 434

Tuchman Tutoring of New York, 188

Tuchman, Max, 188

Tucker, Tanya, 78

Tucker, Richard, 99

Tucker: The Man and His Dream (movie), 83

Tugwell, Rexford Guy, 282

Tunney, Gene, 554

Turcotte, Ron, 551

"Turn the Beat Around" (Robinson), 73, 32

Turner, Ted, 84, 254, 360, 385–386

Turner Communications Group (TCG), 386

Turner Network Television (TNT), 386

Turner, Cecil, 550

The Turning Point (movie), 34, 46, 58–59

Turtle Island (Snyder), 93

Tuskegee Syphilic Study, 417

Tuttle, Holmes, 341

TV Guide, 384

Tweedy, Penney, 538

Twentieth Annual Marlboro Music Festival, 26

20th Century–Fox, 55, 64

Twenty-fifth Amendment, 272

Twenty-sixth Amendment, 149, 217, 255, 274, 320

Twenty-seventh Amendment, 218

Twiggy, 200

Twigs (play), 94

The Twilight Zone, 392

Twilley, Dwight, 31

"Two Centuries of Black American Art", 33

Two Gentlemen of Verona (play), 51, 94

Typhoid, 396

Typhus, 434

Tyrants Destroyed (Nabokov), 31

Tyson, Cicely, 28, 37, 56, 376

U. S. Supreme Court, 106

U.S. Department of Agriculture (USDA), 140

U.S. General Services Administration (GSA), 230

U.S. Labor Department, 107

U.S. Lawn Tennis Association, 544

U.S. National Academy of Sciences, 474

U.S. News & World Report,, 391

U.S. Open, 531, 539, 545

U.S. Open (golf), 545

U.S. Postal Service, 107

U.S. Public Health Service, 350

U.S. Steel, 106–107, 112, 117, 144

U.S. Supreme Court, 106, 107, 113–114, 116, 444–445, 451, 454, 461

UCLA (basketball team), 500–501, 503, 507, 550–551

UCLA Bruins, 520

Udall, Morris, 260

Uggams, Leslie, 376

Ulbricht, Walter, 5

Ultrasound, 413, 429

Ulysses (Joyce), 53, 316

"Uncle Albert/Admiral Halsey" (McCartneys), 27

Uncle Sam, 271

Underclass, 234

Unemployment, 75, 224–225, 229, 234, 251, 258, 262

UNESCO, 29

An Unfinished Woman (Hellman), 91

Unger, Abraham, 317

Unification Church, 446

Unification Theological Seminary, 338, 447

Union Bag–Camp Paper Corporation, 144

Union Leader, 254

Union of Concerned Scientists, 129

Union of Hassidic Rabbis, 469

Union of Orthodox Rabbis, 453

Union Seminary, 469

Unitas, Johnny, 526

United Arab Emirates, 17

United Artists, 95

United Auto Workers (UAW), 106, 123, 127, 134–135, 145

United Automobile Workers (UAW), 127

United Brands, 142

United Canning Company, 110

United Church of Christ, 447, 467–468

United Farm Workers, 333

United Farm Workers (UFW), 107, 114–115

United Farm Workers Union, 351

United Feature Syndicate, 388

United Federation of Teachers of New York City, 169

United Golf Association, 531

United Methodist, 443, 447

United Methodist Board of Church and Society, 444

United Mine Workers (UMW), 106–107, 109–110, 114, 134–136, 142, 145

United Nations (UN), 4, 6–7, 9–10, 12–17, 19, 24, 145 168, 181, 227, 229–232, 234, 277, 280, 420

United Nations Conference on Trade and Development, 16

United Nations Experimental World Campaign for Universal Literacy, 181

United Nations General Assembly, 6, 9, 12–13, 17

United Nations Resolution 242, 458

United Nations Security Council, 9–10, 12, 19

United Presbyterian Church, 447–449

United Press International, 388, 391

United Rubber Workers, 110, 113

United Stated Supreme Court, 264

United States Air Force, 302

United States Census Bureau, 169

United States Circuit Court of Appeals, 152

United States Civil War, 189

United States Commerce Department, 401

United States Congress, 31, 152, 154, 157–159, 172, 176, 180, 186–187, 218–220, 223–224, 226–228, 230, 233–236, 240, 243, 245, 247–250, 252–253, 257–258, 260–267, 269–272, 274, 277 –279, 281, 286–287, 289, 292, 301–306, 308, 312, 314, 367, 376, 396–402, 408, 411, 414–416, 425–426, 433–434

United States Constitution, 60, 149, 166, 178, 287, 290, 292–294, 296–299, 302, 304–310, 312, 314, 316, 397

United States copyright laws, 362

United States daily newspapers, 362

United States Department of Agriculture, 397, 400

United States Department of Defense, 287, 304

United States Department of Education (USOE), 168

United States Department of Health, Education, and Welfare (HEW), 150–152, 154, 167–168,

Vane, Dr. John R., 429

Vanity Fair, 327

Vann, John Paul, 282

Vare Trophy, 531

Vargas Llosa, Mario, 13

Variety, 51

Vasquez, Jacinto, 551

Vass, Joan, 212

Vassar University, 172, 189

Veeck, Bill, 508

Velasco Alvarado, Juan, 15

Velázquez, Delgo, 92

The Velvet Underground, 40, 67, 74

Venturi, Rauch and Scott Brown, 209

Venturi, Robert, 192, 203, 209

Venus, 474, 482

Vera, 204

Verdon, Gwen, 84–85

Vereen, Ben, 27–28, 37, 50, 94, 376

Verlaine, Tom, 75

Vermont Yankee case, 301

Vernon Jordan, 132

Vertigo, 98

Veterans Administration (VA), 160, 424

Vicious, Sid, 75–76, 77, 93

The Victim (Bellow), 81

Vidal, Gore, 32, 52

Videla, Jorge, 16

Videotape, 361

Vienna Folk Opera, 89

Vienna Psychoanalytic Institute, 432

Vietnam Moratorium Committee, 244

Vietnam Veterans Against the War (VVAW), 245–246, 311

Vietnam War, 3–5, 7, 14, 38, 40, 51, 58, 62, 64–65, 70, 118, 125–126, 137, 139, 143, 145, 171–172, 196, 199, 216–217, 220, 223, 225, 234, 236, 240–241, 243–245, 251, 262, 265, 269–271, 274–275, 280–281, 304, 311, 365–366, 368–369, 385, 412, 443, 451–452, 456–457, 461, 464, 479

Vietnamization, 237–239, 241, 243

Viking, 482

Viking 1, 473

Viking 2, 474, 482

Viking Press, 423

Viking probe, 482

Vilas, Guillermo, 552

Village People, 35, 73, 375

Village Voice, 387

Villanova University (basketball team), 501, 503, 520, 550

Vincent, Gene, 99

Virginia Slims, 344

Virginia Slims Championship, 545

Virginia Slims cigarettes, 373–374

Virginia Slims tennis tournament, 527

Virginia Squires, 517

Visconti, Luchino, 21

VisiCalc, 122, 131, 474, 484

Visions of Terror and Wonder (Warrick), 93

Vital Parts (Berger), 26

Vocational Education Act, 168

Vocational Rehabilitation Act, 158

Vogue, 204, 384

Voight, Jon, 28, 35, 59, 63, 95

Volcker, Paul, 137

Volkswagen, 111, 113, 330–331

Volkswagen Beetle, 123, 476

Volvo, 331

Von Braun, Wernher Magnus Maximilian , 497

Von Daniken, Erik, 39

von Euler, Dr. Ulf, 427

von Frisch, Dr. Karl, 427

Vonnegut, Kurt, 32, 53

Vonnegut, Kurt, Jr., 29

Vorster, B. J., 21

Voting Rights Act, 225

Voyager, 482

Voyager 1, 474–475

Voyager 1, 482

Voyager 2, 474

Voyager 2, 482

VW Golf, 331

W. K. Kellogg Foundation, 431

Wade, Henry, 294

Wadkins, Lanny, 510

Waggoner, Porter, 79

Wagner, Lindsay, 374

Wagner, Richard, 98

"Wagon Wheels" (Merk), 189

Wajda, Andrej, 17

Waksman, Dr. Selman A., 435

Wal-Mart, 118, 135, 375

Waldheim, Kurt, 7

Walken, Christopher, 35

Walker, Aaron ("T-Bone"), 99

Walker, Alice, 32, 36, 39, 52

Walker, Charles, 37

Walker, Herbert, 317

Walker, Joseph A., 37, 51, 94

Walker, Kenny, 550

Walking Tall (movie), 65–66

Wall Street Journal, 245, 388, 390

Walla Walla High School, 188

Wallace, George C., 148, 218–219, 235, 254–255, 259–260, 263, 269, 276, 297

Wallace, Irving, 28, 30, 32, 39, 54

Wallach, Michael A., 155

Waller, Fats, 35

Wallington, Jimmy, 392

Walsh, Joe, 70

Walt Disney, 98

Walters, Barbara, 207, 323, 387

Walton, Bill, 506, 518, 521, 550

Walton, Sam, 135

The Waltons, 365, 373, 375, 387

Wambaugh, Joseph, 31

"The Wanderer" (Summer), 89

"War" (Starr), 26, 72

War and Peace (Tolstoy), 80

War and Remembrance (Wouk), 35

War Powers Act, 222, 234, 265

The Ward (Wallace), 28, 74

Ward, Anita, 36

Ward, Clara, 469

Ware v. *Estes*, 187

Warfield, Paul, 526

Warhol, Andy, 74

Warner Brothers (Warner Bros.), 76, 376

Warner Cable Corporation, 363

Warner, Jack, 99

Warner-Lambert Pharmaceuticals, 143

Warren Commission, 272, 282, 312

Warren Court, 292, 305–307, 310

Warren, Earl, 305, 307, 310, 317

Warren, Robert Penn, 94, 282

Warrick, Richard, 93

The Warriors (movie), 48

Warwick, Dionne, 30

Washington, 388

Washington Bullets, 508, 511, 518, 551–552

Washington Drive Junior High School, 188

Washington Plaza, 209

Washington Post, 159, 225, 227, 347, 368, 373, 380–381, 385, 387–389

Washington Redskins, 551

Washington Senators, 512, 514

Washington Star, 380, 389, 391

Washington Times, 338

Washington University, 400

Washington, D.C., 426

Washington, George, 163

Washington, Kermit, 541

Water Pollution Control Act, 1972, 300–301

Williams, Tennessee, 49
Wills, Bob, 99
Willys-Overland, 144
Wilson, Charles E., 145
Wilson, E. O., 492
Wilson, Flip, 87, 392
Wilson, Harold, 4, 11–12, 16
Wilson, Lanford, 50–51
Wilson, Robert W., 45, 50, 492, 495
Wilson, William, 213
Wimbledon, 539, 544
Winchell, Walter, 99, 357, 392
Windows (Druckman), 93
The Winds of War (Wouk), 28, 53
Winfield, Paul, 28, 37, 56
Wings (play), 95
Winn, Dr. Lyman, 430
"Winnie Winkle" (Branner), 390
Winnipeg Jets, 535
Winslow, Don, 391
Winston, Harry, 145
Winter, Edgar, 69
Winter, Johnny, 69
Winter Olympics, 1972, 532
Winter Olympics, 1976, 534
"Winter Soldier Investigations," 246
Wirin, Abraham Lincoln, 317
Wirth, Nicholas, 494
Wishes, Lies, and Dreams (Koch), 187
Wiss, Dr. Edward, 435
"With a Little Luck" (Wings), 35
Withers, Bill, 28, 72
"Without You" (Nilsson), 28
Wittig, George, 495
The Wiz (play), 32, 48, 51, 87, 94
The Wizard of Oz (DC Comics and Marvel Comics), 362
WKRP in Cincinnati, 375
Wodehouse, P. G., 99
Wolfe, Tom, 37, 67, 372
Wolff v. *McConnell*, 296
Woltman, Frederick E., 392
The Woman in Red (movie), 90
Woman on the Edge of Time (Piercy), 32
Woman the Gatherer, 487
A Woman Under the Influence (movie), 57, 62
Woman, Pinky, 212
The Women, 98, 234
Women in Love (movie), 58, 95
Women on the Edge of Time (Piercy), 53
Women's Basketball League, 512
Women's Equity Act, 167

Women's Equity Action League, 294
Women's rights, 5, 13, 20, 23, 233, 264, 281, 290, 292–295, 298, 301, 303, 310, 314
The Women's Room (French), 34, 53
Women's Tennis Association (WTA), 545
Women, Students, and Artists for Black Art Liberation, 42
womenSport, 545
Wonder, Stevie, 29, 34, 72–73, 89–90
Wonder Woman, 374
Wonderlic Personnel Test, 300
Wong Howe, James, 98
Wood, Garfield Arthur, 554
Wood, John, 45
Wood, Natalie, 57
Wood, Rosemary, 431
Wood, Jr., Dr. William Barry, 435
Woodcock, Leonard, 134
Wooden, John, 507, 520
Woodhead, Cynthia, 550
Woodman, Ruth Cornwall, 392
Woodrow Wilson School of Public and International Affairs, 210
Woods, Frederick, IV, 316
Woods, Rose Mary, 222, 249
"Woodstein," 380
Woodstock (movie), 26, 371
Woodward, Bob, 31, 246–247, 368–369, 380–381
Woodward, Joanne, 57
Woodward, Robert Burns, 497
Word Unspoken (Steir), 42
Work in America (Marland), 184
The World According to Garp (Irving), 35, 53
World Almanac, 381
World Championship Tennis (WCT), 539
World Court, 232
World Cup (soccer), 12, 20
World Food Conference, 12
World Health Organization (WHO), 399, 420–421, 429
World Health Organization Public Service Award, 429
World Hockey Association, 535
World Hockey League, 512
The World of Apples (Cheever), 29
World of Krypton (DC Comics), 379
World Series, 361
World Tennis, 540
World Trade Center, 210
World War I, 271, 281

World War II, 127, 131, 144–145, 185, 200–201, 205, 209, 250, 262, 270, 272, 274–275, 281, 411, 424
World's Fair, 210
Worldwide Church of God, 459
Worth, Irene, 94
Wottle, Dave, 533
Wouk, Herman, 28, 35, 39, 53
Wozniak, Steve, 121–122
"The Wreck of the Edmund Fitzgerald" (Lightfoot), 32
Wright, Frank Lloyd, 213
Wright, Henry, 213
Wright, Lee, 211
Wright, Mary Clabaugh, 189
Wright, Syreeta, 90, 93
Wrightson, Berni, 378
Wrigley, Peter, 211
Wrigley, Philip, 145
Writers Guild of America, 87, 378
WTBS (Turner), 360, 386
WTCG (Turner), 360, 386
WTTW (Chicago educational station), 363
Wu, Chien-Shiung, 494
Wuorinen, Charles, 93
Wuthering Heights, 98
WWWW (Women Who Want to be Women), 346
Wyeth, Andrew, 35, 38, 45
Wyman, Jane, 57
Wynder, Dr. Ernst L., 427
Wynette, Tammy, 77, 79
X-Ray Spex, 75
Xenia (Ohio) *Daily Gazette*, 389
Xerox, 109, 111
"Y.M.C.A.," (Village People), 35, 73, 375
Yablonski, Joseph, 106, 115, 136, 142, 145
Yahya Khan, Mohammad, 5–6
Yale Law School, 268, 272
Yale University, 166, 172, 178, 186, 189, 206, 380, 385, 412, 424, 430, 434
Yalow, Dr. Rosalyn S., 424, 428
Yamasaki, Minoru, 209–210
Yamashiro, Dr. Donald H., 426
Yanofsky, Dr. Charles, 428
Yeager, Robert C., 527, 542
Yellow fever, 434–435
Yes, 68
Yippies, 353
Yoder, Edwin M., 389
Yogi, Maharishi Mahesh, 164, 188